REPTILES & AMPHIBIANS

OF AUSTRALIA

REPTILES & AMPHIBIANS

OF AUSTRALIA

HAROLD G. COGGER

Comstock
Cornell

First published by
Reed Books
a division of
Reed International Books
Level 9, North Tower
Chatswood Plaza, 1-5 Railway St,
Chatswood, NSW 2067
in 1975
Revised editions, 1979, 1983, 1986
This 1992 edition published by Reed Books
and
Cornell University Press
124 Roberts Place
Ithaca New York 914850
The text and other information has been completely revised and updated and over 800 species now illustrated in full color

Library of Congress
Cataloging-in-Publication Data
Cogger, Harold G.
Reptiles and amphibians of Australia/
by Harold G. Cogger — 5th ed.
p. cm.
Includes bibliographical references
and index.
ISBN 0-8014-2739-8
1.Reptiles — Australia. 2. Amphibians — Australia.
I. Title.
QL663.A1C63 1992 91-34103
597.6'0994 — dc20 CIP

Edited by Peter Hutton

Designed by Robert Taylor

Typeset in New Zealand by Deadline Typesetting Ltd

Printed in Singapore through Imago Productions (F.E.) Pte Ltd

Contents

List of Currently Recognised Species of Australian Reptiles and Amphibians 7
Preface To The Fifth Edition 19
Preface To The First Edition 20
Acknowledgements 21

Introduction

Descriptions 23
Zoological names 24
Common names 25
Illustrations 25
Distribution 26
Habit 27
Subspecies 27
Making an identification 27
Conservation and protection 29
Location of specimens 30
Collecting methods 31
Localities of Australia's Reptiles and Amphibians 34
Vegetation and Climatic Zones 36
Preservation of specimens 40
Captive specimens 42
Snakebite and its treatment 46

Amphibians

FROGS 50
Diagnostic Characters in Frogs 52
Family Myobatrachidae (Southern Frogs) 53
Family Hylidae (Tree Frogs) 116
Family Microhylidae (Narrow-mouthed Toads) 159
Family Ranidae ('True' Frogs) 168
Family Bufonidae ('True' Toads) 169

Reptiles

CROCODILES 173

Family Crocodylidae (Crocodiles) 173

TURTLES AND TORTOISES 176

Diagnostic Characters in Turtles

Family Cheloniidae (Sea-turtles) 176

Family Dermochelyidae (Leathery Turtle) 184

Family Carettochelydidae (Pitted-shelled Turtle) 186

Family Chelidae (Side-necked Tortoises) 187

LIZARDS 202

Diagnostic Characters in Lizards 203

Family Gekkonidae (Geckos) 204

Family Pygopodidae (Snake-lizards) 277

Family Agamidae (Dragon Lizards) 298

Family Varanidae (Goannas or Monitor Lizards) 356

Family Scincidae (Skinks) 380

SNAKES 585

Diagnostic Characters in Snakes 586

Family Typhlopidae (Blind Snakes) 587

Family Boidae (Pythons) 600

Family Acrochordidae (File Snakes) 615

Family Colubridae (Colubrid Snakes) 617

Family Elapidae (Elapid Snakes) 629

Family Hydrophiidae (Sea-Snakes) 697

Family Laticaudidae (Sea Kraits) 722

The Terrestrial Reptiles of Australia's Indian Ocean Territories 725

Appendix 733

Glossary 742

Selected References 747

Index 765

List of Currently Recognised Species of Australian Reptiles and Amphibians

FAMILY MYOBATRACHIDAE 53

Adelotus 55
brevis 55
Arenophryne 56
rotunda 56
Assa 57
darlingtoni 57
Crinia 57
bilingua 58
deserticola 59
georgiana 59
glauerti 60
insignifera 60
parinsignifera 60
pseudinsignifera 61
remota 61
riparia 61
signifera 62
sloanei 63
subinsignifera 64
tasmaniensis 64
tinnula 65
Geocrinia 65
laevis 66
leai 66
lutea 66
rosea 67
victoriana 68
Heleioporus 68
albopunctatus 70
australiacus 70
barycragus 70
eyrei 71
inornatus 71
psammophilus 72
Lechriodus 72
fletcheri 73
Limnodynastes 73
convexiusculus 75
depressus 75
dorsalis 75
dumerilii 75
fletcheri 76
interioris 76
ornatus 77
peronii 78
salmini 78
spenceri 79
tasmaniensis 80
terraereginae 80
Megistolotus 81
lignarius 81
Metacrinia 82
nichollsi 82
Mixophyes 82
balbus 83
fasciolatus 83
fleayi 83
iteratus 84
schevilli 84
Myobatrachus 86
gouldii 86
Neobatrachus 87
aquilonius 87
centralis 88
fulvus 88
kunapalari 88
pelobatoides 89
pictus 89
sudelli 90
sutor 90
wilsmorei 90
Notaden 91
bennettii 92
melanoscaphus 92
nichollsi 93
weigeli 94

Paracrinia 94
haswelli 94
Philoria 95
frosti 96
kundagungan 96
loveridgei 96
sphagnicolus 97
Pseudophryne 97
australis 98
bibronii 99
coriacea 99
corroboree 101
dendyi 101
douglasi 101
guentheri 101
major 102
occidentalis 103
semimarmorata 103
Rheobatrachus 103
silus 103
vitellinus 104
Taudactylus 104
acutirostris 105
diurnus 105
eungellensis 106
liemi 106
pleione 107
rheophilus 107
Uperoleia 108
arenicola 109
aspera 109
borealis 109
capitulata 109
crassa 110
fusca 110
glandulosa 110
inundata 111
laevigata 111
lithomoda 112
littlejohni 112
marmorata 112
martini 112
micromeles 112
mimula 113
minima 113
mjobergii 113
orientalis 114
rugosa 114
russelli 115
talpa 115
trachyderma 115
tyleri 115

FAMILY HYLIDAE 116

Cyclorana 116
australis 117
brevipes 118
cryptotis 118
cultripes 118
longipes 119
maculosa 119
maini 121
manya 121
novaehollandiae 121
platycephala 121
vagita 122
verrucosa 123
Litoria 123
adelaidensis 127
alboguttata 128
aurea 128
bicolor 129
booroolongensis 129
brevipalmata 130
burrowsae 131
caerulea 132
castanea 132
cavernicola 132
chloris 133
citropa 133
cooloolensis 133
coplandi 134
cyclorhyncha 134
dahlii 135
dentata 135
dorsalis 136
ewingii 136
fallax 137
freycineti 137
genimaculata 138
gilleni 138
gracilenta 139
inermis 139
infrafrenata 140
jervisiensis 140
latopalmata 142
lesueuri 143
longirostris 143
lorica 143
meiriana 143
moorei 144
nannotis 145
nasuta 145
nigrofrenata 146
nyakalensis 146
olongburensis 146
pallida 147
paraewingi 148

peronii 148
personata 148
phyllochroa 150
piperata 151
raniformis 151
revelata 151
rheocola 151
rothii 152
rubella 152
spenceri 153
splendida 155
subglandulosa 155
tornieri 155
tyleri 155
verreauxii 156
wotjulumensis 157
xanthomera 157
Nyctimystes 158
dayi 158

FAMILY MICROHYLIDAE 159

Cophixalus 159
bombiens 160
concinnus 161
crepitans 161
exiguus 162
hosmeri 162
infacetus 162
mcdonaldi 162
neglectus 162
ornatus 163
peninsularis 164
saxatilis 164
Sphenophryne 164
adelphe 165
fryi 165
gracilipes 166
pluvialis 166
robusta 167

FAMILY RANIDAE 168

Rana 168
daemeli 168

FAMILY BUFONIDAE 169

Bufo 169
marinus 169

FAMILY CROCODYLIDAE 173

Crocodylus 173
johnstoni 174
porosus 175

FAMILY CHELONIIDAE 176

Caretta 178
caretta 178
Chelonia 180
mydas 180
Eretmochelys 182
imbricata 182
Lepidochelys 182
olivacea 183
Natator 183
depressus 183

FAMILY DERMOCHELYIDAE 184

Dermochelys 185
coriacea 185

FAMILY CARETTOCHELYDIDAE 186

Carettochelys 186
insculpta 186

FAMILY CHELIDAE 187

Chelodina 188
expansa 189
longicollis 190
novaeguineae 191
oblonga 192
rugosa 192
steindachneri 193
Elseya 193
dentata 194
latisternum 194
Emydura 196
krefftii 196
macquarii 197
signata 199
subglobosa 199
victoriae 199
Pseudemydura 200
umbrina 200
Rheodytes 200
leukops 201

FAMILY GEKKONIDAE 204

Carphodactylus 205
laevis 207
Christinus 207
guentheri 207
marmoratus 208
Crenadactylus 209
ocellatus 209
Cyrtodactylus 210
louisiadensis 210
Diplodactylus 211
alboguttatus 214
assimilis 214
byrnei 215
ciliaris 215
conspicillatus 217
elderi 217
fulleri 218
galeatus 218
granariensis 219
immaculatus 219
intermedius 219
jeanae 220
kenneallyi 221
maini 221
mcmillani 221
michaelseni 222
mitchelli 222
occultus 222
ornatus 223
polyophthalmus 224
pulcher 224
rankini 225
savagei 225
spinigerus 225
squarrosus 226
steindachneri 227
stenodactylus 228
strophurus 228
taeniatus 229
taenicauda 231
tessellatus 231
vittatus 232
wellingtonae 234
williamsi 234
wilsoni 234
wombeyi 234
Gehyra 235
australis 236
baliola 236
borroloola 237
catenata 238
dubia 238
minuta 239
montium 239
mutilata 727
nana 239
occidentalis 240
oceanica 240
pamela 242
pilbara 242
punctata 243
purpurascens 243
robusta 243
variegata 244
xenopus 244
Hemidactylus 246, 728
frenatus 246, 728
Heteronotia 247
binoei 248
spelea 248

Lepidodactylus 248
listeri 728
lugubris 249, 728
pumilus 250
Lucasium 250
damaeum 250
Nactus 251
galgajuga 251
pelagicus 253
Nephrurus 253
asper 254
deleani 255
laevissimus 256
levis 256
stellatus 257
vertebralis 257
wheeleri 257
Oedura 259
castelnaui 260
coggeri 260
filicipoda 261
gemmata 262
gracilis 262
lesueurii 263
marmorata 263
monilis 264
obscura 265
reticulata 265
rhombifer 266
robusta 266
tryoni 266
Phyllurus 268
caudiannulatus 269
cornutus 269
platurus 271
salebrosus 271
Pseudothecadactylus 271
australis 271
lindneri 273
Rhynchoedura 274
ornata 274
Underwoodisaurus 275
milii 275
sphyrurus 276

FAMILY PYGOPODIDAE 277

Aclys 278
concinna 278
Aprasia 278
aurita 279
haroldi 279
inaurita 280
parapulchella 281
pseudopulchella 281
pulchella 281
repens 282
rostrata 282
smithi 282
striolata 283
Delma 284
australis 286
borea 286
butleri 286
elegans 286
fraseri 286
grayii 288
haroldi 288
impar 289
inornata 289
labialis 290
mitella 290
molleri 290
nasuta 291
pax 291
plebeia 292
tincta 292
torquata 292
Lialis 293
burtonis 294
Ophidiocephalus 294
taeniatus 294
Paradelma 295
orientalis 296
Pletholax 296
gracilis 296
Pygopus 297
lepidopodus 297
nigriceps 298

FAMILY AGAMIDAE 298

Amphibolurus 300
muricatus 301
nobbi 301
norrisi 302
Caimanops 303
amphiboluroides 303
Chelosania 304
brunnea 305
Chlamydosaurus 305
kingii 305
Cryptagama 307
aurita 307

Ctenophorus 308
caudicinctus 310
clayi 311
cristatus 311
decresii 312
femoralis 312
fionni 312
fordi 315
gibba 316
isolepis 316
maculatus 317
maculosus 318
mckenziei 318
nuchalis 318
ornatus 320
pictus 320
reticulatus 322
rufescens 323
salinarum 323
scutulatus 326
vadnappa 326
yinnietharra 326
Diporiphora 327
albilabris 328
australis 329
bennettii 329
bilineata 330
convergens 330
lalliae 330
linga 332
magna 332
pindan 332
reginae 333
superba 334
valens 334
winneckei 336
Hypsilurus 337
boydii 337
spinipes 338
Lophognathus 340
gilberti 340
longirostris 341
temporalis 342
Moloch 343
horridus 344
Physignathus 344
lesueurii 345
Pogona 346
barbata 347
microlepidota 347
minima 349
minor 349
mitchelli 349
nullarbor 350
vitticeps 350
Tympanocryptis 350
adelaidensis 351
cephalus 352
diemensis 353
intima 353
lineata 353
parviceps 355
tetraporophora 356
uniformis 356

FAMILY VARANIDAE 356

Varanus 356
acanthurus 359
baritji 361
brevicauda 361
caudolineatus 361
eremius 362
giganteus 362
gilleni 364
glauerti 365
glebopalma 365
gouldii 366
indicus 368
kingorum 368
mertensi 369
mitchelli 369
panoptes 370
pilbarensis 370
prasinus 371
primordius 371
rosenbergi 372
semiremex 372
spenceri 376
storri 376
timorensis 377
tristis 377
varius 379

FAMILY SCINCIDAE 380

Anomalopus 382
brevicollis 383
gowi 384
leuckartii 384
mackayi 385
pluto 385
swansoni 385
verreauxii 386

Calyptotis 386
lepidorostrum 387
ruficauda 387
scutirostrum 388
temporalis 389
thorntonensis 389
Carlia 389
amax 392
coensis 392
dogare 392
gracilis 392
jarnoldae 393
johnstonei 394
longipes 394
munda 395
mundivensis 395
pectoralis 395
rhomboidalis 396
rimula 396
rostralis 397
rubrigularis 398
rufilatus 398
schmeltzii 399
scirtetis 399
storri 399
tetradactyla 401
triacantha 401
vivax 401
Coeranoscincus 402
frontalis 402
reticulatus 402
Cryptoblepharus 403
carnabyi 404
egeriae 728
fuhni 405
litoralis 405
megastictus 405
plagiocephalus 406
virgatus 406
Ctenotus 407
alacer 412
alleni 412
allotropis 413
angusticeps 413
arcanus 413
ariadnae 414
arnhemensis 415
astarte 415
atlas 415
australis 416
borealis 416
brachyonyx 417
brooksi 417
calurus 418
capricorni 418
catenifer 419
coggeri 419
colletti 420
decaneurus 420
delli 421
dux 421
ehmanni 422
essingtoni 423
eurydice 423
eutaenius 424
fallens 424
gagudju 425
gemmula 425
grandis 426
greeri 426
hanloni 426
hebetior 427
helenae 427
hilli 428
impar 428
ingrami 428
inornatus 429
joanae 429
kurnbudj 430
labillardieri 430
lancelini 432
lateralis 432
leae 433
leonhardii 433
mastigura 434
militaris 434
mimetes 435
monticola 435
pallescens 435
pantherinus 436
piankai 437
pulchellus 437
quattuordecimlineatus 438
quinkan 438
rawlinsoni 438
regius 438
robustus 439
rubicundus 440
rutilans 440
saxatilis 441
schevilli 441
schomburgkii 442
septenarius 442
serotinus 442
serventyi 443
severus 443
spaldingi 444
storri 446
strauchii 446
striaticeps 447

taeniolatus 447
tanamiensis 448
tantillus 449
uber 449
vertebralis 449
xenopleura 450
youngsoni 450
zastictus 450
zebrilla 450
Cyclodomorphus 451
branchialis 452
casuarinae 452
maxima 453
Egernia 454
carinata 457
coventryi 457
cunninghami 457
depressa 458
douglasi 460
formosa 460
frerei 461
hosmeri 461
inornata 462
kingii 465
kintorei 465
luctuosa 465
major 465
margaretae 466
mcpheei 467
modesta 468
multiscutata 468
napoleonis 469
pilbarensis 469
pulchra 470
richardi 470
rugosa 470
saxatilis 471
slateri 472
stokesii 472
striata 472
striolata 472
whitii 473
Emoia 475
atrocostata 476, 728
longicauda 477
nativitatis 728
Eremiascincus 477
fasciolatus 477
richardsonii 478
Eroticoscincus 479
graciloides 479
Eugongylus 480
albofasciolatus 480
rufescens 480
Eulamprus 481
amplus 482
heatwolei 483
kosciuskoi 485
leuraensis 485
luteilateralis 485
murrayi 486
quoyii 487
tenuis 487
tigrinus 489
tympanum 489
Glaphyromorphus 490
brongersmai 491
cracens 492
crassicaudis 492
darwiniensis 492
douglasi 492
fuscicaudis 494
gracilipes 495
isolepis 496
mjobergi 496
nigricaudis 496
pardalis 496
pumilus 498
punctulatus 498
Gnypetoscincus 498
queenslandiae 499
Hemiergis 500
decresiensis 500
initialis 500
millewe 502
peronii 502
quadrilineatum 502
Hemisphaeriodon 503
gerrardii 503
Lampropholis 505
amicula 505
caligula 507
delicata 507
guichenoti 507
mirabilis 508
Lerista 508
aericeps 512
allanae 512
allochira 512
ameles 512
apoda 513
bipes 513
borealis 514
bougainvillii 514
carpentariae 515
chalybura 515
christinae 516
cinerea 516
connivens 518
desertorum 518
distinguenda 518
dorsalis 518

elegans 518
flammicauda 519
fragilis 519
frosti 519
gascoynensis 520
gerrardii 520
greeri 520
griffini 521
haroldi 521
humphriesi 521
ips 521
kalumburu 521
karlschmidti 522
kennedyensis 522
labialis 523
lineata 524
lineopunctulata 525
macropisthopus 525
microtis 525
muelleri 526
neander 527
nichollsi 527
onsloviana 528
orientalis 528
picturata 528
planiventralis 529
praefrontalis 530
praepedita 530
punctatovittata 530
separanda 530
simillima 531
stictopleura 532
storri 532
stylis 532
taeniata 533
terdigitata 533
uniduo 534
varia 534
vermicularis 535
vittata 536
walkeri 536
wilkinsi 536
xanthura 536
Lygisaurus 537
aeratus 538
foliorum 539
laevis 539
macfarlani 540
rococo 540
sesbrauna 540
tanneri 540
timlowi 541
Lygosoma 730
bowringii 730
Menetia 541
alanae 542
amaura 542
concinna 542
greyii 543
maini 544
surda 545
Morethia 545
adelaidensis 546
boulengeri 546
butleri 547
lineoocellata 547
obscura 548
ruficauda 548
storri 548
taeniopleura 550
Nannoscincus 552
maccoyi 552
Notoscincus 553
butleri 553
ornatus 553
Ophioscincus 554
cooloolensis 555
ophioscincus 556
truncatus 556
Proablepharus 556
kinghorni 557
reginae 557
tenuis 559
Pseudemoia 559
baudini 561
coventryi 561
duperreyi 561
entrecasteauxii 562
greeni 562
jigurru 563
lichenigera 563
metallica 564
microlepidota 566
ocellata 566
orocrypta 567
palfreymani 567
platynota 567
pretiosa 568
rawlinsoni 569
spenceri 569
trilineata 571
zia 571
Saiphos 571
equalis 572
Saproscincus 572
basiliscus 573
challengeri 574
czechurai 574
mustelina 574
tetradactyla 575
Tiliqua 576
adelaidensis 576

multifasciata 577
nigrolutea 577
occipitalis 579
scincoides 580
Trachydosaurus 583
rugosus 584

FAMILY TYPHLOPIDAE 587

Ramphotyphlops 587
affinis 589
australis 589
bituberculatus 589
braminus 589, 731
broomi 591
centralis 591
diversus 592
endoterus 592
exocoeti 731
grypus 592
guentheri 592
hamatus 593
howi 593
kimberleyensis 593
leptosoma 593
leucoproctus 593
ligatus 593
margaretae 594
micromma 594
minimus 595
nigrescens 595
pinguis 596
polygrammicus 596
proximus 597
tovelli 597
troglodytes 598
unguirostris 598
waitii 598
wiedii 599
yampiensis 599
yirrikalae 599

FAMILY BOIDAE 600

Aspidites 601
melanocephalus 601
ramsayi 602
Chondropython 603
viridis 603
Liasis 604
albertisii 605
childreni 606
fuscus 606
maculosus 606
olivaceus 608
perthensis 608
stimsoni 610
Morelia 610
amethistina 611
bredli 611
carinata 612
oenpelliensis 613
spilota 614

FAMILY ACROCHORDIDAE 615

Acrochordus 615
arafurae 615
granulatus 616

FAMILY COLUBRIDAE 617

Boiga 617
irregularis 618
Cerberus 619
rynchops 619
Dendrelaphis 620
calligastra 620
punctulata 621
Enhydris 623
polylepis 623
Fordonia 624
leucobalia 625
Lycodon 731
capucinus 731
Myron 625
richardsonii 625
Stegonotus 626
cucullatus 627
parvus 627
Tropidonophis 628
mairii 628

FAMILY ELAPIDAE 629

Acanthophis 632
antarcticus 632
praelongus 634
pyrrhus 634
Austrelaps 635
superbus 635
Cacophis 636
harriettae 636
krefftii 637
squamulosus 638
Demansia 638
atra 639
olivacea 640
papuensis 641
psammophis 641
simplex 641
torquata 643
Denisonia 643
devisi 644
maculata 644
Drysdalia 645
coronata 645
coronoides 646
mastersii 647
rhodogaster 647
Echiopsis 648
atriceps 649
curta 649
Elapognathus 649
minor 649
Furina 650
barnardi 651
diadema 651
dunmalli 652
ornata 653
tristis 653
Hemiaspis 654
damelii 654
signata 656
Hoplocephalus 656
bitorquatus 657
bungaroides 658
stephensii 658
Notechis 658
ater 659
scutatus 660
Oxyuranus 660
microlepidota 662
scutellatus 662
Pseudechis 664
australis 664
butleri 665
colletti 665
guttatus 666
porphyriacus 668
Pseudonaja 668
affinis 670
guttata 670
inframacula 670
ingrami 671
modesta 671
nuchalis 672
textilis 675
Rhinoplocephalus 676
bicolor 676
boschmai 677
nigrescens 677
nigrostriatus 679
pallidiceps 679
Simoselaps 680
anomalus 682
approximans 682
australis 682
bertholdi 683
bimaculatus 684
calonotus 684
fasciolatus 684
incinctus 685
littoralis 686
minimus 686
semifasciatus 687
warro 688
Suta 688
fasciata 689
flagellum 689
gouldii 690
monachus 690
nigriceps 691
ordensis 691
punctata 691
spectabilis 693
suta 693
Tropidechis 694
carinatus 694
Vermicella 695
annulata 696
multifasciata 696

FAMILY HYDROPHIIDAE 697

Acalyptophis 698
peronii 698
Aipysurus 699
apraefrontalis 701
duboisii 701
eydouxii 702
foliosquama 702
fuscus 702
laevis 703
tenuis 704
Astrotia 705
stokesii 706
Disteira 706
kingii 707
major 707
Emydocephalus 708
annulatus 708
Enhydrina 709
schistosa 709
Ephalophis 710
greyi 711
Hydrelaps 711
darwiniensis 712
Hydrophis 712
atriceps 714
belcheri 714
caerulescens 714
coggeri 715
czeblukovi 715
elegans 716
gracilis 716
inornatus 717
mcdowelli 717
melanosoma 718
ornatus 718
pacificus 719
vorisi 719
Lapemis 720
hardwickii 720
Parahydrophis 721
mertoni 721
Pelamis 722
platurus 722

FAMILY LATICAUDIDAE 723

Laticauda 723
colubrina 724
laticaudata 724

Preface to the Fifth Edition

Prefaces to the second, third and fourth editions, which are not included here, noted the growth in taxonomic knowledge of the Australian herpetofauna from the 664 species recognised in 1975 through 703 species (1979), 830 (1983), 865 (1986) to the 951 species described in this edition.

This unprecedented growth has resulted largely from those factors identified in the first edition preface reprinted below — the exploration of previously remote areas, increased awareness of the biological and ecological importance of our herpetofauna, and the application of new methods in discriminating biological species.

The format of this edition departs radically from that of its four predecessors. It includes many more photographs, including a much greater use of colour. Moreover it places the illustrations adjacent to the relevant text, and the keys are accompanied by some hundreds of explanatory line drawings. These changes will make the book more reliable and more friendly to use, and ultimately they will enhance its primary objective: the accurate identification of Australia's rich fauna of frogs and reptiles.

Probably the most persistent response from users of earlier editions has been the request to explain the use of different zoological names, in different books, for what is apparently the same animal, and for advice as to which of two or more names is 'correct'.

A corollary of the rapid growth in the naming of new species is that few of them have been subject to rigorous assessment by other herpetologists using a variety of discrimination techniques. Consequently a number of them may well be shown, in the future, to represent no more than variations within a single biological species.

Does this matter? Not at all; indeed, this is the very essence of taxonomic research in which new species are proposed, on the evidence available, so that others later may apply objective tests of their validity.

The importance of distinguishing between species and the names that we apply to them has been stressed elsewhere (p.25). Remember also that whereas most biologists believe that species are natural entities which can be objectively defined with adequate data and tools, genera and higher classifications are intrinsically subjective. Thus, different classifications simply represent different interpretations, by different specialists, of the evolutionary relationships of particular groups of organisms. Despite occasional claims to the contrary, there is no 'correct' classification, only classifications which are perceived to best fit the available data.

The users of biological names (and of the biological classifications which they express) should always bear this last statement in mind, because they will then understand, and hopefully be more tolerant of, the frustratingly frequent scientific name changes and alternative classifications which continue to plague Australian herpetology.

Preface to the First Edition

1975

The primary aim of this book is to provide the means to identify the majority of reptiles and frogs found in continental Australia and Tasmania. Australia's herpetofauna is very rich and varied — about 664 species are described in the following pages. However, new forms are still being found and described, even from the densely populated areas of the eastern seaboard.

In recent years there has been a dramatic increase of interest in reptiles and amphibians. This has resulted not only from a growing appreciation of their diversity of form and habit, of their vital contribution to the diversity and viability of natural systems and of their value as subjects for scientific research, but also from increasing public interest in general natural history.

This public awareness is probably due to the expanding role of biology in primary and secondary education, to the impact of television documentaries and to a burgeoning supply of popular, low-priced books on the subject. It also reflects the growing physical isolation of an urban society from those natural and wild environments in which humans have traditionally refreshed their psyches and been made aware of their transient role in a natural, evolutionary succession.

Those with an advanced knowledge of Australian reptiles and frogs will probably find little use for this book, except perhaps as a catalogue for currently recognised species. It is not intended as a replacement for the excellent regional handbooks listed in the bibliography. Such handbooks contain a wealth of information on the ecology and biology of their subjects, for they are generally the outcome of detailed studies by authors who have spent many years working in particular areas.

The correct identification of any organism is usually the first step to its further study. This is as true for the casual observer as for the scientist. Until recent times the classification of Australian reptiles and frogs was based almost exclusively on a small number of external or internal features which could be readily studied in pickled museum specimens. A gradual awareness of the need to look at an animal as part of a system, rather than as an isolated group of cells, has given a new dimension to the science of classification.

With the application of such modern methods as *in vitro* fertility studies and sonographic analysis of male frog call structure, electrophoretic and immunological studies of protein relationships and the determination of chromosomal complements, a greater understanding of the evolutionary history and relationships of the Australian herpetofauna is slowly emerging. However, concomitant with these studies is a greater awareness of the complexities of such relationships and the frequent inability of classical Linnaean classification to cope with changing concepts.

Consequently, the task of identifying a particular animal becomes increasingly complicated, for one or more pieces of information that may be essential for an accurate identification may be difficult, or even impossible, to obtain.

However, the majority of reptile and frog species in Australia are still defined on the basis of readily observed morphological and anatomical characters — characters which are present whether an individual is dead or alive, in its natural environment or far removed from it.

While this remains the case — and it will undoubtedly remain the case for many years to come — conventional identification manuals such as this one will find a useful place on the naturalist's bookshelf.

Acknowledgments

In order to prepare a book of this kind, I have drawn heavily on the published and unpublished researches of many other workers, living and dead.

As it is not possible, within the available space, to cite full references to every source of information, a list of useful publications is provided in the Selected References on page 747. The books and papers listed are those which, by virtue of their coverage or extensive bibliographies, are thought to provide a broad background to the classification of Australian reptiles and frogs. The omission of any reference does not imply that it is any less important than those listed.

However, where a specific piece of information should be credited to a particular worker or workers, their name follows that information in parentheses. Failure to cite a particular author generally means either that the information is well known to many herpetologists or is here presented as my own observation. I apologise in advance for any omissions.

Nevertheless, special mention should be made of some outstanding recent contributors to Australian herpetology. In the field of systematic herpetology the work of the late F. J. Mitchell, R. Mertens, S. J. Copland and H. W. Parker, and of J. Covacevich, A. E. Greer, G. Ingram, M. King, A. G. Kluge, S. B. McDowell, J. A. Moore, G. M. Storr, M. J. Tyler and R . G. Zweifel stand out among that of many competent workers. Extending into the broader fields of biology and ecology, important contributions have been made in recent years by H. R. Bustard, H. F. Heatwole, M. J. Littlejohn, A. R. Main, A. A. Martin, E. Pianka, P. Rawlinson and R. Shine. The numerous publications of the late Eric Worrell did much to stimulate interest in Australian herpetology.

Many people assisted in the preparation of the various editions of this book by contributing specimens for photography or description, by reading sections of the final draft, by checking distribution maps and by discussing various taxonomic and other problems. Although I am unable to acknowledge all these people by name I am especially indebted to J. Barker, B. Barnett, S.and K. Breeden, R. Cook, J. Covacevich, J. Coventry, H. Ehmann, M. Gillam, G.Gow, A .E. Greer, G. Grigg, M. Hanlon, A. Healy, H. F. Heatwole, the late A. Holmes, T. Houston, H. D. Hughes, G. Ingram, R. Jenkins, M. King, A. G. Kluge, J. M. Legler, D. S. Liem. C. Limpus, M. J. Littlejohn, R. D. Mackay, K. McDonald, K., R. McRae, W. McReaddie, D. Metcalfe, D. Millar, R. Miller, F. Parker, the late U. Peters, M. Peterson, the late P. Rankin, H. Richner, A. Rose, R. Sadlier, G. Shea, R. Shine, K.R. Slater, D. Stammer, D. Stevens, G.M. Storr, S. Swanson, N. Tamiya, R. Taylor,G. Trood, M.J. Tyler, G. Webb, P. Webber, R. Wells, the late G.P. Whitley, G. Witten, J. Wombey, the directors and staffs of the New South Wales National Parks and Wildlife Service, the Forestry, Fisheries, National Parks and Wildlife Branch of the Department of the Northern Territory and the Zoological Parks Board of New South Wales.

For generously providing photographs of species otherwise unavailable to me, I am especially grateful to Stan Breeden, Pavel German, Graeme Gow, Mark Hanlon, Paul Horner, Howard Hughes, Robert Jenkins, Ian Morris, Magnus Peterson, the late Peter Rankin, Ross Sadlier, Glen Shea, Ron and Val Taylor, John Weigel and John Wombey.

Dr J. Calaby and the late Dr H.J. Frith of the CSIRO Division of Wildlife Research and Rangelands, by involving me in several of the Division's faunal surveys in northern Australia, have enabled me to provide a more comprehensive treatment of a previously poorly known fauna than would otherwise have been possible. By virtue of his enthusiasm, help and companionship on many occasions David Lindner supported this project from its inception and I remain especially indebted to him.

Some of the research and fieldwork from which this book is derived has been supported by the Science and Industry Endowment Fund of CSIRO, the Explorers Club (New York), the British Council, the Australian Research Council (through its predecessor the Australian Research Grants Committee), the National Science Foundation through its support of the Alpha Helix programme operated by the Scripps Institute of Oceanography, the Japan Society for the Promotion of Science and the Trustees of the Australian Museum. To the latter, to the Museum's Director Dr D. J. G. Griffin and to the now defunct New South Wales Public Service Board, I am indebted for permission to undertake the preparation of this book.

Data presented in the section on sea-snakes (family Hydrophiidae) are largely extracted from my chapter in *The Biology of Sea Snakes*, a book edited by Professor William Dunson and published in 1975 by University Park Press, Baltimore.

Much of the material on the gekkonid lizard genus *Diplodactylus* and on pygopodid lizards is derived from the monographic publications of A. G. Kluge, while that on the scincid genus *Ctenotus* is largely derived from the extensive publications of G. M. Storr. These and other major sources are identified in the Selected References.

I am grateful to Mrs Alana Thomas, Mrs Caroline Sinclair and my wife Heather, who prepared the original typescript. Brian Bertram generously found time to prepare some of the line illustrations for the original edition in his already overcrowded programme. For their help and advice in producing the first edition I am grateful to Brian Robson and Roger Coates, then of A. H. & A. W. Reed. For this completely revised edition, Bill Templeman and Robert Taylor of Reed Books have been equally patient and helpful.

With the exception of my immediate family, no person has contributed more to this edition than Elizabeth Cameron. Her careful research and eagle eye have together ensured that errors (for which I alone am responsible) have been kept to a minimum. She has also made many indirect contributions to the book's content through her extensive field experience and observations.

Finally, my wife Heather and our children Tim and Sue have become accustomed to having to accommodate their lives to the demands of herpetology — live reptiles and frogs around the house, excursions geared to herpetological collecting or photography and my long absences in the field or darkroom; their original hopes that this situation would be improved following the publication of earlier editions of this book were, I regret, never realised.

Introduction

This introduction explains the way in which the book is organised — its aims, scope and limitations. The manuscript for this edition was completed in March 1990 and with some exceptions the following pages take into account only those research papers published and available to me in Sydney at that time.

DESCRIPTIONS

Because space limitations preclude any possibility of providing comprehensive descriptions of the species listed in the following pages, the descriptions have been limited to brief and diagnostic synopses of salient characteristics. All genera are arranged in alphabetical order within families and all species are arranged in alphabetical order within genera.

To avoid any unnecessary duplication and to ensure that the abbreviated descriptions provide as much information as possible, the descriptions of families, genera and species are constructed on a comparative, hierarchical basis, that is, each description is diagnostic only within the next highest taxonomic category. In this way all genera within a particular family can usually be compared, character for character, so that essential differences between them are obvious. Similarly, the descriptions of all species within a particular genus can be compared to find both differences and similarities.

The combination of characters given in any description is therefore characteristic only of the family, genus or species being described. This means that any individual possessing this combination of characters can only, at least in theory, belong to this particular taxon. However, this unique suite of characters holds true only within the next highest taxonomic category.

Where two or more species are similar in nearly all respects, only one will be described fully; only those features distinguishing the other(s) from this species are described.

Two corollaries of this hierarchical structure are that (1) the descriptions of species in different genera (even where these genera may be closely related) may not be directly comparable and (2) the full diagnostic description of any one species consists not only of the characters cited in the species description, but also those which go to make up the generic and family descriptions.

The size of any given species is given in different ways for different groups: for frogs, a single, unqualified measurement is given at the end of each description; this is the average adult body length of the species unless any comment is made to the contrary. For lizards, the average adult length is usually expressed as snout-vent length. Because many lizards may lose and regenerate their tails, knowledge of total length has little practical advantage in identification. Exceptions are indicated, while relative tail length is provided where this information is important in identification. For snakes, two measurements are frequently given — the average adult total length and the *approximate* maximum total length. This latter measurement is provided because it is so often requested.

In every case the 'average' length quoted is not a statistical mean, but an approximation to indicate to a field worker whether a specimen is at, or near, adult size.

It should also be noted that where all the members of a particular genus have similar habits, then these habits are described in the generic account to avoid repetition in the species descriptions. Where the section on habit is omitted from a particular description, it may be assumed that I can find no published comments on the habit or ecology of the species under discussion, nor do I have personal knowledge of the species in the wild.

ZOOLOGICAL NAMES

Zoological or 'scientific' names provide a standardised international system for labelling particular categories used in the classification of animals. The actual names are usually Latinised names of either classical Greek or Latin words, or of modern words. The way in which these words are used is determined in a set of fairly rigid rules laid down by the International Code of Zoological Nomenclature; these rules are subject to regular review by the International Commission on Zoological Nomenclature. Although changes made periodically by the Commission are intended to facilitate the work of zoological taxonomists and to reflect the views of a majority of practising taxonomists, these aims are not always achieved.

The basic unit of zoological classification is the *species,* which can be roughly defined as a group of animals in which the individuals are free to interbreed and produce normal, fertile offspring. They do not, or are unable, to breed with individuals of another species to produce normal, fertile offspring. This is a simplistic definition which ignores exceptions and glosses over the chemical, physiological and genetic bases of reproductive isolation, but it serves our purpose here.

Closely related species may be grouped into a genus and the combination of specific and generic names together make up the binomial system which is the basis of zoological nomenclature. Hence the zoological names of species in this book consist of a first name (the name of the genus, or generic name, whose first letter is always capitalised) and a second name (the name of the species, or specific name, whose first letter is never capitalised). Both names are, however, italicised. The author, or first describer, of any scientific name immediately follows the name itself. In the case of species the name of the author is sometimes in parentheses. The convention adopted in this book is for authors' names to be placed in parentheses only if the species is now in a different genus from the one in which it was originally described. If the genus/species combination is the same as used by the original describer of the species, then his or her name does not appear in parentheses.

Groups of related genera may be grouped into families, groups of families into orders and groups of orders into classes. Within and between the various categories additional ones may be used from time to time to indicate intermediate groupings of taxa, for example suborders, superfamilies and tribes.

Also the species itself may be divided into subspecies — usually geographically distinct populations which are sufficiently differentiated in some features such as colour, pattern or behaviour to warrant distinguishing them from other populations or subspecies. Subspecies are regarded as incipient species which, depending on the vicissitudes of future changes in climate, topography, vegetation, etc., may ultimately develop into new species or be reabsorbed into a single, more or less homogeneous population. The name of the subspecies may be added to the genus/species combination to form a *trinomen* or *trinomial.*

In this book the only categories used are classes, orders, suborders, families, genera, species and subspecies. An example of a hierarchical classification using these categories is shown below, using one species of knob-tailed gecko, *Nephrurus levis:*

Class:	Reptilia	(reptiles)
Order:	Squamata	(lizards and snakes)
Suborder:	Sauria	(lizards)
Family:	Gekkonidae	(geckos)
Genus:	*Nephrurus:*	(knob-tailed gecko)
Species:	*levis:*	smooth knob-tailed gecko
Subspecies:	*levis:*	
	or *occidentalis:*	
	or *pilbarensis:*	

The classification used in this book is based on that established in Volume 1 of *Zoological Catalogue of Australia: Amphibia and Reptilia,* by Harold G. Cogger, Elizabeth E. Cameron and Heather M. Cogger (Australian Government Publishing Service, Canberra, 1983), with subsequent changes in taxonomy and nomenclature taken into account.

In most cases the names used are those currently accepted by the majority of Australian workers. In cases where competent herpetologists disagree over the status of a particular taxon or the name applied to it, I have made decisions based on my own knowledge of the animal concerned, or on my evaluation of the published opinions.

This has called for some arbitrary decisions on my part and no doubt some of these decisions will be proved wrong in the future. In some cases the material available for comment is inadequate for objective analysis; in other cases I disagree with the published or private opinions of colleagues whose views I respect. In a book of this kind the classification adopted must necessarily reflect the author's opinions and attitudes in contemporary systematic herpetology. Nevertheless, the reader is encouraged, via the bibliography, to enquire further into particular issues. I believe that the ultimate aim of any classification should be to reflect phylogeny — the evolutionary relationships of organisms — and as more genera and species groups are studied this objective will come closer to realisation.

However, this is not a book about classification, nor is it really concerned with either the relationships between the various genera and species described or the particular names to be applied to them. Indeed, as far as names are concerned, this edition, like the previous ones, will be out of date before it appears because the volume of research being undertaken on Australian frogs and reptiles is increasing so rapidly that name changes are likely to continue at a high rate for some considerable time.

What this guide does set out to do is to provide the means to identify most of the species of frogs and reptiles which are currently known from Australia. I would emphasise the distinction between names and species, because it puts scientific names into perspective. The name is important only as part of the language which enables us to communicate our concepts of the relationships between particular animals to other interested people; and although name changes may be made for other reasons, only name changes which result from the refinement of knowledge of Australian frog and reptile species will render this guide obsolete.

COMMON NAMES

Wherever common names have previously appeared in the literature for particular species, these names are given here, unless blatantly inappropriate; and because the nomenclature of Australian reptiles and frogs is in a state of flux (as a result of which one may expect numerous and frequent name changes in the near future) there is an obvious advantage in having a series of non-patronymic common names which can remain stable while scientific names fluctuate. However, because of the size of Australia, and the great variety of local names applied even to the same species, I have not attempted to construct common names where none have previously existed. Following the pattern established in other countries, it is to be hoped that Australian herpetological societies will ultimately compile and formalise a comprehensive list.

ILLUSTRATIONS

In previous editions, all photographs were numbered in a single series according to the sequence of their appearance in the book. However, in this edition all photographs of a particular species are labelled and located on the same or an adjacent page to that on which its description occurs.

Many of the photographs have been selected to demonstrate the range of variation in colour, pattern and form in any particular group and to illustrate the habitats in which they are found; to this end the majority of the photographs are of animals in their natural surroundings.

Line illustrations have been used to explain the terms and characters used in the keys and general text.

All photographs are by the author unless otherwise acknowledged. A list of those photographers who have generously made their photographs available for inclusion in this book is given in the Acknowledgments.

DISTRIBUTION

Although brief comments on distribution are made in the individual species accounts, the principle source of distributional information is the map provided for each species. These do not include spot records; they are intended only as a guide and range limits should be treated as approximations only.

Accurate distributional data are not available for the majority of Australian reptiles and frogs. If a species is found well outside the range shown in its map, one of two explanations is likely; either an interesting range extension has been recorded or the specimen has been misidentified. Both possibilities should be explored, preferably by forwarding the specimen(s) (if permitted), or full descriptions or photographs, to a specialist for confirmation.

One advantage of distribution maps is that they provide a convenient means of constructing tentative faunal lists for any given area. By tracing any map onto transparent paper, marking on it the locality or areas of interest and then using it as an overlay on the maps in the book a species list can be readily drawn up.

It should be emphasised that the distribution of a species is rarely continuous within the range shown on its map. Some species occur only among rocky outcrops, while others may be confined to patches of rainforest; the distribution of animals is a direct response to the numerous features which make up their physical and biological environments.

For terrestrial, ectothermic animals such as frogs and reptiles, distribution is governed by climatic factors, especially those of rainfall and temperature and more especially by vegetation patterns (which themselves constitute another correlate with the physical factors in the environment).

It is possible, therefore, to make generalisations and predictions about the distribution of reptiles and frogs in Australia, so long as one remembers that localised factors can override broader patterns. One should also remember that present distributions are the result not simply of today's climatic patterns but also of climatic conditions prevailing in earlier times.

As this book is concerned largely with identification, discussion of palaeo-climatology and the geographical relationships of different faunal assemblages (the field of zoogeography) would be out of place. Nevertheless these subjects are important to an understanding of the distribution and ecology of Australian reptiles and frogs and I have included references to these topics in the bibliography.

However, it is possible to broadly define a series of more or less common distribution patterns for reptiles and frogs and the maps on pp. 36–37 show a generalised vegetation map of Australia (modified from that in the *Atlas of Australian Resources)* and the twelve broad climatic zones recognised in Australia by Trewartha. By studying the distribution maps scattered throughout this book it can be seen that there is a very real tendency for species to be confined to particular life zones; many species range through more than one zone, and there is also a tendency for areas which are similar in climate and vegetation, but which are geographically isolated from one another, to contain distinct but related faunas.

Nevertheless, knowledge of the principle characteristics of these climatic and vegetation patterns will greatly assist the field herpetologist in studies of the distribution, ecology or biology of species occurring in any given region and the range maps should be used in conjunction with the notes on habits and habitats.

In the notes on distribution the following abbreviations are used for Australian States and Territories:

Qld	Queensland	Vic	Victoria
NT	Northern Territory	Tas	Tasmania
NSW	New South Wales	WA	Western Australia
SA	South Australia		

For the purposes of animal distribution the Australian Capital Territory is treated as an integral part of New South Wales, but has been abbreviated to ACT where necessary.

The term 'central Australia' is sometimes used to denote that central region of the continent which encompasses southern Northern Territory, northern South Australia and adjacent areas of Western Australia.

HABIT

This is not a book about the biology or ecology of the Australian herpetofauna, but merely an aid to its identification. Therefore, the items listed under Habit are intended to summarise only those features of a species' behaviour, ecology or biology which may assist in its identification in the field, or which may be of special interest to the observer.

SUBSPECIES

Professor John Moore once commented that '... a particular "species" category in frogs may occasionally be a fiction, but the "subspecies" is nearly always a myth'. He perhaps overstated the case, but I have largely adopted Moore's philosophy in compiling this book.

There are occasions when the subspecies category is the only one which fits a particular, well-defined situation, but more often than not (and this is specially true in Australia where samples tend to be small and widely scattered) the subspecies is a convenient substitute for lack of knowledge.

Nevertheless, I have given a list of the currently recognised subspecies at the end of each species account; the subspecies are not defined but are simply listed for those who might wish to investigate them further through the literature. Where a subspecies has not received universal or unequivocal acceptance it is not listed.

MAKING AN IDENTIFICATION

There are several ways to set about identifying a specimen. If you are unfamiliar with even the basic groups into which Australian reptiles fall, you should simply thumb through the illustrations until you find the animal that most closely resembles the one you wish to identify. Then check the description of the family (or genus) to which this species belongs and compare the characteristics of your specimen with the diagnostic description. If the family or generic description fits your specimen, then work through the following descriptions of genera or species until you find the one that fits your specimen. Once you have arrived at a decision, double-check your specimen by comparing it with the illustration(s) of the species you have determined (or the species nearest to it).

On the other hand, if your knowledge is sufficient to allow you to recognise immediately the family or genus to which your specimen belongs, go to the descriptions under that category and work through as in the preceding paragraph. Alternatively, once the genus or family grouping is known, you may prefer to look up the distribution maps for that particular group and then list the species known in the area from which your specimen comes. You can then compare your specimen with the descriptions of these species (or genera) to find the correct one, or at least the closest match.

The simplest method of identifying a specimen is to use the 'keys'. Biological keys appear frighteningly complex to people unfamiliar with them. While keys may require specialised knowledge of the scientific terms they contain, it is well worth the effort necessary to learn the meanings of the terms they contain. Unfortunately it is rarely possible to construct a key without using at least some difficult characters, but in this book all such characters are defined in the glossary and/or illustrated in the keys themselves. Let me assure any doubting reader that a little practice in using the keys will be rewarded by the rapid and accurate identification of most Australian reptiles and frogs.

The keys are known as dichotomous keys — that is, at every stage of identification you are presented with two alternate and contrasting characters, or character sets, only one of which should fit the specimen in front of you. If neither fits it maybe either that there is a fault in the key or that you have made an incorrect decision in an earlier couplet. On the other hand, if both of the alternate character sets appear to fit your specimen, again the key may be at fault, and your only option is to follow both paths in the key until you find a character which eliminates one path.

A more unlikely alternative, but a possibility which should not be overlooked, is that the specimen in your hands represents an undescribed species, or one which has been described since this book went to press. New species of reptiles and frogs will certainly continue to be found and described for many years to come, and for this reason, as I have already indicated, if the identity of a specimen is uncertain then either the specimen itself (where permitted) or its description/photograph should be submitted to a competent herpetologist for identification or confirmation.

When making an identification, the following points should always be considered:

1. Many reptiles and frogs are subject to considerable individual or geographic variation in colour and pattern. Although some attempt is made in the descriptions to cover the range of variation encountered, this is not possible in highly variable species. Also, in many species, the total variation is not yet known.
2. Many species show marked sexual dimorphism in colour, pattern, relative proportions and scalation. For example, females generally grow larger than males, males are usually more brilliantly coloured that females, and males tend to have longer tails.
3. There may be considerable differences between juveniles and adults in any given species. The descriptions normally refer to adult features, although known juvenile characteristics are included where known.
4. In many lizards the tail or digits may vary from those described. Regenerated tails may differ greatly from the original tails, especially in geckos, while digits are frequently lost in some groups of skinks.
5. A reptile which is about to shed its skin may undergo marked colour changes. Because the skin becomes cloudy or opaque the underlying pigments may appear different from those described and pattern details may be obscured.
6. Greatly complicating the problems of making identifications in some groups are so-called 'sibling' or 'biological' species. These are two or more species which are virtually identical in appearance (that is, in morphological characters), but which have usually been shown, by one or more of a variety of biochemical, genetic or behavioural techniques, to act towards each other as distinct species. Often, the discovery of such species points the way to physical differences which were previously overlooked, but in many cases the identification

> or differentiation of biological species is just not possible from physical observation or examination of the whole animal. Only when an observer can easily utilise the same character set that was originally used to differentiate the species (for example, the distinctive call of many frogs) is accurate identification possible.
> In the case of frog calls this can be done only when one is present where the frogs are breeding. Non-breeding males, all females and all preserved specimens are virtually unidentifiable. In such cases one can hope to do no more than place a particular specimen within a group of closely allied species .

Finally, the omission of the description of frogs' eggs, tadpoles and most calls is a serious one in a book which purports to provide the means of field identification. However, the eggs and tadpoles of surprisingly few Australian frog species are known in sufficient detail to allow specific identification. The descriptions of eggs and tadpoles, and the recording of the voices of all frog species, remain challenging projects for anyone interested in field studies.

CONSERVATION AND PROTECTION

Varying degrees of statutory protection for reptiles (and sometimes amphibians) now apply in all States and Territories of Australia. Before collecting and/or keeping reptiles or frogs, contact should be made with the appropriate State fauna protection authority to determine the current regulations.

The collection of reptiles and frogs can only be justified if their capture does not endanger the continued existence of wild populations and if the knowledge to be gained from their capture is likely to lead to a better understanding of their biology and ecology, and thus the ultimate management and/or survival of those populations.

Despite, or perhaps because of, a current Australian government ban on the export of native fauna, including reptiles and frogs (except specimens for scientific research), there is an apparently thriving smuggling operation, to judge from the variety and high price of Australian species on foreign pet dealers' lists.

However, with the possible exception of crocodiles and some marine turtles in northern Australia, and some very localised populations of lizards, frogs and tortoises elsewhere, reptile and frog populations in Australia are rarely endangered by direct human exploitation of the animals as a resource, that is, by hunting for skins or for pleasure, or by being captured alive for the local pet, or education market.

For most reptiles and frogs, ultimate survival will depend not on the formality of 'legal' statutory protection but on the survival of the environments in which they live. As I have already stated, Australia is a large country, with vast, untapped natural resources which are daily coming under pressure from developers and exploiters. While human populations continue to grow, so will demands to utilise untapped natural resources. However, more often than not such utilisation involves the irreversible destruction of natural environments, with the result that Australia (and the world) is rapidly losing its rich biotic diversity (biodiversity). Such a loss is of more than academic interest, and as it accelerates it will have catastrophic impacts on human quality of life and survivorship. For this reason, failure to preserve significant and viable samples of as many environments and habitats as possible for future generations is as morally wrong as it is economically myopic.

As yet few quantitative data on the effects of land use and management on populations of reptiles and amphibians are available. Much research is needed to provide the basic data that would allow adequate conservation measures to be determined. However, in a paper in which we examined the sources of reptile and frog mortality in Australia, Harry Ehmann and I conservatively estimated that as a result of the clearing of mallee for agriculture in South Australia and New South Wales over a recent fifteen year period, some 25 million reptiles and frogs were permanently eliminated from the Australian fauna.

I hope that increasing public concern over conservation issues will force both government and business sectors of the community to adopt more enlightened environmental policies, looking beyond short-term economic returns to the survival, welfare and enjoyment of future generations. There seems little reason for optimism.

Because only larger reptiles can be identified on sight, the great majority of reptiles and frogs must be taken in hand if an accurate identification is to be made. However, throughout most parts of Australia reptiles, and sometimes frogs, are protected fauna and it is illegal to interfere with them in any way unless appropriate permits have been obtained. Hence, the following section on the location of specimens, collecting methods, preservation of specimens and care of captive specimens are intended for students, field biologists and others whose work involves the authorised taking of reptiles and frogs for research purposes.

Once collected and identified they should be released back into the same area, unless wanted for later study. It is important that reptiles and frogs, once collected, not be released into areas in which they do not occur naturally; to do so not only seriously jeopardises an animal's chance of surviving, but can play havoc with future distribution records if it becomes established and/or is subsequently recaptured by another person.

LOCATION OF SPECIMENS

Due to the great diversity in habits and habitats of Australian reptiles and frogs, only broad, generalised comments can be made; specific information in the individual descriptions should assist in the search for particular species. While many reptiles will be observed when they are actively foraging or otherwise exploring their environment, most will seek shelter when disturbed or spend long periods of daily or seasonal inactivity in sheltered or protective microhabitats; at such times they have to be searched for in their hiding places.

Rocky environments often have a particularly rich reptile fauna. Apart from some species which live deep in rock crevices most will be found by lifting stones and rock slabs to find the reptiles sheltering under them. Where rocks lie on a deep bed of soil, particularly in arid zones, a garden weeding fork, or some other instrument (a thin, strong twig will do) should be used to rake through the soil under the rock for burrowing species.

Rocks should always be replaced as they were found. An area in which one is collecting should be left as undisturbed as possible as even limited collecting can result in major ecological and aesthetic disturbance of an area that may take years to recover, particularly in arid regions.

As any other cover — debris, logs, loose bark on standing or fallen trees, dense grasses or leaf litter, man-made rubbish tips, building rubble, sheets of timber or iron — may shelter reptiles or frogs, most species must be actively searched for in these situations.

Diurnal animals will usually flee or try to take cover when disturbed. Capturing these specimens is a matter of acquiring enough skill and speed. Goannas which may hide in burrows or hollow logs, or small skinks and dragons which retreat to burrows, may be chopped or dug out. Because many reptiles seek the advantage of roadside homes (loose and piled verge soil for burrows and perches; an open area for feeding and basking) a slow drive along a country road may prove very productive, especially in the early part of the morning.

Similarly, nocturnal reptiles and frogs (especially during or immediately after rain) are attracted to roads with a low traffic flow for residual warmth or open feeding space. They are more easily seen on dark, macadam roads.

Spotlighting is often a successful way of catching nocturnal species, particularly arboreal or aquatic animals. Except where eyeshine is present most species are located when they move. Movement of even small lizards and frogs in leaf litter can be readily heard or located. Driving slowly or walking with a torch or lamp through desert sandhills will usually allow the movement of even small lizards to be picked up, and they must be quickly captured before they can hide in porcupine grass or spinifex, or burrow into the sand.

Most frogs are nocturnal and are readily located by their calls. Breeding congregations produce a chorus which may be heard from a great distance. Many species are ventriloquial however, and individuals may prove extremely difficult to locate, despite the apparent proximity of the voice. In such cases a technique called triangulation will usually prove successful. Ideally, two or more people approach a calling frog from different directions; each faces the spot where he or she thinks the frog is calling and as they walk towards the sound their paths should meet where the frog is located (although they may have to search hard at this point). With torches, the point where the beams (which are pointed towards the call) intersect will be the spot where the frog is calling.

Triangulation can be carried out successfully alone, by taking bearings from two different positions. Practice will soon demonstrate the success of this technique which also depends on the frog's willingness to continue calling when approached or disturbed by light. The most wary frog, will, however, respond to a patient collector.

In sandy areas of Australia, especially in the arid interior, many reptiles and frogs can be located by their tracks. Direction can be determined by the imprint of a lizard's claws or by the build-up of sand on the hind edge of the curve of the track left by a snake or snake-lizard. Follow the tracks to a burrow opening or clump of *Triodia*. The tracks of nesting sea-turtles are obvious and well-known.

Australia's desert areas contain large numbers of burrowing reptiles, only some of which have permanent burrows with well-marked openings. The latter are usually found at the base of a shrub or spinifex clump, and lizard burrows are characterised by ⌂-shaped openings . These should not be confused with the ⌓-shaped opening which usually indicates the burrow of a large scorpion! Many lizards, such as sand-dwelling egernias, have burrow complexes with multiple tunnels, one of which is an escape tunnel which ends a fraction below the surface of the ground some distance away. A second person with a good view of the surroundings is a great help when digging out the burrows of such species.

Finally, some mention should be made of the use of a standard skin-diving mask, flippers and snorkel for locating and catching tortoises in swamps, rivers and lagoons. If the water is clear enough to permit reasonable visibility, this collecting technique is particularly successful and may be supplemented by the subsequent use of nets.

COLLECTING METHODS

A wide variety of collecting techniques can be used to capture reptiles and frogs but only experience in their use will allow the individual collector to assess the most applicable method in any given situation. The majority of smaller frogs and reptiles are literally pounced upon.

Equipment

The following items of equipment may be found useful at one time or another, when collecting or studying reptiles and frogs. Some are basic tools to be taken on all collecting trips, others may be needed only in special circumstances.

Snake sticks or jiggers come in many shapes and forms, each with its own merits. Experience alone will determine the one most suited to you. The simplest is an L-shaped metal angle attached to a strong but light metal or wooden handle about 1–1.5 metres long (page 33); this type of stick can be used not only for pinning down snakes, but also as a hook for lifting captive specimens, lifting light rocks, stripping dead bark from trees, etc. A T-shaped end (page 33) is also useful, but a Y-shaped end, the classic forked stick, is generally unsuitable. It is often convenient to have the end of the snake stick threaded into the handle, so that a variety of useful implements, including a range of angles, hooks or even nets, can be fitted into the one handle.

Pinchbars and crowbars are most useful in rocky environments, and may be the only means of opening up some of the deeper crevices inhabited by lizards. Their weight fortunately discourages extensive use, for they are particularly destructive of some environments and should be used only when no other method is practicable. They may also be used to move large logs, etc.

A shovel may be needed to dig some reptiles from their burrows, while a rake may be useful for sifting the soil beneath stones, logs, etc.

Nooses come in a great variety of forms and may be used to capture a wide range of species. The simplest one is made of cotton, nylon (fine fishing line is excellent) or very fine copper wire. A simple slip noose of any of these materials is attached at its free end to a handle (which may be a permanent piece of equipment, often a telescopic fishing rod, or simply a twig or branch picked up on the spot). The shank of the noose should be as short as possible to prevent it from twisting, being blown about or getting caught in surrounding vegetation. Such a noose is slipped slowly over a lizard's head (which rarely bothers the lizard — indeed it will often attempt to eat the noose!), then jerked upwards. Noosing is most successful with lizards which have a constricted neck and which are relatively heavy for their size, but most species can be captured this way, with practice. The larger the lizard the larger and stronger the noose required and a heavy nylon noose at the end of a telescopic fishing rod is useful for collecting large goannas, particularly arboreal ones.

A number of 'powered' nooses have been devised, and the one illustrated, which is powered by rubber bands, has been used very successfully for the capture of a wide range of small dragons, skinks, goannas, snake-lizards and small snakes. Anyone with a little ingenuity can come up with a design to suit a particular need.

Another noose (page 33) is a useful tool for handling large snakes and lizards in captivity; it is a very old design which has proved successful for many years. The noose itself is a broad strip of pliable leather.

Torches and headlamps are vital to successful collecting. A headlamp is by far the most desirable, as it leaves both hands free for collecting and allows many specimens to be located by their eyeshine. The light should be reasonably powerful (although very strong spotlights are generally undesirable) with a broad, even, central spot. Uneven or dead patches in the beam should be corrected.

Dry cells are the most convenient power source for torches, with the long life of alkaline batteries making them the preferred choice; the convenience and long-term cost benefits of nicad batteries are attractive, but their sudden loss of power when discharged makes it essential for both convenience and safety to have a spare set of batteries always on hand. Many collectors use light, modern, sealed wet-cell motorcycle batteries when recharging facilities are available. A 6 volt, 4 amp hour motorcycle battery will give many nights of use before its charge drops to a level which affects light output. The availability of solar panels or custom-made solar chargers now makes both nicad and wet cells practical power sources for long stints in the field.

Gas and pressure lamps light a wide area and are particularly useful in flat, open areas or when collectors need to share one light.

Nets may be used for a variety of tasks. Standard scoop nets on a long handle are useful for reaching frogs which call from aquatic vegetation or for collecting tadpoles. Seine, drum or gill nets are excellent for collecting chelid tortoises, but the latter two must be checked frequently to prevent the tortoises (or sometimes water rats or platypuses) from drowning. Indeed, the use of nets usually requires special permits and the State Fisheries Department should be consulted before attempting any kind of netting.

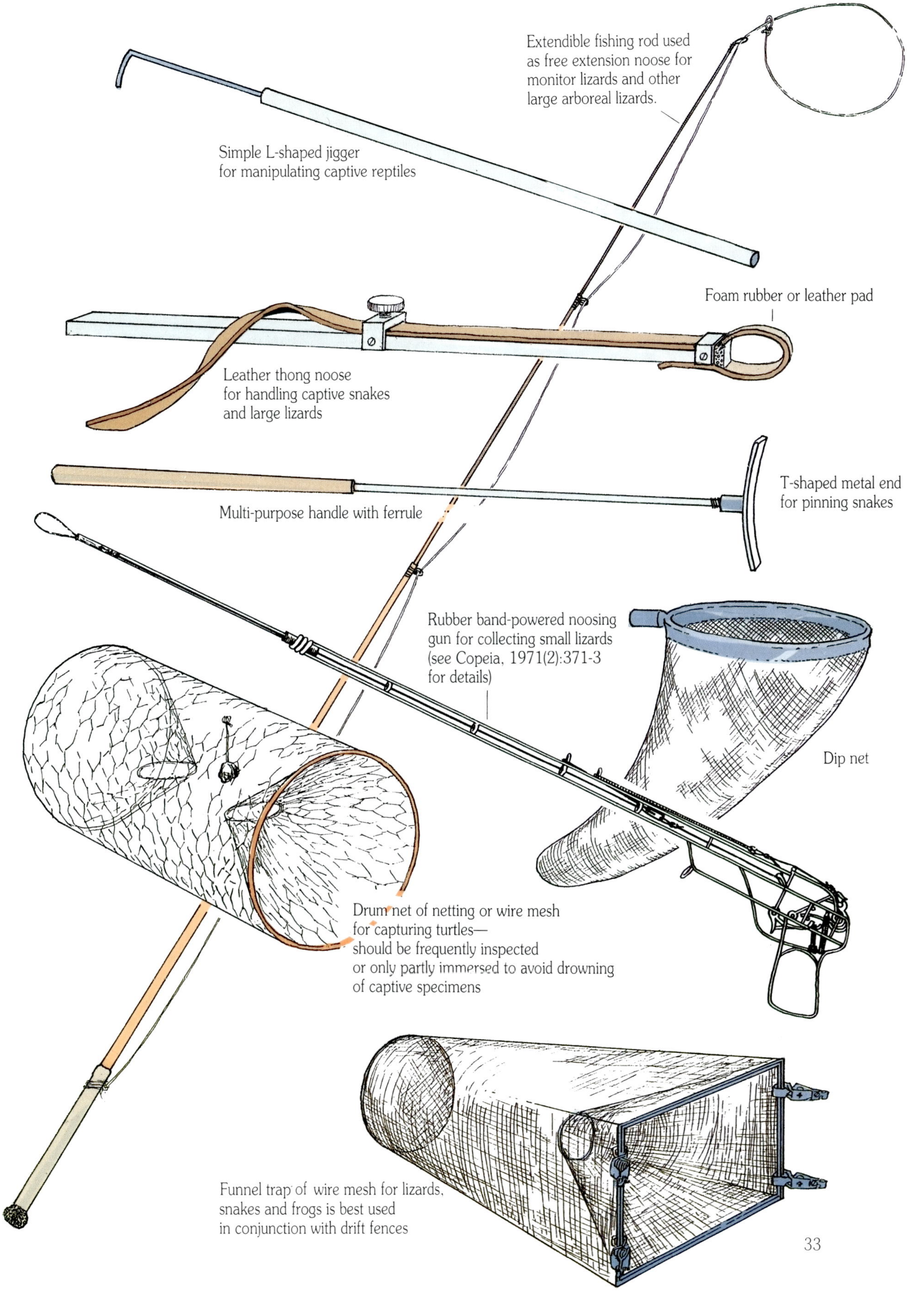
Extendible fishing rod used
as free extension noose for
monitor lizards and other
large arboreal lizards.
Simple L-shaped jigger
for manipulating captive reptiles
Foam rubber or leather pad
Leather thong noose
for handling captive snakes
and large lizards
T-shaped metal end
for pinning snakes
Multi-purpose handle with ferrule
Rubber band-powered noosing
gun for collecting small lizards
(see Copeia, 1971(2):371-3
for details)
Dip net
Drum net of netting or wire mesh
for capturing turtles—
should be frequently inspected
or only partly immersed to avoid drowning
of captive specimens
Funnel trap of wire mesh for lizards,
snakes and frogs is best used
in conjunction with drift fences

Locality Map

Contintental Australia and Tasmania lie between latitudes 10°S and 44°S, and longitudes 113°E and 154°E. They have a total area of 7,682,300 square kilometres and a coastline extending for 36,735 km.

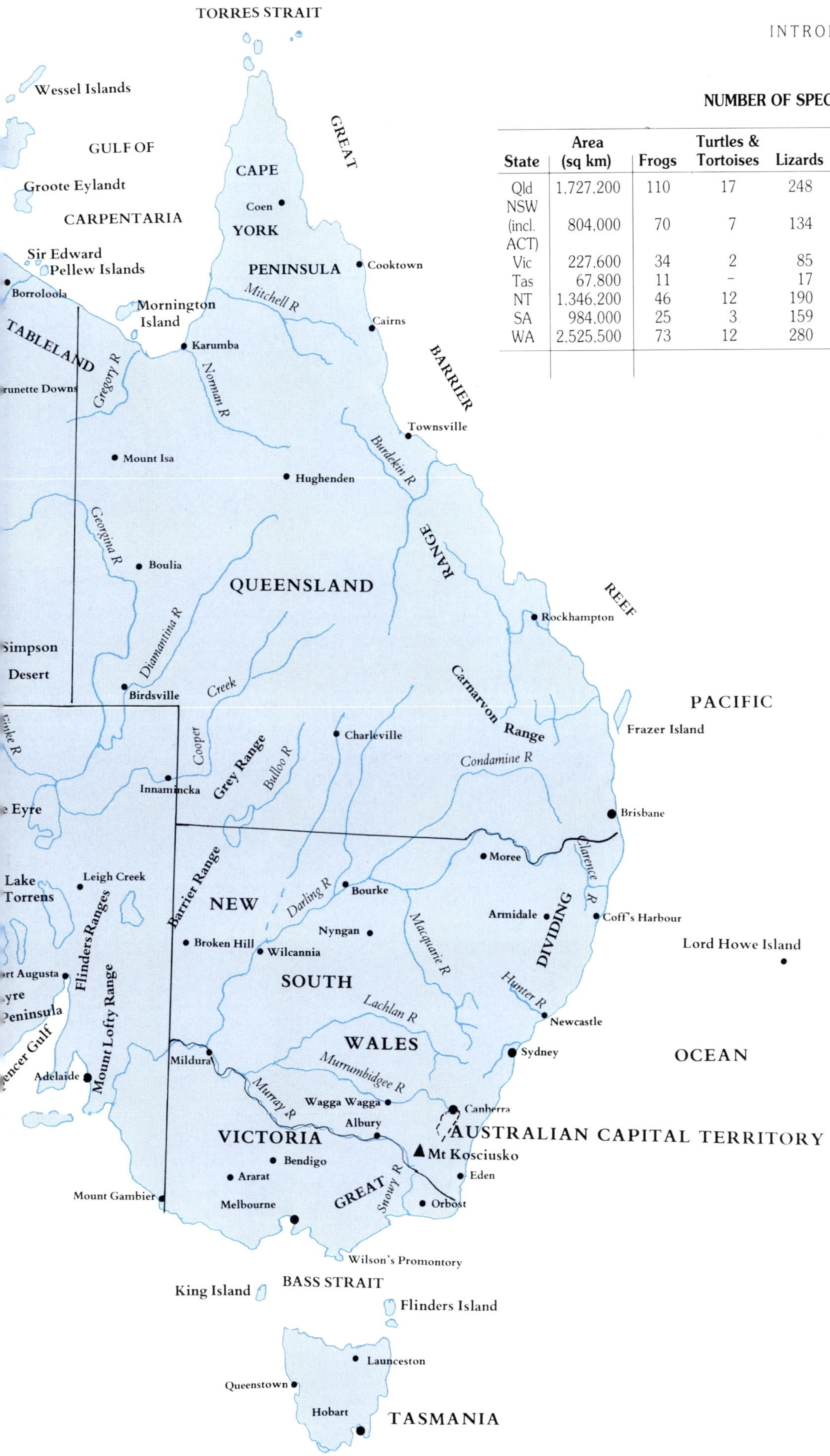

NUMBER OF SPECIES

State	Area (sq km)	Frogs	Turtles & Tortoises	Lizards	Snakes	Crocodiles
Qld	1,727,200	110	17	248	107	2
NSW (incl. ACT)	804,000	70	7	134	56	–
Vic	227,600	34	2	85	27	–
Tas	67,800	11	–	17	3	–
NT	1,346,200	46	12	190	82	2
SA	984,000	25	3	159	43	–
WA	2,525,500	73	12	280	98	2

Vegetation and Climatic Zones

Simplified map of Australia's present vegetation, based on the Third Series of the *Atlas of Australian Resources* (AUSLIG, 1990). Note the large areas now modified for use as pasture and cropping lands, within which many species of frogs and reptiles are mostly restricted to patches of remnant native vegetation.

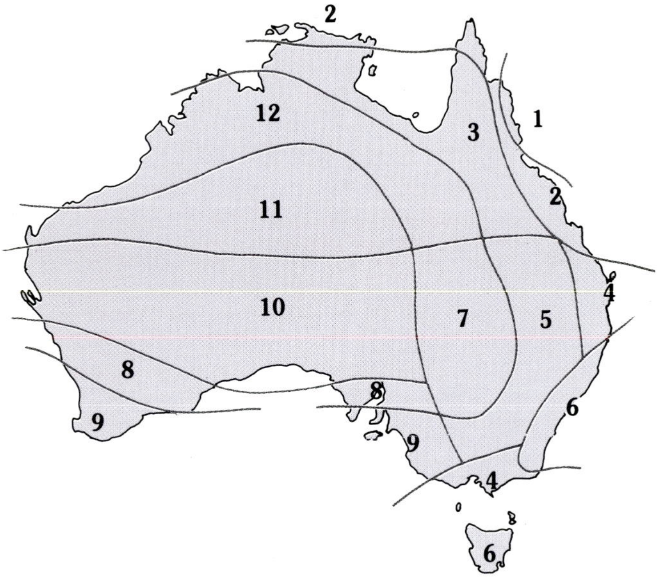

CLIMATIC ZONES

1 Wet; tropical; rainfall abundant in all seasons
2 Humid; tropical; rainfall deficient in winter
3 Sub-humid; tropical; rainfall deficient in winter
4 Sub-humid; mesothermal; rainfall abundant in all seasons
5 Sub-humid; mesothermal; rainfall deficient in all seasons
6 Humid; mesothermal; rainfall abundant in all seasons
7 Semi-arid; mesothermal; rainfall deficient in all seasons
8 Semi-arid; mesothermal; rainfall deficient in summer
9 Sub-humid; mesothermal; rainfall deficient in summer
10 Arid; mesothermal; rainfall deficient in all seasons
11 Arid; tropical; rainfall deficient in all seasons
12 Semi-arid; tropical; rainfall deficient in winter

VEGETATION TYPES

Closed forest
Open forest
Woodland
Open woodland
Scrub & Heath

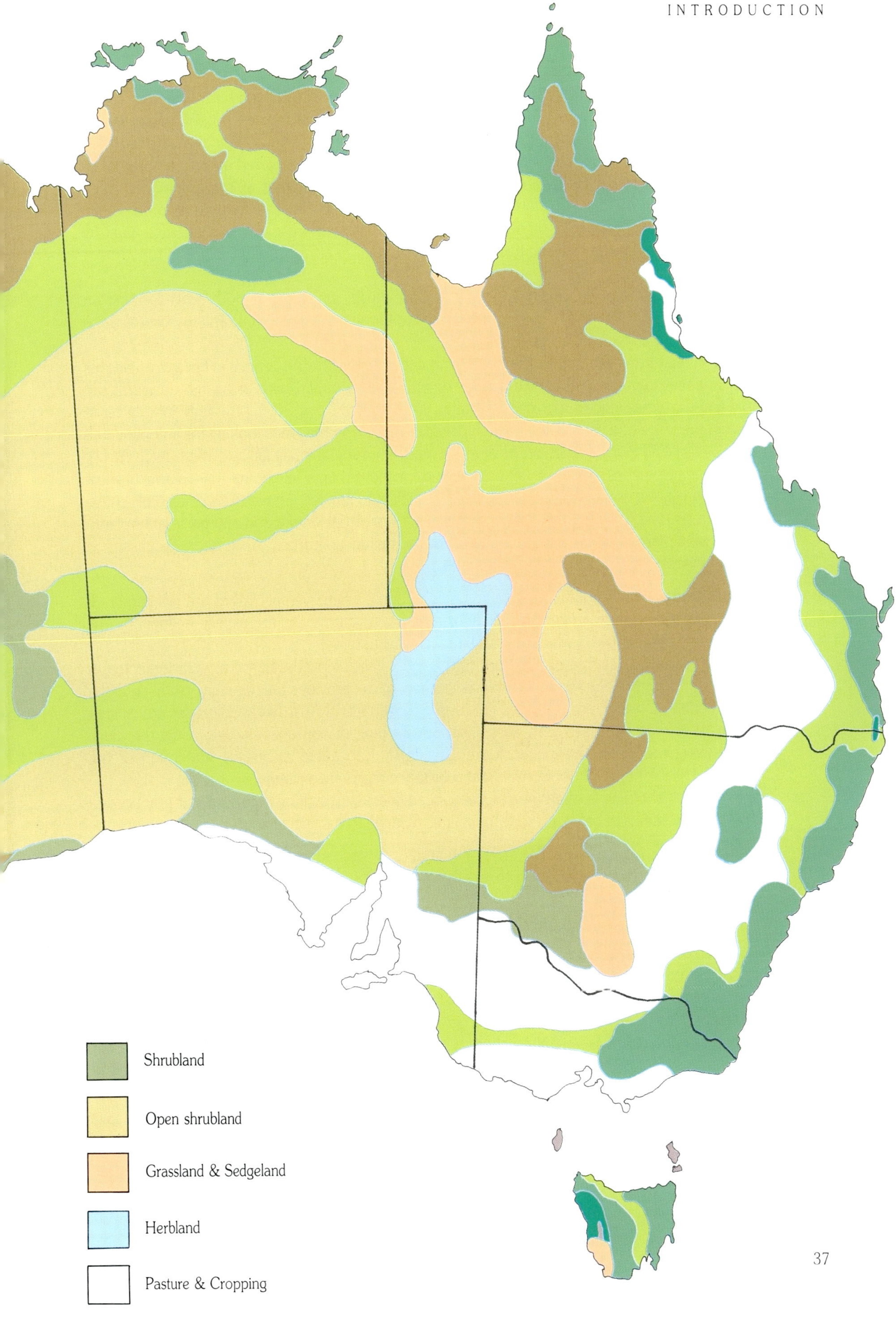
Shrubland
Open shrubland
Grassland & Sedgeland
Herbland
Pasture & Cropping

Traps are seldom used to collect reptiles and frogs except where long-term field studies are being carried out in particular areas. In such cases pit-traps are most frequently used, which vary in size with the species to be caught. Pit-traps generally consist of jars, tins or drums which are buried in the ground with their lips flush with the surface. The openings are covered by a slightly raised lid or stone or other object to keep out predators and prevent trapped animals from becoming overheated (during the day) or drowned (when it rains). To be effective they need to be placed along known 'runs'. The animal simply falls into the trap and can't escape, so that traps must be checked frequently. Pit-traps can be baited with fruit or meat to attract insects, which in turn attract lizards.

Funnel-traps made of solid metal, plastic or wire-mesh, with one or both ends forming an inwards-directed cone (page 39), are very useful in capturing many kinds of lizards or snakes. Like pit-traps, they can be baited if necessary.

Pit-and funnel-traps are most often used in conjunction with drift fences. These are variable lengths of sheet metal or plastic, wire mesh or bituminised paper, with one edge buried in the ground and the whole fence supported by stakes. Reptiles and frogs moving through an area come up against the fence and, finding their way blocked, move along the fence looking for an opening. If pit-traps are placed along the fence, or at either end, then the animals fall into them (with luck!). Neither traps nor fences should be left unattended for more than a few hours. Live mammal traps may occasionally be used effectively to capture lizards and snakes. I have used small, collapsible Sherman traps to collect small diurnal and nocturnal terrestrial skinks in many parts of northern Australia, while large 'bandicoot' or 'possum' traps, baited with meat, have been successful in capturing several of the larger species of goannas.

Pistols and rifles are both useful in some conditions, when live specimens are not required. Solid .22 bullets fired from a rifle will usually bring down a goanna and are usually needed for any large arboreal snake or lizard, which cannot be reached otherwise.

However, it is .22 dust shot or 'rat' shot that is most valuable to the herpetological collector. A multiple shot .22 pistol is the most desirable as its short barrel provides the optimum grouping of the fine shot; pistols, however, are restricted firearms in most parts of Australia and licenses are difficult to obtain. A rifle can be used with dust shot, but its bulk discourages its use, while the close grouping associated with the longer barrel means that to avoid excessive mutilation of the specimen, a collector must shoot from a greater distance than with a pistol.

Nevertheless, shooting is often the only way some specimens can be collected and practice will enable even tiny skinks to be collected with minimal damage to the specimen.

Wading boots are invaluable for collecting aquatic frogs, tadpoles, tortoises and even some swamp-dwelling snakes and lizards. Thigh length boots may be necessary in some situations.

A tape recorder has become an almost essential piece of equipment for the serious herpetologist. The male call is now widely used in the identification of frogs and although the calls of our more common species are well known, the majority have yet to be recorded. Although the quality of recording (and hence the recorder) is important for sonographic analysis, a relatively inexpensive tape recorder will suffice for the average collector, who should also learn to recognise species by call.

Many frogs stop calling when approached so that locating them can be difficult. A tape recorder can be used to encourage such wary specimens to continue calling in response to the playback of the pre - recorded call of the same species, or even the same individual.

Rubber bands have been used by many collectors to stun lizards and frogs. One end of a heavy-duty elastic band, or a band cut from a motor cycle or car inner tube, is held between finger and thumb, then the other end is pulled back with the finger and thumb of the other hand. When released the band (which, with practice, can be aimed with surprising accuracy) flies forward with a force quite sufficient to stun, or even kill, small to moderate lizards. Practise at home with matchboxes lined up in a row! Catapults, using small pebbles as projectiles, can be used for larger lizards such as arboreal goannas.

Containers for live specimens should be chosen on the basis of the numbers of specimens they are to hold and the period of time that specimens will be held in them. Containers for preserved specimens are discussed in the next section.

The most practical temporary containers to use for carrying specimens from field to home or laboratory are calico sacks and plastic bags. For very large specimens such as goannas, pythons or the larger elapids, heavy canvas sacks are preferred, but those made of jute may be used when no others are available. However, jute is generally undesirable because it is less firmly woven, increasing the risk of escape, while its coarse fibres may catch in teeth or claws and damage them.

For the majority of reptiles, sacks made of high-quality, unbleached calico are ideal. The fabric or newly made bags should be washed before use to remove any sizing. The bags should be sewn with French seams (so that they do not fray), and should be two and a half to three times deeper than wide, with a long tie-tape sewn into the side seam at least 10 centimetres below the opening. Drawstrings through a seam around the opening are undesirable and unsafe. These sacks are suitable for all reptiles and frogs, though they should always be kept moist when holding frogs. It is better to hang heavy specimens from a hook or rod, rather than lie them flat and risk packing heavy specimens on top of smaller, delicate ones.

Plastic bags may be used for small lizards and snakes but are not as suitable as cloth bags. They are most suitable for frogs (essential for tadpoles or eggs), for unlike cloth they do not need constant wetting. However, specimens in plastic bags are very susceptible to high temperatures and specimens are easily killed. Moist cloth sacks, on the other hand, are cooled by evaporation and are preferable in hot weather; however, remember that dry cloth sacks act as sponges which can rapidly desiccate and kill frogs and small lizards.

Any clean plastic, glass or metal container is suitable for transporting reptiles and frogs, providing that ventilation is adequate. This can be achieved by drilling a series of small holes in the lid of the container (from the inside to the outside to avoid rough edges) or by tying a cloth over the opening.

All containers should include some light packing material — dry grass, leaf litter, newspaper or paper towelling for reptiles, moss, moist leaf-litter or slightly dampened paper towelling for frogs — to separate specimens when two or more are placed in the same container.

Transporting Specimens

Following are a few hints for collectors when transporting specimens.

1. Never leave specimens or their containers in sunlight.
2. Never overcrowd specimens in their containers, particularly frogs which have toxic secretions.
3. Don't mix specimens of disparate sizes — the larger specimens may actively kill or eat smaller specimens, or simply crush them with their greater weight.
4. To avoid deaths from desiccation, wet down bags containing frogs, small lizards, snakes or tortoises frequently. This is especially important in hot weather.
5. Bags or other containers holding frogs, or even the frogs themselves, should be washed frequently to avoid any build-up of toxins or nitrogenous waste products.
6. Tortoises may seriously damage or scar each other's shells unless each animal is kept in an individual container.
7. Frogs' eggs or tadpoles can be killed by the mechanical action of water sloshing in the container while travelling. To avoid sloshing leave a minimum air space above the water in the jar or plastic bag.
8. Never leave specimens in a stationary vehicle which is standing in the sun, especially when the vehicle is closed. Store all containers (in a low carton or box for convenience) under the vehicle

if stopped for any length of time. Polystyrene cool boxes make excellent containers for storing live specimens.

9. Label all containers with details of their contents, localities, dates of collection, etc. Tie-on labels are undesirable as they are easily detached. Cloth bags should have data written on them directly with a ballpoint pen. When the bags are used again the data can be crossed out and new data added or the writing can usually be removed with methylated spirits. Write on plastic bags with a permanent felt marker pen. A roll of masking tape supplies a seemingly endless number of labels for solid containers, on which data can be written with a ballpoint or felt-tipped pen.
10 Check that all containers are properly closed or sealed. Use two bags, one tied independently within the other, when transporting venomous snakes.
11. Always wash your hands after collecting frogs. Many of their secretions are toxic. If contaminated hands come in contact with eyes or mouth the effect can be painful and distressing.
12. It may be necessary to take along light but sturdy cages for storage of live specimens on an extended field trip.

PRESERVATION OF SPECIMENS

Four distinct stages should be involved in the preservation of specimens.

Killing

All reptiles, large and small, can be killed painlessly by putting them in the freezing compartment of a refrigerator. As the temperature drops they lose mobility and their metabolic rate drops. They subsequently freeze. This method is particularly humane and convenient with tortoises, large lizards and snakes.

Frogs and tadpoles can be killed quickly and painlessly by anaesthetizing them in an 0.5 per cent solution of chlorbutol (chlorotone) or an 0.5 per cent solution of MS 222 (trisodium metasulphonate). Specimens can be left in the latter solution for some time without danger, but the chemical is restricted, expensive and rapidly rendered ineffective by light. Chlorotone, on the other hand, is stable, inexpensive and readily available, but specimens should not be left in the solution any longer than necessary to immobilise them, or they may become set.

All reptiles can be anaesthetized and killed by an injection of sodium pentobarbitone in the region of the heart. But because this drug in normally restricted, it may be necessary to use chloroform. Place the specimen to be killed in a sealable glass or metal container and drop in a paper handkerchief moistened with chloroform. Specimens killed with chloroform must be watched carefully as this anaesthetic can cause muscle contractions and permanent distortion of the specimens.

Labelling

This is a vital stage of preservation and should never be omitted. *Never* rely on your memory for information associated with a particular specimen.

Labels should be of good quality, heavy rag-based paper, doubled where threaded to prevent tearing, and tied securely to the specimen with linen thread. Writing should be in black waterproof ink or HB pencil. Data should include precise locality and date of collection. Collector's name, habitat notes, etc., may be included. Many collectors tie only a number (modern plastic embossing tapes are excellent for this purpose) to the specimen and write the associated data in a field register. The first method is preferred as there is no danger of the data being separated from the specimens, but if large numbers of specimens are involved the second procedure is the only practical one.

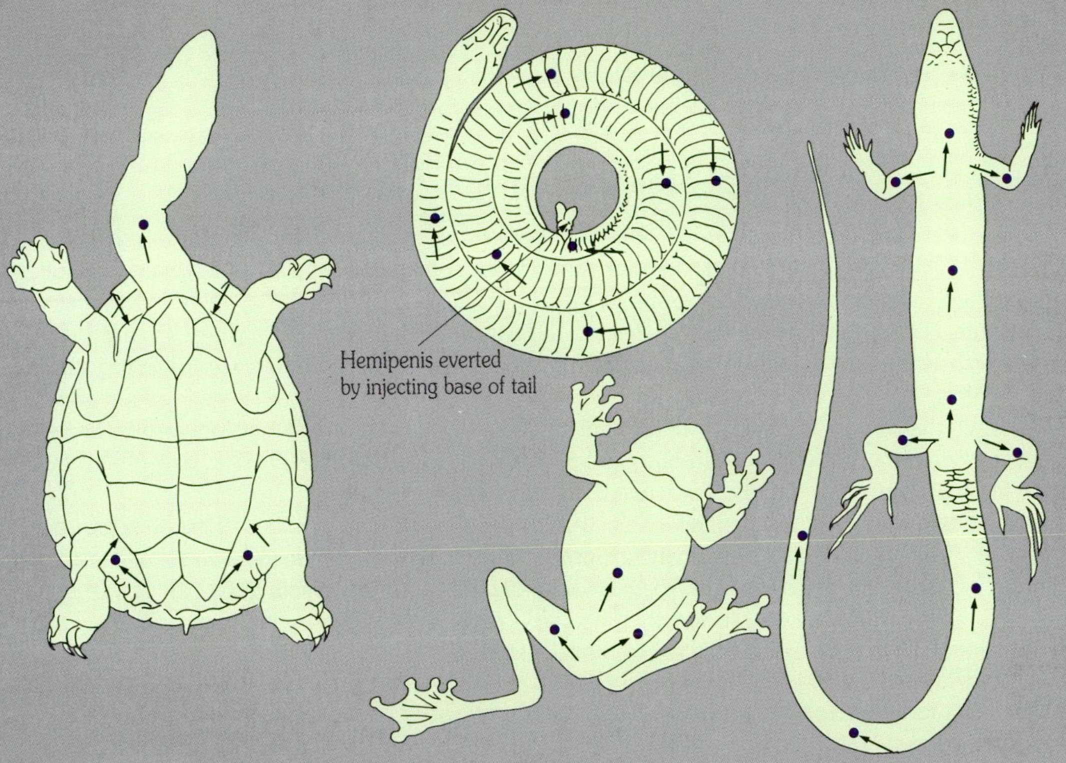

Suggested injecting points and final setting positions for frogs, turtles, lizards and snakes; final fixation should take place with dorsal surface uppermost.

Setting and Fixing

Once killed all specimens should be injected with a 10 per cent formalin solution using a syringe with an appropriate size of needle. The visceral cavity and tail (where appropriate) are the principal injection points, although larger specimens may require injection in the limbs, throat and thoracic cavities. Do not over-inflate and thus distort the specimen. Snakes should be injected at numerous points along their length. Species in which oral characters are important (such as skinks and tortoises) should have their mouths held open by a twig, match or small cork. If injection equipment is not available, a line of longitudinal slits should be cut along the belly and tail to allow fixative to reach the tissues. All specimens should then be set in the most desirable position for later examination and study. To do this, specimens should be laid out in a deep tray on paper towelling saturated with 10 per cent formalin. While still flexible they should be set in the desired position. Setting positions are subject to individual preference, but some typical positions are shown. Reptile hemipenes, which are often of considerable taxonomic interest, can usually be everted by injecting preservative into the base of the tail behind the hemipenes.

After injection, specimens are covered by another layer of paper saturated with formalin, then a cover placed over the tray. After a few hours (for small lizards and frogs) or a day or more (for larger goannas and snakes) the specimens can be removed and immersed in the final fixative. Frogs' eggs and tadpoles go directly into the final fixative and do not go through a setting stage. Incidentally, the setting of specimens, although desirable, is not an essential part of the preservatior process, and may be omitted if time or facilities are inadequate.

Fixing of most specimens will occur during the setting process. Larger specimens may require further immersion of one to several days in 10–15 per cent formalin solution.

Final preservation and storage

This is best carried out in 60–65 per cent ethyl alcohol (for frogs), 70 per cent ethyl alcohol (for geckos) and 75 per cent ethyl alcohol for other reptiles. Because supplies of ethyl alcohol are restricted, commercial methylated spirits may be used in the above strength with less than optimum, but nevertheless satisfactory, results. Dilution of methylated spirits may result in unsightly clouding (which does not affect preservation). Methylated spirits also tends to make specimens hard and brittle.

An alternative final solution is 7–10 per cent formalin, which gives very satisfactory results. Some workers prefer a simple formol-alcohol solution consisting of approximately 9 1/2 parts of alcohol (at the appropriate dilution) to 1/2 part of full-strength formalin solution.

Long-term storage in unbuffered formalin can result in serious decalcification of the body tissues and so if formalin is chosen for permanent storage it is best used in a formol-calcium solution made up as follows: 1 part of full strength (approximately 40 per cent) formalin solution, 1 part of a 10 per cent solution of anhydrous calcium chloride and 8 parts of water; then add powdered calcium sulphate to the mixture until a slight excess remains undissolved.

Frogs' eggs and tadpoles should never be preserved in alcohol, but should be fixed and stored in 5 per cent formalin. Tyler has recommended the following solution for tadpole preservation, but it may be necessary to dilute the solution by up to 50 per cent for the satisfactory preservation of some larvae: formalin (full strength),10 millilitresl; 10 per cent aqueous solution, anhydrous calcium chloride, 4 millilitres; distilled water, 90 millilitres; and cobalt nitrate, 0.2 grams.

Specimens can be stored in any glass or plastic container with an efficient seal. Metal containers should be avoided as they will ultimately be corroded by the preservative. Metal capped jars should never be used for the same reason. Even a slightly inefficient seal will result in evaporation of the preservative, so that containers should be checked regularly and topped up where necessary. This applies especially to small containers.

CAPTIVE SPECIMENS

This subject is largely beyond the scope of this book, for the housing and feeding of frogs and reptiles requires an infinite variety of special considerations depending on the species to be maintained. Some species are such specialised feeders that it is not practicable to keep them; certainly, it is important to try to ascertain the food requirements of a particular specimen or species before attempting to keep it in captivity. Several excellent books on this subject are listed in the Selected References (page 747). However, a few general comments on caring for captive specimens may be helpful.

Frogs

Glass aquaria, large glass jars and the great variety of plastic dishes, bowls and trays available from supermarkets and hardware stores all constitute satisfactory cages for frogs — the size of container depending on the size and number of its intended inmates. In general, the kind of environment set up in the cage should mirror, as closely as possible, the habitat of the species to be maintained. Burrowing species should have at least 10 centimetres depth of moist (not wet) soil or sand, while ground-dwelling species need less soil but adequate leaf-litter, rocks, bark or hollow branches in which to hide. Arboreal or climbing species should be supplied with branches or living plants. Potted plants are specially convenient as they can be kept healthy by alternating them between cage and garden.

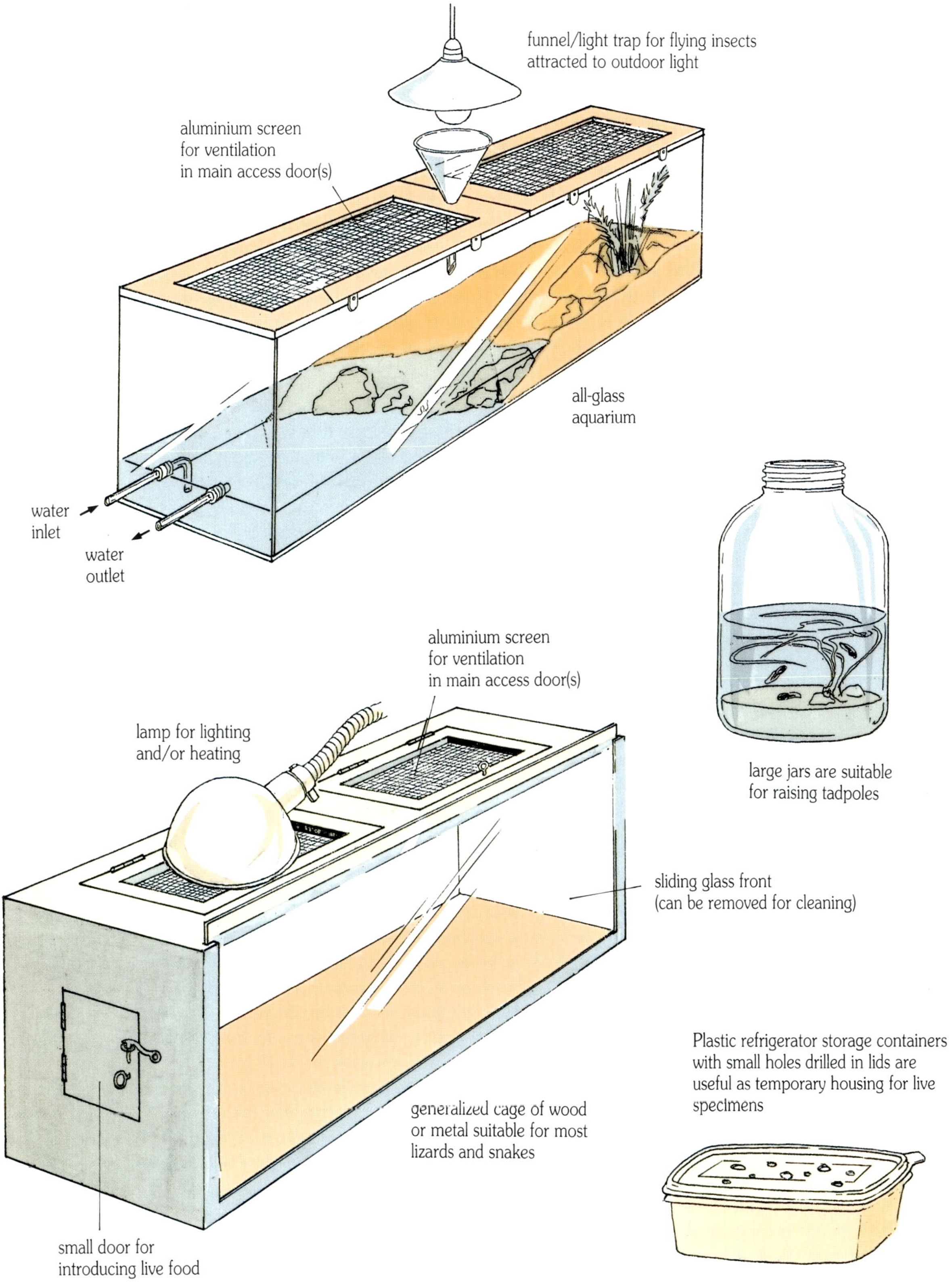

These illustrations are intended only as a source of ideas—the size, shape and internal fittings of individual cages should reflect the specific needs of the animals being housed.

The cage should be sprayed with water from time to time, preferably with a garden hand-held spray which gives a fine mist; a glass or earthenware dish of water should be sunk into the soil with its lip at ground level, replacing the water as necessary to keep it fresh. An alternative system allows the water to be changed regularly: lead polythene tubing from a domestic water tap to a hole in the aquarium, with an outlet or overflow hose at the desired level; both holes can be sealed with corks or rubber stoppers when the water is not being changed. Such a system often stimulates the activity and appetite of the cage's inhabitants, and prevents the build-up of nitrogenous waste products in the water.

Most frogs will feed only on living prey such as worms and insects. An adequate food supply for one or two frogs can be caught by hand, but for larger numbers of specimens the quantity of food required will necessitate either the breeding of food or the use of traps. Mealworms (the larvae of tenebrionid beetles), blowflies, ferment flies *(Drosophila)*, crickets and termites are all relatively easy to breed in captivity.

The simplest insect trap is a large plastic funnel over which a bright light is hung out-of-doors at night. Insects attracted to the light fall into the funnel, the neck of which can drop into a collecting jar (containing dry grass or crumpled paper to stop insects killing or crushing each other) or directly into the frog cage. Such a trap will provide a plentiful supply of food for a large number of frogs throughout the year in tropical Australia, or throughout the summer in southern Australia.

A generalised frog cage with circulating water system and light trap is shown on page 43.

Raising tadpoles is rarely difficult. Shallow dishes or aquaria are most suitable, with well-cured water, preferably from the tadpole collection site. Avoid overcrowding and high temperatures. Feed the tadpoles on algae from natural ponds, or on boiled lettuce or spinach, though some species, especially when nearing metamorphosis, will require small pieces of lean, raw meat. A projecting rock or piece of wood should be supplied for emerging, metamorphosed froglets, while the container needs to be screened to prevent their escape.

Crocodiles

Few private collectors can cope with the requirements of crocodiles in captivity. Although hatchlings will live and feed in large aquaria and ponds, they rarely thrive and their growth is usually stunted. Captive crocodiles are usually fed on raw meat or on live or dead fish.

Turtles and Tortoises

Although hatchling sea-turtles make attractive aquarium pets, they rarely thrive or grow unles offered spacious ponds with circulating seawater. They can generally be maintained only with expensive, specialised equipment.

Freshwater turtles and tortoises generally do well in captivity. Australian species are largely carnivorous and should be fed on chopped raw fish or meat in captivity. Young specimens can be kept successfully in glass aquaria; they should be fed as often as they will take food (seldom or not at all in winter in the south of Australia). The water should be changed whenever itis fouled by decaying food or the animal's excretory products. A built-in water-changing system as described for frogs is ideal.

Larger specimens are best kept in ponds out of doors, provided that the local climate is compatible with that of their native environment; the larger the pond the less risk of the water becoming fouled. A fenced area (with wood, metal or fibro-cement — not wire) surrounding the pond, provided with adequate shade and shelter, gives optimum conditions. Inexpensive, plastic children's swimming pools make excellent homes for freshwater tortoises.

Lizards

Australian lizards vary so greatly in size and habit that it is difficult to give general recommendations for their feeding and housing. Most smaller species (up to about 20 centimetres) are insectivorous. They may be kept in glass aquaria or metal or wooden cages, the design and size of which should be determined by the species being maintained. Cages should have adequate ventilation (without draughts), should generally be dry and easy to clean, and need to have easy and adequate access (without a high risk of escape). Several simple designs are shown on page 43. In general, the height of the cage is unimportant for terrestrial species, whereas taller cages are needed for arboreal species.

The interior of the cage should be set up according to the habitat in which the lizards are found — sand, dry timber and leaves for desert species, moist soil and plants for species from wetter, forested regions. Diurnal species usually require some sunlight (although overheating of the cage must be avoided), whereas nocturnal species can be placed in poorly lit areas. Different species can be kept together provided that their eating habits or relative sizes and aggressiveness are not incompatible; obviously it is absurd to place predator and prey species together.

For larger lizards such as goannas and the larger dragons and skinks, outdoor enclosures are preferable to cages when the lizard comes from a climatic zone similar to that in which the enclosure is situated. Large metal-, brick-or concrete-walled 'pits' (old above-ground swimming pools are excellent), preferably with a wire cover to keep out predators such as cats and kookaburras, are the most popular kind of outdoor enclosure. However if the walls are of a material that the lizards can climb, then either a cover or a continuous inward-projecting overhang are necessary to prevent escapes. Some lizards thrive in all-wire, aviary-type enclosures; however, care should be taken when choosing mesh size, to ensure the lizards cannot escape or injure themselves. All enclosures should contain a pool of water, living vegetation and a sufficient quantity of rock piles, hollow logs, etc., where lizards can hide and shelter from the weather.

Food requirements of lizards are as varied as might be expected in a group displaying such a wide variety of form, habits and size. Most smaller species are insectivorous and require an ample supply of live insects; their needs can be met in the same way as frogs' needs (described earlier). Many of the larger skinks (shingle-backs, blue-tongues, etc.) are omnivorous, feeding in captivity on chopped raw meat, fresh and dried fruits, snails and flowers such as dandelions and clover. Some of the larger dragons also eat meat. Larger captive goannas usually feed readily on raw chopped meat and raw eggs.

Snakes

Housing requirements of snakes are similar to those of lizards except that as a general rule snakes should be kept under very dry conditions. This does not mean that they should be deprived of water — a dish of water should always be available — but that the floor of the cage should be kept clean and dry. Burrowing species are exceptions and should be kept in aquaria with several centimetres of moist sand or soil.

The optimum size and shape of a cage will depend on the size and habit of the captive specimens. Smaller elapid snakes usually thrive in a cage with a floor area up to 1 metre by 0.5 metre, but pythons and larger elapids require at least two to three times this floor area per specimen. Cages for arboreal species should always be about twice as high as long. Snakes, especially venomous species, should be kept away from children and in a secure area which can be locked in the owner's absence. Each individual cage should be solidly constructed and designed with the escapological habits of snakes always in mind, and with locks on all individual cage doors. Keeping venomous snakes in captivity places a great responsibility on the keeper and should not be undertaken lightly. All wire ventilators and covers should be high in the cage where the snakes are not likely to injure themselves by rubbing their snouts.

Most snakes feed only on live prey — from frogs and small lizards to large birds and mammals — and for this reason the maintenance of snakes in captivity places a considerable burden on their keeper in collecting or breeding special food items. Often, the only acceptable food items (small skinks for example) for a particular species of snake, may themselves be protected fauna. In general, only those species that will feed on laboratory mice or rats, or on abundant species of frogs, should be kept in captivity.

It is beneficial to add a multi-vitamin supplement to the diet of all captive reptiles and frogs, preferably on a regular weekly basis. This can be done by adding liquid vitamin supplement to the drinking water, or by periodically placing a drop of the concentrate in the animal's mouth.

SNAKEBITE AND ITS TREATMENT

Although this subject is really beyond the scope of this book, a brief outline is not out of place in an identification manual which may on occasion be used under field conditions.

Snake venom is essentially a complex mixture of proteins, the mixture varying considerably from species to species or family to family. Not all components of snake venom have been studied, or their actions understood, but the major components have been placed into the following broad categories, largely according to their effects:

- *Haemorrhagins* destroy the linings of blood vessels, allowing blood to escape into the surrounding tissues.
- *Haemolysins* destroy red blood cells.
- *Neurotoxins* act on the nervous system, usually causing death by asphyxiation when the nerves controlling the heart and lungs are put out of action.
- *Myotoxins* destroy skeletal muscle which results in the release of the muscle protein *myoglobin,* which in large concentrations can cause kidney failure by blocking the kidney tubules.
- *Thrombase* causes the blood to clot in the blood vessels.
- *Cytolysins* destroy the cells of the blood or those of any other tissues with which they come in contact.
- *Anticoagulins* retard the clotting of blood.

There are several other constituents which, though important, do not usually play a significant role in the dangerously toxic effects of snakebite. They include various enzymes which are important in preparing a snake's food for digestion.

Nor are all of the above components necessarily present in the venom of a particular species. All dangerous Australian snakes are members of the families Elapidae, Laticaudidae and Hydrophiidae, groups with venoms characterised by being particularly rich in neurotoxins, so that their major effect is on the nervous system. Nevertheless, there is considerable variation in the composition (and hence the toxic effects) of Australian snake venoms.

The most modern and effective treatment of snakebite involves the use of snakebite sera (antivenoms or antivenenes). Basically, these are prepared by injecting a horse with gradually increasing doses of venom over a period of time. The initial doses are too small to do the horse any harm. In this way the horse builds up an immunity to the venom by producing antibodies in its blood which destroy the venom. The serum from such a horse is refined to produce an antivenene.

Unfortunately, many people suffer an allergic reaction, of varying severity, to the horse serum which is the basis of the antivenene. A patient is normally tested for allergy to the serum before being given a normal dose, but in snakebite emergencies there is not always time for this precaution. As reaction to the serum can result in fatal anaphylaxis, it is essential that antivenene be administered by a medical practitioner who will be prepared to deal with any shock reactions that develop.

In recent years techniques of partial immunisation against snakebite have been developed and used in some countries, while the production of monoclonal antibodies to individual toxins in snake venom has been achieved in a number of laboratories; when commercial production of these immunoglobulins occurs, horse serum-based antivenoms, with their risks of anaphylaxis, should become obsolete.

The Commonwealth Serum Laboratories produce a series of specific and polyvalent antivenenes for use against Australian snake venoms, but because these sera are themselves unstable under unrefrigerated field conditions, and because they should be administered only under medical supervision, collectors should familiarise themselves with routine first-aid procedures in the case of snakebite.

These have changed dramatically in recent years, largely as a result of research at the Commonwealth Serum Laboratories by Dr Struan Sutherland and his colleagues. The following first-aid procedures were introduced in 1978:

When the bite is on a limb

1. While keeping the limb as still as possible, apply a broad bandage, preferably a crepe (pressure) bandage, over the site of the bite as soon as possible after the bite occurs. Do not remove clothing but roll, push or cut it out of the way if necessary.
2. Apply the bandage as tightly as one would for a sprain and extend it over the entire limb if possible.
3. Use a splint of any rigid material to immobilise the limb.
4. As the most common symptoms are fright and the fear of death, reassure the victim and arrange transport to the nearest hospital as quickly as possible, but without panic, and ideally with the dead snake to confirm identification.
5. Do NOT cut the bitten area or apply Condy's crystals (potassium permanganate).
6 Try to alert the hospital of the victim's pending arrival.

When the bite is on the trunk of the body

There is little one can do except apply firm pressure to the site of the bite and seek antivenom treatment as quickly as possible. Bites to the head and neck cannot be treated by first aid.

Dr Sutherland and his colleagues have also developed diagnostic kits which, using an enzyme immunoassay technique, often permit identification of the snake responsible for the bite from a small sample of the victim's blood, or washings from the site of the bite.

Rheobatrachus silus
Montville, Qld.

Amphibians

Amphibians

(CLASS AMPHIBIA)

At the end of the Devonian Period, about 270 million years ago, the first amphibians evolved from a group of fishes — probably lungfishes — and became the first vertebrates to colonise the world's land surfaces.

Modern amphibians bear only superficial resemblance to these early ancestral groups, and although now a relatively small group of vertebrates in terms of variety of species, they sometimes occur in vast numbers and are of great importance in the food chains of river, swamp and marsh communities.

Typically, amphibians are ectothermal vertebrate animals with soft glandular skins, pentadactyle limbs, and a life cycle which usually involves an aquatic larval stage which eventually undergoes a metamorphosis to become an air-breathing terrestrial adult. The eggs are unshelled and typically laid in water. Particular species have evolved a variety of structural and other modifications which do not conform to all of these generalisations.

There are three major groups of living amphibians. The largest of these — and the only one found in Australia — is the order Salientia, to which belong the world's 2000-odd species of frogs and toads.The order Caudata contains the newts and salamanders; only about 300 species are known, and most are confined to the northern hemisphere. One species — the Axolotl *(Ambystoma mexicanum)* — occurs in Australia as an aquarium pet, but does not occur in wild populations and is therefore excluded from this book.

The third and smallest group of living amphibians is the order Gymnophiona — a group which contains only about 75 species of small, worm-like burrowing animals with such unusual characteristics as small scales in the skin and well-developed copulatory organs. Gymnophionans are found only in the tropics; the nearest to Australia are in South-east Asia.

Frogs

(ORDER SALIENTIA)

Five families of frogs (one of them deliberately introduced in 1935) have long been recognised in Australia. Until recent times, and in most published works on Australian amphibians, these families are the tree frogs (family Hylidae), southern frogs (family Leptodactylidae), true frogs (family Ranidae), narrow-mouthed frogs (family Microhylidae) and the introduced true toads (family Bufonidae). All of these families have long been regarded as being widely distributed in other parts of the world.

However, two proposed changes in recent years have received varying degrees of acceptance by Australian herpetologists. These changes involve the two principal groups of Australian frogs: the southern frogs and the tree frogs.

Recent studies have suggested that the Australian members of these families are not as closely allied to their counterparts in other parts of the world (especially in the Americas) as previously believed, and that consequently these Australian frogs should be more accurately regarded as regional families in their own right.

The result has been the erection of two new frog families:the Myobatrachidae (previously the subfamily Myobatrachinae which encompassed the Australasian members of the family Leptodactylidae) and the Pelodryadidae (previously the Australian members of the family Hylidae). Of these, the first has gained widespread acceptance, the second less so, and consequently only the Myobatrachidae has been adopted in this volume.

Unfortunately it is not always possible to separate members of the different families on external or field characters alone. However, in all areas except Arnhem Land and north-eastern Australia only members of the families Hylidae and Myobatrachidae are found. Most hylids have obvious expanded pads or discs on the tips of the fingers or toes, while most myobatrachids have simple, pointed fingers and toes without any indication of pads. But there are some species in each family with only slightly expanded tips to the fingers and toes, and to determine the family to which such specimens belong it will be necessary to use the Australia-wide key provided below.

This key also must be consulted in those areas cited above where members of other families occur; unless an accurate identification can be made from the illustrations or descriptions, then ultimately dissection or radiography of internal structures will be necessary.

Key

TO THE FAMILIES OF AUSTRALIAN FROGS

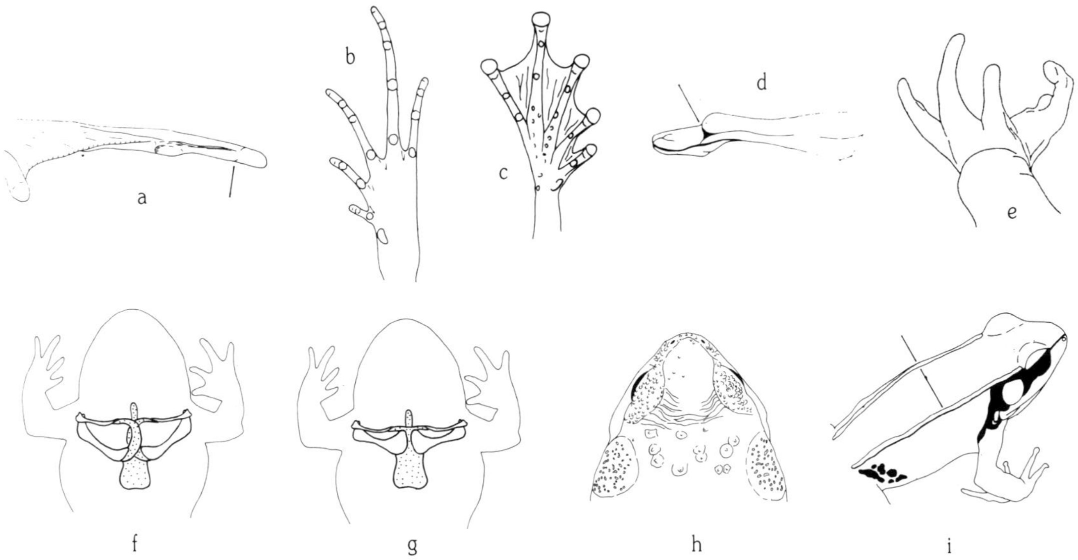

1 Tips of fingers and toes more or less straight in profile, without a distinct notch (a), and without distinct discs or pads (b) in most species; first finger not opposed to remainder..**2**

Tips of fingers and toes with distinct discs or pads (c) in many species and usually with a distinct notch in profile (d) caused by a well-developed intercalary cartilage; if notch is absent, the first finger is opposed to the remainder (e).............................. **Hylidae (Tree Frogs)**

2 Epicoracoid cartilages freely overlapping (f)..................... **3**

Epicoracoid cartilages not overlapping, but firmly united in the midline (g).. **4**

3 Supraocular region warty, separated from interorbital region by a thick fold or ridge of skin (h); maxillary teeth absent (p.52); toes fully webbed (p.52)............................ .... **Bufonidae (True Toads)**

Supraocular region continuous with skin of interorbital

DIAGNOSTIC CHARACTERS IN FROGS

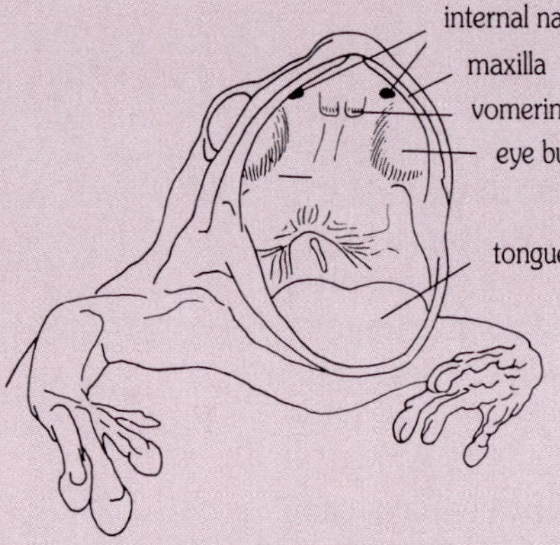

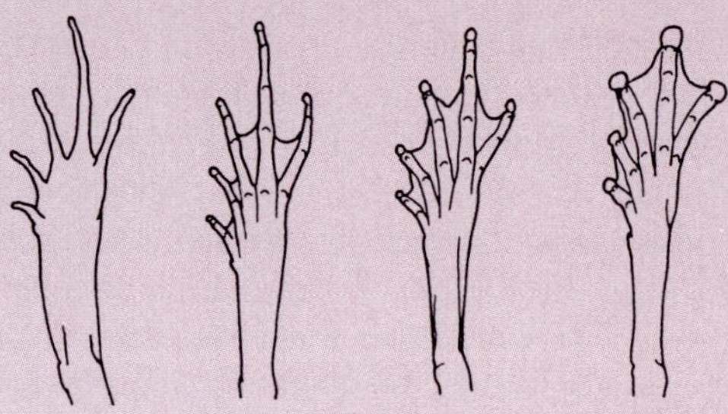

Degrees of webbing on foot, dorsal view

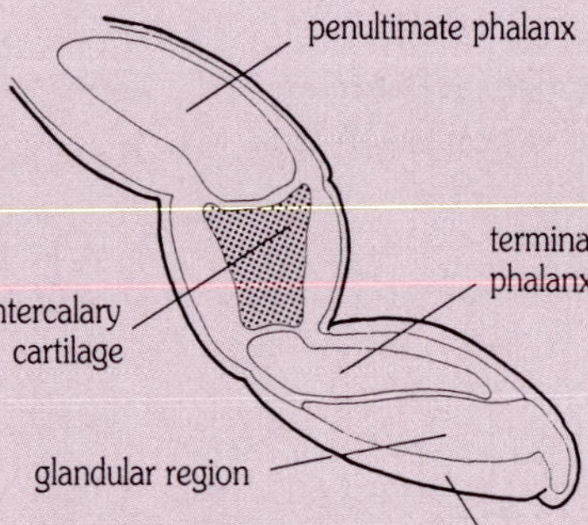

Section through notched tip of digit of the tree frog

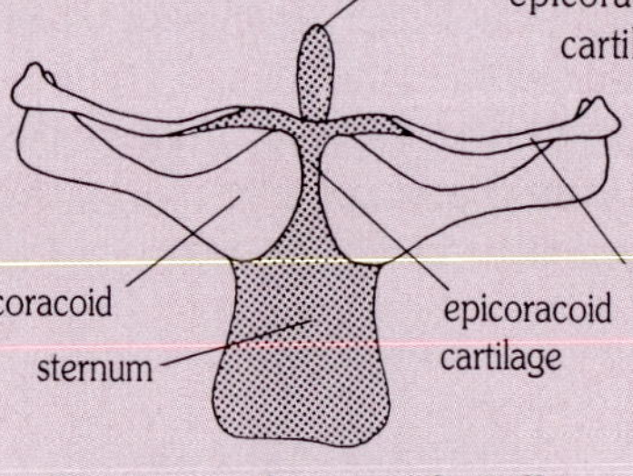

Firmisternal pectoral girdle (epicoracoid cartilages fused in the midline)

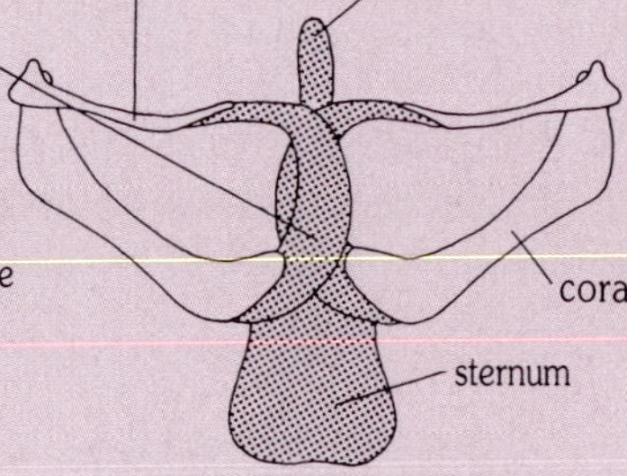

Arciferal pectoral girdle (epicoracoid cartilages free, overlapping)

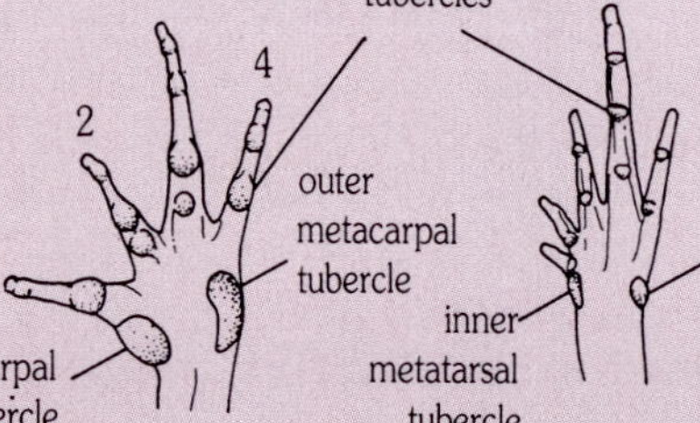

Undersurface of hand and foot

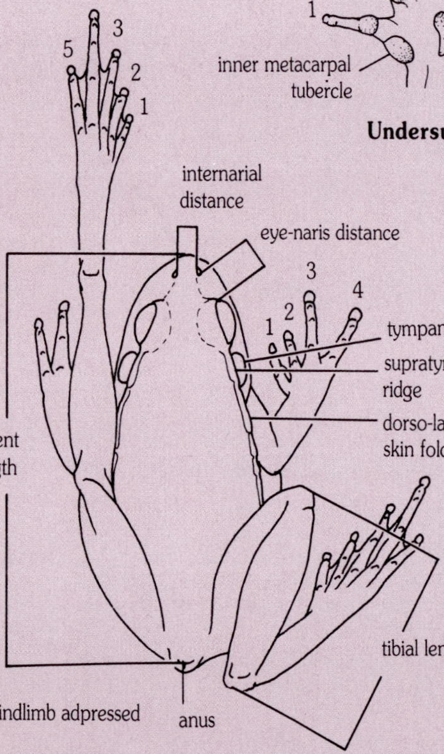

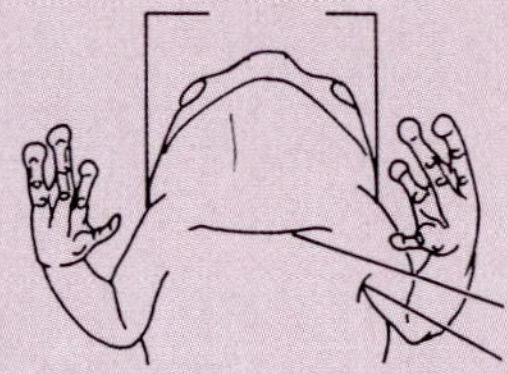

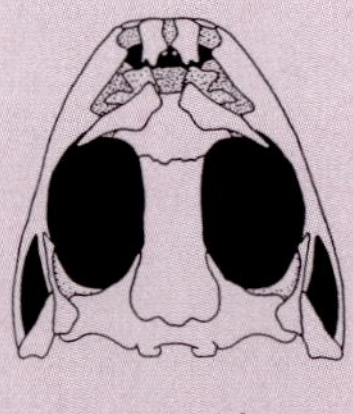

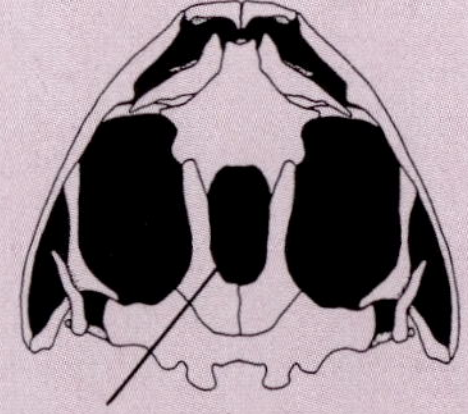

region; maxillary teeth usually present (p.52), but if absent the toes are never more than about half-webbed (p.52) .... **Myobatrachidae (Southern Frogs)**

4 Maxillary teeth present; toes fully webbed; dorso-lateral skin fold from eye to hindlimb (i)... **Ranidae (True Frogs)**

Maxillary teeth absent; toes without webbing; no continuous dorso-lateral skin fold from eye to hindlimb..... .... **Microhylidae (Narrow-mouthed Frogs)**

There is confusion about the use of the names 'frog' and 'toad' in Australia. Technically, true toads are by definition members of the family Bufonidae; hence Australia possesses only one toad — the marine toad of South and Central America (*Bufo marinus*, known here as the Cane Toad) which was introduced into Australia's canefields from Hawaii in 1935 to combat insect pests.

However, because popular usage of the terms 'frog' and 'toad' is based largely on the European experience of Australia's most recent migrants — the western Europeans following the first-fleeters in 1788 — the terms were applied solely on the basis of resemblance of New Holland's amphibian inhabitants to those which occurred 'back home', without any regard for modern phylogenetic relationships. Thus slow, warty, terrestrial forms became 'toads' or 'toadlets' and active, smooth-skinned climbers and jumpers became 'frogs'. Thus the results of early comparisons with a more familiar fauna have today been incorporated in the common names applied to Australia's anuran species.

Family Myobatrachidae

Usually known as Southern Frogs, members of this family are confined to the Australian region. The family is characterised by its arciferal pectoral girdle; intercalary cartilages absent; finger and toe discs small or absent, without lateral grooves; sacral diapophyses more or less dilated; eight presacral vertebrae, the first two fused in some genera; maxillary teeth present or, if absent, the toes never more than about half-webbed.

Members of the family display considerable diversity in morphology, life cycles and ecology. They are found throughout continental Australia and Tasmania, and most are burrowing or terrestrial. Several are found in swift stream/waterfall habitats, while two species appear to be entirely aquatic. None is primarily arboreal. Eggs and larval development range from fully aquatic cycles to fully terrestrial, direct development, with some extraordinary adaptations which include the development of the young in inguinal brood pouches *(Assa)* or in the stomach *(Rheobatrachus)*.

Key

TO THE GENERA OF AUSTRALIAN MYOBATRACHID FROGS

1 Tongue entirely adhering to the floor of the mouth (a)..... **2**

Tongue not adhering to the floor of the mouth posteriorly (b).. **3**

2 Maxillary teeth absent (p.52); small vomerine teeth present (p.52); toes poorly webbed (p.52).................... ***Notaden***

Maxillary teeth present; vomerine teeth absent; toes fully webbed.. ***Rheobatrachus***

3 Tongue large, broadly oval (c); prevomer well-developed, with prominent vomerine teeth (p.52).............................**4**

Tongue small, and/or narrowly oval (d); prevomer much reduced or absent; vomerine teeth vestigial or absent...**11**

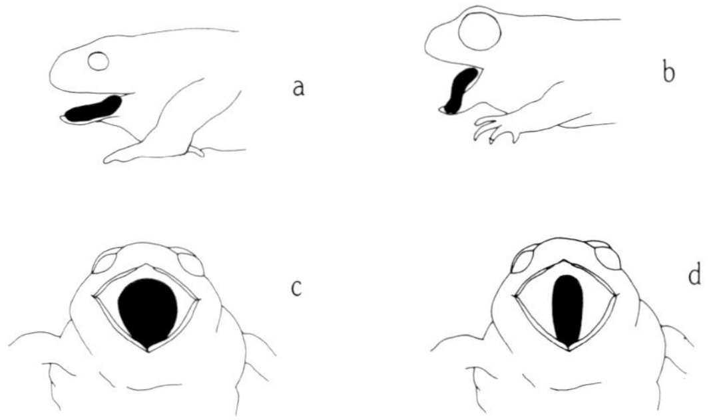

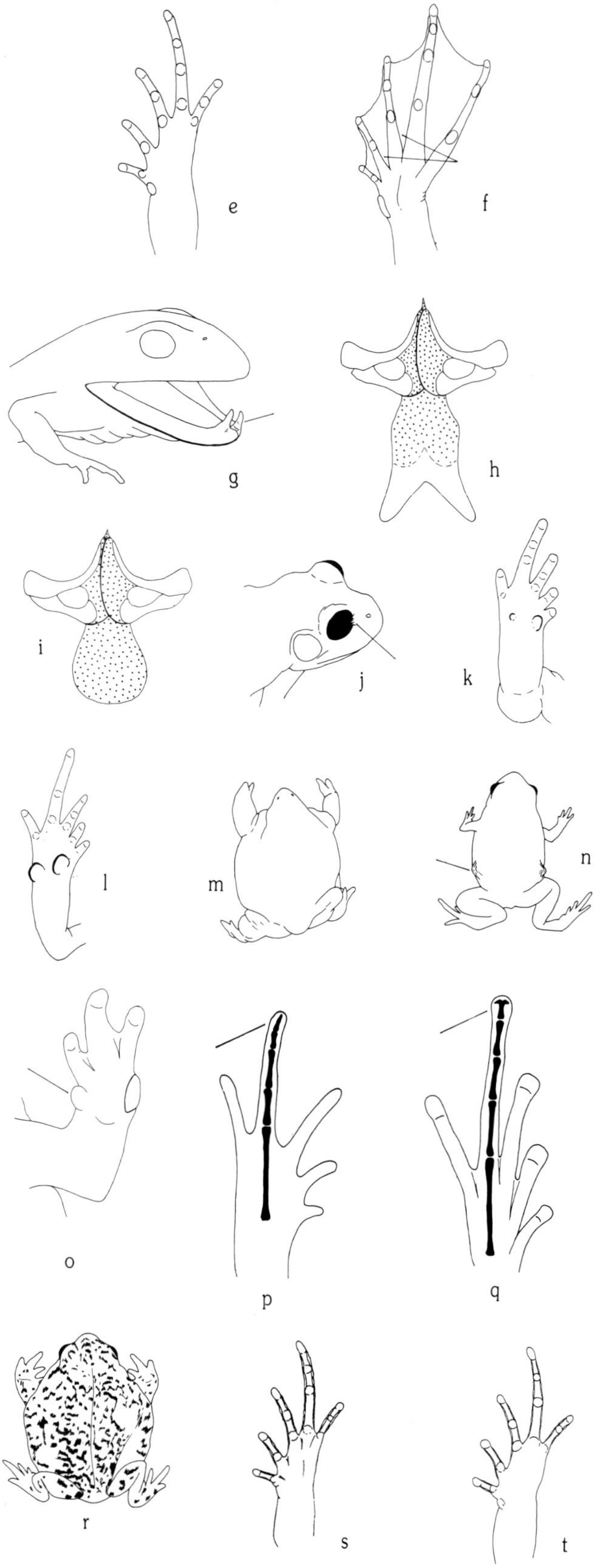

4 Webbing of toes not penetrating between outer metatarsals (e).. **5**

Webbing of toes penetrating between outer metatarsals (f) .... ***Mixophyes***

5 No bright red patch(es) in the groin; no dentary pseudo-teeth.. **6**

One or more bright red patches in the groin; males with two large fang-like dentary pseudo-teeth (g)...... ***Adelotus***

6 Fingers without a trace of webbing (p.52); digits without terminal discs (p.52); a large fronto-parietal foramen in adults (p.52).. **7**

Fingers with distinct basal webbing (p.52); digits with small terminal discs (p.52); no fronto-parietal foramen in adults (p.52)... ***Lechriodus***

7 Vomerine teeth between the choanae (p.52)................... **8**

Vomerine teeth behind the level of the choanae (p.52)..... **9**

8 Inner metatarsal tubercle (p.52) white, unpigmented; adult sternum calcified, bifid posteriorly (h)......... ***Heleioporus***

Inner metatarsal tubercle usually brown or black (always in living specimens); adult sternum cartilaginous, not bifid posteriorly (i).................................... ***Neobatrachus***

9 Toes with at least a distinct basal webbing.................... **10**

Toes free, without a trace of webbing................. ***Philoria***

10 A distinct skin flap with papillae in anterior corner of eye (j) .... ***Megistolotus***

No skin flap or papillae in anterior corner of eye................ .... ***Limnodynastes***

11 Outer metatarsal tubercle, if present, much smaller than inner metatarsal tubercle (k).. **12**

Inner and outer metatarsal tubercles more or less equally developed (l)... ***Uperoleia***

12 Maxillary teeth absent; no terminal discs on fingers or toes **13**

Maxillary teeth present; small terminal discs present or absent... **15**

13 Belly smooth **14**

Belly granular.. ***Metacrinia***

14 Limbs short, but more or less normal, the adpressed hindlimb (p.52) reaching the tympanic region or beyond.... .... ***Pseudophryne***

Limbs very short and stumpy (m), the adpressed hindlimb not reaching the base of the forelimb....... ***Myobatrachus***

15 Dermal brood pouches absent; first finger normal or, if vestigial, there is no dorso-lateral skin fold................... **16**

Dermal inguinal brood pouches present in males (n); first finger vestigial (o); a faint to conspicuous dermal skin fold extending back from the supra-tympanic region, often sharply demarcating the contrasting dorsal and lateral colours.. ***Assa***

16 Terminal phalanges pointed, not T-shaped (p); tips of fingers and toes without distinct discs.......................... **17**

Terminal phalanges T-shaped (q); tips of fingers and toes with small but distinct discs........................ ***Taudactylus***

17 Vomerine teeth absent, or, if present, belly distinctly granular **18**

Vomerine teeth present; belly smooth............. ***Geocrinia***

18 Parotoid glands (p.52) and flank glands absent or not evident externally; skin around body not forming a loose sac extending to knee and elbow................................. **19**

Parotoid and flank glands present and evident externally; skin around body forming a loose sac extending to knee and elbow (r).. ***Arenophryne***

19 Toes broadly fringed (s); vomerine teeth (p.52) conspicuous, behind the level of the choanae; skin smooth or slightly granular on the belly....................... ***Paracrinia***

Toes with or without narrow fringes (t); vomerine teeth absent (usually) or inconspicuous; skin coarsely granular on the belly.. ***Crinia***

Genus *Adelotus* Ogilby, 1907

A monotypic genus whose single species is a small flattened frog readily distinguished by its ventral colouring. Maxillary teeth present. No fronto-parietal foramen in adults. Vomerine teeth in two small clusters behind the choanae. Tongue large, oval. Pupil horizontal. Tympanum indistinct or hidden. Terminal phalanges simple. Tips of digits not dilated. A distinctive red patch in the groin. Males larger than females, with a broad flat head, wider than the body, and with a pair of large dentary pseudo-teeth at the front of the lower jaw.

Adelotus brevis (Günther, 1863)

Tusked Frog

Description: Dark grey or brown above, often with an irregular variegated pattern and infrequently with a narrow light vertebral stripe. Skin usually rough, with low warts and ridges. Limbs barred. Throat dark grey or black with white flecks. Belly smooth, black with white spots (males) or boldly marbled with black and white (females). A bright red patch in the groin and others on the hind edge of the hind leg. Males with two large tusks (dentary pseudo-teeth) at the front of the lower jaw. A brown glandular fold from the eye to the base of the arm. Fingers and toes with only a rudiment of web, without terminal discs. 45 mm.

Distribution: Great Dividing Range and coast from

Adelotus brevis Female, Dorrigo, NSW 45mm

Adelotus brevis
Male, Ourimbah,
NSW

45mm

Adelotus brevis

central-eastern Qld to southern NSW.
Habit: Inhabits rainforest, wet sclerophyll and open grazing country; usually found under logs or stones, or in cavities and crevices, beside puddles, streams, etc. Call a single 'cluck' repeated several times per minute.

Genus ***Arenophryne*** Tyler, 1976

A small, short-limbed, globular, burrowing frog, similar in many respects to *Pseudophryne,* from which it differs in possessing maxillary teeth, a more massive pectoral girdle, reduced digits, colourless and translucent skin on the tip of the snout, and in the absence of extensive areas of dark pigment on the ventral surface. The skin around the body forms a loose sac which extends to elbow and knee.

M. PETERSON

Arenophryne rotunda

Arenophryne rotunda
False Entrance Bay, WA

30mm

Arenophryne rotunda Tyler, 1976

Description: A stout, squat, short-limbed frog, dull cream above stippled with brown, especially on the interorbital region, flanks and dorso-lateral surfaces, Ventrally paler cream with 'small isolated clusters of dark stippling'. Skin smooth and thick above, mostly smooth below. A glandular supratympanic fold. A small inner, but no outer, metatarsal tubercle. 30 mm.
Distribution: Known only from the Shark Bay region and from coastal regions south nearly to Geraldton, WA.
Habit: A burrowing frog, found on coastal sand dunes. Like the Turtle Frog (to which it is related), and unlike most other burrowing frogs, it burrows head-first into the sand.

Genus ***Assa*** Tyler, 1972

A monotypic genus whose single species is characterised by the presence of an inguinal pouch on either side in the males. Maxillary teeth present. A large fronto-parietal foramen in adults. Vomerine teeth absent. Tongue small, oval, free behind. Pupil horizontal. Tympanum hidden. Toes free, without fringes. Terminal phalanges simple, tips of digits slightly expanded.

Assa darlingtoni

Assa darlingtoni
Mt Warning, NSW
30mm

Assa darlingtoni (Loveridge, 1933)

Pouched Frog

Description: Grey, light brown or pinkish-brown to red above, usually with a broad vertebral band commencing between the eyes, narrowing behind the eyes, broadening again on the back, then dividing, each branch running to a groin. In other specimens this band is replaced by a triangular dark patch between the eyes and two ∧ -shaped bars on the back. Sometimes a dark streak, usually broken, from the nostril, through the eye and along the flanks. A pink spot at the base of each arm. Obscure dark bands on the hind limbs. A dark bar beneath the eye. Ventral surface cream-coloured, heavily mottled with brown. Skin smooth above and below. Vomerine teeth absent. Toes with slightly expanded tips, without fringes. 30 mm

Distribution: Known only from the McPherson Ranges and adjacent mountainous areas in the NSW-Qld border region.

Habit: Straughan and Main first recorded the presence of paired, lateral brood pouches in males of this species in which, during late summer, larvae in various stages, including metamorphosing individuals, were found. Adults are found under rocks, leaf-litter, and in or under rotting logs in antarctic beech forests and adjacent rain forest.

Genus ***Crinia*** Tschudi, 1838

A group of small, terrestrial frogs with representatives throughout most parts of Australia except the arid central regions. Maxillary teeth present. A large fronto-parietal foramen in adults. Vomerine teeth usually absent, but present as very small clusters or short rows in some species. Tongue small, narrow, oval, free behind. Pupil horizontal. Tympanum usually hidden but occasionally indistinct. Toes may be fringed, but are without webbing. Phalanges simple, tips of digits not or but very slightly dilated. Belly usually moderately to strongly granular. Females larger than males.

This genus is one in which many sibling species (p.30) have been described on the basis of the analysis of frog calls and experiments on reproductive compatibility between different populations. For this reason several species can be identified only by the call of the male, so that females, non-breeding males and preserved specimens of these species often cannot be identified with any degree of certainty. The key to this genus (below) uses the known distinctions between such species wherever possible, but accurate identification cannot be made in many cases. In such cases the reader should use locality data, etc. to help make an identification but often will have to be satisfied to place a frog within a particular species group.

Key

TO THE AUSTRALIAN SPECIES OF CRINIA

1 Belly distinctly granular, not blotched with pink............... **2**
Belly smooth or only slightly granular, blotched with pink.. .... ***tasmaniensis***

2 Adults with more or less distinct dermal fringes on the toes (a); hind side of thighs not bright pink or red................... **3**
Adults sometimes with lateral seams but without distinct dermal fringes on the toes (b); hind side of thighs bright pink or red.. ***georgiana***

3 No median white line on the throat................................. **4**
A median line of white dots on the throat.............***tinnula***

4 Throat of breeding male dark with white pectoral spots; belly of female boldly blotched with black and white; palm tubercular (c).. **5**
Throat of breeding male white or grey, chin only dark; white pectoral spots inconspicuous or absent; belly of female white, speckled or boldly blotched with black or grey; if boldly blotched then palm of hand smooth........... 6

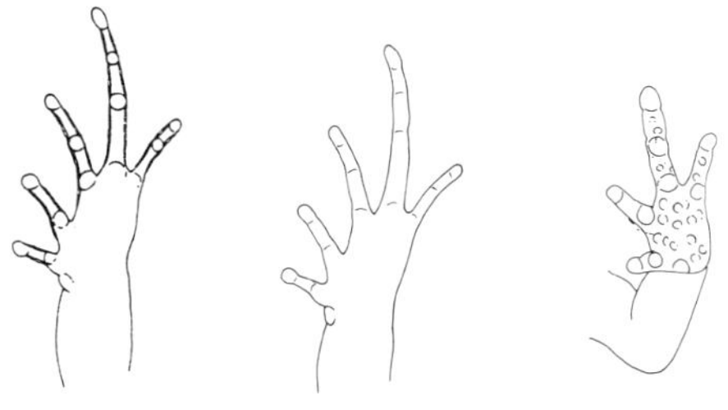

5 Vomerine teeth absent; eastern Australia.......... ***signifera***
Vomerine teeth usually present (p.52); south-western WA. .... ***glauerti***

6 Belly uniform white or grey; flecks, if present, grey and not black.. **7**
Belly with black flecks or mottling................................ **10**

7 Tympanum obscure but distinct..................................... **9**
Tympanum hidden.. ***remota***

8 Belly usually white with at most a few scattered darker flecks; northern Australia and xeric eastern Australia..... **9**
Belly usually grey, sometimes with darker grey flecks; mesic south-eastern Australia................. ***parinsignifera***

9 Adults usually less than 18 mm snout-vent length; pale muddy brown above with at most an obscure dorsal pattern.. ***deserticola***
Adults usually more than 18 mm snout-vent length; medium brown above with well-defined dorsal pattern....... .... ***bilingua***

10 Belly heavily flecked with black..................................... **11**
Belly lightly flecked with black....................................... **13**

11 Western Australia.. **12**
South Australia... ***riparia***

12 Call a harsh squelch or a rapidly repeated series of 'buzzes'; coastal plain of WA from Moore River to Geographe Bay.................................. ***male insignifera***
Call a high-pitched 'bleat'; Darling plateau of south-western Australia, reaching the coast north of the Moore River.. ***pseudinsignifera***

13 Western Australia **14**
South-eastern Australia.. ***sloanei***

14 Males .... ***subinsignifera***
Females .... ***insignifera*** and ***subinsignifera***

Crinia bilingua (Martin, Tyler and Davies, 1980)

Description: Brown above, with a broad, dark brown vertebral zone sometimes finely edged with white and sometimes continuous with a broad, dark triangular bar with its base between the eyes; flanks brown with scattered darker brown dots and, on the lower flanks, with scattered white spots; lips

variegated with dark and pale brown; often a pale glandular stripe from below eye to forearm; limbs with obscure dark brown bands, but the upper forearm pale brownish-orange or fawn. Ventral surfaces whitish, the submandibular area and sometimes the chin densely stippled with dark grey or brown. No red on hind side of thighs. Vomerine teeth absent. Toes fringed. Palm slightly to moderately tubercular. 20 mm
Distribution: Kimberley region WA, through northern NT to lower Gulf of Carpentaria. Possibly also in Cape York Peninsula, Qld.
Habit: Similar to *Crinia signifera.* Call varies from a short to long, bleat or trill.

Crinia deserticola (Liem and Ingram, 1977)

Description: Similar in most respects to *Crinia parinsignifera,* from which it differs in its smaller average size (less than 20 mm snout-vent length), more robust hindlimbs and pale, unspotted belly. It is further distinguished by its characteristic call '...a melodious chirping similar to the call of a young House Sparrow *(Passer domesticus)*' (Liem and Ingram).
Distribution: South-western Qld to adjacent parts of NSW and SA.Also upper NT.
Habit: Normally found in creek beds, soaks and claypans associated with broad river channels throughout its range.

Crinia georgiana Tschudi, 1838

Description: Uniform brown above, or with irregular scattered dark brown spots or marbling, or sometimes with a dark brown dorso-lateral stripe on each side enclosing a lighter vertebral region. A dark stripe from the nostril, through the eye to the groin. Limbs with darker crossbars. Axilla, groin and hind side of thighs bright red. Ventral surface dull white or brownish, often with a white median line. A white spot at the base of each arm. Throat of male dark brown. Skin smooth or with warts and skin folds above, coarsely granular below. Vomerine teeth usually present. Toes without fringes or expanded tips. 40 mm
Distribution: Wide if patchy distribution through coast and adjacent areas of south-western WA, from Carnarvon district in north to Esperance district in south-east.
Habit: Inhabits marshy areas from shallow bogs and marshes to saturated vegetation beside small

J.C. WOMBEY

Crinia bilingua Cannon Hill, NT 20mm

Crinia deserticola Thargomindah, Qld 20mm

Crinia bilingua

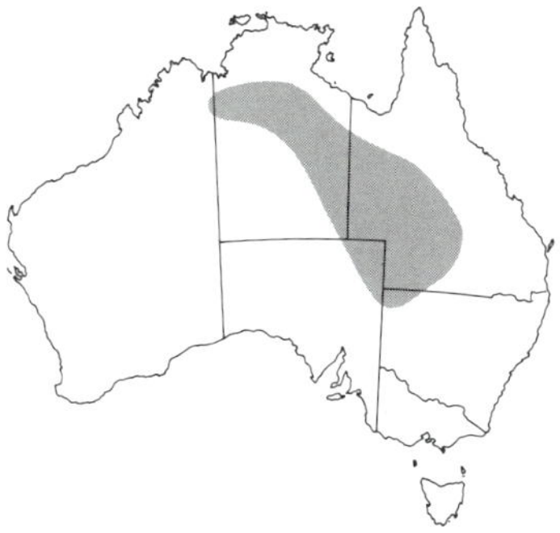

Crinia deserticola

Crinia georgiana

Crinia glauerti

Crinia insignifera

Crinia parinsignifera

Crinia pseudinsignifera

Crinia remota

Crinia riparia

streams, gutters and seeps in forest areas. Main records that the species is a winter-spring breeder and that the call is a 'quack...quack...quack...'.

Crinia glauerti Loveridge, 1933

Description: Similar in most respects to *Crinia signifera*. Vomerine teeth are absent in *signifera* but are usually present, though inconspicuous, in *glauerti*. *C. glauerti* is smaller (less than 20 mm) than *signifera* (35-30 mm). Otherwise these species can be distinguished with certainty only on the basis of locality data. Males often with black throat and chest.
Distribution: Patchy distribution along the coast and adjacent areas of south-western WA, from the Carnarvon district in the north to the Albany district in the south-east.
Habit: Habit similar to that of *C. georgiana*. Call a '...rattle, like pea in a can' (Main).

Crinia insignifera Moore, 1954

Description: Similar in most respects to *C. signifera,* although the two occur in widely separated areas. Male *insignifera* have a white throat, sometimes flecked with brown, and with only the chin dark, whereas male *signifera* have the throat entirely dark. The belly of female *insignifera* is not boldly mottled with black and white, as is generally true of female *signifera*. Ventral white spot at base of arm in signifera is absent or inconspicuous in *insignifera*. 25 mm.
Distribution: Coastal plain of WA, from the Moore River to Geographe Bay.
Habit: Found after rain in and around coastal swamps. At other times shelters under logs, debris etc. Call a 'squelch like drawing a wet finger over a balloon' (Main).

Crinia parinsignifera Main, 1957

Description: Similar in most respects to *Crinia signifera*, from which males of *parinsignifera* can be distinguished almost solely by call. Females of *parinsignifera* have rather uniform belly patterns whereas those of *signifera* are mottled with black and white. The distinction also holds for males of both species from northern populations. The palm of the hand is smooth whereas it is tubercular in *signifera*. 20 mm.

Distribution: Occurs from the Murray River valley to south-eastern Qld, through the central west of NSW. Reaches coastal areas in Qld.
Habit: Similar habitat to that of *C. sloanei.* Call a harsh drawn-out squelch.

Crinia pseudinsignifera Main, 1957

Description: Virtually identical in appearance to *C. insignifera,* from which it can be distinguished with certainty only by male call, which has been described as a high pitched 'bleat'. 30 mm
Distribution: Occurs in south-western WA including '..Darling Plateau in the region of winter rainfall' (Main).
Habit: Shelters under logs, debris, etc. emerging to breed in non-perennial swamps and pools after rain. Call a '... four-pulsed bleat' (Main).

Crinia remota (Tyler and Parker, 1974)

Description: Similar in most respects to *Crinia signifera* and its immediate relatives, from which it differs in lacking any external indication of the tympanum, smooth or only slightly granular skin on the belly, and reduced ventral pigmentation; the throat is usually grey while the belly is white. The throat may be black in some breeding males, with a narrow, pale median line. It is a very small species, the adults not attaining 20 mm in length.
Distribution: Described originally from southern Papua, Tyler and Davies have also recorded it from Qld, Groote Eylandt (NT) and "probably Arnhem Land".
Habit: Similar to *Crinia signifera.* Found in a wide variety of habitats including paperbark and pandanus swamp, flooded grasslands and streamside litter and vegetation. Breeds in a variety of flooded, low-lying country and in roadside pools during the summer wet season.

Crinia riparia Littlejohn and Martin, 1965

Description: Similar in most respects to *Crinia signifera*, from which it differs in lacking a tarsal fold (present in *signifera*), in having a smooth palm (tubercular in *signifera*), and in its call. The latter is an irregularly repeated, long, harsh 'kr-a-a-a-a-ack'. 25 mm
Distribution: Known only from the Flinders Ranges, SA.

Crinia georgiana South-western WA 40mm

R.W.G. JENKINS

Crinia parinsignifera Uriarra Crossing, ACT 20mm

Crinia remota Cannon Hill, NT 20mm

J.C. WOMBEY

Crinia signifera Stanwell Tops, NSW. Shown here are some of the distinctive variations which may occur within a single population of this widespread species.

Crinia riparia Weetootla Gorge, SA 25mm

R.W.G. JENKINS

Habit: Found under rocks beside fast-flowing streams. Tadpoles are torrent-adapted, with flattened bodies and large oral discs. Apparently breeds in spring.

Crinia signifera (Girard, 1853)

Common Eastern Froglet

Description: Extremely variable in colour and pattern, even within a single breeding population. Dorsal ground colour ranges from light grey, fawn or brown to dark grey, dark brown or almost black, while the skin above may be smooth, or with irregular

30mm

small warts, or with raised longitudinal skin folds. Typical dorsal colour patterns are (1) uniform light grey or brown contrasting sharply with black sides; (2) grey or brown with irregular darker patches, and with tubercles and skinfolds tipped with darker or lighter. A pale vertebral stripe is sometimes present; (3) a broad, dark vertebral band commencing between the eyes, bordered on either side by a light brown or grey band from the eye to the groin, below each of which is a black lateral band; (4) light grey or brown with an incomplete darker vertebral band between longitudinal skinfolds and irregular narrow, dark lines following the crests of other skinfolds; sides black. Constant markings associated with all patterns are dark triangular markings on the upper lips and fairly definite darker crossbands on the hindlimbs. Ventral surface granular, ranging from dark grey with scattered fine white spots, through broad black and white marbling, to white with scattered grey and black flecks. Throat very dark brown in males. A small white spot at the base of each arm. Sometimes a white median line on the throat. Hind legs mottled with black and white below. No red on hind sides of thighs. Vomerine teeth absent. Toes fringed. Palm tubercular. 30 mm

Distribution: Widely distributed along the coast, ranges and adjacent western slopes and plains of south-eastern Qld, NSW, Vic and south-eastern SA. Also Tas.

Habit: Occurs in almost every habitat within its range, from supra-littoral soaks behind beaches to drier inland areas. Shelters beneath rocks, logs, thick vegetation, etc., during dry periods, emerging to breed in slow-flowing creeks, claypans, lagoons, gutters, roadside pools, rock holes etc., after rain, calling from within shallow water or fringing grass or leaf-litter. Eggs are usually laid in groups attached to twigs, leaves etc. Call a 'crick-crick-crick...' (Harrison).

Crinia sloanei Littlejohn, 1958

Description: Usually dull grey above with irregular darker flecks or lines usually capping low warts or skinfolds. A white bar, edged above with darker, from below the eye to the base of the forelimb. A black lateral band, usually narrow and incomplete. Skin usually fairly smooth above with a few low, rounded warts and skinfolds. Belly granular. Hindlimbs distinctly banded with darker. Belly dirty white, lightly

Crinia signifera

Crinia sloanei

Crinia sloanei Walgett, NSW 25mm

Crinia subinsignifera Northcliffe, WA 25mm

flecked with black. Throat of breeding male, grey. White spot at base of arm, if present, inconspicuous. No red on hind side of thighs. Vomerine teeth absent. Toes fringed. Palm tubercular. 25 mm
Distribution: Central western plains of NSW from the Murray River (and including adjacent areas of Vic) nearly to the Qld border.
Habit: A cryptic species found usually only after rain, when it calls from grasses within and fringing temporarily inundated areas. Call a single, low 'squelch'.

Crinia subinsignifera Littlejohn, 1957

Description: Virtually identical in appearance to *C. signifera* from which it can be distinguished with certainty only by male call. 25 mm
Distribution: Southern coast and hinterland of extreme south-western WA, from north of Manjimup to Cheyne Bay.
Habit: Habit similar to *C. insignifera.* Call a drawn-out 'squelch'.'

Crinia tasmaniensis (Günther, 1864)

Description: Brown, grey or olive-brown above, with irregular darker spots or stripes, and often with a reddish-brown or orange stripe on each side above a dark brown lateral stripe which starts at the nostril. A dark bar beneath each eye. Lower surfaces marbled white and dark brown anteriorly, dark brown with red or white spots posteriorly. A red spot at the base of

Crinia tasmaniensis Lake St. Clair, Tas 30mm

Crinia tasmaniensis Lake St. Clair, Tas

each arm. Throat of male black. Skin smooth above, or with scattered low tubercles or longitudinal skinfolds, smooth or faintly granular below. Vomerine teeth usually absent, but occasionally slightly discernible. Toes with prominent fringes, but without expanded tips. 30 mm
Distribution: Found throughout Tas, above about 600 m.
Habit: Blanchard records that this species is largely aquatic, breeding during summer.

Crinia subinsignifera

Crinia tasmaniensis

Crinia tinnula Straughan and Main, 1966
Wallum Froglet

Description: Similar in most respects to *Crinia signifera* from which it is reported to differ in having a median line of white dots on the throat, a more pointed over-shot snout (the nostrils equidistant from eye and tip of snout) and a distinctive call. As a light median line occurs on the throat in many southern specimens of *C. signifera* this character has only limited value. The belly of *C. tinnula* is usually white or light brown, only sparsely flecked with darker, whereas the belly of *C. signifera* is usually boldly mottled with black and white.
Distribution: Restricted to coastal areas of southern Qld and northern NSW.
Habit: Straughan and Main record that this species is confined to acid, paperbark swamps of the 'wallum' country, that it is a late winter breeder and that the call is a 'short, high-pitched ringing... tching...tching like the tinkling of a small bell'.

Crinia tinnula

Genus *Geocrinia* Blake, 1973

Small to moderate ground-dwelling frogs confined to the temperate or colder southern parts of Australia. Maxillary teeth present. A large fronto-parietal foramen in adults. Vomerine teeth usually present, though often inconspicuous. Tongue small, narrow, oval, free behind. Pupil horizontal. Tympanum indistinct or hidden. Phalanges simple, tips of digits not or but slightly dilated.Belly smooth, or slightly granular.

Key

TO THE SPECIES OF GEOCRINIA

1 Inner finger and inner toe not reduced, the latter about two-thirds the length of the second toe (a)........................**2**
Inner finger and inner toe much reduced, the latter not more than half the length of the second toe (b), and the inner finger with at most a single very short phalanx....... **4**

2 Toes without terminal expansions and without, or very indistinct, subarticular tubercles....................................**3**
Toes with slight terminal expansions and with distinct

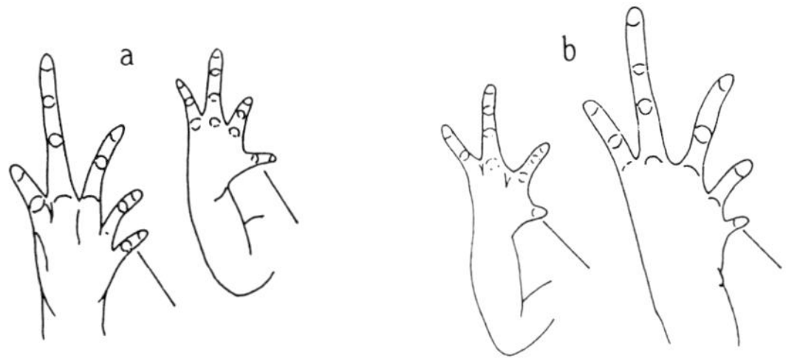

subarticular tubercles (p.52) ; belly brown, yellow-brown or green-grey .... ***leai***
3 Belly pink or reddish.. ***rosea***
Belly light fawn to yellowish-brown........................... ***lutea***

4 Call: cra-a-a-a-a-ack, cra-a-ack, cra-a-ack, cra-a-ack, etc.... .... ***laevis***
Call: cr-r-rack, cr-r-rack, cr-r-rack, pip, pip, pip, pip-pip-pip-pip-pip-pip-pip.. ***victoriana***

Geocrinia laevis (Günther, 1864)

Description: Grey or brown above with scattered, small, black-edged reddish spots and sometimes with irregular darker markings. Ventral surface white or light grey with darker brown or grey flecks or mottling. Lower surfaces of arms and legs usually with patches of pink; a pink spot in each axilla and groin, each outlined or marbled with black. Throat of male bright yellow. Skin smooth above or with scattered low warts, smooth below. Vomerine teeth usually present, but usually only slightly discernible. Tips of toes not expanded. Toes without fringes. Inner finger and toe much reduced, the first toe not more than half the length of the second and the inner finger with at most a single very short phalanx. 35 mm
Distribution: Tas. Littlejohn and Martin have recorded mainland populations from south-western Vic and the Grampians.
Habit: Found in damp locations, beneath vegetation, debris and leaf-litter, often in areas inundated after rain. Breeds in late summer. Call a 'cra-a-a-a-a-ack, cra-a-ack, cra-ack, cra-ack, etc' (Littlejohn and Martin).

Geocrinia laevis
Birdport, Tas
35mm

Geocrinia leai (Fletcher, 1898)

Description: Light yellowish- or pinkish-brown to dark brown above, usually with a broad, irregular darker vertebral band commencing between the eyes and with its hind edge emarginate. Some specimens with numerous tiny blue-white spots, while others may have large, irregular yellow blotches. Ventral surfaces light cream, olive, or yellowish, usually with darker flecks. Throat of males not pigmented. Limbs with dark cross-bars. Skin smooth above and below. Vomerine teeth usually present as two short rows behind the choanae.Toes with slightly expanded tips, usually without fringes, and with distinct subarticular tubercles. 25 mm
Distribution: South-western corner of WA: the Darling Scarp south of the Swan River, extending eastward to the Albany district.
Habit: Inhabits wet, cool, shady areas associated with streams and swamps. Breeds after rain, from autumn until spring. Call a 'chic...chic...chic...chic ...' (Main).

Geocrinia lutea (Main, 1963)

Description: Grey, brown or blackish-brown above usually with a broad dark vertebral band or patch commencing between the eyes and with its hind edge emarginate, and sometimes narrowly pale-edged. Belly white, grey, fawn or yellowish, irregularly peppered with dark brown. Pink spots in groin and on hind side of thighs. Limbs streaked or barred with dark brown or black. Skin smooth or slightly tubercular above, smooth below. Vomerine teeth present. Toes not fringed, the inner finger and toe not reduced, the first toe about two-thirds the length of the second; toes without terminal expansions and without, or with very indistinct, subarticular tubercles. 25 mm
Distribution: South-western corner of WA, in the

Geocrinia lutea
Walpole, WA

25mm

Geocrinia laevis

vicinity of Walpole and Nornalup.
Habit: Similar to that of *Geocrinia rosea* (of which it is sometimes considered to be a synonym), including larval development within the egg-membranes.

Geocrinia rosea (Harrison, 1927)

Description: Brown above, sometimes with faint darker mottling, or with a broad dark vertebral band commencing between the eyes and with its hind edge emarginate. Rosy pink below, often with dark brown flecks. Limbs with darker cross-bars. Throat of male dark brown or black. Skin smooth or slightly tubercular above, and smooth below. Vomerine teeth prominent. Toes not fringed. Inner finger and toe not reduced, the first toe about two-thirds the length of the second. 25 mm

Geocrinia leai

Geocrinia lutea

Geocrinia rosea
Northcliffe, WA

25mm

Geocrinia rosea

Geocrinia victoriana

Distribution: Extreme south-western corner of WA, in the Warren River Valley and adjacent areas.
Habit: Confined to wet karri forest. Found in tunnels under streamside vegetation, or in and under rotting logs. Main records that the larvae develop in broken-down egg capsules and never enter water. Breeds in spring. Call a 'tk...tk...tk...tk' (Main).

Geocrinia victoriana (Boulenger, 1888)

Description: Similar in virtually all respects to *Geocrinia laevis* from which it may be distinguished with certainty only by its call: 'cr-r-rack, cr-r-rack, cr-r-rack, pip, pip, pip, pip-pip-pip-pip-pip-pip-pip-pip' (Blanchard).
Distribution: Vic, south of the Great Dividing Range.
Habit: Similar to that of *G. laevis.*

Genus *Heleioporus* Gray, 1841

Moderate to large, fat globular burrowing frogs, with granular or warty skin, rather stubby limbs and toes with only rudiments of webbing. Fingers without a trace of webbing. Maxillary teeth present. Prominent vomerine teeth between the choanae. Pupil vertical. Tympanum usually distinct. Phalanges simple, tips of digits not dilated. A moderate frontoparietal foramen and calcified sternum in adults, the sternum bifid posteriorly. Inner metatarsal tubercle large, white, unpigmented.

Key

TO THE SPECIES OF HELEIOPORUS

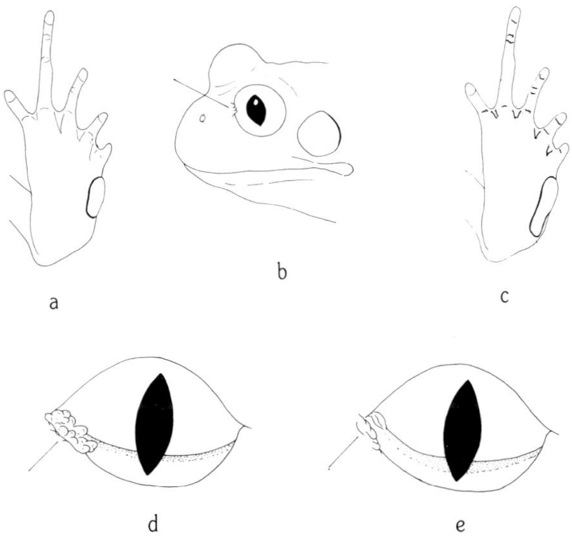

1 Back uniform in colour or with marbled pattern, but never with large white or yellow spots **2**
Back with scattered large white or yellow spots .... ***albopunctatus***

2 Uniform chocolate brown or dark grey with yellow or white spots restricted to the sides **3**
Back with marbled colour pattern or, if uniform, without conspicuous yellow spotting on the back or sides **4**

3 Inner metatarsal tubercle in adults less than half length of fourth toe (a); a small divided flap in the anterior corner of The eye (b) .... ***australiacus***
Inner metatarsal tubercle in adults at least half length of fourth toe (c); two rows of small papillae in anterior corner of eye (d) .... ***barycragus***

4 Tip of fifth toe of adpressed hindlimb (p.52) reaches the tip of the snout or beyond; an inconspicuous fold, sometimes with one or two isolated papillae, in anterior corner of eye (e) **5**
Tip of fifth toe of adpressed hindlimb does not reach

beyond nostril; a distinct flap consisting of at least two papillae in anterior corner of eye (f)................. ***inornatus***

5 Adults often with some yellow markings on back and sides; call, a long, low moan; breeding males without nuptial spines, females often indistinguishable from those of *H. psammophilus*...***eyrei***

Adults usually without any yellow markings on back and sides; call, short, high-pitched, repetitive; breeding males with nuptial spines (g) in northern part of range, without in south...***psammophilus***

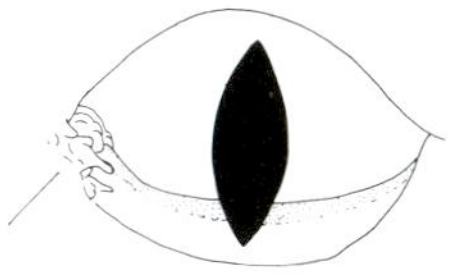

f

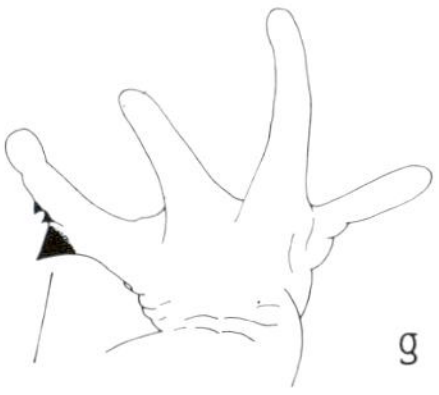

g

Heleioporus albopunctatus

Heleioporus albopunctatus
Pallingup River, WA

80mm

Heleioporus australiacus Sydney, NSW 95mm

Heleioporus australiacus

Heleioporus albopunctatus Gray, 1841

Description: Chocolate brown above, with numerous scattered large (greater than 2 mm in diameter) white or yellow spots over head, back, sides and limbs. A white vertical stripe on the tip of the snout and another below the front edge of each eye. White below. Skin velvety above, smooth below. No flap or group of papillae in the anterior corner of the eye. Tympanum distinct. 80 mm
Distribution: Largely restricted to coast and ranges of south-western Australia from the Murchison River in the north to the vicinity of Hopetoun.
Habit: Breeds in April-June in burrows in non-perennial swamps and creeks. Call 'a short, high-pitched "coo-coo" repeated slowly' (Lee).

Heleioporus australiacus (Shaw and Nodder, 1795)

Giant Burrowing Frog

Description: Dark chocolate-brown above with white or yellowish spots only on the sides, not on the back. White below, with some brown on throat. Skin granular above, with warts capped by black spines on back and sides of adult males. A small divided flap in the anterior corner of the eye. Inner metatarsal tubercle in adults less than half the length of fourth toe. Tympanum prominent. 95 mm
Distribution: Coast and ranges from central coast of NSW to eastern Vic.
Habit: Believed to breed through summer and autumn, apparently in burrows in the banks of small creeks. Call a low-pitched owl-like 'oo-oo-oo' from burrows or in the open.

Heleioporus barycragus

Heleioporus eyrei

Heleioporus barycragus Lee, 1967

Description: Uniform chocolate-brown or dark grey above with small, yellow-capped warts on the sides. White below. Generally similar to *H. australiacus* except that there are no black spines on the back or throat. Two rows of small papillae in anterior corner of eye. Inner metatarsal tubercle in adults at least half the length of the fourth toe. Tympanum prominent. 75 mm
Distribution: Darling Range and foothills east of Perth, WA.
Habit: Breeding habits similar to those of *H. albopunctatus*. Call 'a low-pitched owl-like hoot, slowly repeated' (Lee).

R.W.G. JENKINS

Heleioporus barycragus Forest Field, WA 75mm

Heleioporus eyrei Walpole, WA 60mm

Heleioporus eyrei (Gray, 1845)

Moaning Frog

Description: Brown above, usually with at least some irregular marbling of white, grey or yellow on back and sides. White below, except for some brown on throat. Skin granular on back and sides, smooth below. Tympanum may be indistinct or obvious. Tip of fifth toe of adpressed hindlimb reaches the tip of the snout or beyond. An inconspicuous fold, sometimes with one or two isolated papillae, in anterior corner of eye.This is the only species of *Heleioporus* in which the males lack nuptial spines. Females are not easily distinguished from those of *inornatus*. 60 mm
Distribution: South-western Australia: coastal plain extending into the Darling Range, from just below Geraldton in the north to Esperance in the east.
Habit: Habitat and breeding habits similar to those of *H. inornatus*. Call 'a long, low moan, slowly repeated' (Lee).

Heleioporus inornatus (Lee and Main 1954)

Description: Colour dark brown to dark chocolate above, with or without marblings on the back; the latter, if present, usually brown, but occasionally white, yellow or grey. No conspicuous white spots on the back or sides, although some small spots (less than 1 mm in diameter) may be present on the sides and around the cloaca. White below. Skin granular above, smooth below. A distinct flap consisting of at least two papillae in anterior corner of eye. Tympanum distinct. Tip of fifth toe of adpressed hindlimb does not reach beyond nostril. 70 mm
Distribution: Darling Range, south-western WA.
Habit: Breeds April-June, in burrows in poorly-drained, sandy or peaty bogs and swamps. Call a 'woop, woop, repeated frequently' (Lee).

M. PETERSON

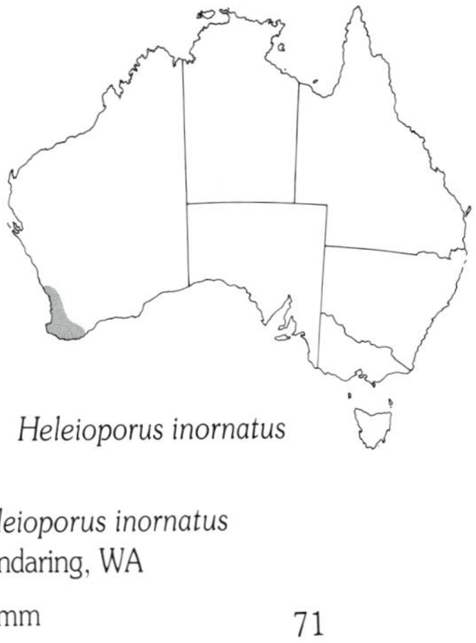

Heleioporus inornatus

Heleioporus inornatus
Mundaring, WA

70mm

Heleioporus psammophilus

(Lee and Main, 1954)

Description: Similar in almost all respects to *H. eyrei*, except that there is rarely any yellow on back or sides. Northern males in breeding season with small nuptial spines, but these are lacking in southern specimens. Females usually indistinguishable from those of *H. eyrei*. Males of these species can only be distinguished with certainty by their calls. 60 mm

Distribution: South-western Australia: coast and western edge of Darling Scarp from Dongara region to Esperance.

Habit: Similar in habitat and breeding habits to *H. eyrei*. Call a long series of short, high-pitched motor-like pulses: put-put-put, etc (Main)

Heleioporus psammophilus
Walpole, WA

60mm

Heleioporus psammophilus

Genus **Lechriodus** Boulenger,1882

A medium-sized frog of moderate build. Maxillary teeth present. No fronto-parietal foramen in adults. Vomerine teeth present as two long straight ridges, one on each side behind the choanae. Tongue large, oval. Pupil horizontal. Tympanum distinct. Terminal phalanges simple, but tips of digits with very small discs which give a hylid-like appearance. No red patch in the groin. Other species occur in New Guinea.

Lechriodus fletcheri Ourimbah, NSW
Male & female in amplexus
50mm

Lechriodus fletcheri

Lechriodus fletcheri (Boulenger, 1890)

Fletcher's Frog

Description: Light grey to rich reddish-brown above with darker flecks or patches, usually a dark transverse bar between the eyes. All limbs distinctly barred with dark grey-brown. A dark temporal streak along the lower edge of the supra-tympanic fold. Sides of face darker brown, while tympanum is same colour as dorsum. Lower surfaces whitish but lower lip brown. Fore and hind sides of thighs silvery-grey. Skin smooth or finely granular above, smooth below, but some distinctive narrow ridges of skin on head, body and limbs. Fingers and toes with a rudiment of webbing. A moderate, rounded, inner metatarsal tubercle but no outer tubercle. 50 mm
Distribution: Rain forest and adjacent wet sclerophyll forests of coast and ranges of northern NSW and south-eastern Qld.
Habit: Breeds in permanent and temporary pools and streams during summer. Tadpoles are notoriously cannibalistic, even in the wild. Call a single, second-long 'g-a-r-r-up' (Moore), repeated at short intervals.'

Genus *Limnodynastes* Fitzinger, 1843

A group of well-built, ground-dwelling and/or burrowing frog with fairly powerful limbs. Maxillary teeth present. A fronto-parietal foramen in adults. Vomerine teeth prominent, behind the choanae and extending laterally beyond their inner borders. Tongue large, oval. Pupil horizontal. Tympanum indistinct or hidden. Phalanges simple, tips of digits without dilations. Second finger not much shorter than first. Toe webbing may be poorly or well developed. Breeding females with one or more inner fingers flanged, for use in "puddling" the egg-mass into a frothy, floating raft.

Limnodynastes fletcheri Euabalong, NSW 50mm

Key

TO THE SPECIES OF LIMNODYNASTES

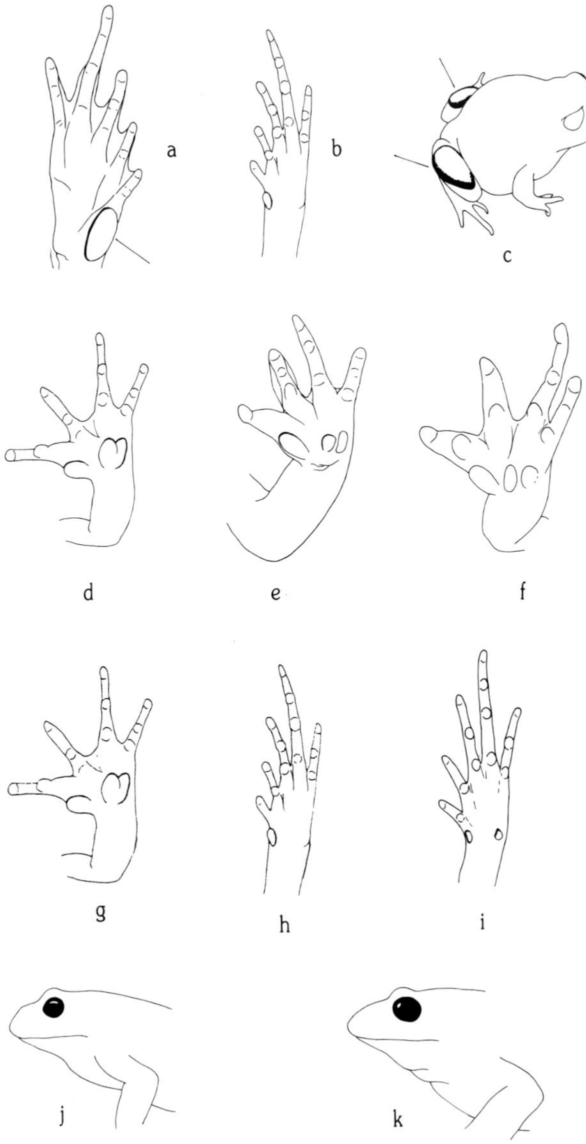

1 Inner metatarsal tubercle large, shovel-shaped (a)........... **2**

Inner metatarsal tubercle small to moderate, not shovel-shaped (b).. **7**

2 A large tibial gland (c).. **3**

No tibial gland **6**

3 Vertebral stripe absent, or if present, groin not suffused with scarlet.. **4**

Vertebral stripe present; groin suffused with scarlet........... .... ***dorsalis***

4 Groin not suffused with scarlet.. **5**

Groin suffused with scarlet....................... ***terraereginae***

5 Toes either with vestigial webbing (p.52) or, if moderately webbed (to about one quarter), the belly has distinct black or grey mottling or reticulations........................ ***dumerilii***

Toes with well-developed (one third to one half) webbing; belly yellow, with or without a few black flecks.................. .... ***interioris***

6 Toes not more than one quarter webbed............. ***ornatus***

Toes at least half webbed................................. ***spenceri***

7 Metacarpal of inner finger equal to, or slightly longer or shorter than that of the second finger (d)........................ **8**

Metacarpal of inner finger much longer than that of second finger (e) **11**

8 A pale glandular fold or ridge from below the eye to the base of the forelimb **9**

No pale glandular ridge or fold from below eye to forelimb. .... ***depressus***

9 First finger equal to or shorter than the second(f).......... **10**

First finger longer than the second (g); a single metatarsal tubercle (h) .... ***salmini***

10 First finger equal to second; a single metatarsal tubercle.... .... ***convexiusculus***

First finger shorter than second (f); usually two metatarsal tubercles (i) .... ***tasmaniensis***

11 Toes with a distinct basal webbing; snout rounded, not prominent (j).. ***fletcheri***

Toes free; snout pointed and prominent (k).......... ***peronii***

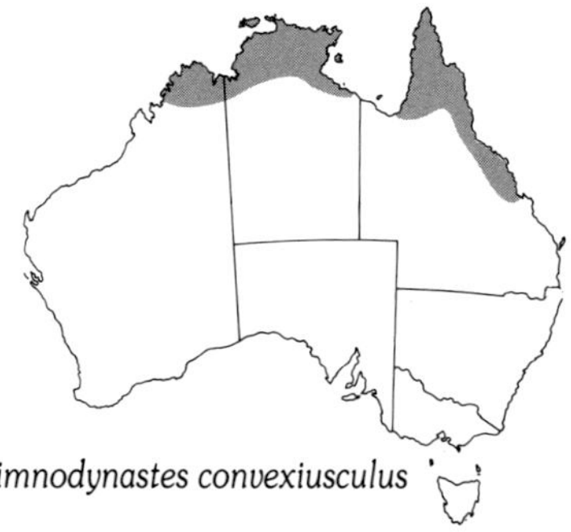

Limnodynastes convexiusculus

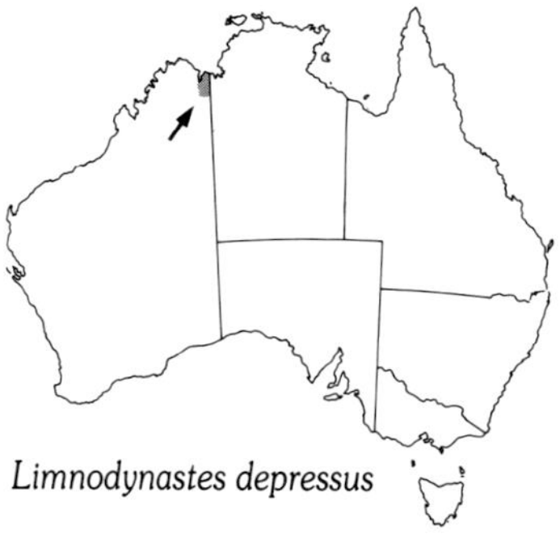

Limnodynastes depressus

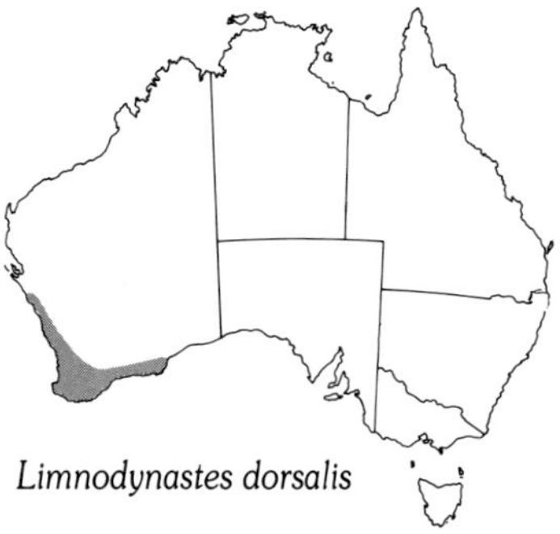

Limnodynastes dorsalis

Limnodynastes convexiusculus Humpty Doo, NT 55mm

Limnodynastes dorsalis Rocky Gully, WA 70mm

Limnodynastes convexiusculus
(Macleay, 1877)
Marbled Frog

Description: Grey, brown, or dark olive above with numerous dark blotches which tend to decrease in size on the flanks. A dark streak along the snout and from the eye, through the tympanum to the base of the forelimb; this streak is bordered below by a white or yellow glandular fold. A dark patch below the eye. Limbs with irregular dark crossbands, spots and marblings. White below except for dark reticulations on throat. Skin above with numerous low, flat glands; smooth below. No tibial gland. Inner metatarsal tubercle not enlarged, shovel-shaped. First finger equal to second. Inner and second metacarpals subequal. A single metatarsal tubercle. Toes with only a rudiment of webbing, not fringed. Tympanum indistinct. 55 mm
Distribution: Coastal and near coastal areas of northern Australia from north-western Australia to Qld. Lowlands of southern New Guinea.
Habit: An inhabitant of savannah woodlands and lowland scrubs. Call a continuous series of single, short, high-pitched 'plonks'.

Limnodynastes depressus Tyler 1976

Description: A somewhat elongate frog with a conspicuously flattened head and prominent shelf-like upper eyelid. No glandular fold from below the eye to the base of the forelimb. Pale grey above with small brown reticulate pattern. Cream below. Skin smooth above and below. No tibial gland. A small inner but no outer metatarsal tubercle. First finger shorter than second. Toes without webbing or fringes. Tympanum hidden. 40 mm.
Distribution: Known only from a site now beneath Lake Argyle, Ord River, WA.

Limnodynastes dorsalis (Gray, 1841)
Western Banjo Frog or Pobblebonk

Description: Grey, olive-brown to dark brown above with a series of large, somewhat irregular blackish patches and marblings, smaller dark blotches on the face and flanks, and a distinct narrow pale white or yellow vertebral stripe from snout to vent. A white glandular stripe from below the eye to above the base of the forelimb.A broad black streak from the eye, through the tympanum to the level of the forearm. A bright patch of red in the groin. Whitish or yellowish below. Skin above smooth or with low, inconspicuous warts; smooth below. A large tibial gland. A large shovel-shaped metatarsal tubercle. First finger slightly shorter than, or equal to, second. Toes with only a trace of webbing. Tympanum more or less hidden. 70 mm
Distribution: Widely distributed throughout the south-western corner of WA.
Habit: Found near permanent water — swamps, streams and farm dams — throughout its range where males call while partly submerged. Call a series of 'plonks' — 'like the plucking of a banjo string' (Main). This and related species in eastern Australia are often known as 'Banjo Frogs', while Main records the name 'Pobblebonk' for the above species.

Limnodynastes dumerilii Peters,1863
Eastern Banjo Frog

Description: Grey or brown above, with blackish marbling, blotches or flecks, and with or without a continuous or broken narrow, vertebral stripe. A pale glandular stripe from below the eye to above the base of the forelimb, bordered above by a broad blackish stripe from the eye through the tympanum. White or yellow in the groin. Sides of thighs often mottled with black and bluish-white. Whitish below, throat

Limnodynastes dumerilii Warrumbungle Mts, NSW 70mm

Limnodynastes interioris Cobar, NSW 90mm

Limnodynastes ornatus Weipa, Qld 45mm

sometimes bright yellow, belly sometimes heavily mottled with dark grey. Skin above smooth or with low, rounded warts; smooth below. A large tibial gland. A large shovel-shaped metatarsal tubercle. First finger slightly shorter than or equal to second. Toe webbing varying from only a trace to about one-quarter. Tympanum more or less hidden. 70 mm
Distribution: Tas; south-eastern SA through Vic and eastern NSW to south-eastern Qld.
Habit: Habits and call similar to those described for *Limnodynastes dorsalis*. A burrowing species found in heaths and sclerophyll forests.
Subspecies: *dumerilii* (south-eastern SA through Vic and NSW to south-eastern Qld); *insularis* (Tas and south-eastern Vic); *variegatus* (south-eastern SA and south-western Vic); *grayi* (central coast of NSW); *fryi* (Snowy Mountains).

Limnodynastes fletcheri Boulenger, 1888

Long-thumbed Frog

Description: Light grey or brown above with scattered, large, dark brown or black blotches interspersed with smaller spots and flecks of the same colour. Usually a small, poorly-defined pink or purplish patch on the hind part of each upper eyelid. A light glandular fold from below the eye. A dark patch below the eye. Limbs with scattered dark spots or irregular cross-bands. White below. Skin above smooth or with low rounded warts; smooth below. No tibial gland. Metatarsal tubercle not shovel-shaped. First finger shorter than second. Inner metacarpal much longer than second. A single metatarsal tubercle. Toes with basal webbing and slight lateral fringes. Tympanum indistinct. 50 mm
Distribution: Western NSW and south-eastern Qld, west of the Great Dividing Range.
Habit: Usually found breeding after rain in inundated grassy areas, where males call from deep within clumps of floating debris, especially burr-bearing grasses. At other times found sheltering under logs, piles of debris, or in ground crevices including yabbie burrows. Call a single dog-like 'bark'.

Limnodynastes interioris Fry, 1913

Giant Banjo Frog

Description: A very large, globular frog varying from a pale yellowish or fawn to brown above, without pattern other than a few small scattered blackish flecks and spots especially posteriorly. A cream, yellow or orange glandular stripe from below the eye to above the base of the forelimb, bordered above by a broad black stripe from the eye through the tympanum, this stripe continued anteriorly as a narrow black stripe along the canthus. A yellow patch on the upper arm. A broad, coppery-orange band along the side, bordered below by an irregular, blackish band, the latter often enclosing numerous white or blue-white flecks and dots. Groin marbled with black and yellow. Bright lemon-yellow below, often lightly speckled with black. Skin smooth or finely granular above, smooth below. A large tibial gland often conspicuously rich brown, copper or orange. A large, shovel-shaped, metatarsal tubercle. First finger slightly shorter than or equal to second. Toes with well-developed webbing. Tympanum more or less hidden. 90 mm

Distribution: Central NSW, west of the great Dividing Range and south to the Murray River.

Habit: Habits and call more or less similar to those of *Limnodynastes dorsalis*. Occurs in a range of dry habitats from woodlands to mallee and semi-arid shrublands. A burrowing species usually seen on the surface only after substantial rains.

Limnodynastes ornatus (Gray, 1842)

Ornate Burrowing Frog

Description: Very variable in colour and pattern ranging from almost uniform dark grey or brown above to pale grey or brown with irregular darker blotches. In many specimens there is a light (grey or yellowish) hour-glass shaped patch in the middle of the back, commencing at a line joining the rear corner of each eye. In other specimens only the front half of this patch is conspicuous, resulting in a U-shaped light patch on the nape, behind the eyes. A light yellow or orange vertebral stripe may be present. Usually a dark temporal band, while the upper lip has several broad, dark bars. The limbs are barred with broad or narrow dark bands. White below. Skin mostly smooth with a few scattered low tubercles and a series of short to long, low skin folds which tend to be longitudinally aligned, except where they follow the pale U-shaped patch on the nape. No tibial gland. Inner metatarsal tubercle shovel-shaped. First and second fingers subequal. Toes only about one quarter webbed. Tympanum very indistinct. Tiny black spicules may cover dorsal surface of males during breeding season. 45 mm

Distribution: Throughout northern half of NSW (from coast to far west), Qld, northern half of NT and north-western Australia.

Habit: Found in a wide range of habitats from coastal rain and wet sclerophyll forests to dry woodlands of

Limnodynastes dumerilii

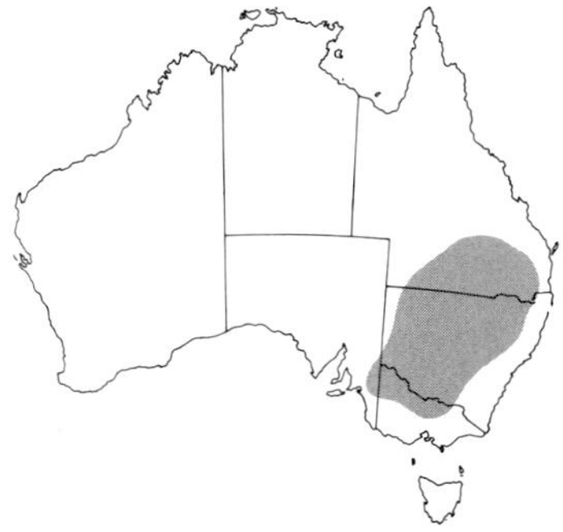

Limnodynastes fletcheri

Limnodynastes interioris

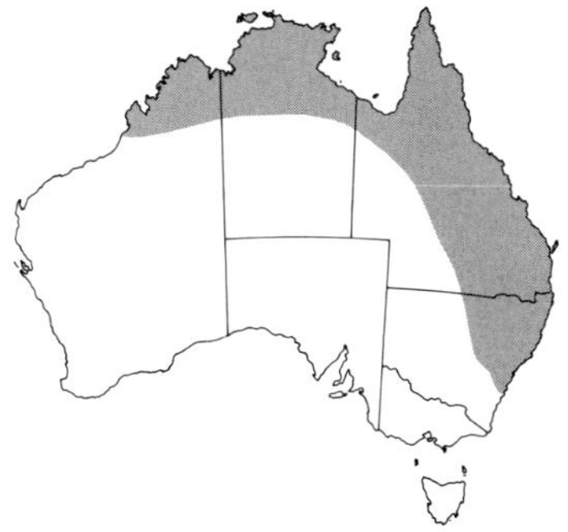

Limnodynastes ornatus

Limnodynastes peronii

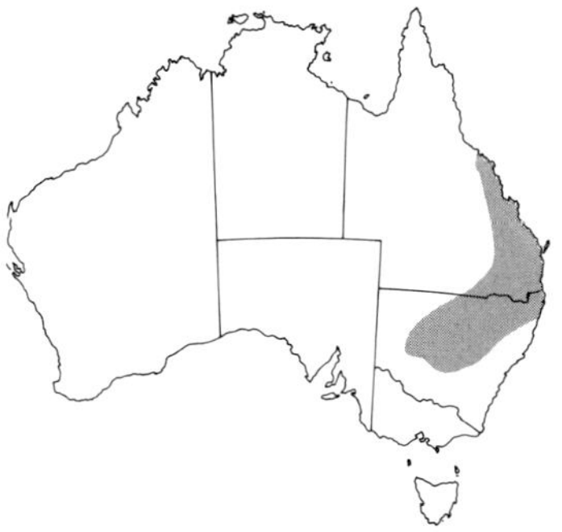

Limnodynastes salmini

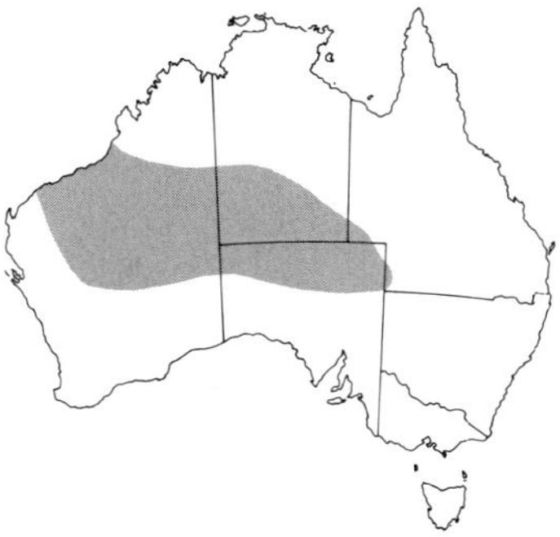

Limnodynastes spenceri

the interior. A burrowing species, it is usually found active after rain, or on warm, humid nights.

Limnodynastes peronii Duméril and Bibron,1841)

Brown-striped Frog

Description: Light brown or grey-brown above with a series of irregular dark brown stripes and spots, usually a broad band from the centre of the head to the vent and another on each side from the eye to the groin. A few scattered dark spots on the flanks. The dark dorsal markings often have lighter centres, while a pale vertebral stripe is often present. A dark band along snout, continued behind the eye, through the tympanum, to the base of the forelimb. This band is bordered below by a white or yellow glandular fold. Limbs with scattered dark spots and irregular cross bands. White below, often with a few brown flecks. Some specimens are much darker brown, with only faint markings, while others have the pale stripes on the body of light red or russet. Such latter specimens superficially resemble *L. salmini*. No tibial gland. Inner metatarsal tubercle not shovel-shaped. First finger slightly shorter than second. A single metatarsal tubercle. Toes without fringes and almost entirely free of web. Tympanum indistinct. 65 mm
Distribution: Tas. Coast and ranges of Vic, NSW and eastern Qld.
Habit: Usually found associated with permanent water throughout its range - slow-moving streams, swamps, marshes, dams and ponds. Especially common under debris on river flats. Also a highly successful urban species which thrives even in small, decorative garden ponds. Call a single loud 'plonk' or 'toc', like a hammer striking an anvil, repeated at intervals of a few seconds. Males call while almost totally submerged in water, often from beneath the floating egg-mass.

Limnodynastes salmini

Steindachner, 1867
Salmon-striped Frog

Description: Brown or grey-brown above, with scattered dark brown spots and blotches. A prominent salmon, pink or red stripe on either side from above the shoulder to the groin. Usually a vertebral stripe of similar colour from the middle of the back to the vent, occasionally complete to snout. A dark band along snout and from eye to tympanum, bordered below by a yellow or red glandular fold. A dark patch below the eye. Limbs spotted or faintly banded with dark brown. Belly and chest whitish, throat heavily spotted with brown. No tibial gland. Inner metatarsal tubercle not shovel-shaped. First finger longer than second. Inner and second metacarpal subequal. A single metatarsal tubercle. Toes with rudimentary webbing, not fringed. Tympanum fairly distinct. 75 mm
Distribution: Central inland of NSW, reaching the coast only in the far north of the State. Coast and near-coastal areas of southern Qld.
Habit: A burrowing frog found above ground only after rain. At such times it shelters by day under logs etc. or in cavities in the ground. Utilizes temporary marshes, roadside ditches etc. for breeding.

Limnodynastes peronii Sydney, NSW 65mm

Limnodynastes peronii Baulkham Hills, NSW. Male guardin

Limnodynastes spenceri Parker, 1940

Description: Status uncertain. Similar in almost all respects to *L. ornatus*. However, the toes are about half-webbed and the proximal tubercle on the fourth toe (present in *L. ornatus*) is lacking in *spenceri*. 50 mm
Distribution: Restricted to the arid areas of central and western Australia.
Habit: A burrowing frog usually restricted to the sandy beds of non-perennial creeks and rivers, in which it breeds after rain. However, it also moves well into hills and ranges after rain, breeding in rock holes.

Limnodynastes tasmaniensis Günther 1858

Spotted Grass Frog

Description: Light brown to rich olive-green above, usually with a series of large, regular dark brown blotches and often with a narrow white, yellow or russet vertebral stripe from snout to vent. A dark band from snout to eye and from eye, through tympanum to base of forelimb. This band is bordered below by a white or yellow glandular fold. Limbs with irregular, dark cross-bars. White below, except for dark throat of adult males. Skin above smooth or with a few low warts, smooth below. No tibial gland. Inner metatarsal tubercle not enlarged, shovel-shaped. First finger shorter than second. Usually two metatarsal tubercles. Toes with only basal webbing and only slight fringes. Tympanum indistinct. 45 mm
Distribution: Widely distributed throughout Tas, Vic, eastern SA (including Eyre Peninsula), NSW and

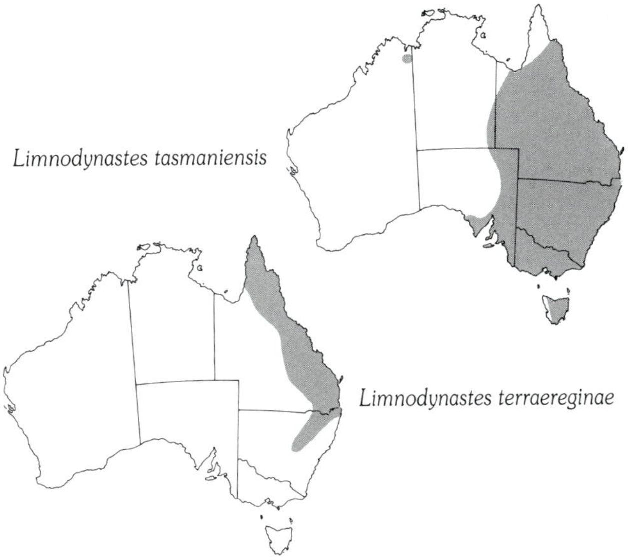

Limnodynastes tasmaniensis

Limnodynastes terraereginae

Limnodynastes spenceri near Mullewa, WA 50mm

M. PETERSON

oam nest. 65mm

Limnodynastes salmini Gulubuga, Qld 75mm

Limnodynastes tasmaniensis Botany, NSW. 45mm
Albino tadpoles and young occur regularly in this species, but they rarely reach adulthood.

Limnodynastes terraereginae Gilgandra, NSW 75mm

Limnodynastes tasmaniensis Mittagong, NSW. Form typical of the eastern coast and ranges, showing distinct pale vertebral stripe. 45mm

Limnodynastes tasmaniensis Sandringham Station, Qld. Typical dry inland form, lacking pale vertebral stripe. 45mm

eastern Qld. In 1978 Martin and Tyler recorded a localised, introduced population at Kununurra, WA. **Habit:** This species is found in a wide variety of habitats from wet coastal areas to the dry interior. It usually shelters under logs and stones on the edge of both permanent and temporary swamps, lagoons and creeks. After rain, it breeds among the shallow, grassy borders of these watercourses. Call ... 'a very rapid uk-uk-uk'...(Moore).

Limnodynastes terraereginae

Fry, 1915
Northern Banjo Frog

Description: Grey or brown above, with obscure darker flecks or blotches, and sometimes a faint vertebral stripe; sides grey. A cream or reddish-orange glandular stripe from below eye to arm, bordered above by a broad black stripe. Often a bright reddish-orange stripe on each flank, and a reddish patch on the upper arm. Groin and hind side of thigh with bright red markings. White or yellow below. Skin smooth or finely granular above, smooth below. A large tibial gland. A large shovel-shaped metatarsal tubercle. First finger slightly shorter than or equal to second. Toes with at most basal webbing. Tympanum more or less hidden. 75 mm
Distribution: Western slopes and ranges of northern NSW through eastern Qld to Cape York Peninsula.
Habit: Habits similar to those of *L. dorsalis*. Call is short and high-pitched. A burrowing frog of dry sclerophyll forests and woodlands, it is usually seen on the surface only after rain.

Genus *Megistolotis* Tyler, Martin and Davies, 1979

A monotypic genus containing a fat, somewhat globular, burrowing frog with granular skin, rather short limbs and toes with at most a rudiment of webbing. Fingers without a trace of webbing. Maxillary teeth present. Prominent vomerine teeth behind the choanae. Pupil vertical. Tympanum distinct. Phalanges simple, tips of digits not dilated. A narrow frontoparietal foramen and calcified sternum in adults, the sternum bifid posteriorly. Inner metatarsal tubercle large, not pigmented. While closely allied to the genus *Limnodynastes*, it resembles the genus *Heleioporus*, with which it shares the possession of pigmented conical spines on the prepollex and first finger of breeding males; absence of flanged fingers in breeding females; production of a floating foam nest; usually conspicuous tympanum; vertically elliptic pupil; unpigmented eggs; extensive, complex skin flap in anterior corner of eye. Tyler, Martin and Davies distinguish *Megistolotis* from *Heleioporus* primarily on its possession of a continuous row of vomerine teeth behind the choanae, its stream-dwelling tadpoles with large, ventral suctorial mouths, and its possession of a vocal sac.

Megistolotis lignarius Tyler, Martin and Davies, 1979

Description: A rather flat-headed species. Rich chocolate-brown above with darker brown variegations covering the head and body; the lighter areas are sometimes white or yellow, giving the impression of irregular, pale, spots on a dark ground colour. Limbs dark brown with irregular, pale, spots. A broken, whitish glandular stripe from below the eye, below the large, conspicuous tympanum almost to the base of the forelimb. Hind side of thighs dark purplish brown. Whitish below, flushed with purplish-brown. Skin granular on head, back and sides, with many small warts capped with minute black spines. A flap containing an irregular cluster of small papillae in the anterior corner of the eye, each papilla capped by a small black spine in breeding males. 50 mm
Distribution: Currently known only from the sandstone hills and gorges of the region between the eastern Kimberleys, WA, and the western escarpment of Arnhem Land, NT.
Habit: Call '...a soft, regularly repeated "tap"...' (Tyler, Martin and Davies). Found on rocky ledges, screes and boulder fields, usually near both perennial and non-perennial small streams in stony hills and escarpments.

Megistolotis lignarius

Megistolotis lignarius
Mt Brockman, NT

30mm

Genus **Metacrinia** Parker 1940

A small, stubby toadlet whose hindlimb when adpressed reaches well beyond the tympanum. No webbing on fingers or toes. Maxillary teeth absent. A large fronto-parietal foramen in adults. Vomerine teeth absent. Pupil horizontal. Tympanum distinct or hidden. Belly granular. Considered by some researchers to be a synonym of *Pseudophryne*.

Metacrinia nichollsi Rocky Gully, WA. Underside, showing distinctive orange patches on chest and legs.

25mm

Metacrinia nichollsi

Metacrinia nichollsi (Harrison, 1927)

Nicholls' Toadlet

Description: Dark brown to black above, sometimes with irregular dark markings and sometimes with tiny pinkish flecks. Grey, bluish or black below, marbled and spotted with white and with a bright yellow or orange glandular spot at the base of each forelimb. Spots of the same colour in front of the thighs and on the hind legs. Males often with darker throats. Skin warty above, granular below. A fold of skin extends back from each eyelid. 25 mm
Distribution: Coast, extending into ranges, of the south-western tip of Australia, centred in Pemberton district.
Habit: A cryptozoic inhabitant of the wet karri forests, where it is usually found under stones and logs. Call a short, grating squelch.

Metacrinia nichollsi Rocky Gully, WA

Genus **Mixophyes** Günther, 1864

Large, well-built frogs with powerful hindlimbs, strongly webbed feet and banded legs. Maxillary teeth present. Prominent vomerine teeth in front of the choanae. Pupil vertical. Tympanum distinct. Characteristically a narrow dark brown or black stripe from the snout to the eye (but interrupted by the nostril) and extending behind the eye over and behind the tympanum, where it usually broadens. All species are terrestrial inhabitants of rain-, antarctic beech or wet sclerophyll forests, feeding on insects and smaller frogs. Females are larger than males.

Key

TO THE SPECIES OF MIXOPHYES

1 Length of inner metatarsal tubercle nearly equal to length of first toe (a); three joints of fourth toe free of web (except for fringe along outer margin) (a)........................ **2**

Length of inner metatarsal tubercle only about half the length of the first toe (b); only two joints of fourth toe free of web (b).. **4**

2 Dark cross-bands on limbs well-defined, widening posteriorly to form dark triangles visible from below (c); a series of conspicuous black spots or blotches on the sides **3**

Dark cross-bands on limbs poorly defined, not forming dark triangles visible from below (d); no conspicuous black spots or blotches on the sides.............................. ***balbus***

3 Upper lip (behind level of nostril) pale creamy-white, without darker blotches in adults .... ***fasciolatus***

Upper lip (behind level of nostril) brownish, with one or more dark purplish-brown blotches in adults........... ***fleayi***

4 Dark cross-bands on limbs as broad as pale interspaces (e); a broad zone of dark spots on the sides........ ***iteratus***

Dark cross-bands on limbs narrower than pale interspaces (f); only a few scattered dark spots on the sides. ***schevilli***

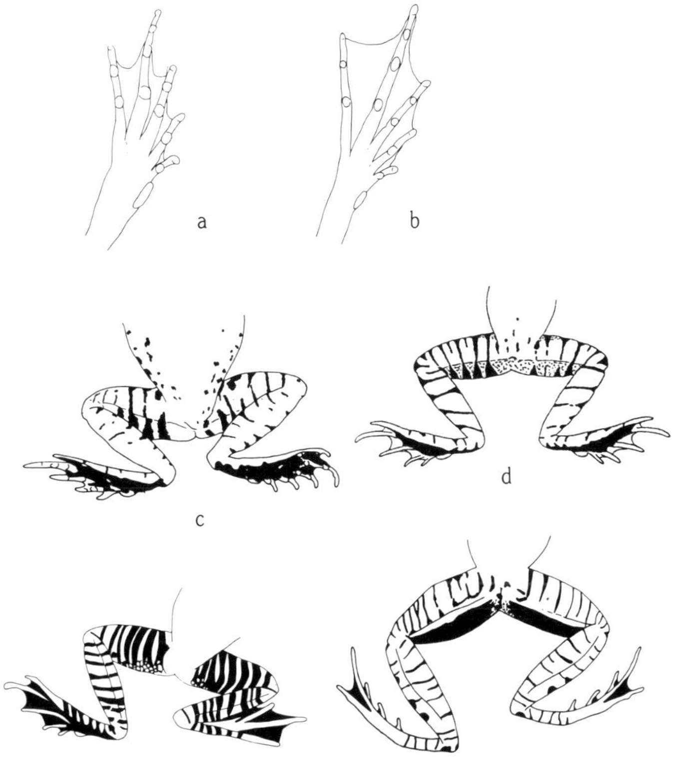

Mixophyes balbus Straughan, 1968

Description: Yellow-grey above, with pattern similar to that of *M. fasciolatus*; dark dorsal surface merging on sides with white of belly, not separated by dark lateral spots. Limbs with very narrow dark crossbars, much narrower than the paler interspaces and often incomplete or indistinct. Hind side of thighs speckled with black. Upper part of iris pale blue. Outer metacarpal tubercle well-developed; inner metatarsal tubercle shovel-shaped, as long as first toe; three joints of fourth toe free of web (except for a lateral fringe). 80 mm
Distribution: From northern NSW, east of the Great Dividing Range, to Vic.
Habit: As for genus.

Mixophyes fasciolatus Günther, 1864

Great Barred Frog

Description: Dark grey or brown above with darker blotches; a dark brown vertebral band, with irregular edges, starting between the eyes; sometimes this band is broken up into a series of blotches. A series of dark spots or blotches on the sides, dividing the dark back from the white belly. Limbs with dark cross-bands which are narrower than the paler interspaces; these dark bands widen on hind edges of limb to form a saw-toothed pattern. Dark flecks on chin and throat. Upper part of iris reddish-brown to black. Outer metacarpal tubercle well-developed; inner metatarsal tubercle as long as first toe; three joints of fourth toe free of web (except for a fringe along outer margins). 80 mm
Distribution: Along Great Dividing Range and coast from Bundaberg, Qld, to south coast of NSW.
Habit: As for genus.

Mixophyes fleayi Corben and Ingram, 1987

Description: Medium to pale brown above with obscure darker blotches, the most conspicuous of which is a darker brown vertebral band, with irregular edges, starting between the eyes; as in other species of *Mixophyes*, this band is sometimes broken up into a series of blotches. A series of dark spots or blotches on the flanks; belly yellowish. Limbs with dark cross-bands which are narrower than the paler interspaces; these dark bands widen on hind edges of limb to form a saw-toothed pattern. Upper part of iris silvery-white to pale blue. Outer metacarpal tubercle well developed; inner metatarsal tubercle as long as first

Mixophyes fleayi Lamington National Park, Qld 80mm

Mixophyes balbus

toe; three joints of fourth toe free of web (except for a fringe along outer margins). 80 mm
Distribution: Along Great Dividing Range and coast from the Conondale Range in south-eastern Qld to about the Clarence River in north-eastern NSW.
Habit: As for genus.

Mixophyes iteratus Straughan, 1968
Giant Barred Frog

Description: Dark olive to black above, with only a faint indication of the pattern described for *M. fasciolatus*. A broad lateral band of dark spots or mottling dividing dark dorsal from white ventral surface. Limbs with dark crossbars which are as wide as the paler interspaces. Hind side of thighs black with a few large, yellow spots. Upper part of iris pale silvery-white to pale gold. Outer metacarpal tubercle flat, poorly developed; inner metatarsal tubercle well-developed, but only half as long as first toe; two joints of fourth toe free of web (except for a lateral fringe). 115 mm
Distribution: Bunya Mts, Qld, and coast and ranges of south-eastern Qld and northern NSW south to about Narooma.
Habit: As for genus.

Mixophyes schevilli Loveridge, 1933
Northern Barred Frog

Description: Yellowish to dark brown above, often with reddish tint, with dorsal pattern similar to that of *M. fasciolatus*. A few scattered dark spots on the sides. Belly white. Limbs with dark cross-bands which are narrower than the paler interspaces, and which merge on the hind side of legs to form a dark horizontal band. Dark flecks on chin and throat. Upper part of iris dark brown to black. Outer metacarpal tubercle flat, poorly developed; inner metatarsal tubercle about half as long as first toe; two joints of fourth toe free of web (except for a lateral fringe). 90 mm
Distribution: Atherton Tableland and coastal ranges north of the Johnstone River, Qld.
Habit: As for genus.

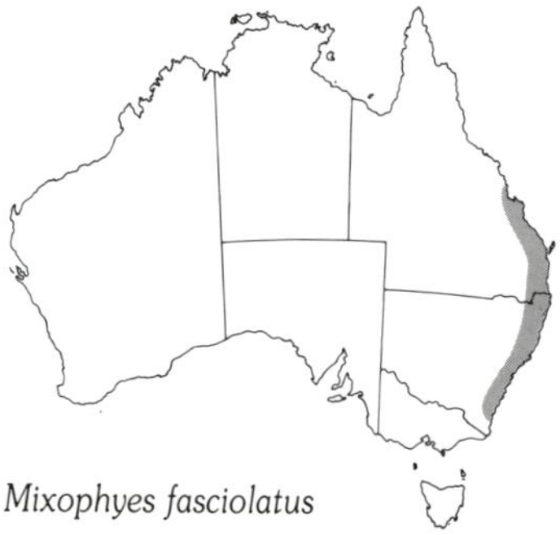

Mixophyes fasciolatus

Mixophyes fleayi

Mixophyes iteratus

Mixophyes schevilli
Thornton Peak, Qld
90mm

Mixophyes fasciolatus
Lamington National Park, Qld
80mm

Mixophyes schevilli

Mixophyes iteratus Ourimbah, NSW
115mm

Genus ***Myobatrachus*** Schlegel, 1850

A single species readily identified by its unique shape with small head and stubby limbs. Maxillary teeth absent. A large fronto-parietal foramen in adults. Prevomer (and hence vomerine teeth) absent. Tongue small. Pupil horizontal to circular. Tympanum hidden. Toes without any webbing. Adpressed hindlimb does not reach base of forelimb.

Myobatrachus gouldii Ongerup, WA 60mm

Myobatrachus gouldii (Gray, 1841)

Turtle Frog

Description: Dull grey or brown above, occasionally with faint darker and lighter variegations, and sometimes with small pink dots and/or a fine vertebral stripe. Dirty white below, sometimes flecked with dark brown. Skin shagreened above, smooth to faintly granular below. A distinctive globular frog, with very small head and short, stubby limbs. 60 mm

Distribution: Extreme south-west of WA, from Geraldton and Houtman Abrolhos in the north to about Esperance in the south.

Habit: A burrowing, termite-eating species often found associated with termite nests. Otherwise found under logs, etc, or on the surface after rain. Eggs believed to develop out of water, having no aquatic tadpole stage. Burrows head-first, using its powerful forelimbs.

Myobatrachus gouldii

Genus ***Neobatrachus*** Peters, 1863

Small to moderate, stout burrowing frogs, with smooth, granular or warty skin, relatively stubby limbs and conspicuous webbing between the toes. Maxillary teeth present. Prominent vomerine teeth between, or slightly in front of, the choanae. Phalanges simple, tips of fingers not dilated. A large fronto-parietal foramen in adults, and a cartilaginous sternum in adults, the sternum notched, but not bifid posteriorly. Inner metatarsal tubercle large, usually black or brown

Key

TO THE SPECIES OF NEOBATRACHUS

1 Toes at least half webbed (p.52) **2**

Toes not more than one third webbed (except in breeding males where the web continues as a tapering fringe to the tip of each toe.. ***pelobatoides***

2 Eye not longer than its distance from the tip of the snout (a); dark blotches or marbling on a light ground.............. **3**

Eye longer than its distance from the tip of the snout ; light bifurcating lines on a dark ground.................... ***wilsmorei***

3 Skin smooth above (may be spinose in breeding males); inner metatarsal tubercle rather narrowly edged with brown or black (b), or occasionally not coloured............ **4**

Skin tubercular or warty above (spinose in breeding males); inner metatarsal tubercle black (c)...................... **7**

4 Skin spinose in breeding males; vomerine teeth in a long row between the choanae (p.52) ; dorsal pattern of small blotches... **5**

Skin not spinose in breeding males; vomerine teeth in a short row between the choanae; dorsal pattern of large blotches.. ***sutor***

5 Foot length/snout-vent length ratio less than 0.4.............. **6**

Foot length/snout-vent length ratio greater than 0.38; sub-tropical arid Australia....................................... ***centralis***

6 Adult size moderate to large, snout-vent length to 42 mm (males), 48 mm (females); diploid chromosome number (2n = 24); North West Cape region of WA .... ***fulvus***

Adult size large, snout-vent length to 55 mm (males), 60 mm (females); tetraploid chromosome number (2n = 48); Kimberley region of WA .... ***aquilonius***

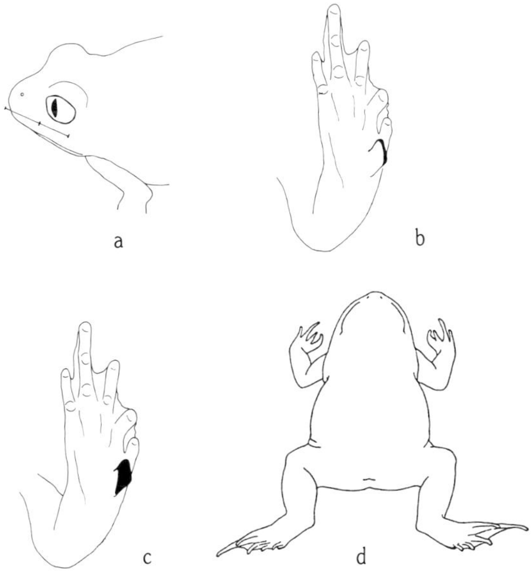

7 Skin in groin often loose, extending from side of body to knee (d); adult size about 40 mm.................................... **8**

Skin in groin not loose, not extending from side of body to knee; adult size to 50 mm...................................... ***pictus***

8 Adult size to about 40 mm; eastern Australia......... ***sudelli***

Adult size to about 60 mm; southern WA...... ***kunapalari***

Neobatrachus aquilonius Tyler, Davies and Martin, 1981

Description: Pale grey (mustard-yellow in life) above, variegated and mottled with dark brown or black, sometimes with a narrow, pale vertebral stripe. Whitish below except for the limbs which are plum-coloured in life. Skin finely tubercular above, smooth below. A conspicuous black inner metatarsal

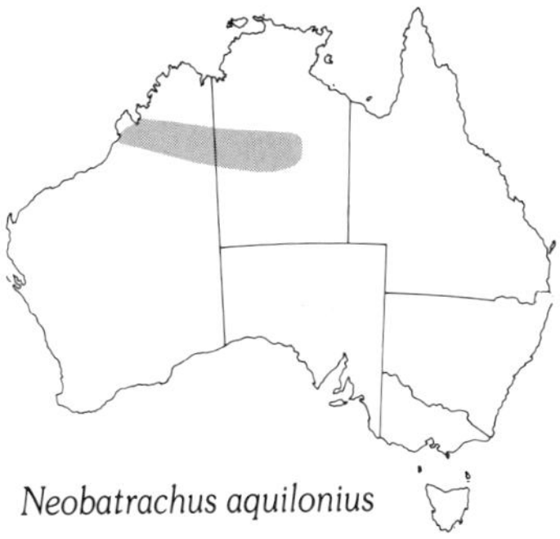

Neobatrachus aquilonius

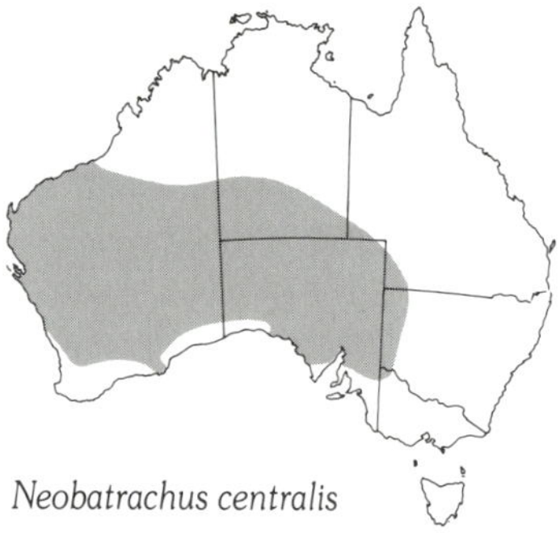

Neobatrachus centralis

Neobatrachus aquilonius Port Hedland, WA 60mm

tubercle. Toes about half webbed. Tympanum hidden. 60 mm
Distribution: Derby-Broome region, WA.
Habit: A burrowing species found above ground only after rain. Call a '...soft, slow rattle' (Tyler, Davies and Martin).

Neobatrachus centralis (Parker,1940)
Trilling Frog

Description: Status uncertain: a member of a complex of species including *N. sudelli* and *N. kunapalari*. Pale brown or yellow, with small irregular darker patches and usually a narrow, pale vertebral stripe. White below. Skin smooth above (spinose in breeding males), smooth below. A compressed inner metatarsal tubercle, narrowly edged with black or brown. Toes more or less fully webbed. Vomerine teeth in a long row between the choanae. Tympanum very indistinct. 55 mm
Distribution: As currently defined this species is widely distributed through central Australia and SA; probably also Vic, north-western NSW, south-western Qld and the far southeast of WA.
Habit: A burrowing species found breeding in flooded claypans after summer and autumn rains. Call a high-pitched trill.

Neobatrachus centralis Woomera, SA 55mm

Neobatrachus fulvus Mahoney and Roberts, 1986

Description: Dark brown above with paler yellowish spots, blotches and variegations and a dark bar between the eyes. White below, except for darker edge to lower jaw and dark sides of throat. Skin more or less smooth above, with at most a few small, low warts; smooth below. The skin in the groin is loose, extending from the side of the body to the knee. A conspicuous, compressed inner metatarsal tubercle, rectangularly shaped with rounded edges and narrowly edged with black. Toes about half webbed. Tympanum hidden. 50 mm
Distribution: Currently recorded only from the North West Cape region of WA.
Habit: A burrowing species recorded from both dunes and open mulga woodland. As with related species it breeds in claypans after summer and autumn rains. Call a high-pitched trill.

Neobatrachus kunapalari Mahoney and Roberts, 1986

Description: Bright yellowish above with numerous dark brown or black spots, blotches and variegations. White below, except for grey throat and dark purplish-brown under hands and feet. Skin above with numerous small warts which are spinose in breeding

M. PETERSON

Neobatrachus pelobatoides Gingin, WA 50mm

Neobatrachus sutor Marchagee, WA 45mm

males; smooth below. A conspicuous, compressed, semicircular-shaped inner metatarsal tubercle, broadly edged with black. Toes almost fully webbed. Tympanum indistinct. 60 mm
Distribution: Widely distributed in southwestern Australia, but the northern and eastern limits of its range are uncertain.
Habit: A burrowing species which like its close relatives breeds in flooded claypans after summer and autumn rains. Call a high-pitched trill.

Neobatrachus pelobatoides

(Werner, 1914)
Humming Frog

Description: Pale grey, yellow or brown to dark brown above, with irregular darker brown or grey-green patches and sometimes with a narrow red vertebral stripe. White or yellowish below, except for darker edge to lower jaw and dark sides of throat. Skin with numerous small warts above, smooth below. A conspicuous, compressed inner metatarsal tubercle, edged with brown. Toes only about one quarter webbed (except for almost complete webbing in freshly metamorphosed specimens and breeding males). Tympanum indistinct. 50 mm
Distribution: South-western WA, from about Geraldton in the north to Esperance in the south.
Habit: A burrowing species usually found after autumn rains, when it breeds in temporarily-flooded claypans. Call '... a long, low-pitched trill or hum' (Main).

Neobatrachus pictus Peters, 1863

Description: Grey, light brown or yellow above with large, irregular dark-brown or olive green patches and usually a thin, light yellowish vertebral stripe. White

Neobatrachus fulvus

Neobatrachus kunapalari

Neobatrachus pelobatoides

Neobatrachus pictus

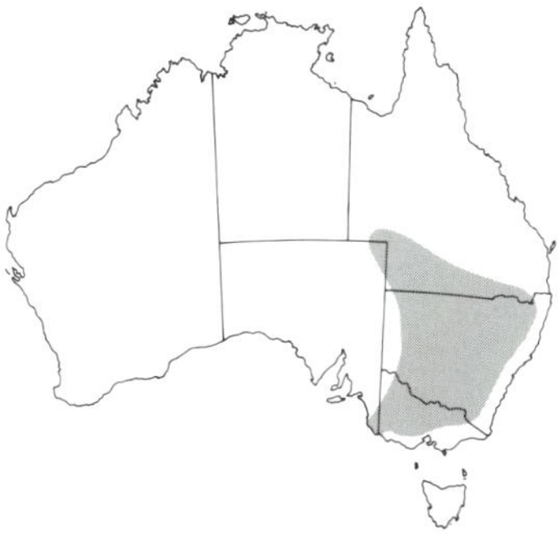

Neobatrachus sudelli

Neobatrachus sudelli Warrumbungle Mts, NSW 40mm

Neobatrachus sudelli Sandringham Station, Qld 40mm

below, except for darker edge to lower jaw and dark sides of throat. Skin with numerous small warts above (spinose in breeding males), the darker warts often tipped with yellow. Smooth below. A large, compressed, black inner metatarsal tubercle. Toes more or less fully webbed. Tympanum indistinct. 50 mm

Distribution: South-eastern SA and probably adjoining areas of Vic and NSW.

Habit: A burrowing species usually found only after summer rains when it breeds in grassy marshes, lagoons, flooded claypans and temporary roadside pools.

Neobatrachus sudelli (Lamb, 1911)

Description: Status uncertain; probably composite as currently recognised. Grey, brown, yellow or reddish-brown above, with large dark brown or olive patches or marbling and usually a narrow, pale, white, cream or yellow vertebral stripe. White below, except for darker throat and edge to lower jaw in breeding males. Skin with numerous small warts above (spinose in breeding males), the darker warts sometimes tipped with yellow. Smooth below. A large, compressed, black inner metatarsal tubercle. Toes more or less fully webbed. Tympanum indistinct. 40 mm

Distribution: The type locality is southern Qld, but specimens from NSW, Vic and extreme south-eastern SA are currently referred to this species by default.

Habit: As for *Neobatrachus pictus.*

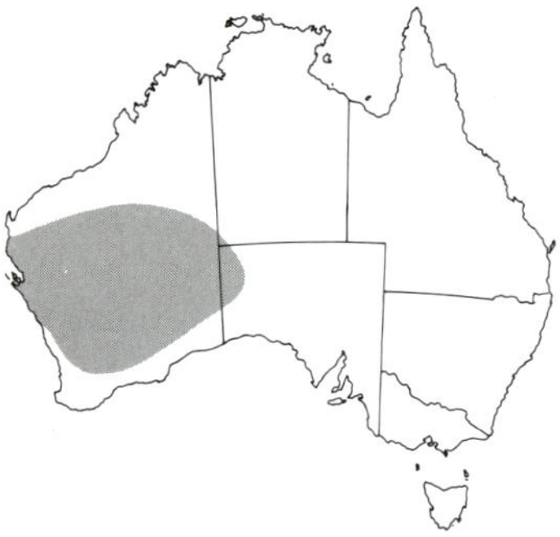

Neobatrachus sutor

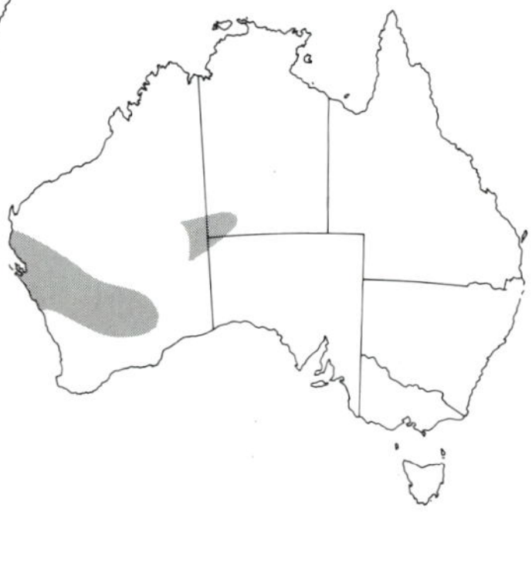

Neobatrachus wilsmorei

Neobatrachus sutor Main, 1957

Shoemaker Frog

Description: Light yellow or golden above with irregular brown blotches. White below. Skin smooth above (not spinose in breeding males), smooth below. A conspicuous, compressed inner metatarsal tubercle edged with brown or black. Toes more or less fully webbed. Vomerine teeth in a very short row between the choanae. Tympanum indistinct. 45 mm

Distribution: Widely distributed throughout the southern half of WA except for the wetter extreme south-western and southern areas and extending into far north-western SA.

Habit: A burrowing species with habits similar to those of *N. centralis.* Call a '...repetitive tapping' (Main).

Neobatrachus wilsmorei (Parker,1940)

Goldfields Bull Frog

Description: Dark chocolate brown above with a

R.W.G. JENKINS

Neobatrachus wilsmorei Wiluna, WA

60mm

bright yellow vertebral stripe and a pair of yellow stripes on each side of the body.Each pair starts at the tympanic region, one stripe running almost to the anus, and the other running obliquely down the groin. Ventral surface white. Skin smooth, but glandular above, smooth below. Inner metatarsal tubercle large, compressed, edged with black. Toes about two-thirds webbed. Tympanum indistinct. 60 mm

Distribution: Drier, southern-central regions of WA, from about Carnarvon in the north to Kalgoorlie in the south-east.

Habit: Similar in habit to *N. centralis* and *N. pelobatoides*. Call a '...plonk...plonk...plonk.. each a distinct single call' (Main).

Genus ***Notaden*** Günther, 1873

A group of medium sized globular frogs with warty bodies and short, stubby limbs. Maxillary teeth absent. A large fronto-parietal foramen in adults. Vomerine teeth present, prominent. Tongue large, oval. Pupil horizontal. Tympanum hidden. Phalanges simple, tips of digits without dilations. Toes with only basal webbing, but with fleshy lateral fringes. All feed on insects, especially ants and termites. All exude a thick, white, smelly poison when aroused, which becomes highly adhesive as it dries to a strong, elastic material.

Key

TO THE SPECIES OF NOTADEN

1 Dorsal surface with black tubercles or blotches; hindlimb short, the ratio of tibia length to snout-vent length (p.52) 0.34 or less........ **2**

Dorsal surface lacking black tubercles or blotches; hindlimb long, the ratio of tibia length to snout-vent length 0.34 or more........ ***weigeli***

2 First finger as long as, or longer than, second (a); inner metatarsal tubercle as long as its distance from the tip of the first toe (b) **3**

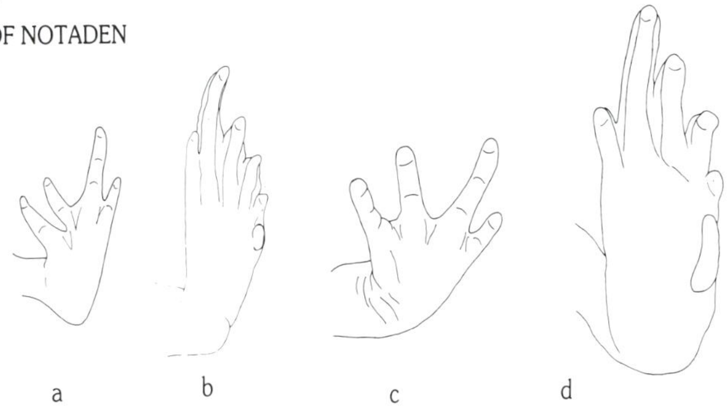

a b c d

First finger shorter than second (c); inner metatarsal tubercle 1.2-2 times as long as its distance from the tip of the first toe (d)... ***bennettii***

3 Inner metatarsal tubercle pale; dorsal tubercles smoothly rounded, not coalescing.................................... ***nichollsi***

Inner metatarsal tubercle black; dorsal tubercles rugose, coalescing to form glandular ridges....... ***melanoscaphus***

Notaden bennettii
55mm

Notaden bennettii Günther, 1873
Crucifix Toad

Description: Adults yellow, olive or green above, with low, rounded dark brown or black warts and scattered white, yellow and red spots arranged in a cruciform pattern. Sides with scattered yellow or white spots. White below. Juveniles bright yellow or brilliant emerald green with markings as described for adults. First finger shorter than second. Metatarsal tubercle pale-coloured. 55 mm
Distribution: Central inland NSW and interior of southern Qld, west of the Great Dividing Range.
Habit: Especially abundant on the black soil flood plains of the large river systems throughout its range, but is also found in savannah woodland and mallee areas. A burrowing frog, usually found above ground only after rain. Breeds in temporary pools. Call a series of long owl-like 'whoo-oos'.

Notaden melanoscaphus Hosmer, 1962
Northern Spadefoot Toad

Description: Dull grey to olive-brown or reddish-brown above with a symmetrical series of large blackish or dark brown blotches — one on the head commencing between the eyes, one on either side of the back above the shoulders, a median one halfway along the mid-dorsal line, and one on either side of the pelvic region. There are also some smaller, scattered, irregular dark blotches. The area between these blotches is yellowish to light brown with irregular flecks and spots of yellow and black, and sometimes red. Flanks and limbs grey, irregularly spotted with white. Limbs sometimes with dark brown bands. White or cream below. Throat of breeding male dark grey with fine white spots. Juveniles sometimes brilliantly marked, the dark blotches surrounded by bright yellow, the remaining areas with numerous,

Notaden bennettii
juvenile
Byrock, NSW

bright red, yellow and black spots. Limbs also with red spots. Dorsal tubercles sometimes very rough, often coalescing to form glandular ridges in the vertebral region. First finger as long as or longer than second. Inner metatarsal tubercle black. 55 mm
Distribution: Known from the Townsville region, the western side of Cape York Peninsula and the northern part of the NT and adjacent parts of WA.
Habit: A burrowing frog found in sparsely timbered savannah and sclerophyll woodland. Found above ground only after rain, or occasionally on humid evenings, usually on low-lying swampy ground which remains saturated or covered with shallow water after rain. Its call is similar to that of *Notaden bennettii* — a series of owl-like 'whoo-oos'.

Notaden nichollsi Parker, 1940

Desert Spadefoot Toad

Description: Brown, grey or olive above with low, rounded brown or black warts and a few scattered white, yellow and russet spots, these markings rarely arranged in a cruciform pattern. Sides with scattered white or yellow spots. White below. First finger as long as or longer than second. Inner metatarsal tubercle pale-coloured. Grows to about 60 mm
Distribution: South Kimberley and Pilbara areas of WA through the southern (desert) half of the NT to western Qld.
Habit: A burrowing frog which lives deep in arid, sandy areas throughout its range. Found above ground only after rain, when it comes to the surface to feed and breed in temporary desert claypans. Call 'oo-oo like cooing of pigeon' (Main).

Notaden melanoscaphus. Koongarra, NT. Typical dull colour of breeding adults. 55mm

Notaden melanoscaphus Koongarra, NT. Typical bright colour and pattern found in juveniles.

Notaden bennettii

Notaden melanoscaphus

Notaden nichollsi

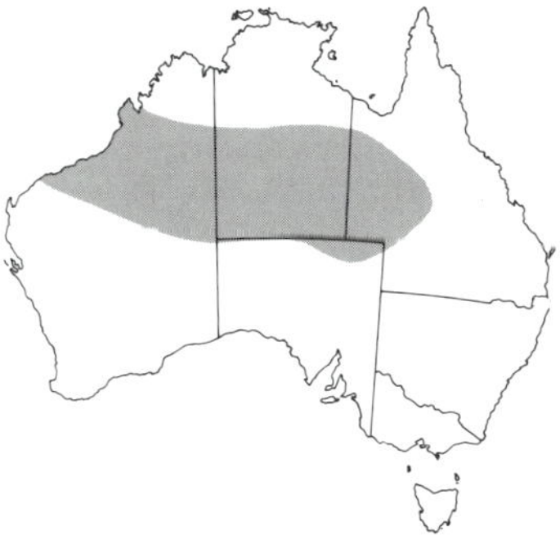

Notaden weigeli

Notaden nichollsi Tanami Desert, NT 60mm

Notaden weigeli Mitchell Falls, WA 70mm J. WEI

Notaden weigeli Shea and Johnston, 1987

Description: Fawn to reddish above with many scattered white-tipped orange tubercles and obscure olive blotches. Limbs grey above, flecked with white (and a few orange flecks on the hindlimbs). Pale grey below. First finger longer than second. Inner metatarsal tubercle pale-coloured. Grows to about 70 mm.
Distribution: North Kimberley region. WA.
Habit: Found in a variety of open woodland, hummock grass and rock outcrop habitats in heavily-dissected sandstone country.

Genus *Paracrinia* Heyer and Liem, 1976

A monotypic genus confined to south-eastern Australia. Maxillary teeth present. A large frontoparietal foramen in adults. Vomerine teeth present (although stated to be absent in the original generic description). Tongue small, narrow, oval, free behind. Pupil horizontal. Tympanum indistinct. Toes fringed, but without webbing. Phalanges simple, tips of fingers not or only very slightly dilated. Belly slightly granular.

Paracrinia haswelli (Fletcher 1894)

Haswell's Frog

Description: Light grey-brown or brown above with irregular darker flecks and often with a faint broad, darker band along the middle of the back, commencing between the eyes. Often a narrow,pale vertebral stripe, at least posteriorly. A black band from the nostril to the eye, and from the eye, below the supratympanic ridge to the flanks. Ventral surface pale brown with paler spots. Patch on the base of each arm, groins and hindside of thighs bright orange-red. Skin smooth or with a few low tubercles above, slightly granular below. Prevomer entire, vomerine teeth in two short rows behind the level of the choanae. Toes fringed. 35 mm
Distribution: Coastal areas from eastern Vic to a little north of Sydney, NSW.
Habit: An inhabitant of wet sclerophyll forests and the marginal vegetation of creeks, swamps and dams within coastal heathlands. Breeds in spring and early summer, calling from grasses and sedges emerging from the water. Sometimes found under stones in rocky creek beds.

Paracrinia haswelli
Stanwell Tops, NSW

35mm

Genus **Philoria** Spencer, 1901

A group of moderate to stout frogs. Maxillary teeth present. A large fronto-parietal foramen in adults. Vomerine teeth present behind the choanae. Tongue large, oval. First finger not opposed to second. Pupil horizontal. Tympanum hidden or indistinct. Terminal phalanges simple. Tips of digits not, or only very slightly, dilated.

Moore placed the two northern species then recognised in a new genus, *Kyarranus,* without defining generic differences. He referred only to an earlier diagnosis of *Philoria* which applies as well to the southern *frosti* as to the northern *loveridgei* or *sphagnicolus;* the latter two are therefore placed in the genus *Philoria* together with the more recently described *kundagungan.*

All species lay large eggs in tunnels in saturated soil or moss, where the larvae develop out of water within the egg capsules, to emerge as metamorphosed frogs.

Key

TO THE SPECIES OF PHILORIA

1 Sides and rump smooth; subarticular tubercles on hands and feet usually much lighter than surrounding colour; no conspicuous parotoid gland (a) **2**

Sides and rump with numerous tiny tubercles, giving a somewhat 'prickly' appearance; subarticular tubercles usually same colour as surrounding areas; usually a conspicuous parotoid gland (b)............................... ***frosti***

a

2 Flanks without a dark band; throat lightly mottled with brown; no dark band across the cloacal region **3**

A brown or black band along each flank; throat heavily mottled with brown; a horizontal brown or black band across the cloacal region.......................... ***sphagnicola***

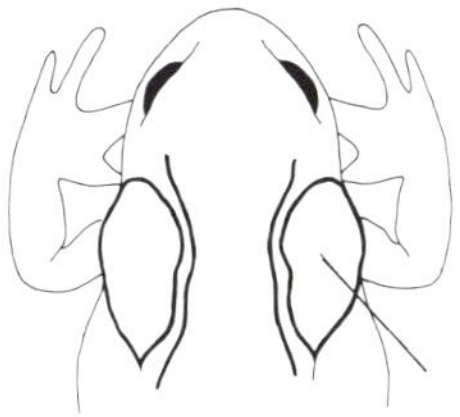

b

3 Body moderate; dark head stripes present; brown or reddish-brown above; skin above with tubercles and/or ridges... ***loveridgei***

Body squat, robust; head stripes absent; bright red to black above; skin above smooth............. ***kundagungan***

Philoria frosti

Philoria kundagungan

Philoria loveridgei

Philoria frosti Mt Baw Baw, Vic 45mm

Philoria frosti Spencer, 1901
Baw Baw Frog

Description: Adults usually dark brown above with a few scattered black flecks and with some irregular lighter patches. A prominent black lobe-shaped parotoid gland on each side, extending back over shoulder. Occasionally a broad white or cream vertebral band, more often this band being confined to the head and the region between the parotoid glands. Ventral surfaces and groin cream or yellowish, heavily mottled and flecked with brown. Upper surface with scattered small low tubercles or warts, especially on the sides and rump, giving a distinct 'prickly' appearance. Belly and throat smooth. Tympanum hidden.45 mm
Distribution: Known only from the higher parts of Mt. Baw Baw, Vic.
Habit: Found beneath streamside logs and rocks, or in tunnels in sphagnum bogs. Call a '...short "clunk" repeated in sequences of up to 30 calls' (Littlejohn). Breeds in late spring.

Philoria kundagungan (Ingram and Corben, 1975)

Description: Bright red to black above, often with two black V-shaped markings on the back above each groin; bright yellow below, except for a red patch on the throat (sometimes the entire throat is red). Skin smooth. Tympanum hidden. 30 mm
Distribution: Mistake Mts to Teviot Falls, south-eastern Qld.
Habit: '... saturated leaf-litter and mud in soaks or small creek beds' (Ingram and Corben), within montane forest.

Philoria loveridgei Parker, 1940
Loveridge's Frog

Description: Colour almost uniform brown above, with a dark brown band along the snout. Another dark band bordered above by a thin white line, from the eye to the base of the forelimb. Edge of upper lip with a few white spots. Upper surfaces of limbs may have faint crossbars. Brown lateral band, if present, indistinct. Belly white, with a few brown flecks; throat heavily dotted with dark brown. Skin smooth or with

Philoria loveridgei
Mt Warning, NSW
30mm

Philoria sphagnicolus Point Lookout, NSW. Pair found beside egg mass in dense mat of sphagnum moss. 35mm

a few low warts or ridges; a supra-tympanic fold. Skin smooth below. Tympanum indistinct. 30 mm
Distribution: Known only from the MacPherson Ranges, on the Qld/NSW border and from Gibraltar Range, NSW.
Habit: An inhabitant of antarctic beech and rainforest, and also wet sclerophyll forests, above about 750 metres. Burrows in loose, moist soil or moss, or sits in mossy cavities beside streams etc. Call a 'slow, guttural "ork"' Moore).

Philoria sphagnicola

Philoria sphagnicola (Moore, 1958)

Sphagnum Frog

Description: Colour varies from cream, through various shades of yellow, orange and russet to black above, usually with a number of irregular flecks and patches. The flecks are often associated with low tubercles, while the most constant markings are a pair of dark stripes which may meet in front. Dark specimens may have a broad, cream-coloured vertebral band. A dark brown or black band along the snout. Another dark band from the eye to the base of the forelimb, while a third dark band occurs along the flank. All three bands are bordered above by a thin white or cream line. Upper surfaces of limbs with faint, dark bars. Sometimes a prominent pale, triangular patch on the side of the face below the dark canthal streak. Belly white; throat lightly to heavily flecked with brown. Skin smooth, or with a few low warts or folds above, smooth below. Tympanum indistinct. 35 mm
Distribution: Known only from ranges near Ebor and Dorrigo to Barrington Tops, NSW.
Habit: Occupies habitat similar to that of *P. loveridgei*. Often found in cracks and other cavities behind and beside both large and small waterfalls where the environment remains saturated with moisture. Call a 'low and soft growl, "gur-r-r-r-r"' (Moore).

Genus *Pseudophryne* Fitzinger, 1843

A group of small, rather stout, short-limbed frogs, some with bright dorsal patterns but all with characteristic black and white marbling on the belly. Maxillary teeth absent. A large fronto-parietal foramen in adults. Vomerine teeth absent. Tongue small, narrowly oval. Pupil horizontal. Tympanum (and middle ear structures) absent. Phalanges simple, tips of digits not dilated. Parotoid glands moderately developed in most species. Toes without webbing. All species have rather similar calls — a short, harsh squelch.

Key

TO THE SPECIES OF PSEUDOPHRYNE

1 Inner metatarsal tubercle large, transverse, often shovel-shaped (a); inner toe with one (b) or two (c) phalanges....**2**

Inner metatarsal tubercle small, low, not shovel-shaped (c); inner toe with two phalanges (c)................................**3**

2 Outer metatarsal tubercle large, shovel-shaped (b); a large inguinal gland (p.52); inner toe with a single phalanx (b)..... .... ***guentheri***

Outer metatarsal tubercle small, conical (c); inner toe with two phalanges (c)..***douglasi***

3 A gland on the distal half of the hinder side of the thigh (d); sometimes obscure in preserved specimens); eastern Australia.. **4**

No gland behind the thigh; Western Australia................... .... ***occidentalis***

4 Snout pointed, prominent; internarial distance (p.52) shorter than the distance between nostril and tip of snout. **5**

Snout rounded, not prominent; internarial distance greater than distance between nostril and tip of snout.................**6**

5 Nostrils directed vertically upwards; belly and throat smooth; lower surfaces of limbs brown, mottled and spotted with white.. ***major***

Nostrils dorso-lateral; belly and throat smooth (females) or very coarsely granular (males); lower surfaces of limbs uniformly flesh-coloured or orange.......***semimarmorata***

6 Dorsal colour pattern not of irregular black and yellow stripes **7**

Dorsal colour pattern of irregular alternate stripes of black and bright yellow.. ***corroboree***

7 Dorsal surface as dark as or darker than sides.................**8**

Dorsal surface reddish, paler than the blackish sides.......... .... ***coriacea***

8 No reddish triangular patch on the crown; a yellow or orange patch on the upper arm....................................... **9**

A bright red or orange triangular patch on the crown; a white patch on the upper arm...........................***australis***

9 A small yellow or orange patch on the base of the upper arm, but not extending to the elbow; no yellow spots or patches on the upper lips or sides of the face; any yellow on the hind side of the thigh confined to femoral gland....... .... ***bibronii***

A bright yellow patch covering the top of the upper arm, and normally extending to the elbow; usually some yellow spots or patches on the upper lips or sides of the face; a bright yellow patch extending from the cloaca along each hind leg, but not usually reaching the femoral gland....... (f) .... ***dendyi***

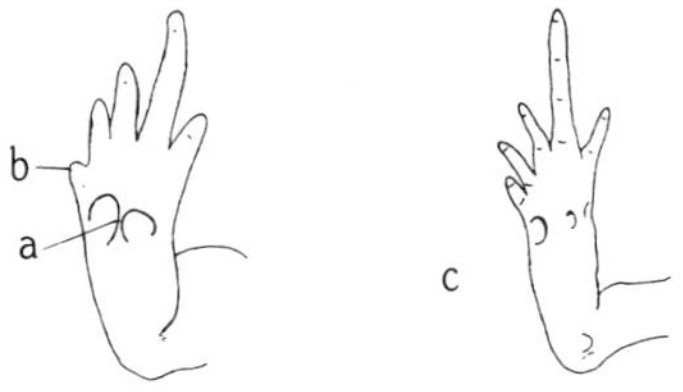

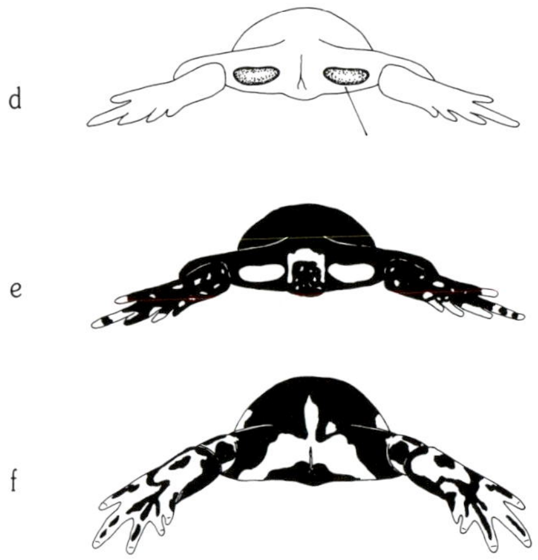

Pseudophryne australis (Gray, 1835)

Red-Crowned Toadlet

Description: Dark brown to black above, often washed with red or with scattered reddish flecks, and with a bright red or orange triangle on the head and a red or orange coccygeal stripe. A white patch on the base of each arm. Ventral surface with large black and white blotches mixed with grey, black and white mottling.Skin smooth or with a few low warts above, smooth below. A large, flat femoral gland on each hindlimb. Inner metatarsal tubercle low, round, not shovel-shaped. Inner toe with two phalanges. 30 mm
Distribution: Found within a radius of about 160 km of Sydney, NSW. However, within this area it is almost totally confined to the Hawkesbury sandstone formation.

Pseudophryne australis
Turramurra, NSW
30mm

When disturbed, many species of *Pseudophryne* will remain immobile as a passive form of defence, even when placed on their backs, Ebor, NSW.

Pseudophryne bibronii Brindabella Range, ACT. Female with eggs beneath thick mat of leaf litter. 30mm

Habit: Breeding congregations occur deep in grass and debris beside non-perennial creeks, gutters etc. in sandstone areas; at other times individuals disperse and are found under rocks, logs etc. on sandstone ridges.

Pseudophryne bibronii Günther, 1858

Brown Toadlet

Description: Brown to almost black above, with scattered darker flecks and sometimes with scattered reddish spots. Often a pale vertical mark on the tip of the snout, a faint yellowish coccygeal stripe and bright yellow area around the anal region. An orange or yellow patch on the base of each arm. Ventral surfaces boldly marbled with white and black. Skin usually with scattered low warts above, smooth or slightly granular below. A large, flat femoral gland on each hindlimb. Inner metatarsal tubercle low, round, not shovel-shaped. Inner toe with two phalanges. 30 mm

Distribution: Widely distributed through south-eastern Qld, the eastern half of NSW, Vic and south-eastern SA. Also Tas.

Habit: Usually found singly under rocks, logs etc. in both wet and dry sclerophyll forest; breeding congregations usually occur in inundated grassy areas beside gutters, small creeks etc. Also occurs in alpine grasslands and mossy bogs.

Pseudophryne coriacea Keferstein, 1868

Red-backed Toadlet

Description: Rich brown to bright red above, with scattered darker flecks, contrasting sharply with a broad black lateral band extending along the side of the head and body to a white patch on the base of each arm, and to the groin. Sometimes a pale patch on each side, in the middle of the black lateral band. Ventral surface broadly marbled with black and white. Skin smooth to velvety, sometimes with scattered low

Pseudophryne australis

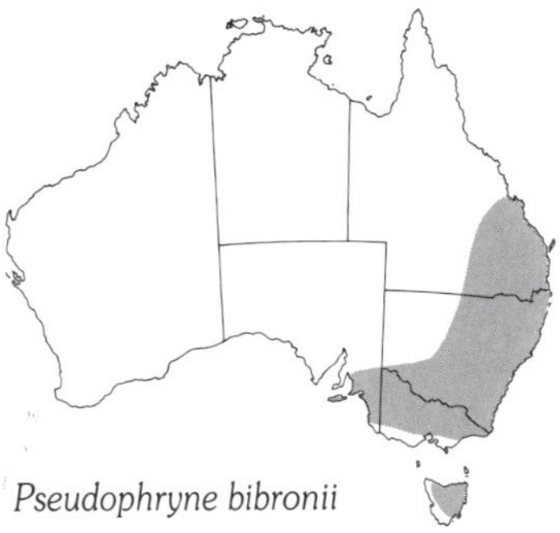

Pseudophryne bibronii

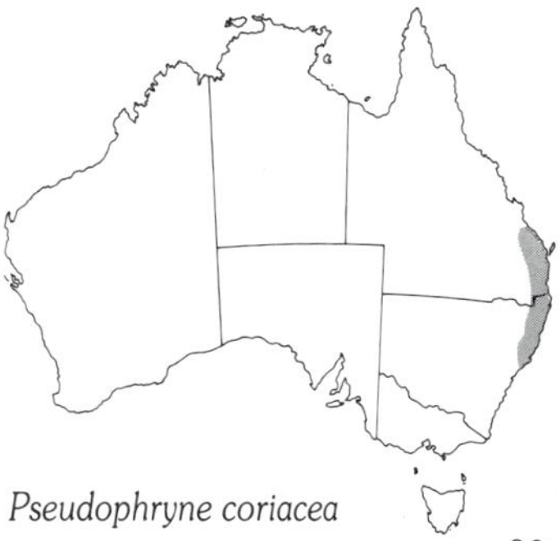

Pseudophryne coriacea

Pseudophryne coriacea Bulahdelah, NSW. Male, with eggs in chamber beneath grass mat at edge of marsh. 35mm

warts. Smooth or faintly granular below. A low femoral gland on each hindlimb. Inner metatarsal tubercle low, round, not shovel-shaped. Inner toe with two phalanges. 35 mm

Distribution: South-eastern Qld and coastal areas of the northern half of NSW.

Habit: An inhabitant of sclerophyll forest and low-lying marshy areas, where it is found under logs or deep in grass beside creeks or at the edge of swamplands.

Pseudophryne corroboree Mt Kosciusko, NSW 30mm

Pseudophryne corroboree Moore, 1953

Corroboree Frog

Description: The most distinctive and easily recognised of all Australian frogs.Bright yellow or greenish-yellow above with shiny longitudinal irregular black stripes, the latter frequently broken and interconnected. This pattern extends over the limbs and flanks. Ventral surface broadly marbled with black and white or black and yellow. Skin slightly granular above with low warts which tend to coalesce to form longitudinal ridges. Smooth below. A large; flat femoral gland on each hindlimb. Inner metatarsal tubercle low, round, not shovel-shaped. Inner toe with a single phalanx. 30 mm
Distribution: The Australian Alps, including the high, alpine country of NSW centred on Mt. Kosciusko, and with an outlier in the high country bordering and entering the ACT (Brindabella and associated mountain ranges).
Habit: Found in grassy marshlands above treeline, or under logs and in vegetation beside creeks, marshes, etc. in wet sclerophyll forest. During breeding season (November to January) Corroboree Frogs are found in alpine sphagnum bogs where they breed in burrows.

Pseudophryne dendyi Lucas, 1892

Description: Status uncertain. Similar in most respects to *P. bibronii,* from which it differs by its shorter limbs (tip of fourth toe of adpressed hindlimb not reaching tip of snout; reaches to tip of snout or beyond in *bibronii*). Typically, bright yellow patches on the upper arm, across the cloacal region and on the 'interocular region'. 35 mm
Distribution: Confined to south-eastern NSW and eastern Vic, where it is almost invariably allopatric to *P. bibronii.*
Habit: Habitat similar to that of *P. bibronii.*

Pseudophryne douglasi Main, 1964

Description: Brown above, often with an orange triangle on the snout and an orange coccygeal stripe. Finely mottled with black and white below. Skin with small, conical warts above, smooth below. Inner metatarsal tubercle large, shovel-shaped; outer metatarsal tubercle small, conical. Inner toe with two phalanges. 30 mm
Distribution: NW Cape-Hamersley Range region of WA.
Habit: Found in '...permanent seeps or deep-shaded, well-vegetated permanent pools in deep gorges and canyons' (Main).

Pseudophryne guentheri Boulenger, 1882

Günther's Toadlet

Description: Grey or brown above, with irregular darker mottling, and usually with a light patch on the snout, another above each shoulder, and a light coccygeal stripe. Lower surfaces white, heavily spotted or marbled with black. Skin with scattered small warts above, smooth below except on the throat, hind part of the belly and lower surfaces of the

Pseudophryne dendyi near Mt Kosciusko, NSW 35mm

Pseudophryne guentheri Northcliffe, WA 30mm

Pseudophryne guentheri

Pseudophryne major Ravenshoe, Qld 40mm

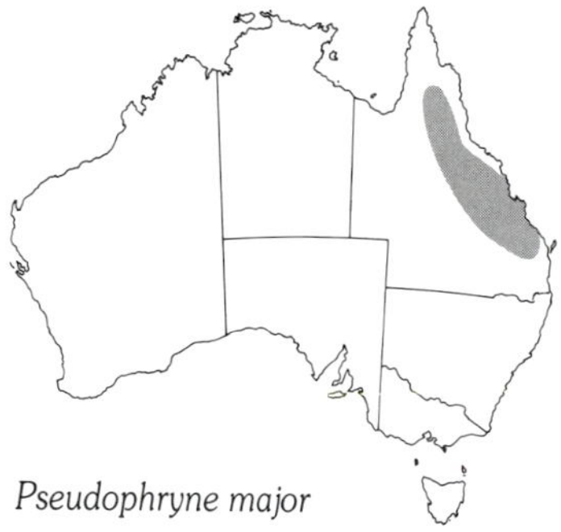

Pseudophryne major

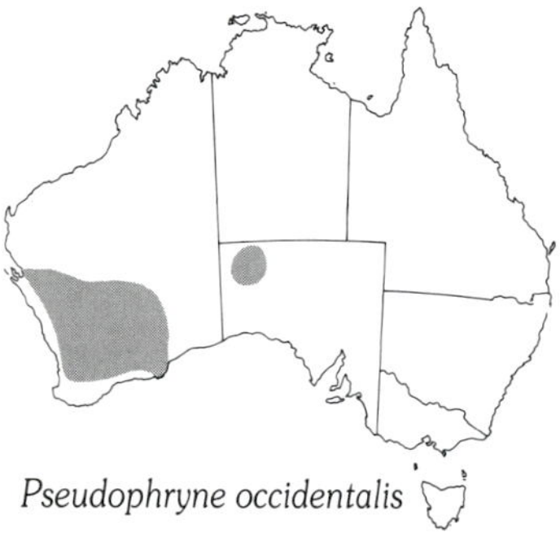

Pseudophryne occidentalis

Pseudophryne semimarmorata

Pseudophryne semimarmorata 30mm
Birdport, Tas

thighs, which are slightly granular. Inner and outer metatarsal tubercles large, shovel-shaped. Inner toe with a single phalanx. 30 mm
Distribution: Widely distributed throughout south-western WA.
Habit: Usually found in moist areas under rocks, logs, dead grass and debris.

Pseudophryne occidentalis Yalgoo, WA 30mm

Pseudophryne major Parker, 1940

Description: Status uncertain. Brown above with irregular darker flecks and marbling. Brown or black below with yellowish marbling. A yellow patch on the base of each forearm. Lower surfaces of limbs brown or black with fine yellow or white spots. Skin with a few warts or ridges above, smooth below. A femoral gland on each hindlimb. Inner metatarsal tubercle small, not shovel-shaped. Inner toe with two phalanges. 40 mm.
Distribution: Recorded from Cape York Peninsula to south-eastern Qld.
Habit: Little known of habitat or biology; generally similar to *P. bibronii*

Pseudophryne occidentalis Parker, 1940

Orange-crowned Toadlet

Description: Rich brown above with an orange triangle on the snout, an orange patch on the base of each forearm and an orange coccygeal stripe. Throat brown, chest and belly boldly marbled with black and white. Skin with scattered small warts above, slightly granular below. No femoral glands. Inner metatarsal tubercle oval, not shovel-shaped. Inner toe with two phalanges. 30 mm
Distribution: Inland parts of south-western WA and north-western SA.
Habit: Found beneath rocks, logs, dried vegetation near waterholes, claypans, etc. or in burrows in damp mud when claypans dry up.

Pseudophryne semimarmorata Lucas, 1892

Southern Toadlet

Description: Dark olive green to dark brown above, with irregular darker flecks. Chest and anterior part of belly boldly marbled with black and white; throat, posterior part of belly and lower surfaces of limbs flesh-coloured to orange. Skin with numerous low warts above, smooth (females) or coarsely granular (males) below. A prominent gland on each hindlimb, usually light brown or orange in colour. Inner metatarsal tubercle small, flat. Inner toe with two phalanges. 30 mm
Distribution: Widely distributed throughout Tas and the wetter parts of Vic.
Habit: Found in a variety of damp situations in sclerophyll forests under logs, leaf-litter etc. where it lives in small tunnels during the breeding season (March-May).

Genus *Rheobatrachus* Liem, 1973

A genus whose two species are both moderate, rather squat, pug-nosed, dull-coloured frogs with only an obscure pattern. Maxillary teeth present, 'fang-like'. A large (*silus*) to moderate (*vitellinus*) fronto-parietal foramen in adults. Vomerine teeth absent. Tongue broad, completely attached to the floor of the mouth. Pupil vertical to vertically rhomboidal. Tympanum hidden. Toes fully webbed. Terminal phalanges with a broad apical knob. Tips of digits with slightly dilated tips.

Key

TO THE SPECIES OF RHEOBATRACHUS

Lower abdomen and undersides of hindlimbs bright yellowish-orange; size large (males to 55 mm, females to 80 mm)............ **vitellinus**

Lower abdomen whitish; undersides of hindlimbs white to orange; size moderate (males to 40 mm, females to 50 mm)..... **silus**

Rheobatrachus silus Liem, 1973

Southern Gastric Brooding Frog (see page 48-49)

Description: Brown or olive-brown to almost black above, usually with some obscure darker blotches on the back, a dark streak from the eye to the forearm, and darker cross-bars on the limbs. Fingers, toes and webbing with pale and dark brown blotches and variegations. Whitish below, except for some bright

Rheobatrachus vitellinus Eungella, Qld

Rheobatrachus silus

Rheobatrachus vitellinus

orange on the limbs. Skin shagreened or finely granular above, smooth below. Snout blunt, the nostrils directed upwards and the eyes also upwards-directed and close together. Fingers free. Toes fully webbed. Fingers and toes with slightly expanded tips. Males to 40 mm, females to 50 mm
Distribution: Known only from the Blackall and Conondale Ranges, south-eastern Qld.
Habit: A nocturnal aquatic frog 'found along rocky mountain streams in wet sclerophyll forest' (Liem). According to Liem it hides submerged under rocks during the day, and sits on rocks or clings to them, partly submerged, at night; it submerges and hides on the bottom or under rocks when disturbed. Its reproductive habits are unique: a gastric brooder, the tadpoles develop in the stomach of the female after the eggs are swallowed and eventually are regurgitated as fully-formed froglets.

Rheobatrachus vitellinus Mahony, Tyler and Davies, 1984

Northern Gastric Brooding Frog

Description: Similar in most respects to *Rheobatrachus silus*, from which it differs in its larger size (males to 55 mm, females to 80 mm) and more brightly coloured (yellow-orange) lower abdomen and undersides of the hindlimbs. Pale brown above with obscure darker brown blotches on the body and limbs; apart from the brightly coloured lower surfaces of hindlimbs and lower abdomen, the remaining ventral surfaces vary from white to brown. Skin granular above, smooth below. Snout blunt, rounded, the nostrils directed upwards as in *R.silus*. Fingers free. Toes fully webbed. Fingers and toes with slightly expanded tips.
Distribution: Known only from the Clarke Range near Eungella, Qld.
Habit: An aquatic species apparently confined to 'shallow sections of fast flowing creeks in rain forest' (Mahony, Tyler and Davies).

Genus *Taudactylus* Straughan and Lee, 1966

Lightly-built, agile frogs distinguished from their nearest relatives only by their possession of T-shaped terminal phalanges, a character not discernible in the field. However, all species live in distinctive mountain stream environments and have limited distributions, so that identification is relatively simple. Vomerine teeth absent. Tips of fingers and toes with distinctive expansions or discs. Toes with at most some basal webbing or fringes.

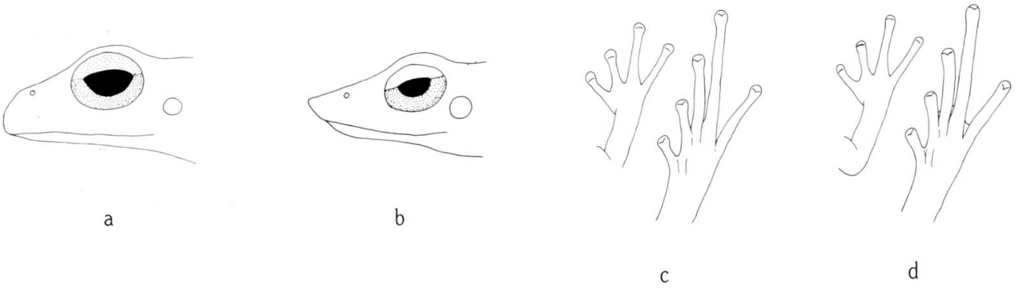

Key

TO THE SPECIES OF TAUDACTYLUS

1 No dorso-lateral skin-fold (p.52); snout rounded, normal, nostril about equidistant from the mouth and the tip of the snout (a) **2**

A distinct dorso-lateral skin-fold present; snout pointed and overslung, the nostrils much nearer the mouth than the tip of the snout (b)................................. ***acutirostris***

2 Head normal, its width (p.52) less than 0.38 times the snout-vent length; fingers with at most low, rounded sub-articular tubercles **3**

Head broad, its width more than 0.38 times the snout-vent length; fingers with prominent, raised sub-articular tubercles..***rheophilus***

3 Discs on fingers and toes noticeably wider than penultimate phalanx (c)...**4**

Discs on fingers and toes only slightly wider than penultimate phalanx (d)..**5**

4 Yellowish-green above, with distinct, irregular, darker markings; ventral surfaces of thighs immaculate yellow..... ....***eungellensis***

Dark olive-green to almost black above, with indistinct irregular darker markings; ventral surfaces of thighs greyish-cream heavily spotted with dark grey...... ***diurnus***

5 Dark interorbital bar triangular, broadest medially; ventral surface whitish with at most some pale brown speckling.... ....***liemi***

Dark interorbital bar more or less uniform in width; ventral surface densely speckled or mottled with dark grey or brown.. ***pleione***

Taudactylus acutirostris Tully Falls, Qld 30mm

Taudactylus acutirostris

Taudactylus diurnus

Taudactylus acutirostris (Andersson, 1916)

Sharp-snouted Torrent Frog

Description: Rich olive-brown above, usually with scattered paler flecks, and one or two V- or W-shaped markings on the back. A broad, black band from the snout, along the side of the head and continuing nearly to the groin, bordered above by a thin light stripe. Legs olive-brown, with faint to conspicuous dark cross-bands. Throat and belly grey-white with scattered black flecks and blotches. A distinctive white patch, edged with black, at the base of each forelimb. Hind part of belly and underside of limbs, olive-yellow. Lower jaw edged with black. Skin smooth above, with a few low tubercles or ridges and a distinct narrow dorso-lateral skin-fold; smooth below. Snout pointed, overslung. Fingers with well-developed subarticular tubercles. Toes fringed, but without webbing. Fingers and toes with only slightly expanded tips. 30 mm

Distribution: Known only from the rainforests of the ranges in the Cairns-Innisfail region of north-eastern Qld.

Habit: Found in debris, vegetation and among rocks in and beside small mountain streams in rain-forest. Summer breeder. 25-40 large eggs are laid as a gelatinous clump in water, among rocks. Call a 'sharp-pitched tapping sound repeated 3-4 times in quick succession' (Liem).

Taudactylus diurnus Straughan and Lee, 1966

Mount Glorious Torrent Frog

Description: Grey or brown above,irregularly mottled with darker. A pale bar between the eyes, bordered behind by a dark brown patch. A pale bar from the eye to the base of the forelimb. A dark, slightly raised, H-shaped mark on the back between the forelimbs. Limbs irregularly banded with black. Throat dark grey with small yellow spots, belly cream

Taudactylus diurnus Mt Glorious, Qld 30mm

Taudactylus eungellensis

Taudactylus liemi

Taudactylus pleione

to bluish, with or occasionally without, large grey spots. Skin smooth, finely granular, or with a few low warts above without dorso-lateral skin folds; more or less smooth below. Fingers without subarticular tubercles. Tips of fingers and toes with wedge-shaped discs, so that this species is easily mistaken for a hylid or microhylid. Toes fringed, but without webbing. 30 mm

Distribution: Known only from rainforest at Mount Glorious, and at Kondalilla, near Montville, both in south-eastern Qld.

Habit: Inhabits rocks or vegetation in or beside mountain streams, entering waterfalls or swift-flowing water when alarmed. This species has a remarkable ability to cling beneath rocks and in crevices within swift torrents. Call a barely audible 'very soft clucking sound, repeated 1-2 or 4-5 times in quick succession' (Liem). Summer breeder.

Taudactylus eungellensis Liem and Hosmer, 1973

Eungella Torrent Frog

Description: Similar in most respects to *Taudactylus diurnus*, from which it differs in having an X-shaped dark marking on the back, behind the head, and immaculate yellow belly and lower thighs. 35 mm

Distribution: Currently known only from the type localities — Eungella and Finch Hatton Gorge, both west of Mackay, Qld.

Habit: Similar in most respects to *Taudactylus diurnus*. Call a 'high-pitched metallic tinkering noise...like a little hammer tapping a metal plate repeated 4-5 times in quick succession' (Liem).

Taudactylus liemi Ingram, 1980

Description: Grey-brown above and on the flanks, with a darker brown or black triangular patch with its base between the eyes and its apex directed posteriorly, sometimes coalescing with a broad, darker, lyre-shaped vertebral zone; a blackish streak from snout, through eye, to ear; side of head otherwise dark brown, the lips barred; a distinct V-shaped mark in front of each hindlimb; an obscure dark streak anteriorly on upper flanks; limbs and digits with narrow, blackish cross-bars; hind side of thighs rich brown, finely dotted with pale yellow. Ventral surfaces cream, peppered with dark brown on the legs. Skin smooth above and below. Snout rounded. Fingers with well-developed subarticular tubercles, without webbing. Toes fringed but without

webbing. Fingers and toes with only slightly expanded tips. 25 mm
Distribution: A small area near Eungella, west of Mackay, Qld.
Habit: A cryptozoic frog recorded from under rocks beside rocky streams and '...inside the rolled-up ends of palm fronds...' in rainforest (Ingram).

Taudactylus pleione Czechura, 1986

Description: Grey above with darker grey flecks, spots and blotches, the most conspicuous of which are a broad bar of more or less uniform width between the eyes, a roughly X-shaped patch between the shoulders, and a large bar or patch above each groin; a broad blackish streak from snout, through eye and ear nearly to forelimb; limbs and digits with conspicuous dark cross-bars; hind side of thighs yellowish, barred and speckled with brown. Ventral surfaces cream, densely speckled or mottled with dark grey or brown. Skin smooth above and below. Snout rounded. Fingers with low rounded subarticular tubercles, without webbing. Toes fringed but without webbing. Fingers and toes with only slightly expanded tips. 25 mm
Distribution: Known only from Kroombit Tops, southeastern Qld.
Habit: Recorded from rocky montane streams and the adjacent forest floor in rainforest.

Taudactylus rheophilus Liem and Hosmer, 1973

Description: Greyish-brown, reddish or dark brown above, with irregular darker markings. A narrow pale greyish streak from above the eye to the groin, bordered below by a broad blackish band whose lower edge breaks up into a marbled or reticulate pattern on the flanks. A faint, pale transverse bar between the eyes. Limbs with irregular blackish cross-bands. A pale glandular patch from the angle of the jaws to the base of the forearm. Digits barred with dark brown and creamy-grey. Brown below, with conspicuous, irregular, creamy-white markings. Skin smooth or finely granular above, without a dorso-lateral skin-fold; smooth below. Fingers with conspicuous subarticular tubercles. Tips of fingers and toes with small but conspicuous discs. Toes fringed but without webbing. 30 mm
Distribution: Currently known from the upland rainforests of the Cairns region, north-eastern Qld.
Habit: Mountain streams in rainforest. Call similar to that of *Taudactylus acutirostris*.

Taudactylus liemi Eungella, Qld 25mm

Taudactylus rheophilus Thornton Peak, Qld 30mm

Taudactylus rheophilus

Genus *Uperoleia* Gray, 1841

Small frogs, superficially resembling members of the genus *Pseudophryne*, but from which they can generally be distinguished by prominent parotoid glands and bright red or orange spots in the groin and in the back of the knee. Like *Pseudophryne* they often have a pale white, yellow or brown patch on the upper arm where it joins the body. Maxillary teeth present or absent. Frontoparietal foramen present or absent. Vomerine teeth absent. Tongue oval, free behind. Pupil rhomboidal. Tympanum hidden. Terminal phalanges simple, tips of digits not dilated.

The following key and descriptions are drawn primarily from the revisory works of Davies, Littlejohn, Martin and Tyler (see references).

Key

TO THE SPECIES OF UPEROLEIA

1 Maxillary teeth (a) present in a continuous well-developed series **2**
Maxillary teeth absent or vestigial, not occurring continuously along the maxilla **7**

2 No tubercle or flap on the heel **3**
A distinctive tubercle or flap on the heel (b) .... ***mjobergii***

3 Chest and abdomen pale, with at most a sparse stippling of darker pigment **4**
Chest and abdomen strongly pigmented **5**

4 Adults small, maximum snout-vent length 25 mm; eastern Australia .... ***laevigata***
Adults large, maximum snout-vent length exceeds 30 mm; north-western WA .... ***marmorata***

5 Parotoid glands (p.52) grossly enlarged, raised well above surface of head and neck **6**
Parotoid glands moderate, not or scarcely raised above surface of head and neck .... ***fusca***

6 Dorsal surface smooth to moderately granular, its colour (including parotoid glands) dark brown with at most obscure darker variegations and few pale flecks or patches .... ***tyleri***
Dorsal surface strongly granular or rugose, its colour (including parotoid glands) brown or grey-brown with numerous pale yellow flecks or patches .... ***martini***

7 Toes without or with at most a trace of basal webbing (p.52) **8**
Toes with at least moderate basal webbing **16**

8 Internarial distance less than eye-naris distance (p.52); maxillary teeth absent **9**
Internarial distance greater than eye-naris distance; a few maxillary teeth present .... ***micromeles***

9 Outer metatarsal tubercle (c) large, raised, conspicuous **10**
Outer metatarsal tubercle small, rounded, inconspicuous (d) .... ***trachyderma***

10 Prominent dorsal colour pattern **11**
Dorsum more or less drab, with little development of colour pattern **13**

11 Ventral surface slightly to conspicuously granular **12**
Ventral surface smooth; parotoid and inguinal glands (p.52) grossly enlarged .... ***capitulata***

12 Belly and abdomen pale, with at most some sparsely-scattered stippling of darker pigment .... ***lithomoda***
Belly and abdomen moderately to strongly pigmented .... ***littlejohni***

13 Dorsal skin smooth or slightly rugose,with a few scattered low tubercles **14**
Dorsal skin coarsely granular or tubercular .... ***minima***

14 A large fronto-parietal foramen (p.52) in adults **15**
A poor to moderate fronto-parietal foramen in adults .... ***mimula***

15 Adults rarely exceed 23 mm snout-vent length ***arenicola***
Adults to 30 mm snout-vent length .... ***inundata***

16 Moderately to extensively webbed toes **17**
Toes with distinct but only basal webbing **21**

17 No indication of pale vertebral stripe **18**
A pale vertebral stripe .... ***orientalis***

18 Toes at least half webbed **19**
Toes less than half webbed **20**

19 Dermal glands, including parotoids, inconspicuous .... ***talpa***
Dermal glands, including parotoids, well-developed and conspicuous .... ***russelli***

20 Thigh and groin markings orange; fourth finger equal to second .... ***borealis***
Thigh and groin markings red; fourth finger longer than second .... ***crassa***

21 Tibia length/snout-vent length ratio (p.52) 0.34 or less **22**
Tibia length/snout-vent length ratio 0.34 or more .... ***glandulosa***

22 Metatarsal tubercles small but prominent (p.52); ventral surface mostly unpigmented; north-western Australia .... ***aspera***
Metatarsal tubercles large (e); ventral surface usually with at least moderate pigmentation; eastern Australia .... ***rugosa***

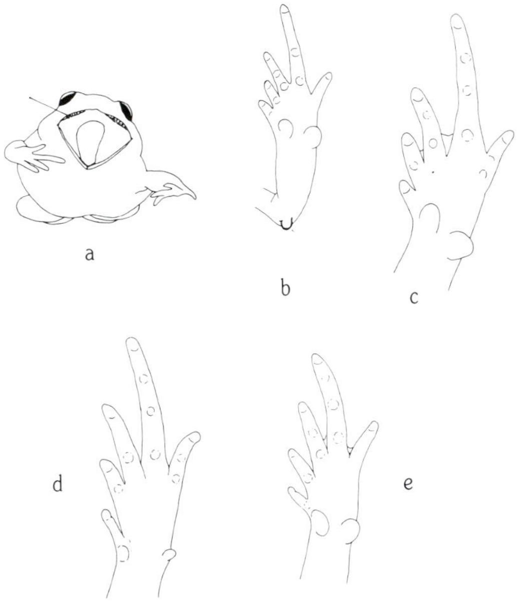

Uperoleia arenicola Tyler, Davies and Martin, 1981

Description: Pale to dark grey or brown above, obscurely variegated or flecked with darker, sometimes forming distinct crossbars on the hindlimbs. The parotoid glands are paler, dull golden-brown. Whitish below. Bright orange-reddish patches in each groin and behind each knee. Skin with low, scattered tubercles above, and with prominent parotoid glands; smooth below. Maxillary teeth absent. Two large metatarsal tubercles. Toes narrowly fringed and without even basal webbing. 25 mm
Distribution: Alligator Rivers region, NT.
Habit: A burrowing frog whose call is 'a rasping note' (Tyler, Davies and Martin).

Uperoleia aspera Tyler, Davies and Martin, 1981

Description: Pale brown above, mottled with darker brown, the top of the head and the dermal glands 'pale yellow marked with brown'. Ventral surfaces whitish, the throat flecked with grey and rimmed with dark grey. No coloured patches in groin or behind knee. Skin above with numerous low tubercles, and with well-developed parotoid glands. Flanks and lower surfaces mostly granular. Maxillary teeth absent. Two large metatarsal tubercles. Toes narrowly fringed and with only a trace of webbing basally. 30 mm
Distribution: Derby-Broome region, WA.
Habit: Grassland. Call '...a sharp, loud click repeated at a rate of 3 calls/sec'(Tyler, Davies and Martin).

Uperoleia glandulosa Mallina, WA 25mm

Uperoleia borealis Tyler, Davies and Martin, 1981

Description: Grey or medium brown above, the parotoid and other dermal glands paler brown or cream. Reddish-orange patches in the groin and behind the knee. Ventral surfaces whitish, with darker grey stippling on the throat. Skin above superficially smooth but with numerous minute tubercles; parotoid glands well-developed and prominent. Ventral surfaces smooth. Maxillary teeth absent. Metatarsal tubercles small but prominent. Toes with broad fringes and about half webbed. 25 mm
Distribution: North-east Kimberley region, WA.
Habit: The call 'is a short, rasping note' (Tyler, Davies and Martin)

Uperoleia capitulata Davies, McDonald and Corben, 1986

Description: Grey-brown above, the parotoid and other dermal glands creamish with scattered fine orange spots. Scarlet patches in the groin and behind the knee. Throat grey, sometimes peppered with white; remainder of ventral surfaces whitish usually with some brown stippling on the belly. Skin above smooth or with numerous low rounded tubercles; parotoid glands highly developed and prominent. Ventral surfaces smooth. Maxillary teeth absent. Metatarsal tubercles prominent. Toes with broad fringes but otherwise unwebbed. 25 mm
Distribution: South-western Qld and north-western NSW.
Habit: Found in a wide variety of dry woodland and

Uperoleia arenicola

Uperoleia aspera

Uperoleia borealis

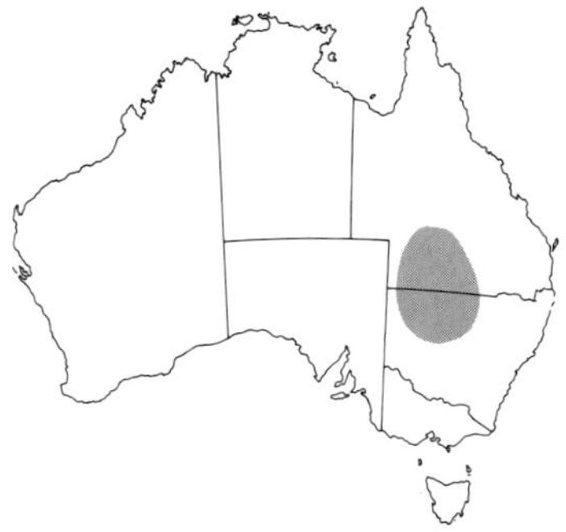

Uperoleia capitulata

Uperoleia crassa

Uperoleia fusca

Uperoleia glandulosa

plains habitats, especially those associated with river overflows; breeds in open grassy areas temporarily flooded by spring and summer rains.

Uperoleia crassa Tyler, Davies and Martin, 1981

Description: Dark brown or grey-brown above, flecked with pale brown, yellow or pink, most densely on the glandular areas. Colour in groin and behind knee not recorded. Ventral surfaces cream, suffused with grey anteriorly. Skin above with scattered low tubercles and with well-developed parotoid glands; ventral surfaces finely granular. Maxillary teeth absent. Two large metatarsal tubercles. Toes slightly fringed and with moderate webbing. 30 mm
Distribution: North-west Kimberley region, WA.
Habit: Original specimens taken in partially flooded clearings in open forest. 'The call is a rasp...' (Tyler, Davies and Martin).

Uperoleia fusca Davies, McDonald and Corben, 1986

Description: Grey-brown above, usually with darker blotches and variegations and scattered paler cream spots and flecks and sometimes a narrow pale vertebral stripe. Reddish, orange or yellow patches in the groin and behind the knee. Ventral surfaces cream, strongly flecked and peppered with dark grey or brown. Skin above with numerous scattered low, rounded tubercles and moderately-developed parotoid glands; ventral surfaces smooth. Maxillary teeth present. Toes with poorly developed fringes and otherwise unwebbed. 30 mm
Distribution: Coast and ranges of eastern Australia, between about latitudes 20° and 33°S.
Habit: Found in a wide variety of forested habitats on the coast and ranges. Usually breeds in grassy depressions which are temporarily flooded after spring and summer rains.

Uperoleia glandulosa Davies, Mahony and Roberts, 1985

Description: Grey or olive-brown above with scattered dark brown or black spots and blotches; usually a broken, narrow pale cream or orange vertebral stripe anteriorly, scattered orange tubercles on the head and a broad dorso-lateral orange zone along each side of the body; glandular areas usually cream-coloured. Reddish-orange patches in the groin

and behind the knee. Ventral surfaces whitish, with scattered grey flecks. Skin above smooth to slightly granular and with well-developed parotoid glands; ventral surfaces smooth to slightly granular. Maxillary teeth absent. Toes with fringes and basal webbing. 25 mm
Distribution: Pilbara region of WA.
Habit: Breeds in claypans and other depressions which are temporarily flooded by summer and autumn rains, where it usually calls from the bases of grasses and sedges. Call '...a sharp click' (Davies, Mahony and Roberts).

Uperoleia fusca Ourimbah, NSW 30mm

Uperoleia inundata Tyler, Davies and Martin, 1981

Description: Grey or grey-brown above, irregularly flecked and mottled with darker brown, the parotoid glands paler than the rest of the dorsum. Orange patches in the groin and behind the knee. Ventral surfaces whitish, finely flecked with grey, especially on the throat. Skin above mostly smooth, with at most a few flat tubercles, becoming more numerous on the flanks. Lower surfaces slightly granular. Maxillary teeth absent. Two large metatarsal tubercles. Toes with narrow fringes but without webbing. 25 mm
Distribution: Far north-eastern NT.
Habit: A burrowing species usually found wherever monsoon rains result in temporarily flooded ground in grassland or woodland. The call 'is a short "rasp"' (Tyler, Davies and Martin).

Uperoleia inundata Koongarra, NT 25mm

Uperoleia laevigata Keferstein, 1867

Description: Brown or olive above with dark brown or blackish spots, bars and reticulations, including a triangular patch on the head and obscure crossbands on the hindlimbs. Grey speckled with dark purplish-brown below. A bright reddish-orange patch in each groin and behind each knee. Skin above with numerous scattered granules and tubercles and with relatively well developed parotoid glands. Smooth below. Maxillary teeth present. Two moderate

Uperoleia inundata

Uperoleia laevigata Sydney, NSW 25mm

metatarsal tubercles, not strongly compressed. Toes fringed, without a trace of webbing. 25 mm
Distribution: Eastern Australia, from Vic to south-eastern Qld.
Habit: A cryptozoic species which emerges to breed in temporarily inundated grassland during spring and summer.

Uperoleia lithomoda Tyler, Davies and Martin, 1981

Description: Grey or grey-brown above, often with a pale median stripe on the head and with darker brown patches on the body, and the dermal glands edged with cream. Ventral surfaces cream, except for a blackish rim below the lower jaw. Colour of patches in groin and behind knee not recorded. Skin above smooth, with scattered tubercles and conspicuous parotoid glands. Ventral surfaces granular. Maxillary teeth absent. Metatarsal tubercles small but conspicuous. Toes without fringes, webbing either lacking or confined to a trace basally. 25 mm
Distribution: East Kimberleys, WA and far north-western NT.
Habit: Found in a variety of woodland and grassy habitats, breeding in temporarily-flooded grassy depressions during the wet season. The call 'is an explosive "tick"' (Tyler, Davies and Martin).

Uperoleia littlejohni Davies, McDonald and Corben, 1986

Description: Grey-brown above with dark brown to black blotches and variegations; the parotoid glands pinkish-orange and many of the smaller tubercles on the dorsum tipped with the same colour. Reddish-orange patches in the groin and behind the knee. Ventral surfaces white or pale grey, usually peppered with brown or dark grey. Skin above with scattered, low rounded tubercles. Ventral surfaces slightly granular. Maxillary teeth absent. Metatarsal tubercles large, conspicuous. Toes fringed, with basal webbing. 30 mm
Distribution: North-eastern and north-central Qld.
Habit: An inhabitant of forest, woodland habitats and savannah habitats where it breeds in flooded depressions after heavy rains.

Uperoleia marmorata Gray, 1841

Description: '... black and green marbled...' above 'leaving a triangular greenish spot on the head...' (Gray). Ventral surfaces grey. Presumably red or orange patches in groin and behind knee. Skin tubercular above, with moderate parotoid glands. Flanks and belly granular. Maxillary teeth present. Two moderately developed metatarsal tubercles, not strongly compressed. Toes without fringes or webbing. 30 mm
Distribution: Kimberley region, WA. Populations from Yule River district, WA, have also been referred to this species.

Uperoleia martini Davies and Littlejohn, 1986

Description: Grey above mottled with yellow and dark brown; colour of pale patches in groin and behind knee not recorded. Throat dark grey, remainder of ventral surface dark brown peppered with white. Skin tubercular above, with highly developed and conspicuous parotoid glands. Ventral surfaces smooth. Maxillary teeth present. Metatarsal tubercles large, prominent. Toes without fringes or webbing. 30 mm
Distribution: Coastal regions of eastern Vic. and southeastern NSW.
Habit: A burrowing species sometimes found under ground debris and logs in dry sclerophyll forests and coastal heaths. Breeds after rain in flooded grassy depressions.

Uperoleia micromeles Tyler, Davies and Martin, 1981

Description: Rich brown above with scattered paler spots and pale, metallic-gold, parotoid glands. Cream coloured patches in groin and behind knee. Ventral surfaces cream-coloured, pale yellow under thighs. Skin above smooth, the parotoid glands not

Uperoleia micromeles
Tanami Desert, NT
25mm

conspicuous. Smooth ventrally. Maxillary teeth absent. Two very large metatarsal tubercles. Toes without fringes and with only basal webbing. 25 mm
Distribution: Tanami Desert, NT.
Habit: A burrowing species found in spinifex/mulga sandplain desert where it emerges after heavy rains to breed in flooded claypans.

Uperoleia mimula Davies, McDonald and Corben, 1986

Description: Brown above with irregular darker brown patches and blotches and paler blotches on the parotoid glands and flanks. Reddish-orange patches in the groin and behind each knee. Cream or dirty-white below, moderately to densely peppered with dark grey or brown. Skin above moderately to strongly tubercular, with well-developed parotoid glands. Ventral surfaces smooth (throat) to slightly granular (belly). Maxillary teeth absent. Metatarsal tubercles well-developed, prominent. Toes fringed, with some basal webbing. 25 mm
Distribution: North-eastern Qld, including Cape York Peninsula and the islands of Torres Strait.
Habit: A cryptozoic species found in a wide range of open woodland and grassland habitats; like most of its relatives it breeds in temporary pools such as claypans, drainage ditches, etc. which are flooded by the summer monsoonal rains.

Uperoleia minima Tyler, Davies and Martin, 1981

Description: Pale brown above, with faint, irregular darker markings; bright red patches in groin and behind knee; ventral surfaces white, suffused with grey on throat, chest and flanks. Skin above densely covered with small tubercles, the parotoid glands moderately prominent; coarsely granular below. Maxillary teeth absent. Two large metatarsal tubercles. Toes without fringes or webbing. 20 mm
Distribution: Mitchell Plateau, Kimberley region, WA.
Habit: '...found in an area of dense grassland subject to seasonal inundation' (Tyler, Davies and Martin).

Uperoleia mjobergii (Andersson, 1913)

Description: Light grey or brown above, with darker patches and with several large, pale yellow or reddish patches, the most conspicuous being a pair on the

Uperoleia laevigata

Uperoleia lithomoda

Uperoleia littlejohni

Uperoleia marmorata

Uperoleia martini

Uperoleia micromeles

Uperoleia mimula

Uperoleia minima

Uperoleia mjobergii

Uperoleia orientalis

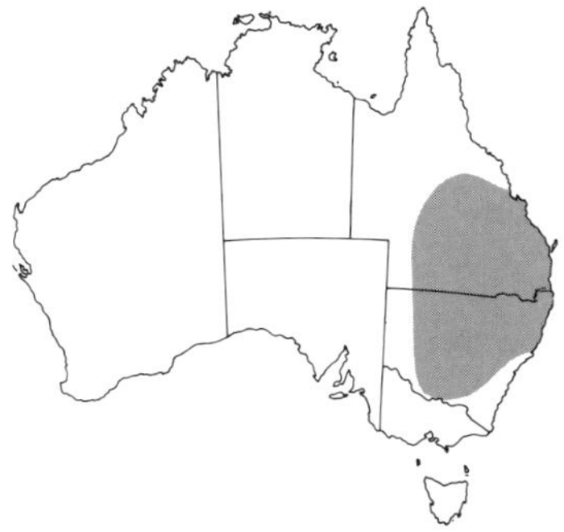

Uperoleia rugosa

Uperoleia russelli

Uperoleia talpa

Uperoleia trachyderma

upper edge of the very prominent parotoid glands. A bright reddish-orange patch in each groin and behind each knee. Whitish below with dark grey around the rim of the lower jaw. Skin moderately to very warty above, smooth on the throat and belly. Maxillary teeth present. A conspicuous tarsal tubercle on the heel. Toes fringed, with only basal webbing. 25 mm
Distribution: Fitzroy River and adjacent regions, WA.
Habit: Call '...a short "rasp" or "creak"...' (Tyler, Davies and Martin).

Uperoleia orientalis (Parker, 1940)

Description: Ground colour light to dark brown, uniform or with lighter or darker tubercles (sometimes reddish) and often with the conspicuous parotoid and supra-inguinal glands much paler than the ground colour. Flanks finely speckled with brown and white. Hind side of thighs with a large bright or dull red patch. Whitish below. Skin finely granular above, with numerous, small, low, flat, rounded tubercles or warts. Maxillary teeth absent. No tarsal tubercle. Toes about one quarter webbed. 30 mm
Distribution: North-eastern parts of NT, including Groote Eylandt.
Habit: A small terrestrial frog which congregates during the wet season in large breeding colonies associated with temporary soaks, swamps and flooded grassy flats. Nocturnal.

Uperoleia rugosa (Andersson, 1916)

Description: Brown above, with irregular darker spots and variegations, including a dark triangular patch on the head. Grey below. A yellow or orange patch in each groin and behind each knee. Skin with low, scattered tubercles above, and with conspicuous parotoid and inguinal glands; smooth or slightly granular below. Maxillary teeth absent. Metatarsal tubercles moderate, not strongly compressed. Toes narrowly fringed and with at most a trace of webbing basally. 30 mm
Distribution: South-eastern Qld and northern NSW, extending into southern NSW west of the Great Dividing Range.
Habit: A burrowing species found primarily in dry sclerophyll forests and open woodlands where it emerges after heavy spring and summer rains to breed in flooded grassland or in billabongs and slow-flowing streams. It calls from a narrow area around the water's edge, often from small cavities at the base of grasses or beneath ground debris, or from within

Uperoleia rugosa Macquarie Marshes, NSW 30 mm

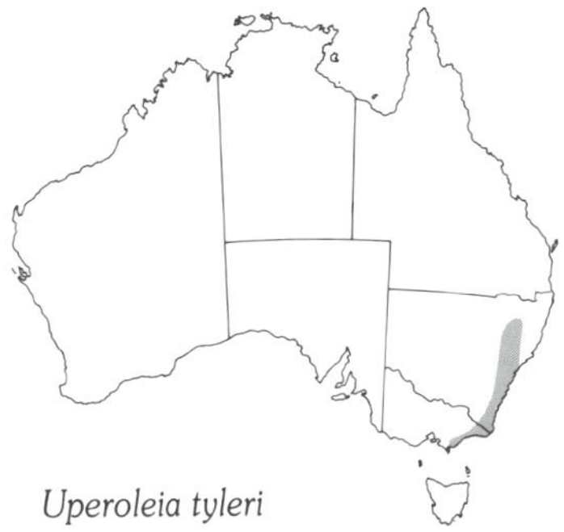

depressions formed by the footprints of livestock in the soft mud.

Uperoleia russelli (Loveridge, 1933)

Description: Brown above, often with two rows of low reddish warts which link a reddish patch on each shoulder with another on each side of the anus. Sometimes a light, reddish vertebral stripe. Yellowish below, the throat sometimes with brown flecking. Skin warty above, granular on the belly. Maxillary teeth absent. No tarsal tubercle. Toes about half webbed. 30 mm
Distribution: 'Gascoyne, Ashburton and Pilbara' regions of WA.
Habit: Breeds in summer. Usually found beside permanent pools in creek and river beds, but is said to be found well away from water after rain. Call a 'short, grating qrk, qrk, qrk' (Main).

Uperoleia talpa Tyler, Davies and Martin, 1981

Description: Bronzy-brown above with irregular blackish dots and streaks, some of them with reddish centres; parotoid and other dermal glands paler brown; groin colour not recorded; ventral surfaces whitish or cream, the lower jaw rimmed with black and dense black stippling on the chest. Skin more or less smooth above, with scattered low tubercles and folds usually coinciding with black markings, smooth below. Maxillary teeth absent. Two very large compressed metatarsal tubercles. Toes broadly fringed and about half webbed. 30 mm
Distribution: Near Derby, WA.
Habit: Recorded only from sandy, sparsely vegetated plains (Tyler, Davies and Martin).

Uperoleia trachyderma Tyler, Davies and Martin, 1981

Description: Pale grey above with scattered darker grey patches, the dermal glands suffused with pale orange as may be the tips of the small, individual tubercles which are scattered over the dorsal surface. A bright red patch in the groin and behind the knee joint. Ventral surfaces creamy grey with darker grey blotches, and a darker grey rim to the throat. Skin above with numerous conical tubercles; inconspicuous parotoid glands; ventral surfaces finely granular. Maxillary teeth absent. Two small and poorly developed metatarsal tubercles. Toes fringed, but without webbing. 25 mm
Distribution: Currently known only from the type locality, nearly 40 km north of Elliott, NT.
Habit: 'The type locality is a flat floodplain of adhesive yellow clay...'; the call is '...a harsh "creak"...' (Tyler, Davies and Martin).

Uperoleia tyleri Davies and Littlejohn, 1986

Description: Dark grey-brown above, the larger glands and smaller tubercles blotched or spotted with cream or yellow. Yellow patches in the groin and behind each knee. Ventral surfaces very dark grey or blue-black, finely spotted with white. Skin slightly to moderately granular above, with greatly enlarged parotoid glands; smooth below. Maxillary teeth present. Metatarsal tubercles well-developed and prominent. Toes with faint to moderate fringes but otherwise unwebbed. 30 mm
Distribution: Coast and adjacent ranges of south-eastern NSW and eastern Vic, extending north in NSW via the ranges to about Tamworth.
Habit: Found in a range of forested habitats and coastal heaths, breeding in grassy depressions and roadside drains temporarily inundated by spring and summer rains.

Family Hylidae

Known broadly as Tree Frogs because of the development, in many species, of large finger and toe pads which have enabled them to become efficient climbers. In addition all species are characterised by an arciferal pectoral girdle; in most species there is an intercalary cartilage between the last two bones of each finger and toe, resulting externally in a distinctive notched profile; finger and toe discs may be well or poorly developed; sacral diapophyses dilated; maxillary teeth present.

Australian members of the family Hylidae vary greatly in form and habit. They range from agile, arboreal species with large adhesive discs on the fingers and toes, to long-limbed terrestrial species with only slightly expanded discs. They are most abundant around the wetter margins of the continent, especially in the north and east, the diversity of species decreasing as one approaches the arid centre, where several wide-ranging and ecologically vagile species are found. The eggs of all Australian species are thought to be laid in water, quickly hatching to produce free-living, aquatic tadpoles.

The Australasian members of this family are sometimes regarded as a distinct regionally endemic family — the Pelodryadidae.

Key

TO THE GENERA OF AUSTRALIAN HYLID FROGS

1 Tips of the digits usually with distinct discs or pads (p.52), but at least with a distinct notch in profile (a) representing the well-developed intercalary cartilage; first finger not opposed to remaining fingers (b).................................... **2**

Tips of digits without discs or pads; intercalary cartilage, if present, small and not indicated by a distinct notch in profile (c); first finger opposed to remaining fingers (d)...... .... ***Cyclorana***

2 Pupil horizontally oriented (e), usually strongly contrasting with a paler iris; upper parts of lower eyelids transparent, without pigmentation... ***Litoria***

Pupil vertically oriented (f), often difficult to distinguish against a dark iris; upper parts of lower eyelids translucent, with a pigmented vein-like pattern (g)............ .... ***Nyctimystes***

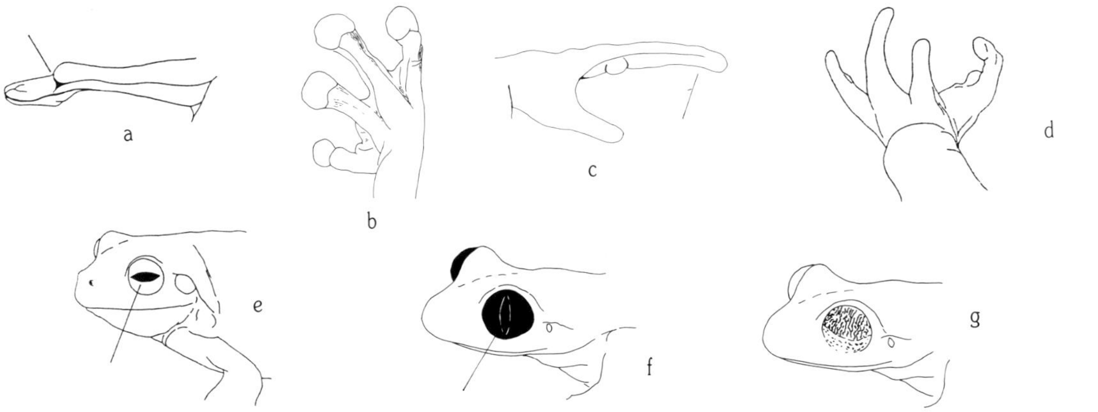

Genus ***Cyclorana*** Steindachner, 1867

A group of well-built ground dwelling and/or aquatic frogs with powerful limbs, and with representatives found throughout most of continental Australia. No fronto-parietal foramen in adults. Vomerine teeth present, largely between the choanae. Tongue large, oval. Pupil horizontal. Tympanum distinct. Phalanges simple, tips of digits without discs. First finger opposed to remainder. Toes webbed.

Key

TO THE SPECIES OF CYCLORANA

1 A distinct straight dorso-lateral skin fold (a); adult snout-vent length usually greater than 70 mm **2**

Usually no more than an indefinite dorso-lateral skin fold; adult snout-vent length less than 70 mm **3**

2 Back of thighs variegated; suborbital bar narrow and not reaching base of maxilla (b); maxilla gently sloping and not expanded laterally .... ***australis***

Back of thighs not variegated; suborbital bar (if present) usually broad and reaching base of maxilla (c); maxilla expanded to form lateral shelf .... ***novaehollandiae***

3 Toes at most about half webbed (p.52) **4**

Toes at least three quarters webbed .... ***platycephala***

4 Toes usually less then half webbed; metatarsal tubercle shorter than its distance from the tip of the inner toe (d); back usually strongly granular, or with at most a few low tubercles; dorsal pattern of large dark blotches on a paler ground **5**

Toes usually about half webbed; metatarsal tubercle as long as or longer than its distance from the tip of the inner toe (e); back usually strongly granular, tubercular or with skin folds; dorsal pattern obscure, with dark flecks and variegations **8**

5 A broad, dark stripe from nostril, through eye and tympanum to insertion of forearm; adult snout-vent length greater than 35 mm **6**

No indication of a dark stripe from nostril along side of head to forearm; adult snout-vent length less than 35 mm.. .... ***manya***

6 Hindlimb relatively long, the tibia length/snout-vent length ratio (p.52) ranging from 0.36-0.45 .... **7**

Hindlimb short, the tibia length/snout-vent length ratio ranging from 0.31-0.38 .... ***maculosa***

7 Eye-naris/internarial distance (p.52) ratio ranging from 0.97-1.19 .... ***brevipes***

Eye-naris/internarial distance ratio ranging from 1.12-.1.36. .... ***longipes***

8 Tympanum distinct, usually prominent **9**

Tympanum usually hidden .... ***cryptotis***

9 A dark stripe on side of head, through eye and tympanum to forelimb **10**

No dark stripe on side of head **11**

10 Skin above 'with raised folds or large tubercles highlighted by being surrounded by dark pigment .... ***verrucosa***

Skin above 'very slightly pitted and raised tubercles on other areas are totally lacking.' .... ***maini***

11 A pale transverse bar across the head, behind the level of the eyes .... ***cultripes***

No pale transverse bar across the head, behind the level of the eye .... ***vagita***

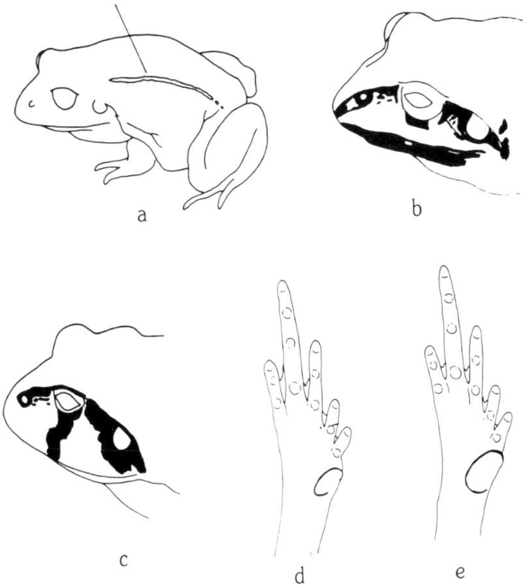

Cyclorana australis (Gray, 1842)

Description: A large, flat-headed frog, ranging in colour from grey through various shades of brown to dull pink above, sometimes with bright green patches; white below except for the throat which may be flecked with brown. Juveniles frequently bright emerald green above. A dark cantho-temporal streak and a black bar below the eye. Groin often flushed with pale blue-green. Hind side of thighs brown or flesh coloured to dark blue. Skin smooth above or with a few scattered warts or short folds; finely granular below. A distinct dorso-lateral skin-fold. Inner metatarsal tubercle shovel-shaped. No outer metatarsal tubercle 100 mm

Distribution: North-western Qld, far northern NT and northern WA.

Habit: A burrowing frog found in a wide range of habitats from coastal floodplains to woodlands and monsoon forests throughout its range. Usually seen above ground only after the onset of the wet season rains.

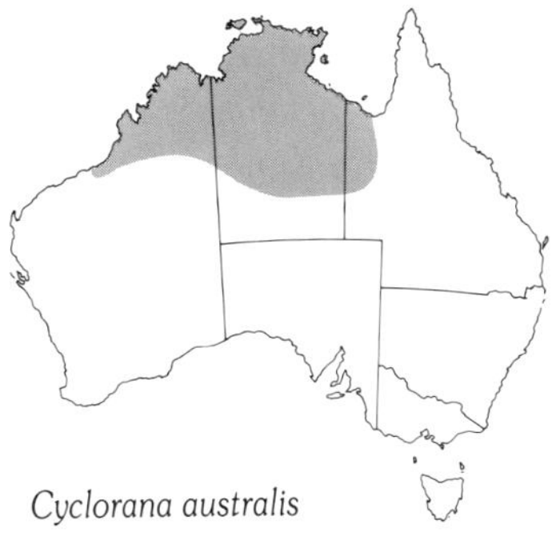

Cyclorana australis

Cyclorana australis Darwin, NT 100mm

Cyclorana brevipes (Peters, 1871)

Description: A small, stout frog, rich brown above and on the sides with broad, pale silvery-brown reticulations and usually with a narrow vertebral stripe of the same colour; dark canthal streak continuing behind the eye; edge of upper lip brown with white flecks. Hind side of thighs dark brown, usually with a few light flecks. Lower surfaces whitish. Skin smooth or slightly granular above, with a few low warts; belly finely granular; throat granular (males) or smooth (females). No dorso-lateral skin fold. Toes less than one quarter webbed. Inner metatarsal tubercle shovel-shaped. No outer metatarsal tubercle. 45 mm
Distribution: Drier parts, including coastal areas, of eastern Qld.
Habit: Primarily an inhabitant of savannah woodland. A burrower, it is usually seen only after rain.

Cyclorana cryptotis Tyler and Martin, 1977

Description: Most similar to *Cyclorana cultripes*, from which it may be distinguished by its hidden tympanum, the latter being completely covered by skin. 40 mm
Distribution: Currently known only from the area between Newcastle Waters and Daly Waters, NT.

Cyclorana cultripes Parker, 1940

Description: A moderate to stout frog, grey-brown to olive-brown or green above with irregular darker patches and usually with a pale vertebral stripe. A faint to strong dark canthal streak continued behind the eye as a broad dark band, of varying intensity,

R.W.G. JENKINS

Cyclorana cryptotis
Mitchell Plateau, WA
40mm

Cyclorana longipes Kununurra, WA 45mm

which merges with the pattern on the sides. Edge of upper lip brown with white flecks. Groin and hind side of thighs light grey-brown mottled with white. Lower surfaces whitish. Skin smooth or slightly warty above lateral fold. Belly coarsely granular; throat finely granular (males) or smooth (females). No continuous dorso-lateral fold but groups of warts sometimes aligned to form a discontinuous dorso-lateral fold. Toes about one-third webbed. Inner metatarsal tubercle shovel-shaped. No outer metatarsal tubercle. 50 mm

Distribution: Lower eastern half of NT to south-western Qld.

Habit: A burrowing frog which is found usually only when it emerges to feed or breed in temporary claypans, ponds and creeks after rain.

Cyclorana longipes Tyler and Martin, 1977

Description: Similar to *Cyclorana brevipes* from which it has been distinguished by its longer call and its tendency to have more narrowly separated nostrils (eye-naris/internarial distance ratio 1.12-1.36 in *longipes*, 0.97-1.19 in *brevipes*). 45 mm

Distribution: Kimberley region of WA and adjacent parts of NT.

Cyclorana maculosa Tyler and Martin, 1977

Description: Status uncertain. Similar in appearance to *Cyclorana brevipes*, from which it differs in its larger adult size (to about 50 mm) and relatively shorter limbs.

Distribution: Top end of NT to north-western Qld.

Cyclorana brevipes

Cyclorana cryptotis

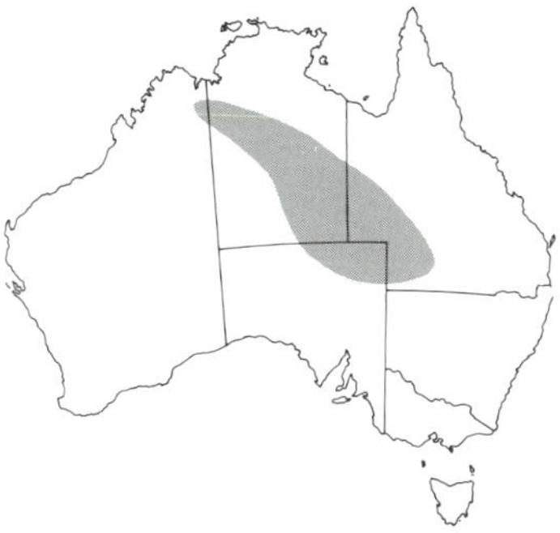

Cyclorana cultripes

Cyclorana longipes

Cyclorana maculosa

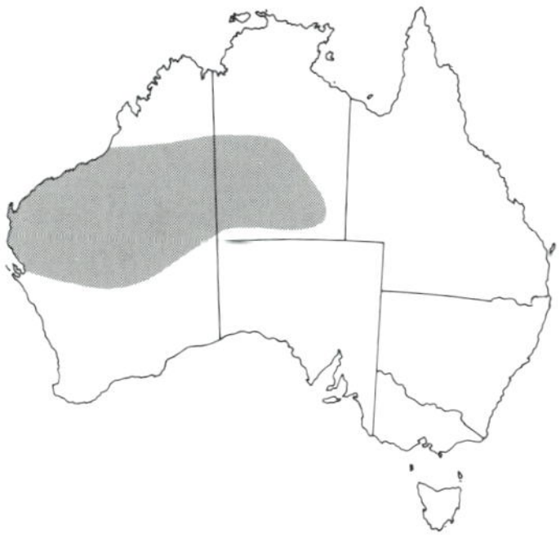

Cyclorana maini

Cyclorana manya

Cyclorana novaehollandiae

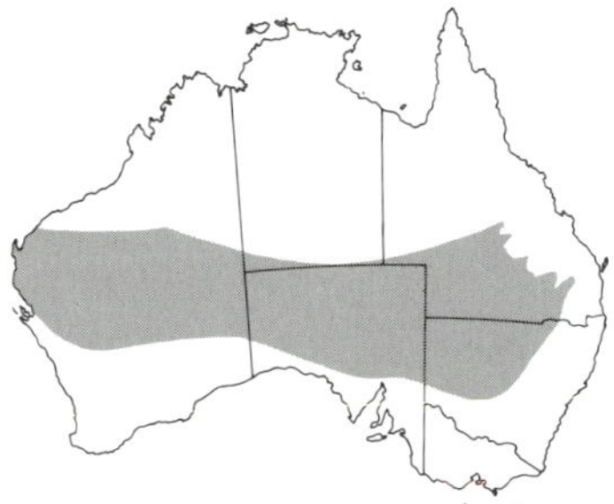

Cyclorana platycephala

S. BREEDEN

Cyclorana brevipes Gin Gin, Qld 45mm

Cyclorana novaehollandiae Weipa, Qld 100mm

R.W.G. JENKINS

Cyclorana maini Alice Springs, NT 45mm

Cyclorana maini Tyler and Martin, 1977

Description: Similar in most respects to *Cyclorana cultripes,* from which it is said to differ by possessing a dark lateral head stripe and a shorter call with a higher pulse repetition rate. It is said to be distinguished from *Cyclorana verrucosa* by lacking 'a dorsal skin with raised folds or large tubercles highlighted by being surrounded by darker pigment', but this feature is present in many living *Cyclorana maini*. 45 mm
Distribution: Southern half of NT through central WA to central western coastal regions.

Cyclorana manya van Buerden and McDonald, 1980

Description: A stout frog, pale grey to brown above, the back and sides with irregular, darker blotches which are smaller and less intense on the flanks and lower back; a pale vertebral stripe from snout to vent; a pale, broad bar across the back of the head; sides of face paler. Ventral surfaces whitish except for darker markings on the throats of males. No indication of loreal or temporal head stripes. Groin and hind side of thigh pale brown with darker brown blotches. Skin warty or granular above, mostly smooth below. No conspicuous dorso-lateral fold. Toes slightly webbed. Inner metatarsal tubercle large, more or less shovel-shaped. No outer metatarsal tubercle. 30 mm
Distribution: Currently known only from central Cape York Peninsula, Qld.
Habit: A burrowing frog which emerges to breed in temporary pools. Call '...a short plaintive bleat of 1.1 to 1.3 sec duration' (van Buerden and McDonald).

Cyclorana novaehollandiae Steindachner, 1867

Description: Similar in most respects to *Cyclorana australis* Pale grey, brown or yellowish above, occasionally with dark brown flecks, blotches or variegations; whitish below except for the throat which may be flecked or lined with grey or brown. A dark brown cantho-temporal stripe on each side of the head and a black or dark brown bar below the eye which usually extends to the mouth. Hind side of thighs usually immaculate grey or bluish. Skin smooth or finely tubercular above, often with a few scattered warts or short skin folds. A distinct dorso-lateral skin fold. Inner metatarsal tubercle shovel-shaped. No outer metatarsal tubercle. 100 mm.
Distribution: Eastern Australia from northern NSW to Cape York Peninsula, Qld.
Habit: A burrowing frog which occurs in a wide range of habitats from coastal floodplains, seasonally-wet scrub and closed forests, woodlands and savannahs. Usually found only during or immediately after heavy summer rains, when it calls from, and breeds in, temporarily inundated areas.

Cyclorana platycephala (Günther, 1873)

Water-holding Frog

Description: A moderate, stout, flat-headed frog, with the eyes usually pointing obliquely upwards. Dull olive-grey or olive-green above, or grey with light green patches, especially on the head. Often a

Cyclorana novaehollandiae Weipa, Qld 100mm

Cyclorana platycephala Nyngan, NSW 60mm

narrow, light green vertebral stripe. Scattered fine, dark flecks over the upper surface, larger brown flecks on the upper lip. Lower surfaces whitish, the throat of breeding males with dark brown flecks. Skin smooth above, or with a few low warts. Lower surfaces smooth or granular. No dorso-lateral skin fold. Toes usually fully webbed. Inner metatarsal tubercle shovel-shaped. No outer metatarsal tubercle. 60 mm
Distribution: Drier inland regions of all mainland states except Vic.
Habit: A burrowing frog which appears above ground after good rains, when it breeds in temporary pools, claypans and creeks. This is the best known of Australia's 'water-holding' frogs; as surface waters dry up it burrows deep into the earth where it makes a 'cocoon'-like chamber, with an impervious lining formed of the sloughed dead outer layers of its skin, while the frog's bladder is filled with water. In this chamber it spends the long, dry periods — sometimes several years in length — characteristic of the areas in which it lives.

Cyclorana vagita Tyler, Davies and Martin, 1981

Description: A relatively stout frog, slate-grey above with scattered, irregular (dull green in life) patches; a narrow white vertebral stripe from snout to vent. An indefinite, sometimes pale edged, dark canthal stripe extending through eye to base of forelimb. Subocular region pale, more or less continuous with a pale glandular region below the angle of the mouth. Throat greyish, remaining ventral surfaces whitish. Skin smooth above, except for some tubercles between the eyes; flanks and belly coarsely granular. No conspicuous dorso-lateral skin fold. Toes slightly webbed. A large oval, inner metatarsal tubercle, no outer metatarsal tubercle. 45 mm
Distribution: Kimberley region, WA.
Habit: Recorded from inundated grassland and a flooded spinifex plain. Call '...an irregularly repeated, quavering, crying sound which we estimate to have a duration of about one second' (Tyler, Davies and Martin).

Cyclorana verrucosa Warialda, NSW 45mm

Cyclorana vagita
near Duncan, NT

45mm

Cyclorana vagita

Cyclorana verrucosa Tyler and Martin, 1977

Description: Similar in most respects to *Cyclorana cultripes*, from which it is said to differ by possessing a 'slightly to extremely warty skin surface' whereas *cultripes* is said to be usually quite smooth'. 45 mm
Distribution: Northern NSW (excluding the coast and ranges) to south-eastern Qld.
Habit: A burrowing frog found primarily in closed and open woodlands throughout its range. Breeds in flooded depressions and billabongs after spring and summer rains.

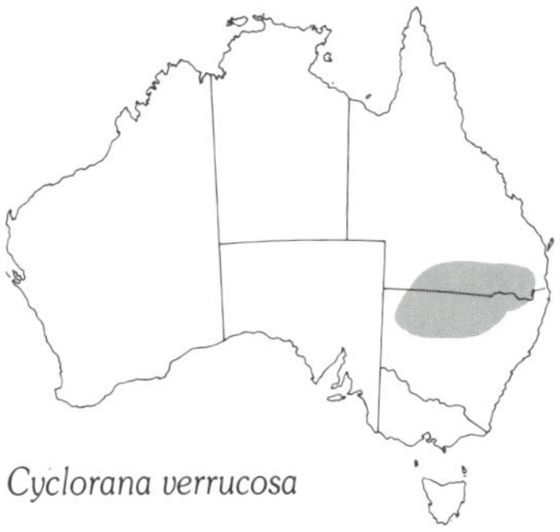

Cyclorana verrucosa

Genus *Litoria* Tschudi, 1838

A large genus containing species with the diversity of body form and habits described under the family; almost certainly it is composite and polyphyletic. Members of the genus *Litoria* are readily distinguished from the only other Australian genus of hylids with large finger and toe pads *(Nyctimystes)* by their possession of a horizontal pupil and the absence of palpebral venation on the lower eyelids.

Members of the genus *Litoria* are found throughout Australia. Extra-limital in the Papuan region.

Key

TO THE AUSTRALIAN SPECIES OF LITORIA

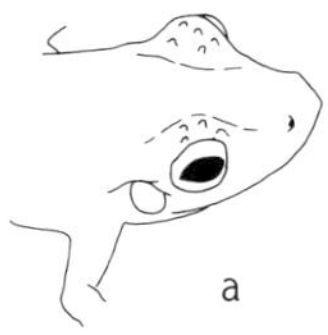

a

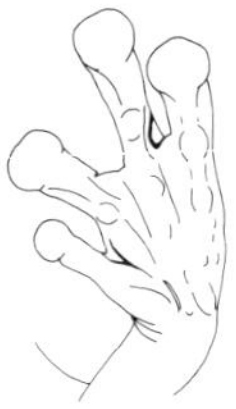

b

c

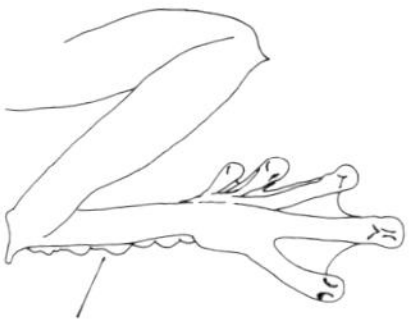

d

e

f

g

1 Vomerine teeth absent (p.52) ... **2**

Vomerine teeth present (p.52) ... **5**

2 Dorsal colour uniform green or fawn, or mixture of green and bronze; skin smooth above; at least one strong pectoral fold (p.52) no tubercles above each eye ... **3**

Variegated dark and light brown dorsally; a row of dorso-lateral tubercles and ridges on each side; no pectoral fold; several conspicuous tubercles above each eye (a) ... ***dorsalis***

3 Brown head streak present; at most a few dark flecks on the dorsal surface; tympanum brown; internarial distance/eye-naris distance (p.52) less than 1.0 ... **4**

Brown head streak absent, dorsal surface with extensive brown spots and reticulations; tympanum green; internarial distance/eye-naris distance greater than 1.0 ... ***cooloolensis***

4 Dorsal surface with broad vertebral band of bronze, bordered on either side by green ... ***bicolor***

Dorsal surface uniform green or fawn, sometimes with darker flecks ... ***fallax***

5 Fingers with conspicuous webbing, reaching at least as far as the base of the penultimate phalanx of the fourth finger (b) ... **6**

Fingers free, or webbed only at the base ... **20**

6 Hind edge of forearm smooth, or with at most a few, low, discontinuous tubercles; hind edge of foot smooth ... **7**

A conspicuous serrated ridge along the forearm (c) and another along the hind edge of the foot (d) ... ***genimaculata***

7 Hind side of the thighs with contrasting black and yellow bars or marbling, at least dorsally (e, f, g) ... **8**

Hind side of thighs more or less uniform, without black and yellow marbling ... **10**

8 Supratympanic ridge dark-edged; groin black or with conspicuous black spots (e) ... **9**

Supratympanic ridge not dark-edged; groin with at the most some small black flecks (g) ... ***tyleri***

9 Fine green spots over dorsal surface; usually groin and hind side of thighs strongly mottled with black and yellow (e) ... ***peronii***

Dorsal surface without fine green spots; usually groin and hind side of thighs with only one or two dark patches or bars on yellow ground, not heavily mottled (f) ... ***rothii***

10 Colour in life usually uniform green above, but ranging on occasion from uniform fawn to blue ... **11**

Colour brown to blackish above, never green, with or without a broad, darker vertebral patch and other contrasting markings ... **18**

11 Webbing reaching or nearly reaching the disc of the fourth finger (h) ... **12**

Webbing reaching no further than the base of the penultimate phalanx of the fourth finger (i) ... **4**

12 Green colour on the forearm extends just beyond elbow to merge with colour of upper arm; skin covering tympanum smooth; lower jaw not edged with white ... **13**

Green colour of forearm stops abruptly, with a sharp edge, at the elbow; skin covering tympanum finely granular; rim of lower jaw, especially anteriorly, narrowly edged with white ... ***gracilenta***

13 Hind side of thighs dark purplish-red or brown, often with a purple or blue iridescent surface ... ***chloris***

Hind side of thighs bright orange ... ***xanthomera***

14 No white stripe along edge of lower jaw ... **15**

A distinctive white stripe along the edge of the lower jaw, extending back to the level of the forelimb ... ***infrafrenata***

15 White, cream or yellow spots, if present, confined to the flanks ... **16**

Small white, cream or yellow spots scattered over entire dorsal surface ... **17**

16 Parotoid gland large, forming a skinfold which partly obscures the upper rim of the tympanum (j); adult snout-vent length greater than 60 mm ... ***caerulea***

Parotoid glands small to moderate, not forming a skinfold which partly obscures the upper rim of the tympanum; adult snout-vent length less than 60 mm ... ***cavernicola***

17 Parotoid glands grossly developed, forming massive fleshy folds on the head (k); adult snout-vent length to 100 mm........ ***splendida***

Parotoid glands moderately developed, forming no more than a fleshy supratympanic fold; adult snout-vent length to 70 mm........ ***gilleni***

18 Dark dorsal patch, if present, inconspicuous and commencing from a line joining the centre of each eye; tympanum covered by skin........ **19**

A broad dark dorsal patch extending from snout to cloacal region; tympanum exposed, not covered by skin........ ***dentata***

19 Webbing reaches the base of the disc of the first toe; ventral surfaces of limbs not reddish-pink........ ***rheocola***

Webbing on first toe reaches only to base of penultimate phalanx, or just beyond; ventral surfaces reddish-pink........ ***nyakalensis***

20 First finger much smaller and shorter than second (l); when pressed together the tip of the first finger reaches no further than the base of the disc of the second finger........ **21**

First finger longer than, equal to, or slightly shorter than(m) second........ **36**

21 Hind edge of vomerine teeth behind the choanae (p.52)........ **22**

Hind edge of vomerine teeth between the choanae (p.52)........ **30**

22 Heel of adpressed hindlimb (p.52) reaches to eye or beyond........ **23**

Heel of adpressed hindlimb reaches only to shoulder or tympanum........ ***rubella***

23 A narrow pale line along at least the posterior edge of the upper jaw, from below the eye to the glandular region behind the angle of the mouth........ **24**

No pale line along posterior edge of upper jaw........ **25**

24 Tympanum distinct; the tympanic annulus clearly visible........ ***citropa***

Tympanum indistinct; the tympanic annulus indistinct........ ***subglandulosa***

25 A narrow pale green, gold or white stripe, sometimes with indefinite edges but always bordered below by dark brown or black along the supratympanic ridge........ **26**

No pale stripe along the supratympanic ridge........ **27**

26 Fingers with scarcely a trace of webbing; a sharp-edged white or gold supratympanic streak........ ***phyllochroa***

Fingers with conspicuous basal webbing; an obscure, narrow, light-green zone along the supratympanic ridge........ ***burrowsae***

27 Outer metacarpal tubercle simple, or with only a shallow notch (n)........ **28**

Outer metacarpal tubercle deeply notched or divided (o)........ ***spenceri***

28 Toes nearly fully-webbed, reaching at least half way along the penultimate phalanx of the fourth toe (p)........ **29**

Toes about two-thirds webbed, reaching only the base of the penultimate phalanx of the fourth toe (q)........ **piperata**

29 Adult snout-vent length less than 40 mm; nostril at edge of snout when viewed from above........ ***lorica***

Adult snout-vent length more than 40 mm; nostrils not at edge of snout when viewed from above........ ***nannotis***

30 Back uniform or with scattered flecks or blotches, but usually without a trace of a broad mid-dorsal patch; hind side of thighs not uniform yellow or orange; a conspicuous white glandular stripe from below eye to above base of forelimb or beyond........ **31**

Usually one or a pair of mid-dorsal patches, darker than the ground colour, extending from a line joining the centre of the eyes; white stripe below eye, if present, not extending beyond anterior edge of base of forelimb........ **33**

31 Toes moderately webbed, the webbing reaching only as far as the base of the penultimate phalanx of the fifth toe; hind side of thighs without red or orange spots........ **32**

Toes extensively webbed, the webbing almost reaching the disc of the fifth toe; hind side of thighs dark brown with bright red or orange spots........ ***adelaidensis***

32 White mandibular streak extends along flank behind forelimb; groin not green or blue-green; snout pointed........ ***olongburensis***

White mandibular streak not extending to flank behind forelimb; groin green or blue-green in life; snout rounded........ ***brevipalmata***

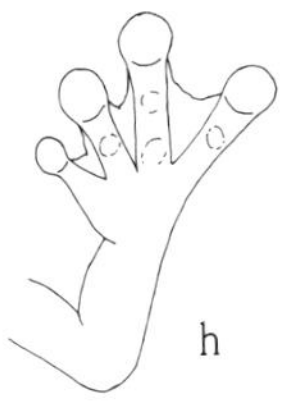
h

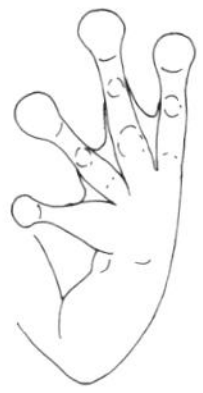
i

j

k

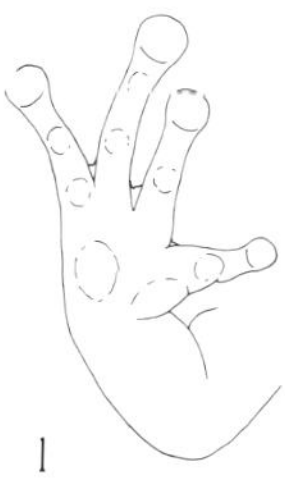
l

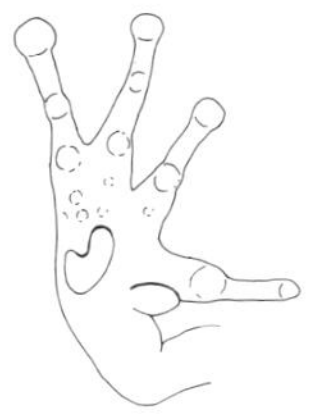

m

33 Flanks and groin with conspicuous black spots or blotches; mid-dorsal patch divided along at least part of its length, including between the eyes (r); finger discs scarcely wider than fingers; **34**

Flanks and groin without conspicuous black spots and blotches; mid-dorsal patch normally undivided, at least between eyes (s); finger discs noticeably wider than fingers; **35**

34 Finger and toe discs not or scarcely broader than the digits........ ***verreauxii***

Finger and toe discs conspicuously broader than the digits........ ***revelata***

35 A conspicuous white or cream stripe from below eye to angle of jaws; disc and two phalanges of fourth toe free of web; webbing reaches about half-way along penultimate phalanx of fifth toe; size small (maximum about 35 mm) .... ***ewingii/paraewingi***

An inconspicuous light area from below eye to angle of jaws; disc and one and a half phalanges of fourth toe free of web; fifth toe webbed almost to disc; size large (maximum about 60 mm)........ ***jervisiensis***

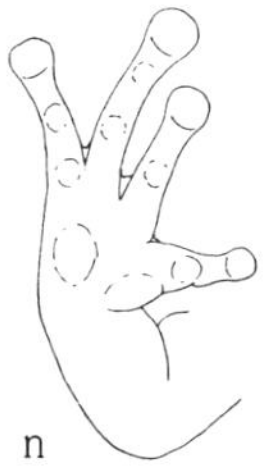

n

36 A small outer metatarsal tubercle present (p.52)........ **37**

No outer metatarsal tubercle........ **50**

37 Dorsal surface smooth, or nearly so, with at most a few low, scattered warts; outer metacarpal tubercle smoothly oval, without a notch or division (n) **38**

Dorsal surface with prominent warts and/or ridges of skin; outer metacarpal tubercle distinctly notched or divided (o)........ **49**

38 Webbing reaches the disc of the fifth toe........ **39**

Webbing not reaching the disc of the fifth toe, but extending no more than halfway along penultimate phalanx........ **42**

39 Dark head stripe, if present, very indefinite........ **40**

A conspicuous, broad, black head stripe, extending from snout, through eye and tympanum to flank, partly interrupted by a light vertical bar immediately in front of the eye (t) .... ***wotjulumensis***

o

40 Second finger slightly longer than first; no gland at the angle of the jaws **41**

Second finger shorter than or almost equal to first; a distinct gland at the angle of the jaws........ ***coplandi***

41 Adult size small (to 25 mm); north-western Australia........ ***meiriana***

Adult size large (to 50 mm); coast and ranges of central-eastern Australia........ ***booroolongensis***

42 Discs on fingers and toes conspicuous, much wider than digits........ **43**

Discs on fingers and toes small and inconspicuous, scarcely wider than digits........ **44**

43 A dark stripe from snout, through eye and tympanum to side of body........ ***personata***

No dark head stripe........ ***longirostris***

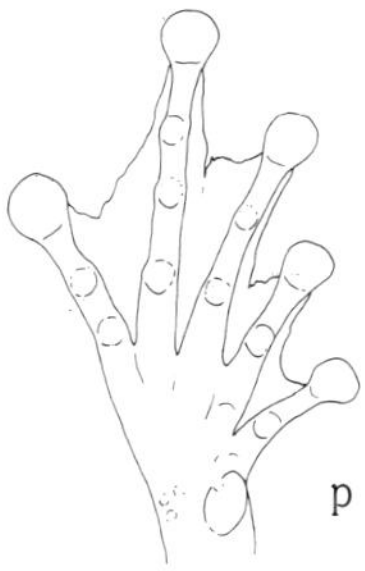

p

44 Anterior black head stripe, when present, interrupted at least in part by a light vertical bar in front of the eye; posterior dark head stripe about as wide as and enclosing the tympanum (u) **45**

Anterior black head stripe present, usually narrow but always continuous, not interrupted by a vertical bar in front of the eye(u); posterior head stripe narrow, no more than half as wide as and not enclosing the tympanum (v)........ ***lesueuri***

45 Dorsum smooth, or with occasional low, small tubercles; dark head stripe usually enclosing whole of tympanum........ **46**

Dorsum with scattered low, rounded tubercles; dark head stripe, if present, not covering whole of tympanum........ ***inermis***

46 Dorsum smooth or with a few low tubercles; adult size small (to 40 mm); posterior part of head stripe (behind level of forelimb) usually much narrower than that part immediately behind the eye **47**

Dorsum smooth; adult size large (to 55 mm); posterior part of head stripe (behind level of forearm) usually as wide as that part immediately behind the eye........ ***nigrofrenata***

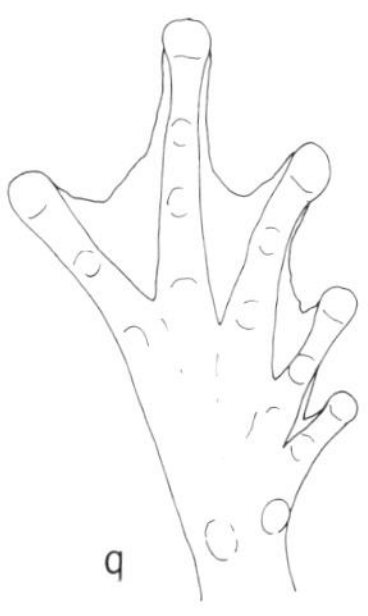

q

47 Dorsum usually marbled or variegated with darker; front edge of thigh with at most a discontinuous series of dark spots or blotches **48**

Dorsum more or less immaculate pale fawn or brown; front edge of thigh with a continuous black stripe........ ***tornieri***

48 Small disc on each finger no wider than the penultimate phalanx........ ***pallida***

Small disc on each finger noticeably wider than the penultimate phalanx........ ***latopalmata***

49 Back usually with longitudinal folds of skin; dorsal pattern longitudinally aligned, continuous from back to tip of snout; markings on hind side of thighs tending to a series of horizontal stripes .... ***nasuta***

Back usually with numerous conspicuous tubercles and short skin folds; dorsal pattern consisting of a series of dark blotches or patches, one of which has an anterior edge forming a straight line between the eyes; markings on hind side of thighs usually irregular, not forming a series of horizontal stripes........ ***freycineti***

50 Groin and lower parts of tibial region not black with large white or yellow spots **51**
Groin and lower tibial region black with large white or yellow spots .... ***cyclorhyncha***

51 Flanks smooth or with a few scattered granules, not contrasting strongly with the skin on the back...... **52**
Flanks strongly granular below a distinct, glandular dorso-lateral skinfold with densely packed, large, rounded, usually pale coloured, granules, contrasting strongly with the smooth or tubercular skin on the back above the skinfold.. **53**

r

52 Skin smooth or shagreened above, usually without any tubercles, granules or skin folds; dark head stripe between eye and tympanum, much narrower than the tympanum.. ***dahlii***
Skin tubercular above, with conspicuous scattered warts and skinfolds; dark head stripe between eye and ear about as wide as the tympanum .... ***alboguttata***

53 Dorsum with a series of large and small low,rounded warts (in life); pale-coloured dorso-lateral skinfold poorly developed or absent; usually a conspicuous pale vertebral stripe.. **54**
Dorsum smooth with at most a few, scattered low, rounded tubercles; a conspicuous yellow or cream dorso-lateral skin fold extending back from the top of the supratympanic fold; usually no indication of a pale vertebral stripe.. ***aurea***

s

54 Larger warts on back usually irregularly scattered; south-eastern Australia **55**
Larger warts on back usually arranged in regular longitudinal rows near the vertebral line; south-western Australia.. ***moorei***

55 Groin with large yellow or cream spots; lower surfaces of hindlimbs with pale yellow spots and/or marbling (w)... ***castanea***
Groin without large yellow or cream spots; lower surfaces of hindlimbs without pale yellow spots and/or marbling.. ***raniformis***

t

u

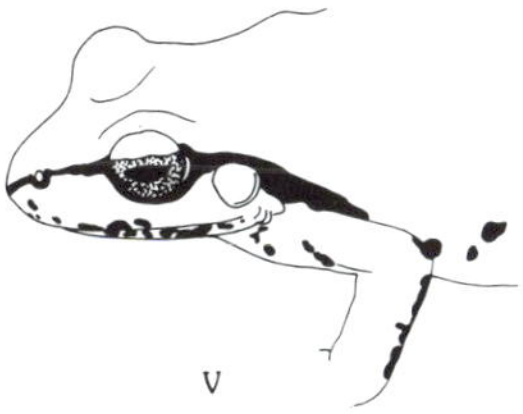
v

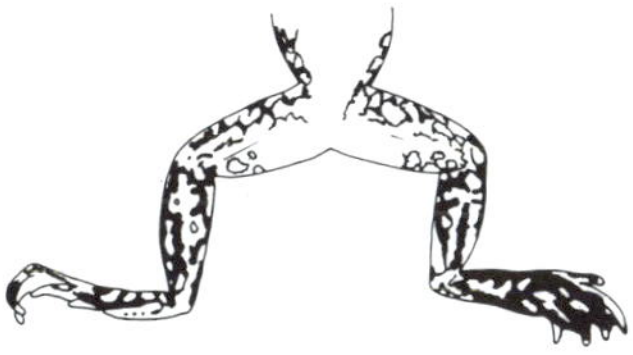
w

Litoria adelaidensis (Gray, 1841)

Slender Tree Frog

Litoria adelaidensis Walpole, WA 60mm

Description: A rather slender frog. Light brown or fawn above, sometimes light green, with dark brown flecks or patches, often arranged in distinct longitudinal lines. A dark brown or black stripe from the tip of the snout below the canthus to the eye and extending from behind the eye, through the tympanum and along the flank. This dark stripe is bordered below by a narrower white stripe from the upper lip, this stripe often breaking up on the side into a series of spots. Hind side of thighs dark brown with orange or reddish spots. Ventral surface whitish to light brown. Skin smooth above, coarsely granular below except for throat, which is smooth. Vomerine teeth prominent between and behind the choanae. A distinct pectoral fold. Finger and toe discs small, not much wider than digits. Fingers with only basal webbing, toes about three quarters webbed. Inner metatarsal tubercle large, no outer. Tympanum distinct. Second finger longer than first. 60 mm
Distribution: South-western WA, in areas of relatively high rainfall (above approximately 500 mm per annum).

Litoria alboguttata Walgett, NSW 65mm

Litoria aurea Myall Lakes, NSW 85mm

Litoria adelaidensis

Litoria alboguttata

Habit: Usually found in vegetation bordering streams and swamps. Breeds in spring. Call a 'harsh grating screech' (Main).

Litoria alboguttata (Günther, 1867)

Striped Burrowing Frog

Description: A relatively slender frog, brown, olive-brown or green above with scattered darker flecks and blotches and often with a light yellowish or green vertebral stripe. A dark canthal streak continued from behind the eye as a broad dark band over the forelimb and along the sides, where it is broken up by paler blotching. Edge of upper lip brown with white spots. Hind side of thighs dark with numerous white spots. Lower surface white, except for throat and chest which may be flecked with brown. Skin with scattered warts above, finely granular on the belly, smooth on the chest and throat. A distinct dorso-lateral skinfold, usually dark in colour. Toes about half webbed. Inner metatarsal tubercle shovel-shaped. No outer metatarsal tubercle. 65 mm
Distribution: Coast and central inland of Qld, as far north as Cape York Peninsula. In NSW it is largely restricted to the western slopes and central plains of the northern half of the State. Also in NT.
Habit: A burrowing frog found in a fairly wide range of environments. Both coastally and inland it is usually found along the grassy edges of temporary (often roadside) ponds after rain. Often active by day.

Litoria aurea (Lesson, 1829)

Green and Golden Bell Frog

Description: Dull olive to bright emerald green above, with large irregular blotches of brown or rich golden-bronze. A cream or yellow dorso-lateral skin fold, sometimes discontinuous, from eye nearly to groin. A narrow blackish canthal stripe from nostril or eye, continued behind the eye as a stripe extending over the conspicuous tympanum and bordering the pale skin fold. Limbs bronzy-brown above. Flanks brown with cream spots and flecks. A white glandular stripe from angle of mouth to base of forearm. Groin and hind side of thighs bright blue or blue-green. Whitish below. Skin smooth, shagreened or finely granular above; flanks with large, flat, smooth tubercles; lower surface granular. Vomerine teeth conspicuous, mostly between the choanae. Pectoral fold present. Finger and toe discs conspicuous but only slightly wider than the digits. Fingers without webbing. Toes nearly fully webbed. A moderate inner

Litoria bicolor Pennefather River, Qld. 30mm
Diurnal resting position in hot sun.

and no outer metatarsal tubercle. Tympanum distinct. Second finger longer than first. 85 mm
Distribution: Eastern and south-eastern NSW and far eastern Vic, principally at lower altitudes.
Habit: A largely aquatic species found among vegetation within or at the edges of permanent water — streams, swamps, lagoons, farm dams and ornamental ponds. Often found under debris on low, oft-flooded river flats. Frequently active by day. A voracious, cannibalistic species. Summer breeder; call a loud, slow guttural four-part 'craw-awk, crawk, crok, crok' (Harrison).

Litoria bicolor (Gray, 1842)

Northern Dwarf Tree Frog

Description: A broad, bronze vertebral band from snout to vent, bordered on either side by green. A dark stripe along the side of the snout, through the eye over the tympanum and along the side, separating the green flanks from the white or green ventral surface. A narrow white stripe along the edge of the upper lip to the corner of the mouth where it widens and continues below the tympanum to the base of the arm. Groin and hind side of thighs pale yellow. Cream or yellowish below, throat of male flecked with darker. Skin satin smooth above, smooth below except for granular belly and femoral region. Vomerine teeth absent. Strong pectoral fold. Finger and toe discs very distinct. Fingers with a trace of webbing, the webbing reaching only about half way along the penultimate phalanx of the first finger. Toes half to three-quarters webbed, fringed, disc and one phalanx free on outer side of fourth toes. Small inner metatarsal tubercle, no outer. Tympanum distinct. Second finger longer than first. 30 mm
Distribution: Coast and adjacent areas of northern Australia, from the Kimberley region to the Proserpine district in the east. Southern coastal areas of New Guinea.
Habit: During the dry season isolated specimens are frequently found in or on vegetation, especially in the leaf axils of *Pandanus* palms or on the exposed upper surfaces of broad-leafed shrubs, even in hot, dry conditions. Breeding conditions are found in aquatic and border vegetation of permanent or temporary lagoons, swamps etc.

Litoria booroolongensis (Moore, 1961)

Booroolong Frog

Description: Dull grey or brown above, with irregular darker flecks and mottling. Hind side of thighs dark brown with small, pale spots. Head stripe usually obscure, but when present widens behind the eye to enclose all of tympanum. White or cream below. Skin smooth, or with scattered low tubercles above. Throat smooth, chest and belly granular. Vomerine teeth largely between the choanae, but extending behind them. Pectoral fold present. Finger and toe discs moderate. Fingers without webbing, toes nearly fully webbed, the webbing reaching the disc of the fifth toe. A prominent inner and a tiny outer metatarsal tubercle. Tympanum distinct. Second finger longer than first. 45 mm
Distribution: Confined to mountain streams of the Great Dividing Range in NSW.
Habit: Usually found on or under boulders and debris in and beside the rocky beds of mountain streams. Breeds in summer. Call a "...soft, slow 'qrk qrk qrk'" (Moore).

Litoria aurea

Litoria bicolor

Litoria booroolongensis

Litoria brevipalmata

Litoria burrowsae

Litoria caerulea

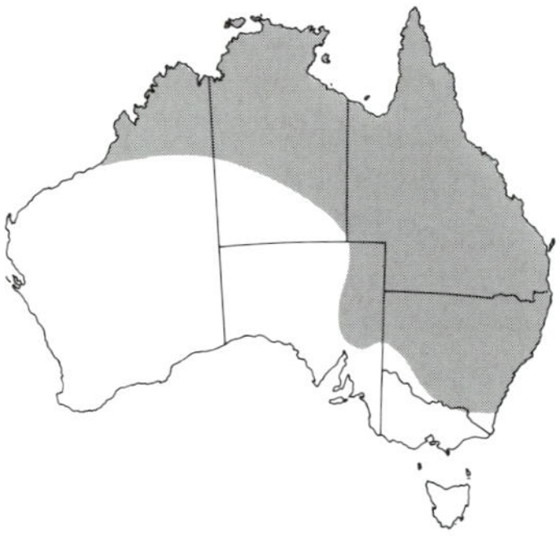

Litoria castanea

Litoria brevipalmata
Ourimbah, NSW.
Pair in amplexus. 40mm

Litoria booroolongensis Ebor, NSW 45mm

Litoria brevipalmata Tyler, Martin and Watson, 1972

Green-Thighed Frog

Description: Rich brown to chocolate brown above, sometimes with scattered small black flecks. A broad, black canthal stripe from snout to eye, continued behind the eye as a broad, black band (almost enclosing the tympanum), extending to the flank and sometimes narrowly bordered above by white or yellow. Upper lip with a narrow white or yellow stripe, even more narrowly edged below with brown, continued as a glandular stripe from the angle of the mouth to the base of the forearm. Lower flanks yellowish with scattered black spots and flecks. Groin and hind side of thighs brilliant light blue, blue-green or green, the former with scattered black spots and blotches. A dark stripe along the front edge of the hindlimb. Whitish to yellow below. Skin smooth or slightly shagreened above, granular below. Vomerine teeth prominent between the choanae. Pectoral fold absent. Finger and toe discs moderate. Fingers free, without webbing; toes about one third webbed. A prominent oval, inner metatarsal tubercle, and an obscure small outer tubercle. Tympanum distinct. Second finger longer than first. 40 mm

Distribution: Known from isolated localities in wet sclerophyll forest along the northern coast of NSW and south-eastern Qld.

Habit: Little known. Breeding aggregations occur around grassy semi-permanent ponds in late spring and summer.

Litoria caerulea Bundaberg, Qld 100mm

Litoria burrowsae (Scott, 1942)

Tasmanian Tree Frog

Description: Uniform light green above, sometimes with scattered light fawn spots, or dark brown with irregular bright green patches and light brown flecks. A narrow, black canthal streak, widening behind the eye to form a broad, dark band extending almost to the groin; this dark band often broken up by groups of irregular white spots and blotches. Pinkish-white below, throat somewhat darker. Groin and hind side of thighs uniform pale brown. Skin smooth above, or with scattered, small tubercles. Chin smooth, remainder of lower surfaces granular. Vomerine teeth between or behind the choanae. Pectoral fold present. Finger and toe discs large. Fingers nearly one third webbed, toes about three-quarters webbed. A large inner and a small outer metatarsal tubercle. Tympanum distinct. Second finger longer than first. 55 mm.
Distribution: Known only from the highlands of Tas.
Habit: Original specimens were collected in January, in alpine grasses at edges of ponds at approximately 900 metres.

Litoria burrowsae Melaleuca Inlet, Tas 55mm

R.W.G. JENKINS

Litoria cavernicola Mitchell Plateau, WA 55mm

Litoria caerulea (White, 1790)

Green Tree Frog

Description: Bright green above, often with scattered white spots on the sides and occasionally on the back. Often an irregular white stripe, or series of white spots, from the angle of the mouth to the base of the forearm. Ventral surface white. Skin smooth or shagreened above, coarsely granular on the sides and ventral surface, somewhat smoother on the throat. A thick, glandular, supratympanic ridge. Vomerine teeth prominent, between and behind the choanae. A pectoral fold. Finger and toe discs large. Fingers about one third webbed and toes nearly three quarters webbed. A large inner and outer metatarsal tubercle. Tympanum distinct. Second finger longer than first. 100 mm
Distribution: Coast to drier interior of north-western WA, NT, Qld, SA and NSW. Also found in southern New Guinea.
Habit: Found in a large variety of habitats and is frequently found in human dwellings, lavatories, water tanks and troughs, windmills, downpipes etc.

Litoria castanea (Steindachner, 1867)

Description: Similar in most respects to *Litoria raniformis*, from which it may be readily distinguished by the presence of large yellow or cream spots in the groin, pale yellow spots and/or marbling on the lower surfaces of the hindlimbs, and completely webbed toes. 80 mm
Distribution: Northern tablelands, NSW.
Habit: Active in the long grass, reeds and sedges of permanent lagoons and marshes; also shelters under ground debris and fallen timber in winter or during dry periods.

Litoria cavernicola Tyler and Davies, 1979

Description: Generally similar in appearance to *Litoria caerulea*. Dull green or greenish-brown above, whitish below. Skin above and below coarsely granular. A narrow non-glandular supratympanic ridge. Vomerine teeth very prominent, mostly behind the choanae. A pectoral fold. Finger and toe discs large. Fingers with basal webbing, the toes nearly three quarters webbed. A large inner and small outer metatarsal tubercle. Tympanum distinct. Second finger longer than first. 55 mm
Distribution: Known only from the Mitchell Plateau, north-west Kimberley region, WA.
Habit: Found in '...large caves in sandstone gorges' (Tyler and Davies).

Litoria chloris Ourimbah, NSW.
Calling male, with vocal sac inflated.
65mm

Litoria cavernicola

Litoria chloris (Boulenger, 1893)

Red-eyed Tree Frog

Description: Uniform bright leaf-green above. White to vivid lemon-yellowish below. Hind side of thighs deep purplish-red or brown, often with some paler iridescent purple patches along the upper edge. Edge of lower jaw green. Inner half of hand white or yellow, but lower part of arm otherwise green, the green extending just beyond the elbow on to the upper arm. Iris golden (centrally) to orange or reddish (outer margins). Skin smoothly shagreened above and on sides, granular below. A serrated ridge along hind edge of forearm. Vomerine teeth in two short, prominent rows between the choanae. A slight pectoral fold. Finger and toe discs large. Fingers about three quarters webbed, toes nearly fully-webbed. Prominent inner, no outer, metatarsal tubercle. Tympanum distinct. Second finger longer than first. 65 mm
Distribution: Coast and adjacent areas of eastern Australia from Gosford district in the south to central-eastern Qld.
Habit: Found in wet sclerophyll/rainforest complexes and regrowth associated with roads and clearings. Also found in open grassed floodplains of coastal rivers.Calls from shrubs and lower branches of trees, eventually congregating to breed around grassy soaks and clearings inundated by heavy spring and summer rains, or in overflow ponds beside streams. Usually encountered only after rain. Call a series of about 9-12 long, drawn-out (each 1-2 secs) aaa-rk's, each series often alternating with several short chirrups.

Litoria citropa Sydney, NSW 65mm

Litoria citropa (Duméril and Bibron, 1841)

Blue Mountains Tree Frog

Description: Except for the green areas described below, virtually all of the exposed dorsal surfaces are light to medium brown, often with scattered, numerous, darker flecks. A dark brown stripe along the canthus, through the eye and extending over the ear and along the flanks almost to the groin. This stripe and another white stripe along the upper lip extend back to the base of the forelimb. Side of the head, much of the forelimb and lower hindlimb, and a broad dorso-lateral patch, bright green. The green areas may disappear under certain conditions of temperature and temperament. Axilla, groin, hind edge of thighs and inner edge of hind foot, bright red or orange. Lower surfaces white. Skin smooth or finely granular above, often with scattered tiny warts; coarsely granular below. Vomerine teeth prominent, mostly behind the choanae. No pectoral fold. Finger and toe discs large. Fingers almost devoid of web, toes nearly half webbed. A large, oval inner metatarsal tubercle, and a small outer. Tympanum distinct. Second finger longer than first. 65 mm
Distribution: Confined to the coast and ranges of NSW and eastern Vic.
Habit: Primarily an inhabitant of heaths and both wet and dry sclerophyll forests. Usually found resting under rocks or in rock crevices; breeds in permanent or semi-permanent pools in spring and summer.

Litoria cooloolensis Liem, 1974

Description: Similar in most respects to *Litoria bicolor* and *Litoria fallax*, from both of which it may be distinguished by (1) the green dorsum, usually with numerous brown spots and reticulations (at most a few scattered flecks in *bicolor* and *fallax*), (2) the green tympanum (brown in *fallax* and *bicolor*), (3) absence of a brown head streak, (present in *bicolor* and *fallax*), (4) a purplish brown streak along the upper thigh (absent or obscure in *bicolor* and *fallax*) and (5) an internarial/eye-naris distance ratio greater

Litoria citropa

Litoria cooloolensis

Litoria coplandi

Litoria cyclorhyncha

Litoria dahlii

Litoria dentata

Litoria dorsalis

than 1.0 (less than 1.0 in *bicolor* and *fallax*). 25 mm
Distribution: Presently known only from Cooloola and nearby Fraser Is., Qld.
Habit: Found in '...sandy freshwater lakes along coastal SE Queensland and on Fraser Island. It occurs in wallum habitats and lowland rainforest' (Liem).

Litoria coplandi (Tyler, 1968)

Saxicoline Tree Frog

Description: Head, body and limbs rich brown above, variegated with darker brown; this colour pattern extends to the middle flanks where it merges (via a pale brown lower lateral zone peppered with white) with the whitish ventral surface. Throat finely peppered with brown. Groin flushed with pale lemon yellow. Hind side of thigh light grey-brown with lemon-yellow flecks and blotches. Skin smooth or finely granular above, with numerous tiny rounded tubercles; granular below. Vomerine teeth in two short, rounded series between the front edge of the choanae. A pectoral fold present. Finger and toe discs moderate, conspicuous. Fingers free, without webbing; toes nearly fully webbed, the webbing reaching the disc of the fifth toe. An oval inner metatarsal tubercle and a small, flat outer tubercle. Tympanum distinct. Second finger shorter than first. 40 mm
Distribution: Kimberley region of WA to Arnhem Land, NT.
Habit: In Arnhem Land an inhabitant of the rocky hills and gorges of the western escarpment, where it shelters by day deep in rock crevices. At dusk it emerges to forage on the large sandstone slopes still hot from exposure to the sun, or frequents temporary and permanent waterholes in the ranges.

Litoria cyclorhyncha (Boulenger, 1882)

Spotted-thighed Frog

Description: Similar in most respects to *Litoria aurea*, from which it differs in having the groin and front side of the thigh, and the lower tibial region black with large white or yellow spots; black reticulations on the ventral surface in most adults; skin with large flat warts above. 80 mm
Distribution: South coast of WA from Cheyne Beach to Israelite Bay.
Habit: Similar in most respects to those of *Litoria aurea*. Call 'like the distant sound of wood being sawn' (Main).

Litoria coplandi McArthur River, NT 40mm

M. PETERSON

Litoria cyclorhyncha Jerramungup, WA 80mm

Litoria dahlii Humpty Doo, NT 70mm

Litoria dentata Ourimbah, NSW. Two males, that on left calling with fully-inflated vocal sac. 45mm

Litoria dahlii (Boulenger, 1896)

Description: A slender frog, olive-brown or olive-grey above with or without irregular darker variegations, and usually at least a faint, pale vertebral stripe. White below. Hind side of thighs mottled, marbled or spotted with white. Skin finely granular or with rich shagreen above, smooth below. No dorso-lateral skin-fold. Toes fully webbed. Inner metatarsal tubercle not shovel-shaped. No outer metatarsal tubercle. 70 mm
Distribution: Widely distributed from Cape York Peninsula, Qld, to the north-western parts of the NT.
Habit: An inhabitant of the savannah woodlands of northern Australia. A predatory, largely aquatic species during the west season, it is usually encountered around the edges of lagoons and swamps.

Litoria dentata (Keferstein, 1868)

Bleating Tree Frog

Description: A broad, rich brown vertebral band of varying width, narrowest over the shoulders, usually from the snout, but sometimes from the level of the eyes. On either side of this band is a broad, paler creamish-brown band from the eye to the groin. A dark canthal stripe on each side through the eye and the tympanum and along the flank. Sides and concealed parts of limbs often lemon-yellow, especially in males. Upper sides of limbs brown with irregular darker flecks, although forearm usually much darker than upper arm. The above colours may have an overall wash of rich olive green. Ventral surface yellowish, breeding males with lemon yellow,

brown or black throat. Skin smooth above, or with a few very small tubercles, granular below except for the throat, which is almost smooth. Vomerine teeth in two small clusters, between and behind the choanae. Finger and toe discs moderate. Fingers nearly one third webbed, toes nearly three-quarters webbed. A prominent inner metatarsal tubercle, no outer. Tympanum very distinct. Second finger longer than first. 45 mm
Distribution: Coast and adjacent upland areas of NSW and southern Qld.
Habit: Often found around swamps and lagoons, especially the paperbark (*Melaleuca*) swamps behind coastal sandhills. Also common in rainforest, wet and dry sclerophyll forests and urban bushland. Breeds in shallow grassy or grass-edged swamps, after summer rains. Call a long, penetrating, wavering bleat.

Litoria dorsalis Weipa, Qld 20mm

Litoria dorsalis Macleay, 1877
Dwarf Rocket Frog

Description: A tiny, slender, agile frog with a sharply pointed snout. Light grey or brown to rich reddish brown above, often irregularly flecked or mottled with darker. Usually a broad, dark band from behind the eye to the groin, and an even darker stripe along the snout, through the eye and over the base of the arm to the flank. Snout and upper surfaces of limbs peppered with dark brown. A conspicuous dark bar along the front edge of the arm. Ventral surface white except for a fine peppering of brown on the throat, chest and limbs. Skin sometimes smooth above but usually with a few low warts or skin folds and almost invariably with several small tubercles over each eye. Skin of throat smooth, belly granular. Vomerine teeth absent. Pectoral fold absent. Finger and toe discs moderate, very distinct. Fingers without a trace of webbing. Toes less than half webbed, disc and nearly two phalanges free on outer side of fourth toe. Prominent inner metatarsal tubercle, no outer. Tympanum usually indistinct. Second finger longer than first. 20 mm
Distribution: Recorded from widely separated areas of northern Australia. Currently known from Cairns district and upper Cape York, Qld and from Arnhem Land and north-western Australia. Also recorded from southern New Guinea.
Habit: Usually found in saturated leaf litter in coastal paperbark swamps and in leaf-litter fringing inland creeks and lagoons. Cairns specimens found among reeds in gutter. A high-pitched penetrating, stridulating call. Breeding habits little known.
Subspecies: *dorsalis* (southern New Guinea); *microbelos* (northern Australia).

Litoria ewingii (Duméril and Bibron, 1841)
Brown Tree Frog

Description: Pale fawn or brown above, usually dotted or flecked with dark brown, and with a conspicuous dark brown mid-dorsal patch commencing between the eyes and extending to the vent. This patch may have a dark edge, but is not divided along the vertebral line. A narrow black stripe along the canthus, continued behind the eye as a broad dark stripe through the ear to the flank; this stripe is sometimes bordered above by a narrow pale stripe, and below by a narrow white glandular stripe from the angle of the jaw to the base of the forearm. Limbs above same as dorsum. No dark spots or blotches in groin. Ventral surfaces white, cream or pale yellow. Hind side of thighs yellow to bright reddish orange. Skin smooth or with low, small tubercles. Throat finely granular, chest and belly coarsely granular. Vomerine teeth small, rounded, between and projecting slightly in front of the choanae. Finger and toe discs small, scarcely wider than digits. Fingers free or occasionally with a trace of webbing. Toes about half-webbed. A small inner, but no outer metatarsal tubercle. Tympanum distinct. Second finger longer than first. 35 mm
Distribution: South-eastern SA, southern and eastern Vic, far south-eastern NSW (with several isolated populations along the coast and ranges of central NSW). Widely distributed in Tas.
Habit: As for *Litoria verreauxii*, except that it does not occur at higher altitudes.

R.W.G. JENKINS

Litoria ewingii Adelaide, SA 35mm

Litoria fallax (Peters, 1880)

Eastern Dwarf Tree Frog

Description: Similar in most respects to *L. bicolor*, from which it differs in being uniform green or fawn above, sometimes with scattered darker flecks; the webbing reaches the base of the disc of the first toe. The groin and hind side of thighs are bright orange. 25 mm

Distribution: Coast and adjacent areas from central-eastern Qld to southern NSW.

Habit: An inhabitant of vegetation, especially reeds and floating plants, in and beside small creeks, dams, lagoons and often swamps. Often found during the day sheltering in the leaf-axils of pandanus, banana and pineapple plants, etc, well away from water. Call a squeaky and high pitched 'wr-e-e-ek, wr-e-e-ek, wr-e-e-ek', continued many times (Moore).

Litoria ewingii

Litoria fallax

Litoria freycineti

Litoria freycineti Tschudi, 1838

Freycinet's Frog

Description: Pale grey-brown to dark brown above, usually with numerous irregular darker blotches, and flecks, the most regular part of the dorsal pattern

Litoria freycineti Sydney, NSW 45mm

Litoria fallax Sydney, NSW 25mm

consisting of a pale triangular patch on the snout, commencing at a line joining the front of the eyes, and enclosing a small to large dark brown central patch. The pale snout is continuous with paler areas extending back over the outer rim of the supraorbital region. A black, canthal stripe, pale-edged above, from the snout to the eye (almost completely interrupted by a pale bar in front of the eye) and continued behind the eye as a broad dark band enclosing the tympanum and extending to the flanks where it is usually broken at about the level of the arm; the front and hind rims of the tympanum usually pale-edged. A pale glandular stripe from below the eye to the base of the forelimb. Edge of jaw brown, lower jaw barred or blotched with brown and white. Whitish below. Skin above with numerous irregularly scattered low tubercles and short folds; granular below, except for the throat which is smooth. Vomerine teeth in two clusters between the choanae. Finger and toe discs small, only slightly wider than the digits. Fingers free, without web; toes with well developed webbing. A small inner and a minute outer metatarsal tubercle. Tympanum distinct. Second finger equal to first. 45 mm

Distribution: Coastal regions from central NSW to south-eastern Qld.

Habit: A terrestrial frog found in a wide variety of heath and forest habitats throughout its range, but usually encountered on warm spring and summer nights after rain.

Litoria genimaculata (Horst, 1883)

Description: Rich grey-brown, silvery, or reddish-brown above, with irregular dark brown mottling, the latter often tending to form longitudinal lines. Often a darker patch between the eyes. Similar colouring on the limbs except that the hind limbs have broad, irregular cross-bands. Groin finely mottled with black and cream. Ventral surface creamish-white, densely peppered with brown on the throat. Iris of eye rich silvery-grey, except for upper quarter which is a rich blue-green. Skin smoothly shagreened above, or with scattered very small tubercles, coarsely granular below. A pale-coloured serrated ridge along hind edge of forearm and a more prominent one along the outer edge of each foot. A small flap on each heel. Vomerine teeth prominent, between and behind the choanae. A slight pectoral fold. Finger and toe discs very large. Fingers about half-webbed, toes nearly fully webbed. An oval inner metatarsal tubercle and a small outer tubercle. Tympanum very distinct. Second finger longer than first. 85 mm

Distribution: Rainforest areas throughout north-eastern Qld from the Atherton Tableland northward. Extra-limital in New Guinea.

Habit: Found in rainforest throughout its range; usually encountered among streamside vegetation or on mossy seepages.

Litoria gilleni (Spencer, 1896)

Centralian Tree Frog

Description: Similar in nearly all respects to *L. caerulea*, of which it has often been regarded as a subspecies. It is geographically isolated from *L. caerulea*, from which it can be distinguished by its more angular snout and the presence of small, creamy-white spots and small blotches over most of the upper surface of the body. 70 mm

Distribution: Mountain ranges and associated rivers and streams of central Australia.

Habit: Usually found on rock surfaces enclosing permanent or semi-permanent streams and waterholes in stony ranges.

Litoria gracilenta (Peters, 1869)

Dainty Green Tree Frog

Description: Bright leaf-green above, usually with a faint lighter, yellowish-green stripe along the canthus, over the eye and along the supratympanic fold. Whole of upper arm and upper and lower surfaces of fingers and toes including webbing bright lemon-yellow. A long, oval shield-shaped patch of green on exposed surface of lower arm. Belly and throat cream to yellow. Hind side of thighs rich purplish-brown, often with an iridescent blue sheen. Iris rich golden or reddish. Skin finely granular or shagreened above, although sometimes with a few small tubercles on the sides and limbs, coarsely granular below. Vomerine teeth prominent, largely between the choanae. No pectoral fold. Finger and toe discs large. Fingers about three-quarters webbed, toes nearly fully webbed. No metatarsal tubercles. Tympanic rim distinct, but tympanum covered with granular skin. Second finger longer than first. 45 mm
Distribution: Coastal and near coastal areas of eastern Australia, from a little north of Sydney to the tip of Cape York Peninsula. Extra-limital in south-western Papua New Guinea.
Habit: Found in a wide variety of moist forest or woodland habitats. Usually encountered after rain on roads or among low vegetation. At other times usually resting on streamside vegetation.

Litoria inermis (Peters, 1867)

Description: A slender frog, grey-brown above with indistinct darker and lighter brown or reddish blotches and flecks, usually covering individual warts. Upper lip flecked with white. Hind side of thighs mottled or blotched with white or yellow and dark brown, rarely forming a fine reticulate pattern. Rarely more than a faint indication of a dark canthal or temporal stripe, which, when present, does not enclose the entire tympanum, and no conspicuous or continuous blackish stripe along the front edge of the tibial region. Lower surfaces white. Throat of male with brown mottling. Skin with numerous small, low warts above, slightly granular on the belly, smooth on the throat and chest. Hindlimbs lightly barred or speckled with brown above. No dorso-lateral fold present. Fingers free, without webbing; toes about

Litoria genimaculata Kuranda, Qld 85mm

Litoria gilleni Simpson's Gap, NT 70mm

Litoria gracilenta near Cairns, Qld. In diurnal resting position. 45mm

Litoria genimaculata

Litoria gilleni

Litoria gracilenta

Litoria inermis

Litoria infrafrenata

Litoria jervisiensis

Litoria latopalmata

three-quarters webbed. Inner metatarsal tubercle small, not shovel-shaped; a small outer metatarsal tubercle present. Tympanum distinct. 35 mm
Distribution: Coast and hinterland of northern Australia, from the Kimberleys in WA to the central coast of Qld.
Habit: A terrestrial species usually found on warm, humid evenings, especially after rain. Primary habitats include coastal and river floodplains, monsoon forest and savannah woodlands.

Litoria infrafrenata (Günther, 1867)

Giant Tree Frog

Description: Uniform bright green or brown above, with an intense white stripe along the lower lip and extending back below the tympanum to above the base of the forelimb. Another white stripe along the hind edge of the hindlimb, including the fifth and most of the fourth toes. Ventral surface whitish. The white stripes on the sides of the head and hindlimbs may become pink at times. Skin finely granular or shagreened above, very coarsely granular on the sides and coarsely granular below, except for throat which is nearly smooth. Vomerine teeth very prominent, between the choanae. No pectoral fold. Finger and toe discs large. Fingers at least half-webbed. Toes nearly fully webbed. A large inner metatarsal tubercle, no outer. Tympanum very distinct. Second finger longer than first. 110 mm
Distribution: Coastal and adjacent areas of north-eastern Qld, north of Townsville and extending around Cape York Peninsula into the Gulf of Carpentaria. Widely distributed throughout New Guinea and its island archipelagos.
Habit: Found in a wide variety of habitats, from rainforest to cultivated areas; frequently inhabits houses, sheds, etc. Forages on humid or wet evenings.

Litoria jervisiensis (Dumeril and Bibron, 1841)

Jervis Bay Tree Frog

Description: Grey-brown or rich light to dark brown above with variable darker flecking and mottling. Usually indications of a dark broad dorsal patch commencing between the eyes. Occasionally a pale vertebral stripe. A dark brown line below the canthus and extending from the eye along a well-developed supra-tympanic fold to the base of the forelimb. Axillas, groins and concealed parts of thighs

dull to bright orange. Sides sometimes with more intense darker flecking or mottling. Cream or yellowish below, throat of male brown. Skin smooth or shagreened above, finely granular below. Vomerine teeth prominent, between the choanae. No pectoral fold. Finger and toe discs large, markedly wider than digits. Fingers with a rudiment of web, toes about two-thirds webbed. A small inner metatarsal tubercle, no outer. Tympanum distinct. Second finger markedly longer than first. 60 mm
Distribution: Coastal areas of NSW from about Wyong in the north to the Victorian border area; extreme eastern Vic.
Habit: Usually found among streamside vegetation in deeply forested gullies in wet sclerophyll forest, and in coastal heaths and swamplands. Exudes a toxic musky skin secretion when molested.

Litoria inermis Pascoe River, Qld 35mm

Litoria infrafrenata Weipa, Qld 110mm

Litoria jervisiensis near Wollongong, NSW 60mm

Litoria latopalmata Brewarrina, NSW 40mm

Litoria lesueuri

Litoria longirostris

Litoria lorica

Litoria meiriana

Litoria latopalmata Günther, 1867

Description: A highly variable frog, probably with more than one species represented under this single name. Pale fawn to dark brown above, immaculate or with a series of darker variegations and blotches similar to those described for *L. freycineti*. A broad black canthal stripe, almost completely interrupted in front of the eye, and continued behind the eye to almost enclose the tympanum and extend to the flanks, where it breaks up into an irregular series of black spots and blotches extending to the groin. A pale glandular stripe from below eye to base of forelimb. Limbs variegated with darker. Lower jaw variegated with brown and pale creamy-white. Hind side of thighs variegated with yellow and dark brown, often forming a reticulum. Whitish below. Skin smooth or with a few small flat warts; remaining ventral surfaces and lower flanks granular. No dorso-lateral skin fold. Finger and toe discs very small, projecting only slightly beyond the lateral edges of the penultimate phalanges. Fingers free, without webbing; toes with well-developed webbing, the webbing not reaching the disc of the fifth toe but extending no further than half way along the penultimate phalanx. A small inner and minute outer metatarsal tubercle. Tympanum distinct. 40 mm

Distribution: Coast, ranges and interior of eastern Australia, from central Qld to central NSW.

Habit: A terrestrial, nocturnal frog, individuals of which appear to forage widely over the forest or woodland floor, or on coastal and river floodplains, even well away from water.

Litoria lesueuri (Duméril and Bibron, 1841)

Leseur's Frog

Description: A composite species as currently recognised. Pale fawn to dark brown above, immaculate, or with a few scattered darker flecks, or with large, irregular dark brown patches covering the dorsal surface; specimens with the latter pattern almost invariably have a dark, transverse bar between the eyes. A narrow black canthal streak from the snout, without interruption to the eye, and continued behind the eye to a point on the flanks near the base of the forelimb; this stripe usually has a narrow pale border above, and does not enclose the pale-rimmed tympanum. Groin yellow, heavily blotched with black; hind side of thigh with black and yellow reticulum. Many specimens are flushed all over with lemon-yellow, while in some juveniles the yellow in the groin and hind thighs is replaced by bright green or blue-green. Whitish below. Skin smooth or shagreened above, smooth on the throat, granular on the belly. No dorso-lateral skin fold. Fingers free, without webbing; toes with well-developed webbing. A moderate inner and a minute outer metatarsal tubercle. Tympanum distinct. 70 mm
Distribution: Coast, ranges and slopes of eastern Australia, from northern Qld to Vic.
Habit: A terrestrial, nocturnal frog found in a wide range of habitats from dry sclerophyll and coastal heathlands to rainforest. Often found long distances from water.

Litoria lesueuri Bellinger River, NSW 70mm

Litoria longirostris Tyler and Davies, 1977

Description: Brown above, with obscure and irregular darker flecks and blotches. Creamy-white below, finely peppered with dark blackish-brown on the throat, with heavy concentrations of stippling on chin, chest and flanks in some specimens. Underside of thighs with irregular brown patches. Hind side of thigh '...brown with irregular fine cream stripes'. Skin smooth above, with a few low tubercles over the eyes; skin smooth below except for some granular skin on lower belly and thighs. Vomerine teeth poorly developed, between the choanae. Fingers without webbing, but with large discs; toes poorly to moderately webbed. A moderate, oval inner and a minute, rounded outer metatarsal tubercle. Tympanum distinct. A distinctive species possibly allied to *L. dorsalis* (from which it differs in its larger size and oval discs) or *L. meiriana* (from which it may be distinguished by its reduced toe webbing). 25 mm
Distribution: McIlwraith Range, eastern Cape York Peninsula, Qld.
Habit: Known only from rainforest.

Litoria lorica Davies and McDonald, 1979

Description: Uniform grey or grey-brown above. Ventral surfaces white, variably peppered with dark brown on the throat. Skin finely tubercular, some large tubercles over the eyes and ears. Lower surfaces granular, except for the throat which is smoother. Vomerine teeth prominent but not extensive, behind the choanae. Usually no pectoral fold (sometimes present in preserved specimens). Finger and toe discs well developed. Fingers with only basal webbing, toes almost fully webbed. A small inner but no outer metatarsal tubercle. Tympanum small, indistinct. Second finger longer than first. 35 mm
Distribution: Known only from Thornton Peak, just north of the Daintree River, Qld.
Habit: Found '...on granite boulders in notophyll vine forest in the splash zone near turbulent, fast flowing water' (Davies and McDonald).

Litoria meiriana (Tyler, 1969)

Description: Two basic colour patterns occur. The common form is irregularly mottled above with metallic fawn, brown or reddish-brown and dark brown, the small low tubercles on the back tending to be light-centred and dark-edged. In the second, less common form, dark brown predominates dorsally, but there is a broad golden-orange dorso-lateral stripe from snout to eye, and continued behind the eye above the tympanum along the body almost to the groin. In both forms the limbs have irregular dark

J.C. WOMBEY

Litoria lorica Windsor Tableland, Qld 35mm

Litoria meiriana Mt Brockman, NT 20mm

Litoria nannotis Kuranda, Qld 65mm

Litoria moorei Perth district, WA 80mm

brown cross-bands, barred lips and the lower surfaces are whitish. The skin is shagreened or finely granular above, with numerous low, rounded tubercles. No pectoral fold. Moderate but conspicuous discs on the fingers and toes. Fingers free; toes with well-developed webbing, the latter reaching the disc of the fifth toe. 20 mm

Distribution: North-eastern WA to Arnhem Land, NT.

Habit: A tiny, agile frog which in Arnhem Land is most active by day. An inhabitant of permanent creeks and waterholes of the rocky hills and gorges of the western escarpment, it escapes when disturbed by hopping across hot rock surfaces to hide in grasses or other vegetation, or by following the stream. Easy to capture at night, when it congregates on floating vegetation or at the water's edge.

Litoria moorei (Copland, 1957)

Western Green and Golden Bell Frog

Description: Externally similar in nearly all respects

Litoria nannotis

Litoria moorei

Litoria nasuta

to *L. raniformis*, from which it may be distinguished by having the larger warts on the back usually arranged in regular longitudinal rows near the vertebral line (these tend to be irregularly scattered in *raniformis*). Some specimens of these two species can be distinguished with certainty only on the basis of geographic location.
Distribution: Coast and hinterland of south-western WA.
Habit: Similar to *Litoria aurea*

Litoria nannotis (Andersson, 1916)
Torrent Tree Frog

Description: Olive, olive-green to almost black above, with extensive irregular darker mottling, often with a bluish metallic sheen on the flanks. Whitish below, often with brown on the throat. Axilla and groin flesh-coloured. Hind side of thighs dark brown. Skin shagreened, finely granular, or with numerous small, scattered warts. Granular below. Vomerine teeth prominent, largely between the choanae. No pectoral fold. Finger and toe discs large. Fingers with strong basal webbing, toes nearly fully webbed. A prominent inner metatarsal tubercle; a small outer. Tympanum indistinct. Second finger longer than first. 65 mm
Distribution: Rainforest areas of north-eastern Qld.
Habit: Found in and beside rocky streams in rainforest. When disturbed it enters waterfalls or swift-flowing water and hides under rocks or in crevices beneath the water.

Litoria nasuta (Gray, 1842)
Rocket Frog

Description: Colour and pattern highly variable. Typically a broad, pale brown to reddish brown, vertebral band from the tip of the snout to the vent, immaculate or enclosing a series of irregular dark brown patches which may be so large as to restrict the pale areas to a pair of stripes joined by transverse bars. A pale stripe runs obliquely from above the eye (continuous with the pale dorsal ground colour), over the tympanum to the flank, where it broadens and breaks up. A dark stripe from the snout to the eye through the nostril, almost completely interrupted by a pale bar in front of the eye, continuing behind the eye as a broad band enclosing the tympanum. This band stops at the level of the forelimb, after which it is continued as a series of irregular blotches. A pale glandular stripe from below the eye to the base of the forelimb, sometimes continued forward as a non-glandular stripe to the snout. Limbs variegated with darker. Hind side of thighs with lines and spots of dark brown on a yellow ground, tending to form alternate horizontal stripes. Whitish below, except for the throat of males which is often peppered with brown. Skin above with numerous low, irregular tubercles and longitudinal folds of skin, the latter more marked in the central dorsal region; throat and chest smooth, belly granular. Vomerine teeth are well-developed and lie between the choanae. Finger and toe discs small, scarcely wider than the digits. Fingers free, without web; toes with moderate webbing, about half webbed. A small inner, with or without a minute outer, metatarsal tubercle. Tympanum distinct, pale

Litoria nasuta Somerset, Qld 50mm

rimmed. First and second fingers subequal. 50 mm
Distribution: Coast and adjacent areas of northern and eastern Australia, from the Kimberleys to the mid-coast of NSW. Extra-limital in southern New Guinea.
Habit: A terrestrial, nocturnal frog usually encountered foraging among the litter on the floor of open forests or around the forested edges of permanent swamps, foraging at night on the open flats exposed by the receding waters. In northern Australia breeds in temporary soaks and waterholes during the wet season, although it may also breed in the permanent swamps which it frequents during the dry season.

Litoria nigrofrenata (Günther, 1867)

Description: Usually immaculate pale fawn or brown above; a conspicuous black stripe from the snout through the nostril to the eye, where it is almost completely broken by a pale vertical bar in front of the eye. This stripe is continued behind the eye as a broad band fully enclosing the tympanum and extending back with almost no loss of width to about the level of the forearm, where it is interrupted before continuing obliquely to the mid-flank. A pale glandular stripe from below the eye to the forearm.
A conspicuous dark brown stripe along the front edge of the tibial region. Lips not spotted or barred. Groin and hind side of thighs pale yellow, spotted and variegated with dark brown. Whitish below. Skin above smooth or shagreened; smooth on the throat, granular on the belly. Vomerine teeth between the choanae. Finger and toe discs small. Fingers free, without web; toes with moderate webbing. A small inner and a minute outer, metatarsal tubercle. Tympanum distinct. First finger slightly longer than second. 50 mm
Distribution: Upper Cape York Peninsula and Torres Strait Islands. Extra-limital in southern New Guinea.
Habit: A terrestrial frog with general habits similar to those of *Litoria latopalmata*; found primarily in seasonally-dry forest and woodland habitats, emerging to forage in moist microhabitats such as creek beds and soaks during the dry season. Congregates around creeks and flooded depressions during the wet season.

Litoria nyakalensis Liem, 1974

Description: Uniform olive-brown or grey-brown above, sometimes the body and limbs with irregular darker olive markings. Cream below with a reddish-pink flush on the limbs and pectoral region and sometimes dotted or flecked with brown. Iris brown. Skin smooth, with scattered low, conical tubercles on the head and back. Dorsal surfaces of limbs smooth, with some scattered tubercles on the tibia and heel, and a row of whitish tubercles along the outer edge of the forearm. Ventral surfaces of head, body and thighs granular. Vomerine teeth in two short, oval, oblique rows just behind the level of the choanae. No pectoral fold. Finger and toe discs relatively large and conspicuous. Fingers with slight but conspicuous webbing, the webbing reaching the base of the penultimate phalanx of the fourth finger; toes more or less fully webbed. A large oval inner metatarsal tubercle, the outer one minute or absent. Tympanum small, indistinct, more or less covered by skin. Second finger longer than first. 30 mm
Distribution: Coastal ranges and scarps of the Cairns region, Qld.
Habit: '... along creeks in rainforest and wet sclerophyll forest; it perches on rocks or on vegetation overhanging creeks' (Liem).

Litoria olongburensis Liem and Ingram, 1977

Description: Light brown to bright green above, with a dark brown loreal streak from nostril to eye, continued behind the eye as a broad dark stripe through the tympanum to the flank; this dark streak is

Litoria nigrofrenata Prince of Wales Island, Qld 50mm

Litoria nigrofrenata

Litoria nyakalensis

bordered below by a creamy white streak from below the eye to the flank. Ventral surface cream, peppered with brown on the throat. Skin smooth or shagreened above, finely granular on the throat, but coarsely granular on the belly. No dorso-lateral skin-fold. Vomerine teeth between the choanae. Fingers webbed at the base; toes moderately webbed. A moderate oval inner and a small rounded outer metatarsal tubercle. Tympanum distinct. 25 mm
Distribution: North-eastern NSW and south-eastern Qld.
Habit: '...along creeks and in marshy or swampy lowland habitats amongst emergent vegetation and reeds...of the wallum.' (Liem and Ingram).

Litoria olongburensis 25mm

Litoria pallida Koongarra, Nt. Male calling, with inflated vocal sac. 35mm

Litoria pallida Davies, Martin and Watson, 1983

Description: Rich brown or grey-brown above, occasionally almost immaculate but usually with a series of irregularly-shaped dark brown or black spots, blotches and variegations including a triangular patch between the eyes. A broad black canthal stripe, almost completely interrupted in front of the eye, but continued behind the eye to enclose the tympanum and extend to a point just above the forelimb. A pale

Litoria peronii Ourimbah, NSW. Calling male, with inflated vocal sac. 50mm

white, brown or golden glandular stripe from below the eye to the base of the forelimb. Lower jaw variegated or barred with dark brown. Hind side of thighs variegated with yellow and dark brown. Throat white (females) to yellow with a dark grey-brown reticulum (breeding males); belly whitish. Skin above smooth or more usually with a few low warts and tubercles; throat smooth but chest, belly and lower flanks slightly granular. No dorso-lateral skin fold. Finger and toe discs very small, not projecting beyond the lateral edges of the penultimate phalanges of the fingers and toes. Fingers free, without webbing; toes with well-developed webbing which reaches about half way along the penultimate phalanx of the fifth toe. A small inner and a minute outer metatarsal tubercle. Tympanum distinct. 35 mm
Distribution: Northern Australia, from Dampier Land in WA to northeastern Qld.
Habit: As for *Litoria latopalmata*. An inhabitant of woodlands and coastal floodplains throughout its range.

Litoria paraewingi Watson, Loftus-Hills and Littlejohn, 1971

A 'biological' or 'cryptic' species similar in most respects to *L. ewingii,* from which it has been distinguished largely on the basis of genetic incompatibility in hybridisation experiments. Subtle differences in mating calls, but identification in the field is difficult.
Distribution: Found in a small area of north-eastern Vic; a detailed distribution map is provided in the original description by Watson, Loftus-Hills and Littlejohn.

Litoria peronii (Tschudi, 1838)
Peron's Tree Frog

Description: Rich grey or brown above (varying in intensity with temperature, temperament etc. of the individual) with irregular darker mottling and reticulations and (in life) with numerous, small, bright emerald green spots. Ventral surface cream or yellowish except for scattered dark brown flecking on the throat. Groin and hind side of thighs mottled black (or dark brown) and bright yellow, the black usually enclosing some irregular yellow patches; this colour pattern usually extends to the webbing of the toes. A similar pattern in the groin. An indefinite light-coloured serrated ridge along the hind edge of the forearm. Iris silvery-grey. Skin rough above, with numerous low, rounded warts or tubercles, granular below. Vomerine teeth prominent, largely between the choanae. A prominent pectoral fold. Finger and toe discs very large. Fingers about half webbed. Toes nearly fully webbed. A large inner metatarsal tubercle, no outer. Tympanum very distinct. Second finger longer than first. 50 mm
Distribution: From coast to drier inland regions of south-eastern Qld, NSW and Vic, and south-eastern SA.
Habit: Found in a wide variety of habitats, often long distances from water. Coastally often found in trees and shrubs,especially among streamside vegetation. In inland regions usually encountered in areas adjacent to rivers, creeks and lagoons, breeding in low-lying areas inundated by summer rains. Away from water lives in trees, but forages on the ground on humid nights. Call a loud, penetrating, long rattling sound.

Litoria personata Tyler, Davies and Martin 1978

Description: Pale grey-brown or fawn above, often with obscure, scattered darker brown flecks; a dark brown head stripe from just in front of nostril, through eye and ear to upper flank just behind forelimb; lips whitish. Ventral surfaces whitish. Skin smooth to very finely tubercular above, coarsely granular below except on the throat. Vomerine teeth in two short clumps between the choanae. Finger and toe discs moderate, wider than digits. Fingers without webbing,

toes about half webbed. A small oval inner, and a smaller outer, metatarsal tubercle. Tympanum distinct. Second finger longer than first. 30 mm
Distribution: Western edge of Arnhem Land, NT.
Habit: Found during the wet season around sandstone rock faces and crevices near permanent and temporary water in stony hills and scarps. During the dry season found among sedges and shrubs bordering small, permanent streams. Tadpoles with distinctive yellow-gold longitudinal stripes.

Litoria personata Mt Brockman, NT 30mm

Litoria phyllochroa Mt Warning, NSW 40mm

Litoria olongburensis

Litoria pallida

Litoria paraewingi

Litoria peronii

Litoria personata

Litoria phyllochroa

Litoria piperata

Litoria raniformis

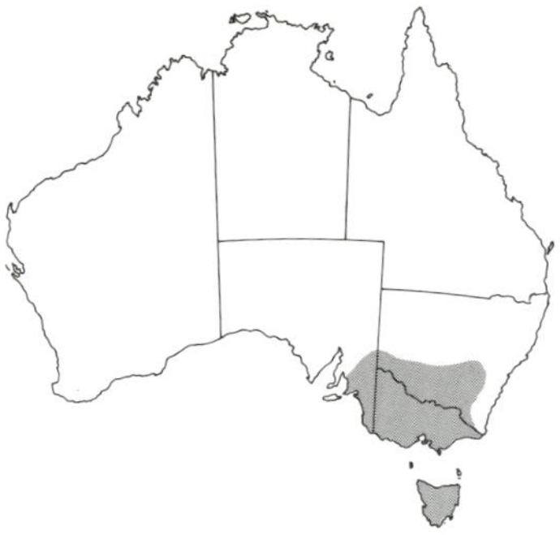

Litoria revelata

Litoria rheocola

Litoria phyllochroa (Günther, 1863)

Leaf Green Tree Frog

Description: Light to dark green above, sometimes becoming dull brown in the same individual. A narrow golden line along the canthus and continuing behind the eye along the supra-tympanic fold to the flanks, where it breaks up into a broad yellowish or white zone which extends almost to the groin. The golden canthal and supra-tympanic line is bordered below by a narrow dark brown stripe. Axilla, groin and concealed surfaces of thighs, dark red. White below, sometimes mottled with darker. Skin smooth or shagreened above, granular below. Vomerine teeth small, mostly behind the choanae. No pectoral fold. Finger and toe discs large. Fingers with only basal webbing, toes about three-quarters webbed. A small but prominent inner metatarsal tubercle, no outer. Tympanum distinct. Second finger longer than first. 40 mm

Distribution: Coast and adjacent areas of NSW and south-eastern Qld. Northern populations often regarded as a distinct species: *Litoria pearsoniana*, Copland 1961.

Litoria raniformis near Melbourne, Vic 80mm

M. PETERSON

Habit: Usually found among vegetation beside small streams, swamps, coastal lagoons and waterholes. Breeds in summer. Call complex: has been described as 'a loud, whirring "wrk-wrk-wrk"' (Moore).

Litoria piperata Tyler and Davies, 1985

Description: Dull olive or grey-green above, with irregular darker brown marbling and flecking, and often peppered with white or cream on limbs and flanks. An obscure dark brown canthal stripe. White or cream below. Skin generally smooth above, but with numerous scattered low tubercles, especially on the head; skin granular below. Vomerine teeth in two small clusters well behind the choanae. Pectoral fold absent. Finger and toe discs well-developed, markedly wider than the digits. Fingers with slight basal webbing; toes about three quarters webbed. A small inner and minute outer metatarsal tubercle. Tympanum distinct. Second finger longer than first. 30 mm.
Distribution: New England Tableland, NSW.
Habit: Usually found among streamside vegetation in a variety of forest habitats.

Litoria raniformis (Keferstein, 1867)

Description: Similar in most respects to *Litoria aurea* from which it may be distinguished by its possession of numerous large warts, tubercles and short skin folds on the back, usually somewhat irregularly arranged, though sometimes longitudinally aligned. Hind side of thighs usually bright bluish. 80 mm
Distribution: South-eastern slopes and plains of NSW through Vic to south-eastern SA; Tas.
Habit: Similar to that of *Litoria aurea*.

Litoria revelata Ingram, Corben and Hosmer, 1982

Description: Pale to dark brown above, usually with a broad darker brown vertebral band which commences between the eyes and extends to the vent, and usually narrowest at the level of the forelimbs. A black stripe along the side of the snout to the eye, continued behind the eye as a broad dark stripe which encloses the tympanum and extends back to the level of the forelimbs. A white stripe along the upper lip from the snout to the angle of the jaw where it becomes distinctly glandular. Groin and hind side of thighs orange, the groin with one or more black spots or blotches, and the hind side of the thighs with black variegations. Cream below, flecked with brown. Skin smooth above, except for a few tubercles between the eyes; granular below. Vomerine teeth conspicuous, in two separate rows on a line with the hind edge of the choanae. Pectoral fold present. Finger and toe discs well developed, markedly wider than the digits. Fingers webbed basally; toes about three-quarters webbed. A small, flat inner and a minute outer metatarsal tubercle. Tympanum distinct. Second finger longer than first. 35 mm.
Distribution: Northeastern NSW to northeastern Qld, apparently in three disjunct populations.
Habit: Coastal swamps to montane forests, breeding in still water. Call '...a series of high pitched whirrings' (Ingram, Corben and Hosmer)

Litoria rheocola Liem, 1974

Description: Dull grey or brown above, with irregular darker markings often tending to form a broad vertebral zone commencing at a line between the eyes. Scattered darker flecks on the other dorsal surfaces. An obscure darker band along the side of the snout, through the eye and ear to the shoulder. Ventral surface white. Skin smooth or with scattered small tubercles above, granular below. Vomerine

Litoria rheocola Thornton Peak, Qld 50mm

Litoria rothii

55mm

teeth in two oval groups mostly behind the choanae. No pectoral fold (an indefinite one may be present in preserved specimens). Finger and toe discs large. Fingers about one third webbed, the toes nearly fully webbed. A large, flat, oval, inner metatarsal tubercle, no outer. Tympanum covered by skin, rim sometimes distinct, about one quarter the diameter of the eye. Second finger longer than first. 50 mm
Distribution: Apparently confined to rainforest areas on the Atherton Tableland, north-eastern Qld.
Habit: Found among rocks and logs in and beside swift running mountain streams and waterfalls into which the frogs will jump when disturbed.

Litoria rothii (De Vis, 1884)

Description: Similar in most respects to *Litoria peronii*, from which it differs largely in colour and pattern. In life it lacks fine green spots on the back, while the upper half of the iris is usually bright rusty-red. Preserved specimens generally paler than *L.peronii*, without the latter's conspicuous darker pattern. There is usually a well-defined, contrasting black stripe over the base of the forearm and entering the axilla. The pattern on the hind side of the thighs is usually no more than an irregular dark bar over bright yellow, without the complex mottling of *peronii*. The pattern in the groin is also simple, consisting of one or two dark brown patches on a yellow ground. 55 mm
Distribution: Coast and near coastal areas from north-western WA to central eastern Qld; specimens found away from the coast are usually associated with larger river systems. Extra-limital in southern New Guinea.
Habit: Similar to those of *L. peronii*

Litoria rubella (Gray, 1842)

Desert Tree Frog

Description: Almost certainly composite. Grey, brown or fawn above, usually with a broad, darker vertebral band, bounded on either side by a lighter brown zone. A blackish stripe along the side of the head, continuing behind the eye, over the base of the forelimb and along the side of the body almost to the groin. Dorsal surface of body and limbs flecked with dark brown or black. Hind side of thighs brown with fine white spots. Groin usually lemon-yellow. Ventral surface white, cream or yellowish. Skin smooth or with numerous tiny granules above, coarsely granular below. Vomerine teeth almost entirely behind the choanae. A prominent pectoral fold. Finger and toe discs large. Fingers with only rudimentary webbing, toes about two-thirds webbed. Inner metatarsal tubercle moderate, elongated; outer tubercle small, rounded. Tympanum very distinct. Second finger longer than first. 35 mm

Distribution: Found throughout Australia except for the far south. In arid regions largely confined to ranges or larger watercourses. Also in southern New Guinea.

Habit: Found in a wide range of habitats from wet eastern coastal forests to central deserts. Usually found calling from trees and shrubs beside watercourses and temporary or permanent swamps and lagoons. Breeds after summer rains.

Litoria rothii

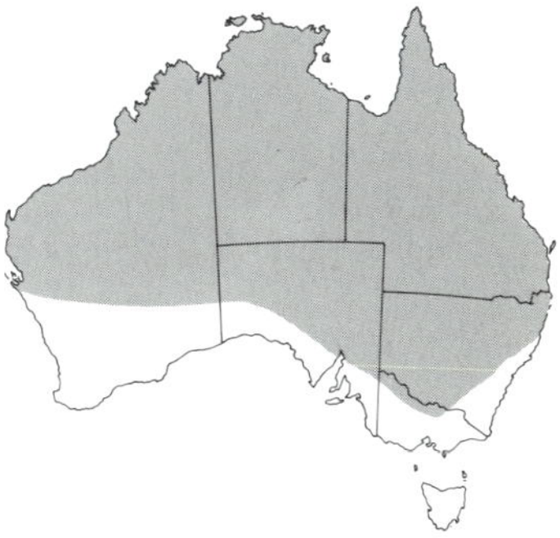

Litoria rubella

Litoria spenceri Dubois, 1984

Description: Until recently known by the unavailable name *Litoria maculata* (Spencer, 1901), this species is grey to olive-green above, with irregular darker mottling or marbling, the latter often forming irregular cross-bands on the limbs. Ventral surface white or yellow. Lower and concealed surfaces of limbs yellowish. Skin shagreened, with a few tiny whitish tubercles on the back becoming numerous on the sides. Skin granular below. Small but prominent

Litoria spenceri

Litoria rubella Brewarrina, NSW 35mm

Litoria spenceri near Mt Kosciusko, NSW 45mm

vomerine teeth, mostly behind the choanae. A slight pectoral fold. Finger and toe discs moderate, only a little wider than digits. Fingers with distinct basal webbing; toes fully webbed. A small but prominent inner metatarsal tubercle, no outer. Tympanum indistinct. Second finger longer than first. 45 mm
Distribution: Known from several widely-scattered locations in eastern Vic, extending to the Mt Kosciusko region in NSW.
Habit: Usually found among boulders or debris in or beside fast flowing mountain streams.

Litoria subglandulosa Willsons Downfall, NSW

Litoria splendida Lake Argyle, WA 100mm

R.W.G. JENKINS

50mm

Litoria tornieri Nourlangie Rock, NT. Note distinctive colour pattern of hindlimbs. 35mm

Litoria subglandulosa Tyler and Anstis, 1983

Description: Superficially similar to *L. citropa*, from which it differs dramatically in size and biology. However, *subglandulosa* may also be distinguished from *citropa* by its hidden tympanum (exposed in *citropa*), broad golden dorso-lateral stripe breaking into patches posteriorly, broad dark lateral stripe, and small size (maximum 50 mm against a maximum of nearly 70 mm for *citropa*).
Distribution: Northern tablelands and highlands of NSW, extending into Qld.

Litoria splendida Tyler, Davies and Martin, 1977

Description: Similar in most respects to *L. caerulea*, from which it differs principally in possessing a massive gland beneath the skin of the head (found also in some *L. caerulea)*, and in having brilliant orange colour on limbs, groins and thighs. 100 mm.
Distribution: Kimberley region, WA.
Habit: As for *Litoria caerulea*

Litoria tornieri (Nieden, 1923)

Description: Similar in most respects to *L. latopalmata*, from which it may be distinguished by its more or less immaculate dorsum, smooth skin with a faint pair of longitudinal dorsal skin folds, and a continuous dark brown stripe along the front edge of the tibial region. It also closely resembles *L. nigrofrenata*, from which it may be distinguished by: its smaller size (to 35 mm); the failure of the head stripe to continue behind the arm as a broad band, being reduced in *tornieri* to a few small scattered spots and blotches; and the pattern on the hind side of the thigh, which in *tornieri* consists of irregular yellow lines and blotches sandwiched, more or less horizontally, between upper and lower horizontal dark brown bars.
Distribution: North-western Australia to Arnhem Land, NT.
Habit: Similar to *L. latopalmata*, although its call is very different from that of *L. latopalmata*

Litoria tyleri Martin, Watson, Gartside, Littlejohn and Loftus-Hills, 1979

Description: Pale grey-brown or fawn above, with scattered small flecks, dots and patches of emerald green; bright lemon-yellow on the axilla, groin and hindside of the thighs, that in the groin and thighs with dark brown mottling and variegations which tend to

Litoria subglandulosa

Litoria splendida

Litoria tornieri

Litoria tyleri

Litoria verreauxii

Litoria wotjulumensis

Litoria xanthomera

be longitudinally aligned on the thighs. Ventral surfaces white, sometimes with a pale yellow wash, and dark brown on throat of breeding males. Skin finely tubercular above, granular below. Vomerine teeth prominent between the choanae. A prominent pectoral fold. Finger and toe discs very large. Fingers about half webbed, toes nearly fully webbed. A small, oval inner metatarsal tubercle, no outer tubercle. Tympanum very distinct. Second finger longer than first. 50 mm.

Distribution: Coast and near-coastal areas from far south-eastern Qld to southern NSW.

Habit: Similar to *L. peronii*. Call a loud, short rattling sound.

Litoria verreauxii (Duméril, 1853)

Description: A highly variable species, usually fawn, brown or reddish-brown above, with scattered darker flecks, but some montane populations with prominent green patches on the dorsum. A dark brown or grey-brown mid-dorsal patch, commencing on a line between the eyes and extending to the vent, partially or completely divided by a narrow vertebral stripe of the ground colour. A narrow dark brown or black stripe on the canthus, continued behind the eye as a broad dark stripe, enclosing the tympanum, to the base of the forelimb where it breaks up into a series of spots on the flanks. This stripe may have a narrow, pale upper border. A white glandular stripe from the angle of the jaws to the base of the forelimb. A series of large black spots or black marbling in the groin. Front and hind side of thighs pale yellow to bright reddish-orange. Limbs above same colour as dorsum. Whitish ventral surfaces. Skin above smooth, shagreened or with small, low, rounded warts. Throat finely granular, remainder of ventral surface coarsely granular. Vomerine teeth small, rounded, between and more or less on a level with the front edge of the choanae. Finger and toe discs small, scarcely wider than digits. Fingers free, occasionally with a trace of basal webbing. Toes about half-webbed. A small inner but no outer metatarsal tubercle. Tympanum distinct. Second finger longer than first. 30 mm

Distribution: Northern tablelands of NSW to central and south coast and ranges of NSW and eastern Vic. Also in south-eastern Qld.

Habit: An abundant species found in a variety of habitats, from coastal swamps and lagoons, wet and dry sclerophyll forests to alpine grassland and bogs. Small or large breeding aggregations occur around ponds, dams, creeks and waterholes where they call from the ground or low vegetation. One of the few species to call throughout the winter months in the

milder parts of its range.
Subspecies: *verreauxii* (coast and ranges); *alpina* (southern Alps).

Litoria wotjulumensis (Copland, 1957)

Description: Immaculate brown or fawn above sometimes very finely peppered with dark brown. A narrow black stripe from the snout, through the nostril to the eye, and continued behind the eye as a broad dark band enclosing the tympanum, continuing obliquely and without interruption to the flanks. A pale glandular stripe from below the eye to the base of the forelimb. Lower lip faintly barred. Whitish below. Skin smooth or shagreened above, smooth on the throat, granular on the belly. Vomerine teeth between the choanae. Finger and toe discs small, scarcely wider than digits. Fingers free, without web. Toes extensively webbed, the webbing reaching the disc of the fifth toe. A small inner and a minute outer metatarsal tubercle. Tympanum distinct. First finger longer than second. 75 mm
Distribution: Kimberley Division of WA to Arnhem Land, NT and north-western Qld.
Habit: A large, ground-dwelling frog with habits similar to those of *Litoria lesueuri*. Frequents open forests and the banks of swamps and streams throughout its range.

Litoria xanthomera Davies, McDonald and Adams, 1986

Description: Bright leaf-, emerald- or lime-green above, white to lemon-yellow or orange below. Hind side of thighs brilliant orange. Edge of lower jaw green. Inner half of hand white or yellow, but lower part of arm otherwise green, the green extending just beyond elbow on to the upper arm. Iris golden with a bright orange outer ring. Skin smoothly shagreened above and on the sides, granular below and on the lower flanks. A serrated pale-coloured ridge along the hind edge of the forearm. Vomerine teeth in two short, prominent rows between the choanae. A slight pectoral fold. Finger and toe discs large. Fingers about three quarters webbed, toes almost fully webbed. Prominent inner metatarsal tubercle but no outer. Tympanum distinct. Second finger longer than first. 55 mm
Distribution: Coastal rainforest areas of far northeastern Qld.
Habit: Similar to *Litoria chloris*, to which this species is very closely related.

Litoria tyleri Ourimbah, NSW 50mm

Litoria verreauxii Mt Kosciusko, NSW. This colour pattern is confined to the southern alps. 30mm

Litoria wotjulumensis Nourlangie Rock, NT 75mm

Genus *Nyctimystes* Stejneger, 1916

A group of tree frogs which have evolved in the New Guinea region and have attained their greatest diversity there.

Although several Australian species have long been recognised, it has recently been shown that only one species occurs in Australia, where it is confined to the rainforests of far north-eastern Qld. Species of *Nyctimystes* are distinguished by their large, dark eyes which have vertically elliptical pupils and a lower eyelid with a characteristic reticulum or palpebral venation of fine, pigmented lines. There is usually a distinct, crenulated skinfold along the hind edge of the forearm and the foot, the heel often having a small flap of skin. Males are usually considerably smaller than females.

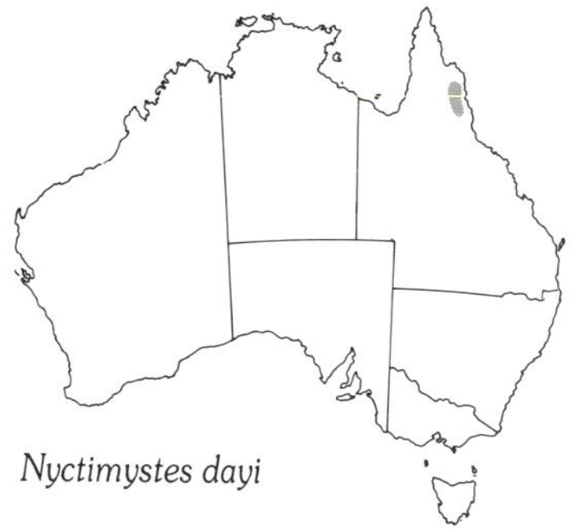

Nyctimystes dayi

Nyctimystes dayi near Cairns, Qld. Upper: in resting position in bromeliad in domestic garden; note closed lower eyelid, with reticulated pattern. Lower: shows same individual alert and with eyes open.

50mm

Nyctimystes dayi (Günther, 1897)

Description: Rich brown or orange-brown above, with or without a series of cream or white fungus-like spots and blotches, sometimes with black centres, on the head, back or limbs. The limbs often with obscure banding or marbling. White, cream or yellowish below, sometimes with sides of throat and undersides of thighs blackish. Skin smooth or finely granular above, coarsely granular on the lower flanks and ventral surfaces. Tympanum indistinct or hidden, although the tympanic annulus is usually distinct. Fingers with well-developed webbing, about half- to nearly fully-webbed. Toe discs usually smaller than finger discs. Palpebral venation in the form of a reticulum, vertically oriented, of thick pearly or golden veins. Dermal flap on heel present or absent. 50 mm

Distribution: Confined to the rainforests of the coast and ranges of north-eastern Qld between Innisfail and Cooktown.

Habit: Arboreal. Apparently confined to rainforest areas.

Family Microhylidae

A large group of frogs occurring throughout the tropical and warm temperate parts of the world. Australian species belong to the subfamily Genyophryninae, a group which has reached its greatest development in New Guinea. Australian species are confined to the wet forests of far north-eastern Queensland and to the drier monsoonal forests of Arnhem Land.

In Australia the family Microhylidae is characterised by: firmisternal pectoral girdle; intercalary cartilages absent; finger and toe discs present or absent, with lateral grooves; sacral diapophyses dilated; maxillary teeth usually absent; toes not webbed; no dorsolateral skin-fold.

Australian species include terrestrial and semi-arboreal forms. All species lay their eggs on land, where all development takes place and fully-formed frogs hatch from the eggs. Egg clusters are often guarded, usually by the male, and in some New Guinean forms the froglets cling to and are carried around on the back of the parent for a lengthy period after hatching.

Identification may be difficult, and the information below is based largely on R.G. Zweifel's 1985 monograph of Australian microhylid frogs.

Key

TO THE GENERA OF THE AUSTRALIAN MICROHYLID FROGS

Pectoral girdle complete, clavicles and procoracoid cartilages present (a); supplementary slip of the intermandibularis muscle narrow, oriented parallel to the mandible (c)................ .... ***Sphenophryne***

Pectoral girdle lacking clavicles and procoracoid cartilages(b); supplementary slip of the intermandibularis muscle broad, oriented more or less transversely across the throat(d)........... .... ***Cophixalus***

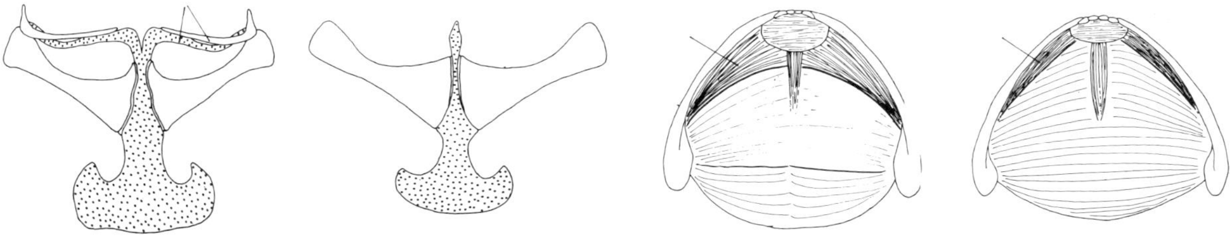

a b c d

Genus ***Cophixalus*** Boettger, 1892

A genus whose members, though distinctive to those familiar with them, may be difficult to identify with certainty without recourse to internal characters.

Distinguished from the only other Australian microhylid genus, *Sphenophryne*, by its lack of clavicles and procoracoid cartilages in the pectoral girdle. Burton has shown that the superficial muscles of the throat are also quite distinctive in the two genera (see generic key above). Tympanum usually obscure, covered by skin. Most species have a distinctive pale golden region in the upper part of the eye.

Largely confined to montane rainforests, where males call from slightly elevated positions on fallen debris or low vegetation, or from leaf litter.

Key

TO THE AUSTRALIAN SPECIES OF COPHIXALUS

1 Disc of third finger at most slightly broader, but usually only as broad as or narrower than that of fourth toe; finger and toe discs sub-circular in outline, the outer edges strongly curved or rounded (a) **2**

Disc of third finger markedly broader than that of fourth toe; finger and toe discs distinctly elliptical in outline, the outer edges only slightly rounded (b)........................... **11**

2 Adult snout-vent length less than 20 mm.........................**3**

Adult snout-vent length 20 mm or more..........................**9**

3 Ratio of eye-naris distance to internarial distance 0.70 or more; maximum snout-vent length of males 15 mm.........**4**

Ratio of eye-naris distance to internarial distance less than 0.70; maximum snout-vent length of males greater than 15 mm... ***peninsularis***

4 First finger at most one third the length of the second, its tip rounded, not flattened, and without any terminal groove...**5**

First finger about half the length of the second, its tip slightly flattened and with at least a weak terminal groove (c).. **8**

5 First finger short but distinctly digit-like.......................... **6**

First finger a stub, not digit-like (d)................... ***crepitans***

6 Ratio of tibia length to snout-vent length 0.43 or more..... **7**

Ratio of tibia length to snout-vent length less than 0.43....... .... ***hosmeri***

7 Finger and toe discs only slightly wider than the digits(e).... .... ***bombiens***

Finger and toe discs markedly wider than the digits (f)....... .... ***infacetus***

8 Snout-vent length of males 15 mm or more, females 18 mm or more .... ***concinnus***

Snout-vent length of males 16 mm or less, females 19 mm or less .... ***exiguus***

9 First finger very short with rounded tip, not flattened, and without any indication of a terminal groove.................. **10**

First finger short but with a slightly flattened, expanded tip and a distinct terminal groove........................ ***concinnus***

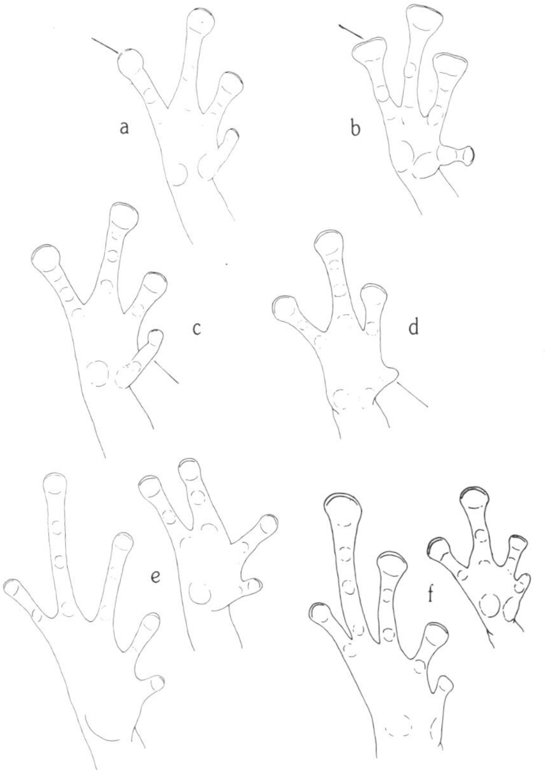

10 Tibia length/snout-vent ratio 0.40 or more; ratio of eye-naris distance to internarial distance 0.78 or more............ .... ***mcdonaldi***

Tibia length/snout-vent ratio less than 0.40; ratio of eye-naris distance to internarial distance less than 0.78........... .... ***neglectus***

11 Adult snout-vent length 30 mm or less; tibia length/snout-vent ratio less than 0.46 .... ***ornatus***

Adult snout-vent length to 35 mm (males) and 46 mm (females); specimens less than 30 mm with tibia length/snout-vent ratio greater than 0.48........... ***saxatilis***

Cophixalus bombiens Zweifel, 1985

Description: Brown to reddish-brown above mottled and flecked with dark brown or black; a blackish streak from behind the eye and over the ear to above the forearm; sometimes a narrow pale cream or golden vertebral stripe; limbs above spotted and flecked with both dark brown and dirty cream; sometimes a pale spot in each groin. Ventral surfaces whitish or grey, with paler flecks. Skin smooth to slightly granular above, with a faint W-shaped skin fold between the shoulders; smooth below. A rather

R.G. ZWEIFEL

Cophixalus bombiens Windsor Tableland, Qld 15mm

squat, moderate-limbed frog, the discs on the fingers and toes only moderately wider than the penultimate phalanges and the disc of the third finger not broader than the disc of the fourth toe. Tibia length/snout-vent length ratio 0.40-0.48. Eye-naris/internarial distance ratio 0.69-0.83. 15 mm
Distribution: Known only from the Mount Windsor Tableland, north-eastern Qld.
Habit: Found in litter on the floor of rainforest, especially where the forest canopy is disrupted by tracks, streams and fallen trees. Call 'a brief buzz, averaging less than one-half second' (Zweifel).

Cophixalus concinnus Tyler, 1979

Description: Uniform grey-brown above, sometimes with obscure paler yellowish or orange patches; sometimes a pale spot in the groin. Ventral surfaces white, yellow or orange, variegated and stippled with dark brown. Smooth above and below. A rather squat, moderate limbed frog with well-developed discs, the discs much wider than the penultimate phalanges and the disc of the third finger slightly narrower to slightly broader than the disc of the fourth toe. Tibia length/snout-vent length ratio 0.37-0.44. Eye-naris/internarial distance ratio 0.76-1.00. 25 mm
Distribution: Currently known from upland rainforests from Mount Finnigan south to Mount Lewis, north-eastern Qld.
Habit: Found in and under logs and leaf litter in montane rainforest. Call 'a short rattle' (Winter).

Cophixalus crepitans Zweifel, 1985

Description: Brown to rusty-brown above, with darker mottling and blotches, including a W-shaped blotch between the shoulders; limbs with obscure darker crossbands. Ventral surfaces brown with paler spots and mottling. More or less smooth above and below, with a weak postocular skin fold. Discs of fingers and toes moderately developed, noticeably wider than the penultimate phalanges but the disc of the third finger not as wide as that of the fourth toe. Tibia length/snout-vent length ratio 0.47-0.54. Eye-naris/internarial distance ratio 0.65-0.78. 15 mm
Distribution: Known only from the McIlwraith Range, eastern Cape York Peninsula, Qld.
Habit: An inhabitant of rainforest. Call '...a rattling sound' (Zweifel).

Cophixalus concinnus
Thornton Peak, Qld
25mm

Cophixalus bombiens

Cophixalus concinnus

Cophixalus crepitans

Cophixalus exiguus

Cophixalus hosmeri

Cophixalus exiguus Zweifel and Parker 1969

Description: Grey-brown to pale yellow above, with an obscure V-shaped dark mark between the eyes and an equally obscure H-shaped mark over the shoulder region. A short dark brown or blackish temporal streak below a slight supra-tympanic fold. A pale ocellus above each groin. Scattered darker flecks and blotches on the lower back and flanks. Sometimes a pale vertebral line or band. Yellowish-brown or brown below, flecked with grey or brown on the throat, chest and limbs and with some scattered white or yellow spots. Smooth above, or with a few tubercles on the hindlimbs. Smooth below. Discs of fingers and toes moderately developed, conspicuously wider than the penultimate phalanges, but the disc of the third finger is narrower than the disc of the fourth toe. Tibia length/snout-vent length ratio 0.40-0.49. Eye-naris/ internarial distance ratio 0.72-0.94. 15 mm
Distribution: Known only from an area a few kilometres south of Cooktown, Qld.
Habit: So far known only from primary rainforest, where the type series was collected under logs, stones and leaf-litter during the day. Call unknown.

R.G. ZWEIFEL

Cophixalus hosmeri Mt Lewis, Qld 15mm

Cophixalus hosmeri Zweifel, 1985

Description: Grey-brown above with obscure darker flecks and blotches, the most consistent being a ∧-shaped mark between the shoulders and a temporal streak; snout and upper eyelids blackish in some specimens; sometimes a pale vertebral band. Throat, chest and sometimes abdomen dark grey with paler stippling; the abdomen and thighs sometimes yellowish. Skin smooth to slightly granular above, smooth below. Discs of fingers and toes moderately developed, conspicuously wider than the penultimate phalanges, but the disc of the third finger narrower than that of the fourth toe. Tibia length/snout-vent length ratio 0.34-0.45. Eye-naris/internarial distance ratio 0.70-0.85. 15 mm
Distribution: Known only from montane rainforest on Mts Lewis and Spurgeon, near Mossman, north-eastern Qld.
Habit: Call '...a series of 15-17 clicks' lasting about a second (Zweifel).

R.G. ZWEIFEL

Cophixalus infacetus Palmerston, Qld 15mm

Cophixalus infacetus Zweifel, 1985

Description: Rich brown above, the back and flanks with dark brown flecks, mottling and other dark markings which typically include a temporal streak, a dark patch beneath each eye, a W-shaped mark between the shoulders and a dark patch, sometimes pale-edged, above each groin. Sometimes a pale vertebral band. Grey ventrally, with paler spots, flecks or stippling. Smooth above and below. Discs of fingers and toes well-developed, conspicuously wider than the penultimate phalanges, and the disc of the third finger as wide as, or only slightly narrower than, that of the fourth toe. Tibia length/snout-vent length ratio 0.43-0.55. Eye-naris/internarial distance ratio 0.72-0.93. 15 mm
Distribution: Low-to mid-montane rainforest in the Cairns-Innisfail region, north-eastern Qld.
Habit: Call 'a series of clicks lasting about 1 second' (Zweifel)

Cophixalus mcdonaldi Zweifel, 1985

Description: Pale to dark brown above with scattered darker markings which typically include a dark streak above each arm, an obscure interorbital bar, dark canthal and temporal streaks and dark facial markings. Ventral surfaces pale with darker stippling and mottling. Smooth above and below, except for a faint supratympanic skin fold. Discs of fingers and toes well-developed, conspicuously wider than the penultimate phalanges, the disc of the third finger about as wide as that of the fourth toe. Tibia length/snout-vent length ratio 0.37-0.44. Eye-naris/internarial distance ratio 0.73-0.95. 25 mm
Distribution: Known only from high up on Mt Elliot, near Townsville, north-eastern Qld.
Habit: Call unknown.

Cophixalus neglectus Zweifel, 1962

Description: Uniform brown or orange-brown above, sometimes with obscure darker flecks on the back and a narrow black bar below a faint supra-tympanic fold; occasionally a narrow pale vertebral

line. Pale below, flecked with brown. Smooth above and below. A rather squat, short-limbed species, with poorly developed discs, the discs scarcely wider than the penultimate phalanges. Tibia length/snout-vent length ratio 0.31-0.42. Eye-naris/internarial distance ratio 0.65-0.88. 25 mm
Distribution: Known only from the Bellenden Ker Range, between Cairns and Innisfail, Qld.
Habit: Rainforest areas above 900 metres. Call '...a buzzing sound with an average duration of about one-half second' (Zweifel).

Cophixalus ornatus Lake Barrine, Qld 25mm

Cophixalus ornatus (Fry, 1912)

Description: A highly variable species, the ground colour ranging from pale fawn to brown, reddish or dark brown. Usually an indistinct dark bar along the side of the snout but a conspicuous short black temporal streak behind the eye (bordering a slight tympanic fold) sometimes extending as a disrupted band to the flanks. Often a dark bar, with pale anterior border, between the eyes and a W-shaped dark bar, also with a pale anterior edge, over the shoulder region. Usually a dark spot, with pale anterior edge forming a distinct ocellus, above each groin. Remainder of dorsal surfaces variably flecked or blotched with darker. In many specimens there is a narrow, pale vertebral stripe which, over the anus, joins pale lines which run along the hind edge of each hindlimb. In still another colour form, the body is dark-coloured with a broad, paler vertebral band from snout to vent, broadest on the head. Many variations of the above colour patterns are found. Grey or brown below, finely peppered with paler and darker flecks, often with a narrow, pale mid-line. Skin above with numerous low rounded tubercles and short skin folds, the latter tending to be concentrated on the dorso-lateral and outer occipital regions. Smooth below. Discs of fingers and toes highly developed, much wider than the penultimate phalanges and the disc of the third finger markedly broader than the disc of the fourth toe. Tibia length/ snout-vent length ratio 0.37-0.48. Eye-naris/internarial distance ratio 0.70-1.00. 25 mm
Distribution: Moist forests of coast and adjacent ranges of north-east Qld, from Townsville to a little north of Cairns.
Habit: Usually found calling at night from shrubs or low trees in rainforests or adjacent secondary forest growth. Call '...a short "beep" lasting about 0.2-0.5 seconds, too rapidly pulsed to be heard as a buzz and not finely enough tuned to be called a peep or whistle' (Zweifel).

Cophixalus infacetus

Cophixalus mcdonaldi

Cophixalus neglectus

Cophixalus ornatus

Cophixalus peninsularis

R.G. ZWEIFEL

Cophixalus saxatilis Black Gap, Qld 40mm

Cophixalus saxatilis

Cophixalus peninsularis Zweifel, 1985

Description: Brown above, with scattered darker markings the most consistent of which are those on the eyelids, snout, side of the face, an obscure patch between the shoulders, a bar behind each arm and faint pale-edged patches above each groin. Ventral surfaces brown with paler spots and mottling. Skin more or less smooth above and below, except for low temporal and scapular skin folds. Discs of fingers and toes well developed, much wider than the penultimate phalanges and the disc of the third finger about as wide as the disc of the fourth toe. Tibia length/ snout-vent length ratio 0.40-0.42. Eye-naris/internarial distance ratio 0.67. 20 mm
Distribution: Known only from rainforest of the Rocky River scrub, McIlwraith Range, eastern Cape York Peninsula, Qld.
Habit: Call unknown.

Cophixalus saxatilis Zweifel and Parker, 1977

Description: Brown above, with irregular darker brown markings which usually include a transverse bar between the eyes, a W-shaped mark between the forelimbs and sometimes a faint ocellate marking above each groin. Creamy-white below, lightly peppered with dark brown or black, but with concentrations on the chin, forelimbs, palms and soles. Skin more or less smooth above with a faint supra-tympanic fold. Discs of fingers and toes well developed, much wider than the penultimate phalanges and the disc of the third finger markedly broader than that of the fourth toe. Tibia length/snout-vent length ratio 0.44-0.50. Eye-naris/internarial distance ratio 0.81-1.00. 40 mm
Distribution: Known only from Black Mountain near Cooktown, Qld.
Habit: The warm and humid cavities below and between the tumbled, gigantic granitic boulders which characterise Black Mountain. Call '...a series of clicks uttered over a period of about 2 to 3 seconds' (Zweifel).

Genus ***Sphenophryne*** Peters and Doria, 1878

A group with its greatest diversity in New Guinea, five species occurring in Australia. As with the genus *Cophixalus*, species of *Sphenophryne* can be identified with certainty only on the basis of internal characters. Distinguished from *Cophixalus* by its possession of well-developed clavicles and procoracoid cartilages and by the superficial throat muscles cited in the generic key. Tympanum usually obscure, covered by skin

Key

TO THE AUSTRALIAN SPECIES OF SPHENOPHRYNE

1 Tibia length/snout-vent ratio 0.43 or more; adult snout-vent length less than 23 mm.. **2**

Tibia length/snout-vent ratio less than 0.43; adult snout-vent length up to 35 mm **3**

2 Top end of Northern Territory............................ ***adelphe***

Cape York Peninsula (extra-limital in New Guinea)............ .... ***gracilipes***

3 Iris dark brown, sometimes with a golden or orange (but not red) upper region; pale canthal stripe absent or inconspicuous.. **4**

Inner rim and upper region of iris red; a conspicuous pale stripe along the upper edge of the canthus, along the edge of the upper eyelid, and sometimes extending along at least part of the body as a dorso-lateral stripe.... ***pluvialis***

4 Call a series of high-pitched peeps or chirps......... ***robusta***

Call a series of brief, whistle-like notes........................ ***fryi***

Sphenophryne adelphe Zweifel, 1985

Description: Identical in size and appearance to *Sphenophryne gracilipes*, from which it can be distinguished only on the basis of its geographic distribution and call, which is a '...moderately rapidly repeated series of high-pitched peeps' (Zweifel) at a rate of more than 200/minute and lasting 2-5 seconds. 20 mm

Distribution: Western and northern Arnhem Land, NT

Habit: Found in ground litter associated with permanent swamps, streams and soaks in both coastal and escarpment savannah woodland, melaleuca swamps and monsoon forests which are subjected to an intense and prolonged dry season followed by torrential monsoonal rains.

Sphenophryne adelphe Brockman Range, NT 20mm

Sphenophryne adelphe

Sphenophryne fryi

Sphenophryne fryi Zweifel, 1962

Description: Rich brown above, with obscure to conspicuous darker brown flecks and blotches. Loreal region darker and a short, dark bar along the poorly developed supra-tympanic fold. Flanks paler, yellowish. Yellowish below, peppered with darker. Skin smooth above and below. Discs on fingers scarcely wider than penultimate phalanges, those of toes only slightly wider. Tibia length/ snout-vent length ratio 0.34 - 0.46. Eye-naris/internarial distance ratio 0.61-0.86. 30 mm

Distribution: Coast and adjacent ranges of far north-eastern Qld, from the Atherton Tableland to Cooktown.

Habit: A terrestrial species usually found under fallen timber or leaf-litter in rain forest. Call '...a series of brief, whistle-like notes' lasting about 2 seconds (Zweifel).

Sphenophryne fryi
Lake Barrine, Qld
30mm

Sphenophryne gracilipes

Sphenophryne pluvialis

Sphenophryne robusta

Sphenophryne gracilipes (Fry, 1912)

Description: Pale to golden-brown above, usually with obscure to conspicuous darker brown flecks or blotches, and often with either a paler or darker, narrow, hair-line vertebral stripe. Sometimes finely dotted with white above. A black canthal streak, sometimes edged above with silvery-white, continued behind the eye and over the ear to the flanks, the lower sides with darker and lighter flecks. In some specimens the entire area below this dark streak is blackish, finely dotted with white. Lower surfaces grey-brown with scattered pale white or yellowish spots. Smooth or shagreened above, smooth below. Distinct discs on fingers and toes, scarcely wider than penultimate phalanges. Tibia length/snout-vent length ratio 0.41-0.51. Eye-naris/internarial distance ratio 0.62-0.85. 20 mm
Distribution: Cape York Peninsula, south to about Cooktown in the east and the Archer River in the west. Extra-limital in southern New Guinea.
Habit: Found in a wide variety of habitats from rain forests to pockets within drier habitats which retain moist litter throughout the dry season: monsoon forest, paperbark swamps, and the lusher growth bordering both perennial and non-perennial streams. Call a series of high-pitched peeps at a rate of no more than 100/second and lasting 10-20 seconds.

Sphenophryne pluvialis Zweifel, 1965

Description: Pale brown or golden brown above, flecked and blotched with dark brown. A pale stripe along the upper edge of the canthus rostralis

Sphenophryne pluvialis Kuranda, Qld 25mm

Sphenophryne robusta
Bobbin Bobbin Falls, Qld
25mm

R.G. ZWEIFEL

extending over the eyes and above the tympanum and sometimes continued as a pale, obscure dorso-lateral band. Side of face dark brown, continuous with a broad, dark brown band along the side, enclosing paler flecks and spots. Brownish below, finely peppered with lighter and darker brown. Skin smooth or shagreened above, smooth below. Distinct discs on fingers and toes, only slightly wider than the penultimate phalanges. Tibia length/ snout-vent ratio 0.40-0.49. Eye-naris/internarial distance ratio 0.64-0.81. 25 mm
Distribution: Known only from the coast and ranges of north-eastern Qld, from about Ingham north to Cooktown. Zweifel cites an unconfirmed northern record from the McIlwraith Ranges.
Habit: Similar to that of *Sphenophryne fryi*. Call '...a short train of relatively high-pitched notes' lasting 1-1.5 seconds (Zweifel).

Sphenophryne robusta (Fry, 1912)

Description: Pale- to reddish-brown above, usually with obscure to conspicuous darker brown flecks or blotches; sometimes with a pale, narrow, hair-line vertebral stripe and more often flecked, dotted or spotted with cream or pale brown above and on the flanks. Side of face black, often continuous with a dark canthal streak that continues behind the eye and through the ear. Lower surfaces dirty white, yellow or orange, mottled with darker brown or grey. Smooth or shagreened above, smooth below. Distinct discs on fingers and toes, scarcely wider than penultimate phalanges. Tibia length/snout-vent length ratio 0.36-0.44. Eye-naris/internarial distance ratio 0.57-0.73. 25 mm
Distribution: Montane rainforest areas of northeastern Qld, from middle of the Atherton Tableland south to the Cardwell Range.
Habit: Usually found in leaf litter on the rainforest floor. Call '...a series of short...high-pitched chirps arranged in couplets' lasting from 1-5 seconds (Zweifel).

Sphenophryne gracilipes Iron Range, Qld 20mm

Rana daemeli

Rana daemeli
Thornton Peak, Qld
80mm

Family Ranidae

The so-called "True" Frogs, members of this family are abundant throughout most parts of the world except Australia, where a single, recently arrived (in geological terms) species of the genus *Rana* has colonised Cape York Peninsula from New Guinea. This species is widely distributed through New Britain, the lowlands of mainland New Guinea, and the Aru Islands.

In Australia the family Ranidae is characterised by: firmisternal pectoral girdle; intercalary cartilages absent; small finger and toe discs present, with lateral grooves; sacral diapophyses cylindrical; maxillary teeth present; toes fully webbed; a dorso-lateral skinfold from eye to hindlimb.

Ranid frogs in other parts of the world display an enormous variety of habit and body form.

Genus ***Rana*** Linnaeus, 1758

Rana daemeli (Steindachner, 1868)

Wood Frog

Description: Pale to rich chocolate brown above, immaculate or with irregular darker flecks and blotches. A dark stripe from snout to eye, continued behind the eye as a broad band enclosing the tympanum and extending back to about the level of the forelimb where it merges with the dark (darker than dorsum) upper lateral zone. A pale stripe from below the eye to the base of the forelimb. Lower sides pale with grey or grey-brown flecks and blotches. Lower arms and hindlimbs brown with dark brown cross-bars. Whitish below, usually heavily speckled with brown. Skin smooth or shagreened above, with a few scattered low tubercles and a distinctive dorsolateral skin fold from the eye, along the upper edge of the dark tympanic stripe, breaking up posteriorly into a row of tubercles. Smooth below. Finger and toe discs small, scarcely wider than digits. Fingers free, without web. Toes fully webbed. A low elongate inner and a smaller, flat, outer metatarsal tubercle. Tympanum distinct. 80 mm

Distribution: North-eastern Qld, including the upper west coast and the east coast, ranges and interior of Cape York Peninsula.

Habit: Rainforest, seasonally-dry monsoon forests and tropical woodlands. A large, agile and predatious ground-dwelling, semi-aquatic frog, usually encountered at night in or beside permanent streams and lagoons. Call a series of sharp yaps or quacks.

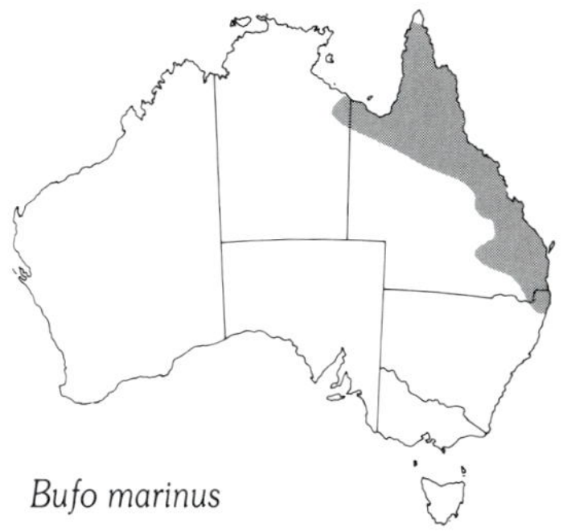

Bufo marinus
South-eastern Qld

150mm

Family Bufonidae

A large family of frogs found throughout most parts of the world, but with no representatives occurring naturally in Australia — the so-called 'True Toads'. One of the largest species in this family — the Marine Toad — was introduced into Australia's Queensland sugar cane fields in 1935 to combat the depredations of the cane beetle and its larvae. The toads thrived, failed to be any more effective than native frogs in controlling the pest insect, and have themselves become a major pest species. The toads' range is being extended each year.

The family Bufonidae in Australia is characterised by an arciferal pectoral girdle; digits without discs or intercalary cartilages; supraocular region warty, separated from the interorbital region by a thick fold or ridge of skin; maxillary teeth absent; toes fully webbed.

Genus ***Bufo*** Laurenti, 1768

Bufo marinus (Linnaeus, 1758)

Marine or Cane Toad

Description: Grey, brown, olive-brown or reddish-brown above, adults rarely with any marked pattern other than dark brown caps to the warts, whereas juveniles have a series of narrow dark bars, dashes or lines on the head and back. Whitish or yellowish below, usually speckled or mottled with dark brown. Skin very warty above, granular below. A grossly enlarged pair of parotoid glands. The supraocular region is warty and is separated from the smooth interorbital region by a high bony ridge, the ridge on each side continuing forward to meet on the snout between the nostrils. Fingers free, toes with a tough leathery webbing. 150 mm (snout-vent).
Distribution: Coast and hinterland of eastern Qld, extending into the northern rivers region of NSW, and extending further west each year into western Qld and the NT. Originally confined to South and Central America this species was introduced in 1935 to Qld from Hawaii, where it had been introduced earlier to control insect pests of sugarcane.
Habit: A ground-dwelling, predacious species, which forages at night in a wide range of habitats, from moist forests to woodlands, grasslands, beach dunes, suburban gardens and roadways. Breeds in any temporary or permanent still or slow-moving waters.

Ctenophorus pictus
Round Hill, NSW

Reptiles

Reptiles

(CLASS REPTILIA)

Reptiles evolved from a group of early amphibians, and reached the peak of their diversity in the Mesozoic Period, about 120 million years ago. At that time reptiles dominated the world's land, seas and skies with an astonishing variety of forms, the best known being the giant dinosaurs. However, for complex and poorly understood reasons, the majority of these reptiles became extinct at the end of the Mesozoic.

Like amphibians, reptiles are typically pentadactyle, air-breathing, terrestrial vertebrates. Also like amphibians, they are ectothermic or cold-blooded animals, that is they have no internal mechanism for producing the vast amounts of metabolic heat needed to maintain a constant body temperature independent of the temperature of their surroundings. Unlike amphibians, however, they have only limited dependence on water. Scaly skins minimise water loss from the body, and generally play no part in respiration. Typically, reptiles are uricotelic, precipitating uric acid in the kidneys, which, together with an efficient mechanism for reabsorbing water in the cloaca, results in the excretion of more or less solid uric acid and solid faeces from which most water has been extracted. This ability to conserve body water has permitted many reptiles to colonise arid regions; aquatic reptiles, on the other hand, have no need to conserve body water and most excrete urea in a fluid urine.

Reptiles were the first really successful colonisers of the earth's land surfaces, for unlike amphibians their eggs are shelled and are laid on land. Together with the shelled egg have developed the amnion, chorion and allantois — the embryonic membranes which serve a variety of functions for the developing embryo. The amnion contains the amniotic fluid in which the embryo develops and is buffered from the shell and its external environment; the allantois acts as a reservoir for the excretory products of the developing embryo; the chorion lies just beneath the shell and, where it fuses with the allantois, acts as a respiratory organ.

In some reptiles varying degrees of viviparity have evolved. The egg may be retained, unshelled, in the oviducts until they hatch; in a few forms a true chorio-allantoic placenta is formed, the embryo linked to the maternal circulation.

Living reptiles, despite their apparent diversity, are but a shadow of their former glory, and only four major groups are recognised. Three of these are represented in Australia — the crocodiles and their relatives (order Crocodilia), the turtles and tortoises (order Testudines) and the snakes and lizards (order Squamata). Although snakes and lizards are closely related and placed together in the same order, together they contain nearly 95% of the 6000-odd species of modern reptiles.

The fourth major group of reptiles is the order Rhynchocephalia, an ancient group whose sole living representative is the lizard-like Tuatara (*Sphenodon punctatus*) of New Zealand.

Crocodiles

(ORDER CROCODILIA)

Family Crocodylidae

Typical crocodiles, together with the alligators, caimans, and gavial, make up the ancient order Crocodilia. Crocodiles are found throughout the world's equatorial regions, and about 21 living species are recognised. Most are more or less similar in appearance, the most obvious difference often being in the shape and configuration of the head. Crocodiles as a group are too well known to warrant a generalised description. Among the most significant features are their size, the development of thick skin enclosing an effective body armour of osteoderms and gastralia, and a four-chambered heart. They are magnificently adapted to an amphibious life, with a secondary palate, valves in nostrils and throat, and a powerful tail for aquatic locomotion. They are fierce predators.

Genus ***Crocodylus*** Laurenti, 1768

Key

TO THE AUSTRALIAN SPECIES OF CROCODYLUS

Snout long and slender (a); in adults the distance from snout to a point midway between the eyes is more than twice the width of the head at the level of the eyes; enlarged nuchal shields in a single row, separated from the smooth-skinned parietal region by fewer than eight granular scales(c)............... .... ***johnstoni***

Snout relatively short and blunt(b); in adults the distance from the snout to a point midway between the eyes is less than twice the width of the head at the level of the eyes; enlarged nuchal shields in two rows, separated from the smooth-skinned parietal region by more than eight granular scales(d)... .... ***porosus***

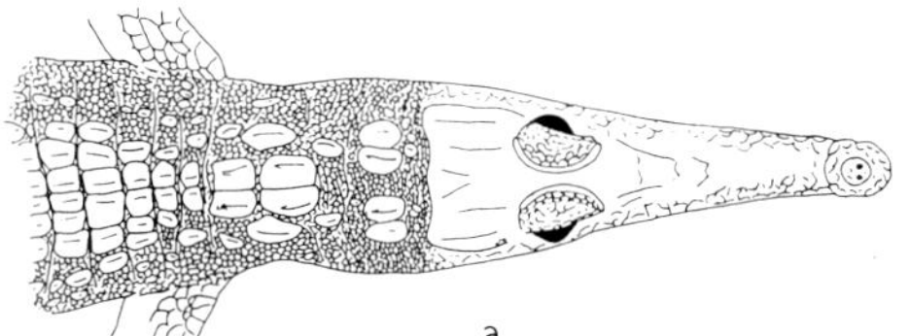

a

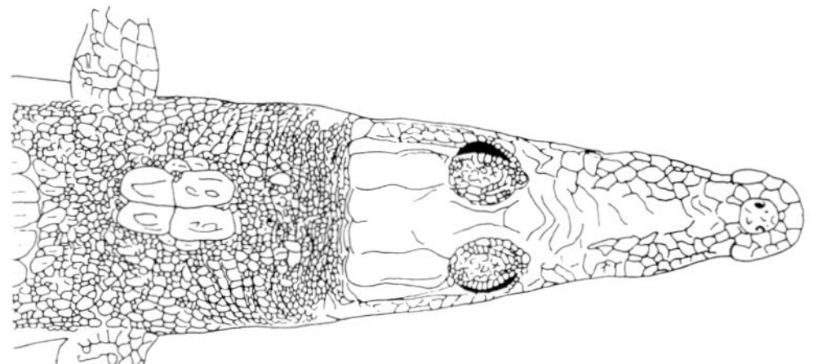

b

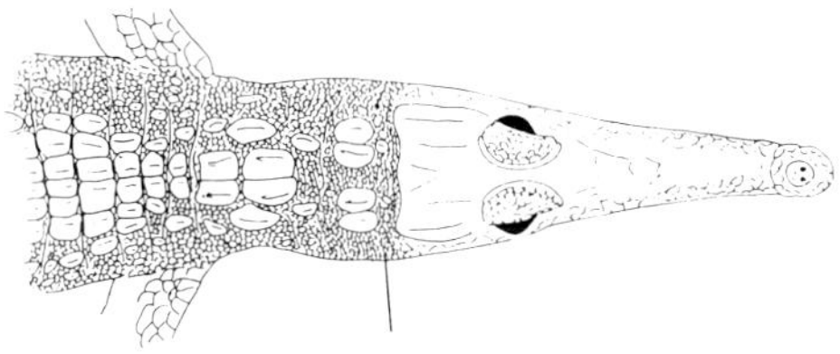

c

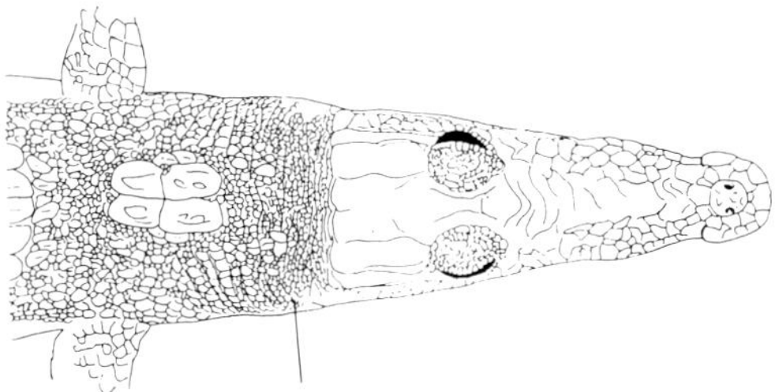

d

Crocodylus johnstoni Jasper Gorge, NT

Crocodylus johnstoni (juvenile)

Crocodylus johnstoni Krefft, 1873

Freshwater Crocodile

Description: Grey or olive-brown above, with irregular darker mottling especially on the flanks. Whitish below. The snout is smooth, long and slender; in adults the distance between the tip of the snout and a point midway between the eyes is more than twice the width of the head at the level of the eyes. Isolated enlarged nuchal shields in a single row, separated anteriorly from the smooth-skinned parietal region by fewer than eight granular scales. 3 metres.
Distribution: Coast and hinterland of northern and north-eastern Australia.
Habit: Generally confined to permanent freshwater rivers, lagoons and billabongs throughout its range. Active by day, but forages mostly at night, feeding on fish, frogs, crustaceans and small reptiles, birds and mammals. About 20 eggs laid towards end of dry season (October-November) in sandbanks.

G. J. W. WEBB

Crocodylus porosus NT In typical basking situation, with mouth agape to assist cooling through evaporation from buccal tissues.

Crocodylus porosus Schneider, 1801

Estuarine or Salt-Water Crocodile

Description: Grey, brown or almost black above, with irregular darker mottling. Whitish below. The snout is relatively broad, granular; in adults the distance between the tip of the snout and a point midway between the eyes is less than twice the width of the head at the level of the eyes. Isolated enlarged nuchal shields in two rows, separated anteriorly from the smooth-skinned parietal region by more than eight granular scales. 7 metres but rarely exceeds 5 metres.
Distribution: Coastal regions of northern and north-eastern Australia. Ranges extra-limitally from islands of western Pacific through Indo-Malaysia to South-east Asia and India.
Habit: An inhabitant of coastal rivers and swamps, though often seen in the open sea, but extending well inland via major rivers and the billabongs in the river floodplains. Largely nocturnal, feeding on crustaceans, fish, reptiles, birds and mammals. About 60 eggs are laid high up on river banks during the wet season.

Crocodylus johnstoni

Crocodylus porosus

Turtles and Tortoises

(ORDER TESTUDINES)

Key

TO THE FAMILIES OF AUSTRALIAN TURTLES

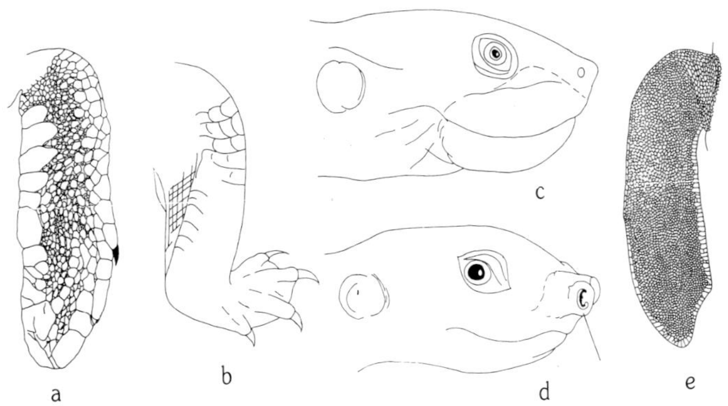

1 Forelimbs and hindlimbs paddle-shaped, without ankle-joints or webbed, clawed feet(a)..**2**

Forelimbs and hindlimbs jointed, not paddle-shaped, with distinct ankle joints and four- or five-clawed webbed feet(b) .... ***Chelidae*** (Side-necked Tortoises)

2 Nostrils level with the surface of the snout; no fleshy proboscis present(c).. **3**

Nostrils at the end of a tubular, fleshy snout or proboscis (d) .... ***Carettochelydidae*** (Pitted-shelled Turtle)

3 Limbs with claws (a) .... ***Cheloniidae*** (Sea Turtles)

Limbs without claws (e).. .... ***Dermochelyidae*** (Leathery Turtle)

Family Cheloniidae

A family which includes all but one of the large sea-turtles. All are more or less confined to tropical and warm temperate seas, although many individuals visit or stray into the colder waters of higher latitudes. Breeding occurs only in the tropics. The eggs are laid on land, but once the hatchlings reach the sea only the females, if they survive, ever return to land to lay their eggs. Most sea-turtles lay several clutches of eggs in a season, but most appear to have 'resting' years when no eggs are laid — typically every third year.

In Australia the family Cheloniidae is characterised by strong, heavy, paddle-shaped limbs without obvious ankle-joints and without webbed, clawed feet; the nostrils are level with the surface of the snout; the limbs have one or more claws on the anterior edge. The shell is bony and well developed, and is covered by large juxtaposed or overlapping plates and sometimes a soft, filmy skin. Cryptodirous (the head is withdrawn under the shell by vertical bends of the neck).

Key

TO THE GENERA OF THE AUSTRALIAN CHELONIID TURTLES

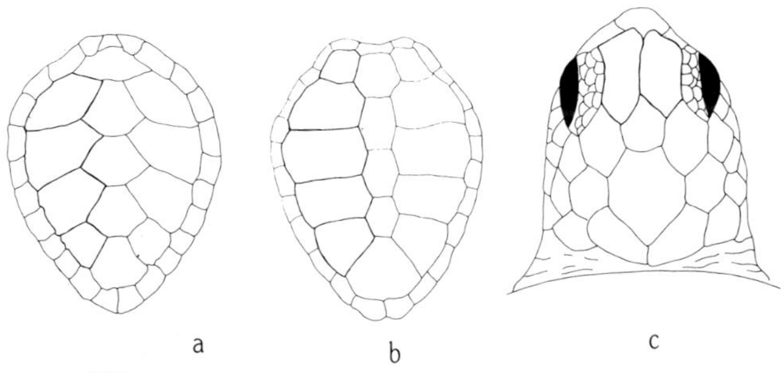

1 Four costal shields on each side(a).................................. **2**

Five or more costal shields on each side(b)...................... **3**

2 One pair of prefrontals(c); tip of upper jaw not projecting forwards and downwards to form a narrow, projecting beak(d).. **4**

Two pairs of prefrontals(e); tip of upper jaw projecting forwards and downwards to form a narrow, projecting beak(f).. ***Eretmochelys***

DIAGNOSTIC CHARACTERS IN TURTLES

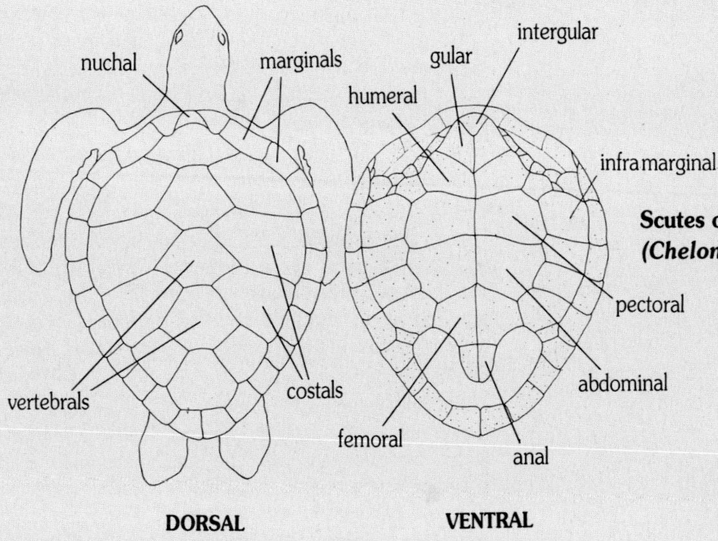

Scutes of the epidermal shell of a cheloniid turtle
(Chelonia mydas)

Plates of the bony shell of a cheloniid turtle
(Chelonia mydas)

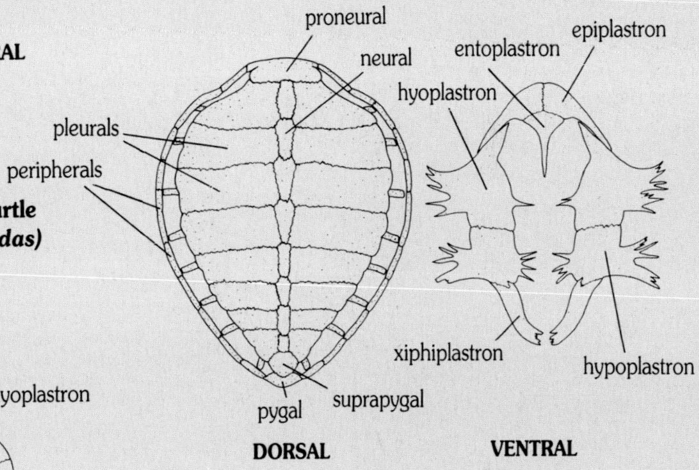

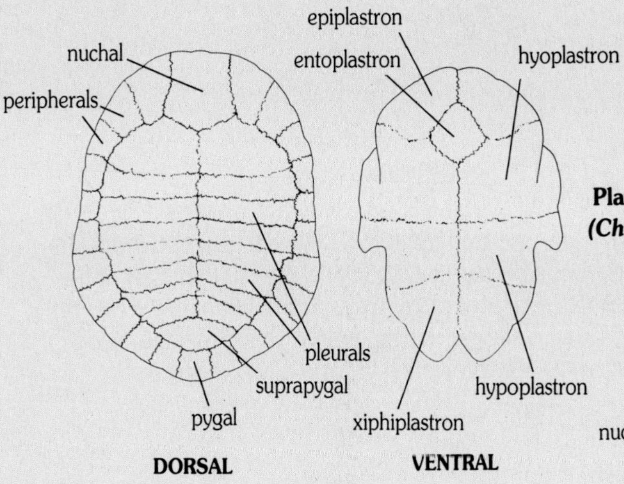

Plates of the bony shell of a chelid turtle
(Chelodina longicollis)

Scutes of the epidermal shell of a chelid turtle
(Chelodina longicollis)

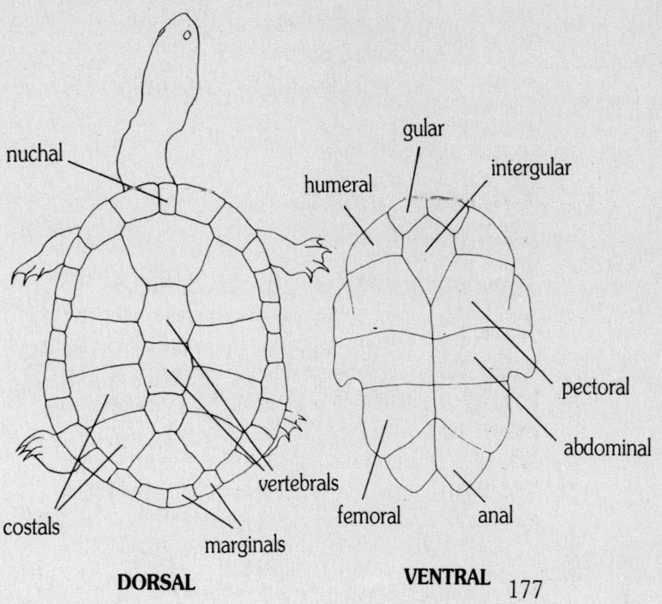

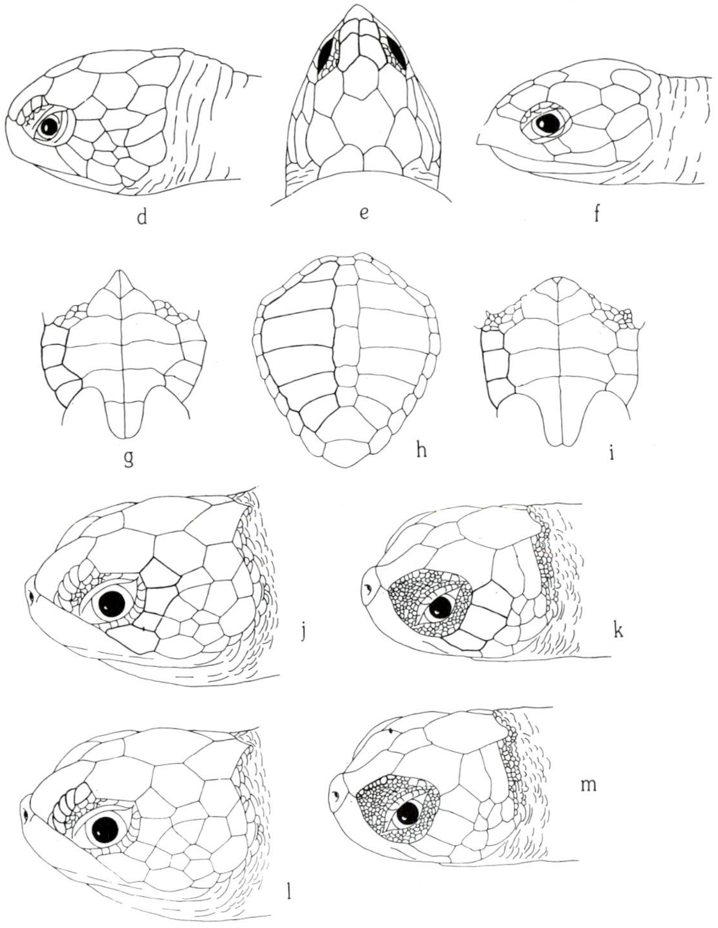

3 Four enlarged inframarginals on the bridge, with or without pores(g); adults olive-grey dorsally, hatchlings almost black; usually six or more costals on each side(h).. ***Lepidochelys***

Usually three enlarged inframarginals on the bridge, without pores(i); adults and hatchlings distinctly reddish-brown dorsally; rarely more than five costals on each side(b).. ***Caretta***

4 Usually four or more postoculars(j); a series of enlarged scales on the upper eyelid, the larger of which are at least half the width of the adjoining prefrontal(l); distal half of forelimb almost entirely covered by enlarged scales, without distinct areas of smaller irregular scales between the phalanges(n).. ***Chelonia***

Three postoculars(k); upper eyelid composed of numerous, small, irregular, subequal scales, the larger of which are much less than one quarter the width of the adjoining prefrontal(m); distal half of forelimb with single rows of enlarged scales extending along phalanges, separated by areas of smaller irregular scales or wrinkled skin(o).. ***Natator***

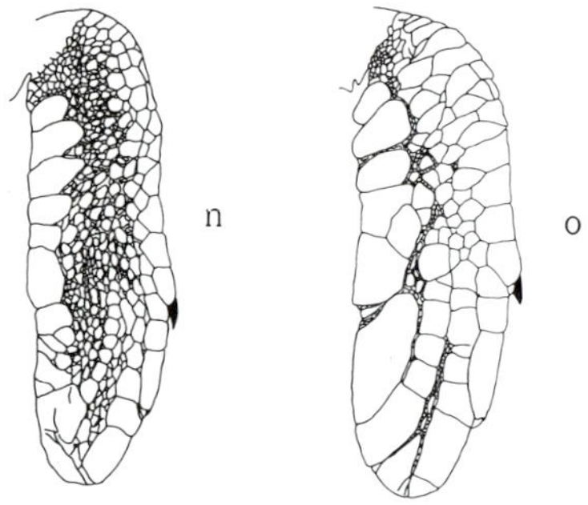

Genus ***Caretta*** Rafinesque, 1814

A monotypic genus whose sole species, the Loggerhead Turtle, is tropicopolitan. In Australia the genus is distinguished from all other sea-turtles by the combination of five costal shields on each side of the carapace; scutes of carapace not overlapping in adults; two pairs of prefrontal scales and three enlarged inframarginal scales on the bridge, usually without pores; upper jaw not noticeably projecting to form a hooked beak.

Caretta caretta (Linnaeus, 1758)
Loggerhead Turtle

Description: Dark brown above, sometimes irregularly speckled with darker brown; top of head dark brown, becoming pale on the sides with irregular darker blotches. White, cream or yellowish below. Hatchlings rich reddish-brown above, dark blackish-brown below. The head of old adults is large and massive. The shell is somewhat elongate and more or less heart-shaped. Five, rarely six, costal shields on each side. 1.5 metres.

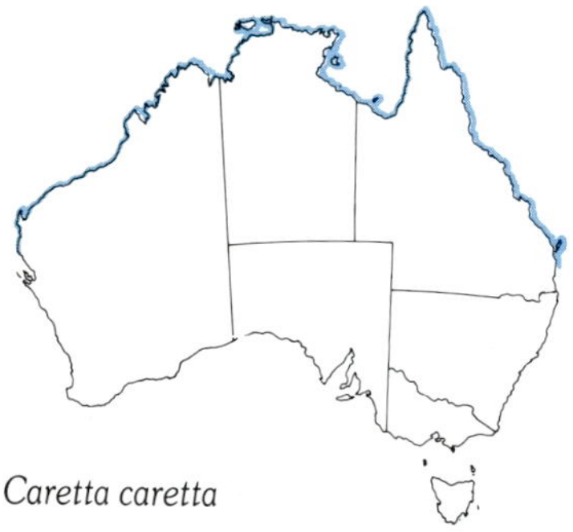

Caretta caretta

Caretta caretta Heron Island, Qld. Female laying eggs.

Distribution: Tropical and warm temperate waters off the Australian coast, including the Great Barrier Reef. Elsewhere throughout tropical waters. Occasional specimens enter southern Australian waters.

Habit: Carnivorous. Appear to forage in deeper water. About 100 small, round parchment-shelled eggs are laid at any time of year, but mainly in the period October-May.
Subspecies: *caretta* (Atlantic Ocean); *gigas* (Indian and Pacific Oceans).

Caretta caretta (hatchling) Heron Island, Qld

Genus *Chelonia* Sonnini and Latreille, 1802

A genus containing a single tropicopolitan species. In Australia the genus is characterised by the combination of: usually four or more postoculars; a series of enlarged scales on the upper eyelid, the larger of which are at least half the width of the adjoining prefrontal; four costal shields; four enlarged inframarginal scales on the bridge, without pores; upper jaw not noticeably projecting to form a hooked beak; distal half of forelimb almost entirely covered by enlarged scales, without distinct areas of smaller irregular scales between the phalanges.

Chelonia mydas Great Barrier Reef, Qld. Two males (above) seeking to mate with the same female. R. TAYLOR

Chelonia mydas (Linnaeus, 1758)

Green Turtle

Description: Olive-green above, usually variegated with brown, reddish-brown and black. Whitish or cream below. Shields on sides of face with distinctive pale-edged sutures. Hatchlings shiny black above, white below. Head moderate. Four or more postoculars. Shell subcircular to heart-shaped, the lateral edges not upturned. Four costal shields on each side. Upper eyelid with a series of enlarged, transverse scales. Distal half of forelimb almost entirely covered by enlarged scales, without distinct areas of smaller irregular scales between the phalanges. 1 metre.

Distribution: Abundant along the tropical coasts of Australia and the Great Barrier Reef. Pan-tropical distribution throughout the world.

Habit: Although carnivorous when young, adults are believed to be almost entirely herbivorous. Breeds throughout its range in Australia; lays about 100 round, smallish, parchment-shelled eggs.

Subspecies: *mydas* (Atlantic Ocean); *agassizi* (eastern Pacific Ocean); *japonica* (Indian and western Pacific Oceans).

Chelonia mydas (hatchling) Groote Eylandt, NT

Chelonia mydas Heron Island, Qld

N. COLEMAN

Genus *Eretmochelys* Fitzinger, 1843

A monotypic genus whose sole species, the Hawksbill Turtle, is tropicopolitan. Distinguished in Australia by: four costal shields on each side; strongly overlapping dorsal scutes (in adults); two pairs of prefrontal scales and enlarged inframarginal scales on the bridge without pores; upper jaw markedly projecting forward to form a parrot-like beak.

Eretmochelys imbricata Heron Island, Qld

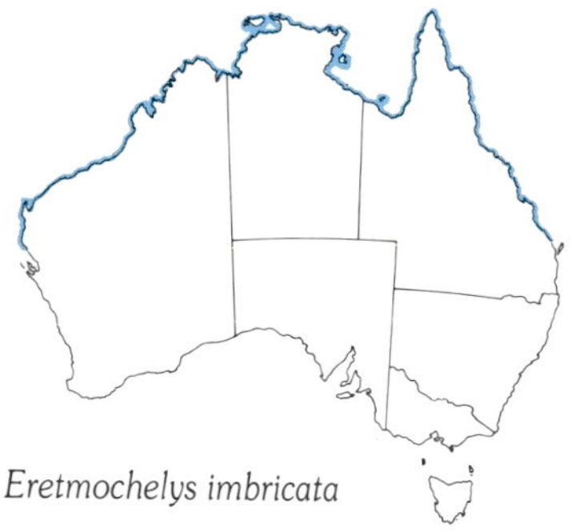

Eretmochelys imbricata

Eretmochelys imbricata (Linnaeus, 1766)

Hawksbill Turtle

Description: Olive-green or brown above, richly variegated with reddish-brown, dark brown and black. Scales of head and face often dark with pale contrasting sutures. Whitish below. Hatchlings blackish above, dark below. Head rather small. Three postoculars. Shell distinctly and somewhat narrowly heart-shaped. Four costal shields on each side. 1 metre.

Distribution: Abundant along the tropical coasts of northern and eastern Australia, from mid-western WA to southern Qld. Found throughout the tropical and warm temperate seas of the world.

Habit: A common species seen frequently foraging on coral reefs. Carnivorous. Breeding rarely observed in Australia, but nesting has been observed in Torres Strait and the Gulf of Carpentaria. About 50 round, smallish, parchment-shelled eggs are laid in a clutch.

Subspecies: *imbricata* (Atlantic Ocean); *squamata* (Indian and Pacific Oceans).

Genus *Lepidochelys* Fitzinger, 1843

A tropicopolitan genus with two species, only one of which is found in Australian waters. Distinguished from other Australian sea-turtles by: six or more costal shields on each side; dorsal scutes not overlapping, and sometimes covered by a soft, thin skin in adults; two pairs of prefrontal scales and four enlarged inframarginal scales on the bridge, each usually pierced by a single pore; upper jaw not markedly projecting to form a beak.

I. MORRIS

Lepidochelys olivacea Elcho Island, NT

Lepidochelys olivacea

Lepidochelys olivacea (Eschscholtz, 1829)

Pacific Ridley

Description: Grey or olive-grey above, usually without any conspicuous markings. Whitish below. Head large and massive. Three or four postoculars. Shell broad and heart-shaped. Usually six or more costal shields. Hatchlings blackish above, dark brown below. 1.5 metres.

Distribution: Apparently occurs commonly in waters along the north coast of Australia, but rarely found in Great Barrier Reef waters.

Habit: Major Australian nesting records from the vicinity of Coburg Peninsula, with isolated records elsewhere. Lays about 100 large round, parchment-shelled eggs.

Genus *Natator* McCulloch, 1908

A regionally endemic Australasian genus previously included within the genus *Chelonia*. It is characterised by the combination of: three postoculars; upper eyelid composed of numerous, small, irregular, subequal scales, the larger of which are much less than one quarter the width of the adjoining prefrontal; four costal shields; four enlarged inframarginal scales on the bridge, without pores; upper jaw not noticeably projecting to form a hooked beak; distal half of forelimb with single rows of enlarged scales extending along phalanges, separated by areas of smaller irregular scales or wrinkled skin.

Natator depressus (Garman, 1880)

Flatback Turtle

Description: Grey or pale grey-green or olive above, the plates of the carapace covered by a thin, fleshy skin in adults. Creamy-yellow below, the ventral colour extending on to the sides of the neck and face. Hatchlings olive-green, the margins of the dorsal scutes broadly outlined in black. Head moderate. Three postoculars. Shell broadly oval, more or less heart-shaped, with upturned lateral edges in adults. Four costal shields on each side. Upper eyelid of

Natator depressus

Natator depressus Sir Edward Pellew Islands, NT. Female leaving nesting beach.

small, irregular, subequal scales. Distal half of forelimb with rows of enlarged scales extending along phalanges separated by areas of small, irregular scales or wrinkled skin. 1.2 metres.

Distribution: Common in coastal waters of northern Australia, from the Kimberley region to Torres Strait; occurs less commonly on the Great Barrier Reef.

Habit: A large, carnivorous turtle occurring commonly in shallow, coastal waters. Breeds throughout its range but patchily along the Great Barrier Reef; lays about 50 large, round, parchment-shelled eggs, the hatchlings almost twice the size of hatchlings of *Chelonia mydas*.

Family Dermochelyidae

A monotypic family of sea-turtles, whose sole highly specialised species occurs throughout the world's tropical and temperate seas, and more than any of the other sea-turtles wanders into the colder waters of higher latitudes. The species rarely breeds in Australia, the nearest known major nesting sites being in the Solomon Islands and the Malayan Archipelago.

It differs from other Australian turtle families in the combination of heavy, paddle-shaped limbs without obvious ankle-joints and without webbed, clawed feet; the nostrils are level with the surface of the snout. The limbs are clawless. The shell is not a fused, bony shield, but is made up of numerous, small, polygonal dermal bones (osteoderms) forming a mosaic embedded in a leathery skin; some of these osteoderms are enlarged and form longitudinal rows which result in a series of high keels along the plastron and carapace. Cryptodirous.

Genus *Dermochelys* Blainville, 1816

Dermochelys coriacea (Vandelli, 1761)

Leathery or Luth Turtle

Description: A very large turtle, dark brown or black above, usually uniform above, but sometimes with paler marbling on the back, or with longitudinal rows of small, fine dots and usually with pale white, pink or cream spots and blotches on the sides; throat and lower sides of neck white, pale cream or pink mottled and blotched with dark brown or black. Whitish or pinkish-white below. Hatchlings rich blue-black trimmed with white, pale below. Hatchlings finely beaded in appearance as a result of the superficial osteoderm mosaic; adult shell covered by a thick, smooth, leathery skin, often pitted and pock-marked in older specimens. A series of seven prominent longitudinal ridges above (including the outer lateral pair) and four ridges along the plastron. 3 metres.

Distribution: All coastal waters of Australia. Most sightings are in temperate waters, less frequently observed in tropical or colder areas. Found in all tropical and temperate seas.

Habit: Known to nest occasionally along a short stretch of the central coast of Qld (Limpus). Most sightings are along the more heavily populated eastern seaboard of Australia where large adults are found, the year round, in larger bays, estuaries and rivers, the number of sightings suggesting that the species actively seeks out temperate feeding grounds, rather than that these specimens have simply strayed so far south. This interpretation is supported by the meagre feeding observations in this country; many casual observers have seen these turtles feeding on unidentified jellyfishes (apparently *Catostylus mosaicus)* and on Bluebottles or Portuguese Man o' War *(Physalia utriculus)* along the coast of NSW.

Dermochelys coriacea (hatchling) Bundaberg, Qld

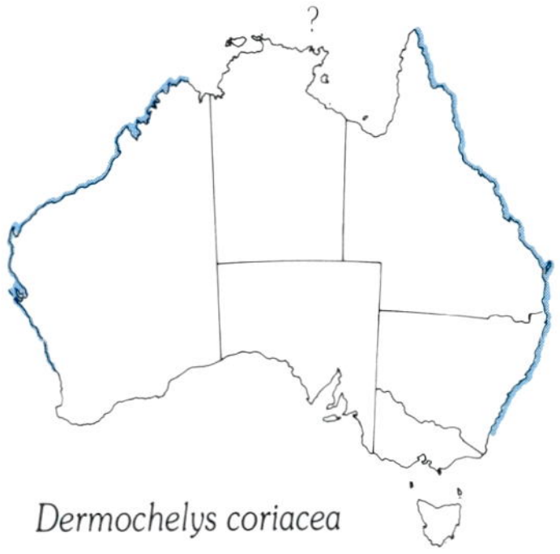

Dermochelys coriacea

Dermochelys coriacea Sydney, NSW. An adult washed up on a beach after drowning in a shark-meshing net.

Family Carettochelydidae

A monotypic family whose sole member was until recently believed to be confined to Papua New Guinea, but which has now been found in widely separated localities in the NT.

It is apparently closely allied to the soft-shelled turtles (Family Trionychidae) of Africa, Asia and North America, but differs in a number of important features. There are no dermal scutes in the shell, the bony carapace being covered with a soft, pitted skin; the limbs are paddle-shaped like those of a sea-turtle, with two claws; nostrils at the end of a prominent, fleshy proboscis. Cryptodirous.

Genus ***Carettochelys*** Ramsay, 1886

Carettochelys insculpta Ramsay, 1886

Pitted-Shelled Turtle

Description: Rich grey, olive-grey or grey-brown above, white, cream or yellowish below. A pale streak behind the eye. A heavy-bodied turtle with bony sutures of carapace indicated by grooves in the skin covering them. Plastron small. The characters cited under the family description — the fleshy proboscis, pitted shell and two-clawed flippers distinguish this species from all other Australian chelonians. 0.7 metres.

Distribution: Known from several rivers in the NT — the Daly, Victoria and Alligator River systems. Extra-limital in Papua New Guinea.

Habit: Found in freshwater and estuarine reaches of rivers, and in large waterholes and lagoons isolated during the dry season. Feeds on snails, fruits (figs and pandanus) and small fish. In New Guinea large numbers of females emerge at night on to high mud and sandbanks towards the end of the dry season (October-November) to deposit about 15 large, round, parchment-shelled eggs in a small hole dug for the purpose. In Australia eggs are laid exclusively in river sandbanks in the late dry season, the embryos when fully-developed entering a dormant stage until the nest is flooded by the rising river after the start of the wet season (Georges).

Carettochelys insculpta Strickland River, PNG. Hatchlings; egg shells in background.

Carettochelys insculpta

Carettochelys insculpta (adult)
Daly River, NT

Family Chelidae

A group of aquatic or semi-aquatic turtles (usually called tortoises in Australia) with representatives confined to Australia (with a few species in New Guinea) and South America. The family is characterised by being pleurodirous (the head and neck are folded under the front edge of the carapace by one or more horizontal folds); the forelimbs and hindlimbs are jointed, not paddle-shaped, with distinct ankle-joints and four- or five-clawed, webbed feet. Barbels well developed in most species. A macrocephalus condition occurs commonly in the adults of some species of *Emydura* and *Elseya*.

Although members of this family are commonly termed 'tortoises' in Australia, to distinguish them from the large marine 'turtles', the distinction is essentially a local custom. In applying common names in the following family I have tended to use the more or less international convention of referring to these side-necked chelonians as 'turtles'.

Chelid turtles in Australia are conservative in many features and their present classification is poorly founded and in drastic need of review. Fortunately, at the time of writing, several workers are involved in various aspects of such a review, and it can be anticipated that major changes will soon be made to the classification presented below. A number of well-known but as yet undescribed species are included within the taxa described below.

Key

TO THE GENERA OF THE AUSTRALIAN CHELID TURTLES

1 Forelimbs each with five claws(a); gular shields entirely separated by the intergular(c)... **2**

Forelimbs each with four claws(b); gular shields meeting in front of the intergular(d).................................. ***Chelodina***

2 Intergular shield not contacting the pectorals(e)................**3**

Intergular shield contacting and partly separating the pectorals(f)... ***Pseudemydura***

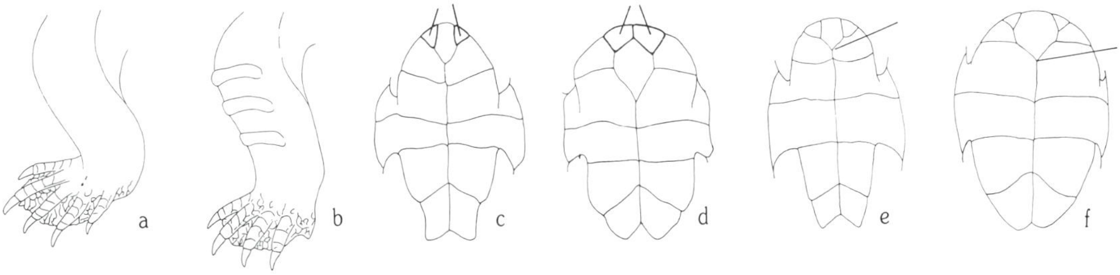

3 Sutures between second and third costals and third and fourth costals contacting seventh and ninth marginals respectively(g)..**4**

Sutures between second and third costals and third and fourth costals contacting sixth and eighth marginals respectively(h).. ***Rheodytes***

4 Skin of temporal region smooth, sometimes broken up into regular, flat scales or tubercles; nuchal shield usually present(i)... ***Emydura***

Skin of temporal region with prominent, low, rounded scales or tubercles which are distinctly raised above the surface of the head; nuchal shield usually absent(j).. ***Elseya***

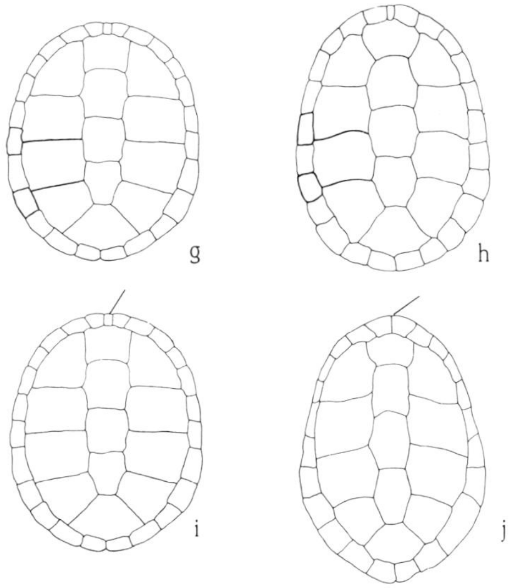

Genus *Chelodina* Fitzinger, 1826

A group of turtles with exceptionally long necks, the extended head and neck usually about as long as or longer than the shell. These Long- or Snake-necked Turtles are distinguished from all other Australian members of their family by the possession of only four claws on the webbed front feet and gular shields which meet in front of the intergular. Many species have well-developed inguinal, and sometimes axillary, musk glands which secrete a milky, viscous, foul-smelling fluid when the turtle is alarmed. Its function is not known.

Found in a wide range of aquatic habitats throughout all but the arid centre of Australia. Not found in Tasmania. All species are largely carnivorous, feeding on fish, molluscs and crustaceans. All species lay up to about 12 elongated, brittle-shelled eggs.

Key

TO THE AUSTRALIAN SPECIES OF CHELODINA

1 Plastron greatly expanded anteriorly, usually only about 1.4-1.7 times longer than broad and widest at about the level of the humerals(a); intergular usually at least twice as long as the suture between the pectorals(c)....................**2**

Plastron narrow, not noticeably expanded anteriorly, usually 1.9 (or more) times as long as broad, and widest at about the level of the bridge(b); intergular usually scarcely longer than the suture between the pectorals(d).............**4**

2 Expanded anterior lobe of plastron moderate, not extending laterally as far as the inner edges of the overlying marginal plates of the carapace(e)....................**3**

Expanded anterior lobe of plastron very broad, extending laterally beyond the inner edges of the overlying marginal plates of the carapace(f)................................ ***longicollis***

3 Carapace very flat, almost circular in outline..................... .... ***steindachneri***

Carapace strongly convex, distinctly oval in outline.......... .... ***novaeguineae***

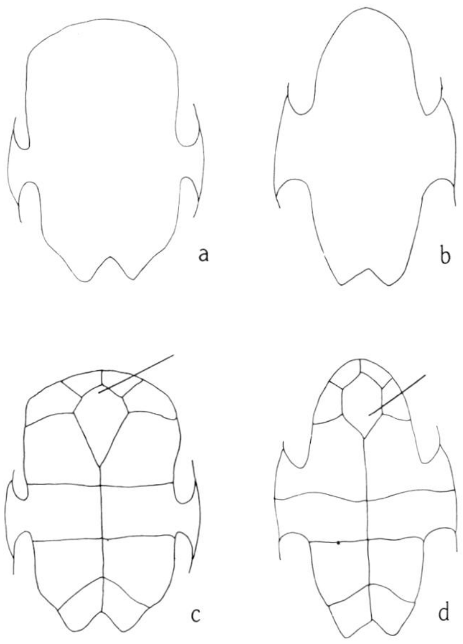

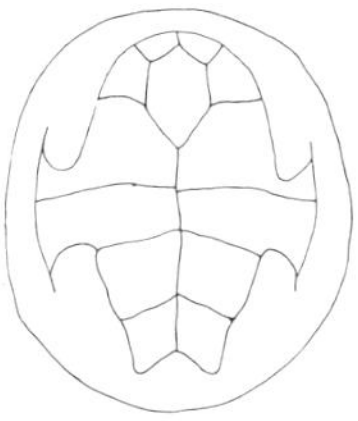
e

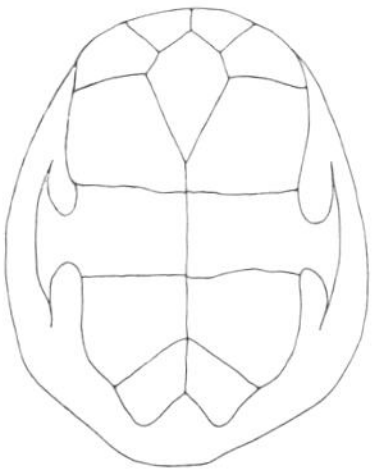
f

4 Carapace broadly oval; plastron moderate, at most twice as long as its width immediately in front of the bridge(g)..**5**

Carapace very narrow, plastron long, slender, more than twice as long as its width in front of the bridge(b) ***oblonga***

5 Second and third vertebrals longer than wide(h); anterior lobe of plastron not beginning to taper immediately in front of bridge(g).. ***expansa***

Second and third vertebrals wider than long(i); anterior lobe of plastron beginning to taper immediately in front of bridge (j) .... ***rugosa***

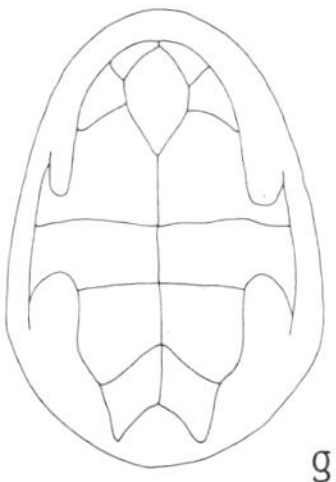
g

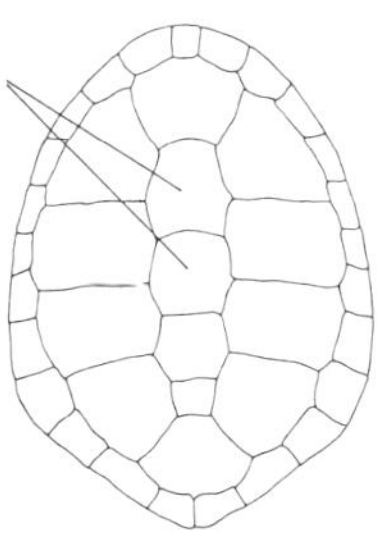
h

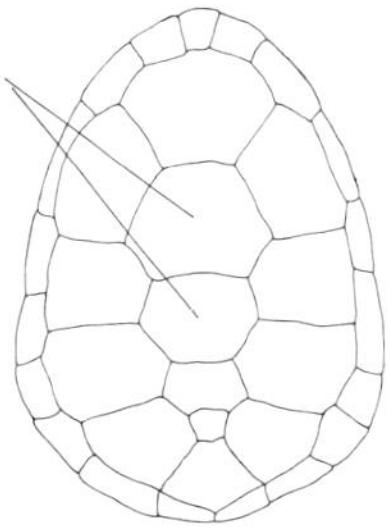
i

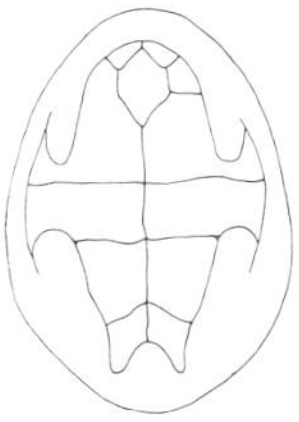
j

Chelodina expansa Gray, 1857

Broad-Shelled River Turtle

Description: Rich brown to blackish-brown above, often with fine dark flecks or reticulations, whitish or creamy-coloured below. Shell broad, oval and flattened above; plastron narrow, not noticeably expanded anteriorly, usually about twice as long as broad, and widest at about the level of the bridge. Intergular shield usually scarcely longer than the suture between the pectoral shields. Second and third vertebrals longer than wide. Anterior lobe of carapace not longer than wide. Anterior lobe of carapace not beginning to taper immediately in front of the bridge. Head broad, strongly depressed, the eyes directed distinctly dorso-laterally. 50 cm (shell length).

Distribution: Murray/Darling River system of south-eastern Australia. Distinctive populations in central and coastal Qld.

Habit: Goode has recorded that this species deposits eggs in autumn, the eggs overwintering and the young hatching in the spring. Inhabits permanent streams and waterholes throughout its range, but essentially a river tortoise.

Chelodina expansa

Chelodina expansa (adult)
Brewarrina, NSW

Chelodina expansa Patho, Vic. Hatchling (inset: lower surface).

Chelodina longicollis (Shaw, 1794)

Eastern Snake-Necked Turtle or Long-Necked Tortoise

Description: Colour variable, from rich brown to dark brown or black above, in lighter-coloured specimens the sutures between the scutes of the carapace outlined in black. White or cream below, the sutures of the plastron and lower margin of carapace broadly edged with black. Hatchlings in some areas with bright orange or red plastron. Shell above moderately broad, slightly expanded posteriorly. Plastron greatly expanded anteriorly, about one and a half times longer than broad, widest at the level of the humerals and the anterior expansion extending

Chelodina longicollis Hunter River, NSW

laterally beyond the inner edges of the overlying marginal plates of the carapace. Intergular shield usually at least twice as long as the suture between the pectorals. Head only moderately depressed, the eyes more or less laterally directed. 25 cm (shell length).
Distribution: Coastal and inland waterways and wetlands of eastern continental Australia, from south-eastern SA to eastern Qld.
Habit: Typically an inhabitant of swamps, oxbow lakes and billabongs, or slow-moving rivers. Sometimes extensive overland migrations occur in summer. Feeds on a variety of aquatic organisms — molluscs, crustaceans, tadpoles and small fishes. Lays up to ten or more eggs in a hole excavated in the bank of its stream or swamp, usually in early summer.

Chelodina longicollis

Chelodina novaeguineae

Chelodina novaeguineae Boulenger, 1888

Description: Brown to almost black above, often mottled or speckled with darker. White or cream below, the sutures of the plastron and submarginal area of the plastron narrowly edged with black. Shell above broad, always oval in outline and somewhat expanded posteriorly. Plastron greatly expanded anteriorly, about one and a half times longer than broad, but the anterior expansion not extending laterally as far as the inner edges of overlying marginal plates of the carapace. Intergular shield usually at least twice as long as the suture between the pectorals. Head only moderately depressed, the eyes more or less laterally directed. 30 cm (shell length).
Distribution: Far north-eastern Qld and northern NT; extra-limital in New Guinea.
Habit: Apparently similar in most respects to that of *Chelodina longicollis*.

Chelodina novaeguineae near Port Moresby, PNG

Chelodina oblonga near Perth, WA

Chelodina oblonga

Chelodina oblonga Gray, 1841
Oblong Turtle

Description: Dark brown to black above, with or without darker flecks and variegations. Whitish below. Shell above very narrowly oval. Plastron long, slender, not noticeably expanded anteriorly, widest at about the level of the bridge, and more than twice as long as its width immediately in front of the bridge. Intergular shield scarcely any longer than the suture between the pectorals. Head strongly depressed, the eyes directed distinctly dorso-laterally. 40 cm (shell length).
Distribution: Permanent waterways of south-western WA.
Habit: Similar in most respects to those of *C. longicollis*.

Chelodina rugosa (hatchling)

Chelodina rugosa Ogilby, 1890
Northern Snake-Necked Turtle

Description: Dark brown to black above, with or without darker flecks, blotches or marbling. Whitish below. Shell above broadly oval, usually somewhat expanded posteriorly. Plastron moderate, at most about twice as long as its width immediately in front of the bridge. Intergular shield scarcely longer than the suture between the pectorals. Second and third vertebrals wider than long. Anterior lobe of plastron beginning to taper immediately in front of the bridge. Head rather broad, rather depressed, the eyes directed dorso-laterally. 40 cm (shell length).
Distribution: Northern Australia, from Cape York Peninsula, Qld, to the Kimberley district, WA.
Habit: An inhabitant of swamps, billabongs, waterholes and slow-flowing rivers throughout its range.

Chelodina rugosa

Chelodina steindachneri

Chelodina rugosa (adult) Port Essington, NT

Chelodina steindachneri Murchison River, WA

Chelodina steindachneri Siebenrock, 1914

Flat-Shelled Turtle

Description: Rich brown above, without any, or rarely with more than a few, darker flecks; whitish below, the sutures between the shields of the plastron and the lower marginals of the plastron narrowly edged with black. Shell above almost circular in outline and scarcely expanded posteriorly. Plastron expanded anteriorly, nearly one and a half times as long as broad and widest at about the level of the humerals, and with a moderately expanded anterior lobe, not extending laterally as far as the inner edges of the overlying marginal plates of the carapace. Intergular shield usually at least twice as long as the suture between the pectorals. Head moderate, only slightly depressed, the eyes directed more or less laterally. 20 cm (shell length).
Distribution: WA, from the De Grey River in the north to the Irwin River in the south.
Habit: Little known.

Genus ***Elseya*** Gray, 1867

Turtles with only moderately long necks, the extended head and neck much shorter than the length of the shell. Closely allied to the genus *Emydura*, from which adult specimens of *Elseya* may be generally (but not always) distinguished by the latter's possession of a horny casque over the head; the skin of the temporal region with prominent low, rounded tubercles or scales which are distinctly raised above the surface of the head. A distinct alveolar ridge sometimes present on the maxilla. Distinguished from *Chelodina* by the possession of five claws on each of the webbed forelimbs and gular shields entirely separated by the intergular, the latter not contacting the pectorals. A nuchal shield may be present or absent even in the same species. Pale temporal stripes absent.

Confined to northern and eastern Australia. All species are omnivorous, feeding on pandanus and other fruits, molluscs, crustaceans and fish. All lay up to about 15 elongated, brittle-shelled eggs.

Key

TO THE AUSTRALIAN SPECIES OF ELSEYA

Intergular shield as wide as or wider than each gular shield(a); neck with conspicuous, sharp-pointed tubercles above; no alveolar ridge on maxilla(c)................................ ***latisternum***

Intergular shield much narrower than each gular shield(b); neck with conspicuous but rounded tubercles above; a distinct alveolar ridge on each maxilla(d).............................. ***dentata***

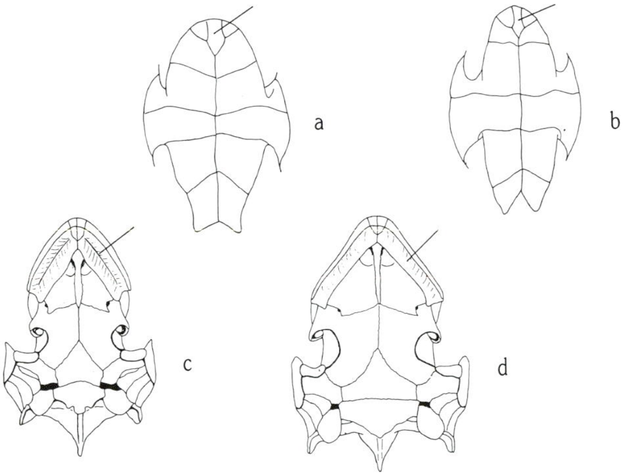

Elseya dentata (Gray, 1863)

Northern Snapping Turtle

Description: Brown to dark brown above, sometimes with scattered darker flecks and blotches. Whitish below. Head without stripes. Tympanum pale coloured. Shell above broadly oval, markedly expanded posteriorly, hind edge serrated in younger specimens. Plastron rather long and relatively narrow, tapering gently in front of and behind the bridge. Intergular shield much narrower than each gular shield. Neck above with conspicuous but rounded tubercles. A distinct alveolar ridge on each maxilla. Macrocephaly common. 35 cm (shell length).
Distribution: Northern Australia, from Cape York Peninsula, Qld, to the Kimberley district, WA.
Habit: An inhabitant of large rivers and their associated overflow lagoons and oxbow lakes.

Elseya latisternum Gray, 1867

Saw-Shelled Turtle

Description: Brown to dark brown above, whitish below, the two colours usually forming a sharply defined line on the side of the face and throat at the level of the angle of the jaws. Sometimes a distinct yellow stripe from the angle of the jaws, especially in the young. Shell above broadly oval, expanded posteriorly, with a serrated hind edge, except in very old specimens. Plastron moderate, nearly twice as long as broad, the front and rear lobes tapering from the bridge. Intergular shield as wide as or wider than each gular shield. Neck above with conspicuous, sharp-pointed tubercles. No alveolar ridge on the maxilla. Macrocephaly does not occur. 20 cm (shell length).
Distribution: Eastern and north-eastern Australia from northern NSW to Cape York Peninsula, Qld.
Habit: A river-dwelling species.

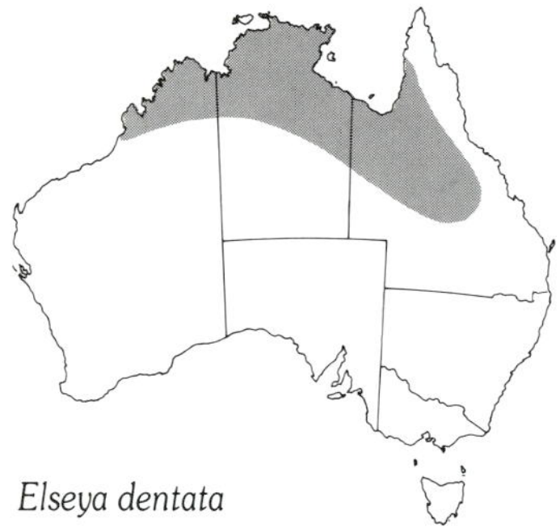

Elseya dentata

Elseya dentata Bullo River, NT

Elseya latisternum (adult) Iron Range, Qld

Elseya latisternum

Elseya latisternum (hatchling) Malanda, Qld

Genus *Emydura* Bonaparte, 1836

Turtles with only moderately long necks, the extended head and neck much shorter than the length of the shell. Head rarely with a horny casque, except in older, larger specimens; the skin of the temporal region smooth, sometimes broken up into regular, flat scales or tubercles. No alveolar ridge on the maxilla. Five claws on each of the webbed forelimbs and gular shields entirely separated by the intergular, the latter not contacting the pectorals. A nuchal shield may be present or absent even in the same species. Pale temporal stripe in most species.

Widely distributed throughout most parts of continental Australia, except for most of the arid centre. Mostly river-dwelling species with habits similar to those of *Elseya*.

Key

TO THE AUSTRALIAN SPECIES OF EMYDURA

1 A continuous, pale-coloured postocular stripe from eye to above ear or beyond (sometimes obscure in old adults)........ **2**

No pale postocular stripe (or occasionally a discontinuous one) from eye to above ear........ **4**

2 Length of mandibular symphysis (a) more or less equal to the horizontal diameter of the tympanum; postocular stripe cream or yellow........ **3**

Length of mandibular symphysis(b) about one and a half times the horizontal diameter of the tympanum; postocular stripe pink, red or salmon........ ***victoriae***

3 Body and shell without bright red or pink markings; postocular stripe cream or light yellow........ ***krefftii***

Lower jaw, sides of neck, limbs, tail and outer lower edges of plastron and carapace with bright red or pink markings; postocular stripe bright yellow........ ***subglobosa***

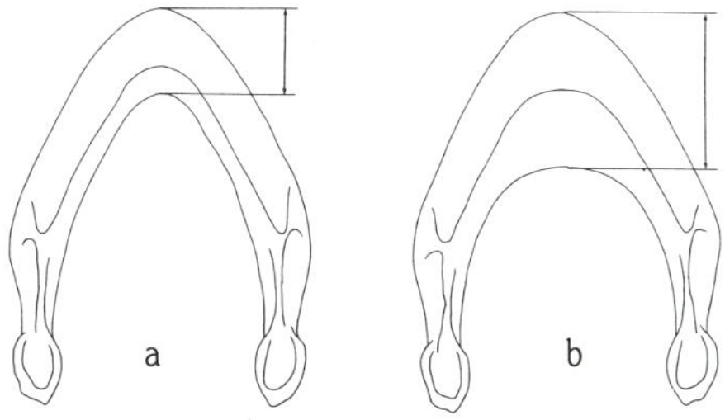

4 Adult size large (to 40 cm carapace length); light head stripe just contacting lower rim of tympanum; rivers of south-eastern Australia, west of Great Dividing Range........ ***macquarii***

Adult size moderate (to 25 cm carapace length); light head stripe enclosing lower portion of tympanum; coastal rivers of south-eastern Australia, east of Great Dividing Range........ ***signata***

Emydura krefftii (Gray, 1871)

Krefft's River Turtle

Description: Brown to dark brown above, with or without darker flecks and blotches. White or cream-coloured below. A conspicuous pale yellow or cream temporal streak and a stripe of the same colour along the lower jaw to the side of the neck. Length of mandibular symphysis more or less equal to the horizontal diameter of the tympanum. Shell above broadly oval, moderately expanded posteriorly, and a serrated hind edge in many juveniles. Plastron moderate, about twice as long as broad, and the front and rear lobes tapering gently from the bridge. Intergular shield a little longer than broad, about as broad as each gular shield. Head usually small to moderate, but macrocephaly common. 25 cm (shell length).

Emydura krefftii (juvenile) near Mt Carbine, Qld

Emydura krefftii (adult) Kennedy River, Qld

Distribution: Rivers of eastern and north-eastern Qld, in both eastern and western drainage systems.
Habit: An inhabitant of larger rivers and the larger waterholes and billabongs of their floodplains.

Emydura krefftii

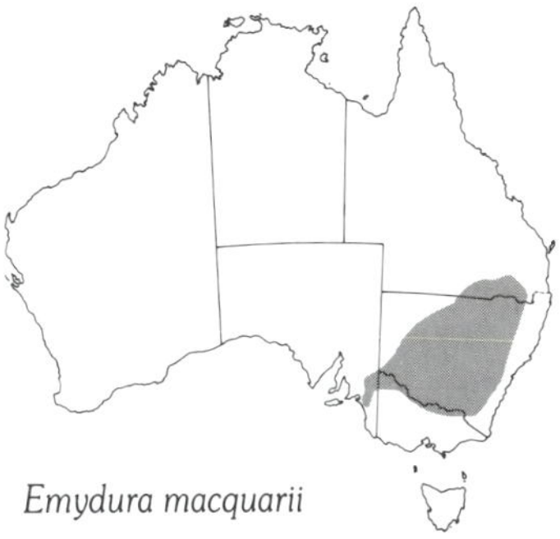

Emydura macquarii

Emydura macquarii (Gray, 1830)

Murray Turtle

Description: Olive, brown or dark brown above, white or yellowish below. No pale temporal stripe, or occasionally a discontinuous one; a pale yellowish

Emydura macquarii Darling River, NSW

J. CANN

stripe along the lower jaw to the side of the neck and just contacting the lower rim of the tympanum. Length of mandibular symphysis more or less equal to the horizontal diameter of the tympanum. Shell above broadly oval, moderately expanded posteriorly and a serrated hind edge in juveniles. Plastron moderate, about twice as long as broad, the front and rear lobes tapering gently from the bridge. Intergular shield a little longer than broad, about as broad as each gular shield. Head rather small. Macrocephaly uncommon. 30 cm (shell length).

Distribution: Murray/Darling River system and associated drainages west of the Great Dividing Range in south-eastern Australia.

Habit: Restricted to larger rivers and associated large waterholes on the floodplains. Summer breeder. About ten elongate, brittle-shelled eggs are laid in a chamber dug high on a river bank. Feeds on crustaceans, molluscs and fishes.

Emydura signata

Emydura subglobosa Jardine River, Cape York Peninsula, Qld

Emydura signata Brisbane R., Qld

J. CANN

Emydura signata Ahl, 1932

Description: Similar in most external features to *Emydura macquarii* from which it differs in its smaller adult size (about 20 cm shell length) and the pale stripe from the lower jaw tends to enclose the lower part of the tympanum.
Distribution: Coastal rivers of northern NSW and adjacent parts of south-eastern Qld.
Habit: Similar to *Emydura macquarii*. It is likely that several species and subspecies are here being lumped together under the one name.

Emydura subglobosa

Emydura victoriae

Emydura subglobosa Krefft, 1876

Description: Generally similar to *Emydura krefftii* in shape, proportions and size but differing from it conspicuously in colour and pattern. There is a bright yellow stripe from the snout to the ear and another (except in older adults) along the upper jaw. A bright reddish stripe along the upper edge of each lower jaw generally continuing as a broken stripe along the length of the neck. Limbs spotted with bright red. Plastron and lower edges of marginal shields usually richly flushed with red. The red colouring described above is most conspicuous in juveniles, fading to a dull pink in older adults. 25 cm (shell length).
Distribution: Abundant and widely distributed in southern New Guinea, but known in Australia from the far tip of Cape York Peninsula (Jardine River drainage).
Habit: An inhabitant of larger rivers and permanent lakes and lagoons.

Emydura victoriae (Gray, 1842)

Description: Brown to blackish-brown above, usually with obscure scattered dark flecks and blotches. Whitish below, faintly or vividly flushed with pink or salmon. A marked (juveniles) to obscure (adults) pale, usually salmon-coloured temporal stripe from the eye and a stripe of the same colour from along the lower jaw to the side of the neck. Length of mandibular symphysis about one and a half times the horizontal diameter of the tympanum. Shell above broadly oval, moderately expanded posteriorly, especially in the young. Plastron moderate, about twice as long as broad, and the front and rear lobes tapering gently from the bridge. Intergular shield only slightly longer than broad, about as broad as each gular shield. Macrocephaly common. 30 cm (shell length).
Distribution: Kimberley region, north-western Australia, northern NT and adjacent border regions of north-western Qld.
Habit: Similar to *Emydura krefftii*.

Emydura victoriae Bullo River, NT. Showing "macrocephaly" the gross enlargement of the head which occurs in adults of some chelid turtles.

Emydura victoriae McArthur River, NT

Genus ***Pseudemydura*** Siebenrock, 1901

A monotypic genus confined to a small area within south-western WA. Characterised by its short neck, the extended head and neck much shorter than the shell; a horny casque. No alveolar ridge on the maxilla. Forelimbs webbed, each with five claws. Gular shields entirely separated by the intergular, the latter contacting and partly separating the pectorals. A nuchal shield normally present. No obvious temporal stripe. Barbels present.

Pseudemydura umbrina Siebenrock, 1901

Western Swamp Turtle

Description: Brown above; whitish, yellowish or olive-brown below. Shell squarish in outline, not much longer than broad, greatly depressed. Plastron flat, broad, almost as wide as the carapace. Head broad, flat, with a horny casque. 15 cm (shell length).
Distribution: Known only from one or two small swamps at Bullsbrook, near Perth, WA. Australia's most endangered reptile.
Habit: Ephemeral *Melaleuca* swamps in dense heath and low *Banksia* woodland (Burbidge).

R. W. G. JENKINS

Pseudemydura umbrina
Ellenbrook Nature Reserve, WA

Pseudemydura umbrina

Genus ***Rheodytes*** Legler and Cann, 1980

A monotypic genus of turtles with a relatively short neck, the extended head and neck much shorter than the length of the shell. Apparently most closely related to the genus *Elseya*, from which it may be distinguished by the following suite of characters: seams between second and third costals and third and fourth costals contacting sixth and eighth marginals respectively; maxilla without an alveolar ridge; a white ring around the iris. Five claws on each webbed front foot. A single pair of barbels on the chin.

A single species found only in the Fitzroy River drainage of eastern Queensland.

J. CANN

Rheodytes leukops Fitzroy River, Qld

Rheodytes leukops Legler and Cann, 1980

Rheodytes leukops

Description: Adults medium to dark brown above, without distinctive or regular markings, but sometimes with scattered darker spots and blotches; ventral surfaces pale yellow or cream, without distinctive darker markings. Exposed fleshy parts dull, olive-grey, except for paler yellowish on underside of head and neck. Hatchlings brown above, with a series of darker spots on the carapace. Pupil black, surrounded by a narrow, white, inner iris ring which contrasts with the dark brown remainder of the iris. Shell above broadly oval, its hind edge serrated in juveniles. Plastron rather long and narrow, tapering fairly gently in front of and behind the bridge. Intergular shield much narrower than each gular. Neck above with scattered large, pointed, conical tubercles. Very large cloacal bursae which Legler and Cann identify as probably having a major respiratory function. 25 cm (shell length).
Distribution: Known only from the Fitzroy River and its tributaries, Qld.
Habit: Legler and Cann record this species as a river turtle preferring fast-flowing water, where it feeds principally on insects and their aquatic larvae.

Lizards

(ORDER SQUAMATA, SUBORDER SAURIA)

Most lizards are easily recognised as such, but problems may arise in trying to distinguish between limbless lizards and snakes. Limbless lizards belong to two families: one, the snake-lizards (Pygopodidae) are universally limbless, though some species possess a single pair of scaly flaps in lieu of hindlimbs; the other is that of the skinks (Scincidae), in which several Australiàn spęcies are totally devoid of limbs.

Certainly, if any kind of limbs are present, no matter how small, then a specimen can be readily identified as a lizard.

Under normal circumstances, the tails in all of these lizards are at least as long as the body, whereas in all snakes the length of the tail is only a small fraction of the body length.

Unfortunately the tails of both skinks and snake-lizards are easily broken off. When this happens regenerative processes eventually result in the growth of a replacement tail, which, although supported only by a cartilaginous rod, usually resembles the original tail in outward appearance. Hence, if a tail has been broken near the vent, the above distinction between snakes and lizards will not hold true until a new tail has grown.

Another feature of value in distinguishing between limbless lizards and snakes is the presence, in many limbless lizards, of a small external ear-opening in the head a short distance behind the eye. Such an opening is universally absent in snakes.

However, as there are a few limbless lizards without an external ear-opening, this character must be used in conjunction with the other characters listed above. Together they should distinguish between snakes and limbless lizards in most cases.

Hence the following points should be remembered:

1 If limbs of any kind are present, no matter how small, then the specimen is a lizard.
2 If the tail is about as long as or longer than the snout-vent length the specimen is a lizard.
3 If an external ear-opening is present, then the specimen is a lizard.

Key

TO THE FAMILIES OF AUSTRALIAN LIZARDS

1 Limbs normally present, though often very small; if limbs are entirely absent, then the eyes are very small and have movable lids.. **2**

No obvious or normal limbs, though a scaly flap or 'fin' may be present in some species; all with snake-like, lidless eyes .... **Pygopodidae** (Snake-lizards)

2 Eyes with or without movable lids; if eyelids are absent then the pupil in daylight is not a narrow, vertical slit and the scales on the dorsum are imbricate (overlapping).............**3**

Eyes snake-like, without movable lids; pupil in daylight a narrow, vertical slit; scales on the dorsum small, juxtaposed (not overlapping) .... **Gekkonidae** (Geckos)

3 Top of head covered with very small, irregular scales(a)....**4**

Top of head covered with large, regular and usually symmetrical, shield-like scales (b) .... **Scincidae** (Skinks)

4 Tongue long, slender, sheathed at its base and deeply forked like that of a snake(c); tongue frequently flicked in and out when lizard is alert .... **Varanidae** (Goannas or Monitor Lizards)

Tongue broad, flat, not sheathed at its base and with only a slight notch in front(d); tongue not normally protruded except for eating and drinking .... **Agamidae** (Agamid or Dragon Lizards)

DIAGNOSTIC CHARACTERS IN LIZARDS

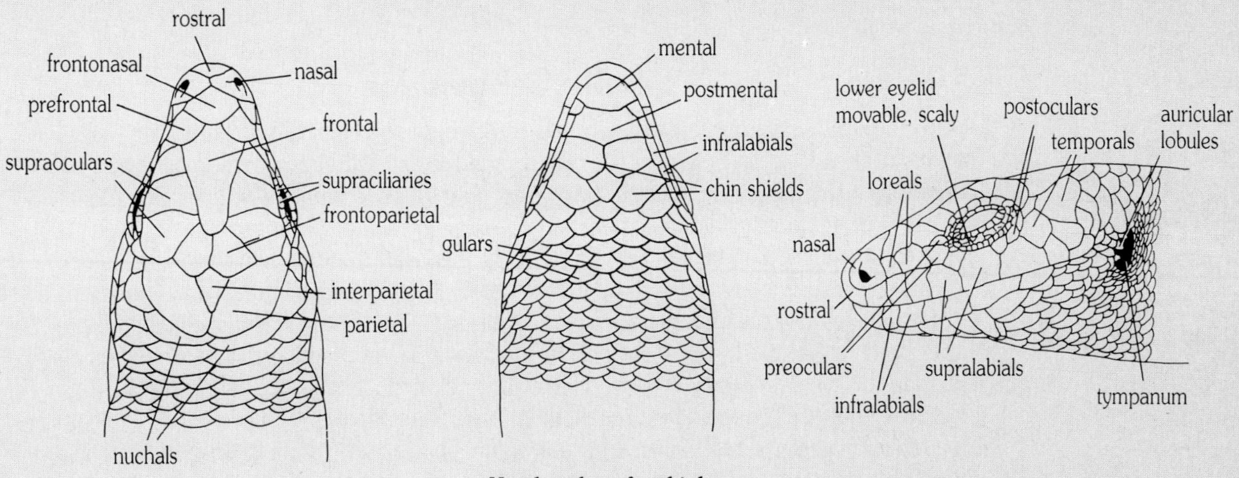

Head scales of a skink

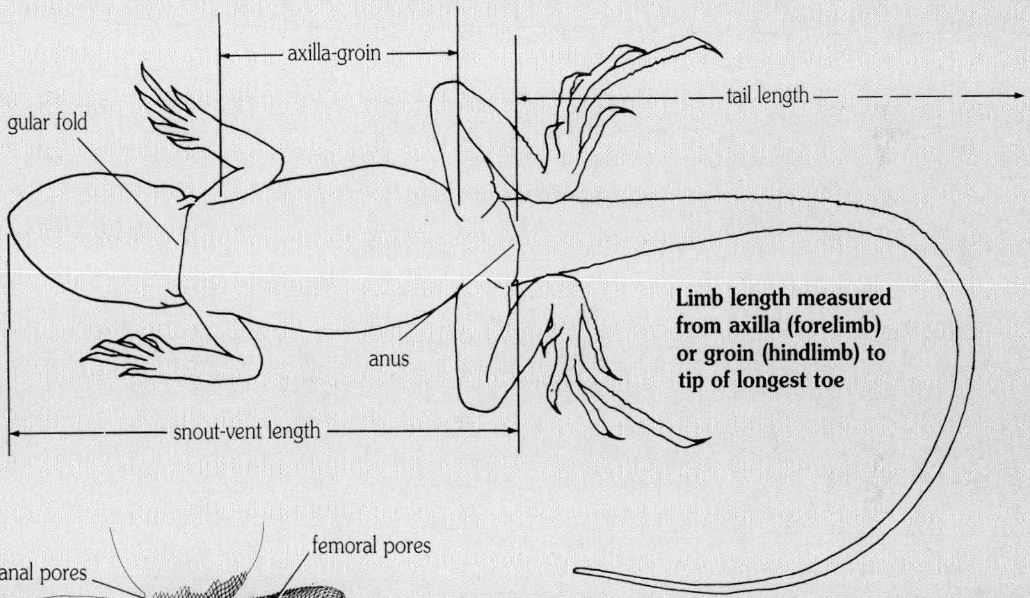

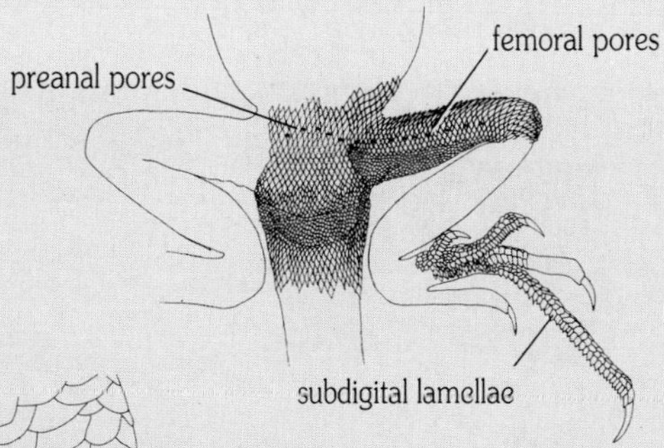

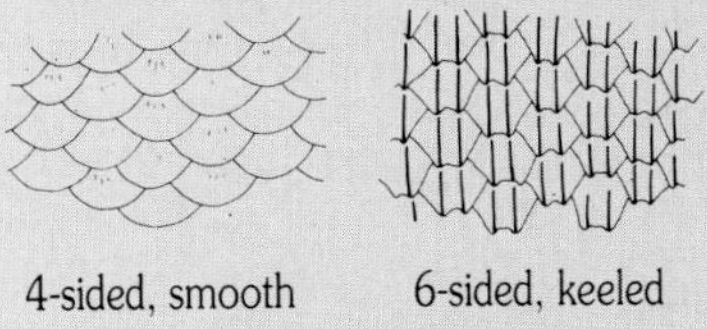

Scales of *Carlia*

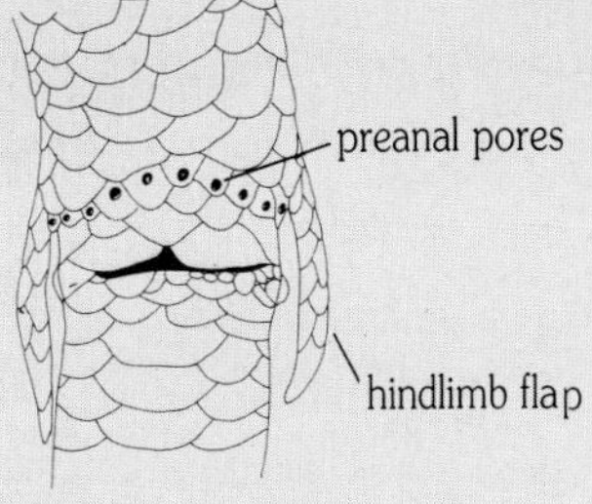

Anal region of pygopodid lizard *(Pygopus lepidopodus)*

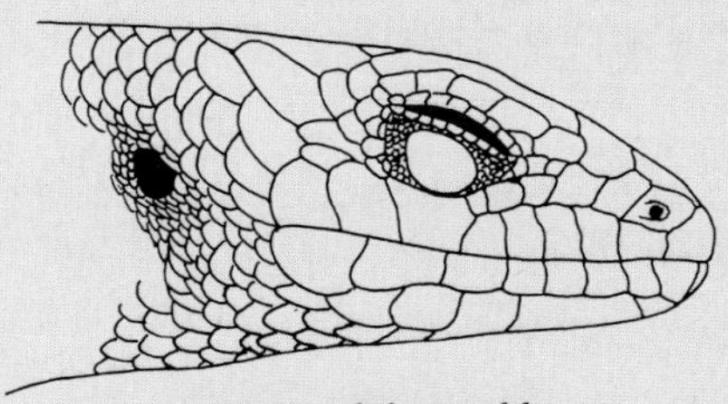

Lower eyelid movable, with transparent disc

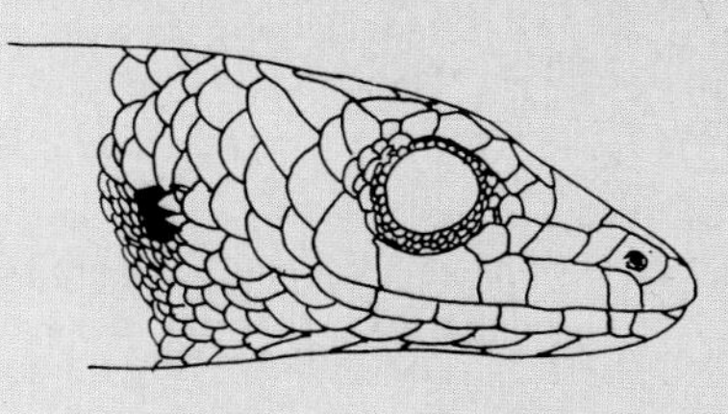

Lower eyelid immovable, fused to form a spectacle

Family Gekkonidae

A large and diverse group of lizards found throughout the tropical and warm temperate regions of the world. In Australia the 60-odd species are rather small, more or less soft-bodied nocturnal lizards with well-developed pentadactyle limbs. The eyes are snake-like, without movable eyelids, the eye being covered by a transparent spectacle, which is shed with the skin. The broad, flat, fleshy tongue is used to keep the lidless eyes clean. The pupil is a vertical slit, or a vertical series of pinhole openings in daylight. The scales of the body are usually juxtaposed. Preanal pores are present in many species, and are either better developed or present only in the males. Males are also characterised by an enlarged, bulbous, postanal region, often with one or more enlarged tubercles on each side. An external ear opening is present in all Australian species.

Geckos may be terrestrial or arboreal, a few species sheltering in shallow burrows during the day. They feed on small arthropods (some larger species eat smaller lizards). All Australian species are oviparous, the majority of species laying two eggs to a clutch.

The digits of many geckos are expanded with specially modified pads which permit the gecko to climb vertical surfaces, or even, in some species, to cling to a surface as smooth as glass, or upside down on the ceiling of a cave or house. In the northern part of Australia several species become 'house geckos', where they feed on the many insects attracted to indoor and outdoor lights.

Autotomy — or voluntary tail loss — is common in members of this family, although once lost the tail can regenerate.

Key

TO THE GENERA OF AUSTRALIAN GEKKONID LIZARDS

1 Digits without any enlarged subdigital tubercles or lamellae(a).. **2**

Digits with at least a pair of enlarged subdigital tubercles or lamellae(b).. **4**

2 Rostral and mental shields rounded(c); labials much larger than adjacent scales(e), or, if subequal, tail not much longer than broad, strongly depressed.. **3**

Rostral and mental shields projecting, beak-like(d); labials and adjacent scales subequal(f); tail long and slender.. ***Rhynchoedura***

3 Tail ending in a globular knob(g); several scales between rostral and nostril(h).. ***Nephrurus***

Tail long and slender, not ending in a knob; rostral contacting nostril or separated from it by only one scale.. ***Lucasium***

4 Digits lying flat, entirely on the substrate when viewed laterally(i); terminal claws, if present, small and lying in a groove between distal lamellae(k) or arising from the upper surface of a large digital expansion(l).. **5**

Digits angular when viewed laterally(j); feet bird-like, their terminal claws conspicuous and free(m).. **12**

5 At least some digits with claws.. **6**

All digits without claws.. ***Crenadactylus***

6 A distal pair of enlarged plates on the lower surface of each digit, quite distinct from and discontinuous with the remaining subdigital lamellae or tubercles(b).. **7**

The enlarged subdigital lamellae in a continuous series(n).. **9**

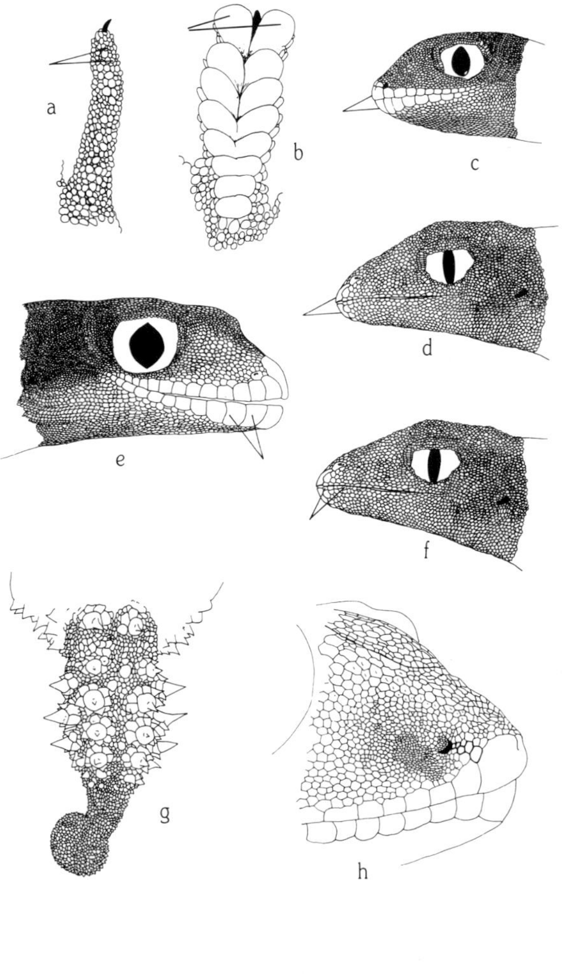

7 Distal subdigital lamellae (excluding enlarged apical plates) single(o).. **8**

Distal subdigital lamellae (excluding enlarged apical plates) paired(b).. ***Oedura***

8 Scales above distal expansions of digits significantly larger than scales above basal parts of digits(p).........***Christinus***

Scales above distal expansions of digits more or less equal in size to those above basal parts of digits(q)... ***Diplodactylus***

9 Claws of digits free, arising from the upper surface of the digital expansion well within the border of the expansion(l). **10**

Claws of digits arising from the edge of the digital expansion(r).. **11**

10 Inner toe of each foot clawless...............................***Gehyra***

Inner toe of each foot clawed.................... ***Hemidactylus***

11 Claws of digits small, sessile and retractile in the distal median groove (r) .... ***Pseudothecadactylus***

Claws of digits large, not retractile in a distal median groove(s)... ***Lepidodactylus***

12 Postmentals greatly enlarged(t); tail long and slender, without large spines.. **13**

Postmentals and adjacent gulars subequal(u); tail swollen, or broad and flattened, or covered in large spines.......... **15**

13 Claw between three scales(v); two rows of lateral scales on digits(y)... ***Heteronotia***

Claw between two scales, the lower deeply notched(w); three rows of lateral scales on digits(z)........................ **14**

14 A lateral skin fold from axilla to groin...... ***Cyrtodactylus***

No lateral skin fold from axilla to groin................. ***Nactus***

15 Claw between two or three scales, body not laterally compressed... **15**

Claw between five scales(x); body laterally compressed... .... ***Carphodactylus***

16 Claw between two scales, the lower deeply notched; digits compressed with three or more rows of lateral scales; tail long, with large spines, or strongly depressed, leaf-shaped, more than twice as broad as thick .... ***Phyllurus***

Claw typically between two scales, but lower scale may be deeply grooved or even divided; digits with two rows of lateral scales; tail without spines, less than twice as broad as thick... ***Underwoodisaurus***

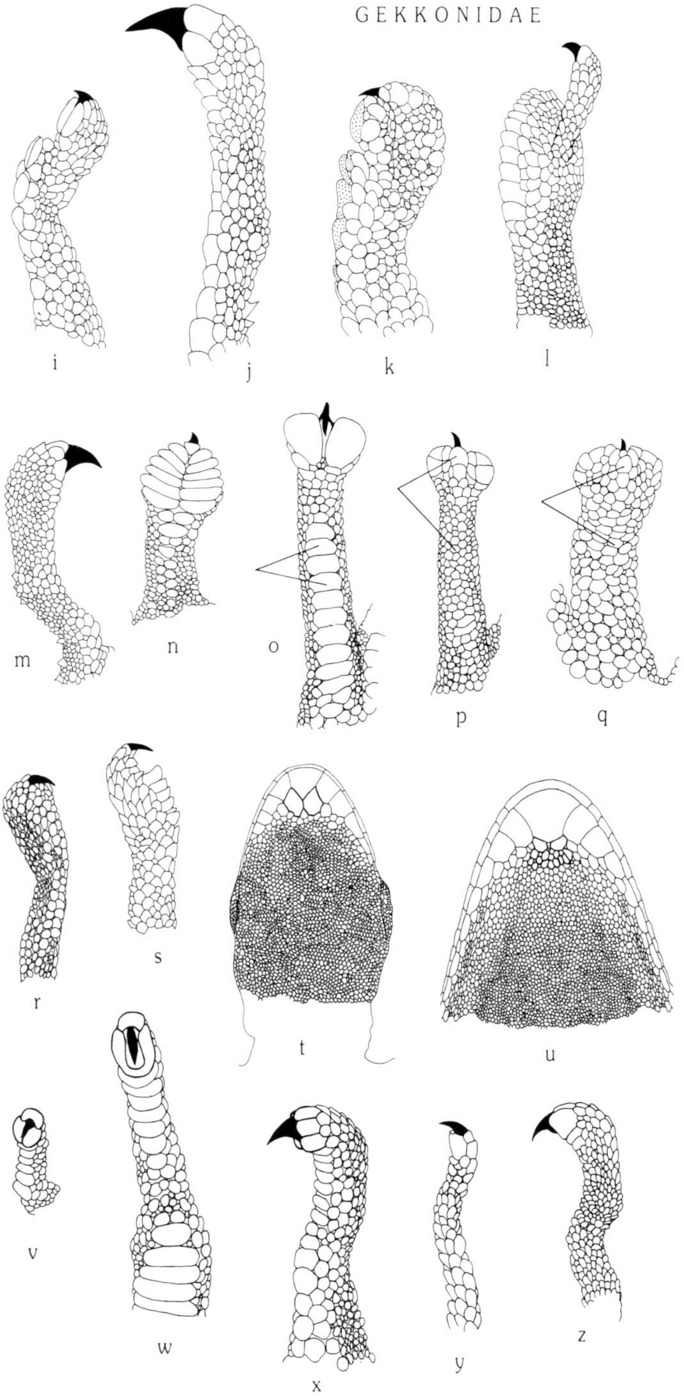

Genus ***Carphodactylus*** Günther, 1897

A monotypic genus confined to Australia. Rostral and mental shields rounded. Labials much larger than adjacent scales. Postmentals and adjacent gulars subequal. Digits long, slender, only slightly compressed distally and without enlarged apical subdigital lamellae, but with a single series of slightly swollen transverse lamellae; feet bird-like, the digits angular when viewed laterally; all digits clawed, the claws conspicuous and free, the base of each claw between five scales. Preanal pores present.

Carphodactylus laevis Lake Barrine, Qld

Carphodactylus laevis Thornton Peak, Qld

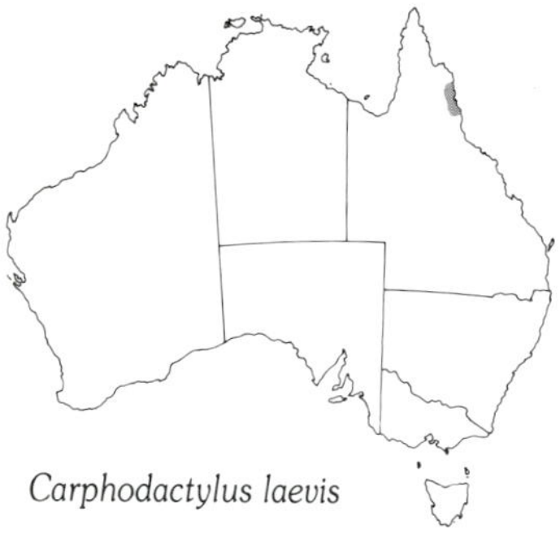

Carphodactylus laevis

Carphodactylus laevis Günther, 1897

Chameleon Gecko

Description: Rich brown above, flecked with obscure, small, paler brown spots and with a series of small black flecks on the back tending to be concentrated along the vertebral line. Snout pale brown above, darker on the top of the head. A broad blackish streak from the snout to the eye, and a narrow black streak above the pale tympanum. A pale labial streak merging with the pale tympanum. Original tail dark brown to black, with four or five complete, narrow, whitish crossbands. Reproduced tails brown speckled with darker. Lower surface purplish-white peppered and freckled with darker grey-brown. A slender, lightly-built lizard with compressed body and tail and a distinctive vertebral ridge from nape to tail. Body scales small, homogeneous. Limbs long and thin. 13 cm (snout-vent).
Distribution: North-eastern Qld, from about Tully north to Cooktown.
Habit: Found only in rainforest areas where it hides in litter by day, emerging at night to climb and forage among low vegetation and debris on the forest floor. Habits otherwise unknown.

Genus *Christinus* Wells and Wellington, 1984

An endemic Australian genus whose two members were until recently assigned to the large tropicopolitan genus *Phyllodactylus*.

Rostral and mental shields rounded. Labials larger than adjacent scales. Postmentals enlarged. Digits rather long, slender, depressed and moderately expanded distally to form distinct pads; a greatly enlarged pair of apical subdigital lamellae, followed by a single series of enlarged, transverse lamellae; scales above the distal expansions of the digits significantly larger than the scales above the basal parts of the digits; digits lying flat on the substrate when viewed laterally; all digits clawed, the claws retractile and lying in a groove between the enlarged apical lamellae. Preanal pores absent.

Key

TO THE AUSTRALIAN SPECIES OF CHRISTINUS

Width of distal expansion of fourth toe at least twice the maximum diameter of the ear-opening; fewer than ten scales on the middle of the back in a distance equal to the diameter of the eye.. ***marmoratus***

Width of distal expansion of fourth toe about equal to the maximum diameter of the ear opening; more than ten scales in the middle of the back in a distance equal to the diameter of the eye... ***guentheri***

Christinus guentheri Nepean Island, off Norfolk Island

Christinus guentheri (Boulenger, 1885)

Description: Pale olive-grey to dark brown above, peppered with dark brown and an obscure series of six paler, W-shaped transverse markings continuous with the paler flanks. Original tail with a dull, russet-red mid-dorsal stripe, often extending forward on to the pelvic region. Whitish or yellowish-brown below, peppered with dark brown. Scales on back smooth, very small and homogeneous, more than ten scales in the middle of the back in a distance equal to the diameter of the eye. Fingers and toes relatively long and slender, the width of the distal expansion of the fourth toe about equal to the maximum diameter of the ear-opening. Body somewhat heavily built, rather depressed. 80 mm (snout-vent).
Distribution: Lord Howe Island and its small satellite islands; satellite islands of Norfolk Island.

Christinus guentheri

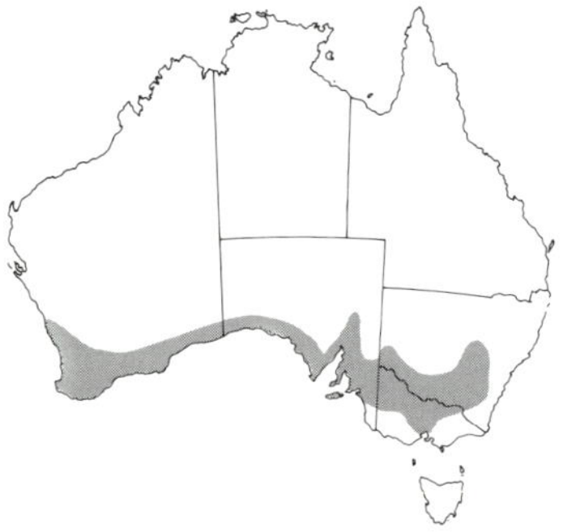

Christinus marmoratus

Habit: An arboreal and rock-dwelling species found on boulder slopes and rock faces, and on trees, especially the White Oak or Norfolk Island Hibiscus *(Lagunaria patersonia)*. Now uncommon on the main island of Lord Howe, where its numbers and range have been reduced by rats and habitat changes, although it is still abundant on the small, rocky, offshore islands on which there are large colonies of sea-birds. On Norfolk Island is has apparently been extinct since before human settlement, and is known only from sub-fossil remains; it is still abundant on the off-shore rocks and islands.

Christinus marmoratus (Gray, 1845)

Marbled Gecko

Description: Grey or brown above, with a complex series of fine blackish markings which tend to form transverse, light-centred bars, but which, almost as often, form a fine reticulated pattern, especially on the head, neck, flanks and limbs. Whitish below. Scales on the back small, but normally fewer than ten scales in the middle of the back in a distance equal to the diameter of the eye. Fingers and toes long and slender, the width of the distal expansion of the fourth toe at least twice the maximum diameter of the ear-opening. Body slender, only slightly depressed. 70 mm (snout-vent).
Distribution: Wetter parts of southern Australia, from central NSW to the coast of WA.
Habit: An arboreal species of dry sclerophyll forests and woodlands, tending to replace *Gehyra variegata* in similar, but colder and wetter, habitats. Lays two brittle-shelled eggs in a clutch.

Christinus marmoratus Warrumbungle Range, NSW

Genus ***Crenadactylus*** Dixon and Kluge, 1964

A monotypic genus confined to Australia. Rostral and mental shields rounded. Labials much larger than adjacent scales. Postmentals enlarged. Digits moderate, fairly strongly depressed, and with a greatly enlarged pair of apical subdigital lamellae followed by a single series of moderately enlarged lamellae; digits lying flat on the substrate when viewed laterally; all digits without terminal claws. Preanal pores present.

Crenadactylus ocellatus McArthur River, NT

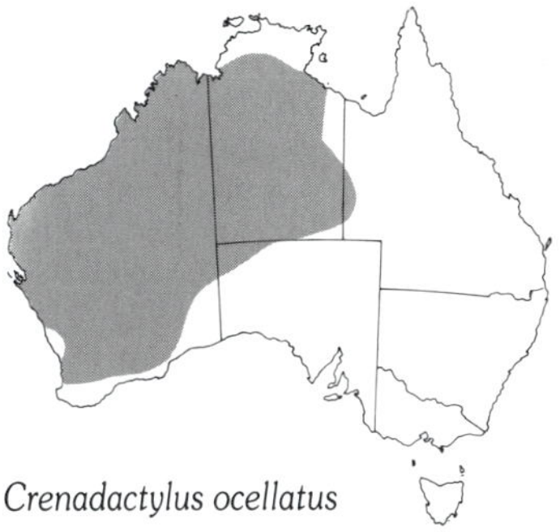

Crenadactylus ocellatus

Crenadactylus ocellatus (Gray, 1845)

Clawless Gecko

Description: Grey-brown or brown above, either with numerous, small, pale, dark-edged ocelli or with a series of narrow, dark brown longitudinal stripes on dorsum and sides, the pale areas between the stripes with somewhat irregular series of tiny whitish dots. Tail long and slender, the colour and pattern of original tail a disrupted version of that on the body. Intermediate patterns are found between these extremes. A dark brown stripe from snout to eye, usually continued behind the eye as a dorso-lateral stripe. Limbs brown dotted with white. Lower surfaces purplish-white, peppered with brown. A small, slender gecko. Body scales homogeneous. 50 mm (snout-vent).

Distribution: Arid, sandy, spinifex-dominated deserts and stony ranges of northern, central and western Australia.

Habit: A nocturnal species which spends most of its life within the shelter of large clumps of *Triodia*. Uncommon, but small, circumscribed, locally abundant populations occur throughout its range.

Subspecies: *ocellatus* (south-western WA); *horni* (arid WA, SA, NT); *rostralis* (southern Kimberleys); *naso* (north-western Kimberleys, WA, to north-eastern NT).

Genus ***Cyrtodactylus*** Gray, 1827

A large genus ranging from south-eastern Europe, through Asia and the Indo-Malayan Archipelago to Australia. Nasal bones paired. No second ceratobranchial rod in the hyoid apparatus. Rostral and mental shields rounded. Labials much larger than adjacent scales. Postmentals enlarged. Digits long, slender, moderately compressed distally with three rows of lateral scales on the digit. No enlarged apical subdigital lamellae but with a series of slightly swollen transverse lamellae; feet bird-like, the digits angular when viewed laterally; all digits clawed, the claws conspicuous and free, the base of each claw between two scales, the lower of which is deeply notched. Preanal pores present.

Cyrtodactylus louisiadensis near Cooktown Qld

Cyrtodactylus louisiadensis (De Vis, 1892) Ring-Tailed Gecko

Description: Spectacularly banded with broad, purplish-brown transverse bands, which may be narrowly edged with white, on a paler brown or olive-brown ground colour. The first of these bands forms a conspicuous collar, stretching on a curve across the nape from eye to eye. Bands on the tail (where the tail is original) almost black and white, except basally. Lips white, sometimes faintly barred. A distinctive, white-edged lateral skinfold. Whitish below. A large, slightly depressed gecko with a broad, flat head and long, slender tail. Body scales small and granular, with numerous scattered small, low, rounded tubercles. Base of tail with large, transverse ventral plates. Males with more than 20 pores. 16 cm (snout-vent).
Distribution: Coast and ranges of north-eastern Qld, as far south as the Atherton Tableland. Extralimital in New Guinea.
Habit: A large, voracious arboreal rainforest gecko. Habits unknown. It has also been recorded from caves and rock fissures in the drier western parts of the Atherton Tableland.

Cyrtodactylus louisiadensis Atherton Tableland, Qld

Cyrtodactylus louisiadensis

Genus ***Diplodactylus*** Gray, 1832

The largest genus of Australian geckos, with all species confined to continental Australia. The genus includes a wide variety of small to moderate terrestrial and arboreal geckos. Rostral and mental shields rounded. Labials larger than or equal to the adjacent scales. Postmentals usually enlarged. Digits moderate to short, round or depressed, and with an enlarged pair of apical subdigital lamellae followed by a single row of transverse enlarged lamellae, or by numerous irregular, small, spinose tubercles; scales above the distal expansions more or less equal in size to those above basal parts of digits; digits lying flat on the substrate when viewed laterally; all digits clawed, the small claws retractile and lying in a groove between the distal lamellae. Preanal pores present or absent.

Key

TO THE SPECIES OF DIPLODACTYLUS

1 Labials reduced to size of granules, more or less equal to or smaller than adjacent loreals(a); dorsal eyelid undifferentiated; mental hemispherical(c); tail strongly depressed. **2**

Labials noticeably larger than adjacent loreals(b); dorsal eyelid well differentiated (poorly so in *pulcher)*; mental lanceolate(d); tail round in cross section......................... **4**

2 Fourth finger and toe lamellae 8 or more and 9 or more respectively; apical plates small or large; colour pattern without large white spots... **3**

Fourth finger and toe lamellae 6-7 and 6-9 respectively; apical plates large; colour pattern consists of large, white spots.. ***savagei***

3 All but first supralabial equal to or smaller than adjacent loreals; colour pattern of dark brown reticulations on a brown ground colour............................. ***conspicillatus***

Supralabials slightly larger than adjacent loreals; colour pattern consists of a pale vertebral zone and white-dotted sides on a dark brown ground colour............ ***kenneallyi***

4 Digits relatively short, wide, obviously depressed; apical plates greatly enlarged; secondary lamellae broad; primary, secondary and tertiary lamellae distinct(e); lateral pair of cloacal bones absent in males............................. **5**

Digits usually moderately long, relatively narrow, not obviously depressed; apical plates not greatly enlarged; secondary lamellae not broad (rarely so in *vittatus*); primary, secondary and tertiary lamellae rarely distinguishable(f); lateral pair of cloacal bones present in males(g) **19**

5 Anterior nasal present, rostral does not border margin of nostril(h); colour pattern consists of obvious dorsal and lateral stripes; dorsal body and caudal scalation homogeneous; preanal pores absent.. **6**

Anterior nasal absent, rostral borders margin of nostril(i); colour pattern rarely consists of both dorsal and ventral body stripes; dorsal body and caudal scalation heterogeneous (except in *taenicauda)*; preanal pores present in males (except in *elderi*).. **9**

6 Nostril usually surrounded by fewer than seven scales.... **7**

Nostril usually surrounded by more than seven scales...... .... ***mcmillani***

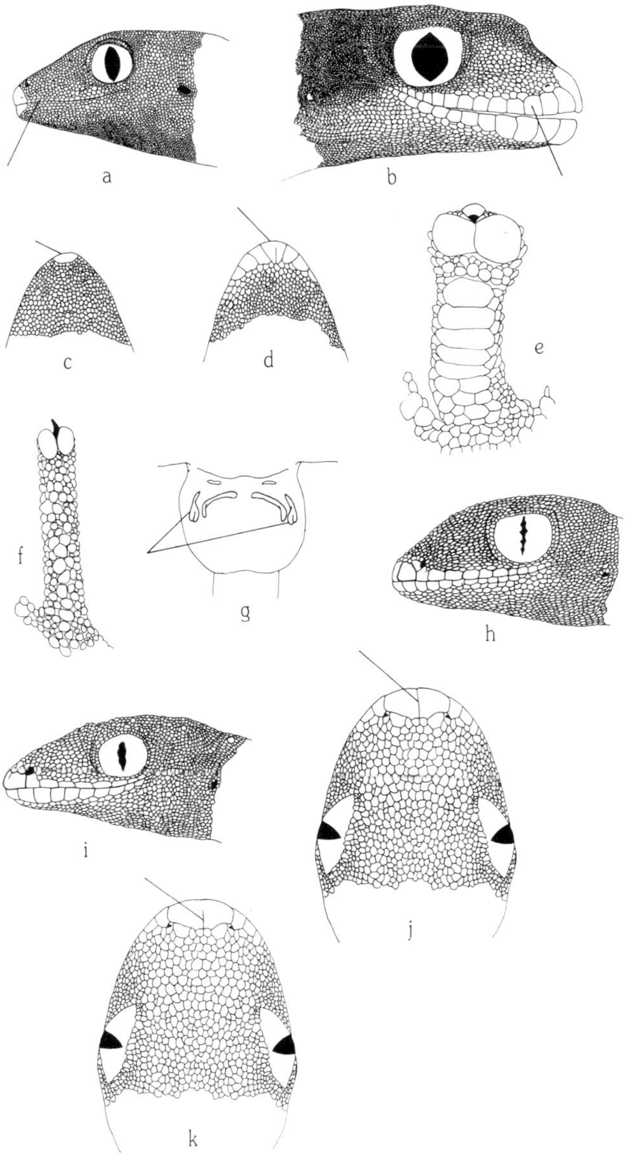

7 Rostral crease almost or completely dividing the rostral(j); a conspicuous pale ventral stripe; body extremely thin and slender.. **8**

Vertical rostral crease incomplete, extending only about half way down the rostral(k); no ventral stripe; body moderate in build.. ***michaelseni***

8 Rostral excluded from nostril.......................... ***taeniatus***

Rostral contacting nostril...................................... ***jeanae***

9 Colour pattern not ocellate; preanal pores present in males(s).. **10**

Colour pattern consists of ocelli (enlarged white tubercles surrounded by rosettes of smaller dark brown or black scales); preanal pores absent in males.................... ***elderi***

10 Dorsal body scalation heterogeneous(l); granules and tubercles or spines present; orange stripe and black spots absent on dorsal surfaces.. **11**

Dorsal body scalation homogeneous(m); bright orange mid-dorsal stripe present over pelvic region and tail, other dorsal surfaces covered with small, irregular dark spots... .... ***taenicauda***

11 Caudal annuli not separated from each other by a band of connective tissue; tubercles or spines not obviously variable in size, generally conical or spinose and generally concentrated on middle one-third of body................... **12**

Caudal annuli separated from each other by a narrow band of white, pink or salmon fibrous connective tissue(n); tubercles extremely variable in size, oval, randomly scattered over dorsal surfaces of head, body and limbs. .... ***strophurus***

12 Caudal spines short to long, blunt or sharp, not in four distinct parallel rows; supraciliaries short to very long; dorsal body tubercles or spines discontinuous or zigzag, rarely in two parallel longitudinal rows.......................... **13**

Caudal spines relatively short, sharply pointed, forming four distinct, parallel, longitudinal rows; supraciliaries short; one or two parallel longitudinal rows of sharply-pointed mid-dorsal body spines........................ ***williamsi***

13 Colour grey and black; prominent dark mid-dorsal body and caudal stripe present; supraciliaries short(o).......... **14**

Colour brown, rarely grey or black; mid-dorsal body and caudal stripe generally absent, indistinct when present; supraciliaries short(o) to extremely long(p).................. **15**

14 Dorsal body and caudal spines long, very pointed, black or black and white... ***spinigerus***

Dorsal body and caudal tubercles short, blunt, brown or orange.. ***assimilis***

15 Supraciliaries almost always long(p); heterogeneous dorsal and body scalation with spines (rarely tubercles); dorsal body spines generally in two parallel longitudinal rows; intracaudals almost always homogeneous(q)................ **16**

Supraciliaries short; heterogeneous dorsal body and caudal scalation with or without tubercles; dorsal body tubercles, when present, in two parallel longitudinal rows; intracaudals distinctly heterogeneous(r)....................... **17**

16 Dorsal tubercles scattered irregularly over back... ***ciliaris***

Dorsal tubercles more or less in two parallel rows............ .... ***wellingtonae***

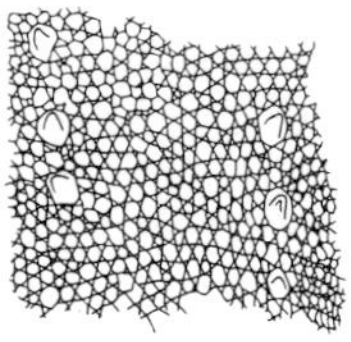

l

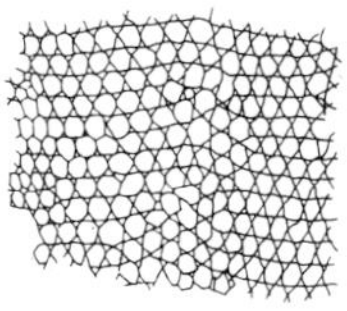

m

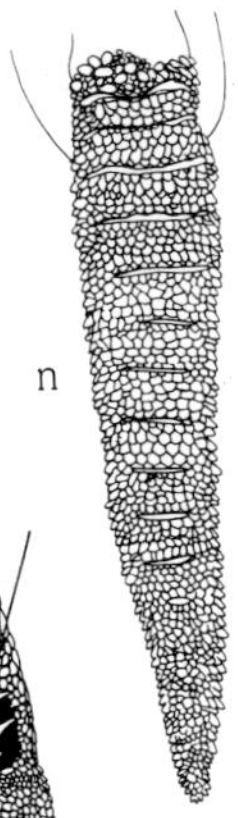

n

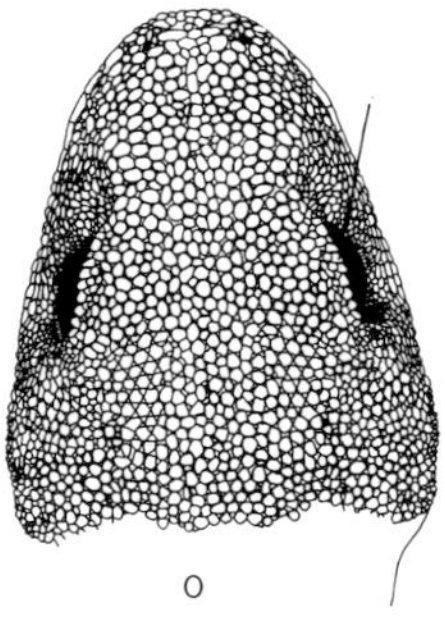

o

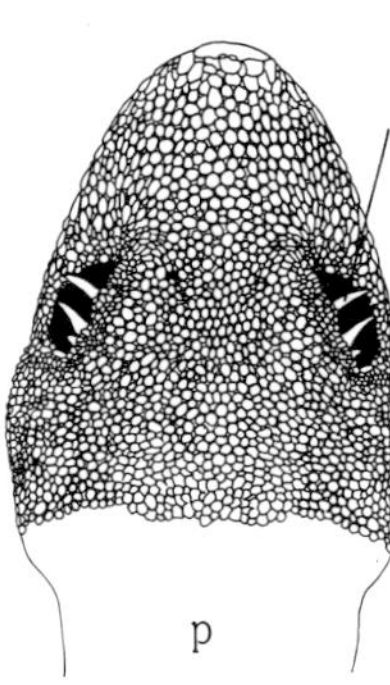

p

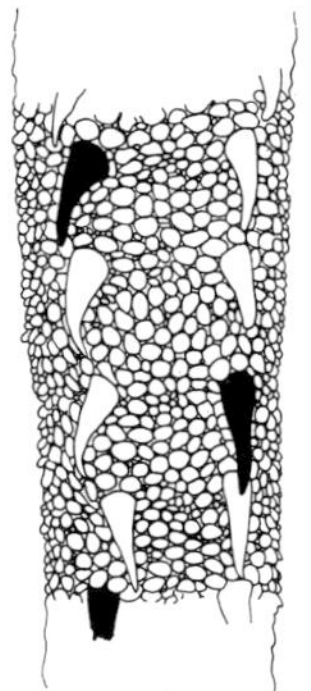

q

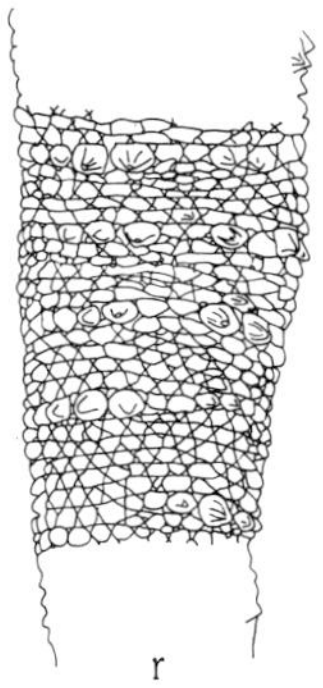

r

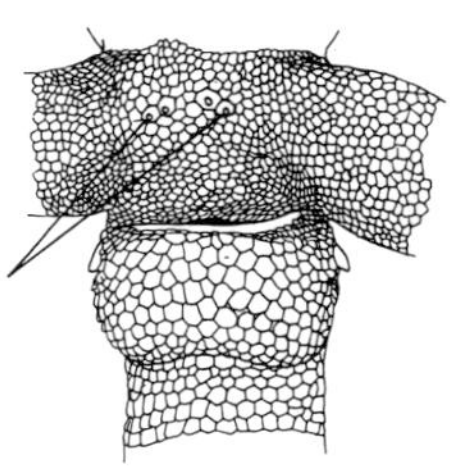

s

17 Dorsal pattern usually obscure, with grey darker markings.. **18**

Dorsal pattern usually strongly contrasting, with black markings.. ***intermedius***

18 A series of slightly enlarged dorso-lateral tubercles along the body; tail about 65% of snout-vent length; colour pattern with broad, dark zigzag vertebral zone......... ***rankini***

No enlarged dorso-lateral tubercles along the body; tail only about 50% of snout-vent length; colour pattern of faint longitudinal stripes...................................... ***wilsoni***

19 Preanal pores present in males(s)................................ **20**

Preanal pores absent in both sexes.............................. **21**

20 Male cloacal spur usually consists of less than three large spines, rarely three(t).. **23**

Male cloacal spur usually consists of more than two spines, rarely two, five to seven common(u)..................... .... ***steindachneri***

21 Male cloacal spur usually consists of less than three large spines, rarely three(t).. **22**

Male cloacal spur usually consists of more than two spines, rarely two, five to seven common(u)................. **27**

22 Back pattern consisting of four large, pale squarish or rhomboidal blotches on a darker ground; northern NT..... .... ***occultus***

Back pattern consisting of an irregular pale vertebral stripe or discontinuous pale vertebral blotches in a zigzag pattern... ***maini***

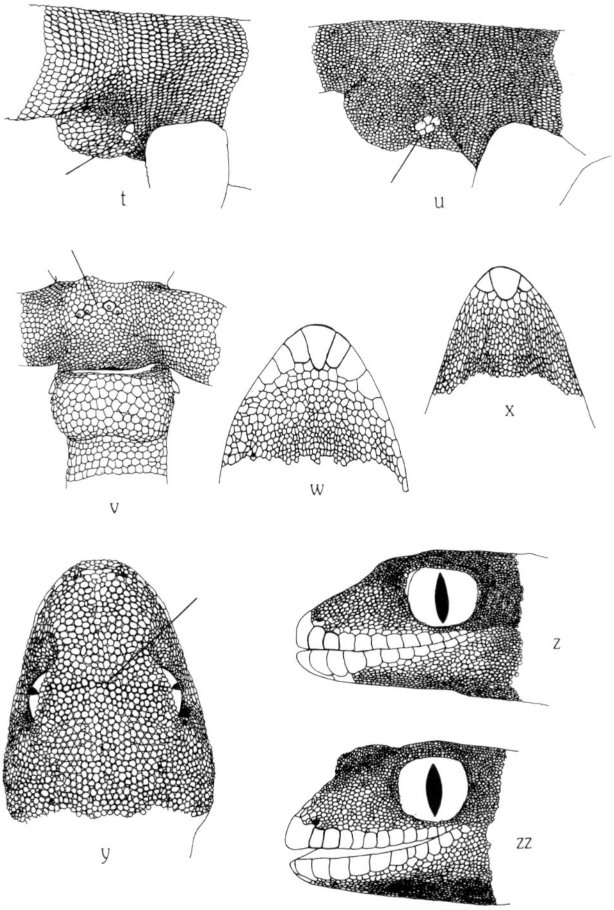

23 Rostral crease almost always present(k); interpore scales(v) in males 1-5 (mean less than 3.5); rostral 1.0-2.9 times wider than deep; mid-dorsals usually equal size of ventrals; dorsal body colour pattern usually consists of a light vertebral stripe (in *alboguttatus* the stripe is broken into five or six irregular white marks), white spots indistinct when present..**24**

Rostral crease absent; interpore scales(v) in males 4-7 (mean 5.4); rostral 2.2-3.0 times wider than deep; mid-dorsals usually conical and much larger than ventrals; dorsal body colour pattern usually consists of three large, star-shaped marks on the midline and numerous distinct small white spots on lateral body surfaces............ ***squarrosus***

24 Anterior nasal usually present, excludes rostral from margin of nostril(h); tail length 59-88% of snout-vent length...... ....**25**

Anterior nasal absent, rostral borders nostril(i); tail length 36-91% of snout-vent length...**26**

25 A pale vertebral stripe separate from pale spots on the back and flanks...................................... ***stenodactylus***

A pale vertebral stripe with a series of lateral extensions forming vertical bars on the back and flanks..................... .... ***immaculatus***

26 Large pale spots on limbs and sides of body..................... ....***alboguttatus***

No large, pale spots on limbs and sides of body; at most with small, pale dots and flecks........................ ***wombeyi***

27 Dorsal body scalation homogeneous(m); rostral crease almost always present(k); anterior nasal absent(i) (except in *pulcher*); rostral even with general contour of snout...... ....**28**

Dorsal scalation heterogeneous, consisting of small,conical granules and enlarged cone-shaped tubercles; rostral crease absent; anterior nasal present, rostral excluded from margin of nostril(h); dorsal margin of rostral bulges beyond general contour of snout.......................... ***byrnei***

28 Mental not noticeably pointed, equal to or only slightly larger than first infralabial(w); first supralabial borders margin of nostril; anterior nasal absent; snout round.... **29**

Mental narrow and long, much larger than first infralabial(x); first supralabial does not border margin of nostril; anterior nasal present, rostral excluded from margin of nostril(h); snout obviously pointed...................... ***pulcher***

29 Dorsal body surfaces usually with an obvious colour pattern; ventral body surfaces uniform in colour; interorbitals(y) usually 23 or more...**30**

Dorsal body surfaces with at most an obscure colour pattern; ventral body surfaces almost always covered with moderately large patches of dark colour; interorbitals usually fewer than 25.................................... ***tessellatus***

30 Length of tail more than 52% of snout-vent length; postocular band usually absent, when present not continuous behind occipital region; dorsum of body without large, enclosed pale diamonds or circles............................... **31**

Length of tail less than 53% of snout-vent length; postocular band of dark colour continuous behind occipital region; four to six large, pale diamond-shaped or circular marks on dorsum of body................................ ***galeatus***

31 Mid-dorsal body scales not enlarged and plate-like, usually only slightly larger than ventrals; interorbitals 23-38....... ....**32**

Mid-dorsal body scales large and plate-like, one and a half to three times larger than ventrals; interorbitals 24-28....... .... ***mitchelli***

32 No indication of a pale, dark-edged vertebral stripe or series of blotches...**33**

A pale, dark-edged vertebral stripe or series of large, pale vertebral blotches; flanks dark, with at most some small, pale spots..**34**

33 Dorsum and flanks dark reddish-brown with scattered paler reddish-brown spots................. ***polyophthalmus***

Dorsum and flanks reddish-brown with an obscure darker reticulum... ***fulleri***

34 Flanks dark brown or black with at most a series of small, pale whitish dots...**35**

Flanks with a series of large, pale white spots or blotches.. .... ***ornatus***

35 First supralabial higher than second(z); flanks almost invariably with small, pale spots which are sometimes dark-edged... ***vittatus***

First supralabial not higher than second (zz); flanks with or without small pale spots which are never dark-edged.... .... ***granariensis***

Diplodactylus alboguttatus
Quobba, WA

R. W. G. JENKINS

Diplodactylus alboguttatus

Diplodactylus assimilis near Yellowdine, WA

M. PETERSON

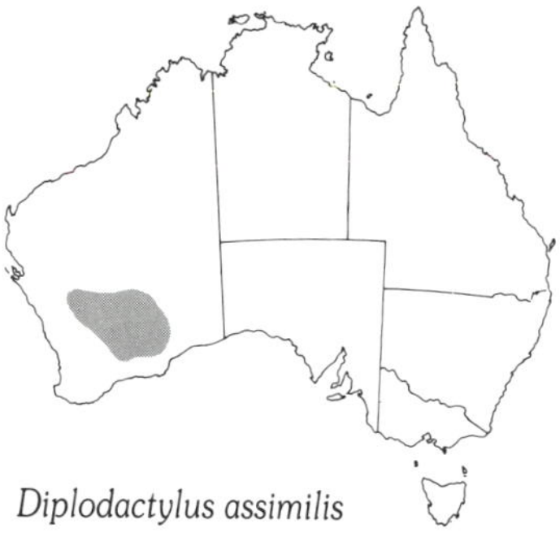

Diplodactylus assimilis

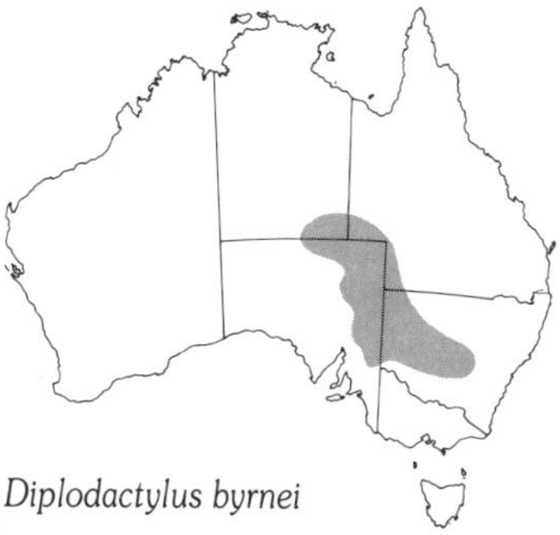

Diplodactylus byrnei

Diplodactylus alboguttatus
Werner, 1910

Description: Pale fawn or brown above; a series of irregular pale blotches on the head and back narrowly edged with darker brown. A dark brown stripe from the snout to the eye, continued behind the eye to the temporal region. Sides grey or grey-brown with one or two series of large whitish spots. Limbs brown above with small white spots and fine brown reticulations over the area between the spots. Whitish below. Body moderate. Tail long (90% of snout-vent), more or less round in section. Dorsal scales small, juxtaposed, homogeneous, slightly larger than ventrals. Rostral partly divided above. Mental lanceolate. Supralabials 7-10, larger than adjacent loreals. Nostril contacting rostral. Preanal pores in males. Postanal tubercles 2-3. Digits long, round, scarcely depressed, with a moderately enlarged pair of subapical lamellae and remaining lamellae small, tubercular and undifferentiated. 55 mm (snout-vent).
Distribution: West coast of WA, south of Shark Bay.
Habit: Terrestrial, primarily in heathlands.

Diplodactylus assimilis Storr, 1988

Description: Grey above with a broad, zigzag, paler grey dorso-lateral zone on either side which may be continuous or arranged as a series of elongated blotches; this zone commences on the canthus, and is sometimes dark-edged. Original tail sometimes with a dark vertebral stripe. Ventral surfaces whitish, with scattered dark grey or brown dots and flecks. Body moderate. Tail slender, long, averaging about 65% of snout-vent length. Dorsal and flank scales heteroge-

neous, the smaller juxtaposed scales interspersed with enlarged, brown or orange tubercles arranged in a more or less zigzag dorso-lateral row on either side of the back, continued on the tail as scattered tubercles arranged roughly in four parallel rows. Rostral usually completely divided. Mental lanceolate. Supralabials 10-16, larger than adjacent loreals. Nostril contacting rostral. Preanal pores present in males. Postanal tubercles 1-4. Digits wide, long, depressed, below with a large pair of apical plates followed by three sets of enlarged lamellae, the largest distal. 70 mm (snout-vent).
Distribution: Southern interior of WA.

Diplodactylus byrnei Lucas and Frost, 1896

Description: Pale creamy-fawn to reddish-brown or dark brown above, with scattered darker flecks and spots and some tiny pale dots, and usually with a distinct series of four or five conspicuous, irregular W-shaped dark brown transverse bars or blotches between nape and hindlimbs. Top of head paler with dark mottling. Tail with a longitudinal series of alternate white and dark brown blotches. Feet pale. Whitish below. Body moderate. Tail long (75% of snout-vent), rather slender, more or less round in section. Dorsal and flank scales heterogeneous, consisting of minute, juxtaposed conical scales, through which are scattered numerous, small, conical tubercles. Rostral greatly enlarged without a median groove. Mental lanceolate. Supralabials 6-9, much larger than adjacent loreals. Nostril separated from rostral by an anterior nasal scale. Preanal pores absent. Postanal tubercles 2-7. Digits long, narrow, slightly depressed below with a moderately enlarged pair of apical lamellae followed by slightly enlarged but otherwise undifferentiated scales. 55 mm (snout-vent).
Distribution: Central and southern interior of NSW and eastern half of SA, extending into adjacent border regions of Qld and NT.
Habit: Terrestrial, hiding in ground litter, holes and ground crevices during the day, and emerging at night to forage in open areas. Found in a wide range of habitats from mallee and open woodland to saltbush and sandy desert.

Diplodactylus ciliaris Boulenger, 1885

Spiny-tailed Gecko

Description: Highly variable in colour. NT specimens vary from almost uniform pale silvery-grey, with a few scattered black and orange-brown scales,

Diplodactylus byrnei Roto, NSW

Diplodactylus ciliaris Alligator Rivers region, NT

Diplodactylus ciliaris Jabiru, NT

Diplodactylus ciliaris

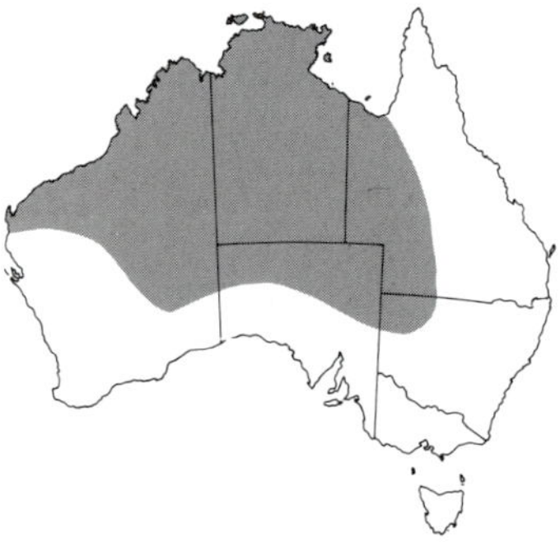

through various shades of grey or grey-brown with only minor darker markings, to rich brown with a broad mottled pattern made up of groups of grey, orange or white scales. Spines or tubercles on back and tail usually orange or orange and black. Whitish below. Colour and pattern of the iris often brilliant and complex. Body moderate. Tail long (about 65% of snout-vent), relatively slender, round or slightly depressed. Dorsal scales heterogeneous, consisting of small, conical, angular scales giving a rasp- or file-like appearance to the skin, with a series of scattered, or in two or more longitudinal rows, low conical tubercles or spines on the body, and with two longitudinal series of tubercles or long spines along the top of the tail. Rostral partially, or completely, divided. Mental usually lanceolate. Supralabials 7-12, larger than adjacent loreals. Nostril contacting rostral. Posterior supraciliaries tubercular or spiny. Preanal pores present in males. Postanal tubercles 1-3. Digits moderate, depressed, below with a pair of apical lamellae, followed by enlarged lamellae in three distinct series. 85 mm (snout-vent).

Distribution: Arid interior of all mainland states (except Vic.) to coastal regions of mid-northern and north-western Australia.

Habit: Normally arboreal, but some populations live in spinifex in arid regions. Found in a wide variety of habitats from tropical coastal forests to the

arid interior. One of a group of *Diplodactylus* able to exude a viscous fluid from the base of spines or tubercles on the tail.
Subspecies: *ciliaris* (northern half of NT to far northern WA); *aberrans* (coast of northwestern WA through arid interior to southern NT, northern SA, western NSW and southwestern Qld).

Diplodactylus conspicillatus

Lucas and Frost, 1897
Fat-Tailed Diplodactylus

Description: Pale fawn to reddish- or dark brown above, finely or coarsely reticulated with darker brown and often with scattered small pale spots. A dark streak between snout and eye, pale-edged above, and sometimes continued for a short distance behind the eye. Lips whitish. Limbs above usually paler than body. Whitish below. Body moderate or somewhat stout. Tail short (about 40% of snout-vent), broad, slightly to strongly depressed. Dorsal and flank scales homogeneous, large, low, juxtaposed. Original tail with large, plate-like scales alternating with regular rings of large, conical tubercles. Rostral without a median groove. Mental hemispherical, wider than long. All but first supralabial small, granular, no larger than adjacent loreals. Nostril separated from rostral by an anterior nasal scale. Preanal pores absent. Postanal tubercles 3-8. Digits short, thick, scarcely depressed, below with a small pair of apical lamellae followed by a series of undifferentiated small scales. 60 mm (snout-vent).
Distribution: Coastal regions to interior of WA and NT, but confined to the drier inland regions of Qld, NSW and SA. Not found in Vic or Tas.
Habit: Terrestrial. Found in a wide variety of habitats, ranging from sandy spinifex-dominated sand deserts to stony hills and ranges.

Diplodactylus conspicillatus White Cliffs Station, WA

Diplodactylus elderi Ethabuka Station, Qld

Diplodactylus elderi Stirling and Zietz, 1893

Jewelled Gecko

Description: Dark brown to velvety grey or black above, with scattered small, dark-edged white spots associated with the enlarged tubercles described below. Dirty white below with scattered darker and paler flecks and spots. Body moderate. Tail moderate (about 55% of snout-vent length), stout, moderately depressed. Scales of back and sides heterogeneous, consisting of small, rounded, juxtaposed scales through which are scattered larger, low, conical white tubercles, each tubercle the centre of a rosette of small, blackish scales. Rostral partly divided above. Mental lanceolate. Supralabials 5-8, larger than adjacent loreals. Nostril contacting rostral. Preanal pores absent. Postanal tubercles 1-3. Digits long, wide, moderately depressed, below with a large pair of apical lamellae followed by three series of well-differentiated lamellae. 45 mm (snout-vent).
Distribution: Arid regions of north-western Australia, through central and southern Australia to the Murray River mallee of SA.
Habit: Appears to be confined to various species of

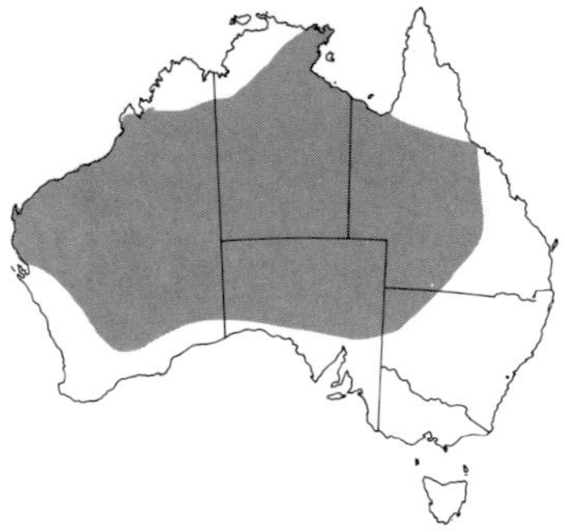

Diplodactylus conspicillatus

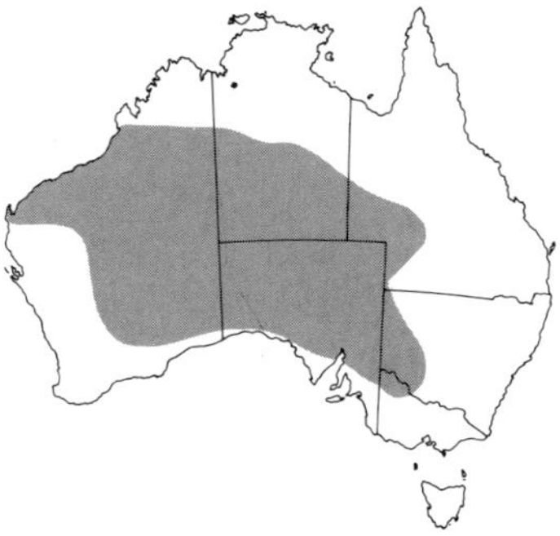

Diplodactylus elderi

Diplodactylus fulleri

Diplodactylus galeatus

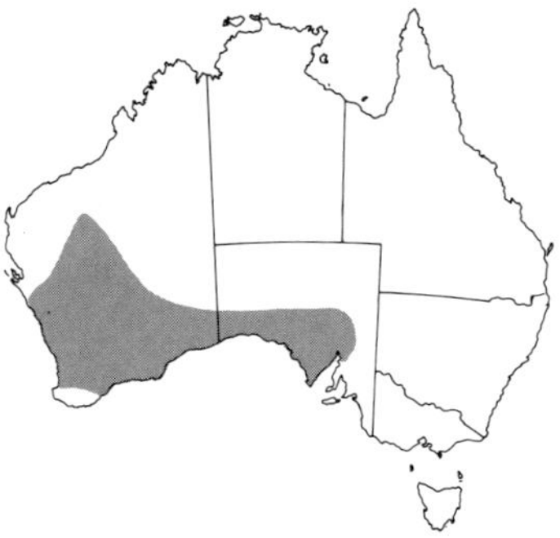

Diplodactylus granariensis

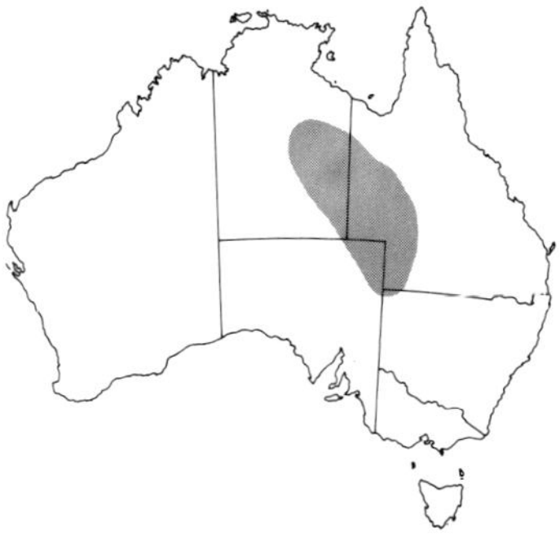

Diplodactylus immaculatus

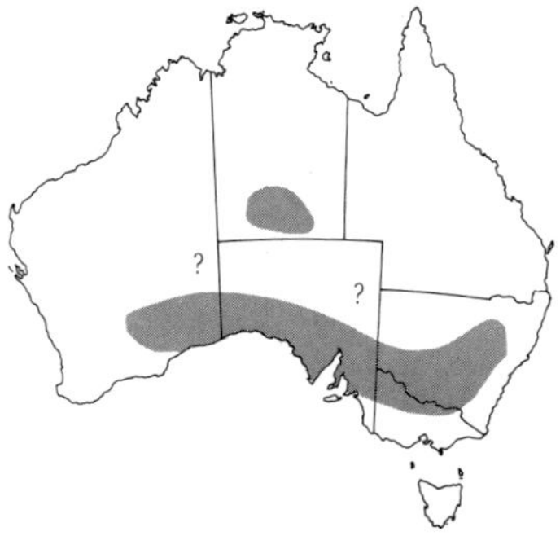

Diplodactylus intermedius

spinifex (*Triodia* spp.) throughout most parts of its range, within a broad range of arid habitats from mallee and sand desert to stony hills. One of the group of species able to exude fluid from its tail.

Diplodactylus fulleri Storr, 1978

Description: Pale reddish-brown above and on the flanks, with an indistinct darker brown reticulum; tail with a series of irregular dark brown cross-bands. Ventral surfaces whitish. Body moderate. Tail moderate, somewhat bulbous basally, about 65% of snout-vent length. Dorsal scales granular, more or less homogeneous, slightly larger than ventrals but much smaller than the large, rectangular, plate-like caudals. Rostral partly divided above by a median groove. Supralabials 9, larger than adjacent loreals. Nostril contacting rostral. Preanal pores absent. Postanal tubercles five. Digits long, slender, slightly depressed, below with a pair of enlarged apical plates followed by undifferentiated conical granules. 50 mm (snout-vent).
Distribution: Currently known only from the type locality, Lake Disappointment, WA.

Diplodactylus galeatus Kluge, 1963

Description: Pale to rich brown or reddish above, with a series of four or five pale transverse blotches, each narrowly edged with dark brown. Head pale, narrowly edged with dark brown which forms a curved line around the occiput from eye to eye. Sometimes some smaller pale spots on the neck or sides, but the latter almost invariably finely dotted with white. Original tail with four pale blotches similar to those on the back. Whitish below. Body moderate. Tail relatively short (about 50% of snout-vent length), slightly depressed. Dorsal and flank scales homogeneous, relatively large, low, juxtaposed or separated by minute granules. Rostral with or without a median groove above. Mental lanceolate. Supralabials 8-10, larger than adjacent loreals. Nostril contacting rostral. Preanal pores absent. Postanal tubercles 5-8, in males only. Digits long, narrow, depressed, below with a large pair of apical lamellae followed by moderately enlarged lamellae in two groups. 50 mm (snout-vent).
Distribution: Mountain ranges and hills of central Australia.
Habit: Appears to be confined to rocky spinifex-covered hills, where it is usually found sheltering under large rock slabs.

Diplodactylus granariensis
Storr, 1979

Description: Similar in colour and pattern to *Diplodactylus vittatus* except that the head may be darker and the pale spots on the flanks are often absent. Body moderate. Tail moderate, not or but slightly depressed. Dorsal and flank scales small, homogeneous, scarcely larger than ventrals. Rostral usually partly divided above by a median groove. Mental lanceolate, usually longer than broad. Supralabials 7-12, larger than adjacent loreals. Nostril contacting rostral. Preanal pores absent. Postanal tubercles long, pointed, 4-14. Digits long, slightly depressed, below with a relatively large pair of apical plates followed by at least two series of enlarged scales, diminishing in size proximally. 50 mm (snout-vent).
Distribution: Southern Pilbara region of WA to Eyre Peninsula, SA.
Habit: A ground-dwelling species.
Subspecies: *granariensis* (south of about 28°S); *rex* (north of about 28°S).

Diplodactylus galeatus Alice Springs, NT

Diplodactylus granariensis near Jerramangup, WA

Diplodactylus immaculatus
Storr, 1988

Description: Reddish-brown above with a pale brown or creamy-white vertebral stripe which commences as canthal and temporal stripes, on either side of the head, which converge into a single stripe on the nape; the pale vertebral stripe has a series of lateral extensions on the back which form a series of disrupted, pale vertical bars on the back and flanks, often alternating with pale flecks and spots. The pale vertebral stripe continues on to original tails as a broad zigzag stripe. Body moderate to slender. Tail long, slender, round in section and nearly as long as the snout-vent length. Dorsal and flank scales homogeneous, small, low, rounded, about same size as the ventrals. Rostral with or without a median groove. Mental lanceolate, longer than wide. Supralabials 9 12, larger than adjacent loreals. Nostril not contacting the rostral. 2 preanal pores present in males. Postanal tubercles 1-2 on each side. Digits long, slender, scarcely depressed, below with a pair of moderately enlarged apical plates followed by a series of moderately-enlarged granules. 75 mm (snout-vent).
Distribution: North-western Qld and adjacent arid interior of NT.
Habit: A terrestrial gecko found in spinifex grassland on sandy soils and on stony ranges throughout its range.

Diplodactylus intermedius Round Hill, NSW

Diplodactylus intermedius Ogilby, 1892
Eastern Spiny-Tailed Gecko

Description: Grey or grey-brown above with scattered black scales usually forming a fine dark reticulum over the body. Original tail usually with black variegations along the vertebral line. Whitish below,

with numerous scattered darker dots and flecks. Body moderate. Tail long (about 65% of snout-vent length), round or only slightly depressed. Dorsal and flank scales heterogeneous, the smaller juxtaposed, conical scales interspersed with enlarged, conical, brown tubercles which tend to form two longitudinal rows, one on either side of the back, and more or less continuous with the two rows of tubercles on the tail. Rostral completely divided. Mental lanceolate. Supralabials 7-10, larger than adjacent loreals. Nostril contacting rostral. Preanal pores present in males. Postanal tubercles 1-4. Digits long, wide, depressed, below with a large pair of apical plates followed by three sets of enlarged lamellae, the largest distal. 65 mm (snout-vent).
Distribution: South-eastern WA, through southern SA and NT, to north-western Vic and western NSW.
Habit: Dry sclerophyll forest, eucalypt and Callitris woodland, and mallee, extending into areas of hummock grassland. Typically arboreal, but often found sheltering in spinifex or foraging on the ground in the more arid parts of its range.

M. PETERSON

Diplodactylus maini Dedari, WA

Diplodactylus jeanae Storr, 1988

Description: Whitish, pale cream or brown above, the top of the head darker brown and usually continuous with a dark brown or orange-brown vertebral stripe. A single faint to conspicuous dorsolateral and ventro-lateral dark brown, orange-brown or grey stripe on either side, the upper of which passes forward through the eye and along the canthus, and the lower of which usually extends forward through the lower part of the eye and along the lips. Limbs variegated with dark grey or brown.

Diplodactylus mcmillani Mitchell Plateau, WA

Pale below, with a broad, dark mid-ventral stripe, at its widest point up to half the width of the belly, and often enclosing a secondary yellow or orange stripe; sometimes an additional stripe on the side of the throat. As in *Diplodactylus taeniatus* the pale areas between the dark stripes may be uniform, but more typically are pale fawn or grey enclosing a pale yellow or orange stripe. Body pattern continuous on tail. Body very slender, limbs spindly. Tail long (about 90% of snout-vent length), slender, more or less round in section. Dorsal and flank scales homogeneous, moderate, low, rounded, juxtaposed, about as large as ventrals. Rostral usually completely divided by a median groove. Mental lanceolate, longer than wide. Supralabials 9-14, larger than adjacent loreals. Rostral bordering nostril. Preanal pores absent. Postanal tubercles 1-2. Digits long, wide, depressed, below with a very large pair of apical lamellae followed by three series of lamellae, diminishing in size proximally. 45 mm (snout-vent).
Distribution: Arid regions of NT and northern WA.
Habit: As for *Diplodactylus taeniatus*, i.e., an inhabitant of various species of spinifex (*Triodia* and *Plechtrachne*) and other desert grasses, where it moves in a distinctive fashion resembling that of certain stick insects. It also belongs to that group of *Diplodactylus* which exudes a viscous fluid from the tail when alarmed.

below with a small pair of apical lamellae followed by a series of undifferentiated small scales. 48 mm (snout-vent).
Distribution: Currently known from a single specimen from the type locality: a stony hill near Lake Buchanan, WA.
Habit: Terrestrial.

Diplodactylus maini Kluge, 1962

Description: Brown above, with an irregular, pale vertebral zone or series of pale discontinuous dorsal blotches in a more or less zigzag pattern. Head pale above with scattered dark brown flecks, and enclosed behind by a broad, curved, dark occipital zone from eye to eye. Sides with scattered dark flecks and irregular pale spots. Whitish below. Body moderate. Tail long (about as long as head and body combined), slender, only slightly depressed. Dorsal scales homogeneous, small, juxtaposed, low and conical, about as large as ventrals. Rostral with or without a slight median division above. Mental lanceolate. Supralabials 7-9, larger than adjacent loreals. Nostril in contact with rostral. Preanal pores absent. Postanal tubercles 1-2. Digits long, slender, round, below with a slightly enlarged pair of apical lamellae followed by small, tubercular undifferentiated scales. 45 mm (snout-vent).
Distribution: Coast and interior of southern WA.
Habit: A terrestrial species found in a variety of woodland, mallee and heath associations.

Diplodactylus kenneallyi Storr, 1988

Description: Brown above, somewhat paler along a broad vertebral zone, the flanks chocolate-brown dotted with white. A faint dark streak between snout and eye, continued for a short distance behind the eye. Lips whitish. Limbs above usually paler than body. Whitish below. Body moderate or somewhat stout. Tail short (about 40% of snout-vent) slightly swollen and depressed. Dorsal and flank scales homogeneous, large, low, juxtaposed. Tail with regular rings of large, plate-like scales. Rostral without a median groove. Mental hemispherical, wider than long. All but first supralabial small, granular, scarcely larger than adjacent loreals. Nostril separated from rostral by an anterior nasal scale. Preanal pores absent. Digits short, thick, scarcely depressed,

Diplodactylus mcmillani Storr, 1978

Description: Olive-grey above, sometimes with four lines of dark brown dots along the back; a broad whitish upper lateral stripe from snout to tail, usually narrowly edged with dark brown; a narrower, pale, midlateral stripe between the limbs, below which is a dark lower lateral stripe; the darker areas of the head and body often give the impression of a series

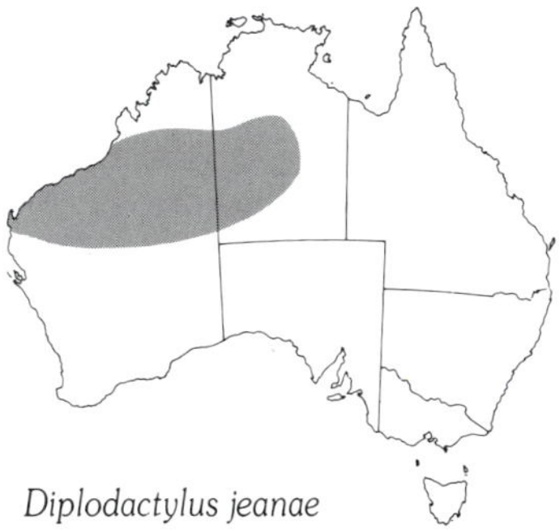

Diplodactylus jeanae

Diplodactylus kenneallyi

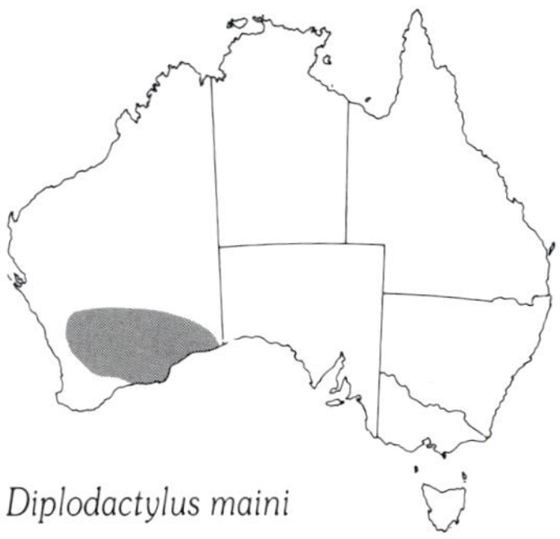

Diplodactylus maini

of pale-centred longitudinal stripes. Ventral surfaces whitish with faint darker longitudinal stripes. Body pattern continuous on tail. Dorsal and flank scales small, homogeneous. Rostral partially divided above by a median groove. Supralabials 12-17, larger than adjacent loreals. Nostril separated from rostral by an anterior nasal. Preanal pores absent. Postanal tubercles 1-2. Digits long, wide, depressed below with a very large pair of apical lamellae followed by three series of lamellae, diminishing in size proximally. 50 mm (snout-vent).
Distribution: North-western Kimberleys, WA.
Habit: '...in *Triodia* growing on sandstone.' (Storr).

Diplodactylus michaelseni
Werner, 1910

Description: Olive-grey above, browner on the head and limbs. A pale brownish-white vertebral stripe from occiput to tail, and a dorso-lateral and mid-lateral stripe of the same colour on either side. Whitish below, with scattered dark brown dots and flecks. Body moderate. Tail moderate (about 70% of snout-vent length), scarcely or not depressed.

Diplodactylus michaelseni Port Hedland, WA

Dorsal scales homogeneous, small, juxtaposed, low and conical. Rostral completely divided medially. Supralabials 7-9, larger than adjacent loreals. Nostril separated from rostral by an anterior nasal scale. Preanal pores absent. Postanal tubercles 1-2. Digits moderate, wide, depressed, below with a pair of very large apical lamellae followed by three series, diminishing in size proximally, of lamellae. 50 mm (snout-vent).
Distribution: Central coast and adjacent interior of WA.
Habit: Storr and Ford found this species in '...clumps of soft spinifex (*Plectrachne* sp.) growing in red undulating sandy country' and '...in sedge tussocks near the edge of an open flat'.

Diplodactylus mitchelli Kluge, 1963

Description: Yellow to dark reddish-brown above, usually with an irregular, pale, whitish vertebral zone, bordered by dark brown, but entire dorsum sometimes with darker reticulations, spots and flecks. A dark temporal stripe sometimes present. Whitish below, lightly peppered with brown. Body moderate. Tail relatively short, broad, moderately depressed. Dorsal scales homogeneous, rather large, flat and juxtaposed. Rostral with or without a partial median division above. Mental lanceolate, longer than wide. Supralabials 7-8, larger than adjacent loreals. Nostril contacting rostral. Preanal pores absent. Postanal tubercles 6-10. Digits long, narrow, depressed, below with a pair of large apical lamellae followed by two series of lamellae diminishing in size proximally. 60 mm (snout-vent).
Distribution: Apparently confined to the Hammersley-North West Cape regions of WA.
Habit: Primarily on spinifex-covered stony flats and hills.

Diplodactylus occultus King, Braithwaite and Wombey, 1982

Description: Dark brown above, reddish on the head; four large, squarish pale brown blotches along back; a dark brown occipital band from eye to eye; whitish spots scattered on flanks and limbs; tail mottled with reddish- and dark brown; labials and ventral surfaces white. Body moderate, tail long, slender and round in section. Dorsal scales homogeneous, small, round and granular, slightly smaller than the flatter ventrals. Rostral divided by a median groove. Mental large and spade-shaped. Supralabials 10, larger than adjacent loreals. Nostril may or may not contact the rostral. Preanal pores absent. Postanal tubercles 2. Digits moderate, scarcely depressed, below with a large pair of apical plates followed by 3 pairs of secondary lamellae and 9 enlarged tertiary lamellae. 40 mm (snout-vent).
Distribution: Alligator Rivers region, NT.
Habit: The only known specimens were taken under grass and ground litter in eucalyptus woodland.

J. WEIGEL

Diplodactylus mitchelli Mt Barnett Station, WA

Diplodactylus ornatus Gray, 1845

Description: Grey, grey-brown or brown above, with a broad, often broken, pale, ragged-edged vertebral stripe which divides on the neck to become a pair of pale stripes extending over eyes to snout, bordered below by a broad, sometimes broken, blackish upper lateral band from snout to tail, enclosing a few pale spots and dots; lower flanks speckled with dark brown. Ventral surface whitish, lightly peppered with dark grey. Body moderate. Tail moderate, at most slightly depressed. Dorsal and flank scales more or less homogeneous, small, scarcely larger than ventrals. Rostral partly divided above by a median groove. Mental lanceolate, about as long as wide. Supralabials 8-11, larger than adjacent loreals. Nostril contacting rostral. Preanal pores absent. Postanal tubercles long, pointed, 3-9. Digits long, slightly depressed, below with relatively large apical plates, usually followed by at least two series of enlarged scales, diminishing in size proximally. 50 mm (snout-vent).
Distribution: Mid-western coast and hinterland, WA.
Habit: Terrestrial; usually found under debris, logs and rocks in open woodlands and heathlands.

Diplodactylus mcmillani

Diplodactylus michaelseni

Diplodactylus mitchelli

Diplodactylus occultus

Diplodactylus ornatus

Diplodactylus polyophthalmus

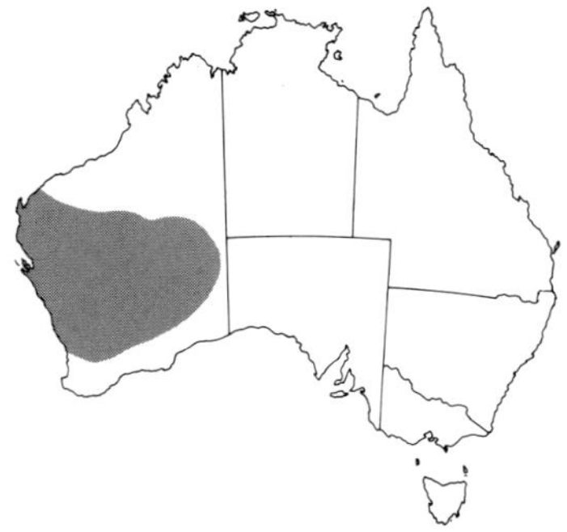

Diplodactylus pulcher

Diplodactylus rankini

Diplodactylus savagei

Diplodactylus spinigerus

Diplodactylus polyophthalmus

Günther, 1867

Description: Reddish-brown above, with scattered pale reddish dots, spots and blotches tending to be smaller and more sharply defined on the flanks; sometimes the paler spots on the dorsum coalesce to form transverse blotches; a dark stripe from snout, through eye, continuous with dark upper lateral zone. Ventral surfaces white, finely peppered with dark brown. Body moderate. Tail moderate, slightly depressed. Dorsal and flank scales small, homogeneous, scarcely larger than ventrals. Rostral partly divided above by a median groove. Mental lanceolate, about as long as wide. Supralabials 8-11, larger than adjacent loreals. Nostril contacting rostral. Preanal pores absent. Postanal tubercles long, pointed, 5-14. Digits long, slightly depressed, below with a relatively large pair of apical plates followed by at least two series of enlarged scales, diminishing in size proximally. 50 mm (snout-vent).
Distribution: Far south-western WA.
Habit: Terrestrial; usually found under debris, logs and rocks in open woodlands and heathlands.

Diplodactylus pulcher (Steindachner, 1870)

Description: Colour pattern highly variable. Usually light brown above, usually with a broad, dark-edged pale vertebral stripe from the pale crown of the head to the tail, or with the stripe replaced by a series of discontinuous, pale irregular blotches. Sides and limbs with scattered white spots and flecks. Whitish below. Body moderate. Tail moderate (about 60% of snout-vent length), more or less round in section. Dorsal scales homogeneous, large, flat, juxtaposed, larger than ventrals. Rostral with a median groove above. Mental large, lanceolate, longer than broad. Supralabials 9-13, the first greatly enlarged but all larger than adjacent loreals. Nostril usually separated from the rostral by an anterior nasal scale. Preanal pores absent. Postanal tubercles 3-13. Digits long, narrow, slightly depressed, below with a pair of moderately enlarged apical lamellae followed by uniform small scales. 50 mm (snout-vent).
Distribution: Coast and interior of central and southern WA.
Habit: Terrestrial, occupying a wide range of dry forest, woodland and scrubland habitats throughout its range.

Diplodactylus rankini Storr, 1979

Description: Pale grey above, with a broad, darker grey mid-dorsal zone which is delineated by a somewhat darker zigzag dorso-lateral line on either side, which usually contains some darker tubercles. White or grey below, with or without darker flecks. Body moderate. Tail relatively slender, about 65% of snout-vent length. Rostral partially or completely divided by a median groove. Supralabials 8-10, larger than adjacent loreals. Nostril in contact with rostral. Preanal pores 4-6. Postanal tubercles three. Digits long, wide, depressed, below with a large pair of apical lamellae followed by four or five transverse lamellae then 1-3 rows of small scales. 60 mm (snout-vent).
Distribution: Coastal area south of North West Cape, WA.
Habit: 'Active at night in trees and shrubs on white coastal dunes.' (Storr).

R. W. G. JENKINS

Diplodactylus occultus Kapalga, NT

M. PETERSON

Diplodactylus ornatus Shark Bay region, WA

Diplodactylus savagei Kluge, 1963

Description: Dark brown above, with numerous irregular, small to large, white spots on back and sides, some spots merging to form larger blotches. Head above with pale flecks and blotches. Supralabials and canthus rostralis usually white. Whitish below. Body moderate. Tail short, fat, only slightly depressed. Dorsal and flank scales homogeneous, small, low, conical, juxtaposed; mid-dorsals slightly imbricate, about as large as ventrals. Rostral large, without a median groove. Mental hemispherical, wider than deep. All but first supralabial small, granular, no larger than adjacent loreals. Nostril separated from rostral by an anterior nasal. Preanal pores absent. Postanal tubercles 5-14. Digits long, wide, very depressed, below with a large pair of apical lamellae followed by a series of uniformly small, undifferentiated scales. 45 mm (snout-vent).
Distribution: Apparently confined to the Pilbara district, WA.
Habit: Terrestrial. Spinifex-covered stony hills and ranges.

Diplodactylus spinigerus Gray, 1842

Western Spiny-Tailed Gecko

Description: Pale grey to brown or almost black above, with numerous scattered dark brown or black scales forming flecks, spots or fine lines, few on the flanks. Usually a broad, dark vertebral stripe from head to tail, with either straight or irregular edges. Whitish, grey or brown below, peppered with darker. Body moderate to slender. Tail long (about 70% of snout-vent length), slender, slightly depressed. Dorsal and flank scales heterogeneous, consisting of small, flat or low conical, juxtaposed scales through which are scattered large, spinose tubercles forming two parallel longitudinal rows which continue along the length of the tail as two rows of long, slender spines. Rostral almost or completely divided by a median groove. Supralabials 7-11, larger than adjacent loreals. Nostril in contact with rostral. Preanal pores 0-8. Postanal tubercles 2-5. Digits long, wide, depressed, below with a large pair of apical lamellae followed by three series of lamellae, diminishing in size proximally. 70 mm (snout-vent).

Diplodactylus polyophthalmus
Mundaring Weir, WA

Distribution: Lower western coast and south-western coast and interior of WA.
Habit: Primarily arboreal, in heath and open woodland.
Subspecies: *spinigerus* (lower west coast and adjacent hinterland of WA); *inornatus* (south-east coast and interior of WA)

Diplodactylus squarrosus Kluge, 1962

Description: Brown to reddish-brown above with darker reticulations and with a series of four large, irregular, pale whitish spots or blotches along the

Diplodactylus pulcher Point Kidman, WA

Diplodactylus rankini
Maud Hill, WA

Diplodactylus spinigerus Mundaring Weir, WA

Diplodactylus savagei near Pannawonnica, WA

M. PETERSON

midline of the body and seven on the tail. Limbs and flanks with large white spots. The darker reticulations form a distinct collar, curving around the occiput from eye to eye. Whitish below. Body moderate. Tail long (about 80% of snout-vent length), slender, more or less round in section. Dorsal and flank scales homogeneous, the mid-dorsals moderate to large, low or conical, juxtaposed, larger than ventrals. Rostral without or with only a slight median groove above. Mental lanceolate, longer than wide. Supralabials 6-9, larger than adjacent loreals. Nostril separated from the rostral by an anterior nasal scale. Preanal pores present. Postanal tubercles 1-3. Digits long, slender, slightly depressed, below with a moderately enlarged pair of apical lamellae followed by undifferentiated, small tubercular scales. 50 mm (snout-vent).
Distribution: Central coast and interior of WA.
Habit: Terrestrial. Found primarily in heaths and woodlands.

Diplodactylus steindachneri

Boulenger, 1885

Description: Pale to dark brown above, typically with a distinctive set of pale dorsal markings consisting of two narrow, pale, dark-edged stripes, one from above each eye to the base of the tail, and broadly connected at three points on the body, so as to enclose oval or rhomboidal patches of darker ground colour. A pale patch on the snout. Sides with scattered pale flecks, spots or short transverse lines. Tail above with a series of irregular pale blotches along the midline. Whitish below. Body moderate. Tail long (about 70% of snout-vent length), slender, more or less round in section. Dorsal and flank scales homogeneous, very small, conical, juxtaposed, about equal to or smaller than ventrals. Rostral with a well-developed median groove above. Mental lanceolate, longer than wide. Supralabials 6-10, larger than adjacent loreals. Nostril separated from rostral by an anterior nasal scale. Preanal pores present. Postanal tubercles 2-9. Digits long, narrow, scarcely depressed, below with a moderately enlarged pair of apical lamellae followed by slightly enlarged but otherwise undifferentiated scales. 55 mm (snout-vent).
Distribution: Interior of NSW through inland Qld to the north-eastern coastal regions of Qld.
Habit: A terrestrial gecko which shelters by day in ground litter or, more usually, in ground crevices or holes, especially the vertical openings of abandoned insect nests and spider burrows. It is found in a wide variety of habitats from mallee through savannah woodland to dry sclerophyll forests in the north.

M. PETERSON

Diplodactylus squarrosus
Mullewa, WA

Diplodactylus squarrosus

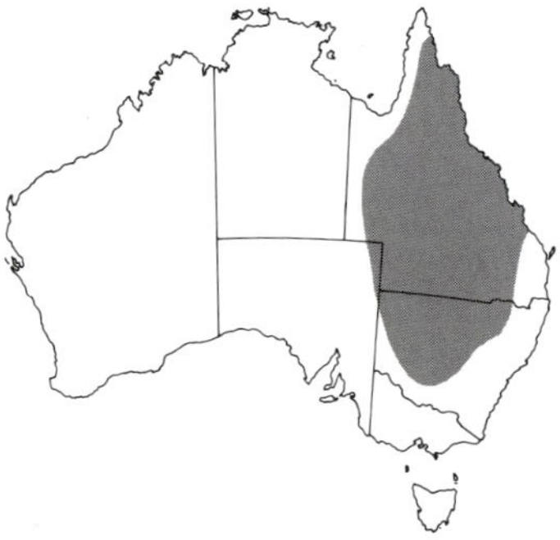

Diplodactylus steindachneri

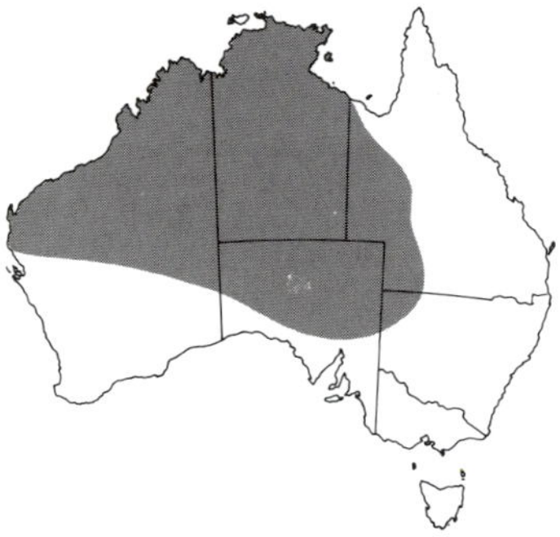

Diplodactylus stenodactylus

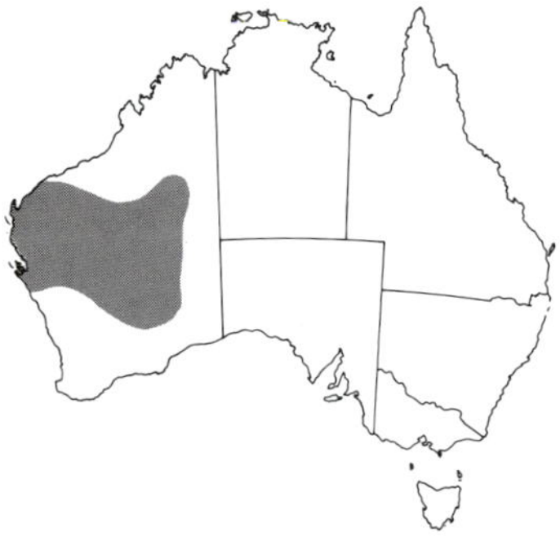

Diplodactylus strophurus

Diplodactylus stenodactylus

Boulenger, 1896

Description: Brown or reddish-brown above, with a variable pattern. Typically a dark-edged pale cream or yellow vertebral stripe commencing as separate pale stripes from each eye which converge and fuse on the nape. Sides and limbs with scattered large and small pale spots. Top of head with pale variegations. A dark bar may be present or absent on the snout and behind the eye. Pale vertebral stripe may be obscure or absent in some specimens. Whitish below. Body moderate. Tail long (about 80% of snout-vent length), slender, scarcely depressed. Dorsal and flank scales homogeneous, small to moderate, low and rounded. Rostral varies from having no median groove to a completely divided condition. Mental lanceolate, longer than wide. Supralabials 7-10, larger than adjacent loreals. Nostril either contacting rostral or separated from it by an anterior nasal scale. Preanal pores present. Postanal tubercles 1-3. Digits long, slender, scarcely depressed, below with a pair of slightly enlarged apical lamellae, followed by undifferentiated small, tubercular scales. 50 mm (snout-vent).
Distribution: Widely distributed from the coast of WA through northern, central and southern Australia to north-eastern NT.
Habit: Found in a wide range of habitats from sandy deserts to savannah woodland. Terrestrial, usually encountered at night foraging in open sandy or grassy areas.

Diplodactylus strophurus (Duméril and Bibron, 1836)

Description: Pale grey to almost black above, with or without irregular darker variegations which tend to be longitudinally aligned on the head and neck. Variable below, ranging from whitish with darker flecks or reticulations to almost black, and with or without a dark mid-ventral stripe. Body moderate. Tail moderate (about 60% of snout-vent length), slightly depressed. Dorsal and flank scales heterogeneous, consisting of moderate, low to conical, juxtaposed scales through which are scattered moderate to large conical tubercles. Tail with distinctive narrow bands of connective tissue separating groups of scales which themselves form regular rings. Rostral partly divided by a median groove above. Mental lanceolate, longer than wide. Supralabials 6-9, larger than adjacent loreals. Nostril contacting rostral. Preanal pores usually present. Postanal tubercles 2-3. Digits long, wide, depressed, below with a pair of very large apical lamellae, followed by three series of

lamellae, diminishing in size proximally. 70 mm (snout-vent).
Distribution: Central coast and interior of WA.
Habit: Primarily arboreal, in arid shrublands throughout its range.

Diplodactylus taeniatus (Lönnberg and Andersson, 1913)

Description: Whitish, pale cream or brown above, the top of the head darker brown and usually continuous with a dark brown vertebral stripe. A single dorso-lateral and ventro-lateral dark brown stripe on either side, both of which may be continuous or discontinuous with a dark postocular streak. Limbs variegated with dark brown. Pale below, with a dark mid-ventral stripe, and sometimes with an additional stripe on the side of the throat. Pale areas between dark stripes may be uniform, but more typically are pale fawn or grey enclosing a pale yellow or orange stripe. Body pattern continuous on tail. Body very slender, limbs spindly. Tail long (about 80% of snout-vent length), slender, more or less round in section. Dorsal and flank scales homogeneous, moderate, low, rounded, juxtaposed, about as large as ventrals. Rostral completely divided by a median groove. Mental lanceolate, longer than wide. Supralabials 7-9, larger than adjacent loreals. Nostril separated from

Diplodactylus steindachneri
Wenlock River, N Qld

Diplodactylus stenodactylus
Omicron Station, SW Qld

Diplodactylus strophurus Giles Meteorological Station, WA

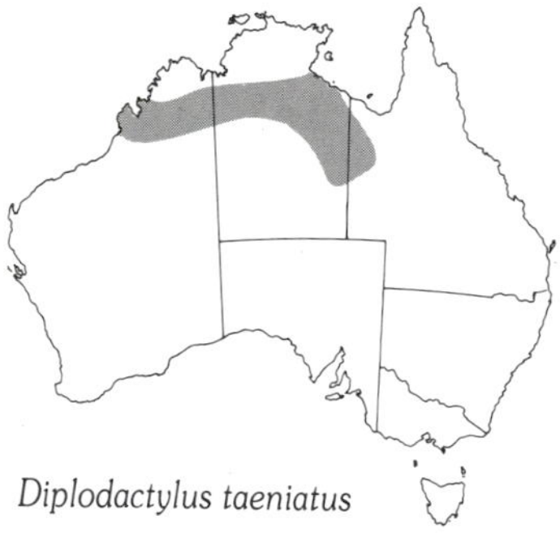

Diplodactylus taeniatus

Diplodactylus taeniatus McArthur River, NT

rostral by an anterior nasal. Preanal pores absent. Postanal tubercles 1-2. Digits long, wide, depressed, below with a very large pair of apical lamellae followed by three series of lamellae, diminishing in size proximally. 50 mm (snout-vent).

Distribution: Seasonally dry areas of northern Australia, from the Kimberley region of WA through the top end of the NT to north-western Qld.
Habit: An inhabitant of various species of spinifex *(Triodia)* and other dry-adapted grasses, where it

moves in a distinctive jerky, slow-motion fashion resembling certain grasshoppers and phasmids. It belongs to that group of *Diplodactylus* which exudes a viscous fluid from the tail when alarmed.

Diplodactylus taenicauda

De Vis, 1886

Golden-Tailed Gecko

Description: The entire dorsal and lateral surfaces of head and body grey, the grey forming a finely reticulated pattern enclosing small to large spots and blotches of black. A distinctive bright orange or orange-brown mid-dorsal stripe on the tail, extending on to the hind part of the body. Remainder of tail black, with numerous scattered white scales forming an irregular pattern. Greyish below, peppered with darker. As in several related species the iris is bright orange, the vertical pupil edged with white. Body moderate. Tail long (about 70% of snout-vent length), slender, more or less round in section. Dorsal and lateral scales homogeneous, small, flat, juxtaposed, about equal to ventrals. Rostral partly divided by a median groove above. Mental lanceolate, longer than broad. Supralabials 8-11, larger than adjacent loreals. Nostril contacting rostral. Preanal pores present in males. Postanal tubercles 1-4. Digits long, wide, depressed, below with a very large pair of apical lamellae, followed by three series of lamellae, diminishing in size proximally. 70 mm (snout-vent).

Distribution: Darling Downs to coastal regions of central and north-eastern Qld.

Habit: Arboreal. Dry sclerophyll forests and eucalyptus and cypress woodlands. A member of the group capable of exuding a viscous fluid from the tail.

Diplodactylus tessellatus Günther, 1875

Tessellated Gecko

Description: Varies from pale grey to rich reddish-brown above, with a highly variable pattern. Specimens may be uniform above, but more often there is an irregular series of darker markings forming either obscure reticulations or marbling. In addition many specimens may have an irregular series of pale yellowish and blackish spots, often in pairs, along the mid-dorsal region of the body and tail. Whitish below, with a series of scattered, irregular dark grey or brown spots on all ventral surfaces. Body moderate.

Diplodactylus taenicauda Condamine River, Qld

Diplodactylus taenicauda

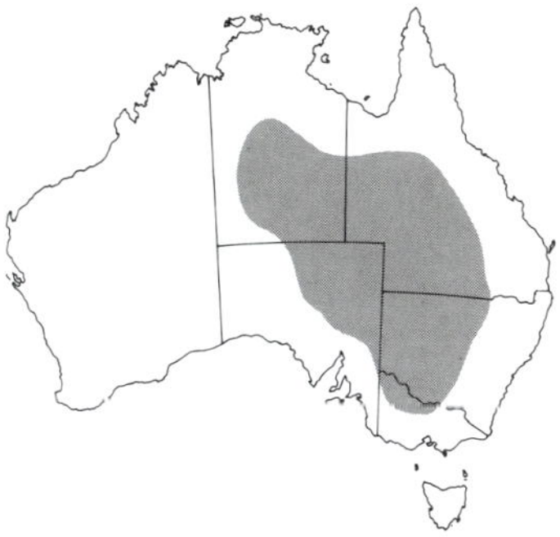

Diplodactylus tessellatus

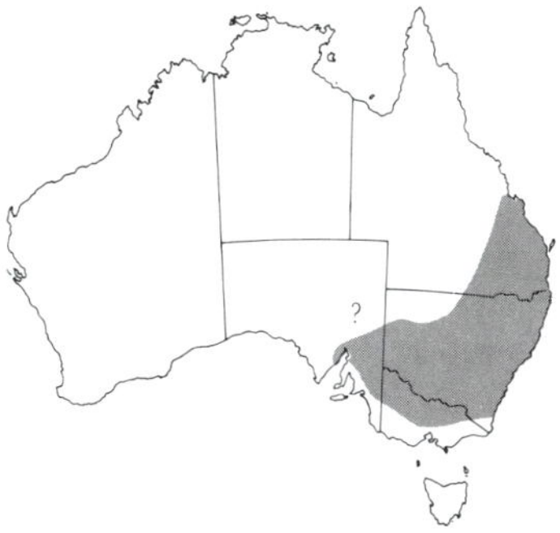

Diplodactylus vittatus

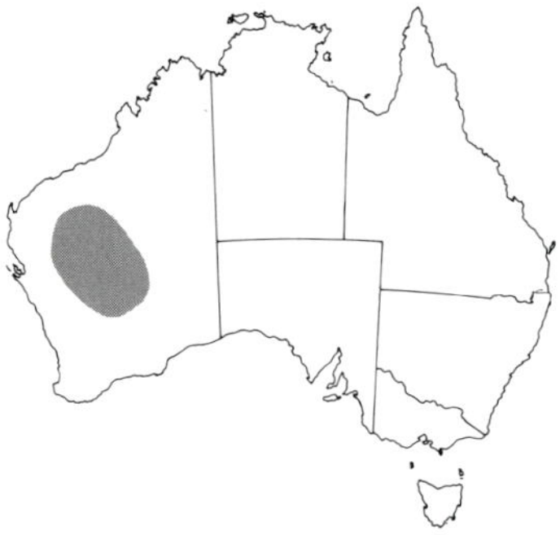

Diplodactylus wellingtonae

Diplodactylus williamsi

Diplodactylus wilsoni

Diplodactylus wombeyi

Diplodactylus tessellatus Bourke, NSW

Tail moderate to short (40-50% of snout-vent length), fat, only slightly depressed. Dorsal and flank scales homogeneous, the mid-dorsals large, low, rounded, juxtaposed. Scales on tail heterogeneous, with regular rings of large, conical scales (sometimes larger and spinose near the tip), alternating with smaller, low, conical scales. Rostral partly divided by a median groove above. Mental lanceolate, longer than broad. Supralabials 6-8, larger than adjacent loreals. Nostril contacting rostral. Preanal pores absent. Postanal tubercles 4-13. Digits long, narrow, slightly depressed, below with a large pair of apical lamellae, followed by slightly enlarged but otherwise undifferentiated scales. 50 mm (snout-vent).
Distribution: Widely distributed throughout the drier interiors of NT, Qld, NSW, Vic and SA.
Habit: A terrestrial species which may be found during the day in ground cracks and crevices or in or under fallen timber and other ground debris. Emerges at night to forage in open areas. Especially abundant on the black soil floodplains of the larger inland rivers.

Diplodactylus vittatus Gray, 1832

Wood Gecko

Description: Light to dark brown or blackish above, typically with a pale grey, cream or brown, dark-edged, zigzag vertebral stripe from nape to tail, and along the tail where the latter is original. Top of the head pale (often with a dark brown central region) and continuous with the vertebral stripe. Lateral and dorso-lateral regions with scattered, small, pale spots and blotches. Ventral surfaces white, finely peppered with dark brown. Body moderate. Tail moderate (about 60% of snout-vent length), fat, only slightly depressed. Dorsal and flank scales homogeneous, small, scarcely larger than ventrals. Rostral partly divided by a median groove above. Mental lanceolate, longer than wide. Supralabials 6-10, larger than adjacent loreals. Nostril contacting rostral. Preanal pores absent. Postanal tubercles 2-10. Digits long, slightly depressed, below with a relatively large pair of subdigital lamellae, usually followed by at least two series of enlarged scales, diminishing in size proximally. 50 mm (snout-vent).
Distribution: Southern SA to Vic, NSW and south-eastern Qld.
Habit: Found in a wide variety of habitats from arid scrubs to wet sclerophyll forest. Terrestrial, usually found during the day in or under fallen timber, stones and litter.

Diplodactylus vittatus Nymagee, NSW

Diplodactylus williamsi Goondiwindi, Qld

Diplodactylus wellingtonae Storr, 1988

Description: Pale to dark grey above, sometimes with no more than a few scattered dark grey and orange-brown scales, but more often with an obscure, pale, sometimes dark-edged dorso-lateral zone or series of elongate blotches. Spines or tubercles on back and tail usually orange or brown. Whitish below. Colour and pattern of the iris silvery-grey with a black reticulum. Body moderate. Tail long (about 70% of snout-vent), relatively slender, round or slightly depressed. Dorsal scales heterogeneous, consisting of small, conical angular scales giving a rasp- or file-like appearance to the skin, with a series of two parallel, longitudinal rows, low conical tubercles or spines on the body, and with two or more longitudinal series of long, orange spines along the top of the tail. Rostral partially, but more often completely, divided. Mental usually lanceolate. Supralabials 10-15, larger than adjacent loreals. Nostril contacting rostral. Posterior supraciliaries spiny. Preanal pores present in males. Postanal tubercles 1-3. Digits moderate, depressed, below with a pair of apical lamellae, followed by enlarged lamellae in three distinct series. 75 mm (snout-vent).
Distribution: Arid parts of WA from the Pilbara to the southern interior.
Habit: Normally arboreal, but some populations living in spinifex (*Triodia* spp.) in desert regions. One of a group of *Diplodactylus* able to exude a viscous fluid from spines or tubercles on the tail.

Diplodactylus williamsi Kluge, 1963

Description: Pale to dark grey above, usually with numerous scattered black scales, which may sometimes form an obscure reticulate pattern. Whitish below, peppered with dark brown or black. Body moderate. Tail long (about 65% of snout-vent length), slender, more or less round in section. Dorsal and flank scales homogeneous, with four longitudinal rows of brown or yellow conical tubercles emerging from the smaller, low, conical, juxtaposed scales covering the remaining dorsal surfaces. The tubercles on the back continuous with four rows of longer, spinose tubercles on the tail. Rostral partly or completely divided by a median groove. Mental lanceolate, longer than wide. Supralabials 7-11, larger than adjacent loreals. Nostril contacting rostral. Preanal pores present in males. Postanal tubercles 1-15. Digits long, wide, depressed, below with a pair of very large apical lamellae, followed by three series of enlarged lamellae, diminishing in size proximally. 60 mm (snout-vent).
Distribution: North-eastern interior of NSW, through inland Qld to the north-eastern coast.
Habit: An arboreal species usually found sheltering in hollow limbs or under loose bark of standing or fallen trees. Found at night foraging on the trunks of trees, or occasionally on the ground. Found in a wide variety of habitats from savannah woodland to dry sclerophyll and *Callitris* forests.

Diplodactylus wilsoni Storr, 1983

Description: Grey-brown above, with scattered blackish scales tending to form narrow longitudinal stripes which themselves are the black edges of faint, wider, pale stripes, especially on the head, neck and anterior part of the body. Whitish below, with scattered darker flecks sometimes forming longitudinal lines. Dorsal and flank scales more or less homogeneous, those on tail heterogeneous. Rostral partly divided. Supralabials 10-12, larger than adjacent loreals. Nostril contacting rostral. Preanal pores absent. Postanal tubercles 1-2. Digits long, wide, depressed, below with a large pair of apical plates, followed by 5-7 enlarged and usually undivided lamellae. 60 mm (snout-vent).
Distribution: 'Arid mid-western interior of Western Australia' (Storr).
Habit: All known specimens were 'found in vertical crevices in dolerite and quartz sandstone' (Storr).

Diplodactylus wombeyi Storr, 1978

Description: Reddish-brown above, with a series of darker reddish-brown markings tending to form a series of broken cross-bands or reticulations; canthus and lips usually paler than remainder of head; flanks and limbs usually finely spotted with white. Ventral surfaces white. Dorsal and flank scales small, more or less homogeneous, low and rounded. Rostral partly divided by a median groove. Supralabials 9-11, larger than adjacent loreals. Nostril contacting rostral. Preanal pores present, one on each side. Postanal tubercles present, 1-4 on each side. Digits long, slender, moderately depressed, below with a large pair of apical lamellae, followed by flat granules which tend to be arranged in pairs. 50 mm (snout-vent).
Distribution: Pilbara region, WA.
Habit: A rock-dwelling species found on spinifex-covered stony hills, ranges and escarpments.

Genus ***Gehyra*** Gray, 1834

A large genus ranging from Madagascar through Asia and the Indo-Malayan Archipelago to Australia and the islands of the Pacific Ocean.

Rostral and mental shields rounded. Labials much larger than adjacent scales. Postmentals enlarged. Digits moderately long, depressed, greatly expanded distally to form large subcircular pads; apical subdigital lamellae not enlarged but continuous with a series of single, notched or divided, long, narrow transverse lamellae extending across the full width of the pad; digits lying flat on the substrate when viewed laterally; all digits but the inner one on each foot clawed, the claws free and arising from the upper surface of the digit well within the border of the expanded pad. Preanal pores present.

Although Australian species have received considerable attention in recent years, relationships are still obscure, due, partly to inadequate collections from many parts of the continent, but also to strong correlations between habitat and morphology apparently independent of geographic relationships.

Key

TO THE AUSTRALIAN SPECIES OF GEHYRA

1 Subapical lamellae on fourth toe usually undivided, but sometimes with a medial depression or notch (a)............ **2**

Subapical lamellae on fourth toe usually divided or at least deeply grooved (b).. **6**

2 Basal webbing only between the third and fourth toes, or entirely free **3**

Marked webbing between third and fourth toes (c) .... ***oceanica***

3 9-11 subdigital lamellae under dilated portion of fourth toe. **4**

7-8 subdigital lamellae under dilated portion of fourth toe... ....***catenata***

4 Rostral scale oblong, almost twice as wide as high, with at most a slightly angular upper edge, and bordered above (between the nostrils) by only two large internasal scales (d)... **5**

Rostral scale at most about 1.5 times wider than high, angular above, and bordered above (between the nostrils) by three internasal scales: two large outer and a small medial (e).. ***dubia***

5 Grey or grey-brown above, immaculate or with a pattern consisting of faint reticulations or cross-bands of pale spots with black anterior margins...................... ***australis***

Orange- or reddish-brown above with alternate irregular cross-bands of black and off-white spots............. ***robusta***

6 No cutaneous fold along the hind edge of the hindlimb.... **7**

A cutaneous fold along the hind edge of the hindlimb (f)..... .... ***baliola***

7 Basal subdigital lamellae divided, but each half usually in contact, or separated by no more than a single small granule (g).. **8**

Basal subdigital lamellae divided, each half separated from its partner by a wedge-shaped series of small granules (h).. .... ***xenopus***

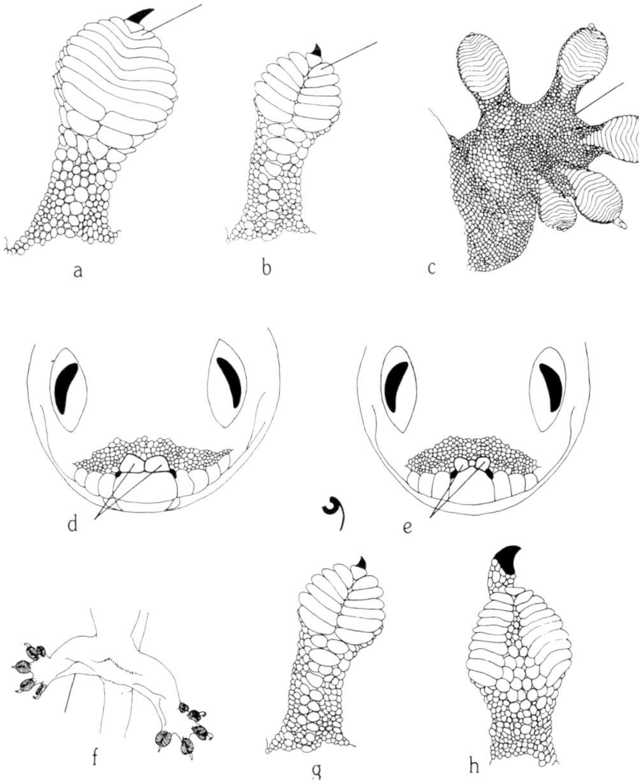

8 Usually fewer than 9 divided subdigital lamellae under dilated portion of fourth toe..**9**

Usually 9 or more divided subdigital lamellae under dilated portion of fourth toe..**15**

9 Body pattern with irregular but distinct spotting............**10**

Body pattern variegated but without distinct spotting....**13**

10 Dark and pale spots on back tending to be aligned in transverse rows... **11**

Spots on back scattered irregularly, not usually aligned in transverse rows... ***punctata***

11 Rostral scale oblong, almost twice as wide as high, with at most a slightly angular upper edge, and usually bordered above (between the nostrils) by only two large (and an occasional small third) internasal scales (d)................... **12**

Rostral scale at most about 1.5 times wider than high, angular above, and bordered above (between the nostrils) usually by three or more (occasionally only two) internasal scales (e).. ***minuta***

12 Dorsal colour in life essentially reddish- or orange-brown; stony ranges of central Australia....................... ***montium***

Dorsal colour in life essentially pinkish-grey; rocky habitats across northern Australia............................ ***nana***

13 Grey or brown with darker mottling.............................. **14**

Pale orange or russet-brown with darker cross-markings... .... ***pilbara***

14 Usually 11 or fewer preanal pores in males; rostral scale oblong, almost twice as wide as high, with a straight or at most a slightly angular upper edge (d)....... ***purpurascens***

Usually 11 or more preanal pores in males; rostral scale at most about 1.5 times wider than high, angular above (e).... .... ***variegata***

15 19 or more preanal pores in males................................ **16**

Fewer than 19 preanal pores in males............ ***borroloola***

16 Rostral scale oblong, almost twice as wide as high, with at most a slightly angular upper edge, and usually bordered above (between the nostrils) by only two large (and an occasional small third) internasal scales (d).......... ***pamela***

Rostral scale at most about 1.5 times wider than high, angular above, and bordered above (between the nostrils) usually by three or more (occasionally only two) internasal scales (e).. ***occidentalis***

Gehyra australis Gray, 1845

Northern Dtella

Description: Pale to dark grey or grey-brown above, usually without any discernible pattern (especially when active at night), but occasional specimens have a faint to conspicuous pattern of darker brown blotches or reticulations on the back and snout and temporal streaks. White, pink or grey below, varying in individuals with temperature and activity. A heavily built gecko covered above and below with small homogeneous scales. Tail distinctly depressed at its base. 9-12 undivided subdigital lamellae under the fourth toe. Third and fourth toes usually free, but occasionally a trace of webbing. Anterior chin shields contacting only the first, and not the second, infralabials. 70 mm (snout-vent).
Distribution: Far northern Australia, from East Kimberley to the NT/Qld border.
Habit: Primarily arboreal, in a variety of woodlands and coastal and riverine forests, but frequents buildings and human habitations.

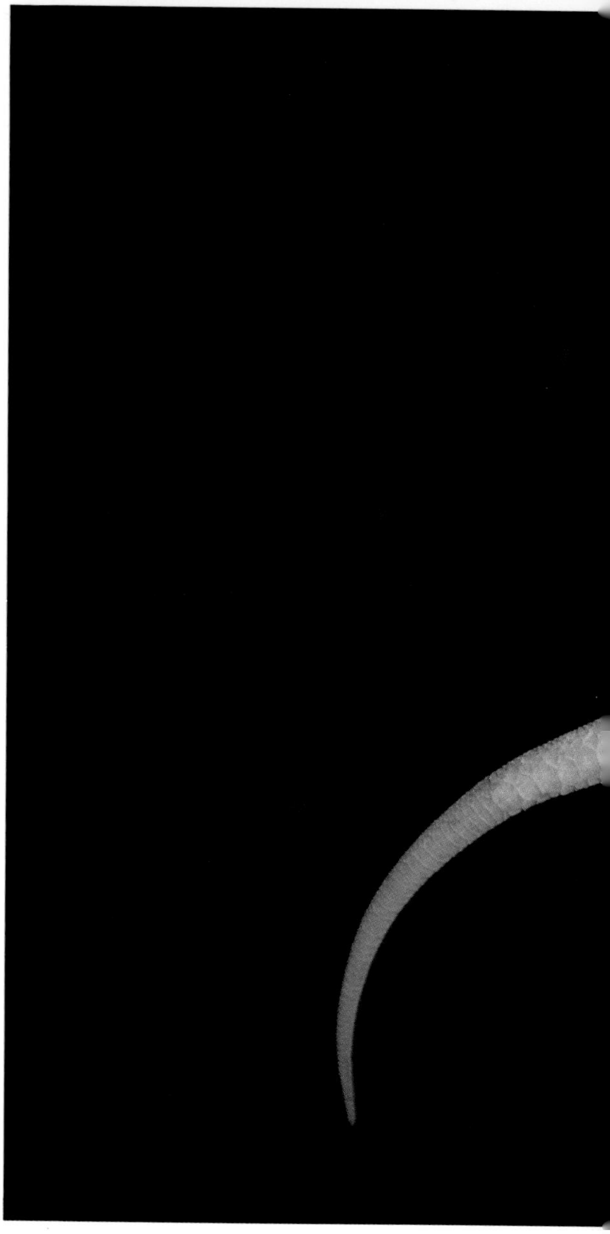

Gehyra australis Brockman Range, NT

Gehyra baliola (Duméril and Duméril, 1851)

Description: Status in Australia uncertain. Similar in most respects to *Gehyra australis*, from which it differs in having divided distal subdigital lamellae and a distinct cutaneous (skin) fold along the hind edge of the hindlimb. 70 mm (snout-vent).
Distribution: Eastern islands of Torres Strait (Darnley and Murray Islands, and their smaller satellite islands). Also in New Guinea.
Habit: Similar to *Gehyra australis*, sheltering during the day in crevices or under the bark of standing or fallen trees, or among boulders and crevices.

Gehyra borroloola King, 1983

Description: Grey-brown or brown above, with a faint to conspicuous pattern consisting of a dark head stripe extending from the snout, through the eye to the temporal region and scattered dark brown and pale cream spots which tend to be aligned transversely on the body and tail; whitish or pale yellow below. A heavily-built gecko covered above and below with small homogeneous scales and with a tapering tail which is fat and distinctly depressed at its base. 10-12 divided subdigital lamellae under the fourth toe. Third and fourth toes free, without webbing. Anterior chin shields contacting only the first infralabial on each

Gehyra baliola Murray Island, Torres Strait

side. 65 mm (snout-vent).
Distribution: Coast and adjacent interior of lower Gulf of Carpentaria region of NT.
Habit: A rock-dwelling species found on stony hills, ranges and rocky escarpments. Oviparous: two eggs per clutch.

Gehyra catenata Low, 1979

Description: Pale to dark grey above, with a relatively obscure pattern consisting of a pair of dark brown zigzag paravertebral stripes from the eye to the base of the tail, sometimes joined by a series of dark transverse bars resulting in a vertebral series of pale rhomboidal blotches. Head, flanks and limbs speckled and streaked with dark brown. Ventral surfaces whitish. Body large, fairly heavily built. Pads of fingers and toes with lamellae undivided, occasionally grooved. Third and fourth toes free, without webbing. 55 mm (snout-vent).
Distribution: Interior of central-eastern and southern Qld.
Habit: Arboreal, in tall open and savannah woodlands. Oviparous: two eggs per clutch.

Gehyra dubia (Macleay, 1877)

Description: Grey-brown or grey to almost pale cream above, with or without obscure darker blotches, variegations or marbling and scattered paler spots. Whitish to rich lemon-yellow below. Usually at least some indication of an irregular, narrow temporal stripe, sometimes continued forward as a narrow black stripe on the canthus rostralis. A well-built gecko, covered above with small, homogeneous smooth scales and with a relatively slender tail which is distinctly depressed at the base. Subdigital lamellae usually undivided, though sometimes deeply notched or grooved; however Bustard records some populations with divided lamellae, which may be distinguished from *Gehyra variegata* by the larger number (9-11) of lamellae under the expanded part of the pad (only 7-8 in *Gehyra variegata*). At most some basal webbing between the third and fourth toes, but usually free. Sometimes a slight cutaneous fold along the hind edge of the hindlimb. 80 mm (snout-vent).
Distribution: Widely distributed throughout eastern Australia, from Cape York Peninsula south to central NSW.
Habit: A nocturnal, arboreal gecko of dry sclerophyll forests and savannah woodlands. Bustard

regards the production of two eggs in a clutch as characteristic of this species and its near relatives.

Gehyra minuta King, 1982

Description: Pale orange-or reddish-brown above, sometimes almost uniform but more usually with a faint to conspicuous pattern of darker brown and pale cream spots or blotches which tend to form irregular, alternate darker and paler cross-bands on the back and tail; usually a dark streak from snout, through eye to temporal region. Cream or white below. Body moderate, tail long and tapering, slightly depressed at the base. 6-8 divided subdigital lamellae under the fourth toe. Third and fourth toes free of webbing. Anterior chin shields in contact with first and second infralabials. 45 mm (snout-vent).
Distribution: South-western edge of the Barkly Tableland, NT.
Habit: Found 'under rock exfoliations, or blocks, in minor rock outcrops confined to a narrow band of red soil country' (King).

Gehyra montium Storr, 1982

Description: Reddish-brown above with scattered dark brown and pale cream spots tending to form irregular cross-bands on the body and tail. Side of head with one or two dark brown streaks, and sometimes with other longitudinal dark streaks on the head and neck. White or cream below. Tail relatively long, tapering, slightly depressed at its base. 6-8 divided subdigital lamellae under the fourth toe. Third and fourth toes free, without a trace of webbing. Anterior chin shields in contact with the first and second infralabials. 50 mm (snout-vent).
Distribution: Ranges, hills and rocky outcrops of central Australia.
Habit: A rock-dwelling species found in crevices or under boulders and exfoliating rock slabs.

Gehyra nana Storr, 1978

Description: Reddish-brown above, with scattered dark brown and pale pinkish spots, the latter usually more numerous and smaller than the former, and all the spots tending to form transverse rows. No dark temporal markings. Ventral surfaces white. A small, rather slender gecko with moderately depressed head and relatively long, slender tail. Subdigital

R. W. G. JENKINS

Gehyra borroloola Balbirini Junction, NT

R. W. G. JENKINS

Gehyra catenata Yandaburra, Qld

Gehyra borroloola

Gehyra catenata

Gehyra dubia

Gehyra minuta

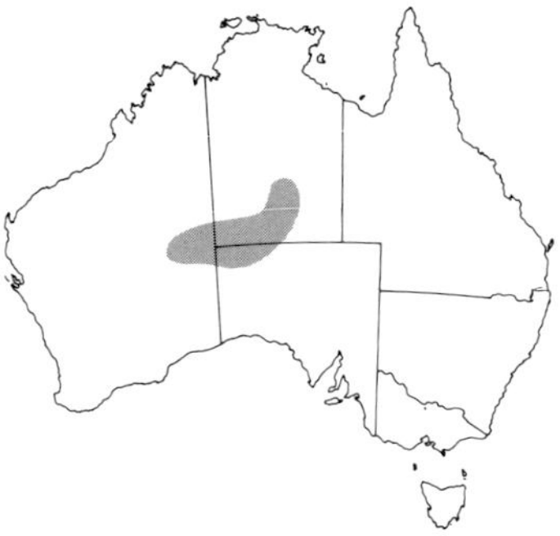

Gehyra montium

Gehyra nana

Gehyra occidentalis

Gehyra oceanica

Gehyra pamela

lamellae divided. Third and fourth toes free, without webbing. 50 mm (snout-vent).
Distribution: Northern Kimberley region, WA, to northern Qld.
Habit: A rock-dwelling species found under exfoliating rock slabs or in crevices and caves of rocky hills and ranges, or of the large sandstone escarpments which are found throughout much of its range.

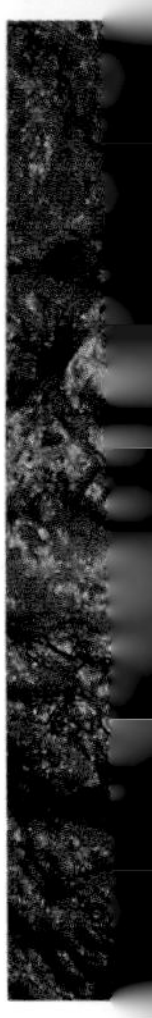

Gehyra occidentalis King, 1984

Description: Rich brown above, with scattered darker brown and pale whitish spots which tend to form alternate darker and paler cross-bands on body and tail, and with the spots often coalescing to form transverse bars; head with two dark brown streaks on either side; whitish below. Tail relatively long, tapering, slightly depressed at its base. 9-10 divided subdigital lamellae under the fourth toe. Third and fourth toes free, without a trace of webbing. Anterior chin shields in contact only with the first infralabial. 65 mm (snout-vent).
Distribution: West Kimberley region, WA.
Habit: A rock-dwelling species of stony hills and ranges.

J. WOMBEY

Gehyra oceanica (Lesson, 1830)

Oceanic Gecko

Description: Grey, grey-brown or brown above, paling to nearly white at night, with or without dark brown or black flecks, spots or variegations. Whitish below. A large, fleshy gecko with greatly depressed head and body, with small, homogeneous scales and a moderately long, rather fat tail. Pads of fingers and toes very large, with undivided subdigital lamellae and indications of a claw on the inner digits of large specimens. Conspicuous webbing present between the third and fourth toes. 120 mm (snout-vent).
Distribution: Recorded from some of the islands of Torres Strait, but currently considered to be restricted to the islands of Oceania (King). Has been recorded erroneously in the literature as being found on Lord Howe and Norfolk Islands.
Habit: An agile and voracious arboreal gecko, usually found in wet, lowland forests.

R. W. G. JENKINS

Gehyra dubia Somerset, Qld

R. W. G. JENKINS

Gehyra minuta

Gehyra montium WA

J. WEIGEL

Gehyra occidentalis Napier Range, WA

Gehyra nana Mitchell Plateau, WA

Gehyra oceanica Kadavu Island, Fiji

Gehyra pamela King, 1982

Description: Reddish-grey above with a pattern of pale spots aligned transversely to form about a dozen irregular cross-bands, the intervening areas with obscure darker brown lines and variegations; a dark temporal streak on each side of the head; white or cream below. A large, well-built gecko, covered above with small, homogeneous, smooth scales. Tail moderate, usually depressed at the base. 9-11 deeply notched or grooved (but seldom divided) subdigital lamellae under the expanded portion of the fourth toe; toes usually free of webbing. 70 mm (snout-vent).
Distribution: Currently known only from western Arnhem Land, NT.
Habit: A common, nocturnal, rock-dwelling gecko, found among sandstone plateaux, escarpments and outliers throughout its range.

Gehyra pilbara Mitchell, 1965

Pilbara Dtella

Description: Bright reddish-brown or pale orange

Gehyra pamela Cannon Hill, NT R.W.G. JENKINS

Gehyra pilbara Port Hedland, WA R.W.G. JENKIN

above, with irregular darker lines and spots forming irregular cross-bands, sometimes obscure, between which are irregular transverse rows of pale cream or yellowish spots. Lower surfaces whitish or pale yellow. Body moderate, depressed, with small, homogeneous scales and moderately long, slender tail. Pads of fingers and toes with divided subdigital lamellae. Third and fourth toes free without webbing. Anterior chin shields in contact only with first infralabials. 40 mm (snout-vent).
Distribution: Pilbara Plateau, WA, east to the Tanami Desert, NT.
Habit: According to Mitchell this species lives characteristically within the tunnels of the giant mounds of termites of the genus *Eutermes*. Certainly this is the only habitat in which I found this species in the Tanami Desert. The geckos are active on the surface of the termitaria at night, retiring to crevices in the surface and also through openings into the interior of the mound during the day.

Gehyra punctata (Fry, 1914)
Spotted Dtella

Description: Almost certainly a composite species as currently recognised. In this as in other 'species' of *Gehyra*, King has recently demonstrated a number of chromosomal variants which probably represent distinct species. Variable in colour, from dull grey or brown to rich reddish-brown above, with irregular dark, narrow crossbands, or transverse rows of blackish spots and blotches alternating with transverse or scattered groups of conspicuous or obscure pale-coloured spots. Whitish to pale yellow below. Body moderate, depressed, with small homogeneous scales and moderately long, slender tail. Pads of fingers and toes with divided subdigital lamellae. Third and fourth toes free, without webbing. Anterior chin shields in contact with only the first infralabials. 40 mm (snout-vent).
Distribution: Saxicoline habitats from the southern Kimberley region and the Pilbara region south to the Yalgoo region, WA.
Habit: This name is applied to numerous isolated, but morphologically similar populations occupying rocky habitats - caves, crevices and exfoliating rock surfaces - throughout the range cited above. All are similar in habit, and are usually encountered at night foraging on open rock faces. A single egg in a clutch.

Gehyra purpurascens Storr, 1982

Description: Pale to dark grey above, usually with faint to conspicuous dark brown or blackish streaks or blotches tending to form reticulations over the back and tail; usually with a dark streak on each side of the head; whitish below. A moderately-built body with small, homogeneous scales. Tail relatively long, tapering, slightly depressed at its base. 6-9 divided subdigital lamellae under the fourth toe. Third and fourth toes free, without a trace of webbing. Anterior chin shields in contact with the first but not the second infralabials. 60 mm (snout-vent).
Distribution: Arid regions of Western and central Australia.
Habit: An arboreal species found in a range of arid scrublands and woodlands.

Gehyra robusta King, 1983

Description: Orange- or reddish-brown above with numerous scattered blackish and pale cream spots or streaks which tend to form alternate darker and

Gehyra punctata near Gascoyne Junction, WA M. PETERSON

Gehyra purpurascens Kulgera, NT R. W. G. JENKINS

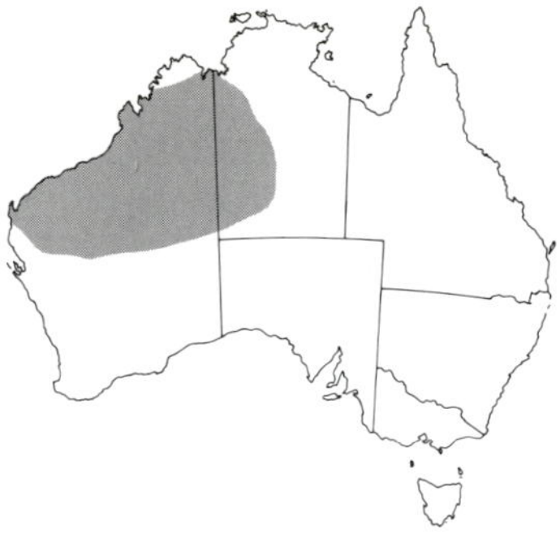

Gehyra pilbara

Gehyra punctata

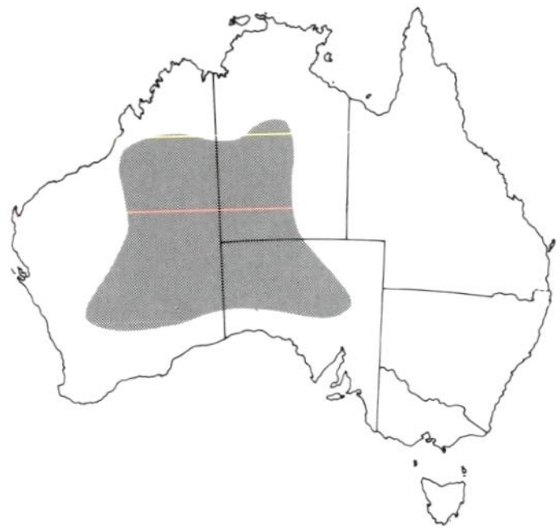

Gehyra purpurascens

Gehyra robusta

Gehyra xenopus

Gehyra robusta Dajarra, Qld

R. W. G. JENKINS

paler transverse bands; an indefinite blackish head stripe from snout to ear; lower surfaces cream to yellow. A solidly built body with small, homogeneous scales. Tail relatively long, tapering, depressed at its base. 9-12 notched, but undivided, subdigital lamellae under the fourth toe. Third and fourth toes free, without a trace of webbing. Anterior chin shields in contact with the first but not the second infralabials. 75 mm (snout-vent).
Distribution: Arid north-west of Qld.
Habit: A rock-dwelling species found in stony hills and ranges.

Gehyra variegata (Duméril and Bibron, 1836)

Tree Dtella

Description: A highly variable gecko probably encompassing more than one species under the present name. Grey or grey-brown above, with numerous scattered, irregular blackish and pale flecks, blotches and marblings, often forming an irregular reticulate pattern over the entire dorsal surface. Usually a conspicuous, dark temporal streak. Whitish below. Body moderate, depressed, with small, homogeneous scales and relatively long tail, which is markedly depressed at its base. Pads of fingers and toes with divided subdigital lamellae. Third and fourth toes free, without webbing. Anterior chin shields in contact with only first infralabials. 45 mm (snout-vent).
Distribution: Widely distributed throughout the inland of eastern and south-eastern Australia, except for most coastal regions; a distinct population in southern WA, except for the far south-western corner.
Habit: Usually an arboreal species, retiring during the day within crevices or under loose bark of standing or fallen trees. Found on exfoliating rocks on granite outcrops throughout eastern Australia, and probably invades similar habitats elsewhere in its range. A single egg in a clutch (Bustard).

Gehyra xenopus Storr, 1978

Description: Grey-brown or brown above, with scattered darker and paler spots and flecks, those on the back tending to be aligned transversely; lower lips and chin brown. Ventral surfaces whitish. Body large, heavily built and with a long, pointed, somewhat turned-up snout and large prominent eyes. Pads of fingers and toes with divided lamellae, the basal pairs separated by a wedge-shaped series of granules.

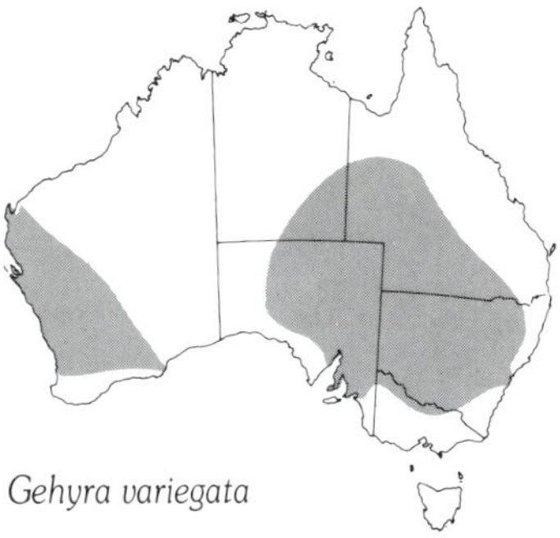

Gehyra variegata

Gehyra variegata Round Hill, NSW

Third and fourth toes free, without webbing. 70 mm (snout-vent).
Distribution: North-western Kimberley region, WA.

Habit: A rock-dwelling species found in crevices and caves of the extensive sandstone escarpments which are found within its range.

Gehyra xenopus near Halls Creek, WA

J. WEIGEL

Genus ***Hemidactylus*** Gray, 1825

A large tropicopolitan genus with only a single species reaching Australia, probably accidentally introduced by man. Most are relatively small, arboreal species. Rostral and mental shields rounded. Labials much larger than adjacent scales. Postmentals enlarged. Digits moderately long, depressed, expanded distally to form broad pads; apical subdigital lamellae not enlarged but are continuous with a series of narrow transverse lamellae, extending across the full width of the pad; digits lying flat on the substrate when viewed laterally; all digits clawed, the claws free and arising from the upper surface of the digit well within the border of the expanded pad. Preanal pores present.

Hemidactylus frenatus Duméril and Bibron, 1836

House Gecko

Description: Pale creamy-white to dark grey or brown above, with or without scattered dark blackish-brown flecks, spots or lines. Whitish below. A moderately built lizard, above with small, smooth scales through which are scattered small, tubercular scales. Tail moderately long, distinctly depressed, with a lateral flange along each side and, when original, with numerous small tubercles among the smaller scales. Subdigital lamellae 7-10. Preanal and femoral pores 20-40. 60 mm (snout-vent).
Distribution: Various settlements around the northern coast of Australia, from about Darwin to Cairns. No longer present in abandoned settlements where it once occurred, suggesting a dependence on man for its distribution in this country.
Habit: The agile, arboreal, common house gecko is found in much of Indo-Malaysia, New Guinea and many Pacific islands. In Australia, almost entirely confined to human settlements in Australia where it usually lives in and around buildings, emerging at night to feed on insects attracted to indoor and outdoor lights. Its distinctive 'chuck-chuck-chuck' call is quite loud and may be made both during the day and at night. Lays two brittle- shelled eggs.

Hemidactylus frenatus (eggs)
Cocos (Keeling) Islands, Indian Ocean. Many females lay their two eggs in communal nesting sites, which may contain eggs at all stages of development as well as old egg shells.

Hemidactylus frenatus Yam Island, Torres Strait

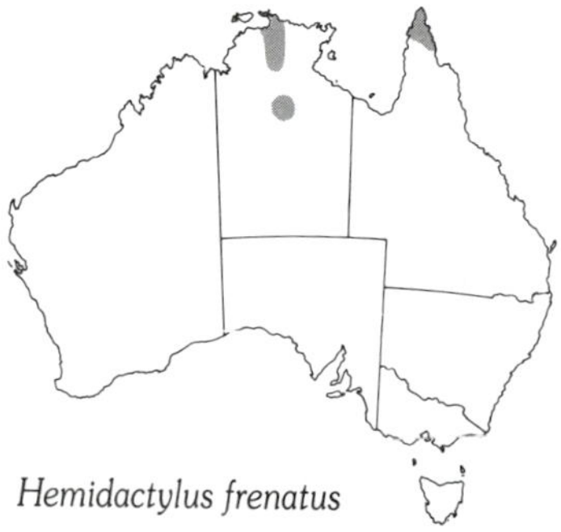

Hemidactylus frenatus

Genus ***Heteronotia*** Wermuth, 1965

An endemic Australian genus, currently with only two species. Rostral and mental shields rounded. Labials much larger than adjacent scales. Postmentals enlarged. Digits long, slender, slightly compressed distally, with two rows of lateral scales on the digits; no enlarged apical subdigital lamellae, but with a single series of slightly swollen transverse lamellae; feet bird-like, the digits angular when viewed laterally; all digits clawed, the claws conspicuous and free, the base of each claw between three scales. Preanal pores present.

Key

TO THE SPECIES OF HETERONOTIA

Dorsal tubercles small (more than 25 in paravertebral row between axilla and groin), lying in very regular longitudinal rows; body strongly banded..***spelea***

Dorsal tubercles large (fewer than 25 in paravertebral rows between axilla and groin), not in very regular longitudinal rows; body pattern variegated or banded..............................***binoei***

Heteronotia binoei Muttaburra, Qld

Heteronotia binoei (Gray, 1845)

Bynoe's Gecko

Heteronotia binoei

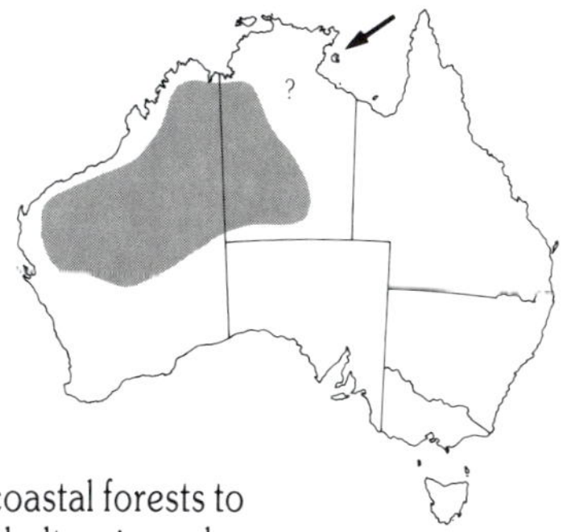

Heteronotia spelea

Description: Highly variable in colour, ranging from pale grey through dull brown to bright reddish-brown to almost black, typically with scattered darker and paler flecks, spots and blotches which may be distributed irregularly over the back and tail, but are more usually aligned transversely, making a pattern of conspicuous to obscure broken bands. Usually at least some indication of a dark temporal streak and another dark streak along the canthus rostralis. Lips whitish, lightly flecked with dark brown. Whitish below, finely peppered with dark brown. A slender gecko with a long, tapering tail which is more or less round in section. Skin above finely granular, with numerous scattered trihedral tubercles, sometimes arranged in fairly uniform longitudinal rows, usually fewer than 25 in a paravertebral row between the axilla and the groin. 50 mm (snout-vent).
Distribution: Found throughout most parts of continental Australia, except for the more humid areas of the south-west and the south-east.
Habit: A small, common, terrestrial lizard found in a wide variety of habitats from wet coastal forests to the deserts of the centre. Usually shelters in rock crevices, or among ground litter and debris, emerging to forage in open areas at night. Lays two brittle-shelled eggs. A number of all-female (parthenogenetic), triploid populations occur in central and western Australia (Moritz).

Heteronotia spelea Mt Doreen, NT

Heteronotia spelea (Kluge, 1963)

Desert Cave Gecko

Description: Strongly banded above, with four or five broad, dark brown crossbands, sometimes dark-edged, alternating with pale fawn- or cream-coloured bands about equal in width to the darker bands. The first dark band forms a collar, extending around the nape from eye to eye; occasionally a dark bar across the back of the head. Original tails strongly banded; regrown tails brown. Body shape similar to that of *Heteronotia binoei*. Skin above finely granular with numerous small, scattered trihedral tubercles, arranged in regular longitudinal rows, with more than 25 in a paravertebral row between the axilla and groin. 50 mm (snout-vent).

Distribution: Described from the Pilbara region of WA, but extends north and east into the rocky hills and outcrops of the Tanami Desert region. Recorded from Groote Eylandt by Gow.

Habit: An inhabitant of subterranean cavities such as caves and mine shafts, but specimens have also been found in caves and rock crevices well up in stony desert hills. Found at night foraging about the entrances of such caves and crevices.

Genus *Lepidodactylus* Fitzinger, 1843

A large genus ranging from East Asia through the Indo-Malayan Archipelago to New Guinea and the islands of Oceania, but with only two species reaching Australia. Its limited and patchy distribution on mainland Australia suggests that it might have been accidentally introduced by man, although it was first recorded as early as the 1870's. Rostral and mental shields rounded. Labials much larger than adjacent scales. Postmentals enlarged. Digits moderately long, somewhat depressed, and expanded distally to form broad pads; apical subdigital lamellae not enlarged but continuous with a single or double series of narrow transverse lamellae extending across the full width of the pad; digits lying flat on the substrate when viewed laterally; all digits clawed, the large claws rising from the edge of the expanded pad, and not retractile in a distal median groove. Preanal pores present.

Key

TO THE AUSTRALIAN SPECIES OF LEPIDODACTYLUS

Subdigital lamellae undivided (a).............................. ***pumilus***
Subdigital lamellae divided (b).................................. ***lugubris***

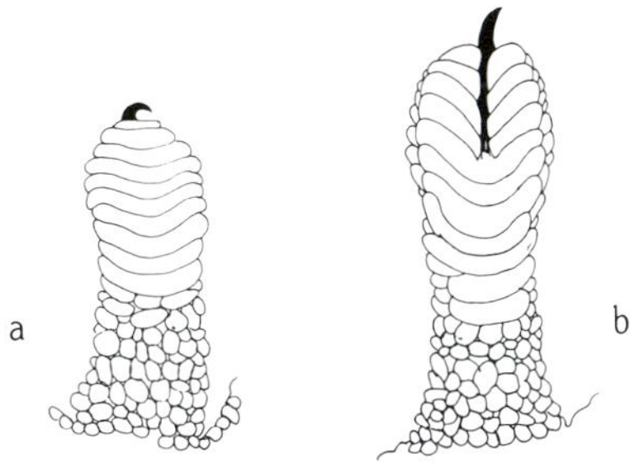

Lepidodactylus lugubris

Lepidodactylus lugubris Cocos (Keeling) Islands, Indian Ocean

Lepidodactylus lugubris (Duméril and Bibron, 1836)

Mourning Gecko

Description: Usually pale creamy-fawn above, with darker brown flecks and mottling especially on the sides. A series of obscure W-shaped markings down the centre of the back and tail, each angular base of the W usually with a small blackish spot. A narrow dark brown stripe along the canthus rostralis, continued behind the eye, with a pale upper edge, to about the level of the forearm. Body covered with small, smooth, homogeneous scales. Tail relatively long, depressed, covered above with homogeneous scales but with a lateral flange on each side often consisting of a row of small, spinose scales and sometimes including some slightly enlarged, spinose scales. 50 mm (snout-vent).
Distribution: Known only from several coastal localities between Innisfail and Port Douglas, Qld, and from many islands in Torres Strait. Extra-limital in Indo-Malaysia, New Guinea and the islands of Oceania.

Lepidodactylus lugubris Cocos (Keeling) Islands, Indian Ocean. A hatchling and several pairs of eggs, each one of a pair attached to each other and the substrate. Each pair of eggs is produced by a different female.

Habit: A small arboreal gecko normally living in the crowns of palms and in other low vegetation, especially in coastal and beach situations, but is also a common inhabitant of buildings and other man-made structures. Eggs are soft and adherent when laid, hardening soon after to become connected to each other and to the substrate on which they are laid.

Lepidodactylus pumilus (Boulenger, 1885)

Description: Superficially similar to *Lepidodactylus lugubris,* from which it may be readily distinguished by its undivided subdigital lamellae and more cylindrical tail.
Distribution: Known only from the islands of Torres Strait.
Habit: An arboreal species found in closed forests (including mangroves) and adjacent humid woodland.

Lepidodactylus pumilus Prince of Wales Island, Torres Strait

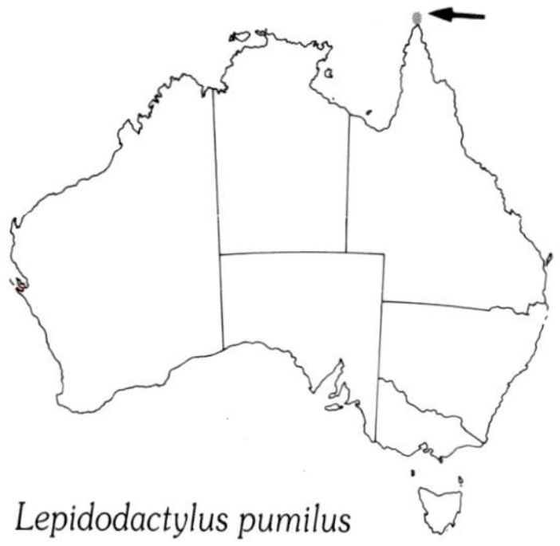

Lepidodactylus pumilus

Genus *Lucasium* Wermuth, 1965

A monotypic, endemic Australian genus. Similar in most respects to *Diplodactylus,* of which it is sometimes regarded as a synonym. Differs from *Diplodactylus* in the absence of even a slightly enlarged pair of apical subdigital lamellae, the digits covered below by numerous irregular, small, spinose tubercles.

Lucasium damaeum (Lucas and Frost, 1896)

Beaded Gecko

Description: Rich reddish-brown above, with a broad pale cream or fawn vertebral band which has a ragged or zigzag edge on either side, or which may be broken up into a series of rhomboidal or diamond-shaped blotches in some specimens. Sides and limbs with numerous pale spots, usually a single longitudinal series of larger spots on the sides, surrounded by scattered smaller spots. The reddish-brown ground colour of the sides and limbs with obscure, fine, dark brown reticulations. Snout and crown of head pale with reddish-brown flecks and reticulations. Rim of upper eyelid white or cream. Original tails with a continuation of the body pattern, reproduced tails plain brown or spotted with darker brown. Whitish below. Digits usually whitish. Body scales small, smooth, homogeneous. 50 mm (snout-vent).
Distribution: Drier interior of all mainland states of Australia.
Habit: A common, small, terrestrial gecko, found in a wide variety of xeric habitats from savannah woodland and mallee to the spinifex-covered sandhills and ranges of the centre. Usually found foraging in open sandy areas at night, by day sheltering in shallow, sub-surface burrows dug by the lizard itself, or more commonly in abandoned lizard, spider or insect burrows, including the vertical openings to ant nests, in which it sits during the day with its head almost at ground level.

Lucasium damaeum Round Hill, NSW

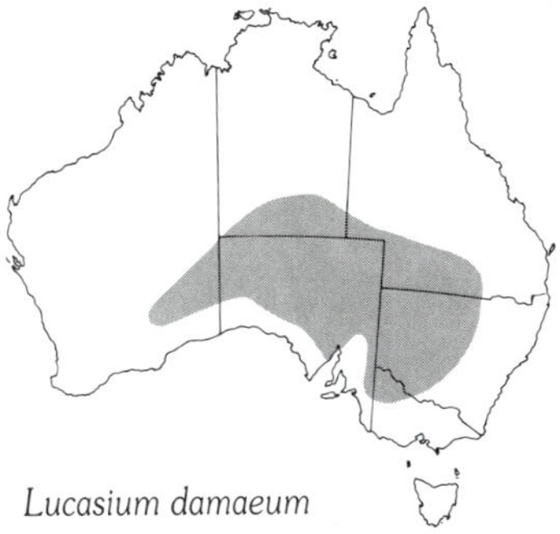

Lucasium damaeum

Genus ***Nactus*** Kluge, 1983

Similar in most external features to *Cyrtodactylus*, from which it is distinguished by the internal features of fused nasal bones (paired in *Cyrtodactylus*) and possession of a second ceratobranchial rod in the hyoid apparatus (absent in *Cyrtodactylus*). Australian species in these two genera can be readily distinguished by the presence (*Cyrtodactylus*) or absence (*Nactus*) of a lateral skin fold from axilla to groin.

Key

TO THE AUSTRALIAN SPECIES OF NACTUS

Preanal and femoral regions with slightly enlarged scales (a); fewer than 13 longitudinal rows of enlarged tubercles on back and flanks..***galgajuga***

Preanal and femoral regions without enlarged scales (b); more than 13 longitudinal rows of enlarged tubercles on back and flanks..***pelagicus***

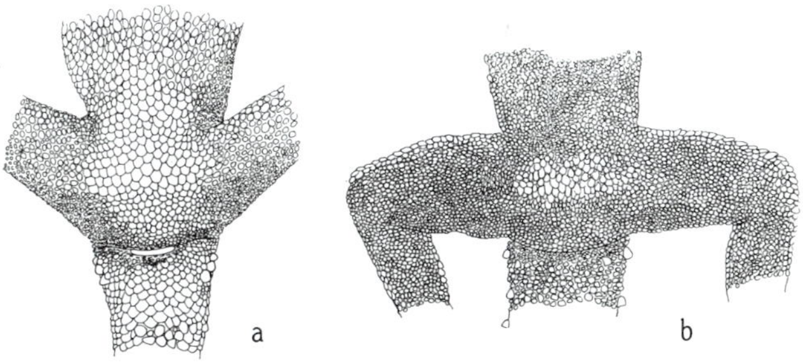

a b

Nactus galgajuga (Ingram, 1978)

Description: Dark purplish-brown above, with a series of narrow, pale cream cross-bands on the body, tail and limbs, the pale bands much narrower than the darker interspaces; bands break up on lower flanks into cream and purplish-brown variegations; labials dark. Ventral surfaces pale brown, the palmar surfaces and subdigital lamellae dark brown. A lightly built, spindly-legged gecko with long, slender tail. Body scales small and granular, with ten longitudinal rows of enlarged, pointed tubercles on the back. Base of tail without large, transverse ventral plates.

Nactus galgajuga

Nactus galgajuga Black Mountain, Qld

Nactus pelagicus Weipa, Qld

Preanal and femoral pores presumed to be present in males. 50 mm (snout-vent).
Distribution: Known only from the Trevathan Range, near Cooktown, Qld.
Habit: A rock-dwelling species apparently confined to the black boulder ranges which characterise the type locality.

Nactus pelagicus

Nactus pelagicus (Girard, 1858)
Pelagic Gecko

Description: Resembles some specimens of *Heteronotia binoei,* with which it can be confused where the two are sympatric. Brown, dark brown or blackish above, with or without a series of dark-edged darker blotches which tend to form broken transverse bands, especially on the tail. Lips whitish, lightly barred with dark brown. Whitish below, finely peppered with brown. No lateral skin fold. A small, moderately built lizard, with long, slender tail. Body scales small and granular, with numerous tubercular scales arranged in more than a dozen longitudinal rows along the body and sides. Base of tail without large, transverse ventral plates. Males with fewer than 20 pores. 80 mm (snout-vent). The specific name of this species is currently in dispute, with some herpetologists using the earlier, forgotten name *Nactus arnouxii.*
Distribution: Cape York Peninsula. Extra-limital in New Guinea and throughout the islands of the western Pacific Ocean.
Habit: A nocturnal terrestrial gecko usually found hiding under ground debris. Sometimes found at night foraging on the forest floor. Occurs in both wet and dry forests and tropical woodlands.

Genus ***Nephrurus*** Günther, 1876

A distinctive endemic Australian genus whose members are all characterised by their large heads and short, fat tails terminating in a small knob. All are essentially arid-adapted terrestrial species.

Rostral and mental shields rounded. Labials larger than the adjacent scales. Postmentals not enlarged. Digits short, round, without enlarged apical subdigital lamellae, and covered below by numerous irregular, small, spinose tubercles; all digits clawed. Preanal pores absent.

Key
TO THE SPECIES OF NEPHRURUS

1 Scattered tubercles on the flanks.................................... **2**
Flanks smooth, without tubercles................ ***laevissimus***

2 Flank tubercles each contain a single, conical scale (a); fewer than eight interorbital scales (b)............................. **3**
Flank tubercles each contain several conical scales (c); more than eight interorbital scales (d)...................... ***asper***

3 No broad, dark transverse bands; transverse bands, if present, narrow, pale and irregular on a darker ground colour... **4**
Four or five broad, dark bands across body and tail........... .... ***wheeleri***

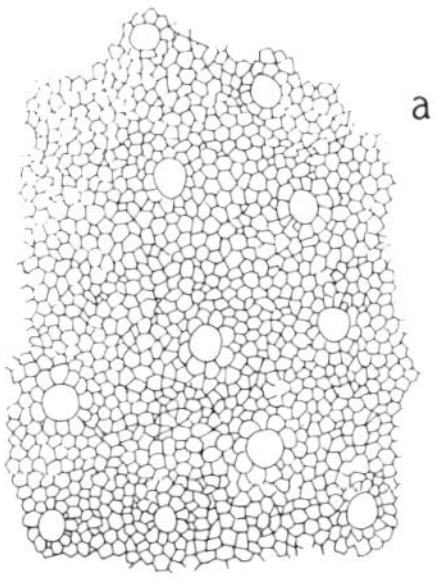

a

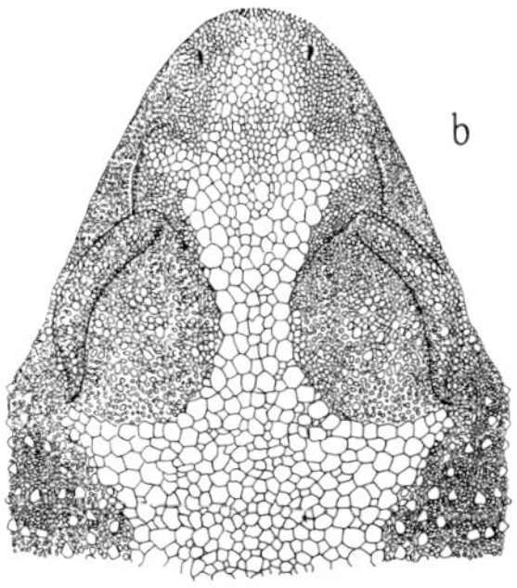

b

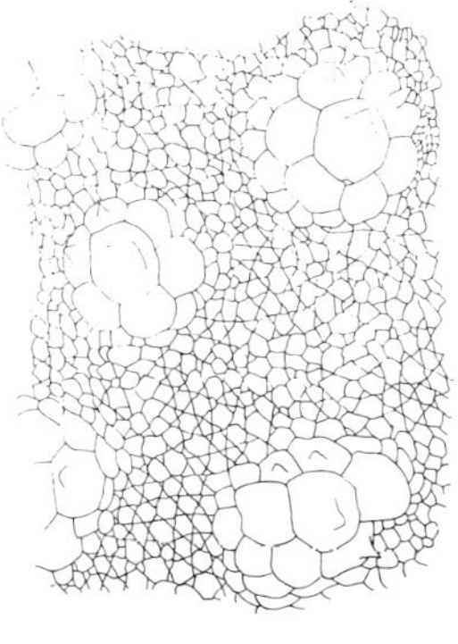

c

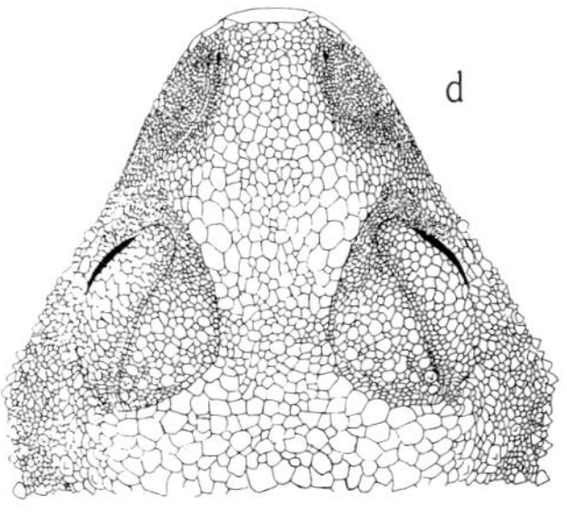

d

4 Vertebral stripe absent in adults; if present in juveniles, then nine or more longitudinal rows of enlarged tubercles on the tail.. **5**

A prominent pale, vertebral stripe in adults; fewer than nine longitudinal rows of enlarged tubercles on the tail; tail narrow and slightly depressed........................***vertebralis***

5 Tail narrow and only slightly depressed........................... **6**

Tail broad and flat; white spots on back, if present, represented only by white tubercles................................. ***levis***

6 Most enlarged tubercles on back surrounded by a ring of scales which are noticeably larger than the other body scales between the tubercles; back and flanks with numerous white spots, each much larger than central tubercle (e)... ***stellatus***

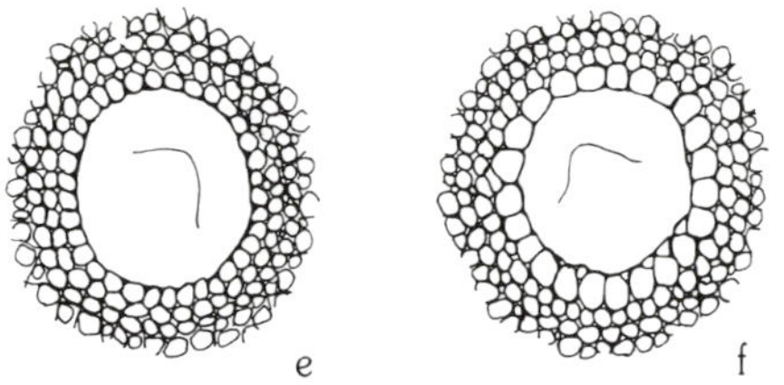
e f

Enlarged tubercles on back surrounded by a ring of scales which are not noticeably larger than the other body scales between the tubercles (f); white spots, if present, largely confined to the flanks.. ***deleani***

Nephrurus asper Rockhampton, Qld

Nephrurus asper (tail) Rockhampton, Qld

Nephrurus asper Günther, 1876

Description: Pale grey to rich brown, olive-brown or reddish-brown above, with a series of obscure to conspicuous narrow, irregular blackish cross-bands, alternating with irregular transverse rows of white spots, each spot covering one of the rosettes of tubercles described below, and the spots irregularly crowding the flanks. Top and sides of head covered with a fine dark brown or black reticulation. Limbs above the same ground colour as the dorsum, mottled with darker and paler brown. Whitish below. Head very large and massive, with more than eight interorbital scales. Body above and on the sides covered with small, flat scales through which are scattered numerous rosettes of enlarged scales, each rosette consisting of a ring of rounded tubercular scales enclosing one (on the back) or more (on the sides and throat) larger and higher conical tubercular scales. Smooth below, except on the throat which has numerous small tubercular rosettes. Tail very short, only a little longer than broad, with about eight or nine transverse rows of enlarged tubercular scales or rosettes, ending in a fairly large knob. 100 mm (snout-vent).

Distribution: North-western Australia, through northern and central Australia to drier parts of Qld, almost to the east coast near Townsville.

Habit: Little known. Usually found in rocky habitats where it lives in crevices between larger outcrops or under larger slabs on a soil or sandy substrate.

Nephrurus deleani Harvey, 1983.

Description: Pale brown or purplish-brown above with a series of narrow blackish streaks or bars forming reticulations on the head (including a dark temporal streak on each side of the head) and a series of V-shaped bars, often interrupted on the midline, on the neck and body; between these dark bars on the body are narrow pale fawn bars and spots; often a pair of longitudinal dark streaks over the pelvic region; sometimes a pale vertebral stripe; tail dark brown with transverse rows of white enlarged tubercles. Ventral surfaces white. Head moderate, with fewer than eight interorbital scales. Body covered above with small flat scales, throughout which are scattered low, conical tubercles. Smooth below. Tail narrow, slightly depressed, and with 14-18 transverse rows of enlarged tubercles and ending in a small knob. 85 mm (snout-vent).

Distribution: SA, north of Spencer Gulf, where it has been found 'only from the *Acacia* vegetated sand hills immediately north and west of Pernatty Lagoon' (Harvey).

Habit: On vegetated sand dunes.

Nephrurus deleani Mt Gunson, SA

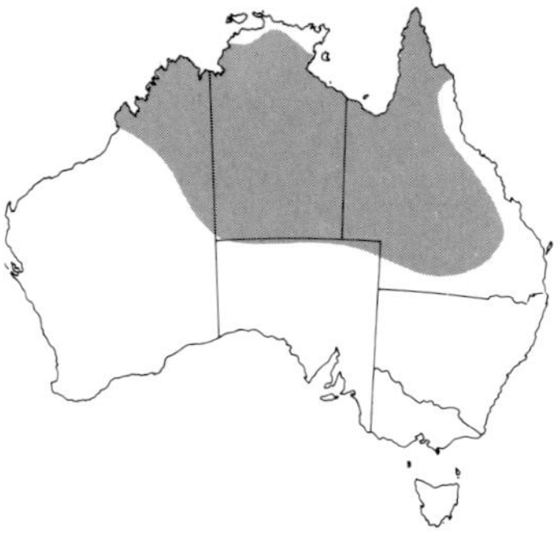

Nephrurus asper

Nephrurus deleani

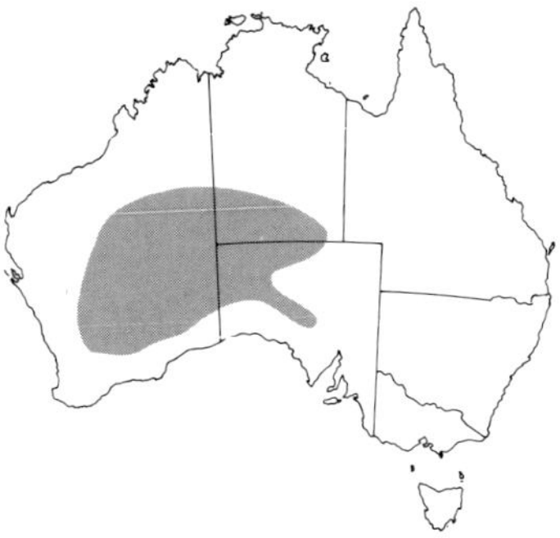

Nephrurus laevissimus

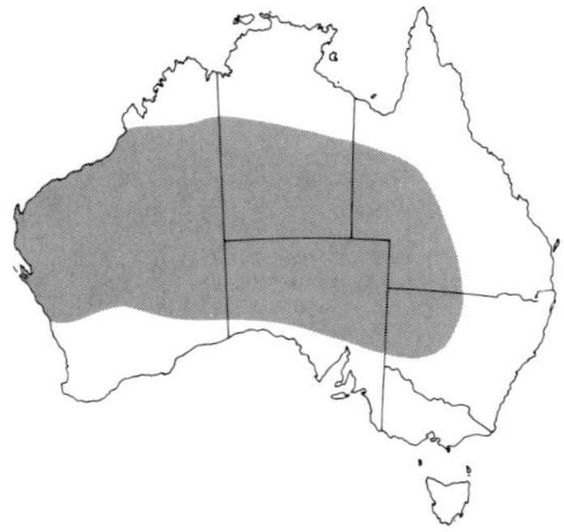

Nephrurus levis

Nephrurus stellatus

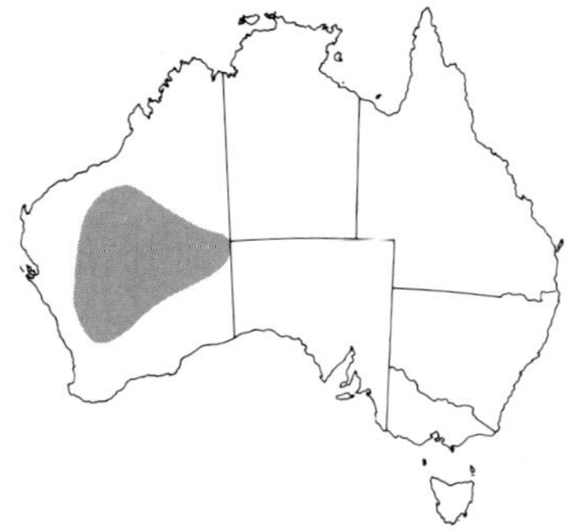

Nephrurus vertebralis

Nephrurus wheeleri

Nephrurus laevissimus Mertens, 1958

Description: Dorsally pale pink or pinkish-grey, with a black or dark brown bar from behind each eye and extending across the occipital, another dark bar across the neck, and a third crossing the back from forelimb to forelimb; there is also a dark bar along each side of the sacrum, while there may be dark spots or patches on the head and over the sacral region. White below. Head moderate, with fewer than eight interorbital scales. Body mostly smooth, especially on the neck and most of the back and flanks, with scales or low tubercles along the midline and increasing over the sacral region. Tail narrow, above with about six regular longitudinal series of conical tubercles each surrounded by a group of slightly enlarged granules, and ending in a small knob. Ventral surface covered by small granular scales. Average snout-vent length 65 mm, maximum about 80 mm.
Distribution: South-eastern WA, extending into north-western SA and southern parts of the NT.
Habit: Associated with spinifex-covered sand dunes throughout its range.

Nephrurus levis De Vis, 1886

Description: Light to dark purplish-brown above usually with a light-coloured bar from eye to eye across the occiput, a second light bar across the neck and a third across the back from forelimb to forelimb; each of these light bars is dark-edged so that the dark edging may be more prominent on specimens with a pale ground colour. Remainder of body with a series of small spots, bars or transverse lines consisting of groups of individual white tubercles. Head moderate, with fewer than eight interorbital scales. White below. Body covered above with small, juxtaposed scales through which are scattered single, low conical tubercles, each of which is surrounded by a ring of scales similar to those occurring between the tubercles. Tail narrow to wide, depressed above with usually eight or more longitudinal rows of tubercles, each of which is surrounded by a group of slightly enlarged granules, and ending in a small knob. Ventral surface covered by small granular scales. 80 mm (snout-vent).
Distribution: Found in a broad belt from central coast of WA to the arid parts of all mainland states except Vic.
Habit: Found in a wide range of arid and semi-arid habitats, from open woodland and arid scrubs to spinifex-covered desert sandplains and dunefields. A

nocturnal terrestrial lizard which apparently lives during the day in burrows which it either excavates itself or which have been made previously by insects, other lizards or small mammals. Forages at night in open areas.
Subspecies: *occidentalis* (central coast of WA); *pilbarensis* (Pilbara region, WA); *levis* (remainder of range).

Nephrurus stellatus Storr, 1968

Description: Reddish- or purplish-brown above, the back, sides and tail with numerous scattered white spots, most spots covering the site of one of the enlarged tubercular scales described below. Three broken transverse pale lines across the neck between the occiput and the shoulders. A white streak below the eye and a large, pale patch in front of the eye. Rim of eyelid cream or yellow. Whitish below. Head moderate, with fewer than eight interorbital scales. Body covered above with small, flat scales through which are scattered small rosettes (consisting of a ring of slightly enlarged scales enclosing a larger, pointed conical scale), or single enlarged conical scales. Tail narrow and only slightly depressed with about thirteen transverse rows of enlarged tubercles, and ending in a smallish knob. 80 mm (snout-vent).
Distribution: South-eastern WA to Eyre Peninsula, SA.
Habit: Arid scrublands and heaths. Otherwise similar to *Nephrurus levis*.

Nephrurus vertebralis Storr, 1963

Description: Similar in most respects to *Nephrurus levis*, from which it differs in having a conspicuous, pale vertebral stripe from the occiput to the end of the tail, and a narrower and less depressed tail, with tubercles arranged in more regular, but usually fewer (7-8) longitudinal rows. 80 mm (snout-vent).
Distribution: Lower central interior of WA to SA.
Habit: Arid scrub- and shrub-lands throughout its range. Otherwise similar to *Nephrurus levis*.

Nephrurus wheeleri Loveridge, 1932

Description: Pinkish- or purplish-brown above, with four or five broad, dark-brown cross-bands on the body and tail, each dark band nearly as wide, or as wide, as the paler interspaces. Head pale with brown reticulations on the snout and sides. Whitish below.

Nephrurus laevissimus near Mt Olga, NT

Nephrurus levis Bourke, NSW

Nephrurus stellatus Mt Holland, WA

M. PETERSON

Nephrurus wheeleri Dandaraga Station, WA

M. PETERSON

Nephrurus vertebralis Great Victoria Desert, WA

Head large, with fewer than eight interorbital scales. Body covered with small, flat scales through which are scattered numerous small rosettes, each consisting of a ring of slightly enlarged scales enclosing a much larger, raised conical scale; these enlarged tubercles extend on to the nape, flanks, tail and throat. Tail much longer than wide, depressed, ending in a smallish knob. 80 mm (snout-vent).
Distribution: Largely restricted to the Murchison and Fortescue River districts, WA.
Habit: A terrestrial species inhabiting arid scrublands, rocky outcrops and spinifex-covered stony ranges.
Subspecies: *wheeleri* (Murchison district, WA); *cinctus* (Fortescue River district, WA).

Genus ***Oedura*** Gray, 1842

An endemic Australian genus with species found throughout most parts of continental Australia. Rostral and mental shields rounded. Labials larger than adjacent scales. Postmentals enlarged. Digits moderately long, depressed, moderately expanded distally to form a distinct pad; a greatly enlarged pair of apical subdigital lamellae, followed by a series of enlarged transverse lamellae, divided distally, single proximally; digits lying flat on substrate when viewed laterally; all digits clawed, the claws small, retractile and lying between the enlarged apical lamellae. Preanal pores present.

Key

TO THE SPECIES OF OEDURA

1 Dorsal scales flat, round, juxtaposed, about as large as ventrals.. **2**

Dorsal scales minute, granular, usually much smaller than the ventrals.. **10**

2 Hindlimbs mottled, spotted or variegated above, but without regular, pale, dark-edged ocelli; dorsal pattern of cross-bands, irregular mottling or ocelli; the latter, if present, are larger than the eye and tend to occur in pairs..... **3**

Hindlimbs with regular, small, pale, dark-edged ocelli; dorsal pattern typically of regular, small ocelli, each smaller than the eye; occasionally these ocelli may coalesce to form irregular or broken cross-bands............................. **9**

3 Digits without conspicuous lateral fringes (a)................... **4**

Digits with conspicuous lateral fringes caused by laterally-expanded subdigital lamellae (b)...................... ***filicipoda***

4 Size large, snout-vent length to 100 mm; white spots, if present on the back, not confined to the paler alternate cross-bands.. **5**

Size small, snout-vent to about 65 mm; white spots, if present on the back, confined to the paler alternate cross-bands.. ***obscura***

5 Enlarged apical lamellae of fourth toe followed by four or more pairs of large, divided lamellae (c).......................... **6**

Enlarged apical lamellae of fourth toe followed by only two pairs of large, divided lamellae (d)........................***gracilis***

6 Body colour pattern of distinct (though sometimes broken) cross-bands or large ocelli...................................... **7**

Body colour pattern of small whitish or yellowish flecks, dots or spots on a black or dark brown groundcolour........ .... ***gemmata***

7 Body typically with five or six distinct, light-coloured cross-bands, extending to the white ventral surface on each side; where these bands are broken up the resulting patches have no regular shape and size; the dark streak through each eye almost invariably meets on the nape to form a dark collar... **8**

Body typically with five or six pairs of dark ocellate markings having a dark edge and being at least as large as the eye; occasional specimens with an odd number of ocelli, or with the pairs of ocelli coalescing; the dark streaks through each eye never meet on the nape to form a dark collar...... .... ***monilis***

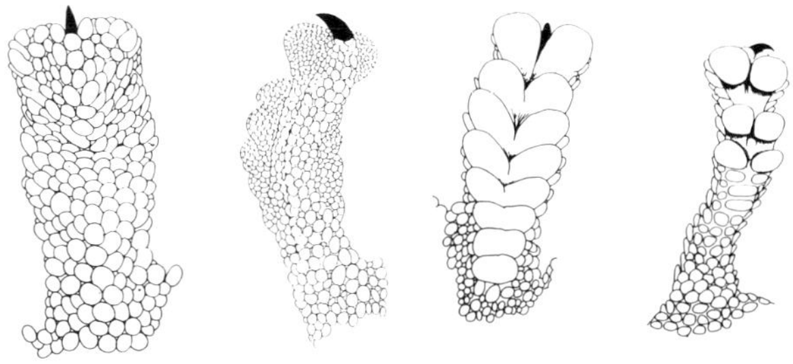

a b c d

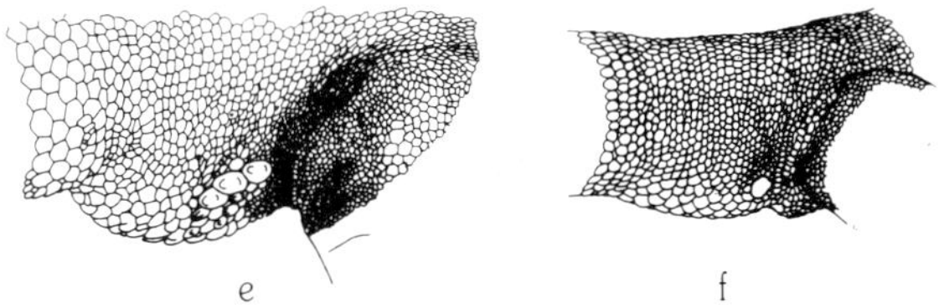

e f

8 A series of five or six light cross-bands between snout and vent; these bands may be sharp and regular or may be broken up into a series of spots in a curved line, but are only about one-quarter the width of the darker interspaces; head usually with scattered white flecks.. ***marmorata***

A series of five light crossbands between snout and vent; these bands are almost invariably sharp in outline and almost as wide as the darker interspaces; head without numerous scattered white flecks.................... ***castelnaui***

9 Interorbitals generally 18-19 or more; mid-body scale rows generally exceed 95; only rarely will one or other count be lower than those cited; southern Qld or northern NSW..... .... ***tryoni***

Interorbitals generally 18 or fewer; mid-body scale rows generally fewer than 95; only rarely will one or other count exceed those cited; north-eastern Qld.................. ***coggeri***

10 Two or more enlarged postanal tubercles on each side (e). **11**

A single enlarged postanal tubercle on each side (f)........... .... ***reticulata***

11 A continuous, broad, lighter-coloured vertebral band enclosed on each side by a darker zigzag dorso-lateral band.......... **12**

A dark dorso-lateral band on each side extending from the eye to the tail, the two bands being joined by a series of five or six transverse bars (the first across the occiput), so as to enclose a series of large, light-coloured, dorsal blotches.......... ***robusta***

12 Grey or dark brown above, with continuous mottling along the vertebral region; this mottling is enclosed on each side by a thin, irregular, dark zigzag line; sides and limbs with small, light-coloured spots; tail depressed.......... ***lesueurii***

Uniform light brown along the vertebral region, with an irregular dark brown line running from each eye laterally along the body; sides and limbs with very small dark spots; tail usually cylindrical.......... ***rhombifer***

Oedura castelnaui (Thominot, 1889)

Northern Velvet Gecko

Description: Deep purplish-brown above, usually with a series of pale white or yellowish transverse bands between snout and vent. Each of these pale cross-bands may enclose some darker brown scales, but the bands are about as wide as the darker interspaces. Juveniles are strongly banded but in old adults the dark ground colour may contain numerous yellow scales, sometimes so numerous as to reduce the ground colour to the borders of the pale cross-bands. Snout and crown of head pale, continuous with the first (and sometimes second) pale cross-bands. First dark cross-band forming a collar across the nape from eye to eye. Limbs specked or mottled with yellow and brown. Whitish below. Dorsal scales flat, round, juxtaposed and homogeneous, about as large as the ventrals. A single postanal tubercle on each side. The tail is relatively long and moderately depressed. 90 mm (snout-vent).

Distribution: Cape York Peninsula, approximately north of latitude 18° south.

Habit: Woodland. Typically arboreal, but often found under bark on fallen trees and among natural and man-made debris on the ground. Lays two parchment-shelled eggs.

Oedura castelnaui Mitchell River, Qld

Oedura coggeri Bustard, 1966

Northern Spotted Velvet Gecko

Description: Rich orange-brown above, with an irregular series of pale ocelli or short transverse bars each bordered with dark purplish-brown and sometimes coalescing to form irregular cross-bands. Areas between the ocelli mottled with dark brown. The pale ocelli and bars may themselves contain

Oedura coggeri Lappa Junction, Qld

some dark brown scales. Usually a complete or broken pale, dark-edged nuchal band, the dark edge more or less continuous with a dark brown stripe along the side of the face. Hindlimbs with distinct, pale, dark-edged ocelli. Snout and top of head pale, with obscure darker mottling. Juveniles dark purplish-brown with numerous small yellow spots. Whitish below. Dorsal scales flat, round, juxtaposed and homogeneous, about as large as the ventrals. A single postanal tubercle on each side. The tail is moderately long and slender, only slightly depressed. 70 mm (snout-vent).
Distribution: Cape York Peninsula, approximately north of latitude 18°S.
Habit: Woodland. Usually found under exfoliating granite wherever rocky outcrops or hills occur throughout its range, but sometimes found under bark on fallen trees. Emerges at night to forage over the open rock faces.

Oedura castelnaui

Oedura coggeri

Oedura filicipoda

Oedura filicipoda King, 1984

Description: Dark brown above with small fawn or yellowish spots scattered over face, head, limbs and back, except where the neck and back are traversed by five narrow, paler brown cross-bands. The cross-bands may be obscure to prominent, and individual bands may occasionally coalesce. Original tails blue-black with several broad blackish cross-bands spotted with bright yellow; reproduced tails blackish mottled with yellow; ventral surfaces whitish, with

Oedura filicipoda Mitchell Plateau, WA

Oedura gemmata Brockman Range, NT

Oedura gracilis King Leopold Range, WA

Oedura lesueurii Tenterfield, NSW

Oedura marmorata

darker brown or grey dots, flecks or mottling, especially on the throat. Dorsal scales small, flat, juxtaposed and homogeneous, almost as large as ventrals. Usually 4 postanal tubercles on each side in males. Tail large, swollen, depressed. 100 mm (snout-vent).
Distribution: Known only from the Mitchell Plateau, Kimberley region of WA.
Habit: Inhabits caves in heavily dissected sandstone country.

Oedura gemmata King and Gow, 1983

Description: Very dark brown to black above, the head and body covered with numerous small, irregularly scattered cream, yellow and pale brown flecks, dots and spots; original tails black with a series of narrow whitish cross-bands and scattered white spots; ventral surfaces white or grey. Dorsal scales small, flat, juxtaposed and homogeneous, about as large as the ventrals. Usually 2-3 postanal tubercles on each side. Tail relatively long, sometimes rather slender but more usually rather fat and distinctly depressed. 100 mm (snout-vent).
Distribution: Western escarpment of Arnhem Land, NT, and its outliers.
Habit: A rock-dwelling species found active at night in caves and on rock faces throughout its range.

Oedura gracilis King, 1984

Description: Dark yellow-brown above with a series of about eight paler yellow-brown cross-bands from nape to base of tail, these bands being about twice as wide as the darker interspaces. A blackish canthal streak continuing through the eye and above the ear on either side of the head, then narrowing to form a continuous blackish collar across the nape. Edge of eyelid yellow. Lips whitish. Whitish below. Dorsal scales flat, round, juxtaposed and homogeneous, almost as large as the ventrals. Three postanal tubercles on each side. The tail is long and slender, more or less round in section, almost as long as the head and body. 85 mm (snout-vent).
Distribution: Currently known only from the Mitchell Plateau, Kimberley region of WA.
Habit: The only known specimens were taken from rock outcrops and overhangs in heavily-dissected sandstone country.

Oedura marmorata McArthur River, NT. Juvenile, showing strongly banded pattern which usually becomes more obscure as the individual grows.

Oedura lesueurii (Duméril and Bibron, 1836)

Lesueur's Velvet Gecko

Description: Pale grey to brown above, with a broad, dark-edged vertebral band, sometimes reduced to a series of connected or disconnected (especially on the tail) rhomboidal patches. The edges of the band are deeply notched to form a zigzag pattern. Sides and limbs dark grey or brown with numerous small, dark-edged spots or blotches, or merely specked and mottled with paler and darker brown. Snout and top of head pale, with obscure darker mottling. Whitish below. Skin finely granular above, the dorsal scales minute and homogeneous, usually much smaller than the ventrals. Two or more postanal tubercles on each side. The tail is moderately long and markedly depressed. 80 mm (snout-vent).
Distribution: Coast and ranges of NSW and south-eastern Qld.
Habit: Usually found living in caves or crevices, or under exfoliating slabs on large rock slopes and ridges. Forages on the open rock faces, but more usually among ground litter at the edges of the rock faces. Lays two parchment-shelled eggs in a clutch.

Oedura marmorata Lightning Ridge, NSW

Oedura marmorata Gray, 1842

Marbled Velvet Gecko

Description: The most variable and widely distributed member of its genus, and probably composite as currently recognised. Typically rich purplish-brown above, with five or six pale white or yellow cross-bands between snout and vent. The cross-bands are frequently dark-centred and are

Oedura monilis Warrumbungle Range, NSW

usually less than half the width of the darker interspaces; the latter may enclose numerous scattered white or yellow scales; flanks spotted or mottled with white or yellow on brown. The first pale transverse band is more or less continuous with a pale stripe along the lips. In some older specimens nearly all pattern may be lost. Hindlimbs brown, speckled with white or yellow; if spotted the spots are not in the form of dark-edged ocelli. Juveniles are black or dark purplish-brown above, with well-delineated white or yellow cross-bands. Whitish below. Dorsal scales flat, round, juxtaposed and homogeneous, about as large as the ventrals. Usually two postanal tubercles on each side, but a single tubercle in some central and northern populations. The tail may vary from long, slender and only slightly depressed (southern populations), to short and greatly depressed or even globular (Arnhem Land). 90 mm (snout-vent).

Distribution: Eastern, central and northern Australia, excluding north-eastern Qld.

Habit: Largely arboreal in eastern populations, sheltering in crevices or under the loose bark of standing or fallen trees, or tree stumps; saxicolous in many of the central and northern populations, living by day in crevices, caves or overhangs, or under exfoliating slabs of rock, and emerging at night to forage on the open rock faces. Found primarily in savannah woodlands in the east and north, but more or less confined to spinifex- and scrub-covered stony hills in central Australia.

Oedura obscura Mitchell Plateau, WA

R. W. G. JENKINS

Oedura monilis De Vis, 1888

Ocellated Velvet Gecko

Description: Pale yellow-brown above, with numerous dark purplish-brown or blue-brown scales, forming fine mottling or reticulations. A series of five

or six pairs of large white, cream or bluish-white ocelli along the centre of the back between snout and vent. Each ocellus is dark-edged and at least as large as the eye, but the two members of a pair of ocelli frequently merge to form an 8-shaped mark or a short transverse bar. In northern populations (central Qld) the blackish edges of the ocelli frequently coalesce to form longitudinal markings, especially anteriorly. A dark streak below the canthus rostralis continued a short distance behind the eye. Limbs mottled with yellow and brown. Juveniles above deep purplish-black, with the pairs of ocelli strongly contrasting in yellow. Whitish below. Dorsal scales flat, round, juxtaposed and homogeneous, about as large as the ventrals. A single postanal tubercle on each side. Tail long and relatively slender, only slightly depressed. 80 mm (snout-vent).
Distribution: Western slopes and ranges of central and northern NSW to central-eastern Qld.
Habit: An arboreal species of dry sclerophyll forests and of eucalyptus and Callitris woodlands, usually found under bark or in crevices of standing or fallen trees.

Oedura obscura King, 1984

Description: Fawn above, with a dark brown canthal streak and a series of about 12 irregular, narrow, dark brown cross-bands between the nape and the base of the tail, each dark band narrower than the paler interspaces and lacking the white spots and dots which are scattered over the paler interspaces and the head. Whitish below. Limbs mottled fawn and dark brown, dotted with white. Original tail colour and pattern similar to dorsum; reproduced tail fawn with three longitudinal dark brown streaks. Dorsal scales flat, round, juxtaposed, almost as large as ventrals. Three postanal tubercles on each side. Tail long, slender, more or less round in section, almost as long as head and body. 60 mm (snout-vent).
Range, Kimberley region of WA.
Habit: Type specimen 'found under flat boulders...of sandstone' (King).

Oedura reticulata Bustard, 1969

Reticulated Velvet Gecko

Description: Rich brown above, with darker brown flecks and dots, and with a broad, paler brown vertebral stripe with relatively straight edges. Whitish below. Skin finely granular above, the dorsal scales

Oedura gemmata

Oedura gracilis

Oedura lesueurii

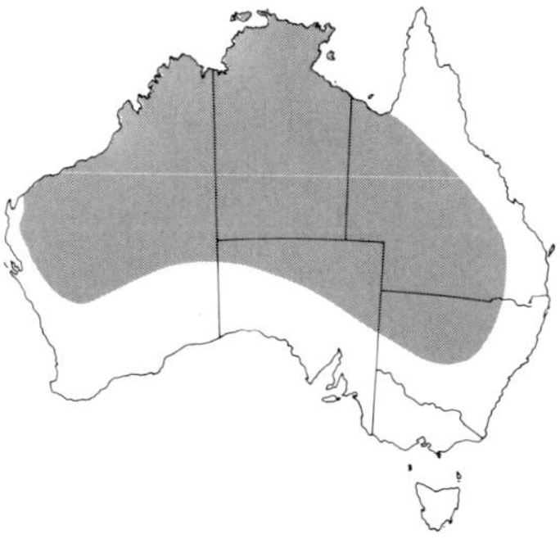

Oedura marmorata

Oedura monilis

Oedura obscura

Oedura reticulata

Oedura reticulata Lake Cronin, WA R. W. G. JENKINS

minute and homogeneous, usually much smaller than the ventrals. A single postanal tubercle on each side. Tail relatively long and slender, only moderately compressed. 70 mm (snout-vent).
Distribution: South-western WA.
Habit: An arboreal species found primarily in woodland areas where it is said to be virtually restricted to smooth-barked eucalyptus.

Oedura robusta Boulenger, 1885
Robust Velvet Gecko

Description: Pale grey or blue-grey above, darker on the sides, with a distinctive dorsal pattern consisting of a series of pale, squarish, mid-dorsal blotches, enclosed in a black or dark brown ladder-shaped longitudinal marking. The outer edges of the 'ladder' continue forward to the eye, so that the top of the head is pale bluish-grey, while the transverse 'rungs' of the 'ladder' are sometimes broken. The limbs above are finely speckled and mottled with dark brown and pale grey. Whitish below. Skin finely granular above, the dorsal scales minute and homogeneous, usually much smaller than the ventrals. A small cluster of 2-5 postanal tubercles on either side. Tail relatively long and wide, usually strongly depressed. 80 mm (snout-vent).
Distribution: North-eastern quarter of NSW to the Atherton Tableland, northern Qld.
Habit: An arboreal species of dry sclerophyll forests and woodlands. It normally shelters by day within hollow limbs and trunks of gum trees, but is sometimes found under loose bark. Forages at night about the limbs and trunk only of its 'home' tree. Occasionally found in human dwellings.

Oedura rhombifer Gray, 1845

Description: Rich brown above, the sides and limbs speckled with darker and paler brown. A broad, pale brown or cream vertebral band, with a ragged, zigzag edge on either side, and sometimes dark-edged. The pale vertebral stripe divides on the nape to continue forward as a pale temporal stripe on either side of the head, enclosing a darker brown patch on the crown. A dark brown or blackish stripe along the side of the snout and continued behind the eye. Whitish below. Skin finely granular above, the dorsal scales minute and homogeneous, usually much smaller than the ventrals. Two or more postanal tubercles on each side. Tail long and slender, more or less round in section, but sometimes slightly depressed. 80 mm (snout-vent).
Distribution: Northern Australia, excluding most of the drier interior. An outlying population, apparently introduced in recent years to the Alice Springs region (Gillam).
Habit: Largely confined to tropical woodlands. Usually arboreal, sheltering during the day under the loose bark of standing or fallen trees. However, often hides in ground litter, especially man-made dumps. Also frequents buildings.

Oedura tryoni De Vis, 1884
Southern Spotted Velvet Gecko

Description: Reddish-brown to chocolate-brown above, with numerous, scattered, small cream or yellow spots, each edged with black or dark brown. These ocelli are usually small, smaller than the eye, occasionally coalescing to form pale, dark-edged transverse bars (especially on the nape) or, in older individuals, to form pale reticulations. Hindlimbs almost invariably with small, dark-edged ocelli. Juveniles rich chocolate-brown with small bright yellow or white spots. Whitish below. Dorsal scales flat, round, juxtaposed and homogeneous, about as large as the ventrals. A single postanal tubercle on each side. Tail long and relatively slender, only slightly depressed. 80 mm (snout-vent).
Distribution: North-eastern NSW and south-eastern Qld.
Habit: Largely restricted to granite outcrops and ranges in dry sclerophyll forest, where it shelters by day in crevices or under exfoliating slabs of rock. Lays two parchment-shelled eggs.

Oedura rhombifer McArthur River, NT

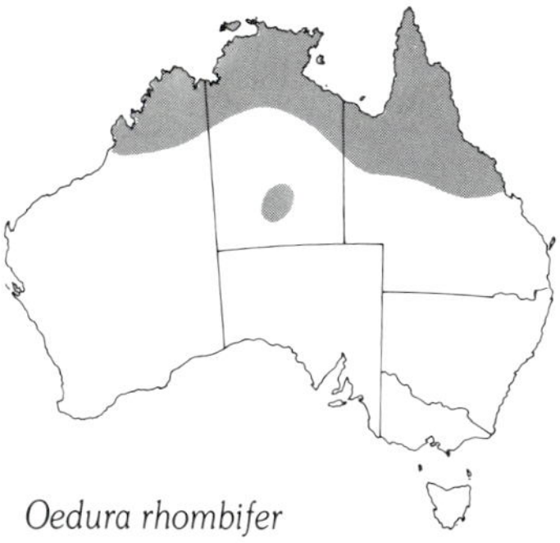

Oedura rhombifer

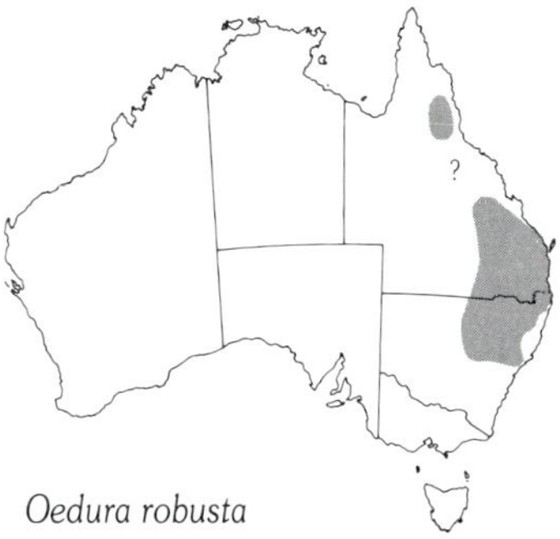

Oedura robusta

Oedura robusta
Laurieton, NSW

Oedura tryoni

R.W.G. JENKINS

Oedura tryoni Stanthorpe, Qld

Genus *Phyllurus* Schinz, 1822

An endemic Australian genus containing one of the largest Australian geckos. All but one species with a broad, flat, leaf-shaped tail.

Rostral and mental shields rounded. Labials larger than adjacent scales; postmentals and adjacent gulars subequal. Digits long, slender, moderately compressed, and with three or more lateral rows of scales; no enlarged apical, subdigital lamellae, but with a single series of slightly swollen transverse lamellae; feet bird-like, the digits angular when viewed laterally; all digits clawed, the claws conspicuous and free, the base of each claw between two scales, the lower of which is deeply notched. Preanal pores absent.

Key

TO THE SPECIES OF PHYLLURUS

1 Tail strongly depressed, leaf-shaped, more than twice as broad as thick, rarely more than twice as long as broad .. **2**

Tail moderately depressed to more or less cylindrical in section, more than four times as long as broad .... ***caudiannulatus***

2 Lateral fold, between axilla and groin, with a series of long, curved, spinose tubercles which are surrounded by a rosette of smaller tubercles which are much larger than the adjacent scales (a) **3**

Lateral fold, between axilla and groin, with a few low, rounded tubercles; conical tubercles on flanks surrounded by scales which are scarcely or not differentiated fro those adjacent to them (b) .... ***platurus***

3 Throat with numerous scattered tubercles ... ***salebrosus***

Throat smooth or with a few scattered tubercles .... ***cornutus***

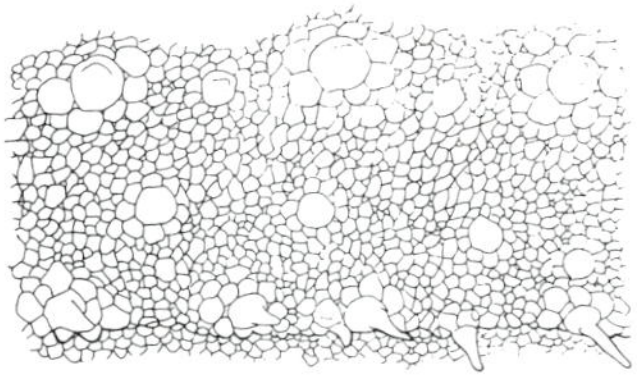

a

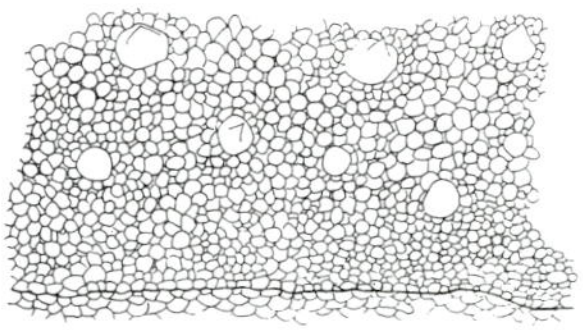

b

Phyllurus caudiannulatus
Eungella National Park, Qld

Phyllurus cornutus Atherton Tableland, Qld

Phyllurus caudiannulatus Covacevich, 1975

Description: Brown, grey or grey-brown above, with darker and paler flecks giving a salt and pepper appearance, or with more definite darker blotches (often longitudinally aligned) and paler spots (usually transversely aligned); tail same colour as dorsum but with a series of four to six narrow, transverse, pale bars. Whitish below. Head, body and limbs covered with small, flat, granular scales above, among which are interspersed numerous enlarged, low, conical tubercles, which are largest on the flanks. Head large, triangular, flat. Body strongly depressed. Tail long, cylindrical (Bulburin region), or basally depressed and narrowly leaf-shaped (Eungella region). Limbs long and spindly. 80 mm (snout-vent).
Distribution: Two, apparently isolated, populations in central Qld.
Habit: An arboreal species largely restricted to rainforest and adjacent wet sclerophyll forests, where it forages at night on the trunks of trees and in the canopy.

Phyllurus cornutus (Ogilby, 1892)

Northern Leaf-Tailed Gecko

Description: Olive-green or brownish above, usually with a series of four or five paler, dark-edged,

Phyllurus cornutus Lake Barrine, Qld

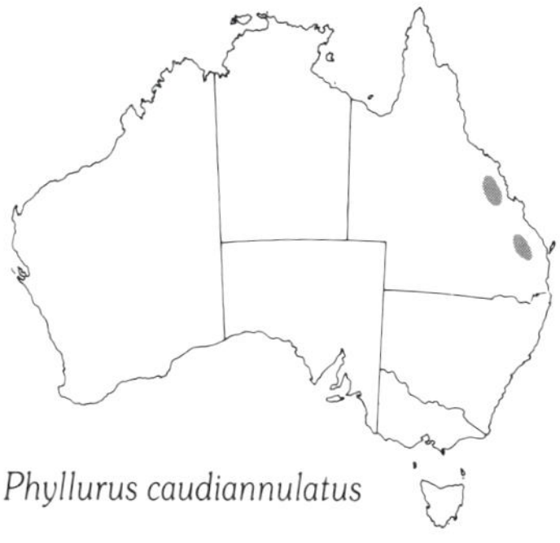

Phyllurus caudiannulatus

Phyllurus platurus Turramurra, NSW

Phyllurus cornutus

Phyllurus platurus

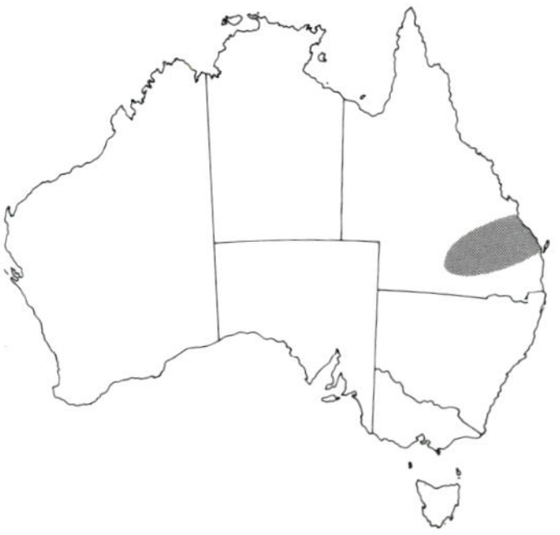

Phyllurus salebrosus

transverse blotches along the centre of the back, the remaining areas of the back, flanks and limbs with dark brown flecks, mottling and reticulations. Often a distinct russet-red vertebral stripe, especially in the young. Head above with two or more W- or M-shaped dark brown markings and irregular lines and reticulations. Whitish below, often peppered with brown. Scales on the dorsal surface small, flat, granular, through which are scattered numerous rosettes formed by circles of slightly enlarged flat scales enclosing a single, enlarged, pointed tubercle. A distinct lateral skin fold along each flank, between axilla and groin, with a series of long, curved spinose scales arising from circles of scales which are much larger than the adjacent body scales. Head large, triangular, flat. Body strongly depressed. Tail broad, flat, leaf- or shield-shaped, original tails ending in a short, spinose, slender tip. Limbs long and spindly. 16 cm (snout-vent).

Distribution: Lower Cape York Peninsula, Qld, with isolated populations along the eastern coast and ranges to the central coast of NSW.

Habit: A large, arboreal gecko of rainforest and adjacent beech or wet sclerophyll forest. Often found at night on the trunks of both large trees and small saplings. It commonly forages on the trunks or among the protective foliage of stinging trees (*Laportia*).

Phyllurus platurus (White, *ex* Shaw, 1790)

Southern Leaf-Tailed Gecko

Description: Pale grey to rich brown above, finely or coarsely peppered with dark brown and black on all dorsal surfaces. Whitish below. Back of head, body, limbs and tail (when original) covered by very small, flat, granular scales, through which rise numerous enlarged, low, pointed tubercles, each of which is surrounded by a circle of slightly enlarged scales. A distinct lateral skin fold from axilla to groin, with a few low, conical tubercles, which are surrounded by scales which are scarcely or not differentiated from the adjacent body scales. Head, large, triangular, flat. Body strongly depressed. Tail broad, flat, leaf- or heart-shaped. Limbs long and spindly. 80 mm (snout-vent).
Distribution: Central coast and ranges of NSW
Habit: An inhabitant of sandstone caves, overhangs and crevices in wet and dry sclerophyll forests and heathland. Also found under smaller exfoliating rocks on sandstone ridges. Frequently enters garages and houses in suburban areas.

Phyllurus salebrosus Covacevich, 1975

Description: Superficially similar to *Phyllurus cornutus*, from which it may be distinguished by its extremely tubercular throat (mostly without tubercles in *cornutus*) and the longer spinous tip of original tails.
Distribution: Mid-eastern and south-central Qld.
Habit: An arboreal, cavernicolous or rock-dwelling species, found in a variety of habitats ranging from dry rocky scrublands to moister closed forests.

Genus *Pseudothecadactylus* Brongersma, 1936

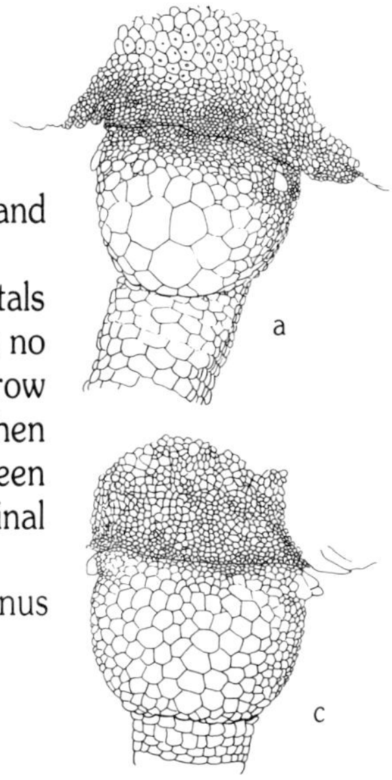

A distinctive genus containing two large species, and confined to northern Australia and the islands of Torres Strait. Probably occurs in southern New Guinea.

Rostral and mental shields rounded. Labials larger than adjacent scales. Postmentals enlarged. Digits long, depressed, strongly expanded distally to form large, oval pads; no enlarged pair of subdigital apical plates, but a continuous double series of long, narrow lamellae extending across the full width of the pad, digits lying flat on the substrate when viewed laterally; all digits clawed, the claws small and retractile within a groove between the apical lamellae. Preanal pores present. Tail more or less prehensile, the terminal subcaudals modified to form adhesive lamellae.

Bauer has recently placed this genus in the synonymy of the New Caledonian genus *Rhacodactylus*.

Key

TO THE SPECIES OF PSEUDOTHECADACTYLUS

A single postanal tubercle on each side in males (a); rostral scarcely broader than high (b); ear opening minute, about equal to nostril.. ***australis***

Three to four postanal tubercles on each side in males (c); rostral much broader than high (d); ear opening large, at least five times larger than nostril....................................... ***lindneri***

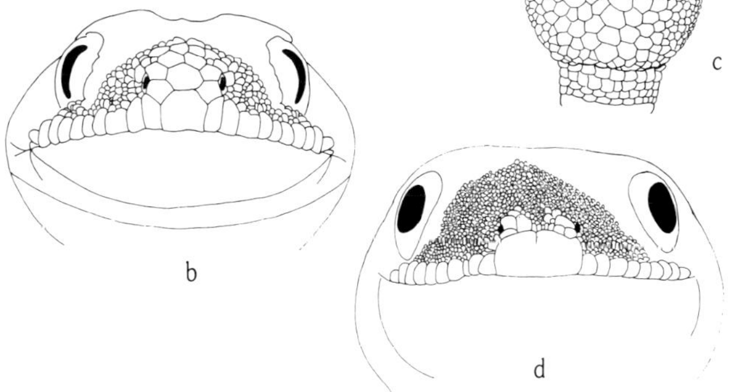

Pseudothecadactylus australis (Günther, 1877)

Description: Brown above, finely mottled or peppered with darker brown, and with a series of about six pale, dark-edged, transverse blotches between snout and vent, some blotches occasionally divided to form a pair of ocelli, especially on the nape. Flanks with or without obscure pale blotches, which may be continuations of the pale dorsal patches. A poorly defined dark brown bar along the side of the snout, continued behind the eye and extending to about the level of the forelimb. This dark area is bordered below by a contrasting white or pale brown

Pseudothecadactylus australis Iron Range, Qld

Pseudothecadactylus australis Weipa, Qld

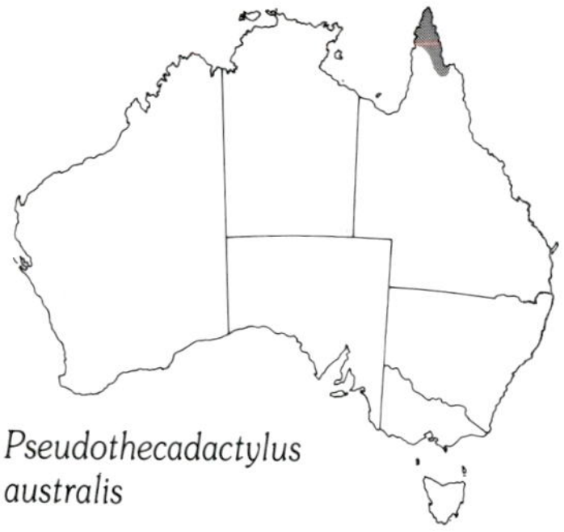

Pseudothecadactylus australis

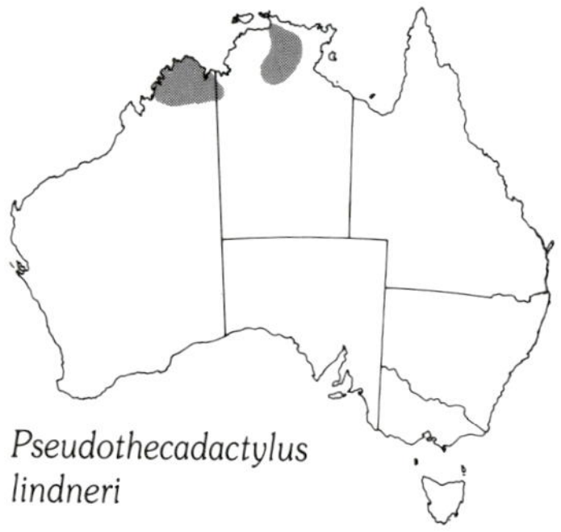

Pseudothecadactylus lindneri

area which starts at the upper labials and extends back along the side of the neck (enclosing the ear-opening) to about the level of the forearm. Lower labials white with dark sutures. Whitish below, speckled and flecked with dark brown, especially on the throat. Scales above small, smooth, juxtaposed and homogeneous. Scales on snout large, about ten scales along median line between the rostral and the anterior margin of the eyes. Ear-opening small, scarcely larger than the nostril. Rostral scale scarcely broader than high. A distinct lateral skin fold between axilla and groin. A single postanal tubercle on each side in males. Tail long, slender, more or less cylindrical. 120 mm (snout-vent).

Distribution: Northern and north-eastern coast and ranges of Cape York Peninsula, Qld; islands of Torres Strait.

Habit: A powerful, arboreal gecko found primarily in tropical woodlands but also on the edges of closed monsoonal forests and mangroves. Found at night foraging on the trunks of large trees, but by day occupies hollow limbs. It's presence is often revealed when it calls from its hollow, during the day, when disturbed by a person walking or riding past its home tree!

Pseudothecadactylus lindneri

Cogger, 1975
Giant Cave Gecko

Description: Rich dark purplish-brown above, with a series of irregular, poorly defined, narrow to broad, pale cream or yellow cross-bands, often disrupted on the mid-line (in Arnhem Land), or with a series of six or seven well-defined, broad, pale cross-bands, each band about as wide as the darker interspaces and often with a secondary dark band in its centre (Kimberleys). Head dark purplish-brown with obscure paler blotches, or pale with a coarse, dark brown reticulate pattern. Limbs above with pale yellow and dark brown variegations or brown with small yellow spots. Original tail ringed with dark brown and pale yellow; regrown tail uniform brown. Scales above small, smooth, juxtaposed and homogeneous, shagreened; upper lateral scales slightly enlarged and tubercular in some populations. Scales on snout small, 20-25 scales along a median line between the rostral and the anterior margins of the eyes. Ear-opening large, at least five times larger than the nostril. Rostral scale much broader than high. A slight lateral skin fold between axilla and groin. A cluster of three to four post-anal scales on each side in males. Tail long, slender, more or less cylindrical. 100 mm (snout-vent).
Distribution: Western Arnhem Land, NT, and Kimberleys, WA. A large, powerful gecko inhabiting caves, crevices and overhangs in the deeply dissected sandstone hills and escarpments of the Kimberleys and the western escarpment of Arnhem Land.
Habit: Most active on drizzly evenings during the wet season, when the geckos emerge on to open rock faces to feed on insects, spiders and other geckos. At other times they forage around the openings of caves and crevices.
Subspecies: *lindneri* (Arnhem Land, NT); *cavaticus* (Kimberley district, WA).

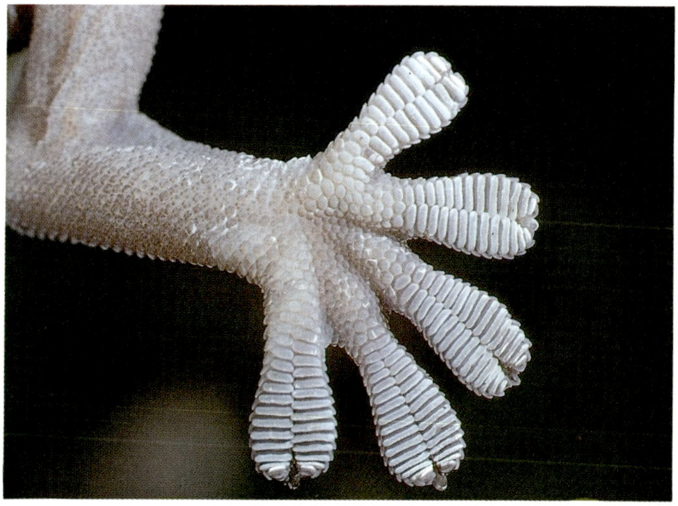

Pseudothecadactylus lindneri Brockman Range, NT. Underside of hind foot, showing arrangement of lamellae.

Pseudothecadactylus lindneri Brockman Range, NT

Genus ***Rhynchoedura*** Günther, 1867

A monotypic, endemic genus whose sole species is a small, terrestrial, deserticolous gecko.

Rostral and mental shields projecting, forming a small but distinctive beak. Labials and adjacent scales subequal. A cluster of moderately enlarged postmentals. Digits moderate, slender, round in section; a small pair of enlarged, apical, subdigital lamellae followed by numerous, irregular, small, spinose tubercles; digits slightly angular when viewed laterally, but tending to lie flat on the substrate; all digits clawed, the claws more or less free. Preanal pores present.

Rhynchoedura ornata Günther, 1867
Beaked Gecko

Description: Reddish-brown to red above, specked or finely reticulated with darker brown, and with numerous small, white, cream or yellow spots over the back and flanks; these spots tend to be in two series, one larger than the other, while original tails have two rows of large spots along the upper surface. Crown of head paler grey or brown. A white or cream stripe along the upper labials to below the eye. Upper eyelid rimmed with white or cream, at least in front of and behind the eye. Immaculate white below. Scales above small, smooth, juxtaposed, homogeneous. A small, lightly-built lizard with long, slender tail, round in section. 50 mm (snout-vent).
Distribution: Drier interior of all mainland states of Australia.

Habit: A terrestrial gecko found in a wide variety of dry or arid life zones, from open savannah woodlands and grasslands, through mallee and mulga scrubs to the spinifex-dominated sandhills and sandy deserts of the centre. Habits similar to those of *Lucasium damaeum*, the two species commonly encountered together.

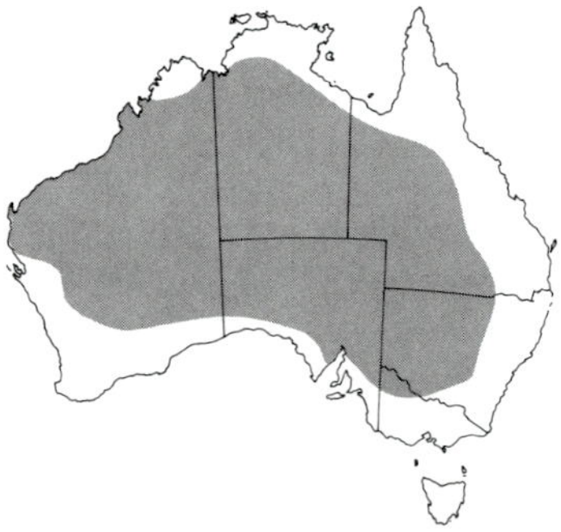
Rhynchoedura ornata

Rhynchoedura ornata Round Hill, NSW

Genus ***Underwoodisaurus*** Wermuth, 1965

An endemic Australian genus (although it originally included a New Guinea species).

Rostral and mental shields rounded. Labials larger than adjacent scales. Postmental and adjacent gulars subequal. Digits long, slender, slightly compressed, with only two lateral scale rows; no enlarged, apical, subdigital lamellae, but a single continuous series of slightly swollen transverse lamellae; feet bird-like, the digits angular when viewed laterally; all digits clawed, the claws conspicuous and free; the base of each claw typically between two scales, but the lower scale may be deeply notched or occasionally divided. Preanal pores absent.

Bauer has recently (1990) placed this genus in the synonymy of *Nephrurus*.

Key

TO THE AUSTRALIAN SPECIES OF UNDERWOODISAURUS

Anterior loreals minute, granular, strongly differentiated from posterior loreals (a).. ***milii***

Anterior and posterior loreals more or less subequal, without marked differentiation anteriorly (b)..................... ***sphyrurus***

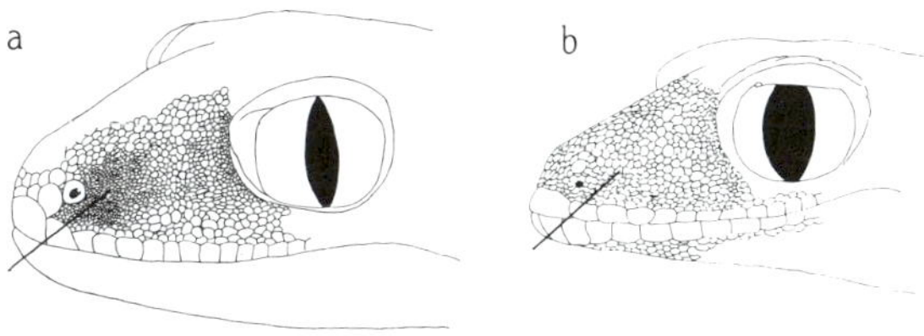

Underwoodisaurus milii (Bory de Saint-Vincent, 1825)

Thick-Tailed Gecko

Description: Dark purplish-black (juveniles) to deep purplish- or reddish-brown on the head, back and limbs with numerous scattered small white or yellow spots tending to be arranged in transverse rows on the back, interspersed with tiny blackish spots. Both dark and pale spots centred on the small enlarged tubercles described below. The yellow spots on the occiput and nape tend to form two or three discontinuous pale, curved lines across the occiput, nape and/or shoulders, the one on the occiput more or less continuous with some larger yellowish spots on the cheek and loreal region. Original tail black, with five or six narrow, white cross-bands; regrown tail uniform brown. Lower surfaces white, sometimes suffused with purplish-brown. Head relatively deep, only moderately depressed. Scales minute, granular above, interspersed with numerous small conical tubercles on the back of the head, body, limbs and original tail. Anterior loreals minute, granular, strongly differentiated from the posterior loreals. Original tail relatively long, but broad and depressed, carrot-shaped in outline. 80 mm (snout-vent).

Distribution: Southern Australia, from the eastern to western coasts, with a possibly isolated population in central Australia.

Habit: A nocturnal terrestrial lizard, found in a range of habitats from wet coastal heathlands and wet sclerophyll forests to the arid scrubs. Shelters under litter

Underwoodisaurus milii Hornsby, NSW

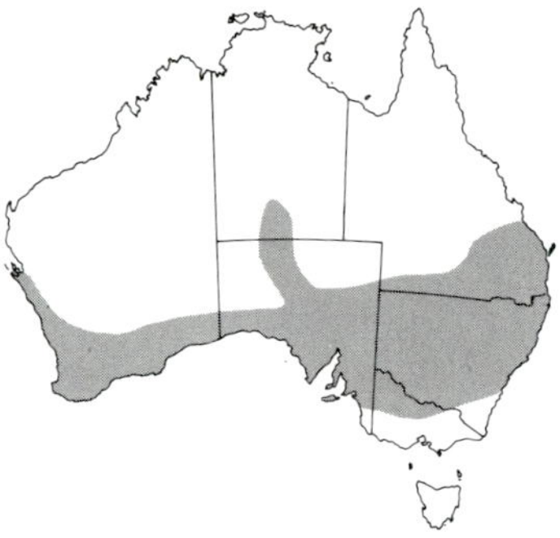

Underwoodisaurus milii

Underwoodisaurus sphyrurus

and debris, or in crevices or under loose bark at the bases of standing trees, emerging at night to forage in open grassed or sandy areas.

Underwoodisaurus sphyrurus

(Ogilby, 1892)

Description: Pale fawn to brown above, with faint darker brown flecks and reticulations, and with numerous very small white spots scattered over the head, neck, back, sides and limbs, each spot centred on one of the small tubercles described below, and the spots tending to be aligned transversely. Some obscure darker reticulations on the head. Original tail dark grey-brown to almost black, with obscure alternate dark and pale cross-bands formed by rows of enlarged tubercles. White below, sometimes peppered with brown. Scales small, granular above, interspersed with numerous scattered, small, conical tubercles. Original tail with regular longitudinal rows of enlarged conical or spinose tubercles; such tails are rectangular, fat and depressed proximally, with a thin, tapering, round terminal section. 70 mm (snout-vent).
Distribution: Northern slopes and tablelands of NSW and adjacent border regions of southern Qld.
Habit: Little known. Terrestrial. Appears to be confined to the northern granite belt, where it is closely associated with exfoliating rocky outcrops and stony hills in eucalyptus woodland.

Underwoodisaurus sphyrurus Copeton Dam, NSW

Family Pygopodidae

A group of about thirty snake- and worm-like lizards confined to the Australian region, with only two species (in New Guinea) occurring beyond continental Australia. Indeed, it is the only reptile family endemic to the Australian region.

Pygopodid lizards are closely allied to the geckos (family Gekkonidae); a recent monographic revision by A. G. Kluge increased the number of species recognised from fourteen to thirty, and much of the material which follows draws heavily on Dr. Kluge's revision. More recently, Kluge has placed these lizards in the family Gekkonidae, with the diplodactyline geckos.

Forelimbs absent, the hindlimbs not obvious or normal, but represented by a scaly flap just above the vent; the eyes are lidless and snake-like, covered by an immovable spectacle. An external ear-opening is present in some species but not in others. All pygopodid lizards are oviparous, summer breeders and, according to Kluge, all species lay two elongate parchment-shelled eggs in a clutch, except for *Lialis burtonis* which may occasionally lay one or three eggs (Patchel and Shine). Most species are insectivorous, but some feed primarily on spiders or scincid lizards.

The tail of a pygopodid lizard is readily broken at any point, and regeneration is fairly rapid. Regenerated tails are rarely as long as the original (depending largely on the point of breakage), so that comments regarding relative tail length in the descriptions that follow are based on original, complete tails.

Key

TO THE GENERA OF PYGOPODID LIZARDS

1 Head covered with enlarged, symmetrical shields (a)....... **2**
Head covered with small, irregular shields (b).......... ***Lialis***

2 Ventral scales smooth... **3**
Ventral scales keeled....................................... ***Pletholax***

3 Preanal pores present (c)... **4**
Preanal pores absent... **5**

4 Eight or more preanal pores.............................. ***Pygopus***
Four preanal pores...................................... ***Paradelma***

5 Parietal scales present (d)... **6**
Parietal scales absent (e).................................... ***Aprasia***

6 Anterior nasals in contact (f), or fewer than 20 mid-body scale rows... **7**
Anterior pair of nasals separated by rostral (g), and 20 mid-body scale rows.. ***Aclys***

7 External ear-opening present and obvious; more than eight scales along a line across the top of the head joining the angle of the mouth on each side (h)................. ***Delma***
External ear-opening very small and hidden by overlying temporal scales; fewer than eight scales along a line across the top of the head joining the angle of the mouth on each side (i)... ***Ophidiocephalus***

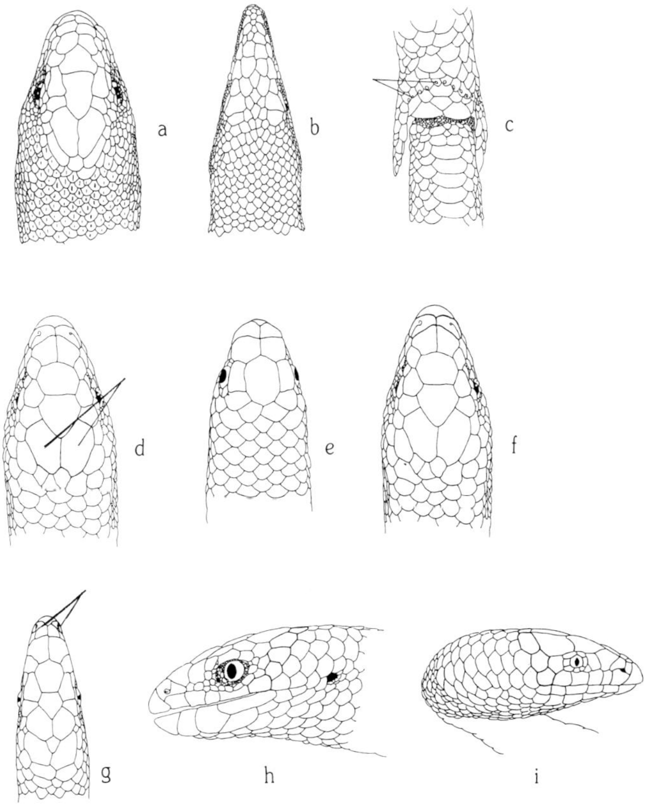

Genus **Aclys** Kluge, 1974

A small, slender, long-tailed legless lizard with well-developed hindlimb flaps and an external ear-opening. Confined to a small part of the coast of south-western Australia, this distinctive genus was first described in mid-1974.

Head scales, including parietals, enlarged and symmetrical. Scales (including ventrals) in 20 rows at mid-body. Snout long and pointed. Nasals separated by rostral. Preanal pores absent. Dorsal and ventral scales smooth.

M. PETERSON

Aclys concinna
Mt Peron, WA

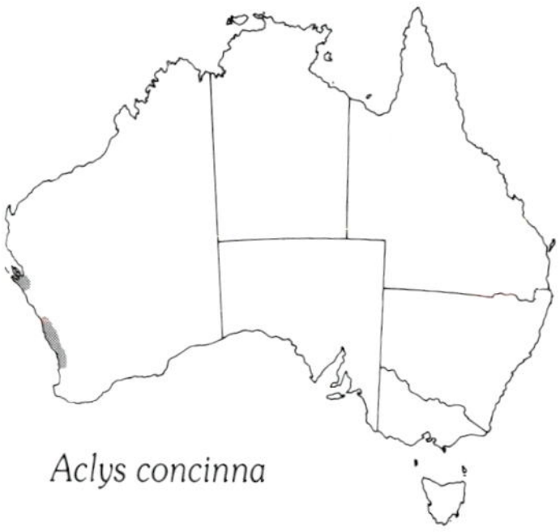

Aclys concinna Kluge, 1974

Description: Grey with narrow, darker longitudinal stripes along the back and sides of the body and tail, uniform below. Body slender. Tail about four times as long as the snout-vent length. Body and ventral scales smooth, in 20 rows at mid-body. Snout long, pointed. Head shields, including the parietal shields, enlarged. Rostral separating anterior nasal scales. Nostril bordered by two scales. External ear-opening present. Ventral scales not noticeably larger than adjacent body scales. Preanal pores absent. Three enlarged preanal scales. 75 mm (snout-vent).
Distribution: Coastal sandplain of lower west coast of WA, with an apparently isolated population in the Shark Bay region.
Habit: Coastal heath and woodland, on a sandy substrate.
Subspecies: *concinna* (lower west coast of WA); *major* (Shark Bay region).

Genus **Aprasia** Gray, 1839

A group of very small worm-like, burrowing, legless lizards with poorly-developed hindlimb flaps and no obvious external ear-opening. Widely distributed throughout the drier parts of southern Australia, although one or two species enter wetter sclerophyll forests. All species burrow freely in loose sand and soil, often being found in association with the litter below, and the root systems of, arid shrubs. They are sometimes found under ground debris and logs, or in ant and termite nests.

Anterior head scales enlarged and symmetrical, but enlarged parietal scales absent. Scales (including ventrals) in 14 or fewer rows at mid-body, the ventrals not noticeably wider than the adjacent body scales. Snout relatively short and blunt. Nasal scales in contact. Preanal pores absent. Dorsal and ventral scales smooth. Tail shorter than body.

Key

TO THE SPECIES OF APRASIA

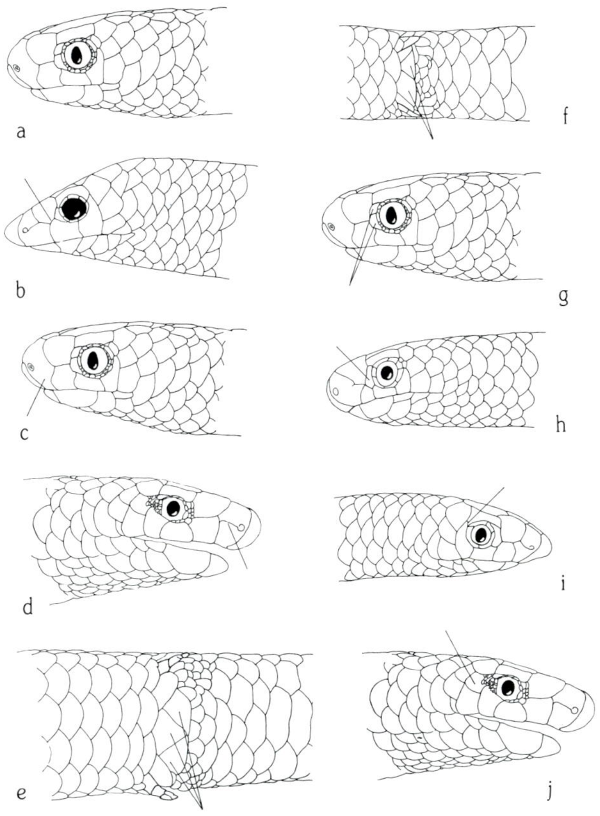

1 External ear-opening absent... **2**
External ear-opening present, but partly hidden beneath a temporal scale... ***aurita***

2 Prefrontal not in contact with the subocular labial (a)...... **3**
Prefrontal in contact with the subocular labial (b)............. .... ***haroldi***

3 Colour of head and tail-tip not contrasting with colour of remainder of body... **4**
Head and tail-tip colour contrasting strongly with colour of remainder of body.. ***smithi***

4 Nasal and first supralabial completely or partially fused posterior to the nostril (c).. **5**
Nasal and first supralabial not fused posterior to the nostril (d)... **7**

5 Three preanal scales (e)... **6**
Two preanal scales (f)..................................... ***pulchella***

6 Usually two preocular scales present (g); lateral head pattern absent.. ***parapulchella***
A single preocular scale (h); faint lateral head pattern often present..................................... ***pseudopulchella***

7 Twelve mid-body scale rows... **8**
Fourteen mid-body scale rows.. **9**

8 Postocular scale absent, the fourth supralabial contacting the supraocular (i)... ***repens***
A single postocular scale separating the fourth supralabial from the supraocular (j).................................... ***striolata***

9 Two preanal scales (f); snout long, pointed and projecting when viewed dorsally and laterally...................... ***rostrata***
Usually three preanal scales (e); snout rounded, not projecting when viewed dorsally and laterally...... ***inaurita***

Aprasia aurita Kluge, 1974

Description: Moderately pigmented (brown) above, each scale with a dark median longitudinal bar tending to form a series of longitudinal dark lines above; whitish below (including the supralabials). Body slender. Tail shorter than body. Body and ventral scales smooth, in 14 rows (including ventrals) at mid-body. Nostril in a semi-divided scale formed by the fusion of nasal and first supralabial scales anterior to the nostril. A single postocular scale. External ear-opening present but almost entirely covered by a notched scale. Three enlarged preanal scales. 110 mm (snout-vent).
Distribution: Recorded only from Ouyen and Woomelang, north-western Vic.
Habit: As for genus.

T.M.S. HANLON

Aprasia haroldi False Entrance Well, WA

Aprasia haroldi Storr, 1978

Description: Pale grey-brown above, each scale with an obscure short, dark-edged streak, tending to

Aprasia inaurita Jim-Jimerick, Vic

form a series of obscure dark, longitudinal lines above; lips and chin pale yellowish-white; a dark, wavy streak from snout to temple. Belly pale greyish-brown, underside of tail white. Body slender. Tail shorter than body. Body and ventral scales smooth,in 14 rows (including ventrals) at mid-body. Snout rounded but projecting. Nostril in a semi-divided scale formed by fusion of nasal and first supralabial anterior to the nostril. No postocular scale between the third supralabial and supraocular. Usually two enlarged preanal scales. 110 mm (snout-vent).
Distribution: Shark Bay region, WA.
Habit: As for genus.

Aprasia parapulchella Canberra, ACT

Aprasia inaurita Kluge, 1974

Description: Pale olive-brown or grey-brown above, head and neck reddish-brown; terminal part of tail bright reddish-orange; whitish below. Body slender. Tail shorter than body. Body and ventral scales smooth, in 14 rows (including ventrals) at mid-body. Nostril in a semi-divided scale, formed by the fusion of nasal and first supralabial scales anterior to the nostril. A single postocular scale. External ear-opening absent. Usually three enlarged preanal scales. 120 mm (snout-vent).
Distribution: Far south-eastern corner of WA and southern SA to north-western Vic and south-western NSW.

Aprasia pseudopulchella Mt Bryan, SA

Habit: A burrower in sandy arid habitats (e.g. mallee) in at least the eastern part of its range.

Aprasia parapulchella Kluge, 1974

Description: Head and nape dark brown, gradually merging with the pale grey or grey-brown body and basal portion of tail, which in turn merges with the pinkish- or reddish-brown terminal half of the tail; each dorsal scale with a median longitudinal dark bar, giving an overall impression of longitudinal lines of dots along the body and tail; whitish below, including the labial regions. Body slender. Tail nearly as long as the body. Body and ventral scales smooth, in 14 rows (including ventrals) at mid-body. Snout blunt, rounded. Nostril in a single scale formed by the fusion of the nasal and first supralabial scales. A single postocular scale. External ear-opening absent. Three enlarged preanal scales. 140 mm (snout-vent).
Distribution: Known only from the type locality, Coppins Crossing, Molonglo River, ACT, and from near Tarcutta and Bathurst, NSW.
Habit: Type specimens found under weathered granite rocks on a grazed, grassy riverside slope.

Aprasia pseudopulchella Kluge, 1974

Description: Similar in most respects to *Aprasia parapulchella*, from which Kluge distinguishes it principally by its greater average number of ventral scales (166-193 compared with 158-184 in *parapulchella*), two preorbital scales (usually three in *parapulchella*), and frequent presence of a faint lateral head pattern (absent in *parapulchella*, but present in some specimens I have examined).
Distribution: Flinders Ranges, SA.
Habit: As for genus.

Aprasia pulchella Gray, 1839

Description: Colour and pattern similar to that of *Aprasia parapulchella*, except that the pattern on the neck often extends to the top and sides of the head, tending to form a dark temporal streak. Body slender. Tail shorter than body. Body and ventral scales smooth, in 14 rows (including ventrals) at mid-body. Snout blunt, rounded. Nostril in a single scale formed by the fusion of the nasal and first supralabial scales. A single postocular scale. External ear-opening absent. Two enlarged preanal scales. 110 mm (snout-vent).

Aprasia aurita

Aprasia haroldi

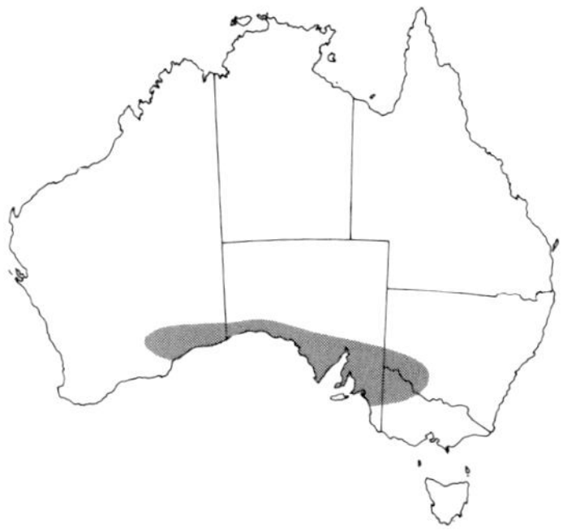
Aprasia inaurita

Aprasia parapulchella

Aprasia pseudopulchella

Aprasia pulchella

Aprasia repens

M. PETERSON

Aprasia repens Perth, WA

Distribution: Extreme south-western corner of WA.
Habit: Found under granitic and lateritic stones and boulders embedded in soil.

Aprasia repens (Fry, 1914)

Description: Pale grey-brown above, each scale with a central dark dot or median streak, forming overall a series of dark, longitudinal stripes or lines of dots. Whitish below. Body slender. Tail shorter than body. Body and ventral scales smooth, usually in 12 rows (including ventrals) at mid-body. Snout rounded but somewhat projecting. Nostril in a semi-divided scale formed by the fusion of the nasal and first supralabial anterior to the nostril. No postocular scale between the fourth supralabial and supraocular. Usually two enlarged preanal scales. 110 mm (snout-vent).
Distribution: South-western corner of WA.
Habit: As for genus.

Aprasia pulchella Mt Dale, WA

M. PETERSON

Aprasia rostrata Parker, 1956

Description: Pale brown above, with a broad dark stripe on either side of the neck, each of which breaks up on the body into three fine lines. Head finely reticulated with darker brown. Three dark fine lines on the nape. A dark vertebral line on the tail. Whitish below, with a fine brown line on each side of the belly. Body slender. Tail shorter than body. Body and ventral scales smooth, in 14 rows (including ventrals) at mid-body. Snout relatively pointed and distinctly projecting. Nostril in a semi-divided nasal formed by the fusion of the nasal and the first supralabial anterior to the nostril. A postocular scale between the supraocular and the fourth supralabial. Two enlarged preanal scales. 95 mm (snout-vent).
Distribution: Known only from Hermite Island, Monte Bello Islands and the Exmouth Gulf region, WA.
Habit: As for genus.
Subspecies: *rostrata* (Monte Bello Islands, WA); *fusca* (Exmouth Gulf region,WA).

Aprasia smithi Storr, 1970

Description: Head and adjacent neck region and tip of tail, black. Body above ranges from orange-yellow anteriorly to fawn posteriorly, whitish below. Six longitudinal series of dorsal and dorso-lateral spots, one spot to a scale (Storr). Body slender. Tail shorter than body. Body and ventral scales smooth, in 12 rows (including ventrals) at mid-body. Snout distinctly pointed and projecting. Nostril in a semi-divided scale formed by the fusion of the nasal and first supralabial anterior to the nostril. No postocular scale between the fourth supralabial and the supraocular. Two enlarged preanal scales. 110 mm (snout-vent).
Distribution: WA, from Shark Bay to Yuna.
Habit: A burrowing species, the holotype being dug from very dry and moderately hard ground (Kluge).

Aprasia striolata Lütken, 1863

Description: Pale brown, olive-brown or grey above, usually with a series of narrow, blackish stripes on the top of the head, but which tend to fade out on the neck, and a conspicuous series of narrow, black dorso-lateral and lateral stripes along the body and tail, the most conspicuous commencing at the snout and passing through the eye. In some populations (WA and Kangaroo Island) the stripes are either absent or present as lines of dots. Whitish below. Body slender. Tail shorter than body. Scales in 12 rows at mid-body (including ventrals). Snout relatively blunt and rounded. Nostril in a semi-divided scale formed by the fusion of the nasal and the first supralabial anterior to the nostril. A single postocular scale between the fourth supralabial and the supraocular. Usually three enlarged preanal scales. 120 mm (snout-vent).
Distribution: Apparently three isolated populations: one in south-western WA; another extending from Eyre Peninsula, SA to western Vic; and another represented by a single record from Mt. Buring, NT.
Habit: A burrowing species found in a wide variety of habitats with sandy or loamy soils.

Aprasia rostrata

Aprasia smithi

Aprasia striolata

Aprasia striolata Fleurieu Peninsula, SA

Genus ***Delma*** Gray, 1831

A group of moderate-sized, terrestrial, legless lizards with well-developed hindlimb flaps and conspicuous external ear-openings. Widely distributed throughout most parts of continental Australia except for the south-eastern coastal regions.

Head scales, including the parietals, enlarged and symmetrical. Scales (including ventrals) usually in fewer than 18 rows at mid-body, the ventrals scarcely to noticeably wider than the adjacent body scales. Anterior nasal scales nearly always in contact. Preanal pores absent. Dorsal and ventral scales smooth. Tail about three times as long as body. All species are oviparous, most laying two eggs in a clutch (Patchell and Shine).

Key

TO THE SPECIES OF DELMA

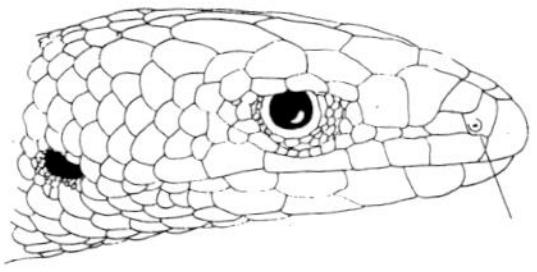

a

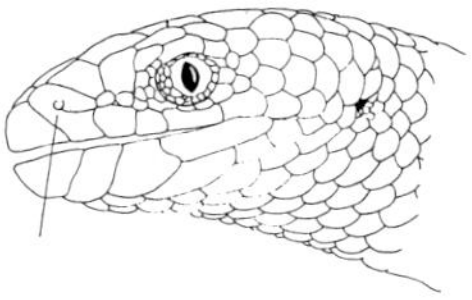

b

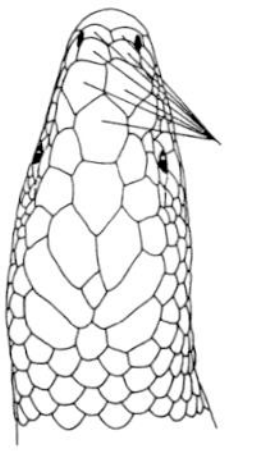

c

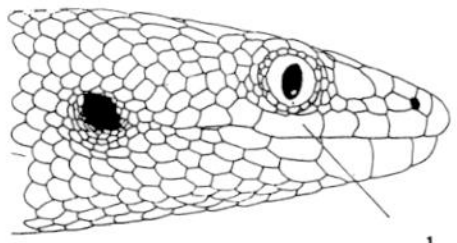

d

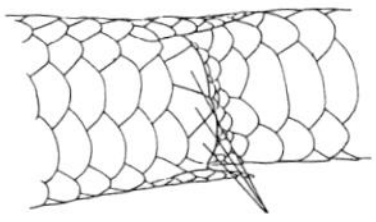

e

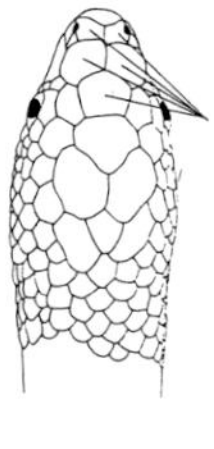

f

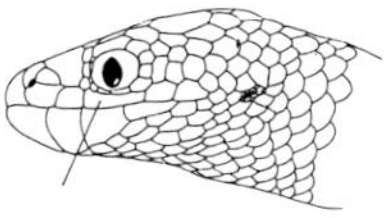

g

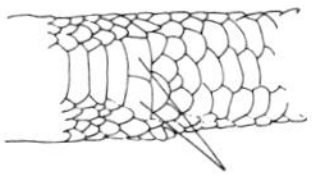

h

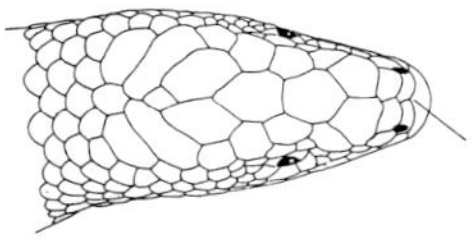

i

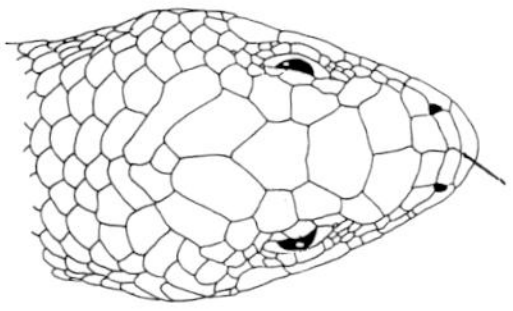

j

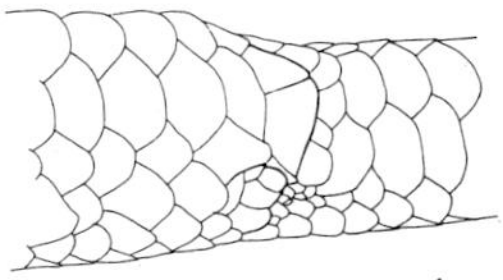

k

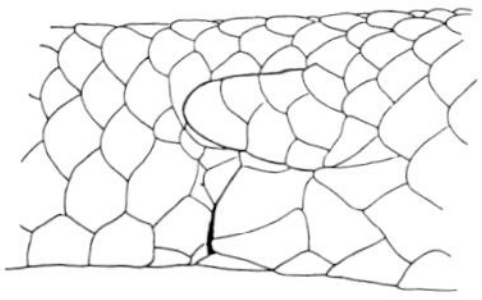

l

1 Pale stripes absent on body and tail; nasal and first supralabial not fused anterior to nostril (a).............................. **2**

One or two narrow dorso-lateral whitish stripes on body and tail; nasal and first supralabial fused anterior to nostril (b).. ***impar***

2 Two broad dark transverse bands, sometimes obscure in large adults, posterior either to parietal scales or to any dark transverse band fully or partly enclosing the parietal scales.. **3**

One or no dark transverse bands posterior either to parietal scales or to any dark transverse band fully or partly enclosing the parietal scales.. **4**

3 Seven scales on top of snout between rostral and frontal (c); fourth supralabial below eye (d); three preanal scales (e)... ***elegans***

Five scales on top of snout between rostral and frontal (f); third supralabial below eye (g); two preanal scales (h)....... .... ***torquata***

4 Rarely as few as 14 mid-body scale rows; if fewer than 18 mid-body scale rows then seven scales on top of snout between rostral and frontal (c)....................................... **5**

Rarely more than 14 mid-body scale rows present; five scales on top of snout between rostral and frontal (f)........ .... ***tincta***

5 Rarely other than 18 mid-body scale rows; usually five scales on top of snout between rostral and frontal (f)... **6**

Usually fewer than 18 mid-body scale rows; usually seven scales on top of snout between rostral and frontal (c)..... **7**

6 Ventral scales usually scarcely wider than adjacent body scales; dark reticulations usually present on throat........... .... ***australis***

Ventral scales conspicuously wider than adjacent body scales; no dark pigmentation on throat................ ***molleri***

7 Usually three preanal scales (e); lateral lip pattern and dorsal head bands present or absent.............................. **8**

Usually two preanal scales (h); conspicuous lateral lip pattern present; dorsal head bands absent.............. ***plebeia***

8 Fourth (d) or fifth supralabial usually below eye; dark pigmentation on throat or venter present or absent............ **9**

Third supralabial usually below eye (g); dark pigmentation absent from throat and venter.................................. ***pax***

Hind limb flap of a *Delma*

9 Conspicuous cross-bands present on top of head and nape..**10**

Conspicuous dorsal head bands absent........................**13**

10 Rarely a conspicuous dark lateral stripe present posteriorly; rostral noticeably projecting between anterior pair of supranasals (i)...**11**

Usually a conspicuous dark lateral stripe posteriorly, sharply demarcating the dark lateral from the pale ventral surfaces; rostral not or scarcely projecting between the anterior pair of supranasals(j)..............................***mitella***

11 Dark pigmentation usually absent on throat; usually fewer than six infralabials and three hindlimb scales (k).........**12**

Dark pigmentation usually present on throat; usually more than five infralabials and three hindlimb scales (l) present..***fraseri***

12 Pale bands on head and neck straight in outline; no additional pale bands on side of head between pale dorsal bands...***borea***

Pale bands on head and neck wavy in outline; usually some additional narrow, pale bands on the side of the head between the pale dorsal bands...................***haroldi***

13 Ventral scales with or without dark edges; usually 16 scales along a line across the top of the head and usually 17 scales along a line across the throat, each line extending from the angle of the mouth on each side................**14**

Ventral scales without dark edges; usually fewer than 16 scales along a line across the top of the head and usually fewer than 17 scales along a line across the throat, each line extending from the angle of the mouth on each side.... ....**15**

14 Dorsal scales dark brown finely edged with blackish; ventral scales without dark edges...............................***butleri***

Dorsal scales pale brown spotted and flecked with darker brown; ventral scales usually dark-edged.............***nasuta***

15 Conspicuous lateral lip pattern; ventral surfaces cream to bright lemon-yellow in life...**16**

No conspicuous lip pattern; ventral surfaces flesh-coloured in life..***inornata***

16 Hindlimb scales 4-6 (l); no dark dorso-lateral stripe extending from posterior body to tail.......................***grayii***

Hindlimb scales 3; a dark dorso-lateral stripe extending from posterior third of body to tail.......................***labialis***

Delma australis Musgrave Ranges, SA

Delma australis Kluge, 1974

Description: Rich brown above, whitish below, the top of the head, throat and ventral surface with black variegations and reticulations, while the sides of the head and neck have a series of narrow, vertical black bars. Tail about twice as long as body. Scales (including ventrals) in 16-20 rows, usually 18, at mid-body. Snout short, rounded. Five scales on upper snout between rostral and frontal shields . Nasal and first supralabial scales distinct. Three scales bordering nostril. Fourth supralabial below the eye. 10-15 scales along a line across the top of the head joining the angle of the mouth on each side. Ventral scales not noticeably wider than the adjacent body scales. 2-5 scales along the lower margin of hindlimb flap. Usually three enlarged preanal scales. 80 mm (snout-vent).
Distribution: Widely distributed through the southern part of WA, the southern end of the NT, SA, western NSW and north-western Vic.
Habit: Found in a wide variety of habitats, under rocks and logs, and in clumps of spinifex (*Triodia*) in sandy arid areas.

Delma borea Kluge, 1974

Description: Dark transverse head bands usually present, the most conspicuous being a broad band across the parietal region and a second one on the nape. Throat usually unpigmented. Body brown or grey-brown above, whitish below. Tail two to three times longer than body. Scales (including ventrals) in 14-16 rows, usually 16, at mid-body. Snout moderate, rounded. Seven scales on upper snout between rostral and frontal shields . Nasal and first supralabial scales distinct. Four scales bordering nostril. Fourth supralabial below the eye. 11-14 scales along a line across the top of the head which joins the angle of the mouth on each side. Ventral scales paired, noticeably wider than the adjacent body scales. 2-3 scales along lower margin of hindlimb flap. Usually three enlarged preanal scales. 80 mm (snout-vent).
Distribution: Widely distributed across northern Australia, from western Qld to north-western WA.
Habit: Found in wide variety of habitats, from coastal monsoon and sclerophyll forests to arid rocky hills and plains with scattered clumps of porcupine grass.

Delma butleri Storr, 1987

Description: Brown or olive-brown above, the hind edges of individual scales dark brown to black, so that the body appears to have a fine reticulate pattern; sides of head and neck with (usually) or without pale spots or blotches, often vertically aligned to form a series of alternating dark and pale vertical bars; ventral surfaces pale white, grey or yellow. Tail 2.5 to 3.5 times longer than body. Scales (including ventrals) in 15-18 rows, usually 16, at mid-body. Snout moderate, rounded. Seven scales on upper snout between rostral and frontal shields . Nasal and first supralabial scales distinct. Four scales bordering nostril. Usually fourth, but sometimes fifth, supralabial below the eye. 15-20 scales along a line across the top of the head which joins the angle of the mouth on each side. Ventral scales paired, noticeably wider than the adjacent body scales. 3-5, usually 4 scales along lower margin of hindlimb flap. Usually three enlarged preanal scales. 90 mm (snout-vent).
Distribution: Southern half of WA, through SA and north-western Vic. to the interior of NSW.
Habit: Found in a variety of habitats ranging from hummock grasslands to arid *Acacia* scrubs, mallee and savannah woodlands; found commonly in spinifex.

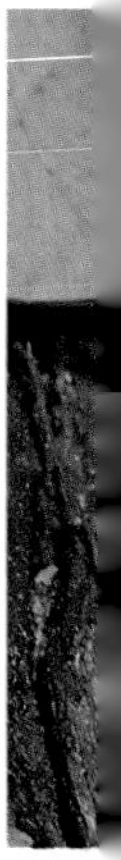

Delma elegans Kluge, 1974

Description: Dark transverse head bands present, the most conspicuous being a broad band across the parietal region and two narrower ones on the nape, each band extending to the ventro-lateral region. Body brown, the individual scales dark-edged. Dark reticulations or bars usually present on throat. Tail about three times as long as body. Scales (including ventrals) in 17-18 rows, usually 18, at mid-body. Snout moderate, rounded. Seven scales on upper snout between rostral and frontal shields . Nasal and first supralabial scales distinct. Four scales bordering nostril. Fourth supralabial below eye. 14-17 scales along a line across the top of the head which joins the angle of the mouth on each side. Ventral scales paired, noticeably wider than the adjacent body scales. Four scales along lower margin of hindlimb flap. Three enlarged preanal scales. 90 mm (snout-vent).
Distribution: Vicinity of Hamersley Ranges, WA.
Habit: Type locality consists of porcupine grass on stony hillsides. Kluge records a sloughed skin in an old and abandoned termitarium.

Delma fraseri Gray, 1831

Description: Dark transverse head bands usually present, the most conspicuous being a broad one across the parietal region and a narrower one on the

Delma grayii Perth, WA

Delma borea McArthur River, NT

Delma fraseri Ravensthorpe, WA

Delma butleri Round Hill, NSW

Delma impar Gungahlin, ACT

R. W. G. JENKINS

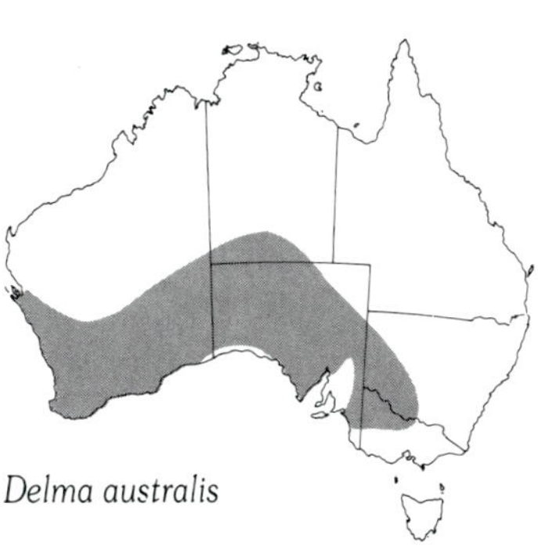

Delma australis

Delma borea

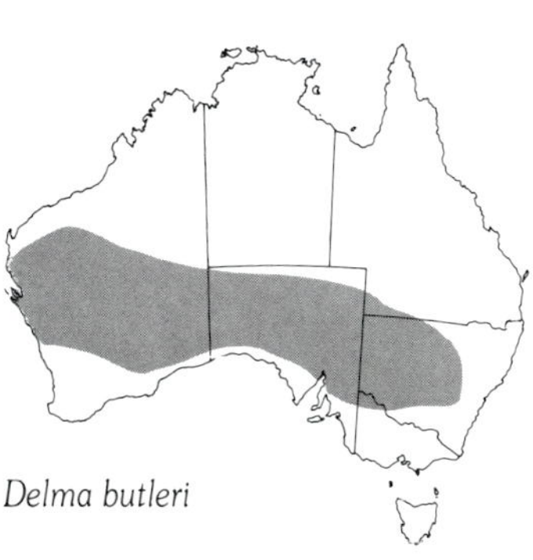

Delma butleri

Delma elegans

Delma fraseri

Delma grayii

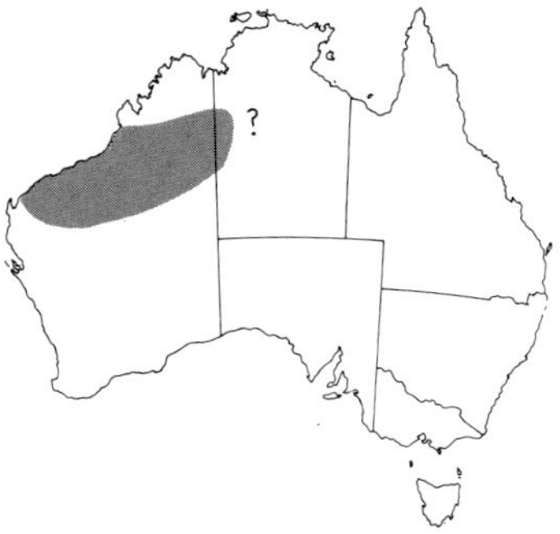

Delma haroldi

Delma impar

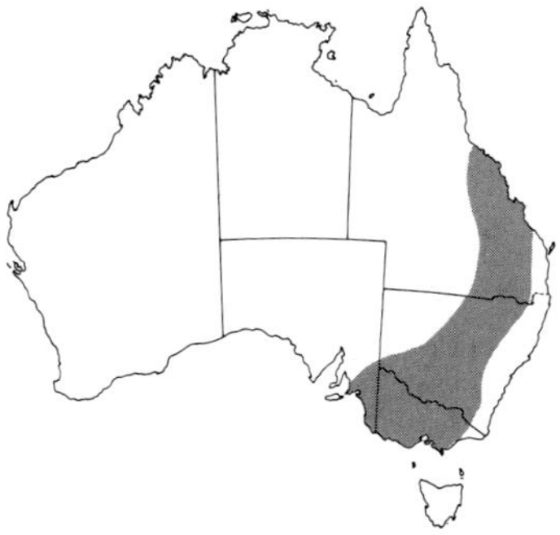

Delma inornata

Delma labialis

nape, each band extending to the ventro-lateral region. Body more or less uniform brown or grey-brown above, paler, with dark-edged scales, below. Dark bars or reticulations usually present on throat. Scales (including ventrals) in 15-17 rows, usually 16, at mid-body. Snout relatively elongate. Seven scales on upper snout between rostral and frontal shields. Nasal and first supralabial scales distinct. Four scales bordering nostril. Fourth supralabial below eye. 12-16 scales along a line across the top of the head which joins the angle of the mouth on each side. Ventral scales paired, noticeably wider than the adjacent body scales. 2-5 scales along the lower margin of the hindlimb flap. Usually three enlarged preanal scales. 120 mm (snout-vent).
Distribution: South-western WA and at least one isolated population in southern SA.
Habit: A terrestrial species found in a wide variety of habitats, where it is usually found under rocks, logs or ground debris. Ranges from wetter coastal forests to arid sandy or stony inland areas. Feeds primarily on insects and spiders (Patchell and Shine).

Delma grayii Smith, 1849

Description: Olive-green, grey or grey-brown above, the body scales often with darker margins, and usually a series of obscure darker lateral bars on the head and anterior part of the body. Yellowish below. Scales (including ventrals) in 15-18 rows, usually 16, at mid-body. Snout moderate. Seven scales on upper snout between rostral and frontal shields. Nasal and first supralabial scales distinct. Four scales bordering nostril. Fourth supralabial below eye. 12-16 scales along a line across the top of the head joining the angle of the mouth on each side. Ventral scales paired, noticeably wider than the adjacent body scales. 4-6 scales along the lower margin of hindlimb flap. Three enlarged preanal scales. 110 mm (snout-vent).
Distribution: West coast and hinterland of south-western WA.
Habit: Usually found in grasstree heathland and Banksia woodland (Maryan), under fallen logs and other surface debris on both sandy and hard clay soils (Kluge).

Delma haroldi Storr, 1987

Description: Pale brown above, each scale edged with dark brown; darker brown on the head; a pale whitish band across the back of the head and another on the neck, extending on to the sides of the head and neck where there are several other pale vertical

G. SHEA

Delma inornata near Yass, NSW

bars; whitish below. Tail three to four times longer than body. Scales (including ventrals) in 16-18 rows, usually 16, at mid-body. Snout moderate, rounded. Seven scales on upper snout between rostral and frontal shields. Nasal and first supralabial scales distinct. Four scales bordering nostril. Usually fourth supralabial below the eye. 13-17 scales along a line across the top of the head which joins the angle of the mouth on each side. Ventral scales paired, noticeably wider than the adjacent body scales. 2-3 scales along lower margin of hindlimb flap. Usually three enlarged preanal scales. 70 mm (snout-vent).
Distribution: Arid regions of northern WA to adjoining regions of NT.
Habit: 'Shelters in hummocks of Trioda grass' (Wilson and Knowles).

Delma impar Fischer, 1882

Description: Pale grey-brown above, but usually with a series of dark brown or blackish dorso-lateral and lateral longitudinal stripes along the length of the body and tail, commencing on the neck. Each stripe is made up of individual black-centred scales, and the lower stripes tend to consist of lines of dark spots. Whitish below. Scales (including ventrals) in 13-16 rows at mid-body. Snout relatively blunt. Five scales on top of snout between rostral and frontal shields. Nasal and first supralabial scales fused anterior to the nostril, so that the nostril lies in a single, semi-divided scale. Fourth supralabial below eye. 9-11 scales along a line across the top of the head joining the angle of the mouth on each side. Ventral scales paired, usually noticeably wider than adjacent body scales. 2-4 scales along the lower margin of the hindlimb flap. Two enlarged preanal scales. 90 mm (snout-vent).
Distribution: Extreme south-eastern SA, Victoria and south-eastern NSW west of the Great Dividing Range.
Habit: Usually found under logs, rocks and ground debris in a variety of forest and woodland habitats.

Delma inornata Kluge, 1974

Description: Grey, grey-brown or olive-brown above, the individual scales often dark-edged. Whitish below. Scales (including ventrals) in 15-18 rows, usually 16, at mid-body. Snout moderate. Usually seven, but occasionally five scales on top of snout between rostral and frontal shields. Nasal and first supralabial scales distinct. Nostril usually bordered by three scales. Fourth supralabial below eye. 11-16 scales along a line across the top of the head joining the angle of the mouth on each side. Ventral scales paired, noticeably wider than adjacent body scales. 3-5 scales along the lower margin of the hindlimb flap. Usually three enlarged preanal scales. 125 mm (snout-vent).
Distribution: Widely distributed throughout south-eastern Australia, west of the Great Dividing Range, with isolated records from central and northern Qld.
Habit: Found in a wide variety of habitats, from the wetter forests of the ranges and slopes to the drier plains, woodlands and mallee communities in the western part of its range. Often seen feeding in porcupine grass or other grass tussocks, it is usually found sheltering under logs and other surface debris. Feeds almost exclusively on insects and spiders (Patchell and Shine).

Delma molleri near Clare, SA

Delma nasuta Tomkinson Ranges, SA

G. SHEA

Delma pax near Cane River crossing, WA

R. W. G. JENKINS

Delma labialis Shea, 1987

Description: Rich red-brown or grey-brown above, immaculate cream below; the top of the head is uniform brown, but the lips and sides of the head and neck with a series of alternating cream and yellow-brown vertically-aligned bars. The throat and ventral surfaces are immaculate cream. Tail about four times longer than the body. Scales (including ventrals) in 16-18 rows at mid-body. Snout moderate, rounded. Seven scales on upper snout between rostral and frontal shields. Nasal and first supralabial scales distinct. Four scales bordering nostril. Fourth supralabial below the eye. 16 scales along a line across the top of the head joining the angle of the mouth on each side. Ventral scales paired, noticeably wider than the adjacent body scales. 3 scales along the lower margin of hindlimb flap. Usually three enlarged preanal scales. 100 mm (snout-vent).

Distribution: Vicinity of Townsville, Qld, including adjacent islands.

Habit: Recorded by Shea from a variety of dry to wet open and forest habitats, including those adjacent to beaches.

Delma mitella Shea, 1987

Description: Reddish-brown above, pale yellow to white below, the top of the head darker and with four narrow pale cream cross-bands, irregularly edged with black, which extend to the level or edges of upper lips; lower lips,throat and ventral surface without darker markings. Relative length of tail not known. Scales (including ventrals) in 16 rows at mid-body. Snout short, rounded. Seven scales on upper snout between rostral and frontal shields
Nasal and first supralabial scales distinct. Three scales bordering nostril. Fourth supralabial below the eye. 12-13 scales along a line across the top of the head joining the angle of the mouth on each side. Ventral scales paired, noticeably wider than the adjacent body scales. 5 scales along the lower margin of hindlimb flap. Three enlarged preanal scales. 80 mm (snout-vent).

Distribution: Eastern side of Atherton Tableland, Qld.

Habit: Not recorded.

Delma molleri Lutken, 1863

Description: Pale grey-brown above, the individual scales usually with dark margins. Usually two conspicuous dark head bands, a broad one across the

Delma plebeia Injune, Qld

parietal region and a second across the neck. Throat and ventral scales whitish, but the ventral scales with darker margins. Scales (including ventrals) in 16-18 rows, usually 18, at mid-body. Snout moderate. Five scales on top of snout between rostral and frontal shields. Nasal and first supralabial scales distinct. Nostril bordered by three scales. Fourth supralabial below eye. 12-15 scales along a line across the top of the head joining the angle of the mouth on each side. Ventral scales paired, noticeably wider than adjacent body scales. 3-4 scales along lower margin of the hindlimb flap. Three enlarged preanal scales. 100 mm (snout-vent).
Distribution: South-eastern SA.
Habit: An inhabitant of semi-arid shrublands and woodlands.

Delma nasuta Kluge, 1974

Description: Rich brown or olive-brown above, the body scales often with darker margins or sometimes with darker centres forming a reticulate pattern. Ventral surface whitish, the scales often with darker margins. Scales (including ventrals) in 14-18 rows, nearly always 16, at mid-body. Snout elongated and rather pointed. Seven scales on top of snout between rostral and frontal shields. Nasal and first supralabial scales distinct. Nostril bordered by three or four scales. Fourth supralabial below eye. 12-19 scales along a line across the top of the head joining the angle of the mouth on each side. Ventral scales paired, noticeably wider than adjacent body scales. 2-6 scales along the lower margin of the hindlimb flap. Usually three enlarged preanal scales. 90 mm (snout-vent).
Distribution: The northern arid zone of Australia, from the coast of WA through the NT to western Qld.
Habit: Appears to be closely associated with porcupine grass (Triodia) in a variety of sandy and stony desert conditions, as well as in arid mulga and related scrubs. Feeds almost exclusively on insects and spiders (Patchell and Shine).

Delma pax Kluge, 1974

Description: Brown above, the individual scales often with darker centres, and usually with dark head bands — the most conspicuous being a broad one across the parietal region and a narrow one on the neck. Ventral surfaces whitish. Scales (including ventrals) in 15-16 rows, almost invariably 16, at mid-body. Snout relatively elongate. Seven scales on top

Delma mitella

Delma molleri

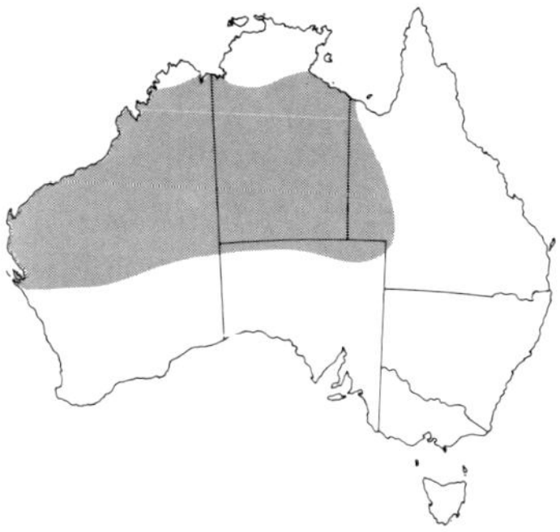

Delma nasuta

Delma pax

Delma plebeia

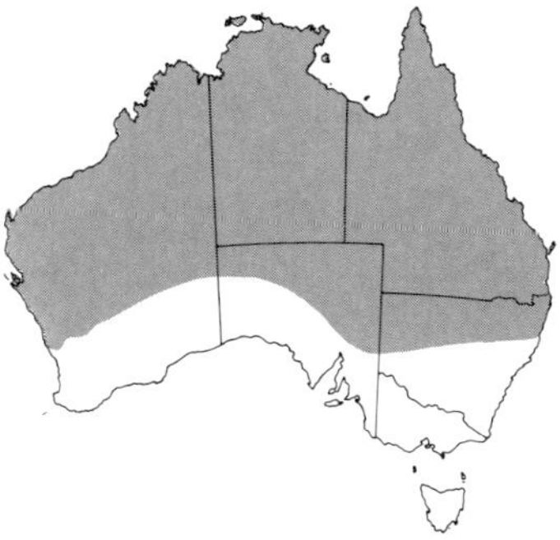

Delma tincta

Delma torquata

Delma tincta Muttaburra, Qld

of snout between rostral and frontal shields. Nasal and first supralabial scales distinct. Nostril usually bordered by four scales. Nearly always third supralabial below eye. 12-14 scales along a line across the top of the head joining the angle of the mouth on each side. Ventral scales paired, noticeably wider than adjacent body scales. 3-4 scales along lower margin of hindlimb flap. Three enlarged preanal scales. 90 mm (snout-vent).
Distribution: Hamersley Plateau, WA.
Habit: Kluge records two specimens collected in leaf-litter in stream beds.

Delma plebeia De Vis, 1888

Description: More or less uniform brown or grey-brown above, usually uniform whitish below; some darker bars on the lips. Head darker than body (black in the young); sides of neck sometimes bright rusty-brown (more conspicuous in the young), often extending back along the anterior part of the body as a series of narrow faint, reddish-brown stripes through the centres of the lateral scale rows. Scales (including ventrals) in 14-16 rows, usually 16, at mid-body. Snout moderate. Usually seven, sometimes eight or five, scales on top of the snout between the rostral and frontal shields. Nasal and first supralabial scales distinct. Nostril usually bordered by four, sometimes three, scales. Fourth supralabial below eye. 10-14 scales along a line across the top of the head joining the angle of the mouth on each side. Ventral scales paired, noticeably wider than adjacent body scales. 2-4 scales along the lower margin of hindlimb flap. Usually two enlarged preanal scales. 110 mm (snout-vent).
Distribution: South-eastern Qld and north-eastern NSW.
Habit: An inhabitant of leaf-litter and ground debris in dry sclerophyll forests and savannah woodland.

Delma tincta De Vis, 1888

Description: More or less uniform grey or grey-brown above, immaculate white below. Usually well-developed dark bands on the head, with pale cream or yellow interspaces; the most conspicuous is a broad dark band across the parietal region and a somewhat narrower one on the neck. Scales (including ventrals) in 12-16 rows, usually 14, at mid-body. Snout moderate. Nearly always five scales on the top of the snout between the rostral and frontal shields. Nasal and first supralabial scales distinct. Nostril bordered by three scales. Third supralabial below eye. 10-13 scales along a line across the top of the head joining the angle of the mouth on each side. Ventral scales paired, noticeably wider than adjacent body scales. 2-3 scales along lower margin of hindlimb flap. Usually three enlarged preanal scales. 80 mm (snout-vent).
Distribution: Ranges widely across the northern half of Australia.
Habit: Found in a very wide range of habitats, from wet coastal forests to the arid interior. Usually, found under rocks, logs or other ground debris, or in vegetation, it sometimes burrows into the surface layers of the soil.

Delma torquata Kluge, 1974

Description: More or less uniform brown above, paler below but the ventral shields with darker margins. Head strongly banded, the most conspicuous being a broad band across the parietal region , with two additional bands on the neck, and the paler interspaces cream or yellow. Throat with coarse dark reticulations. Scales (including ventrals) in 16 rows at mid-body. Snout relatively short and blunt. Five scales on top of snout between rostral and frontal shields. Nasal and first supralabial scales distinct. Nostril bordered by three scales. Third supralabial below eye. 10-12 scales along a line across the top of the head joining the angle of the mouth on each side. Ventral scales paired, usually noticeably wider than adjacent body scales. Two scales along lower margin of hindlimb flap. Two enlarged preanal scales. 60 mm (snout-vent).
Distribution: South-eastern Qld.
Habit: Recorded from a number of disturbed habitats. Found under rocks, logs and other ground cover. Apparently a burrowing species, the type found about 15 cm below the surface (Kluge).

M. PETERSON

Delma torquata near Brisbane, Qld

Genus *Lialis* Gray, 1835

A group of rather large terrestrial snake-like lizards with poorly-developed hindlimb flaps and conspicuous external ear-openings. A single widely-distributed Australian species (*burtonis*) which also occurs in New Guinea, and an endemic New Guinean species (*jicari*) are the only two members of the genus.

Head scales small, fragmented and irregular. Scales (including ventrals) in 18 or more rows at mid-body, the ventrals noticeably wider than the adjacent body scales (*burtonis*). Nasal scales not in contact. Preanal pores present. Dorsal and ventral scales smooth.

Lialis burtonis Round Hill, NSW

Lialis burtonis Brinerville, NSW

Lialis burtonis

Lialis burtonis Gray, 1835

Burton's snake-lizard

Description: Highly variable in colour and pattern, the number of combinations and permutations being so great that they cannot be described briefly here. Ground colour ranges from pale grey or cream through various shades on brown, russet to almost black. Pattern may be totally absent, while combinations of dark and pale spotted scales may result in an overall spotted pattern or, if longitudinally aligned, in continuous or interrupted stripes. Often a dark zone along the side of the snout, face and neck, which may be bordered below by a narrow white or cream stripe. Ventral surface usually heavily pigmented, the individual scales with small dark and pale spots and flecks which tend to be longitudinally aligned. The head is greatly elongated, the snout sharply angular and wedge-shaped. Head scales small, fragmented, irregular. Scales (including ventrals) in 18-22 rows at mid-body. 13-21 supralabial scales. Ventral scales paired, usually noticeably wider than adjacent body scales. Hindlimb flap very small, triangular, usually with one, occasionally two scales along the lower margin. Usually four preanal pores. 250 mm (snout-vent).

Distribution: The most widely distributed member of its family, occurring virtually throughout continental Australia and the islands of Torres Strait. Extra-limital in New Guinea.

Habit: A terrestrial species found in low vegetation, or in ground debris in a broad spectrum of habitats from wet coastal forests to the deserts of the interior. Active both by day and night, but especially in the early morning and late afternoon, the species feeds largely on small lizards, especially skinks.

Genus ***Ophidiocephalus*** Lucas and Frost, 1897

A monotypic genus of legless lizards, until recently known only from the type specimen collected at Charlotte Waters in about 1890 but rediscovered near Abminga in SA. Hindlimb flaps small; external ear-opening small, hidden beneath a temporal scale.

Head scales, including the parietals, enlarged and symmetrical. Scales (including ventrals) in 16 rows at mid-body, the ventrals not noticeably wider than the adjacent body scales. Anterior nasal scales in contact. Preanal pores absent. Dorsal and ventral scales smooth. Tail longer than body.

Ophidiocephalus taeniatus Lucas and Frost, 1897

Description: Rich fawn above, pale grey on the head; a broad, dark brown, lateral band from snout to tip of tail, sharply demarcated above from the dorsal colour but merging into the grey-brown ventral surface; the ventral and lower lateral surfaces with a reticulated pattern formed by the white free margins of the scales. Major features have been described under the genus. 102 mm (snout-vent).

Distribution: Known only from the vicinity of the

type locality, Charlotte Waters, NT.
Habit: Found '...in loose soil blanketed by undisturbed leaf-litter, all overlying cracking clay loams' (Ehmann).

Ophidiocephalus taeniatus
Abminga, SA

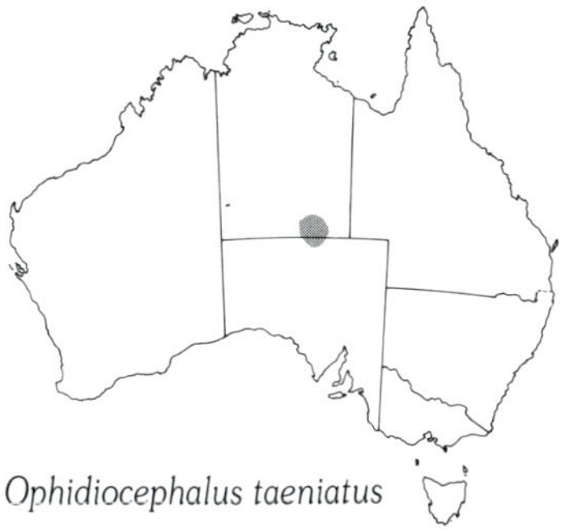

Ophidiocephalus taeniatus

Genus *Paradelma* Kinghorn, 1926

A monotypic genus of terrestrial legless lizards with moderate hindlimb flaps and a conspicuous external ear-opening, known only from central Qld.

Head scales, including parietals, enlarged and symmetrical. Scales (including ventrals) in 18-20 rows, usually 18, at mid-body, the ventrals paired and usually noticeably wider than the adjacent body scales. Nasal scales in contact. Four preanal pores present. Dorsal and ventral scales smooth. Tail nearly twice as long as body.

Paradelma orientalis Cracow, Qld

Paradelma orientalis (Günther, 1876)

Description: Glossy brown or dark grey above, usually with a milky opaqueness; white below, the individual scales often with darker centres so that a faint longitudinal striped pattern may be present, especially on the sides. A conspicuous black bar across the neck, behind a broad pale zone which extends to the throat. See generic description for other characteristics. 160 mm (snout-vent).
Distribution: Central-eastern Qld.
Habit: An essentially terrestrial lizard usually found sheltering under logs and ground debris in eucalyptus woodland. It has also been observed to climb, usually

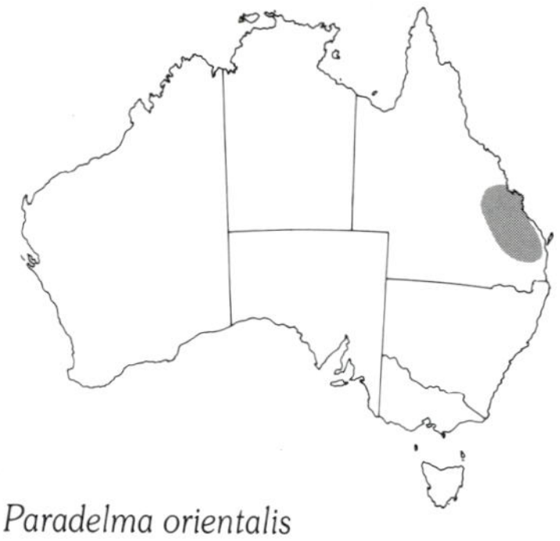

Paradelma orientalis

in the early morning or evening, well off the ground to 'perch' on the rough back of *Acacia* trees — possibly to scan a wider area for prey (Tremul)

Genus *Pletholax* Cope, 1864

A monotypic genus of burrowing legless lizards with small hindlimb flaps and minute external ear-opening, known only from a small area of south-western WA.

Head scales, including parietals, enlarged and symmetrical. Scales (including ventrals) in 16 rows at mid-body, the ventrals not noticeably wider than the adjacent body scales. Nasal scales in contact. Preanal pores absent. Dorsal and ventral scales strongly keeled. Tail much longer than body.

Pletholax gracilis Greenhead, WA

M. PETERSON

Pletholax gracilis Cope, 1864

Description: Pale grey to brown above, the head somewhat darker brown. Sides of head darker, with

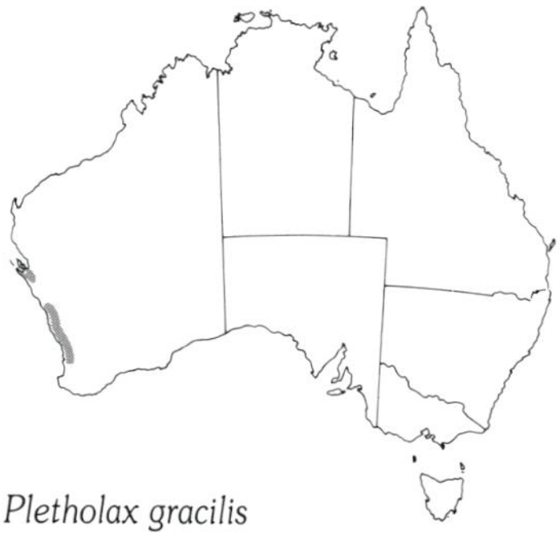

Pletholax gracilis

a blackish stripe from the snout, below the eye, to the side of the neck, contrasting sharply with the pale labial region. Throat and chest lemon-yellow in breeding males (Glauert). Many of the body scales with small dark or pale flecks, with a narrow dorsolateral stripe formed by a longitudinal line of dark-centred scales. See generic description for other characteristics. 75 mm (snout-vent).
Distribution: Western coastal regions of south-western WA.
Habit: A burrowing species found in sandy coastal woodland (Kluge), but extending into a variety of other habitats in its range.
Subspecies: *gracilis* (lower west coast of WA); *edelensis* (Shark Bay region, WA).

Genus **Pygopus** Merrem, 1820

A genus of large, heavily built legless lizards with large hindlimb flaps and conspicuous external ear-openings, found throughout most parts of continental Australia.

Head scales, including parietals, enlarged and symmetrical. Scales (including ventrals) in 21 or more rows at mid-body, the ventrals paired and noticeably wider than the adjacent body scales. Anterior nasal scales in contact. Eight or more preanal pores present. Dorsal scales smooth or, more usually, keeled; ventral scales smooth. Tail about twice as long as body.

Key

TO THE SPECIES OF PYGOPUS

Scales strongly keeled; no dark bars across head or neck...... .... ***lepidopodus***

Scales smooth to moderately keeled; usually at least one dark bar across head or neck.............................. ***nigriceps***

Pygopus lepidopodus Round Hill, NSW

Pygopus nigriceps Mt Davies, SA

Pygopus lepidopodus (Lacépède,1804)

Common Scaly-Foot

Description: Highly variable in colour and pattern, ranging from uniform grey, brown or russet above, to a complex pattern of dark, pale-edged dorsal and lateral stripes; these stripes may be continuous or broken up into lines of dark pale-edged spots or blotches. Ventral surface usually pigmented, often with a complex spotted pattern formed of darker and paler flecks. Lips usually with a few dark bars which may be more or less continuous with some oblique dark bars on the side of the neck. In eastern populations the head and tail may be a grey which contrasts sharply with the body colour. The body is relatively heavily built, with 21-25 rows of scales (including ventrals) at mid-body, the dorsal body scales strongly keeled. Ventral scales paired, noticeably wider than adjacent body scales. Hindlimb flap large, with 5-9 scales along its lower margin. 230 mm (snout-vent).
Distribution: Ranges widely across southern parts of continental Australia, from south-eastern Qld to Shark Bay, WA.
Habit: Found in a wide variety of habitats from wet sclerophyll coastal forests and coastal heaths and dunes to semi-arid mallee associations of the inland. A terrestrial, largely diurnal species, it is usually encountered foraging under or in low vegetation. At other times found under fallen timber and other ground litter. Feeds primarily on spiders, but also takes insects (Patchell and Shine).

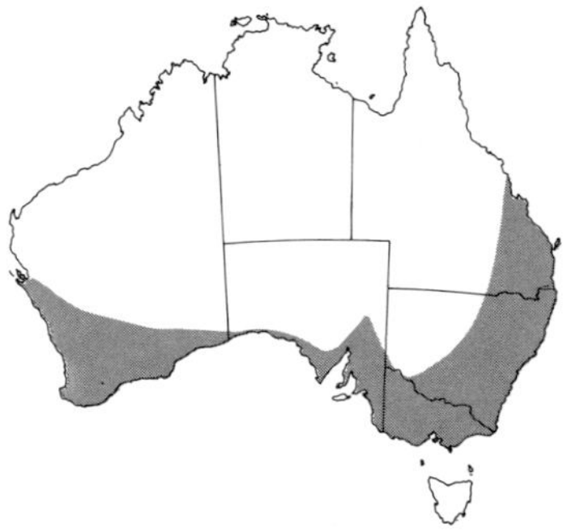

Pygopus nigriceps (Fischer, 1882)

Hooded Scaly Foot

Description: Pale grey to rich reddish-brown above, usually immaculate whitish below. The body scales may be dark-edged, forming an overall reticulated pattern, or individual paler and darker scales may form a vague longitudinal pattern. Head usually with two dark cross-bands, the first a narrow one at the level of the eyes, the second a broad, dark collar. In older specimens these bars may merge into a single dark hood, or may become obscure. Similar in most other respects to *P. lepidopodus*, from which it differs in having smooth or feebly-keeled scales. 180 mm (snout-vent).
Distribution: More or less throughout continental Australia except for the wetter coastal and highland regions of southern and south-eastern Australia.
Habit: Similar to *Pygopus lepidopodus*, except that it is largely crepuscular and nocturnal, probably as a response to high daytime temperatures throughout much of its range. However, unlike *P. lepidopodus* which feeds mainly on spiders, *P. nigriceps* feeds mostly on insects (Patchell and Shine).

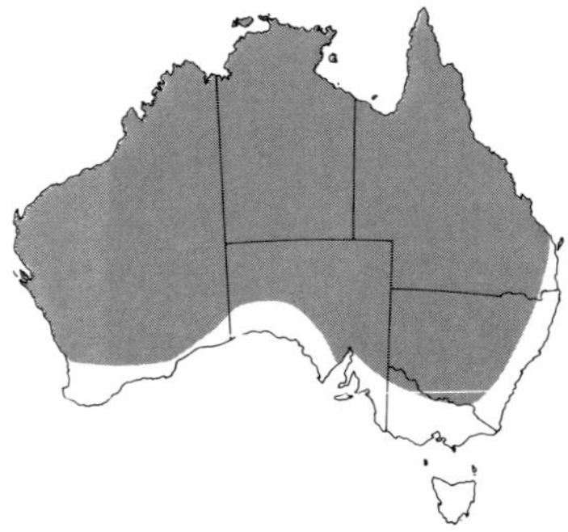

Subspecies: *nigriceps* (western Australia); *schraderi* (eastern Australia).

Family Agamidae

A large family of lizards which extends from the western Pacific, through Australia, Indo-Malaysia and Asia to Africa.

About 60 species are found in Australia, where there has been marked radiation in the arid parts of the continent. They are usually active, diurnal lizards, mainly terrestrial but with a few arboreal species. They are characterised by their juxtaposed body scales, often with greatly enlarged tubercles and spines. The limbs are well-developed, while the tongue is broad, flat and fleshy, slightly notched in front and not sheathed at its base.

All agamids are oviparous, laying from two to more than 20 eggs in a clutch, according to species. Autotomy does not occur, although some species have limited powers of regeneration if part of the tail is damaged or lost. Femoral and/or preanal pores are present in most species.

Most agamid lizards feed on insects and other small arthropods, but some larger species feed on reptiles, nestling birds and small mammals, and occasionally wildflowers and other plant material.

Key

TO THE GENERA OF AUSTRALIAN AGAMID LIZARDS

1 Body without very large conical spines or a spiny nuchal hump **2**

Body covered above with large conical spines, each much larger than the eye; nape with a large spiny hump (a).......... ***Moloch***

2 No large skin 'frill' around neck.......... **3**

A large, loose 'frill' of skin around neck (b) .... ***Chlamydosaurus***

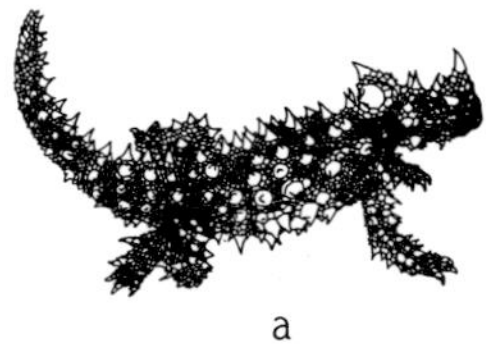
a

b

3 Femoral and/or preanal pores absent.............................. **4**

Femoral and/or preanal pores (c) present, at least in males **5**

4 Transverse gular fold absent; tail about one and one quarter times as long as body.............................. ***Chelosania***

Transverse gular fold present (d); tail at least twice as long as head and body.. ***Hypsilurus***

5 Tail at most slightly laterally compressed, without a strongly differentiated dorsal keel.................................... **6**

Tail strongly compressed with a strongly differentiated dorsal keel... ***Physignathus***

6 A vertebral series of enlarged scales (e) present or absent on the back; if absent, three or more femoral pores present on each side... **7**

No vertebral series of enlarged scales along the back (f); 0-2 femoral pores on each side....................... ***Diporiphora***

7 Femoral pores present.. **8**

Femoral pores absent.................................. ***Caimanops***

8 Nuchal crest and/or series of enlarged, keeled vertebral scales (g) present or absent; if latter, present along at least anterior two-thirds of body; enlarged, strongly keeled or spinose scales are present elsewhere on dorsum (g)........ **9**

A distinct nuchal crest present (h), continuous with a series of enlarged, keeled scales forming a distinct vertebral series along at least the anterior two-thirds of the body; enlarged dorsal scales (excluding vertebrals) never strongly keeled or spinose (i)............................ ***Lophognathus***

9 Spinose scales on sides of base of tail present or absent, but in a single linear row (j) if present............................ **10**

Sides of base of tail with a series of irregularly scattered spinose scales (k).. ***Pogona***

10 Lower edge of supralabials straight or at most slightly curved, forming a more or less straight or even edge to the upper lip (l)... **11**

Lower edge of supralabials strongly curved, forming a distinctly crenellated or fringed edge to the upper lip (m)........ .... ***Cryptagama***

11 No row of enlarged scales from below eye to above ear (n); dorsal scales of body heterogeneous, with distinctive vertebral and paravertebral rows of enlarged, keeled or spinose scales.. **12**

A row of enlarged scales from below the eye to above the ear (o); dorsal scales of body more or less homogeneous with at most a few slightly enlarged scattered tubercles.. ***Ctenophorus***

12 Tympanum exposed, the external ear-opening prominent (p); no enlarged spinose scales along each side of the base of the tail (q)... ***Amphibolurus***

External ear-opening either absent (r), with the tympanic region covered by skin, or, if present, a series of enlarged spinose scales along each side of the base of the tail (j)...... .... ***Tympanocryptis***

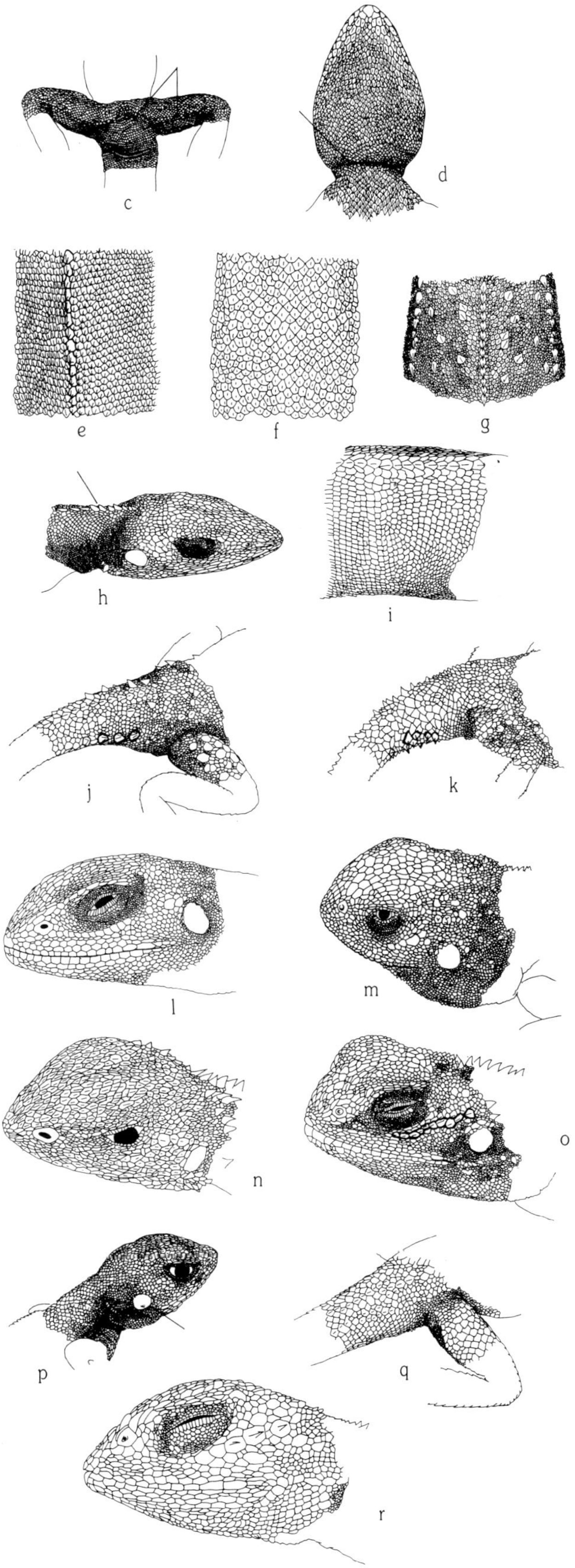

Genus *Amphibolurus* Wagler, 1830

Until recently the largest endemic genus of Australian dragon lizards, the genus *Amphibolurus* has recently been redefined more narrowly to encompass a small group of closely-related species. It appears to be most closely related to *Lophognathus* and *Tympanocryptis*.

Amphibolurus is characterised by the presence of heterogeneous dorsal scalation, usually with vertebral and paravertebral rows of enlarged mucronate tubercles or spines; an exposed tympanum; a nuchal crest and/or vertebral keel is usually present; and the absence of enlarged spinose scales along each side of the base of the tail. All species are semi-arboreal, regularly foraging on the ground but more often seen resting or perching in shrubs or on tree-trunks and low branches. All are egg-layers which produce clutches of about 6-10 eggs.

Key

TO THE SPECIES OF AMPHIBOLURUS

1 Dorsal and lateral body scales (excluding longitudinal rows of enlarged keeled scales) strongly heterogeneous in shape and size; lining of mouth bright yellow in life.......... **2**

Dorsal and lateral body scales (excluding longitudinal rows of enlarged keeled scales) homogeneous or subequal; lining of mouth flesh-coloured or pink in life................ ***nobbi***

2 Dark canthal stripe, if present, extends only from snout to nostril; transverse dark markings on the snout in the internarial region... ***muricatus***

Dark canthal stripe extending from snout to eye; no transverse dark markings on the snout in the internarial region. .... ***norrisi***

Amphibolurus nobbi Round Hill, NSW

Amphibolurus muricatus

P. GERMAN

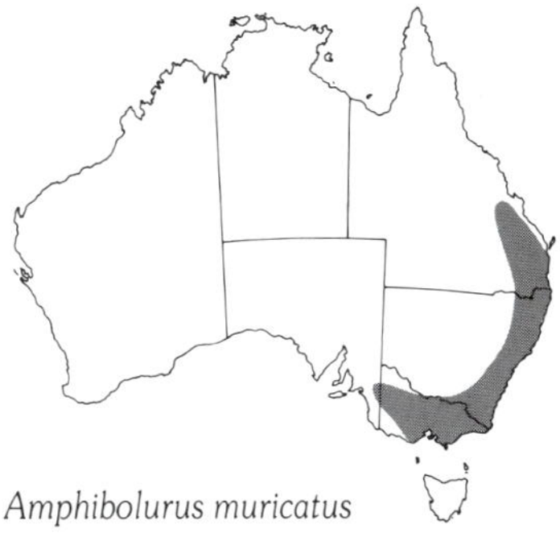

Amphibolurus muricatus

Amphibolurus muricatus (White, ex Shaw, 1790)
Jacky Lizard

Description: Pale grey to dark brown above, usually mottled with darker brown on the flanks and sometimes with a narrow, pale, dark-edged lateral stripe from above arm to groin. A series of large, angular, blackish patches along the middle of the back, often divided or displaced along the vertebral line, and bordered below by a broad, pale, dorso-lateral stripe from the nape to the base of the tail. This stripe may be broken up into a series of lozenge-shaped bars by downward extensions of the dark mid-dorsal blotches. The dark dorsal blotches usually continue on to the tail as a series of irregular cross-bands. Usually a dark brown bar between the eye and the ear. Often some narrow transverse bars on the top of the head. Lips and lower jaws often conspicuously paler than remainder of head. Whitish to pale yellowish-brown below, with or without darker flecks. Dorsal body scalation strongly heterogeneous; scales of dorsum and flanks keeled, very variable in size, and with numerous scattered enlarged, strongly keeled scales or tubercles, especially on the flanks and hindlimbs. The enlarged scales on the dorsum tend to form distinct longitudinal series; a nuchal crest continuous with a vertebral series of enlarged scales; a paravertebral series from the nape to the base of the tail, separated by two or three scales from the vertebral series, and a dorso-lateral series on each side. Numerous spinose scales on the sides of the neck. Scales on throat and neck feebly to strongly keeled. Marginal scales of lower eyelid not forming a fringe. Tympanum moderate and conspicuous. Canthus angular, the nostril sub-circular and facing outwards in an enlarged nasal scale lying well below the canthal ridge. 100 mm (snout-vent). Adpressed hindlimb reaches to about the eye, the hindlimb about 75%, the tail about 200% of the snout-vent length. Preanal and femoral pores 10-20, widely spaced and widely separated on the midline, extending only about halfway along each thigh. Lining of mouth usually bright yellow.
Distribution: South-eastern continental Australia, from south-eastern SA along the coast and ranges to northern NSW and south-eastern Qld.
Habit: An inhabitant of dry sclerophyll forests, rocky ridges and coastal heathlands, where it feeds opportunistically on insects and other small arthropods. Often found in shrubs and other low vegetation.

Amphibolurus nobbi Witten, 1972
Nobbi

Description: Similar in most respects to *Amphibolurus muricatus*, from which it differs in having more uniform and homogeneous scalation, fewer femoral than preanal pores (femoral pores greater than preanal in *muricatus*), and colour. In *nobbi* the dorsal and lateral scales (except for the longitudinal rows of strongly keeled scales) are subequal and without scattered enlarged scales. The pale dorso-lateral stripe is often bright yellow, while the rump and base of the tail are often flushed with pink or red. The lining of the mouth is pink. 75 mm (snout-vent).
Distribution: From north-western Vic and adjacent border regions of SA through southern inland areas of NSW to south-eastern Qld.
Habit: As for *A. muricatus*, except that *A. nobbi*

Amphibolurus nobbi

Amphibolurus norrisi

extends into mallee and related arid scrubs.
Subspecies: *nobbi* (ranges of northern NSW to coast and ranges of south-eastern Qld); *coggeri* (south and west of the Warrumbungle Mountains, NSW).

Amphibolurus norrisi Witten and Coventry, 1984

Description: Grey or grey-brown above, darker on the flanks, and with a dark vertebral stripe which has lateral extensions which may sometimes reach the dark flanks and therefore enclose a series of paler dorso-lateral blotches. A dark canthal stripe from snout to eye and a more intensely dark stripe from the eye to the tympanum, bordered above by a narrow pale stripe. Lower labials pale grey or white. Tail with a series of darker blotches at its base, gradually becoming cross-bands further back on the tail. Whitish to pale brown below. Dorsal body scalation strongly heterogeneous, with a distinct nuchal crest, continuous with a vertebral series of enlarged scales. A paravertebral series of enlarged scales on either side of the vertebral line, and a further continuous dorso-lateral series of enlarged scales on either side of the body. Dorsal scales strongly keeled, the keels running more or less parallel to the vertebral line. Dorsum with numerous scattered, enlarged, keeled scales. Gular scales smooth or feebly keeled. Marginal scales of lower eyelid not forming a fringe. Tympanum moderate and conspicuous. Canthus angular, the nostril subcircular and facing outwards in an enlarged nasal scale lying well below the canthal ridge. 110 mm (snout-vent). Adpressed hindlimb reaches to about the eye, the hindlimb about 75% of snout-vent length, the tail about 200% of snout-vent length. Preanal and femoral pores 8-20. Lining of mouth pale yellow.
Distribution: Western Vic and adjacent regions of SA; an isolated population in Eyre Peninsula and coastal areas of the Great Australian Bight.
Habit: Mallee heath.

R. MILLER

Amphibolurus norrisi (female), Big Desert, Vic

Genus ***Caimanops*** Storr, 1974

A monotypic genus whose single species is a moderate, rather elongate, short-limbed terrestrial lizard with a distinctly long, wedge-shaped snout. It is characterised by its lack of femoral pores and the presence of five longitudinal rows of enlarged keeled scales along the back, the median one commencing as a strong nuchal crest of spinose scales. Gular fold present.

Caimanops amphiboluroides Wiluna, WA

Caimanops amphiboluroides

(Lucas and Frost, 1902)

Description: Pale fawn above with a broad, dark brown, dorso-lateral stripe from angle of jaws above forelimb to base of tail; this stripe is separated by a pale fawn zone from a narrower brown stripe which reaches from the groin nearly to the axilla. A dark brown bar from eye to ear. Often a narrow dark brown stripe along the canthus and sometimes a narrow, V-shaped dark brown mark between the eyes, and a narrow dark brown bar running back to the

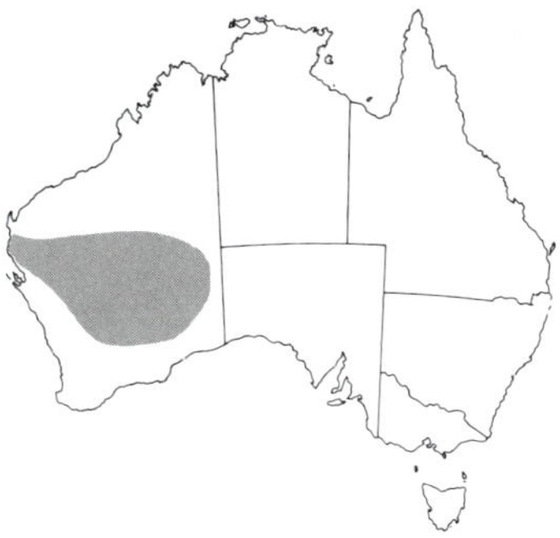

Caimanops amphiboluroides

nape from above each eye. Throat and belly white, sometimes with faint, often broken, dark longitudinal lines. Snout very angular. A marked nuchal crest continuous with a vertebral row of enlarged scales. Another series of discontinuous enlarged keeled scales on either side of the vertebral line and separated from the vertebral row by several scale rows. A dorso-lateral series of discontinuous enlarged scales from above the ear to the base of the tail. Remaining dorsal and lateral scales with low keels, but not uniform in size. Gulars smooth. Ventral scales with low keels. Caudal scales strongly keeled. Adpressed hind-limb reaches to just beyond the shoulder, the hind-limb about 55%, the tail about 160% of snout-vent length. Two small preanal pores on each side. 90 mm (snout-vent).

Distribution: Southern interior of WA, extending to coastal regions between Shark Bay and Exmouth Gulf.

Habit: A diurnal species associated with mulga and other Acacia shrublands. Reported to be a slow-moving species which relies on crypsis rather than flight to avoid predators; terrestrial to semi-arboreal.

Genus ***Chelosania*** Gray, 1845

A monotypic genus whose sole member is confined to the woodlands of north-western Australia to Arnhem Land and the north-western corner of Qld. It is characterised by an exposed tympanum, slender compressed body, absence of either a transverse gular fold or preanal and femoral pores, and a short tail scarcely more than one and a half times as long as the head and body.

Chelosania brunnea Jim Jim, NT

Chelosania brunnea Gray, 1845
Chameleon Dragon

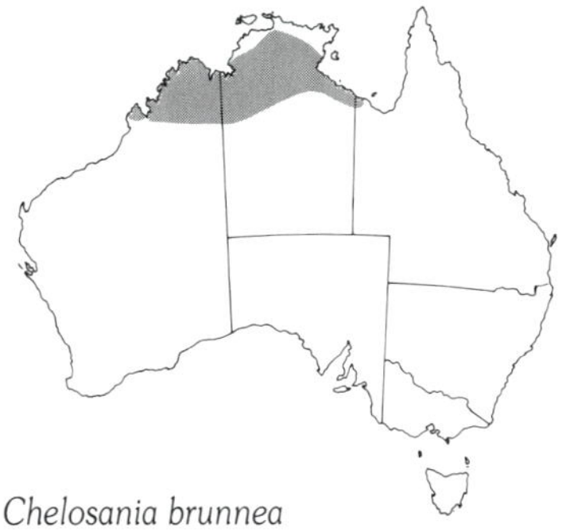
Chelosania brunnea

Description: Pale grey to bright yellowish above, with or without narrow, dark brown variegations. Almost always two narrow, longitudinal brown bars on the nape and scattered dark flecks on the head, and a distinctive dark brown patch of small scales behind the tympanum within the auricular circle. The scales around the tympanic margin cream-coloured, and a series of narrow, oblique dark lines on the side of the neck corresponding with the skin between oblique rows of scales. Tail with broad, dark brown bands, as wide as or narrower than the paler interspaces. A series of narrow, brown longitudinal lines on the throat, all converging on the chest. A few grey-brown flecks on the vent, otherwise whitish. Body scalation homogeneous, the dorsal and lateral scales subequal, keeled. A low but distinct nuchal crest continuous with a low dorsal crest which extends along the basal half of the tail. Gular scales smooth or feebly keeled, ventrals strongly keeled. A distinctive series of slightly raised scales surrounding the equally distinctive wedge- or sector-shaped ear-opening. A unique series of oblique furrows on the side of the neck. Canthus curved, the nostril circular and facing outwards and upwards in an enlarged nasal scale lying on the canthal ridge. Adpressed hindlimb reaches to about the shoulder, the hindlimb about 55%, the tail about 150% of snout-vent length. 90 mm (snout-vent).
Distribution: Kimberley region, WA, through north-eastern NT to north-western Qld.
Habit: Found in savannah woodland, usually on the ground or perched on debris, fallen timber or low vegetation. Moves slowly and deliberately, with a distinct chameleon-like action. Lays two or three eggs per clutch.

Genus *Chlamydosaurus* Gray, 1825

A monotypic genus which is characterised by the presence of a large, loose 'ruff' or 'frill' around the neck, which, though lying in folds around the neck and shoulders when the lizard is at rest, can be erected by opening the mouth when the lizard is alarmed. The frill on each side overlaps on the crown of the head. The tympanum is exposed, while femoral and preanal pores are present. The frill is small and poorly developed in hatchlings. Occurs in Australia and southern New Guinea.

Chlamydosaurus kingii Gray, 1825
Frilled Lizard

Description: Grey to brown or orange-brown or nearly black above, usually with obscure darker brown variegations or mottling on the dorsum and flanks which, when it reaches the tail, often forms irregular cross-bands. Sometimes a broad, blackish, dorso-lateral band between forelimbs and hindlimbs, in which individual white or yellow scales form obscure vertical bars. Pattern on lower flanks sometimes a series of large, pale ocelli or rhombs. Lips and lower jaw dark brown with numerous pale flecks. Frill yellow to black, often variegated with orange. Off-white or yellowish below, male with pale

Chlamydosaurus kingii Port Keats, NT

Chlamydosaurus kingii McArthur River, NT

chest but black belly. Terminal portion of tail sometimes blackish. Dorsal scalation heterogeneous, the vertebrals small,the paravertebrals much larger, but contrasting suddenly with the tiny dorso-lateral scales which in turn give way to the larger scales on the flanks. Scattered slightly enlarged scales, usually white or yellow, among the minute dorso-lateral scales. A row of slightly enlarged nuchal scales, but no dorsal crest. Nearly all dorsal scales, including those on the frill, keeled. Gular and ventral scales keeled. Canthus acutely angular, the nostril round and facing outwards and downwards in an enlarged nasal scale lying below the canthal ridge. Adpressed hindlimb reaches to between the ear and the eye, the hindlimb about 80%, the tail about 200% of snout-vent length. Preanal and femoral pores 6-20, widely spaced and not extending more than halfway along the thigh. 220 mm (snout-vent).

Distribution: Kimberley district, WA, through 'top end' of NT to Cape York Peninsula and eastern Qld. Extra-limital in southern New Guinea.

Habit: An arboreal, diurnal lizard living in dry sclerophyll forests or woodlands, where it takes to trees when alarmed. Frequently forages on the ground where it feeds on insects and small vertebrates. Well-known for its bipedal locomotion when running, and for the erection of its large frill when confronting an enemy.

Chlamydosaurus kingii Townsville, Qld

Chlamydosaurus kingii

P. HORNER

Cryptagama aurita Wave Hill, NT

Genus ***Cryptagama*** Witten, 1984

A terrestrial monotypic genus confined to arid north-eastern WA. The tympanum is present and exposed, while there are 10-18 preanal and femoral pores. Tail shorter than snout-vent length. Scattered enlarged, keeled tubercles over the dorsal surface. The supralabial scales form a distinctive fringe along the upper lip.

Cryptagama aurita (Storr, 1981)

Description: Pale reddish-brown above suffused with pale brownish-grey on the head and back; sometimes a series of small, dark brown blotches on neck and back on either side of the midline; tail irregularly banded with dark brown, the dark bands about equal in width to the paler interspaces. Ventral surfaces whitish. Neck not much narrower than head. Supralabials 16-20. Scales on head slightly rugose or with a single low keel. Scales on back and flanks very small and more or less smooth, with numerous scattered enlarged keeled scales. Gular and ventral scales smooth or slightly keeled. 45 mm (snout-vent), the hindlimb about 60%, the tail about 75% of snout-vent length. 10-18 femoral and preanal pores.

Distribution: Arid north-eastern WA.

Habit: Some specimens found '... in bulldozed Triodia on lateritic plain' (Storr).

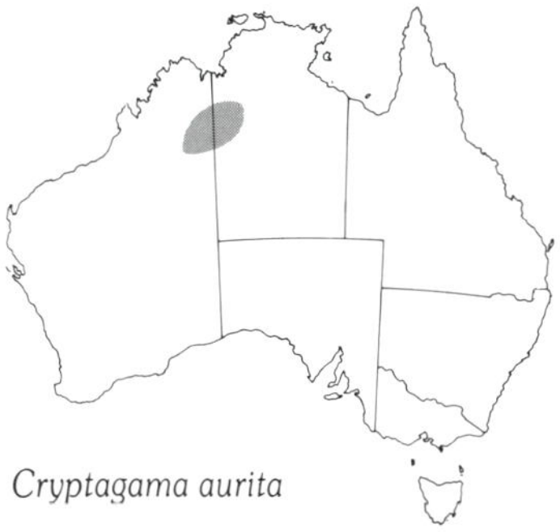

Cryptagama aurita

Genus *Ctenophorus* Fitzinger, 1843

A composite genus of essentially terrestrial lizards found throughout most of continental Australia and characterised by small dorsal scales, homogeneous or with at most slightly enlarge tubercles; absence of distinct rows of paravertebral or dorso-lateral spinose scales; a row of enlarged scales from below the eye to above the ear; tympanum exposed; tail long, slightly to much longer than head and body; femoral and preanal pores present in males; males usually with distinctive black or dark grey markings on throat and/or chest.

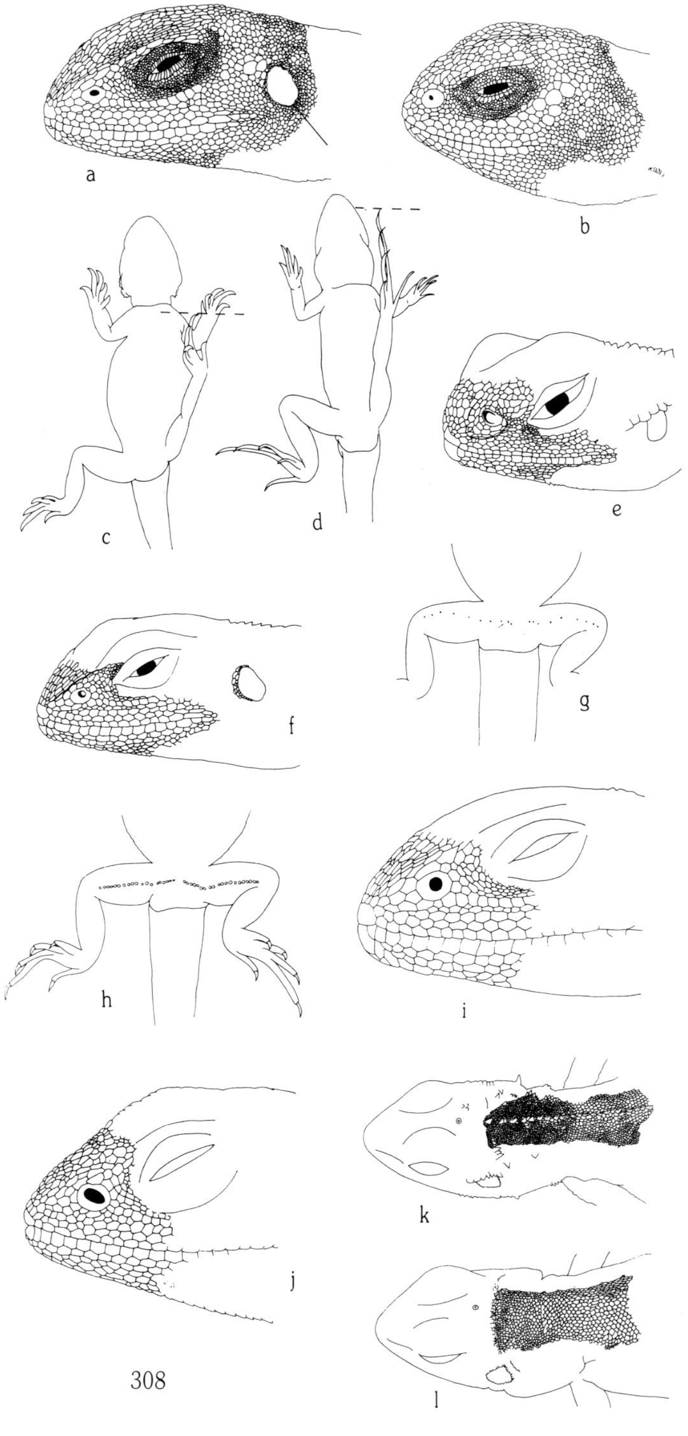

Key

TO THE SPECIES OF CTENOPHORUS

1 Tympanum exposed (a) **2**
Tympanum hidden, covered by skin (b) .... ***maculosus***

2 Hindlimb usually reaching no further than tympanum when adpressed (c); tail usually less than one and a half times as long as head and body **3**
Hindlimb usually reaching to eye or beyond when adpressed (d); tail usually much more than one and a half times as long as head and body **8**

3 Nasal region swollen, the nostril lying on or above the curved canthal ridge (e) **4**
Nasal region not swollen, the nostril lying below an angular canthal ridge (f) **5**

4 Femoral pores widely spaced along a curve which lies along the inner half of the thigh (g) .... ***nuchalis***
Femoral pores closely spaced along a more or less straight line along the outer half of the thigh (h) .... ***reticulatus***

5 Pores more than 25; nostril circular or broadly elliptical (i). **6**
Pores fewer than 15; nostril slit-like or narrowly elliptical (j) .... ***clayi***

6 No linear series of dark spots or blotches along each side of the tail **7**
A series of 20-30 dark spots or blotches along each side of the tail .... ***gibba***

7 Dorsal scalation homogeneous, without scattered enlarged scales on the back and sides .... ***pictus***
Dorsal scalation heterogeneous, with numerous low, enlarged scales on the back and sides .... ***salinarum***

8 Canthus rostralis angular or moderately swollen but nostrils, when viewed from above, face outwards **9**
Canthus rostralis swollen, the nostrils when viewed from above face distinctly upwards .... ***caudicinctus***

9 A distinct nuchal crest; a series of enlarged keeled scales form a distinct vertebral series along at least the anterior two-thirds of the body (k) **10**
At most a few enlarged keeled scales on the nape; a series of enlarged vertebral scales, if present, forming a distinct linear series only to about the level of the forelimbs (l) .. **12**

10 Dorsal, caudal and hindlimb scales homogeneous; a dark brown zigzag dorso-lateral streak along each side of the tail, which is never banded........ **11**

Dorsal, caudal and hindlimb scales heterogeneous, with scattered, enlarged, keeled scales, especially along the dorso-lateral skin-fold; tail without dark dorso-lateral streaks, usually banded distally........ ***cristatus***

11 Fewer than 30 subdigital lamellae under fourth toe; dorsal pattern dark brown with narrow, broken, pale vertebral and dorso-lateral stripes joined by pale, broken transverse bars........ ***mckenziei***

More than 32 subdigital lamellae under fourth toe (m); dorsal pattern of paired dark brown blotches on a pale brown ground colour........ ***scutulatus***

12 Dorsal and even small dorso-lateral scales with distinct sharp central keels forming continuous ridges running obliquely towards vertebral line; scales on the chest strongly keeled........ **13**

Dorsal scales at most with low, irregular keels which do not form distinct continuous ridges; dorso-lateral scales and those on the chest smooth, or with low, blunt ridges........ **16**

13 Pores more than 32 and extend to more than halfway along thigh (n); black on throat at least in males........ **14**

Pores 32 or fewer, extending no more than halfway along thigh (o); no black on throat........ ***femoralis***

14 Preanal pores not arching forward in the mid-line (p); black throat markings, when present, not in a single undivided band and black on chest of males not extending to abdomen (q)........ **15**

Preanal pores arching forward to an apex on the mid-line (n); a single, broad undivided throat marking in males and black on chest of males extends back to abdomen (r)........ ***isolepis***

15 Pores extending almost to knee (s); a solid black chevron on throat of males (t)........ ***maculatus***

Pores not extending to distal quarter of thigh (p); throat spotted with black, the spots often arranged in a chevron-shaped zone (q)........ ***fordi***

16 Nostril subcircular, in a normal nasal scale lying below an acute canthal ridge (u); scales on anterior and posterior surfaces of tibial region subequal (v)........ **17**

Nostril elliptical in a swollen nasal scale lying on a swollen canthal ridge (w); tibial region with a series of anterior proximal scales which are very much larger than those on posterior surface (x)........ **20**

17 Upper head scales between and in front of eyes rarely coarsely wrinkled, usually with simple longitudinal keels or almost smooth; vertebral row of keeled scales absent or not extending part way down back........ **18**

Upper head scales between and in front of eyes coarsely wrinkled, not simply keeled; vertebral row of keeled scales extending at least part-way along back........ ***vadnappa***

18 Scales on side of body homogeneous, without scattered tubercles........ **19**

Sides of body with few to many scattered, slightly enlarged tubercles, each usually pale in colour and contrasting with

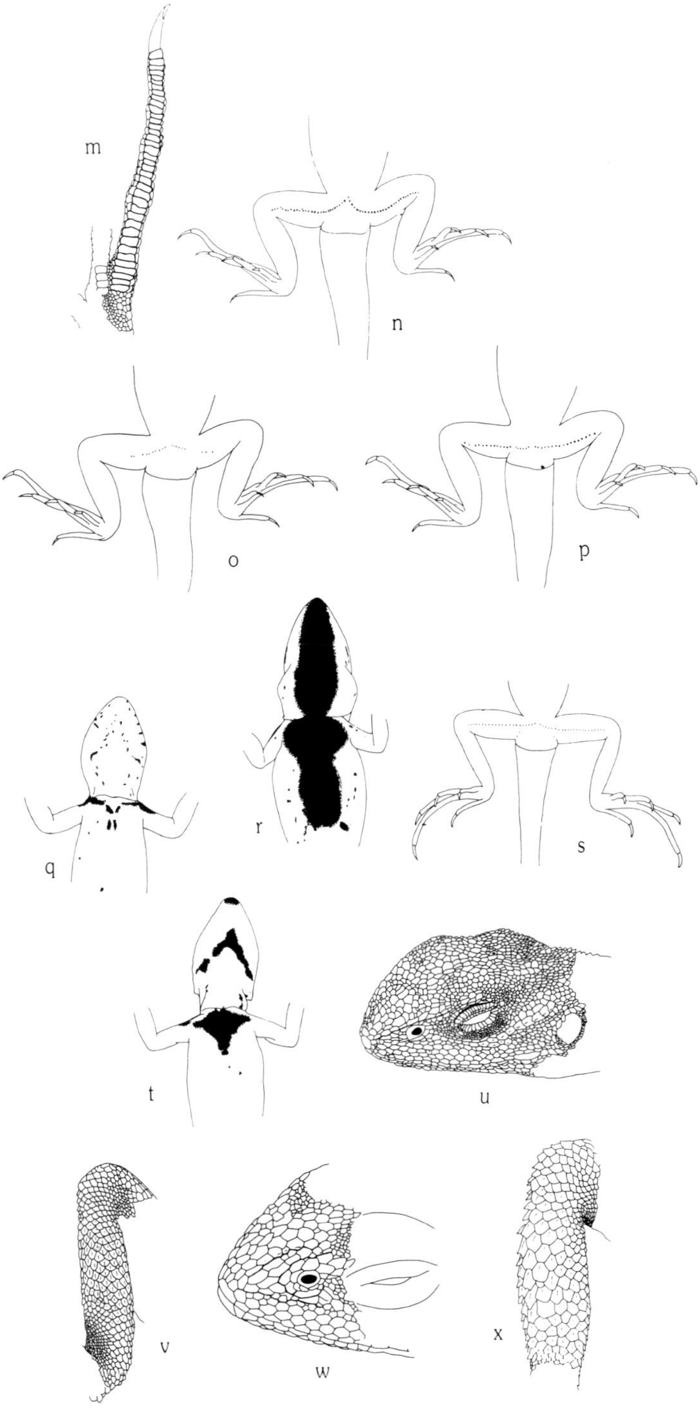

the darker ground colour........ ***decresii***

19 Normally 26 or fewer lamellae under fourth toe, between its junction with the third toe and its tip........ ***fionni***

Normally 27 or more lamellae under fourth toe, between its junction with the third toe and its tip........ ***rufescens***

20 Tail banded throughout its length........ ***ornatus***

Tail banded only on posterior portion; basal third unbanded........ ***yinnietharra***

Ctenophorus caudicinctus Mt Isa, Qld

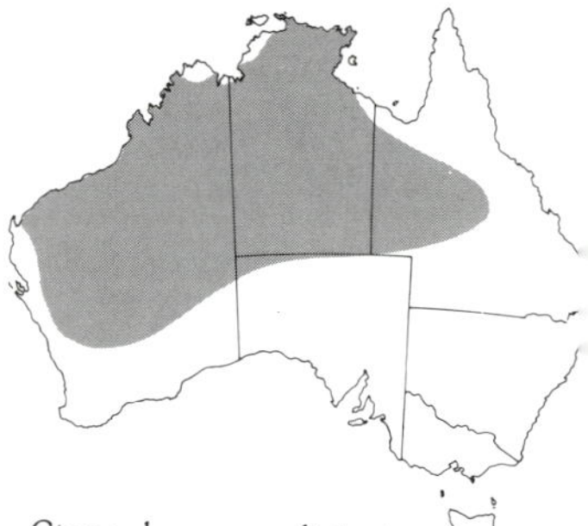

Ctenophorus caudicinctus

Ctenophorus caudicinctus (Günther, 1875)

Ring-Tailed Dragon

Description: A highly variable species ranging from pale fawn or orange-brown to bright brick-red. Typically with a series of dark spots along each side of the mid-dorsal line and scattered dark flecks and small pale spots, tending to form irregular transverse bands. Often with darker and paler variegations on lower flanks. Tail with dark brown or black rings, often obscure or absent basally. Whitish to yellow below, males with dark reticulations on the throat and a black patch, geographically variable in size and intensity, on the chest. Dorsal markings may become obscure in old adults. Dorsal body scalation homoge-

Ctenophorus caudicinctus McArthur River, NT

neous, the scales imbricate, each with a single keel, largest mid-dorsally. A low nuchal crest; no dorsal crest, but vertebral scales with larger and higher keels, forming a distinct dorsal ridge. Throat and ventral scales smooth or weakly keeled. Tympanum exposed. Canthus rostralis slightly swollen, the oval nostril on or below it and facing slightly forwards and upwards. 100 mm (snout-vent). Adpressed hindlimb reaches almost to snout or beyond, the hindlimb about 90%, the tail about 170-240% of snout-vent length. Preanal and femoral pores 22-42.
Distribution: Far-western Qld through NT and northern SA to most of WA, excluding the south and south-west.
Habit: A saxicoline diurnal lizard, one of our swiftest lizards. Usually encountered on rocks or boulders on large, open, rocky slopes, where it forages for insects. When disturbed it drops from its perch and shelters in crevices or under large rocks, often dashing long distances before taking cover.
Subspecies: *caudicinctus* (Pilbara region and offshore islands, WA); *mensarum* (Murchison and East Murchison Goldfields, WA); *infans* (Mt. Margaret Goldfield, WA); *graafi* (far eastern interior of WA); *slateri* (ranges of southern NT); *macropus* (Arnhem Land, NT).

Ctenophorus clayi (Storr, 1966)

Description: Pale brown to reddish-brown above, usually with a series of dark brown blotches on each side of a pale vertebral stripe, the blotches alternating with obscure pale transverse bars. All of these markings may become obscure in old adults. A distinctive black spot on either side of the gular fold, sometimes joined by a narrow black bar along the gular fold. Whitish below. Dorsal scalation more or less homogeneous, small, sub-imbricate, weakly keeled, largest mid-dorsally. No nuchal crest, but some larger tubercular scales on the midline. Scales on throat smooth, those on chest and belly weakly keeled. Tympanum exposed. Canthus rostralis fairly acute, the narrowly oval or slit-like nostril facing forwards and downwards. 50 mm (snout-vent). Adpressed hindlimb reaching almost to the tympanum, the hindlimb about 65%, tail about 150% of snout-vent length. Preanal and femoral pores 4-10.
Distribution: From Exmouth Gulf region of WA through the eastern deserts of WA to south-western NT.
Habit: A diurnal, terrestrial inhabitant of sandy deserts, several specimens having been taken from burrows similar to those of *C. nuchalis*.

Ctenophorus clayi near Exmouth, WA

Ctenophorus cristatus (Gray, 1841)

Crested Dragon

Description: Brown, fawn or reddish-brown on the head and neck, with dark brown to black variegations and a broad, irregular, blackish streak on either side of the neck usually extending backwards as a narrow broken stripe along the dorso-lateral skin fold, or as a series of large blotches. Sometimes a dorsal series of short transverse black bars on the anterior half of the body. Middle and hind parts of body darker brown, with obscure darker and paler flecks and variegations, especially on the flanks. Forelimbs above with irregular blackish variegations or cross-bands, hindlimbs with scattered darker flecks. Males below with a broad median wedge-shaped black bar on the throat, bordered by dark longitudinal lines; chest and under

Ctenophorus clayi

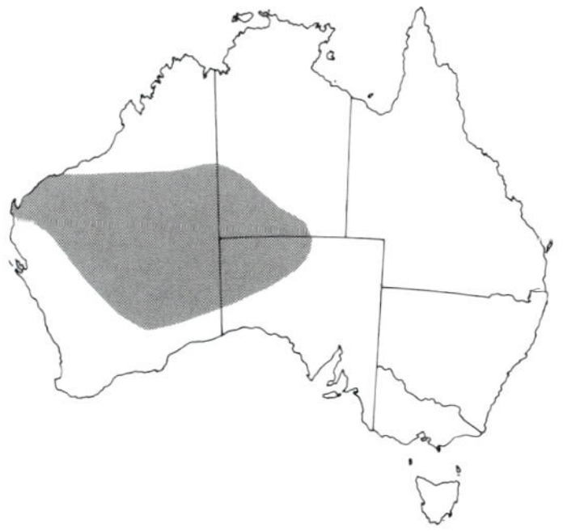

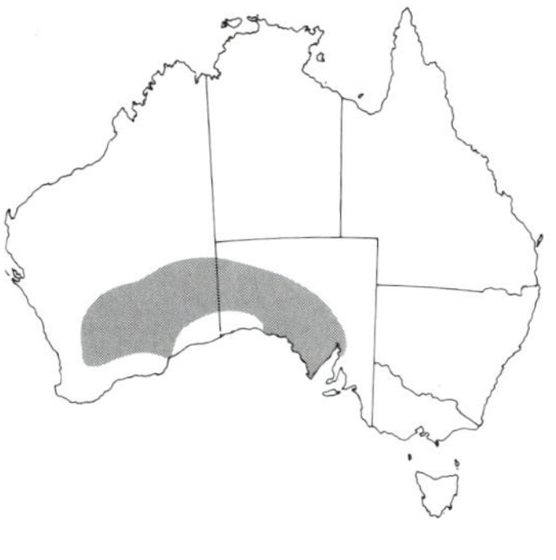

Ctenophorus cristatus

surfaces of all limbs black, remainder brown or whitish. Dorsal body scalation heterogeneous; a strong nuchal crest of long, compressed scales continued along the back as a series of enlarged scales with low spines; head scales keeled; a series of short folds on the neck with scattered spinose scales; usually a narrow, dorso-lateral skin fold; body scales largest dorsally, grading to the smallest on the lower flanks, throughout which are scattered enlarged, strongly keeled scales. Gular and ventral scales smooth or with low blunt keels. A moderate marginal fringe on the lower eyelid. Tympanum large and conspicuous. Canthus angular, the nostril circular and facing outwards in an enlarged nasal scale lying below the canthal ridge. 100 mm (snout-vent). Adpressed hindlimb reaches well beyond tip of snout, the hindlimb about 100%, tail about 250% of snout-vent length. Preanal and femoral pores 50-65, in two concave curves meeting on the midline, and extending to the inside of the knee.
Distribution: Drier parts of southern WA to south-western SA.
Habit: Found primarily in semi-arid open scrublands such as mallee and myall, and in low chenopod shrublands. A diurnal, fast-moving, terrestrial lizard which feeds largely on insects.

Ctenophorus decresii (Duméril and Bibron, 1837)

Description: A variable species in which there is marked sexual dichromatism. Males above typically with brown head, grey or grey-brown body. Usually a pale labial stripe extending almost to the forelimb. Lips and lower jaw may be bright blue or yellow, throat yellow. Often a series of cream, yellow or orange spots and blotches on the sides of the neck. A broad, black, lateral stripe from the neck almost to the groin, bordered above (at least anteriorly) by a pale stripe. Throat with a dark reticulum; chest, lower forelimbs and sometimes hindlimbs blackish. Females brown or grey-brown above, usually with a broad, black, lateral stripe anteriorly and marbled, flecked or mottled with black. Dorsal scalation more or less homogeneous, the scales small and each with a low keel, but usually some scattered, slightly enlarged and usually pale, tubercles on the flanks. A few enlarged, strongly keeled scales in a line on the nape, but no enlarged vertebral row on the body. A series of skin folds around the neck, each with some enlarged spinose scales. Usually a narrow dorso-lateral skin fold, at least anteriorly. Gular and ventral scales smooth. Marginal scales of lower eyelid not forming a fringe. Tympanum moderate and conspicuous. Canthus angular, the nostril circular or slightly elliptical, and facing outwards in an enlarged nasal scale lying just below the canthal ridge. 75 mm (snout-vent). Adpressed hind-limb reaches between the eye and the tip of the snout, the hindlimb about 80%, tail about 200% of snout-vent length. 33-50 preanal and femoral pores, in two slightly concave series from the inside of the knee, slightly broken in the midline.
Distribution: Kangaroo Island and the southern Mt Lofty Ranges, SA; northern Mt Lofty Ranges and Flinders Ranges, SA, with outliers extending east to Mootwingee, NSW.
Habit: Usually closely associated with rocky habitats.

Ctenophorus femoralis (Storr, 1965)

Description: Pale brick-red above, finely flecked or spotted with dark brown. A whitish mid-lateral stripe from above forearm to groin and continued behind the groin along the basal half of the tail where it is bordered above by a dark brown stripe. Usually a narrow, discontinuous, grey dorso-lateral stripe from above the eye to the base of the tail. The brown flecks on the back tend to be more intense above each of the pale dorso-lateral stripes. Whitish below, adult males with a black patch on the chest which extends on to the base of each forearm. Dorsal body scalation homogeneous, the scales in the middle of the back largest and becoming gradually smaller on the flanks, each dorsal scale with a low but sharp keel. No indication of nuchal or vertebral crests. Gular scales smooth or feebly keeled. Ventral scales keeled. Marginal scales of lower eyelid not forming a fringe. Tympanum large and conspicuous. Canthus moderately angular, the nostril oval and facing outwards and backwards in an enlarged nasal scale lying on or just below the canthal ridge. 55 mm (snout-vent). Adpressed hindlimb reaches beyond tip of snout, the hindlimb about 100%, tail about 280% of snout-vent length. 18-32 preanal and femoral pores, disrupted in the midline and scarcely extending more than half way along the thighs.
Distribution: Confined to the vicinity of Exmouth Gulf, WA.
Habit: Spinifex-covered sand dunes and interdunes.

Ctenophorus fionni (Proctor, 1923)

Description: Morphologically similar to *Ctenophorus decresii,* from which it differs in always lacking pale enlarged scales or tubercles on the

Ctenophorus cristatus near Balladonia, WA

Ctenophorus decresii Kangaroo Island, SA

Ctenophorus femoralis Giralia, WA

R. W. G. JENKINS

Ctenophorus fionni (male) Paney Station, SA

Ctenophorus fionni (female) Burra Creek Gorge, SA

flanks. Males with small spots or blotches, often aligned to form irregular or obscure transverse bars, and never with the bright blue colouring which is often found on the throat of *decresii* males. Female colour pattern essentially similar to that of *decresii* females.
Distribution: Eyre Peninsula, including Gawler Ranges and many offshore islands, SA.
Habit: Similar to *A. decresii.*

Ctenophorus fordi (Storr, 1965)

Mallee Dragon

Description: Orange-brown to rich reddish-brown above, with a white or grey dorso-lateral stripe from the nape to the base of the tail. A pale mid-lateral stripe from above forearm to groin, bordered below by a blackish stripe. The pale lateral stripe continues behind the groin along the side of the tail and is bordered above by a dark brown or blackish stripe. Head and body flecked above with dark brown or black, with larger dark markings bordering the pale dorso-lateral stripe. The darker zones between the pale lateral and dorso-lateral stripes and below the lateral stripe often with white or cream flecks or spots. Limbs above rich brown, speckled or variegated with darker brown. White below, males with black flecks or an obscure ∧- shaped black mark on the throat and a black transverse bar across the chest extending on to each forelimb. Dorsal body scalation homogeneous, the scales in the middle of the back largest, smallest on the flanks, each scale

.TERSON

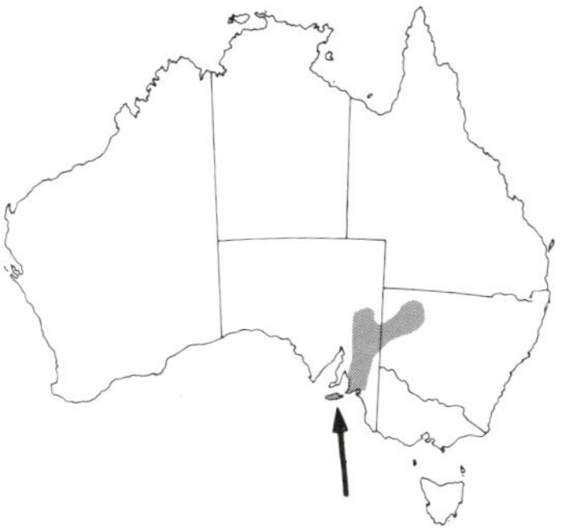

Ctenophorus decresii

Ctenophorus femoralis

Ctenophorus fionni

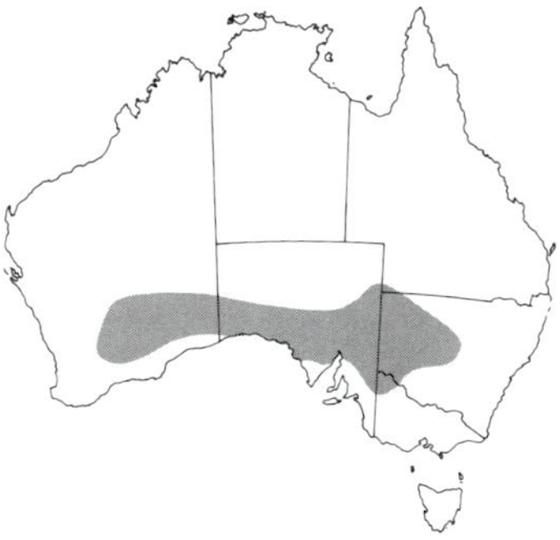

Ctenophorus fordi

Ctenophorus gibba

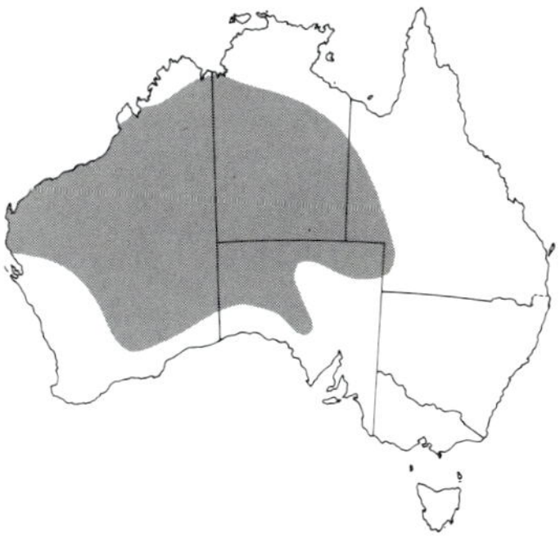

Ctenophorus isolepis

Ctenophorus maculatus

Ctenophorus fordi Nymagee, NSW

with a low but sharp keel. No indication of nuchal or vertebral crests. Gular scales smooth, ventrals feebly keeled. Marginal scales of lower eyelid not forming a noticeable fringe. Tympanum moderate and conspicuous. Canthus moderately angular, the nostril oval and facing outwards in an enlarged nasal scale lying on or just below the canthal ridge. 50 mm (snout-vent). Adpressed hindlimb reaches beyond tip of snout, the hindlimb about 90%, tail about 230% of snout-vent length. 32-42 preanal and femoral pores, disrupted and slightly arched forward on the midline, and extending about three-quarters of the way along each thigh.
Distribution: Widely distributed through south-eastern WA and southern SA, with outlying populations in western Vic and western NSW.
Habit: Appears to be confined to mallee and related arid scrubs, where it occurs only in the presence of porcupine grass (*Triodia* spp.). Feeds almost solely on ants.

Ctenophorus gibba (Houston, 1974)

Description: Pale brown to rich reddish-brown above, usually with scattered darker flecks and usually with 6-8 pairs of blackish spots on the back, each spot lying to one side of the vertebral line. Tail with a series of 20-30 spots along each side. White or yellowish below, usually with a median small black patch on the chin, a median large grey or black patch on the throat, and a grey to black patch on the chest. Dorsal body scalation homogeneous, the scales small and smooth on the back. A few enlarged median scales on the nape, but none on the back. Gular and ventral scales smooth except those under the tail. A few enlarged scales on skin folds of the neck. Marginal scales of lower eyelid elongated, forming a distinctive fringe. Tympanum small but conspicuous. Canthus subangular, slightly swollen, the nostril oval and facing outwards in an enlarged nasal scale lying just below the canthus. 75 mm (snout-vent). Adpressed hindlimb reaches to about the eye, the hindlimb about 80%, tail about 140% of snout-vent length. 26-35 preanal and femoral pores, well-spaced in a more or less continuous series extending almost to the end of each thigh.
Distribution: North-eastern SA.
Habit: An '...inhabitant of...barren, stone-strewn gibba plains...' (Houston).

Ctenophorus isolepis (Fischer, 1881)

Military Dragon

Description: Pale buff or yellowish to rich reddish-brown above, with a pattern ranging from a mixture of dark brown and pale spots or blotches to irregular darker and paler flecks. These markings may occasionally be arranged in transverse series or, more often, in longitudinal lateral and dorso-lateral series. In addition to these markings most specimens possess a narrow, pale, dorso-lateral stripe from the nape to the base of the tail, and a narrow, pale, mid-lateral stripe from above the forearm to the groin. Both of these stripes may be broken or obscure, while the flanks between the stripes are black in some populations. Whitish below. Adult males with intense black markings ventrally, their extent varying geographically. Usually a wedge-shaped median black bar on the throat and at least a large black patch on the chest; in some populations the black extends over the entire chest and most of the abdomen, and to the limbs. Dorsal body scalation homogeneous, the scales in the middle of the back largest, keeled, but becoming smaller and smooth on the flanks. Occasionally a few enlarged median scales on the nape but none on the back. Gular scales vary from smooth to strongly keeled. Scales on the chest usually strongly keeled; those on the abdomen smooth to strongly keeled. Marginal scales on lower eyelid not especially acute, not forming a noticeable fringe. Tympanum moderate and conspicuous. Canthus angular, the nostril oval and facing outwards in an enlarged nasal scale lying only just below the canthal ridge. 75 mm (snout-vent). Adpressed hindlimb reaches beyond the tip of the snout, the hindlimb about 90%, tail about 200-250% of snout-vent length. A continuous line of 40-70 preanal pores, each side forming a concave curve and arching forward to meet on the midline, and extending as far as the inside of each knee.
Distribution: From central coastal regions of WA through the arid interior to Central Australia and

Ctenophorus isolepis Mount Isa, Qld

western Qld.
Habit: A swift, diurnal ground-dwelling lizard found in a variety of arid and desert habitats, but usually closely associated with spinifex or porcupine grass (*Triodia* spp.) in which it takes cover when alarmed.
Subspecies: *isolepis* (northern WA and NT); *citrinus* (southern interior of WA); *gularis* (central and southern interior of WA and central Australia); *rubens* (Exmouth Gulf region, WA).

Ctenophorus maculatus (Gray, 1831)

Spotted Dragon

Description: Grey, grey-brown or reddish-brown above, usually with a pale white to grey-brown dorso-lateral stripe from neck to base of tail; this stripe is often broken into a series of short bars. Another pale stripe from above forearm to groin, this stripe also often broken up into a series of pale blotches, but continued behind the groin as an uninterrupted pale stripe along the side of the tail. Between the pale dorsal and dorso-lateral stripes is a dark brown to black zone, usually in the form of a series of 5-7 dark blotches; these continue on the tail as a continuous dark dorso-lateral stripe. Back with dark flecks and spots, often concentrated along the pale dorso-lateral stripe. In some females most of the above pattern may be lost. Whitish below, sometimes yellow on the throat and chest, but adult males with a median ∧-shaped black mark on the throat and a black bar across the chest. Dorsal body scalation homogeneous, without distinct nuchal or vertebral series, the mid-dorsals largest and keeled, the laterals smallest and smooth. Gular and ventral scales smooth or keeled. Marginal scales of lower eyelid not forming a fringe. Tympanum moderate and conspicuous. Canthus angular, the nostril oval and facing outwards in an enlarged scale lying just below the canthal ridge. 55 mm (snout-vent). Adpressed hindlimb reaches beyond tip of snout, the hindlimb about 85%, the tail about 220-270% of snout-vent length. 35-60 preanal and femoral pores in a more or less continuous series, usually arched forward slightly and disrupted on the midline, and extending as far as the inside of each knee.
Distribution: Central coast of WA through south-western Australia (excluding extreme south-western corner) to south-eastern WA and south-western SA.
Habit: A small, swift-moving, diurnal lizard found on coastal and inland sand dunes and flats with low vegetation, especially spinifex, and arid scrubs.
Subspecies: *maculatus* (west coast of WA south of

Ctenophorus maculatus
Shark Bay, WA

Shark Bay); *badius* (coast and interior of WA between Shark Bay and Exmouth Gulf); *griseus* (south-western interior of WA); *dualis* (south-eastern WA and extreme south-western SA).

Ctenophorus maculosus (Mitchell, 1948)

Lake Eyre Dragon

Description: Whitish or very pale grey above, with two longitudinal series of five intense black spots or blotches, one on either side of the back and converging on the base of the tail. Usually a few small black spots on the back and tail, especially along the vertebral line. Ventral surfaces white or pale yellow, with a blackish median streak on the throat (intense in males, obscure in females). Dorsal body scalation homogeneous to feebly heterogeneous, with flat, slightly tuberculate and enlarged scales scattered among the small, smooth dorsals. Gulars smooth, small and granular; ventrals smooth. Marginal scales of lower eyelid greatly elongated to form a long fringe. Tympanum hidden, being completely covered by scaly skin. Canthus rounded, the nostril oval and facing downwards and backwards, in an enlarged nasal scale lying on, or slightly below, the canthal curve. 70 mm (snout-vent). Adpressed hindlimb reaches to about the tympanic region, the hindlimb about 50%, the tail about 100-120% of snout-vent length. Usually a total of 12 pores, widely spaced and interrupted by almost the entire preanal region and extending along the thigh almost to the level of the inner knee.
Distribution: Lake Eyre Basin, SA.
Habit: A highly specialised lizard which lives on the vegetation-free, salt-encrusted margins of parts of Lake Eyre and other dry salt lakes in the region, sheltering in the sand below the salty crust. A comprehensive study of the biology and ecology of this species by F.J. Mitchell is cited in the Selected References.

Ctenophorus mckenziei (Storr, 1981)

Description: Blackish-brown above, paler on the head and with a series of pale greyish-white spots, dashes and lines, which tend to form indefinite, narrow, paravertebral and dorso-lateral stripes from head to base of tail, connected to each other by a series of indefinite, pale transverse bars; some pale upper lateral spots and an indefinite pale mid-lateral stripe. Ventral surfaces whitish, except for a dark grey patch on the throat and another on the chest in the males, or densely stippled with dark grey in females. Dorsal body scalation more or less homogeneous, the dorsal scales small and sharply keeled, those on the tail and legs larger and more strongly keeled. A distinct nuchal series of enlarged scales, more or less continuous with a vertebral series of slightly enlarged scales. Some small spinose scales in clusters on a skinfold on the neck. Gular and ventral scales smooth. Tympanum conspicuous. Canthus angular, the nostril oval and facing outwards in an enlarged nasal scale lying below the canthal ridge. 65 mm (snout-vent). The adpressed hindlimb reaches to about the eye or just beyond, the hindlimb about 85% the tail about 230% of snout-vent length. Preanal and femoral pores 36-48, curving forward but well-separated on the midline.
Distribution: Currently known only from a small area inland from Israelite Bay, WA.
Habit: The only known specimens were taken in '...bluebush-saltbush steppe with scattered eucalypts...' and in '... low, open eucalypt woodland over low, open shrubbery and leaf litter...' (Storr).

Ctenophorus nuchalis (de Vis, 1884)

Central Netted Dragon

Description: Pale brown to bright orange-brown or reddish-brown, with a fine dark chocolate-brown

R. W. G. JENKINS

Ctenophorus maculosus Lake Eyre, SA

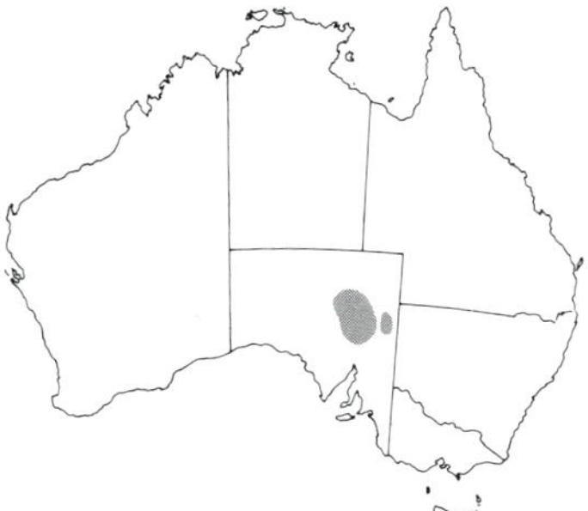

Ctenophorus maculosus

M. PETERSON

Ctenophorus mckenziei Colona Station, SA

Ctenophorus mckenziei

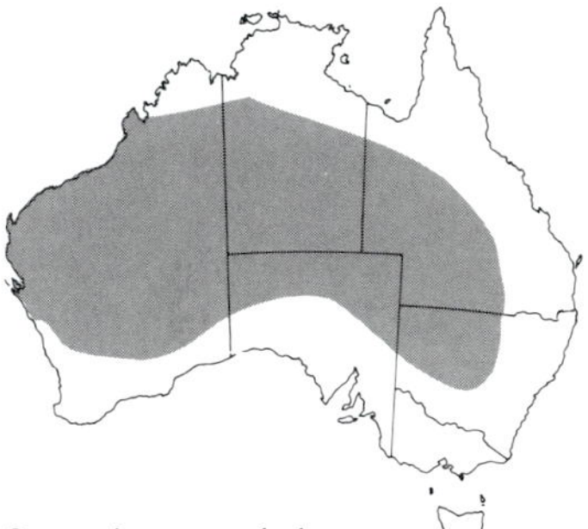

Ctenophorus nuchalis

reticulum covering the head and body. No further pattern may be present in older specimens, but usually there is a distinctive narrow, pale, vertebral stripe from the head to the base of the tail, and a series of pale spots which are most conspicuous on the back of the head and along the back, where they often tend to be aligned transversely. Snout and supraocular region sometimes paler than remainder of dorsum. Usually a pale, dark-edged bar between eye and ear, and some obscure barring on the lips. Limbs variegated or barred with dark brown. Tail with or without obscure dark bars, especially on the sides. Whitish below, the throat often with an obscure grey reticulum, and breeding males flushed with bright orange. Head deep and blunt, massive in old adults. Dorsal body scalation homogeneous to somewhat heterogeneous, with slightly enlarged, often paler, tubercular scales scattered or arranged in irregular transverse rows. Nape with a median row of enlarged scales, but no distinct vertebral series on the body. Sides of neck with scattered spinose scales on folds of skin or swollen ridges. Dorsal and flank scales smooth to feebly keeled, largest dorsally, smallest on the flanks. Throat and ventral body scales smooth to feebly keeled. Marginal

Ctenophorus nuchalis near Ayers Rock, NT

scales of lower eyelid long and spinose, forming a conspicuous fringe, pale with light brown tips. Tympanum large and conspicuous. Canthus rounded, swollen, the nostril round and facing distinctly upwards in an enlarged nasal scale lying on or just below the canthal ridge. 100 mm (snout-vent). Adpressed hindlimb scarcely reaches beyond shoulder, the hindlimb about 55%, the tail about 120% of snout-vent length. Preanal and femoral pores 12-35, widely spaced in two straight lines or convex curves separated on the midline, and extending almost to the knees. Tips of claws pale-coloured.
Distribution: Central and northern coasts of WA, through the drier parts of central and northern Australia to central Qld and western NSW.
Habit: A diurnal, ground-dwelling lizard found in the open even at very high temperatures. Usually found perched on a rock, log, roadside verge or other vantage point, close by a short, usually shallow, burrow into which it runs when alarmed or when the heat becomes excessive. Usually found in open country on sandy or loamy soils.

Ctenophorus ornatus (Gray, 1845)
Ornate Dragon

Description: Males black above, the head brown or olive with black variegations or spots. A broad, irregular, yellowish mid-dorsal stripe which is more often broken up into a series of irregular yellow spots or blotches. Sides with a series of small yellowish spots or bars tending to be aligned in irregular transverse bands. Limbs with transverse rows of pale scales which form obscure cross-bands. Tail strongly banded with black and yellow, the bands more or less equal in width. Whitish below, often with black or grey spots on the throat and sometimes a conspicuous black stripe from the angle of the jaw to the side of the neck, and often with a pale labial stripe extending to the forearm. A large black patch on the chest. Females with less conspicuous pattern, usually brown rather than black above, and lacking the black patch on the chest. Dorsal body scalation heterogeneous, the dorsal and lateral scales strongly to feebly keeled and the sides with scattered enlarged, sometimes spinose, scales which tend to correspond with the pale spots. A distinct nuchal series of slightly enlarged scales, at least on the anterior part of the body. Numerous spinose scales in clusters on skin folds on the neck. Gular and ventral scales keeled. Marginal scales of lower eyelid not noticeably elongate or forming a fringe. Tympanum moderate and conspicuous. Canthus swollen, the nostril subcircular and facing outwards and slightly upwards in an enlarged nasal scale lying just below the canthal ridge. 80 mm (snout-vent). Adpressed hindlimb reaches to between eye and tip of snout, the hindlimb about 90%, the tail about 200% of snout-vent length. Preanal and femoral pores 40-66, closely spaced and in two convex curves almost meeting on the midline and extending to the inside of each knee. Both the head and the base of the tail are distinctively depressed in *Ctenophorus ornatus*.
Distribution: South-western WA.
Habit: Essentially a rock-dwelling species living in crevices and under exfoliating rock slabs on the extensive rock outcrops and stony hills which occur throughout its range.

Ctenophorus pictus (Peters, 1866)
Painted Dragon

Description: Blue-grey to reddish-brown above, with marked sexual dichromatism. Usually a vertebral series of black blotches which may be disrupted on the mid-line to form pairs of paravertebral black spots. Between the blotches are narrow cream or yellow, dark-edged transverse bars or rows of pale spots. Flanks spotted, variegated or reticulated with dark brown and with scattered, pale, dark-edged spots which sometimes tend to be aligned transversely. Limbs variegated. Pattern on tail obscure, the base usually with obscure broad dark bands. Whitish below, except breeding males in which there may be

Ctenophorus ornatus Darling Ranges, WA

Ctenophorus ornatus Cue, WA

Ctenophorus pictus Round Hill, NSW

a bright blue flush on the throat and flanks, and bright yellow or orange on the chest. Males with grey on the hind part of the throat and a large black patch on the chest and black on the forearm. Dorsal scalation homogeneous; the dorsal and lateral scales are smooth or feebly keeled, subequal. A low nuchal crest often present, and usually a distinct vertebral series of slightly enlarged scales along the back. Gular and ventral scales smooth. Marginal scales of lower eyelid moderately obtuse and forming a moderate fringe. Tympanum large and conspicuous. Canthus slightly angular, the nostril round and facing outwards in an enlarged nasal scale lying below the canthal ridge. 70 mm (snout-vent). Adpressed hindlimb reaches to between the ear and the eye, the hindlimb about 70%, the tail about 180% of snout-vent length. Preanal and femoral pores 32-45, closely spaced and in two concave curves which arch forward slightly and meet on the midline, and which extend as far as the inner knee.

Distribution: Drier parts of south-eastern WA through SA to north-western Vic and central-western NSW.

Habit: A swift-moving, diurnal lizard usually found on sandy soils, where it occupies short burrows. Especially fond of low vegetation (especially the dense litter around the bases of shrubs) and ground debris such as fallen logs and branches; it perches on the latter, from which it forages in surrounding areas, and among which it shelters when alarmed.

Ctenophorus reticulatus (Gray, 1845)

Western Netted Dragon

Description: Similar in most respects to *Ctenophorus nuchalis*, from which it differs in having 31-55 closely-spaced preanal and femoral pores, interrupted on the midline and extending almost to the knee, but which tend to lie along the posterior half of the thigh (anterior half in *nuchalis*). The enlarged marginal scales on the lower eyelid and the tips of the claws are blackish. In females and many adult males the dorsal pattern includes a dorso-lateral series of pale, irregular spots and blotches. Tail longer than in *nuchalis* (about 150% of snout-vent length).

Distribution: Throughout most of the southern half of WA and northern SA.

Habit: '...favours heavy, stony soils...Found under logs and other natural debris, rubbish, fallen fence posts, cowturds and isolated stones and boulders, with or without a short burrow. They also shelter under exfoliating granite and behind the bark of fallen trees' (Storr).

Ctenophorus rufescens (Stirling and Zietz, 1893)

Description: Generally similar in form and scalation to *Ctenophorus decresii* from which it differs in colour and pattern, in its higher number of lamellae (27 or more under the fourth toe between its tip and its junction with the third toe; 26 or fewer in *decresii*), and in having homogeneous body scales. Brown or orange-brown above, with a series of dark brown mid-dorsal blotches which may be disrupted or displaced on the midline to form two series of paravertebral blotches. A series of blackish blotches dorso-laterally, which when contiguous form a broad, dark zone. Flanks broadly variegated with dark brown, the variegations sometimes enclosing obscure pale spots. Head, limbs and tail speckled and flecked with dark brown. Whitish below, with brown spots and variegations on the throat. Preanal and femoral pores 50-60, in a more or less continuous series. 90 mm (snout-vent). Adpressed hindlimb reaches to about tip of snout, the hindlimb about 90%, the tail about 230% of snout-vent length.
Distribution: Arid mountain ranges of north-western SA.
Habit: Found under exfoliating rock slabs on stony ranges with few trees but extensive cover of porcupine grass.

Ctenophorus salinarum (Storr, 1966)

Description: Blue-grey to grey-brown or reddish-brown above, usually a vertebral series of transverse black bars or blotches which may be disrupted on the midline to form pairs of paravertebral black spots. Between the blotches are narrow cream or yellow, dark-edged, transverse bars or rows of pale spots. Flanks with scattered, pale, dark-edged spots which tend to be aligned transversely and each of which corresponds with an enlarged scale. Limbs variegated, usually with pale spots. Tail the same ground colour as the dorsum, and with scattered, pale cream-coloured scales tending to coalesce to form irregular, disrupted, narrow, pale cross-bands. Whitish below, except breeding males in which there may be dark grey patches on the throat and chest. Dorsal scalation slightly heterogeneous; the dorsal and lateral scales are smooth or feebly keeled, with scattered, enlarged (usually pale-coloured) scales which tend to be aligned in transverse rows. A low nuchal crest sometimes present and usually a distinct vertebral series of slightly enlarged scales along the back. Gular and ventral scales smooth. Marginal scales of lower eyelid moderately obtuse and forming a moderate

Ctenophorus ornatus

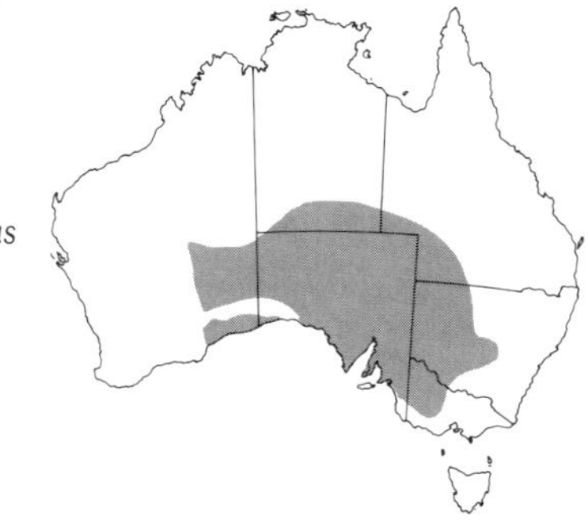
Ctenophorus pictus

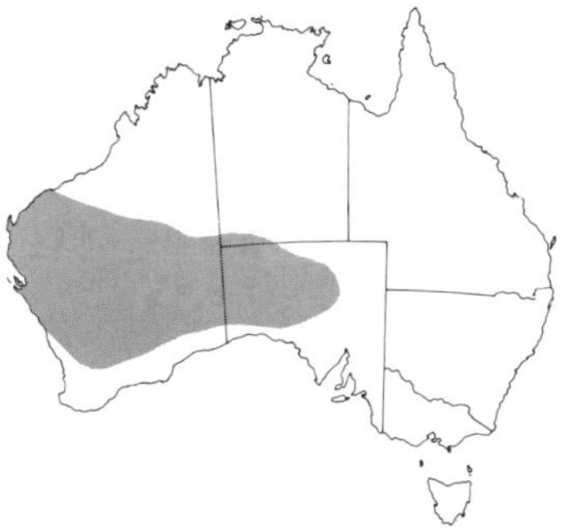
Ctenophorus reticulatus

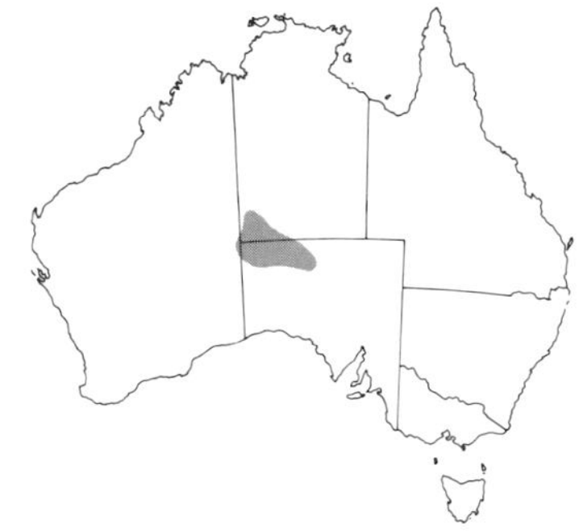
Ctenophorus rufescens

Ctenophorus salinarum

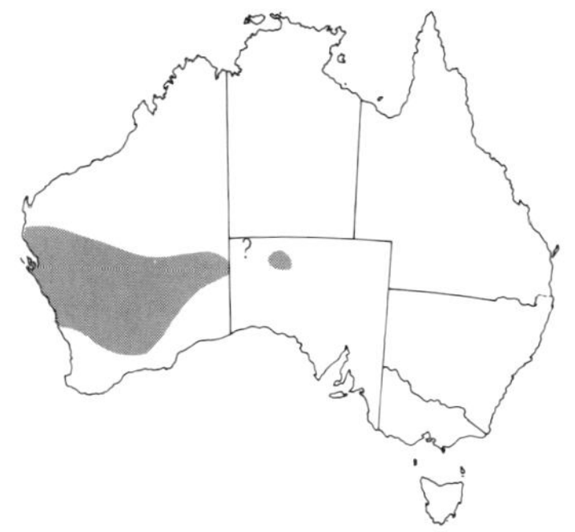

Ctenophorus scutulatus

Ctenophorus vadnappa

Ctenophorus salinarum
near Yellowdine, WA

Ctenophorus reticulatus near Welbourne Hill, SA

Ctenophorus yinnietharra (male)
Yinnietharra Stn, WA

Ctenophorus scutulatus Hamelin Pool, WA

M. PETERSON

M. PETERSON

Ctenophorus rufescens Musgrave Ranges, SA

Ctenophorus vadnappa Flinders Ranges, SA

fringe. Tympanum large and conspicuous. Canthus slightly angular, the nostril round and facing outwards in an enlarged nasal scale lying below the canthal ridge. 70 mm (snout-vent). Adpressed hindlimb reaches to between the ear and the eye, the hindlimb about 70%, the tail about 180% of snout-vent length. Preanal and femoral pores 36-56, closely spaced and in two concave curves which arch forward slightly and meet on the midline, and which extend as far as the inner knee.
Distribution: Interior of southern WA, extending to coastal regions near the western edge of the Great Australian Bight.
Habit: A swift-moving, diurnal lizard usually found on sandy soils, where it shelters in short burrows and forages from raised mounds and low perches on fallen timber and vegetation. Found '...in shrub steppe (saltbush, samphire etc.) especially around salt-lakes' (Storr).

Ctenophorus scutulatus (Stirling and Zietz, 1893)

Lozenge-Marked Dragon

Description: Brown or reddish-brown above, with a median series of four or five blackish transverse bars on the nape, neck and shoulders. A broad, pale, dorso-lateral stripe from neck to base of tail, which in most specimens is broken up on the back to form a series of dark-edged ocelli or rhomboidal blotches, the intervening areas sometimes black with white edges. These dorso-lateral markings extend on to the tail where they usually continue as a pale, dark-edged, zigzag stripe. Flanks with obscure zigzag longitudinal markings. A broad, pale, brown vertebral zone, usually with a narrow median dark brown stripe, often broken up. A broad dark brown stripe, sometimes pale-centred, from eye to ear. Ventral surface whitish, immaculate or flecked and speckled with dark brown. Males with a median, wedge-shaped dark bar on the throat and a long black patch covering the chest and anterior abdomen. Dorsal body scalation homogeneous, keeled, largest mid-dorsally and smallest on the flanks. A very low nuchal crest continuous with a distinct vertebral series of slightly enlarged keeled scales. A few spinose scales on skin folds on the neck. Gular and ventral scales smooth or feebly keeled. Marginal scales of lower eyelid not forming a noticeable fringe. Tympanum large and conspicuous. Canthus angular, the nostril oval and facing outwards in an enlarged nasal scale lying below the canthal ridge. 100 mm (snout-vent). Adpressed hindlimb reaches to eye or just beyond, the hindlimb about 80%, the tail about 250% of snout-vent length. Preanal and femoral pores 40-60, closely spaced in a more or less continuous series which arches forward slightly on the midline, extending as far as the knee.
Distribution: Exmouth Gulf region south-east through the interior to the eastern goldfields of the Kalgoorlie region, WA and north-western SA.
Habit: Found in habitats '...dominated by various species of Acacia and chenopodeaceous shrubbery...' but not observed '...in sandplain and sandridge habitats with triodia grass' (Pianka).

Ctenophorus vadnappa (Houston, 1974)

Description: Morphologically similar to *Ctenophorus decresii*, from which it differs in possessing coarsely wrinkled scales on top of the snout (usually simple longitudinal keels in *decresii* and the related *fionni*) and in possessing a distinct vertebral series of scales with longitudinally aligned keels on the anterior part of the body. Adult males with orange or reddish spots or blotches on the sides of the body which tend to be aligned transversely, but never extending on to a broad, immaculate vertebral zone. Females similar to those of *C. decresii*, except that the dark variegations on the sides tend to form irregular vertical bars.
Distribution: Northern Flinders Ranges, and their outlying Willouran Ranges, SA.
Habit: Similar to *Ctenophorus decresii:* found under exfoliating rock slabs, among boulder slopes and in rock crevices.

Ctenophorus yinnietharra (Storr, 1981)

Description: Males dull reddish-brown above, suffused with bluish-grey in life; eyelids very pale brown; a dark brown or black streak from below eye to ear, and a dark vertical patch on the side of the neck; last two-thirds of tail orange-brown with four broad, black bands; ventral surfaces pale orange-brown, paler on the chest and throat. Females with similar dorsal colour, but with dark grey on back, flanks and limbs, that on the vertebral line formed of a series of pale-centred blotches; end of tail not strongly banded; ventral surfaces whitish. Dorsal body scalation homogeneous, the dorsal scales small and keeled, the keels converging on the midline, the scales on the limbs and tail larger and more strongly keeled. A distinct nuchal series of slightly enlarged scales. Numerous spinose scales in clusters on skin folds on the neck. Gular and ventral scales smooth. Tympanum con-

spicuous. Canthus swollen, the nostril subcircular and facing outwards and upwards in an enlarged nasal scale lying on the canthal ridge. 80 mm (snout-vent). Adpressed hindlimb reaches to between eye and tip of snout, the hindlimb about 90%, the tail about 200% of snout-vent length. Preanal and femoral pores 40-50, curving forward but well-separated on the midline.
Distribution: Currently known only from the Yinnietharra district, WA.
Habit: Associated with granite outcrops and the intervening stony flats.

Ctenophorus yinnietharra

Genus ***Diporiphora*** Gray, 1842

A genus of essentially terrestrial lizards (although many climb on low shrubs or timber), with members widely distributed throughout many parts of Australia, with one species reaching New Guinea. The tympanum is exposed while preanal (and rarely two femoral) pores are present. Several species complexes are currently under review, and it can be anticipated that significant changes in the classification and composition of the genus will be made in the near future.

Key

TO THE SPECIES OF DIPORIPHORA

1 Keels of dorsal scales parallel to the vertebral line (a)....... **2**
Keels of dorsal scales converging on the vertebral line (b).. .... ***convergens***

2 Gular scales smooth; ventrals smooth to weakly keeled.. **3**
Gular and ventral scales (excluding chin shields) weakly to strongly keeled.. **4**

3 Grey vertebral stripe and longitudinal ventral stripes present; preanal pores usually absent in both sexes.................. .... ***winneckei***
No grey vertebral or ventral stripes present; preanal pores present in males and some females.......................... ***linga***

4 Gular fold present (c).. **5**
Gular fold absent (d).. **10**

5 Dorsal scales heterogeneous, including a longitudinal series of enlarged scales along the outer edge of the paravertebrals.. **6**
Dorsal scales homogeneous, more or less equal in size.... **7**

6 Vertebral and paravertebral scales much smaller than adjacent (inner) rows of enlarged dorsals (e).... ***albilabris***
Vertebral scales not or scarcely smaller than inner rows of enlarged dorsals (f).. ***australis***

7 Posterior lateral scales in rows which are aligned upwards and backwards, converging on the dorsals...................... **8**
Posterior lateral scales in rows which are aligned more or less parallel to the dorsals...................................... ***lalliae***

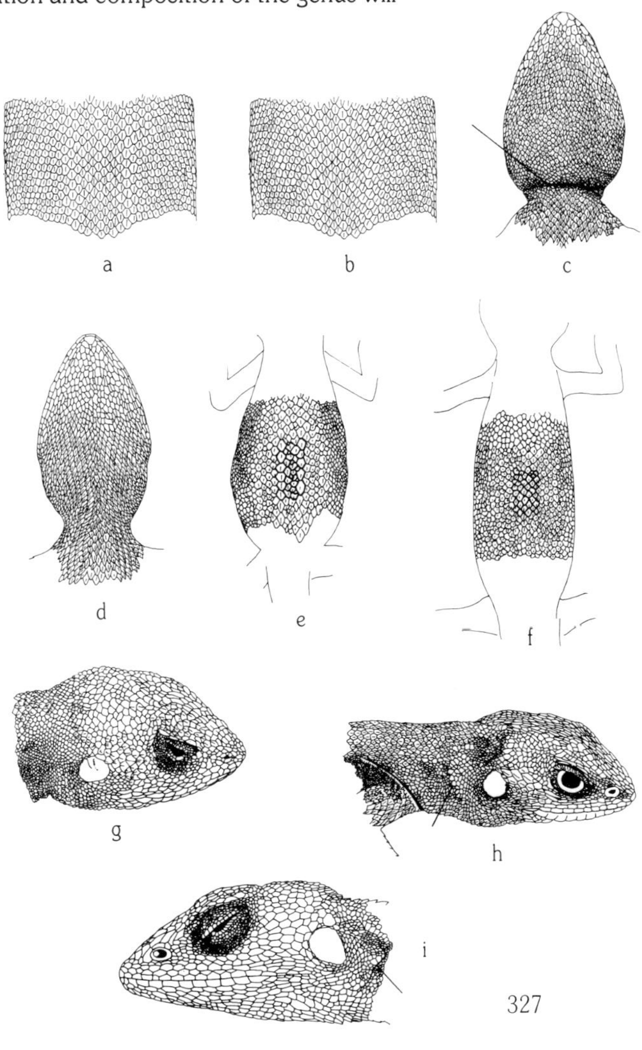

8 Usually no post-auricular fold or spines (g)...................... **9**
A distinct spinose post-auricular fold (h)........... ***bennettii***
9 Femoral pores absent... ***valens***
A femoral pore on each side................................ ***reginae***
10 At most a very short, weak fold behind the ear............. **11**
A long, strong fold behind the ear (i)...................... ***magna***
11 No indication of spines or a fold behind the ear (g)........ **12**
One, or occasionally more, short, whitish spines behind the ear.. **13**
12 Brown above, the dorsal pattern usually including a pale dorso-lateral stripe on each side.......................... ***pindari***
Usually greenish above, without pale dorso-lateral stripes.. .... ***superba***
13 Dorsal scales homogeneous, without any indication of a dorso-lateral row of slightly enlarged keeled scales............ .... ***magna***
Some indication of a dorso-lateral row of slightly enlarged, keeled scales... ***bilineata***

Diporiphora albilabris Storr, 1974

Description: Brown or reddish-brown above, uniform or with a pattern consisting of a faint, narrow, grey vertebral stripe; a pale dorso-lateral stripe on each side, palest and most conspicuous anteriorly and interrupting a series of five or six dark brown transverse bands across the body; lips whitish. Tail and limbs obscurely banded with dark brown. Whitish below, usually with two or three grey ∧ - shaped marks on the throat. Dorsal scalation heterogeneous, with longitudinal series of enlarged keeled scales on each side, adjacent to the small paravertebrals, and enlarged, keeled dorso-lateral scales. Vertebrals and paravertebrals subequal. Gular and ventral scales keeled. Gular fold present. 50 mm (snout-vent). Adpressed hindlimb usually reaches to about the eye. The hindlimb about 60-80%, the tail about 160-230% of snout-vent length. 2-6 preanal pores.
Distribution: 'North-west coast and adjacent plateaux of the Kimberley Division, WA', and the 'hilly north-western interior' of NT (Storr).
Habit: Found on the ground or among low vegetation in tropical woodlands, especially on stony hills and escarpments which have a dense rock and grass substrate.

Diporiphora albilabris Mt Barnett Station, WA

J. WEIGEL

M. PETERSON

Diporiphora australis Brisbane, Qld

Diporiphora albilabris

Diporiphora australis

Diporiphora australis (Steindachner, 1867)

Description: Status uncertain, with several species included under this one name. Similar in most respects to *D. bilineata* from which it supposedly differs in possessing a gular fold. Usually flecked with brown on the throat, and the remaining ventral surfaces strongly speckled with dark brown. Tail relatively shorter than in *bilineata*, being about 200% of snout-vent length.
Distribution: Coast and hinterland of north-eastern Australia.
Habit: A wide range of habitats are occupied by the populations included in this species: coastal dunes, open woodland, *Melaleuca* swamplands and other seasonally dry forests and wetlands. A semi-arboreal lizard which perches on low shrubs and the branches of smaller trees, dropping to the ground to feed on the insects which it observes from its perch.

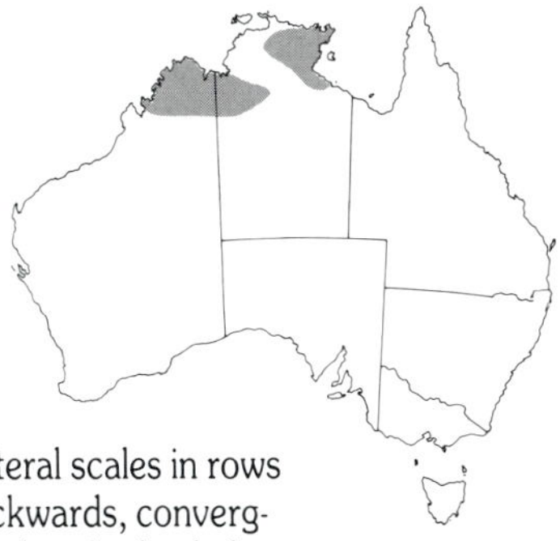

Diporiphora bennettii

Diporiphora bennettii (Gray, 1845)

Description: Brown or grey-brown above, young and sub-adults usually with a narrow, pale, dorso-lateral stripe on each side, interrupting a series of narrow, dark brown cross-bands; often a distinct grey vertebral stripe; sides dark brown dotted with grey, white or yellow and often a large, dark blotch above the base of the forelimb. All pattern may be lost in adults except for the dark patch above the insertion of the forelimb. Tail obscurely banded. Whitish below. Dorsal scales strongly keeled, homogeneous except for a low nuchal crest. Posterior lateral scales in rows which are aligned upwards and backwards, converging on the dorsals. Gular and ventral scales keeled. Gular fold present, sometimes disrupted in the midline. 65 mm (snout-vent). Adpressed hindlimb reaches to about the tip of the snout or beyond, the hindlimb 60-80%, the tail 150-300% of snout-vent length. 2-6 preanal pores. A single femoral pore on each side in NT populations.
Distribution: Kimberley region of WA to Arnhem Land, NT.
Habit: Found on the ground or in low vegetation in the tropical woodlands associated with stony hills and escarpments throughout its range.
Subspecies: *bennettii* (Kimberleys to adjacent NT); *arnhemica* (southern Kimberleys to Arnhem Land, NT); the latter is often regarded as a distinct species.

Diporiphora bennettii Mitchell Plateau, NT

Diporiphora bennettii McArthur River, NT

Diporiphora bilineata Gray, 1842

Two-Lined Dragon

Description: Pale grey to brown or reddish-brown above, uniform or more typically with a conspicuous pattern consisting of a pale grey vertebral stripe and a narrow white or yellow dorso-lateral stripe on either side from the nape to the base of the tail. Between the dorso-lateral and vertebral stripes is a series of dark brown angular blotches which are sometimes confluent across the pale vertebral stripe, but which more often are slightly displaced on either side of the stripe. The dorsal blotches merge on the tail and eventually become a series of obscure bands. Flanks pale brown to blackish with scattered white dots and flecks. Head above with transverse brown markings, especially over the eyes. Often a black patch on the side of the neck near the base of the forearm. White or yellow below, usually with a series of narrow, pale brown lines on the throat which continue over the venter to the vent. Dorsal scalation mostly homogeneous, except for a dorso-lateral series of slightly enlarged, keeled scales on each side. Sometimes a few enlarged, median, nuchal scales, but no indication of a distinct vertebral series. All ventral scales keeled. No distinct gular fold. 50 mm (snout-vent) but some populations (probably representing distinct species) to 100 mm. Adpressed hindlimb reaches to between ear and eye, the hindlimb about 75%, the tail about 230% of snout-vent length. Usually two preanal pores on each side, rarely discernible in females.
Distribution: Coast and adjacent hinterland of northern and north-eastern Australia. Extra-limital in southern New Guinea.
Habit: Found in a wide variety of habitats, from coastal sanddunes to savannah woodland and both wet and dry sclerophyll forest. Diurnal and largely terrestrial, it nevertheless climbs into low vegetation or on to fallen timber from where it forages for small insects. Often found at night sleeping on the branch of a she-oak or small shrub.

Diporiphora convergens Storr, 1974

Description: Brown or grey-brown above, uniform, or with a series of faint, dark, transverse bands on the back which are broken on the vertebral line. Dorsal scales keeled, more or less homogeneous. No nuchal crest. Posterior lateral scales in rows which converge on the dorsals. Gular and ventral scales weakly keeled. Gular fold present. Currently known only from the holotype which has a snout-vent length of 34 mm. Hindlimb 89%, tail 204% of snout-vent length. Number of pores not known.
Distribution: Known only from Crystal Creek, Admiralty Gulf, north-western WA.

Diporiphora lalliae Storr, 1974

Description: Pale brown above with a series of squarish dark brown bands across the back, interrupted by a broad grey vertebral stripe. A narrow pale brown or white dorso-lateral stripe and sometimes an obscure pale mid-lateral stripe. Whitish below, sometimes faintly streaked with grey. Dorsal scales keeled, homogeneous except for the usual presence of a low nuchal crest. Posterior lateral scales in rows which are more or less parallel to the dorsals. Gular and ventral scales keeled. Gular fold present. 65 mm (snout-vent). Adpressed hindlimb reaches to about the ear or eye, the hindlimb about 55-80%, the tail about 200-300% of snout-vent length. 2-6 preanal pores.

Diporiphora bilineata
Daly River, NT

Diporiphora bilineata complex Weipa, Qld

Diporiphora bilineata

Diporiphora convergens

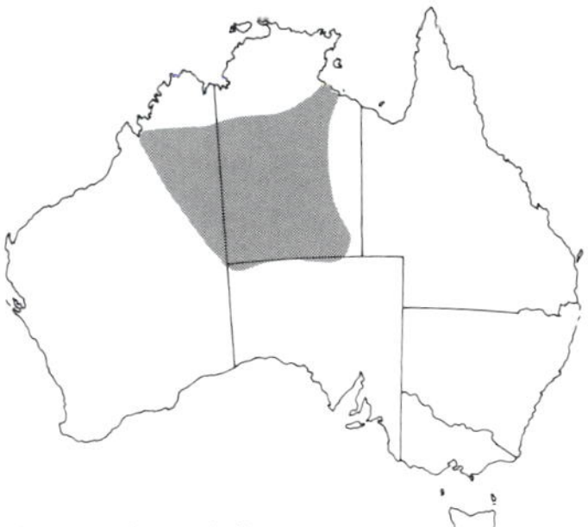

Diporiphora lalliae

Diporiphora lalliae Mt Elizabeth Stn, Kimberleys, WA

Distribution: Northern interior of WA and interior of NT.
Habit: Found primarily among spinifex on stony plains and hills, from arid shrublands in the south to tropical woodlands in the north.

Diporiphora linga Houston, 1977

Description: Superficially similar to *Diporiphora winneckei*, from which it may be distinguished by the presence, in males (and usually females) of preanal pores (usually absent in *winneckei)*, and by the absence of a grey vertebral stripe or longitudinal ventral stripes (both present in *winneckei*).
Distribution: Southern SA, excluding the south-east.
Habit: Inhabits hummocky grass clumps in mallee/sandridge country.

Diporiphora magna Storr, 1974

Description: Brown or grey-brown above, juveniles and sub-adults usually with a series of narrow, dark brown, transverse bands interrupted by a pale grey vertebral stripe and a narrow, pale dorso-lateral stripe on each side; sides brown, dotted with white or cream and sometimes with an obscure, pale mid-lateral stripe. Whitish below. Dorsal pattern obscure or absent in adults, in which the only markings may be a large black patch above the base of each forelimb. Dorsal scales strongly keeled, more or less homogeneous. Posterior lateral scales in rows which are parallel to or diverge from the dorsals. Gular and ventral scales keeled. Gular fold absent, but a long, strong fold behind the ear. 80 mm (snout-vent). Adpressed hindlimb reaches to between the ear and the eye, the hindlimb about 60-80%, the tail about 200-300% of snout-vent length. 2-6 preanal pores.
Distribution: Kimberley region of WA through the NT to eastern Arnhem Land and extending into north-western Qld.
Habit: Open eucalypt forest and mixed woodlands, on stony hills and plains; also found on coastal dunes.

Diporiphora pindan Storr, 1979

Description: Dark reddish-brown above, usually with a broad, pale grey vertebral stripe from nape to

Diporiphora magna near Mt Barnett Station, WA

level of hindlimbs, and on each side a narrower pale grey or cream dorso-lateral stripe from nape to basal portion of tail; a faint, pale, mid-lateral stripe above a white or speckled lower lateral zone; the pale dorso-lateral stripe on each side interrupting a series of dark brown transverse bars or blotches; lips white; a whitish stripe from eye to ear, bordered above and below by equally wide dark brown bars. Ventral surfaces white except for darker striations on the throat in some specimens. Body scalation more or less homogeneous, all scales moderately keeled. No indication of nuchal or dorsal crests. No gular or auricular folds. Marginal scales of lower eyelid not forming a fringe. 60 mm (snout-vent). Adpressed hindlimb reaches to about the eye or slightly beyond, the hindlimb about 70%, tail about 300% of snout-vent length. Preanal pores, when present, no more than six.

Distribution: Dampier Land and adjacent coast and hinterland, WA.
Habit: Found '...mainly in pindan (a thicket, mostly of *Acacia* spp. growing on light red soils)' (Storr).

Diporiphora reginae Glauert, 1959

Description: Olive-brown above, somewhat greyer on the head, with a bright yellow dorso-lateral stripe on either side of the back from nape to tail. Males with a bright reddish patch on either side of the base of the tail. Ventral surfaces whitish. Dorsal scalation more or less homogeneous, the scales strongly keeled, the keels forming continuous lines running obliquely back to converge on the vertebral line. Chin shields smooth, but gular scales strongly keeled.

Diporiphora linga

Diporiphora magna

Diporiphora pindan

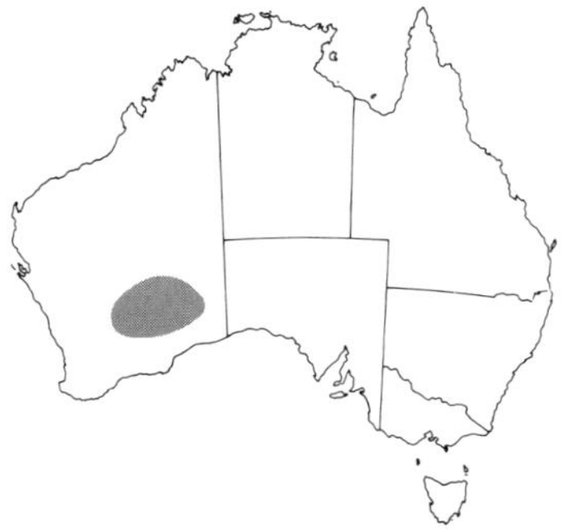

Diporiphora reginae

Diporiphora superba

Diporiphora valens

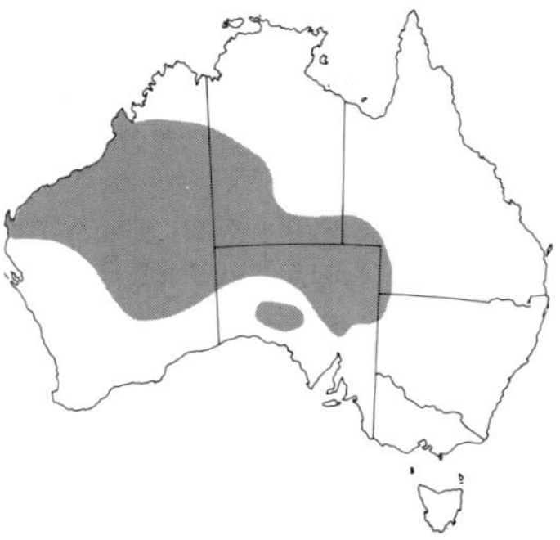

Diporiphora winneckei

Ventral scales keeled. Gular fold present. 70 mm (snout-vent). Adpressed hindlimb reaches nearly to the eye, the hindlimb about 65-80%, the tail about 220-250% of snout-vent length. No pores recorded in type series but four (two on each side) preanal pores in other specimens examined. Storr records a single femoral pore on each side.
Distribution: Southern interior of WA.
Habit: Spinifex/heathland. 'Basks on Triodia hummocks, sheltering in them when disturbed' (Wilson and Knowles).

Diporiphora superba Storr, 1974

Description: Living specimens are uniformly green above, yellow below; sometimes a brown vertebral stripe may be present. Dorsal scales keeled, more or less homogeneous. Posterior lateral scales in rows which are aligned more or less parallel to the dorsals. Gular and ventral scales keeled. Gular fold absent. 80 mm (snout-vent). Adpressed hindlimb reaches to about the eye, the hindlimb about 70-100% of snout-vent length, the tail about 300-400% of snout-vent length. Four preanal pores.
Distribution: North-western Kimberley region, WA.
Habit: A semi-arboreal species found in association with acacias and spinifex on sandstone hills and scarps.

Diporiphora valens Storr, 1979

Description: Grey-brown or reddish-brown above, with a broad, pale grey vertebral stripe from nape to base of tail and on either side a narrow, pale grey dorso-lateral stripe from nape to tail; the pale, longitudinal stripes interrupting a series of about eight transverse dark brown blotches on the back and upper flanks; sometimes a pale temporal streak; a white mid-lateral stripe on each side. Ventral surfaces white, sometimes with faint grey longitudinal stripes. Body scalation homogeneous, all scales moderately keeled. No indication of nuchal or dorsal crests. A strong gular fold and usually some indication of an auricular fold. Marginal scales of lower eyelid not forming a fringe. 60 mm (snout-vent). Hindlimb when adpressed reaches to eye or beyond, the hindlimb about 90%, the tail about 300% of snout-vent length. Preanal pores, if present, no more than four.
Distribution: Pilbara region of WA.
Habit: 'Favours shrublands and low woodlands over ground cover of hummock grasses' (Wilson and Knowles).

J. WEIGEL

Diporiphora pindan
Derby, WA

G. SHEA

Diporiphora superba Mitchell Plateau, NT

M. PETERSON

Diporiphora reginae
Buningonia Spring, WA

Diporiphora winneckei SA

Diporiphora winneckei Lucas and Frost, 1896

Description: Pale grey-brown or brown above, with a broad, grey vertebral band and a pale white or yellow dorso-lateral stripe on each side from the neck to the base of the tail. Between the vertebral and dorso-lateral stripes is a series of dark brown angular blotches which may be obscure or very conspicuous. A white or yellow stripe, obscure in some specimens, from the groin forward almost to the axilla. A white stripe along the upper jaw, from the snout, below the ear to the neck, bordered above by a broader brown stripe between the eye and the ear. Tail with faint cross-bands. Whitish below, immaculate or with three broad, blue-grey stripes on the throat, the median one continuing on to the chest where it divides into two broad stripes which run the length of the ventral surface. Body scalation more or less homogeneous, the scales keeled but with some indication of a dorso-lateral fold or row of enlarged scales in some specimens. No indication of nuchal or dorsal crests. Gular scales smooth or feebly keeled, ventral scales keeled. Gular fold present or absent, but usually some indication of its presence on the lower sides of the neck. Marginal scales of lower eyelid not forming a fringe. 70 mm (snout-vent). Adpressed hindlimb reaches nearly to ear, the hindlimb about 65%, the tail about 240-300% of snout-vent length. Usually no preanal pores present.

Distribution: From the region around the junction of the Qld/NSW/SA borders, through central Australia apparently to the coast of WA.

Habit: A swift diurnal lizard usually encountered among ground litter or porcupine grass on desert sandhills and other sandy or loamy soils.

Genus **Hypsilurus** Peters, 1867

A group of dragon lizards, previously included within the South-east Asian genus *Gonocephalus*, but whose separate status has been proposed in an as yet unpublished thesis by Moodie. Widely distributed and rich in variety throughout the Papuo-Malayan Archipelago, this genus is poorly represented in Australia. While three species have been recorded from Australia, one is a widely-distributed Melanesian species *(Hypsilurus godeffroyi)*, which ranges from the Solomons to the Philippines, and whose Australian record, almost certainly erroneous, is based on a single specimen described from Cape York in 1877.

Australian *Hypsilurus* are confined to the rainforests and adjacent moist forest communities of the east coast, and clearly represent a relatively recent migrant stock from New Guinea. Most members of the genus are large, arboreal lizards with heavy angular heads; the tympanum is exposed, femoral and preanal pores are absent; there is a transverse gular fold, and the tail is at least twice as long as the head and body.

Key

TO THE AUSTRALIAN SPECIES OF HYPSILURUS

1 No median longitudinal row of grossly enlarged scales on the throat (a).. ***spinipes***

A median longitudinal row of grossly enlarged scales (similar to those in the nuchal crest) on the throat (b)... ***boydii***

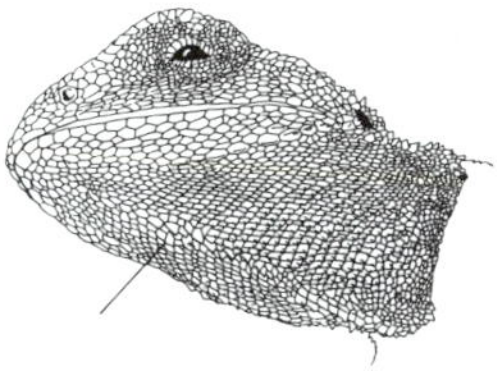

a

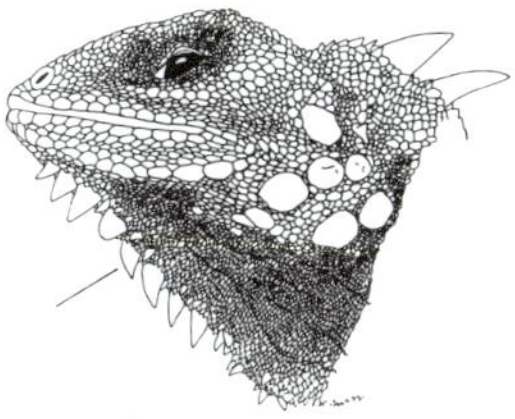

b

Hypsilurus boydii (Macleay, 1884)

Boyd's Forest Dragon

Hypsilurus boydii Kuranda district, Qld

Description: Rich chocolate-brown above, tending to become black on the flanks. Sometimes the entire dorsum with a green flush. The enlarged plates on the cheek, enlarged scales on the gular pouch and long, flat scales in the nuchal crest are yellow. One or two short, oblique, yellow or cream bars on the skin fold below the nuchal crest, while there is a yellow stripe on either side of the neck. A series of yellow scales on the flanks tend to be aligned in transverse rows. Pale brown or whitish below, except for the throat which may be darker brown. Dorsal scalation heterogeneous. A very high nuchal crest atop a fleshy fold, and discontinuous with a high dorsal crest of compressed scales which extends on to the basal portion of the tail. Cheek with a series of large, flat plates. A deep gular pouch with a median series of enlarged flat spines. Body scales largest dorsally, contrasting strongly with the small scales of the flanks, all keeled. Scattered, enlarged, keeled or spinose scales on the flanks, tending to form transverse rows. Gular scales smooth, ventrals and caudals strongly keeled. Head

Hypsilurus boydii Kuranda district, Qld

large, wedge-shaped, with a thick angular canthus rostralis continuous with a supraocular ridge. Tympanum large and superficial. Nostril oval, facing outwards and distinctly downwards in an enlarged nasal scale lying well below the canthal ridge. 150 mm (snout-vent). Adpressed hindlimb reaches almost to the tip of the snout, the hindlimb about 100%, the tail about 200% of snout-vent length.
Distribution: Rainforest areas of north-eastern Qld.
Habit: A diurnal, arboreal lizard confined to areas of tropical rainforest. Well camouflaged, it is usually only seen when foraging on roadsides, tracks or stream edges.

Hypsilurus boydii

Hypsilurus spinipes (Duméril and Duméril, 1851)

Southern Angle-Headed Dragon

Description: Grey, grey-brown or chocolate-brown above, often suffused with green. Immaculate or with dark brown flecks, spots or variegations and sometimes with obscure dark transverse bands across the top of the back and tail. Whitish or dirty brown below. Usually a broad, dark brown bar from the eye to the ear, and some darker bars on the jaws. Body scales heterogeneous, the scales on the dorsum

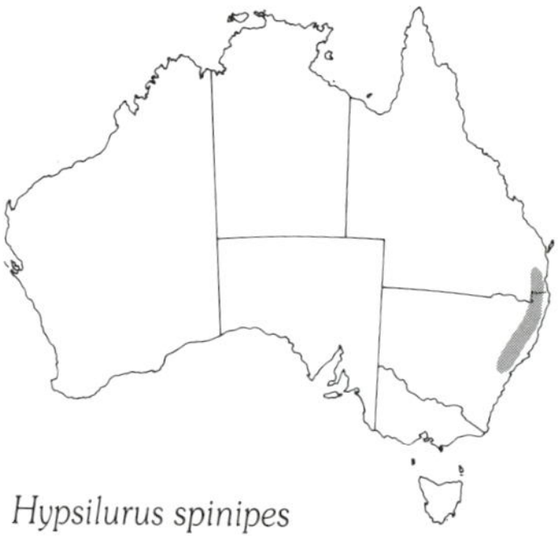

Hypsilurus spinipes

Hypsilurus spinipes (adult)
Brinerville, NSW

Hypsilurus spinipes (adult) Brinerville, NSW

Hypsilurus spinipes (hatchling and eggs) Brinerville, NSW

and flanks small and keeled, but with scattered, enlarged, strongly keeled or spinose scales, often aligned to form irregular transverse rows. A series of enlarged spinose scales on the upper surfaces of the limbs. A fairly strong nuchal crest continuous with a low but conspicuous dorsal crest. Gulars keeled with

a few scattered, larger, keeled scales, especially on the midline. Remaining ventral and caudal scales strongly keeled. Head large, wedge-shaped, with a thick, angular canthus rostralis which continues as an acute supraocular ridge. Tympanum large and superficial. Nostril subcircular, facing outwards and slightly backwards and downwards in an enlarged and somewhat swollen nasal scale lying below the canthal ridge. 110 mm (snout-vent). Adpressed hindlimb reaches to between eye and tip of snout, the hindlimb about 90%, the tail about 200% of snout-vent length.
Distribution: Rainforests and adjacent wetter forests of south-eastern Qld and north-eastern NSW.
Habit: Similar to *H. boydii.*

Genus ***Lophognathus*** Gray, 1842

A small genus of dragons with representatives in northern Australia, New Guinea and Tanimbar. It is very closely allied to certain members of the genus *Amphibolurus*, with which it may more properly belong. All species are somewhat slender and largely arboreal. The body is slightly compressed, and although they may possess a nuchal crest and a row of keeled vertebral scales (at least anteriorly), as well as one or more dorso-lateral rows of slightly enlarged, keeled scales, there are no other regular or scattered, enlarged, spinose or strongly keeled scales on the back or sides. Tympanum exposed. Femoral and preanal pores present. The tail at most moderately compressed, but without a strong dorsal keel.

Key

TO THE SPECIES OF LOPHOGNATHUS

a b c d

1 Keels of dorsal scales forming ridges running obliquely to the vertebral scale row (a)..**2**
Keels of dorsal scales forming ridges running parallel to the vertebral scale row (b)................................. ***gilberti***

2 Nostril about equidistant from snout and eye (c); light labial stripe does not include supralabials and several scale rows above them; small white spot on black posterior margin of ear.. ***longirostris***
Nostril nearer snout than eye (d); light labial stripe includes supralabials and several scale rows above them; posterior margin of ear without a small white spot............
.... ***temporalis***

Lophognathus gilberti Gray, 1842

Description: Pale fawn or grey to rich reddish-brown above, with a conspicuous pale cream or white dorso-lateral stripe commencing narrowly behind the eye and expanding on the body, where it is four or five scales wide and continues to the base of the tail. In life this stripe is subject to rapid changes in intensity in the same individual. The dorso-lateral stripe may sometimes be interrupted by dark brown blotches which may occasionally form complete but irregular transverse bars across the dorsum, especially in females. The entire dorsum between the dorso-lateral stripes may be immaculate or speckled with darker or paler spots, especially on the nape. A broad, dark brown bar between the eye and the ear. Upper and lower jaws white, cream or yellow, forming a broad labial stripe from the snout to the rear of the lower jaw. Flanks dark brown, uniform or with darker and paler flecks. Tail obscurely banded. Whitish below,

Lophognathus gilberti near Windorah, Qld

females with dark grey flecks, especially on the throat. Dorsal scalation more or less homogeneous. A low nuchal crest continuous with a vertebral ridge. A dorso-lateral skin fold marked by slightly enlarged keeled scales. Of the remaining dorsal scales the largest are in the paravertebral rows, smallest on the flanks, and dorsal scales keeled and their keels running parallel to the vertebral series. Some enlarged, spinose scales on the cheeks and neck. Gular scales smooth, ventrals feebly keeled. Marginal scales of lower eyelid not forming a fringe. Tympanum large and conspicuous. Canthus acutely angular, the nostril oval and facing outwards in an enlarged nasal scale lying below the canthal ridge. 100 mm (snout-vent). Adpressed hindlimb reaches between the eye and the tip of the snout or just beyond, the hindlimb about 90%, the tail about 300% of snout-vent length. Preanal and femoral pores 8-16, widely separated and not usually extending beyond the basal portion of the thigh.
Distribution: Widely distributed throughout northern Australia from coastal regions to the arid interior.
Habit: An arboreal species usually observed perched on limbs of trees, termitaria, etc., from which it forages in the surrounding area. Found in a variety of habitats from coastal sand dunes to savannah woodland and stream- or swamp-edge vegetation.

Lophognathus longirostris Boulenger, 1883

Description: Fawn to dark reddish-brown above, with a pale white, cream or yellow dorso-lateral stripe on each side from the nape to the base of the tail. The area between the dorso-lateral stripes uniform or anteriorly with a series of transverse black blotches or entirely black. A black patch behind the ear, in which is always a distinctive, small white spot. A narrow, pale, mid-lateral band from the groin forward, about halfway along the flank. A white or cream stripe along the lower jaw only to the rear of the lower jaw. White to pale brown below, often with darker flecks on the throat. Dorsal scalation homogeneous. A low to conspicuous nuchal crest more or less continuous with a low vertebral ridge. Dorsal scales largest near the mid-line, smallest on the flanks, all keeled, the keels forming lines which run obliquely to the vertebral ridge. Some enlarged, spinose scales on the jowls. Gular scales smooth or feebly keeled, remaining ventral scales strongly keeled. Marginal scales of lower eyelid not forming a fringe. 90 mm (snout-vent). Adpressed hindlimb reaches to the tip of the snout or beyond, the hindlimb about 90%, the tail about 350% of snout-vent length. Femoral and preanal pores 14-22, widely separated, the femoral distinct from the

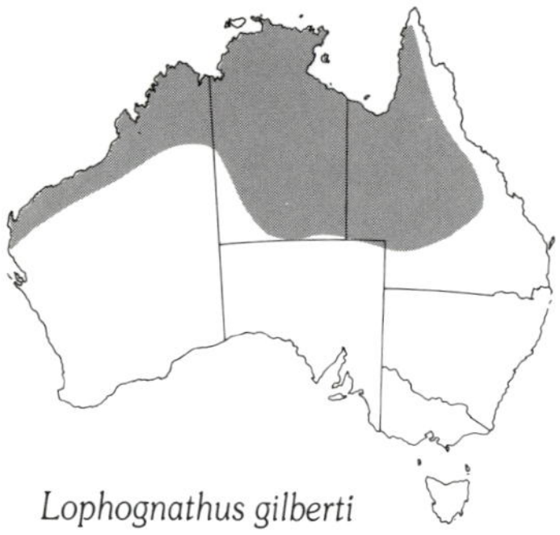

Lophognathus gilberti

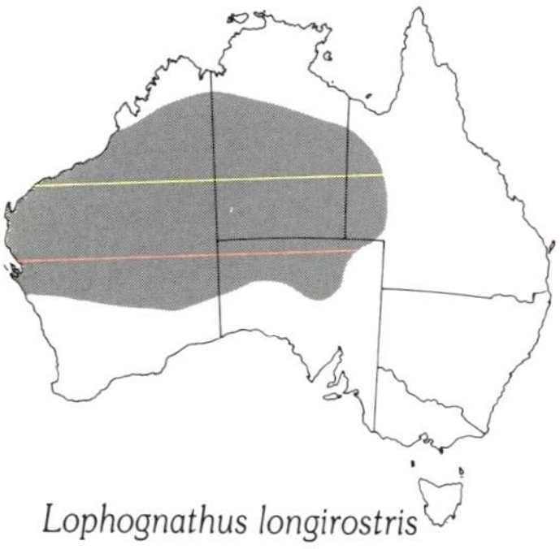

Lophognathus longirostris

Lophognathus temporalis

Lophognathus longirostris Tanami Desert, NT

Lophognathus temporalis Weipa, Qld

preanal series and extending about halfway along each thigh.

Distribution: Arid regions of northern Australia, from the coast of WA through central Australia to western Qld.

Habit: A swift-moving arboreal lizard usually found in trees or shrubs, or among rocks or ground debris, along watercourses.

Lophognathus temporalis (Günther, 1867)

Description: Fawn to reddish-brown above, with a broad, pale, dorso-lateral stripe from the nape to the base of the tail. This stripe is more or less continuous with a broad, pale stripe from the tip of the snout along the upper jaw to the side of the neck. The intensity of the dorso-lateral stripe is subject to rapid changes in living individuals, and is usually more intense anteriorly. Dorsal surface between the dorso-lateral stripes rich brown, with a series of transverse blackish bars which become more obscure or disappear posteriorly. Top of head flecked and spotted with dark brown. Flanks mottled with paler and darker spots and flecks. Limbs obscurely mottled or barred with dark brown. Usually a dark bar between the eye and the ear. Throat white, immaculate or flecked with grey, or entirely grey. Ventral surfaces whitish, speckled with grey. Dorsal scalation homogeneous. A low (in juveniles and females) to very high (in males) nuchal crest and a conspicuous vertebral ridge which forms a distinct crest in adult males. Dorsal and lateral scales subequal, all keeled, the keels forming lines which run obliquely to the vertebral ridge. Sometimes a dorso-lateral skin fold anteriorly. Some enlarged, spinose scales on the jowls. Gular scales smooth, remaining ventral scales strongly keeled. Marginal scales of lower eyelid not forming a fringe. 100 mm (snout-vent). Adpressed hindlimb reaches the tip of the snout or beyond, the hindlimb about 100%, the tail about 300% of snout-vent length. Preanal and femoral pores 8-12, widely separated and not extending beyond base of thigh.

Distribution: Coastal areas of north-western Australia and the NT; Cape York Peninsula, Qld. Extra-limital in southern New Guinea.

Habit: A semi-arboreal species found in a range of habitats from coastal dunes to tropical woodlands and monsoon forests; usually associated with paperbark swamps, lagoons, creeks and riverine vegetation.

Genus **Moloch** Gray, 1841

A distinctive, monotypic, endemic Australian genus, immediately identifiable by the large, conical spines covering the fat, depressed body, a large spiny nuchal hump or appendage, a large curved spine above each eye, and a short (shorter than head and body) spinose tail. A terrestrial, deserticolous lizard with specialised internal and external structures and feeding habits.

Moloch horridus Hermannsburg, NT

Moloch horridus Alice Springs, NT

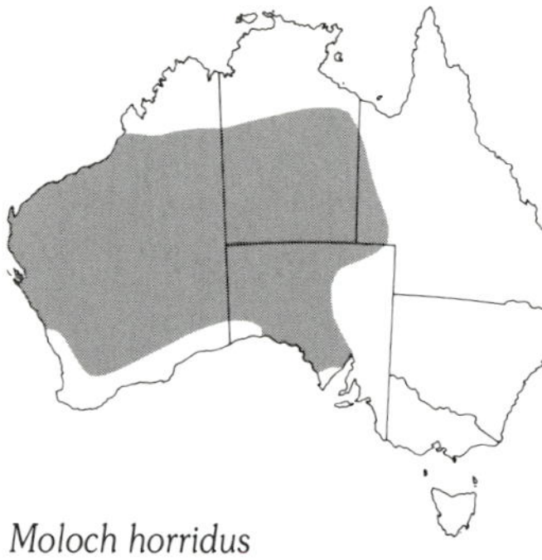

Moloch horridus

Moloch horridus Gray, 1841

Thorny Devil or Moloch

Description: An unmistakable lizard, unique in scalation and form. Head short and wide, body globular, limbs and tail short. 90 mm (snout-vent). Pale grey-brown, fawn to rich reddish-brown above, usually with a series of black-edged, darker reddish-brown markings which are symmetrical on either side of a pale vertebral stripe on neck and back. Typically these markings consist of the following series: a Y-shaped mark on the head, each arm of the Y extending on to a large spine over each eye and continuing with a divided patch on the nuchal hump; an elongate pair from behind the nuchal hump; a large pair midway along the body; a series of small pairs from the rump nearly to the end of the tail. A broad, black-edged, reddish band from the eye, through the ear to the shoulder where it divides, one branch running along the front edge of the upper arm, the other extending along the flank, where it may break up into a series of blotches. Often a canthal stripe. Entire ventral surface more or less marbled with black-edged, reddish patches. Scalation strongly heterogeneous, the smaller granular scales interspaced with longitudinal series of grossly enlarged spines on all dorsal and lateral surfaces; the largest of these spines are those on the flanks, one over each eye, and a pair on a large hump on the nape. Scales of ventral surfaces granular, interspersed with numerous low spines.

Distribution: From the coast of WA, through much of the interior of that state, to the arid lower half of the NT, and most of SA to far western Qld.

Habit: A slow-moving diurnal lizard, found in a variety of habitats from the sand and spinifex deserts of central Australia to the arid scrubs of southern WA. Feeds only on ants. 'Clutch size varies from three to ten, with a mode of eight' (Pianka and Pianka), the eggs being laid in November/December.

Genus *Physignathus* Cuvier, 1829

Represented in Australia by a single species which is widely distributed along the eastern seaboard and adjacent hinterland. The tympanum is exposed, preanal and femoral pores are present, and the tail is long, strongly compressed and with a strong dorsal keel.

Physignathus lesueurii Nepean River, NSW

Physignathus lesueurii Sydney, NSW

Physignathus lesueurii (Gray, 1831)

Eastern Water Dragon

Description: Grey or grey-brown above, typically with a series of obscure, blackish, transverse bars which may be confined to the upper surface in adults and extend on to the tail where they become a series of rings or cross-bands. A series of irregular, narrow, white, cream or yellow cross-bands on the body and basal part of the tail and on the hindlimbs, formed by transverse rows of pale individual scales. Often a broad, black stripe from the eye, enclosing the ear to the side of the neck. Lips distinctly barred in younger specimens. Yellow-brown below, heavily flecked with darker on the chest and throat. In some populations the chest and anterior abdomen are richly suffused with dark red. In other populations there is a rich green flush over the chest, head and throat, while in some southern populations the throat is strikingly blotched or striped with orange, red, blue, green and yellow. Dorsal scalation heterogeneous. A high nuchal crest of compressed scales continuous with a strong vertebral crest which extends along the length of the tail; on the terminal portion of the tail the crest divides into a low double ridge. Dorsal and flank scales very small, subequal, keeled, with scattered, enlarged, spinose scales tending to form transverse series on the flanks, tail and hindlimbs. Some enlarged, spinose scales on the cheeks. Gular scales smooth, remaining ventral scales feebly to strongly keeled. Marginal scales of lower eyelid not forming a fringe. 200 mm (snout-vent). Adpressed hindlimb reaches to between the eye and the tip of the snout, the hindlimb about 95%, the tail about 250% of snout-vent length. No preanal pores. Femoral pores 12-22 on each side, each series extending almost as far as the inside of the knee.

Distribution: Ranges and slopes of eastern Australia, from Cape York Peninsula , Qld, to eastern Vic. Extra-limital in southern New Guinea.

Habit: A semi-aquatic, arboreal lizard, usually seen perched on tree branches overhanging the water in creeks and rivers into which the lizard will drop from a considerable height when disturbed. Feeds on a variety of insects and aquatic organisms, including frogs, as well as other small terrestrial vertebrates. Also feeds on fruits and berries. A common species in some coastal areas where it forages in the rocky littoral and supra-littoral zones.

Physignathus lesueurii

Subspecies: *lesueurii* (central NSW to Cape York Peninsula); *howittii* (eastern Vic to south-eastern NSW).

Genus *Pogona* Storr, 1982

A genus of terrestrial and semi-arboreal lizards found throughout most parts of Australia and characterised by their relatively large size, broad triangular head, heterogeneous body scales, generally depressed body, and relatively short tail which has a distinctive lateral series of spinose scales on either side of its base. The tympanum is exposed, while preanal and femoral pores are present.

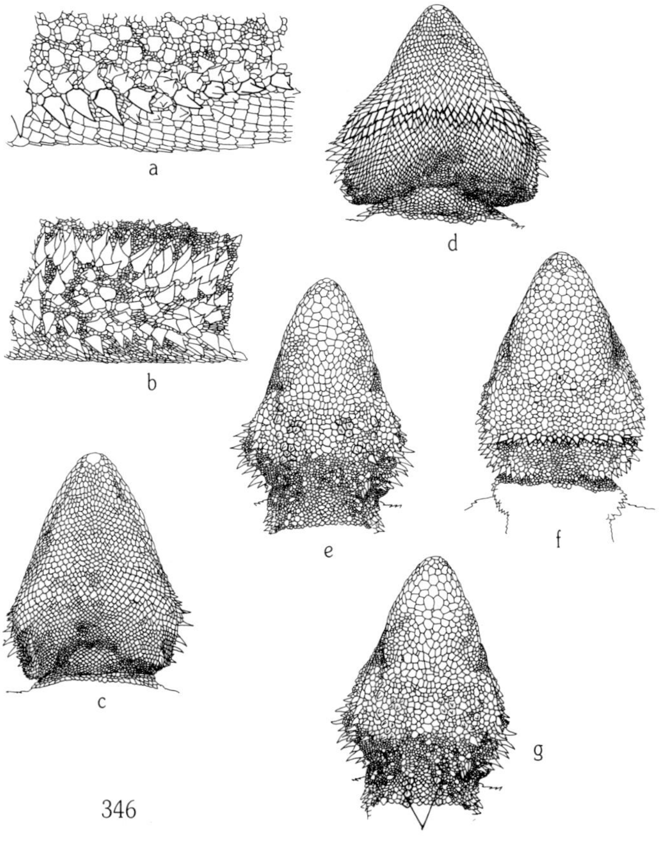

Key

TO THE SPECIES OF POGONA

1 Dorso-ventral margin of body demarcated by an orderly row of enlarged conical spines (a) **2**

Dorso-ventral margin of body with several rows of spines widening to a broad band anteriorly behind the axilla (b). **5**

2 No enlarged gular spines in centre of throat (c) **3**

Enlarged gular spines across centre of throat (d) .... ***vitticeps***

3 Spine rows of head with smaller spines that are usually not contiguous (e) **4**

Spine rows of head strongly defined with contiguous,stout, conical spines (f) .... ***mitchelli***

4 An additional nuchal row of spines parallel to the vertebral column on each side (g) .... ***minimus***

No nuchal row of spines parallel to the vertebral column, at most only a clump of spines at termination of transverse nuchal row (e) .... ***minor***

5 Enlarged gular spines across centre of throat (c) **6**

No enlarged gular spines in centre of throat (d) .... ***microlepidota***

6 Conspicuous narrow white bands across back and tail .... ***nullarbor***

No conspicuous white bands on back and tail..... ***barbata***

Pogona barbata (Cuvier, 1829)

Bearded Dragon or Jew Lizard

Description: Variable in colour from pale grey to fawn or brown, reddish-brown or almost black above. Typically with a series of pale oblong blotches in two longitudinal series, one on either side of the mid-dorsal line, the blotches sometimes coalescing to form two pale, longitudinal, parallel, paravertebral stripes, but adult specimens are frequently more or less uniform in colour with only obscure darker markings. Usually a dark postocular stripe, edged above with paler and continued forward for a short distance in front of the eye. Tail often banded. Whitish below, the throat sometimes brown or black, and usually with a series of dark ocellate markings on the chest and belly. Lining of mouth bright yellow. Head and body heavily built, depressed. Tail short, mostly round, but moderately depressed at the base. Dorsal body scalation heterogeneous with small, low, keeled, imbricate scales through which are scattered enlarged, keeled scales. A series of large, spinose scales above the ear, on the occiput and behind the angle of the mouth. Enlarged, strongly keeled or spinose scales scattered over the sides of the base of the tail. Throat with well-developed pouch or 'beard' in adults, its hind edge bordered by long, spiny scales. A transverse series of enlarged spines across the throat. Gular and belly scales keeled. Tympanum exposed. Canthus rostralis moderate, the oval nostril lying below it and facing outwards. 25 cm (snout-vent length). Adpressed hindlimb reaches to about the shoulder, the hindlimb about 55%, tail about 130% of snout-vent length. Preanal and femoral pores 10-30.
Distribution: Eastern and south-eastern Australia, excluding Cape York Peninsula, Qld, and Tas.
Habit: Semi-arboreal, being seen during the day perched on fallen timber, stumps, fence posts or roadside verges where they forage for insects. Frequently feed on flowers and soft herbage. A common species encountered basking on roads.

Pogona microlepidota (Glauert, 1952)

Description: Similar in most respects to *Pogona barbata,* from which it differs in its smaller adult size and the absence of a transverse series of enlarged spines across the throat. It differs from *Pogona minima* in lacking nuchal rows of spines parallel to the vertebral column, while it may be distinguished from *Pogona minor* in that the occipital row of spines on each side fails to meet the temporal row of spines. 14 cm (snout-vent).
Distribution: Known only from Drysdale River region, WA.
Habit: Open woodland with spinifex and other ground cover.

Pogona barbata Pearl Beach, NSW

Pogona barbata

Pogona microlepidota

Pogona minima

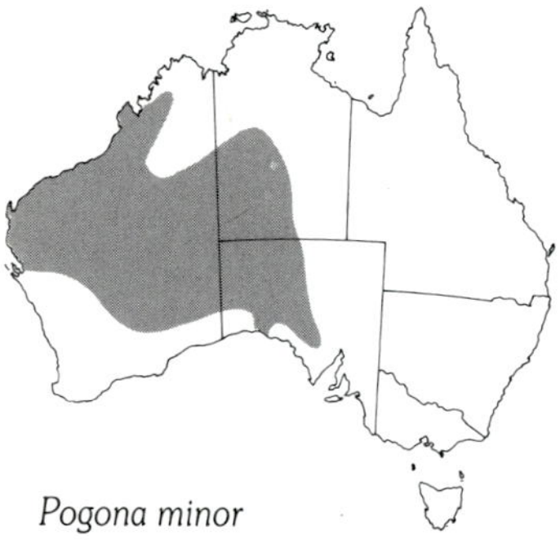

Pogona minor

Pogona minima Norseman, WA

Pogona nullarbor Eucla, WA

Pogona vitticeps Mt Olga, NT

Pogona minima (Loveridge, 1933)

Western Bearded Dragon

Description: Status uncertain; sometimes regarded as a race of *Pogona minor,* from which it differs in having a nuchal row of spines on each side of the head, parallel to the vertebral column. 16 cm (snout-vent).
Distribution: South-western WA, extending far into the arid interior.
Habit: Occupies a range of habitats from coastal dunes to the arid shrublands of the interior.

Pogona minor (Sternfeld, 1919)

Dwarf Bearded Dragon

Description: Similar in most respects to *Pogona barbata,* from which it differs in its smaller adult size and the absence of a transverse series of enlarged spines across the throat. It differs from *Pogona minima* in lacking nuchal rows of spines parallel to the vertebral column, while it may be distinguished from *Pogona microlepidota* in having the occipital row of spines on each side meeting the temporal row of spines. 16 cm (snout-vent).
Distribution: Central coast of WA through central Australia and SA to Eyre Peninsula.
Habit: A semi-arboreal species found in a wide range of habitats, from coastal dunes, heathlands, eucalypt forest, open woodlands and arid scrubs with spinifex.

Pogona mitchelli (Badham, 1976)

Description: Sometimes regarded as a subspecies of *Pogona minor*, to which it is similar in most respects, but from which it may be distinguished by having contiguous, stout, conical spines in the spine rows of the head (smaller spines, rarely contiguous, in *P. minor*). 14 cm (snout-vent).
Distribution: Lower NT to north-western WA.
Habit: Dry woodland to arid scrubs.

Pogona vitticeps near Kulgera, NT

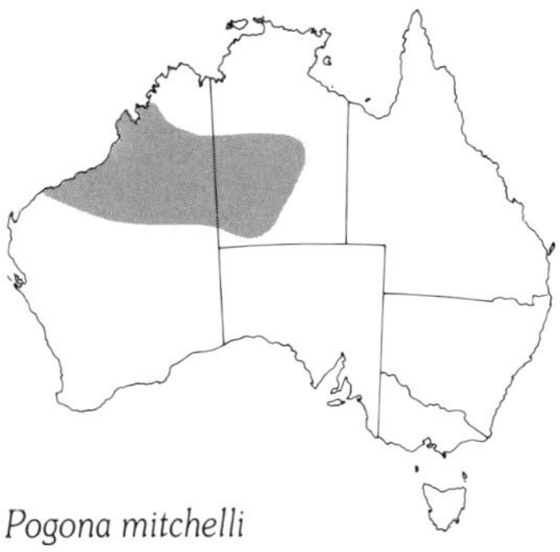

Pogona mitchelli

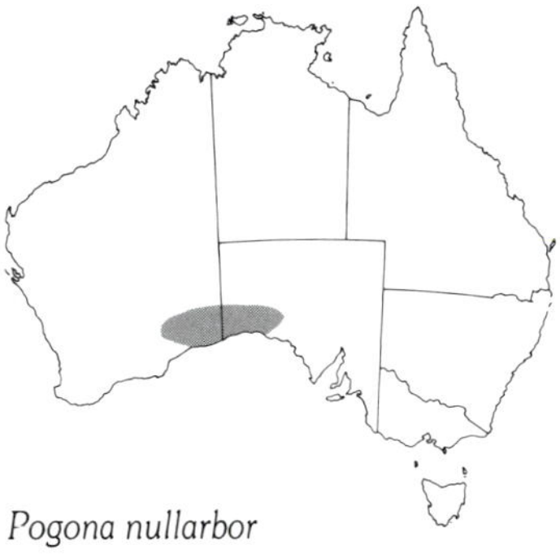

Pogona nullarbor

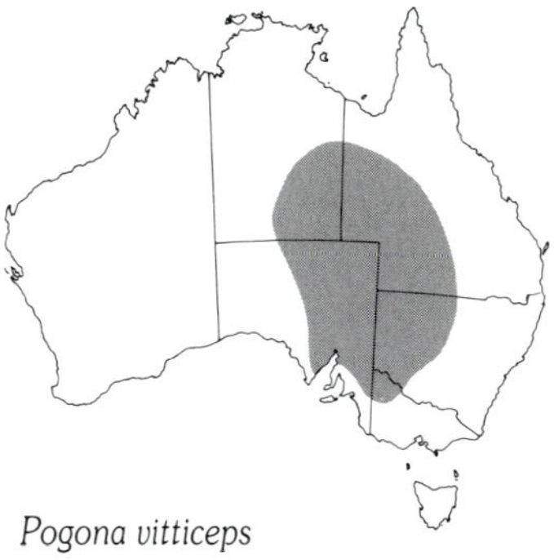

Pogona vitticeps

Pogona nullarbor (Badham, 1976)

Description: Similar in most respects to *Pogona barbata*, from which it may be distinguished by having conspicuous narrow white bands across the back and tail (these are absent in *P. barbata*). 13 cm (snout-vent).
Distribution: Nullarbor Plain in SA and WA.
Habit: A semi-arboreal species found in open eucalypt woodland, low chenopod shrublands and coastal dunes.

Pogona vitticeps (Ahl, 1926)

Description: Similar in most respects to *Pogona barbata*, from which it may be distinguished in its more robust body and the possession of an orderly row of spines along the lateral edge of the body, which continues over the forearm (several rows widening to a broad band behind the axilla in *P. barbata*). 20 cm (snout-vent).
Distribution: Interior of all eastern continental states to the eastern half of SA and south-eastern NT.
Habit: Found in a very wide range of habitats, from the dry sclerophyll forests and eucalypt and *Callitris* woodlands in the south-east of its range, through mallee and arid *Acacia* scrubs to the gibber, sandplain and sandridge deserts of the interior. Semi-arboreal, it is often seen perched on raised roadside verges, fallen timber, fence posts or trees from which it forages for the insects which make up the bulk of its diet. At other times it shelters under fallen timber, in the litter beneath shrubs,or in spinifex.

Genus *Tympanocryptis* Peters, 1863

An endemic Australian genus of small, primarily terrestrial lizards, recently redefined but still composite (polyphyletic). Most members of the genus are characterised by the absence of external ear structures, the tympanic region being covered by scaly skin; at least some of the dorsal scales are enlarged and raised, keeled or spinose. The earless species of *Tympanocryptis* are also characterised by a reduction in the phalangeal formula of the hind foot to 2. 3. 4. 5. 3. (normally 2. 3. 4. 5. 4.).

Key

TO THE SPECIES OF TYMPANOCRYPTIS

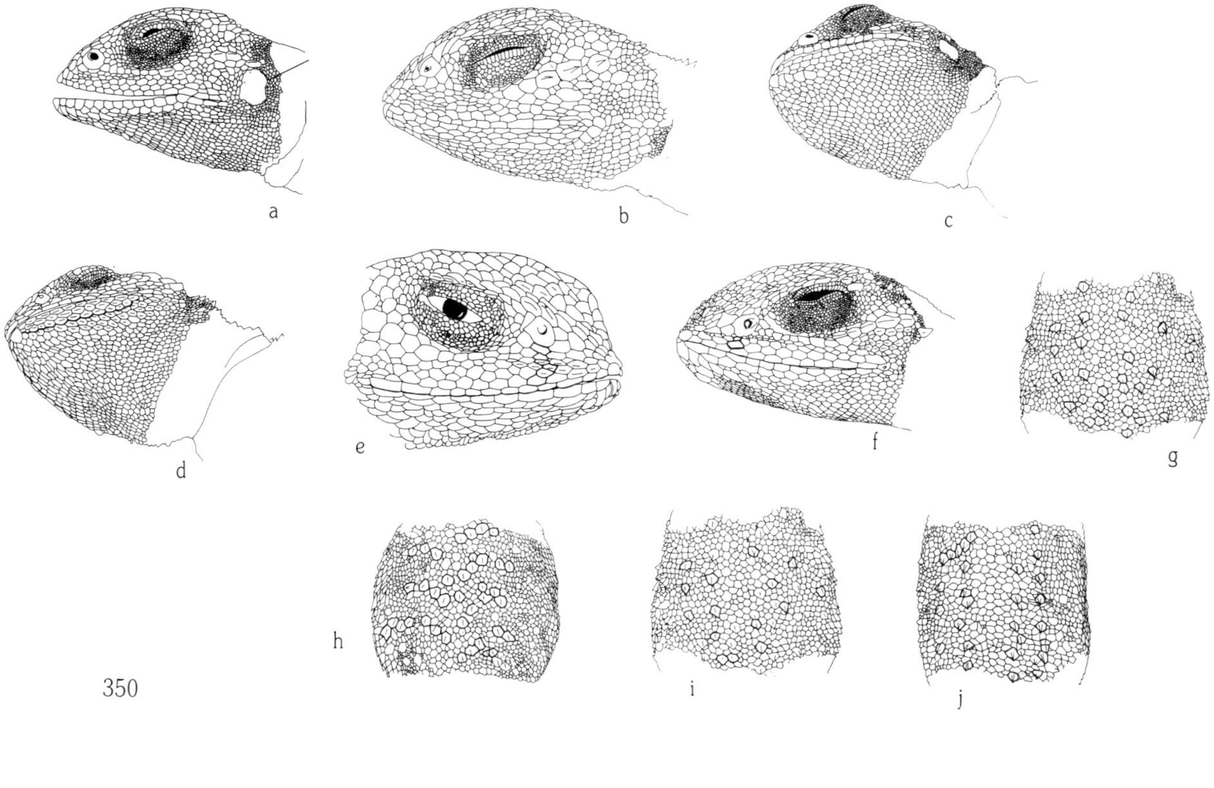

1 Tympanum distinct (a)...**2**
Tympanic region covered by scaly skin (b).................... **3**
2 Gular scales strongly keeled, not terraced (c)... ***adelaidensis***
Gular scales smooth, terraced (d)................. ***diemensis***
3 4-8 rows of scales between nasal and labials (e)..............**4**
2-3 rows of scales between nasal and labials (f).. ***parviceps***
4 Dorsal tubercles scattered irregularly or aligned longitudinally (g)..**5**
Dorsal tubercles tend to be arranged in transverse or oblique ridges (h)... ***cephalus***
5 Pale vertebral, dorso-lateral and lateral lines obscure or absent...**6**
Pale vertebral, dorso-lateral and sometimes lateral lines conspicuous.. ***lineata***
6 Dorsal tubercles scattered irregularly (i)........................ **7**
Dorsal tubercles more or less aligned in four longitudinal rows (j).. ***intima***
7 Tail tapers rapidly from its base; tail only about one and a half times as long as head and body................ ***uniformis***
Tail tapers gradually from its base; tail at least twice as long as head and body......................... ***tetraporophora***

Tympanocryptis adelaidensis
(Gray, 1841)

Description: Pale grey or fawn above, uniform or more often with four longitudinal series of dark, pale-edged blotches, those on either side converging on the pelvic region and continuing on either side of the base of the tail. A broad, pale vertebral zone and a narrow, pale dorso-lateral line (coinciding with a narrow skin fold). Head and nape with blackish markings usually arranged symmetrically. Lips faintly to strongly barred. Limbs with dark cross-bars. Whitish below, males with dark brown or black lines or reticulations on the throat, and a black patch on the chest continuing on the belly as a median blackish line or, or in some specimens, extending as a broad reticulum over the entire ventral region. Dorsal body scalation keeled and heterogeneous; no nuchal or vertebral crest or distinct, enlarged, vertebral scale row, but the dorsal scales much larger than those of the flanks; scattered, enlarged, keeled scales among the smaller ones on the dorso-lateral skin fold from the neck to the base of the tail. Gular scales usually smooth, ventrals smooth to keeled. Strongly keeled

Tympanocryptis adelaidensis Perth, WA

Tympanocryptis adelaidensis

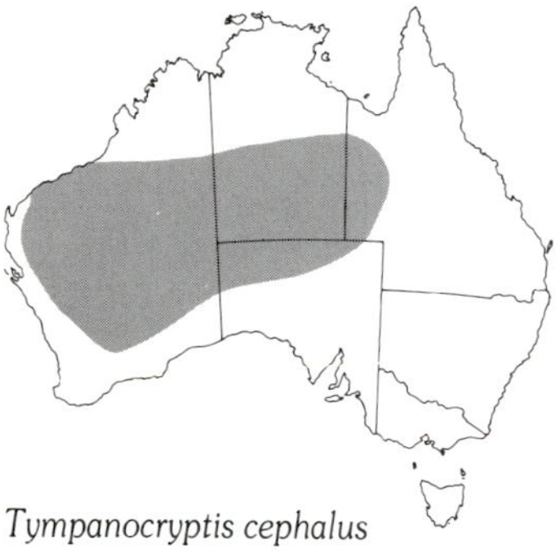

Tympanocryptis cephalus

Tympanocryptis cephalus Mt Isa, Qld

or spinose scales on either side of the base of the tail. No dentate marginal fringe on lower eyelid. Tympanum conspicuous. Canthus angular, the nostril slightly elliptical and facing outwards in an enlarged nasal scale lying just below the canthal ridge. 50 mm (snout-vent). Adpressed hindlimb reaches to about the eye, the hindlimb about 70%, tail about 160% of snout-vent length. Preanal and femoral pores 18-34, more or less in a straight line extending about two-thirds of the way along the thighs.
Distribution: Southern SA to south-western WA, north to Exmouth Gulf.

Habit: A small terrestrial lizard usually found among low vegetation in heaths and woodlands on paler sandy soils.
Subspecies: *adelaidensis* (lower west coast of WA); *chapmani* (remainder of range).

Tympanocryptis cephalus Günther, 1867

Description: Bright reddish-brown above, often with

Tympanocryptis diemensis Dharug National Park, NSW

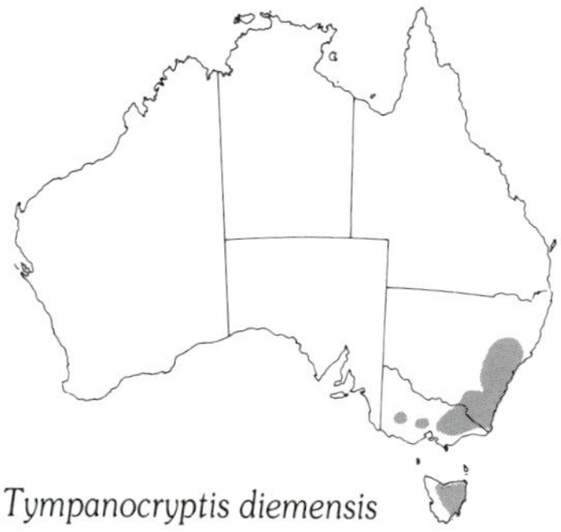

Tympanocryptis diemensis

a short, narrow, pale vertebral stripe from the neck on to the anterior part of the body, on either side of which is an equally short and narrow pale dorso-lateral stripe. A broad, dark chocolate-brown band across the neck between the forelimb and a series of three, very obscure, broad, dark bands on the body. Flanks sometimes grey or blue-grey. Tail with a series of 8-12 broad, dark cross-bands, widest distally, which are generally as wide as or wider than the paler interspaces. Limbs obscurely barred with dark brown. Whitish below. Head short and deep, the neck narrower than the head. Nasal separated from labials by 5-6 scales. Supralabials 12-16. Scales on top of head conical or with high blunt keels. Scales on back keeled, with enlarged, spinose scales which tend to be aligned in transverse or oblique rows. Gular and chest scales feebly keeled, those on the abdomen smooth or keeled. 50 mm (snout-vent), the hindlimb about 65%, the tail about 110% of snout-vent length. Usually only males with a single preanal pore on each side.
Distribution: Central coast of WA through southern and central interior of that state to central Australia and western Qld.
Habit: A small terrestrial lizard found in a variety of arid habitats, especially spinifex-dominated stony/lateritic plains, breakaways, stony hills and ranges.

Tympanocryptis diemensis (Gray, 1841)

Mountain Dragon

Description: Pale grey to dark brown above with a series of irregular darker variegations or blotches usually arranged in four longitudinal series on the back, but which may also tend to form obscure transverse bands, especially on the base of the tail. Limbs and head brown with paler and darker flecks. Ventral surface white or cream, uniform, or lightly to heavily flecked with brown and black. Dorsal body scalation strongly heterogeneous; scales on back variable in size, but tending to be largest dorsally and smallest on the flanks, but with numerous, enlarged, spinose scales scattered over the back (including the tail) and sides. Some of these spinose scales are aligned longitudinally to form four rows — a zigzag row on either side of the midline, and a more or less straight dorso-lateral row corresponding with a narrow skin fold. Scales of head, throat and remaining ventral surfaces keeled. A series of enlarged, spinose scales on either side of the base of the tail. Marginal scales of lower eyelid not forming a fringe. Tympanum small but conspicuous. Canthus angular, the nostril subcircular, facing outwards in an enlarged and somewhat swollen nasal scale lying just below the canthal ridge, 75mm (snout-vent). Adpressed hindlimb reaches to between shoulder and ear, the hindlimb about 70%, tail about 150-200% of snout-vent length. 12-24 preanal and femoral pores, in two short series disrupted in the midline and extending about halfway along each thigh.
Distribution: Uplands of south-eastern Australia, reaching the coast in the vicinity of Sydney, NSW; eastern Tas.
Habit: An inhabitant mainly of dry sclerophyll forests and heathlands, it is a diurnal lizard usually encountered among rocks or ground litter, or in low vegetation. Adults achieve a greater size in southern populations.

Tympanocryptis intima Mitchell, 1948

Description: Pale grey-brown to bright reddish-brown above, without paler dorso-lateral stripes, but the body usually with four obscure darker brown blotches on either side of the vertebral line. A greyish bar across the nape. Tail usually distinctly banded with dark brown, the dark bands about as wide as the paler interspaces. Ventral surfaces whitish, sometimes finely spotted with brown on the throat and chest. Neck narrower than the head. Nasal separated from the labials by 4-6 scales. Supralabials 13-16. Scales on top of the head smooth, or slightly rugose. Scales on back more or less smooth, with widely scattered, enlarged, spinose tubercles tending to be aligned in four longitudinal rows. Gular and ventral scales smooth. 50 mm (snout-vent), the hindlimb about 70%, the tail about 130% of snout-vent length. Usually only males with a single preanal pore on each side.
Distribution: Arid interior of northern and north-eastern SA and adjoining states.
Habit: '...inhabits the open gibber deserts and spinifex flats of the Eyrean Basin' (Mitchell).

Tympanocryptis lineata Peters, 1863

Description: Pale grey or fawn to reddish-brown above, usually with a broad, pale vertebral stripe ending on the rump. Two narrower pale grey or white stripes on each side, a lateral and a dorso-lateral. These longitudinal stripes are partly or wholly interrupted by a series of four or five dark transverse bars and another 12-20 on the tail. Limbs with conspicuous or obscure darker transverse bands. Usually a narrow, pale bar between the anterior

Tympanocryptis lineata Wilcannia, NSW

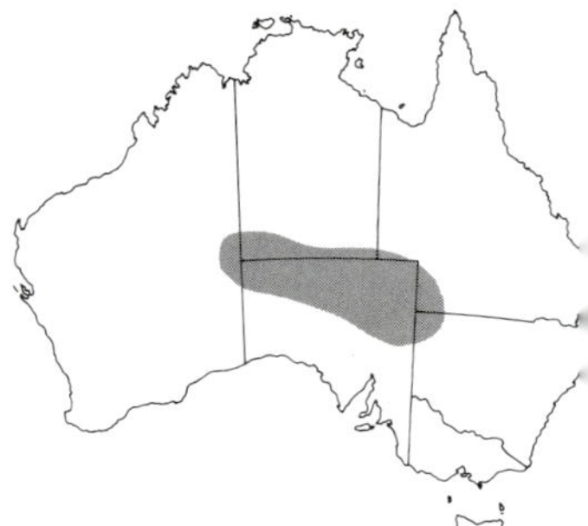

Tympanocryptis intima

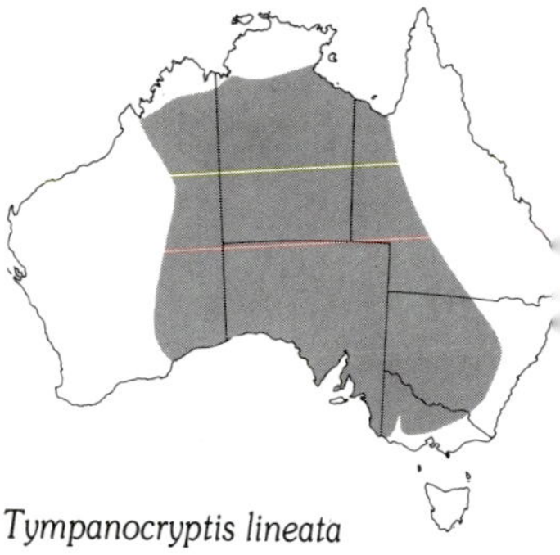

Tympanocryptis lineata

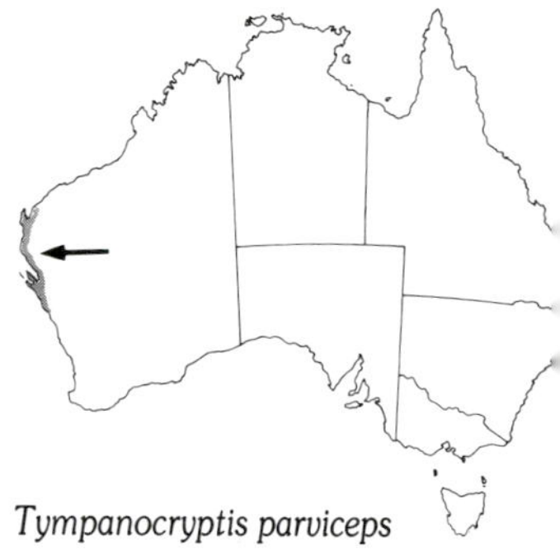

Tympanocryptis parviceps

Tympanocryptis intima Sandringham Station, Qld

corners of the eyes. Whitish below, sometimes flecked with grey, brown or black. Neck narrower to broader than the head. Nasal separated from labial by 4-6 scales. Supralabials 11-16. Scales on top of head, keeled. Scales on back keeled, with scattered, enlarged, sharply keeled scales, or spinose tubercles. Gular and ventral scales smooth or keeled. 50 mm (snout-vent). The hindlimb about 60%, the tail about 150% of snout-vent length. Usually only males with one preanal pore on each side and occasionally with one femoral pore on each side.
Distribution: From eastern and south-eastern WA through the interior of all mainland states to the western slopes of NSW and southern Vic.
Habit: Found in a wide variety of terrestrial habitats, from desert sandhills and *Triodia* through gibber and black-soil plains to open woodland. Usually found living in earth cracks, grasses or ground litter.
Subspecies: *lineata* (south-eastern part of range); *centralis* (deserts regions of eastern WA, northern SA, and NT to western Qld and NSW); *houstoni* (Kimberleys and northern NT); *macra* (Nullarbor Plain); *pinguicolla* (Vic and south-eastern NSW).

Tympanocryptis parviceps Storr, 1964

Description: Pale grey- brown above, palest as a broad vertebral band; flanks and sides of tail darker brown with a series of narrow, hourglass-shaped bars extending upwards to meet the pale vertebral band. Limbs uniformly or obscurely banded with brown. Whitish below, except for some grey or black marbling on the throat. A relatively slender lizard with small head and the neck narrower than the head. Nasal separated from the labial by two, occasionally three, scales. Supralabials 8-12. Scales on the head strongly keeled. Scales on centre of back, tail and upper surfaces of limbs more or less uniform, strongly keeled and sometimes spinose, those on the sides smaller and variable in size. Gular scales feebly

Tympanocryptis parviceps Maud Hill, WA

Tympanocryptis tetraporophora near Tibooburra, NSW

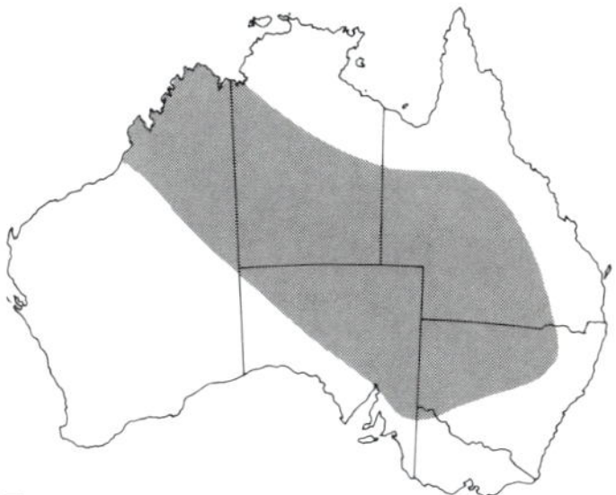

Tympanocryptis tetraporophora

Tympanocryptis uniformis

to strongly keeled, remaining ventral scales feebly keeled on abdomen, strongly keeled on chest. 45 mm (snout-vent), the hindlimb about 70%, the tail about 150% of snout-vent length. A small, distinct, dorso-lateral skin fold. Males with 8-10 preanal, 16-25 femoral pores. The chin is distinctively ridged on each side, just below the infralabials.
Distribution: Coast of WA between Exmouth Gulf and Shark Bay.
Habit: '...restricted to coastal dunes...' (Storr).
Subspecies: *butleri* (Edel Land, WA); *parviceps* (remainder of species' range).

Tympanocryptis tetraporophora
Lucas and Frost, 1895

Description: Status uncertain. Similar in most respects to *Tympanocryptis lineata*, from which it differs in having the pale vertebral and dorso-lateral stripes scarcely distinct or absent. The neck is narrower than the head, and the hindlimb is relatively longer than in *lineata* (about 75% of snout-vent length).
Distribution: Eastern central Australia and arid interiors of Qld, NSW and SA.
Habit: Barren gibber plains and low arid shrublands and hummock grasslands, especially on stony plains and hills. Also found in earth cracks on the extensive inland river floodplains and overflows that characterise much of its range.

Tympanocryptis uniformis Mitchell, 1948

Description: Generally similar to *Tympanocryptis cephalus*. Grey above, with a series of obscure, darker grey cross-bands on body and tail, each about as wide as the paler interspaces. A broad dark grey or black vertebral band from the nape to the base of the tail and much fainter, dark, narrow, dorso-lateral and lateral lines on each side, usually disrupted and obvious only where they cross the dark cross-bands. Limbs with obscure dark brown bars. Whitish below, except for some darker flecks around the jaws. Head large, short and deep, the neck narrower than the head. Nasal separated from labials by 5-6 scales. Supralabials 15. Scales on top of head strongly keeled. Scales on back keeled, with scattered, enlarged spinose tubercles tending to be aligned in four longitudinal rows, two on either side of the dark vertebral band. Gular scales smooth or feebly keeled, remaining ventral scales feebly keeled. 50 mm (snout-vent), the hindlimb about 60%, the tail about 150% of snout-vent length. Usually only males with a single preanal pore on each side.
Distribution: North-western NT.

Family Varanidae

A group of about 30 lizards found from Africa, through Asia and the Indo-Papuan Archipelago, to Australia. All are egg-laying, diurnal, raptorial lizards, and the group includes the world's largest lizard (the Indonesian Komodo Dragon, *Varanus komodoensis* growing to more than three metres) and Australia's largest lizard (the Perentie, *Varanus giganteus*). The limbs are well-developed and powerful, the eyes have well-developed movable lids, the scales on top of the head are small and fragmented, while the tongue is deeply forked like that of a snake and is flicked in and out constantly when the lizard is alert. Generally known in Australia as goannas, elsewhere they are usually known as monitor lizards.

One widespread Asian species, the Asian Water Monitor *(Varanus salvator)* has been recorded from the islands of Torres Strait, almost certainly in error.

Genus *Varanus* Merrem, 1820

All Australian members of the Family Varanidae belong to the genus *Varanus*.

Key

TO THE AUSTRALIAN SPECIES OF VARANUS

1 Tail strongly laterally compressed except at the base; a distinct median double keel dorsally along the posterior half of the tail (a)..**2**

Tail only moderately laterally compressed or not at all; no obvious median double keel dorsally along the tail (b)... **10**

2 Caudal scales not arranged in regular rings, as ventral caudal scales are larger than the dorsal caudals (c)......... **3**

Caudal scales arranged in regular rings (d), occasionally incomplete on the sides of the tail.................................**6**

3 Nostrils directed laterally (e); caudal keel moderate, low.... ....**4**

Nostrils directed upwards (f); a very high strong caudal keel... ***mertensi***

4 All supraoculars small, irregularly distributed (g)............**5**

A series of a few distinctly broader or enlarged scales among the supraoculars (h)................................ ***indicus***

5 A row of enlarged scales forming a ridge on the inner edge of the basal part of the fourth toe (i)...................... ***varius***

No ridge of enlarged scales on the fourth toe (j)................ .... ***giganteus***

6 Tail at least 1.3 times as long as head and body; scales on upper side of basal portion of tail not rugose (k)............. **7**

Tail no more than 1.2 times as long as head and body; scales on upper side of basal portion of tail rugose (l)......... .... ***spenceri***

7 Scales on the head and body small (m): 70-100 scales across the top of the head from the angle of the mouth on one side to that on the other; 140-220 scales around the body...**8**

Scales on the head and body fairly large (n): 40-60 scales across the top of the head from the angle of the mouth on one side to that on the other; 90-130 scales around the body... ***mitchelli***

8 Dorsal pattern without transverse rows of large, dark spots; ventrally uniformly pale with dark bands or reticulations, or randomly scattered dark spots.......................... **9**

Dorsal pattern consisting of alternating transverse rows of small, pale spots and large, dark spots; ventrally with transverse rows of small dark spots aligned with the dark spots on the back.. ***panoptes***

9 Neck with transverse dark bands; end of tail banded or uniformly dark; ventrally with grey cross-bands or reticulations.. ***rosenbergi***

Neck without transverse dark bands; end of tail uniform pale yellow or white; ventrally with randomly scattered dark spots... ***gouldii***

10 Tail round in section or somewhat dorso-ventrally compressed, at the most very slightly laterally compressed in the last half.. **11**

Last two-thirds of tail moderately laterally compressed...... .... ***semiremex***

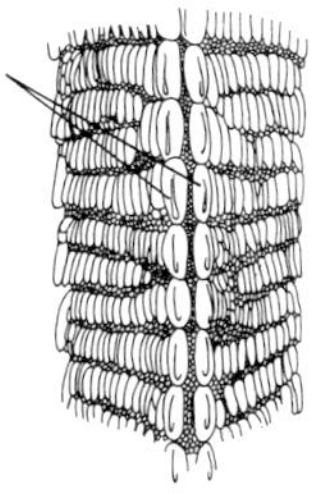
a

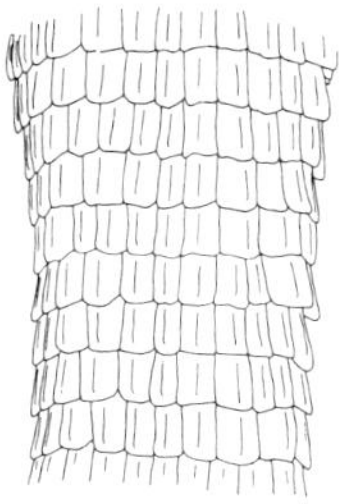
b

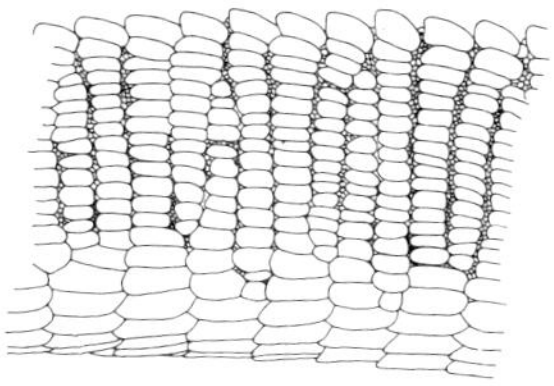
c

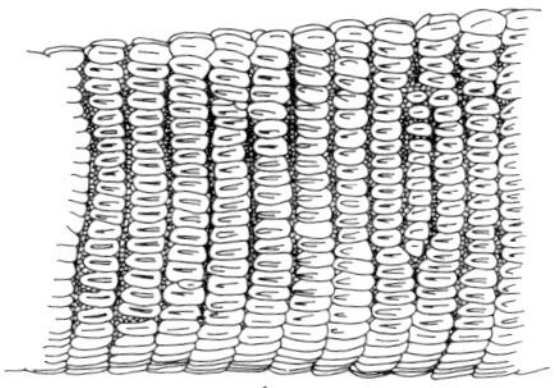
d

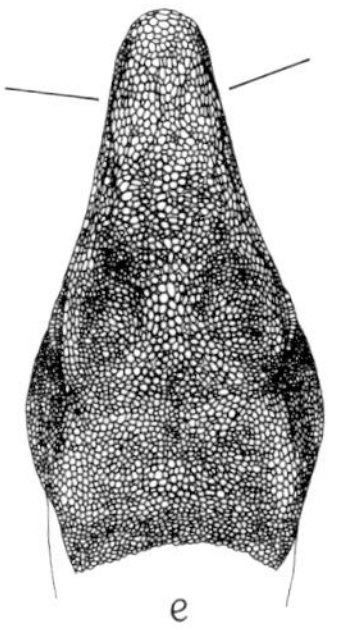
e

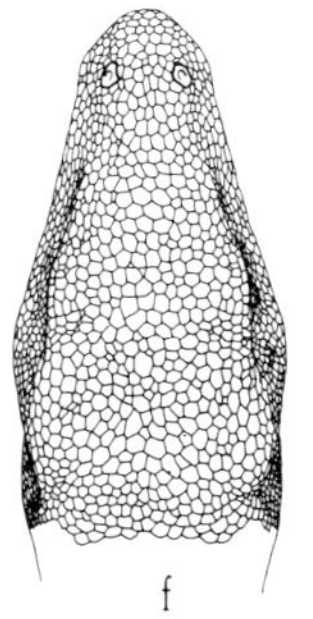
f

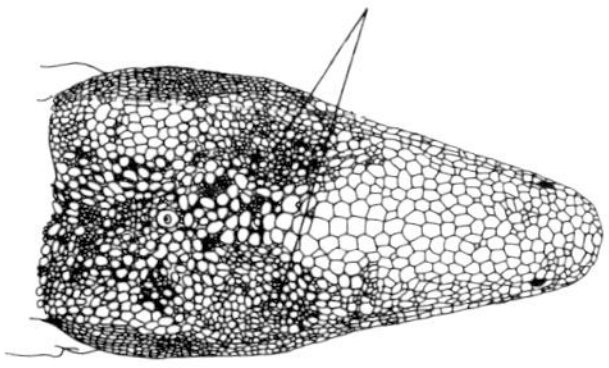
g

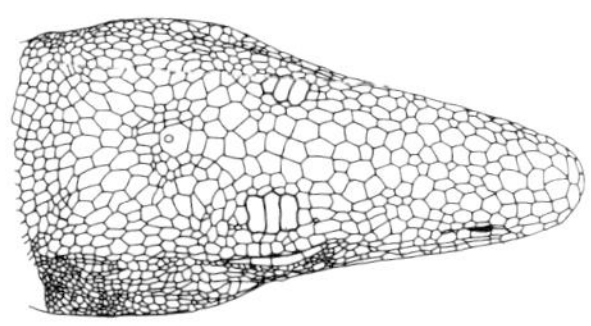
h

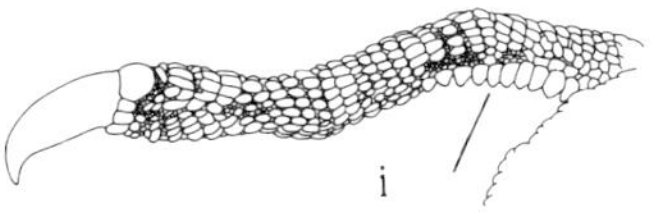
i

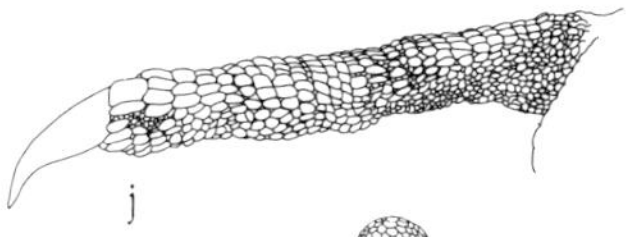
j

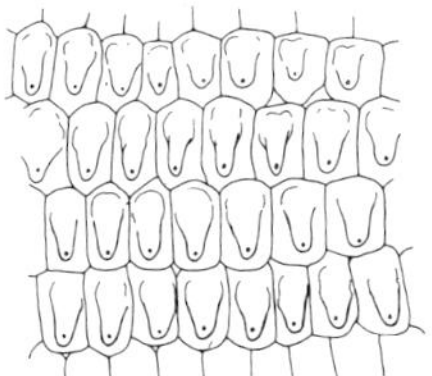
k

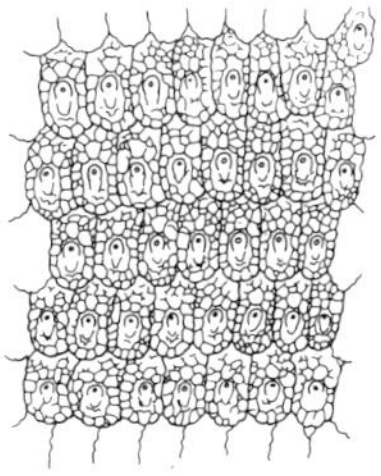
l

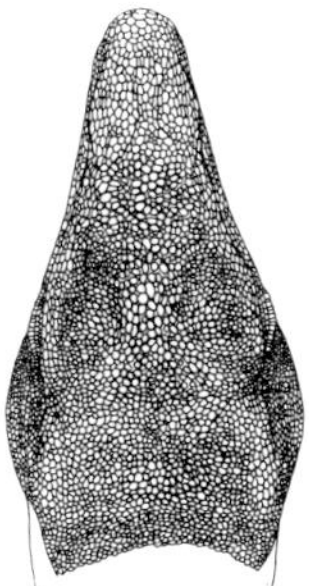
m

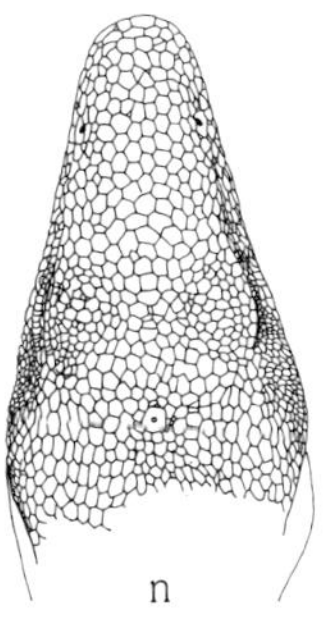
n

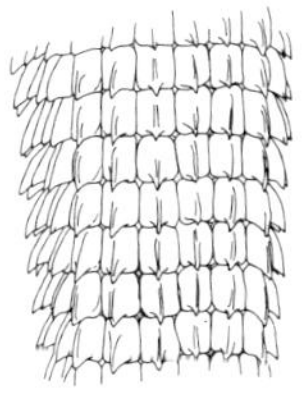
o

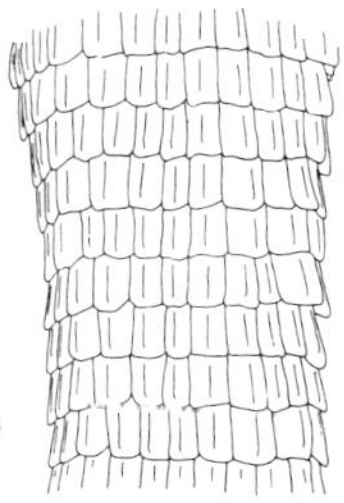
p

q

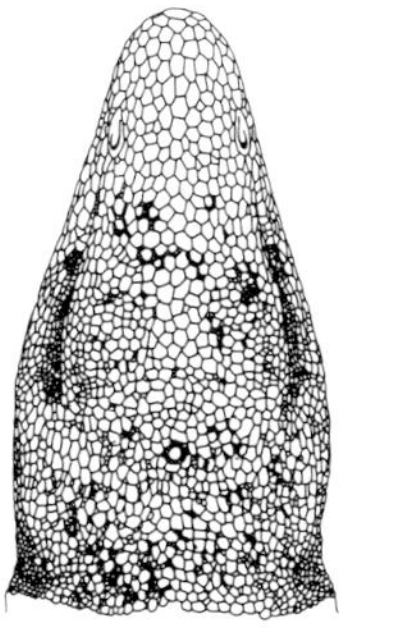
r

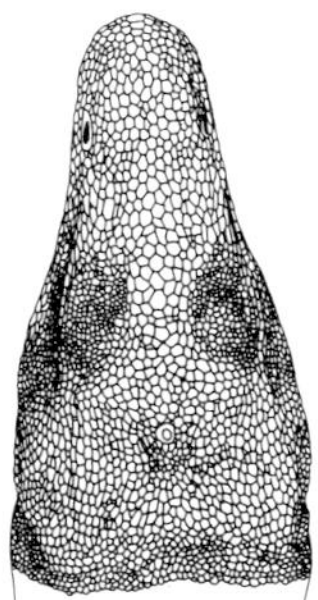
s

11 Supraocular scales subequal (g)....................................**12**
A median series of transversely enlarged supraocular scales (h).. ***prasinus***

12 The keels of the dorsal and lateral caudal scales spinose (o)...**13**
The keels of the caudal scales sometimes very strong, but never spinose (p)... **16**

13 Tail less than 1.8 times as long as head and body; back without a distinct pattern of ocelli................................. **14**
If tail less than 1.8 times as long as head and body, the back with distinct pattern of ocelli................ ***acanthurus***

14 More than 70 rows of scales around the body.............. **15**
Fewer than 70 rows of scales around the middle of the body..***primordius***

15 Size small, snout-vent length to about 130 mm; dark facial stripes absent; 70-94 mid-body scale rows.............. ***storri***
Size moderate, snout-vent length to about 250 mm; dark facial stripes present; 80-112 mid-body scale rows...***baritji***

16 Tail longer than head and body..................................... **17**
Tail shorter than head and body.................. ***brevicauda***

17 Scales on top of head smooth....................................... **18**
Scales on top of head keeled.............................. ***eremius***

18 Tail with longitudinal stripes or bars distally................. **19**
Tail pattern, if present, transversely aligned distally...... **20**

19 Body and base of tail with narrow purplish-brown cross-bands.. ***gilleni***
Body and base of tail with randomly scattered dark brown spots... ***caudolineatus***

20 Tail patterned or uniform in colour throughout its length.. **21**
About last half of tail creamy white; tubercles on lower surfaces of feet large and glossy black (q).... ***glebopalma***

21 Last half of tail without alternate black and white bands.. **22**
Last half of tail with conspicuous alternate black and white bands.. ***glauerti***

22 Supraoculars gradually merging with the larger interoculars (r); males with or without ventro-lateral rows of moderately enlarged keeled scales on each side behind the vent... **23**
Supraoculars very small, sharply differentiated from the larger interoculars (s); males with a ventro-lateral cluster of strong spines on each side behind the vent (t)..... ***tristis***

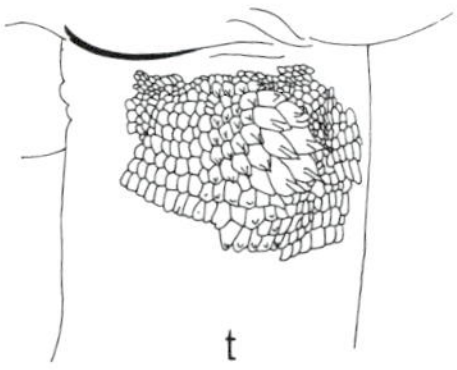
t

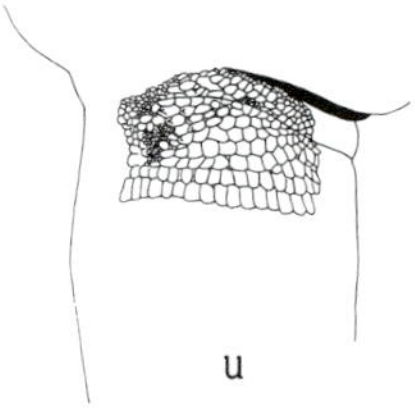
u

23 Several ventro-lateral rows of enlarged keeled scales on each side behind the vent (u).. **24**
No series of enlarged keeled scales on each side behind the vent.. ***kingorum***

24 Dorsal and lateral caudal scales feebly keeled; ground colour reddish-brown; nostril latero-dorsal; snout-vent length less than 180 cm................................ ***pilbarensis***
Dorsal and lateral caudal scales moderately to strongly keeled; ground colour dull grey, brown or blackish; nostril lateral; snout-vent length to 270 cm................***timorensis***

Varanus acanthurus Mt Isa, Qld

Varanus acanthurus Boulenger, 1885

Ridge-Tailed Monitor

Description: Body above with a reticulated pattern of rich dark brown enclosing numerous small dull to bright yellow spots, lines or cream ocelli — many of the ocelli with one or two dark brown scales in their centres. Head brown, spotted with yellow or cream, often tending to longitudinal stripes on the neck. A dark brown stripe along the snout, through the eye

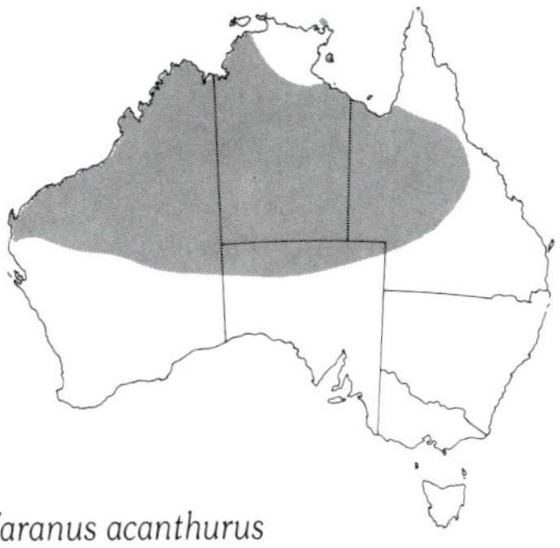

Varanus acanthurus

Varanus baritji Umbrawarra Gorge, NT G. HUSBAND

Varanus brevicauda Port Hedland, WA

and continued as a broad temporal stripe which is bordered above and below by light yellow stripes or rows of spots. Another yellow stripe runs back from the lower jaw. Tail dark brown with rings, often indefinite, formed of light brown or yellow scales. White or cream below. Head scales small, smooth. Nostril lateral, about halfway between eye and tip of snout. 70-115 rows of smooth scales around the middle of the body. Tail more or less round in section, or slightly depressed, without any indication of a dorsal keel, about 1.3-2.3 times longer than head and body. Dorsal and lateral caudal scales with strong spinose keels. Grows to about 70 cm (total length).
Distribution: Found throughout the arid and seasonally dry regions of northern Australia wherever suitable habitats occur.
Habit: Found among rocky outcrops, or on stony ranges, breakaways and scarps where it lives under boulders or in deep crevices. Occasionally found sheltering in spinifex. Feeds mainly on insects and lizards.
Subspecies: *acanthurus* (north-western Australia); *brachyurus (*throughout remaining mainland range of species); *insulanicus* (Groote Eylandt).

Varanus baritji King and Horner, 1987

Description: Reddish-brown above, with numerous scattered, small dark brown or blackish spots which tend to be aligned transversely on the flanks. A dark canthal streak, usually pale-edged, from nostril to eye and continued as a temporal stripe behind the eye and over the ear to the nape; sometimes another dark stripe from the angle of the jaws through the ear to the side of the neck. Limbs and tail brown above, spotted, flecked or mottled with dark brown and dirty-white, tending to form alternate dark and pale bands on the basal portion of the tail. Whitish to fawn below, except yellow on the throat. Head scales small, smooth. Nostril dorso-lateral, about halfway between eye and tip of snout or slightly nearer the snout than the eye. 80-112 rows of slightly (dorsum) to strongly (flanks) keeled scales around the middle of the body. Tail more or less round to somewhat triangular in section, without a true dorsal keel but with a double row of enlarged, keeled scales, about 1.7 times longer than head and body. Dorsal and lateral caudal scales with strong spinose keels. Grows to about 60 cm (total length).
Distribution: Northern NT.
Habit: An inhabitant of stony hills and dissected ranges and scarps.

Varanus brevicauda Boulenger, 1898

Description: Head and body pale yellowish-brown to pinkish- brown or fawn, with numerous small flecks of dark brown or creamy-white scattered over the head, body, limbs and tail; the darker flecks tend to be larger on the sides of the body and tail. A faint dark temporal stripe often present. White below. Head scales small, smooth. 70-100 rows of scales around the middle of the body. Nostril lateral, about halfway between eye and tip of snout. Tail more or less round in section, without any indication of a dorsal keel, and nearly as long as the head and body. Dorsal and lateral caudal scales tricarinate, with moderate keels. Grows to about 25 cm (total length).
Distribution: Arid regions of northern WA and southern NT to western Qld.
Habit: A ground-dwelling inhabitant of sandy desert areas, where it lives in spinifex (*Triodia*) or litter; it has been dug up from burrows beneath spinifex.

Varanus caudolineatus Boulenger, 1885

Description: Grey-brown above, with numerous irregularly scattered dark brown spots and flecks on the head and body. Tail grey with dark brown spots and blotches on its basal part, which gradually merge

Varanus baritji

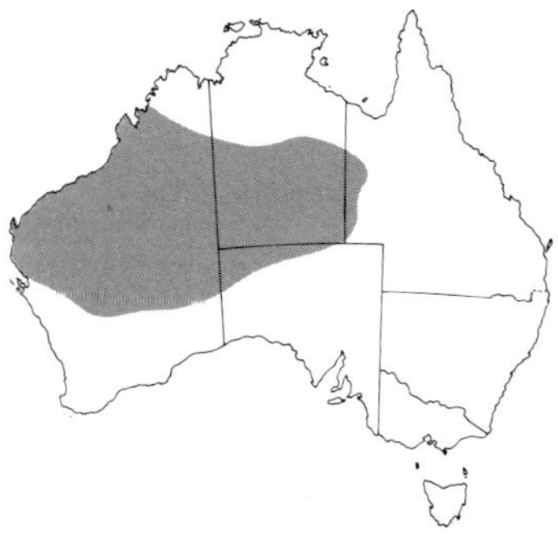

Varanus brevicauda

Varanus caudolineatus

to form a series of dark brown longitudinal stripes along the hinder part of the tail. A dark brown temporal stripe. Creamy-white below, lightly flecked with dark brown. Head scales small, smooth. 80-110 scales around the middle of the body. Nostril lateral, about halfway between eye and tip of snout. Tail more or less round in section, without any indication of a keel, and about 1.5 times as long as head and body. Caudal scales strongly keeled, slightly spinose. Grows to about 30 cm (total length).
Distribution: Coast and interior of central WA.
Habit: Mainly arboreal, living under bark or in crevices of mulga and gum trees; however, Pianka has taken it from under rocks and in crevices of exfoliating granite outcrops. Feeds on insects and small lizards.

Varanus eremius Great Victoria Desert, WA

Varanus eremius Lucas and Frost, 1895

Description: Pale to dark reddish-brown above, with numerous irregularly scattered dark brown or black flecks and spots mixed with smaller flecks and spots of pale yellow or cream. Tail with alternating longitudinal stripes of cream and dark brown, the stripes often broken up into blotches on the base of the tail. A conspicuous black stripe from snout to eye, and a faint temporal stripe. A thin cream stripe from the angle of the jaws, below the ear to the base of the forelimb. White below, except for grey mottling on the throat. Head scales small, keeled. 85-110 scales around the middle of the body. Nostril lateral, much nearer the tip of the snout than the eye. Tail more or less round in section, with a faint indication of a dorsal keel near the tip and about 1.5 times longer than the head and body. Caudal scales strongly keeled but not spinose. Grows to about 50 cm (total length).
Distribution: Central coastal regions of WA to desert areas of SA and the NT.
Habit: A ground-dwelling inhabitant of sandy and loamy desert country, where it is found in and around spinifex *(Triodia)*. Feeds on insects and small lizards.

Varanus giganteus (Gray, 1845)

Perentie

Description: Rich brown above, the back and sides with a series of large creamish or yellowish spots or blotches which tend to be aligned in transverse rows across the body and tail. Each light spot is edged with dark brown or black, while the black edgings of the spots on the neck run together to form a conspicuous reticulated pattern on the sides of the neck and face and on the throat. The limbs are darker brown, spotted with cream or yellow. White or cream below. The above pattern is brilliant and contrasting in juveniles, gradually becoming more obscure with increasing size. No indication of a temporal stripe. Head scales including the supraoculars small, smooth, irregular. Nostril lateral, about twice as far from the eye as from the tip of the snout. 240-290 scales around the middle of the body. Tail strongly laterally compressed, except at the base, with a distinct median dorsal double keel along its hinder half. Tail about 1.3 times longer than the head and body. Caudal scales are not keeled, and because the lower scales are larger than the upper scales, the caudal scales are not arranged in regular rings. Averages about 1.6 metres in total length, but specimens exceeding 2 metres have been found, making this Australia's largest lizard.
Distribution: Arid interior of Australia from far western Qld through central Australia to the coast of WA.
Habit: Essentially a ground-dwelling lizard which inhabits deep crevices and burrows in rocky outcrops throughout its range, it nevertheless forages widely in adjacent sandy desert and claypans and will sometimes climb a tree when disturbed. Feeds on insects, reptiles, birds, small mammals and carrion.

Varanus caudolineatus near Gascoyne Junction, WA

Varanus giganteus near Finke, NT

Varanus gilleni Lucas and Frost, 1895
Pygmy Mulga Monitor

Description: Rich grey-brown above, fading to grey on the sides with a series of narrow, irregular, dark reddish-brown or maroon cross-bands made up of spots and short bars which sometimes coalesce to form continuous bands; these cross-bands often contain scattered, light grey scales. Head and limbs grey-brown with dark brown flecks and reticulations. Tail grey with dark brown scales forming narrow cross-bands basally but gradually forming a series of dark longitudinal stripes on the hinder part of the tail. White below, with numerous grey flecks, especially on the throat. Head scales small, irregular, smooth. 90-125 scales around the middle of the body. Nostril lateral, about halfway between eye and tip of snout. Tail more or less round in section, without any indication of a dorsal keel, and about 1.4 times as long as head and body. Grows to about 30 cm (total length).
Distribution: Desert areas of SA and the NT through the interior of WA to the north-west coast.
Habit: An arboreal lizard usually found under bark or in cracks or crevices of mulga, gum or desert oak trees. Feeds on insects and small lizards.

Varanus gilleni Tomkinson Ranges, SA

Varanus glauerti Kununurra, WA

G. HUSBAND

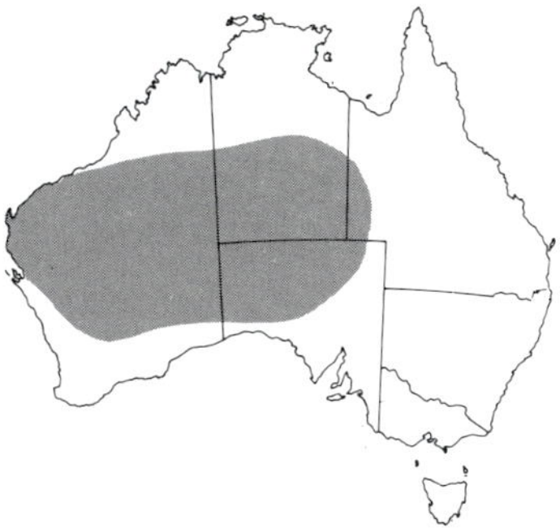

Varanus eremius

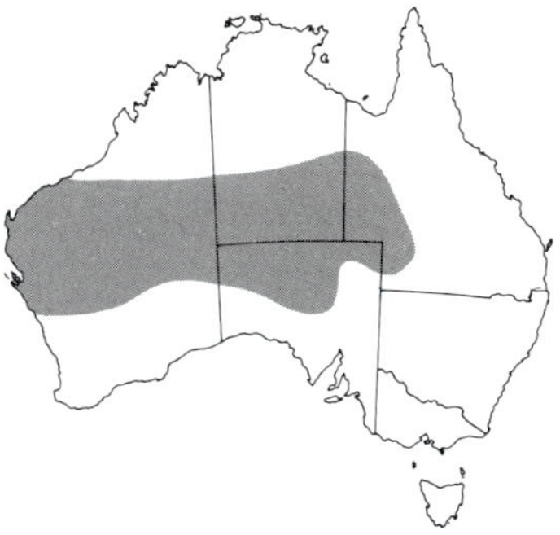

Varanus giganteus

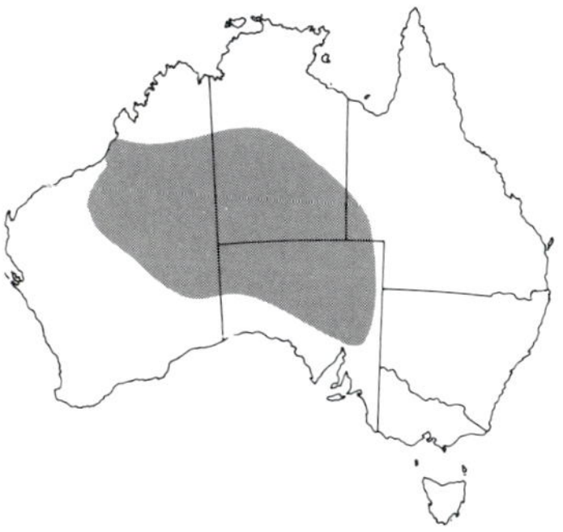

Varanus gilleni

Varanus glauerti

Varanus glauerti Mertens, 1957

Description: Head, body and limbs blackish or dark brown above, the body with obscure transverse rows of large, lighter spots and the hindlimbs with transverse rows of small spots. A contrasting, sharply-defined, white temporal stripe. Tail with alternate light and dark cross-bands. Throat and belly whitish. Head scales small, irregular, smooth. Nostril lateral, a little nearer the tip of the snout than the eye. 120-160 scales around the middle of the body. Tail more or less round in section, without any indication of a dorsal keel, nearly twice as long as the head and body. Scales smooth on the base of the tail, moderately keeled on the distal part. Grows to about 80 cm (total length).
Distribution: Known only from the Kimberley region of WA.
Habit: Rock-dwelling.

Varanus glebopalma

Varanus gouldii

Varanus glebopalma Mitchell, 1955

Long-Tailed Rock Monitor

Description: Dorsally black with individually fawn-coloured scales which form a reticulum on the flanks

Varanus indicus

Varanus glebopalma Kimberley Ranges, WA J. WEIGEL

(where they predominate over the black) or small black-centred ocelli on the midline (where black predominates). Top of head and upper surfaces of limbs black with small cream or fawn flecks and spots, clustering to form larger spots on the limbs. Anterior half of tail mostly black above, posterior half creamy-yellow. Throat white with a broad reticulum of light purplish-fawn extending on to the sides of the throat, but forming bars on the lower lips. Belly and chest white with vague transverse bars of light purplish-fawn. Tail and limbs creamy-yellow below. Palms and soles with rounded, shiny, dark brown scales. Head scales small, irregular, smooth. Nostril lateral, much nearer to the tip of the snout than the eye. 130-170 scales around the middle of the body. Tail more or less round in section without any indication of a dorsal keel, but somewhat compressed near the tip, more than twice as long as head and body. Caudal scales smooth or with low keels. Grows to about 1 metre (total length).
Distribution: Found in suitable habitats throughout the tropical north of Australia, from the Kimberley region of WA to western Qld.
Habit: An agile, shy species found in rocky outcrops, hills and ranges where it shelters in crevices and caves and under large boulders. Although active by day, it is commonly crepuscular and can often be disturbed foraging just after sundown. Feeds largely on insects.

Varanus gouldii (Gray, 1838)
Gould's Goanna or Sand Monitor

Description: A widespread species subject to considerable geographic variation in colour, pattern and size. Dorsal ground colour ranges from light yellow to almost black, usually with numerous small, scattered, lighter and darker flecks and spots, which tend to be aligned transversely to form irregular, narrow crossbands. Sometimes the light cream or yellow markings are in the form of distinct, dark-centred ocelli. The limbs are usually finely spotted with white, cream or yellow. There is usually a well-defined black temporal stripe edged above and below with white or cream. The tail, except for its tip, is light brown to black with light- coloured scales tending to form narrow rings; the last several centimetres of the tail are almost invariably white, cream or yellow. Whitish below, usually with scattered dark flecks and spots. Head scales small, irregular, smooth. Nostril lateral, much nearer

Varanus gouldii Alice Springs, NT

the tip of the snout than the eye. 130-220 scales around the middle of the body. Tail strongly laterally compressed, except at the base, with a distinct median dorsal double keel along the distal half of the tail, and about 1.5 times longer than the head and body. Caudal scales with low keels. Grows to about 1.6 metres (total length).

Distribution: Found throughout most parts of continental Australia except the extreme south-east and those forests of the east coast subject to very high rainfall. Extra-limital in the seasonally dry savannahs of southern New Guinea.

Varanus gouldii Lizard Island, Qld. Ritual fighting in two males; one will eventually give way and leave the area.

B. GOLDMAN

Varanus indicus Murray I. Qld

Habit: A ground-dwelling species found in a wide variety of habitats from coastal sclerophyll forest to the sandy deserts of the interior. Shelters in burrows (its own or those of other animals), hollow logs, dense litter, etc. Ranges over large areas when foraging for the insects, reptiles, birds, mammals and carrion on which it feeds. Larger specimens raise themselves on a 'tripod' formed by hind legs and tail to obtain a view of their surroundings, or when on the defensive.
Subspecies: *gouldii* (continental Australia except arid interior); *flavirufus* (arid interior of Australia).

Varanus indicus (Daudin, 1802)

Mangrove Monitor

Description: Dark purplish-brown to black above, with numerous scattered small flecks and spots of cream, yellow or yellow-green. White or cream below. Head scales small, smooth, except for a distinct series of broader, enlarged scales among the small supraoculars. Nostrils lateral, each slightly nearer the tip of the snout than the eye. 110-180 scales around the middle of the body. Belly scales smooth. Tail strongly compressed, with a low, moderate median dorsal keel, about 1.4 to 1.8 times as long as head and body. Caudal scales smooth or with low keels, not in complete rings as the lower scales are larger than the upper scales. Grows to about 1 metre (total length).
Distribution: Rainforest and coastal mangrove habitats of eastern Cape York Peninsula and the islands of Torres Strait; recorded from coastal mangrove forests of Arnhem Land, NT. Also found in New Guinea and other parts of the Indo-Papuan Archipelago.
Habit: A species which forages for insects, fish, reptiles, birds and mammals in or near forest streams and tidal mangrove areas. An able swimmer and climber, it usually takes to the water when alarmed.

Varanus kingorum Storr, 1980

Description: Reddish-brown above, dotted dorsally and laterally with black, the dots sometimes forming a reticulate pattern. Pale cream or white below, the throat and belly dotted with dark brown. Head scales small, smooth. 97-108 rows of scales around the middle of the body (Storr). Nostril dorso-lateral, about halfway between eye and tip of snout. Tail slightly

Varanus kingorum near Lake Argyle, WA

compressed except basally, without any indication of a dorsal keel, at least twice as long as head and body. Dorsal and lateral caudal scales large, with low, moderately sharp keels (Storr). Grows to about 40 cm (total length).
Distribution: Known only from a small area, taking in the eastern Kimberley region of WA and the adjacent part of north- western NT.
Habit: A species living in crevices and under exfoliating sandstone slabs throughout its range. Presumably insectivorous.

Varanus mertensi Glauert, 1951

Mertens' Water Monitor

Description: Rich dark brown to black above, with numerous scattered tiny, light cream or yellow spots.

Lower lip speckled or barred with dark grey. Lower surfaces white to yellowish, with grey mottling on the throat and a series of blue-grey cross-bars on the chest. Head scales moderate, regular and smooth. Nostrils on the upper part of the snout directed upwards, about twice as far from the eye as the from the tip of the snout. 150-190 scales around the middle of the body. Tail very strongly compressed with a high median dorsal keel, about 1.5 times as long as head and body. Caudal scales with low keels, not in complete rings as the lower scales are larger than the upper scales. Grows to about 1 metre (total length).
Distribution: Coastal and inland waters of far northern Australia, from north-western Australia to central Qld and the western side of Cape York Peninsula.
Habit: An aquatic lizard usually seen basking on rocks or logs, or on tree trunks or branches overhanging rivers, swamps and lagoons throughout its range. It usually drops into the water when disturbed and can remain submerged for long periods. Feeds largely on fish, frogs and carrion, but will eat insects and terrestrial vertebrates when available.

Varanus mitchelli Mertens, 1958

Mitchell's Water Monitor

Description: Dark brown to blue-black or blackish above, the head with scattered cream or yellow flecks, the body with numerous yellowish flecks, spots, or small, black-centred ocelli. A poorly defined yellowish temporal stripe, while the throat and sides of the neck are bright lemon-yellow with black flecks and blotches and black barring on the lower lips. Lower edge of orbit bright yellow. Limbs black above with scattered yellow spots. Tail black with numerous small yellow or cream flecks. Ventral surfaces cream-coloured tinged with green. Head scales moderate, smooth. Nostrils on the canthus facing upwards and outwards, a little nearer the tip of the snout than the eye. 90-130 scales around the middle of the body. Tail strongly laterally compressed, except at the base, with a distinct median dorsal double keel along the last half of the tail, and 1.7 to 2.2 times longer than the head and body. Caudal scales in regular rings occasionally incomplete on the sides. Grows to about 60 cm (total length).
Distribution: Aquatic habitats throughout the northern parts of the NT and northern WA.
Habit: An aquatic species usually seen basking on rocks or trees in or beside rivers and lagoons. Feeds largely on insects, fish and frogs.

Varanus mertensi Brockman Range, NT

Varanus panoptes Storr, 1980

Description: Similar in general size and build to *Varanus gouldii*. Dark brown to reddish-brown above, usually with a dorsal pattern consisting of alternating transverse rows of small pale spots and large dark spots, this pattern extending on to the basal portion of the tail. Limbs above with numerous pale spots. A white-edged dark temporal stripe and another pale-edged dark streak along each upper lip. End of tail pale with darker bands, though the latter may disappear in older specimens from some areas. White or cream below with small dark spots in transverse rows aligned with the dark spots on the back. Scalation similar to that of *Varanus gouldii*. 175-245 scales around the middle of the body. Grows to about 1.2 metres (total length).
Distribution: Kimberley and arid western regions of WA and the NT.
Habit: A large, ground-dwelling monitor, feeding largely on insects and small, terrestrial vertebrates.
Subspecies: *panoptes* (Kimberleys and NT); *rubidus* (Pilbara and adjacent and regions).

Varanus pilbarensis Storr, 1980

Description: Pale to medium reddish-brown above, the head and neck flecked with dark reddish-brown, sometimes forming irregular cross-bands on the neck. Back with pale-centred, dark brown spots tending to be aligned transversely. Limbs spotted above. Tail irregularly and narrowly banded with dark reddish-brown and pale grey. Sometimes an obscure dark temporal streak. Whitish below, finely flecked or irregularly banded with grey. Head scales small, smooth. Nostril latero- dorsal, facing upwards and outwards, about halfway between eye and tip of snout. 110-135 scales around the middle of the body. Tail more or less round in section, without any indication of a dorsal keel, about 1.7 to 2.1 times as long as the head and body. Dorsal and lateral caudal scales with low keels. Grows to about 50 cm (total length).
Distribution: Pilbara region, WA
Habit: Rock-dwelling.

M. PETERSON

Varanus mitchelli Bullo River, NT

Varanus mertensi Mt Isa, Qld. This species spends most of its active life in or beside water.

Varanus prasinus (Schlegel, 1839)

Emerald Monitor

Description: Dull blackish or dark brown to bright emerald-green above, with individual black scales forming obscure narrow transverse cross-bands, which may be joined by narrower longitudinal series to form transverse rows of small ocellate markings. The black transverse bands are most conspicuous in the shoulder region. Palmar surfaces black, remaining ventral surfaces whitish to yellow or pale green. Head scales moderate, smooth, some supraoculars transversely enlarged, scarcely differentiated from the interoculars. Nostril more or less on the canthus and facing upward and outward, slightly nearer the tip of the snout than the eye. 75-90 scales around the middle of the body. Tail slightly compressed laterally, posteriorly without a distinct keel and about twice as long as the head and body. Caudal scales each with a low keel, in regular rings. 75 cm (total length).
Distribution: Found in the northern Torres Strait islands and northern Cape York Peninsula, Qld. Extra-limital in New Guinea.
Habit: Found in a variety of habitats, from monsoon, rain and palm forests to lagoons and mangroves.

Varanus primordius Mertens, 1942

Description: Pale to dark reddish-brown above, with numerous scattered dark brown to blackish scales which sometimes form a vague reticulum. A faint dark temporal streak. Lower surfaces and lower sides of neck white or cream. Head scales small, irregular, smooth. Nostrils lateral, slightly nearer the tip of the snout than the eye. Fewer than 70 scales around the middle of the body. Tail round in section, without any indication of a dorsal keel, about 1.4 times longer than head and body. Caudal scales strongly keeled, each keel ending in a low but distinct spine. Grows to about 30 cm (total length).

Varanus panoptes near Mt Isa, Qld M. PETERSON

Distribution: Far north of the NT.
Habit: An inhabitant of rocky places, where it is found in crevices and under slabs of stone. Presumably largely insectivorous, but little is known of its biology.

Varanus rosenbergi Mertens, 1957

Description: Similar in most respects to *Varanus gouldii*, from which it differs mainly in colour pattern: blackish above, finely dotted with yellow or white, with about fifteen, narrow, black bands on the neck and body, those on the neck curving forward. A pale-edged black temporal stripe. Tail more or less alternately banded with blackish-brown and pale yellow, either extending to the end of the tail, or the latter uniformly dark. Whitish below, reticulated with black or grey. Head scales small, smooth. Nostril lateral, nearer tip of snout than eye. 160-210 scales around the middle of the body. Tail strongly laterally compressed, except at the base, with a distinct median double dorsal keel along the distal half of the tail, 1.3 to 1.8. times as long as head and body. Caudal scales with low keels. Grows to about 1 metre (total length).
Distribution: Far south of WA and SA, with isolated populations in Vic. and coastal NSW.
Habit: Coastal heaths, humid woodlands and both wet and dry sclerophyll forests. A mostly terrestrial species which shelters in burrows (which it digs for itself), hollow logs and rock crevices.

Varanus semiremex Peters, 1869

Rusty Monitor

Description: Grey-brown above, with numerous scattered blackish flecks and spots forming a fine reticulum over the dorsal surface. White or cream below. Head scales small, irregular, smooth. Nostrils lateral, slightly nearer the tip of the snout than the eye. 85-105 scales around the middle of the body. Tail round in section at the base, but the last two-thirds

Varanus prasinus Fly River, PNG

Varanus kingorum

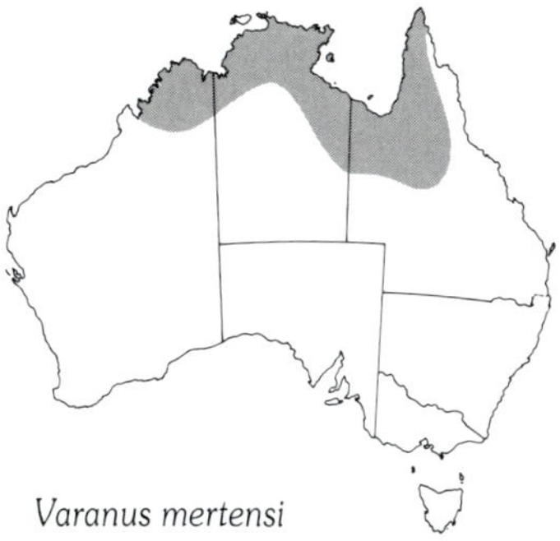

Varanus mertensi

Varanus mitchelli

Varanus semiremex Yepoon, Qld

Varanus primordius
Goodparla, NT

Varanus rosenbergi
South-western WA

Varanus spenceri (juvenile) Barkly Tableland, NT

Varanus spenceri (adult)
Headingly Station, Qld

Varanus storri Charters Towers, Qld

R. W. G. JENKINS

Varanus timorensis
Silver Plains Stn, Cape York Peninsula, Qld

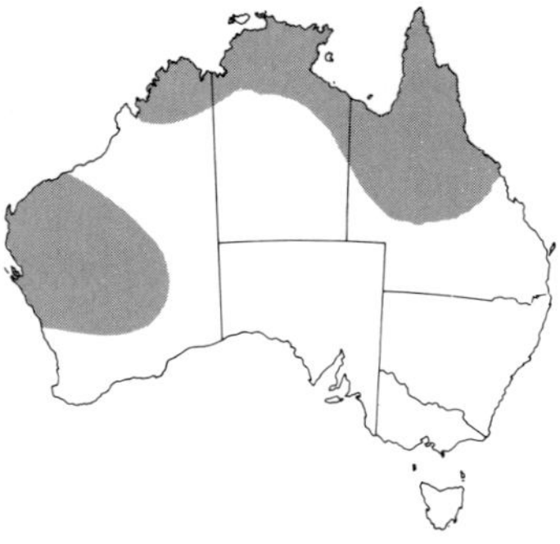

Varanus panoptes

Varanus pilbarensis

Varanus prasinus

Varanus primordius

Varanus rosenbergi

Varanus semiremex

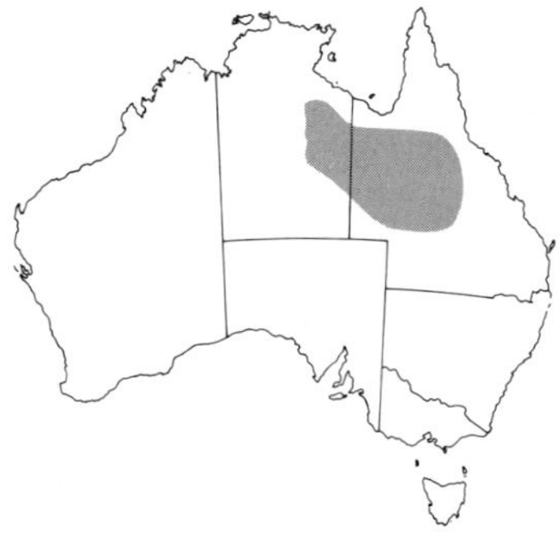

Varanus spenceri

moderately but distinctly laterally compressed though lacking a median keel; tail about 1.6 times longer than head and body. Grows to about 60 cm (total length).
Distribution: Coast and adjacent river systems of eastern and northern Qld. Worrell records it from 'northern Australia', while Mertens has recorded it from the Ord River in north-western Australia.
Habit: Commonly found living in holes in mangrove trees in tidal estuarine situations along the foreshores of small islands, where it feeds on fish, crabs, insects and lizards. It has also been recorded from vegetation bordering freshwater streams and swamps.

Varanus spenceri Lucas and Frost, 1903

Spencer's Monitor

Description: Ground colour typically light grey-brown but ranging from pale dirty-cream to darker rusty-brown, with scattered dark brown and cream spots and flecks and irregular, narrow, light yellowish or grey cross-bands on the neck, body and tail. Lips distinctly barred. Lower surfaces cream-coloured, flecked with dark grey or brown, especially on the throat. Head scales irregular, smooth. Nostrils lateral, much nearer the tip of the snout than the eye. 150-175 scales around the middle of the body. Tail more or less round in section at the base, but its last half distinctly laterally compressed with a double median dorsal keel; tail scarcely longer than head and body. Grows to about 1.2 metres (total length).
Distribution: Black-soil plains of north-western Qld, extending across the Barkly Tableland to the eastern parts of the NT.
Habit: A ground-dwelling species apparently confined to the black-soil plains, where it shelters in burrows and large soil cracks, foraging widely on the open grassy plains.

Varanus storri Mertens, 1966

Description: Similar in size, colour and pattern to *Varanus primordius,* from which it differs in having more than 70 scales around the middle of the body. However, as geographic and morphological intermediates occur between *V. primordius* and *V. storri,* the status of the latter has yet to be resolved. About 30 cm (total length).
Distribution: Vicinity of Charters Towers, Qld. Isolated populations occur as far west as the Kimberleys, WA.
Habit: An inhabitant of crevices in rocky ranges and

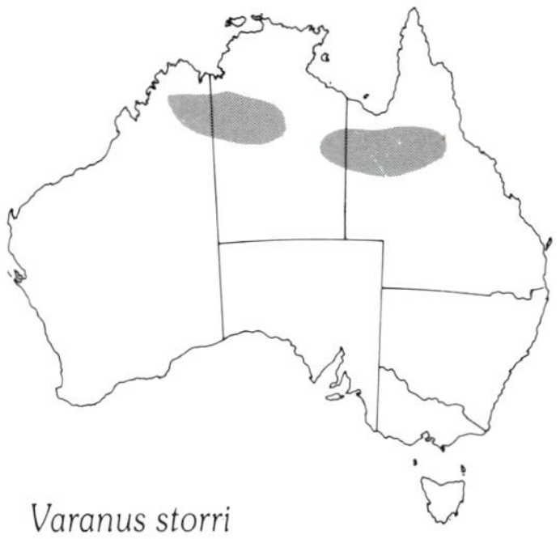

Varanus storri

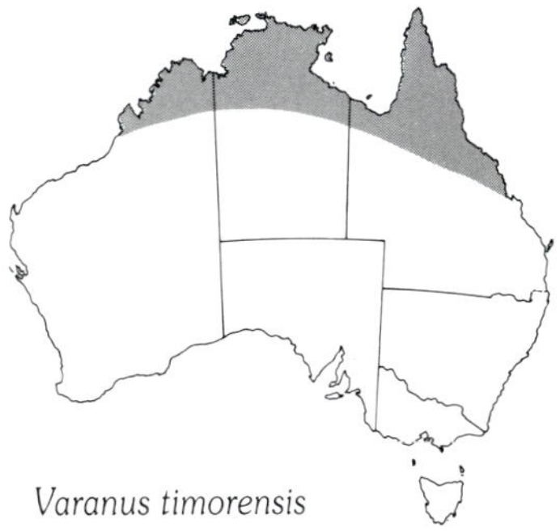

Varanus timorensis

hills. Presumably largely insectivorous.
Subspecies: *storri* (Qld); *ocreatus* (Kimberleys, WA, and adjacent parts of the NT).

Varanus timorensis Gray, 1831

Spotted Tree Monitor

Description: Highly variable, but usually grey to black above, with a series of white or yellowish flecks and spots, the latter often forming distinct, dark-centred ocelli. In some specimens the ocelli form a distinct 'leopard-skin' network, while in others they tend to form transverse rows; in still other specimens the pattern is obscure. Usually a black, temporal stripe, edged below with white. Limbs spotted with white or cream. Tail grey to black with regular or irregular rings made up of whitish scales. Head scales small, smooth, the smaller supraoculars more or less merging with the somewhat larger interoculars. Nostrils lateral, only slightly nearer the tip of the snout than the eye. 95-135 scales around the middle of the body. Tail more or less round in section, without any indication of a median dorsal keel, and about 1.5 times as long as head and body. 60 cm (total length).
Distribution: Northern Australia, from the Kimberley region of WA to the coast of Qld. Also found extra-limitally in Timor and southern New Guinea.
Habit: An arboreal lizard usually seen basking or foraging on the trunks and branches of trees, from which it sometimes descends to feed on insects and lizards on the ground. Shelters in hollow limbs, holes or under loose bark.
Subspecies: *timorensis* (Timor); *scalaris* (north-western Australia); *similis* (NT and Qld).

Varanus tristis (Schlegel, 1839)

Description: Pale grey to dark brown or black above, with numerous small dirty-cream or white elongated ocelli, each with a dark centre. The ocelli are often obscure or absent in adults, or may be reduced to a faint reticulum. The head and neck may be uniformly blackish (*V. tristis tristis*). Limbs and tail blackish with scattered small, creamy spots, sometimes forming narrow irregular rings on the tail. Lower surfaces whitish. Head scales small, smooth, the supraoculars minute and sharply differentiated from the larger interoculars. Nostrils lateral, a little nearer the tip of the snout than the eye. 105-155 scales around the middle of the body. Tail more or less round in section, without any indication of a dorsal keel and about 1.5 to 2.3 times as long as head and body. Grows to about 80 cm (total length).
Distribution: Coast to arid interior of northern Australia, extending as far south as northern NSW in the east and south- western WA in the west.
Habit: Normally an arboreal lizard with habits similar to those of *Varanus timorensis*, it is often found living in crevices etc. in rocky hills and outcrops throughout the more arid parts of its range.

Varanus tristis Brunette Downs, NT

Varanus varius (adult) northwestern NSW

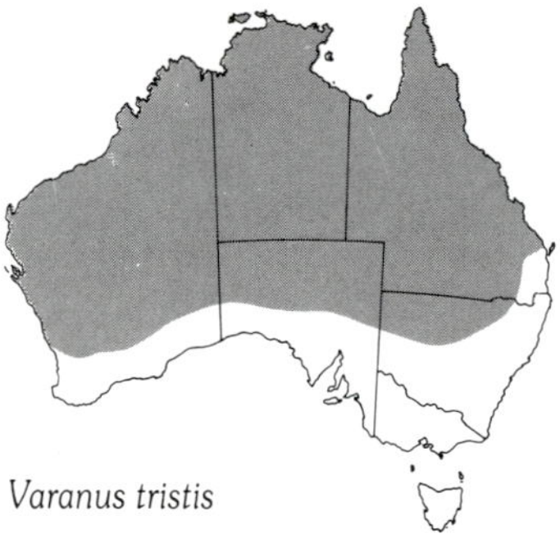

Varanus tristis

Varanus varius (hatchlings) Warrumbungle Range, NSW

Varanus varius (adult)
Sydney, NSW

Subspecies: *tristis* (western and central Australia); *orientalis* (northern and north-eastern Australia).

Varanus varius (White, ex Shaw, 1790)
Lace Monitor

Description: Typically dark blue above, with numerous scattered white, cream or yellow scales or groups of scales forming larger spots and blotches. In the young, these light spots tend to be confined to lighter areas between dark cross-bands, but all signs of body bands tend to be lost in adult specimens. However, a banded adult phase occurs in parts of northern NSW and south-eastern Qld, in which broad bands of black and yellow occur along the body and tail, and on the limbs. Usually there are black bars across the snout, chin (resulting in barred lips) and throat. Tail usually with irregular yellow cross-bands. Head scales moderate, smooth, the supraoculars subequal. Nostril lateral, about twice as far from the eye as from the tip of the snout. About 200 scales around the middle of the body. A distinctive row of enlarged scales forming a ridge on the inner edge of the basal part of the fourth toe. Tail strongly laterally compressed, except at the base, with a distinct median dorsal double keel, and about 1.8 times as long as head and body. Averages about 1.5 metres but may grow to more than 2 metres (total length).
Distribution: Coast, ranges, slopes and adjacent plains of eastern and south-eastern Australia, from south-eastern SA to Cape York Peninsula, Qld.
Habit: A large arboreal lizard which feeds on insects, reptiles and small mammals, but is a major predator of nestling birds. It also feeds on carrion, and many lace monitors may be seen feeding on the same carcase. Often forages on the ground, but will take to a tree when disturbed. Like so many arboreal lizards it spirals upwards around a tree trunk when pursued, always keeping to the opposite side of the tree from the observer. It generally lays about 6-12 eggs, often within the protection of a hole dug into a termite nest; the termites seal up the hole, and while the young can usually manage to burrow their way out of the nest there are reports of the female returning to the nest about 6-8 weeks after laying the eggs to free her hatchlings.

Varanus varius

Family Scincidae

The largest family of Australian lizards, encompassing species with an enormous variety of body form, size and habits. Although most are diurnal, many are nocturnal or crepuscular. Some larger species are omnivorous, but the majority of smaller forms are insectivorous. Reproduction ranges from egg- laying to live-bearing, and in many of the latter species well-developed chorio-allantoic placentation occurs.

Limbs are usually present, but are absent in a few species; if limbs are entirely absent then the eyes are very small and usually have moveable eyelids. In those species in which the eyelids are fused to form a snake-like spectacle over the eye, the pupil in daylight is not a narrow vertical slit and the scales on the body are imbricate. The scales on top of the head are large, regular and usually symmetrical and shield-like. The tongue is short, relatively broad and fleshy.

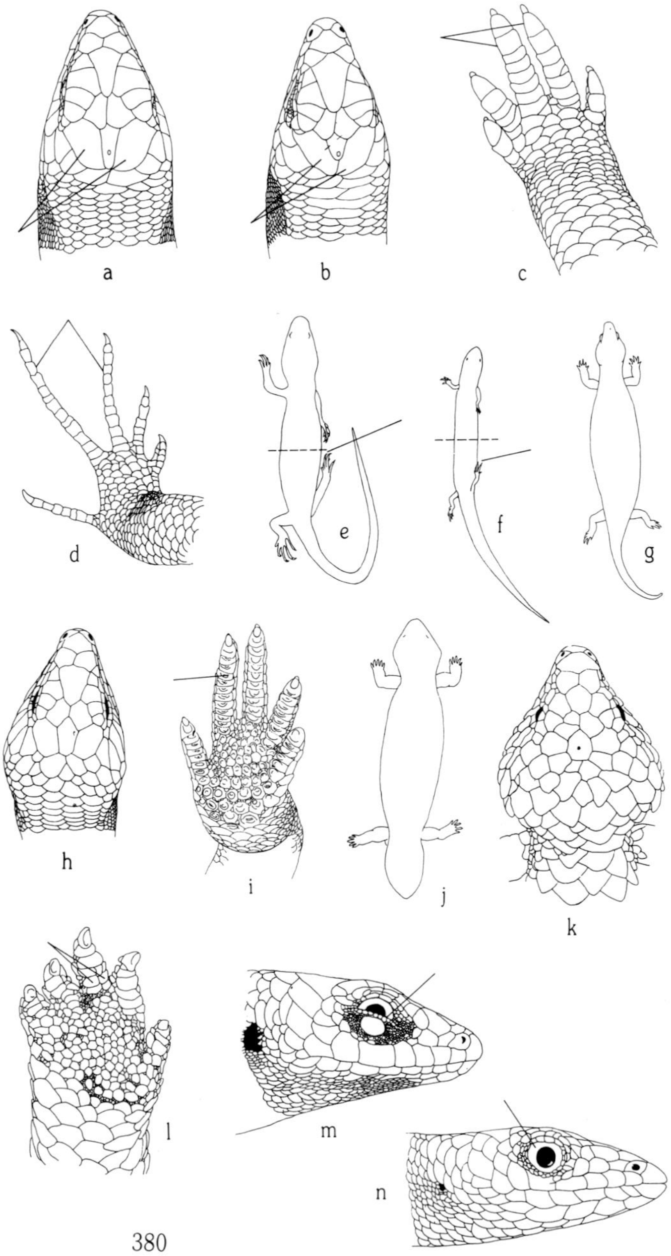

Key

TO THE GENERA OF AUSTRALIAN SCINCID LIZARDS

1 Parietal shields (if unfragmented) nowhere in contact, being separated behind by the interparietal (a)................**2**

Parietal shields in contact behind the interparietal (b)..... **6**

2 Third and fourth toes subequal or the third slightly longer than the fourth (c)...**3**

Fourth toe markedly longer than the third (d)..... ***Egernia***

3 Tail long, from nearly as long as to longer than snout-vent length...**4**

Tail short, at most about 60% of snout-vent length..........**5**

4 Head broad, conspicuously broader than neck; more than 29 mid-body scale rows; adpressed hind limb reaches at least to middle of axilla-groin or beyond (e)...................... .... ***Hemisphaeriodon***

Head narrow, scarcely wider than neck; fewer than 29 mid-body scale rows; adpressed hind limb falls far short of middle of axilla-groin (f).................... ***Cyclodomorphus***

5 Tail moderate to long, tapering (g); dorsal scales moderate, smooth; head shields smooth, entire, symmetrical (h); subdigital lamellae undivided (i)........................... ***Tiliqua***

Tail short, depressed, blunt-ended (j); dorsal scales grossly enlarged, strongly rugose; head shields broken up, only vaguely symmetrical (k); subdigital lamellae divided, at least basally (l).................................... ***Trachydosaurus***

6 Lower eyelid with a transparent disc and either moveable (m) or fused (n) to form a permanent spectacle............. **7**

Lower eyelid moveable, scaly (o) or with an opaque disc... ....**22**

7 Lower eyelid moveable, or partly (open slit along upper edge) or totally fused to form a permanent spectacle; if the lower eyelid is fused the prefrontals are small and widely separated (p) or absent (q)..................................**8**

Lower eyelid fused to form a permanent spectacle; prefrontals large (r), in contact or narrowly separated....... **18**

8 Supranasals present, or nasals divided (s)......................**9**

Supranasals absent and nasals undivided (t)................**10**

9 Frontoparietals paired (u) or single (v); fewer than 30 lamellae under fourth toe; anterior auricular lobules present(w)..***Pseudemoia***

Frontoparietals united to form a single shield (v); more than 30 lamellae under fourth toe; anterior auricular lobules absent (x)...***Emoia***

10 Limbs well developed, meeting or overlapping when adpressed (y), or else separated by one or two scale lengths; ear opening prominent.....................................**11**

Limbs short, separated by at least several scale lengths when adpressed (z); ear-opening small to minute, or hidden **15**

11 Fingers four; ear-opening with one or more obvious lobules (w)..**12**

Fingers five, or if four, ear-opening without lobules.......**13**

12 Ten or more scales along the top of the fourth toe (aa)...... ....***Carlia***

Fewer than ten scales along the top of the fourth toe (bb).. ....***Lygisaurus***

13 Nasals usually widely separated (cc).............................**14**

Nasals usually narrowly separated (dd).......***Pseudemoia***

14 Frontoparietals fused (v)..........................***Lampropholis***

Frontoparietals paired (u)......................... ***Saproscincus***

15 Nasals small to moderate, usually separated (cc)..........**16**

Nasals enlarged, usually in contact medially (ee)...***Lerista***

16 Forelimbs with 2-5 fingers, but if 4 fingers present then hindlimb with at most 4 toes..**17**

Forelimbs with 4 fingers and hindlimbs with 5 toes............ ....***Eroticoscincus***

17 2-5 fingers, 2-5 toes; ear-opening hidden in specimens with 5 fingers and 5 toes...***Hemiergis***

5 fingers and 5 toes; ear-opening minute, punctiform, but distinct..***Nannoscincus***

18 Fingers and toes five..**19**

Fingers four, toes five... ***Menetia***

19 Frontoparietal single (v) or paired (u), but always distinct from the interparietal (ff); ear-opening absent, or smaller than eye if present..**20**

Frontoparietal and interparietal fused to form a single shield (gg); ear-opening approximately same size as eye. **22**

20 Frontoparietals paired (u)...................... ***Proablepharus***

Frontoparietals fused to form a single shield (v)................ .... ***Notoscincus***

21 Upper eyelid with three or four scales much larger than granules surrounding remainder of eye (hh); frontal and prefrontals subequal (ii)......................***Cryptoblepharus***

Eye more or less surrounded by a circle of uniformly small granules (jj); frontal much larger than prefrontals (kk)....... .... ***Morethia***

22 Supranasals absent and nasals undivided (t).................**23**

Supranasals present (s), although sometimes partially fused with nasals.. ***Eugongylus***

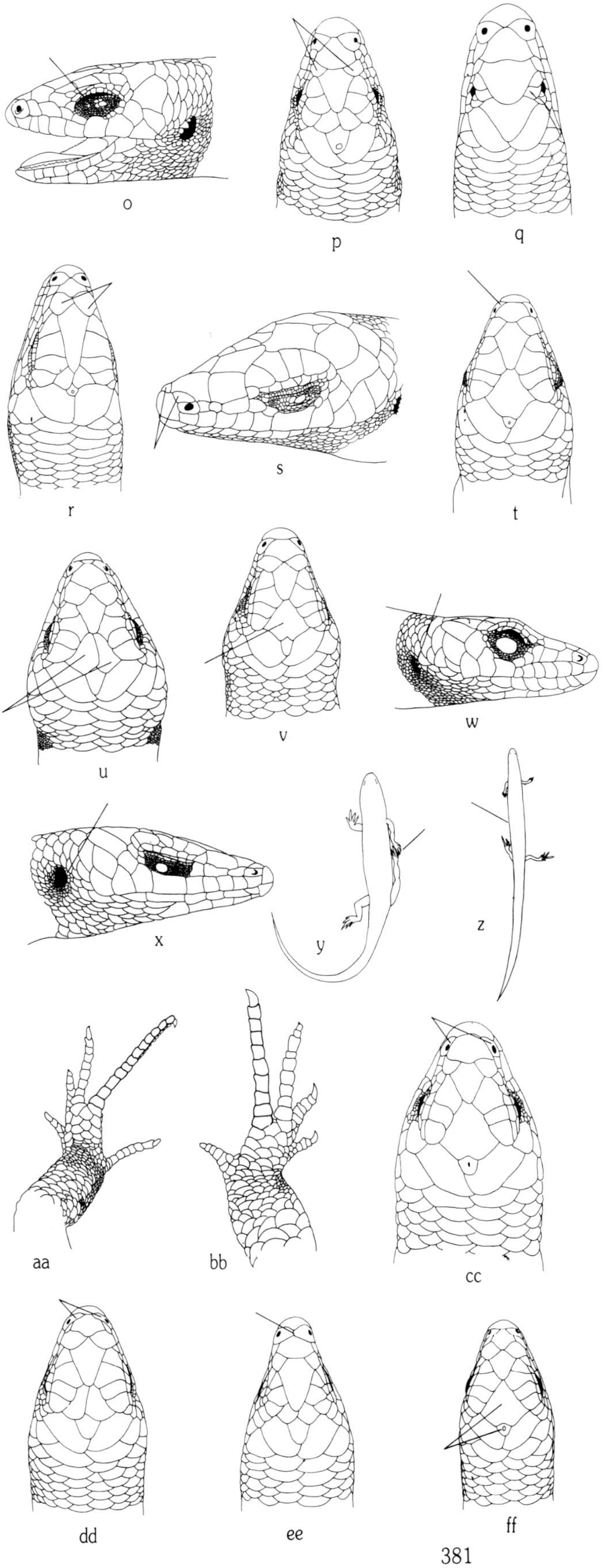

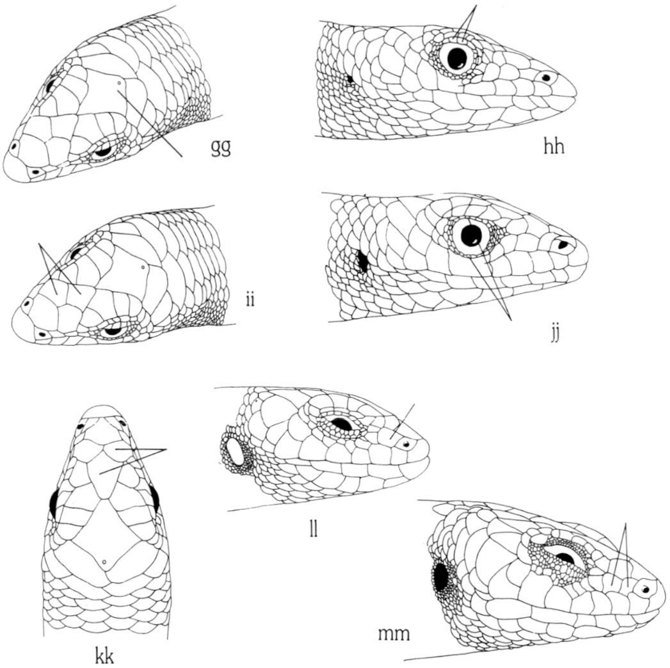

gg hh ii jj kk ll mm

23 Dorsal scales moderate, smooth or with a faint median keel..**24**

Dorsal scales very small, each with a sharp keel...............
....***Gnypetoscincus***

24 Fingers and toes five..**25**

Fingers and toes fewer than five....................................**29**

25 Ear lobules absent (x); pattern usually transversely aligned or of irregularly scattered spots and variegations..
....**26**

Conspicuous ear lobules present (w); pattern usually of dorsal and/or lateral longitudinal stripes.......... ***Ctenotus***

26 Dorsal and upper caudal scales smooth........................**27**

Scales on the rump and the base of the tail, and sometimes on the remaining dorsals, with distinct median 'humps' or low keels forming a series of continuous longitudinal ridges............ ....***Eremiascincus***

27 Hindlimb short to moderate, its length contained at least 2.5 times in the snout-vent length...................................**28**

Hindlimb long, its length contained less than 2.5 times in the snout-vent length....................................***Eulamprus***

28 Fourth toe lamellae fewer than 16; a single loreal scale(ll)..
....***Calyptotis***

Fourth toe lamellae usually more than 16 but, if fewer, then 2 or more loreal scales are present (mm).................
....***Glaphyromorphus***

29 If limbs tridactyle, scales in 23 or more rows.................**30**

Limbs tridactyle; mid-body scales in fewer than 23 rows....
....***Saiphos***

30 With or without limbs; limbed forms with only 1 or 2 digits on each limb; limbless forms without prefrontals (q), or with prefrontals at most moderately developed and widely separated (p); 5 or 6 supralabials.............................**31**

With or without limbs; limbed forms with 3 digits on each limb; limbless forms with large prefrontals, contacting (r) or only narrowly separated ; 6 supralabials ....
....***Coeranoscincus***

31 Either 6 supralabials and 2-4 supraoculars or 5 supralabials and 2 supraoculars...............................***Anomalopus***

5 supralabials and 3 supraoculars............***Ophioscincus***

Genus ***Anomalopus*** Duméril and Duméril, 1851

A genus of small to medium-sized, smooth-scaled, burrowing skinks, with greatly reduced or absent limbs, the limbs when present with fewer than three digits. The parietal shields are in contact behind the interparietal; the lower eyelid is movable and scaly; the nasals are undivided and there are no supranasals; ectopterygoid process present. Usually the scales of the snout — the rostral, mental, nasals and first labials — are covered by a thickened, milky dermis. Oviparous.

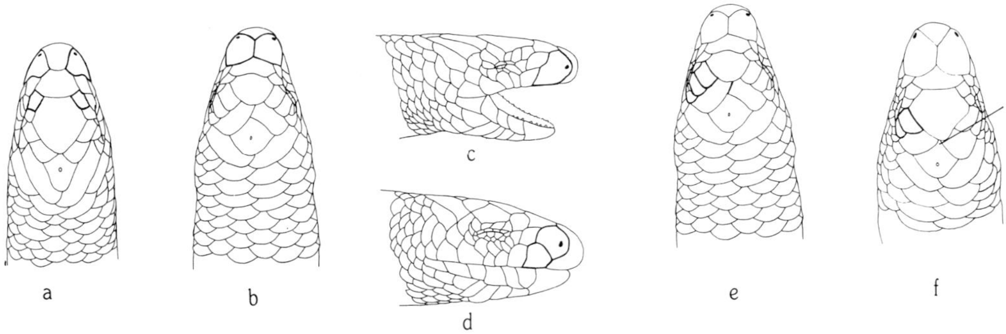

a b c d e f

Key

TO THE SPECIES OF ANOMALOPUS

1 Limbs absent **2**
Limbs present **5**

2 Nasals usually separated and prefrontals present (a) **3**
Nasals in contact and prefrontals absent (b) **4**
Nasal fused to first supralabial, thus extending to lip (c) .... ***pluto***
Nasal separated from lip by first supralabial (d) .... ***swansoni***

4 Usually three supraoculars and frontoparietals in contact (e); fewer than 105 paravertebral scale rows; six supralabials .... ***brevicollis***
Two supraoculars and frontoparietals usually separated (f); more than 105 paravertebral scale rows; five supralabials .... ***gowi***

5 Front limbs each with three toes **6**
Front limbs each with two toes .... ***leuckartii***

6 Hind limbs styliform, each with a single toe .... ***verreauxii***
Hind limbs each with two toes .... ***mackayi***

Anomalopus brevicollis Greer and Cogger, 1985

Description: Pale brown above, darker on the head and tail; scales other than those on the belly with dark brown spots or flecks which tend to be longitudinally aligned to give the impression of faint longitudinal striations along the length of the body. Chin and throat spotted with dark brown. Whitish or flesh-coloured below. Snout more or less rounded. Nasals in contact. Prefrontals absent. A single loreal, deeper than long. Postmental usually in contact with two infralabials (occasionally one only) on each side. Ear-opening hidden, its position indicated by a depression. 18-20 mid-body scale rows. Limbs entirely absent. Preanals moderately enlarged. 80 mm (snout-vent).
Distribution: Central-eastern Qld.
Habit: A burrowing species found in a wide range of habitats from dry sclerophyll to rainforest.

Anomalopus brevicollis near Rockhampton, Qld 80mm

Anomalopus gowi Woodstock, Qld

Anomalopus gowi Greer and Cogger, 1985

Description: Uniform rich brown above, sometimes with a darker brown region across the top of the head. The brown pigment tends to be concentrated in the centre of each scale, resulting in paler margins to the scales. Ventral surfaces pale brown or cream, but all scales pigmented. Snout somewhat bulbous. Nasal broadly in contact. Prefrontals small, widely separated. A single loreal on each side. Two supraoculars (a small anterior supraciliary and a small supraocular could each be interpreted as a preocular). Postmental in contact with one or two infralabials on each side. Ear hidden, its position indicated by a depression. 18-22 mid-body scale rows. Limbs entirely absent. Preanals moderately enlarged. 50 mm (snout- vent).
Distribution: Drier parts of central-eastern to north-eastern Qld.
Habit: A burrowing species found in woodland and vine scrub, where it is usually found sheltering beneath rocks and fallen timber.

Anomalopus leuckartii Warrumbungle Range, NSW

Anomalopus leuckartii (Weinland, 1862)

Description: More or less uniform grey-brown, purplish-brown or brown above, the individual scales pale-edged; white or flesh-coloured below. Rarely a faint, paler bar across the nape. Snout moderate, more or less rounded. Nasals separated. Prefrontals small, widely separated. Two loreals on each side. Three or four supraoculars. Postmental in contact with two infralabials on each side. Ear hidden, its position indicated by a depression. 20-22 mid-body scale rows. Limbs present, the forelimb didactyle, the hind-

Anomalopus mackayi
Wallangarra, NSW

limb with a single short style. Preanals moderately enlarged. 100 mm (snout-vent).
Distribution: South-eastern Qld and western slopes and ranges of northern NSW.
Habit: A burrowing lizard found under rocks and fallen timber in dry sclerophyll forest and eucalypt and *Callitris* woodland.

Anomalopus mackayi Greer and Cogger, 1985

Description: Similar in nearly all respects to *Anomalopus leuckartii*, from which it differs in possessing a distinctly didactyle hindlimb. Dark brown above, the individual scales each with a central dark spot, more conspicuous in northern populations. Yellow-green below, heavily flecked with darker posteriorly. 100 mm (snout-vent).
Distribution: Western slopes of north-western NSW and south-eastern Qld.
Habit: Similar to *Anomalopus leuckartii*.

Anomalopus pluto Ingram, 1977

Description: Brown, the tail darker. Nasals widely separated. Prefrontals small and widely separated (regarded as the first supraciliaries in the original description). A single loreal. Two supraoculars. Postmental in contact with one infralabial on each side. Ear hidden, its position indicated by a depression. 20 mid-body scale rows. Limbs entirely absent. Two enlarged preanals. This species is readily distinguished from other limbless members of the genus *Anomalopus* by the fusion of the nasal with the first supralabial. 70 mm (snout-vent).
Distribution: Known only from the north-east tip of Cape York Peninsula, Qld.
Habit: A burrowing species living in the soil beneath leaf-and other ground litter in monsoon forest and heath/woodland.

Anomalopus swansoni Greer and Cogger, 1985

Description: Brown or pinkish-brown above, each scale with a darker brown centre. Ventral surface whitish or flesh- coloured. Distal portion of tail darker, often blackish near the tip. Snout more or less rounded. Nasals separated or narrowly in contact.Prefrontals small and widely separated. Two loreals on each side. Postmental in contact with two infralabials on

Anomalopus brevicollis

Anomalopus gowi

Anomalopus leuckartii

Anomalopus mackayi

Anomalopus pluto

Anomalopus swansoni

Anomalopus verreauxii

Anomalopus pluto near Heathlands, Cape York Peninsula, Qld

Anomalopus verreauxii Bulburin, Qld

Anomalopus swansoni Newcastle, NSW

each side. Ear-opening hidden, its position indicated by a depression. 22-26 mid-body scale rows. Limbs entirely absent. Preanals moderately enlarged. 100 mm (snout- vent).
Distribution: Central coast and hinterland of NSW, from the Hawkesbury River to the Hunter River valley.
Habit: A burrowing lizard usually found under stones or fallen timber on sandy soils in coastal dunes and heathlands and in dry sclerophyll forest on sandstone hills and ridges.

Anomalopus verreauxi (Duméril and Duméril, 1851)

Description: Similar in most respects to *Anomalopus leuckartii*, from which it differs in its larger average size and in possessing a pale cream to yellow collar (sometimes obscure in old adults), and in having three digits on each forelimb. 150 mm (snout-vent).
Distribution: Coast and ranges of north-eastern NSW and south-eastern Qld.
Habit: Similar to *Anomalopus leuckartii*, except that it occurs in more humid habitats including wet sclerophyll forest, rainforest margins, vine thickets and coastal scrubs.

Genus *Calyptotis* De Vis, 1886

A group of small, fossorial lizards characterised by: pentadactyle limbs; smooth scales; anterior ear lobules absent; supranasals absent; nasals undivided; lower eyelid movable, scaly; parietal scales in contact behind the interparietal; fourth toe scarcely longer than third; lower surfaces of rump and tail usually flushed with bright red or pink. Oviparous.

Key

TO THE SPECIES OF CALYPTOTIS

1	External ear-opening present	**2**
	External ear-opening absent	**3**
2	Prefrontals present (a); two or more rows of supradigital scales (b)	***ruficauda***
	Prefrontals absent (c); a single row of supradigital scales (d)	***temporalis***
3	Prefrontals present (a)	**4**
	Prefrontals usually absent (c)	***scutirostrum***
4	Ear a scaly, conical depression	***lepidorostrum***
	Ear a scaly, superficial disc	***thorntonensis***

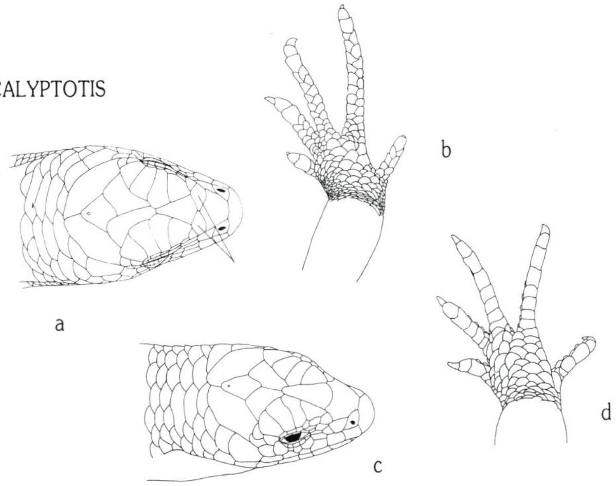

M. PETERSON

Calyptotis lepidorostrum Cooloola National Park, Qld

Calyptotis lepidorostrum Greer, 1983

Description: Pale to dark brown above, with scattered darker brown spots, flecks and blotches which tend to form longitudinal stripes through the centres of the four vertebral scale rows; a broad, dark dorsolateral stripe extends from the snout, through the eye and along the body to the side of the tail. Limbs and flanks flecked and spotted with dark brown. Lips and cheeks spotted or barred with dark brown. Ventral surfaces of body white to bright yellow, but often with the anal region, thighs and base of the tail flushed with bright pink. Nasals separated. Prefrontals usually present and widely separated. Four supraoculars. Six supralabials. Postmental contacting only the first infralabial on each side. Ear-opening hidden, but marked by a scaly, conical depression. Scales smooth, in 20-24 rows at mid-body. Limbs short, separated when adpressed, the hindlimb 20-30% of snout-vent length. 8-14 rounded or ridged lamellae under the fourth toe, which is scarcely longer than the third toe. 50 mm (snout- vent).
Distribution: Coast and ranges of central and south-eastern Qld.
Habit: A burrowing species found under surface litter and other debris in rainforest and adjacent wet sclerophyll forests.

Calyptotis ruficauda Greer, 1983

Description: Brown above, usually with scattered darker brown to black spots, flecks and streaks which tend to form four longitudinal stripes on the back, each running through the centres of the four vertebral scale rows. A distinct to obscure blackish dorso-lateral stripe from the snout, through the eye and along the body to the tail, most distinct anteriorly. Flanks paler grey-brown, liberally spotted with a mixture of dark brown and pale whitish spots. Lips with dark brown bars or variegations. Ventrally cream to pale yellow, the base of the tail, preanal region and thighs usually flushed with bright pink or red. Nasals separated. Prefrontals present and narrowly separated. Four supraoculars. 6-8, usually 7, supralabials. Postmental contacting only the first infralabial on each side. Ear-opening large, the tympanum superficial and vertically elliptic. Scales smooth, in 20-24 rows at mid-body. Limbs short, separated when adpressed, the hindlimb about 25-35% of snout-vent length. 10-15 rounded or ridged lamellae under the fourth toe, which is scarcely longer than the third toe. 50 mm (snout-vent).

Calyptotis ruficauda Brinerville, NSW

Calyptotis scutirostrum Mt Nebo, Qld

M. PETERSON

Calyptotis lepidorostrum

Calyptotis ruficauda

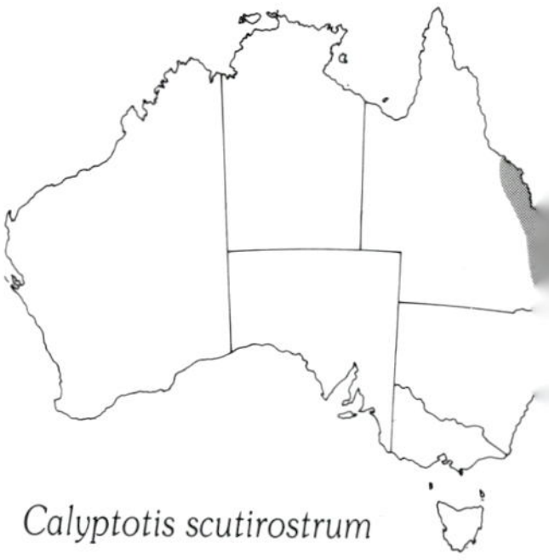

Calyptotis scutirostrum

Calyptotis temporalis

Calyptotis thorntonensis

Distribution: Coast and lower altitudes of the adjacent ranges from the lower north coast of NSW south almost to the Hunter River.
Habit: A burrowing species found under logs, stones and other surface litter in moist situations in wet and dry sclerophyll forests and adjacent rainforest. Oviparous.

Calyptotis scutirostrum (Peters, 1873)

Description: Pale brown to rich brown above, uniform, or the individual scales with a blackish spot or median streak; sometimes these markings are more conspicuous on the two mid- dorsal scale rows, forming two narrow dark lines along the back and tail. Usually a narrow, dark brown dorso-lateral stripe

from the nostril through the eye to the forepart of the body, sometimes extending to the tail. Flanks with numerous scattered dark and pale flecks, becoming paler below where the colour merges with the white or cream ventral surface. Lips and cheeks spotted or barred with dark brown. Throat with scattered brown dots. Tail sometimes heavily spotted with brown below, often with a rich pink or reddish flush over its entire ventral surface. Nasals separated. Prefrontals absent, although a large anterior supraciliary has variously been regarded as a small prefrontal or small first supraocular. Four supraoculars. Six supralabials. Postmental contacting a single infralabial on each side. Ear-opening hidden, its position indicated by a depression. Scales smooth in 20-24 rows at mid-body. Limbs short, separated when adpressed, the hindlimb about 20-30% of snout-vent length. 9-12 smooth, undivided lamellae under the fourth toe, the latter scarcely longer than the third. 45 mm (snout-vent)
Distribution: Coast and ranges of central and south-eastern Qld and adjacent border regions of NSW.
Habit: A burrowing species found in moist soil under logs and in leaf-litter.

Calyptotis temporalis Greer, 1983

Description: Brown above, with scattered darker brown flecks, spots and streaks which tend to form narrow longitudinal stripes through the centres of the four vertebral scale rows. A dark brown dorso-lateral stripe from snout, through eye and along the body to the side of the tail, but most distinct anteriorly. Flanks paler brown, flecked and spotted with dark brown. Lips more or less barred with dark brown. Ventral surfaces white to yellow, often with a bright pink flush to the preanal region, thighs and base of the tail. Nasals separated. Prefrontals absent. Four supraoculars. Six supralabials. Postmental contacting only the first infralabial on each side. Ear-opening large, the tympanum circular. Scales smooth, in 20-22 rows at mid-body. Limbs short, separated when adpressed, the hindlimb about 20-30% of snout-vent length. 8-10 rounded or ridged lamellae under the fourth toe, which is scarcely longer than the third toe. 35 mm (snout-vent).
Distribution: Central-eastern Qld.
Habit: A burrowing species found under logs, stones and surface litter in rainforest and adjacent wet sclerophyll forests of the coast and ranges.

Calyptotis thorntonensis Greer, 1983

Description: Medium to dark brown above, with numerous scattered darker flecks and spots making a generally mottled pattern. A blackish dorso-lateral stripe from snout, through eye and along the body to the tail, but most conspicuous anteriorly. Labial sutures edged with dark brown. Flanks pale brown with darker mottling. Ventral surfaces whitish, with brown flecking on the throat and tail. Nasals separated. Prefrontals present and moderately separated. Four supraoculars. Six supralabials. Postmental contacting only the first infralabial on each side. Ear-opening absent, represented by a circular scaly depression. Scales smooth, in 24 rows at mid-body. Limbs short, separated when adpressed, the hindlimb about 25-30% of snout-vent length. 8-10 rounded or ridged lamellae under the fourth toe, which is scarcely longer than the third toe. 35 mm (snout-vent).
Distribution: Known only from Thornton Peak, north-eastern Qld.
Habit: A burrowing species found beneath rocks and logs in rainforest and along rainforest margins.

Genus *Carlia* Gray, 1845

A group of small, terrestrial, diurnal lizards with well-developed limbs. The forelimbs are tetradactyle, the hindlimbs pentadactyle. The parietal shields are in contact behind the interparietal. The lower eyelid possesses a conspicuous, transparent disc and is movable. All species are oviparous, with two eggs per clutch. More than one clutch of eggs may be laid in a season. All species are active, basking, diurnal skinks. Most species tend to be found in litter about the bases of trees, logs, stones, etc.

Key

TO THE AUSTRALIAN SPECIES OF CARLIA

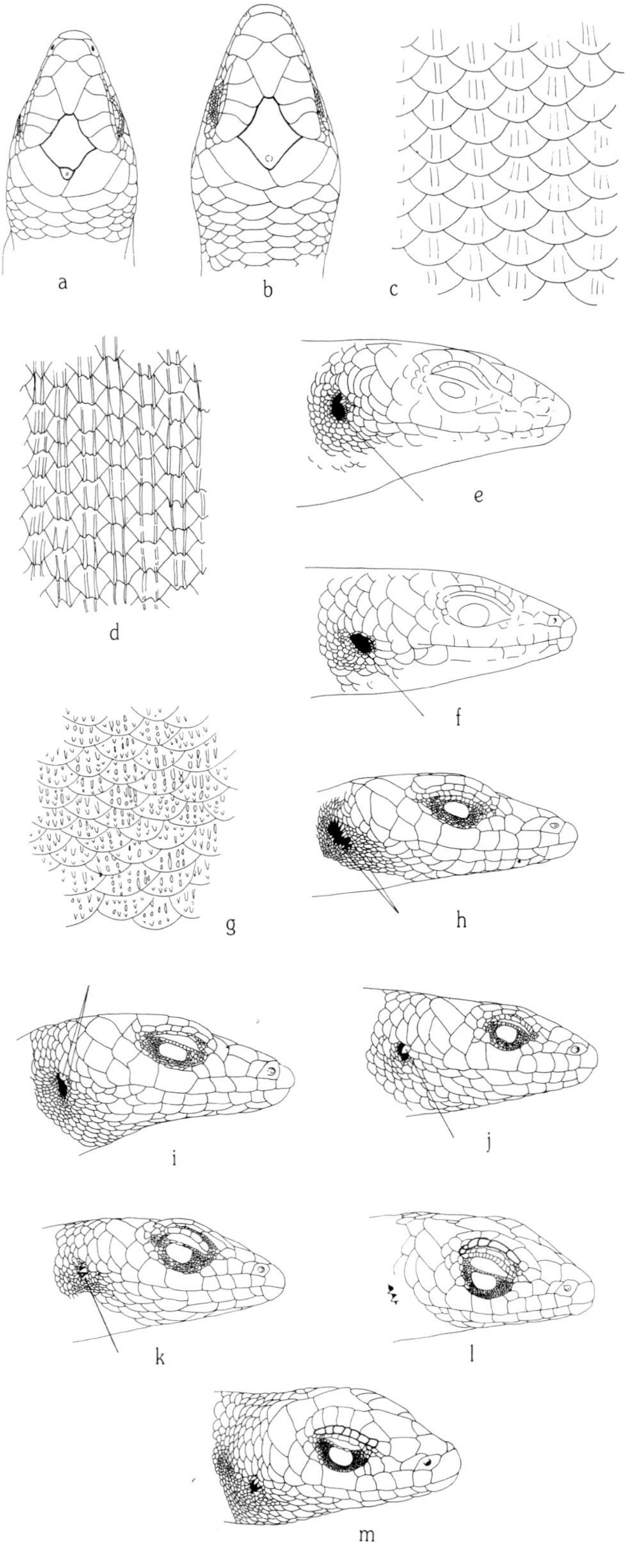

1 Interparietal distinct (a).. **3**
Interparietal fused to frontoparietals (b)........................... **2**

2 Neck, throat, chin and lower sides of head pink in life........ .... ***rubrigularis***
Neck, throat, chin and lower sides of head blue in life........ .... ***rhomboidalis***

3 Dorsal scales 4-sided, each with a smoothly curved posterior edge (c); smooth, striated or feebly keeled.............. **4**
Dorsal scales 6-sided, each usually with an angular posterior or free edge and moderately to strongly keeled (d).... .... **10**

4 Ear-opening round or vertically elliptic (e); pale mid- lateral stripe, if present, not split or displaced by ear-opening... .... **5**
Ear-opening horizontally elliptic (f); pale midlateral stripe, split and displaced by the ear-opening................. ***munda***

5 Dorsal scales each with longitudinal rows of low, rounded tubercles (g).. **6**
Dorsal scales smooth or keeled, but never with rows of raised tubercles **8**

6 Scales in more than 35 rows at mid-body......................... **7**
Scales in fewer than 35 rows at mid-body............. ***rimula***

7 Ear lobules pointed (h)....................................... ***scirtetis***
Ear lobules rounded (i).. ***coensis***

8 One or more acute, pointed, ear lobules (h).................... **9**
A small, rounded, anterior ear lobule (j)...... ***tetradactyla***

9 Males with black throat and broad black upper lateral stripe from eye to hindlimb; females with a conspicuous pale dorso-lateral stripe..................................... ***rostralis***
Males without black throat and with black upper lateral stripe from eye only to forelimb; females without a pale dorso-lateral stripe.. ***longipes***

10 Dorsal scales mostly bicarinate, or when occasionally tricarinate, the ear-opening is surrounded by acute, pointed lobules (k).. **11**
Dorsal scales mostly tricarinate; ear-opening not completely surrounded by long, acute pointed lobules......... **16**

11 Throat whitish, gular scales without black margins....... **12**
Scales of throat edged with black.................. ***johnstonei***

12 Ear-opening surrounded by acute, pointed lobules (k).. **13**
Ear opening usually with no more than one or two lobules anteriorly (j).. **14**

13 28-33 mid-body scale rows; usually six supraciliaries (l)...... .... ***storri***
34-40 mid-body scale rows; usually seven supraciliaries..... .... ***mundivensis***

14 Ear-opening round or vertically elliptic (e)..................... **15**
Ear-opening horizontally elliptic (f).......................... ***amax***

15 Males with two reddish lateral stripes; females with a pale vertebral stripe; usually 28 or more lamellae under the fourth toe.. ***dogare***

Males with a single lateral reddish stripe or band; females lacking a pale vertebral stripe; usually fewer than 29 lamellae under the fourth toe.................................. ***vivax***

16 Palpebral disc occupying at most scarcely more than half of lower eyelid (n)..**17**

Palpebral disc occupying much more than half of lower eyelid (o)..**18**

17 Supraciliaries usually seven (m); ear-opening as large as palpebral disc, vertically elliptic....................... ***schmeltzii***

Supraciliaries usually five; ear-opening usually smaller than palpebral disc, horizontally elliptic................ ***gracilis***

18 Ear-opening circular or vertically elliptic (e); supraciliaries usually fewer than seven.. **19**

Ear-opening horizontally elliptic (f); supraciliaries usually seven.. **20**

19 Prefrontals usually in contact (p) or narrowly separated (q); dorsal scales triscuspid, the keels not well-aligned with those of the following scales so that the keels do not form continuous lines along the body (r); usually six supraciliaries; NT and northern WA............. ***triacantha***

Prefrontals narrowly (q) to widely (s) separated; dorsal scales tricarinate, the keels well aligned to form more or less continuous lines along the body (t); usually five supraciliaries; eastern Qld.............................. ***pectoralis***

20 Males with 5-7 black longitudinal stripes along the back; females with a conspicuous, black-edged, white stripe from supralabials to groin; north-eastern Australia............ .... ***jarnoldae***

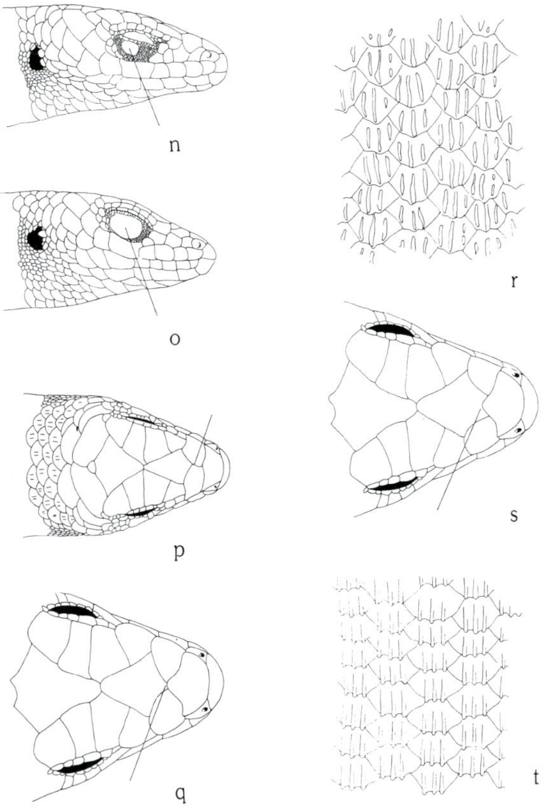

Back dotted with black, never with longitudinal stripes; white lateral stripe, if present, not extending back beyond forelimb; north-western Australia...................... ***rufilatus***

Carlia amax McArthur River, NT

Carlia amax Storr, 1974

Description: More or less uniform brown above, except for a narrow white edge to the ear-opening and a pale greenish-white line under the eye. Whitish below. Head in breeding males bright coppery green, and the flanks may be flushed with red. Prefrontals in contact or narrowly separated. Supraciliaries 5-8, usually 6. Ear-opening horizontally elliptic, much smaller than the palpebral disc and usually with only one very small anterior lobule. Dorsal scales 6-sided, each usually with an angular free edge, and mostly bicarinate with two strong mucronate keels which are not well aligned with keels of following scales. Scales in 26-35 rows at mid-body. 19-28 lamellae under the fourth toe. 35 mm (snout-vent).
Distribution: Far north-western Qld through the northern NT to northern WA.
Habit: Usually found foraging in leaf-litter around the bases of trees, logs and rocks, usually associated with stony hills and ranges.

Carlia coensis (Mitchell, 1953)

Description: Dark brown to black above, the head bronzy-brown and with a broad continuous or discontinuous pale bluish vertebral stripe. A dorso-lateral series of pale blue rectangular spots, commencing as a continuous streak,from the eye to the base of the tail, and a mid-lateral series of similar spots from the ear to the groin. Whitish below. Pattern may be obscure in older specimens. Prefrontals usually separate, sometimes in contact. Supraciliaries usually seven. Ear-opening circular, about equal to palpebral disc, and about four tubercular lobules anteriorly. Dorsal scales 4-sided, each with 3-5 longitudinal rows of low, rounded tubercles and a curved free edge. Scales in 35-45 rows at mid-body. 32-36 lamellae under the fourth toe. 50 mm (snout-vent).
Distribution: Ranges east of Coen, Cape York Peninsula, Qld.
Habit: A rock-dwelling species found on boulder slopes, rock faces and creek beds, especially where these are associated with rainforest and thick monsoonal scrub.

Carlia dogare Covacevich and Ingram, 1975

Description: Brown above, darker on the head and usually with some indication of a narrow white streak from below the eye to the ear. Lips speckled with brown. Ear blackish. Dorsum often with scattered dark brown flecks and black-edged pale spots. Breeding males with reddish-orange upper and lower lateral stripes from about the level of the forelimb to the groin. Whitish below. Adult females often with distinct pale vertebral, dorso-lateral and mid-lateral stripes. Prefrontals usually separated. Supraciliaries usually five. Ear-opening vertically elliptic, smaller than palpebral disc, and with two small rounded lobules anteriorly. Dorsal scales moderately bicarinate, 6-sided, each with an angular free edge. Scales in 28-34 rows at mid-body. 27-35 lamellae under the fourth toe. 45 mm (snout-vent).
Distribution: Lizard Island and adjacent mainland of Cape York Peninsula, Qld.
Habit: Heath and woodland, especially in the presence of dense grass and low shrub cover.

Carlia gracilis Storr, 1974

Description: Coppery-brown to grey-brown above, dark anteriorly; often a narrow white streak over the ear and sometimes extending forward to below the eye, and occasionally a pale mid-lateral stripe. Whitish below. Breeding males with coppery forelimbs and anterior flanks. Prefrontals usually separated, Supraciliaries usually five, occasionally six or seven. Ear-opening usually horizontally elliptic, smaller than palpebral disc, and with 0-3 (usually 1) small anterior lobules. Dorsal scales 6-sided, each with an angular free edge and mostly tricarinate, the three well-developed keels arranged in a median cluster. Scales in 24-32 rows at mid- body. 19-27 lamellae under the fourth toe. 35 mm (snout-vent).
Distribution: Northern WA and northern NT.
Habit: '...well-watered habitats, such as vine thickets and monsoon forests along creek and river margins...' (Wilson and Knowles), where it forages among grasses and ground litter.

Carlia coensis Pascoe River, Qld

Carlia dogare
Lizard Island, Qld

Carlia jarnoldae (male above, and female) Townsville district, Qld

Carlia jarnoldae Covacevich and Ingram, 1975

Description: A species with striking sexual dimorphism. Breeding males brown above, with four to six narrow black stripes (sometimes broken) from nape to base of tail; a broad, black upper lateral zone commencing as a loreal streak and continuing behind the eye to the base of the tail; on the body this zone contains scattered small blue spots and is bordered below by a broad, reddish-orange mid-lateral stripe; lips and throat pale green with a series of black striations on the side of the throat; limbs reddish-brown speckled with dark brown; cream below. Females dark brown above, pale coppery-brown on the head; dorsum uniform, with scattered black and white flecks tending to form longitudinal series; a brilliant white mid-lateral stripe from the labials to the groin, bordered above by a broad, black stripe and below by an indefinite black stripe; in some specimens an indefinite, narrow, pale, dorso-lateral stripe; limbs above same colour as dorsum; whitish below. Prefrontals usually separated. Supraciliaries usually seven. Ear-opening horizontally elliptic, smaller than palpebral disc, and usually with a single pointed lobule anteriorly. Dorsal scales moderately tricarinate, 6-sided, each with an angular free edge. Scales in 26-32 rows at mid- body. 22-28 lamellae under the fourth toe. 40 mm (snout-vent).
Distribution: North-eastern Qld.
Habit: Dry sclerophyll forest and tropical woodlands. Forages among leaf and other ground litter, climbing onto logs, stumps and low branches.

Carlia amax

Carlia coensis

Carlia dogare

Carlia gracilis

Carlia jarnoldae

Carlia johnstonei

Carlia longipes

Carlia johnstonei Storr,1974

Description: Olive to dark blackish-brown above, uniform or with black flecks; flanks often darker, flecked with brown or white. Head and anterior part of body black flecked with white in breeding males. Ventral surfaces whitish to bluish-grey, many of the scales of the chin and throat edged with grey- brown or black. Prefrontals usually separated, occasionally in contact. Supraciliaries 6-8. Ear-opening round or, either vertically or horizontally elliptic, with a single large lobule anteriorly and numerous smaller lobules around remaining margins, smaller than the palpebral disc. Dorsal scales six-sided, each with an angular free edge and mostly strongly bicarinate, with the keels well-aligned to form continuous longitudinal lines. Scales in 30-40 rows at mid- body. 20-26 lamellae under the fourth toe. 40 mm (snout-vent).
Distribution: North-eastern Kimberley region of WA.
Habit: Tropical woodlands, especially in denser vegetation in gullies and bordering creeks and lagoons.

Carlia longipes (Macleay, 1877)

Description: Pale to rich brown above, immaculate or with a broad, blackish lateral zone enclosing a series of white or yellow spots at least anteriorly. The head is usually paler and more bronzy than the body, while there are usually some scattered darker and paler spots on the dorsum. Flanks reddish-brown in adults. In juveniles and sub-adults there is typically a broad, blackish upper lateral zone from eye to groin, bordered above by an obscure, narrow, pale dorsolateral stripe and below by a white mid-lateral stripe from below the eye to the groin. Lower flanks with white dots or flecks. Whitish below. Tail pale brown. Prefrontals usually separated. Supraciliaries usually 7. Ear-opening circular or vertically elliptic, about equal to palpebral disc, and with one or more pointed lobules sometimes surrounding the ear. Dorsal scales 4-sided, smooth, striated or feebly tricarinate, the free edge of each scale rounded. Scales in 28-36 rows at mid-body. 22-34 lamellae under the fourth toe. 55 mm (snout- vent).
Distribution: Northern Qld and the islands of Torres Strait. An (apparently) outlying population in eastern Arnhem Land, NT, and Groote Eylandt.
Habit: Found in a variety of habitats from grassed and wooded beach dunes and mangrove margins, rainforest margins and clearings, monsoon scrub and vine thickets, paperbark swamps and Pandanus groves, and tropical woodlands on both stony and sandy substrates. An active diurnal forager which is

usually seen among leaf and other ground litter, it also climbs onto logs, stumps and low vegetation.

Carlia munda (De Vis, 1885)

Description: Highly variable in colour, from pale grey to olive or dark grey-brown above, dotted or flecked with black and pale brown or white. A narrow white stripe from below the eye to the top of the ear, continued from the bottom of the ear to form a mid-lateral stripe, which may extend to the groin but usually cuts out on the neck or anterior part of the body. The stripe is usually bordered above by a broader blackish upper lateral zone, at least anteriorly, which in some specimens is in turn bordered above by a faint, pale dorso-lateral stripe. Whitish below, the throat and chest in breeding males bluish-grey to blackish, the scales often with black margins. Breeding males also with a red upper lateral zone. Prefrontals usually separated. Supraciliaries 5-7. Ear-opening horizontally elliptic, much smaller than palpebral disc, and with one or two small lobules anteriorly. Dorsal scales smooth to feebly tricarinate, 4-sided, each with a rounded free edge. Scales in 26-34 rows at mid-body. 19-30 lamellae under the fourth toe. 40 mm (snout-vent).
Distribution: Northern half of WA, NT and northern and eastern Qld.
Habit: Seasonally dry woodlands and monsoon scrubs; dry sclerophyll forest and well-vegetated beach dunes.

Carlia mundivensis (Broome, 1898)

Description: More or less black above and on the sides, with scattered pale flecks and usually some indication of a pale dorso-lateral stripe. Whitish below. Prefrontals usually separated. Supraciliaries 6-8, usually seven. Ear-opening circular, usually about equal to palpebral disc and surrounded by short, pointed lobules. Dorsal scales six-sided, each usually with an angular free edge and either bi- or tri- carinate. Scales in 34-40 rows at mid-body. 23-26 lamellae under the fourth toe. 50 mm (snout-vent).
Distribution: Eastern Qld.
Habit: A rock-dwelling species.

Carlia pectoralis (De Vis, 1885)

Description: Colour and pattern similar in most respects to *Carlia vivax*, except that there is never

J. WOMBEY

Carlia gracilis Kapalga, NT

Carlia longipes Weipa, Qld

Carlia mundivensis Charters Towers, Qld

Carlia munda Prince of Wales Island, Torres Strait

Carlia pectoralis Forty-mile Scrub S of Mt Garnet, Qld

any indication of a pale dorso-lateral stripe, while the pale mid-lateral stripe rarely extends beyond the level of the forelimb. Breeding males with a well-defined, bright red mid-lateral stripe; throat blackish. Prefrontals usually separate. Supraciliaries usually five. Ear-opening vertically elliptic, smaller than palpebral disc, and with one or two lobules anteriorly. Dorsal scales 6-sided, each with an angular free edge and mostly strongly tricarinate. Scales in 24-30 rows at mid-body. 24-28 lamellae under the fourth toe. 40 mm (snout-vent).
Distribution: Eastern Qld, excluding Cape York Peninsula.
Habit: Open eucalypt forest and woodlands.

Carlia rhomboidalis (Peters, 1869)

Description: Dark grey-brown above, with numerous scattered darker and paler flecks. Sometimes a narrow pale dorso-lateral stripe commencing over the eye and extending to the tail in females, but absent, or present only anteriorly, in adult males. Flanks darker, finely speckled with black and pale brown. Sometimes a pale mid-lateral stripe present. Head paler than body, usually rich bronzy-brown, and the sides of the neck richly flushed with red in breeding males. Whitish below. Prefrontals in contact or narrowly separated. Supraciliaries usually seven. Ear-opening more or less circular, about equal

Carlia rhomboidalis Rockhampton, Qld

Carlia rostralis Hervey Range, near Townsville, Qld

to the palpebral disc and with 1-3 enlarged lobules anteriorly and a series of small, rounded lobules around remaining margin. Dorsal scales 4-sided, each usually with a curved free edge and mostly smooth or feebly tricarinate. Scales in 32-38 rows at mid-body. 20-30 lamellae under the fourth toe. 50 mm (snout-vent).
Distribution: North-eastern Qld.
Habit: Mesic habitats throughout its range, including rainforest, monsoonal scrub and creek margins.

Carlia rimula Ingram and Covacevich, 1980

Description: Blackish-brown above, often flecked with pale brown or white and with a pale metallic dorso-lateral stripe on each side, from above the eye to the base of the tail, and usually a similar pale metallic mid-lateral stripe from forelimb to hindlimb; a pale grey-brown vertebral zone from nape to base of tail. Pale ventrally. Prefrontals separate. Supraciliaries usually seven. Ear-opening vertically elliptic, usually smaller than palpebral disc and surrounded by pointed lobules. Dorsal scales 4-sided, each with 4-5 weak keels formed by series of individual small points and each with a curved free edge. Scales in 25-30 rows at mid-body. 24-30 lamellae under the fourth toe. 35 mm (snout-vent).
Distribution: Coast and adjacent interior near Coen, Cape York Peninsula, Qld.
Habit: 'Rocks and associated leaf-litter in open and vine forest, usually along creeks' (Ingram and Covacevich).

Carlia rostralis (De Vis, 1885)

Description: Body and limbs rich brown above, becoming grey-brown or olive-brown on the head; the dorsal colour may be uniform or with scattered black flecks and dots on the anterior part of the body, but sometimes these occur more densely and extend over the entire back and base of the tail. A narrow, pale, creamy dorso-lateral stripe, narrowly edged with black above, from above and behind the eye to the level of the forelimb or a little beyond; this stripe lies above a broad blackish band which extends from the snout, through the eye and ear, to about the level of the forelimb; sometimes this dark band is bordered below by a narrow, broken white stripe which may extend back along the body as a pale mid-lateral stripe. Flanks, at least anteriorly, bright russet, this colour often extending onto the upper forelimb. Lips whitish, barred or flecked with black at least posteriorly; throat white, cream or pale blue, with dense black flecks, lines and reticulations in males; belly whitish. Prefrontals separated. Supraciliaries usually 7. Ear-opening vertically elliptic, usually larger than palpebral disc, and with one or more pointed lobules sometimes surrounding the ear, the largest anteriorly. Dorsal scales 4-sided, smooth, striated or feebly tricarinate, the free edge of each scale rounded. Scales in 30-38 rows at mid-body. 26-36 lamellae under the fourth toe. 65 mm (snout-vent).
Distribution: Far north-western Qld and lower Cape York Peninsula, south to about Townsville.
Habit: '. . . a ground-dweller in grasslands and woodlands but not in rainforests . . .' but may be '. . . found in association with rocks and vine thickets. . . .' (Ingram and Covacevich).

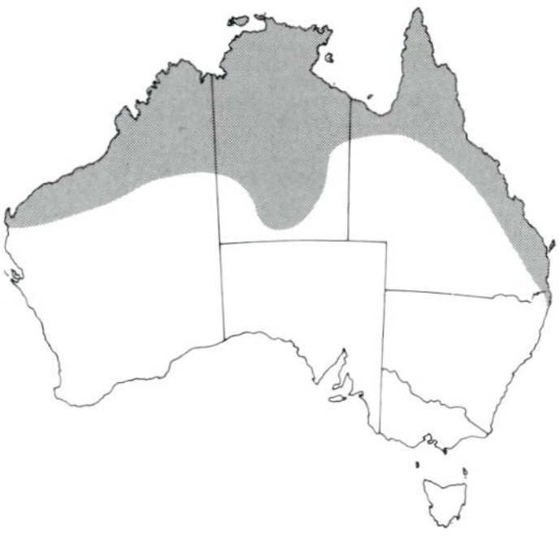

Carlia munda

Carlia mundivensis

Carlia pectoralis

Carlia rhomboidalis

Carlia rimula

Carlia rostralis

Carlia rubrigularis

Carlia schmeltzii near Rockhampton, Qld

Carlia rubrigularis Ingram and Covacevich, 1989

Description: Dark grey-brown above, with numerous scattered darker and paler flecks. Sometimes a narrow pale dorso-lateral stripe commencing over the eye and extending to the tail in females, but absent, or present only anteriorly, in adult males. Flanks darker, finely speckled with black and pale brown. Sometimes a pale mid-lateral stripe present. Head paler than body, usually rich bronzy-brown, and the sides of the neck richly flushed with red in breeding males. Whitish below. Prefrontals narrowly separated. Supraciliaries 6-8, usually seven. Ear-opening more or less circular, about equal to the palpebral disc and with 1-2 enlarged lobules anteriorly and a series of small rounded lobules around remaining margin. Dorsal scales smooth and 4-sided, each with a smoothly-curved free edge. Scales in 28-37 rows at mid-body. 24-35 lamellae under the fourth toe. 50 mm (snout-vent).
Distribution: Rainforests of north-eastern Qld, from Cooktown south to Townsville.
Habit: Rainforest, especially edge habitats beside tracks, clearings and streams.

Carlia rufilatus Storr, 1974

Description: Dark olive to brown above, dotted or flecked with black. Often a pale stripe from below the eye to above the ear and sometimes continued from below the ear to the forelimb. A red mid-lateral stripe in breeding males. Whitish below, Prefrontals usually separated. Supraciliaries 5-7. Ear opening horizontally elliptic, much smaller than palpebral disc and with at most one small lobule anteriorly. Dorsal scales 6-sided,each usually with an angular free edge and mostly moderately tricarinate, the keels more or less regularly aligned longitudinally. Scales in 28-32 rows at mid-body. 21-31 lamellae under the fourth toe. 35 mm (snout-vent).
Distribution: Far northern WA and north-western NT.
Habit: Tropical seasonally-dry woodlands and more humid microhabitats associated with streams, lagoons and rocky gullies.

Carlia rufilatus Daly River, NT

Carlia scirtetis Pascoe River, Qld

Carlia schmeltzii (Peters, 1867)

Description: Olive-brown or grey-brown above, paler bronzy- brown on the head, the back with scattered darker and paler flecks. Usually some indication of a pale brown dorso-lateral stripe and a dark upper lateral zone with darker flecks. Lower flanks paler brown with scattered pale spots. Limbs above similar to dorsum. Usually a narrow black loreal streak. Whitish below. Flanks of breeding males flushed with red. Prefrontals separated. Supraciliaries usually seven. Ear opening vertically elliptic, about equal to palpebral disc and usually two, short, rounded lobules anteriorly. Dorsal scales strongly tricarinate, 6-sided, each with a free edge. Scales in 32-38 rows at mid-body. 22-30 lamellae under the fourth toe. 50 mm (snout-vent).
Distribution: North-eastern Qld, including the lower half of Cape York Peninsula.
Habit: Open eucalypt forest and woodland, especially among rock outcrops and stony hills.

Carlia scirtetis Ingram and Covacevich, 1980

Description: Dark blackish-brown above, with scattered paler scales sometimes aligned longitudinally to give the impression of stripes; ventral surfaces dark grey, tinged with bluish, heavily flecked with dark brown on the throat and underside of limbs and tail. Limbs above blackish, spotted with pale blue. Prefrontals separate. Supraciliaries 6-8, usually seven. Ear-opening vertically elliptic, about equal to palpebral disc, and with many long, pointed lobules around its margin. Dorsal scales four-sided, each with three or four weak keels consisting of a row of smaller points. Scales in 40-45 rows at mid-body. 30-40 lamellae under the fourth toe. 60 mm (snout-vent).
Distribution: Known only from the Black Trevathan Range, near Cooktown, Qld.
Habit: An agile, diurnal, rock-dwelling lizard which lives among the large caverns formed by the enormous, tumbled, dark granite boulders which characterise its habitat.

Carlia storri Ingram and Covacevich, 1989

Description: Brown or pale olive-brown above, the males uniform or dotted above with dark brown, sometimes with a narrow, whitish dorso-lateral stripe from above the eye to the tail. Females with a narrow pale brown vertebral stripe, a white or cream dorso-lateral stripe and a white or cream mid- lateral stripe from ear to groin. Lower flanks, neck, lips and ventral surfaces, white or cream. Limbs above pale brown flecked with dark brown. Breeding males flushed with dark orange posteriorly. Prefrontals separated. Supraciliaries usually 5-6. Ear-opening circular or vertically elliptic, about equal to palpebral membrane, surrounded by small pointed lobules. Dorsal scales 6-sided, strongly bicarinate, each with an angular free edge. Scales in 26-34 rows at mid-body. 27-35 lamellae under the fourth toe. 40 mm (snout-vent)

Carlia storri Torres Strait, Qld

Distribution: North-eastern Qld, including the islands of Torres Strait. Extra-limital in southern New Guinea.
Habit: Found in a variety of habitats, including rainforest edges, secondary regrowth, coastal scrubs and tropical eucalypt woodlands, where it forages among grasses and ground litter. Prefers shaded, humid microhabitats.

Carlia rufilatus

Carlia schmeltzii

Carlia scirtetis

Carlia storri

Carlia tetradactyla

Carlia triacantha

Carlia vivax

Carlia tetradactyla Warrumbungle Range, NSW

J. WOMBEY

Carlia triacantha Kapalga, NT (male in breeding colours)

J. WOMBEY

Carlia tetradactyla (O'Shaughnessy, 1879)

Description: Rich brown above, flecked with black and paler brown, the flecks tending to be concentrated in a broad vertebral zone and an upper lateral zone, resulting in a pale dorso-lateral stripe. Upper flanks brown, lower flanks and sides of neck very pale brown, cream or, in breeding males, rich blue-green. Breeding males also with a pair of rich reddish-orange lateral stripes. Whitish to pale green below. Limbs brown, spotted and flecked with black. Prefrontals usually separated. Supraciliaries usually seven. Ear-opening circular or vertically elliptic, about equal to palpebral disc with a single, enlarged, anterior lobule. Dorsal scales smooth, 4-sided, the free edge of each scale smoothly rounded. Scales in 30-34 rows at mid-body. 18-26 lamellae under the fourth toe. 50 mm (snout-vent).
Distribution: Eastern Australia, from northern Vic to south-eastern Qld.
Habit: Dry sclerophyll forest and eucalypt, *Casuarina* and *Callitris* woodland; a ground-dwelling species which forages in leaf litter and grasses around rock outcrops and fallen timber.

Carlia triacantha (Mitchell, 1953)

Description: Grey-brown above, usually with an iridescent sheen which is coppery blue-green on the head in breeding males; numerous grey-black flecks or dots on the dorsum, tending to form longitudinal series posteriorly. A reddish stripe along the flanks in breeding males. Whitish below. Prefrontals usually in contact. Supraciliaries 4-7, usually six. Ear-opening usually circular, smaller than palpebral disc and with one enlarged anterior lobule and often a number of small, pointed lobules around remaining margins. Dorsal scales 6-sided each, with an angular free edge and mostly tricarinate, the three strong keels on each scale not well aligned with keels of following scales. Scales in 28-36 rows at mid-body. 21-30 lamellae under the fourth toe. 45 mm (snout-vent).
Distribution: Northern WA and northern NT. Storr also records this species from the southern desert of NT through the arid interior of WA to the coast between Exmouth Gulf and Broome.
Habit: Ranges from seasonally-dry tropical woodlands to the arid scrubs and spinifex-covered ranges of central Australia. Forages among litter and spinifex, especially on broken stony ground.

Carlia triacantha Jabiru, NT
(non-breeding colours)

Carlia vivax (De Vis, 1884)

Description: Brown above, head paler bronzy-brown. A series of pale brown spots or flecks on the back, sometimes black edged, sometimes tending to form longitudinal series. Usually some indication of a narrow, pale dorso-lateral stripe from above shoulder to base of tail. A narrow cream or white mid-lateral stripe from the mid-loreal region under the eye and through the ear to the tail. Whitish to pale bluish below. Breeding males uniform brown or with black flecks above, flanks with a poorly to well-defined pinkish stripe. Prefrontals usually separated. Supraciliaries usually five. Ear-opening vertically elliptic, smaller than palpebral disc and with 1-2 lobules anteriorly. Dorsal scales 6-sided, each with an angular free edge and mostly strongly bicarinate. Scales in 26-34 rows at mid-body. 22-28 lamellae under the fourth toe. 40 mm (snout-vent).
Distribution: Eastern Australia, south to the Hunter River Valley, NSW.
Habit: Drier habitats throughout its range: predominantly dry sclerophyll forest and tall woodland.

Carlia vivax (female) Oakey, Qld

J. WEIGEL

Genus ***Coeranoscincus*** Wells and Wellington, 1984

Similar in most respects to *Anomalopus,* from which it may be distinguished by lacking an ectopterygoid process (present in *Anomalopus*) and in having tridactyle limbs when limbs are present (limbs, when present, with only one or two digits in *Anomalopus*) and, in limbless forms, large prefrontals which are in contact or only narrowly separated (prefrontals small to moderate and widely separated in limbless *Anomalopus*).

Key

TO THE SPECIES OF COERANOSCINCUS

Limbs present.. ***reticulatus***
Limbs absent..***frontalis***

Coeranoscincus frontalis (De Vis, 1888)

Description: Medium to dark chocolate-brown above with obscure darker flecks over the dorsum, and in some specimens an obscure, broad blackish collar. A series of dark spots following the line of the lower jaw and continuous with a dark brown streak from the angle of the jaw, along the throat and then extending upwards and backwards to form a grey-brown mid-lateral stripe along the length of the body. This stripe may be separated from dorsal colour in some specimens by a narrow, pale line, while in others it may be totally absent. A dark patch or series of spots around and below the eye and extending on to the upper and lower labials. In juvenile specimens the above pattern is conspicuous and contrasting. The dark streak on the throat may be joined to the dark dorsal colouring by a vertical bar through the ear region and is sometimes discontinuous. The lateral stripe becomes a series of broken bars on the tail. Except for the throat the remaining ventral surfaces are white or cream. Snout rather pointed, wedge-shaped. Nasals separated. Prefrontals large, narrowly separated or in contact. Two loreals on each side. Three supraoculars. Postmentals in contact with two infralabials on each side. Ear hidden, its position indicated by a depression. 28-32 mid-body scale rows. Limbs entirely absent. Preanals greatly enlarged. 250 mm (snout-vent).
Distribution: Atherton Tableland and its escarpment, north- eastern Qld.
Habit: A large, burrowing skink, usually found under fallen timber or in decaying logs in rainforest.

Coeranoscincus frontalis Cairns district, Qld

Coeranoscincus reticulatus (Günther, 1873)

Description: Adults pale fawn to dark brown above, the individual scales flecked and streaked with dark brown. Usually some indication of a black collar and often some small, scattered, dark brown spots on the dorsum. Lower lateral and ventral scales paler brown, with the dark streaks on the scales tending to form series of narrow, longitudinal lines. Ventral scales of some specimens edged with dark brown, forming a fine, reticulated pattern. Throat with dark brown streaks. Sides of face and neck paler than dorsal colour. Juveniles distinctly patterned, with a broad, dark brown patch on the head having a forward extension on either side over and including each eye; another on the nape, and a conspicuous series of narrow and irregular dark brown transverse bars across the anterior part of the body, gradually fading to an obscure flecked pattern posteriorly; flanks minutely dotted with brown; a few dark brown spots on the throat. Snout distinctly wedge-shaped and pointed. Nasals separated. Prefrontals moderate, separated. Usually a single, elongate loreal, but sometimes two

Coeranoscincus reticulatus Richmond River, NSW

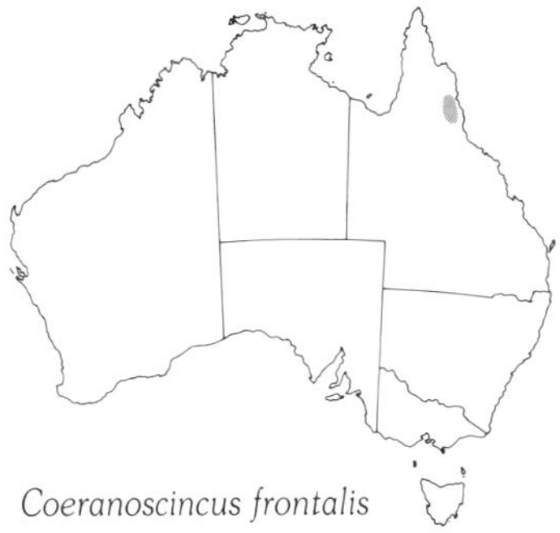

Coeranoscincus frontalis

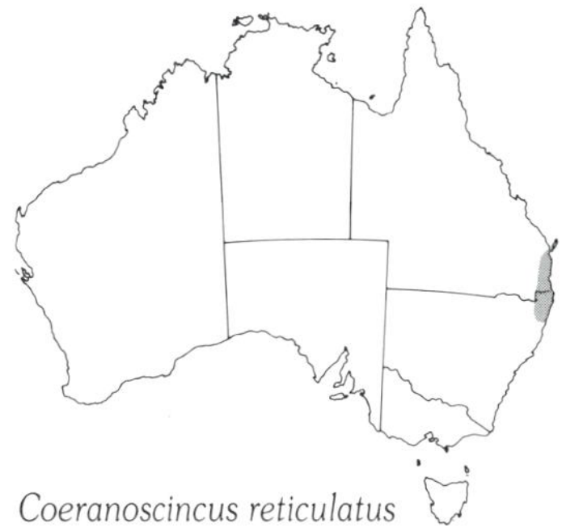

Coeranoscincus reticulatus

on each side. Three supraoculars. Postmental normally in contact with two infralabials on each side. Ear hidden, its position indicated by a depression. 24-28 mid-body scale rows. Limbs very short, all tridactyle. Preanals moderately enlarged. 180 mm (snout-vent). Tail tip tapering, more or less ending in a point.

Distribution: Forest areas of coast and adjacent ranges of the northern rivers district, north-eastern NSW and south-eastern Qld.
Habit: Apparently an inhabitant of rainforest and adjacent wet sclerophyll forests, where it is usually found in rotting logs or in soil under fallen timber.

Genus *Cryptoblepharus* Wiegmann, 1834

A widely distributed genus of small, active, diurnal lizards with six species occurring in Australia, although some currently recognised subspecies are almost certainly distinct species. Characterised by a fused, immovable, lower eyelid forming a spectacle over the eye; upper eyelid with three or four scales much larger than the granules surrounding the remainder of the eye; frontal shield more or less equal in size to each of the large prefrontals; frontoparietal and interparietals fused to form a single large shield; ear-opening more or less equal to the nasal scale; all limbs pentadactyle; parietal shields in contact behind the interparietal.

Usually arboreal, but one species (*litoralis*) is found only in a variety of foreshore habitats and two species, *megastictus* and *fuhni*, are primarily rock dwellers.

Key

TO THE AUSTRALIAN SPECIES OF CRYPTOBLEPHARUS

1 Pale dorso-lateral stripe, if present, not bordered above by a sharp-edged, continuous black stripe; five or six supraciliaries; maximum snout-vent length may exceed 40 mm........ **2**

A well-defined, pale dorso-lateral stripe bordered above by a sharp-edged continuous black stripe; supraciliaries normally five; maximum snout-vent length rarely exceeding 40mm........ ***virgatus***

2 Subdigital lamellae smooth or only bluntly keeled basally; posterior plantar scales rounded....................................**3**

Subdigital lamellae finely keeled; posterior plantar scales sharply pointed.. ***carnabyi***

3 Lower surfaces of hands and feet very dark brown or black; supraciliaries usually five......................................**4**

Lower surfaces of hands and feet pale brown or whitish; supraciliaries usually six...**5**

4 Dorsal pattern of pale spots and dashes aligned longitudinally; no continuous pale dorso-lateral stripe...........***fuhni***

Dorsal pattern of irregularly scattered darker and paler flecks and spots on a dark background; a ragged but continuous pale dorso-lateral stripe from above eye to tail...... .... ***litoralis***

5 Usually at least some indication of a longitudinal pattern of stripes or pigment zones; darker on the back; a pale dorso- lateral stripe, at least anteriorly, and a dark upper lateral zone; arboreal; widespread in Australia................. .... ***plagiocephalus***

No indication of a longitudinal pattern of stripes or pigment zones; paler and darker flecks, spots and dashes scattered irregularly over body or aligned transversely; saxicoline; Kimberleys to eastern NT ....***megastictus***

Cryptoblepharus carnabyi Storr, 1976

Description: Grey-brown above, usually with some indication of a ragged-edged, pale dorso-lateral stripe from above eye to tail; this stripe is usually bordered above by a series of dark spots and blotches which merge with the scattered pale and dark mid-dorsal flecks and spots; usually a dark upper lateral zone with scattered darker and paler flecks and spots; limbs above similar to mid-dorsal region; ventral surfaces, including lower surfaces of hands and feet, whitish. Nasals separated. Prefrontals in contact. Four supraoculars, the second largest. Usually five supraciliaries, the second largest. 7-8 supralabials, usually 7. 14-22 finely keeled lamellae under the fourth toe. 22-28 mid-body scale rows. 40 mm (snout-vent).

Distribution: Interior of eastern Australia to the coast and interior of WA, excluding arid central regions.

Habit: Occupies a very wide range of habitats from coastal dunes and rocky shores, through dry scler-

Cryptoblepharus carnabyi Goodooga, NSW

R. W. G. JENKINS

ophyll forests and woodlands to mallee and a variety of arid scrubs. Semi- arboreal, being most often seen on tree trunks and shrubs, but also common among rocks on stony hills and screes.

Cryptoblepharus fuhni Covacevich and Ingram 1978

Description: Blackish above, with pale brownish-white flecks and spots on the head and with numerous pale spots and dashes on body and tail tending to form cross-bands. Remaining ventral surfaces cream, except for lower surfaces of hands and feet which are black. Nasals separated. Prefrontals in contact. 4 supraoculars, the second largest. 5 supraciliaries, the first largest. 7 supralabials. 22-26 smooth lamellae under fourth toe. 23-26 mid-body scale rows. 45 mm (snout-vent).
Distribution: Currently known only from Melville Range, Cape Melville, Qld.
Habit: Found among exposed black boulders.

Cryptoblepharus litoralis (Mertens, 1958)

Description: Dark grey-brown to greenish-black above, usually with a ragged-edged, pale olive to cream dorso-lateral stripe from above the eye to the tail, which is usually narrowly edged with black on the head and neck; mid-dorsal region with numerous scattered, pale grey-green or whitish flecks and spots; a dark upper lateral zone with scattered paler flecks; metallic whitish-grey below, except for the lower surfaces of the hands and feet which are shiny black. Nasals separated. Prefrontals in contact. 4 supraoculars,the second largest. Usually 8 supralabials. 17-24 lamellae under the fourth toe. 22-28 mid-body scale rows. 55 mm (snout-vent).
Distribution: Coast of north-eastern Qld and islands of Torres Strait and the northern NT coast; extra-limital in New Guinea.
Habit: Found among ground litter and herbage in beach dune situations, in mangroves and among crevices and boulders of rocky foreshores. Commonly forages for amphipods and other small marine animals in the intertidal zone at low tide.

Cryptoblepharus megastictus Storr, 1976

Description: Rich metallic-brown above, flecked, spotted and striated with dark brown and creamy-white; rarely any indication of a pale dorso-lateral

Cryptoblepharus litoralis Portland Roads, Qld

Cryptoblepharus megastictus McArthur River, NT

Cryptoblepharus plagiocephalus near Elliott, NT

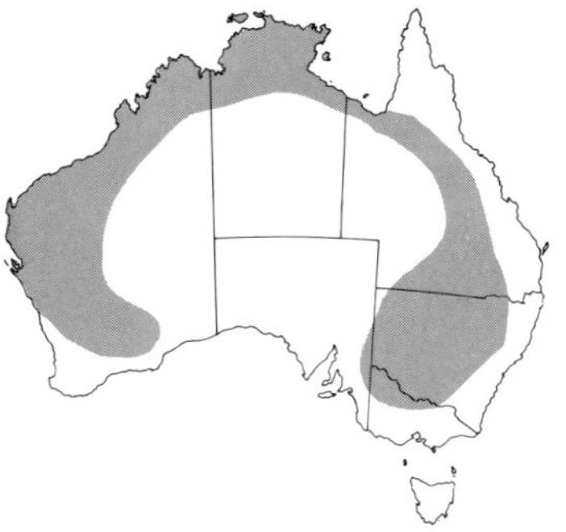

Cryptoblepharus carnabyi

Cryptoblepharus fuhni

Cryptoblepharus litoralis

Cryptoblepharus megastictus

Cryptoblepharus plagiocephalus

Cryptoblepharus virgatus

stripe or of a dark upper lateral zone; colour and pattern of flanks and limbs similar to that of dorsum; ventral surfaces whitish; lower surfaces of hands and feet pale. Nasals separated. Prefrontals in contact. 4 supraoculars, the second usually largest. Supraciliaries 4-6, the first or second largest. Usually 7 supralabials. 17-20 lamellae under the fourth toe. 24-28 mid-body scale rows. 40 mm (snout-vent).
Distribution: Stony hills, plateaux and escarpments of far northern Australia from the Kimberleys, WA , to the Gulf of Carpentaria, NT.
Habit: An agile, rock-dwelling species sheltering in crevices, caves or under rocks and boulders; seen by day basking on exposed rocky areas, especially in areas with deep litter or with spinifex cover.

Cryptoblepharus plagiocephalus

(Cocteau, 1836)

Description: Brownish or greyish above, usually with some indication of a narrow, ragged-edged, pale dorso-lateral stripe or zone from above eye to tail; this stripe usually bordered above by an irregular series of dark spots and blotches which rarely coalesce to form a very ragged dark stripe; mid-dorsal region and limbs flecked, spotted or striated with white and dark brown; a dark upper lateral zone with scattered paler and darker dots and spots; ventral surfaces whitish or pale metallic blue; lower surfaces of hands and feet brownish. Nasals separated. Prefrontals in contact. 4 supraoculars, the second largest. Supraciliaries 5-6, usually 6, the third usually largest. Usually 7 supralabials, occasionally 8. 14-22 smooth or callose lamellae under the fourth toe. 22-30 mid- body scale rows. 45 mm (snout-vent).
Distribution: Virtually Australia-wide, except for the east and south-east.
Habit: Found in a wide variety of habitats from tropical woodlands and eucalypt forests to temperate woodlands, mallee, and the arid eucalypt and Acacia scrublands of central Australia. Primarily arboreal, being found in crevices or under the bark of trees when not active. Commonly inhabits buildings and other man-made structures.
Subspecies: *plagiocephalus* (range excluding west Kimberleys,WA); *ruber* (west Kimberleys, WA).

Cryptoblepharus virgatus (Garman, 1901)

Description: Silvery-grey to pale brown above, with a conspicuous white, cream or silvery dorso-lateral stripe from above eye to base of tail; this stripe is bordered above by a distinctive black stripe and below by a broad dark grey or brown upper lateral zone (becoming paler ventrally), which commences as a stripe from the nostril and contains numerous pale dots and spots; ventral surfaces white or pale metallic blue; lower surface of hands and feet whitish. Nasals separated. Prefrontals in contact. 4 supraoculars, the second largest. 5 supraciliaries, the second usually largest. Usually 7 supralabials. 16-22 smooth lamellae under the fourth toe. 20-28 mid-body scale rows. 40 mm (snout-vent).

Distribution: Far southern and eastern Australia.

Habit: Occupies a variety of habitats from wet and dry sclerophyll forests to heathlands and woodlands. Usually arboreal, sheltering in crevices or under the bark of trees; commonly inhabits human dwellings, other buildings, rock retaining walls, bridge footings, etc.

Genus ***Ctenotus*** Storr, 1964

A large group of moderate-sized, active, diurnal lizards with long, slender, pentadactyle limbs. They are characterised by the conspicuous anterior ear lobules; a colour pattern which usually consists of dorsal and/or lateral longitudinal stripes or markings otherwise aligned longitudinally; smooth or faintly keeled scales; the absence of supranasal scales or divided nasals; a scaly movable lower eyelid; parietal scales in contact behind the interparietal.

This genus of skinks is almost confined to Australia (one species occurs in New Guinea), where species diversity is greatest in desert regions and the seasonally-dry tropics. Virtually all species are terrestrial, and many species are active at very high temperatures; most are opportunistic feeders on a wide variety of insects. All species are oviparous.

Key

TO THE SPECIES OF CTENOTUS

1 Pattern on back, flanks and hindlimbs includes at least some small, white, black-edged ocelli; nasal usually strongly grooved (a)........ **2**

Pattern, if present, of longitudinally aligned stripes, or series of spots, but never with black-edged white ocelli on back, flanks and hindlimbs together; nasal not, or weakly, grooved........ **3**

2 Prefrontals usually in contact (b); subdigital lamellae sharply keeled (e); usually more than 30 mid-body scale rows........ ***pantherinus***

Prefrontals usually separated (c); subdigital lamellae bluntly keeled (f); 30 or fewer mid-body scale rows........ ***angusticeps***

3 Top and/or sides of body with alternate series of longitudinal stripes, never with prominent spots, except occasionally in juveniles........ **4**

Top of body either striped or plain, sides of body either plain or a combination of stripes and prominent spots, at least anteriorly........ **22**

4 Vertebral stripe present........ **5**

Vertebral stripe absent........ ***quinkan***

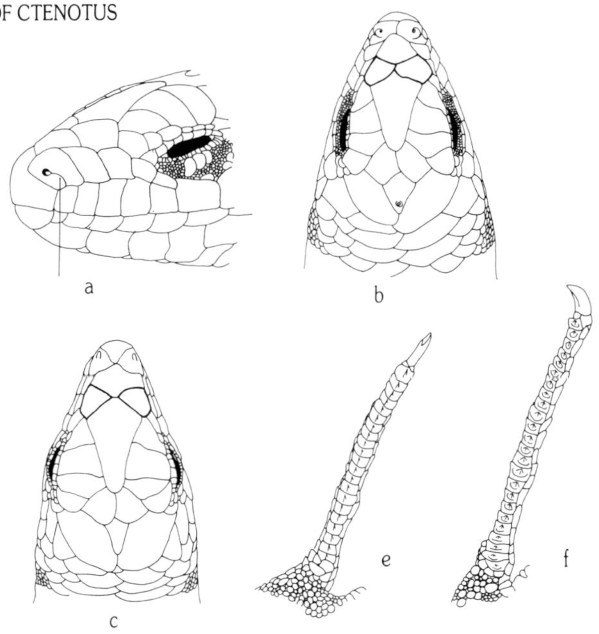

5 A pale vertebral stripe (sometimes enclosing a dark median line anteriorly) **6**

A dark vertebral stripe **8**

6 Eight supraciliaries (i), 9 or 10 pale stripes on back and flanks; northern Australia **7**

Six or seven supraciliaries; 11 pale stripes on back and flanks; south-western Australia .... ***impar***

7 Uppermost auricular lobule larger than any others (j);pale paravertebral stripes coalescing for at least part of their length .... ***storri***

Uppermost auricular lobule not largest in series (k); paravertebral stripes not coalescing .... ***decaneurus***

8 Eight or more pale longitudinal stripes on body and sides **9**

Six pale stripes on body and sides .... ***piankai***

9 Ten or eight pale stripes on back and sides at level of mid-body **10**

More than ten pale stripes on back and sides at level of mid-body **20**

10 Subdigital lamellae mucronate (e) **11**

Subdigital lamellae smooth (h), callose (g) or bluntly keeled (f) **15**

11 Tail not blue above; no black markings under tail or toes; no enlarged keeled scales on sole **12**

Tail blue above, with transverse black markings below basal portion; series of enlarged keeled scales on sole opposite fourth toe (l) .... ***calurus***

12 Ear lobules two, occasionally three, the upper much larger than the others; first supraocular larger than second (m) **13**

Ear lobules 2-5, graded in size; first supraocular usually smaller than second (n) **14**

13 Prefrontals usually in contact (b); fewer than 27 mid-body scale rows; dark dorsal stripes much narrower than dark dorso- lateral stripe .... ***colletti***

Prefrontals usually widely separated (c); more than 27 mid-body scale rows; dark dorsal stripes about as wide as a dark dorso-lateral stripe .... ***striaticeps***

14 Mid-body scales in fewer than 27 rows; tail red above, pink below .... ***leae***

Mid-body scales in more than 27 rows; tail dark brown above, whitish below .... ***zebrilla***

15 Four narrow pale stripes on back between and including those commencing above the eyes **16**

Six pale stripes on back between and including those commencing above the eyes **19**

16 No indication of a pale stripe between pale dorso-lateral and mid-lateral stripes; nasals usually separated (o) **17**

Usually at least an obscure narrow pale stripe between the pale dorso-lateral and mid-lateral stripes; nasals usually in contact (p) **18**

17 Fewer than 30 subdigital lamellae under the fourth toe .... ***ingrami***

More than 30 subdigital lamellae under the fourth toe .... ***rawlinsoni***

18 A conspicuous pale lower lateral stripe, extending forward from forelimb to ear aperture .... ***atlas***

Pale lower lateral stripe, if present, not extending anteriorly forward to forelimb .... ***lateralis***

19 Usually seven supralabials (q); prefrontals usually separated (c); pale stripe between pale paravertebral and pale dorso-lateral stripe on each side markedly wider than the others .... ***taeniolatus***

Usually eight supralabials (r); prefrontals usually in contact (b); pale stripe between pale paravertebral stripe and pale dorso-lateral stripe on each side scarcely wider than the others .... ***eutaenius***

20 More than sixteen pale stripes **21**

Sixteen or fewer pale stripes... ***quattuordecimlineatus***

21 Eighteen pale stripes on body and sides, the lateral pattern indistinct or obscure, especially anteriorly .... ***ariadnae***

Twenty pale stripes on body and sides, the lateral pattern reasonably distinct anteriorly .... ***dux***

22 Body uniformly coloured without dorsal or lateral pattern **23**

Dorsal and/or lateral pattern present **24**

23 Fewer than 33 mid-body scale rows .... ***helenae***

More than 33 mid-body scale rows .... ***rubicundus***

24 Frontoparietals paired (s) **25**

Frontoparietals fused to form a single shield (t) .... ***gagudju***

25 Four supraoculars of which only two are usually in contact with the frontal; three presuboculars (u) **26**

Three or four supraoculars; if four supraoculars usually three are in contact with the frontal; two presuboculars (v) **31**

26 A continuous white dorso-lateral stripe; abdomen yellow **27**

White dorso-lateral stripe broken into a series of short dashes; abdomen white **29**

27 Pale mid-lateral stripe well developed, conspicuous anteriorly **28**

Pale mid-lateral stripe not, or but poorly, developed, not distinct anteriorly .... ***youngsoni***

28 Hindlimb reddish; south-western WA .... ***labillardieri***

Hindlimb yellowish; confined to Lancelin Island, WA .... ***lancelini***

29 Usually fewer than eight supralabials; hindlimb olive-grey dotted with blackish-brown **30**

Eight supralabials; hindlimb yellowish-brown, boldly marked with black and white .... ***gemmula***

30 Back dark brown, unpatterned between narrow, black, dorso- lateral stripes .... ***delli***

Back olive-grey, usually with some trace of a dark vertebral stripe and a broad black dorso-lateral stripe usually enclosing a series of white dots .... ***catenifer***

31 Subdigital lamellae each with a fine, sharp keel usually ending in a mucronate spine (e) **32**

Subdigital lamellae smooth (h), callose (g) or obtusely keeled (f) **38**

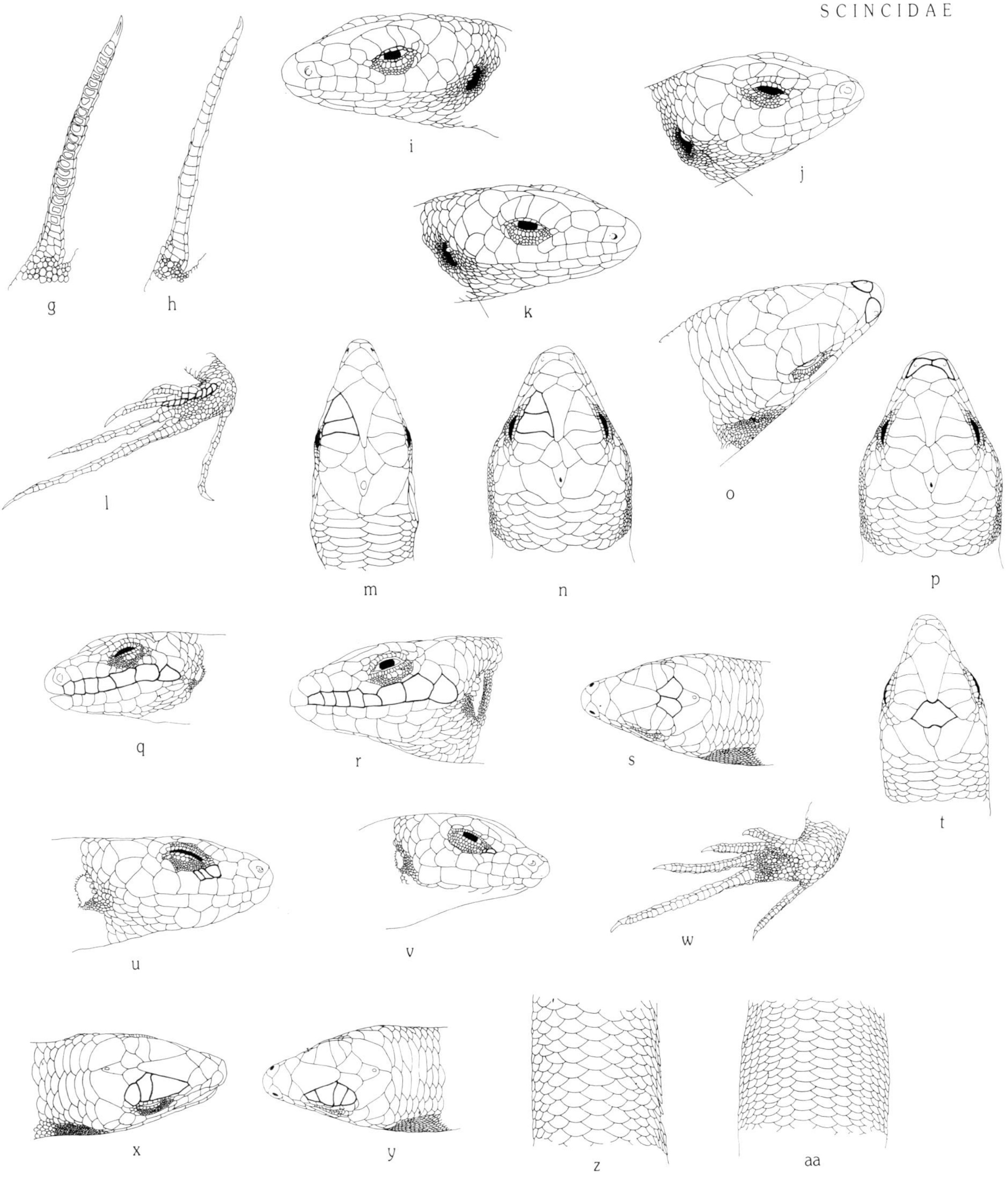

32 Nasals usually in contact (p); prefrontals narrowly to widely separated (c); hindlimb usually 45% or less of snout-vent length.. **33**

Nasals usually separated (o); prefrontals in contact (p) or narrowly separated (c); hindlimb usually more than 45% of snout-vent length.. **36**

33 Multiple dark dorsal stripes, when present, terminate just beyond rump; ear lobules 1-4, the first sometimes the largest but not much larger than the second..................... **34**

Multiple dark dorsal stripes usually extend along at least anterior half of tail; ear lobules two, the upper much larger than the lower.. ***ehmanni***

34 Basal subdigital lamellae pale-coloured with narrow keels.. .... **35**

Basal subdigital lamellae blackish with fairly wide keels...... .... ***allotropis***

35 Uppermost auricular lobule largest in series; upper lateral zone enclosing scattered, small pale spots......... ***tantillus***

Uppermost auricular lobule not largest in series; upper lateral zone usually enclosing a single series of large pale blotches.. ***strauchii***

36 White dorso-lateral and mid-lateral stripes well developed; black vertebral stripe always present; prefrontals usually narrowly separated; plantar scales uniformly granular (w). **37**

White dorso-lateral and mid-lateral stripes indistinct or absent; black vertebral stripe often absent in adults; prefrontals usually in contact; plantar scales opposite fourth toe enlarged and keeled (l).......... ***brooksi***

37 Mid-body scale rows usually fewer than 28; lower NT, SA, NSW and WA.......... ***schomburgkii***

Mid-body scale rows usually 28 or more; upper NT.......... ***pallescens***

38 Three supraoculars (x).......... **39**

Normally four supraoculars (y).......... **40**

39 Toes strongly compressed.......... ***mastigura***

Toes not, or but weakly, compressed.......... ***spaldingi***

40 Continuous pale mid-lateral stripe (as against a discontinuous longitudinal series of spots) absent or barely distinguishable in adults; sometimes a disrupted stripe in juveniles.......... **41**

A distinct dark-edged, continuous, pale mid-lateral stripe usually present on at least the posterior half of the body.......... **52**

41 Scales in vertebral pairs of scale rows not noticeably wider than adjacent paravertebral scales (z); sides of face and neck variegated without distinct small white dots.......... **42**

Scales in vertebral pairs of scale rows noticeably wider than adjacent paravertebral scales (aa); small white dots on sides of face and neck.......... ***pulchellus***

42 No obvious dark upper lateral zone; sides grey with numerous small, pale spots tending to form vertical bars.......... **43**

A distinct upper lateral zone, noticeably demarcated from the back either by its darker colour or by a pale dorso- lateral stripe, and enclosing paler spots or blotches.......... **46**

43 Flanks with conspicuously pale spots or flecks.......... **44**

Flanks without or with only faint pale spots or flecks.......... ***vertebralis***

44 Prefrontals usually in contact (b); hindlimbs with pale and dark spots and flecks, not striped.......... **45**

Prefrontals usually separated (c); hindlimbs not spotted or flecked with whitish, but with obscure darker brown stripes.......... ***astarte***

45 Nasals usually separated (o); pale spots on flanks aligned vertically.......... ***grandis***

Nasals usually in contact (p); pale spots on flanks not aligned vertically.......... ***hanloni***

46 Dark upper lateral zone, when it extends on to tail, forms a continuous stripe along side of tail.......... **47**

Dark upper lateral zone extends along side of tail as a series of blackish blotches.......... ***kurnbudj***

47 A narrow blackish vertebral stripe from nape to base of tail; pale spots on sides not usually aligned to form vertical bars.......... **48**

A discontinuous dark vertebral zone of spots and flecks forming a distinct stripe only on the nape; pale spots on sides aligned to form vertical bars.......... ***schevilli***

48 Head and neck not coppery-red.......... **49**

Head and neck coppery-red.......... ***rutilans***

49 Hindlimbs brown with darker brown or blackish stripes.......... **50**

Hindlimbs brown with darker brown or blackish spots and flecks.......... ***borealis***

50 Nasals usually in contact (p); dark vertebral stripe broader than dark dorso-lateral stripe, the latter not enclosing any pale spots.......... **51**

Nasals usually separated (o); dark vertebral stripe narrower than dark dorso-lateral stripe, the latter enclosing a series of pale spots.......... ***uber***

51 Lips usually uniformly coloured; six sharply demarcated pale stripes between and including the narrow, pale dorso-lateral stripes.......... ***militaris***

Lips barred with dark brown; only four poorly demarcated pale stripes between and including the broad pale dorso-lateral zone.......... ***serotinus***

52 Toes moderately to slightly compressed, the subdigital lamellae narrowly callose or bluntly keeled (f).......... **53**

Toes not, or slightly, compressed, the subdigital lamellae smooth (h) or broadly callose (g).......... **68**

53 At least one dark stripe or zone on body.......... **54**

No dark stripes on body, pattern consisting solely of longitudinal series of whitish dots and dashes.......... ***tanamiensis***

54 A dark vertebral stripe from nape to base of tail.......... **55**

Vertebral stripe absent or confined to nape.......... **65**

55 Six or fewer pale longitudinal stripes between and including the pale dorso-lateral stripes on each side, commencing on the supraciliaries.......... **56**

Eight pale longitudinal stripes between and including the pale dorso-lateral stripes on each side, commencing on the supraciliaries.......... ***septenarius***

56 Black back, with six pale continuous longitudinal stripes between and including the pale dorso-lateral stripe on each side, commencing on the supraciliaries.......... **57**

Back olive or brown, with at most four pale continuous longitudinal stripes between and including the pale dorso-lateral stripe on each side, commencing on the supraciliaries.......... **59**

57 Pale mid-lateral stripe extending forward to side of snout.......... **58**

Pale mid-lateral stripe present only posteriorly... ***hebetior***

58 Usually eight supralabials (r).......... ***alacer***

Usually seven supralabials (q).......... ***xenopleura***

59 White mid-lateral stripe, if present, breaking into a series of spots before reaching as far forward as the level of the forelimb.......... **60**

White mid-lateral stripe extending forward to side of snout.......... **61**

60 Outer dorsal region (above pale dorso-lateral stripe) with a series of pale dots or streaks.......... ***greeri***

Outer dorsal region (above pale dorsolateral stripe) without pale dots or streaks.................................. ***leonhardii***

61 Blackish vertebral stripe distinctly pale-edged; prefrontals usually in contact (b).. **62**

Blackish vertebral stripe only faintly pale-edged; prefrontals usually separated (c).. **64**

62 Back with broad brown stripes contrasting with the narrower black vertebral and dorso-lateral stripes............. **63**

Back black, with contrasting narrow whitish stripes; at most a few brown spots or flecks in the black dorso-lateral stripe... ***zastictus***

63 Nasals usually in contact (p); north-western Australia........ .... ***serventyi***

Nasals usually separated (o); interior of eastern states....... .... ***regius***

64 Usually seven supralabials (q); nasals usually separated (o).. ***monticola***

Usually eight supralabials (r); nasals usually in contact(p).. .... ***joanae***

65 Toes strongly compressed... **66**

Toes not, or but weakly, compressed................ ***mimetes***

66 Pale dorso-lateral stripe bordered above by a narrow, often faint (especially posteriorly) blackish stripe.......... **67**

Pale dorso-lateral stripe bordered above by a conspicuous and equally broad blackish stripe.............................. ***hilli***

67 Uppermost auricular lobule largest in series; usually 28 or fewer mid-body scale rows........................... ***essingtonii***

Uppermost auricular lobule not largest in series; usually more than 28 mid-body scale rows................. ***mastigura***

68 Dark vertebral stripe present, not noticeably pale-edged... .... **69**

Dark vertebral stripe, if present, noticeably pale-edged. **71**

69 A prominent pale dorso-lateral stripe............................ **70**

Little or no indication of a pale dorso-lateral stripe............ .... ***helenae***

70 Pale mid-lateral stripe extends forward to lips; south-eastern SA and western Vic......................... ***brachyonyx***

Pale mid-lateral stripe, anteriorly obscure, extends forwards to ear; southern WA................................. ***severus***

71 Dark vertebral stripe absent or very obscure in adults; or restricted to the nape.. **72**

Dark vertebral stripe from nape to base of tail.............. **75**

72 Dark upper lateral zone with one or more distinct series of pale spots or blotches along the body....................... **73**

Dark upper lateral zone obscurely mottled or uniform with at most a few pale spots anteriorly......................... **74**

73 Fewer than 25 lamellae under the fourth toe; supralabials 7-8, usually 7 (q); prefrontals separated (c); south-eastern Qld.. ***arcanus***

More than 25 lamellae under the fourth toe; supralabials 8-9, usually 8 (r); prefrontals usually in contact (b); south-western WA.. ***alleni***

74 Pale mid-lateral stripe passes over the hindlimb to continue along the tail..................................... ***inornatus***

Pale mid-lateral stripe extends to groin, then continues along the front edge of the hindlimb..................... ***coggeri***

75 A distinct narrow pale stripe between the pale paravertebral and the pale dorso-lateral stripes, at least anteriorly.. **76**

No pale stripe between the pale paravertebral and pale dorso-lateral stripes... **79**

76 Pale spots in dark upper lateral zone extend to rear of body... **77**

Pale spots in dark upper lateral zone confined to anterior part of body... ***eurydice***

77 Eight (r) or nine supralabials; prefrontals usually in contact (b).. **78**

Usually seven supralabials (q); prefrontals usually separated (c); northern NT....................... ***arnhemensis***

78 Western WA.. ***australis***

Eastern Qld.. ***capricorni***

79 Pale mid-lateral stripe more or less continuous from eye to groin... **80**

Pale mid-lateral stripe reaches no further forward than ear before breaking up into a series of spots or mottling.......... .... ***saxatilis***

80 Western WA; white mid-lateral stripe from behind eye to tail.. ***fallens***

NT, SA, Qld, NSW and Vic; white mid-lateral stripe from snout to tail... ***robustus***

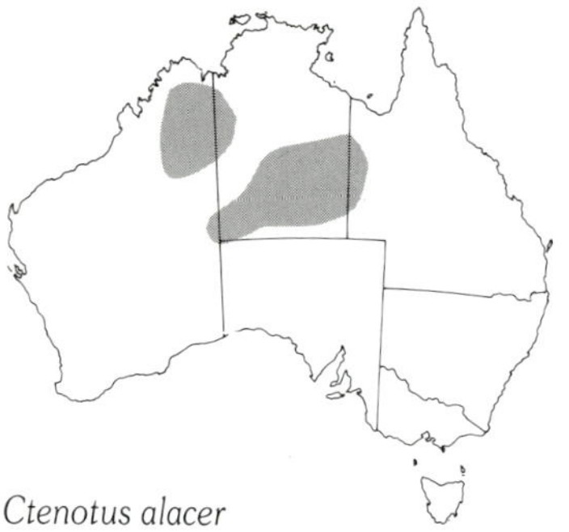

Ctenotus alacer

Ctenotus alleni

Ctenotus alacer Alice Springs, NT

Ctenotus alacer Storr, 1970

Description: Body black above, with six white longitudinal lines tinged with green, yellow or brown; head olive-brown, paler on snout; a black upper lateral stripe from eye to tail, enclosing a series of white, elongate spots that tend to coalesce anteriorly to form a stripe which turns down behind the ear to join the mid-lateral light stripe; the latter runs from nostrils to groin, but is interrupted by the ear and tends to be discontinuous between ear and arm; a white lower lateral stripe from ear to arm, sometimes represented on flanks by a series of coalescing spots; limbs above streaked with reddish- brown; lower surfaces white. 28-32 mid-body scale rows. Nasals narrowly separated or in contact. Prefrontals usually separated, occasionally in contact. Four supraoculars. Eight supralabials. Five, occasionally four, ear lobules. 20-28 lamellae under the fourth toe, each with a narrow brown callus or blunt keel. 60 mm (snout-vent).

Distribution: Central Australia and north-eastern WA.

Habit: Spinifex-covered rock outcrops, screes and ranges.

M. PETERSON

Ctenotus alleni Storr, 1974

Description: Olive-brown above, darker on the head and paler on the tail. Occasionally a short, narrow, black vertebral stripe on the nape. A narrow white dorso-lateral stripe from the eye to the base of the tail, bordered above by a narrow black stripe commencing above the eye, and below by a blackish upper lateral zone enclosing one or two series of small, white spots or short dashes. A white mid-lateral stripe extending forward from above the groin nearly to the arm and backwards nearly to the end of the tail. Lower flanks blackish-brown with one or two irregular series of short, pale dashes. Ventral surfaces whitish. 24-28 mid-body scale rows. Nasals separated. Prefrontals in contact. Four supraoculars. Supralabials 8-9, usually 8. Ear lobules 4-7. 27-34 lamellae under the fourth toe, each with a narrow to moderately wide callus. 90 mm (snout-vent).

Distribution: 'Far-northern interior of South-West Division,' WA (Storr).

Habit: Open arid woodlands and low shrublands.

Ctenotus alleni Eurardy Station, WA

G. SHEA

Ctenotus arcanus Kroombit Tops, Qld

Ctenotus allotropis Storr, 1981

Description: Similar in most respects to *Ctenotus strauchii*, from which it differs in almost always lacking a dark vertebral stripe, in having black subdigital keels which become blunter near the base of the digit, and in having the second supraocular not narrower than the third. 55 mm (snout- vent).
Distribution: South-eastern Qld to central-western NSW.
Habit: Mallee, dry open eucalypt and *Callitris* woodland and arid acacia scrublands, where it forages among leaf and other litter, especially around the bases of trees.

Ctenotus angusticeps Storr, 1988

Description: Olive-grey above, mottled and variegated with black and dirty-white or cream; a series of longitudinally-aligned whitish, dark-edged spots or short bars, especially on the upper and lower flanks, more obscure on the back; usually some indication of a dark mid-dorsal stripe; whitish below. 28-30 mid-body scale rows. Nasals in contact or narrowly separated. Prefrontals narrowly separated. Four supraoculars. 7-8 supralabials. Ear lobules 3-4. Lamellae under fourth toe 19-22, each with "a moderately wide callus". 70 mm (snout- vent).
Distribution: Known only from Airlie Island, WA.

Ctenotus arcanus Czechura and Wombey, 1982

Description: Olive-brown above, with a conspicuous pale-edged black vertebral stripe in juveniles which is reduced or lost in adults. A pale dorso-lateral stripe from above the eye to the tail, usually bordered above by a blackish stripe and below by a broad, dark brown or blackish upper lateral zone containing a single series of pale spots or blotches. A broad, pale, mid-lateral stripe from upper lip to groin, below which the flanks have obscure grey variegations. White below. 26-28 mid-body scale rows. Nasals usually separated but occasionally in narrow contact. Prefrontals separated. Four supraoculars. 8, rarely 7, supralabials. Ear lobules 3-5. Lamellae under fourth toe 20-23, each with a narrow callus. 90 mm (snout-vent).

Ctenotus allotropis Round Hill, NSW

Ctenotus ariadne Sandringham Station, Qld

R. W. G. JENKINS

Ctenotus arnhemensis Jabiluka, NT

Distribution: South-eastern Qld.
Habit: 'Eucalyptus dominated open forest and woodland in coastal areas or adjacent upland areas...or rocky outcrops.' (Czechura and Wombey)

Ctenotus ariadnae Storr, 1969

Description: Body black or dark brown above, with 18 pale longitudinal stripes which are well defined dorsally, but more poorly defined on the sides; head olive-grey or brown; tail and limbs pale reddish-brown; white mid-lateral stripe narrow and indistinct, not reaching the axilla or beyond; white ventro-lateral stripe indistinct or absent, not reaching the axilla; whitish below. 29-34 mid-body scale rows. Nasals in contact. Prefrontals in contact. Four supraoculars. Eight supralabials. 4-7 ear lobules. 20-24 lamellae under the fourth toe, each with a narrow brown callus or blunt keel. 60 mm (snout-vent).
Distribution: Central-eastern interior of WA.
Habit: Spinifex dominated sand dunes and interdunes. Recorded as feeding primarily on insects and spiders, but especially termites.

Ctenotus astarte Diamentina Lakes, Qld

Ctenotus arnhemensis Storr, 1981

Description: Brown above, with a moderate black, white-edged vertebral stripe from nape to base of tail; a narrow, white dorso-lateral stripe from eye to tail, bordered above by a narrow, black or dark brown stripe and below by a broad dark upper lateral zone which encloses a series of white spots between eye and hindlimb and which continues behind the hindlimb as a white lateral stripe; a white mid-lateral stripe from ear to tail; limbs pale brown with longitudinal dark brown streaks. Whitish below. 23-27 mid-body scale rows. Nasals separated. Prefrontals separated. Four supraoculars. Seven supralabials. Ear lobules 5-7. 20-23 lamellae under the fourth toe, each with a moderately wide callus. 55 mm (snout- vent).
Distribution: Western Arnhem Land.
Habit: Seasonally-dry woodlands and grassy floodplains.

Ctenotus astarte Czechura, 1986

Description: Brown or grey-brown above, the back with an irregular series of dark brown or blackish blotches intermixed with pale brown or creamy dots, spots and dashes; usually little indication of a dark mid-dorsal stripe; a pale, dark edged temporal stripe from above eye to above ear, and usually some indication of a narrow, pale dorso-lateral stripe, below which the brown upper flanks are peppered with white dots which tend to be aligned transversely, and which drastically decrease in numbers and intensity on the greyish lower flanks; upper labials with darker margins and several conspicuous whitish spots in the temporal region; limbs brown above with obscure pale longitudinal stripes. Ventral surfaces whitish. 32-37 mid-body scale rows. Nasals separated or narrowly contacting. Prefrontals separated. Four (occasionally five) supraoculars. Supralabials 8-9. Ear lobules 4-6. 25-27 lamellae under the fourth toe, each with a blunt keel or narrow callus. 80 mm (snout-vent).
Distribution: Far western Qld.
Habit: A ground-dwelling species living in crevices or under ground debris on a variety of arid substrates.

Ctenotus atlas Storr, 1969

Description: Back and sides dark brown or black, with eight or sometimes ten white or pale brown longitudinal stripes; head, tail and upper surfaces of limbs rich dark brown; vertebral stripe black; no more than a single fully-developed white stripe between the

Ctenotus allotropis

Ctenotus angusticeps

Ctenotus arcanus

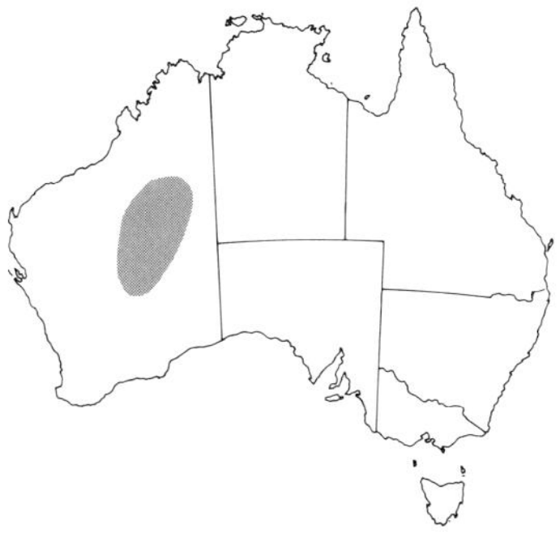
Ctenotus ariadnae

Ctenotus arnhemensis

Ctenotus astarte

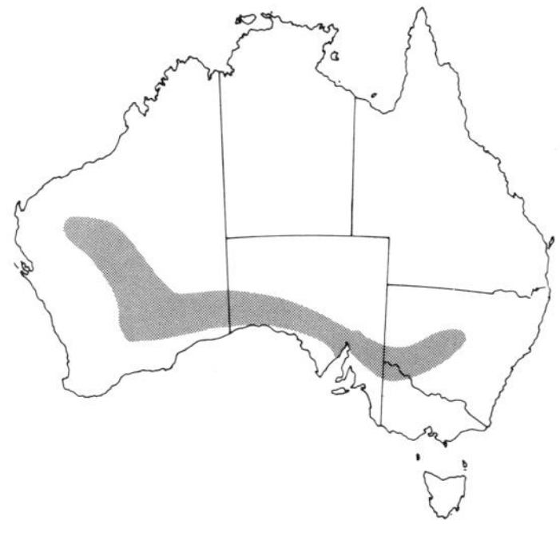
Ctenotus atlas

white dorso-lateral and mid-lateral stripes; lower surfaces white; 28-34 mid-body scale rows. Nasals usually in contact. Prefrontals usually in contact. Four supraoculars. Eight, occasionally nine, supralabials. 2-7 ear lobules. 21-27 lamellae under the fourth toe, each with a narrow, dark brown callus. 70 mm (snout-vent).
Distribution: Central and southern interior of WA, through southern SA to the mallee regions of western NSW and Vic.
Habit: In the eastern part of its range this species is confined to certain mallee associations, where it lives within the clumps of porcupine grass (*Triodia)*, emerging to feed on cockroaches and other insects, usually in the early to mid- morning and late afternoon.

Ctenotus australis (Gray, 1838)

Description: Brown or olive-brown above, with a black vertebral stripe from nape to tail edged with white or pale brown; a whitish dorso-lateral stripe from nape to tail, bordered above and below by black; upper lateral stripe dark grey, brown or black, and enclosing a series of large, pale spots or blotches; a broad, whitish mid-lateral stripe from behind axilla to tail, continuing forward to axilla and side of neck as a series of pale blotches; limbs longitudinally streaked with dark brown; whitish below. 26-32 mid-body scale rows. Nasals separated or occasionally contacting. Prefrontals contacting or occasionally separated. Four supraoculars. Eight or nine supralabials. Ear lobules 4-7. 19-24 lamellae under the fourth toe, each with a broad, flat, pale callus. 100 mm (snout-vent).
Distribution: Coastal regions of southern WA, north from Perth.
Habit: Coastal dunes and heaths.

Ctenotus borealis Horner and King, 1986

Description: Fawn, brown or olive-brown above, usually with some indication of a black vertebral stripe from nape to base of tail, sometimes narrowly edged on either side by a narrow white or cream stripe. Usually a narrow, pale, dorso-lateral stripe or series of discontinuous spots from above the eye to the base of the tail, bordered below by a broad dark brown upper lateral zone, commencing behind the eye and enclosing one or two series of small, obscure pale spots or blotches. A pale mid-lateral stripe extending

Ctenotus atlas Euabalong, NSW

Ctenotus australis Perth, WA

forward from the groin; it usually breaks up before reaching the forelimb, but in some specimens it is distinctly continuous with a pale subocular stripe. Below the pale mid-lateral stripe is a pale grey region with obscure brown variegations and mottling. Labials narrowly margined with brown. Ventral surfaces whitish. 28-33 mid-body scale rows. Nasals usually separated but occasionally in narrow contact. Prefrontals usually in broad contact. Four supraoculars. 7-8 supralabials. Ear lobules 5-7. Lamellae under the fourth toe 20-25, each with a broad, low callus. 115 mm (snout-vent).
Distribution: North-western NT.
Habit: A fast-moving diurnal species found in a variety of habitats from *Pandanus*-dominated grassy coastal dunes to open savannah woodland on floodplains and stony hills; shelters in burrows or rocky crevices.

Ctenotus brachyonyx Storr, 1971

Description: Olive-grey to brown above, with a relatively broad, black vertebral stripe from nape to base of tail; little or no indication of a pale edge to the vertebral stripe; an indistinct pale dorso-lateral stripe, bordered above by a narrow black stripe; upper lateral region with or without scattered black and whitish flecks and dots; an indistinct pale mid-lateral stripe, represented anteriorly by a short, narrow line below the eye; lower lateral zone pale brown or cream; lower surfaces whitish. 30-32 mid-body scale rows. Nasals narrowly separated. Prefrontals usually in contact. Four supraoculars. Eight or nine supralabials. 2-5 ear lobules. 22-24 lamellae under the fourth toe, each with a broad callus. 80 mm (snout-vent).

Ctenotus brachyonyx Hattah, Vic M. PETERSON

Distribution: Arid parts of north-western Vic and south- western NSW to the Murray River Valley in SA.
Habit: Mallee/*Triodia* associations and semi-arid eucalypt and acacia scrubs.

Ctenotus brooksi (Loveridge, 1933)

Description: Pale brown or fawn to reddish-bronze or crimson above, with or without a narrow, pale-edged, black vertebral stripe from nape to tail, and sometimes with an additional black stripe or scattered dark flecks on either side of the vertebral stripe; upper lateral zone pale with a series of small blackish blotches or black with an irregular series of enclosed pale spots and blotches; the latter may continue forward as a narrow dark streak through eye to

Ctenotus australis

Ctenotus borealis

Ctenotus brachyonyx

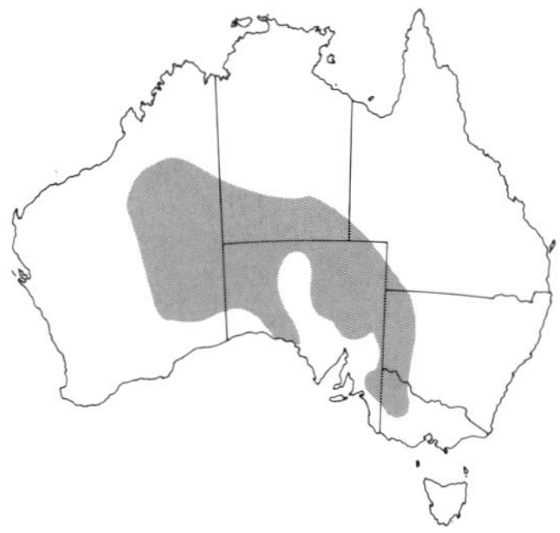

Ctenotus brooksi

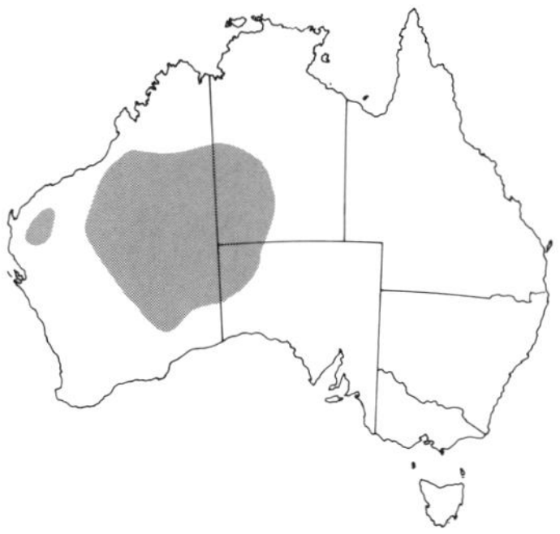

Ctenotus calurus

Ctenotus capricorni

Ctenotus catenifer

snout; with or without a broad, white mid-lateral stripe from ear to groin; limbs above with grey to black streaks and variegations; supralabials whitish with faint barring; ventral surfaces whitish. 24-28 mid-body scale rows. Nasals separated or narrowly contacting. Prefrontals in contact or narrowly separated. Four, occasionally five, supraoculars. Seven or eight supralabials. 2-5 ear lobules. 18-28 lamellae under the fourth toe, each with a fine, dark brown keel which may end in a fine spine. A single presubocular. A series of enlarged, keeled plantar scales opposite fourth toe. 50 mm (snout-vent).
Distribution: Sandy deserts of south-eastern WA and adjacent desert areas of SA and NT; north-eastern SA and adjacent parts of NT, Qld and NSW, western Vic and adjacent parts of SA.
Habit: A species inhabiting sandridge deserts throughout its range (Pianka).
Subspecies: *brooksi* (eastern deserts of WA, adjacent desert regions of south-western NT and western SA); *aranda* (Simpson Desert south to Lake Eyre basin); *taeniatus* (Lake Torrens basin); *euclae* (coastal areas of Great Australian Bight); *iridis* (western Vic and adjacent parts of SA).

Ctenotus calurus Storr, 1969

Description: Back and sides black with eight longitudinal white stripes; vertebral stripe black; head coppery-brown above flecked with dark brown; tail bright blue (juvenile) to grey-blue (adult), especially posteriorly; basal part of tail with transverse black markings, especially on the lower sides; lips and under-surfaces whitish. 24-28 mid-body scale rows. Nasals usually in contact, sometimes narrowly separated. Prefrontals in contact. Four supraoculars. Seven supralabials. 3-5 ear lobules. 20-24 lamellae under the fourth toe, each with a fine, sharp keel. A series of enlarged, keeled plantar scales opposite the fourth toe. 50 mm (snout- vent).
Distribution: Widely distributed throughout the desert regions of mid-eastern WA and adjacent desert areas of SA and NT.
Habit: A sand-swimming species which lives in the soil beneath spinifex and other grasses and shrubs in spinifex-dominated sandridge desert, living both on the dunes and interdunes.

Ctenotus capricorni Storr, 1981

Description: Brown above; narrow black vertebral stripe, narrowly edged with pale brown; a narrow,

indistinct pale brown dorsal stripe; a narrow white dorso-lateral stripe bordered above by a narrow, black stripe and below by a dark-brown upper lateral zone enclosing a series of white dots and dashes; a white mid-lateral stripe becoming faint or broken anteriorly; lower lateral zone pale grey-brown; limbs brown, flecked with darker brown; ventral surfaces whitish. 30-32 mid-body scale rows. Nasals narrowly separated. Prefrontals contacting or narrowly separated. Four supraoculars. Eight supralabials. Ear lobules 4-5, second or third largest. Lamellae under fourth toe 21-23, each with a moderately wide callus. 60 mm (snout- vent).
Distribution: Known only from near Jericho, Qld.
Habit: "Sandy areas supporting Triodia, often in association with shrub and woodland communities..." (Wilson and Knowles).

Ctenotus brooksi Flinders Ranges, SA

Ctenotus catenifer Storr, 1974

Description: Olive-grey above, flecked with black. Sometimes an irregular black vertebral stripe. A narrow, white, dorso- lateral stripe from above the eye to the tail, usually broken into a series of short dashes, bordered above by a ragged- edged black stripe enclosing a series of pale dots, below by a broad, black, upper lateral zone enclosing a series of white dots. Lower flanks with scattered white flecks. Ventral surfaces whitish. 24-30 mid-body scale rows. Nasals separated. Prefrontals separated. Four supraoculars. 7, occasionally 8, supralabials. Ear lobules 3-6. 21-25 lamellae under the fourth toe, each with a dark, blunt keel or narrow callus. 50 mm (snout-vent).
Distribution: South coast and hinterland of south-western WA.
Habit: Coastal heaths and low shrublands.

Ctenotus catenifer Stirling Range National Park, WA M. PETERSON.

Ctenotus coggeri Sadlier, 1985

Description: Brown or olive-brown above, without vertebral stripes. A broad, white, dorso-lateral stripe extending from above the eye to the base of the tail, and bordered above, at least anteriorly, by a narrow black stripe, and below by a broad, black, upper lateral zone containing several pale spots anteriorly. A white mid-lateral stripe from ear to groin, below which is some obscure grey and black mottling. Cream to yellow below, the yellow confined to the chest and belly. 28-32 mid-body scale rows. Nasals separated. Prefrontals narrowly separated or contacting. Four supraoculars. 8, rarely 7, supralabials. Ear

Ctenotus coggeri

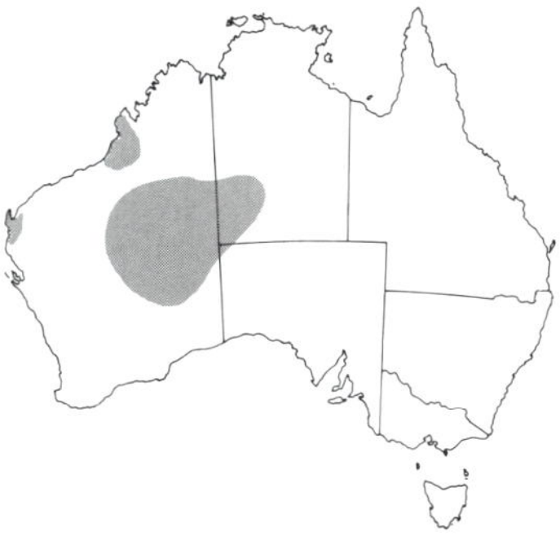

Ctenotus colletti

Ctenotus coggeri Brockman Range, NT

Ctenotus colletti Giralia, WA

lobules 3-4. Lamellae under fourth toe 24-28, each with a moderate to broad dark callus. 80 mm (snout-vent).
Distribution: Western escarpment of Arnhem Land, NT, and its outliers.
Habit: A ground-dwelling species found in open woodland associated with the sandstone massifs and outcrops of western Arnhem Land.

Ctenotus colletti (Boulenger, 1896)

Description: Back and sides very dark brown to black with eight to twelve pale longitudinal stripes; head yellowish- brown with darker brown flecks and streaks; tail pale brown above; lips and lower surfaces whitish. 22-27 mid-body scale rows. Nasals usually in contact. Prefrontals usually in contact. Four supraoculars. Four, occasionally three, ear lobules, the upper one greatly enlarged. 22-30 lamellae under the fourth toe, each with a fine dark mucronate but fairly weak keel. 45 mm (snout-vent).
Distribution: Great Victoria Desert and adjacent desert areas of NT; south-western Kimberley region, WA.
Habit: Spinifex-dominated red sand dunes and inter-dune areas.
Subspecies: *colletti* (south-west Kimberleys); *nasutus* (Great Victoria Desert); *rufescens* (Exmouth Gulf region, WA).

Ctenotus decaneurus Storr, 1970

Description: Back and sides blackish-brown, with usually ten white longitudinal stripes; head greyish-

brown; upper surfaces of limbs reddish-brown streaked with dark brown; a white vertebral stripe formed by the fusion of the paravertebrals, occasionally separated on the nape by a short, black vertebral stripe; whitish below. 24-32 mid-body scale rows. Nasals in contact or separated. Prefrontals usually widely separated. Four supraoculars. Supralabials 7-8. 4-6 ear lobules. 18-24 lamellae under the fourth toe, each with a moderately wide brown callus. 50 mm (snout-vent).
Distribution: North-west coast and hinterland of NT and bordering regions of WA.
Habit: Stony hills and ranges.
Subspecies: *decaneurus* (northern Kimberleys, WA and NT); *yampiensis* (Yampi Sound, west Kimberleys, WA).

Ctenotus delli Storr, 1974

Description: Dark olive-brown above, more or less uniform; a broken, narrow, white dorso-lateral stripe from above eye to tail, bordered above by a narrow, indistinct black stripe and below by a broad blackish upper lateral zone enclosing one or more series of white dots. A broken, white mid-lateral stripe extending forward as a series of short dashes to below the eye. Lower flanks dark grey flecked with white. Ventral surfaces whitish. 28-36 mid-body scale rows. Nasals usually separated, sometimes narrowly in contact. Prefrontals separated. Four supraoculars. Seven, occasionally eight, supralabials. Ear lobules, small, 3–5. 23-29 lamellae under the fourth toe, each with a narrow dark callus. 55 mm (snout- vent).
Distribution: 'The north Darling Range' (Storr), south- western WA.
Habit: Dry sclerophyll forest on stony hills and ranges.

Ctenotus dux Storr, 1969

Description: Back and sides black with about 16-20 white (in smaller specimens) to brown (older adults) longitudinal stripes; a pale-edged, black vertebral stripe; head olive- brown above with darker flecks; tail and limbs brown above, the latter streaked with dark brown; lower lateral light stripes extend forward to sides of face and neck; lips lightly barred; lower surfaces whitish. 28-32 mid-body scale rows. Nasals in contact or slightly separated. Prefrontals in contact. Four supraoculars. Eight, occasionally nine, supralabi-

Ctenotus decaneurus Kunnunurra, WA J. WEIGEL

Ctenotus delli Mt Dale, Darling Ranges, WA

Ctenotus essingtonii Daly River, NT

Ctenotus decaneurus

Ctenotus delli

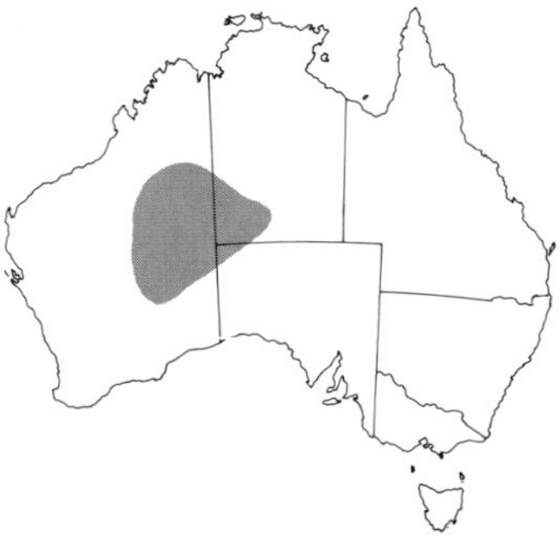

Ctenotus dux

als. 2-6 long, acute ear lobules. 22-30 lamellae under fourth toe, each with a dark brown narrow callus or blunt keel. 65 mm (snout- vent).
Distribution: Sandy deserts around the junction of WA, SA and NT borders, extending well into WA.
Habit: Spinifex-dominated red sand dunes.

Ctenotus ehmanni Storr, 1985

Description: Back and sides very dark brown to black, with six narrow, pale longitudinal stripes on the back; an upper lateral series of white spots and dashes from the eye to above the hindlimb; a broad, whitish mid-lateral stripe from the loreal region, through the ear to the groin and a broad whitish lower lateral stripe anteriorly; tail brown above with a series of pale longitudinal stripes; lips and lower surfaces whitish. 28-32 mid-body scale rows. Nasals in contact. Prefrontals separated. Four supraoculars. Two ear lobules, the upper one greatly enlarged. 21-24 lamellae under the fourth toe, each with a fine dark mucronate

Ctenotus dux Condun Well, WA

Ctenotus eurydice Yarrowitch, NSW

but fairly weak keel. 40 mm (snout-vent).
Distribution: North-west Kimberley region, WA.
Habit: '...sandy (soil) with outcropping and embedded quartzite and sandstone boulders. The vegetation was eucalypt woodland with sparse ground cover.' (Storr).

Ctenotus essingtonii (Gray, 1842)

Description: Brown to reddish-brown above, darker on the head, usually without a dark vertebral stripe but occasionally with a pale-edged narrow black stripe, especially anteriorly; tail and limbs reddish above, the latter streaked and variegated with dark brown; a white dorso-lateral stripe from above the eye to the base of the tail, bordered above by a darkish brown stripe; upper lateral zone dark brown or black, sometimes enclosing a few paler spots, especially anteriorly; a narrow, white mid-lateral stripe from ear to groin; lower lateral zone pale brown, spotted with white; whitish below. 24-28 mid-body scale rows. Nasals separated or contacting. Prefrontals separated or occasionally contacting. Four supraoculars. Seven or occasionally eight supralabials. 2-5 ear lobules. 20-26 lamellae under the fourth toe, each with a moderately wide dark callus. 60 mm (snout-vent).
Distribution: North coast and islands of NT and Qld, extending inland from the Gulf of Carpentaria and across CapeYork Peninsula.
Habit: Seasonally-dry tropical woodlands and coastal dunes and shrublands, extending into the spinifex-dominated stony plains, hills and ranges of the interior.
Subspecies: *essingtoni* (northern and north-eastern NT); *brevipes* (Qld).

Ctenotus eurydice Czechura and Wombey, 1982

Description: Olive-brown above, with a series of contrasting dark and pale stripes: a black vertebral stripe bordered on either side by a narrow pale stripe;

Ctenotus ehmanni

Ctenotus essingtoni

Ctenotus eurydice

Ctenotus eutaenius

Ctenotus fallens

Ctenotus gagudju

Ctenotus gemmula

a whitish dorso-lateral stripe from above the eye to the tail, bordered above by a narrow black stripe and below by a broad, black upper lateral zone containing a few pale spots or blotches anteriorly; a whitish stripe from the lips to the ear, where it is slightly displaced to continue along the side of the body to the groin and along the hindlimb; this stripe in turn is bordered below by a broad, black mid-lateral stripe, below which is a pale lower lateral stripe. White below. 24-28 mid-body scale rows. Nasals separated or narrowly in contact. Prefrontals separated. Four supraoculars. 7 or 8 supralabials. Ear lobules 3-4. Lamellae under fourth toe 12-23, each with a moderate to broad dark callus. 75 mm (snout-vent).
Distribution: South-eastern Qld and north-eastern NSW.
Habit: Eucalypt woodland, sclerophyll forests and rainforest edges.

Ctenotus eutaenius Storr, 1981

Description: Black above and on the sides, with ten pale brown or white narrow longitudinal stripes; the five pale stripes on each side consist of one paravertebral from nape to tail, one dorsal from nape to base of tail, a dorso-lateral from eye to tail, an upper lateral from temple to tail and a wider mid-lateral from below eye to tail. Lower surfaces white. 30 mid- body scale rows. Nasals separated or just contacting. Prefrontals in contact. Four supraoculars. Eight supralabials. Ear lobules 4-5. 20-22 lamellae under the fourth toe, each with a broad callus. 90 mm (snout-vent).
Distribution: North-eastern Qld, centred on Townsville.
Habit: Rock outcrops and stony hills in coastal and near- coastal woodlands.

Ctenotus fallens Storr, 1974

Description: Olive-green, brown or blackish above; a black vertebral stripe edged with pale brown or white, which in turn is sometimes edged with black; a white dorso-lateral stripe from above eye or from nape to tail, bordered above and below with black; dark upper lateral zone encloses a series of pale spots or blotches; a white mid-lateral stripe sometimes present, edged above and below with black. Ventral surfaces whitish. 26-36 mid-body scale rows. Nasals usually separated. Prefrontals usually in contact. Four supraoculars. 7-9, usually eight, supralabials. Ear lobules 3-7. 17-25 lamellae under the fourth toe,

Ctenotus eutaenius near Charters Towers, Qld

each with a broad pale callus. 90 mm (snout-vent).
Distribution: West coast and hinterland of WA.
Habit: Coastal dunes and heaths; low shrublands.

Ctenotus gagudju Sadlier, Wombey and Braithwaite, 1986

Description: Brown above, usually unpatterned but occasionally with a narrow, dark, vertebral stripe anteriorly; a white dorso- lateral stripe from above the eye to the tail, broadly bordered above with black; upper lateral zone blackish-brown, enclosing a series of small, pale, elongate spots; a white mid-lateral stripe extending forward from groin and usually breaking up into a series of spots or dashes on the flanks and neck; lower flanks rusty-brown with a series of white spots; whitish below. 28-32 mid-body scale rows. Nasals in contact. Prefrontals separated. Four supraoculars. Frontoparietals fused to form a single scale, a character unique within its genus. Seven supralabials. 4-5 ear lobules. 21-28 lamellae under the fourth toe, each with a blunt, dark brown keel. 50 mm (snout-vent).
Distribution: Alligator Rivers region, NT.
Habit: '...mixed eucalypt woodland on a hard lateritic substrate' (Sadlier, Wombey and Braithwaite).

Ctenotus gemmula Storr, 1974

Description: Olive-grey above, more or less uniform with a broken narrow, white dorso-lateral stripe from above the eye to the base of the tail, narrowly bordered above by black and below by a broad, blackish upper lateral zone with or without a series of white spots. This dark upper lateral zone continues forward as a broken stripe through the eye nearly to the tip of the snout. A white mid-lateral stripe, irregular, or broken into a series of short dashes. Lower lateral zone dark grey flecked with white. Limbs above yellowish-brown with bold black and white markings. 24-28 mid-body scale rows. Nasals usually separated, occasionally in narrow contact. Prefrontals usually separated. Four supraoculars. Eight supralabials. Ear lobules small, 2-5. 23-27 lamellae under the fourth toe, each with a blunt, dark keel. 50 mm (snout-vent).
Distribution: South coast and hinterland of south-western WA.
Habit: Coastal heaths and semi-arid woodlands.

Ctenotus gagudju Jabiru, NT

Ctenotus grandis Laverton, WA

Ctenotus grandis Storr, 1969

Description: Pale to dark brown, olive or reddish above, with a dark brown or black vertebral stripe from nape to tail, with an additional four dark brown conspicuous (juveniles) to broken or faint (adults) dorsal longitudinal stripes from nape to tail; head and tail somewhat paler than back; sides of body dark greyish-brown flecked or finely spotted with white, the latter tending to form vertical bars; limbs reddish-brown above, the hindlimbs variegated with dark and pale brown; lips pale, barred with brown; whitish below. 28-34 mid-body scale rows. Nasals separated or contacting. Prefrontals usually in contact, but occasionally separated. Four supraoculars. Eight, occasionally seven or nine, supralabials. 4-8 ear lobules. 19-26 lamellae under the fourth toe, each with a dark brown blunt keel (juveniles) or pale, flat callus (adults). 100 mm (snout-vent).
Distribution: Mid-western coast of WA through arid interior to Tanami Desert, NT.
Habit: Coastal low shrublands to spinifex-dominated sand ridge and sandplain deserts of the interior.
Subspecies: *grandis* (Tanami, Great Sandy, Gibson and Great Victoria Deserts); *titan* (Pilbara and adjacent regions, WA).

Ctenotus greeri Storr 1979

Description: Dark brown above, paler on the head, neck and tail; a broad, blackish vertebral stripe, narrowly edged with white; a narrow white dorso-lateral stripe from above eye to tail, the dark brown area above it enclosing a series of white dots and dashes which tend to form a broken pale dorsal stripe; dark upper lateral zone enclosing one or more series of white dots; a white mid-lateral stripe which breaks up into a series of spots anteriorly. Limbs pale brown with darker brown longitudinal stripes. Ventral surfaces whitish. 24-26 mid-body scale rows. Nasals contacting or separated. Prefrontals usually narrowly separated. Four supraoculars. Eight supralabials. Ear lobules 5-7, third usually largest. 23-27 lamellae under the fourth toe, each with a narrow callus or blunt keel. 50 mm (snout-vent).
Distribution: Great Victoria Desert, WA.
Habit: An inhabitant of red, sandy soils in spinifex/mallee/mulga associations (Storr).

Ctenotus hanloni Storr, 1980

Description: Rich reddish-brown in adults, olive-

Ctenotus gemmula Melaleuca Park, WA

M. PETERSON

Ctenotus hanloni
Gnaraloo Station, WA

green in juveniles, head paler olive-brown; a blackish vertebral stripe, a narrow blackish dorsal stripe on each side, and a whitish dorso-lateral stripe from behind eye to tail, edged above with blackish and below by dark olive flanks enclosing numerous white spots and flecks tending to be aligned horizontally rather than vertically. Limbs brown with dark brown flecks and longitudinal stripes. Ventral surfaces whitish. 30-32 mid-body scale rows. Nasals in contact. Prefrontals in contact or narrowly separated. Four supraoculars. Supralabials eight or nine, usually eight. Ear lobules 4-7, third usually largest. Lamellae under fourth toe 19-27, each with a blunt keel or narrow callus. 70 mm (snout- vent).
Distribution: Coast of north-western WA to Great Sandy,Tanami and Great Victoria Deserts.
Habit: Sand ridge and sandplain deserts dominated by hummock grasses.

Ctenotus hebetior Storr, 1978

Description: Brownish above, with a very narrow and indistinct blackish vertebral stripe and, on each side of the back, an equally narrow and indistinct blackish dorsal stripe, all from nape to tail; a whitish dorso-lateral stripe from above eye to tail, bordered above by a wide blackish stripe and below by a dark upper lateral zone enclosing two series of white flecks or spots; a narrow, white mid-lateral stripe, if present, distinct only posteriorly, breaking up anteriorly into a series of spots; lower lateral zone a paler reddish-brown with obscure paler spots. Limbs pale brown with darker brown flecks and longitudinal stripes. Ventral surfaces whitish. 30 mid- body scale rows. Nasals separated or in contact. Prefrontals separated or in contact. Four supraoculars. Eight supralabials. Ear lobules 4-5. 22-28 lamellae under the fourth toe, each with a moderately wide callus. 60 mm (snout-vent).
Distribution: Central interior of Qld and adjacent parts of NT.
Habit: '...on grassy flats (including *Triodia*)' (Storr).

Subspecies:*hebetior* (Central Qld); *schuettleri* (north- western Qld and adjacent areas of NT).

Ctenotus helenae Storr, 1969

Description: Pale to dark brown or olive-brown above, with a dark brown or black vertebral stripe from nape to tail, sometimes pale-edged; occasionally pale dorso-lateral and mid- lateral stripes present, each narrowly edged with black; sides greyish, with irregularly scattered dark and pale flecks and dots; whitish below, sometimes suffused with grey or bluish-grey and with black flecks under the tail. Some specimens uniform in colour, virtually lacking any pattern. 26-32 mid- body scale rows. Nasals usually widely separated, but occasionally contacting. Prefrontals usually in contact, occasionally separated. Normally four supraoculars. Eight, occasionally seven or nine, supralabials. 2-6 ear lobules. 17-25 lamellae under the fourth toe, each with a narrow or broad callus, or smooth. 90 mm (snout-vent).
Distribution: From the northern coast of WA through the arid interior and adjacent desert regions of north-western SA and the NT.
Habit: An inhabitant of the sandy central deserts, where it is found in close association with *Triodia*.

Ctenotus hebetior near Charters Towers, Qld

G. SHEA

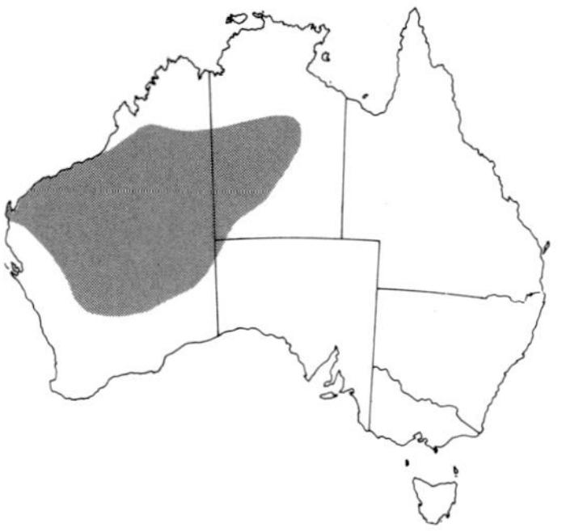
Ctenotus grandis

Ctenotus greeri

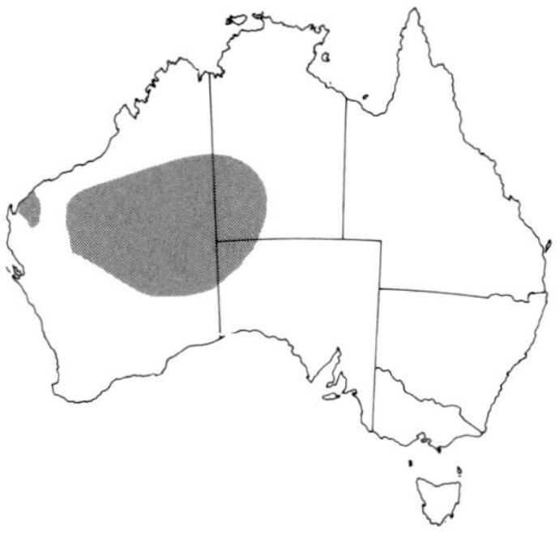
Ctenotus hanloni

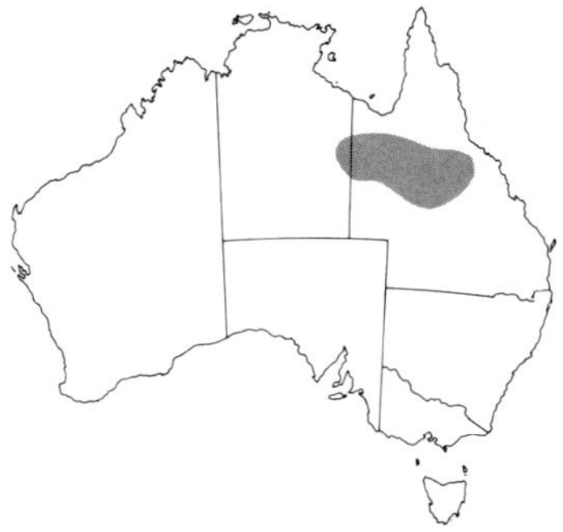
Ctenotus hebetior

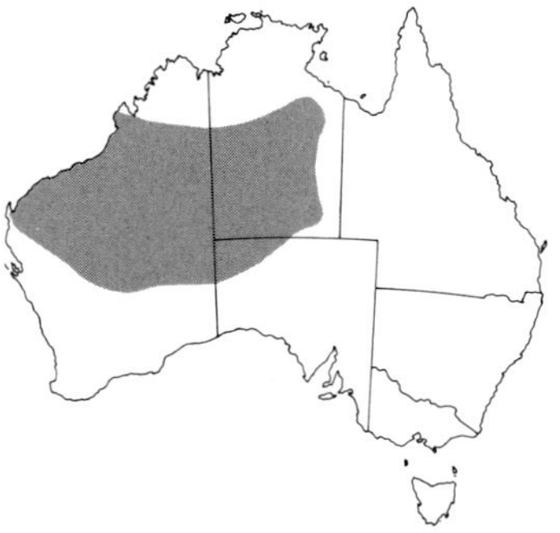
Ctenotus helenae

Ctenotus hilli

Ctenotus impar

Ctenotus hilli Storr, 1970

Description: Brown above, usually unpatterned but occasionally with a narrow, dark vertebral stripe anteriorly; a white dorso- lateral stripe from above the eye to the tail, broadly bordered above with black; upper lateral zone blackish-brown enclosing a series of small pale elongate spots; a white mid-lateral stripe from arm to groin, continued on the neck as a series of spots or dashes; lower sides usually without pattern, occasionally brown with white spots; whitish below. 30-34 mid-body scale rows. Nasals in contact. Prefrontals widely separated. Four supraoculars. Seven or eight supralabials. 4-6 ear lobules. 22-28 lamellae under the fourth toe, each with a blunt, dark brown keel. 50 mm (snout-vent).
Distribution: Islands, coast and adjacent hinterland of NT.
Habit: Seasonally-dry open woodlands and vegetated coastal dunes.

Ctenotus impar Storr, 1969

Description: Back and sides black, with 11 pale whitish or brown longitudinal stripes: a broad, pale vertebral stripe occasionally split by a thin black line; two pale dorsal stripes on each side; a pale dorso-lateral stripe from above ear to tail; pale mid-lateral stripe extends forward to ear, where it branches, but is continued after its interruption as a labial stripe; pale lower lateral stripe; head, tail and limbs brown; whitish below. 26-28 mid-body scale rows. Nasals separated. Prefrontals separated, Four supraoculars. Seven, occasionally six or eight, supralabials. 2-5 ear lobules. 18-26 lamellae under the fourth toe, each with a wide, dark brown callus. 65 mm (snout-vent).
Distribution: Far south-western WA.
Habit: Coastal heathlands, mallee and low eucalypt woodland.

Ctenotus ingrami Czechura and Wombey, 1982

Description: Olive-brown above, with a pattern of contrasting dark and pale stripes: a black, pale-edged vertebral stripe; a whitish dorso-lateral stripe from above the eye to the tail, edged above by a narrow black stripe and below by a broad black or brown upper lateral zone; a broad, whitish mid-lateral stripe from the upper lip, through the ear to the groin and along the hindlimb; this in turn is bordered below by a broad black stripe which is itself bordered below by a

pale lower lateral stripe. Whitish below. 24-28 mid-body scale rows. Nasals separated, rarely in narrow contact. Prefrontals separated. Four supraoculars. 8 supralabials. Ear lobules 3-5. Lamellae under fourth toe 19-25, each with a moderate to broad callus. 80 mm (snout-vent).
Distribution: Western slopes and plains of central Qld and central-northern NSW.
Habit: Acacia and eucalyptus woodland.

Ctenotus helenae Ethabuka Station, SW Qld

Ctenotus inornatus Gray, 1845

Description: Pale olive-brown to dark brown above, with (usually juveniles) or without (adults) a narrow, complete or incomplete blackish stripe from nape to tail, rarely pale-edged; a narrow pale dorso-lateral stripe from above eye to tail, usually narrowly edged above with dark brown; upper lateral zone dark brown with darker and/or lighter flecks and dots; pale mid-lateral stripe either conspicuous (juveniles) or obscure (adults); lower sides greyish-brown, with or without lighter and darker flecks; whitish below. 26-34 mid-body scale rows. Nasals separated or contacting. Prefrontals usually in contact, occasionally separated. Four, occasionally three, supraoculars. Eight, rarely seven to nine, supralabials. 3-7 ear lobules. 18-26 lamellae under the fourth toe, each with a wide, flat callus. 90 mm (snout-vent).
Distribution: Coast and hinterland of northern Australia from the Kimberley region to the lower Gulf of Carpentaria.
Habit: In Arnhem Land this species is an inhabitant of the Triodia-covered sandstone hills of the western escarpment.

Ctenotus impar near Albany, WA

Ctenotus joanae Storr, 1970

Description: Pale olive above, with a broad black vertebral stripe from nape to tail, with only a faint indication of a narrow pale edge; a narrow white dorso-lateral stripe from above eye to tail, broadly edged above with black; upper lateral zone olive-brown with small, indistinct, pale spots; a pale mid lateral stripe from side of snout to tail; a pale lower lateral stripe from below and behind ear to tail; faint indications of a pale ventro-lateral stripe; whitish below. 26 mid-body scale rows. Nasals in contact. Prefrontals separated. Four supraoculars. Eight supralabials. 2-3 ear lobules. 19-20 lamellae under the fourth toe, each with a narrow, dark callus. 50 mm (snout-vent).
Distribution: Currently known from Newcastle

Ctenotus inornatus near Drysdale River crossing, WA

R. W. G. JENKINS

J. WOMBEY

Ctenotus kurnbudj near Kapalga, NT

Waters, NT, and adjacent regions, to central Qld. **Habit:** Tussock grasslands of the black soil complexes of the Barkly Tableland, central Qld and the Channel Country.

Ctenotus kurnbudj Sadlier, Wombey and Braithwaite, 1986

Description: Medium brown to rich ochrous-brown above. Dark vertebral stripe absent, the darker lateral edges of the dorsal scales forming a series of narrow dark brown longitudinal lines on the back. A narrow, whitish dorso-lateral stripe from behind the eye to the basal portion of the tail, usually edged above with a broad, dark brown or black stripe either enclosing, or broken up by, a series of paler brown spots or blotches; below the pale dorso-lateral stripe is a broad, dark brown upper lateral zone containing one to three series of small white spots or flecks. A cream or very pale brown stripe from the groin forward along the flanks, where it usually breaks up into a series of spots well before reaching the arm; this stripe continues behind the groin as a narrow, pale lateral stripe on the tail. Usually scattered white spots on the side of the neck and cheeks; ear lobules pale; lips spotted or barred; limbs above with dark brown streaks and scattered pale spots. Ventral surfaces white. 26-30 mid-body scale rows. Nasals narrowly contacting or narrowly separated. Prefrontals usually separated, occasionally in point contact. Four supraoculars. 23-28 lamellae under the fourth toe, each with a narrow brown callus or blunt keel. 50 mm (snout-vent).
Distribution: Alligator Rivers region, NT.
Habit: Open eucalypt woodland.

Ctenotus lancelini Lancelin Island, WA

M. PETERSON

Ctenotus labillardieri Walpole, WA

Ctenotus labillardieri (Duméril and Bibron, 1839)

Description: Variable in colour and pattern. Olive-

brown or dark brown above, uniform or flecked with darker brown; sometimes an irregular, blackish vertebral stripe. A narrow, white dorso-lateral stripe from above the eye to the base of the tail, bordered above by a narrow to broad blackish stripe which sometimes encloses a series of white spots, and below by a broad, blackish upper lateral zone. This zone may be immaculate or may contain up to three series of small white spots. A white mid-lateral stripe from below the eye, through the ear and over the forearm to the groin, continued behind as a stripe along the tail. Lower flanks blackish variegated with white or with an obscure whitish lower lateral stripe from axilla to groin. Limbs above rich brown, spotted or streaked with black. Ventral surface cream to yellow. 24-31 mid-body scale rows. Nasals separated, rarely in contact. Prefrontals usually separated. Four supraoculars. Seven or eight supralabials. 2-6 small ear lobules. 20-30 lamellae under the fourth toe, each with a wide, dark callus. 60 mm (snout-vent).
Distribution: Southern coastal regions and offshore islands of south-western WA.
Habit: Essentially a rock-dwelling species found around and under exfoliating rocks, rock outcrops, etc. in heathlands and eucalypt forests. Also found under decaying logs, bark, etc.

Ctenotus ingrami

Ctenotus inornatus

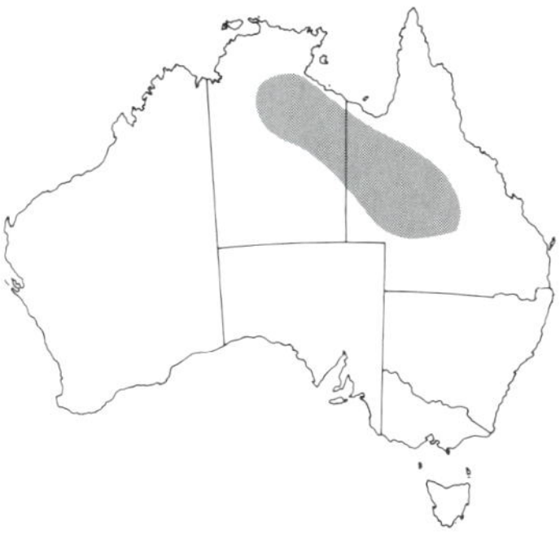

Ctenotus joanae

Ctenotus kurnbudj

Ctenotus labillardieri

Ctenotus lancelini

Ctenotus lateralis

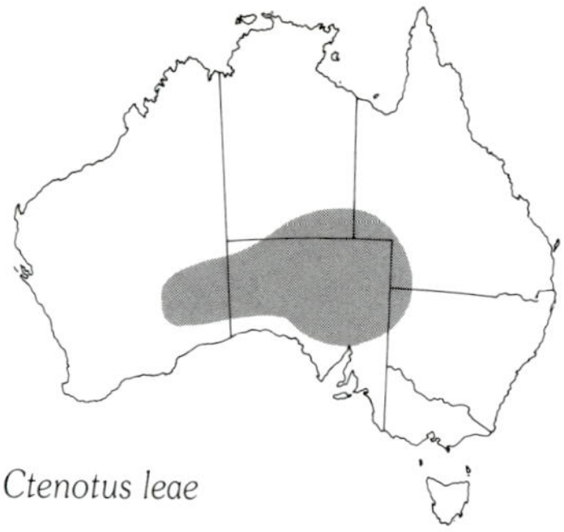

Ctenotus leae

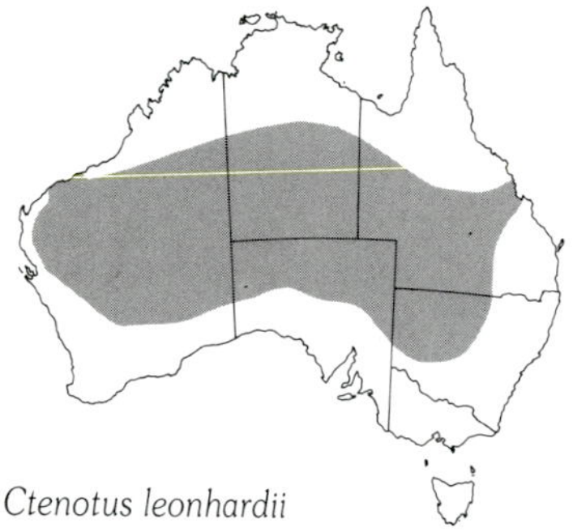

Ctenotus leonhardii

Ctenotus mastigura

Ctenotus militaris

Ctenotus lateralis Mayne Junction, W Qld

Ctenotus leae Ethabuka Station, SW Qld

Ctenotus lancelini Ford, 1969

Description: Closely allied to *Ctenotus labillardieri* from which it may be distinguished by its larger size (to 80 mm snout-vent length), paler brown dorsal colour, speckled back, and yellow legs spotted and streaked with blackish-brown. 24 mid-body scale rows.
Distribution: Known only from Lancelin Island, WA.
Habit: '...limestone outcrops...' (Wilson and Knowles). Otherwise similar to *Ctenotus labillardieri.*

Ctenotus lateralis Storr, 1978

Description: Greyish-brown to reddish-brown above, with a narrow black, usually pale-edged, vertebral stripe from nape to base of tail; a pale brown to white dorso-lateral stripe from above eye to base of tail, narrowly edged above with black; a dark brown upper lateral zone divided by an indefinite, narrow, paler longitudinal stripe which may break up into a series of dots and dashes anteriorly; a narrow whitish mid-lateral stripe commencing brokenly on snout and

passing through ear and above forelimb and hindlimb to tail; lower lateral zone paler grey, sometimes with a pale lower lateral stripe. Ventral surfaces whitish. 28-32 mid-body scale rows. Nasals usually narrowly separated. Prefrontals usually in contact. Four supraoculars. Supralabials 8-9, usually 8. Ear lobules 3-5. 20-25 lamellae under the fourth toe, each with a broad, dark callus. 80 mm (snout-vent).
Distribution: Arid interior of northern and north-western Qld.
Habit: Found among '...stony hills and ridges' (Storr), dominated by a ground cover of *Triodia*.

Ctenotus leae (Boulenger, 1887)

Description: Back and sides with alternating pale and dark stripes; a black vertebral stripe from nape to tail, narrowly bordered with white to pinkish-brown; a dark dorso-lateral stripe on either side from nape to tail, bordered below by white; dorso- lateral stripe commencing above eye; a dark upper lateral stripe from above eye to tail, and a dark lower lateral stripe from axilla to groin, but branching in front of forelimb, bordered above by a white mid-lateral stripe from lips to groin; tail bright reddish-brown, especially distally; whitish below. 20-26 mid-body scale rows. Nasals in contact. Prefrontals usually in contact. Four supraoculars. Eight supralabials. 2-5 ear lobules. 24-30 lamellae under the fourth toe, each with a sharp, mucronate, dark brown keel. 60 mm (snout-vent).
Distribution: Great Victoria Desert region of WA and SA to far western Qld and NSW.
Habit: Red sand ridges and interdunes with spinifex as the dominant ground cover.

Ctenotus leonhardii (Sternfeld, 1919)

Description: Pale brown to rich ochrous-brown above. A pale- edged, dark brown vertebral stripe sometimes present, otherwise the darker lateral edges of the dorsal scales result in a series of narrow dark brown longitudinal lines on the back. A narrow, whitish dorso-lateral stripe from behind the eye to the basal portion of the tail, usually edged above with dark brown; below the pale dorso-lateral stripe is a broad dark brown lateral stripe containing one to three series of small white spots. A cream or very pale brown stripe from the groin forward along the flanks, where it breaks up into a series of spots well before reaching the arm; this stripe continues behind the groin as a narrow, pale lateral stripe on the tail. Usually scattered white spots on the side of the neck

Ctenotus leonhardii Ethabuka Station, SW Qld

Ctenotus mimetes

Ctenotus monticola

Ctenotus pallescens

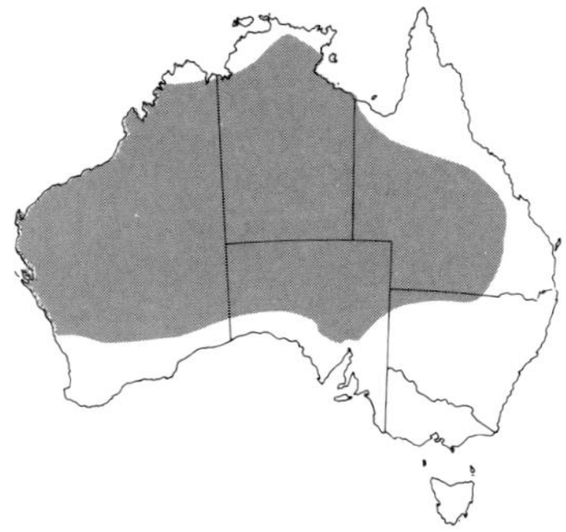

Ctenotus pantherinus

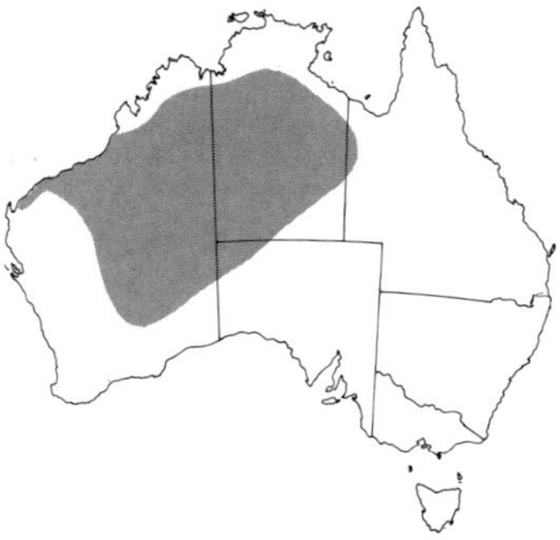

Ctenotus piankai

Ctenotus pulchellus

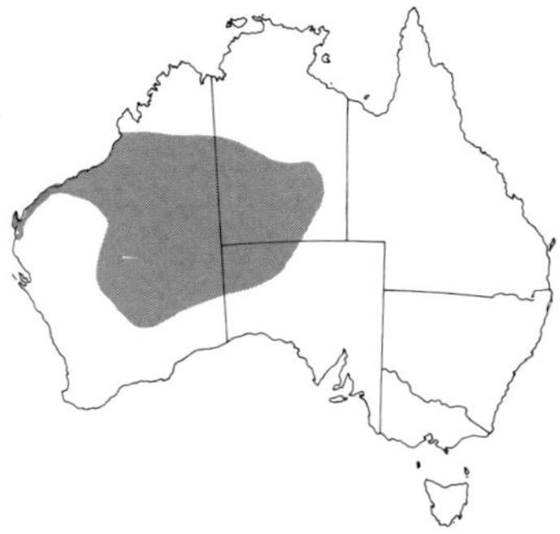

Ctenotus quattuordecimlineatus

and cheeks; ear lobules pale; lips spotted or barred; limbs above with dark brown streaks and scattered pale spots. Ventral surfaces white. 26-33 mid-body scale rows. Nasals usually in contact, rarely narrowly separated. Prefrontals usually separated, but sometimes in narrow contact. Four supraoculars. 21-30 lamellae under the fourth toe each with a narrow brown callus or blunt keel. 70 mm (snout-vent).
Distribution: From the central western coast of WA, through the lower half of the NT and northern SA to Qld and NSW.
Habit: Found in a variety of arid habitats, from stony situations associated with the centralian ranges to sandridge and sandplain deserts with spinifex (porcupine grass) the dominant ground cover.

Ctenotus mastigura Storr, 1975

Description: Dark, iridescent olive-brown above, with a narrow, blackish, pale-edged vertebral stripe; a narrow but conspicuous white dorso-lateral stripe on each side, narrowly edged with black; upper flanks brownish-grey above a narrow, whitish, dark-edged mid-lateral stripe. Whitish below. 29-32 mid-body scale rows. Nasals separated. Prefrontals usually in contact. Three or four supraoculars. Seven or eight supralabials. 4-6 moderate ear lobules. 21-31 lamellae under the fourth toe, each smooth or bluntly callused. 60 mm (snout- vent).
Distribution: Coast and hinterland of the Kimberley region, WA. 'An apparently related population occurs on the Arnhem Land Plateau' (Storr).
Habit: Seasonally-dry tropical eucalypt woodlands.
Subspecies: *mastigura* (north Kimberleys); *burbidgei* (north-west Kimberleys).

Ctenotus militaris Storr, 1975

Description: Pale brown above, darker on the head; a narrow, dark vertebral stripe lacking pale edges; a pale brown or white dorso-lateral stripe from above eye to tail, bordered above by black; on each side between this black stripe and the vertebral stripe is another blackish dorsal stripe from nape to tail; a dark reddish-brown upper lateral zone enclosing one or more series of pale dots or dashes; no pale mid-lateral stripe; lower lateral zone pale grey-brown; limbs brown above with longitudinal dark brown stripes. Ventral surfaces whitish. 30-40 mid-body scale rows. Nasals in contact. Prefrontals usually separated. Four supraoculars. Supralabials 7-9, usually eight. 3-7 ear lobules. 20-25 lamellae under the fourth toe, each with

Ctenotus mimetes Galena, WA

a blunt, brown keel. 60 mm (snout-vent).
Distribution: East Kimberleys, WA.
Habit: Seasonally-dry open woodland.

Ctenotus mimetes Storr, 1969

Description: Brown above, brighter and redder posteriorly. Labials narrowly edged with brown. A narrow, white dorso- lateral line from above the eye to the basal portion of the tail, bordered above by a narrow dark brown stripe, below by a broad, dark lateral zone enclosing large, pale irregular spots or short, vertical bars. The dark lateral zone is more or less divided by a narrow, pale mid-lateral stripe, from the loreal region to the groin. This stripe continues behind the groin as a conspicuous lower lateral stripe. Limbs above with black- brown reticulations. Ventral surfaces white. 26-32 mid-body scale rows. Nasals usually widely separated. Prefrontals usually in contact. Four supraoculars. 7-9 supralabials. Ear lobules 3-6, usually four. 23-31 lamellae under the fourth toe, each with a narrow dark brown callus or blunt keel. 80 mm (snout-vent).
Distribution: Arid and semi-arid parts of south-western WA.
Habit: Arid low shrublands and eucalypt and *Acacia* woodlands.

Ctenotus monticola Storr, 1981

Description: Brownish above, flushed with olive on the back and reddish on the tail; upper labials barred with dark brown. A narrow, black vertebral stripe, itself narrowly edged with white; a narrow white dorso-lateral stripe from eye to rump, narrowly edged above with black and below by a broad, blackish upper lateral zone enclosing series of pale dots which tend to form vertical bars; sometimes a narrow, dark dorsal stripe is present, especially anteriorly; a narrow, pale midlateral stripe; lower flanks dark brown with pale spots. Limbs olive- brown with dark brown longitudinal streaks. Ventral surfaces whitish. 24-28 mid-body scale rows. Nasals separated. Prefrontals separated. Four supraoculars. Seven supralabials. Ear lobules 2-4, first usually largest. 17-19 lamellae under the fourth toe, each with a narrow to moderately wide callus. 65 mm (snout-vent).
Distribution: Atherton Tableland, Qld.
Habit: Open woodland.

Ctenotus pallescens Storr, 1970

Description: Brown above, sometimes suffused with reddish; an indistinct and sometimes incomplete black vertebral stripe; a narrow white, dorso-lateral stripe

Ctenotus pantherinus Ethabuka Station, SW Qld

from above eye to tail, bordered above by a dark zone enclosing a series of short, pale transverse bars and bordered below by a dark upper lateral zone enclosing a series of pale, metallic-brown vertical bars; a white mid-lateral stripe from upper lip to hindlimb; from ear to groin a lower lateral series of greyish blotches. Limbs brown, striped or reticulated with dark brown. Ventral surfaces whitish. 28-30 mid-body scale rows. Nasals narrowly separated. Prefrontals separated. Four supraoculars. Seven supralabials. Ear lobules 2-5, first usually largest. 18-22 lamellae under the fourth toe, each with a fine, dark, sharp mucronate keel. 45 mm (snout-vent).
Distribution: Arid northern part of NT.
Habit: 'Hard to stony soils vegetated with low woodlands and hummock grasses...' (Wilson and Knowles).

Ctenotus pantherinus (Peters, 1866)

Description: Grey, olive-brown or brown above, with a series of small, white or yellow spots (usually a single scale) on the back and base of the tail, each spot with a black edge, or, more commonly, a short black bar on each side. South- western populations with a blackish-brown vertebral stripe, while some populations from the upper NT are virtually devoid of pattern. Flanks and sides of tail with scattered small, black-edged white spots (the white usually occupying several scales), becoming more obscure towards the vent and on the side of the neck. Forelimb with dark brown streaks, hindlimb with scattered small ocelli. Labials with narrow, dark brown margins, usually one or two pale spots below the eye. Ventral surfaces pale silvery-grey or pale olive-grey. 31-38 mid-body scale rows. Nasals in contact. Prefrontals usually in contact. Four supraoculars. 7-9 supralabials, usually eight. Ear lobules 3-7. 21-29 lamellae under the fourth toe, each with a fine, sharp, brown keel. 90 mm (snout-vent).
Distribution: Widely distributed from south-western WA through most drier parts of that state and the more xeric parts of northern SA, NT and western Qld.
Habit: A swift-moving, diurnal lizard usually closely associated with porcupine grasses in a wide variety of sandy and deserticolous habitats.
Subspecies: *pantherinus* (south-western WA); *acripes* (arid north-western Qld and Barrow Island, WA); *calx* (northern Australia from the Kimberleys to north-western Qld); *ocellifer* (remainder of species range).

Ctenotus pulchellus Mt Isa, Qld

Ctenotus piankai Storr, 1969

Description: Pattern consisting solely of six longitudinal white stripes contrasting with the brown ground colour, except in juveniles, which may possess fine white spots in the dark upper lateral zone. Brown above, darkest on the back and palest on the snout and tail. A narrow pale stripe from neck to base of tail along each of the two mid-dorsal scale rows. A narrow whitish dorso-lateral stripe from above the eye, on either side, to the middle of the tail. A white mid-lateral stripe from the ear to the groin, continuing behind the groin along the basal portion of the tail. Labials white. Ventral surfaces white. 24-26 mid-body scale rows. Nasals in contact. Prefrontals usually in contact. Four supraoculars. Eight supralabials. Ear lobules 1-5. Lamellae under the fourth toe 19-26, each with a narrow dark brown callus. 45 mm (snout- vent).
Distribution: Widely distributed through the interior of WA and the more arid parts of NT and western Qld.
Habit: Found in a variety of desert habitats, usually in association with spinifex (porcupine grass).
Subspecies: *piankai* (north-western and eastern WA, NT, SA and Qld); *duricola* (coast and hinterland of north-western WA).

Ctenotus pulchellus Storr, 1978

Description: Rich brown above, darker and more bronze on the head, with a narrow, black vertebral stripe edged with pale brown and a narrow, black dorsal stripe on either side, all extending from the nape to the tail. A narrow, pale brown or cream dorso-lateral stripe from above each eye to the tail, narrowly bordered by black above and broadly bordered by black below. Sides of face, neck and body bright reddish, with numerous scattered white spots which sometimes are vertically aligned and which often extend into the black upper lateral zone. Whitish below. Limbs longitudinally striped with dark and pale brown. 30-34 mid-body scale rows. Nasals in broad contact. Prefrontals separated. Four supraoculars. Eight supralabials. Ear lobules 5-6. 22-28 lamellae under the fourth toe, each with a narrow to broad, dark callus. 65 mm (snout- vent).
Distribution: Currently known only from western Qld and eastern NT.
Habit: Stony hill and breakaways with spinifex as the major ground cover.

Ctenotus quattuordecimlineatus Condun Well, WA

Ctenotus quattuordecimlineatus (Sternfeld, 1919)

Description: Dark brown to blackish on the body and flanks, paler brown on the head, limbs and tail. Body with 18 or 16 pale longitudinal lines, whitish on the sides but usually very pale brown dorsally; usually a narrow pale stripe along each of the adjacent scale rows; a broader dorso-lateral pale stripe from above the eye to the base of the tail where it is joined by two narrow pale stripes commencing above and behind the ear; a pale mid-lateral stripe from below the eye, through the ear and over the forearm to the groin, continuing along the groin and over the base of the tail; a lower lateral stripe from below the ear, interrupted by the arm and continuing almost to the groin. Ventral surfaces whitish. 26-30 mid-body scale rows. Nasals usually in contact. Prefrontals usually in contact. Four supraoculars. 7-9 supralabials, usually eight. Ear lobules 2-7. Lamellae under the fourth toe 21-28, each with a dark brown callus or blunt keel. 70 mm (snout-vent).
Distribution: Central-western WA, through adjacent desert regions of north-western SA and south-western NT.
Habit: Mostly found in spinifex dominated red sandridge and sandplain deserts.
Subspecies: *quattuordecimlineatus* (north-western to south-eastern WA); *iapetus* (coastal north-western WA).

Ctenotus quinkan Ingram, 1979

Description: Olive-brown above, without pattern on the back; a narrow, pale dorso-lateral stripe from above the eye to the tail, bordered below by a broad, blackish, upper lateral zone without enclosed pale flecks or spots; a whitish midlateral stripe from ear to hindlimb extending in front of ear as a labial stripe; a black lower lateral stripe breaking up into irregular blotches in front of forelimb; lips pale, mottled with dark brown. Limbs pale brown with dark brown longitudinal stripes. Ventral surfaces white. Only known specimen has 28 mid-body scale rows. Nasals separated. Prefrontals narrowly separated. Four supraoculars. Eight supralabials. Ear lobules 5-6. Lamellae under the fourth toe 32, each with a moderate callus. 81 mm (snout-vent).
Distribution: Currently known only from the sandstone escarpments in the Cooktown-Laura area, Qld.
Habit: '...open forest, sometimes with a heath understorey. The substrate is decomposed sandstone with small to large sandstone rocks' (Ingram).

Ctenotus rawlinsoni Ingram, 1979

Description: Brown above, with a black pale-edged vertebral stripe from nape to tail; a whitish dorso-lateral stripe from above eye to tail, edged above by a narrow black stripe and below by a broad, dark upper lateral zone without paler flecks or spots; a white mid-lateral stripe from ear to hindlimb; the dark stripe below the white mid-lateral stripe breaks up anteriorly (i.e., from well behind the forelimb) into a series of dark blotches on flanks and neck. Ventral surfaces whitish. 25-28 mid-body scale rows. Nasals separated. Prefrontals narrowly separated. Four supraoculars. Eight supralabials. Ear lobules 6-8. 33-34 lamellae under the fourth toe, each with a moderate callus. 80 mm (snout-vent).
Distribution: Known only from the type locality, near Cape Bedford, Cape York Peninsula, Qld.
Habit: An inhabitant of sandy coastal heath.

Ctenotus regius Storr, 1971

Description: Brown above, with a narrow, white-edged, blackish-brown vertebral stripe from nape to base of tail. A narrow, white dorso-lateral stripe from above eye to about middle of tail, widely or narrowly edged above with blackish-brown, sometimes enclosing a series of small, pale spots or bars. Upper lateral zone dark brown or reddish-brown, with one or two series of small whitish spots or bars aligned longitudinally, continuing on the tail as a pale, dark-edged stripe. A white mid-lateral stripe from the loreal region, through the ear and over the arm to the groin, continuing over the groin and along the side of the tail.

Lower lateral region brown, sometimes enclosing some pale spots. Ventral surfaces whitish. 24-28 mid-body scale rows. Nasals usually separated. Prefrontals in contact. Four supraoculars. 7-9 supralabials, usually eight. Ear lobules 3-6. Lamellae under the fourth toe 23-30, each with a narrow, dark brown callus or blunt keel. 70 mm (snout-vent).
Distribution: Central and eastern SA to western NSW, south- western Qld and southern NT.
Habit: Similar to *C. leonhardii*. Often found on clay and loamy soils with sparse ground cover.

Ctenotus robustus Sandy Hollow, NSW

Ctenotus robustus Storr, 1970

Description: Fawn, brown or olive-brown above, with a conspicuous broad, black vertebral stripe from nape to base of tail, narrowly edged on either side by a narrow white or cream stripe. A conspicuous pale dorso-lateral stripe from above the eye to about half-way along the tail, bordered above by a blackish-brown stripe and below by a broad, dark brown upper lateral zone, commencing behind the eye and enclosing one or two series of small, pale spots or blotches. A pale mid- lateral stripe extending forward from the groin; it usually breaks up before reaching the forelimb, but in some specimens it is distinctly continuous to the loreal region. This stripe continues behind the groin as a lower lateral stripe along the tail. Below the pale mid-lateral stripe is a region of obscure brown variegations. Labials narrowly margined with brown. Ventral surfaces whitish. 26-32 mid-body scale rows. Nasals just contacting or narrowly separated. Prefrontals in broad contact. Four supraoculars. 7-9 supralabials. Ear lobules 3-7. Lamellae under the fourth toe 18-27, each with a broad, low callus. 110 mm (snout-vent).
Distribution: Widely distributed from south-eastern SA through Vic, eastern NSW and Qld and the upper NT to north- western WA.

Ctenotus regius Wilcannia, NSW

Ctenotus quinkan

Ctenotus schevilli Muttaburra, Qld

Ctenotus rawlinsoni

Habit: A large, active, diurnal species found in a wide variety of habitats, from coastal beach dunes and heaths, through wet and dry sclerophyll forests and rocky situations to the savannah and mallee woodlands of the more mesic interior. Often takes refuge when disturbed in short, shallow burrows under ground debris.

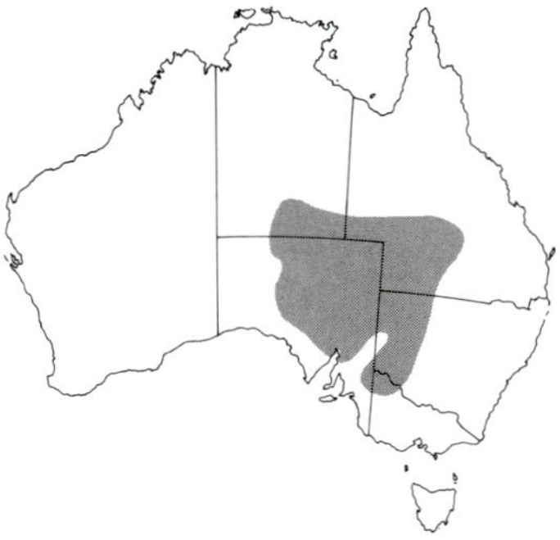

Ctenotus regius

Ctenotus robustus

Ctenotus rubicundus

Ctenotus rubicundus Storr, 1978

Description: Reddish-brown to olive-brown above, paler on snout, face and sides. Ventral surfaces whitish. Otherwise without pattern. 34-36 mid-body scale rows. Nasals in contact. Prefrontals in contact. Four supraoculars. Eight supralabials. Ear lobules 3-5. Lamellae under the fourth toe 19-22, each with a moderately narrow callus. 100 mm (snout-vent).
Distribution: Pilbara region of WA.
Habit: Stony hill country with spinifex.

Ctenotus rutilans Storr, 1980

Description: Brown above, the head, neck and forelimbs coppery-red; a narrow, blackish vertebral stripe edged with pale brown; a narrow, pale dorso-lateral stripe from nape to tail, bordered above by a wide dark stripe enclosing a series of pale spots, and bordered below by a dark upper lateral zone enclosing

Ctenotus saxatilis Jabiru, NT

scattered, pale reddish-brown flecks and spots; pale midlateral stripe virtually absent, being confined to an area just in front of the hindlimb, where it breaks up anteriorly into a series of spots; lower lateral zone reddish-brown with scattered pale dots. Ventral surfaces whitish. 34-40 mid-body scale rows. Nasals in contact or separated. Prefrontals separated. Four supraoculars. Supralabials eight. Ear lobules 5-7. Lamellae under the fourth toe 31-33, each with a dark, narrow callus or blunt keel. 55 mm (snout-vent).
Distribution: Pilbara region, WA.
Habit: Triodia and arid scrubs on a stony substrate.

Ctenotus saxatilis Storr, 1970

Description: Similar in most respects to *Ctenotus robustus*, from which it differs in lacking a pale subocular stripe, and in having a narrow, dark vertebral stripe, 8-10 supralabials and fewer nuchals (2-3, as against three, usually four, in *robustus*). 80 mm (snout-vent).
Distribution: Mountain ranges, stony hills and rock outcrops of central Australia to coast of WA.
Habit: Hummock grasses on rocky substrates.

Ctenotus schevilli (Loveridge, 1933)

Description: Brown above, with a series of dark

Ctenotus rutilans

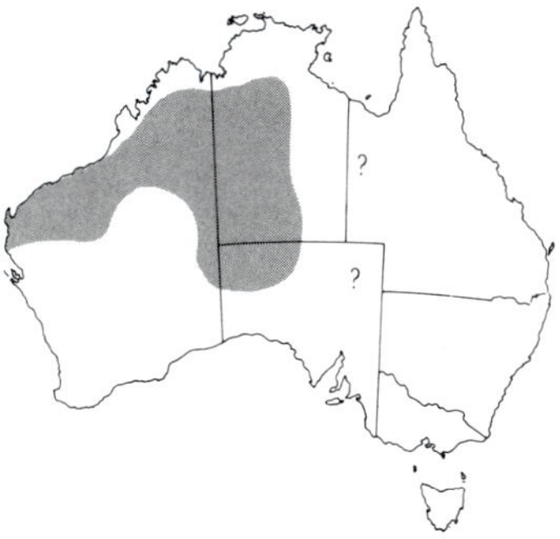

Ctenotus saxatilis

Ctenotus schevilli

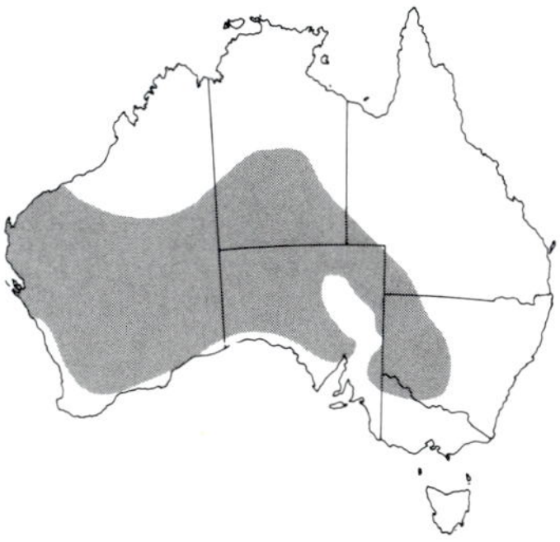

Ctenotus schomburgkii

brown to blackish flecks forming a broad vertebral stripe from the neck to the base of the tail. A darker brown upper lateral zone, darkest along its upper edge where it tends to form a narrow dorso-lateral stripe enclosing numerous small pale spots which form more or less vertical bars. Ventral surfaces whitish. 36-44 mid-body scale rows. Nasals usually in contact. Prefrontals separated or in narrow contact. Four supraoculars. Eight supralabials. Ear lobules short, small, 3-7. Subdigital lamellae 22-26, each moderately compressed and smooth to bluntly keeled. 80 mm (snout-vent).
Distribution: Known only from the interior of Qld.
Habit: Cracked black soil tussock-grassed plains, where it lives in earth cracks or under fallen timber and other ground debris.

Ctenotus schomburgkii (Peters, 1863)

Description: A variable species, usually a rich bronzy-brown or coppery-brown gradually merging with olive-brown or bronzy- green colouring on the rump and tail. Typically with a narrow black vertebral stripe from nape to basal half of tail, and a narrow, black paravertebral stripe on either side from neck to base of tail. A narrow white or cream dorso-lateral stripe from above the eye to the base of the tail, narrowly edged above with blackish-brown and bordered below by a broad, black upper-lateral zone commencing as a narrow streak along the canthus and enclosing a single series of brown or orange-brown spots or blotches. A pale white mid-lateral stripe commencing on the loreal region and extending through the ear, over the forearm to the groin, continuing behind the groin as a lower lateral stripe on the tail. Below this on the flanks is a dark lower lateral zone with obscure, poorly defined pale spots, especially anteriorly. Limbs above spotted and streaked with blackish-brown. Ventral surfaces white. In some western and northern populations the dorsal stripes may be obscure or absent. 24-30 mid-body scale rows. Nasals usually separated or in very narrow contact. Prefrontals narrowly separated or in contact. Four supraoculars. Seven, rarely eight supralabials. Ear lobules 1-5. Lamellae under the fourth toe 17-26, each with a fine, dark, sharp mucronate keel. 45 mm (snout-vent).
Distribution: Widely distributed throughout the southern half of WA, through SA and the southern NT to central western NSW.
Habit: Usually found among porcupine grass on sandy soils, usually in association with mallee communities and other arid scrubs.

Ctenotus schomburgkii Round Hill, NSW

Ctenotus septenarius King, Horner and Fyfe, 1988

Description: Rich reddish-brown above with a pale dorso- lateral stripe on each side which extends from above the eye to the tail; on the back between these two pale stripes are seven dark stripes, the outer of which may contain a series of pale spots anteriorly; a broad, dark brown upper lateral zone enclosing one or two series of pale brown or whitish spots and flecks, and bordered below by a continuous or broken pale mid- lateral stripe from the groin forward to the ear, and then extending below the eye to the loreal region; the lower flanks mottled dark brown and white; limbs above reddish-brown with dark brown longitudinal stripes and streaks. Ventral surfaces white. 28-30 mid-body scale rows. Nasals usually separated or occasionally in very narrow contact. Prefrontals narrowly separated or in contact. Four supraoculars. Eight supralabials. Ear lobules 3-5. Lamellae under the fourth toe 26-32, each with a narrow, dark brown callus. 65 mm (snout- vent).
Distribution: South-western NT.
Habit: A burrowing species found on the lower slopes of stony hills and rock outcrops.

Ctenotus serotinus Czechura, 1986

Description: Olive-brown above, with a blackish vertebral stripe narrowly and obscurely edged with pale brown, and the darker lateral edges of the other

Ctenotus severus near Menzies, WA

dorsal scales tending to form obscure longitudinal lines; a broad, pale dorso-lateral zone commencing as a narrow pale stripe over the eye; upper lateral zone dark olive-brown enclosing several series of small whitish dots or spots aligned more or less transversely; an obscure, pale mid-lateral stripe between axilla and groin, merging with a greyish lower lateral zone mottled with whitish; a disrupted pale loreal/subocular streak; limbs brown with darker brown longitudinal stripes. Ventral surfaces whitish. 29-33 mid-body scale rows. Nasals narrowly separated or in narrow contact. Prefrontals narrowly separated. Four supraoculars. Eight supralabials. Ear lobules 4-5. Lamellae under the fourth toe 22-27, each smooth or bluntly keeled. 50 mm (snout-vent).
Distribution: South-western Qld.
Habit: Original specimens found on 'gravelly downs and sand- dune interface" and 'on a sandhill' (Czechura).

Ctenotus serventyi Storr, 1975

Description: Brown above; a narrow, black vertebral stripe from nape to tail, edged with pale brown or white; a narrow, whitish dorso-lateral stripe from above eye to tail, bordered above by black; on each side between this black stripe and the black vertebral stripe is another black or dark brown dorsal stripe; dark brown upper lateral zone enclosing one or two series of pale brown or whitish dots and dashes; a narrow, pale mid-lateral stripe commencing on the snout and extending around the ear to the tail; limbs brown with longitudinal dark stripes. Ventral surfaces whitish except for tail, which is sometimes suffused with pink. 24-28 mid-body scale rows. Nasals usually in contact. Prefrontals contacting or separated. Four supraoculars. Eight supralabials. Ear lobules 3-7. Lamellae under the fourth toe 18-24, each with a blunt dark keel or narrow callus. 50 mm (snout-vent).
Distribution: Coastal plains, islands and hinterland of north-western WA.
Habit: Coastal and inland sandy areas associated with semi- arid woodlands and shrublands.

Ctenotus severus Storr, 1969

Description: Grey, brown or reddish-brown above; an obscure dark vertebral stripe may be present, but usually only on the neck; a narrow, pale dorso-lateral stripe from above the eye to the tail, bordered above by a broad black stripe and separated below from the dark upper lateral zone by a narrow zone of paler ground colour; upper lateral zone enclosing scattered, pale dots and spots; a pale mid-lateral stripe from ear to hindlimb. Ventral surfaces whitish. 28-32 mid-body scale rows. Nasals usually separated. Prefrontals usually in contact. Four supraoculars. 8-9, usually eight, supralabials. Ear lobules 3-7. Lamellae under the fourth toe 18-23, each smooth or with a flat callus. 80 mm (snout-vent).
Distribution: Coast and interior of southern WA, except for south and south-west.
Habit: Mulga and other *Acacia* scrubs, especially on stony substrates.

Ctenotus spaldingi (Macleay, 1877)

Description: Basic colour and pattern similar to that of *Ctenotus robustus*, although the dorsal stripes may become obscure or almost absent in some eastern populations. 28-30 mid-body scale rows. Nasals in contact or widely to narrowly separated. Prefrontals in contact. Only three supraoculars. Seven, rarely eight, supralabials. Ear lobules 3-5. Lamellae under the fourth toe 18-24, each with a broad, low callus. 100 mm (snout-vent).
Distribution: Upper NT through coastal and adjacent regions to Cape York Peninsula, Qld, and the islands of Torres Strait. Extra-limital in southern New Guinea.

M. PETERSON

Ctenotus strauchii Mootwingee National Park, NSW

Ctenotus striaticeps near Mt Isa, Qld

M. PETERSON

Ctenotus storri Jabiru, NT

Ctenotus spaldingi near Torrens Creek, Qld

Ctenotus taeniolatus near Mt Garnet, Qld

Ctenotus septenarius

Ctenotus serotinus

Ctenotus serventyi

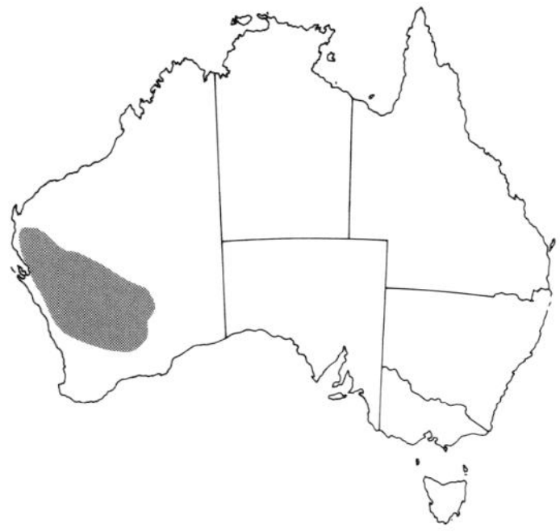

Ctenotus severus

Ctenotus spaldingi

Ctenotus storri

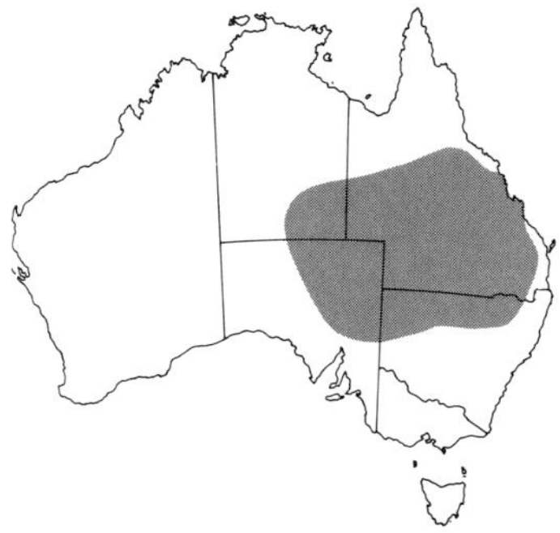

Ctenotus strauchii

Habit: Similar to *Ctenotus robustus*, usually observed foraging among grasses and other low vegetation in savannah woodland, especially where rock outcrops, and on grassy coastal dunes, monsoon scrub and heathland. Usually takes cover in ground litter and debris, or in shallow burrows, when disturbed.

Ctenotus storri Rankin, 1978

Description: Yellowish-brown above, with the following series of paler longitudinal stripes: on each side a fairly obscure pale paravertebral and an equally obscure dorsal extending from nape to tail (the paravertebrals on each side merging on the rump), a dorso-lateral from above the eye to the tail, and a whitish mid-lateral stripe from the lips over the ear to the hindlimb; dark upper lateral zone without enclosed paler spots or flecks. Limbs pale brown with dark brown longitudinal stripes. Ventral surfaces white. 24-26 mid-body scale rows. Nasals in contact. Prefrontals widely separated. Four supraoculars. Supralabials 6-7. Ear lobules 1-5. Lamellae under the fourth toe 21-24, each with a narrow brown callus. 40 mm (snout-vent).
Distribution: Coastal and river plains of northern and north- western NT.
Habit: Found in open forest and woodland habitats.

Ctenotus strauchii (Boulenger, 1887)

Description: Reddish-brown to almost chocolate-brown above, without any indication of mid-dorsal stripes. Usually a narrow, white dorso-lateral stripe from above the eye to the base of the tail, bordered above by a linear series of small blackish blotches and below by a broad, blackish vertebral zone which encloses series of small white or pale brown spots which tend to be aligned transversely, and which may sometimes divide the dark lateral zone into a series of dark rhomboidal blotches. Usually a narrow white stripe from below the eye, through the ear and along the mid-flank to the groin, passing over the groin to continue as a white lower lateral stripe along the side of the tail; this pale stripe may be broken up into a series of spots or short bars between the ear and the forelimb. Lower flanks brown with obscure pale spots. Ventral surfaces white. 24-32 mid-body scale rows. Nasals usually in contact. Prefrontals usually separated. Four supraoculars. 8-9 supralabials. Ear lobules small, 2-3. Lamellae under the fourth toe 16-20, each with a fine, dark, sharp mucronate keel. 50 mm (snout-vent).

Distribution: Widely distributed through the interior of NSW and southern Qld, extending deeply into adjacent regions of SA and the NT.
Habit: Usually found in leaf-litter or among fallen timber and other ground debris in savannah woodland, mallee and grassland plant communities. It appears to avoid porcupine grass, even when found in areas where this grass is abundant.

Ctenotus striaticeps Storr, 1978

Description: Blackish above, with eight conspicuous broad white stripes from snout to tail; on each side a paravertebral joining its opposite number on the snout, a dorso-lateral from above the eye to the tail, a mid-lateral from lips to tail and a lower lateral between fore- and hindlimbs. Limbs white, with dark longitudinal stripes. Ventral surfaces whitish. 28 mid-body scale rows. Nasals in broad contact. Prefrontals widely separated. Four supraoculars. Seven supralabials. Ear lobules two, first largest. Lamellae under the fourth toe 24-28, each with a fine mucronate keel. 50 mm (snout-vent).
Distribution: Arid north-western Qld.
Habitat: Spinifex-covered hills, ranges, rock outcrops and stony flats.

Ctenotus taeniolatus (White, *ex* Shaw, 1790)

Copper-Tailed Skink

Description: Pattern consisting entirely of contrasting longitudinal stripes, without spots. Rich brown above, paler on the limbs and tail, the latter sometimes bright orange or reddish in colour. Usually a short black bar between the eyes, narrowly edged with white or cream. A broad black vertebral stripe from the nape to the basal part of the tail, edged on either side by a narrow cream or yellow stripe. The latter is itself narrowly edged with black. A narrow pale brown or cream dorso-lateral stripe, narrowly bordered above by black and below by a broad black upper lateral stripe commencing as a narrow stripe along the canthus, ultimately extending along the side of the tail. Below this is a conspicuous white mid-lateral stripe from the loreal region, through the ear and along the flank to the groin and continued behind the groin along the side of the tail. This stripe is in turn bordered below by a black stripe commencing on the labials and extending to the groin. Below this is a white stripe from the angle of the jaws to the upper arm; it is continued behind the arm from the axilla to the groin, and is bordered below by a narrow black

Ctenotus striaticeps

Ctenotus taeniolatus

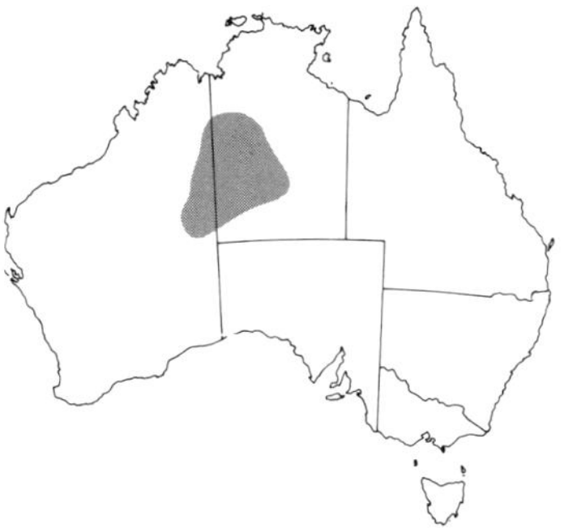
Ctenotus tanamiensis

Ctenotus tantillus

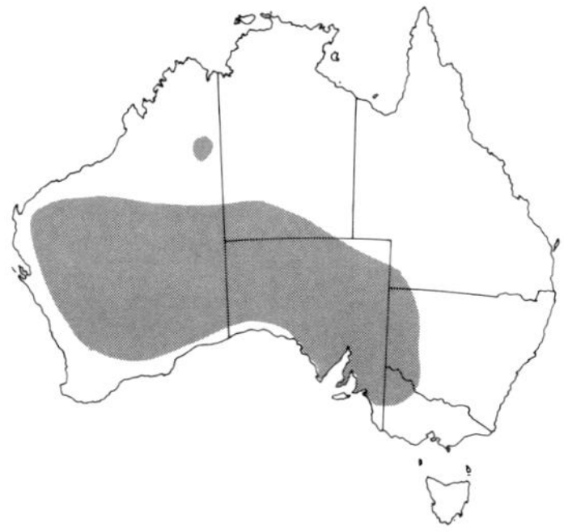
Ctenotus uber

Ctenotus vertebralis

Ctenotus xenopleura

Ctenotus uber Wyangala Dam, NSW

Ctenotus youngsoni

Ctenotus zastictus

Ctenotus zebrilla

stripe. Limbs streaked with black or dark brown. White below. 26-34 mid-body scale rows. Nasals separated or narrowly in contact. Prefrontals usually separated. Four supraoculars. Seven supralabials. 2-5 small ear lobules. Lamellae under the fourth toe 18-22, each with a blunt keel. 80 mm (snout-vent).
Distribution: From northern Vic through eastern NSW and Qld to Cape York Peninsula.
Habit: Found in a variety of habitats, from coastal heathlands to wetter montane forest, dry sclerophyll forest and woodlands, but mostly in rocky situations where the lizards shelter in crevices or under logs or exfoliating rock slabs.

Ctenotus tanamiensis Storr, 1970

Description: Dark reddish-brown above, much paler on the head, lower flanks and tail; a narrow, pale, paravertebral stripe on each side enclosing a vertebral stripe of the ground colour. Remainder of back and flanks with seven or eight series of small, pale dots and dashes, smallest in the middle series, the latter often aligned as vertical bars. A narrow, white subocular streak. Labials barred with white and brown. Ventral surfaces whitish. 29-32 mid-body scale rows. Nasals in contact or narrowly separated. Prefrontals usually separated. Four supraoculars. Ear lobules 4-7. Lamellae under the fourth toe 24-30, each

with a narrow dark callus or blunt keel. 90 mm (snout-vent).
Distribution: Tanami Desert, NT.
Habit: *Triodia*-dominated sandplain desert.

Ctenotus tantillus Storr, 1975

Description: Similar in many respects to *Ctenotus schomburgkii*; pale greenish-brown above, sometimes with a dark vertebral stripe; a narrow, whitish dorso-lateral stripe from above the eye to the tail, sometimes broken up into a series of dashes and sometimes bordered above by black; sometimes a narrow black dorsal stripe on either side of the back; dark brown upper lateral zone enclosing a series of white flecks or spots; a white mid-lateral stripe present or absent, continuous or broken, but when distinct, commences on the snout. Ventral surfaces whitish. 26-30 mid-body scale rows. Nasals in contact. Prefrontals separated. Four supraoculars. Supralabials 7-8, usually eight. Ear lobules 1-4, the first largest. Lamellae under the fourth toe 18-23, each finely keeled. 45 mm (snout-vent).
Distribution: Northern Kimberleys, WA.
Habit: Seasonally-dry tropical woodlands.

Ctenotus uber Storr, 1969

Description: Pale sandy-fawn to golden-brown above, with a narrow to moderate blackish-brown vertebral stripe from nape to base of tail, pale-edged in eastern populations and sometimes fading before reaching the rump. A narrow, dark brown paravertebral stripe on each side from the nape to about halfway along the body. A narrow, whitish dorso-lateral stripe from above the eye nearly to the base of the tail, narrowly edged above with blackish-brown and below by a broad blackish- brown upper lateral zone enclosing numerous small white spots which tend to be aligned transversely. Below the dark upper lateral zone is a broad lower lateral region with obscure darker variegations sometimes enclosing paler spots. Lips with pale brown spots and bars. Limbs streaked with dark brown above. Ventral surfaces whitish. 26-34 mid-body scale rows. Nasals separated. Prefrontals separated or contacting. Four supraoculars. 7-9 supralabials, usually eight. Ear lobules 3-7. Lamellae under the fourth toe 19-31, each with a brown callus or blunt keel. 65 mm (snout-vent).
Distribution: Eastern interior of southern WA, through SA and central Australia to far western parts of Qld, NSW and Vic with an isolated population in north-eastern WA.
Habit: Found in a variety of arid habitats, from chenopod shrublands to arid scrubs and open woodland. Often associated with small rock outcrops on open sandy and stony plains.
Subspecies: *uber* (WA); *orientalis* (WA, NT, Qld, NSW, Vic).

Ctenotus vertebralis Rankin and Gillam, 1979

Description: Pattern obscure; olive or bronzy-brown above, paler grey on the head; a conspicuous pale-edged, black vertebral stripe; a white dorso-lateral stripe, most conspicuous anteriorly, but often broken

Ctenotus youngsoni False Entrance Bay, WA

M. PETERSON

Ctenotus zastictus near Denham, WA

into an obscure series of dots or dashes; usually only an obscure dark upper lateral zone with faint, enclosed, pale flecks and sometimes a faint, pale midlateral stripe from ear to hindlimb. Lips whitish, flecked with olive-brown. Limbs pale brown, with or without faint dark brown stripes or flecks. Ventral surfaces whitish. 24-26 mid-body scale rows. Nasals usually separated. Prefrontals narrowly separated or in contact. Four supraoculars. Supralabials 7-8. Ear lobules 3-6. Lamellae under the fourth toe 20-25, each with a dark, slightly compressed callus. 55 mm (snout-vent).
Distribution: Western edge of Arnhem Land, NT.
Habit: Found primarily in woodland habitats where stony hills and escarpments meet adjacent plains.

Ctenotus xenopleura Storr, 1981

Description: Ground colour black above, except for the head which is much paler brown or olive; a series of pale coppery- white stripes consisting of paravertebral, dorsal, dorso- lateral, mid-lateral and lower-lateral; the dark upper lateral zone contains a series of spots and longitudinal streaks commencing immediately behind the eye; tail pale brown with fairly obscure dark stripes continuing from those on the body. Limbs pale brown with black longitudinal stripes. Ventral surfaces whitish. 26-30 mid-body scale rows. Nasals separated. Prefrontals narrowly separated or in contact. Four supraoculars. Supralabials 6- 8, usually seven. Ear lobules 2-6. Lamellae under the fourth toe 20-26, each with a weak, obtuse keel. 50 mm (snout-vent).
Distribution: Semi-arid interior of south-western WA.
Habit: Primarily mallee/*Triodia* associations.

Ctenotus youngsoni Storr, 1975

Description: Similar in most respects to *Ctenotus labillardieri*, from which it may be distinguished by having little or no indication of a pale mid-lateral stripe. Ground colour of back and sides olive-grey, the blackish-brown spots on the flanks tending to form vertical bars. Limbs olive- brown, spotted with darker. 28-30 mid-body scale rows.
Distribution: Known only from Dirk Hartog Island and adjacent mainland, WA.
Habit: Apparently similar to *Ctenotus labillardieri*.

Ctenotus zastictus Storr, 1984

Description: Blackish above, except for the head and tail which are dark brown. A broad black vertebral stripe, narrowly edged with white; a narrow, white dorso-lateral stripe from above the eye to the tail, bordered below by a broad black upper lateral zone containing a series of pale spots or blotches; a narrow, pale upper lateral stripe from ear to groin, and separated from a pale lower lateral stripe by a black zone which may sometimes contain another whitish stripe. Limbs brown, striped with paler brown. Whitish below. 24-26 mid-body scale rows. Nasals contacting. Prefrontals narrowly separated or contacting. Four supraoculars. 8 supralabials. Ear lobules 3-4. Lamellae under fourth toe 24-25, each with a narrow to moderate callus. 60 mm (snout-vent).
Distribution: Shark Bay region, WA.
Habit: 'Confined to an isolated belt of *Triodia* and *Eucalyptus* on red sand' (Storr).

Ctenotus zebrilla Storr, 1981

Description: Black above, with a series of eight narrow white stripes: on each side a paravertebral and dorsal extending from the nape, a dorso-lateral from above the eye, and a mid- lateral extending over the ear aperture to the upper labials. Limbs with dark brown longitudinal stripes. Whitish below. 29-30 mid-body scale rows. Nasals in contact. Prefrontals widely separated. Four supraoculars. 6-7 supralabials. Ear lobules 3-7. Lamellae under the fourth toe 17-21, each with a fine, dark keel. 40 mm (snout-vent).
Distribution: Western section of north-eastern highlands, Qld.
Habit: Tall open woodland on stony hills and ranges.

Genus ***Cyclodomorphus*** Fitzinger, 1843

A group of medium-sized to largish lizards related to the blue-tongued skinks, but with slender heads, necks and bodies. Anterior ear lobules usually present; scales smooth, subequal; no supranasals or divided nasal scales; a scaly, movable lower eyelid; parietal scales not in contact behind the interparietal; third and fourth toes subequal or the third toe slightly longer than the fourth; subdigital lamellae undivided; tail long and slender, usually at least as long as the body. All species are viviparous (livebearing) and are crepuscular or nocturnal in habit. Found only in continental Australia and Tasmania.

Key

TO THE SPECIES OF CYCLODOMORPHUS

1 Post-narial groove present (a).. **2**
Post-narial groove absent (b)......................... ***casuarinae***

2 Maximum snout-vent length about 12 cm...... ***branchialis***
Maximum snout-vent length about 22 cm........... ***maxima***

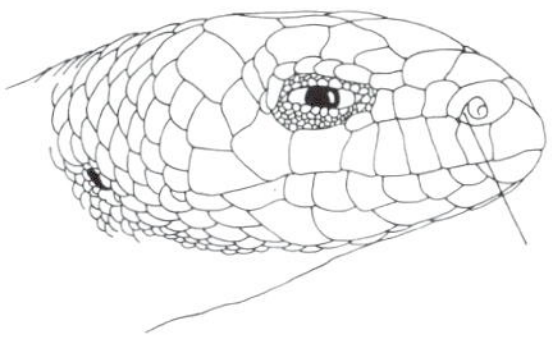

a

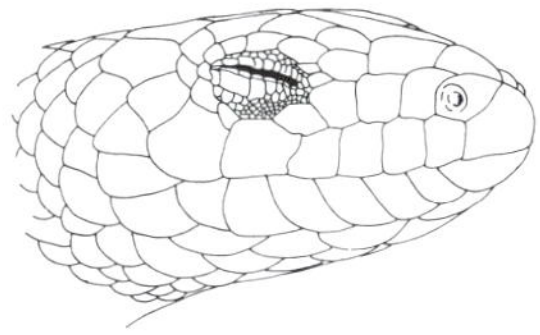

b

Cyclodomorphus branchialis Musgrave Ranges, SA. Female with large new-born twins.

Cyclodomorphus branchialis

(Günther, 1867)

Description: A slender, short-limbed lizard. Considerable geographic variation in colour pattern. Typically grey-brown to rich olive-brown above, paler on the flanks, the individual scales with darker brown margins and sometimes with a blackish central spot. Some populations with three large, blackish blotches on either side of the neck. Lips sometimes pale grey or whitish. Throat grey in males (sometimes with paler spots), white in females; remaining ventral surfaces whitish. Young may be heavily dotted with white or cream. Nasals in contact. Prefrontals usually separated. Four, occasionally three, supraoculars. Anterior temporals not noticeably elongated. No enlarged hexagonal scales between the parietals and the normal nuchal scales. Post-narial groove present. Ear-opening conspicuous, with a small anterior lobule. 24-28 mid-body rows of smooth scales. Limbs short, the hindlimbs about 20-25% of snout-vent length. 100 mm (snout-vent).
Distribution: Most of WA, NT and SA to western Qld.
Habit: A ground-dwelling lizard of largely crepuscular and nocturnal habit, sheltering by day in porcupine grass, leaf- litter and under fallen timber. Produces two or three large, living young.

Cyclodomorphus branchialis

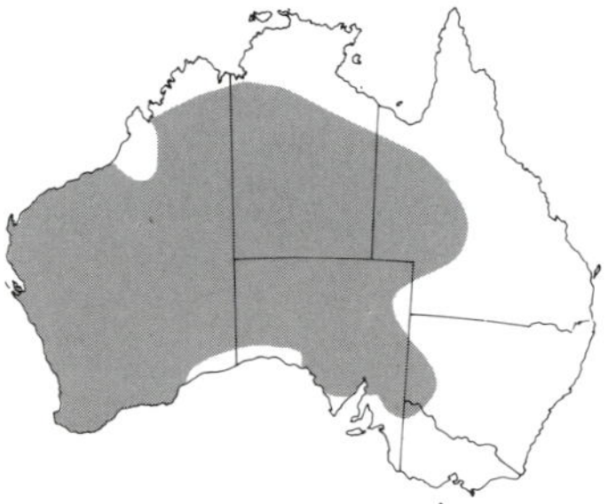

Cyclodomorphus casuarinae

Cyclodomorphus maxima

Cyclodomorphus casuarinae

(Duméril and Bibron, 1839)
Oak Skink

Description: A very slender, short-limbed lizard. Pale grey, fawn to olive-brown or even reddish-brown above, paler on the head and flanks. Narrow, dark, lateral edges to dorsal scales result in a series of narrow, longitudinal dark lines, while individual dark-edged scales, sometimes with pale centres, form an obscure, variegated, pattern which is sometimes aligned transversely, especially on the flanks. Usually an obscure dark bar below the eye. Pale silvery-grey to olive-green ventrally. The throat immaculate or with scattered dark flecks. Chest, abdomen and tail with a conspicuous series of dark-edged scales forming obscure transverse markings. Juvenile with a broad black nuchal collar from ear to ear. Nasals usually in contact. Prefrontals separated or narrowly contacting. Three supraoculars. Anterior temporals not or moderately elongated. No enlarged hexagonal scales between the parietals and the normal nuchal scales. Post-narial groove absent. Ear-opening conspicuous, without enlarged anterior lobules. 22-28 mid-body rows of smooth scales. Limbs short, the hindlimb 15-20% of snout-vent length. 130 mm (snout-vent). Tail long and slender, 90-120% of snout-vent length.
Distribution: Coast and ranges of eastern NSW and Vic. Widely distributed in Tas.
Habit: Found in a variety of habitats from coastal heaths and sand dunes to the dry sclerophyll forests of the ranges. Common in coastal grazing lands. Normally crepuscular or nocturnal, it is usually found during the day in leaf-litter or under fallen timber. Produces about six living young (Worrell).

Cyclodomorphus maxima (new-born) Barnett River Gorge, WA

Cyclodomorphus casuarinae Sydney district, NSW

Cyclodomorphus maxima (Storr,1976)

Description: Similar in appearance and scalation to *Cyclodomorphus branchialis*, but grows to more than 20 cm (snout-vent).
Distribution: North-western Kimberley region, WA.
Habit: Apparently confined to the rugged sandstone plateaux within its range.

Cyclodomorphus maxima (adult) Barnett River Gorge, WA

Genus *Egernia* Gray, 1838

A group of moderate to large lizards with well-developed limbs, and characterized by parietal shields which are not in contact behind the interparietal, and a fourth toe which is much longer than the third. The head is moderate while the tail is also moderate, thick and tapering. The scales range from smooth to sharply keeled, the rough-scaled species generally inhabiting rocky environments. Most are diurnal, but some desert species are crepuscular or even nocturnal. All species are viviparous, the number of young produced usually six or fewer. Widely distributed throughout continental Australia, with one species reaching Tasmania and another New Guinea.

Key

TO THE SPECIES OF EGERNIA

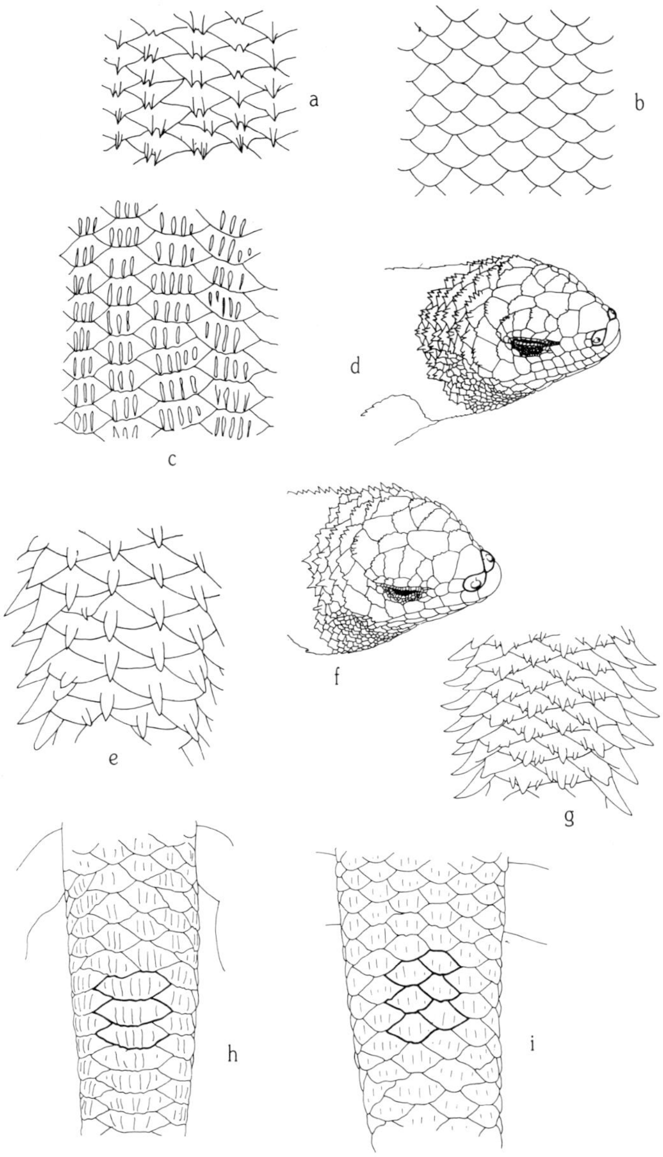

1 Dorsal and caudal scales, especially the latter, strongly spinose (a).......... **2**
Dorsal and caudal scales smooth (b) or keeled (c), but never strongly spinose.......... **5**

2 Nasal scales not in contact (d); caudal scales each with a single spine, although occasionally with two minute lateral spines (e).......... **3**
Nasal scales in contact (f); caudal scales each with three well-developed spines, the central one largest (g).......... ***depressa***

3 More than 30 mid-body scale rows.......... **4**
30 or fewer mid-body scale rows.......... ***hosmeri***

4 Tail flattened, much shorter than head and body. ***stokesii***
Tail more or less cylindrical, almost as long as, or longer than, head and body.......... ***cunninghami***

5 A series of expanded upper caudals on base of tail (h)..... **6**
No expanded upper caudals on base of tail (i).......... **8**

6 Dorsals moderately to strongly keeled; dark brown or black above with darker striations and a broad blackish upper-lateral zone, if present, usually confined to the neck and anterior part of the body and not strongly contrasting with the throat which is heavily speckled and mottled with dark brown.......... **7**
Dorsal scales striated or with low keels; grey above with distinct blackish striations and a broad black upper-lateral zone on each side, contrasting sharply on the neck with the pale whitish throat.......... ***striolata***

7 Lips and side of face and neck prominently spotted and speckled with white; usually fewer than 30 mid-body scale rows; ear lobules moderate, rounded (j).......... ***mcpheei***
Lips and side of face without prominent spots and flecks;usually more than 30 mid-body scale rows; ear lobules long,rugose (k).......... ***saxatilis***

8 One or more supralabials in contact with granules of lower eyelid (l); subocular series, if present, with its smallest members no larger than adjacent granules of the lower eyelid.......... **9**
A continuous row of enlarged suboculars, the smallest of which is much larger than the adjacent granules of the lower eyelid (m).......... **15**

9 Median supraciliaries much larger than the underlying (adjacent) palpebrals (n); no more than five supraciliaries in contact with outer margins of second, third and fourth supraoculars (o).. **10**

Median supraciliaries equal to or only slightly larger than the underlying palpebrals (p); at least six supraciliaries in contact with outer margins of second, third and fourth supraoculars (q)... ***kingii***

10 Dorsal scales smooth or at most striated....................... **11**

Dorsal scales distinctly keeled...................................... **13**

11 Back with or without darker spots and flecks; a distinct dark brown or black upper lateral stripe, at least anteriorly **12**

Uniformly dark reddish-brown on the back, without conspicuous darker spots and flecks and without any definite dark upper lateral stripe.................... ***pilbarensis***

12 Back with numerous dark spots and flecks, sometimes aligned longitudinally.. ***formosa***

Back uniform brown, without darker spots and flecks........ .... ***douglasi***

13 No distinct pale dorso-lateral stripe or zone.................. **14**

A distinct pale dorso-lateral stripe or zone..... ***napoleonis***

14 Southern WA.. ***carinata***

Northern NT... ***richardi***

15 Fewer than 30 mid-body scale rows; side of head dark brown or black with a conspicuous white stripe through the labials, extending almost to the ear.......................... **16**

More then 30 mid-body scale rows, or if fewer than 30 mid-body scale rows, side of head not black or dark brown with a conspicuous white labial stripe........................... **17**

16 Usually a continuous dark paravertebral stripe on each side of the back; a long post-narial groove extending to the top of the nostril (r)... ***coventryi***

Dorsum spotted, the spots forming a discontinuous dark paravertebral stripe on each side of the back; a short post-narial groove not extending more than half way up the nostril(s).. ***luctuosa***

17 A conspicuous post-narial groove meeting the labial on a level with or behind the hind edge of the nostril (t)......... **18**

Post-narial groove, if present, joining the labial at a point below the centre of the nostril (u)................................ **20**

18 Seven or more supraciliaries (v); parietals and frontoparietals intact (w)... **19**

Six or fewer supraciliaries (x); parietals (and sometimes frontoparietals) broken up into several irregular scales (y). .... ***rugosa***

19 Dorsal colour light brown with darker lateral regions .... ***frerei***

Dorsal and lateral colour uniform dark brown or black, ocasionally with a few white spots laterally.......... ***major***

20 Snout blunt; distance between outer edges of parietals equal to or greater than the distance from the snout to the hind edge of the frontal.. **21**

Snout rather pointed; distance between outer edges of parietals less than the distance from the snout to the hind edge of the frontal.. **24**

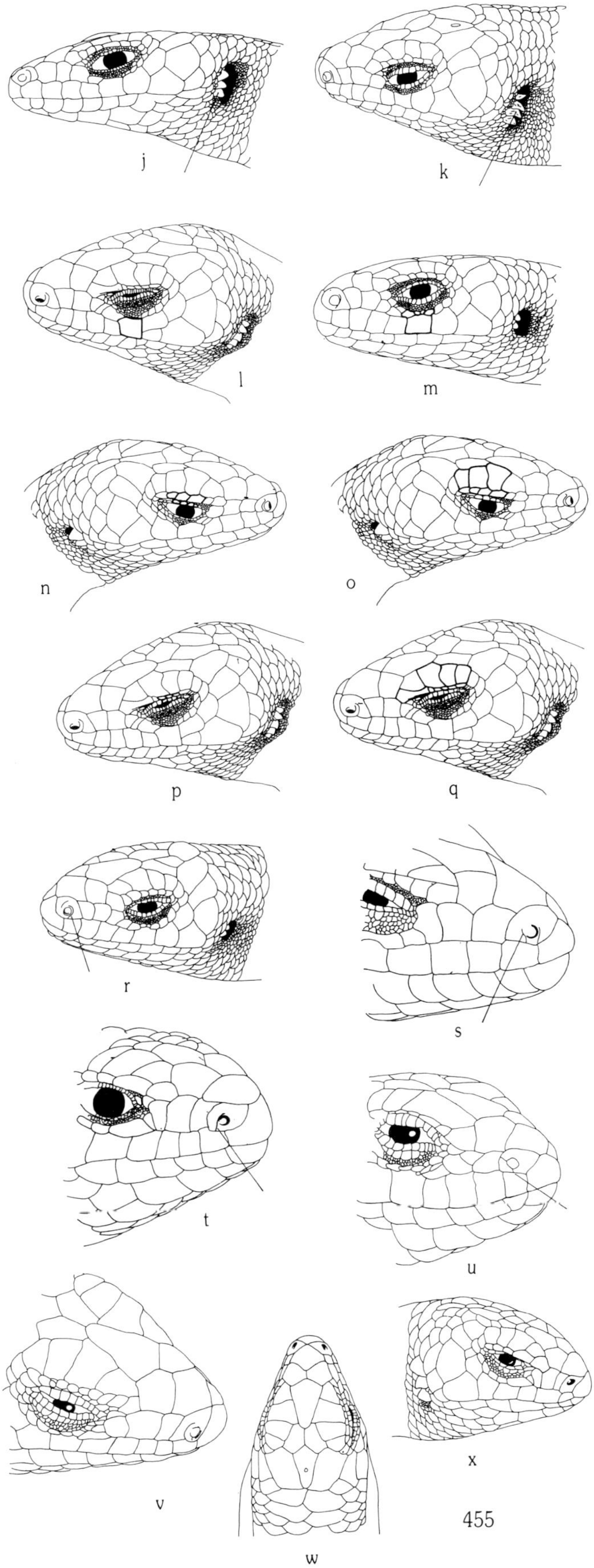

21 Ventral surface uniform creamish-white; dark brown or black dorsal pattern present or absent, but sides not flecked with white.. **22**

Throat, chest and belly pale bluish; one or more narrow dark brown or black longitudinal stripes dorsally; sides flecked with white.. ***slateri***

22 Total absence of any dark brown or black markings...... **23**

Sides, and sometimes back, spotted and flecked with black or dark brown, tending to form irregular vertical bars on the sides... ***inornata***

23 Adults with snout-vent length less than 120 mm; pupil much narrower than high; back with faint, narrow, red-brown longitudinal lines; dorsal colour merging with the duller lateral colour... ***striata***

Adults with snout-vent length greater than 150 mm; pupil only slightly narrower than high; back without red-brown striations; russet dorsal colour sharply demarcated from blue- grey lateral colour...................................... ***kintorei***

24 Dorsal scales smooth.. **25**

Dorsal scales keeled... ***pulchra***

25 Subdigital lamellae smooth or with one or two series of pale or dark brown longitudinal calli or keels (z); soles and palms smooth or with small white or dark tubercles...... **26**

Conspicuous black callus along free edge of subdigital lamellae (aa); scales of soles and palms each with a prominent black tubercle............................ ***margaretae***

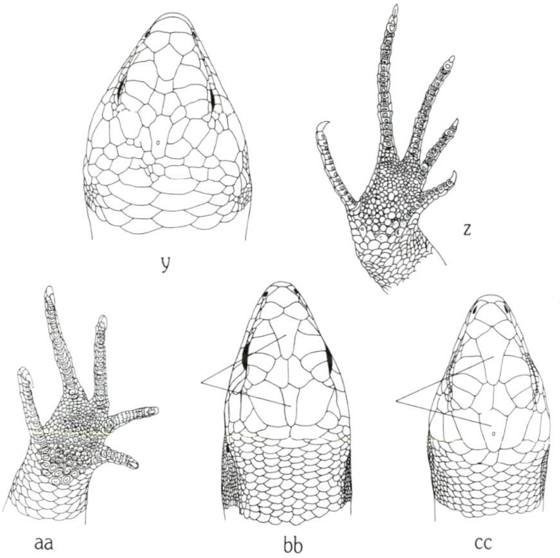

26 Interparietal much narrower than frontal in adults (bb) (slightly narrower or as wide in juveniles)...................... **27**

Interparietal slightly narrower or wider than frontal in adults (cc) (much wider in juveniles).......... ***multiscutata***

27 A pale supralabial streak and/or a dark dorso-lateral stripe enclosing pale spots; almost invariably some spotting on flanks.. ***whitii***

No pale supralabial streak; no dark dorso-lateral stripe or pale spots; flanks usually without pattern........... ***modesta***

Egernia coventryi Mornington Peninsula, Vic

Egernia carinata

Egernia carinata Eucla, WA

Egernia carinata Smith, 1939

Description: Dark grey-brown, olive-brown or brown above with numerous blackish, often pale-edged, dashes forming a series of eight narrow, discontinuous, longitudinal stripes. A dark temporal streak usually continuous with a blackish upper lateral zone with scattered pale scales. Upper labials pale brown or whitish, sometimes with darker sutures. Ventral surfaces pale, often flushed with pale orange on the chest and abdomen, and grey on the throat. Scales in 28-34 rows at mid- body, mid-dorsals usually with 3 or 4 moderate keels. Base of tail without expanded upper caudal scales. 2-4 ear lobules. 5-7 supraciliaries. A moderately strong post-narial groove. Head shields regular, unfragmented. Nasals usually narrowly separated or in point contact. Interparietal narrower than the frontal. 18-24 smooth, undivided lamellae under the fourth toe. 100 mm (snout-vent), the tail about 110% of snout-vent length.
Distribution: Interior of southern WA and southern SA.

Egernia coventryi Storr, 1978

Description: Pale greenish-brown, olive-brown or yellow-brown above, many or all of the dorsal scales with a black anterior margin, and some with black lateral edges coalescing to form a conspicuous, black dorso-lateral stripe on each side, from the nape to the base of the tail. Another black stripe from above the ear to the base of the tail, widening on the body to become a broad, black upper lateral zone enclosing some paler scales. Head and limbs above usually flecked and streaked with blackish. Limbs with scattered pale spots. A pale labial stripe. Throat and lower flanks often flushed with olive- green. Ventral surfaces whitish. 20-24 mid-body scale rows, the dorsals faintly striated. Base of tail without enlarged upper caudal scales. Two moderate ear lobules. 5-7 supraciliaries. Well-developed post-narial groove present. Head shields regular, unfragmented. Nasals in contact or narrowly separated. Interparietal narrower than frontal. Subdigital lamellae 17-22 under the fourth toe. 100 mm (snout- vent), the tail about 150% of snout-vent length.
Distribution: Southern Vic, probably just extending into SA and the extreme south-eastern corner of NSW.
Habit: Low-lying marshes and lagoon margins, in paperbark swamps, sedges and ti-tree *(Melaleuca)* thickets.

Egernia cunninghami (Gray, 1832)
Cunningham's Skink

Description:A highly variable species complex, subject to considerable geographic colour and pattern variation. Grey- brown, olive-brown, through various shades of brown to black, above. Head often somewhat paler than body, particularly in the young, and often with scattered whitish spots. Dorsum may be uniform in pattern or may have a conspicuous pattern made up of dark brown scales and white or cream flecks or spots. In many specimens the darker markings tend to be aligned transversely to form a series of narrow and irregular transverse bands, while

Egernia coventryi

Egernia cunninghami

Egernia depressa

Egernia douglasi

Egernia formosa

Egernia frerei

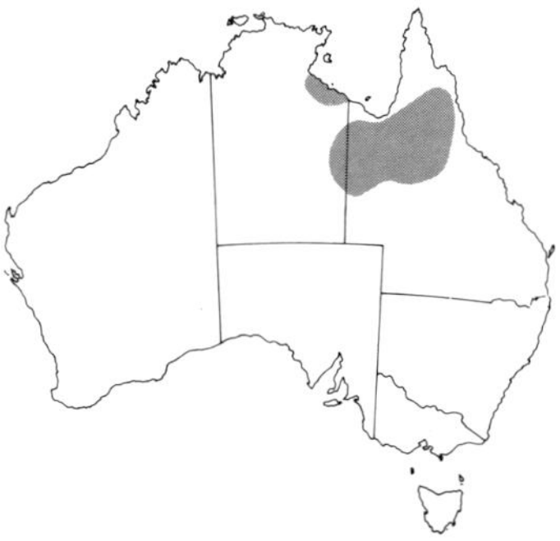

Egernia hosmeri

in other specimens the pale spots predominate. Tail usually ringed with darker brown, the paler interspaces being the same colour as the dorsum in adults, but often white in the young. Whitish below, usually with dark brown transverse bars or variegations on the throat, which in the young continue over the whole ventral surface, but which in adults are usually reduced to a series of scattered dark brown spots or obscure transverse bars on chest and abdomen. Many labial scales with conspicuous white or yellow spots. Marginal scales of each eyelid white or cream. Auricular lobules pale-coloured. Scales in 36-44 rows at mid-body, the scales on the back, flanks and tail each with a single, sharp, spinose keel, highest posteriorly and on the tail. Base of the tail without noticeably expanded upper caudal scales. 3-5 moderate ear lobules. 7-8 supraciliaries. Post-narial groove present. Head shields regular, unfragmented. Nasals usually separated. Interparietal narrower than the frontal. Subdigital lamellae 16-22. 150 mm (snout-vent), the tail more or less round in section, tapering gently, about 100% of snout-vent length.

Distribution: Mt Lofty Ranges in SA; slopes and ranges of Great Dividing Range from western Vic through NSW to south- eastern Qld; extends to the coast in the vicinity of Sydney, NSW.

Habit: A species living in rock crevices or under large exfoliating rock slabs throughout its range. Much of its diet consists of fruit and seeds, but arthropods and small vertebrates are also eaten. Usually produces 4-6 young in a single litter.

Egernia depressa (Günther, 1875)

Pygmy Spiny-Tailed Skink

Description: Pale fawn to bright orange-red above, with a series of dark brown to black irregular transverse markings forming obscure cross-bands. Dorsal pattern is obscure on the head and shoulders, becoming much more conspicuous on the body and tail. A dark brown streak from the eye, through the ear and over the base of the forelimb, which fades out a short distance along the flanks. This is bordered below by a white or cream labial zone which is continuous with paler colouring on the lower flanks. Cream-coloured below, usually with some brown flecks or short bars on the throat, often extending on to the chest or abdomen. Irregular darker flecks and variegations almost invariably present on the lower surfaces of the tail and limbs. Limbs above with irregular darker spots or cross- bands. Nasal scales usually in contact, usually much paler than the rest of the head. Scales in 28-38 rows at mid-body, most of

Egernia cunninghami Sydney district, NSW

Egernia depressa Port Hedland district, WA

Egernia formosa Python Pool, WA

the scales on the back and tail with three strong, spinose keels, the median one largest. Base of the tail without noticeably expanded upper caudal scales. 1-6, but usually 2-3, small ear lobules. 4-6 supraciliaries. Head shields regular, unfragmented. Nasals in broad contact. Interparietal about as wide as the frontal. Subdigital lamellae 8-18. 100 mm (snout-vent), the tail strongly depressed, only about 35% of snout-vent length.
Distribution: Central-western coastal regions of WA through much of the arid interior of that state.
Habit: Rocky outcrops and stony hills and ranges; mulga and other arid scrubs.

Egernia douglasi Glauert, 1956

Description: Dark olive-brown or reddish-brown above, with a pair of darker brown or blackish dorsal stripes anteriorly, each starting on the head and extending back to about one third of the way along the body, where it becomes more obscure and ragged-edged and may extend to the base of the tail. A dark brown to black streak from the snout through the eye and temporal region to just behind the forelimb, where it becomes more obscure and ragged-edged. Upper labials pale cream, the sutures edged with dark brown. Pale below. Scales in 26-28 rows at mid-body, the mid-dorsal with 3-7 striations. Base of tail without expanded upper caudal scales. 3-4 ear lobules. 6-7 supraciliaries. A distinct post-narial groove. Head shields regular, unfragmented. Nasals usually separated. Interparietal about as wide as frontal. 15-20 smooth subdigital lamellae under the fourth toe. 160 mm (snout-vent), the tail about 100% of snout-vent length.
Distribution: North-western Kimberley region, WA.
Habit: '...rocky areas (possibly extending into adjacent woodlands...' (Wilson and Knowles).

Egernia formosa Fry, 1914

Description: Similar in most respects to *Egernia striolata,* from which it differs in lacking expanded upper caudal scales. The pale dorso-lateral stripes and dark temporal stripe tend to be much more conspicuous than in *striolata.* Scales in 28-30 rows at mid-body, mid-dorsals smooth or faintly striated. 3-4 moderate ear lobules. 6-7 supraciliaries. A weak post-narial groove. Head shields regular, unfragmented. Nasals usually separated. Interparietal narrower than the frontal. 17-22 smooth or faintly keeled lamellae under the fourth toe. 80 mm (snout-vent), the tail about 140% of snout-vent length.
Distribution: Arid interior of WA, from edges of Great Sandy Desert and Nullarbor Plain to the Pilbara region.
Habit: A rock-dwelling and arboreal skink (like many of its nearest relatives) found in mulga and other arid scrublands.

Egernia frerei Günther, 1897
Major Skink

Description: Pale fawn to rich chocolate-brown above, the scales on the back each with a darker brown median streak, which together form a series of narrow, longitudinal lines or stripes from the neck to the base of the tail. The dorso-lateral, and sometimes the dorsal, scales may be finely peppered with yellow. Top of the head with irregular flecks and blotches. Usually a dark upper lateral zone becoming paler on the flanks and enclosing a few scattered pale dots, or, more often, a series of pale, black-edged spots. Lips white to rich yellow in colour, sometimes speckled or barred with brown. Ear lobules white or cream. Ventral surfaces white to yellow, often with contrasting creamy colour on the throat and tail. Throat sometimes flecked with brown. Palmar surfaces flesh-coloured. Scales in 32-36 rows at mid-body, the scales with low multiple keels. Base of tail without enlarged and expanded upper caudals. 3-6 short, moderate ear lobules. 8-12 supraciliaries. Post-narial groove present. Head shields regular, unfragmented. Nasals separated. Interparietal narrower than, to almost as wide as, frontal. Subdigital lamellae 17-22 under the fourth toe. 180 mm (snout- vent), the tail round, tapering, about 130% of snout-vent length.
Distribution: North-eastern NSW to Cape York Peninsula and the islands of Torres Strait. An apparent isolate in Arnhem Land, NT. Extra-limital in southern New Guinea, being the only member of the genus occurring outside Australia.
Habit: A shy, diurnal lizard usually found basking or foraging within or at the edge of thick ground cover such as vines, grass, fallen timber, around the buttresses of larger trees, or among well-vegetated rock outcrops in well-watered forested country or seasonally dry woodland.

Egernia hosmeri Kinghorn, 1955
Hosmer's Skink

Description: Pale fawn to reddish-brown above, darker brown on the head and neck. A series of pale brown or cream spots and blotches on the head, neck

Egernia frerei Yam Island, Torres Strait

and labials, with a few scattered pale spots and dark brown spots on the back, flanks and limbs and sometimes on the tail. Ventral surfaces white, cream or yellowish, sometimes with brown flecks and blotches on the throat. Scales in 24-28 rows at mid-body, the dorsal scales with 3-4 sharp, spinose keels (2-3 on flank scales) and the upper caudals each with a long spine. Base of the tail without enlarged and expanded upper caudals. 3-7 long, rugose, pale-coloured ear lobules almost concealing the ear. 5-6 supraciliaries. Post-narial groove present. Head shields regular, unfragmented. Nasals usually separated. Interparietal about as wide as frontal. Subdigital lamellae 15-18 under the fourth toe. 180 mm (snout-vent), the tail round, tapering, about 60% of snout-vent length.

Distribution: Drier parts of northern Qld and the adjacent border region of the NT.

Habit: A diurnal, rock-dwelling species found on the drier ranges, rock outcrops and stony hills throughout its range, where it lives in crevices, under exfoliating boulders and among the tumbled rocks of scree slopes.

Egernia inornata Rosén, 1905

Desert Skink

Description: Pale fawn to bright reddish-brown above, usually with some mixed pale and dark streaks on the back of the head. Individual scales on dorsum have darker brown lateral edges so that there is a series of narrow, faint, longitudinal striations. Many of the dorsal scales have white hind edges, while in some

Egernia hosmeri near Charters Towers, Qld

Egernia hosmeri
McArthur River, NT

Egernia inornata
Round Hill, NSW

Egernia kingii
South-western WA

Egernia kintorei Tanami Desert, NT — H. HUGHES

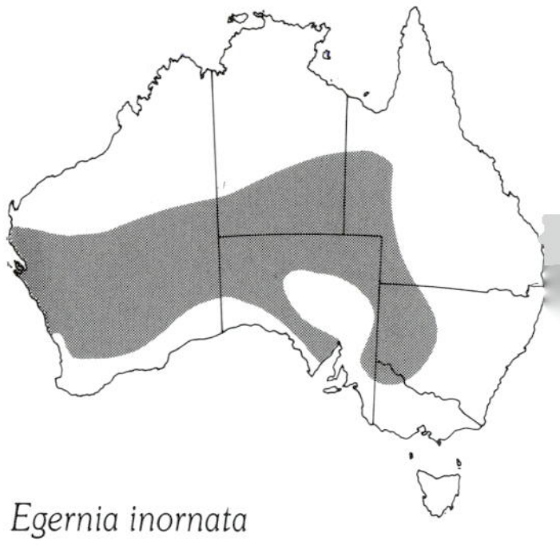

Egernia inornata

Egernia kingii

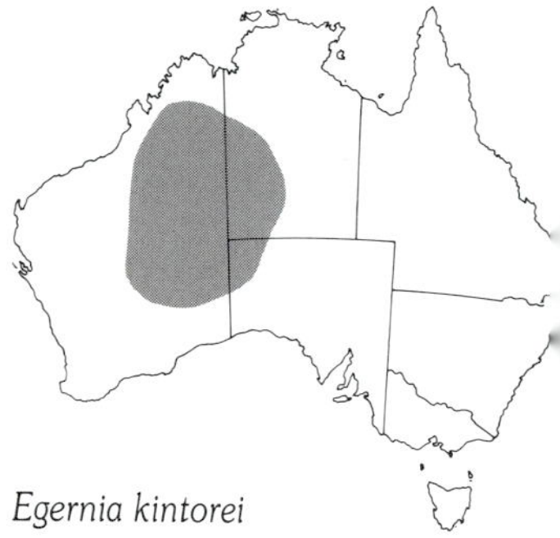

Egernia kintorei

Egernia luctuosa Perth, WA — M. PETERSON

specimens scattered black flecks and spots may be present. Flanks a mixture of black, white and brown scales, sometimes aligned transversely to form alternate pale and dark bars. Lips and cheeks with dark brown bars and blotches, auricular lobules white or cream. Limbs above usually a paler brown than the dorsum. Hindlimbs with a few white spots. Ventral surface white. Colour and pattern of tail continuous with body. Scales in 34-44 rows at mid-body. Base of tail without a median series of enlarged and expanded upper caudals. 3-6 ear lobules. 5-9 supraciliaries. Usually a faint post-narial groove. Head shields regular, unfragmented. Nasals usually separated. Interparietal nearly as wide as, or wider than, the frontal. Subdigital lamellae under the fourth toe 19-28, smooth to strongly callose, usually notched or divided basally. 75 mm (snout-vent), the tail round and tapering and about 120% of snout-vent length.

Distribution: Widely distributed through the southern half of WA, SA and lower NT to western Qld, western NSW and north- western Vic.

Habit: A burrowing, diurnal lizard found in a wide variety of xeric habitats with softer sandy and loamy soils. Usually constructs a relatively shallow burrow complex at the base of a shrub or clump of porcupine grass, from the entrance of which it forages for insects.

Egernia kingii (Gray, 1838)

King's Skink

Description: Olive-brown to blackish above, usually paler on the flanks and side of the neck. Young usually with white or cream spots on the back and sides, but these are usually reduced in the adult to some obscure pale spots on the flanks, limbs and side of the neck, and some pale longitudinal striations on the back caused by paler centres of the dorsal scales. White, grey or olive-yellow below, with dark brown spots or reticulations on the throat. Scales in 32-46 rows at mid-body, the scales (including caudals) relatively strongly bi- or tricarinate. Base of tail without enlarged, expanded upper caudals. 3-6 small, short ear lobules. 5-9 supraciliaries. Post-narial groove present. Head shields regular, unfragmented. Nasals usually separated. Interparietal about as wide as frontal. Subdigital lamellae 22-28 under the fourth toe, smooth. 200 mm (snout-vent), the tail round, tapering, about 130% of snout-vent length.
Distribution: South-western WA and its offshore islands.
Habit: Among the rocks and crevices and low coastal heaths and strand plants of rocky islands and mainland coasts, as well as rock outcrops further inland.

Egernia kintorei Stirling and Zietz, 1893

Great Desert Skink

Description: Pale fawn to rich reddish-brown above, flanks and side of neck pale grey or blue-grey. Lateral edges of dorsal scales rich, darker brown, forming a series of narrow, dark, longitudinal lines from the nape to the base of the tail. Sides of neck, body and tail with a series of dark brown or blackish scales usually aligned transversely to form dark vertical bars, the pale grey interspaces with scattered, obscure, white spots. Limbs grey-brown above. Ear lobules whitish. Ventral surfaces white or cream. Scales in 43-52 rows at mid-body, the scales smooth or faintly tricarinate. Base of tail without a median series of enlarged and expanded upper caudals. 4-6 ear lobules. 7-10 supraciliaries. Usually a faint post-narial groove. Head shields regular, unfragmented. Nasals separated. Interparietal nearly as wide, as or wider than, the frontal. Subdigital lamellae 17-23 under the fourth toe, more or less smooth and sometimes divided basally. 200 mm (snout- vent), the tail round, tapering, about 110% of snout-vent length.
Distribution: Eastern interior of WA, and adjacent regions of south-western NT and north-western SA.
Habit: A burrowing species in which large and complex burrow systems may be occupied by family groups. As in *Egernia stokesii,* regular defecating spots are used (on the surface) and generally indicate occupied burrow systems. Found in a variety of desert habitats on sandy, clay and loamy soils.

Egernia luctuosa (Peters, 1866)

Description: Dark brown to almost black above, often with a pale, broad dorso-lateral stripe from nape to base of tail. Sides dark brown to black with numerous scattered white or cream scales. A white or cream labial stripe from snout to ear, while in others the entire dorsum may be dark blackish- brown with no indication of longitudinal stripes. Limbs brown above with irregular paler spots and flecks. Whitish below, the individual scales sometimes edged with dark brown, or the entire ventral surface with obscure grey-brown variegations. Scales in 22-28 rows at mid-body, the scales striated. Base of tail without expanded upper caudals. Usually two ear lobules. 7-9 supraciliaries. A short post-narial or sub-narial groove present. Nasals usually in contact. Interparietal nearly as wide as the frontal. Subdigital lamellae under the fourth toe 21-28, undivided. 120 mm (snout-vent), the tail about 200% of snout-vent length.
Distribution: South-western WA.
Habit: Like its close relative, *Egernia coventryi*, it is primarily an inhabitant of dense ground cover on the margins of swamps, lakes and streams.

Egernia major (Gray, 1845)

Land Mullet

Description: Shiny black or very dark brown above and on the sides, young specimens with scattered white dots on the flanks, which either disappear or become very obscure in adults. White to lemon-yellow or orange on the ventral surfaces. Scales in 26-30 rows at mid-body, the scales with multiple low, blunt keels. Base of the tail without enlarged and expanded upper caudals. 2-3 large pointed ear lobules. 10-12 supraciliaries. Post-narial groove present. Head shields regular, unfragmented. Nasals separated. Interparietal narrower than, to as wide as, the frontal. Subdigital lamellae 17-22 under the fourth toe, divided basally. 300 mm (snout-vent), the tail about 120% of snout-vent length.
Distribution: South-eastern Qld and the north coast of NSW almost as far as the Hawkesbury River.
Habit: Rainforest and adjacent wet sclerophyll forests. Otherwise similar to *Egernia frerei*.

Egernia major Central coast, NSW

Egernia luctuosa

Egernia major

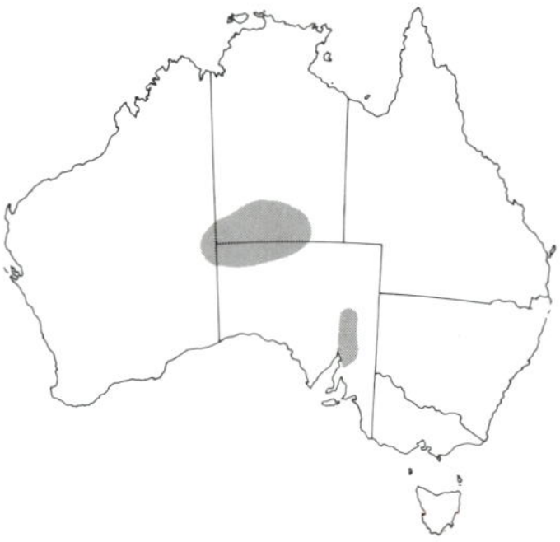

Egernia margaretae

Egernia margaretae Storr, 1968

Description: Closely allied to *Egernia whitii*. Brown above, grey or grey-brown on the sides, usually with a series of dark brown or black spots on the back; these may be scattered or aligned longitudinally. Dark lateral edges to the dorsal scales may also form faint longitudinal striations. Ear lobules white or cream. Sometimes some black spots or flecks on the flanks which tend to form irregular vertical bars. Labials and chin shields sometimes with brown margins. Throat spotted or streaked with pale grey-brown. Remaining ventral surfaces white, pale grey or cream. Scales smooth, in 34-43 rows at mid-body. Base of tail without expanded and enlarged upper caudals. 2-5 moderate, blunt ear lobules. 7-9 supraciliaries. Nasals separated. Interparietal much narrower than, to nearly as wide as, the frontal. Subdigital lamellae 20-26 under the fourth toe, each with a conspicuous black callus along its free edge. 90 mm (snout-vent), the tail round, tapering and about 160% of snout-vent length.
Distribution: Stony hills and ranges of central

Egernia margaretae Mann Ranges, SA

Australia and eastern SA.
Habit: A diurnal lizard usually seen basking or foraging on open rock surfaces and among leaf-litter near crevices, rockslopes and exfoliating rock slabs, among which the lizard shelters when alarmed.
Subspecies: *margaretae* (central Australia); *personata* (Flinders Ranges, SA).

Egernia mcpheei Wells and Wellington, 1984

Description: Similar in most respects to *Egernia saxatilis intermedia*, from which it is said to differ in its larger size; possession of fewer, more obtuse auricular lobules; smoother body scales; and fewer mid-body scale rows (28:no variation is cited in the original

Egernia mcpheei near Bellingen, NSW

Egernia mcpheei

Egernia modesta

Egernia multiscutata

Egernia napoleonis

Egernia pilbarensis

Egernia pulchra

Egernia richardi

description). 130 mm (snout-vent).
Distribution: Coastal NSW, north of the Hunter River, to south-eastern Qld.
Habit: 'primarily wet sclerophyll forests and the adjacent dry sclerophyll ecotone' (Wells and Wellington).

Egernia modesta Storr, 1968

Description: Pale olive-brown to brown. Individual scales of dorsum with darker brown lateral edges forming a series of narrow, dark brown, longitudinal striations from nape to base of tail. Flanks greyish-brown, often with obscure, small pale spots on the sides of the neck and anterior part of the body. Auricular lobules white or cream, and usually some white or cream spots on the cheeks and posterior labials. Tip of snout orange-brown merging into the more olive colouring of the head. Head shields narrowly outlined with dark brown. Margins of eyelids white or cream. Ventral surface whitish. Scales in 33-40 rows at mid-body, smooth or with faint striations. Base of tail without expanded upper caudal scales. 2-5 ear lobules. 7-9 supraciliaries. Post-narial groove very faint or absent. Head shields regular, unfragmented. Nasals usually separated, sometimes in narrow contact. Interparietal much narrower than the frontal in adults, only slightly narrower in juveniles. Subdigital lamellae under the fourth toe 21-26, smooth to bluntly callose, divided basally. 100 mm (snout-vent), the tail about 160 % of snout-vent length.
Distribution: Slopes and ranges of north-eastern NSW and south-eastern Qld, extending to the coastal plain of the Hunter River Valley in NSW. An apparently isolated population in the hills north of Roto, NSW.
Habit: A swift, diurnal lizard found in a variety of dry sclerophyll and open woodland habitats, where it forages about the fallen timber and rocky slopes in which it shelters when disturbed.

Egernia multiscutata Mitchell and Behrndt, 1949

Description: Generally similar to *Egernia whitii*, from which it may be distinguished by having the interparietal as wide as, or wider than, the frontal (even in adults), bicarinate subdigital lamellae, and two or three series of small white or yellow spots enclosed in the dark dorso-lateral stripe. Flanks with obscure pale and dark scales, rarely forming the ocelli which are present in *Egernia whitii*. Scales in 37-46

smooth rows at mid-body. 80 mm (snout-vent).
Distribution: Western Vic, Kangaroo Island and Eyre and Yorke Peninsulas of SA to coastal regions of southern WA, including many offshore islands.
Habit: Coastal dunes and open heathlands, and the complex of open forest and low open woodlands which characterise much of its range, especially where rock outcrops.
Subspecies: *multiscutata* (Greenly I., SA); *bos* (remainder of range).

Egernia modesta Sandy Hollow, NSW

Egernia napoleonis (Gray, 1839)

Description: Dark grey-brown, olive-brown or brown above with scattered blackish spots and dashes tending to form three longitudinal lines; a broad, paler, dorso-lateral zone free of black markings. A blackish temporal streak usually extending forward to the snout and posteriorly to a black upper lateral zone, usually with scattered paler scales. Upper labials pale brown or whitish, often with darker sutures. Ventral surfaces pale, usually flushed with orange or salmon on the chest and abdomen and grey on the throat. Scales in 32-42 rows at mid- body, mid-dorsals moderately to strongly bi-, tri- or quadricarinate. Base of tail without expanded upper caudal scales. 2-6 ear lobules. 4-8 supraciliaries. A strong post-narial groove. Head shields regular, unfragmented. Nasals usually separated. Interparietal narrower than frontal in adults, only slightly or not narrower in juveniles. 19-28 smooth undivided lamellae under the fourth toe. 120 mm (snout-vent), the tail about 140% of snout-vent length.
Distribution: Coast and adjacent hinterland of south-western WA.
Habit: Heath, open forest and woodland.

Egernia multiscutata near Israelite Bay, WA

Egernia napoleonis Boxer Island, WA

Egernia pilbarensis Storr, 1978

Description: Rich reddish-brown above, with an indistinct darker zone extending from the snout through the eye and temple to just behind the forelimb; flanks sometimes with paler scales which may be scattered or vertically aligned. Upper labials and ventral surfaces pale creamy-brown. 32-34 mid-body scale rows, the dorsals smooth or faintly striated. Base of tail without expanded upper caudal scales. 4-6 bluntly pointed ear lobules. 7-8 supraciliaries. Post-narial groove present. Head shields regular, unfragmented. Nasals separated or narrowly contacting. Interparietal narrower than, to as wide as, frontal. Subdigital lamellae 13-16 under the fourth toe.

Egernia pilbarensis
Port Hedland region, WA

Egernia pulchra (female) Augusta, WA

120 mm (snout-vent), the tail about 140% of snout-vent length.
Distribution: Coast and hinterland of Pilbara region, WA.
Habit: An agile, diurnal, rock-dwelling skink found in spinifex and scrub on stony hills, breakaways and ranges.

Egernia pulchra Werner, 1910

Description: Generally similar to *Egernia whitii*, from which it may be distinguished by its keeled scales (in 33-39 rows at mid-body, the scales each with 2-4 keels). The tail ranges from about 150% to 220% (the latter in the long-tailed subspecies *longicauda*) of snout-vent length.
Distribution: Lower west coast and south-western corner of WA.
Habit: Similar to *Egernia whitii*.
Subspecies: *pulchra* (range exclusive of that of *longicauda*); *longicauda* (islands of Jurien Bay).

Egernia richardi (Peters, 1869)

Description: Status uncertain. Similar in almost all respects to *Egernia carinata* (over which name *richardi* would have priority if the two are conspecific), and of which it may be an example from an erroneous locality.
Distribution: Recorded only from the type locality: 'Alligator River, N. Australia'.

Egernia rugosa De Vis, 1888
Yakka Skink

Description: A broad dark brown to blackish mid-dorsal stripe from nape to base of tail, the individual scales within the stripe variegated with dark and medium brown. The dark mid- dorsal stripe bordered on either side by a narrow (1-2 scales wide), pale fawn, dorso-lateral stripe, obscure or absent in some specimens. Flanks with a mixture of dark brown, pale brown and/or reddish-brown scales forming a faintly variegated orange-brown pattern. Labials usually paler fawn or cream contrasting with darker head colouring. Throat creamy-yellow, often with blackish flecks and spots. Chest and abdomen yellow-orange, more or less uniform; orange under the tail. Scales in 26-30 rows at mid-body, the dorsal and caudal scales each with four or five low, blunt keels and the two mid-dorsal rows largest. Upper caudal scales on base

Egernia rugosa Condamine district, Qld

of tail not noticeably expanded. 2-3 large, rugose ear lobules. Six or fewer supraciliaries. A conspicuous post-narial groove meeting the labial on a level with or behind the hind edge of the nostril. Parietal (and sometimes frontoparietal) shields partly fragmented. Nasals separated. Interparietal not wider than the frontal. Subdigital lamellae 16-24 under the fourth toe. 200 mm (snout-vent), tail about 100% of snout-vent length.
Distribution: Coast and hinterland of eastern Qld.
Habit: Poorly known. Usually found in open dry sclerophyll forest or woodland throughout its range. Ground-dwelling, it usually takes cover among dense ground vegetation, fallen timber and other debris.

Egernia rugosa

Egernia saxatilis

Egernia saxatilis Cogger, 1960
Black Rock Skink

Description: Similar in most respects to *Egernia striolata*, from which it differs in its larger size (to 130 mm snout- vent), its more obscure pattern and usually more rugose scalation. The dorsal surface is

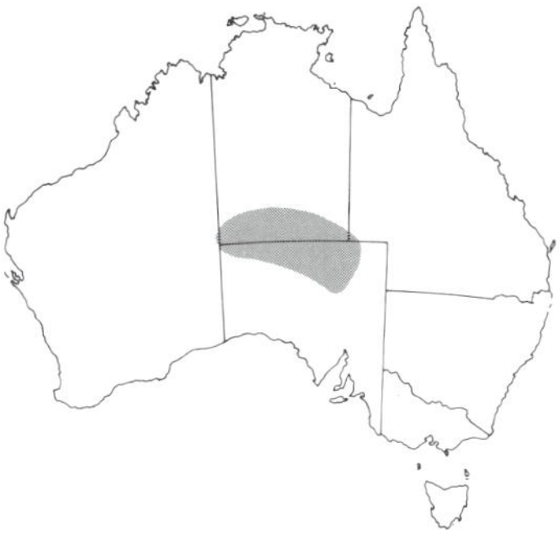

Egernia slateri

dark blackish-brown, with occasional faint indications of longitudinal stripes and an obscure, dark upper lateral zone. Labial scales mottled with brown, their margins edged with dark brown. The throat moderately to strongly variegated with dark brown. Auricular lobules whitish, variegated with brown. Chest and abdomen usually immaculate and often brilliant lemon-yellow or orange in life. Head and body sometimes with numerous, pale brown spots and flecks. Palmar surfaces black or dark brown. Scales in 27-40 rows at mid-body, the scales moderately to strongly multicarinate. Ear lobules 3-4, strongly rugose or spinose. 115 mm (snout-vent).
Distribution: Highlands and outlying hills and ranges of south-eastern Australia, from western Vic to northern NSW.
Habit: Typically a rock-dwelling lizard found on boulder slopes and in crevices under exfoliating slabs on exposed rock faces, basking and foraging in the immediate area around its shelter. Sometimes taken in low timber and fallen trees.
Subspecies: *saxatilis* (Warrumbungle Mountains); *intermedia* (remainder of range).

Egernia slateri Storr, 1968

Description: Similar in most respects to *Egernia inornata*, from which it may be distinguished by its duller and darker grey-brown ground colour, paler olive-brown on the head, and black-centred dorsal scales forming a series of conspicuous, black, longitudinal striations on the back, and in southern populations, a black vertebral stripe. 85 mm (snout-vent).
Distribution: Southern NT and northern SA.
Habit: Mulga and other arid *Acacia* scrubs, and low open eucalypt woodland. Otherwise similar to *Egernia inornata*.
Subspecies: *slateri* (southern NT); *virgata* (northern SA).

Egernia stokesii (Gray, 1845)
Gidgee Skink

Description: Olive-brown to rich reddish-brown above, sometimes with scattered paler brown scales and scattered scales with darker brown posterior edges tending to form obscure transverse bars. These dark-edged scales tend to be more numerous posteriorly, and are often especially conspicuous on the tail. White, cream or yellow below. The plantar region somewhat darker. Scales in 32-38 rows at mid-body, the scales generally with a single, large spinose keel, but the caudals sometimes with a small lateral keel on either side of the enlarged median keel. Base of tail without a median series of enlarged and expanded upper caudals. 1-4 moderate to rugose ear lobules. 4-7 supraciliaries. Post-narial groove conspicuous. Head shields regular, unfragmented. Nasals almost invariably separated, occasionally in point contact. Interparietal nearly as wider as the frontal. Subdigital lamellae under the fourth toe 12-20, each smooth or with a blunt median keel, undivided. 180 mm (snout-vent). The tail strongly depressed and about 35% of snout-vent length.
Distribution: Coast of WA through arid interior, through central Australia and SA to south-western Qld and north- western NSW.
Habit: Found among rocky outcrops, stony hills and mountain ranges, where it shelters in deep crevices or under large boulders, basking and foraging within easy reach of its rocky shelter. Like several other large members of this genus, its presence in an area can often be determined from its habit of using particular defecating sites, where small piles of faeces accumulate. Feeds largely on insects.
Subspecies: *stokesii* (Houtman Abrolhos, WA); *aethiops* (Baudin Island, Shark Bay, WA); *badia* (mainland WA).

Egernia striata Sternfeld, 1919

Description: Similar in most respects to *Egernia inornata*, from which it may be distinguished by the total absence of black on the back or flanks, the pattern consisting of a series of faint, pale brown longitudinal striations on the back, and a slightly darker brown upper lateral zone enclosing some mixed, paler scales. Often the flanks suffused with pale bluish-grey. Similar in appearance to some juvenile specimens of *Egernia kintorei*, from which it is distinguished by its fewer mid-body scale rows (36-46 in *striata*, 43-53 in *kintorei*). 100 mm (snout-vent). The pupil is distinctively vertically elliptic.
Distribution: Widely distributed through the interior of WA to south-western NT and north-western SA.
Habit: Spinifex sandplains and spinifex/arid scrub associations. Otherwise similar to *Egernia inornata*.

Egernia striolata (Peters, 1870)
Tree skink

Description: A species complex in which relationships are uncertain. Typically dark blackish-

brown to grey-brown above, usually with a broad, pale, dorso-lateral stripe from the top of the head to the base of the tail. These dorso-lateral stripes may be indistinct posteriorly where dark-centred scales may obscure the pattern. Between the pale dorso-lateral stripes is a darker zone made up of black scales or scales with blackish median bars, which are sometimes arranged as disrupted, longitudinal stripes. In many specimens the dorsum contains scattered, small, white spots and flecks. Scales of head with narrow, dark brown or black margins and sometimes a few scattered white spots. Labials white or cream, their margins edged with dark brown. Auricular lobules white. The broad, dark upper lateral band from eye to groin usually contains scattered, pale scales which tend to form transverse bars. White or silver-grey below, with obscure, transverse dark brown bars or scattered flecks on the throat, and dark brown speckling on the chest and lower flanks; this speckling sometimes extends on to the lower abdomen, and in some specimens forms a dark, narrow, median stripe on the chest and/or abdomen. Ventral surfaces of limbs and tail whitish or grey, speckled with dark brown. Ventral surface often flushed with lemon-yellow or pale orange in living specimens. Palmar surfaces pale brown. Scales in 27-34 rows at mid-body, the scales smooth or more usually with striations or low keels. Base of tail with a median series of enlarged and expanded upper caudals. 2-4 small to moderate ear lobules. 5-7 supraciliaries. Post-narial groove conspicuous. Head shields regular, unfragmented. Nasals usually separated. Interparietal nearly as wide as the frontal. Subdigital lamellae 17-23 under the fourth toe, smooth and undivided. 100 mm (snout-vent), the tail round, tapering, about 120% of snout-vent length.
Distribution: Eastern and central Qld, through NSW (excluding the coast and higher parts of the Great Dividing Range) to Vic and eastern SA.
Habit: Typically an arboreal species found in hollow limbs and cracks or under bark of standing trees. Also found in fallen timber and, in some parts of its range, under exfoliating slabs on granite and other rock outcrops.

Egernia whitii (Lacépède, 1804)

White's Skink

Description: A highly variable species complex, subject to considerable geographic variation in colour and pattern. Pale fawn to rich chocolate-brown above, some specimens uniform above or with a few blackish flecks, but typically with a series of longitudinal markings consisting of a pale vertebral

Egernia saxatilis Kanangra Walls, NSW

Egernia stokesii Alice Springs, NT

Egernia striata Condun Well, WA

Egernia striolata Euabalong, NSW

Egernia whitii
Sydney district, NSW

stripe bordered on either side by an equally wide blackish stripe from nape to base of tail, and enclosing series of small, white, cream or yellow spots. This stripe is bordered below by a paler dorso-lateral stripe which may enclose some pale, black-edged spots anteriorly. Flanks dark blackish-brown above, merging below with the grey-white ventral surface and enclosing a series of small, pale (white and brown) spots. Dark lateral edges to dorsal scales often resulting in a narrow, dark, vertebral stripe, especially on the neck. Typically a dark bar enclosing one or more white spots above the base of the forearm. Usually a narrow, pale, subocular stripe narrowly edged above with black and often a dark temporal streak. Auricular lobules white, and usually one or two white, dark-edged spots along the hind margin of the ear. Marginal scales of eyelids white or cream. Ventral surface silvery-grey to white, usually with some obscure, pale spots along the lower jaw and cheek. Limbs with obscure pale, dark-edged spots. Scales in 30-44 rows at mid-body, the scales smooth with faint striations. Base of tail without enlarged, expanded upper caudals. 2-5 moderate ear lobules. 5-9 supraciliaries. Post- narial groove faint or absent. Head shields regular, unfragmented. Nasals separated. Interparietal usually much narrower than frontal in adults, nearly as wide as frontal in juveniles. Subdigital lamellae 16-28, smooth or slightly callose, single, notched or sometimes divided basally. 95 mm (snout-vent), the tail round, tapering and about 160% of snout-vent length.

Distribution: Eyre Peninsula in SA, through Vic and eastern NSW to extreme south-eastern Qld. Also Tas and the islands of Bass Strait.

Habit: A swift-moving, diurnal lizard found in a wide variety of habitats, from coastal heath and grasslands through dry sclerophyll forests to open woodland of the western slopes of the Great Dividing Range. Often closely associated with rocky situations, where it shelters under exfoliating rock slabs and in crevices, but also found in and around fallen timber and any other ground cover.

Subspecies: *whitii* (known range excluding coastal NSW); *moniligera* (coastal and adjacent areas north of Nowra, NSW).

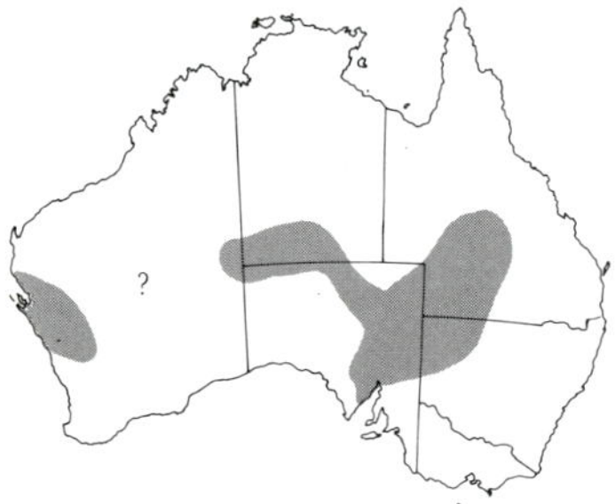

Egernia stokesii

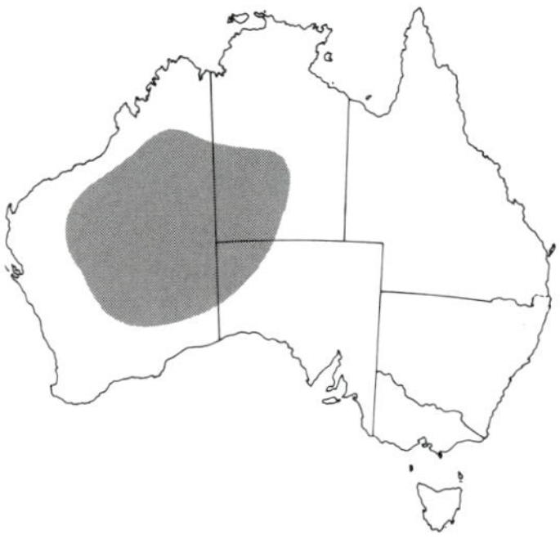

Egernia striata

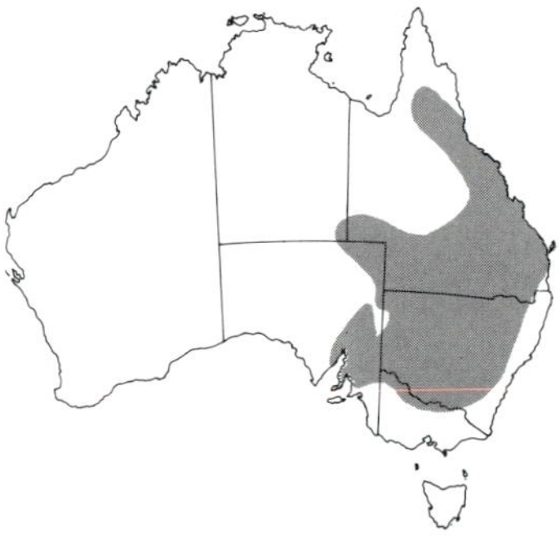

Egernia striolata

Egernia whitii

Genus **Emoia** Gray, 1845

A group of small to moderate smooth-scaled, active, diurnal lizards with well-developed pentadactyle limbs Characterised by the presence of supranasals (sometimes regarded as divided nasals), frontoparietals united to form a single shield; parietals in contact behind the interparietal; and a movable lower eyelid with a large transparent disc. Australian species have more than 30 lamellae under the fourth toe and lack anterior auricular lobules.

This genus attains its greatest diversity in the Indo-Pacific region, and in Australia is represented by only two widely distributed species-complexes whose ranges just encompass the islands of Torres Strait and the tip of Cape York Peninsula.

Key

TO THE AUSTRALIAN SPECIES OF EMOIA

Lamellae under fourth toe fewer than 55 and lamellae under distal phalanges not differentiated from those under basal phalanges (a); snout moderate............................ ***atrocostata***

Lamellae under fourth toe more than 55 and lamellae under distal phalanges normal, sharply differentiated from the wide, narrow lamellae under the basal phalanges (b); snout depressed.. ***longicauda***

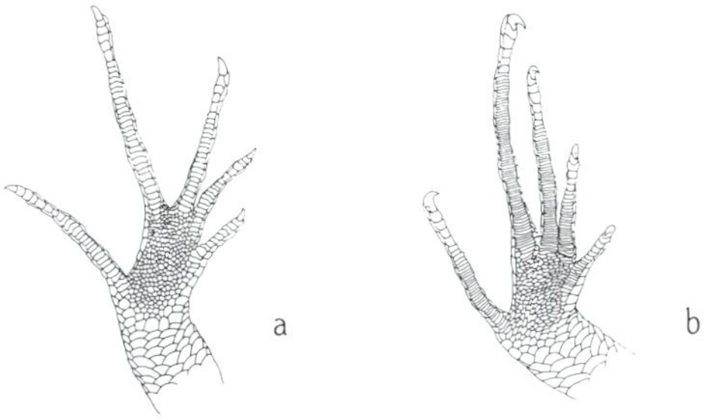

Emoia atrocostata Christmas Island, Indian Ocean

Emoia longicauda Murray Island, Torres Strait

Emoia atrocostata

Emoia longicauda

Emoia atrocostata (Lesson, 1830)

Description: Dark brown to blackish above, often paler on the head, sometimes with some scattered, paler scales on the flanks. Limbs brown with obscure, scattered, paler and darker flecks. White or cream below, individual scales sometimes edged with darker brown, especially on the thorax, resulting in a pale brown ventral surface. Juveniles and sub-adults usually with a broad, dark upper lateral zone enclosing series of small, pale spots. Back often with pale and dark brown variegations or irregular transverse bands. Snout moderate, pointed but not noticeably depressed. Nostril surrounded by the nasal, a small supranasal and a small postnasal. Prefrontals well developed, usually separated. Four supraoculars. Scales smooth, in 32-42 rows at mid-body. Limbs well developed, the hindlimb about 50% of snout-vent length. Subdigital lamellae under the fourth toe 32-42, smooth, normal; those under basal phalanges not sharply differentiated from those under the distal phalanges. 100 mm (snout-vent).

Distribution: Poorly known. Some of the islands of Torres Strait and the northern tip of Cape York Peninsula, Qld. Extra-limital in New Guinea and islands to the east and west.

Habit: Restricted to lowland forests and coastal scrubs and grasslands and beach situations. Especially abundant on the littoral and supra-littoral zones of rocky foreshores, where it hops with agility from boulder to boulder. A common mangrove species in some areas, including many parts of its Australian range .

Emoia longicauda (Macleay, 1877)

Description: Australian specimens glossy greenish-bronze on back and sides, rather more bronze on the top of the head. Individual dorsal scales with dark grey or blackish flecks. Loreals and lips pale green, with some black spots along the upper edges of the supralabials. Entire ventral surface bright green or yellowish-green, merging with the dorsal colouring on the lower flanks. Limbs with scattered blackish flecks above. Palmar surfaces yellowish. Reproduced tails brown. Marginal scales of eyelids pale green. A narrow, broken, dark streak between the eye and the ear in some specimens. Snout pointed, depressed. Nostril surrounded by the nasal, a small supranasal and a small postnasal. Prefrontals well developed, narrowly separated or in contact. Four supraoculars. Scales smooth in 24-26 rows at mid-body. Limbs well developed, the hindlimb nearly 50% of snout-vent length. Subdigital lamellae under the fourth toe 55-70, those under the basal phalanges very wide and short, smooth, sharply differentiated from the normal lamellae under the distal phalanges. 80 mm (snout-vent).
Distribution: Islands of Torres Strait and the northern parts of Cape York Peninsula.
Habit: An agile, diurnal, arboreal lizard, found most often in rainforest edges and clearings, secondary growth and dense streamside vegetation. Usually seen basking on low shrubs and trees, but often descending to the ground to forage. Readily able to jump short distances from branch to branch. Especially abundant in gardens in forest clearings, where the lizards forage on the trunks of pawpaw trees and bananas, and hide among the dead, trailing leaves of the latter.

Genus *Eremiascincus* Greer, 1979

A genus containing only two closely related species of sharp-snouted, arid-zone, sand-swimming lizards. Both species are glossy scaled, with moderately developed pentadactyle limbs. Ear lobules absent; colour pattern usually consisting of dark transverse cross-bands on body and tail; scales usually faintly keeled or rugose on the posterior part of the body, becoming more strongly rugose on the base of the tail; supranasals absent and nasals undivided. Lower eyelid movable, scaly. Parietal scales in contact behind the interparietal.

Key

TO THE SPECIES OF EREMIASCINCUS

Bands on back and tail usually much narrower than paler interspaces (a); ten or more bands on body and 35-40 bands on the tail.. ***fasciolatus***

Bands on back and tail as wide as, or nearly as wide as, paler interspaces (b); 14 or fewer bands on body and 19-32 bands on the tail... ***richardsonii***

a

b

Eremiascincus fasciolatus (Günther, 1867)

Narrow-Banded Sand Swimmer

Eremiascincus fasciolatus Carnarvon, WA

Description: Highly variable in colour and pattern, ranging from almost uniform pale, creamy-brown or orange-brown to dark brown, with 10-19 irregular, narrow, dark cross-bands on the body and 35-40 narrow, dark cross-bands on the tail. The bands on the body may be absent above and obvious only on the flanks. Lower flanks very pale, merging with the

Eremiascincus richardsonii Wanaaring, NSW

white or cream ventral colour. Nasals separated. Prefrontals large, narrowly separated or in short contact. Four supraoculars. Seven or eight supralabials. Postmental contacting one or two infralabials. Ear-opening small, sub-circular, as large as or smaller than the nasal. Body scales smooth to faintly keeled, except over the rump and on the base of the tail, where the scales are almost invariably keeled and form a series of continuous ridges. 28-36 mid-body scale rows. Limbs well developed, the hindlimb about 30-45% of snout-vent length. 17-30 lamellae under the fourth toe, divided basally, tubercular. 80 mm (snout-vent).

Distribution: Central coast of Qld, through south-western Qld, western NSW, north-western Vic and the NT to the northern half of WA.
Habit: A nocturnal, burrowing lizard found in a wide variety of arid or drier habitats, usually in sandy or loamy soils. Usually found by day sheltering in shallow burrows under logs, stones or litter. Its habit, when disturbed, of instantly burrowing into the soil with a snake-like movement, has earned it the name 'sand-swimmer'; this form of locomotion in loose sand or soil occurs in a wide variety of unrelated desert lizards throughout the world.

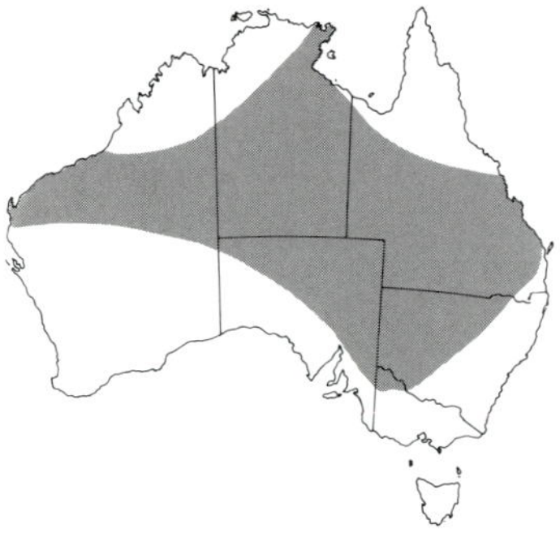

Eremiascincus fasciolatus

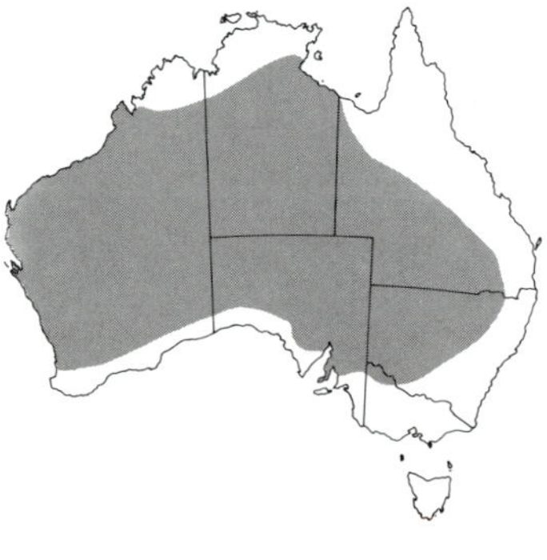

Eremiascincus richardsonii

Eremiascincus richardsonii (Gray, 1845)

Broad-Banded Sand Swimmer

Description: Similar in most respects to *Eremiascincus fasciolatus*, from which it is distinguished in having '... caudal bands fewer (19-32 v. 35-40), wider and less regular (often oblique and branching). Dorsal pattern generally stronger; dark bands generally fewer (8-14 v. 10-19) and wider (up to as wide as the interspaces), sharper edged and more strongly contrasting with the pale ground colour. Tail longer (131-171% of snout- vent length, v. 114-142%)' (Storr). 100 mm (snout-vent).
Distribution: Most of WA, SA and the NT to NSW (except the coast and ranges) and south-eastern Qld.
Habit: Similar to that of *Eremiascincus fasciolatus*.

Genus **Eroticoscincus** Wells and Wellington, 1984

A monotypic genus containing a small, cryptic species found in wet forest habitats. The sole Australian species occurs in south-eastern Qld. Characterised by: moderate limbs which just fail to meet when adpressed; supranasals absent; nasals small, undivided and widely separated; prefrontals absent; parietal shields in contact behind the interparietal; lower eyelid movable, with a small transparent disc; ear-opening minute, circular; preanals enlarged; forelimbs tetradactyle, hindlimbs pentadactyle.

Eroticoscincus graciloides Maleny, Qld

Eroticoscincus graciloides Lönnberg and Andersson, 1913)

Description: Rich brown above, individual scales striated with dark brown and with dark brown edges. Paler on sides, individual scales finely peppered with dark brown. A dark brown, narrow dorso-lateral streak from a little in front of the hindlimb to the basal half of the tail. Lips distinctly barred with dark brown. White below, some of the scales, especially near the vent, on the limbs and under the tail, finely dotted with dark brown. Prefrontals absent. Four supraoculars. Scales smooth, in 20 rows at mid-body. Forelimb tetradactyle, hindlimb pentadactyle, the fourth toe conspicuously longer than the third. Hindlimb about 20-30% of snout-vent length. 35 mm (snout-vent).

Distribution: Extreme south-eastern corner of Qld.
Habit: Found under logs, stones and ground litter in rainforest and associated wet sclerophyll forests.

Genus **Eugongylus** Fitzinger, 1843

A small group of rather heavily built, ground-dwelling lizards with relatively short limbs. Characterised by their possession of a movable, scaly lower eyelid; parietal scales in contact behind the interparietal; supranasals present (sometimes regarded as divided or partly divided nasals). Found throughout the New Guinea region; although two species have been recorded from the islands of Torres Strait and the northern tip of Cape York Peninsula, only one has been found in the area in recent times. The taxonomy of the genus is also in need of revision.

Key

TO THE AUSTRALIAN SPECIES OF EUGONGYLUS

Scales smooth, in more than 32 rows.......... ***albofasciolatus***
Scales smooth or keeled, in fewer than 32 rows....... ***rufescens***

Eugongylus albofasciolatus
(Günther, 1872)

Description: Status in Australia uncertain. Similar in most respects to *Eugongylus rufescens* from which it differs largely in its higher number of mid-body scale rows (34-38), which are always smooth.
Distribution: Northern Cape York Peninsula; possibly also found in some Torres Strait islands. Extra-limital in New Guinea.

Eugongylus albofasciolatus

Eugongylus rufescens (Shaw, 1802)

Description: Juveniles iridescent dark purplish-brown with numerous narrow, irregular, white cross-bands on neck, body and tail, the bands joining the whitish ventral surface. A pale stripe across the snout. Lips conspicuously barred with dark brown, bars extending backwards as a series of dark streaks on the throat. Limbs irregularly banded with white. Adults uniformly iridescent grey-brown, brown or

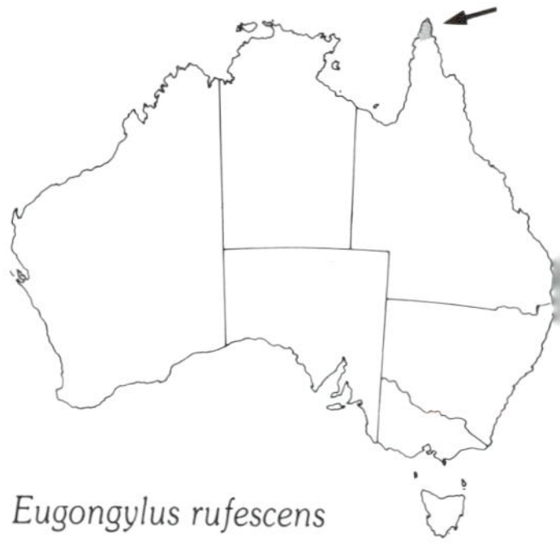
Eugongylus rufescens

Eugongylus rufescens (adult)
Murray Island, Torres Strait

dark brown, sometimes with obscure or faint paler cross-bands, paler on the sides; ventral surfaces cream or yellow; lips distinctly barred with dark brown; some specimens have some obscure brown streaks on the throat and chest. Ventral surfaces cream to bright yellow. Body scales smooth, or each with a low, median keel, in 28-30 rows at mid-body. Prefrontals moderate, separate. Frontoparietals paired, distinct from interparietal. Ear-opening conspicuous, oval, with a few short anterior lobules. Preanals not enlarged. Limbs relatively short, not meeting when adpressed (except in juveniles), the hindlimb about 25-35% of snout-vent length. 16-21 lamellae under the fourth toe. 150 mm (snout-vent).
Distribution: Northern Cape York Peninsula and the islands of Torres Strait. Extra-limital in New Guinea and the Moluccas.
Habit: Found in a variety of monsoon and rainforests, usually under fallen timber and leaf-litter at the edge of clearings and paths, although specimens have been found living high off the ground in tree hollows and tall root buttresses. Nocturnal and crepuscular, foraging about the forest floor as soon as light levels fall in the early evening.

Eugongylus rufescens (juvenile) Murray Island, Torres Strait

Genus ***Eulamprus*** Fitzinger, 1843

A group of largish, active and primarily diurnal lizards characterised by: pentadactyle limbs; smooth scales; anterior ear lobules absent; supranasals usually absent (except in *amplus*); lower eyelid movable, scaly; parietal scales in contact behind the interparietal; fourth toe much longer than third; lower surfaces of tail and rump not flushed with red or pink; hindlimb long, at least 40% of snout-vent length; viviparous.

Key

TO THE AUSTRALIAN SPECIES OF EULAMPRUS

1 Supranasals absent (a).. **2**
Supranasals present (b)...................................... ***amplus***

2 Base of fourth toe broad, with three or more granules or lamellae between the lateral scales and all or some of the lamellae, including the distal ones, divided (c).................**3**
Base of fourth toe moderate, with no more than two granules or lamellae between the lateral scales, and basal lamellae sometimes divided, but all distal lamellae undivided(d)..**8**

3 Throat with conspicuous dark grey or black streaks and/or reticulations..**4**
Throat immaculate or at most with a few pale grey spots or streaks..**5**

4 Top of head heavily spotted or flecked with black; cheeks and/or temples usually spotted with white ...... ***heatwolei***
Top of head immaculate or with at most a few scattered dark flecks.. ***quoyii***

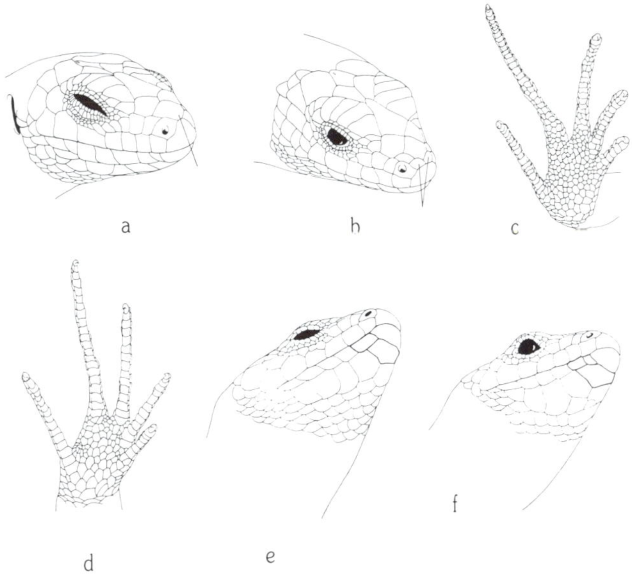

5 Dorsum with one or more dark longitudinal stripes.........**6**
Dorsum without dark longitudinal stripes............... ***quoyii***

6 Ground colour of dorsum mid-brown, strongly contrasting with narrow blackish longitudinal stripes.......**7**
Ground colour of dorsum very dark brown or black, strongly contrasting with narrow pale longitudinal stripes.. ....***leuraensis***

7 Venter immaculate cream, white or pale yellow ***kosciuskoi***
Venter with pale grey blotches or mottling.....***tympanum***

8 Palmar surfaces and subdigital lamellae mostly unpigmented; postmental in contact with a single infralabial on each side (e); a broad, lateral, dark grey or grey-black zone dotted with white; lower flanks usually darker than dorsum.. **9**
Palmar surfaces and subdigital lamellae with dark brown pigmentation; postmental in contact with two infralabials on each side (f); a broken, dark upper lateral zone but lower flanks as pale as or paler than the dorsum........... **10**

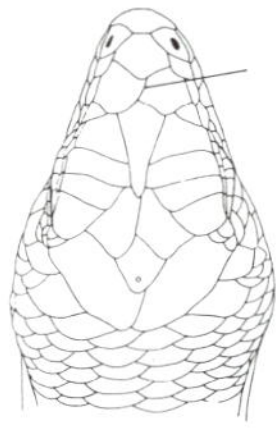
g

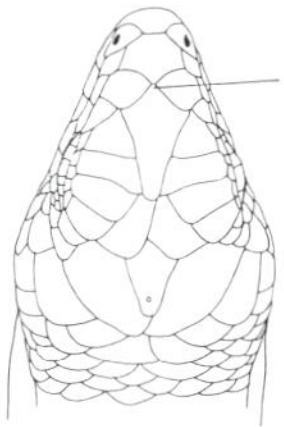
h

9 Flanks dark grey to black, dotted with white....... ***murrayi***
Flanks orange, dotted with white............... ***luteilateralis***

10 Prefrontals broadly in contact and frontal narrow (g); eye-bulge prominent... ***tigrinus***
Prefrontals usually separated or in point contact and frontal broader (h); eye-bulge not prominent......... ***tenuis***

Eulamprus amplus (Covacevich and McDonald, 1980)

Description: Rich, glossy, olive-brown above with scattered paler brown scales which tend to be aligned transversely to form a series of narrow, irregular cross-bands on body and tail. Lips, chin and sides of neck blue-grey, the labials and chin shields edged with dark brown. Ventral surfaces creamish, flushed with lemon in life. Nasals separated by one or two pairs of supranasals, at least one pair in contact. Prefrontals in contact. Five supraoculars. Seven supralabials. Postmental contacting one infralabial on each side. Ear opening conspicuous, much larger than the nasal. Scales smooth, 40-52 at mid-body. Limbs moderate, overlapping when adpressed, the hindlimb about 40% of snout-vent length. 22-26 lamellae under the fourth toe. 110 mm (snout-vent).
Distribution: Montane rainforests in the Proserpine and Eungella districts, Qld.
Habit: Usually found among rocks or at the base of trees beside streams in rainforest. Diurnal.

Eulamprus amplus Eungella, Qld

Eulamprus amplus

Eulamprus heatwolei

Eulamprus kosciuskoi

Eulamprus heatwolei Cronulla, NSW

Eulamprus kosciuskoi Point Lookout, New England National Park, NSW

Eulamprus heatwolei Wells and Wellington, 1984

Description: Olive-brown above, the top of the head usually heavily spotted or flecked with black, usually conspicuous white spots on temples and/or cheeks, and with scattered black spots on the body and tail which sometimes tend to form longitudinal series. A narrow, pale golden or yellowish dorso-lateral stripe from above the eye and extending at least along the anterior part of the body. This pale stripe or zone is usually bordered below by a broad, blackish, upper lateral zone enclosing several series of pale yellow or cream spots. Lower flanks creamy-yellow with numerous scattered small blackish spots. Lower lips and chin shields with scattered blackish spots or margined with black, and usually a series of dark grey or blackish longitudinal lines on the throat which may extend on to the chest and belly. Limbs above olive-brown spotted with black. Rarely any pale streak from behind eye to above ear. Nasals separated. Four supraoculars. Usually seven supralabials. Postmental contacting two or three infralabials on each side. Ear-opening conspicuous, larger than the nasal. Scales smooth in 36-44 rows at mid-body. Limbs well developed, strongly overlapping when adpressed, the hindlimb about 40-50% of snout-vent length. 24-34 smooth lamellae under the fourth toe, many or all of which are divided; base of fourth toe broad, with three or more lamellae or granules between the lateral scales. 80 mm (snout-vent).
Distribution: Northeastern Vic. through coast and tablelands of south-eastern NSW to northern tablelands of NSW.
Habit: A ground-dwelling inhabitant of open upland forests and grasslands, where it is usually found in close association with wet microhabitats such as the margins of swamps, lagoons and creeks.

Eulamprus leuraensis Wentworth Falls, NSW

A. HATTON

Eulamprus luteilateralis Eungella, Qld

Eulamprus kosciuskoi (Kinghorn, 1932)
Alpine Water Skink

Description: Similar in most respects to *Eulamprus tympanum*, except that there is no pale streak from above the eye, but a narrow, pale, black-edged dorso-lateral stripe from the neck to at least halfway along the body. Black spots on the dorsum are usually arranged as continuous dorsal stripes. No pale spots or streaks on the cheeks. Ventral surface usually white or cream, with only a few scattered grey spots on the throat and occasional black flecks on the chest and belly. 80 mm (snout-vent).
Distribution: Mt Kosciusko region of the Australian Alps to northern tablelands of NSW.
Habit: Among rocks and fallen timber beside creeks in montane forests and woodlands, and in alpine bogs and marshes.

Eulamprus leuraensis Wells and Wellington, 1984

Description: A broad, black, vertebral stripe narrowly edged with gold or yellow; a narrow, pale, golden-yellow or cream dorso-lateral stripe from neck to rump, the region between this stripe and the pale paravertebral stripe black, with scattered pale flecks or spots; flanks blackish, with several series of pale yellow or cream spots which sometimes coalesce to form streaks or bars, gradually merging with black and cream mottling on the lower flanks. Head dark brown above with black variegations. Upper labials mostly black, especially posteriorly, and contrasting strongly with the white or greenish-white lower labials. A pale streak over the ear and another below the ear, more or less continuous with the pale lower lip stripe. Limbs above black, speckled with gold or fawn. Metallic greenish-white below, speckled with dark brown. Nasals separated. Prefrontals usually in contact. Four supraoculars. Seven supralabials. Postmental contacting two infralabials on each side. Ear-opening larger than the nasal. Scales smooth, in 28-32 rows at mid-body. Limbs well developed, strongly overlapping when adpressed; the hindlimb about 45% of snout-vent length. 20-24 lamellae, many or all or which are divided, under the fourth toe. 80 mm (snout-vent).
Distribution: Central Blue Mountains, NSW.
Habit: Riparian and swampy areas in montane forests and heaths.

Eulamprus luteilateralis (Covacevich and McDonald, 1980)

Description: Rich brown above, with scattered darker brown scales, or scales edged with darker brown; a conspicuous blackish patch above the insertion of the forelimb, and one or two smaller blackish patches on the side of the head and neck between the ear and the forelimb. Lips whitish and sides of head and neck dirty white. Flanks between

Eulamprus murrayi
Dorrigo, NSW

Eulamprus leuraensis

Eulamprus luteilateralis

Eulamprus murrayi

Eulamprus quoyii

Eulamprus tenuis

Eulamprus tigrinus

Eulamprus tympanum

forelimbs and hindlimbs dull to bright orange with numerous scattered white dots. Ventral surfaces whitish. Nasals separated. Prefrontals just contacting or separated. Usually four supraoculars. Six supralabials. Postmental contacting one infralabial on each side. Ear-opening large, much larger than the nasal. Scales smooth, in 36-42 rows at mid-body. Limbs well developed, strongly overlapping when adpressed, the hindlimb about 35-40% of snout-vent length. 17-22 smooth lamellae under the fourth toe. 90 mm (snout-vent).
Distribution: Known only from Clarke Range, west of Mackay, Qld.
Habit: Diurnally active among litter and fallen timber in montane rainforest. Live-bearing. Covacevich and McDonald record five young in a litter.

Eulamprus murrayi (Boulenger, 1887)

Description: Rich brown to chocolate-brown above, many scales with darker brown edges and/or paler centres to give an overall variegated effect. Head scales narrowly margined with darker brown. Lips and cheeks dark brown to blackish with pale cream or yellow bars or spots. Side of neck and body dark purplish-brown or blackish, with numerous very small white dots and scattered larger pale spots and blotches. Throat cream or yellow, chin shields broadly margined with dark brown, with a series of brown variegations on the throat and chest sometimes tending to form longitudinal streaks. Belly creamy-yellow variegated with brown where it meets the lower flanks. Usually some brown spots or flecks before the vent. Lower limbs and tail finely to strongly flecked with brown. Nasals separated. Prefrontals separated or in point contact. Four supraoculars, although an enlarged anterior supraciliary sometimes regarded as a fifth prefrontal. Usually six supralabials. Postmental contacting a single infralabial on each side. Ear-opening conspicuous, much larger than the nasal. Scales smooth in 30-34 rows at mid-body. Limbs well developed, strongly overlapping when adpressed, the hindlimb about 40-45% of snout-vent length. 16-22 smooth lamellae under the fourth toe, divided only at the base of the toe where there are no more than two lamellae or granules between the lateral scales. 85 mm (snout-vent).
Distribution: North-eastern NSW and south-eastern Qld.
Habit: Found in rainforest and wet sclerophyll forests of the coast and ranges where it forages by day among leaf-litter and around logs and other fallen timber. Live-bearing, producing 3-5 young usually in late January.

Eulamprus quoyii Tia, New England, NSW

Eulamprus quoyii (Duméril and Bibron, 1839)

Eastern Water Skink

Description: Olive-brown above, usually with some scattered darker flecks on the head and scattered black spots on the body and tail, which in some specimens tend to form longitudinal series. A narrow, pale golden or yellowish dorso- lateral stripe from above the eye and extending at least along the anterior part of the body. Bordered below by a broad, blackish, upper lateral zone enclosing several series of pale yellow or cream spots which sometimes form obscure transverse bars. Lower flanks creamy-yellow with numerous scattered small blackish spots. Lower lips and chin shields with scattered blackish spots or margined with black, and often a series of dark grey or blackish longitudinal lines on the throat which may extend on to the chest and belly. Limbs above olive-brown spotted with black. Rarely any pale streak from behind eye to above ear. Nasals separated. Four supraoculars. Usually seven supralabials. Postmental contacting two or three infralabials on each side. Ear-opening conspicuous, larger than the nasal. Scales smooth in 36-44 rows at mid-body. Limbs well developed, strongly overlapping when adpressed, the hindlimb about 40-50% of snout-vent length. 24-34 smooth lamellae under the fourth toe, many or all of which are divided; base of fourth toe broad, with three or more lamellae or granules between the lateral scales. 100 mm (snout-vent).

Distribution: Coast and ranges of eastern Australia from northern Qld to southern NSW, extending inland via the Darling River system to north-western Vic and south-eastern SA.

Habit: Rainforest, wet and dry sclerophyll forests, coastal and mountain heaths, woodland, coastal and inland wetlands and riverine vegetation along larger inland rivers. A diurnal lizard usually seen basking on rocks or logs, or foraging among vegetation beside small creeks, larger streams and rivers. Sometimes seen on rocky ridges well away from water. Takes to rock crevices, hollow logs or the water when alarmed. Omnivorous. Viviparous, usually producing two or three young in a litter.

Eulamprus tenuis (Gray, 1831)

Description: Pale fawn to grey-brown above, variegated with dark brown flecks and blotches. In some specimens the variegations may be restricted to

Eulamprus tenuis

Eulamprus tigrinus Windsor Tableland, Qld

the mid-dorsal region. A dark brown upper lateral zone commencing as a dark streak below the canthus and extending to the base of the tail. This zone has ragged edges and is usually broken up into a series of large, black blotches on the hind portion of the body. Lower flanks cream, liberally spotted and flecked with dark brown. Lips barred with dark brown. Ventral surface cream to yellow, chin shields edged with dark brown, and a series of dark brown flecks on the throat, sometimes extending to the chest. Palmar tubercles dark brown. Nasals separated. Prefrontals usually separated, sometimes in narrow contact. Four supraoculars. Usually only seven supralabials. Postmental contacting two infralabials on each side. Ear-opening conspicuous, larger than the nasal. Scales smooth, in 26-34 rows at mid-body. Limbs well developed, overlapping when adpressed, the hindlimb about 40% of snout-vent length. 19-26 smooth or bluntly keeled lamellae under the fourth toe, divided only at the base of the toe where there are one or two lamellae or granules between the lateral scales. 70 mm (snout- vent).

Distribution: Central coast and ranges of NSW through eastern Qld to Cape York Peninsula.

Habit: An agile, diurnal or crepuscular, essentially arboreal skink, but often found in rock slopes, retaining walls, etc. Found primarily in rainforest, and in wet and dry sclerophyll forests.

Subspecies: *tenuis* (NSW and southern Qld); *brachysoma* (northern Qld).

Eulamprus tigrinus (De Vis, 1888)

Description: Rich brown or coppery-brown above, with a dorso- lateral series of dark brown bars or patches on the neck and body. A few dark brown flecks and spots on the back, tending to be concentrated along the vertebral line. An obscure dark brown canthal streak and usually a conspicuous, short, dark brown temporal streak from the eye; sometimes another short streak or series of spots on the cheek. Flanks and limbs flecked and spotted with dark brown, and usually a series of small, dark spots along the side of the tail. Lips lightly barred with dark brown. Throat sometimes variegated with pale grey-brown. Remaining ventral surfaces white or cream. Palmar tubercles dark brown. Nasals separated. Prefrontals in broad contact. Four supraoculars. Seven or eight supralabials. Postmental usually in contact with two infralabials on each side. Ear-opening conspicuous, oval, at least as large as the nasal scale. Scales smooth in 28-32 rows at mid-body. Limbs well developed, the hindlimb about 40-50% of snout-vent length. 24-28 lamellae under the fourth toe, the base of the latter only slightly swollen. 80 mm (snout-vent).
Distribution: Known only from the rainforests of north- eastern Qld.
Habit: Diurnal/crepuscular; basks in patches of sunlight in rainforest.

Eulamprus tympanum (Lönnberg and Andersson, 1913)

Description: Olive-brown above, head variegated with black and usually with few to many scattered black scales on the dorsum. A broad, dark upper lateral zone from below the eye to the base of the tail, enclosing scattered small white or cream spots and bordered above, at least anteriorly, by a pale streak from above the eye to about the shoulder. Lower flanks whitish, with numerous scattered black scales, sometimes tending to be aligned transversely. Lower labials whitish, continuous with a whitish streak running from the angle of the jaw and below the ear to the base of the forelimb. Usually a pale streak or series of pale spots from behind the eye to above the ear. Limbs above variegated with black, and the throat spotted with black. In some specimens there is a series of broad, black longitudinal stripes on the throat. Ventral surface white or cream, the chin shields often broadly margined with black. Nasals separated. Prefrontals usually separated, occasionally in narrow contact. Four supraoculars. Usually seven supralabials. Postmental contacting two infralabials on each side. Ear-opening larger than nasal. Scales smooth, in 34-44 rows at mid-body. Limbs well-developed, overlapping strongly when adpressed; the hindlimb about 45-50% of snout-vent length. 20-28 lamellae under the fourth toe, many or all of which are divided; base of fourth toe broad, with three or more lamellae or granules between the lateral scales. 80 mm (snout-vent).
Distribution: Southern and eastern Vic and south-eastern NSW, with isolated populations in the Fleurieu Peninsula, SA.
Habit: An agile, diurnal lizard, most commonly encountered along small creeks, where it is usually seen basking on rocks, logs, etc. Readily takes to the water when alarmed.

Eulamprus tympanum Smiggin Holes, Kosciusko National Park, NSW

Genus *Glaphyromorphus* Wells and Wellington, 1984

A group of moderate, cryptozoic, nocturnal or crepuscular lizards characterised by: pentadactyle limbs; smooth scales; anterior ear lobules absent; supranasals absent; lower eyelid movable, scaly; parietal scales in contact behind the interparietal; fourth toe markedly longer than third; lower surfaces of rump and tail not flushed with red or pink; hindlimb moderate, usually less than 40% of snout-vent length; oviparous.

Key

TO THE AUSTRALIAN SPECIES OF GLAPHYROMORPHUS

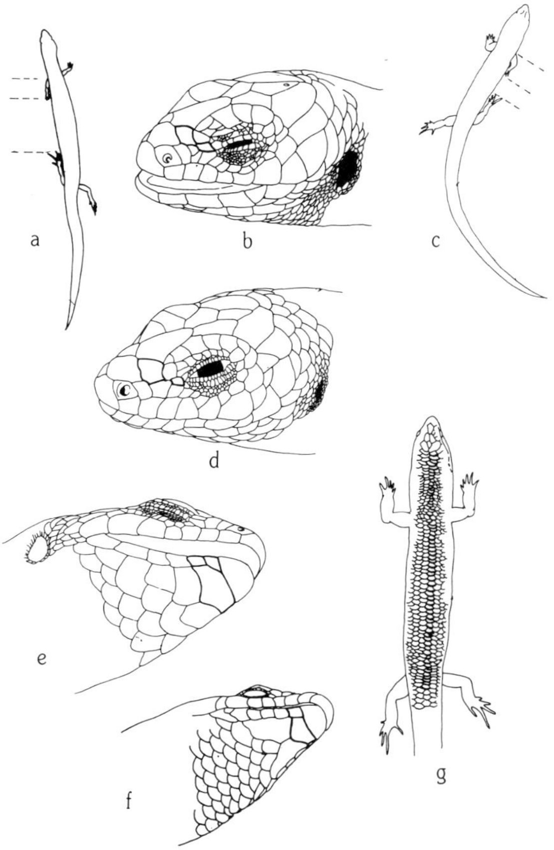

1 Adpressed limbs separated by noticeably more than the length of the forelimb (a); 24 or fewer mid-body scale rows; prefrontal contacting first preocular (b) **2**

Adpressed limbs overlapping or separated by at most the length of the forelimb (c); 22 or more mid-body scale rows; prefrontal not contacting first preocular (d)..................... **9**

2 Postmental usually contacting two infralabials (e)......... **3**

Postmental usually contacting only one infralabial (f) **5**

3 Flanks not spotted or dotted with white; northern Australia.. **4**

Flanks spotted or dotted with white; south-western Australia... ***gracilipes***

4 More than 65 scales along the vertebral line between the parietal scales and the posterior edge of the thigh (g)......... .... ***cracens***

Fewer than 65 scales along the vertebral line between the parietal scales and the posterior edge of the thigh............. .... ***darwiniensis***

5 A broad dark upper lateral stripe along body, its lower edge sharply differentiated from the paler lower flanks.... **6**

A broad, dark upper lateral zone, if present, with its lower edge merging with the colour on the lower flanks............ **7**

6 Ear-opening minute, not or scarcely larger than the nostril. .... ***pumilus***

Ear-opening small, but noticeably larger than the nostril .... ***crassicaudus***

7 Lamellae under the fourth toe 15 or fewer; no indication of a dark vertebral stripe or paired dark vertebral lines of dots; limbs short, the axilla-groin/hindlimb ratio usually more than three **8**

Lamellae under fourth toe rarely as low as 15, but if so there is usually some indication of a dark vertebral stripe; limbs moderate, the axilla-groin/hindlimb ratio usually less than three .... ***darwiniensis***

8 Upper flanks heavily mottled or blotched with dark brown, especially anteriorly; size large (to 100 mm snout-vent); 22-24 mid-body scale rows .... ***mjobergi***

Upper flanks finely dotted with dark brown, but without obvious dark blotches or mottling; size small (to 60 mm snout-vent); 18-22 mid-body scale rows....... ***punctulatus***

9 Postmental in contact with two infralabials on each side (e) **10**

Postmental in contact with a single infralabial on each side (f) **11**

10 60 or more scales along the vertebral line between the parietal scales and the posterior edge of the thigh; sides of neck and anterior flanks blackish, enclosing a series of irregular pale cream or yellow spots and blotches............. .... ***fuscicaudis***

Fewer than 60 scales along the vertebral line between the parietal scales and the posterior edge of the thigh; sides of neck and anterior flanks brown, with irregular darker brown flecks, mottling or vertical bars.......... ***nigricaudis***

11 Adpressed limbs overlap or almost touch; mid-dorsal and mid-ventral scales subequal.. **12**

Adpressed limbs fail to overlap by at least six rows of scales; mid-dorsal scale rows conspicuously broad and larger than the mid-ventrals .... ***pardalis***

12 Usually six supralabials; dorsal pattern and/or colour differentiated from that of flanks.................................. **13**

Usually seven supralabials; dorsal and lateral colour and pattern not noticeably differentiated.................... ***isolepis***

13 A solid black dorso-lateral stripe at least anteriorly, enclosing a series of small white dots; flanks and sides of neck reddish-brown or reddish and with numerous, scattered, small white dots; dorsal surface dark brown...... .... ***douglasi***

Dark dorso-lateral streak irregular, flecked with white; flanks pale brown, thickly dotted with dark brown or black; dorsal surface pale to moderately dark reddish-brown.. ***brongersmai***

Glaphyromorphus crassicaudis Darnley Island, Torres Strait

Glaphyromorphus brongersmai

(Storr, 1972)

Description: Pale to moderately dark reddish-brown above, uniform or with longitudinal series of blackish streaks through the dorsal scales. An irregular, dark dorso-lateral streak, commencing on the snout and extending through the eye to the forepart of the body, and dotted with white behind the ear. Flanks pale brown, thickly dotted or flecked with dark brown or black to the dorso-lateral line, contrasting strongly with the dorsal surface. Supralabials edged with brown. Ventral surfaces whitish. Nasals separated. Prefrontals separated. Four supraoculars. Six supralabials. Postmental contacting a single infralabial on each side. Ear-opening conspicuous, as large as or larger than the nasal. Scales smooth, in 26-31 rows at mid-body. Limbs well developed, nearly meeting or overlapping when adpressed, the hindlimb about 25-35% of snout-vent length. 20-25 lamellae under the fourth toe, not noticeably swollen. 90 mm (snout-vent).

Distribution: Northern Kimberley region, WA.

Habit: In moist microhabitats among boulders and fallen timber, usually beside streams or at the bases of rock slopes and cliffs.

Glaphyromorphus cracens (Greer, 1985)

Description: Pale fawn or brown above, dotted and flecked with blackish on the head and neck and on the tail; back immaculate; a broad, black upper lateral stripe from the snout, through the eye and ear and over the limbs to the base of the tail; the neck and lower flanks grey, with numerous darker flecks and dots aligned to form obscure longitudinal striations. Ventral surfaces whitish or cream, except the tail which is brown. Nasals separated. Prefrontals moderate, separated. Four supraoculars. Postmental contacting two labials on each side. Ear-opening minute, nearly twice as large as nostril. Scales smooth, in 20-22 rows at mid-body. Limbs short, widely separated when adpressed, the hindlimb about 20-25% of snout-vent length. 13-17 smooth, undivided lamellae under the fourth toe. 50 mm (snout-vent).
Distribution: North-eastern Qld.
Habit: Usually found under ground litter or rocks in open woodland and vine scrub.

Glaphyromorphus crassicaudus (Duméril and Duméril, 1851)

Description: Pale fawn to rich chocolate-brown above, immaculate or flecked with dark brown, or usually with a dark vertebral zone. This zone may consist simply of two continuous narrow black lines, or two discontinuous lines of flecks and short streaks along the two mid-dorsal scale rows; in other specimens the area between these two lines may be solid black or dark brown. A broad, black upper lateral zone, sharply delineated as a stripe, or its edges indefinite, with or without smaller pale dots. This zone usually commences as a blackish streak below the canthus, passing through the eye and temporal region. Lower flanks pale grey-brown, usually dotted with dark brown. Lips faintly to strongly barred with dark brown. White, cream or pale yellow below, sometimes with dark brown spots and flecks. Nasals separated. Prefrontals separated. Four supraoculars. Supralabials 6-8, usually seven. Postmental contacting one infralabial on each side. Ear-opening small, round, distinctly larger than the nostril. Scales smooth, in 20-22 rows at mid-body. Limbs short, widely separated when adpressed, the hindlimb about 20-30% of snout-vent length. 15-22 lamellae under the fourth toe, undivided and more or less smooth. 50 mm (snout-vent).
Distribution: North-eastern Qld and the islands of Torres Strait. Extra-limital in New Guinea.
Habit: Occurs in a variety of forest and coastal dune habitats, where it is found under logs and stones, or in rotting leaf-litter and decaying logs. Common under stones at the bases of stony hills and rocky outcrops, especially in the beds of non-perennial creeks.

Glaphyromorphus darwiniensis (Storr, 1967)

Description: Grey-brown, dark brown or chocolate-brown above, usually immaculate or flecked with dark brown, or with a dark vertebral stripe or zone which may be a single broad stripe or two continuous narrow black lines separated by a narrow pale vertebral stripe, at least anteriorly. Usually a broad, ill-defined dark upper lateral zone, with scattered darker and paler brown flecks and dots. Lower flanks pale brown, with scattered darker flecks. Lips whitish, strongly barred with dark brown. White or cream below, sometimes with dark brown spots on the base of the tail. Nasals separated. Prefrontals separated. Four supraoculars. Supralabials 5-7. Postmental contacting 1 or 2 infralabials on each side. Ear-opening small, round, slightly sunken and distinctly larger than the nostril. Scales smooth, in 20-22 rows at mid-body. Limbs short, widely separated when adpressed, the hindlimb about 20-30% of snout-vent length. 15-22 lamellae under the fourth toe, undivided, and more or less smooth. 55 mm (snout-vent).
Distribution: Extreme northern WA, through northern NT.
Habit: Seasonally-dry woodlands and monsoon forest, under rocks, logs, dense leaf-litter and flood debris.
Subspecies: *darwiniensis* (north-western NT and north Kimberleys, WA); *arnhemicus* (Arnhem Land, NT).

Glaphyromorphus douglasi (Storr, 1967)

Description: Brown to dark brown above, with scattered dark brown or blackish flecks and spots on the back and base of the tail. A broad, blackish dorso-lateral streak from above the ear to at least the level of the forelimb, but sometimes extending back almost to the hindlimbs; this encloses scattered, tiny, white dots. An obscure dark brown streak below the canthus and continued behind the eye as a series of flecks which may be continuous with the dorso-lateral streak. Labials edged with brown. Sides of neck and flanks pale brown to rich reddish-brown, with scattered, small, white dots and dark brown flecks. Ventral surfaces white or cream, except for some

short, oblique brown bars from the lips. Nasals separated. Prefrontals usually separated, occasionally in narrow contact. Four supraoculars. Six, occasionally seven, supralabials. Postmental contacting a single infralabial on each side. Ear-opening conspicuous, as large as or larger than the nasal. Scales smooth, in 26-32 rows at mid-body. Limbs well developed, nearly meeting or overlapping when adpressed, the hindlimb about 25-35% of snout-vent length. 17-25 lamellae under fourth toe, divided basally; base of fourth toe not noticeably swollen. 80 mm (snout-vent).
Distribution: Western Arnhem Land to the coast of Van Diemen's Gulf and Melville Island, NT.
Habit: Similar to *Glaphyromorphus isolepis*, the two species found together over a wide area of sympatry in western Arnhem Land.

Glaphyromorphus douglasi Mt Brockman, NT

Glaphyromorphus fuscicaudis Lake Barrine, Qld

Glaphyromorphus brongersmai

Glaphyromorphus cracens

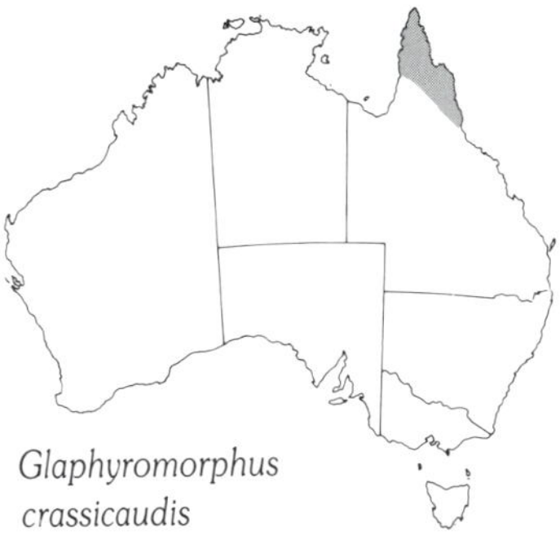

Glaphyromorphus crassicaudis

Glaphyromorphus gracilipes Two People Bay, WA

M. PETERSON

Glaphyromorphus isolepis Brockman Range, NT

Glaphyromorphus darwiniensis

Glaphyromorphus douglasi

Glaphyromorphus fuscicaudis

Glaphyromorphus fuscicaudis

(Greer, 1979)

Description: Rich brown above, darker on the base of the tail, with scattered darker scales which sometimes tend to form transverse bars on the neck region; flanks and sides of neck with numerous, scattered, dark brown or black flecks and dots interspersed with numerous, pale cream or yellow spots or patches, most intense anteriorly where they form a contrasting reticulum and/or series of pale dorso-lateral blotches. Limbs brown above with darker flecks and variegations. Lips lightly barred. White below, often flushed with yellow in life. Sometimes a pale pink flush to the cloacal region and to the lower base of the tail. Nasals separated. Prefrontals usually separated. Four supraoculars. Seven supralabials. Postmental usually in contact with two infralabials on each side. Ear-opening conspicuous, at least as large as nasal. Scales smooth, in 27-30 rows at mid-body. Limbs moderate, separated by no more than the length of the forelimb when adpressed, the hindlimb about 25-35% of snout-vent length. 18-24 bluntly keeled lamellae under the fourth toe. 90 mm (snout-vent).
Distribution: Lowland and montane rainforests from the Atherton Tableland north nearly to Cooktown, Qld.
Habit: Typically an inhabitant of rainforest, where it is active among the debris of the forest floor, but also extends into cleared areas within or beside rainforest. Oviparous.

Glaphyromorphus mjobergi near Tully Falls, Qld

Glaphyromorphus nigricaudis Murray Island, Torres Strait

Glaphyromorphus gracilipes

(Steindachner, 1870)

Description: Dark brown above, sometimes paler, usually minutely flecked with black; the black flecks tend to be concentrated on the two mid-dorsal scale rows to form two broken, longitudinal lines along the back. A poorly defined or obscure black dorso-lateral stripe, commencing on the snout and continuing on the tail as a broad lateral zone. Flanks olive-grey, finely spotted and flecked with black and white, the white spot often extending into the black dorso-lateral stripe. Lips barred with dark brown or black. White or cream below, the throat sometimes spotted and streaked with dark grey, the chest and belly sometimes bright yellow, turning yellow-green under the tail, which is heavily blotched with black. Nasals separated. Prefrontals usually separated. Four supraoculars. Usually seven supralabials. Postmental contacting two infralabials on each side. Ear-opening large, much larger than the nasal. Scales smooth, in 19-22 rows at mid-body. Limbs short, not meeting when adpressed, the hindlimb about 15-30% of snout-vent length. 16-23 smooth lamellae under the fourth toe, occasionally divided. 80 mm (snout-vent).
Distribution: South-western WA.
Habit: A burrowing skink usually found under stones, logs, etc. on moist soil in a variety of heathland and forest habitats.

Glaphyromorphus gracilipes

Glaphyromorphus isolepis

Glaphyromorphus mjobergi

Glaphyromorphus isolepis

(Boulenger, 1887)

Description: Pale brown to rich orange-brown above, liberally flecked with darker brown, the flecks sometimes aligned longitudinally. Flanks similar to dorsum, but usually more heavily speckled with dark brown above to form an obscure, darker, dorso-lateral zone. Labials edged with dark brown. Scattered whitish flecks on the side of the neck. Limbs and tail speckled with dark brown. Ventral surfaces white or cream. Nasals separated. Prefrontals usually separated, occasionally in contact. Four supraoculars. Usually seven supralabials, occasionally six or eight. Postmental contacting a single infralabial on each side. Ear-opening conspicuous, as large as or larger than the nasal. Scales smooth, in 25-32 rows at mid-body. Limbs well developed, nearly meeting or overlapping when adpressed, the hindlimb about 25-35% of snout-vent length. 19-25 lamellae under the fourth toe, divided basally; base of fourth toe not noticeably swollen. 70 mm (snout-vent).
Distribution: Eastern Arnhem Land and the south-western Gulf of Carpentaria through the northern NT to north-western WA as far south as Exmouth Gulf.
Habit: Found in seasonally-dry woodlands and coastal shrublands. A nocturnal, ground-dwelling lizard usually found under fallen timber, leaf-litter, stones and any man-made debris lying on sandy or loamy soils. Often seen at night foraging in litter, grass or around the base of trees, especially on the edge of soaks, swamps and billabongs.

Glaphyromorphus mjobergi

(Lönnberg and Andersson, 1915)

Description: Rich brown above, uniform, or the individual scales each with a dark brown spot. An upper lateral zone containing numerous dark brown or blackish spots, which in some specimens tend to form a dark dorso-lateral streak, especially anteriorly. Lower flanks pale brown, gradually merging with the white or cream ventral surface. Sometimes an obscure dark streak below the canthus. Nasals separated. Prefrontals usually separated. Four supraoculars. Six supralabials. Postmental contacting a single infralabial on each side. Ear-opening conspicuous, about as large as the nasal. Scales smooth, in 22 rows at mid-body. Limbs short, widely separated when adpressed, the hindlimb about 15-20% of snout-vent length. 12-15 smooth, undivided lamellae under the fourth toe. 90 mm (snout-vent).
Distribution: Known only from rainforests and related habitats of the Atherton Tableland, Qld, and its eastern escarpment.
Habit: A burrowing species usually found in moist soil under logs, stones or leaf-litter in shaded forest situations.

Glaphyromorphus nigricaudis

(Macleay, 1877)

Description: Rich brown above and on the sides, immaculate or with irregular, small, dark brown flecks or spots on the anterior half of the body, sometimes aligned transversely across the shoulders. No indication of a dark dorso-lateral zone. Lips barred with dark brown. White or cream ventral surfaces, sometimes with a few dark brown flecks or streaks on the throat. Terminal portion of tail sometimes heavily spotted with black. Nasals separated. Prefrontals usually separated, occasionally in narrow contact. Four supraoculars. Usually seven supralabials. Postmental in contact with two infralabials on each side. Ear-opening conspicuous, at least as large as nasal. Scales smooth in 26-28 rows at mid-body. Limbs moderate, separated by no more than the length of the forelimb when adpressed, the hindlimb about 25-35% of snout-vent length. 18-24 smooth or bluntly keeled lamellae under the fourth toe. 75 mm (snout-vent).
Distribution: North-eastern Qld and the islands of Torres Strait. Extra-limital in New Guinea.
Habit: Found in a wide variety of habitats including marginal rainforest, monsoon forest and vine thickets, vegetated coastal dunes and heaths, and tropical woodlands. A nocturnal, burrowing species usually found sheltering by day under rocks, fallen timber, and dense leaf- and other litter.

Glaphyromorphus pardalis

(Macleay, 1877)

Description: Rich brown above, with a dark dorso-lateral zone consisting of a narrow temporal streak and a large number of individual black spots or short vertical bars which may or may not form a continuous streak along the dorso-lateral line. Flanks fawn, spotted with black or dark brown. Usually a few dark brown spots on rear of head and conspicuous dark brown labial bars extending on to lower jaw as a series of short, oblique bars. Ventral surface otherwise immaculate. Pale brown dorsal region may be uniform, but more often contains scattered dark brown scales which may be largely confined to the two mid-dorsal scale rows. Sides of tail heavily

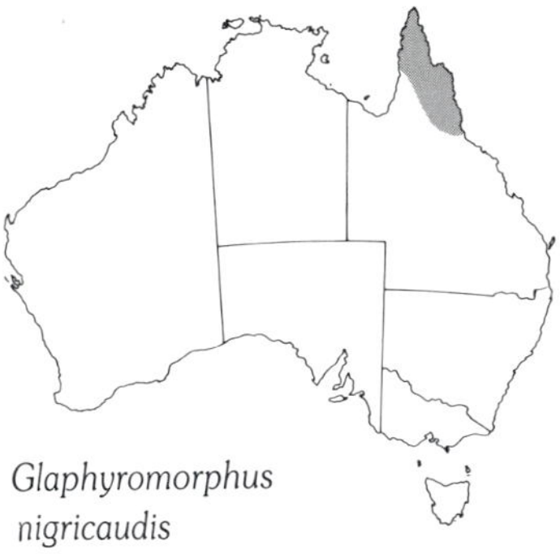

Glaphyromorphus nigricaudis

J. WOMBEY

Glaphyromorphus pardalis Edward River, Qld

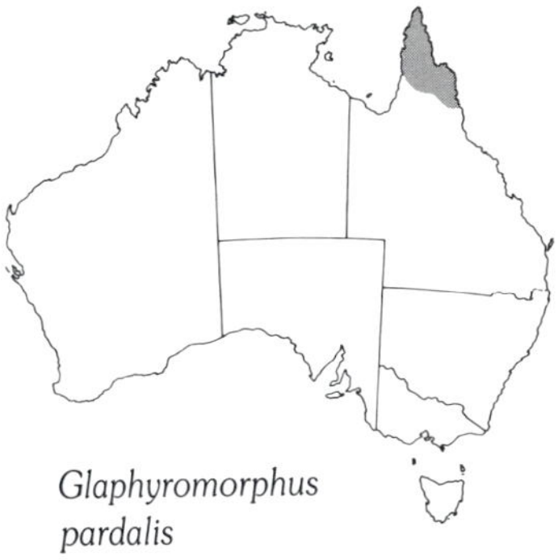

Glaphyromorphus pardalis

Glaphyromorphus pumilus near Mareeba, Qld

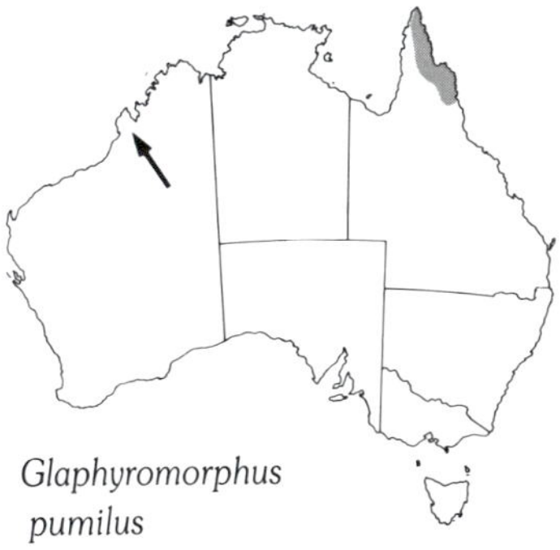

Glaphyromorphus pumilus

Glaphyromorphus punctulatus Mt Morgan, Qld

Glaphyromorphus punctulatus

spotted or variegated with brown. Nasals separated. Prefrontals separated. Four supraoculars. Postmental in contact with a single infralabial on each side. Usually seven supralabials, but only five infralabials. Ear-opening small, scarcely as large as the nasal. Scales smooth, in 22-26 (usually 24) rows at mid-body. Limbs short or moderate, separated by at least six rows of scales when adpressed, the hindlimb about 25-30% of snout-vent length. 17-24 smooth, undivided lamellae under the fourth toe. 70 mm (snout-vent).
Distribution: Cape York Peninsula, Qld.
Habit: A burrowing, cryptozoic lizard, usually found in softer soils under logs, stones and man-made debris in a variety of habitats ranging from monsoon forest to savannah woodland and associated grasslands.

Glaphyromorphus pumilus
(Boulenger, 1877)

Description: Pale fawn or brown above, many of the individual scales with a dark brown or blackish dot; the dots on the two mid-dorsal scale rows largest and usually forming two fine, longitudinal lines along the back and tail. Lips and head flecked and speckled with dark brown. Flanks and sides of neck and tail speckled and dotted with dark brown, tending to form an indefinite, dark upper lateral zone. Ventral surfaces cream or yellowish. Nasals separated. Prefrontals large but separated. Four supraoculars. Postmental contacting one labial on each side. Ear-opening minute, scarcely or not larger than the nostril. Scales smooth in 20 rows at mid-body. Limbs short, widely separated when adpressed, the hindlimb about 20-25% of snout-vent length. 16-20 smooth, undivided lamellae under the fourth toe. 50 mm (snout-vent).
Distribution: Eastern Cape York Peninsula, Qld.
Habit: A small, burrowing lizard found under rocks and logs in seasonally-dry forests and woodlands.

Glaphyromorphus punctulatus
(Peters, 1871)

Description: Rich brown above, the individual scales on the dorsum and flanks flecked and streaked with darker brown, pale-edged. In some specimens the scales on the upper flanks are more heavily flecked, resulting in an indefinite dark upper lateral zone. Lips and side of face heavily spotted with brown. Ventral surfaces cream or yellow, with some dark brown dots on the chin and throat which tend to form longitudinal striations on the sides of the throat, a few small brown dots laterally and near the vent, and heavy brown spotting on the tail. Nasals separated. Four supraoculars. Usually seven supralabials. Postmental contacting one or two infralabials on each side. Ear-opening small, round, scarcely as large as the nasal. Scales smooth, in 18-20 rows at mid-body. Limbs very short, widely separated when adpressed, the hindlimb about 15-20% of snout-vent length. 11-14 smooth, undivided lamellae under the fourth toe. 55 mm (snout-vent).
Distribution: Central-eastern Qld.
Habit: Found under rocks, fallen timber and dense leaf-litter in tall woodland and seasonally-dry forest habitats.

Genus ***Gnypetoscincus*** Wells and Wellington, 1984

A distinctive genus whose sole Australian species is readily distinguishable from all other Australian skinks. Limbs well developed, pentadactyle; ear-opening large without anterior lobules; scales small (ventrals largest), strongly keeled; no supranasals or divided nasal scales; lower eyelid movable, scaly; parietal scales in contact behind the interparietal; tail moderate to long, tapering.

One Australian species confined to north-eastern Qld. Relationships uncertain.

Gnypetoscincus queenslandiae Atherton, Qld

Gnypetoscincus queenslandiae

Gnypetoscincus queenslandiae

(De Vis, 1890)

Description: Brown to rich purplish-brown or blackish above, uniform, or more often with obscure and irregular pale cross-bands; these cross-bands usually much narrower than the darker, and sometimes confined to the flanks. Lips and throat dark brown with irregular pale spots and streaks. Remaining ventral surfaces pale cream or yellowish, spotted or flecked with brown and sometimes with an indefinite, dark brown mid-ventral stripe. Tail below barred or blotched with brown. Dorsal and lateral scales small, each with a high median keel; scales of throat tubercular, keeled; ventrals larger than dorsals, each with a low keel. 32-36 mid-body scale rows. Nasals separated. Prefrontals moderate, separated by a conspicuous azygous scale. Five supraoculars. Frontal complete, or divided anteriorly to form three shields. Postmental in contact with two infralabials on each side. Fourth toe with 20-28 smooth lamellae. Preanals greatly enlarged. 80 mm (snout-vent).

Distribution: Apparently confined to the rainforests of the Cooktown-Cardwell region, Qld.

Habit: A nocturnal, cryptozoic lizard, usually found in a semi-torpid condition in or under rotting logs deep in rainforest. Little is known of its biology.

Genus ***Hemiergis*** Wagler, 1830

A group of cryptozoic and fossorial small, slender, smooth-scaled lizards characterised by: short limbs, which fail to overlap by at least several scale rows when adpressed; supranasals absent; nasals small to moderate, usually separated; prefrontals absent, or, when present, moderate to large, often forming a median suture; parietal shields in contact behind the interparietal; lower eyelid movable, with a transparent disc; ear-opening usually absent, its position usually indicated by a slight depression (a minute opening in one species); preanals enlarged.

Members of the genus are confined to continental Australia.

Key

TO THE SPECIES OF HEMIERGIS

1 Five fingers **2**
Fewer than five fingers... **3**

2 11 or fewer lamellae under the fourth toe; supralabials separated from eye by a series of subocular scales (a)...... .... ***initialis***
12 or more lamellae under the fourth toe; fifth labial contacting the eye (b)... ***millewe***

3 Limbs each with two, three or four digits; if tridactyle, the third toe is much longer than the second (c) **4**
Limbs each with three digits; second toe slightly longer than third (d) .... ***decresiensis***

4 Limbs each with two digits.................... ***quadrilineatum***
Limbs each with three or four digits...................... ***peronii***

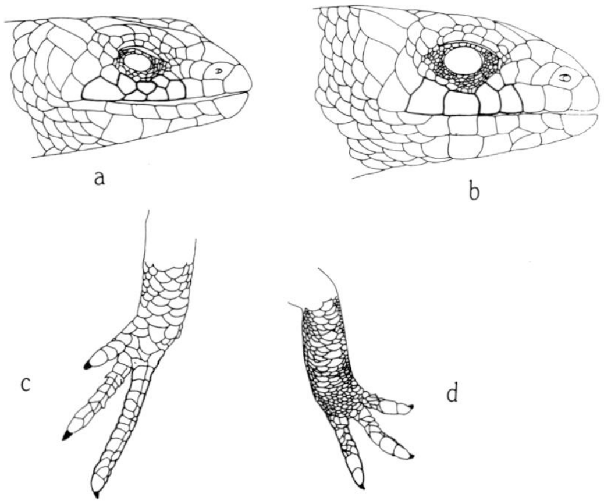

Hemiergis decresiensis (Cuvier, 1829)

Description: Rich brown above, with a series of narrow, dark brown stripes or series of spots, sometimes confined to a paravertebral and a dorso-lateral pair, the latter invariably the most conspicuous. Flanks grey-brown, with darker flecks tending to form longitudinal series of dots. A narrow dark brown stripe along the canthus and through the eye, usually continuous with the dark dorso-lateral stripe. Often some dark longitudinal streaks on the side of the neck. Ventral surface cream to yellow. Scales of throat usually margined with brown. Underside of tail usually heavily spotted with dark brown. Prefrontals moderate, separated. Four supraoculars. 18-26 mid-body rows of smooth scales. Forelimb tridactyle; hindlimb also tridactyle, the second toe slightly longer than the third. Hindlimb about 15-20% of snout-vent length. 50 mm (snout-vent).
Distribution: South-eastern SA through Vic to the eastern highlands and tablelands of NSW.
Habit: A burrowing species usually found under stones or fallen timber in wet and dry sclerophyll forests. Confined to the ranges in the northern part of its range, but found at lower altitudes in the south.
Subspecies: *decresiensis* (Kangaroo Island, SA); *continentis* (mainland SA); *talbingoensis* (southern NSW and Vic); *davisi* (central and northern Great Dividing Range, NSW).

Hemiergis initialis Werner, 1910

Description: Medium to dark brown above, with a pair of fine, blackish lines along the vertebral region formed by individual, small, black dots on each of the scales in the two mid-dorsal rows. Sometimes also an outer pair of fine lines and dots. A narrow, blackish dorso-lateral stripe on each side, bordered above by an obscure, pale stripe (paler brown than the mid-dorsum). Flanks paler grey-brown. Throat white, the individual scales narrowly edged with black. Chest,

belly and underside of tail yellowish. Prefrontals usually absent. Four supraoculars. 20-22 mid-body scale rows. Fore- and hindlimbs pentadactyle, the third toe longer than the fourth, hindlimb about 20% of snout-vent length. 40 mm (snout-vent). Ear-opening absent, indicated by a depression.
Distribution: South-western WA.
Habit: A burrowing lizard found in soil under fallen timber, stones, etc. in heathland, shrublands, mallee and dry sclerophyll forest habitats.
Subspecies: *initialis* (south-western WA); *brookeri* (south-eastern WA).

Hemiergis initialis Ravensthorpe, WA

Hemiergis decresiensis Tarana, NSW

Hemiergis millewae near Blanchetown, SA

Hemiergis decresiensis

Hemiergis initialis

Hemiergis millewae

Hemiergis peronii

Hemiergis quadrilineatum

Hemiergis millewe Coventry, 1976

Description: Uniform dark olive-brown above, usually with a burnt orange dorso-lateral stripe, two scales wide, from above the ear to the level of the hindlimbs; lower flanks whitish; mostly pale yellow on the ventral surfaces; tail whitish below, heavily spotted with dark brown. Prefrontals moderate to large, separated. Four supraoculars. 22 mid-body scale rows, smooth. All limbs pentadactyle, failing to meet when adpressed. Hindlimb about 20-30% of snout-vent length. 50 mm (snout-vent).
Distribution: Southern WA, SA and far western Vic.
Habit: Reported to live under clumps of *Triodia* in mallee.

Hemiergis peronii (Gray, 1831)

Description: Brown or olive-brown above, usually with a series of small blackish spots on the scales which tend to form longitudinal series. A narrow, blackish dorso-lateral stripe from the canthus, through the eye and along the body to the tail. This stripe may be bordered above by a pale golden stripe. Flanks grey-brown, with scattered darker brown and pale flecks tending to form an obscure variegated pattern. Lips spotted with brown. Ventral surfaces cream to yellow, the individual scales heavily spotted or edged with dark brown to form a conspicuous reticulated pattern. Prefrontals moderate, separated. Four supraoculars. 18-22 mid-body rows of smooth scales. Forelimb and hindlimb with 2-4 digits, the third toe much longer than the others in tetradactyle forms. Hindlimb about 20-25% of snout-vent length. 55 mm (snout-vent).
Distribution: From south-western WA to southern SA and far western Vic.
Habit: Similar to that of *Hemiergis decresiensis*, but found in drier habitats associated with offshore islands and coastal heaths and scrubs.

Hemiergis quadrilineatum
(Duméril and Bibron, 1839)

Description: Pale brown to golden-brown or dark brown above, the individual scales each with a median dark brown streak resulting in longitudinal lines of dots from nape to tail. A narrow dark dorso-lateral stripe from above the ear to the tail, bordered below by a grey-brown lateral region, darker in colour than the dorsum. Ventral surfaces cream or yellow. Prefrontals well developed, narrowly contacting or separated. Four supraoculars. 18-20 mid-body rows of smooth scales. Forelimbs didactyle; hindlimbs didactyle, the second toe much longer than the first. Hindlimb about 15-20% of snout-vent length. 55 mm (snout-vent).
Distribution: Coastal regions of WA, from about 'Geraldton to Bunbury' (Glauert).
Habit: A burrowing species found in sandy coastal and near-coastal heaths and scrubs.

Hemiergis peronii Eyre Peninsula, SA

Genus ***Hemisphaeriodon*** Peters, 1867

A monotypic genus whose sole member has been associated with both the blue-tongued skinks (*Tiliqua*) and more recently, by G. Shea, with the slender skinks of the genus *Cyclodomorphus*. Like the blue tongued skinks it has a relatively broad, angular head and short limbs, but the body is relatively slender and the tail is long and prehensile.

Anterior ear lobules usually present; scales smooth, subequal; no supranasals or divided nasal scales; a scaly, movable lower eyelid; parietal scales not in contact behind the interparietal; third and fourth toes subequal or the third toe slightly longer than the fourth; subdigital lamellae undivided; tail long and slender, prehensile and usually nearly as long as the body. Viviparous, and mostly nocturnal or crepuscular. Found only in eastern continental Australia.

Hemisphaeriodon gerrardii (Gray, 1845)

Pink-Tongued Lizard

Description: Silvery-grey to fawn or rich brown above, occasionally immaculate, but typically with a pattern consisting of a series of dark brown transverse cross-bars running obliquely backwards on the flanks. These cross-bars are about as wide as, or narrower than, the paler interspaces and are

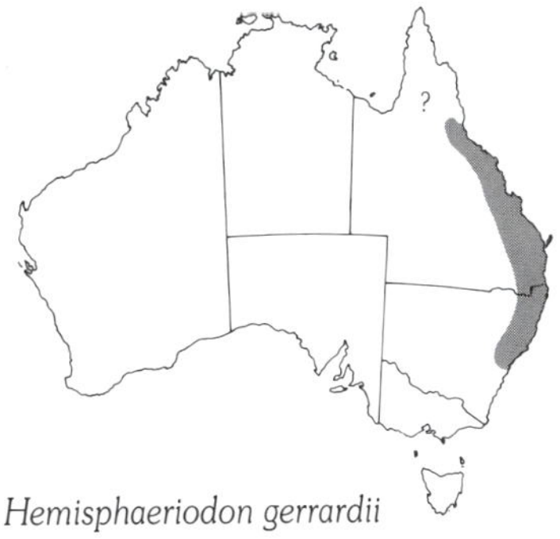

Hemisphaeriodon gerrardii

Hemisphaeriodon gerrardii Port Macquarie, NSW

sometimes narrowly edged behind with white or cream. A series of dark, purplish-brown spots may be present on the head and temporal region and one or two conspicuous dark bars below the eyes and extending to throat. A few labial scales with dark margins. Limbs above spotted or streaked with dark brown or black. Pale purplish-brown below, with two or three obscure, broad, transverse bars on the throat. Tail with about 8-12 broad, black bands, each about equal to the paler interspaces. The scales on chest and abdomen with pale posterior margins. In specimens with broader, dark cross-bands there may be obscure secondary pale cross-bands within the darker ones. Nasals separated. Prefrontals in contact. Three supraoculars. Anterior temporals not elongated. No enlarged hexagonal scales between the parietal and the normal nuchal scales. Post-narial groove absent. Ear-opening conspicuous, with one or two indistinct, small, anterior lobules. 30-34 mid-body rows of smooth scales. Limbs moderate, the hindlimb about 25-30% of snout-vent length. Tail about 110-140% of snout-vent length. 200 mm (snout-vent).

Distribution: Coast and ranges of eastern Australia from the Blue Mountains, west of Sydney, NSW, to lower Cape York Peninsula, Qld.

Habit: An essentially ground-dwelling species, but often climbs low vegetation using its prehensile tail. Mostly crepuscular or nocturnal, but sometimes seen foraging during the day. Usually found in wet sclerophyll or rainforest, but not uncommon in monsoon and dry sclerophyll forest in northern parts of its range. Produces up to 25 live young in a litter. Feeds on insects and other small arthropods.

Genus *Lampropholis* Fitzinger, 1843

A group of small, diurnal, crepuscular or cryptozoic skinks largely restricted to moister, or at least well-watered, habitats in eastern Australia. Limbs pentadactyle in all but one species, the latter with tetradactyle forelimbs, and usually overlapping when adpressed; ear-opening small to moderate, lower eyelid movable, with a transparent disc.

Superficially very similar to some members of the genus *Pseudemoia*, from which genus it has been distinguished by A.E. Greer, primarily on its possession of what he termed a 'beta palate': a palate in which there is a distinctive rear-projecting process on the anterior inner edge of each pterygoid bone. (These processes are lacking in *Pseudemoia:* an 'alpha palate'.) The only four-fingered member of this genus *(tetradactyla)* could easily be mistaken for a species of *Carlia*, but it may be distinguished from all *Carlia* by its possession of a series of subocular scales separating the eye from the upper labials.

Key

TO THE SPECIES OF LAMPROPHOLIS

1 No dark vertebral stripe; dark lateral band not bordered below by well-defined narrow light-coloured band........... **2**

An irregular dark vertebral stripe; dark lateral band bordered below by a well-defined, narrower band, lighter in colour than the dorsal surface.................... ***guichenoti***

2 Fewer than 29 mid-body scale rows; fewer than 27 lamellae under the fourth toe... **3**

29 or more mid-body scale rows; 27 or more lamellae under the fourth toe .... ***mirabilis***

3 4 supraoculars (a); usually 7 supralabials..........................**4**

3 supraoculars (b); usually 6 supralabials............. ***caligula***

4 Usually only 5 supraciliaries (c).......................... ***amicula***

Usually 7 supraciliaries (d).................................. ***delicata***

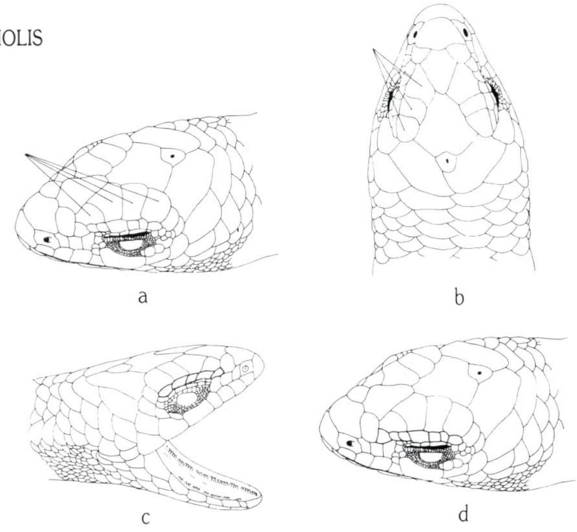

Lampropholis amicula Ingram and Rawlinson, 1981

G. SHEA

Lampropholis amicula Moggill State Forest, Qld

Description: Brown or grey-brown above, darker on the head, and sometimes obscurely flecked with black; a narrow, pale yellow or cream dorso-lateral stripe on each side, from nape to base of tail, narrowly edged with black below. Side of head and upper flanks black, merging with the paler grey lower flanks which are dotted with paler and darker scales. Ventral surfaces white or pale grey, with a few scattered black flecks. Limbs black above. Palmar surfaces and subdigital lamellae black. Scales smooth, in 19-23 rows at mid-body, but the mid-dorsals with 3-4 striations. Suture between rostral and frontonasal wider than the frontal. Supraciliaries 5-6, usually five. Frontoparietals fused. Transparent disc of lower eyelid smaller than the eye. Subdigital lamellae

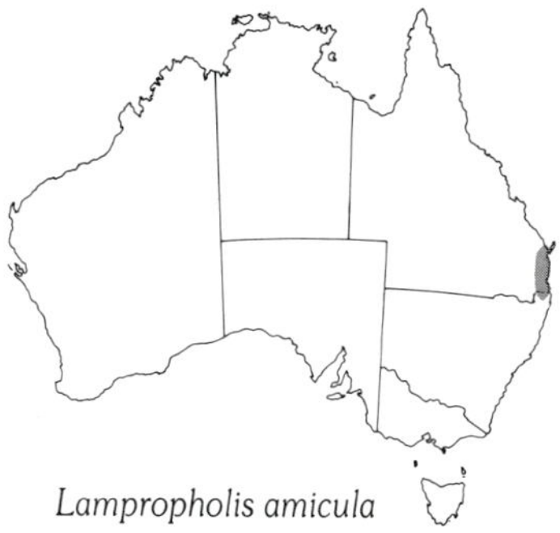

Lampropholis amicula

Lampropholis caligula Stewart's Brook State Forest, NSW

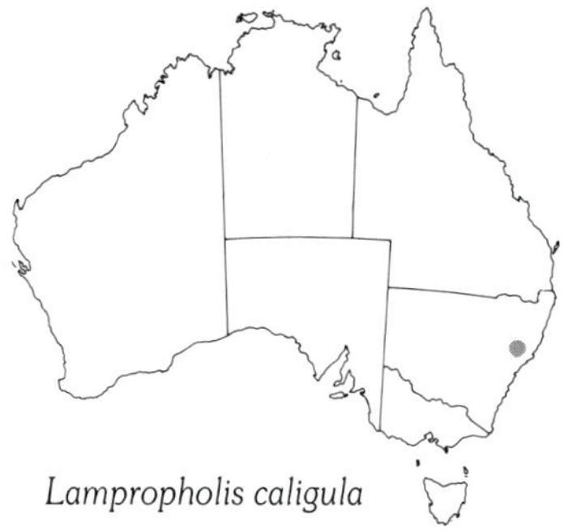

Lampropholis caligula

Lampropholis delicata Kuranda, Qld

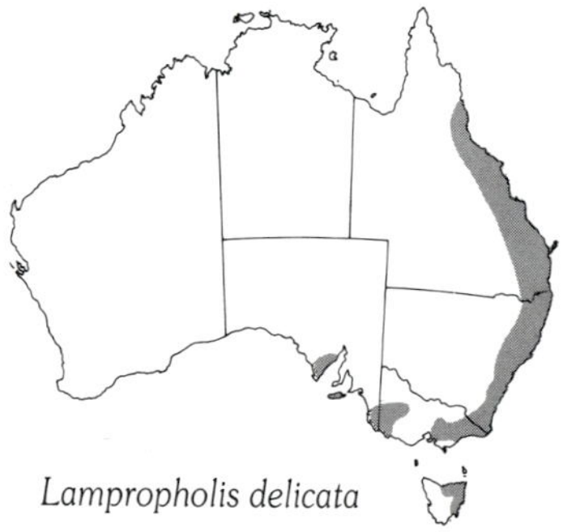

Lampropholis delicata

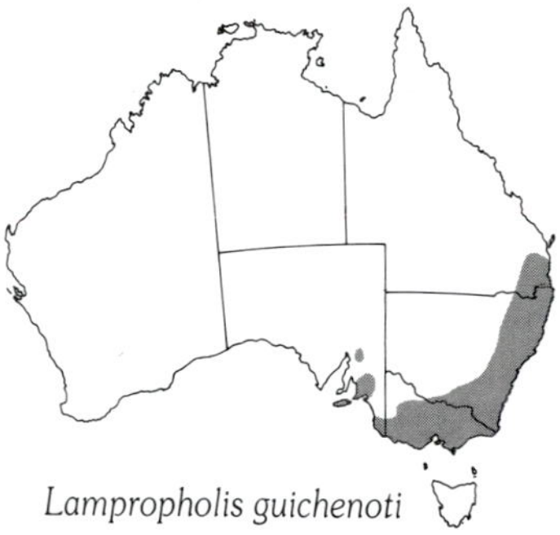

Lampropholis guichenoti

Lampropholis guichenoti Turramurra, NSW

smooth, 17-21 under the fourth toe. 30 mm (snout-vent), the tail about 130% of snout-vent length. Adpressed limbs just overlapping.
Distribution: Far south-eastern Qld.
Habit: '...occurs in open forest and heath' (Ingram and Rawlinson).

Lampropholis caligula Ingram and Rawlinson, 1981

Description: Superficially similar to *L. delicata* and *L. amicula.* Brown or grey-brown above, sometimes with a few darker flecks. Often a narrow, pale creamy, dorso-lateral stripe from nape to base of tail. Side of head, neck and upper flanks black, merging with paler grey lower flanks in which there are scattered darker and paler scales. Sides of tail with 2-3 narrow black stripes. Ventral surfaces pale creamy-grey, sometimes with a few scattered dark brown flecks. Scales smooth, in 19-23 rows at mid-body, but the mid-dorsals with 3-4 striations. Suture between the rostral and frontonasal wider than the frontal. Supraciliaries 5-6, usually five. Frontoparietals fused. Transparent disc of lower eyelid smaller than the eye. Subdigital lamellae smooth, 17-22 under the fourth toe. 45 mm (snout-vent), the tail about 120% of snout-vent length. Adpressed limbs usually overlap.
Distribution: Barrington Tops region, NSW.
Habit: A ground-dwelling species found in litter or in open snow-grass areas in upland wet sclerophyll forests and woodlands.

Lampropholis guichenoti (eggs) Turramurra, NSW. Communal nesting site in old bricks.

Lampropholis delicata (De Vis, 1888)

Description: Similar in form, size and scalation to *Lampropholis guichenoti,* from which it can be distinguished largely by its colour pattern. Grey-brown to rich bronze-brown above, usually immaculate but sometimes with a faint or disrupted, narrow, dark brown vertebral stripe. A dark brown upper lateral zone from the side of the neck to the base of the tail. This zone is sometimes narrowly bordered above with pale brown, and rarely below by a pale mid-lateral stripe from side of neck to groin. The pale dorso-lateral stripe is itself sometimes narrowly bordered above with black, especially anteriorly. Whitish below, often with brown flecks which tend to form longitudinal striations on the throat. 40 mm (snout-vent).
Distribution: South-eastern SA through southern Vic and eastern NSW to north-eastern Qld. Also found in eastern Tas.
Habit: Found in a wide variety of habitats from rainforest edges, wet and dry sclerophyll forests, coastal heaths and woodlands, where it forages among leaf-litter and other ground debris. Builds up large populations in suburban gardens.

Lampropholis guichenoti (Duméril and Bibron, 1839)

Description: Grey-brown, olive-brown or brown above, usually with a faint to conspicuous darker brown vertebral stripe from the neck to the base of the tail. Usually some scattered whitish or pale brown scales on the dorsum, while other scales may be flecked with dark brown. A dark brown upper lateral stripe commencing on the canthus and extending from behind the eye to the base of the tail. This stripe narrowly bordered above and below by a pale stripe, the lower one usually more conspicuous and commencing at the ear. Lower flanks pale brown, spotted with darker brown, gradually merging with a whitish or silvery-grey ventral surface. 24-30 mid-body scale rows, the scales usually smooth but sometimes with faint striations. Suture between the rostral and frontonasal about as wide as the frontal. Supraciliaries 5-8, usually six. Frontoparietals fused to form a single shield. Transparent disc of lower eyelid moderate, much smaller than the eye. Subdigital lamellae smooth, 18-26 under the fourth toe. 40 mm (snout-vent), the tail about 160% of snout-vent length. Adpressed limbs slightly separated to slightly overlapping.
Distribution: South-eastern SA through Vic and eastern NSW to south-eastern Qld.

G. HUSBAND

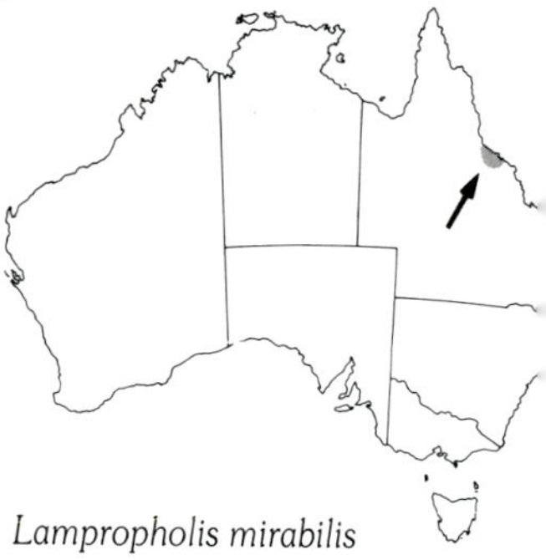

Lampropholis mirabilis

Lampropholis mirabilis
Magnetic Island, Qld

Habit: A diurnal lizard usually seen basking or foraging for ants and other small insects in leaf-litter, grass and rock piles in wet and dry sclerophyll forests, moister woodlands and in coastal and mountain heaths. One of the most abundant species in suburban gardens in eastern Australia.

Lampropholis mirabilis Ingram and Rawlinson, 1981

Description: Olive-brown above, with scattered darker brown and white spots or blotches, the dark brown spots on the flanks tending to coalesce to form vertical bars. Head bronze; ventral surfaces white. Scales smooth, in 29-33 rows at mid-body. Suture between the rostral and frontonasal about as wide as the frontal. Supraciliaries 7-8, usually seven. Frontoparietals fused. Transparent disc of lower eyelid small, much smaller than the eye. Subdigital lamellae smooth, 27-32 under the fourth toe. 50 mm (snout-vent), the tail about 160% of snout-vent length. Adpressed limbs overlap.
Distribution: Magnetic Island and parts of adjacent mainland, Qld.
Habit: A rock-dwelling species found among granitic rocks at the edges of, or in clearings in, rain- and monsoon forest, vine thickets and denser woodland habitats.

Genus *Lerista* Bell, 1833

A group of elongated, smooth-scaled cryptozoic or fossorial lizards in which the limbs may range from a well-developed pentadactyle condition, through various degrees of reduction in length and digits, to a minute style or even a total absence in the case of the forelimbs, but always separated by at least several scale lengths when adpressed. Supranasals absent. Nasals enlarged, usually in contact medially. Prefrontals small and widely separated, or absent. Parietal shields in contact behind interparietal. Lower eyelid with a transparent disc, and either movable or fused above to form a permanent spectacle like that of a snake. Ear-opening small but always distinct. A single pair of enlarged preanals. Intraspecific and local variation in the size of the limbs and the number of digits complicates identification and the key below is modified accordingly.

Members of the genus are confined to continental Australia. Most are burrowing species which are usually found in loose soil or sand beneath stones, logs, termite mounds, etc., where they feed on ants, termites and other small insects. At night, they emerge to feed on the surface, immediately 'diving' into the loose sandy substrate when disturbed. This behaviour results in the distinctive, disrupted wavy tracks which often criss-cross sand dunes and sandy flats, roads and tracks.

Key

TO THE SPECIES OF LERISTA

1 Forelimbs present.. **2**
Forelimbs absent.. **37**

2 Forelimbs and hindlimbs pentadactyle............................**3**
Forelimbs and hindlimbs with fewer than five digits......... **4**

3 Four supraoculars (a); six supraciliaries (b); hindlimb about as long as distance from snout to forelimb.. ***microtis***
Three supraoculars (c); five supraciliaries (d); hindlimb shorter than distance from snout to forelimb.. ***bougainvillii***

4 Forelimbs and hindlimbs tetradactyle.............................. **5**
Forelimbs and hindlimbs with fewer than four digits...... **16**

5 Lower eyelid movable (e)..**6**
Lower eyelid fixed to form permanent spectacle (f)......... **9**

6 Ear-opening about twice as large as nostril; north-western WA.. **7**
Ear-opening at most as large as nostril; central and southern Australia...**8**

7 Dark upper lateral stripe sharp-edged and more than one scale wide.. ***flammicauda***
Dark upper lateral stripe not sharp-edged below and less than one scale wide.. ***chalybura***

8 Usually little or no development of dark longitudinal dorsal stripes or lines of dots; dark upper lateral stripe not sharp-edged below, but merging with colour of lower flanks.. ***frosti***
Dark dorsal stripes or lines of dots usually well developed; lower edge of dark upper lateral stripe sharp-edged.. ***dorsalis***

9 Scales in 16 rows at mid-body....................................... **10**
Scales in 18 or more rows at mid-body.......................... **11**

10 A conspicuous dark paravertebral stripe on either side of the back.. ***christinae***
No conspicuous paravertebral stripes, the paravertebral scales with dark central spots or flecks................ ***elegans***

11 Nasals usually in contact (g); north-eastern and northern Australia.. **12**
Nasals usually separated (h); south-western Australia... ***distinguenda***

12 No dark upper lateral stripe.. **13**
A conspicuous dark upper lateral stripe on either side of the body... **14**

13 Two preoculars (i)... ***xanthura***
One preocular (j)... ***aericeps***

14 Hindlimb more than 30% of snout-vent length............... **15**
Hindlimb less than 30% of snout-vent length.... ***orientalis***

15 Two preoculars (i); four supraciliaries (k)....... ***separanda***
One preocular (l); five supraciliaries (d).............. ***taeniata***

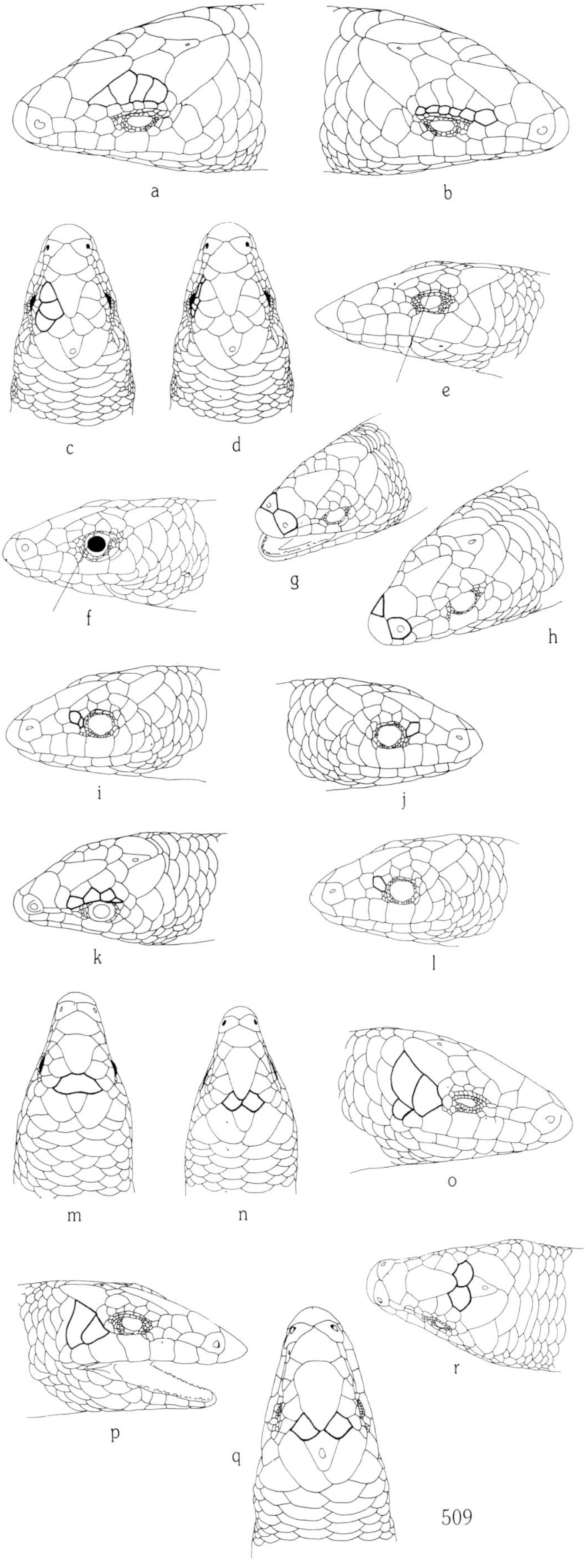

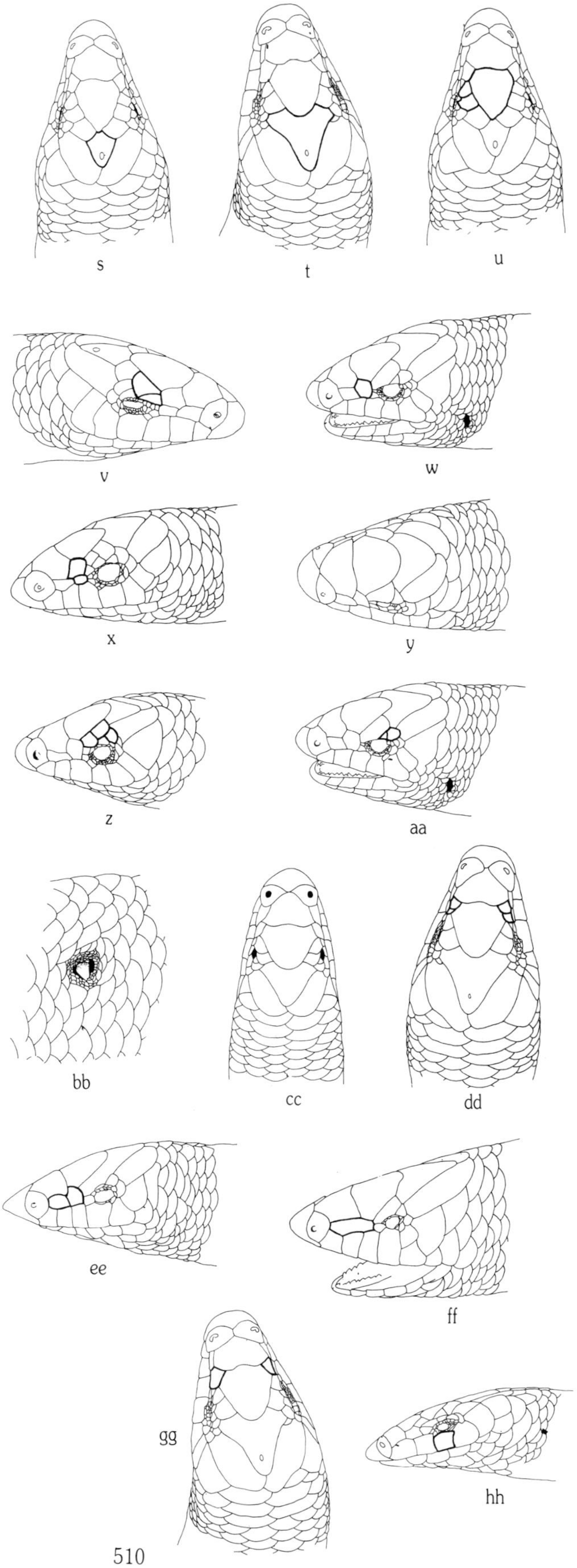

16 Forelimb tridactyle.. **17**
Forelimb with fewer than three fingers.......................... **20**

17 Lower eyelid fixed to form a permanent spectacle........ **18**
Lower eyelid movable.. **19**

18 A prominent dark brown or black upper lateral stripe along the body.. ***muelleri***
Little or no indication of a dark upper lateral stripe along the body..***haroldi***

19 Hindlimbs tridactyle; frontoparietals fused (m)......***fragilis***
Hindlimbs tridactyle; frontoparietals paired (n)... ***terdigitata***

20 Forelimb didactyle... **21**
Forelimb monodactyle or stylar.................................... **30**

21 Hindlimb tridactyle... **22**
Hindlimb didactyle... **27**

22 Lower eyelid movable.. **24**
Lower eyelid fixed to form a permanent spectacle **23**

23 16 mid-body scale rows; frontoparietals separated; a conspicuous dark dorso-lateral stripe on body...... ***lineata***
19-20 mid-body scale rows; frontoparietals fused to form a single shield; dark dorso-lateral stripe, if present, restricted to tail.. ***allochira***

24 Temporals 1 + 2 (o); no ventro-lateral keel................... **25**
Temporals 1 + 1 (p); a strong ventro-lateral keel... ***planiventralis***

25 No longitudinal stripes or broken lines.......................... **26**
A dark upper lateral stripe and paravertebral lines present.. ***desertorum***

26 Frontoparietals not in contact (q)........ ***macropisthopus***
Frontoparietals in contact forming a median suture (r)... ***borealis***

27 Frontoparietals paired (n).. **28**
Frontoparietals fused (m)..................................... ***walkeri***

28 Nasals separated (h)... **29**
Nasals in contact (g)... ***picturata***

29 Dorsal and upper lateral surfaces spotted.......... ***neander***
No obvious colour pattern.................. ***macropisthopus***

30 Hindlimb tridactyle... **31**
Hindlimb didactyle.. **32**

31 18 mid-body scale rows............................... ***kalumburu***
20 or more mid-body scale rows.......... ***macropisthopus***

32 Interparietal distinct from paired frontoparietals (s)...... **34**
Interparietal fused with frontoparietals (t)..................... **33**

33 Lower eyelid a fixed spectacle.................. ***kennedyensis***
Lower eyelid movable........................ ***lineopunctulatus***

34 Lower eyelid movable... **35**
Lower eyelid fixed to form a permanent spectacle.. ***stictopleura***

35 Nasals usually in contact (g)... **36**
Nasals usually separated (h)............................. ***gerrardii***

36 First and second supraoculars in broad contact with the frontal (u); no continuous dark upper lateral stripe from the snout to the base of the tail............ ***punctatovittata***

Enlarged second supraocular excluding (v) or nearly excluding the first supraocular (which is sometimes regarded as a supraciliary) from contact with the frontal.... .... ***picturata***

37 Hindlimbs absent.. **38**

Hindlimbs present... **39**

38 Lower eyelid movable; frontoparietals and interparietal distinct (s)... ***ameles***

Lower eyelid fixed to form a permanent spectacle; frontoparietals and interparietal fused to form a single shield (t).. .... ***apoda***

39 Hindlimb didactyle.. **40**

Hindlimb monodactyle or styliform.............................. **55**

40 Lower eyelid fixed to form a permanent spectacle........ **41**

Lower eyelid movable... **45**

41 Usually fewer than four supraciliaries; second loreal often fused to prefrontal (i.e. only two scales between eye and nasal) (w)... **42**

Usually 4 supraciliaries; second loreal rarely fused to prefrontal (i.e. usually three scales between eye and nasal) (x) .... ***nichollsi***

42 Supraciliaries 2 or more... **43**

No supraciliaries (y).................................... ***vermicularis***

43 Usually 3 supraciliaries (z).. **44**

Usually 2 supraciliaries (aa)........................... ***onsloviana***

44 Size large (snout-vent to 70 mm) and stout; dark dorsal stripe sharp and intense; 20-22 mid-body scale rows.......... .... ***gascoynensis***

Size moderate (snout-vent to 60 mm) and slender; dark dorsal stripe usually somewhat diffuse; 18-20 mid-body scale rows.. ***uniduo***

45 Interparietal fused with frontoparietals (t).................... **46**

Interparietal distinct (s)...................................... ***wilkinsi***

46 Distinct groove present where forelimb would otherwise be (bb).. **47**

No groove present... **49**

47 Usually at least some indication of dark vertebral and/or upper lateral stripes; usually 4 supraciliaries................. **48**

No striped pattern; usually 5 supraciliaries........................ .... ***lineopunctulata***

48 Dorsal and lateral stripes strongly developed; 20-24 mid-body scale rows, usually 22............................ ***connivens***

Dorsal and lateral stripes moderately to very poorly developed; 18-22 mid-body scale rows, usually 20............ ***varia***

49 Two supraoculars contacting frontal (u); one or two supraciliaries... **50**

One supraocular contacting frontal (v); no supraciliaries... .... ***labialis***

50 Prefrontals absent (cc)... **51**

Prefrontals present, each divided (dd)....... ***praefrontalis***

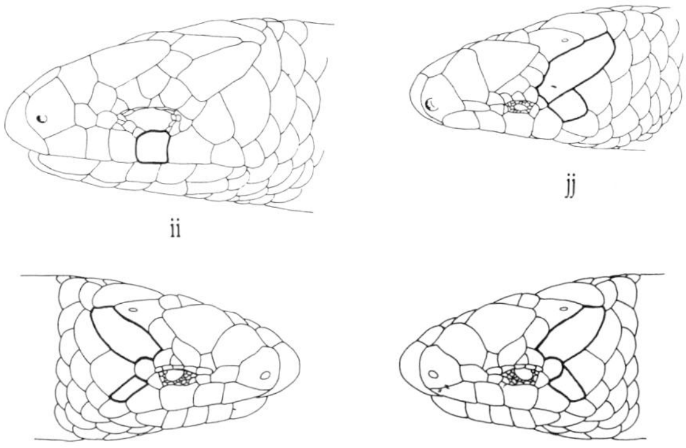

ii jj kk ll

51 A dark upper lateral stripe; two or more loreal scales (ee). **52**

No dark stripes on body; a single loreal scale (ff).......... ***ips***

52 Supraciliaries present.. **53**

Supraciliaries absent (y)................................. ***simillima***

53 Usually five supralabials... **54**

Usually six supralabials.. ***greeri***

54 Body slender; two loreals between nasal and small preocular... ***bipes***

Body stout; one loreal between nasal and large preocular.. .... ***griffini***

55 Interparietal fused with frontoparietals(t)...................... **56**

Interparietal distinct from frontoparietals (s)................. **58**

56 Prefrontals absent (cc); no anterior limb groove............ **57**

Prefrontals widely separated but present (gg); distinct groove where otherwise forelimb would be....................... .... ***lineopunctulata***

57 Six labials; two loreals (ee); temporals 1 + 1 (p); one supraciliary.. ***humphriesi***

Five labials; one loreal (ff); temporals 1 + 2 (o); no supraciliaries.. ***praepedita***

58 Third supralabial entering eye (hh)............................... **59**

Fourth supralabial entering eye (ii)....................... ***allanae***

59 Prefrontals absent (cc).. **60**

Prefrontals present... ***cinerea***

60 A broad dorsolateral stripe on each side from snout to tail, much wider and more prominent than any other longitudinal stripes on the back or flanks............................. **61**

Numerous narrow longitudinal dorsal and lateral stripes; hindlimb as long as five or more adjacent scales............ **63**

61 First temporal in broad contact with the parietal (jj)...... **62**

First temporal not (kk) or in only narrow contact with the parietal (ll)... ***vittata***

62 Two supraoculars; 18 mid-body scale rows............. ***stylis***

Three supraoculars; 16 mid-body scale rows.................... .... ***carpentariae***

63 First temporal in broad contact with the parietal (jj).......... .... ***karlschmidti***

First temporal not (kk) or in only narrow contact (ll) with the parietal... ***storri***

Lerista aericeps

Lerista aericeps Storr, 1986

Description: Status uncertain; closely allied to *Lerista xanthura.* Colour very variable: southern specimens with head, body and tail silvery-brown or pale bronze, the individual scales on the back with a central dark brown spot resulting in five fine dark longitudinal lines along the back; a dark brown loreal streak from the snout, through the eye and continuing along the flank as a series of dark brown dots; Qld and eastern NT specimens rich metallic-bronze, deeper orange on the head, neck and tail, and only faint darker peppering on the dorsum and almost no indication of a dark loreal/temporal/lateral stripe. White or cream below, the individual scales often dark-edged. Forelimbs and hindlimbs tetradactyle, the forelimb about 15%, the hindlimb about 30%, of snout-vent length. Lower eyelid fused above to form a fixed spectacle. 18 mid-body scale rows. Nasals in contact or narrowly separated. Frontoparietals paired, distinct from and smaller than the interparietal. Prefrontals small and widely separated. Three supraoculars. 50 mm (snout-vent).
Distribution: Arid eastern interior of NT, south-eastern Qld and western NSW.
Habit: Sandridge and sandplain desert dominated by spinifex. Otherwise as for genus.

Lerista allanae (Longman, 1937)

Description: Grey or grey-brown above, the individual scales with darker margins forming five longitudinal lines of dark spots. Sides paler, the individual scales finely spotted with dark brown. Ventral surfaces whitish, the scales on the throat (and sometimes the chest and belly) dark spotted. Forelimbs absent, but with a faint groove on each side marking their position; hindlimbs, each with a single digit, about 10% of snout-vent length. Lower eyelid movable. 18 mid-body scale rows. Nasals broadly in contact. Frontoparietals paired, distinct from the interparietal. Prefrontals small and widely separated. Three supraoculars. Six supralabials. 90 mm (snout-vent).
Distribution: Central Qld.
Habit: Found under rocks and logs in open woodland. Otherwise as for genus.

Lerista allochira Kendrick, 1989

Description: Olive or olive-brown above, each scale with a small black spot; dark dorso-lateral stripe, if present, confined to the tail; white or pale grey below, dotted and flecked with black; labials barred with dark brown or black. Forelimbs didactyle, about 15% of snout-vent length; hindlimbs tridactyle, about 25% of snout-vent length. Lower eyelid immovable, forming a fixed spectacle over the eye. 19-20 mid-body scale rows. Nasals in moderate contact. Frontoparietals fused into a single shield, distinct from the interparietal. Prefrontals small and widely separated. Three supraoculars, second largest, the first two contacting the frontal. Six supralabials. 25mm (snout-vent).
Distribution: North West Cape region, WA.
Habit: '... gorges, slopes, and crests' of a '...heavily dissected limestone plateau, sparsely vegetated with *Triodia,* shrubs, and low eucalypts; gorges are more heavily vegetated' (Kendrick).

Lerista ameles Greer, 1979

Description: Dark grey or brown above, the scales of the six mid-dorsal rows each with a median, longitudinal darker brown bar; flanks and lower surfaces dark brown, darker than the dorsum; thickened scales on snout milky-grey. Limbs absent. Lower eyelid movable. 18 mid-body scale rows. Nasals broadly contacting. Frontoparietals paired, distinct from the large interparietal. Prefrontals small, widely separated. Two supraoculars. Five supralabials. Only known specimen 58 mm (snout-vent).
Distribution: Known only from the type locality: about 30 km east of Mt Surprise, Qld.
Habit: Woodland. Otherwise as for genus.

Lerista apoda Storr, 1976

Description: Pale above, with four longitudinal series of faint brown dots along the back and tail; sides and ventral surfaces dark brown, with even darker spots and flecks, except for whitish areas on the throat, preanal scales and anterior half of tail. Distinguished from all but one other member of the genus by the complete absence of limbs. Lower eyelid immovable, forming a transparent scale over the eye. 16 mid-body scale rows. Nasals in broad contact. Frontoparietals fused with interparietal to form a single large shield. Prefrontals absent. Four supralabials. 75 mm (snout-vent).
Distribution: Western Kimberley region, WA.
Habit: '...*Acacia*-dominated transition zone between consolidated coastal dunes and open Pindan country' (Wilson and Knowles). Otherwise as for genus.

Lerista allanae near Charters Towers, Qld

Lerista ameles near Mt Surprise, Qld

Lerista bipes (Fischer, 1882)

Description: Pale fawn to reddish-brown above, usually with a series of dark brown dots or longitudinal dashes on each paravertebral scale, forming two narrow, dark, broken longitudinal lines from the nape to the tail; a broad pale to dark brown stripe from the snout, through the eye, to the tail; lips, lower lateral and ventral surfaces whitish. Forelimbs absent, without any indication of a groove; hindlimbs each with two digits; hindlimbs about 17% of snout-vent length. Lower eyelid movable. 18-20 mid-body

Lerista bipes Goldsworthy, WA

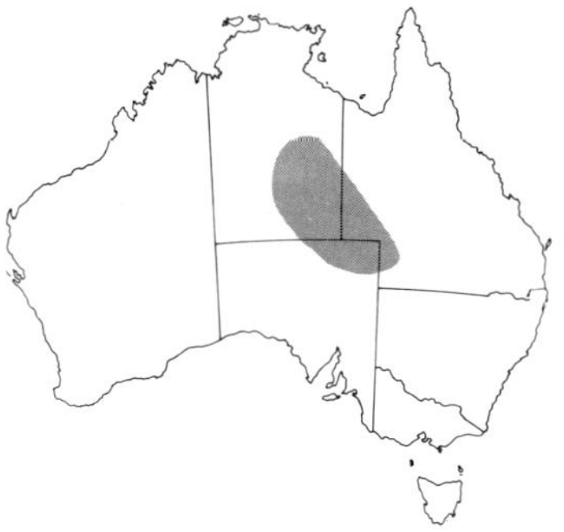

Lerista aericeps

Lerista allanae

Lerista allochira

Lerista ameles

Lerista apoda

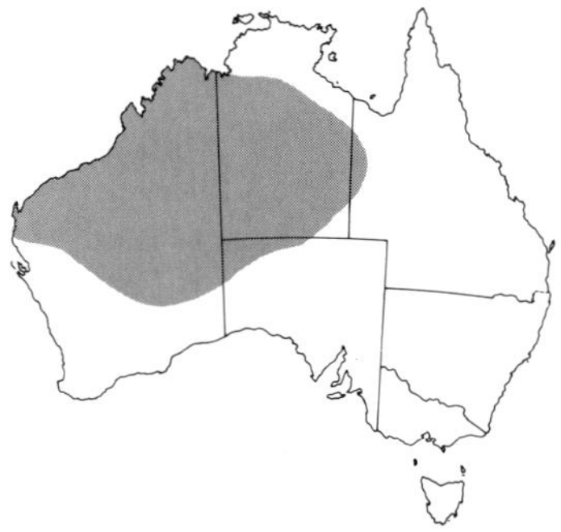

Lerista bipes

Lerista borealis

scale rows. Nasals narrowly separated or contacting. Frontoparietals and interparietal fused to form a single large shield. Prefrontals absent. Two, or usually three, supraoculars. Normally five, occasionally six, supralabials. Grows to about 60 mm (snout-vent).
Distribution: Widely distributed through northern and middle WA through north-western SA and the arid parts of the NT to far western Qld.
Habit: Hummock grasslands on both sand plains and sand ridge desert and coastal dunes. Otherwise as for genus.

Lerista borealis Storr, 1971

Description: Reddish- or greyish-brown above, flecked or dotted with dark brown; supralabials may be heavily barred; pale brown below, the underside of the tail flecked with dark brown. Forelimbs each with two digits, hindlimbs each with three digits; forelimb about 8%, and hindlimb about 17%, of snout-vent length. Lower eyelid movable. 20-22 mid-body scale rows. Nasals narrowly separated or in contact. Frontoparietals paired, in contact; interparietal distinct. Prefrontals widely separated. Three supraoculars. Six supralabials. Grows to about 50 mm (snout-vent).
Distribution: Kimberley district of WA.
Habit: Woodlands and semi-arid shrublands. Otherwise as for genus.

Lerista bougainvillii (Gray, 1839)

Description: Pale silvery-grey to pale grey-brown above, immaculate, or the individual scales with a dark brown dot, resulting in longitudinal lines of dots along the back. A broad, black upper lateral zone, commencing as a stripe from the nostril, through the eye and over the arm to the base of the tail, where it breaks up into a series of dark variegations on the side of the tail. Lower flanks whitish, flecked and streaked with black. Ventral surfaces white or cream. Forelimbs and hindlimbs short, pentadactyle, forelimb about 15%, hindlimb about 25%, of snout-vent length. Lower eyelid movable. 22-24 mid-body scale rows. Nasals in contact. Frontoparietals paired, broadly in contact; interparietal distinct. Prefrontals small and widely separated. Four supraoculars. Usually seven supralabials. 70 mm (snout-vent).
Distribution: South-eastern SA through Vic to south-eastern NSW. Islands of Bass Strait and eastern and northern Tas.
Habit: Heaths, dry sclerophyll forests and tall

woodlands, under rocks, logs and leaf litter. Otherwise as for genus.

Lerista carpentariae Greer, 1983

Description: Pale fawn to reddish-brown above, with a dark brown streak down the centre of each scale of the two vertebral series forming two dark paravertebral lines down the length of the body and tail. A broad, dark brown lateral stripe from the snout, through the eye, to the tail. Head and many of the paler scales flecked or mottled with dark brown. Immaculate white below. Forelimbs absent, without any indication of a groove; hindlimb monodactyle or stylar, from 2·5% of snout-vent length. Lower eyelid movable. 16 mid-body scale rows. Nasals large, in broad contact. Frontoparietals paired and distinct from the interparietal. Prefrontals absent. Three supraoculars. Five supralabials. 70 mm (snout-vent).

Lerista borealis Bullo River, NT

Lerista bougainvillii Yea, Vic

Distribution: Currently known only from Groote Eylandt and the Sir Edward Pellew Islands, NT.
Habit: Low coastal shrubland and adjacent low woodland, usually on rocky areas. Otherwise as for genus.

Lerista chalybura Storr, 1985

Description: Brown above, the individual scales with slightly darker edges producing a slightly reticulated effect, but otherwise unmarked; tail greyish, heavily

Lerista bougainvillii

Lerista carpentariae

Lerista chalybura

Lerista christinae

Lerista cinerea

Lerista connivens

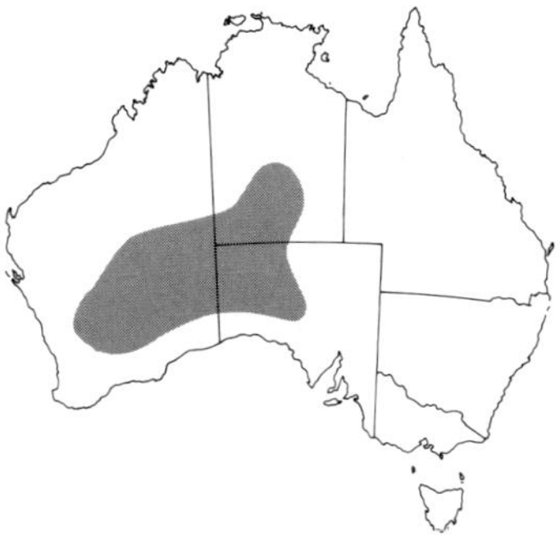

Lerista desertorum

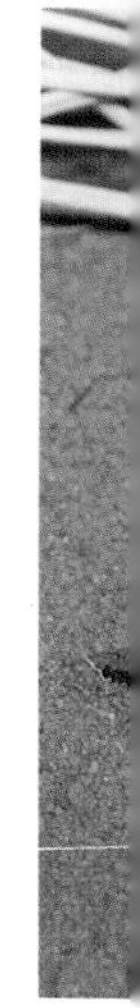

spotted and flecked with dark brown; a narrow, dark brown upper lateral stripe from above eye to base of tail, sharply delineated from the pale dorsal surface but merging with the darker brown flanks. Ventral surfaces whitish, sometimes spotted with dark brown. Forelimbs and hindlimbs each with four digits; the forelimb about 15%, the hindlimb about 20%, of snout-vent length. Lower eyelid movable. 20-22 mid-body scale rows. Nasals separated or narrowly in contact; interparietal distinct. Prefrontals small, widely separated. Three supraoculars. Usually six supralabials. 50 mm (snout-vent).
Distribution: Pilbara region, WA
Habit: '...strongly associated with major drainage systems, especially gorges' (Wilson and Knowles). Otherwise as for genus.

Lerista christinae Storr, 1979

Description: Pale olive-grey above, browner on the tail, with six blackish or dark brown stripes; on each side a paravertebral commencing on the nape and extending well along the tail, a dorso-lateral from the eye to the base of the tail extending forward as a narrow dark stripe to the snout, and a narrow lower lateral from neck to hindlimb. Limbs pale grey-brown variegated with dark brown. Whitish below. Both fore- and hindlimbs each with four digits; forelimb about 20%, and hindlimb about 30%, of snout-vent length. Lower eyelid immovable. 16 mid-body scale rows. Nasals in contact. Frontoparietals paired, in contact; interparietal distinct. Three supraoculars. 35 mm (snout-vent).
Distribution: Known only from a sandplain near Badgingarra, WA.
Habit: Heath. Otherwise as for genus.

G. SHEA

Lerista cinerea Greer, McDonald and Lawrie, 1983

Description: Grey-brown above, each of the dorsal scales with dark brown median streaks which tend to form a series of dark brown lines along the length of the body. Head with dark brown flecks and variegations. Whitish below, although one of the type specimens was recorded as having an orange tail in life. Forelimbs absent, without any indication of a groove; hindlimb monodactyle, about 5% of snout-vent length. Lower eyelid movable. 18 mid-body scale rows. Nasals large, in broad contact. Frontoparietals paired and distinct from the interparietal. Prefrontals present, but small and widely separated. Two supraoculars. Five supralabials. 70 mm (snout-vent).
Distribution: Vicinity of Charters Towers, Qld.
Habit: Found in a variety of open forest and woodland habitats, and seasonally-dry vine thicket. Otherwise as for genus.

G. SHEA

Lerista connivens near Overlander Roadhouse, Shark Bay, WA

Lerista desertorum Mt Olga, NT

Lerista distinguenda Perth, WA

Lerista dorsalis near Gawler, SA

Lerista elegans Yardie Creek, WA

Lerista fragilis Moura, Qld

Lerista frosti SA

Lerista connivens Storr, 1971

Description: Similar in most respects to *Lerista nichollsi,* from which it differs in having a movable eyelid, a wider, rougher-edged vertebral stripe, and greater size (to 80 mm snout-vent).
Distribution: Mid-western coast and adjacent islands of WA.
Habit: Arid shrublands. Otherwise as for genus.

Lerista desertorum (Sternfeld, 1919)

Description: Pale grey-brown above, with a pair of narrow, longitudinal lines along the back formed by lines of dots through the centre of each paravertebral scale; a dark brown or black stripe from the snout, through the eye to the tail; head spotted with black; scales on tail each with a transverse blackish spot; lips, lower lateral and ventral surfaces whitish, except for dark brown spots under the tail. Forelimbs each with two digits, hindlimbs each with three digits; forelimb about 4%, hindlimb about 15%, of snout-vent length. Lower eyelid movable. 20-22 mid-body scale rows. Nasals separated. Frontoparietals paired, usually separated; interparietal distinct. Prefrontals widely separated. Three supraoculars. Six supralabials. 90 mm (snout-vent).
Distribution: South-eastern interior of WA extending to the south-western and north-western desert areas of the NT and SA respectively.
Habit: Mulga and other arid *Acacia* scrubs and eucalypt woodlands, often with a ground cover of spinifex. Otherwise as for genus.

Lerista distinguenda (Werner, 1910)

Description: Pale grey-brown above, with or without two or four longitudinal series of blackish dots; head finely blotched with black; a blackish upper lateral stripe from canthus, through the eye to the tail; a white lateral stripe from the supralabials to the tail, clearly differentiated from a greyish ventro-lateral region. Whitish below, except that the tail may be flushed with russet and flecked or spotted with brown. Forelimbs and hindlimbs each with four digits; forelimb about 15%, hindlimb about 25%, of snout-vent length. Lower eyelid fused, immovable. 18-20 mid-body scale rows. Nasals usually separated, sometimes narrowly in contact. Frontoparietals paired, in contact; interparietal distinct. Prefrontals moderately to widely separated. Three supraoculars. Usually six supralabials. 40 mm (snout-vent).
Distribution: Coast and adjacent regions of south-western Australia, from Geraldton to the Great Australian Bight.
Habit: Coastal heaths, woodlands and sclerophyll forest. Otherwise as for genus.

Lerista dorsalis Storr, 1985

Description: Shiny olive-brown above, usually with two or four longitudinal series of narrow blackish stripes or longitudinal series of black dots, dashes or spots on the back; an obscure pale, dorso-lateral stripe from above the eye to the base of the tail, bordered below by a prominent black upper lateral stripe from the snout, through the eye and ear to the base of the tail; flanks whitish, usually with 1-3 (usually 2) narrow, black, longitudinal stripes or lines of dots. Ventral surfaces whitish, the individual scales sometimes edged with darker; tail pinkish. Forelimbs and hindlimbs each with four digits; the forelimb about 10%, the hindlimb about 25%, of snout-vent length. Lower eyelid movable. 16-22 mid-body scale rows. Nasals separated or narrowly in contact; interparietal distinct. Prefrontals small, widely separated. Three supraoculars. Supralabials 6-7. 65 mm (snout-vent).
Distribution: Coast and hinterland of southern Australia, from south-eastern WA to the Flinders Ranges and the lower Murray River, SA.
Habit: Coastal heathland, chenopodous shrublands and a variety of semi-arid and more mesic woodlands. Otherwise as for genus.

Lerista elegans (Gray, 1845)

Description: Grey-brown above, the paravertebral scales each with darker centres forming longitudinal rows of dots; head darker than body; a dark brown stripe from the snout, through the eye to the tail, and narrowly bordered below with white; ventro-lateral surfaces and sometimes ventral surfaces flushed with grey. Tail flecked with grey-brown below. Forelimbs and hindlimbs each with four digits; forelimb about 15%, hindlimb about 30%, of snout-vent length. Lower eyelid fused, immovable. Usually 16, sometimes 18, mid-body scale rows. Nasals broadly in contact. Frontoparietals paired, in contact; interparietal distinct. Prefrontals moderately to widely separated. Three supraoculars. Usually six supralabials. 40 mm (snout-vent).
Distribution: Coastal regions and offshore islands of WA from Barrow Island to Perth.
Habit: Heath, low shrubland and dry sclerophyll forest. Otherwise as for genus.

Lerista flammicauda Storr, 1985

Description: Rich bronzy-brown above, the back immaculate, but with an obscure, narrow, paler dorso-lateral streak from snout to base of tail, bordered below by a broad, black upper lateral stripe from snout to base of tail; lower flanks pale brown, sometimes with one or two longitudinal series of blackish dots; tail deep reddish-orange. Ventral surfaces (except for tail) whitish. Forelimbs and hindlimbs each with four digits; the forelimb about 15%, the hindlimb about 20%, of snout-vent length. Lower eyelid movable. 20-22 mid-body scale rows. Nasals in contact; interparietal distinct. Prefrontals small, widely separated. Three supraoculars. Supralabials 6-7. 50 mm (snout-vent).
Distribution: Pilbara region, WA.
Habit: Humid microhabitats such as gorges and watercourses in arid stony hills and ranges. Otherwise as for genus.

Lerista fragilis (Günther, 1876)

Description: Olive or grey-brown above, the individual scales each with a blackish dot or central blackish streak, resulting in a series of more or less continuous fine, dark lines along the length of the dorsum. Flanks darker than the back, tending to form a narrow, black dorso-lateral stripe above. Ventral surfaces white or cream, dotted with black. Forelimbs and hindlimbs tridactyle, the third toe the longest, the forelimb about 5%, and hindlimb about 15-20%, of snout-vent length. Lower eyelid movable. 20 mid-body scale rows. Nasals in contact. Frontoparietals fused to form a single shield distinct from interparietal. Prefrontals small, widely separated. Three supraoculars. Usually six supralabials. 60 mm (snout-vent).
Distribution: South-eastern Qld.
Habit: Dry sclerophyll forests and woodlands. Otherwise as for genus.

Lerista frosti (Zietz, 1895)

Description: Pale grey-brown or fawn above, with or without two narrow blackish dorsal stripes from nape to tail; a dark blackish-brown upper lateral stripe from the canthus, through the eye to the tail, sometimes white-edged on the body; sides pale fawn or whitish, with or without two or three narrow, dark brown rows or lines of fine spots. Lips faintly barred with dark brown. Whitish below, except that the tail may be flushed with russet or orange. Forelimbs and

Lerista distinguenda

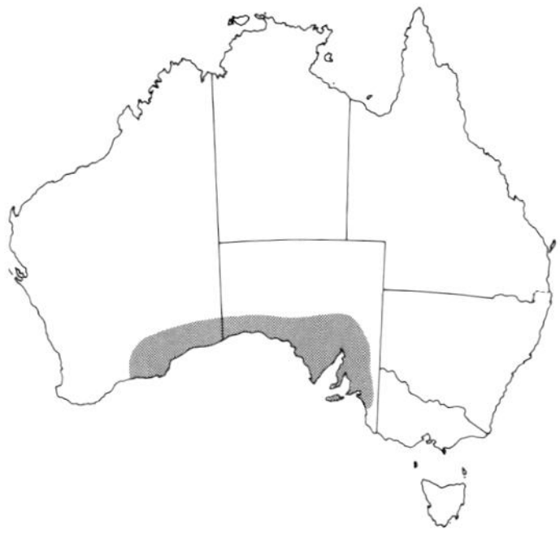
Lerista dorsalis

Lerista elegans

Lerista flammicauda

Lerista fragilis

Lerista frosti

Lerista gascoynensis

hindlimbs each with four digits; the forelimb about 10%, the hindlimb about 25%, of snout-vent length. Lower eyelid movable. 18-20 mid-body scale rows. Nasals separated or narrowly in contact. Frontoparietals paired, in contact; interparietal distinct. Prefrontals small, widely separated. Three supraoculars. Usually six supralabials. 50 mm (snout-vent).
Distribution: Central Australia.
Habit: Humid microhabitats such as gorges and watercourses in spinifex-covered stony hills and ranges and adjacent stony plains. Otherwise as for genus.

Lerista gascoynensis Storr, 1986

Description: Pale brown above, with a prominent dark brown or black vertebral stripe, often with a paler brown centre; head shields with darker brown margins and flecks; lips barred with dark brown; a broad, blackish upper lateral stripe from snout, through the eye and ear and along the body to nearly the full length of the tail; lower flanks and ventral surfaces whitish. Forelimbs absent (although their positions may be indicated by a groove), hindlimbs each with two digits; hindlimb about 15-20% of snout-vent length. Lower eyelid fused, immovable. 20-22 mid-body scale rows. Nasals in contact. Frontoparietals and interparietal fused to form a single shield. Prefrontals small and widely separated. Three supraoculars. Six supralabials. 65 mm (snout-vent).
Distribution: Gascoyne River basin, WA.
Habit: Semi-arid shrublands. Otherwise as for genus.

Lerista gerrardii (Gray, 1864)

Description: Pale brown above and on the sides, darker on the head and tail, with a dark brown or black vertebral stripe from nape to tail; a dark brown or black stripe from snout, through eye to tail. Lips, lower lateral and ventral surfaces whitish. Forelimbs somewhat stylar, usually each with one (but occasionally two) digits, hindlimbs each with two digits; forelimb about 3%, hindlimb about 15%, of snout-vent length. Lower eyelid movable. Nasals narrowly separated; interparietal distinct. Prefrontals widely separated. Usually three supraoculars. Six supralabials. 80 mm (snout-vent).
Distribution: South-western WA.
Habit: Semi-arid woodlands and shrublands. Otherwise as for genus.

Lerista greeri Storr, 1982

Description: Pale brown or reddish-brown above, the scales of the two vertebral series each with a dark

Lerista gascoynensis near Gascoyne Junction, WA

M. PETERSON

brown median streak or line of dots which tend to form two narrow, dark, paravertebral lines along the body from nape to tail. A broad, dark brown lateral stripe from the snout to the tail. Head with brown flecks and variegations. Pale scales on dorsum sometimes flecked with dark brown. Ventral surfaces white. Forelimbs absent, without any indication of a groove; hindlimbs each with two toes, 15-20% of snout-vent length. Lower eyelid movable. 19-20 mid-body scale rows. Nasals in contact or narrowly separated. Frontoparietals and interparietal fused to form a single large shield. Prefrontals absent. Three supraoculars. Six supralabials. 65 mm (snout- vent).
Distribution: Drier parts of northern WA.
Habit: Semi-arid shrubland with hummock grasses. Otherwise as for genus.

Lerista griffini Storr, 1982

Description: Brown or reddish-brown above, the scales of the two vertebral series each with a dark brown median streak or line of dots which tend to form two narrow, dark, paravertebral lines along the body from nape to tail. A broad, dark brown lateral stripe from the snout to the tail. Head with brown flecks and variegations. Pale scales on dorsum sometimes flecked with dark brown. Ventral surfaces white. Forelimbs absent, without any indication of a groove; hindlimbs each with two toes, 10-20% of snout-vent length. Lower eyelid movable. 20-21 mid-body scale rows. Nasals in contact or narrowly separated. Frontoparietals and interparietal fused to form a single large shield. Prefrontals absent. Three supraoculars. Five supralabials. 65 mm (snout-vent).
Distribution: Apparently two isolated populations: one in Dampier Land, WA, and the other around the top end of the WA/NT border region.
Habit: Seasonally-dry eucalypt woodlands and semi-arid shrublands. Otherwise as for genus.

Lerista haroldi Storr, 1983

Description: Pale yellow-brown above, the head and body finely dotted and flecked with darker brown; an obscure darker brown streak along side of snout; tail with darker brown mottling, tending to be arranged transversely. Ventral surfaces whitish. Forelimbs and hindlimbs present, both tridactyle. Hindlimb about 25% of snout-vent length. Lower eyelid fused, immovable. 20 mid-body scale rows. Nasals in contact. Frontoparietals paired and distinct from the interparietal. Prefrontals present. Three supraoculars. Six supralabials. 40 mm (snout- vent).
Distribution: Currently known only from the type locality, Gnaraloo Homestead, on the upper western coast of WA.
Habit: Coastal dunes. Otherwise as for genus.

Lerista humphriesi Storr, 1971

Description: Pale brown or fawn above, the head flecked with darker brown, the supralabials barred and with a pair of narrow, dark, brown broken stripes from the nape to the tail formed by lines through the paravertebral scales; a broad, dark brown stripe from side of snout, through eye to tail; scales between paravertebral and upper lateral stripes with lines of dark brown dots; three longitudinal series of dark brown dots below upper lateral stripe; lower surfaces whitish. Forelimbs absent, without any indication of a groove; hindlimb stylar, about 2% of snout-vent length. Lower eyelid movable. 16 mid- body scale rows. Nasals in contact. Frontoparietals and interparietal fused to form a single shield. Prefrontals absent. Three supraoculars. Six supralabials. 60 mm (snout- vent).
Distribution: Known only from Murchison River district, mid- western WA.
Habit: 'Acacia-dominated sand plains...' (Wilson and Knowles). Otherwise as for genus.

Lerista ips Storr, 1980

Description: Pinkish-brown above, the scales of the eight uppermost scale rows each with a faint brown spot; tip of snout whitish; a faint brown streak on either side of the head; ventral surfaces whitish. Forelimbs absent; hindlimbs each with two digits, about 17% of snout-vent length. Lower eyelid movable. 20 mid-body scale rows. Nasals separated. Frontoparietals and interparietal fused into a single large shield. Prefrontals absent. Two supraoculars. Six supralabials. 60 mm (snout-vent).
Distribution: Great Sandy Desert, WA and lower western NT.
Habit: Red sand dunes and interdune plains dominated by spinifex. Otherwise as for genus.

Lerista kalumburu Storr, 1976

Description: Brown above, each scale with a brown spot tending to form longitudinal lines on the flanks; lips paler, barred with dark brown; whitish below.

Lerista gerrardii

Lerista gerrardii WA

Forelimb with a single digit, hindlimb with three digits; forelimb about 2%, hindlimb about 13%, of snout-vent length. Lower eyelid movable. 18 mid-body scale rows. Nasals in broad contact. Frontoparietals paired, separated; interparietal distinct. Three supraoculars. 50 mm (snout-vent).
Distribution: Known only from 'vicinity of Napier Broome Bay, North Kimberley, WA, (Storr).
Habit: As for genus.

Lerista karlschmidti (Marx and Hosmer, 1959)

Description: Olive-brown or grey-brown above, somewhat paler on the lower flanks. Each body scale with a median blackish streak, resulting in a series of more or less continuous narrow, blackish lines along the body and tail, becoming obscure or disappearing

Lerista karlschmidti Woolwonga, NT

on the lower flanks and venter. Forelimb absent; hindlimb present, monodactyle, clawed, about 5% of snout-vent length. Lower eyelid movable. 16 mid-body scale rows. Nasals separated. Frontoparietals paired and usually separated, distinct from interparietal. Prefrontals usually separated. Three supraoculars. Five supralabials. 70 mm (snout-vent).
Distribution: North-eastern Qld to the northern NT.
Habit: Monsoon forest, gully and gorge vegetation and seasonally-dry woodlands usually associated with rock outcrops, stony hills, ranges and scarps. Otherwise as for genus.

Lerista kennedyensis Kendrick, 1989

Description: Pale pinkish-grey to orange or salmon-coloured above, whitish below; a narrow, dark brown paravertebral stripe on each side of the vertebral line, formed by scales bearing one or two dark brown spots or streaks; a dark brown dorso-lateral stripe from snout, through eye, to tail, formed by two rows of dark-spotted scales; labials barred with dark brown. Forelimb stylar, clawless, about 1-2% of snout-vent length; hindlimb didactyle, about 20-25% of snout-vent length. Lower eyelid immovable, forming a fixed spectacle over the eye. 21-22 mid-body scale rows. Nasals large, narrowly contacting. Frontoparietals and interparietal fused to form a single large shield. Prefrontals small, widely separated, each fused with the second loreal. Three supraoculars, the first two in contact with the frontal. Six supralabials. A distinct ventro-lateral keel anteriorly. 55mm (snout-vent).
Distribution: Kennedy Range, WA.
Habit: Crests and slopes of red sandridges sparsely vegetated with *Triodia* and shrubs (Kendrick).

Lerista labialis Storr, 1971

Description: Similar in most respects to *Lerista bipes*, from which it differs in only having one supraocular in contact with the frontal (two supraoculars in contact in *bipes*) and no supraciliaries (one or two supraciliaries in *bipes*). Usually two, rarely three, supraoculars. 60 mm (snout-vent).
Distribution: From Houtman Abrolhos to south-eastern interior of WA, through southern and central Australia to arid interiors of Qld, NSW and north-western Vic.

Lerista greeri

Lerista griffini

Lerista haroldi

Lerista humphriesi

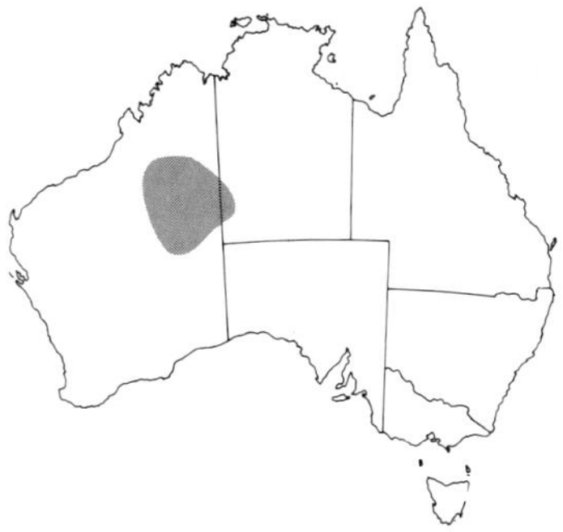

Lerista ips

Lerista kalumburu

Lerista karlschmidti

M. PETERSON

Lerista kennedyensis
Kennedy Range, WA

Habit: Found in a wide range of arid habitats from coastal dunes, mulga and other arid scrublands and red sandridge and sandplain deserts dominated by hummock grasses. Otherwise as for genus.

Lerista lineata Bell, 1833

Description: Grey-brown above, with two narrow, black, paravertebral lines from the nape to the tail, the area between these lines darker than the rest of the dorsal surface; a blackish stripe from the snout, nostrils or eye to tail; a whitish mid-lateral stripe from the lips to the tail; head and lips blotched with black; remaining surfaces, but especially lower lateral areas and underside of tail, with greyish flecks or dots. Forelimbs each with two digits and hindlimbs each with three digits; forelimb about 7%, hindlimb about 22%, of snout-vent length. Lower eyelid fused, immovable. 16 mid-body scale rows. Nasals narrowly separated or in contact. Frontoparietals paired, in contact; interparietal distinct. Prefrontals widely separated. Three supraoculars. Usually six supralabials. 50 mm (snout-vent).
Distribution: Found only near Fremantle, WA, and adjacent islands.
Habit: Coastal heaths and low shrublands. Otherwise as for genus.

Lerista labialis Wanaaring, NSW

Lerista lineopunctulata (Duméril and Bibron, 1839)

Description: Pale grey or brown above, with or without longitudinal black bars on some or all scales; sometimes these black bars are so numerous as to form six narrow, broken, longitudinal lines along the back and upper lateral zone; head often darker than body; lips barred with dark brown; lower surfaces whitish. Forelimbs may be absent, tubercular or stylar, but when absent their positions are always marked by a groove; hindlimbs each with one or two digits; forelimb about 0.5%, hindlimb about 10%, of snout-vent length; lower eyelid movable. 18-22 mid-body scale rows. Nasals in contact. Frontoparietals and interparietal fused to form a single large shield. Prefrontals widely separated. Usually three supraoculars. Six supralabials. 100 mm (snout-vent).
Distribution: Lower western coast of WA.
Habit: Coastal low shrublands. Otherwise as for genus.

Lerista macropisthopus (Werner, 1903)

Description: Uniform purplish-grey above and on the sides, with slight darkening on the sides of the face; lips, lower lateral and ventral surfaces whitish. Forelimbs each with two (sometimes one) digits, and hindlimbs normally each with three (sometimes two) digits; forelimb about 4%, hindlimb about 15%, of snout-vent length. Lower eyelid movable. 20-22 mid-body scale rows. Nasals narrowly separated or in contact. Frontoparietals paired, separated; interparietal distinct.Prefrontals widely separated. Usually three supraoculars. Five or six supralabials. 90 mm (snout-vent).
Distribution: South-western interior of WA.
Habit: Woodlands and semi-arid scrubs. Otherwise as for genus.

Lerista microtis (Gray, 1845)

Description: Uniform grey-brown above; a dark brown or black dorso-lateral stripe on either side from the eye to the tail, below which is a white stripe from the upper labials to the tail, and below this is a blackish lower lateral stripe from the level of the ear to about the vent, this lower stripe broken by the limbs. Whitish below, except for an orange or reddish flush under the tail. Forelimbs and hindlimbs each with five digits, the forelimb about 20%, the hindlimb

Lerista kennedyensis

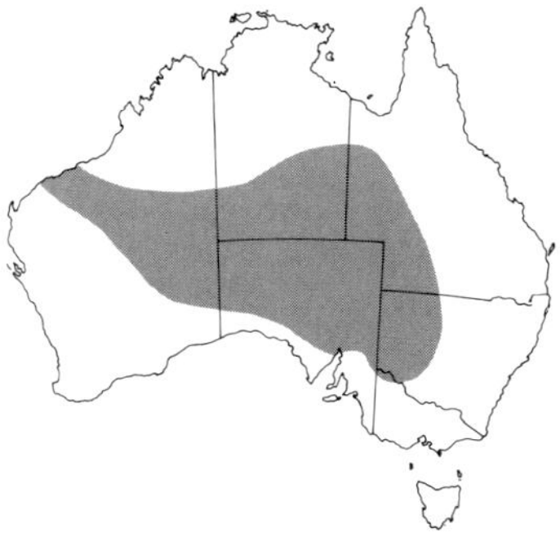

Lerista labialis

Lerista lineata

Lerista lineopunctulata

Lerista macropisthopus

Lerista microtis

Lerista lineata Singleton Beach, WA

M. PETERSON

Lerista lineopunctulata near Lancelin, WA

about 30%, of snout-vent length. Lower eyelid movable. 18-20 mid-body scale rows. Nasals narrowly separated or just contacting. Frontoparietals paired, in contact; interparietal distinct. Prefrontals small, widely separated. Four supraoculars. Usually seven supralabials. 50 mm (snout-vent).
Distribution: Coastal areas of southern Australia from Scott River, WA, to Eyre Peninsula, SA.
Habit: Coastal heaths, low shrublands, woodland and eucalypt forest. Otherwise as for genus.
Subspecies: *microtis* (south-western Australia); *arenicola* (Great Australian Bight).

Lerista muelleri (Fischer, 1881)

Description: Grey, brown or bronze above, with or without four narrow, longitudinal lines (sometimes a series of dots) along the back; usually a dark brown or black stripe from the snout, through the eye to the tail, but this stripe may be reduced to a dark zone formed by a concentration of blackish flecks; sides of body uniform pale brown or with scattered blackish flecks; whitish below. Forelimbs and hindlimbs each with three digits; limb lengths very variable, the forelimb about 12%, and hindlimb about 25%, of snout-vent length. Lower eyelid fused, immovable. 18-22 mid-body scale rows. Nasals usually contacting, occasionally separated. Frontoparietals either fused or paired, in contact; interparietal distinct. Prefrontals widely separated. Three supraoculars. Usually six supralabials. 45 mm (snout-vent).
Distribution: From the central coastal regions of WA, through SA and central Australia to the drier interiors of Qld, NSW and Vic.
Habit: Found in a wide variety of habitats from dry sclerophyll forests and woodlands, mallee, low shrublands, river floodplains and overflows, and arid scrublands. Otherwise as for genus.

Lerista muelleri near Lake Cargelligo, NSW

Lerista neander Storr, 1971

Description: Grey-brown above, with eight dorsal and upper lateral longitudinal series of squarish, blackish-brown spots, each spot in the centre of a scale; spots on the enlarged nuchals coalesce to form transverse bars; head, face and lips blotched with blackish-brown. Lower surfaces whitish, underside of tail spotted with dark brown. Forelimbs and hindlimbs each with two digits (sometimes reduced, according to Storr); forelimb about 4%, hindlimb about 13%, of snout-vent length. Lower eyelid movable. 18-20 mid-body scale rows. Nasals separated. Frontoparietals paired, sometimes separated; interparietal distinct. Prefrontals separated or in contact. Three supraoculars. Six supralabials. Snout depressed, markedly overhanging the mouth. 80 mm (snout-vent).

Lerista macropisthopus Galena, WA

T. M. S. HANLON

Lerista microtis Albany, WA

Distribution: Known only from Ophthalmia Range, WA.
Habit: Spinifex and open scrubs on stony hills and adjoining plains. Otherwise as for genus.

Lerista nichollsi (Loveridge, 1933)

Description: Pale grey, brown or fawn above, with a darker brown vertebral stripe from nape to tail, lying between two paravertebral series of dark brown dots; a dark brown or black stripe from side of snout, through eye to tail. Lower lateral and ventral surfaces whitish. Forelimbs tubercular or absent (though their positions indicated by grooves), hindlimbs each with two digits; hindlimb about 17% of snout-vent length. Lower eyelid fused, immovable. 18-20 mid-body scale rows. Nasals in contact. Frontoparietals and interparietal fused to form a single, large shield. Prefrontals normally present, small and widely separated, often fused to second loreal. Three supraoculars. Six supralabials. 60 mm (snout-vent).
Distribution: Mid-western coast and adjacent interior of WA.
Habit: Coastal low shrublands and open semi-arid scrublands. Otherwise as for genus.
Subspecies: *nichollsi* (Shark Bay region, WA); *petersoni* (mid-western interior of WA).

Lerista onsloviana Storr, 1984

Description: Pale brown or fawn above, with a narrow, dark, vertebral stripe enclosing two closely spaced longitudinal lines formed by two series of dark brown dots or streaks. Head with dark brown variegations. A dark brown lateral stripe from snout to tail, its lower edge ragged. Ventral surfaces whitish. Forelimbs absent, though their position indicated by a groove; hindlimbs each with two digits. Hindlimb about 15-20% of snout-vent length. Lower eyelid normally fused and immovable, although Storr records a single specimen with movable eyelids. 20 mid-body scale rows. Nasals usually in contact, but occasionally narrowly separated. Frontoparietals and interparietal fused to form a single shield. Prefrontals small and widely separated. Three supraoculars. Six supralabials. 70 mm (snout-vent).
Distribution: Coastal plain in the vicinity of Exmouth Gulf, WA.
Habit: Coastal dunes and low shrublands. Otherwise as for genus.

Lerista orientalis McArthur River, NT

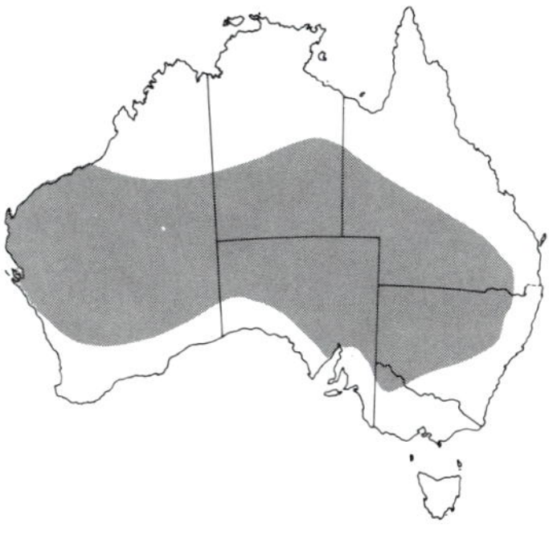

Lerista muelleri

Lerista neander

Lerista nichollsi

Lerista onsloviana

Lerista orientalis

Lerista picturata

Lerista planiventralis

Lerista praefrontalis

Lerista orientalis (De Vis, 1889)

Description: Bronzy-brown above, each of the dorsal body scales with a black dot, resulting in four fine, longitudinal rows of dots on the back and base of the tail. A broad, blackish upper lateral stripe from eye to tail. Lower flanks pale brown, merging with the whitish ventral surface. Forelimbs and hindlimbs tetradactyle, the forelimb about 10%, the hindlimb about 20%, of snout-vent length. Lower eyelid fused above to form a fixed spectacle. 18-20 mid-body scale rows. Nasals in contact. Frontoparietals paired, distinct from the interparietal. Prefrontals small and widely separated. Three supraoculars. Five or six supralabials. 45 mm (snout-vent).
Distribution: North-eastern NT and north-western Qld.
Habit: Low shrublands and heath to seasonally-dry woodlands and lightly-wooded floodplains. Otherwise as for genus.

Lerista picturata (Fry, 1914)

Description: Pale brown or fawn above, with or without four narrow, blackish lines from nape to tail; head flecked with black; a conspicuous to faint black

Lerista picturata near Menzies, WA

Lerista neander near Kumarina, WA

stripe from the snout, through the eye to the tail; lips, lower lateral and ventral surfaces whitish. Forelimbs stylar, or each with one or two digits, hindlimbs each with one or (usually) two digits; forelimb about 1%, hindlimb about 15%, of snout-vent length. Lower eyelid movable. 18-22 mid-body scale rows. Nasals normally in contact. Frontoparietals paired, separated; interparietal distinct. Prefrontals widely separated. Three supraoculars. Six supralabials. 85 mm (snout-vent).

Distribution: Southern interior of WA to south-western corner of SA.

Habit: Coastal heaths and low shrublands, semi-arid woodlands and arid scrubs. Otherwise as for genus.

Subspecies: *picturata* (southern interior of WA); *baynesi* (south-eastern WA and south-western SA); *edwardsae* (southern SA).

Lerista planiventralis (Lucas and Frost, 1902)

Description: Grey or brown above, darker on the head; with four narrow, dark brown or black stripes from the nape to the tail, the outer pair often breaking up into a series of dots; a dark brown or black stripe from the snout, through the eye to the tail; sides pale

T. M. S. HANLON

Lerista planiventralis False Entrance Well, WA

brown or fawn; whitish below. Forelimbs each with two digits, hindlimbs each with three digits; forelimb about 8%, hindlimb about 25%, of snout-vent length. Lower eyelid movable. 20-24 mid-body scale rows. Nasals widely separated. Three supraoculars. Six or seven supralabials. A distinctive ventro-lateral keel distinguishes this species from most other species of *Lerista*. 60 mm (snout-vent).

Distribution: Mid-western coastal regions of WA.

Habit: Coastal consolidated dunes and low shrubland. Otherwise as for genus.

Subspecies: *planiventralis* (upper west coast of WA); *decora* (mid-west coast of WA).

Lerista praefrontalis Greer, 1986

Description: Pale fawn, with a series of dark brown dots or longitudinal dashes on each paravertebral scale, forming two narrow, dark, broken longitudinal lines from the nape to the tail; a broad, pale to dark brown stripe from the snout, through the eye, to the tail; lips, lower lateral and ventral surfaces whitish. Forelimbs absent, without any indication of a groove; hindlimbs each with two digits; hindlimbs about 12% of snout-vent length. Lower eyelid movable. 20 mid-body scale rows. Nasals narrowly separated or contacting. Frontoparietals and interparietal fused to form a single large shield. Prefrontals present, each divided. Three supraoculars. Five supralabials. Grows to about 70 mm (snout-vent).
Distribution: Currently known only from a single specimen from King Hall Island, Kimberley region, WA.
Habit: '...in litter among sand at base of cliff'.

Lerista praepedita (Boulenger, 1887)

Description: Pale olive-grey above, with two longitudinal series of blackish-brown dots on the paravertebral scales; a dark brown or black stripe from the side of the snout, through the eye to the tail; lower lateral, ventral and subcaudal scales greyish-white, edged anteriorly with dark brown. Forelimbs absent, without any indication of a groove; hindlimb stylar, about 2% of snout-vent length. Lower eyelid movable. Usually 16 mid-body scale rows. Nasals in contact. Frontoparietals and interparietal usually fused to form a single shield. Prefrontals absent. Normally two, sometimes three, supraoculars. Five supralabials. 60 mm (snout-vent).
Distribution: Western coast and islands of WA, south of Houtman Abrolhos.
Habit: Heath, low shrublands and woodland. Otherwise as for genus.

Lerista praepedita Swanbourne, WA

Lerista punctatovittata (Günther, 1867)

Description: Pale fawn to brown above, individual scales with dark brown to black hind edges forming four to six series of longitudinal spots. Paler on the flanks, which gradually merge with the whitish ventral surface. Many of the scales on the lower flanks with dark hind edges or dark centres. Upper lips obscurely barred with brown, and often an obscure, dark brown or blackish streak through the eye and over the temporal region. Underside of tail usually strongly flecked and spotted with dark brown. Forelimbs very short, monodactyle, about 2-5% of snouth-vent length (didactyle in some southern populations). Hindlimb didactyle, short, about 10% of snouth-vent length. Lower eyelid movable. 18 mid-body scale rows. Nasals in broad contact. Frontoparietals paired, separated, distinct from interparietal. Prefrontals very small and widely separated. Three supraoculars. Usually six supralabials. 100 mm (snout-vent).
Distribution: South-eastern SA, through north-western Vic and inland NSW to southern interior of Qld.
Habit: A burrowing lizard which is usually found only after rain in the surface layers of moist soil underneath logs, stones, etc., in a wide variety of habitats, from dry sclerophyll forest and mulga and mallee scrubs to open savannah woodland. Otherwise as for genus.

Lerista separanda Storr, 1976

Description: Status uncertain. 'Upper surface pale pinkish-buff, each scale finely edged with brown. A brown spot in centre of frontonasal, frontoparietals and interparietal, and a brown median streak on frontal, nape and foreback. Dark brown upper lateral stripe from tip of snout back through orbit to base of tail. Under surface whitish' (Storr). Forelimbs and hindlimbs tetradactyle, the forelimb about 20%, and the hindlimb about 35%, of snout-vent length. Lower eyelid fused above to form a fixed spectacle. 18 mid-body scale rows. Nasals in contact. Frontoparietals paired, distinct from and smaller than the interparietal. Three supraoculars. 30 mm (snout-vent).
Distribution: Dampier Land, Kimberley Division, WA.

Lerista stictopleura Mt Augusta Station, WA

Lerista punctatovittata Mt Hope, NSW

Lerista stylis Nhulunbuy, NT

Habit: Consolidated coastal dunes.Otherwise as for genus.

Lerista simillima Storr, 1984

Description: Pale brown above, with two paravertebral series of dark brown dots or streaks. Head flecked and variegated with dark brown. A broad, dark brown, lateral stripe from snout, through eye, to tail. Ventral and lower lateral surfaces white. Forelimbs absent, without any indication of a groove. Hindlimbs about 15-20% of snout-vent length, each with two digits. Lower eyelid movable. 20-21 mid-body scale rows. Nasals in contact or narrowly separated. Frontoparietals and interparietal fused to form a single shield. Prefrontals small and widely separated. Two supraoculars. Six supralabials. 55 mm (snout-vent).
Distribution: 'Semi-arid south Kimberley', WA (Storr).
Habit: All known specimens from localities where 'the soil is red sandy loam and the vegetation pindan' (Storr).

Lerista praepedita

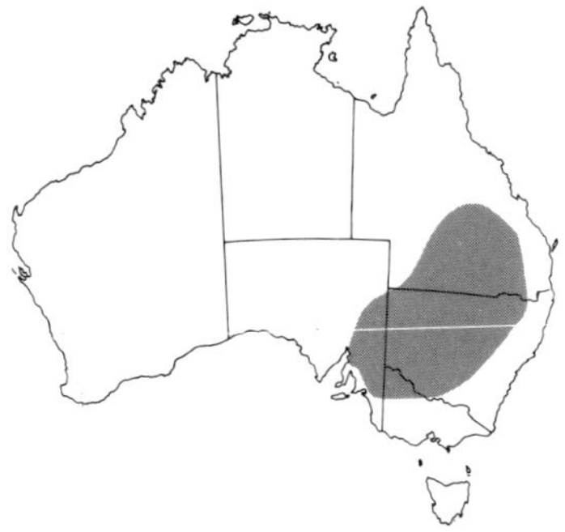

Lerista punctatovittata

Lerista separanda

Lerista simillima

Lerista stictopleura

Lerista storri

Lerista stylis

Lerista stictopleura Storr, 1985

Description: Brown above, back with four series of dark brown dashes forming four fine, longitudinal lines from nape to tail; a prominent, pale, orange-brown dorso-lateral stripe from above eye to base of tail, and bordered below by a sometimes obscure, narrow, black upper lateral stripe from snout, through eye and across temporal region to tail; upper labials barred, with dark brown margins; upper flanks rich reddish-brown, with several series of vertically-aligned blackish spots and flecks, both colour and pattern becoming less intense on the lower flanks, merging with whitish ventral surfaces. Forelimbs monodactyle, hindlimbs didactyle, the forelimb about 5%, and the hindlimb about 20%, of snout-vent length. Lower eyelid fused above to form a fixed spectacle. 20-22 mid-body scale rows. Nasals narrowly separated or in narrow contact. Frontoparietals paried and distinct from the interparietal. Prefrontals present, widely separated. Three supraoculars. Supralabials 5-6. 55 mm (snout-vent).
Distribution: Known only from the vicinity of Mt Augustus, WA.
Habit: Arid scrubland. Otherwise as for genus.

Lerista storri Greer, McDonald and Lawrie, 1983

Description: Pale grey or grey-brown above, the individual scales with central dots or longitudinal streaks which result in the appearance of fine, dark, longitudinal lines along the length of the body. Head flecked and variegated with darker brown. Ventral surfaces whitish. Forelimbs absent, without any indication of a groove. Hindlimbs each with a single digit. Hindlimb about 2-3% of snout-vent length. Lower eyelid movable. 18-20 mid-body scale rows. Nasals in contact. Frontoparietals paired and distinct from the interparietal. Prefrontals absent. Two supraoculars. Five supralabials. 70 mm (snout-vent).
Distribution: Dry western edge of the Atherton Tableland, Qld.
Habit: Found in open eucalyptus woodland. Otherwise as for genus.

Lerista stylis (Mitchell, 1955)

Description: Grey-brown, pale fawn or rich brown above, the scales in the two mid-dorsal rows each with a median blackish streak, resulting in two more or less continuous, narrow, black lines down either side of the middle of the back. Sometimes the next

Lerista terdigitata Moonta, SA

two scale rows each with a faint, broken, longitudinal line, especially anteriorly. A broad, black, upper lateral stripe, commencing at the nostril and passing through the eye along the body and tail. Lower flanks white, sometimes flecked with dark brown. Ventral surfaces white. Forelimbs absent. Hindlimbs very small, stylar, usually without a claw, about 1% of snout-vent length. Lower eyelid movable. 16-20 mid-body scale rows. Nasals in broad contact. Frontoparietals paired, widely separated, distinct from interparietal. Prefrontals absent. Three supraoculars. Five supralabials. 60 mm (snout-vent).
Distribution: Eastern Arnhem Land, NT, and the coast and offshore islands of the lower western Gulf of Carpentaria.
Habit: Coastal dunes, coastal shrublands and seasonally-dry woodlands, especially where rock outcrops. A burrowing species, usually found under fallen timber, stones and old termitaria. Otherwise as for genus.

Lerista taeniata Storr, 1986

Description: Status uncertain. Metallic-brown above, with a paler dorso-lateral zone bordered below by a broad, blackish, upper lateral stripe which continues forward through the ear and eye to the snout; scales of back finely dotted with darker, tending to form a series of four fine, dark, longitudinal lines along the back; head and neck bright bronzy-orange, finely flecked with dark brown. Ventral surfaces whitish, the individual scales dark-edged. Forelimbs and hindlimbs tetradactyle, the forelimb about 15%, the hindlimb about 30%, of snout-vent length. Lower eyelid fused above to form a fixed spectacle. 20 mid-body scale rows. Nasals in contact. Frontoparietals paired, distinct from and smaller than the interparietal. Prefrontals small and widely separated. Three supraoculars. 40 mm (snout-vent).
Distribution: Tanami Desert, NT.
Habit: Spinifex-dominated sandplain desert, especially associated with rock outcrops and stony hills. Otherwise as for genus.

Lerista terdigitata (Parker, 1926)

Description: Grey to olive-brown above, with four longitudinal series of blackish dots along the back; a dark brown or black stripe from the snout, through the eye to the tail; lower lateral and ventral surfaces whitish, with numerous small, blackish flecks and spots arranged in longitudinal series. Forelimbs and hindlimbs each with three digits; forelimb about 11%, and hindlimb 23%, of snout-vent length. Lower eyelid movable. 18-22 mid-body scale rows. Nasals moderately contacting to narrowly separated. Frontoparietals paired, occasionally not contacting; interparietal distinct. Prefrontals widely separated.

Lerista uniduo Denham, WA G. SHEA

Lerista varia Monkey Mia, WA M. PETERSON

Lerista wilkinsi Torrens Creek, Qld

Lerista xanthura Ethabuka Station, SW Qld

Four supraoculars. Usually six supralabials. 55 mm (snout-vent).
Distribution: Islands, coast and hinterland of the Great Australian Bight to north-western SA.
Habit: Mulga and other arid *Acacia* scrubs, mallee, low shrublands, spinifex sandplain desert, especially at the bases of stony hills and ranges. Otherwise as for genus.

Lerista uniduo Storr, 1984

Description: Pale brown or fawn above, with a darker vertebral stripe enclosing two or four closely spaced longitudinal lines formed by two or four series of dark brown dots or streaks. Head with dark brown variegations. A dark brown lateral stripe from snout to tail, its lower edge ragged. Ventral surfaces whitish to yellow. Forelimbs absent, though their position indicated by a groove; hindlimbs each with two digits. Hindlimb about 15-20% of snout-vent length. Lower eyelid fused and immovable. 18-20 mid-body scale rows. Nasals usually in contact, but occasionally narrowly separated. Frontoparietals and interparietal fused to form a single shield. Prefrontals small and widely separated. Three supraoculars. Six supralabials. 55 mm (snout-vent).
Distribution: Mid-western coastal regions of WA.
Habit: Coastal dunes and low shrublands to spinifex/ *Acacia* scrublands. Otherwise as for genus.

Lerista varia Storr, 1986

Description: Pale brown or fawn above, with or without a broad, dark, vertebral zone from nape to tail made up 2 or 4 longitudinal series of dark brown spots; a faint, dark, loreal streak, sometimes continued behind the eye to the temporal region; an obscure, pale, dorso-lateral zone, not or scarcely

Lerista vittata near Mt Cooper, Qld

M. PETERSON

Lerista walkeri Mt French, WA

differentiated from the pale yellowish-brown flanks; sometimes a faint indication of a dark upper lateral stripe; ventral surfaces whitish, with dark brown dots; a dark brown or black stripe from side of snout, through eye to tail. Lower lateral and ventral surfaces whitish. Forelimbs absent (though their positions indicated by a groove), hindlimbs each with two digits; hindlimb about 15% of snout-vent length. Lower eyelid movable. 18-22 mid-body scale rows. Nasals in contact. Frontoparietals and interparietal fused to form a single, large shield. Prefrontals normally present, small and widely separated, often fused to second loreal. Three supraoculars. Six supralabials. 70 mm (snout-vent).
Distribution: Shark Bay region, WA.
Habit: Low coastal shrublands. Otherwise as for genus.

Lerista vermicularis Storr, 1982

Description: Pale reddish-brown or fawn above, with up to four narrow, blackish lines of dots from nape to tail. A broad, dark brown or black lateral stripe, sometimes obscure in places, from snout to tail. Head flecked or streaked with dark brown. Ventral surfaces whitish. Forelimbs absent, without any trace of a groove. Hindlimbs each with two digits. Hindlimb about 15-20% of snout-vent length. Lower eyelid fused and immovable. 16-18 mid-body scale rows. Nasals separated. Frontoparietals and

Lerista taeniata

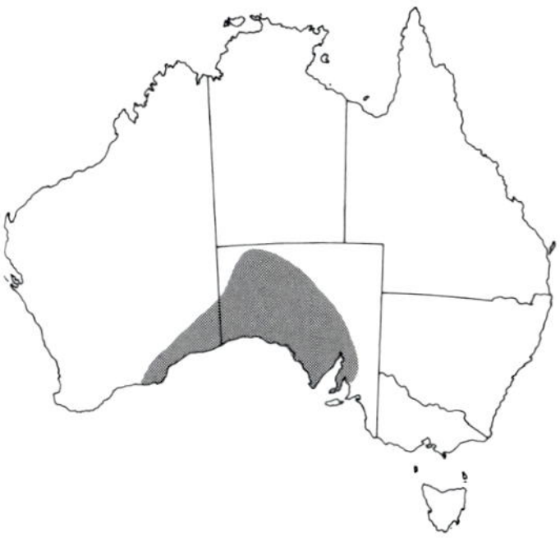

Lerista terdigitata

Lerista uniduo

Lerista varia

Lerista vittata

Lerista vermicularis

Lerista walkeri

Lerista wilkinsi

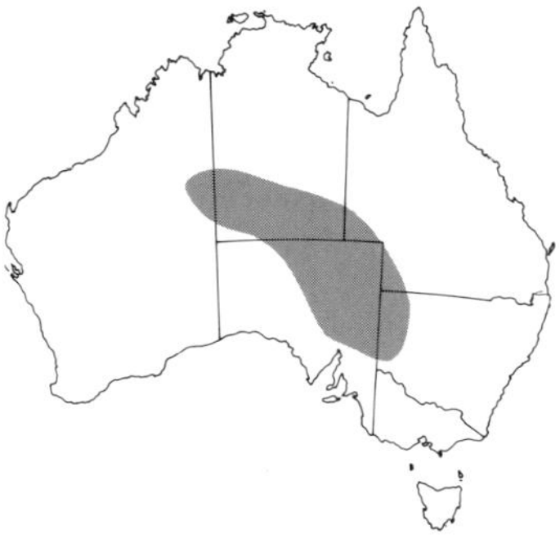
Lerista xanthura

interparietal fused to form a single shield. Prefrontals absent. Two supraoculars. Five supralabials. 40 mm (snout-vent).
Distribution: Great Sandy Desert, WA.
Habit: Red sand ridge desert dominated by hummock grasses. Otherwise as for genus.

Lerista vittata Greer, McDonald and Lawrie, 1983

Description: Pale grey or grey-brown above, with faint darker brown flecks on the head and dorsum, and a broad, dark brown lateral stripe from snout to tail. Ventral surfaces whitish. Forelimbs absent, without any indication of a groove. Hindlimbs each with a single digit. Hindlimb about 5% of snout-vent length. Lower eyelid movable. 18 mid-body scale rows. Nasals in contact. Frontoparietals paired and distinct from the interparietal. Prefrontals absent. Two supraoculars. Five supralabials. 65 mm (snout-vent).
Distribution: Currently known only from a small area south-east of Charters Towers, Qld.
Habit: All known specimens from 'deciduous vine thicket' (Greer, McDonald and Lawrie). Otherwise as for genus.

Lerista walkeri (Boulenger, 1891)

Description: Grey, grey-brown or metallic pale brown above, each scale with a central blackish dot, resulting in a series of fine, longitudinal lines of dots along the body and tail. Several of these lines merge on the temporal region to form a dark temporal streak. Labials and top of head with dark brown spots and marbling, or with dark-edged sutures. Ventral surfaces whitish. Forelimbs and hindlimbs each with two digits; forelimb about 8%, and hindlimb about 15%, of snout-vent length. Lower eyelid movable. 20 mid-body scale rows. Nasals in contact. Frontoparietals fused; interparietal distinct. Prefrontals widely separated. Three supraoculars. Six supralabials. 60 mm (snout-vent).
Distribution: Coast and adjacent hinterland of the western and northern Kimberley districts of WA.
Habit: Seasonally-dry woodlands, especially associated with rock outcrops and stony hills and scarps. Otherwise as for genus.

Lerista wilkinsi (Parker, 1926)

Description: Pale silvery-grey or grey-brown above, the scales on the back and sides each with a dark brown dot or fleck, resulting in a series of longitudinal lines of dots. These tend to be more conspicuous on the sides and tail. Head shields narrowly edged with dark brown, and usually an obscure, dark brown streak from the nostril through the eye to the side of the body. Ventral surface white, immaculate, except for the tail which is heavily spotted with brown. Forelimbs absent, hindlimbs each with two digits, the outer more than twice as long as the inner; hindlimb about 6-10% of snout-vent length. Lower eyelid movable. 18-20 mid-body scale rows. Prefrontals small or absent. Nasals in broad contact. Frontoparietals paired, not, or scarcely, in contact, distinct from the interparietal. Three supraoculars (four, counting the widely separated 'prefrontals'). Five supralabials. 75 mm (snout-vent).
Distribution: Central Qld.
Habit: Open woodland and deciduous scrubs. Otherwise as for genus.

Lerista xanthura Storr, 1976

Description: 'Upper surface pale pinkish-buff, each scale finely edged with brown. Lower surface whitish' (Storr). Tail bright yellow in living specimens. Forelimbs and hindlimbs tetradactyle, the forelimb about 15%, the hindlimb about 30%, of snout-vent length. Lower eyelid fused above to form a fixed spectacle. 18 mid-body scale rows. Nasals in contact. Frontoparietals paired, distinct from and smaller than the interparietal. Prefrontals small and widely separated. Three supraoculars. 45 mm (snout-vent).

Distribution: Gibson Desert, WA, to south-western NSW.

Habit: Dry open woodlands, grassed alluvial sands and dunes, spinifex-dominated red sand plain desert. Otherwise as for genus.

Genus ***Lygisaurus*** De Vis, 1884

A genus of small, slender, short-limbed, four-fingered skinks previously included within the genus *Carlia*, from which *Lygisaurus* may be distinguished by the combination of separated prefrontals, single presubocular, adult snout-vent length usually less than 40 mm (more than 40 mm in most species of *Carlia*), fewer than 10 supradigital scales on the fourth toe (10 or more in *Carlia*), and usually 15 premaxillary teeth (usually 13 in *Carlia*). The only four-fingered species in *Lampropholis (tetradactyla)* can be distinguished from the species of *Lygisaurus* by its possession of a series of subocular scales separating the eye from the upper labial scales.

Most species are diurnal or crepuscular litter-dwelling inhabitants of forests and open woodlands; although primarily heliothermic, they tend to be most active in heavily shaded areas and dappled sunlight. The following key and descriptions are based in large part on the 1988 revision of this genus by Ingram and Covacevich.

Key

TO THE AUSTRALIAN SPECIES OF LYGISAURUS

1 Lower eyelid partially or completely fused above, immovable, forming a fixed spectacle covering the eye (a) **2**
Lower eyelid movable (b) **3**

2 Interparietal distinct (c) .... ***foliorum***
Interparietal fused to the frontoparietal (d) .... ***timlowi***

3 Margin of ear-opening with a more or less continuous series of enlarged, sharply-projecting lobules (e) **4**
Margin of ear-opening with at most a series of low, flat, lobules which do not project, or at most project low and bluntly, into the ear-opening itself (f) **6**

4 Projecting ear lobules more or less subequal in size and continuous around margin of ear-opening (g) **5**
Anterior ear lobules distinctly larger than the posterior ones (h) .... ***sesbrauna***

5 Ear-opening horizontally elliptic, much smaller than the palpebral disc (i) .... ***aeratus***
Ear-opening round, more or less equal in size to the palpebral disc (j) .... ***laevis***

6 Ear lobules if present, flat, low and not projecting into the ear-opening (k) **7**
Usually at least one low, blunt projecting ear lobule anteriorly (l) .... ***macfarlani***

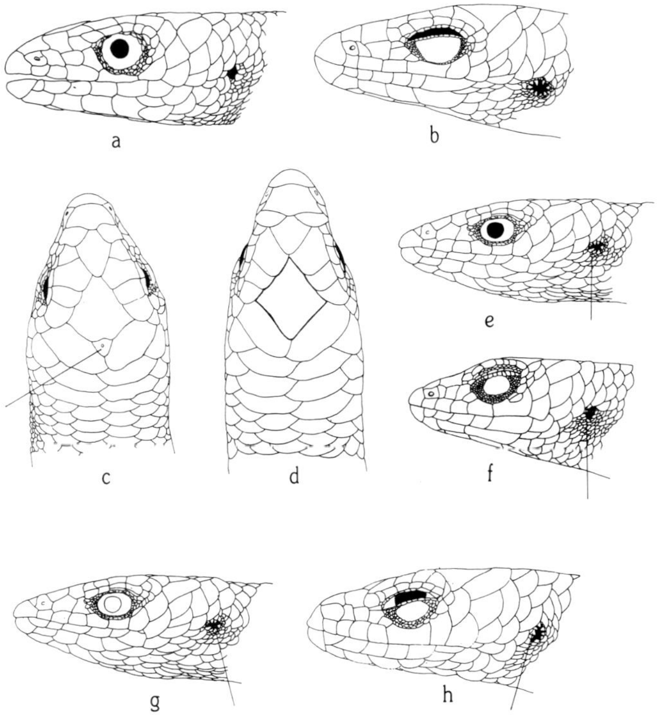

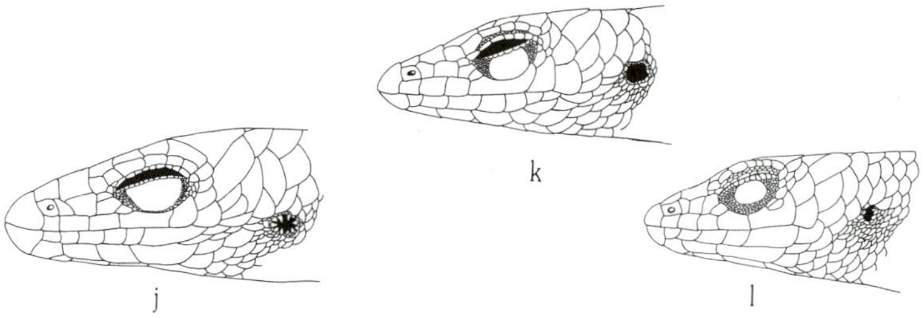

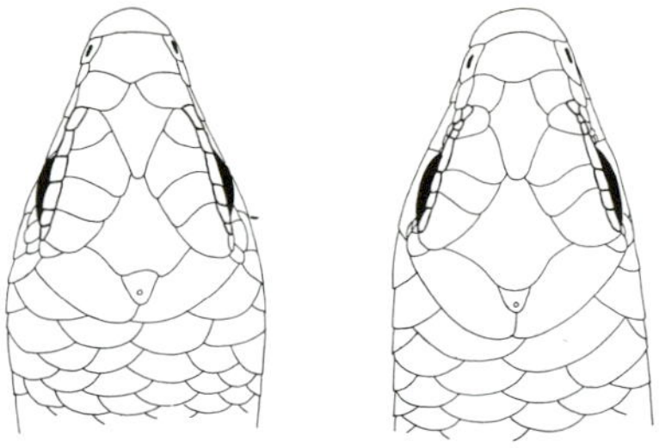

7 Mid-body scale rows 27 or more; usually six supraciliaries (m).. ***rococo***

Mid-body scale rows 27 or fewer; usually seven supraciliaries (n)... ***tanneri***

Lygisaurus macfarlani Murray Island, Torres Strait

Lygisaurus aeratus (Garman, 1901)

Description: Pale to dark olive-brown above, the individual scales finely flecked with black and pale brown. Head often copper-coloured, while the flanks and limbs are often finely dotted with white. Lips pale brown, with darker brown barring, and usually with a series of white flecks forming an obscure, whitish labial stripe to below the ear. Throat, limbs and tail often rich reddish-brown in breeding males. White to cream below, sometimes with scattered, dark brown flecks forming a series a fine longitudinal lines. Eyelid movable, with a large palpebral disc. Prefrontals separate. Supraciliaries usually six. Supralabials 5-7,

Lygisaurus foliorum Kuranda, Qld

usually 6. Interparietal distinct from the single frontoparietal. Ear-opening horizontally elliptic, much smaller than palpebral disc and surrounded by subequal pointed lobules.Dorsal scales 4-sided, the free edge evenly rounded, smooth or faintly striated. Scales in 19-24 rows at mid-body. 18-24 lamellae under the fourth toe. 35 mm (snout-vent).
Distribution: North-eastern Qld, from Prince of Wales Island south nearly to Townsville.
Habit: Tropical woodlands and monsoon forests. Otherwise as for genus.

Lygisaurus foliorum De Vis, 1884

Description: Pale to dark brown above, the individual scales finely flecked or streaked with black and pale brown. Flanks and limbs finely dotted with white. Lips pale brown, flecked or variegated with dark brown. Tail often rich reddish-brown. Whitish below, sometimes with scattered dark brown flecks. The lower eyelid mostly fused above and immovable. Prefrontals separate. Supraciliaries usually six. Interparietal distinct from the single frontoparietal. Ear-opening circular or horizontally elliptic, much smaller than palpebral disc, and surrounded by pointed lobules (northern populations), or with only a few minute, flat lobules (southern populations). Dorsal scales 4-sided, the free edge evenly rounded, smooth or faintly striated. Scales in 21-25 rows at mid-body. 17-23 lamellae under the fourth toe. 35 mm (snout-vent).
Distribution: Eastern Australia, from about Townsville, Qld south to Sydney, NSW.
Habit: Wet and dry sclerophyll forests, moister woodlands and montane heaths. Otherwise as for genus.

Lygisaurus laevis (Oudemans, 1894)

Description: Brown above, sometimes darker on the head and flanks, and often some indication of a paler brown dorso- lateral stripe on each side. Many dorsal and lateral scales pale-centred, but with darker flecks or dots, often resulting in longitudinal lines of dots on the back and flanks. Limbs brown, dotted with pale brown and black. Lips pale brown, spotted or flecked with dark brown. Whitish below, sometimes flecked with dark brown. Breeding males often with rich reddish-brown on the throat and tail. Prefrontals separate. Supraciliaries 6-8, usually seven. Interparietal distinct from the single frontoparietal. Ear-opening circular or longitudinally oval, about

Lygisaurus aeratus

Lygisaurus foliorum

Lygisaurus laevis

Lygisaurus macfarlani

Lygisaurus rococo

Lygisaurus sesbrauna

Lygisaurus tanneri

equal to the palpebral disc, and surrounded by a series of sharp, subequal lobules. Dorsal scales 4-sided, each with its free edge evenly rounded, smooth or faintly striated. Scales in 23-26 rows at mid-body. 18-25 lamellae under the fourth toe. 35 mm (snout-vent).
Distribution: Rainforest areas between Cooktown and the Atherton Tableland, north-eastern Qld.
Habit: As for genus.

Lygisaurus macfarlani (Günther, 1877)

Description: Rich brown above, darker on the head. Usually some indication of a paler brown dorso-lateral stripe on each side, sometimes black edged. Many dorsal scales, especially on the tail, flecked or dotted with black, often resulting in longitudinal lines of dots on the back and flanks. Limbs brown, dotted with pale brown and black. Lips pale brown, spotted or flecked with dark brown. Occasionally a faint, pale mid-lateral stripe. Whitish below, sometimes flecked with dark brown. Breeding males more or less uniform olive-brown, with rich reddish-brown on the throat, limbs and tail. Prefrontals separate. Supraciliaries 6-8, usually seven. Interparietal distinct from the single frontoparietal. Ear-opening more or less circular, smaller than palpebral disc, and usually with one or more bluntly pointed lobules anteriorly. Dorsal scales 4-sided, each with its free edge evenly rounded, smooth, or faintly striated. Scales in 22-30 rows at mid-body. 20-26 lamellae under the fourth toe. 35 mm (snout-vent).
Distribution: Far north-eastern Qld, including islands of Torres Strait. Possibly extra-limital in New Guinea.
Habit: Rainforest edges and clearings, monsoon forests, secondary regrowth and denser growth beside streams and in rocky gullies; some moist woodlands habitats. Otherwise as for genus.

Lygisaurus rococo Ingram and Covacevich, 1988

Description: More or less uniform dark brown above, head often copper-coloured; the individual body scales faintly dark-edged, giving a finely-reticulate pattern on the dorsum. Grey below, the lower surfaces of the feet black. Eyelid movable, with a large palpebral disc. Prefrontals separate. Supraciliaries usually six. Supralabials usually seven. Interparietal distinct from the single frontoparietal. Ear-opening round, much smaller than palpebral disc, and its margin with low, flat lobules which do not project into the ear-opening. Dorsal scales 4-sided, the free edge evenly rounded, smooth, or faintly striated. Scales in 27-30 rows at mid-body. 23-26 lamellae under the fourth toe. 35 mm (snout-vent).
Distribution: Currently known only from limestone rock outcrops near Chillagoe, north-eastern Qld.
Habit: Ground litter which has accumulated between rock outcrops (Ingram and Covacevich).

Lygisaurus sesbrauna Ingram and Covacevich, 1988

Description: Brown above, often flushed with red or lemon, the individual scales finely flecked with black and pale brown.Top of head blackish. Often a narrow, dark, vertebral stripe and several fine dark paravertebral lines. An obscure, pale dorso-lateral stripe with poorly-defined darker edges. The flanks and limbs may be finely dotted with white. Lips pale brown, with darker brown flecks or barring. Limbs and tail often rich reddish-brown in breeding males. White to cream below, sometimes with scattered dark brown flecks forming a series a fine longitudinal lines. Eyelid movable, with a small palpebral disc. Prefrontals separate. Supraciliaries 6-8, usually seven. Supralabials 6-7, usually seven. Interparietal distinct from the single frontoparietal. Ear-opening round, about the same size as the palpebral disc and surrounded by subequal pointed lobules.Dorsal scales 4-sided, the free edge evenly rounded, smooth, or faintly striated. Scales in 22-26 rows at mid-body. 21-26 lamellae under the fourth toe. 30 mm (snout-vent).
Distribution: Eastern Cape York Peninsula, south to about Princess Charlotte Bay.
Habit: Monsoon forest, moist microhabitats within tropical woodland, especially those associated with gullies and creeks. Otherwise as for genus.

Lygisaurus tanneri Ingram and Covacevich, 1988

Description: Mid- to dark-brown above, the individual scales finely flecked with black and pale brown; the flanks and limbs are often finely dotted with white, cream or very pale brown. Lips pale brown, with darker brown barring, and usually with a series of white flecks forming an obscure, narrow whitish labial stripe. Throat, limbs and tail often rich reddish-brown in breeding males. White to cream below, sometimes with scattered dark brown flecks. Eyelid movable, with a small palpebral disc.

Prefrontals separated. Supraciliaries 6-7, usually seven. Supralabials 6-7, usually seven. Interparietal distinct from the single frontoparietal. Ear-opening round, smaller than palpebral disc, and surrounded by low, flat lobules which do not normally project into the ear-opening. Dorsal scales 4-sided, the free edge evenly rounded, smooth, or faintly striated. Scales in 22-27 rows at mid-body. 20-24 lamellae under the fourth toe. 30 mm (snout-vent).
Distribution: Coastal north-eastern Qld in a small area centred on the Cooktown region.
Habit: As for genus.

Lygisaurus timlowi

Lygisaurus timlowi (Ingram, 1977)

Description: Pale to dark brown above, the individual scales finely flecked or streaked with black and pale brown. Flanks and limbs finely dotted with white, but with a distinctly darker brown upper lateral zone. Lips pale brown, flecked or variegated with dark brown. Tail often rich reddish-brown. Whitish below, sometimes with scattered dark brown flecks, especially under the tail. The lower eyelid fused above to form an immovable spectacle. Prefrontals separated. Supraciliaries 5-6, usually five. Interparietal fused with the frontoparietal to form a single large shield. Ear-opening very small, circular, much smaller than palpebral disc, and without obvious auricular lobules. Dorsal scales 4-sided, the free edge evenly rounded, smooth, or faintly striated. Scales in 18-20 rows at mid-body. 15-19 lamellae under the fourth toe. 25 mm (snout-vent).
Distribution: Eastern Qld.
Habit: Dry sclerophyll forest and woodland. Otherwise as for genus.

Genus ***Menetia*** Gray, 1845

A genus of small, cryptozoic lizards, characterised by: short limbs which fail to overlap by at least several scale rows when adpressed; fingers four, toes five; supranasals absent; parietal shields in contact behind interparietal; prefrontals large, usually narrowly separated; lower eyelid immovable, fixed above to form a permanent spectacle; ear-opening very small but distinct; preanals scarcely enlarged.

Key

TO THE SPECIES OF MENETIA

1 Two or more supraciliaries **2**
A single supraciliary (a) .... ***amaura***

2 Second supraciliary much larger than first, contacting prefrontal and separating first supraciliary from first supraocular (b).......... **3**
Second supraciliary not, or scarcely, larger than first and not contacting prefrontal; first supraciliary and first supraocular in contact (c) **5**

3 Two presuboculars (d); pale mid-lateral stripe present or absent **4**
One presubocular (e); pale mid-lateral stripe present, at least anteriorly .... ***greyii***

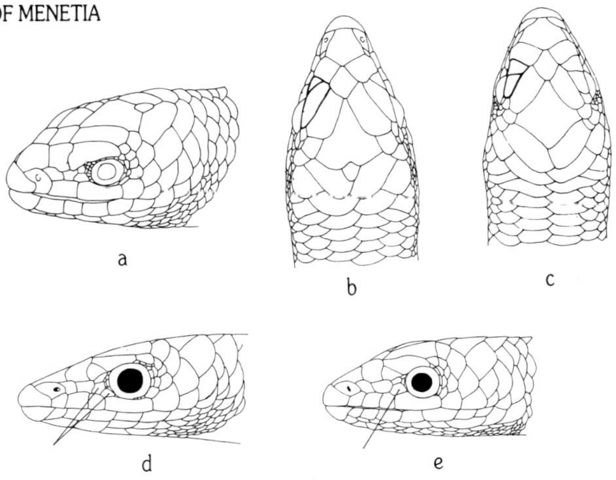

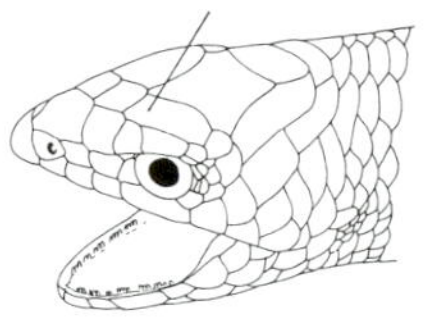

f

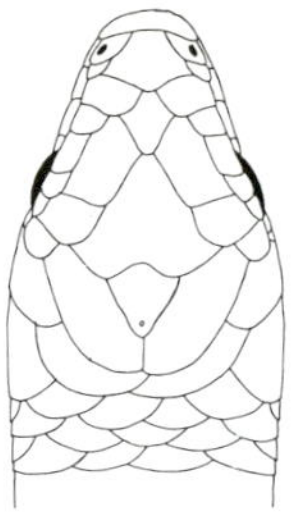

g

4 No indication of a pale mid-lateral stripe; 22-24 mid-body scale rows .... ***alanae***

A pale mid-lateral stripe present, at least anteriorly; 20 mid-body scale rows .... ***concinna***

5 First supraocular at least 2.5 times as long as wide (f); ear aperture present, though often minute .... ***maini***

First supraocular about twice as long as wide (g); ear opening absent .... ***surda***

Menetia alanae Rankin, 1979

Description: Pale brown above, the two rows of mid-dorsal scales with a few darker brown flecks tending to form obscure, longitudinal lines down the middle of the back; dorsal colour merging with or slightly delineated from the dark grey-brown or black upper lateral zone; no pale mid-lateral stripe; lips whitish, flecked with dark brown; ventral surfaces whitish, except for pale yellow under tail. Nasals separated. Frontoparietals fused to form a single large shield, distinct from the small interparietal. Two supraoculars, the first a little more than twice as long as wide. Usually three supraciliaries, the second much larger than the first and in contact with prefrontal. 17-20 lamellae under the fourth toe. 22-24 mid-body scale rows. 25 mm (snout-vent).
Distribution: Coast and nearby hinterland of north-western NT.
Habit: Found in leaf-litter in coastal forest and woodland.

Menetia amaura Storr, 1978

Description: Blackish-brown above, paler on tail and flanks; lips pale brown flecked with darker brown; ventral surfaces whitish. Nasals separated. Frontoparietals fused to form a single large shield, distinct from the small interparietal. Two supraoculars, the first not much more than twice as long as wide; a single supraciliary. 15 lamellae under the fourth toe. 22 mid-body scale rows. 25 mm (snout-vent).
Distribution: Only a single specimen currently known from Carrarang Station, Edel Land, Shark Bay, WA.
Habit: Low shrubland on coastal sands.

Menetia concinna Sadlier, 1984

Description: Grey-brown above, with up to four

Menetia alanae Munmarley Station, NT

J. WOMBEY

Menetia alanae

J. WOMBEY

Menetia concinna Nourlangie, NT

Menetia amaura

Menetia concinna

Menetia greyii Jabiru, NT

Menetia greyii

narrow, dashed, longitudinal lines along the back. A broad, dark brown or black lateral stripe from snout, through the eye, to the hindlimb and continuing weakly on the tail. This dark lateral stripe is bordered below by a narrow white stripe which commences on the upper lip and passes through the ear and over the forelimb to the groin, becoming more obscure posteriorly, and bordered below by a mottled brown and cream zone. Ventral surfaces whitish. Nasals separated. Frontoparietals fused to form a single shield, distinct from the small interparietal. First of the two supraoculars about twice as long as wide. Three supraciliaries, the second much larger than the first and contacting the prefrontal. 16-19 lamellae under the fourth toe. 20 mid-body scale rows. 30 mm (snout-vent).

Distribution: Western Arnhem Land, NT.
Habit: An inhabitant of ground litter in eucalyptus woodland.

Menetia greyii Gray, 1845

Description: Bronzy-brown or grey-brown above, often with four narrow, broken (made up of a series of dashes), dark lines from the nape to the base of the tail. A blackish-brown dorso-lateral stripe, widest anteriorly, from nostril to tail. This stripe is bordered above by an obscure, narrow, pale zone, while below it is bordered anteriorly by a creamy-white stripe from the snout to just behind the forelimb. Flanks the same

G. SHEA

Menetia surda Billabong Roadhouse, WA

colour as the dorsum. Lower lips and chin speckled with dark brown, as is the underside of the tail. Ventral surfaces cream to rich yellow, usually paler on the throat and sometimes with fine, longitudinal lines of dark brown. Nasals widely separated. Frontoparietals fused to form a single large shield, distinct from the small interparietal. Two large, elongate supraoculars, distinctively oblique, the first nearly three times as long as wide. Second supraciliary much larger than first and in contact with prefrontal. 12-23 lamellae under the fourth toe. 20-24 mid-body scale rows. Other characters as for genus. 30 mm (snout-vent).
Distribution: Widely distributed throughout most parts of continental Australia except the northern, eastern and south-eastern perimeters.
Habit: Found in a wide variety of habitats from dry sclerophyll forest and temperate and tropical woodlands, to mallee, Acacia and other arid scrubs and hummock grasslands. A diurnal lizard usually seen scuttling in leaf-litter or grasses.

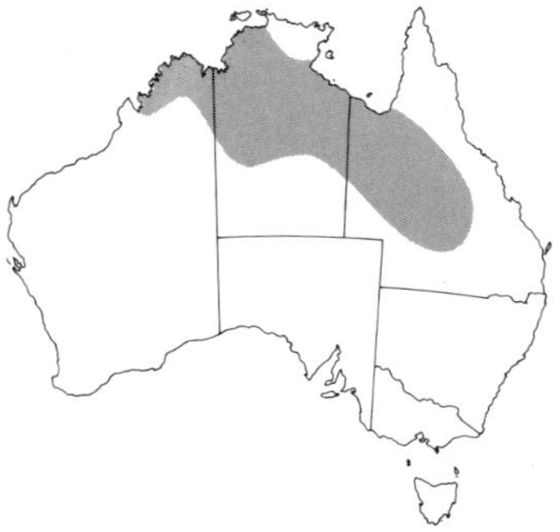

Menetia maini

Menetia surda

Menetia maini Storr, 1976

Description: Metallic- brown above and on the sides, the individual scales sometimes with a dark brown median streak (especially on the back), or flecked with dark brown (especially on the flanks); creamy-white below, many of the individual scales dark-edged. Nasals separated. Frontoparietals fused to form a single large shield distinct from the small interparietal. First supraocular nearly three times as long as wide. Three supraciliaries, the second supraciliary not much larger than the first and not contacting the prefrontal. 16-21 lamellae under the fourth toe. 18-26 mid-body scale rows. 25 mm (snout-vent).
Distribution: North-western coastal regions of the Kimberley Division, WA, to northern NT and central Qld.
Habit: Seasonally-dry tropical woodlands and scrubs to spinifex-dominated sandplain desert, rock outcrops and stony hills and ranges.

Menetia surda Storr, 1976

Description: Olive-brown above, the individual scales sometimes with a faint, dark brown longitudinal streak; an obscure, dark, upper lateral zone sometimes present; upper labials pale; ventral surfaces whitish. Nasals separated. Frontoparietals fused to form a single large shield, distinct from the small interparietal. Two supraoculars, the first not much more than twice as long as wide. Three to four supraciliaries, the second largest and not in contact with the prefrontal. 20-24 lamellae under the fourth toe. 20-24 mid-body scale rows. 30 mm (snout-vent).
Distribution: Middle western coastal regions of WA, extending well inland.
Habit: Coastal low shrublands to arid scrubs and open Acacia woodland.

Genus *Morethia* Gray, 1845

A group of small, terrestrial, diurnal skinks characterised by: pentadactyle limbs; smooth scales; fused frontoparietal and interparietal scales; large prefrontals in contact or narrowly separated; lower eyelid fused above to form an immovable spectacle; eye surrounded by a continuous or interrupted circle of uniformly small granules; frontal much larger than prefrontals; nasal usually divided to form a distinct supranasal which may be distinct from, or fused with, a small postnasal. All are oviparous.

Key

TO THE SPECIES OF MORETHIA

1 Ear-opening usually without any obvious anterior lobules (a); ground colour of back and sides brown to black, with two or more conspicuous pale stripes on either side; palpebral slit absent **2**

Ear-opening usually with conspicuous anterior lobules (b); ground colour of back and sides grey or brown, with or without darker and lighter stripes, flecks and spots; a distinct palpebral slit present (c) **4**

2 Supranasals distinct from nasals (d) **3**

Each supranasal fused at least anteriorly to nasal (e) .... ***storri***

3 A narrow, pale dorso-lateral stripe on each side, each separated from the other by six rows of scales .... ***taeniopleura***

A broad, pale dorso-lateral stripe on each side, each separated from the other by five or fewer rows of scales ... . ***ruficauda***

4 Subdigital lamellae strongly keeled and palmar tubercles strongly pointed **5**

Subdigital lamellae smooth or with low, blunt keels **6**

5 Usually five supraciliaries, the last three largest and deeply penetrating between the supraoculars (f) .. ***adelaidensis***

Usually six supraciliaries, the first largest, and all forming a straight-sided series in which there is no penetration of the supraoculars (g) .... ***butleri***

6 Fourth supraciliary not smaller than third (h) **7**

Fourth supraciliary much smaller than third (i) .... ***boulengeri***

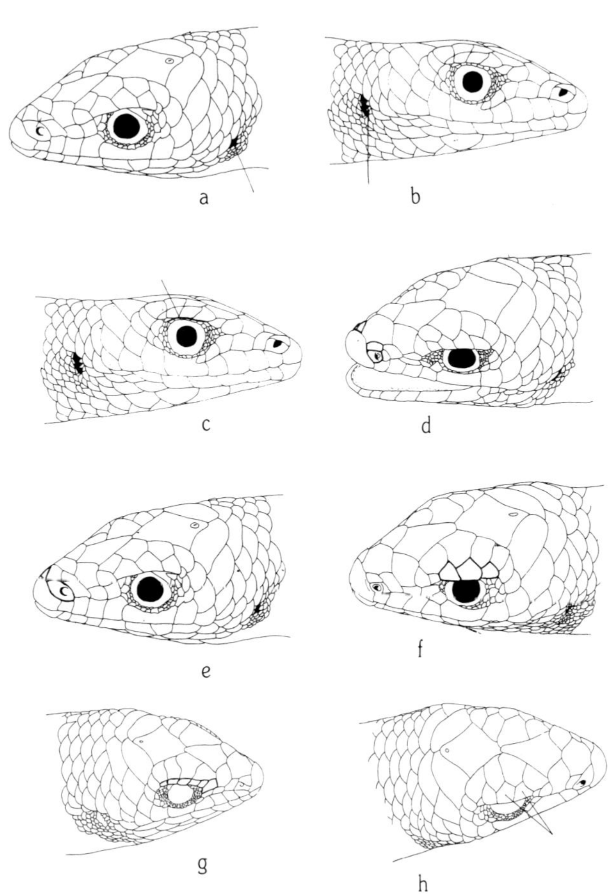

7 Fifth supraciliary penetrating deeply between supraoculars (h); supranasal often fused to nasal; dorsal spots and lateral white stripe usually well developed .... ***lineoocellata***

Fifth supraciliary not penetrating deeply between supraoculars (j); supranasal and nasal distinct; dorsal spots and mid-lateral white stripe absent or obscure .... ***obscura***

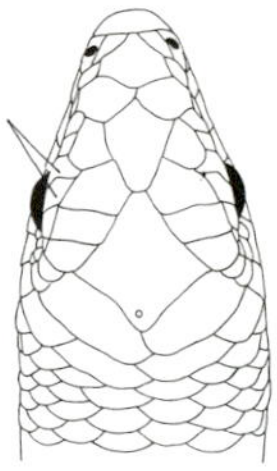

i

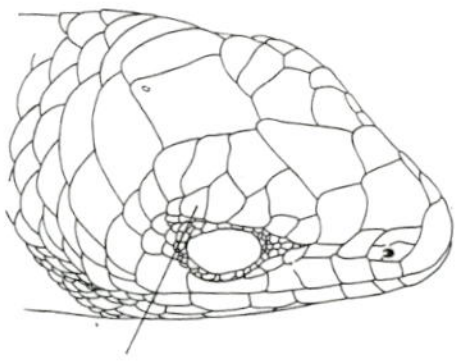

j

Morethia adelaidensis Adelaide district, SA

Morethia adelaidensis Peters, 1874

Description: Grey, brown or olive-brown above, often with scattered dark spots and flecks tending to form broken, longitudinal lines. Usually a vague, interrupted, pale dorso-lateral band from above the eye to the base of the tail; this band occasionally bordered above by an obscure darker band and usually bordered below by a dark upper lateral band in which there are numerous, scattered, darker and lighter flecks. Below this in turn is a narrow, often broken, whitish mid-lateral stripe from the upper labials to the hindlimb, while below this is a poorly defined dark brown band. Ventral surface white, though flushed with orange-pink in breeding males. All lateral markings may be obscure in some specimens. 26-34 mid-body scale rows. Usually five supraciliaries, the last three subequal and larger than the first two and penetrating between the supraoculars. Lamellae under the fourth toe 17-24. Subdigital lamellae and palmar tubercles with one or three sharp keels. Ear-opening with distinct anterior lobules which may be partly hidden by overlying scales. 45 mm (snout-vent).

Distribution: South-eastern WA through arid parts of SA to western NSW and Qld and north-western Vic.

Habit: Principally an inhabitant of ground litter and fallen timber in open woodland, low chenopod shrubland, mallee and in mulga and other arid Acacia scrublands. Oviparous.

Morethia boulengeri (Ogilby, 1890)

Description: Grey or brown above, usually with scattered, darker and lighter flecks, the former often tending to form broken, longitudinal lines. Tail usually

Morethia boulengeri Mayne Junction, W Qld

richer brown or even russet, brightest in juveniles. A conspicuous narrow white stripe from the upper labials to the groin; this is bordered above by a well-defined, broader, blackish upper lateral stripe and below by a more obscure dark area. Ventral surface white, but the throat and tail may be flushed with bright orange-pink apparently independent of season. Mid-body scales in 26-32 rows. Usually six supraciliaries, the first and third largest and both penetrate between the supraoculars. Lamellae under fourth toe 15-23. Subdigital lamellae and palmar tubercles rounded or with a single, blunt keel. Ear-opening with several small but obvious anterior lobules. 45 mm (snout-vent).

Distribution: From southern Qld and NSW, west of the Great Dividing Range through western Vic, SA and the lower end of the NT to the eastern interior of WA.

Habit: Found among ground litter and fallen timber in a wide variety of habitats from dry sclerophyll forest, woodlands, mallee, low shrublands and arid scrublands. Often shelters under the bark of fallen or standing dead, ring-barked trees.

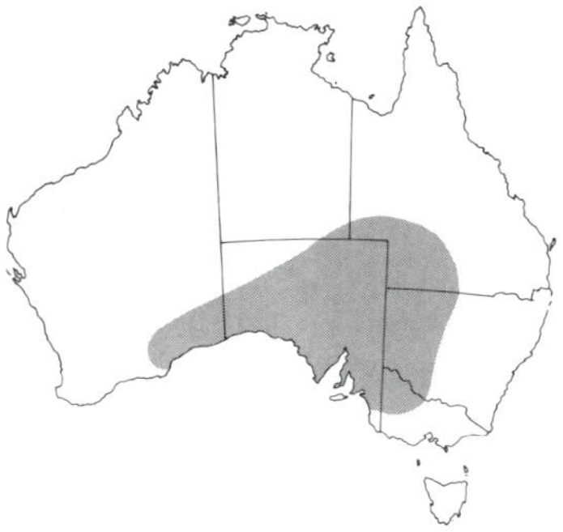

Morethia adelaidensis

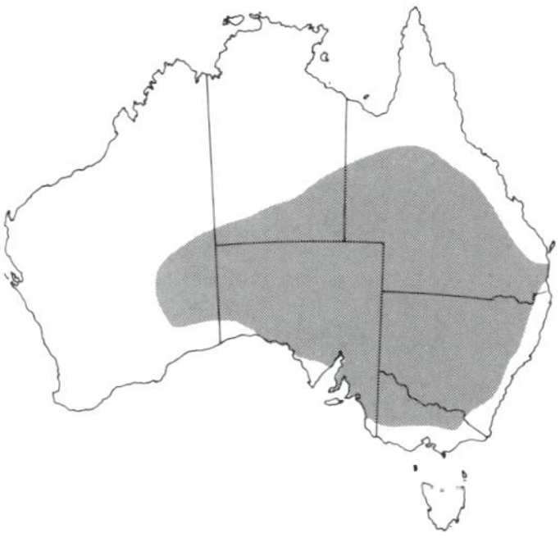

Morethia boulengeri

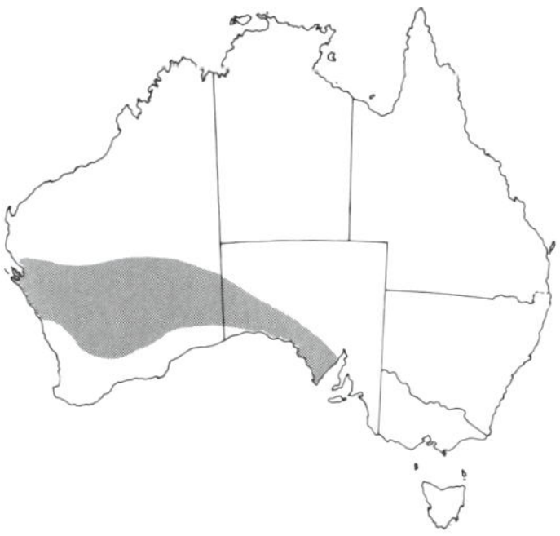

Morethia butleri

Morethia butleri (Storr, 1963)

Description: Similar in colour and pattern to *Morethia boulengeri*, except that the back is usually uniform. Distinguished from *M. boulengeri* by having

Morethia butleri near Norseman, WA

usually six supraciliaries, the first of which is the largest, and all of which fail to penetrate between the supraoculars and hence form a straight or curved-edged series. Lamellae under the fourth toe 19-27 (Storr). Subdigital lamellae and palmar tubercles sharply keeled. In other respects similar to *M. boulengeri*.
Distribution: Drier parts of southern WA to the Nullarbor Plain and the Eyre Peninsula, SA.
Habit: Woodland and low shrubland.

Morethia lineoocellata (Duméril and Bibron, 1839)

Description: Colour and pattern similar in most respects to *Morethia adelaidensis*, except that the back typically has a pattern of distinct, scattered ocelli formed by individual black scales with white centres. As in *M. adelaidensis*, dorsal and lateral patterns may be obscure to the point of absence. Throat orange-pink in some adults. Mid-body scales in 24-32 rows. Usually six supraciliaries, the fourth largest and the third and fourth penetrating between the supraoculars. Lamellae under the fourth toe 14-26. Subdigital lamellae and palmar tubercles smooth, or with low, blunt keels. Ear-opening with distinct anterior lobules. 45 mm (snout-vent).
Distribution: Central and lower coastal areas of WA.
Habit: Low coastal shrublands and heaths to adjacent woodland habitats.

Morethia obscura Storr, 1972

Description: Sometimes similar in colour and pattern to *Morethia lineoocellata*, except that the dorsal ground colour is darker and the lateral pattern more obscure or, in some specimens, body virtually devoid of pattern. Scalation and size also similar to those in *M. lineoocellata*, except that, although there are usually six supraciliaries and the fourth is largest, the fifth does not penetrate between the supraoculars, so that the last three supraciliaries form a straight line junction with the supraoculars.
Distribution: Southern WA, extending through southern SA to north-western Vic and western NSW.
Habit: Coastal heathlands, mallee/spinifex associations, semi-arid scrubs and woodlands.

Morethia ruficauda (Lucas and Frost, 1895)

Description: Generally similar in colour, pattern and scalation to *Morethia taeniopleura*, from which it may be distinguished by its broader, pale, dorso-lateral stripes separated from each other by only 3-5 scales (by six scales in *taeniopleura*) and by its five large supraciliaries (four large supraciliaries and sometimes a tiny fifth in *taeniopleura*). 26-30 mid-body scale rows. 35 mm (snout-vent).
Distribution: North-western quarter of continental Australia, from coasts to central arid region.
Habit: Seasonally-dry tropical woodlands, arid scrublands and desert spinifex/*Acacia*/eucalypt associations on rock outcrops and stony hills and ranges, especially where vegetation is richest in gullies or near creeks and waterholes.
Subspecies: *ruficauda* (central, northern and north-western Australia); *exquisita* (mid-western WA).

Morethia storri Greer, 1980

Description: Rich brown to bright reddish above, most intense on the back, hindlimbs and end of tail, and the individual scales on the back often darker-edged, giving the appearance of longitudinal striations; a white dorso-lateral stripe from the snout above the eye to the base of the tail, and another pale mid-lateral stripe from the lips to the base of the hindlimb; the area between these two pale stripes is dark brown or black. Ventral surfaces white, except

Morethia lineoocellata Cape Naturaliste, WA

Morethia ruficauda Cannon Hill, NT

for the chin and throat which may be flushed with reddish-orange. Mid-body scales in 24-28 rows. Five supraciliaries. 17-26 bluntly keeled lamellae under the fourth toe. Ear-opening without lobules. 35 mm (snout-vent).

Distribution: Coast and hinterland of northern Australia from Dampier Land, WA, to about the NT/Qld border.

Habit: Coastal grasslands and woodlands to the edges of stony hills and scarps, where it is a diurnal inhabitant of ground litter.

Morethia lineoocellata

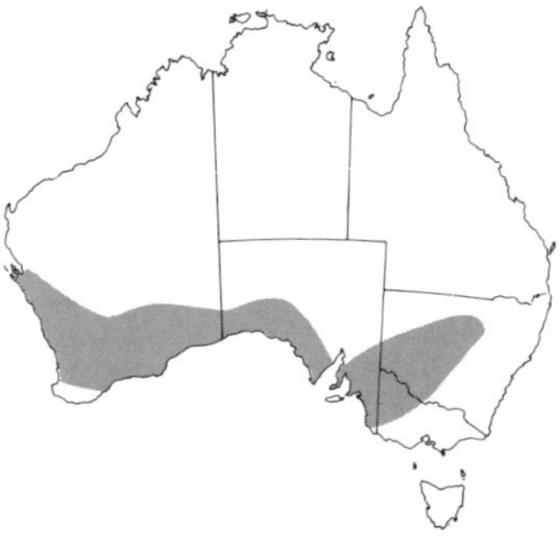

Morethia obscura

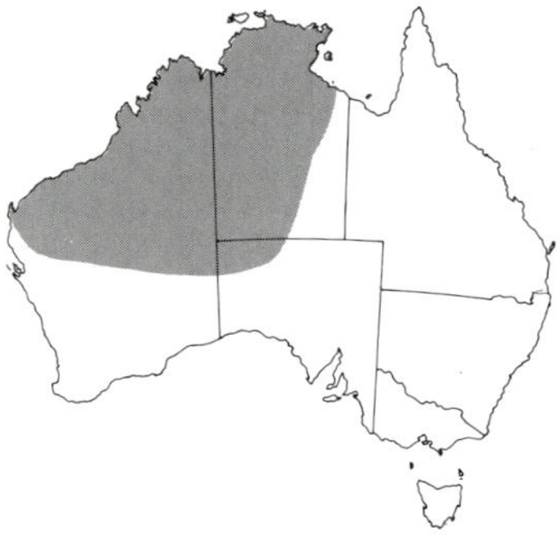

Morethia ruficauda

Morethia taeniopleura Peters, 1874

Fire-Taled Skink

Description: Dorsal ground colour rich grey-brown to glossy black, lighter specimens flecked with darker brown; a brilliant, narrow, cream, light brown or white dorso-lateral streak on either side from the canthus, above the eye and along the body to the level of the hindlimbs or beyond; this white stripe is bordered below by a broad, glossy black, upper lateral stripe from the snout, through the eye to the level of the hindlimb, while this black stripe is, in its turn, bordered below by a broad white stripe from the labials to the groin. Below this is yet another narrow, black stripe. In some populations there is a conspicuous, whitish, vertebral stripe. Ventral surfaces white. The tail varies from dull russet to orange or brilliant red. Mid-body scales in 26-34 rows. Four of five supraciliaries, the fifth, if present, minute. Lamellae under the fourth toe 15-25. Subdigital lamellae and palmar tubercles smooth to finely keeled. Ear-opening usually without obvious lobules, sometimes with a few small inconspicuous ones. 35 mm (snout-vent).

Distribution: Coast and hinterland of eastern Qld.

Habit: Found in a variety of habitats, from open woodland in coastal and near coastal areas, to rocky hills and ranges in the interior. Commonly seen in dense leaf-litter.

Morethia obscura Round Hill, NSW

Morethia storri

Morethia taeniopleura

Morethia storri McArthur River, NT

Morethia taeniopleura Brockman Range, NT

Genus ***Nannoscincus*** Günther, 1872

A New Caledonian genus which in Australia contains a small, fossorial and litter-dwelling species restricted to cool, moist forests in upland areas of south-eastern Australia. Characterised by: moderate limbs which just fail to meet when adpressed; supranasals absent; nasals small, undivided and separated; prefrontals normally absent; parietal shields in contact behind the interparietal; lower eyelid movable, with a small transparent disc; ear-opening present, minute; preanals enlarged; limbs pentadactyle.

Nannoscincus maccoyi Jamberoo, NSW

Nannoscincus maccoyi (Lucas and Frost, 1894)

Description: Rich brown above, uniform, or with a pale vertebral stripe and usually with some scattered dark flecks and obscure pale-centred scales. A narrow, dark brown dorso-lateral stripe along the canthus and continuing above, behind the eye, along the body to the base of the tail, and with a notch above the ear. Flanks may be paler than the dorsum or much darker, in the latter forming a well-defined, dark lateral zone. Throat whitish, uniform, or heavily spotted with dark brown. Prefrontals normally absent. Four supraoculars. 20-22 mid-body scale rows. Forelimbs and hindlimbs pentadactyle, the third toe longer than the fourth. Hindlimb about 15-20% of snout-vent length. Ear-opening minute, punctiform. 50 mm (snout-vent).

Distribution: Southern and eastern Vic and south-eastern NSW.

Habit: Found in moist soil under rocks, logs and litter associated with rocky screes and fallen timber in rainforest and wet sclerophyll forests throughout its range.

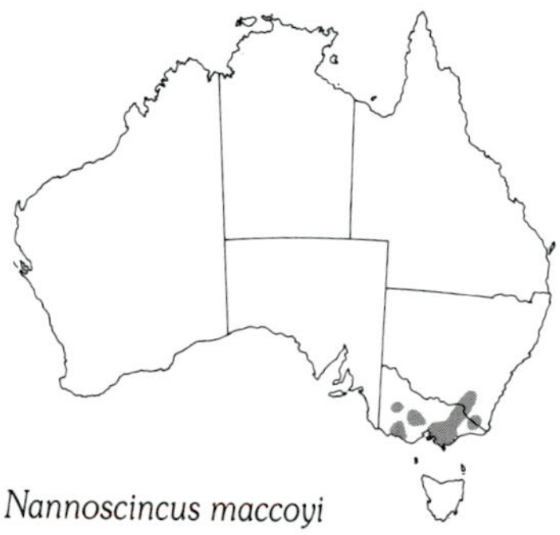

Nannoscincus maccoyi

Genus *Notoscincus* Fuhn, 1969

Small, terrestrial, cryptozoic but diurnal snake-eyed skinks. Limbs moderate, slightly separated to slightly overlapping when adpressed; limbs pentadactyle; ear-opening very small; supranasals absent and nasals undivided; prefrontals large, in contact or narrowly separated; parietal shields in contact behind the interparietal; frontoparietals fused to form a single shield, distinct from the interparietal; lower eyelid totally fused to the upper eyelid to form a permanent spectacle.

Confined to northern and eastern Australia. Little is known of the biology, ecology or relationships of the members of this genus.

Key

TO THE SPECIES OF NOTOSCINCUS

Colour pattern of bold, alternating pale and dark longitudinal stripes .... ***butleri***

Colour pattern not consisting of bold, alternating pale and dark longitudinal stripes .... ***ornatus***

Notoscincus ornatus Bullo River, NT

Notoscincus butleri Storr, 1979

Description: Pale brown above, with seven blackish, longitudinal stripes; a vertebral from nape to tail, where it breaks into a series of spots, and on each side a dorso-lateral (extending from above each eye to tail), an upper lateral and a lower lateral. Pale mid-lateral stripe extending forward over lips. Limbs pale brown with dark brown variegations. Whitish below. Nasals separated. Prefrontals in contact. Three supraoculars. Ear-opening small, with 2-4 small ear lobules. Adpressed limbs meet or overlap. Scales smooth, in 28-32 rows at mid-body. 40 mm (snout- vent).

Distribution: Known only from near Dampier, Pilbara region, WA.
Habit: Stony areas dominated by spinifex ground cover.

Notoscincus ornatus (Broom, 1896)

Description: Olive-brown above, reddish-brown on the tail, immaculate or with a series of darker flecks tending to form longitudinal lines of dots. Usually a vertebral series of larger, brown, widely spaced spots

Notoscincus butleri

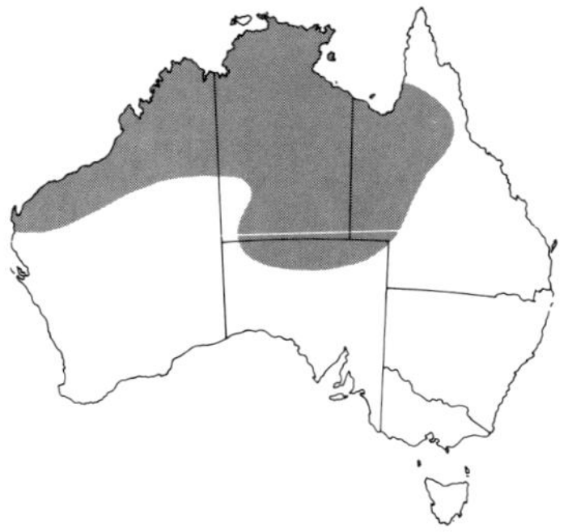

Notoscincus ornatus

on the back and extending along the length of the tail, most conspicuous posteriorly. A dark upper lateral zone extending from behind the eye to the base of the tail, and enclosing a series of small, pale spots or bars which may sometimes divide the dark zone into a series of dark upper lateral blotches. The dark upper lateral zone is continued along the tail as a series of dark brown spots. A narrow, pale mid-lateral stripe from the eye to above the ear to the base of the hindlimb. Lower flanks with a few obscure brown spots and streaks. Lips whitish, with the labials narrowly edged with pale brown. White below, with some obscure, dark brown longitudinal streaks along the throat. Limbs above, pale brown with dark brown spots and streaks. Nasals separated. Prefrontals in contact. Four supraoculars. Ear-opening small, without anterior lobules. Adpressed limbs meet or overlap. Scales smooth in 26-32 rows at mid-body. 30 mm (snout-vent).

Distribution: Far northern Qld, WA and NT, to the coast and islands of the Gulf of Carpentaria and south to central Australia.

Habit: Poorly known. Specimens have been taken in the grassy edges of samphire swamps, among spinifex-covered stony ranges, on vegetated sand dunes and in well-grassed tropical woodlands.

Subspecies: *ornatus* (range excluding north coast and hinterland); *wotjulum* (tropical north coast and hinterland).

Genus ***Ophioscincus*** Peters, 1873

A genus of small, smooth-scaled, burrowing skinks with limbs either absent or styliform. The parietal shields are in contact behind the interparietal; the lower eyelid is movable and scaly; the nasals are undivided, and there are no supranasals. Scales of the snout covered by a thickened, milky epidermis. Oviparous. Most similar to the genus *Anomalopus*, from which it may be distinguished by lacking an ectopterygoid process (present in *Anomalopus*) and in possessing only five supralabials and three supraoculars (usually six supralabials in *Anomalopus* but, when only five are present there are only two supraoculars).

Key

TO THE SPECIES OF OPHIOSCINCUS

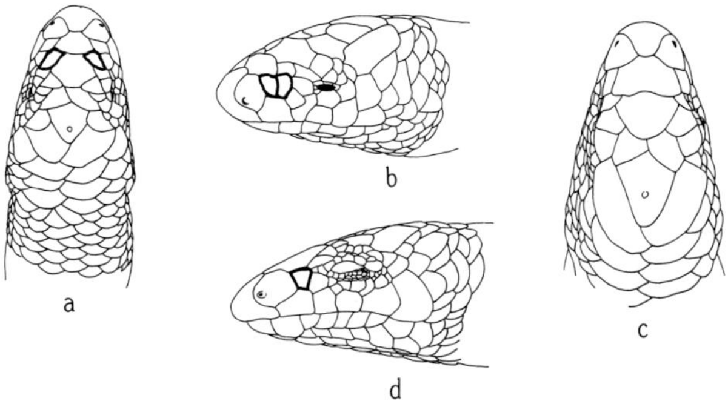

1 Limbs absent **2**
Limbs present .... ***truncatus***

2 Prefrontals present (a); two loreals (b); 20-24 mid-body scale rows .... ***ophioscincus***
Prefrontals absent (c); a single loreal (d); 18-19 mid-body scale rows .... ***cooloolensis***

Ophioscincus ophioscincus Bulburin, Qld

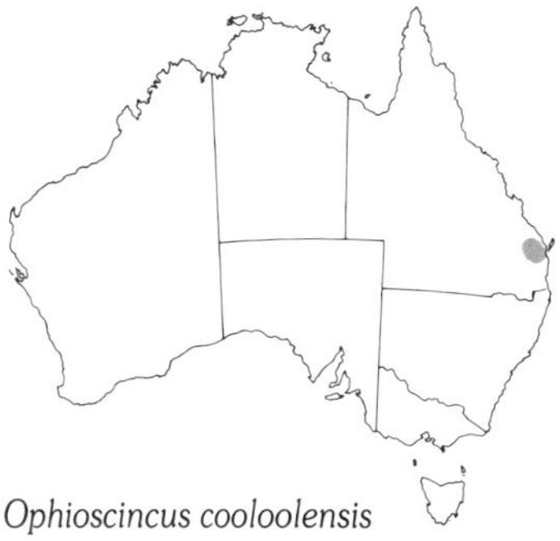

Ophioscincus cooloolensis

Ophioscincus ophioscincus

M. PETERSON

Ophioscincus truncatus Lamington National Park, Qld

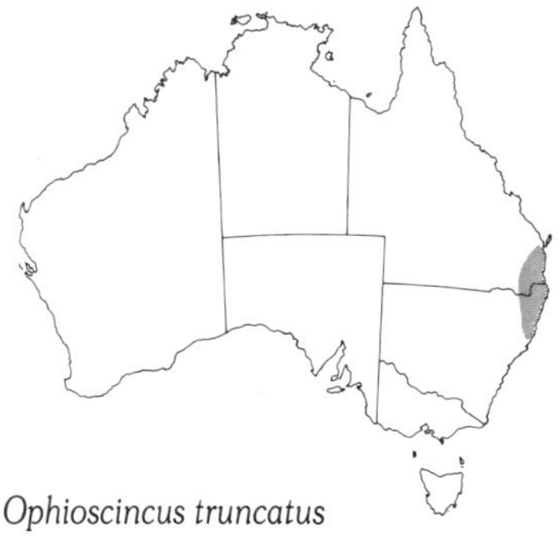

Ophioscincus truncatus

Ophioscincus cooloolensis Greer and Cogger, 1985

Description: Medium to pale brown above, each scale with a dark brown spot, the spots aligned longitudinally to form dark striations along the body and tail. A broad, dark brown, lateral stripe which starts as heavy mottling on the head and neck and extends along the body and tail, where it joins a dark brown region at the end of the tail. Chin and throat spotted with dark brown. Remaining ventral surfaces whitish to pale brown or orange. Snout more or less rounded. Nasals separated. Prefrontals absent. A single loreal on each side. Two or three supraoculars. Postmental usually in contact with two infralabials (occasionally only one). Ear hidden, its position indicated by a depression. 18-19 mid-body scale rows. Limbs entirely absent. Preanals moderately enlarged. 70 mm (snout-vent).
Distribution: Fraser Island and the adjacent

mainland, Qld.
Habit: A burrowing species recorded from wallum and rainforest.

Ophioscincus ophioscincus
(Boulenger, 1887)

Description: Pale fawn to rich brown above, each scale in the four or six dorsal rows with a blackish dot at its base, resulting in four or six longitudinal rows of dots from the back of the head almost to the end of the tail. Each scale also minutely flecked with dark brown. A broad, dark brown or blackish, lateral stripe from behind the ear (though sometimes continuing forward to the snout) to the end of the tail. Ventral surface lemon or orange (except for the throat which may be dotted with dark brown, or entirely black, and the black posterior portion of the tail). Snout moderate, more or less rounded. Nasals separated. Prefrontals moderate, separated. Two loreals on each side. Three supraoculars, scarcely differentiated from supraciliaries. Postmental in contact with a single infralabial on each side. Ear hidden, its position indicated by a depression. 22-24 mid-body scale rows. Limbs entirely absent. Preanals moderately enlarged. 80 mm (snout-vent). Tail ending bluntly.
Distribution: Coast and adjacent ranges and slopes of central-eastern and south-eastern Qld.
Habit: A burrowing lizard usually found in moist soil under logs, rocks, etc. in rainforest and adjoining wet sclerophyll forest.

Ophioscincus truncatus (Peters, 1876)

Description: Grey-brown or brown above, the individual scales flecked or dotted with dark brown; in some specimens the dark brown pigment is concentrated in a small spot in each scale which results in a series of longitudinal lines of dots along the dorsum. Upper flanks as for dorsum, lower flanks paler, merging with the cream or yellow ventral surface. Throat brown or spotted with brown. End of tail entirely blackish. Snout more or less rounded. Nasals separated. Prefrontals small and widely separated. A single loreal on each side. Postmental in contact with two infralabials on each side. Ear-opening hidden, its position indicated by a depression. 18-20 mid-body scale rows. Limbs extremely short, both fore- and hindlimbs stylar or with a single digit. Preanals moderately enlarged. 60 mm (snout-vent).
Distribution: Extreme south-eastern Qld and adjacent regions of NSW.
Habit: A burrowing species found in moist soil under logs and stones in pockets of moist scrub in dry sclerophyll forest, coastal heathland, rainforest and associated wet sclerophyll forests.
Subspecies: *truncatus* (islands of Moreton Bay); *monswilsonensis* (McPherson Ranges).

Genus ***Proablepharus*** Fuhn, 1969

A poorly known genus of small, terrestrial and cryptozoic lizards whose affinities are uncertain. Limbs moderate to short, not meeting when adpressed; limbs pentadactyle; ear-opening very small; supranasals absent and nasals undivided; prefrontals large, in contact or separated; frontoparietals fused or paired, distinct from the interparietal; lower eyelid immovable, partially fused to the upper eyelid to form a permanent spectacle.

Confined to northern and western Australia.

Key

TO THE SPECIES OF PROABLEPHARUS

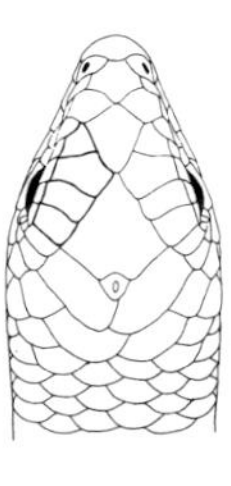
a

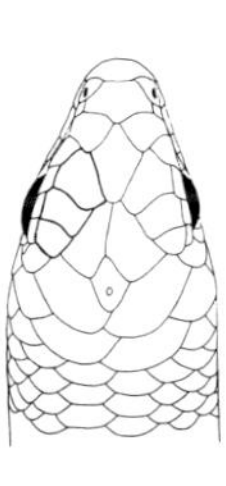
b

1 Four supraoculars (a) **2**
Three supraoculars (b) .... ***tenuis***
2 Frontoparietals paired (c) .... ***reginae***
Frontoparietals fused to form a single shield (d) ***kinghorni***

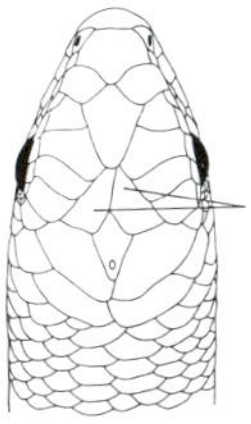

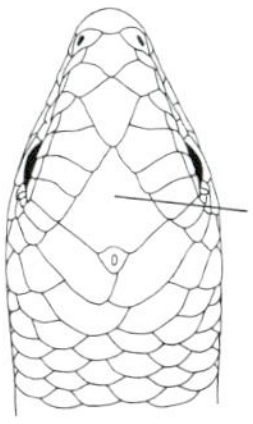

Proablepharus kinghorni Brunette Downs, NT

Proablepharus kinghorni (Copland, 1947)

Description: Usually a series of narrow, white, longitudinal stripes running through the centre of each dorsal and lateral scale row and alternating with brown, the brown stripes more or less equal in width to the pale ones. The lowest distinguishable stripe is a mid-lateral one from the axilla to the groin. Whitish below. Nasals separated. Prefrontals separated. Frontoparietals fused to form a single shield. Four supraoculars. Ear-opening small, without anterior lobules. Adpressed limbs fail to meet. Scales smooth, in 22 rows at mid-body. 45 mm (snout-vent).
Distribution: Known from Darling River, NSW, through inland Qld to eastern NT.

Habit: Cracked black soil tussock-grass plains, where it is lives in earth cracks and in or under fallen timber.

Proablepharus reginae (Glauert, 1960)

Description: Dark olive above, the base of each scale paler. The pale areas are largest on the flanks, where the scales appear to be spotted with white. Head, limbs and tail brown. Lips pale. A distinct white patch behind the eye. Ventral surfaces whitish. Nasals widely separated. Prefrontals large, separated. Frontoparietals paired, distinct from the interparietal.

Proablepharus reginae
Ormiston Gorge, NT

Proablepharus tenuis McArthur River, NT

Four supraoculars. Ear-opening very small, no larger than an adjacent scale. Scales smooth, in 28 rows at mid-body. 40 mm (snout-vent).
Distribution: Recorded from the type locality, Queen Victoria Spring, WA, to central and north-western Australia.
Habit: A tiny lizard usually found in leaf-litter or around the bases of fallen timber, etc., in wide variety of woodland and spinifex-dominated arid or desert habitats, especially in stony hills and ranges.

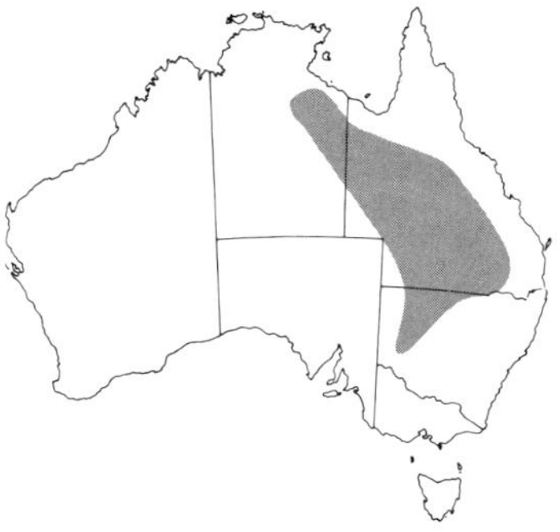

Proablepharus kinghorni

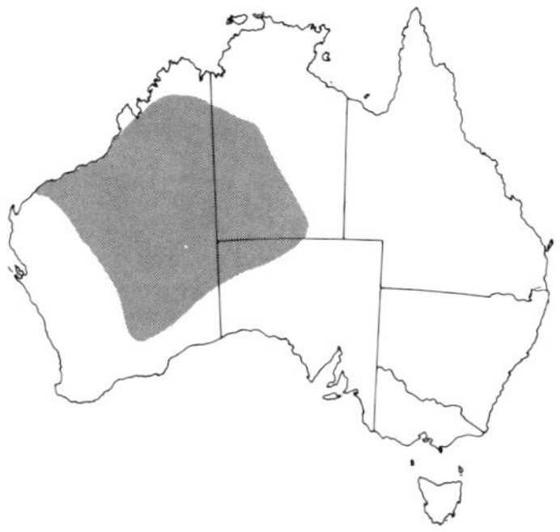

Proablepharus reginae

Proablepharus tenuis

Proablepharus tenuis (Broom, 1896)

Description: Dark brown above, more or less uniform, but a dark median area on each of the dorsal and lateral scales resulting in a series of faint, longitudinal striations. The latter are more pronounced on the flanks, resulting in an obscure, darker, lateral zone. More or less uniform white or cream below. Nasals widely separated. Prefrontals large, widely separated or almost touching. Frontoparietals paired, distinct from the interparietal. Three supraoculars. Ear-opening small, no larger than an adjacent scale. Scales smooth, in 22-24 rows at mid-body. 30 mm (snout-vent).
Distribution: Coast and hinterland of northern Australia, from northern Qld to western Kimberleys, WA.
Habit: A small, cryptozoic lizard usually found under leaf-litter, fallen timber or stones in dry sclerophyll forest or savannah woodland.

Genus ***Pseudemoia*** Fuhn, 1967

Usually included in the polyphyletic genus *Leiolopisma,* this is a group of small to moderate, active, mostly diurnal, smooth-scaled lizards characterised by: moderate to well developed limbs which meet or overlap when adpressed, or which fail to meet by no more than one or two scale lengths; limbs pentadactyle; ear-opening prominent; supranasals present or absent; parietal shields in contact behind the interparietal; lower eyelids movable, with a transparent disc. The generic name *Pseudemoia* has sometimes been more restrictively applied to one or two members of this genus.

This genus is itself polyphyletic, with recent research by Hutchinson and Donnellan showing that several genera are represented under this name. Occurs extra-limitally in New Zealand and in some south-western Pacific islands. Otherwise confined to southern and eastern Australia and Tas.

Key

TO THE AUSTRALIAN SPECIES OF PSEUDEMOIA

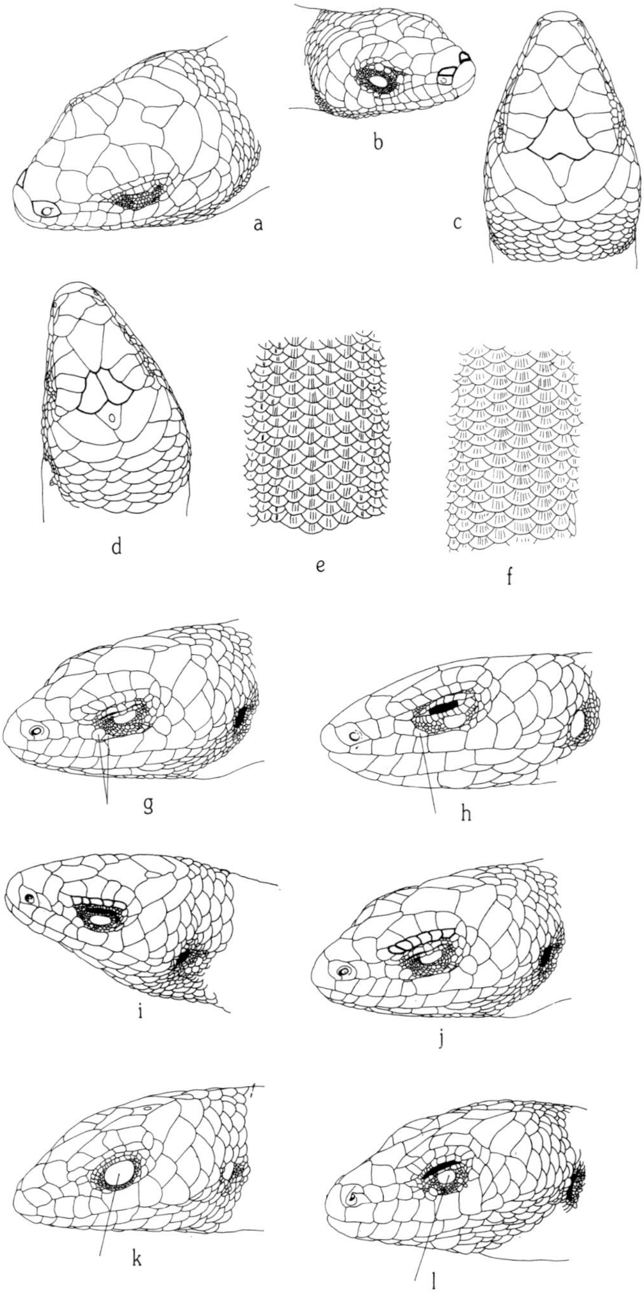

1 Supranasal scales absent (a) **2**
Supranasal scales present (b) **18**

2 Frontoparietal scales fused to form a single shield (c) ... **3**
Frontoparietal scales paired (d) **14**

3 Fewer than 45 rows of scales at mid-body **4**
45 or more rows of scales at mid-body .... ***ocellata***

4 At least some indication of one or more pale longitudinal stripes **5**
Usually no indication of pale longitudinal stripes **10**

5 Pale mid-lateral stripe obscure or absent **6**
A conspicuous, pale, mid-lateral stripe **7**

6 Supraciliaries 5-7, but usually 6 or more; south-eastern Australia .... ***metallica***
Supraciliaries 5-7, but usually 5; south-western Australia .... ***trilineata***

7 Scales in 28 or more rows at mid-body; if fewer than 31 rows, usually 6 or more supraciliaries **8**
Scales in 30 or fewer rows at mid-body; usually 5 supraciliaries .... ***duperreyi***

8 Back without scattered white dots or flecks **9**
Back usually with scattered white dots or flecks .... ***pretiosa***

9 Usually two presubocular scales (g); usually more than 30 mid-body scale rows .... ***microlepidota***
One presubocular scale (h); usually fewer than 32 mid-body scale rows .... ***orocrypta***

10 Dark brown or black upper lateral stripe present **11**
Dark brown or black upper lateral stripe absent **13**

11 Paravertebral and adjacent dorsal scales subequal (e) **12**
Paravertebral scales transversely enlarged, wider than adjacent dorsal scales (f) .... ***metallica***

12 24-32 mid-body scale rows; 5 supraciliaries (i) .... ***platynota***
30-44 mid-body scale rows; 6-7 supraciliaries (j) .... ***microlepidota***

13 More than 35 mid-body scale rows .... ***greeni***
Fewer than 30 mid-body scale rows .... ***zia***

14 Transparent disc in lower eyelid large, almost filling the eyelid (k) **5**
Transparent disc in lower eyelid much smaller than the eyelid (l) **16**

15 Fewer than 25 subdigital lamellae; usually a well-defined pale mid-lateral stripe **17**
More than 25 subdigital lamellae; no continuous mid-lateral stripe, but a series of prominent, elongate pale blotches along the mid-lateral line .... ***jigurru***

16 Fewer than 30 mid-body scale rows .... ***coventryi***
More than 30 mid-body scale rows .... ***lichenigera***

17 Pale dorso-lateral stripe on fourth, or third and fourth, scale row from the mid-line of the back .... ***entrecasteauxii***
Pale dorso-lateral stripe on third scale row from the mid-line of the back .... ***rawlinsoni***

18 Frontoparietals paired (d) **19**
Frontoparietals fused to form a single shield (e) .... ***palfreymani***

19 Fewer than 30 mid-body scale rows .... ***baudini***
More than 35 mid-body scale rows .... ***spenceri***

Pseudemoia baudini (Greer, 1982)

Description: Olive brown above, with a dark-edged, pale, dorso-lateral stripe from the neck to the tail and another dark-edged, pale, mid-lateral stripe commencing on the labials, and extending back through the ear (where it may be slightly disrupted) and over the forearm to the groin. Dorsal scales dark edged, giving the appearance of a series a fine, dark, longitudinal lines on the back. Ventral surfaces whitish. 26 mid-body scale rows, the scales with 3 or 4 striations or low keels. Suture between rostral and frontonasal much narrower than the frontal. Supraciliaries 6-7. Frontoparietals paired. Supranasals present. Transparent disc of lower eyelid large, almost as large as the eye. Subdigital lamellae smooth, 22-23 under the fourth toe. 50 mm (snout-vent), the tail about 150% of snout-vent length. Adpressed limbs meeting or overlapping.
Distribution: Known only from the region near Point Culver on the Great Australian Bight, WA.
Habit: The only known specimen was 'found on the ground in an open sandy area within a few feet of a vegetated dune immediately behind the beach' (Greer).

Pseudemoia coventryi (Rawlinson, 1975)

Description: A somewhat nondescript metallic-brown above, with occasional darker flecks, the individual scales often with 3 or 4 fine, black longitudinal streaks; a broad, black upper lateral band from snout to base of tail, usually bordered above by a narrow (half-scale wide) pale, bronzy, dorso-lateral stripe; lower lateral zone flecked with dark brown and pale creamy yellow; ventral surfaces creamy-grey, with scattered black spots and flecks; palms and soles black. 25-27 faintly keeled mid-body scale rows. Suture between the rostral and the frontonasal narrower than the frontal. Supraciliaries 6-7. Frontoparietals paired. A large, transparent disc in the lower eyelid, about as large as the ear-opening. Subdigital lamellae rough, 19-23 under the fourth toe. 50 mm (snout-vent).
Distribution: Highlands of south-eastern Australia, from the Blue Mountains to the Grampians.
Habit: Usually associated with decaying stumps and logs in wet and dry sclerophyll forests. Viviparous

Pseudemoia duperreyi (Gray, 1838)

Description: Similar in most respects to *Pseudemoia trilineata*, from which it differs in having the colour pattern more conspicuous, with sharply contrasting stripes on back or flanks, and more paravertebral scale rows (54-61 in *trilineata*, 57-66 in *duperreyi*). Throat usually flushed with orange-pink.
Distribution: South-eastern Australia, from south-eastern SA, through southern Vic to the highlands of southern NSW. Also found in Tas and the islands of Bass Strait

Pseudemoia coventryi Mt St Leonard, Vic

Pseudemoia baudini

Habit: Found on the ground in open habitats such as woodland, shrubland or heath; may climb low grass tussocks or shrubs to bask. Oviparous, with clutches of 3-8 eggs (Greer, Rawlinson).

Pseudemoia coventryi

Pseudemoia duperreyi

Pseudemoia entrecasteauxii

Pseudemoia greeni

Pseudemoia lichenigera

Pseudemoia jigurru

Pseudemoia entrecasteauxii

(Duméril and Bibron, 1839)

Description: Grey-brown, olive, or brown above, usually with a narrow, dark brown, vertebral stripe from the nape to the base of the tail. A narrow, white or cream, dorso-lateral stripe from the temporal region to the base of the tail, bordered above by a broader, dark brown stripe and below by a broad dark brown zone, which usually encloses a faint, median, paler stripe. Labials whitish, continuing as a pale stripe, usually dark-edged above, to above the ear, and more or less continuous with a white mid-lateral stripe that extends to the groin. Silvery-grey, olive or whitish below. Juveniles with a very conspicuous pattern, often including additional, narrow dark dorsal lines; older adults often with entire pattern obscure and just a few pale dots on the flanks. 28-34 mid-body scale rows, the scales smooth or with faint multiple striations. Suture between the rostral and frontonasal much narrower than the frontal. Supraciliaries 5-7. Frontoparietals paired. Transparent disc of lower eyelid large, almost as large as the eye. Subdigital lamellae smooth, 16-22 under the fourth toe. 50 mm (snout-vent), the tail about 150% of snout-vent length. Adpressed limbs usually meeting or overlapping.
Distribution: South-eastern SA, Vic and the highlands of NSW; Tas and the islands of Bass Strait.
Habit: Found in a variety of forest and grassland habitats throughout its range; usually seen on or around fallen timber, or foraging in leaf-litter. Viviparous.

Pseudemoia greeni (Rawlinson, 1975)

Description: Black above, many individual scales with a grey-green central spot or patch. Grey-green below. 40-44 faintly keeled mid-body scale rows. Suture between rostral and frontonasal much narrower than the frontal. Supraciliaries 7-8. Frontoparietals fused. A conspicuous transparent disc in the lower eyelid. Subdigital lamellae smooth, 20-25 under the fourth toe. 60 mm (snout-vent).
Distribution: Alpine regions of Tasmania.
Habit: Rawlinson reports that this species is 'restricted to the rocky banks of streams and swamps' above the tree line.

M. PETERSON

Pseudemoia duperreyi Oberon, NSW

Pseudemoia entrecasteauxii Snowy Mountains, NSW

Pseudemoia greeni Ben Lomond National Park, Tas

R. SADLIER

Pseudemoia jigurru Mt Bartle Frere, Qld

Pseudemoia jigurru (Covacevich, 1984)

Description: Rich metallic brown above, with scattered, dark brown, flecks and streaks on the head; back and tail with numerous scattered, pale brown and dark brown flecks and spots, the dark spots tending to be aligned longitudinally and the pale spots transversely, except on the tail where the dark spots predominate, and are arranged transversely; a narrow blackish streak from snout to eye, continued behind the eye as a broad lateral stripe which extends to the hindlimb, and which encloses a series of pale spots or blotches along its lower half; ventral surfaces metallic-cream or pale green. 30 mid-body scale rows, the scales with slight striations. Suture between the rostral and frontonasal about as wide as frontal. Supraciliaries 7. Frontoparietals paired. Transparent disc of lower eyelid large. Subdigital lamellae 26. 70 mm (snout-vent), the tail nearly twice as long as snout-vent. Adpressed limbs overlapping.

Distribution: Known only from the top of Mount Bartle Frere, north-eastern Qld.
Habit: Found ' amongst granite boulders which occur as large 'fields' surrounded by dense rainforest near the mountain summit' (Covacevich).

Pseudemoia lichenigera
(O'Shaughnessy, 1874)

Description: Rich metallic-bronze or olive above, the dorsum sometimes immaculate, but more often with numerous small brown flecks or streaks aligned longitudinally. Head above with or without brown spots. Usually a pale golden dorso-lateral stripe from above the eye to the base of the tail, bordered below by a broad, darker brown, upper lateral zone, usually enclosing some irregular pale spots and darker brown flecks. Lower flanks pale brown with darker flecks,

Pseudemoia lichenigera Lord Howe Island

gradually merging with the white or lemon-yellow chest and abdomen. Throat white or grey, usually with some dark greyish-brown flecks. Limbs above variegated with pale and dark brown. Reproduced tail a rich reddish-brown. 36-46 mid-body scale rows, the scales smooth. Suture between the rostral and frontonasal much narrower than the frontal. Supraciliaries seven. Frontoparietals paired. Transparent disc of lower eyelid smaller than the eye. Subdigital lamellae smooth, 15-21 lamellae under the fourth toe. 80 mm (snout-vent), the tail about 100% of snout-vent length. Adpressed limbs fail to meet.
Distribution: Lord Howe Island and its outliers, including Balls Pyramid, Norfolk Island.
Habit: Originally found under rocks, boulders and fallen timber on most parts of Lord Howe Island, it is now uncommon on the main island. Still abundant on the offshore islands, where it is usually found under stones on grassy slopes. Apparently largely diurnal in winter, specimens having been seen rolling seabird eggs over rocks until they break, then feeding on the contents. In summer, large numbers of lizards move about the littoral and supra-littoral zones at night, feeding on amphipods, insects and other small organisms. With similar habits, the distinctive Norfolk Island population now appears to be restricted to Philip Island, a large degraded satellite island several kilometres off the main island.

Pseudemoia metallica (O'Shaughnessy, 1874)

Description: A variable species subject to marked geographic variation in colour pattern. Brown above, sometimes immaculate, but more often with a series of dark brown and pale brown flecks and streaks, or with a series of narrow, dark brown longitudinal stripes (a vertebral and two paravertebral, the latter sometimes broken up into a series of spots, on each side). A dark brown, upper lateral zone extending from the eye to the base of the tail, sometimes pale-centred or with a series of dark and pale brown flecks. This zone may be bordered above by a narrow pale dorso-lateral streak. In some specimens there is a distinct or indefinite whitish mid-lateral streak from

Pseudemoia metallica Mt St Leonard, Vic

Pseudemoia ocellata Lake St Clair, Tas

the ear to the groin. Lower flanks and neck flecked with dark brown. Whitish below, often with some dark flecks on throat, chest and tail. 24-28 mid-body scale rows, the scales smooth or with faint multiple keels. Suture between the rostral and frontonasal much narrower than the frontal. Supraciliaries 5-7. Frontoparietals fused to form a single shield. Transparent disc of lower eyelid moderate, much smaller than the eye. Subdigital lamellae smooth, 16-22 under the fourth toe. 50 mm (snout-vent), the tail about 150% of snout-vent length. Adpressed limbs meeting or slightly overlapping.

Distribution: Southern Vic, islands of Bass Strait and Tas.

Habit: Found in a wide variety of habitats, from coastal dunes and heaths to dry and wet sclerophyll forests and montane woodlands. Viviparous.

Pseudemoia metallica

Pseudemoia microlepidota

Pseudemoia ocellata

Pseudemoia orocrypta

Pseudemoia palfreymani

Pseudemoia platynota

Pseudemoia pretiosa

Pseudemoia microlepidota

(O'Shaughnessy, 1874)

Description: Grey, olive-brown or brown above, sometimes with a conspicuous, dark brown, vertebral stripe from the nape to the base of the tail, and narrow dark paravertebral stripes on either side. Remainder of the dorsum flecked and speckled with dark brown, but never with white. A broad, dark brown, upper lateral zone commencing as a narrow stripe on the canthus and extending to the base of the tail. This zone may be uniform, but more often contains scattered, small, whitish spots and is usually bordered above, at least anteriorly, by a narrow white or cream dorso-lateral stripe. Lower flanks and neck mottled with dark brown, and rarely a prominent white mid-lateral stripe between axilla and groin. Limbs above with small white spots and brown mottling. Upper labials sometimes spotted brown. Ventral surfaces whitish, never flushed with red. 30-44 mid-body scale rows, the scales smooth or with faint striations or multiple keels. Suture between the rostral and frontonasal much narrower than the frontal. Supraciliaries 7-9. Frontoparietals fused to form a single shield. Transparent disc of lower eyelid much smaller than the eye. Subdigital lamellae smooth, 18-25 under the fourth toe. 50 mm (snout-vent), the tail about 130% of snout-vent length. Adpressed limbs meeting or overlapping.
Distribution: Highlands of central and southern Tas.
Habit: Found only in alpine areas.

Pseudemoia ocellata (Gray, 1845)

Ocellated Skink

Description: Black to dark bronzy-brown above, usually paler on head, flanks, limbs and tail. Head spotted and variegated with black or brown. Dorsal pattern consisting of small cream or yellow spots aligned longitudinally in the mid-dorsal region. A dorso-lateral series of somewhat larger spots from above the eye to the base of the tail; sides of neck and flanks with numerous pale, dark-edged spots. An obscure, pale, streak from below the eye to the ear, often broken into a series of spots or variegations. Whitish or olive-grey below, sometimes with a few dark flecks or striations on the throat. Plantar surfaces sometimes dark brown. Marginal scales of eyelids brown or cream. Lips usually with a few brown spots. In some specimens the pale dorsal spots coalesce to form an indefinite, variegated pattern. 45-56 mid-body scale rows, the scales smooth or with faint striations. Suture between the rostral and the

frontonasal much narrower than the frontal. Supraciliaries 7-9. Frontoparietals fused to form a single shield. Transparent disc of lower eyelid much smaller than the eye. Subdigital lamellae smooth, 20-26 under the fourth toe. 60 mm (snout-vent), the tail about 120% of snout-vent length. Adpressed limbs overlapping.
Distribution: Tas and eastern Bass Strait islands.
Habit: A ground-dwelling, diurnal lizard found in lowland forests and heaths. Viviparous.

Pseudemoia orocrypta (Hutchinson, Schwaner and Medlock, 1988)

Description: Brown above, with a continuous, or broken, black mid-dorsal stripe, and scattered darker flecks, the dark lateral edges of the remaining dorsal scales often forming narrow, dark, longitudinal lines along the back; a pale, golden-brown, dorso-lateral stripe from above the eye to the base of the tail, bordered below by a broad, blackish upper lateral zone with a few paler flecks along its lower margin; a prominent white mid-lateral stripe from axilla to groin; lower flanks variegated and speckled blackish and whitish; a broken white or cream loreal/subocular stripe to the ear. Ventral surfaces white, although specimens with the venter flushed with red have been recorded. 28-32 mid-body scale rows, the scales smooth, or with faint striations. Suture between the rostral and the frontonasal much narrower than the frontal. Supraciliaries 6-7. Frontoparietals fused to form a single shield. Transparent disc of lower eyelid much smaller than the eye. Subdigital lamellae smooth, 20-24 under the fourth toe. 60 mm (snout-vent), the tail about 150% of snout-vent length. Adpressed limbs overlapping.
Distribution: Highlands of south-western Tas.
Habit: Recorded from alpine heaths and woodlands, where they were found basking on the lower branches of trees and shrubs.

Pseudemoia palfreymani Rawlinson, 1974

Description: Similar in most respects to *Pseudemoia spenceri* from which it differs in having the frontoparietals fused to form a single shield and in always having a small postnasal scale distinct from the nasal. Colour and pattern similar to that of *Pseudemoia spenceri*, except that the pale vertebral stripe is absent and the pale dorso-lateral stripe may also be absent. 75 mm (snout-vent), the tail about 120% of snout-vent length.
Distribution: Confined to Pedra Branca Rock, a small, wave-swept, rocky islet less than 60 m above sea level, off the southern coast of Tas.
Habit: Pedra Branca is devoid of vegetation other than a low samphire, the lizards living in burrows under rocks and in crevices, and basking on exposed rock surfaces. Rounsevell, Brothers and Holdsworth found that the preferred food is '. . . the flesh of dead Jack Mackeral (*Trachurus declivis*) which litter the seabird colony . . .' on the island. Viviparous.

Pseudemoia platynota (Peters, 1881)

Red-Throated Skink

Description: Similar in scalation and size to *Pseudemoia trilineata*, but differing markedly in colour pattern. Pale silvery-grey to brown above, the outer edges of the dorsal scales sometimes with black

Pseudemoia palfreymani
Pedra Branca Island, Tas

Pseudemoia rawlinsoni

Pseudemoia spenceri

Pseudemoia trilineata

Pseudemoia platynota Adaminaby, NSW

G. SHEA

Pseudemoia pretiosa Chappell Island, Bass Strait

margins, producing longitudinal lines or a fine reticulum. Head bronze-brown. A broad, black, upper lateral stripe from the snout, through the eye, to the base of the tail, sometimes with a pale upper margin. Usually some blackish spots on posterior supralabials. Flanks silvery-grey, merging with white ventral surface. The throats of living males sometimes bright pinkish-red.
Distribution: Eastern Vic and the coast, ranges and western slopes of NSW.
Habit: A ground-dwelling diurnal lizard, usually seen foraging in leaf-litter and around fallen timber and rock crevices and exfoliating rock slabs in coastal and montane heaths, dry sclerophyll forests and woodlands. Oviparous.

Pseudemoia pretiosa (O'Shaughnessy, 1874)

Description: Grey, olive-brown or brown above, sometimes with a conspicuous, dark brown, vertebral stripe from the nape to the base of the tail. Remainder of the dorsum flecked and speckled with dark brown and (usually) whitish. A broad, dark brown, upper lateral zone commencing as a narrow stripe on the canthus, and extending to the base of the tail. This zone may be uniform, but more often contains scattered small, whitish spots and is usually bordered above, at least anteriorly, by a narrow white or cream dorso-lateral stripe. Lower flanks and neck mottled with dark brown, and usually a prominent, whitish,

Pseudemoia zia

Pseudemoia spenceri Mt Kosciusko, NSW

mid-lateral stripe from axilla to groin. Limbs above with small white spots and brown mottling. Upper labials sometimes spotted brown. Ventral surfaces whitish, often flushed with red; usually some fine, dark brown flecks on the throat tending to form longitudinal lines. 33-40 mid-body scale rows, the scales smooth or with faint striations or multiple keels. Suture between the rostral and frontonasal much narrower than the frontal. Supraciliaries 7-9. Frontoparietals fused to form a single shield. Transparent disc of lower eyelid much smaller than the eye. Subdigital lamellae smooth, 18-24 under the fourth toe. 50 mm (snout-vent), the tail about 130% of snout-vent length. Adpressed limbs meeting or overlapping.
Distribution: Tas and the islands of Bass Strait.
Habit: Wet and dry sclerophyll forests and montane woodlands.

Pseudemoia rawlinsoni
(Hutchinson and Donnellan, 1988)

Description: Grey-brown, olive, or brown above, with a narrow, dark brown vertebral stripe from the nape to the base of the tail. A narrow, white or cream, dorso-lateral stripe from the temporal region to the base of the tail, bordered above by a broader dark brown stripe and below by a broad, dark brown zone, which usually encloses a faint, median, paler stripe. Labials whitish, continuing as a pale stripe, usually dark-edged above, to above the ear, then continuing below and behind the ear as a prominent white mid-lateral stripe. Silvery-grey or whitish below. 23-30 mid-body scale rows, the scales weakly to moderately tricarinate. Suture between the rostral and frontonasal much narrower than the frontal. Supraciliaries 5-8. Frontoparietals paired. Transparent disc of lower eyelid large, almost as large as the eye. Subdigital lamellae smooth, 17-23 under the fourth toe. 50 mm (snout-vent), the tail about 170% of snout-vent length. Adpressed limbs usually meeting or overlapping.
Distribution: Currently known only from a range of alpine and lowland localities in south-eastern continental Australia and from Cape Barren Island in Bass Strait.
Habit: Reported to be confined to humid microhabitats such as marshlands and the margins of creeks, swamps and lakes. Livebearing, producing 4-8 young.

Pseudemoia spenceri (Lucas and Frost, 1894)

Description: Dark brown to black above, the head variegated and spotted with pale brown or bronze. Usually a pale, olive-brown, vertebral stripe, with irregular margins and a paravertebral series of pale spots. A conspicuous, pale silver or golden, dorso-lateral stripe from the temple to the base of the tail. Below this is a broad, blackish upper lateral zone from the snout to the base of the tail, enclosing tiny, scattered pale spots. Usually a pale midlateral stripe from ear to groin, sometimes continued forward to below the eye. Supralabials barred or spotted with brown. Lower flanks blackish with scattered pale flecks. Ventral surface whitish. 37-48 mid-body scale rows, the dorsal and lateral scales smooth or very faintly keeled, with 2-4 keels per scale. Supralabials 8-11, usually 9. Ear-opening small but conspicuous, with 2-3 slightly enlarged anterior lobules. Frontoparietals paired. A small postnasal scale sometimes distinct

Pseudemoia trilineata Albany, WA

Pseudemoia zia Dorrigo National Park, NSW

from the nasal. Subdigital lamellae 20-28, all smooth and undivided. 55 mm (snout-vent), the tail about 120% of snout-vent length.
Distribution: Highlands of south-eastern Australia, with peripheral or outlying populations on the Blue Mountains, west of Sydney, NSW, and in the Gisborne region and Otway Ranges of Vic.
Habit: '...restricted to dead trees or rocky outcrops in montane, wet sclerophyll forests and rocky outcrops in subalpine woodlands' (Rawlinson). Diurnal, these lizards are usually seen basking on trees and bare rock faces, even at very low ambient temperatures. Produce 1-3 live young.

Pseudemoia trilineata

(Gray, 1838)

Description: Colour and pattern similar to *Pseudemoia entrecasteauxii,* except that the broad upper lateral zone tends to be dark-centred rather

than pale-centred. Often some dark brown spots and streaks on the head. 26-30 mid-body scale rows, the scales smooth or faintly striated. Suture between the rostral and frontonasal much narrower than the frontal. Supraciliaries 5-7. Frontoparietals fused to form a single shield. Transparent disc of lower eyelid much smaller than the eye. Subdigital lamellae smooth, 18-24 under the fourth toe. 60 mm (snout-vent), the tail about 150% of snout-vent length. Adpressed limbs usually fail to meet.
Distribution: Southwestern WA, with an apparently disjunct population in Eyre Peninsula, SA.
Habit: Moist forest and wetland habitats. Oviparous.

Pseudemoia zia (Ingram and Ehmann, 1981)

Description: Brownish above, flecked with black and pale brown; a pale brown, dorso-lateral stripe from head to base of tail, bordered below by a blackish upper lateral zone which commences as a black stripe from the snout, through the eye and temporal region; this dark upper lateral zone merges into a paler lower lateral zone which is flecked with black. A black, vertical, mid-rostral bar. Ventral surfaces whitish, the area from chest to vent bright yellow in life and with black spotting on the throat. End of tail rich reddish-brown. Scales smooth, in 22-26 rows at mid-body, the mid-dorsals each with 3-5 striations. Suture between rostral and frontonasal much wider than the frontal. Supraciliaries 6-9, usually 7-8. Frontoparietals paired. Transparent disc of lower eyelid moderate, but smaller than eye. Subdigital lamellae rough, undivided, 14-17 under the fourth toe. 50 mm (snout-vent), the tail about 140% of snout-vent length. Adpressed limbs overlap.
Distribution: Rainforests of north-eastern NSW and south-eastern Qld.
Habit: Recorded from '...moist areas in rainforests, including antarctic beech *(Nothofagus moorei)* forests.' (Ingram and Ehmann). Oviparous.

Genus *Saiphos* Gray, 1831

As here recognised, a monotypic genus whose relationships are obscure, having been placed in a variety of genera and associated with a variety of other species in recent years. Appears to be closely allied to those members of the genus *Hemiergis* which have

Saiphos equalis Pearl Beach, NSW

been sometimes placed together in the New Caledonian genus *Anotis*. Limbs very short, widely separated when adpressed; limbs tridactyle; ear-opening hidden, its presence indicated by a depression; supranasals absent and nasals undivided; prefrontals absent, although the enlarged first supraciliary is sometimes regarded as a small prefrontal; parietal shields in contact behind the interparietal; frontoparietals paired, distinct from the interparietal; lower eyelid movable, scaly. South-eastern Australia.

Saiphos equalis (Gray, 1825)

Description: Brown above, usually with some minute, dark brown dots tending to form longitudinal series along the body and tail. Sides of face, neck, body and tail dark brown to black, contrasting sharply with the paler dorsal surface. Usually some paler flecks on sides of face and on lower flanks, often forming longitudinal series on the lower neck. Chin shields with pale brown margins, usually some additional brown flecks on the throat. Occasionally the entire throat blackish. Remainder of ventral surface pale yellow to bright yellowish-orange. 18-20 mid-body scale rows. Four supraoculars. Postmental in contact with two infralabials on each side. A series of suboculars between labials and eye. Six supralabials. Limbs tridactyle, the digits very short and subequal, the hindlimb about 10% of snout-vent length. Other characters as for genus. 70 mm (snout-vent).

Saiphos equalis

Distribution: Coast and adjacent ranges of NSW and far south-eastern Qld.

Habit: A burrowing lizard usually found under rocks, logs and other ground cover in heathland, wet and dry sclerophyll forests and rainforest. Abundant, large numbers may be taken from a single compost heap or garden plot. Produces large eggs with advanced embryos which hatch within a week or two of being laid.

Genus *Saproscincus* Wells and Wellington, 1984

A group of small, diurnal or crepuscular lizards found primarily in moist forest habitats in eastern Australia. Most closely related to the genus *Lampropholis,* from which it may be distinguished by its paired frontoparietal scales (fused in *Lampropholis*) and six supralabials, the fourth usually subocular (seven supralabials, the fifth subocular in *Lampropholis*). A characteristic pale rust-coloured Y-shaped mark over the rump. All species are believed to be oviparous.

Key

TO THE SPECIES OF SAPROSCINCUS

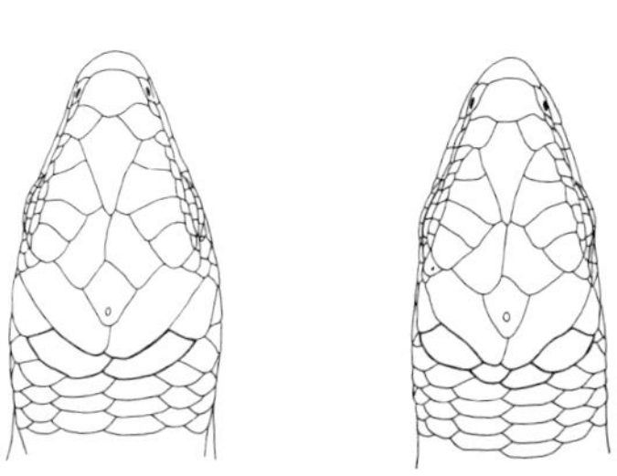

a b

1 Forelimbs pentadactyle **2**
Forelimbs tretadactyle .... ***tetradactylus***

2 Usually only 2 nuchals contacting parietals (a)................. **3**
Usually more than 2 nuchals contacting parietals (b)....... **4**

3 Dorsal pattern relatively uniform; a dark-edged white or cream streak below and behind the eye, sometimes extending to ear-opening; a pale orange or red dorso-lateral band on each side begins over rump and extends on to the tail .... ***mustelinus***

Dorsal pattern variegated; no dark-edged white streak below and behind the eye; usually no dorso-lateral band extending from above hindlimbs on to tail; limbs strongly overlapping when adpressed .... ***challengeri***

4 Snout pointed (c); canthus rostralis very concave; no indication of a black stripe from nostril to flank.................. .... ***czechurai***

Snout blunt (d); canthus rostralis not or but slightly concave; usually some indication of a black stripe from nostril to flank .... ***basiliscus***

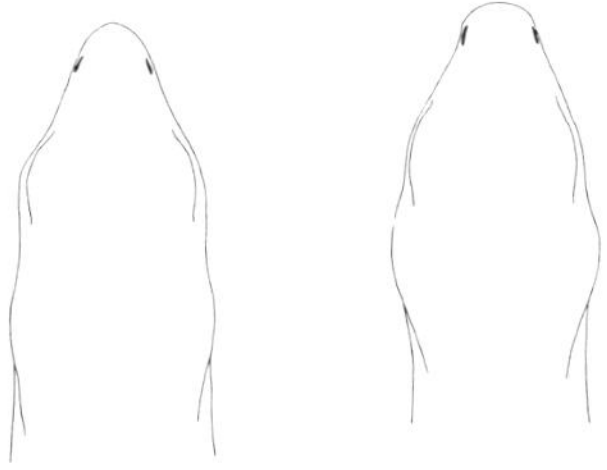

c d

Saproscincus basiliscus (Ingram and Rawlinson, 1981)

Description: Pale brown to deep reddish-brown above and on the upper flanks, with or without blackish and paler brown flecks and spots; often a blackish stripe from nostril, through eye to upper flank a short distance behind forelimb, and sometimes an obscure, dark-edged, pale dorso-lateral stripe on each side; lower flanks paler brown. A distinctive dark-edged, pale spot at the posterior base of each hindlimb. Ventral surfaces creamy-yellow, often with scattered dark brown flecks and spots. Scales smooth, in 21-28 rows at mid-body, but the mid-dorsal scales with 2-4 striations. Suture between rostral and frontonasal narrower than the frontal. Supraciliaries 5-8, usually seven. Frontoparietals paired. Transparent disc of lower eyelid small, smaller than the eye. Subdigital lamellae with a central groove, 16-25 under the fourth toe. 40 mm (snout-vent), the tail about 150% of snout-vent length. Adpressed limbs overlap.

Distribution: Two apparently isolated populations; one ranges from near Cooktown to Townsville, Qld, the other in the Eungella-Proserpine district, Qld.

Habit: An inhabitant of ground litter in rainforest.

Saproscincus challengeri Brinerville, NSW

Saproscincus mustelinus Turramurra, NSW

Saproscincus challengeri (Boulenger, 1887)

Description: Grey-brown to rich ochrous-brown above, uniform or with numerous pale brown and dark brown scales forming either a variegated pattern, or in some specimens transversely aligned to form obscure cross-banding. A dark brown streak along the canthus continuing behind the eye and over the ear as a broad, dark, dorso-lateral zone, usually broken by pale blotches. Anteriorly this streak is often bordered above by a narrow, pale golden stripe. Flanks spotted and variegated with pale brown and dark brown. Lower lip finely spotted with brown. Ventral surface white or yellow, sometimes spotted and flecked with brown, the flecks often forming narrow, continuous, longitudinal lines. 24-28 mid-body scale rows. Suture between the rostral and the frontonasal about as broad as the frontal. Supraciliaries 6-8, usually seven. Frontoparietals paired. Transparent disc of lower eyelid much smaller than the eye. Subdigital lamellae smooth, mostly undivided, 20-28 under the fourth toe. 50 mm (snout-vent), the tail about 170% of snout-vent length. Limbs strongly overlapping when adpressed.
Distribution: Coast and ranges of eastern Australia from northern NSW to Cape York Peninsula, Qld.
Habit: A diurnal lizard usually found in rainforest or adjacent wet sclerophyll forests, where it forages among leaf-litter, fallen timber and other ground debris.

Saproscincus czechurai (Ingram and Rawlinson, 1981)

Description: Fawn to dark reddish-brown above and on the flanks, with scattered, blackish and paler brown or white flecks, spots and dashes which sometimes coalesce to form wavy, longitudinal lines on the back. Sides of head and neck jet black in breeding males. Sometimes an obscure, black-edged, pale dorso-lateral stripe. A distinctive, dark-edged, pale spot at the posterior base of each thigh. Ventral surfaces cream, irregularly flecked with brown. Scales smooth, in 22-24 rows at mid-body, but each mid-dorsal scale with 3-4 striations. Suture between the rostral and frontonasal about as wide as the frontal. Supraciliaries 6-8, usually seven. Frontoparietals paired. Transparent disc of lower eyelid small, much smaller than the eye. Subdigital lamellae with a central groove, 15-19 under the fourth toe. 40 mm (snout-vent), the tail about 120% of snout-vent length. Adpressed limbs generally overlap.
Distribution: Atherton Tablelands north nearly to Cooktown, Qld.
Habit: Found in ground litter in rainforest.

Saproscincus mustelinus
(O'Shaughnessy, 1874)
Weasel Skink

Description: Pale fawn to rich russet-brown above, usually with some scattered, paler brown scales and darker flecks on the dorsal surface. Sometimes a darker upper lateral zone is clearly delineated from the dorsum by a narrow line, but more often the dorsal colour merges with that on the flanks. Usually a short, narrow, pale streak edged above with dark brown from the hind corner of the eye. Often a series of dark brown streaks on the lower flanks results in a series of dark longitudinal lines which are continuous with a similar series of lines on the ventral surface. In some specimens these lines are confined to the throat and tail, or continue on to the chest and abdomen as

Saproscincus czechurai near Ravenshoe, Qld

Saproscincus tetradactylus near Kuranda, Qld

a series of isolated flecks. Usually a pale orange to reddish dorso-lateral streak commencing above the rump and converging with its opposite number on the base of the tail. The upper surface of the tail usually much paler and brighter than the back. Ventral surfaces white to bright lemon-yellow. 22-26 smooth mid-body scale rows. Suture between the rostral and the frontonasal about as broad as the frontal. Supraciliaries 6-8. Frontoparietals paired. Transparent disc of lower eyelid much smaller than eye. Subdigital lamellae smooth, 15-22 under the fourth toe. 45 mm (snout-vent), the tail about 200% of snout-vent length. Limbs not, or scarcely, overlapping when adpressed.
Distribution: Coast and ranges of NSW and eastern and southern Vic.
Habit: A diurnal inhabitant of leaf-litter in a variety of habitats ranging from coastal heathland to the wet and dry sclerophyll forests of the Great Dividing Range. Common in suburban gardens.

Saproscincus tetradactylus
(Greer and Kluge, 1980)

Description: Medium to dark brown above, usually with a few darker brown flecks or longitudinal dashes anteriorly, a dark brown W-shaped mark on the head, and a series of dark brown dashes forming an obscure dorso-lateral stripe; lips barred with whitish and dark brown; flanks usually darker brown than the dorsum, with scattered paler flecks. A distinctive, dark-edged white spot at the posterior base of each thigh. Ventral surfaces whitish, usually with a few, scattered, dark brown spots and usually flushed with lemon-yellow from the chest to the base of the tail in living adults. Scales smooth in 22-26 rows at mid-body. Suture between the rostral and frontonasal wider than the

Saproscincus basiliscus

Saproscincus challengeri

Saproscincus czechurai

Saproscincus mustelina

Saproscincus tetradactyla

frontal. Supraciliaries 7-8. Frontoparietals paired. Transparent disc of lower eyelid small, much smaller than the eye. A series of small subocular scales between the eye and the upper labials. Subdigital lamellae with a central groove, 15-18 under the fourth toe. Forelimbs with only four digits. 30 mm (snout-vent), the tail about 120% of snout-vent length. Adpressed limbs usually overlap.
Distribution: Coast and adjacent ranges of north-eastern Qld from about Townsville to Cairns.
Habit: An inhabitant of rainforest and its marginal, ecotonal areas.

Genus *Tiliqua* Gray, 1825

A group of large lizards, usually known as blue-tongued lizards, with relatively short, pentadactyle limbs and short tails. At least one species occurs in most parts of Australia. Anterior ear lobules usually present; scales smooth, subequal; no supranasals or divided nasal scales; a scaly, movable, lower eyelid; parietal scales not in contact behind the interparietal; third and fourth toes subequal, or the third toe slightly longer than the fourth; subdigital lamellae undivided; tail moderate, tapering, usually much shorter than the body. All species are viviparous (live-bearing) and primarily diurnal in habit.

Except for one species *(gigas),* which occurs from New Guinea west to Sumatra, all species are confined to Australia.

Key

TO THE AUSTRALIAN SPECIES OF TILIQUA

1 Anterior temporal scales more or less equal to others, not much longer than broad (a) **2**
Anterior temporal scales much larger than others, being much longer than broad (b) .... ***scincoides***

2 More than 32 mid-body scale rows.......... **3**
32 or fewer mid-body scale rows .... ***nigrolutea***

3 Body with distinct cross-bands; 2-4 rows of enlarged hexagonal scales between the interparietal and the smaller body scales on the neck (c) **4**
Body without cross-bands; at most a single row of enlarged scales between the interparietal and the smaller body scales on the neck (d) .... ***adelaidensis***

4 Up to six broad, dark cross-bands on the body .... ***occipitalis***
Nine or more narrow, irregular, brown cross-bands on the body .... ***multifasciata***

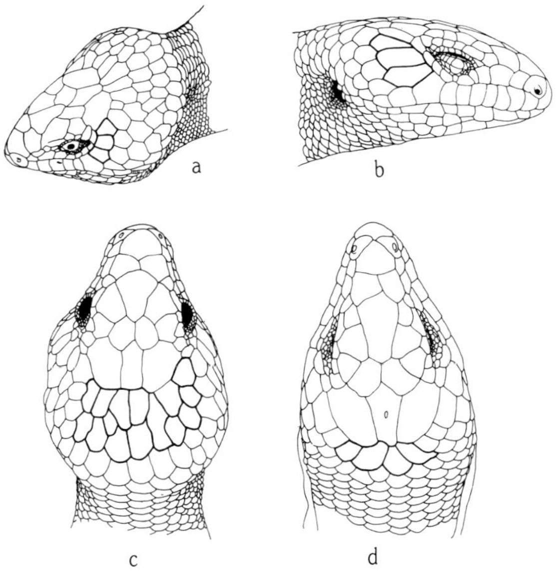

Tiliqua adelaidensis (Peters, 1863)

Description: Grey or grey-brown above, paler on the flanks. Dorsum, limbs and tail with scattered, darker spots and blotches mixed with paler scales, sometimes aligned to form irregular, narrow, transverse bars. Ventral scales margined with pale brown, otherwise white or cream. Nasals in contact or narrowly separated. Prefrontals in contact. Three supraoculars. Anterior temporals not noticeably elongated or differentiated from other temporals. One or two rows of enlarged hexagonal scales between the parietals and the normal nuchal scales. Post-narial groove present. Ear-opening conspicuous, with a single anterior lobule. 36-42 mid-body rows of smooth scales. Limbs short, the hindlimb about 20% of snout-vent length. Tail compressed, about 50-75% of snout-vent length. 90 mm (snout-vent).
Distribution: Not known. Most specimens from the general region of Adelaide, SA. Possibly extinct.

Tiliqua multifasciata Jasper Gorge, NT

Habit: Believed to be a terrestrial/cryptic inhabitant of '. . . compacting . . . soils carrying mallee scrub and chenopodiaceous understorey . . . and . . . a user of relatively short and hard-rimmed refuges in wood and stone . . .; a diet generalist . . . taking a wide range of mostly invertebrate and some plant material; not an active forager but rather an ambush predator.' (Ehmann)

Tiliqua multifasciata Sternfeld, 1919

Centralian Blue-Tongued Lizard

Description: Pale grey or grey-brown above, with a series of broad, pale orange-brown cross-bands on the neck, body and tail, which are much wider than the paler interspaces, but narrowest on the mid-dorsal region. A broad, wedge-shaped, black, temporal streak from the eye to above the ear. Upper and hind surfaces of hindlimb black, contrasting with the pale grey-brown anterior surface. Hindlimbs with obscure, orange-brown crossbands. White or cream below. Nasals narrowly separated. Prefrontals usually in contact, sometimes narrowly separated. Two or three supraoculars. Anterior temporals not elongated or differentiated from other temporals. Three or more rows of enlarged hexagonal scales between the parietals and the normal nuchal scales. Postnarial groove present. Ear-opening large and conspicuous, with several blunt, anterior lobules. 38-46 mid-body rows of smooth scales. Limbs short, the hindlimb about 20-25% of snout-vent length. Tail about 40-55% of snout-vent length. 300 mm (snout-vent).

Distribution: Northern half of WA, through northern SA and the NT to western Qld.

Habit: A ground-dwelling, diurnal lizard found in a variety of arid and semi-arid habitats including stony, *Triodia*-covered hills and sandy deserts. Produces up to about ten living young in a litter.

Tiliqua nigrolutea (Quoy and Gaimard, 1824)

Blotched Blue-Tongued Lizard

Description: Rich chocolate-brown to black above, with a series of pale cream to salmon-pink blotches, which may be irregular, aligned in longitudinal rows, or which may form obscure, transverse bands, especially on the tail; a variegated or reticulated pattern on flanks, chest and abdomen, becoming more obscure in older adults. Sometimes an obscure, dark brown to black temporal streak from above eye to above ear. Head paler than dorsum, usually finely peppered with black. Lips pale grey, sometimes peppered with black. Limbs above speckled with

Tiliqua multifasciata
McArthur River, NT

Tiliqua nigrolutea Oberon, NSW

black and white. Throat white, or with a few darker flecks. Nasals separated. Prefrontals separated or in narrow contact. Four supraoculars. Anterior temporals not elongated or differentiated from other temporals. Two or more rows of enlarged hexagonal scales between the parietals and the normal nuchal scales. Post-narial groove present. Ear-opening moderate, with one or two small anterior lobules. 28-32 mid body rows of smooth scales. Limbs short, the hindlimb about 20% of snout-vent length. Tail about 40-50% of snout-vent length. 250 mm (snout-vent).
Distribution: South-eastern SA, through southern Vic to the highlands of southern and central NSW. Eastern and northern Tas and the islands of Bass Strait.
Habit: A diurnal, ground-dwelling lizard with habits more or less similar to those of *Tiliqua scincoides,* though active at much lower temperatures. Found in wet and dry sclerophyll forests, montane woodlands and coastal heathlands.

Tiliqua occipitalis (Peters, 1863)
Western Blue-Tongued Lizard

Description: Top of head pale brown, body above pale yellowish-brown with a series of 4-6 broad, dark brown bands on the body. These dark bands sometimes enclose scattered, pale scales or transverse rows of pale scales, and are usually about twice as wide as the paler interspaces. Tail with a further 3-5 dark bands, usually darker than those on the body. A broad, blackish, temporal streak from the eye to above the ear. Flanks somewhat paler than the dorsum. Limbs brown above, speckled or streaked with dark brown; hindlimb sometimes black. Ventral surfaces whitish, the dark bands extending on to the ventral surface of the body, more or less complete under the tail. Nasals narrowly separated. Prefrontals usually in contact, sometimes narrowly separated. Two or three supraoculars. Anterior temporals not elongated or differentiated from other temporals.

Tiliqua occipitalis Round Hill, NSW

Tiliqua adelaidensis

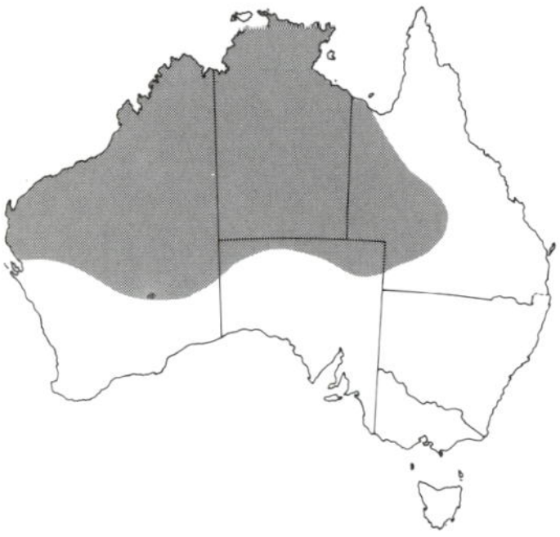

Tiliqua multifasciata

Tiliqua nigrolutea

Three or more rows of enlarged hexagonal scales between the parietals and the normal nuchal scales, Post-narial groove present. Ear-opening conspicuous, with several large, blunt, anterior lobules. 38-42 mid-body rows of smooth scales. Limbs short, the hindlimb about 20-25% of snout-vent length. Tail about 40-55% of snout-vent length. 300 mm (snout-vent).

Distribution: Drier parts of southern Australia, from the coast of WA to SA, to the far south of the NT, central-western NSW and north-western Vic.

Habit: Found in a variety of xeric habitats, often in close association with mixed mallee/*Triodia* communities. Otherwise similar to *Tiliqua multifasciata*.

Tiliqua scincoides (White, ex Shaw, 1790)

Eastern Blue-Tongued Lizard

Description: Pale silvery-grey to brown above, usually with a series of 7-9 irregular, darker brown, transverse cross-bands on the body and 7-10 on the tail, often displaced on the mid-line, oblique on the flanks. The scales on the paler interspaces usually with dark lateral edges resulting in a series of narrow, longitudinal, dark brown lines. The darker cross-bands often contain some small, white, dark-edged

Tiliqua scincoides Western Arnhem Land, NT

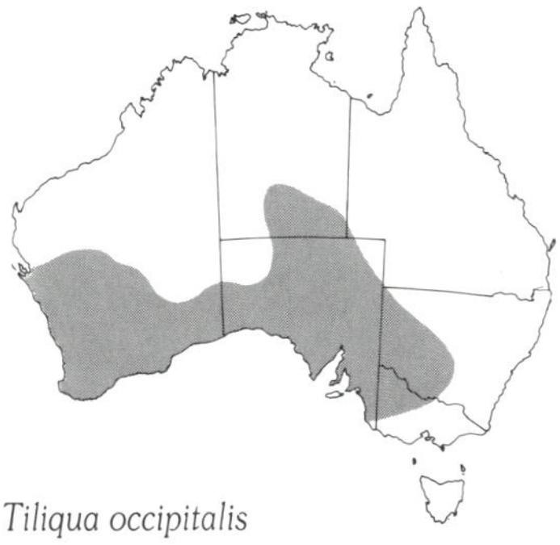

Tiliqua occipitalis

Tiliqua scincoides

Tiliqua scincoides McArthur River, NT

Tiliqua scincoides Turramurra, NSW

spots or paler brown centres. A broad, dark brown or black temporal streak from the eye to above the ear, sometimes continuous with a short dark bar on the side of the neck. Ventral surfaces white, grey or pale yellow. The northern race *(intermedia)* is distinct in colour and pattern from southern populations: rich brown above, usually with some obscure pale transverse markings on the dorsum and a series of large, blackish, oblique, dorso-lateral bars alternating with a series of large, cream to orange, lateral blotches; head pale brown, and dark temporal streak typical of southern populations may be obscure or absent. Nasals separated. Prefrontals in contact. Four supraoculars. Anterior temporals much larger than others, being much longer than broad. Two or more rows of enlarged hexagonal scales separating the parietals from the normal nuchal scales. Post-narial groove present. Ear-opening conspicuous, with 2-3 large anterior lobules. 34-40 mid-body rows of smooth scales. Limbs short, the hindlimb about 20% of snout-vent length. Tail about 50-75% of snout-vent length. 300 mm (snout-vent).

Distribution: South-eastern SA through Vic, eastern NSW and most of Qld to the northern NT and north-western WA.

Habit: Found in a wide variety of habitats from coastal heaths, forests and woodlands, to montane forests and the woodlands and grasslands of the less arid interior. A diurnal, ground-dwelling lizard, it feeds on a variety of insects, snails, carrion and wildflowers, native fruits and berries. Shelters at night in hollow logs, ground debris, etc. Live-bearing, it produces up to 25 young in a litter.

Subspecies: *scincoides* (southern and eastern Australia); *intermedia* (northern Australia).

Genus ***Trachydosaurus*** Gray, 1825

A monotypic genus closely allied to the Blue-tongued Lizards and whose single species is one of the most distinctive and abundant of Australian lizards, immediately recognisable by its short, rounded, depressed tail and grossly enlarged, rugose dorsal scales. Limbs short, pentadactyle. Lower eyelid movable, scaly; parietal scales (when intact; often fragmented) not meeting behind the interparietal; third and fourth toes subequal or the third toe slightly longer than the fourth; subdigital lamellae mostly divided. More or less confined to the southern half of continental Australia.

Trachydosaurus rugosus near Kingoonya, SA

Trachydosaurus rugosus Round Hill, NSW

Trachydosaurus rugosus Gray, 1825

Shingle-Back

Description: Subject to considerable geographic variation in colour and pattern. Typically dull reddish-brown, dark brown or blackish above, with scattered cream or yellow spots or blotches, especially on the flanks, and whitish below. In western populations these markings tend to form irregular cross-bands. Other specimens are uniform dark brown above and below, while in some eastern populations the overall colour is off-white, with only a few, small, dark brown spots or blotches. Scales on tail and upper body grossly enlarged, rugose, distinctly like a pine cone in appearance. Head shields rugose, usually at least partly fragmented. Post-narial groove present. Ear-opening conspicuous, without anterior lobules. 20-30 mid-body scale rows. Limbs short, the hindlimb about 20% of snout-vent length. Tail short, depressed, rounded, more slender and slightly longer in males than females, about 20-25% of snout-vent length. 250 mm (snout-vent).

Distribution: Widely distributed over the southern half of continental Australia, except for the coast and ranges of the east and south-east.

Habit: A slow-moving, diurnal lizard found in a wide range of habitats from coastal heaths, dry sclerophyll forest, woodlands, mallee, chenopod shrublands, arid Acacia and eucalypt scrublands and gibber plains and spinifex-dominated sandy deserts. It feeds on insects and other arthropods, snails, carrion, flowers, fruit and berries. Produces one, two or rarely three large young in a litter. Shelters under fallen timber, leaf-litter, spinifex and other grasses, etc., when inactive.

Subspecies: *rugosus* (western Australia); *asper* (eastern Australia); *konowi* (Rottnest Island, WA).

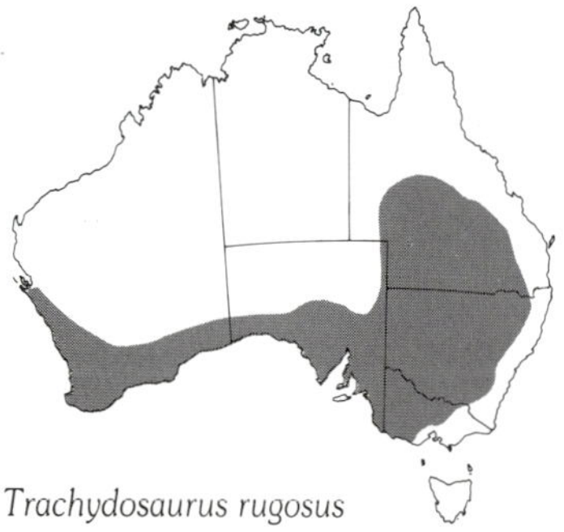

Trachydosaurus rugosus

Snakes

(ORDER SQUAMATA, SUBORDER SERPENTES)

Key

TO THE FAMILIES OF AUSTRALIAN SNAKES

1 Tail more or less cylindrical, not flattened and paddle-shaped (a).. **2**

Tail strongly vertically compressed and paddle-shaped (b). **6**

2 No enlarged ventral scales, the scales on the belly more or less equal in size to those on the back and sides.............. **3**

A single row of enlarged ventral scales which are at least three times as wide as those on the back and sides......... **4**

3 More than 80 mid-body scale rows; body scales rough, strongly keeled; eyes well-developed ....**Acrochordidae (File Snakes)**

Fewer than 40 mid-body scale rows; body scales smooth; eyes vestigial, consisting of dark spots beneath scales of head............................**Typhlopidae (Blind Snakes)**

4 Fewer than 30 mid-body scale rows................................. **5**

More than 30 mid-body scale rows... **Boidae (Pythons)**

5 One or more loreal scales present (c), or, if absent, 23 or more mid-body scale rows and a divided anal shield........... ....**Colubridae (Colubrid Snakes)**

No loreal scales (d); anal single if mid-body scales in 23 or more rows........................**Elapidae (Elapid Snakes)**

6 Ventral scales large, at least three times as wide as the adjacent body scales (e); nasals separated by internasals (f).................................... **Laticaudidae (Sea Kraits)**

Ventral scales small or large; if large (2-3 times as wide as the adjacent body scales) then the nasals are in contact (g) ....**Hydrophiidae (Sea Snakes)**

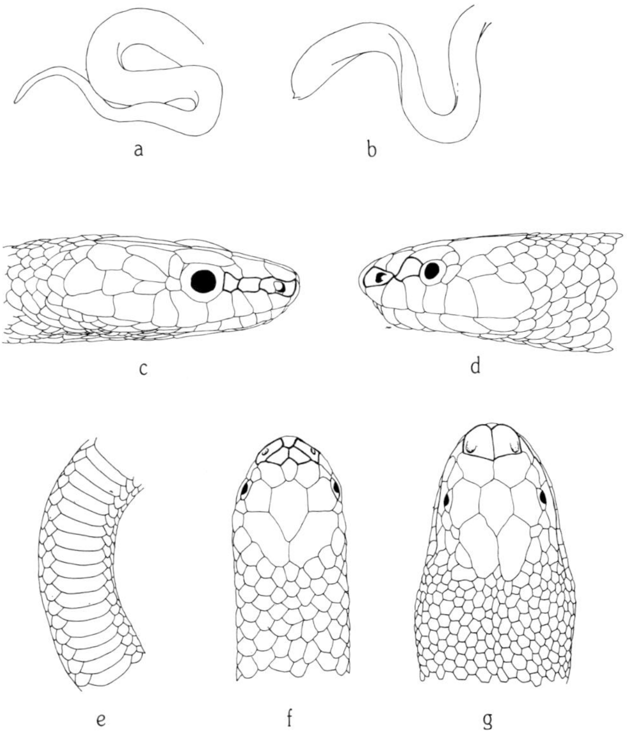

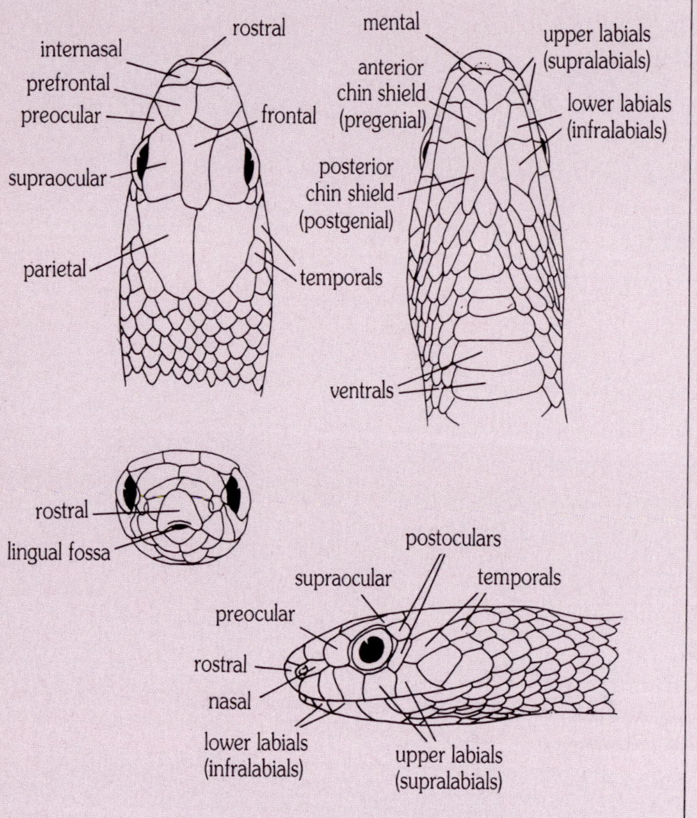

Head of *Demansia psammophis*

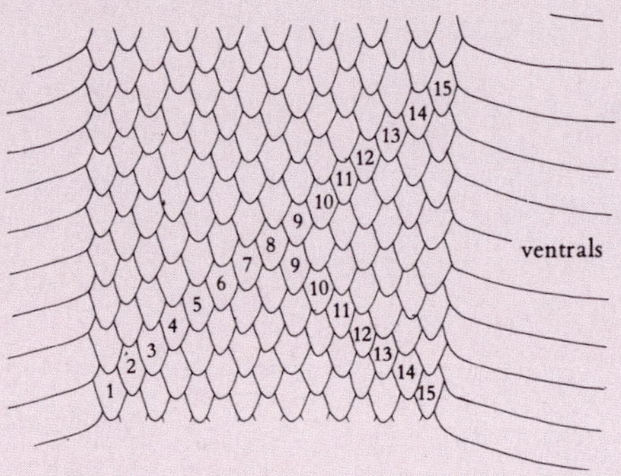

Methods of counting number of scale rows

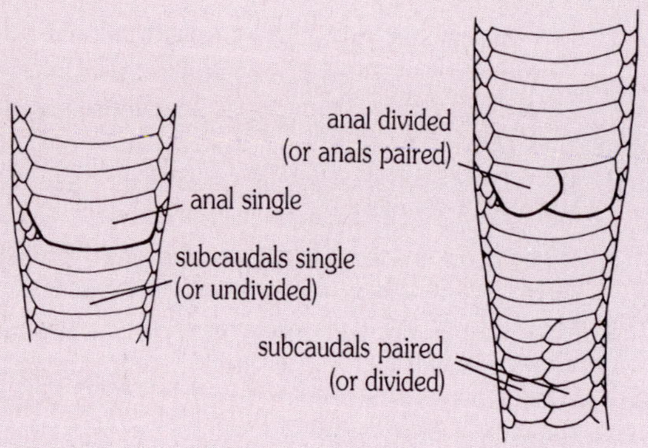

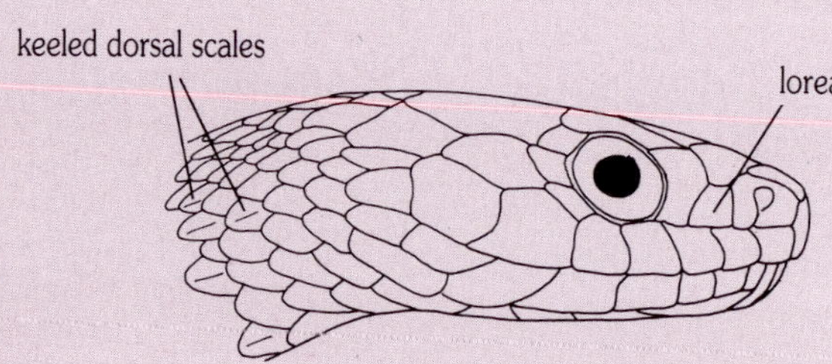

Head of *Tropidonophis mairii*

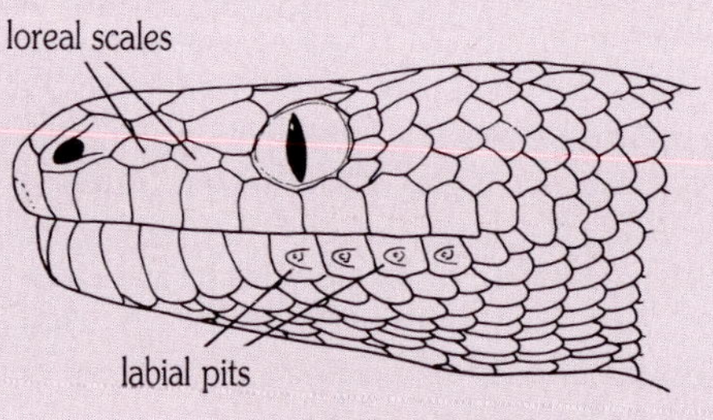

Head of a python

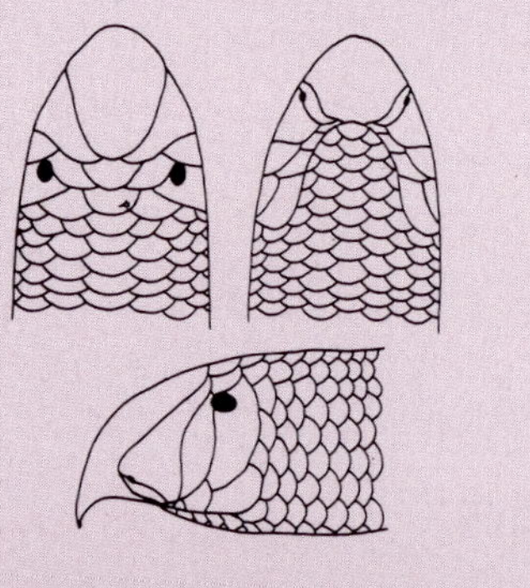

Ramphotyphlops grypus
(nasal cleft joining first labial)

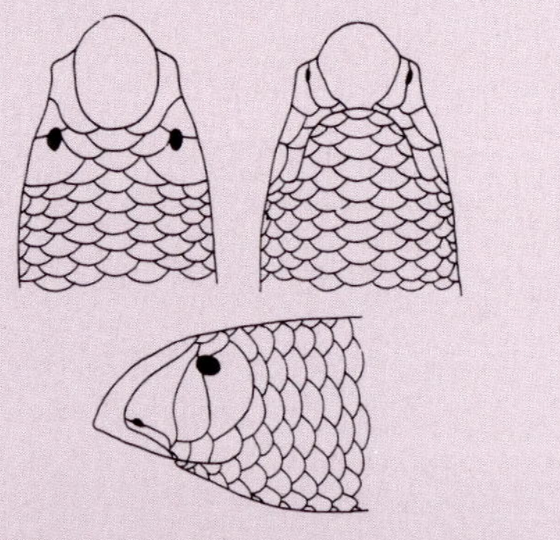

Ramphotyphlops bituberculatus
(nasal cleft joining second labial)

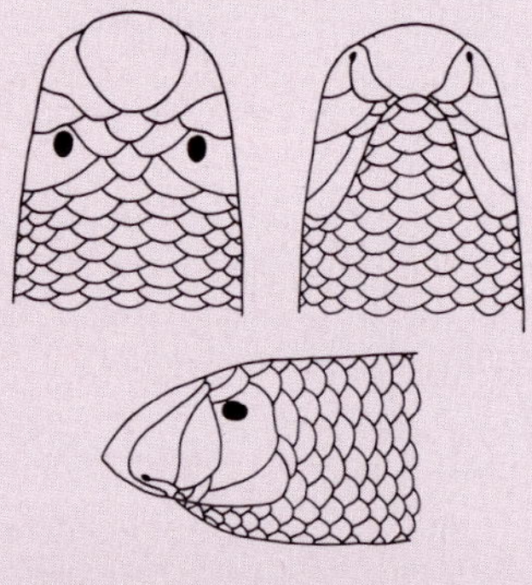

Ramphotyphlops endoterus
(nasal cleft joining preocular)

Family Typhlopidae

Genus ***Ramphotyphlops*** Fitzinger, 1843

A group of small, worm-like, burrowing snakes, all of which are more or less similar in appearance, varying externally only in minor features of scalation, colour and relative proportions. All have smooth, shiny scales which are similar in size around the body (i.e., there are no broad belly shields). The eyes are reduced to small dark spots under the scales of the head, while the small, curved mouth is well behind and below the tip of the snout, rather like that of a shark. The body is uniform in thickness along its length, while the tail is very short and ends in a short, conical spine.

Blind snakes are non-venomous and harmless; they are oviparous and feed principally on ants and termites, the distribution of many species being closely correlated with the distribution of the termites on which they feed. When aroused, they often emit a strong and objectionable odour from well-developed anal glands. Except when dug from the ground or termite nests, or uncovered by moving rocks or logs, blind snakes are usually seen only when moving about the surface of the ground at night, especially in warm weather and/or after rain.

Current knowledge of the classification of Australian Blind Snakes is little changed from that established by E. R. Waite in the early part of this century, and that presented here is no more than a minor modification of Waite's scheme, taking into account recent work on New Guinea blind snakes by S. B. McDowell and on Western Australian species by G. M. Storr. Although this classification relies heavily on the disposition of certain head scales, including the position of the nasal cleft (p 586), this character is much more variable than has been generally conceded.

Key

TO THE AUSTRALIAN SPECIES OF RAMPHOTYPHLOPS

1 Nasal cleft usually joining first supralabial (a) **2**

Nasal cleft usually joining second supralabial (b) or preocular (c) **6**

2 22 or more mid-body scale rows **3**

20 or fewer mid-body scale rows .... ***proximus***

3 24 mid-body scale rows **4**

22 mid-body scale rows .... ***nigrescens***

4 Head rounded from above (d); rostral without a sharp transverse keel, so that the head is smoothly rounded in profile (e) **5**

Head bluntly trilobed from above (f); rostral with a sharp transverse keel, so that the head is angular in profile (g).... .... ***unguirostris***

5 Rostral narrow, about twice as long as broad when viewed dorsally (h) .... ***ligatus***

Rostral broad, less than one and a half times as long as broad when viewed dorsally (i) .... ***yirrikalae***

6 Nasal cleft usually joining second supralabial (b) **7**

Nasal cleft usually joining preocular (c) **27**

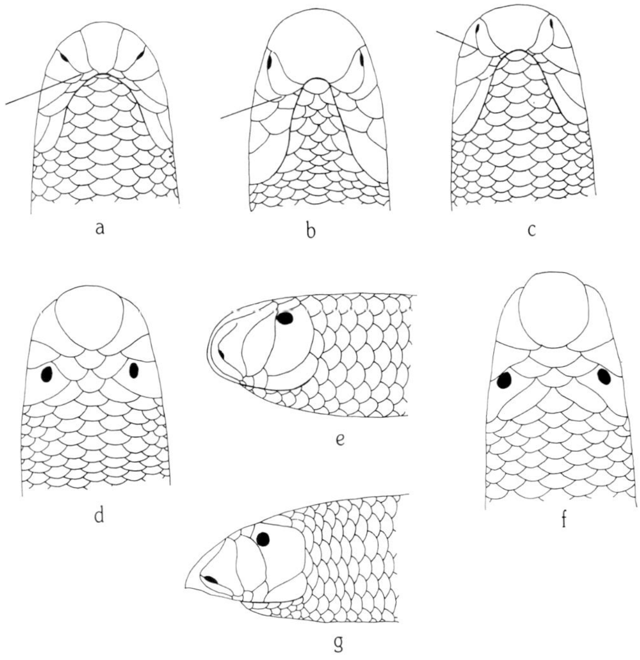

h

i

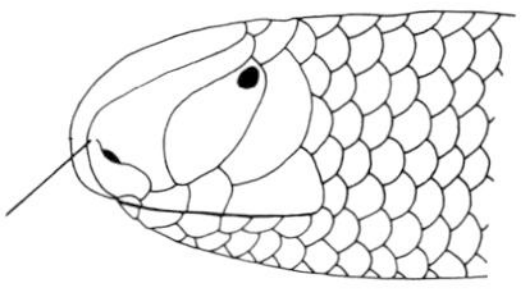
j

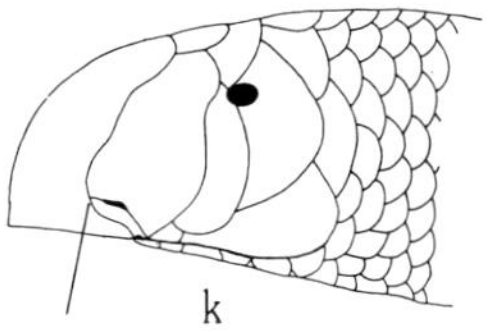
k

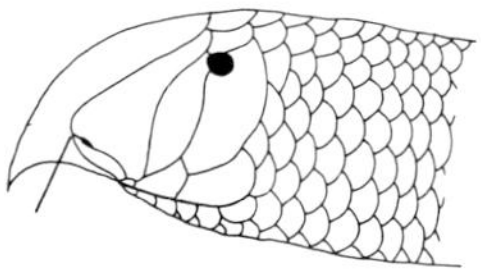
l

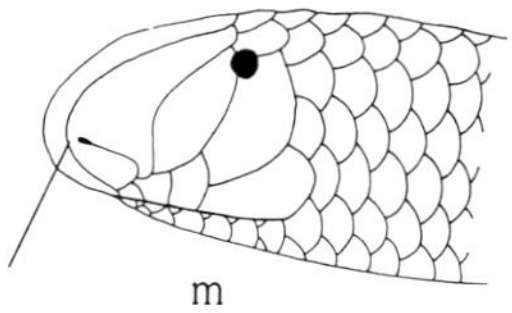
m

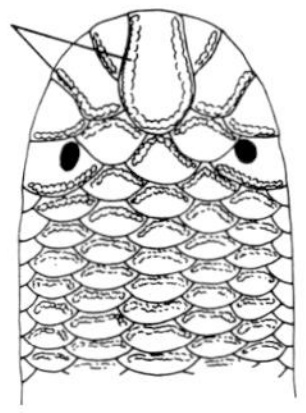
n

7 Fewer than 20 mid-body scale rows **8**
20 or more mid-body scale rows **16**

8 16 mid-body scale rows **9**
18 mid-body scale rows **10**

9 Snout blunt; nasal cleft not extending to rostral (j); head and/or tail blackish; dorsum with distinct, dark longitudinal lines .... ***minimus***
Snout angular; nasal cleft reaching the rostral (k); more or less uniform brown above............................. ***leptosoma***

10 Nasal completely divided (l) **11**
Nasal not divided (m)...................................... ***guentheri***

11 Snout smoothly rounded in profile (e)........................... **12**
Snout bluntly to strongly angular in profile (g) **13**

12 Nasal cleft visible from above .... ***micromma***
Nasal cleft not visible from above .... ***howi***

13 Rostral without a sharp transverse keel (e) **14**
Rostral with a sharp transverse keel forming a distinct cutting edge to the snout (g) **15**

14 Head distinctly trilobed when viewed from above (f) .... ***margaretae***
Head more or less bluntly rounded when viewed from above (d) .... ***affinis***

15 Tail black .... ***grypus***
Tail not black .... ***leptosoma***

16 20 mid-body scale rows.. **17**
22 or more mid-body scale rows **23**

17 Head smoothly rounded in outline from above (d) **18**
Head not smoothly rounded in outline from above **21**

18 Ventral surface markedly paler than dorsum **19**
Ventral surface as dark as dorsum .... ***leucoproctus***

19 Nasal not completely divided (m).................................. **20**
Nasal completely divided (l) .... ***broomi***

20 Snout rounded in profile, the leading edge of the rostral curved and lacking a downturned transverse keel (e) .... ***wiedii***
Snout angular in profile, the leading edge of the rostral with a sharp, downturned transverse keel (g) ... ***centralis***

21 Head strongly trilobed in outline from above (f) **22**
Head feebly or bluntly trilobed in outline from above .... ***pinguis***

22 More than 500 ventrals.. ***waitii***
Fewer than 500 ventrals......................... ***bituberculatus***

23 Nasal cleft extending well on to upper surface of head, visible from above.. **24**
Nasal cleft not extending on to upper surface of head, not visible from above... **26**

24 Nasal cleft fails to completely divide nasal scale (m).......**25**
Nasal cleft completely divides nasal scale (l).. ***troglodytes***

25 Rostral widest anteriorly......................... ***kimberleyensis***
Rostral narrowest anteriorly .... ***polygrammicus***

26 Snout rounded in profile (e); rostral without transverse keel .... ***australis***
Snout angular in profile (g); rostral with a transverse keel .. .. ***hamatus***

27 20 or more mid-body scale rows **28**
18 mid-body scale rows .... ***yampiensis***

28 20 mid-body scale rows **29**
22 mid-body scale rows ....***endoterus***

29 Body length less than 50 times its diameter.................. **30**
Body length more than 50 times its diameter...... ***diversus***

30 Head scales covered with numerous small tubercles; prominent whitish glands between the scales of the head (n)... ***braminus***
Head scales with at most a few scattered tubercles; no prominent glands between the scales of the head... ***tovelli***

Ramphotyphlops australis Round Hill, NSW

Ramphotyphlops affinis (Boulenger, 1889)

Description: Dark brown above, somewhat paler on the head, merging on the lower flanks with the pale yellow, pale yellowish-cream or pinkish-white ventral colour. Snout bluntly rounded when viewed from above, bluntly angular in profile. Nasal cleft meeting the second supralabial, and extending forward through the nostril (but not above it) to completely divide the nasal scale, not visible from above. Rostral broadly oval from above, scarcely longer than broad. Scales in 18 rows at mid-body. Body diameter 45-60 times in its length. Average length about 15 cm, maximum about 22 cm.
Distribution: Northern and eastern Australia. McDowell regarded a specimen from the Solomon Islands as belonging to this species.
Habit: As for genus.

Ramphotyphlops australis (Gray, 1845)

Description: Brown, grey-brown or purplish-brown above, merging raggedly on the lower flanks with the whitish ventral surface. Snout bluntly rounded from above, rounded but projecting in profile. Nasal cleft usually joining the second supralabial, but ending a little in front of the nostril. Rostral subcircular, nearly as broad as long. Scales in 22 rows at mid-body. Body diameter 25-50 times in its length. Average length about 25 cm, maximum about 50 cm.
Distribution: Drier parts of southern Australia, from inland NSW to WA.
Habit: As for genus.

Ramphotyphlops bituberculatus (Peters, 1863)

Description: Brown to almost black above, creamish-white to pinkish-white below. Snout strongly trilobed from above, angular in profile. Nasal cleft not dividing nasal, not visible from above, and contacting the second labial below. Rostral shield-shaped from above, longer than broad. Scales in 20 rows at mid-body. Body diameter 40-90 times in its length. Average length 30 cm, maximum about 45 cm.
Distribution: Southern continental Australia.
Habit: As for genus.

Ramphotyphlops braminus (Daudin, 1803)

Description: A small, slender blind snake, adults usually mistaken for juveniles of other species. Dark

Ramphotyphlops affinis

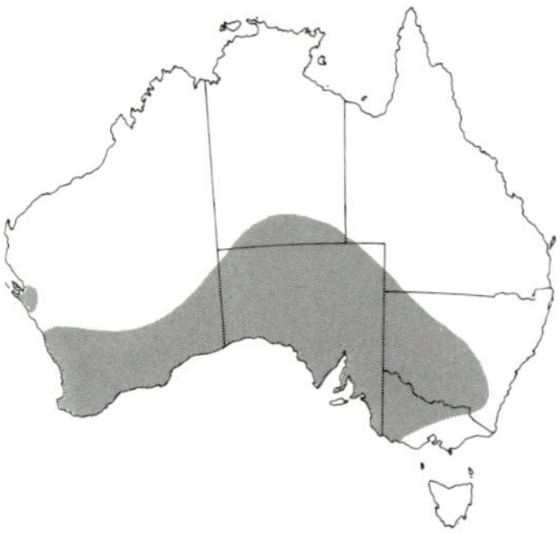

Ramphotyphlops australis

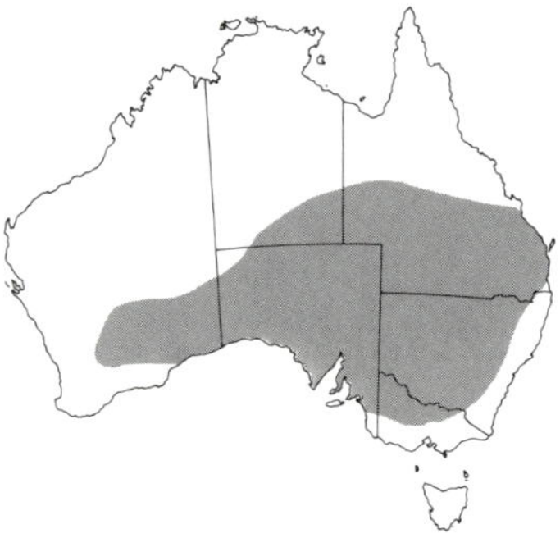

Ramphotyphlops bituberculatus

Ramphotyphlops braminus

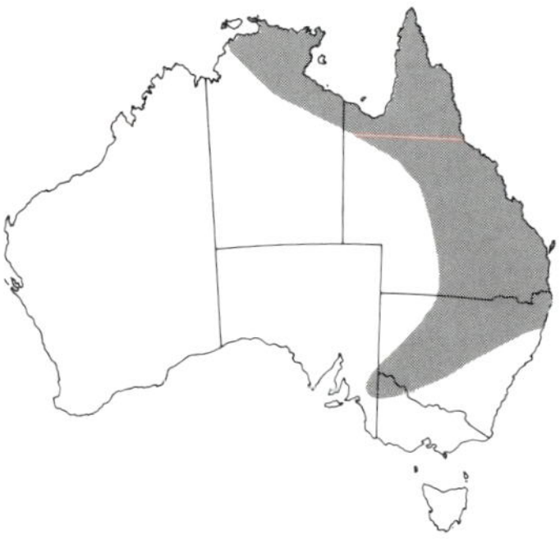

Ramphotyphlops broomi

Ramphotyphlops centralis

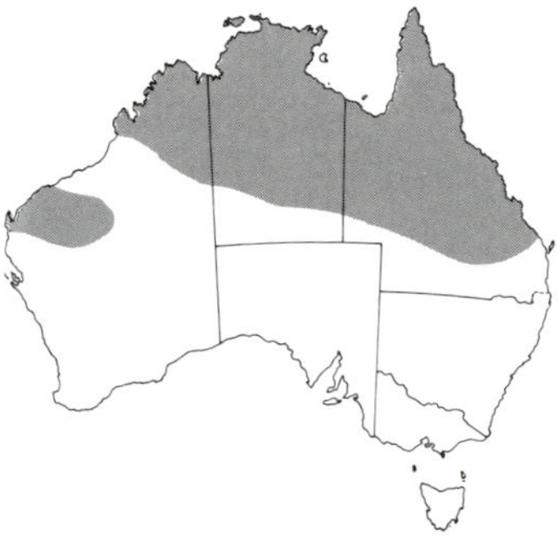

Ramphotyphlops diversus

Ramphotyphlops bituberculatus Wilcannia, NSW

purplish-brown above, merging on the lower flanks with the pale brown ventral surface. Head scales with distinctive tiny tubercles and rows of whitish glands in the sutures between the scales. Snout evenly rounded from above and in profile. Nasal cleft joining preocular and extending upwards to the rostral to divide the nasal, visible from above. Scales in 20 rows at mid-body. Body diameter 40-60 times in its length. Average length about 12 cm, maximum about 17 cm.
Distribution: Known in Australia only from the Darwin area, NT (Storr), where it was probably introduced by man, and Torres Strait. Widely distributed in Asia, Indo-Malaysia and New Guinea.
Habit: As for genus. McDowell found that all known

Ramphotyphlops braminus Christmas Island, Indian Ocean

J. WOMBEY

Ramphotyphlops endoterus Mulgaria Station, WA

specimens are females, which presumes that this species reproduces by parthenogenesis.

Ramphotyphlops broomi (Boulenger, 1898)

Description: Light brown above, the dark brown centred dorsal scales resulting in a series of reddish-brown longitudinal streaks. Snout bluntly rounded from above and in profile. Nasal cleft dividing nasal, not or scarcely visible from above, and joining the second labial below. Rostral subcircular from above, slightly longer than broad. Scales in 20 rows at mid-body. Body diameter 30-60 times in its length. Average length 18 cm, maximum about 25 cm.
Distribution: Widely distributed from northern Australia to eastern Australia.
Habit: As for genus.

Ramphotyphlops centralis Storr, 1984

Description: Purplish-brown above, merging on the lower flanks with the pale ventral surface. Snout rounded from above, but with a slightly hooked, recurved 'beak' in profile. Nasal cleft joining second supralabial and extending only slightly beyond the nostril, not visible from above. Scales in 20 rows at

mid-body. Average length about 25 cm, maximum about 32 cm.
Distribution: Central Australia.
Habit: As for genus.

Ramphotyphlops diversus
(Waite, 1894)

Description: Brown or blackish-brown above, whitish below. Snout entirely rounded from above and in profile. Nasal cleft joining the preocular, continuing in front of the nostril and often dividing the nasal. Rostral elliptical from above, and relatively narrow and sometimes constricted anteriorly. Scales in 20 rows at mid-body. Body diameter 40-70 times in its length. Average length about 25 cm, maximum about 35 cm.
Distribution: Known from widely scattered localities throughout northern Australia.
Habit: As for genus.
Subspecies: *diversus* (northern Australia, except Pilbara region, WA); *ammodytes* (Pilbara region, WA).

Ramphotyphlops endoterus
(Waite, 1918)

Description: Brown or reddish-brown above, white or cream below. Snout bluntly rounded or obscurely trilobed from above, bluntly angular in profile. Nasal cleft joining preocular, not extending forward beyond the nostril. Rostral broadly oval, slightly broader than long. Scales in 22 rows at mid-body. Body diameter 40-60 times in its length. Average length about 25 cm, maximum about 40 cm.
Distribution: Central Australia.
Habit: As for genus.

Ramphotyphlops grypus (Waite, 1918)

Distribution: Light brown above, creamish below; snout pale, remainder of head and neck blackish; tail usually darker than remainder of body, often blackish. Snout elongate, bluntly angular from above with a strongly hooked, recurved 'beak' in profile. Nasal cleft not or scarcely visible from above, usually contacting the second labial below. Rostral elongate from above, much longer than broad. Scales in 18 rows at mid-body. Body diameter 60-130 times in its length. Average length 35 cm, maximum about 45 cm.
Distribution: Known from widely scattered localities across northern Australia.
Habit: As for genus.

Ramphotyphlops guentheri (Peters, 1865)

Description: Brown to almost black above,

Ramphotyphlops grypus Gordon Downs, WA

creamish below, tail blackish. Snout bluntly rounded from above and in profile. Nasal cleft not visible from above, contacting the second labial below. Rostral subcircular from above, scarcely longer than broad. Scales in 18 rows at mid-body. Body diameter 40-90 times in its length. Average length 25 cm, maximum about 40 cm.
Distribution: North-western Australia.
Habit: As for genus.

Ramphotyphlops hamatus Storr, 1981

Description: Brownish-black above, whitish below. Snout weakly trilobed from above, angular with a slightly recurved 'beak' in profile. Nasal cleft usually contacting the second labial and extending to nostril or a little beyond, but not visible from above. Rostral large, oval, longer than wide. Scales in 22 rows at mid-body. Body diameter about 60 times in its length. Average length about 25 cm, maximum about 42 cm.
Distribution: Western WA, in arid and semi-arid regions.
Habit: As for genus.

Ramphotyphlops howi Storr, 1983

Description: Dark brown above, merging on the lower flanks with the paler brown ventral surface. Head and tail tip darker than the body. Snout rounded from above and in profile. Nasal cleft joining second supralabial and extending upward to the rostral to divide the nasal, but not visible from above. Scales in 18 rows at mid-body. Total length of only known specimen 21 cm.
Distribution: Currently known only from the type locality: Walsh Point, Kimberley region, WA.
Habit: As for genus.

Ramphotyphlops kimberleyensis Storr, 1981

Description: Dark brown above, whitish below, snout pale. Snout smoothly rounded from above and in profile. Nasal cleft not completely dividing nasal, but clearly visible from above, and contacting the second supralabial below. Rostral elongate, much longer than wide, and broadest anteriorly. Scales in 22 rows at mid-body. Length of two known specimens 22 cm and 29.6 cm.
Distribution: 'Subhumid north-west Kimberley' WA (Storr).
Habit: As for genus.

Ramphotyphlops leptosoma Robb, 1972

Description: Purplish-brown above, grey-white below. Snout rounded or faintly trilobed from above, bluntly angular in profile. Nasal cleft completely dividing the nasal, not visible from above, contacting the second supralabial. Rostral large, subcircular, about as wide as long. Scales in 16 or 18 rows at mid-body. Body diameter 70-80 times in its length. Average length about 25 cm, maximum about 40 cm.
Distribution: So far known from the lower Murchison River district and adjacent coastal regions, WA.
Habit: As for genus.

Ramphotyphlops leucoproctus (Boulenger, 1889)

Description: Superficially similar in most respects to *Ramphotyphlops braminus*, from which it may be distinguished by its larger size, its incompletely divided nasal shield and its nasal cleft joining the second supralabial. The distinctive whitish glands between the head scales, which are so obvious in *Ramphotyphlops braminus*, are also conspicuous in *Ramphotyphlops leucoproctus*. Body diameter 40-70 times in its length. Average length about 18 cm, maximum about 25 cm.
Distribution: Eastern islands of Torres Strait; Cape York Peninsula, Qld. Extra-limital in southern New Guinea.
Habit: As for genus.

Ramphotyphlops ligatus (Peters, 1879)

Description: Brownish above, creamish-white below, snout pale. Snout smoothly rounded from above and in profile. Nasal cleft visible from above, almost dividing the nasal and contacting the first labial below. Rostral narrow, elongate from above, much longer than broad. Scales in 24 rows at mid-body. Body diameter 20-40 times in its length. Average length 30 cm, maximum 50 cm.
Distribution: Widely distributed throughout eastern

Australia, but with isolated records from north-western Australia.
Habit: As for genus.

Ramphotyphlops margaretae
Storr, 1981

Description: Purplish-grey above, pale grey below, snout pale. Snout strongly trilobed from above and sharply angular in profile. Nasal cleft joining the second labial and extending only a little beyond the nostril, not visible from above. Rostral broadly oval, longer than wide. Scales in 18 rows at mid-body. Length of only known specimen 30.6 cm.
Distribution: Known only from Lake Throssell, WA.
Habit: As for genus.

Ramphotyphlops micromma
Storr, 1981

Description: Colour unknown. Snout rounded from above and in profile. Nasal cleft extending from second supralabial through nostril to completely divide the nasal scale; visible from above. Rostral large, oval, widest posteriorly, much longer than broad. Scales in 18 rows at mid-body. Length of only known specimen 20.5 mm.
Distribution: Known only from Leopold Downs, WA.
Habit: As for genus.

Ramphotyphlops ligatus Forty-mile Scrub, S of Mt Garnet, Qld

Ramphotyphlops endoterus

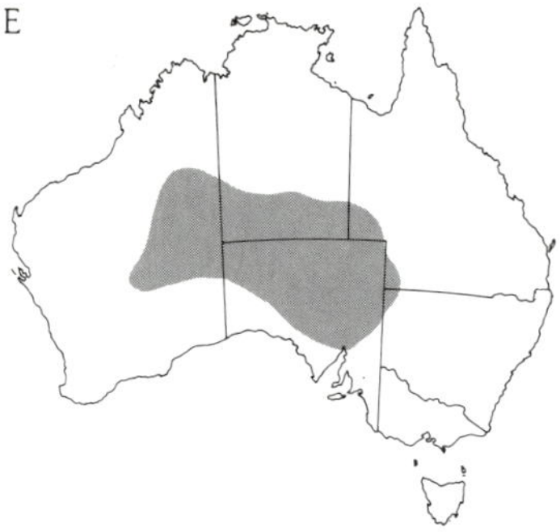

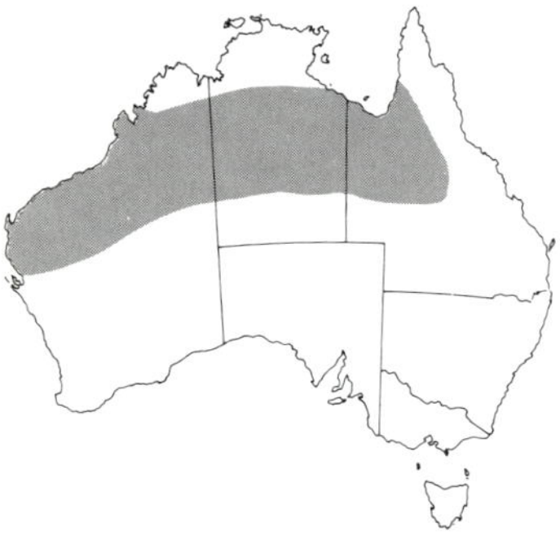

Ramphotyphlops grypus

Ramphotyphlops guentheri

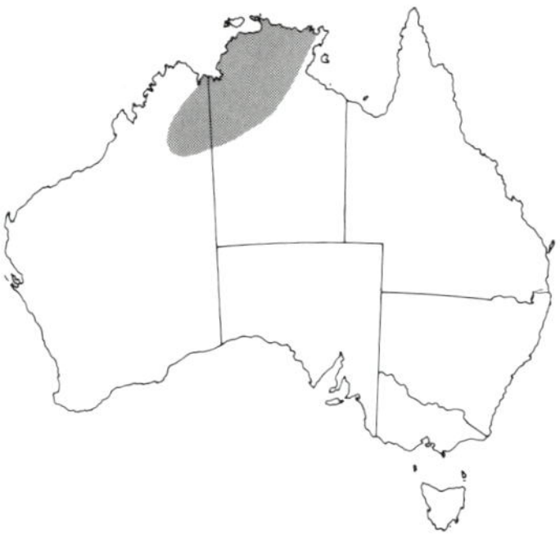

Ramphotyphlops hamatus

Ramphotyphlops howi

Ramphotyphlops kimberleyensis

Ramphotyphlops leptosoma

Ramphotyphlops minimus
(Kinghorn, 1929)

Description: Pale brown or reddish-brown above, whitish below, the head and tail, or just the tail, blackish. Snout rounded from above and in profile. Nasal cleft joining the second labial, extending forward only a short distance beyond the nostril. Rostral from above, large and subcircular, only slightly longer than broad. Scales in 16 rows at mid-body. Body diameter about 70 times in its length. Average length about 20 cm.
Distribution: Groote Eylandt, western Gulf of Carpentaria.
Habit: As for genus.

Ramphotyphlops nigrescens
(Gray, 1845)

Description: Purplish pink-brown to nearly black above, cream or pinkish below; tail with often a dark patch on either side of vent. Snout smoothly rounded from above and in profile. Nasal cleft visible from above, joining the first supralabial, and extending forward and upward from the nostril to partially divide the nasal. Rostral broadly oval, slightly longer than broad. Scales in 22 rows at mid-body. Body diameter 30-60 times in its length. Average length 38 cm, maximum about 75 cm.
Distribution: Eastern Australia, from southern Qld to Vic.
Habit: As for genus.

Ramphotyphlops leucoproctus

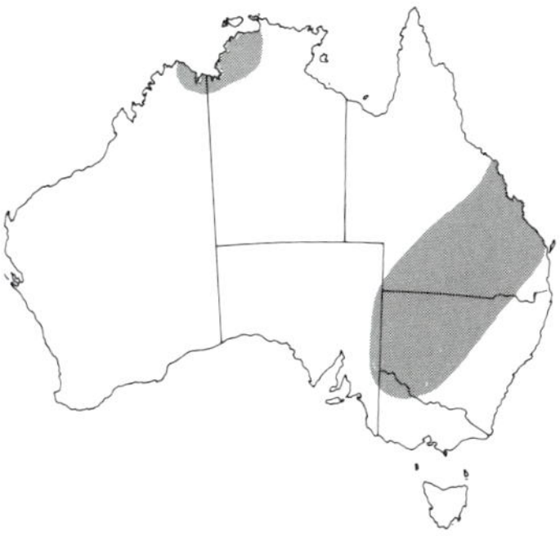

Ramphotyphlops ligatus

Ramphotyphlops margaretae

Ramphotyphlops micromma

Ramphotyphlops nigrescens Sydney, NSW

Ramphotyphlops minimus

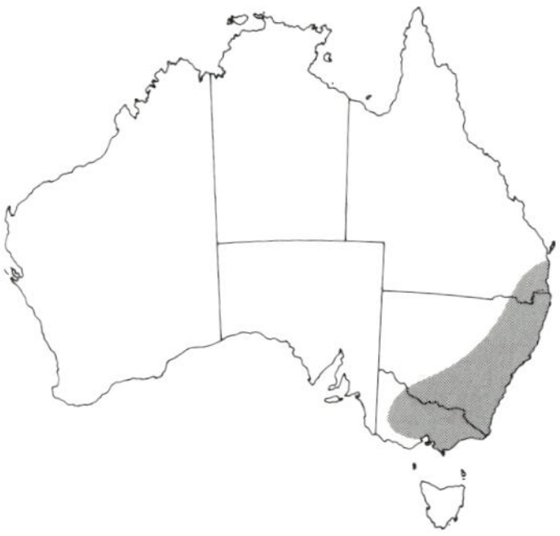

Ramphotyphlops nigrescens

Ramphotyphlops pinguis

Ramphotyphlops polygrammicus

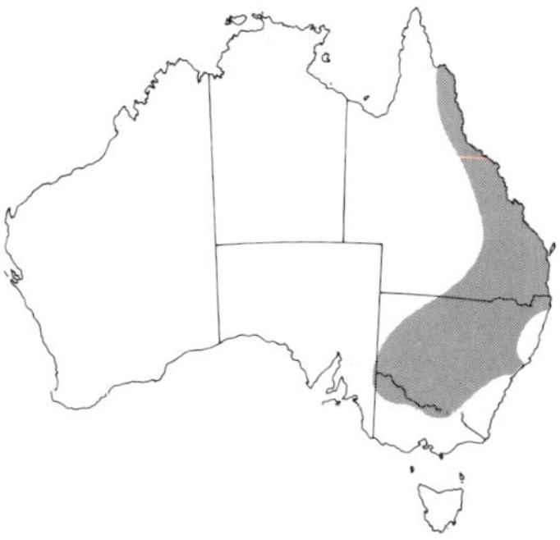

Ramphotyphlops proximus

Ramphotyphlops tovelli

Ramphotyphlops troglodytes

Ramphotyphlops pinguis (Waite, 1897)

Description: Brown to almost black above, creamish-white below. Snout slightly or very bluntly trilobed from above, bluntly angular in profile. Nasal cleft not dividing nasal, not visible from above, and contacting the second labial below. Rostral roughly circular from above, sometimes with a median constriction. Scales in 20 rows at mid-body. Body diameter only 20-30 times in its length. Average length 35 cm, maximum about 55 cm.
Distribution: South-western and south-eastern Australia.
Habit: As for genus.

Ramphotyphlops polygrammicus (Schlegel, 1839)

Description: Brown above, yellowish below, the rostral shield, mouth and tail tip yellowish. Snout rounded from above and in profile. Nasal cleft joining the second supralabial or the suture between the between the first and second labials, projecting forward and upward to partially divide the nasal, visible from above. Rostral large, oval or elliptical, much longer than broad. Scales in 22 rows at mid-body. Body diameter 35-60 times in its length. Average length about 25 cm, maximum about 40 cm.
Distribution: Islands of Torres Strait and north-eastern Qld. Extra-limital in New Guinea, Indonesia and Timor.
Habit: As for genus.

Ramphotyphlops polygrammicus Cairns, Qld

R. W. G. JENKINS

M. PETERSON

Ramphotyphlops pinguis Canning Dam, WA

Ramphotyphlops proximus (Waite, 1893)

Description: Rich dark brown above, fading to creamish-white below, sometimes with a small dark patch on either side of the vent. Snout very bluntly trilobed from above, angular in profile. Nasal cleft visible from above, joining the first labial below. Rostral subcircular from above, about as long as broad. Scales in 20 rows at mid-body. Body diameter 20-40 times in its length. Average length 50 cm, maximum about 75 cm.
Distribution: Eastern Australia from northern Qld to Vic.
Habit: As for genus.

Ramphotyphlops tovelli (Loveridge, 1945)

Description: Status uncertain. Rich brown above, each scale with a darker median streak resulting in a series of faint, longitudinal, dark lines or striations. Ventral surface white, its junction with the darker dorsal colour irregular. Snout rounded from above, bluntly angular and projecting in profile. Nasal cleft meeting the preocular, scarcely extending forward beyond the nostril, not visible from above. Rostral oval, longer than broad. Scales in 20 rows at mid-body. Body diameter 30-40 times in its length. Larger of the two known specimens is 12 cm (total length).
Distribution: Known only from the vicinity of Darwin, NT.
Habit: As for genus.

Ramphotyphlops proximus Clarence Town, NSW

G. SHEA

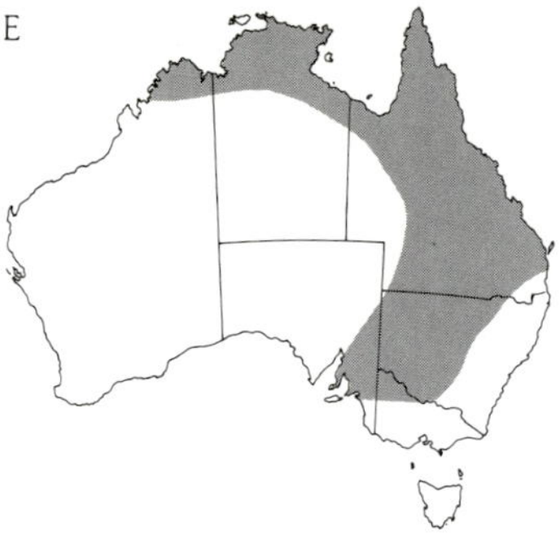

Ramphotyphlops unguirostris

Ramphotyphlops waitii

Ramphotyphlops wiedii

Ramphotyphlops yampiensis

Ramphotyphlops yirrikalae

Ramphotyphlops troglodytes
Storr, 1981

Description: Dark brown above, paler on the snout and tail tip, whitish below. Snout rounded from above and in profile. Nasal cleft visible from above, extending from second labial to rostral, completely dividing the nasal. Rostral somewhat egg-shaped, broadest anteriorly. Scales in 22 rows at mid-body. Length of only known specimen 40.2 cm.
Distribution: Known only from Tunnel Cave, Napier Range, Kimberley Division, WA.
Habit: As for genus.

Ramphotyphlops unguirostris
(Peters, 1867)

Description: Brownish above, creamish-white below. Snout bluntly trilobed from above, sharply angular in profile. Nasal cleft not, or scarcely, visible from above, contacting the first labial below and sometimes completely dividing the nasal. Rostral oval from above, longer than broad. Scales in 24 rows at mid-body. Body diameter 40-70 times in its length. Average length 40 cm, maximum 70 cm.
Distribution: Known from widely scattered localities throughout eastern and northern Australia.
Habit: As for genus.

Ramphotyphlops waitii (Boulenger, 1895)

Description: Dark purplish-brown above, whitish below. Snout strongly trilobed from above, sharply angular with a slight, recurved 'beak' in profile. Nasal cleft usually extending from second labial, not visible from above and not completely dividing the nasal. Rostral broadly oval, longer than wide, broadest anteriorly. Scales in 20 rows at mid-body. Body diameter about 80 times in its length. Average length

Ramphotyphlops wiedii Manilla, NSW

J. WOMBEY

Ramphotyphlops tovelli
South Alligator River, NT

about 35 cm, maximum about 60 cm.
Distribution: Southern half of WA.
Habit: As for genus.

Ramphotyphlops wiedii (Peters, 1867)

Description: Brown or blackish-brown above, creamish-white below. Snout bluntly rounded from above and in profile. Nasal cleft not dividing nasal, visible from above and joining the second labial below. Rostral almost circular from above. Scales in 20 rows at mid-body. Body diameter 30-80 times in its length. Average length 20 cm, maximum about 30 cm.
Distribution: Known widely from scattered localities throughout continental Australia. Also occurs in New Guinea.
Habit: As for genus.

G. SHEA

Ramphotyphlops yampiensis
Storr, 1981

Description: Dark brown above, paler on snout but darker on head, neck and tail, whitish below. Snout rounded from above and in profile. Nasal cleft extending from preocular to rostral, completely dividing the nasal scale but not visible from above. Rostral oval, much longer than broad. Scales in 18 rows at mid-body. Length of only known specimen 12.8 cm.
Distribution: Known only from Koolan Island, Yampi Sound, WA.
Habit: As for genus.

Ramphotyphlops yirrikalae
(Kinghorn, 1942)

Description: Brown above, whitish below. Snout rounded from above and in profile. Nasal cleft joining the first labial and continued only a short distance in front of the nostril. Rostral oval, longer than broad. Scales in 24 rows at mid-body. Body diameter about 60-70 times in its length. 20 cm.
Distribution: Known only from the north-eastern tip of Arnhem Land, NT.
Habit: As for genus.

Family Boidae

This family, which includes the boas and the pythons, contains the largest living snakes. In Australia the only representatives of the family are about ten species of python, including the Amethystine or Rock Python, which has been recorded as exceeding eight metres in length.

All pythons are rather bulky, relatively slow-moving snakes which feed largely on birds and mammals, although some species feed on reptiles. All Australian pythons lay eggs, which they 'incubate' and protect by coiling around the eggs almost continuously until they hatch. Pythons are mostly nocturnal, but are frequently found basking during the day.

Pythons are non-venomous constrictors, that is, they kill their prey by coiling around it and squeezing until it suffocates. As in most other snakes, kinesis in the skull is very great, and this, together with its extensile skin, allows a python to swallow prey with a diameter much greater than that of its own body.

Other characteristics of pythons include the possession of a pair of cloacal spurs, one on either side of the vent, larger in males than females, which are the external parts of vestigial hindlimb and pelvic structures. In Australian species the mid-body scale rows are never fewer than 30; the ventrals are enlarged, much broader than the adjacent body scales; the tail in most species is strongly prehensile.

The classification and relationships of Australian pythons have been subject to many different interpretations in recent years, resulting in many confusing name changes.

While it is now generally agreed that, with the exception of the genus *Aspidites*, all remaining Australian pythons are very closely related, generic limits are obscure. The classification presented below is a temporary compromise between the various schemes put forward by different researchers. A 1990 paper by Underwood and Stimson presented a new classification of pythons, but was too late to be incorporated in this book; however it is listed in the Selected References.

Key

TO THE GENERA OF AUSTRALIAN BOID SNAKES

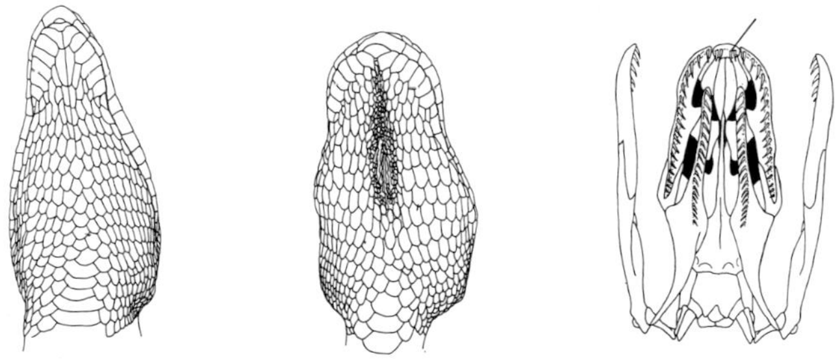

a b c

1 Mental grove bordered by scales which are more or less equal in size to the other gular scales (a)..................... **2**
Mental groove bordered by granular scales (b)............... .... ***Chrondropython***

2 Premaxilla with teeth (c).. **3**
premaxilla without teeth............................ ***Aspidites***

3 Scales, at least on rear of body, with one or two apical pits .... ***Liasis***
Most scales, including those on rear of body, without apical pits.................................... ***Morelia***

Genus **Aspidites** Peters, 1876

An endemic Australian genus of terrestrial pythons characterised by the absence of teeth on the premaxilla, enlarged symmetrical shields on the top of the head, and the absence of pits in the rostral or labial scales. Oviparous.

Key

TO THE SPECIES OF ASPIDITES

Head glossy black.. ***melanocephalus***

Head pale olive or brown, same colour as body ground colour. .... ***ramsayi***

Aspidites melanocephalus (Krefft, 1864)

Black-Headed Python

Description: Light to dark brown above, often lighter on the sides, with numerous darker brown, reddish-brown or blackish cross-bands which are usually narrower than the lighter interspaces. Head, neck and throat shiny jet black. Belly cream to yellow, sometimes with darker blotches. Scales smooth, in 50-65 rows at mid-body. Ventrals 315-355. Anal single. Subcaudals 60-75, mostly single, but posterior ones divided, often irregularly. Average length 1.5 metres, maximum about 2.5 metres.
Distribution: Northern half of Australia, except for extremely arid regions.

Aspidites melanocephalus Charters Towers, Qld

Aspidites ramsayi Harts Range, NT

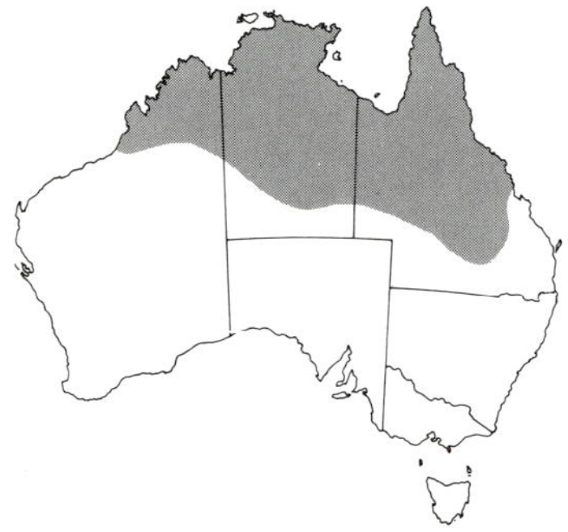

Aspidites melanocephalus

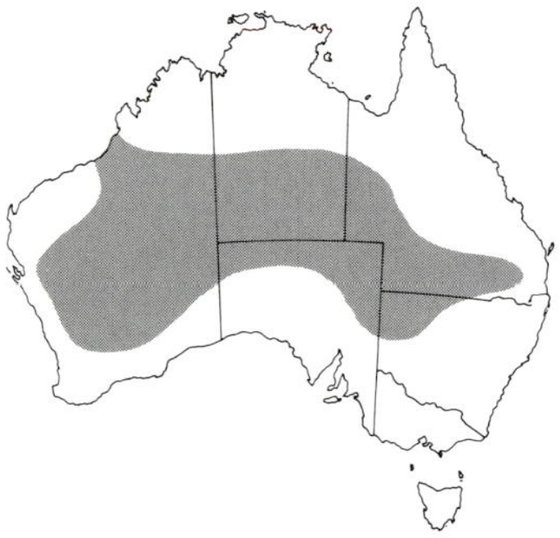

Aspidites ramsayi

Habit: Found in a wide range of habitats from humid coastal forests and seasonally-dry tropical woodlands to the arid interior. Nocturnal. Feeds on small mammals, ground birds and reptiles, including venomous snakes.

Aspidites ramsayi (Macleay, 1882)

Woma

Description: Grey, olive, brown or rich reddish-brown above, often lighter on the sides, and usually with numerous, darker, olive, brown to black cross-bands which are normally narrower than the lighter interspaces. These bands may almost disappear with age. The head is the same colour as the body ground colour, although juveniles may have patches of black on the snout or supraocular regions. Belly (including throat) cream to yellow, with numerous pink or brown blotches. Scales smooth, in 50-65 rows at mid-body. Ventrals 280-315. Anal single. Subcaudals 45-55, mostly single, but a few posterior ones divided, often irregularly. Average length 1.5 metres, maximum about 2.7 metres.

Distribution: The desert and adjacent areas of the central parts of Australia.

Habit: Restricted to arid areas, including desert sandhills of the centre. A nocturnal, terrestrial snake which shelters in hollow logs, animal burrows or thick herbage during the day. Feeds on small mammals, ground birds and reptiles.

Genus *Chondropython* Meyer, 1874

A monotypic genus confined to New Guinea and north-eastern Australia, characterised by granular scales bordering the mental groove , irregular small scales on the head, and the presence of pits in some of the labial scales. Oviparous.

Chondropython viridis (adult) Tifalmin, PNG

Chondropython viridis (Schlegel, 1872)
Green Python

Description: Adults bright to dull emerald-green above, with a complete or broken series of white or yellow scales along the vertebral line, and a few scattered white scales on the sides. A series of short, light blue bars extending out from the vertebral line. Belly cream to bright yellow. Juveniles bright lemon-yellow, gold or orange, often with a dark purplish-brown, white-centred streak through the eye and a vertebral stripe of the same colour, with short bars of brown extending out from the vertebral line. The change from the juvenile to the adult colour may be completed within a few weeks and without any sloughing. Scales smooth, in 50-75 rows at mid-body. Ventrals 225-260. Anal single. Subcaudals 90-110, all, or most, divided. 1.2 metres (total length), maximum nearly 2 metres.
Distribution: Rainforest areas of eastern Cape York Peninsula, Qld. Extra-limital in New Guinea.
Habit: A nocturnal, arboreal python which normally shelters in tree hollows, epiphytic ferns, etc., during the day. Feeds on small mammals and birds.

Chondropython viridis

Chondropython viridis (juvenile) PNG. The young vary in colour from pale yellow to red, but this is the most common form. This photograph also shows the typical resting position.

Genus ***Liasis*** Gray, 1842

A group of pythons found in Australia, New Guinea and parts of Indonesia. Characterised by the presence of teeth on the premaxilla, head covered by large, symmetrical shields, and the presence of pits in some of the labial scales. Members of the genus occupy a wide range of habitats. Oviparous.

Key

TO THE AUSTRALIAN SPECIES OF LIASIS

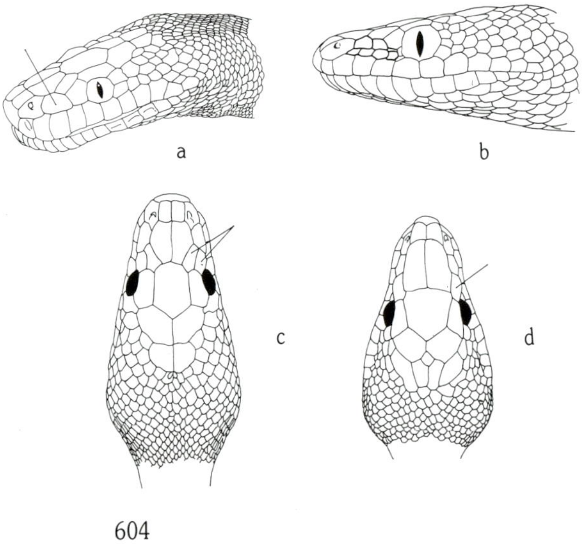

1 A single loreal (a) **2**
Two or more loreals (b) **4**

2 Two pairs of prefrontals (c).. **3**
A single pair of prefrontals (d)........................... ***albertisii***

3 40-55 mid-body scale rows..................................... ***fuscus***
60-80 mid-body scale rows.............................. ***olivaceus***

4 Mid-body scale rows 35 or more, and/or ventrals more than 250 .... **5**
Mid-body scale rows 35 or fewer; ventrals fewer than 250 .. .. ***perthensis***

5 Body with prominent pattern of contrasting dark brown transversely-aligned blotches, transverse bars or irregular cross-bands on a pale brown or reddish-brown ground colour; with or without a conspicuous pale stripe along the lower part of the neck and anterior part of the body........**6**
Body usually without a prominent pattern of darker

blotches; the latter, if present, usually not strongly differentiated from ground colour except anteriorly, and tending to be arranged in longitudinal series; usually little or no indication of a pale stripe along the lower part of the neck and anterior part of the body .... ***childreni***

6 Dorsal pattern of ragged-edged dark blotches which tend to coalesce on the anterior and posterior parts of the body; pale stripe along lower part of neck obscure or absent .... ***maculosus***

Dorsal pattern of smooth-edged blotches, and/or bars and/or irregular cross-bands; pale stripe along lower part of neck usually well developed .... ***stimsoni***

Liasis albertisii Madang, PNG

Liasis albertisii Peters and Doria, 1878

Description: 'Australian' specimens grey-brown, the young sometimes with darker heads. Lips pale cream, the sutures outlined in brown and the labials specked with darker. Creamy-white below. Anterior labials pitted. Parietal shields normal, undivided. A single loreal on each side. Scales smooth in 45-55 rows at mid-body. Ventrals 260-290. Anal single. Subcaudals 60-80, divided. Average length about 2 metres, maximum about 3 metres.
Distribution: Known only from the northern islands of Torres Strait, lying close to the New Guinea mainland. Extra-limital in southern New Guinea. The relationship of this form to the smaller, brown, black-headed form from northern New Guinea is obscure.
Habit: Found in a variety of forested habitats, from primary monsoon forests to secondary regrowth and coastal palm swamps.

Liasis childreni Gray, 1842

Children's Python

Description: Typically light brown to reddish-brown above, but paler on the lower sides, often without any distinct pattern, but sometimes with a series of

R. W. G. JENKINS

Liasis childreni Camooweal, Qld

irregular, darker, smooth-edged brown blotches or transverse bars along the back and longitudinal series of lateral and lower lateral blotches, of the same colour as those of the dorsum. Head uniform light brown or with darker flecks or blotches; a dark streak through each eye; lips pale, with or without dark vertical barring. Usually little or no indication of a pale stripe along the lower part of the neck and anterior part of the body. Ventral surfaces opalescent creamy-white. Anterior supralabials not deeply pitted. Parietal shields normal, undivided. Two or more loreals on each side. Scales smooth, in 36-49 rows at mid-body. Ventrals 250-300. Anal single. Subcaudals 35-60, most divided, but usually (but not always) with a few single ones anteriorly. Average length 75 cm, maximum about 1 metre.
Distribution: Coastal and inland regions of northern Australia, from the Kimberleys in WA to the Gulf of Carpentaria in Qld.
Habit: A nocturnal snake, mainly terrestrial, but often arboreal or in caves and rock crevices. Found in a wide range of habitats, from coastal woodlands and monsoon forests to the arid interior. Feeds upon small mammals, birds and reptiles.

Liasis fuscus Peters, 1873
Water Python

Description: Uniform, iridescent dark, blackish-brown above, bright to dull yellow below, the latter colour extending to the lower three or four rows of lateral body scales. Underside of tail, dark blackish-brown. Cloacal spurs yellow on the base, dark brown distally. Throat, creamy white. Upper labials a lighter grey-brown finely peppered with dark brown or black. Anterior supralabials pitted. Parietal shields normal, undivided. A single loreal on each side. Scales smooth, in 40-55 rows at mid-body. Ventrals 270-300. Anal single. Subcaudals 60-90, divided. Average length about 2 metres, maximum about 3 metres.
Distribution: Coast and hinterland of northern and north-eastern Australia, from the Kimberley region of WA to eastern Qld.
Habit: Usually found in the immediate vicinity of streams, dams, lagoons and billabongs, taking to the water when alarmed. Nocturnal, feeding on a variety of vertebrates.

Liasis maculosus Peters, 1873

Description: Typically pale to medium brown above, but paler on the lower flanks, and with a strongly contrasting pattern of ragged-edged dark brown blotches and/or transverse bars which tend to coalesce on the front and rear parts of the body to form zigzag vertebral stripes. Head uniform light brown or with darker flecks or blotches; a dark streak through each eye; lips paler, usually blotched or barred with darker brown. Little or no indication of a pale stripe on the lower neck and anterior part of the body. Ventral surfaces opalescent white or yellowish. Anterior supralabials not deeply pitted. Parietal shields normal, undivided. Two or more loreals on each side. Scales smooth, in 35-45 rows at mid-body. Ventrals 245-290. Anal single. Subcaudals 30-45, most divided, but usually (but not always) with a few single ones anteriorly. Average length 75 cm, maximum about 1 metre.
Distribution: Eastern and north-eastern Australia, from Cape York Peninsula, Qld, to far northern NSW.
Habit: Like *L. childreni* this is a nocturnally-active snake found as often on the ground or in trees and shrubs, especially around stony hills and outcrops. It

Liasis fuscus Kakadu National Park, NT

Liasis albertisii

Liasis childreni

Liasis fuscus

Liasis maculosus Yetman, NSW

Liasis olivaceus Brockman Range, NT

is also found in a wide range of habitats, from wet coastal forests to seasonally dry woodlands in the north and dry savannah west of the Great Dividing Range in the south. Feeds primarily upon small mammals, birds and reptiles.

Liasis olivaceus Gray, 1842

Olive Python

Description: Pale fawn to rich brown or dull olive-brown above, merging on the lower flanks with the white or cream ventral surface. Lips paler, finely dotted with pale grey or brown. Anterior labials pitted. Parietal shields normal, undivided. A single loreal on each side. Scales smooth, in 55-80 rows at mid-body. Ventrals 340-415. Anal single. Subcaudals 90-110, divided. Average total length about 2.5 metres, maximum about 4 metres.
Distribution: Coast and hinterland of northern Australia, from north-western WA to western Qld.
Habit: Found in a variety of habitats from monsoon forest to savannah woodland. Especially abundant in rocky hills and ranges.

Subspecies: *olivaceus* (Kimberleys, WA, to Qld); *barroni* (Pilbara region, WA).

Liasis perthensis Stull, 1932

Description: Similar in appearance to *L. childreni,* from which it differs in its smaller size and body and ventral scale counts, both of which may represent one extreme of the range of variation for *L. childreni.* Scales smooth, in 31-35 rows at mid-body. Ventrals 205-255. Anal single. Subcaudals 30-45, mostly divided, but usually a few anterior ones single. Average total length 40 cm, maximum about 60 cm.
Distribution: Mid-western WA, centred on the Pilbara region.
Habit: Little known of habits, presumably similar to those of *L. childreni.* Mitchell found specimens inhabiting the tunnels of the giant termitaria of *Eutermes triodiae*, where they fed on a gecko (*Gehyra pilbara*) which also inhabited the tunnels. He regarded this as a distinctive habitat of *L. perthensis,* but I have found *L. stimsoni* in identical circumstances in the Tanami Desert, NT.

Liasis perthensis southern WA

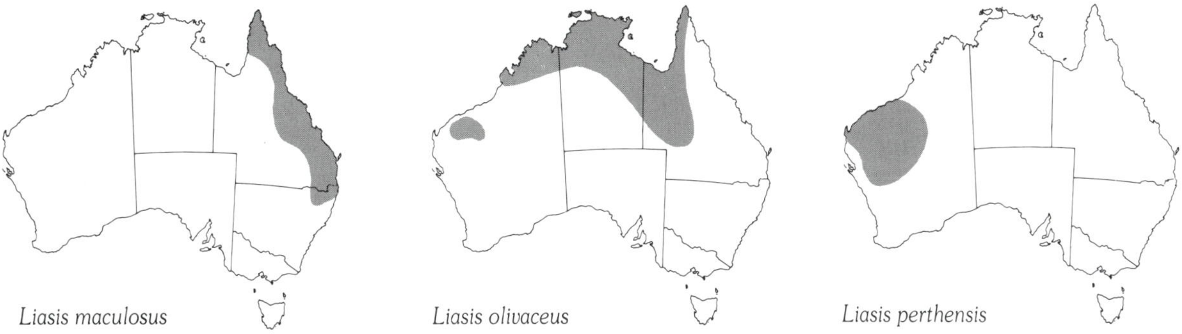

Liasis maculosus *Liasis olivaceus* *Liasis perthensis*

Liasis stimsoni Wilcannia, NSW

Liasis stimsoni Smith, 1985

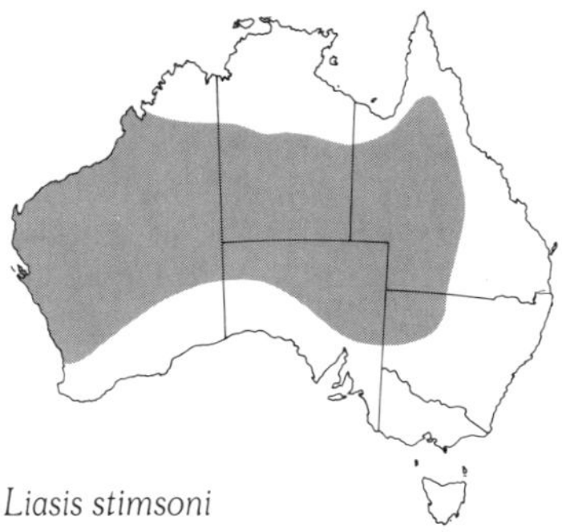

Liasis stimsoni

Description: Rich light brown above, paler on the lower flanks, and with a strongly contrasting pattern consisting either of a series of smooth edged, irregular, darker brown blotches, often transversely elongate, along the back and sides, or with a series of irregular, transverse bars which present a strongly banded appearance. Head pale brown, usually with darker flecks, blotches or streaks; a dark streak through each eye. Usually a pale stripe along the lower part of the neck and anterior part of the body. Ventral surfaces opalescent white or cream. Anterior supralabials not deeply pitted. Parietal shields normal, undivided. Two or more loreals on each side. Scales smooth, in 35-49 rows at mid-body. Ventrals 240-305. Anal single. Subcaudals 30-45, most divided, but usually (but not always) with a few single ones anteriorly. Average total length 75 cm, maximum about 1 metre.
Distribution: Widely distributed throughout Australia, except the far north and the extreme south/south-east.
Habit: Found in a wide range of arid environments, where it is most often associated with topographic features such as rock outcrops and stony ranges, but on sandy plains and dunefields it is as likely to be associated with isolated larger trees or those on the margins of dry watercourses, or even large termite mounds and larger clumps of spinifex.

Genus *Morelia* Gray, 1842

A genus of python with species found in most of continental Australia and in New Guinea. Characterised by the presence of teeth on the premaxilla, head covered by small, irregular, broken shields or symmetrical large shields, and the presence of pits in some of the labial scales. Tail prehensile. Oviparous.

Key

TO THE AUSTRALIAN SPECIES OF MORELIA

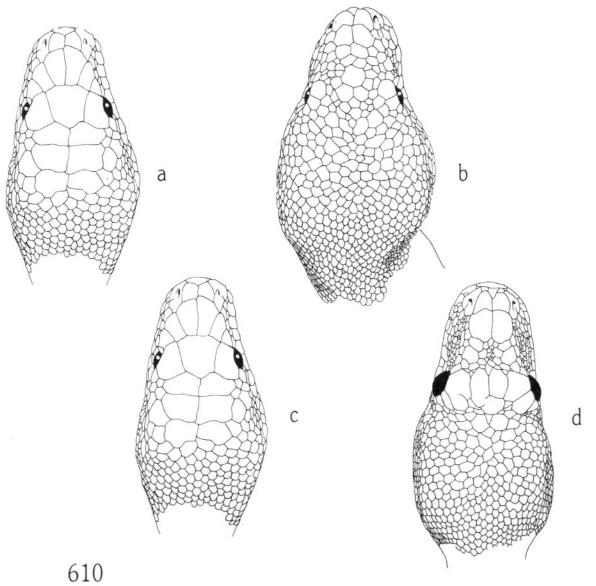

1 Body scales smooth **2**
Body scales bluntly keeled .... ***carinata***

2 Central head shields large, regular, with at least a distinct frontal shield (a) **3**
Central head shields small, fragmented, without a distinct frontal shield (b) **4**

3 Fewer than 60 mid-body scale rows; parietal shields not fragmented (c) .... ***amethistina***
More than 60 mid-body scale rows; parietal shields fragmented (d) .... ***oenpelliensis***

4 Fewer than nine scales across the top of the head, between the centre of the eyes .... ***spilota***
More than nine scales across the top of the head, between the centre of the eyes .... ***bredli***

Morelia amethistina Innisfail, Qld

Morelia amethistina (Schneider, 1801)

Amethystine Python

Description: Shagreened, iridescent olive-yellow or olive-brown above, with numerous dark brown or black irregular and broken transverse bands, sometimes forming a reticulum, and usually connected along the lower flanks to form one or more longitudinal, lower lateral 'stripes'. Head uniform or spotted and streaked with dark brown. The dorsal pattern is often more pronounced anteriorly, becoming obscure posteriorly. White or cream on the ventral surface. Anterior supralabials deeply pitted. Two or more loreals on each side. Parietal shields divided into four squarish shields. Scales smooth in 35-50 rows at mid-body. Ventrals 270-340. Anal single. Subcaudals 80-120, mostly divided. Average length 3.5 metres; Worrell records a giant specimen of 8.5 metres.
Distribution: North-eastern Qld and the islands of Torres Strait. Extra-limital in New Guinea.
Habit: Found in a variety of habitats, from rainforest to open savannah woodland, monsoon forest, secondary regrowth and scrubby vegetation on coral cays. Feeds on a wide variety of vertebrates.

Morelia bredli (Gow, 1981)

Description: Closely allied to *Morelia spilota.* Brown or reddish-brown above, with an extremely variable pattern of paler, dark-edged spots, blotches, longitudinal bars and stripes, and transverse cross-bars. Head with darker brown flecks and variegations, the lips paler and barred with dark brown. Ventral surfaces white or cream or yellow, variegated with dark brown or grey. Anterior labials with shallow pits. Parietal shields and most other shields of the head (except for the prefrontal region) fragmented, small and irregular in shape. Numerous small loreals on each side. Scales smooth, in 52-54 rows at mid-body. Ventrals 280-310. Anal single. Subcaudals 85-95, divided. Average length about 2 metres.
Distribution: Arid southern parts of NT.
Habit: '...normally arboreal, inhabiting ranges and

Morelia amethistina

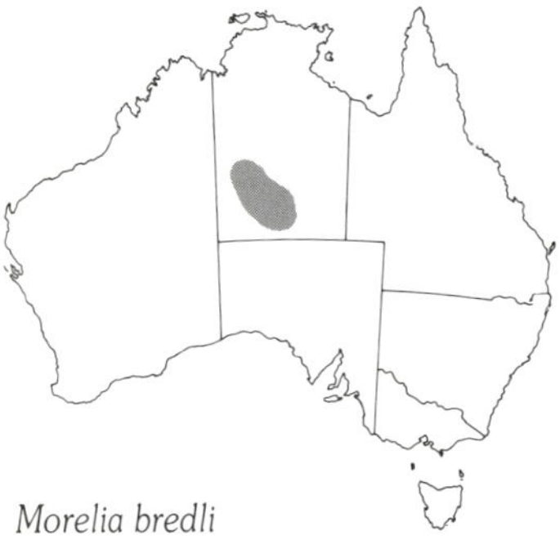

Morelia bredli

R. W. G. JENKINS

Morelia bredli Alice Springs, NT

rock outcrops. In flatter country it may be located in trees or shrubs, particularly those bordering river banks' (Gow).

Morelia carinata (Smith, 1981)

Description: Very pale brown above, with a series of dorsal and lateral darker brown streaks, blotches and variegations tending to be aligned transversely; head more or less without pattern, except for two obscure whitish streaks on the temporals; lips paler. Ventral surfaces whitish, with faint darker brown markings. Anterior labials with shallow pits. Parietal shields and most other shields on the head (except on the prefrontal region) fragmented, small and irregular in shape. Numerous small loreals on each side. Scales bluntly keeled or rugose, at least dorsally, in 45 rows at mid-body. Ventrals 298. Anal single. Subcaudals 83, mostly divided. 2 metres (total length).
Distribution: Currently known only from Mitchell River Falls, north-western Kimberley region, WA.

Morelia carinata

Morelia oenpelliensis

Morelia oenpelliensis Brockman Range, NT

Morelia spilota Gosford, NSW. This is the subspecies *(spilota)* known as the Diamond Python.

Morelia oenpelliensis (Gow, 1977)

Description: Fawny-brown above, becoming pale grey on the sides. A series of irregular, dark brown blotches along the length of the back and sides, tending to be aligned in four or five longitudinal rows. A dark brown temporal streak on each side. Many individual scales tipped or edged with dark brown, giving a reticulated pattern on the tail. Whitish below. Anterior labials deeply pitted. Numerous small loreal scales and granules. Parietal shields not distinct, but broken up into numerous small scales and granules. Scales smooth, in 70 rows at mid-body. Ventrals 429-445. Anal single. Subcaudals 155-163, mostly divided. Average length 2 metres.
Distribution: Known only from western Arnhem Land, NT.
Habit: Seasonally-dry tropical woodlands. Closely associated with the Kombalgie sandstone gorges and massifs of the western Arnhem Land escarpment.

Morelia spilota Brinerville, NSW

Morelia spilota Brinerville, NSW. This is one of many forms of the Carpet Python, subspecies *variegata*.

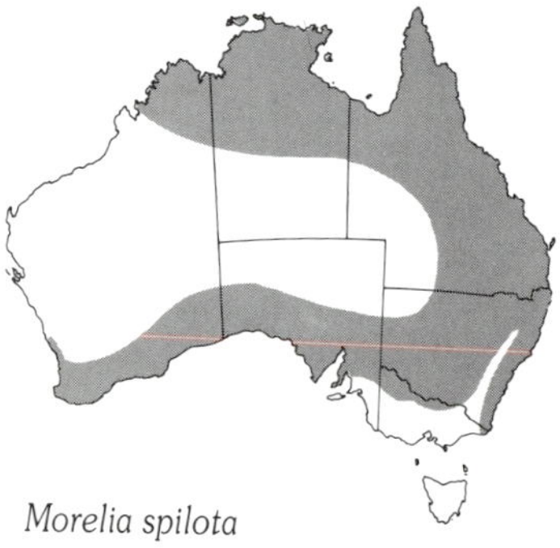

Morelia spilota

Morelia spilota (Lacépède, 1804)

Carpet and Diamond Pythons

Description: The subspecies listed below have very distinctive colour patterns, two of them (*variegata* and *imbricata*) being subject to enormous variation in colour and pattern. The races *variegata* and *spilota* appear to hybridise in the northern rivers district of NSW providing still further variation. Typical forms of both subspecies and their hybrids are illustrated. The Diamond Python (*spilota*) is typically glossy olive-black above, with cream or yellow spots on many of the individual scales, forming a variegated or vague series of diamond-shaped patterns. Lips cream, barred with black. Ventral surface cream or yellow, variegated with dark grey. The Carpet Pythons (*variegata* and *imbricata*) range from pale to dark brown, with blackish (sometimes paler-centred) blotches or variegations, which may form obscure cross-bands or even longitudinal markings enclosing blotches of the ground colour. Ventral surfaces as in the Diamond Python. Anterior labials with shallow pits. Parietal shields, and most other shields of the head (excluding the prefrontal region), fragmented, small and irregular. Numerous small loreals on each side. Scales smooth, in 40-65 rows at mid-body. Ventrals 240-310. Anal usually single. Subcaudals 60-95, divided. Average length about 2 metres, maximum about 4 metres.

Distribution: Continental Australia, except southern Vic and arid centre and west. Extra-limital in New Guinea.

Habit: Found under an enormous variety of conditions, from rainforest on the east and north-east coasts to a variety of semi-arid coastal and inland habitats. Often arboreal, but in many areas lives in burrows made by other animals. Mostly nocturnal and crepuscular. Feeds on a variety of terrestrial vertebrates.

Subspecies: *spilota* (coastal NSW); *imbricata* (southern WA); *variegata* (remainder of range).

Family Acrochordidae

A family containing a single genus and only three species, one of which ranges from South-east Asia through the Indo-Malayan Archipelago to Australia. All are aquatic snakes with small, finely keeled and pointed scales which have the texture of a coarse file or rasp; these small scales are more or less continuous around the body, so that there are no enlarged belly scales. More than 80 scales around the middle of the body. A series of loreal scales. Tail prehensile. Non-venomous, solid-toothed snakes.

Genus *Acrochordus* Hornstedt, 1787

Key

TO THE AUSTRALIAN SPECIES OF ACROCHORDUS

11-14 scales between nasal and eye; 9-11 scales between lip and eye.. ***arafurae***

5-7 scales between nasal and eye; 5-7 scales between lip and eye... ***granulatus***

Acrochordus arafurae McDowell, 1979

Arafura File Snake

Description: Grey to dark brown above, with broad darker brown to black reticulations extending from a broad vertebral band, to form either vague cross-bands or a series of circular or oblong blotches along the upper surface of the body. Whitish below, the dark reticulations of the dorsal surface extending on to the belly. The skin is very loose and flabby. Scales small, granular, but strongly keeled, and are coarsely file-like in appearance and to touch; in 120-180 rows at mid-body. No conspicuous mid-ventral fold and no enlarged ventral, anal or subcaudal scales. Average length 1.5 metres, maximum about 2.5 metres.
Distribution: Coastal and adjacent areas of

Acrochordus arafurae Lake Murray, PNG

Acrochordus arafurae Lake Murray, PNG

northern Australia (extra-limital in New Guinea).
Habit: Largely restricted to freshwater streams and lagoons, wherever monsoonal floods permit them to enter permanent waters; however, they freely enter estuarine waters and the sea. Strictly aquatic, and although extremely agile in water they are virtually helpless and defenceless on land. Feed almost exclusively on fish. Largely nocturnal. Live-bearing.

Acrochordus granulatus (Schneider, 1799)
Little File Snake

Description: Grey, brown or almost black, with numerous narrow, indefinite whitish or fawn-coloured cross-bands, fading gradually on the belly. The skin is not flabby as in *A. arafurae*, but the scales are small, granular and keeled, and the skin is coarsely file-like in appearance and to touch. Scales in 90-160 rows at mid-body. A distinct mid-ventral fold, but no enlarged ventral, anal or subcaudal scales. Average length 60 cm, maximum about 1.2 metres.
Distribution: Coast of north-eastern and northern Australia (and north to south-eastern Asia)
Habit: An aquatic marine and estuarine snake. It forages principally in the intertidal zone, where it feeds on small crabs and fishes. Specimens are sometimes seen on the surface of inshore waters in depths of up to about 18 metres. Live-bearing. Kinghorn records litters of 6-12 young.

Acrochordus granulatus Weipa, Qld

Acrochordus arafurae

Acrochordus granulatus

Family Colubridae

This is the dominant family of snakes in all parts of the world except Australia. It includes an enormous array of snakes with a wide range of characteristics and habits. The classification of this family has been the subject of numerous studies, and no system has yet gained universal acceptance.

Two subfamilies are currently recognised as having Australian representatives. These are:

Subfamily Colubrinae: a group embracing both solid-toothed, non-venomous snakes and venomous, rear-fanged forms (the latter sometimes placed in a separate subfamily, Boiginae). In Australia the Green Tree Snakes *(Dendrelaphis)*, Brown Tree Snake *(Boiga irregularis)* and Freshwater Snake *(Tropidonophis mairii)* belong in this subfamily.

Subfamily Homalopsinae: this is a group of venomous, rear-fanged, oriental water snakes, which in Australia includes the Bockadam *(Cerberus rhynchops)*, Macleay's Water Snake *(Enhydris polylepis)*, White-bellied Mangrove Snake *(Fordonia leucobalia)* and Gray's Mangrove Snake *(Myron richardsonii)*.

Australian members of the family Colubridae are distinguished from all other Australian snakes by the following unique combination of characters: tail more or less cylindrical; a single row of enlarged ventral scales; fewer than 30 mid-body scale rows; loreal shield present or, if absent, 23 or more mid-body scale rows and a divided anal scale.

Key

TO THE GENERA OF AUSTRALIAN COLUBRID SNAKES

1 Scales strongly keeled.......................................**2**
Scales smooth or feebly keeled.......................................**3**

2 23 or more mid-body scale rows.......................***Cerberus***
15 or 17 mid-body scale rows.................***Tropidonophis***

3 Ventrals fewer than 225, and/or 17 or fewer mid-body scale rows.......................................**4**
Ventrals more than 225, and/or 19 or more mid-body scale rows.......................................**5**

4 17 mid-body scale rows.......................***Stegonotus***
13 mid-body scale rows.......................***Dendrelaphis***

5 Anal divided (a).......................................**6**
Anal single (b).......................................***Boiga***

6 Nasals not in contact (c).......................................**7**
Nasals in contact (d).......................................***Enhydris***

7 Loreal present (e); scales feebly keeled.................***Myron***
Loreal absent (f); scales smooth.......................***Fordonia***

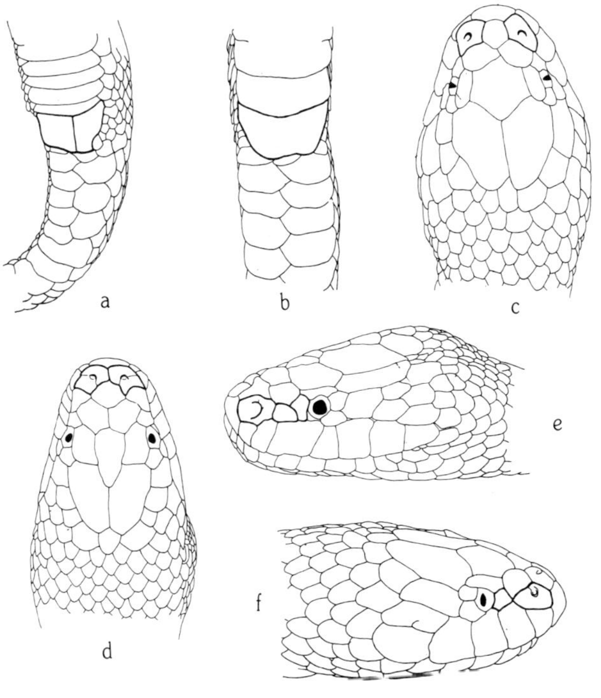

Genus ***Boiga*** Fitzinger, 1826

Venomous, rear-fanged tree snakes with a single Australian species confined to northern and eastern Australia. In Australia the genus is characterised by its broad head and large eyes (the latter with a narrow, vertical pupil), 19-23 mid-body scale rows, smooth scales, undivided anal scale and the presence of a loreal scale on each side.

Boiga irregularis Rocky River, Cape York Peninsula, Qld

Boiga irregularis Brockman Range, NT

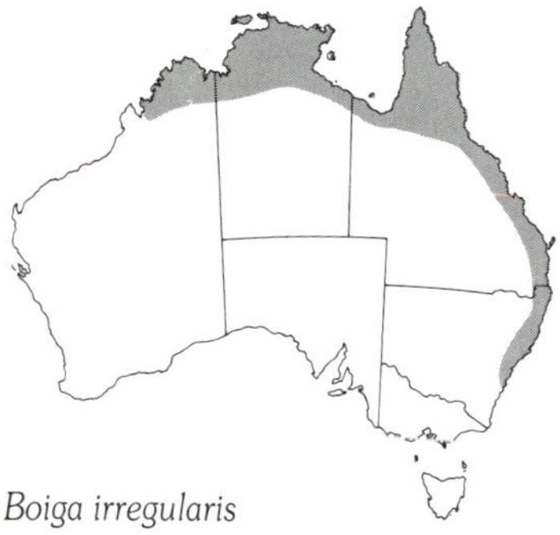

Boiga irregularis

Boiga irregularis (Merrem, 1802)
Brown Tree Snake

Description: Brown to bright reddish-brown above with numerous narrow, irregular, dark cross-bands (eastern Australia) or cream to light reddish-brown with numerous broad, irregular, bright red or reddish-brown cross-bands. Many of the scales slightly edged with black or patches of black skin between the scales. Belly cream to salmon-coloured. In some

specimens there is a distinct dark bar through the eye and along the side of the head. Scales smooth, in 19-23 rows at mid-body. Ventrals 225-265. Anal single. Subcaudals 85-130, all divided. Average length 1.4 metres, maximum about 2 metres.
Distribution: Coast and adjacent areas of northern and eastern Australia (also New Guinea and Indonesia).
Habit: Found in a range of habitats from rainforests and mangroves to both wet and dry sclerophyll forests, paperbark swamps and coastal heaths. Nocturnal and arboreal, but frequently forages on the ground. Shelters in tree hollows or hollow logs, rock crevices, caves, and occasionally under stones. Feeds on small mammals, birds and their eggs, and lizards. Very aggressive when aroused, throwing forepart of body into a series of S-shaped loops from which it strikes accurately and savagely, often with mouth agape. Oviparous; McPhee records a clutch of 12 eggs. Although venomous, it is not regarded as dangerous to humans. Australian specimens never attain the great size of the Indo-Pacific specimens, and their recognition as an endemic Australian species *(Boiga fusca)* may ultimately prove to be warranted.

Genus ***Cerberus*** Cuvier, 1829

A venomous, rear-fanged, broad-headed, aquatic snake with small beady eyes, ranging from northern Australia to South-east Asia. Scales keeled, in 23 or 25 rows at mid-body. Loreal scale present.

Cerberus rynchops (Schneider, 1799)
Bockadam

Description: Light grey to reddish-brown, above with a series of irregular, darker cross-bars and occasionally longitudinal bars. A dark streak through the eye. Sides sometimes flushed with pink or salmon. Belly whitish, salmon or yellow, with regular dark cross-bands and lateral blotches. Head relatively broad with beady eyes directed upwards and valvular nostrils on the upper surface of the snout. Scales keeled, in 25 (occasionally 23) rows at mid-body.

Cerberus rynchops Darwin, NT

Ventrals 140-160. Anal divided. Subcaudals 45-60, all divided. Average length 60 cm, maximum to 1.2 metres.
Distribution: Coast of northern and north-western Australia, from the Gulf of Carpentaria to the western Kimberley region, WA. Extra-limital in Indo-Malaysia.
Habit: An aquatic snake usually encountered in estuaries or coastal mangrove flats, where it feeds on small crabs and fish. It is quite muscular, being a powerful swimmer and climber. Rear-fanged and venomous, but not regarded as dangerous to humans. Live-bearing, litter size ranging from 8-26 (Loveridge).

Cerberus rynchops

Subspecies: Australian populations are sometimes referred to a distinct subspecies, *australis*

Genus ***Dendrelaphis*** Boulenger, 1890

A group of slender, agile tree snakes with whip-like tails. Two species occur in Australia, and others in New Guinea and Indo-Malaysia. Scales smooth, in 13 (rarely 15) rows at mid-body, and with the vertebral scale row enlarged. Loreal scale present. The skin between the scales, normally concealed but exposed when a snake inflates its body during display, is pale to dark blue.

These diurnal tree snakes spend most of their active lives in trees or shrubs, but frequently forage on the ground. Food consists of frogs and birds, although reptiles and occasionally small mammals are eaten. Green tree snakes usually shelter in tree hollows, under rocks, in crevices and caves, or even in houses, and in winter small colonies are frequently found in caves, rock-retaining walls, etc. Oviparous, with recorded clutch sizes varying from 5 (Worrell) to 12 (Worrell, McPhee).

Key

TO THE AUSTRALIAN SPECIES OF DENDRELAPHIS

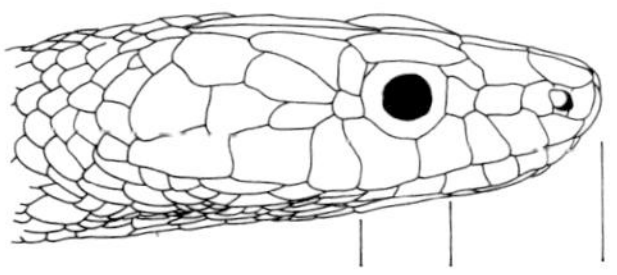

a

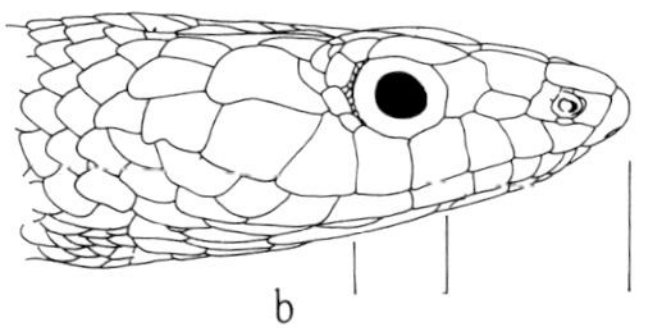

b

A dark streak along the side of the head, following the upper edge of the labials to the eye, then continuing more or less to the angle of the mouth; distance from snout to anterior edge of the eye much less than twice diameter of eye (a).. ***calligastra***

No dark streak along the side of the head; distance from snout to anterior edge of eye about twice diameter of eye (b)............ .... ***punctulata***

Dendrelaphis calligastra (Günther, 1867)

Northern Tree Snake

Description: Similar in most respects (including scalation) to *D. punctulata*, though less variable in colour. Differs from *D. punctulata* in its larger eye (distance from snout to anterior edge of eye much less than twice the diameter of the eye) and in the presence of a dark streak from the snout, through the eye, to the side of the neck. This streak contrasts sharply with the bright yellow labials. Olive to rich brown above, the belly (and sometimes the lateral scales) yellow, often flecked with darker. Scalation and size as for *D. punctulata*. Average length 0.8 metre, maximum about 1.2 metres.
Distribution: Eastern side of Cape York Peninsula, Qld, and islands of Torres Strait (also found in New Guinea).
Habit: Rainforest, mangroves, dense secondary

Dendrelaphis calligastra Murray Island, Torres Strait

regrowth, and tropical woodlands with a dense shrub layer — especially along tracks, stream beds and around clearings. See generic description for general habits.

Dendrelaphis calligastra Murray Island, Torres Strait

Dendrelaphis punctulata (Gray, 1827)

Common Tree Snake

Description: Colour subject to considerable geographic variation. Varies from grey and olive-green through various shades of brown to almost black or even blue above, the skin between the scales (displayed when the snake is aroused and vertically flattens its neck and body) light blue. The head of light-coloured specimens is often grey or brown,

Dendrelaphis punctulata Boggabri, NSW

Dendrelaphis punctulata Port Essington, NT

Dendrelaphis calligastra

Dendrelaphis punctulata

Dendrelaphis punctulata Humpty Doo, NT

contrasting strongly with the body colour. Belly usually lemon-yellow, more intense in colour under the throat, but varies from white to olive, yellow, green or even bluish. No dark streak from the snout and through the eye. Distance from snout to anterior edge of eye about twice the diameter of the eye. Scales smooth, in 13 (rarely 15) rows at mid-body. Ventrals 180-230. Anal divided. Subcaudals 100-150, all divided. Average length 1.2 metres, maximum about 2 metres.
Distribution: Coast and adjacent areas of northern and eastern Australia (also New Guinea).
Habit: Found in a wide range of habitats: rainforest, mangroves, wet and dry sclerophyll forests, coastal heaths, riverine vegetation of inland rivers. See generic description for general habits.

Genus ***Enhydris*** Sonnini and Latreille, 1802

A genus of mildly venomous, rear-fanged snakes, with one species found in northern Australia. Characterised by small eyes, smooth scales in 21 rows at mid-body, nasals in contact, divided anal scale, and the presence of a loreal scale on each side.

Enhydris polylepis (Fischer, 1886)
Macleay's Water Snake

Description: Dark olive-brown to olive-black above, this colour extending about halfway down the flanks to within three or four scale rows of the ventrals. The lower flanks spotted or speckled with black and cream, but more often the lower flanks are whitish, with a pale grey stripe along the lowest body scale row on each side (i.e., the scale row adjacent to the ventrals). Sometimes a pale grey mid-ventral stripe on the body, but almost invariably a dark grey or black stripe under the centre of the tail. Lips pale cream or brown. Scales in 21-23 rows at mid-body. Ventrals 140-165. Anal divided. Subcaudals 35-50, divided. Average length 60 cm, maximum about 80 cm.
Distribution: North-eastern Qld. to northern NT. Extra-limital in New Guinea.
Habit: An aquatic snake, usually found in creeks, clear swamps and larger rivers, especially in the overflow waterholes left behind riverbanks by receding floodwaters during the wet season. Grassy banks, or those with dense aquatic vegetation fringing

Enhydris polylepis

Enhydris polylepis Daly River, NT

the banks, are especially favoured. Feeds on a variety of aquatic vertebrates. Ovoviviparous, producing about a dozen live young.

Its common name is derived from an obsolete scientific name for this species (*Hypsirhina macleayi* Ogilby); this is an example of the problems which can arise when patronymic colloquial names are applied to animals.

Genus *Fordonia* Gray, 1842

A genus, usually regarded as monotypic, whose sole species ranges from South-east Asia to northern Australia. Characterised by its blunt head, small eyes, smooth scales, separated nasals, divided anal scale, 23-29 mid-body scale rows and the absence of a loreal scale.

Fordonia leucobalia

Fordonia leucobalia Daru Island, PNG

Fordonia leucobalia Darwin, NT

Fordonia leucobalia (Schlegel, 1837)

White-Bellied Mangrove Snake

Description: Glossy black, brown, yellow or even reddish above, merging on the lower flanks with the white ventral surface. Dorsum occasionally immaculate, but usually with numerous, scattered, white, cream, yellow, pink, reddish or pale grey scales. Sometimes the pale scales form patches or irregular, transverse bands, while in some specimens the white scales predominate over the black. Lips mostly white. Underside of tail, dark grey or with a dark median stripe. Scales smooth in 23-29 rows at mid-body. Ventrals 130-160. Anal divided. Subcaudals 25-45, usually all divided. Average length about 60 cm, maximum about 1 metre.
Distribution: North coast of Australia, from northern WA to Cape York Peninsula, Qld.
Habit: Found on exposed mudbanks at low tide, usually at night,and in fringing mangrove swamps where it shelters and forages among the mangrove roots and in the intertidal channels which penetrate the mangroves. Feeds on small fish and crabs.

Genus **Myron** Gray, 1849

A mangrove snake found in northern Australia and New Guinea. Characterised by its small eyes, feebly keeled scales in 21-23 rows at mid-body; nasals separated; divided anal scale; and the presence of a loreal scale on each side.

Myron richardsonii Gray, 1849

Description: Grey, brown or olive-brown above, the head darker, and with numerous irregular, dark brown or blackish cross-bands on the body and tail, the dark bands more or less equal to the interspaces and often extending to the cream or yellow ventral surface. Scales with blunt keels, in 21-23 rows at mid-body. Ventrals 130-145. Anal divided. Subcaudals 30-40, all divided. Average length 40 cm, maximum about 60 cm.
Distribution: Northern WA and the NT.
Habit: Usually found in the littoral or supra-littoral zones of mangrove flats and mangrove-lined creeks and estuaries. Worrell records this species as a crab eater.

Myron richardsoni

Myron richardsoni Darwin, NT

Genus ***Stegonotus*** Duméril, Bibron and Duméril, 1854

A group of non-venomous, solid-toothed, dark-coloured, terrestrial/arboreal snakes found elsewhere through parts of Indo-Malaysia and New Guinea. Two species currently recognised in Australia. Scales smooth, in 17 rows at mid-body. Loreal scale present.

Key

TO THE AUSTRALIAN SPECIES OF STEGONOTUS

A wide, conspicuous diastema between the third and fourth maxillary teeth from the rear (a)................................. ***parvus***

Diastema between third and fourth maxillary teeth from rear inconspicuous or absent (b)................................. ***cucullatus***

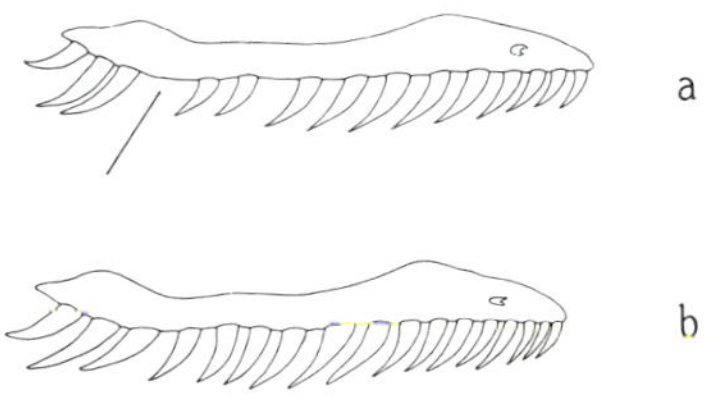

Stegonotus cucullatus (Duméril, Bibron and Duméril, 1854)

Slaty-Grey Snake

Description: Uniform brown to leaden-grey or black above, belly white or cream, sometimes with black flecks and blotches, especially on lateral edges of ventrals, and more marked posteriorly. Scales smooth, in 17, occasionally 19, rows at mid-body. Ventrals 170-225. Anal single. Subcaudals 65-105, all divided. Diastema between third and fourth maxillary teeth from rear inconspicuous or absent. 1.3 metres (total length).

Stegonotus cucullatus

Stegonotus parvus

R. W. G. JENKINS

Stegonotus cucullatus Fogg Dam, NT

Distribution: Coast and adjacent wetter areas of northern and north-eastern Australia. Doubtfully recorded from north-western Australia. Extra-limital in New Guinea.
Habit: A nocturnal snake often frequenting human habitations. An able climber, but normally forages on the ground for the frogs on which it mainly subsists. Extremely aggressive when aroused, biting fiercely and exuding a strong odour from anal glands. Oviparous. Found in a range of habitats from coastal dunes to rocky creek beds and rainforest. Often closely associated with streams, lagoons or even water tanks in buildings and outhouses.

Stegonotus parvus (Meyer, 1874)

Description: Similar in most respects to *Stegonotus cucullatus* from which it may be distinguished by its pale upper lip and its possession of a conspicuous, wide diastema between the third and fourth maxillary teeth from the rear. 80 cm (total length).
Distribution: McDowell records this species from Murray Island, Torres Strait. Otherwise known only from New Guinea.
Habit: Similar to that of *Stegonotus cucullatus*.

Genus ***Tropidonophis*** Jan, 1863

A group of non-venomous, solid toothed, rough-scaled, semi-aquatic snakes found in the Philippines, the Moluccas and New Guinea (and its island archipelagos to the east), with a single species reaching Australia. They are characterised by strongly keeled scales, in 15-17 rows at mid-body and without any reduction on the neck or posterior trunk; many subcaudal scales, each with a single pit; loreal scale present.

Tropidonophis mairii (Gray, 1841)

Keelback or Freshwater Snake

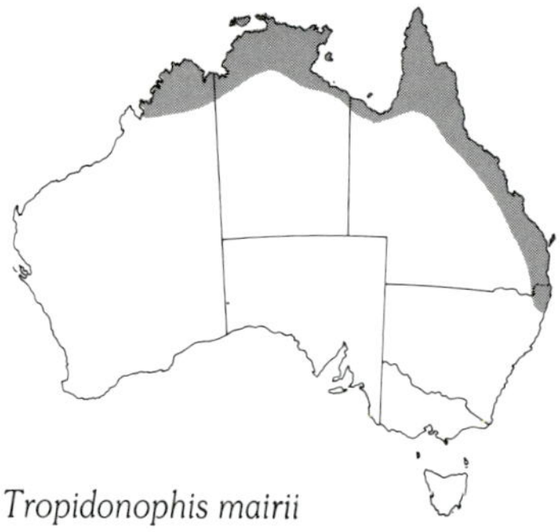

Tropidonophis mairii

Description: Various shades of grey, brown, olive, reddish to black above, often with numerous narrow, irregular, darker cross-bands formed by dark-tipped scales or patches of dark skin between the scales. These bands may at times be reduced to scattered dark flecks. Belly cream, olive-green, brown or even salmon-coloured. Scales strongly keeled, in 15 (rarely 17) rows at mid-body. Ventrals 130-165. Anal divided. Subcaudals 50-85, all divided. Average length 50 cm, maximum about 1 metre.
Distribution: Coastal areas of northern and north-eastern Australia, from north-western Australia to Clarence River, NSW (also New Guinea).
Habit: A semi-aquatic species almost invariably found in close proximity to streams, swamps and lagoons, where it feeds on frogs. Active both by day or night, but is usually more often encountered at night. Non-venomous, harmless. Oviparous; Worrell records clutch sizes of 5-12.
Subspecies: *mairii* (Australia and south-eastern New Guinea); *brongersmai* (central-southern New Guinea).

Tropidonophis mairii Daly River, NT

Family Elapidae

Australia's venomous snakes, both terrestrial and marine, are termed proteroglyphous — a term which means that they possess fixed (i.e.,immovable) fangs at the front of the upper jaw (maxilla). Other proteroglyphous snakes include the well-known and highly venomous African mambas, the African and Asian cobras, the Asian kraits and the New World coral snakes. Nowhere are these 'fixed front-fanged' snakes more diverse than in Australia.

Until relatively recently all of the terrestrial proteroglyphous snakes were included in a single family, the Elapidae, while the marine forms, including both the viviparous 'true' sea snakes and the oviparous banded sea snakes (or 'sea kraits') were included in a second family, the Hydrophiidae.

The evolutionary relationships of the various subgroups of proteroglyphous snakes have been the subject of intense study in recent years, in part because of the medical importance of these snakes and in part because recent advances in genetic and biochemical techniques have permitted a more rigorous multi-disciplinary study of their relationships. Results to date indicate that there are six major groups of proteroglyphs:

Mambas	Cobras, kraits and related Afro-Asian snakes
American coral snakes	Australian 'elapids'
Viviparous sea snakes	Oviparous 'sea kraits'

Most recent studies have convincingly shown that Australian 'elapids' are most closely related to the viviparous sea snakes, and formal proposals to include these together in the family Hydrophiidae have gained wide acceptance. However, the nature of the relationships of the other four groups of proteroglyphs to this group are far from clear and, like many others, I have opted to treat each of the three groups represented in Australia as separate families until their phylogenetic relationships become clearer. It is important to stress that the family-level taxa, like genera, are conceptually highly subjective.

Consequently the family Elapidae, as used here in its traditional sense, is a family of venomous snakes which contains some of the most dangerous snakes in the world. In Australia the majority of land snakes belong to this family, but fortunately most species are only mildly venomous and are not regarded as being dangerous to man. The family is characterised by the possession of a pair of relatively short, hollow fangs, each lying at the front of the maxillary bone and connected at the base to a duct which leads to the venom gland. Although the fangs are effectively hollow, like a hypodermic needle, the hollow is formed by the infolding over an anterior groove as the fang develops. The venom of Australian elapid snakes is largely neurotoxic in its effects, although other components may be significant (see discussion of snake venom and snakebite, page 46). In Australian Elapidae the scales are usually in fewer than 23 rows at mid-body, and there are no loreal scales present. About 65 species are known from Australia, usually with at least one species present in any part of mainland Australia and Tasmania. Many species are oviparous, while others are ovoviviparous or viviparous, the latter with a well-developed chorio-allantoic placenta.

Key

TO THE GENERA OF AUSTRALIAN ELAPID SNAKES

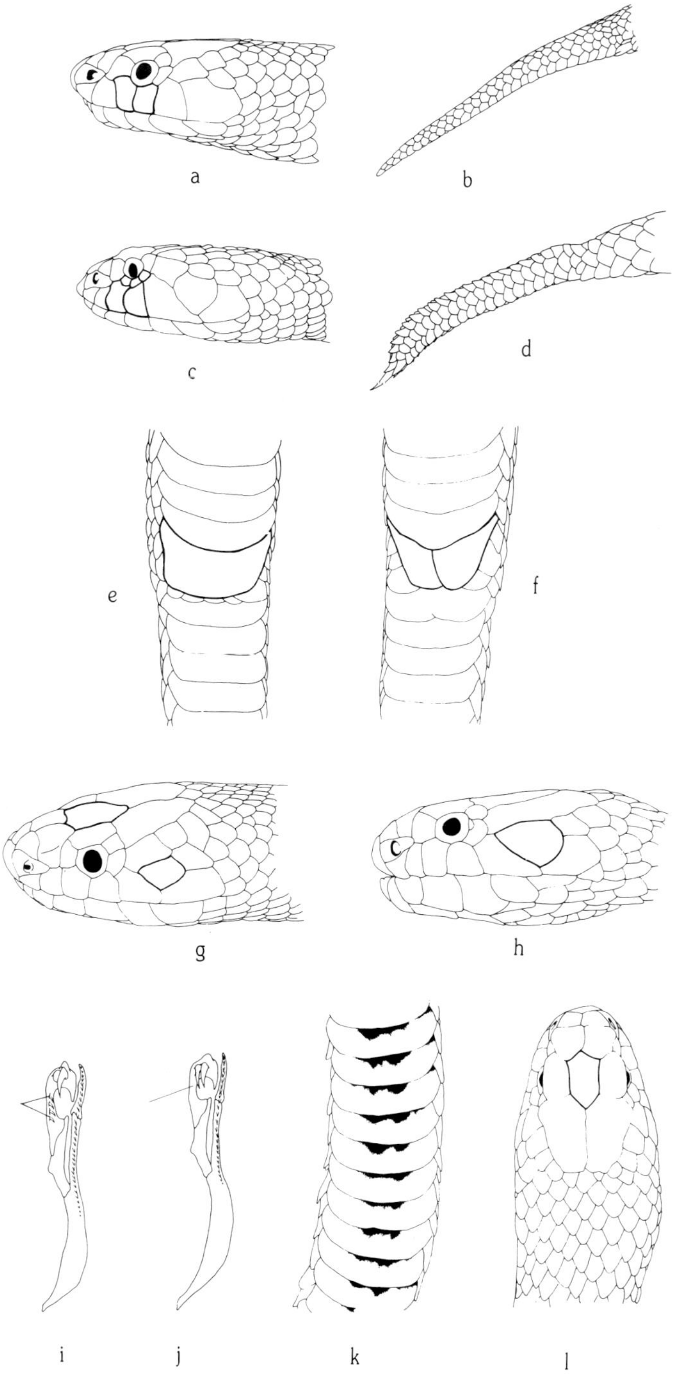

1 No suboculars (a); no specialised curved soft spine on the tip of the tail (b) **2**

Suboculars (c); a curved soft spine on the tip of the tail (d) .... ***Acanthophis***

2 All subcaudals normally undivided **3**

At least some subcaudals divided **13**

3 Dorsal scales smooth **4**

Dorsal scales strongly keeled .... ***Tropidechis***

4 Anal normally single (e) **5**

Anal normally divided (f) .... ***Hemiaspis***

5 Scales in 13-21 rows at mid-body; if in 19 or more rows, ventrals more than 140 or head not jet-black above contrasting with brown body colour **6**

Scales in 19 rows at mid-body; ventrals fewer than 140 or head jet-black above contrasting with paler brown body colouring .... ***Echiopsis***

6 Frontal shield longer than broad; where frontal is only slightly longer than broad, lower anterior temporal shield is shorter than frontal (g) **7**

Frontal shield not, or scarcely, longer than broad; lower anterior temporal about as long as or longer than the frontal (h) .... ***Notechis***

7 Scales in 15-21 rows at mid-body; ventrals not keeled or notched; if 19 or more, ventrals fewer than 190 .... **8**

Scales in 19-21 rows at mid-body; ventrals keeled or notched; ventrals 190 or more .... ***Hoplocephalus***

8 Three or more solid maxillary teeth following the fang (i); belly without a series of crescent-shaped transverse black bars **9**

No maxillary teeth following the fang (j); belly with a median series of crescent-shaped transverse black bars (k) .... ***Elapognathus***

9 Frontal less than one and a half times as broad as the supraocular (l) **10**

Frontal more than one and a half times as broad as the supraocular (m) **11**

10 Lateral scales adjoining ventrals not noticeably enlarged (n) .... ***Drysdalia***

Lateral scales adjoining ventrals noticeably enlarged (o). .... ***Austrelaps***

11 Scales in 15-21 rows at mid-body; upper labials uniformly pale, without darker bars **12**

Scales in 17 rows at mid-body; upper labials strongly barred .... ***Denisonia***

12 Scales in 15 rows at mid-body; head and body usually uniformly coloured above, or sides of body and face a paler pink in one species (*nigrostriata*) .... ***Rhinoplocephalus***

Scales in 15-21 rows at mid-body; head with a dark, contrasting hood or with strongly contrasting darker spots and streaks .... ***Suta***

13 Anal normally divided; 21, or usually fewer, mid-body scale rows **14**

Anal normally single; 21 or more mid-body scale rows ... . ***Oxyuranus***

14 Subcaudals 35 or more **15**

Subcaudals fewer than 35 .... **19**

15 Nasal and preocular scales in contact (p) **16**

Nasal and preocular scales widely separated (q) .... ***Furina***

16 Scales in 17 or more rows at mid-body **17**

Scales in 15 rows at mid-body **18**

17 Nearly always a single temporal scale between the fifth upper labial and the parietal scale (r); usually all subcaudals divided or at most a few anterior ones undivided .... ***Pseudonaja***

Nearly always two temporal scales between the fifth upper labial and the parietal scale (s); usually at least anterior 20% of subcaudals undivided, remainder divided .... ***Pseudechis***

18 Diameter of eye markedly greater than its distance from the mouth (t) .... ***Demansia***

Diameter of eye about equal to or less than its distance from the mouth (u) .... ***Cacophis***

19 Colour pattern not consisting of alternate black and white bands **20**

Colour pattern consisting of black and white bands from head to tail .... ***Vermicella***

20 Body with or without cross-bands; if unbanded, the ventral surface is immaculate white or cream .... ***Simoselaps***

Body without cross-bands; ventral surface coloured and/or patterned .... ***Cacophis***

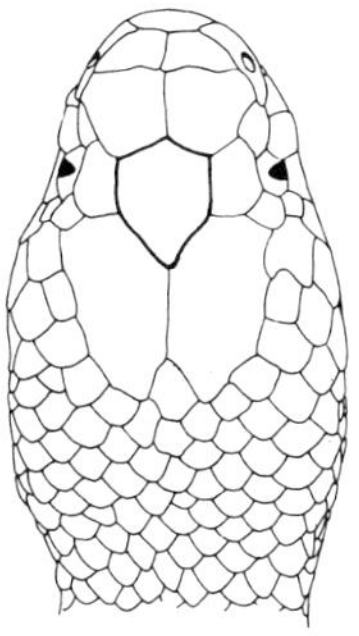

m

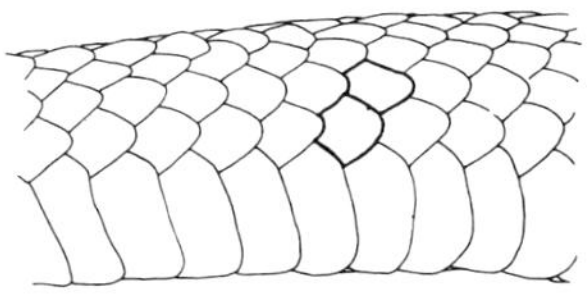

n

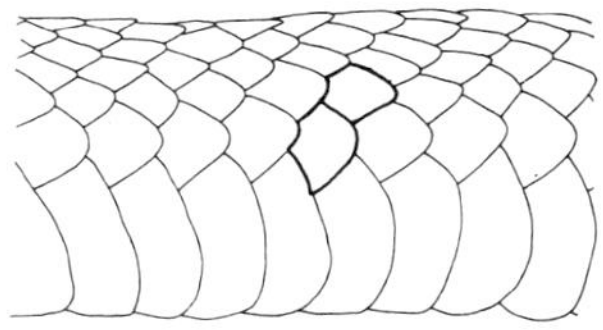

o

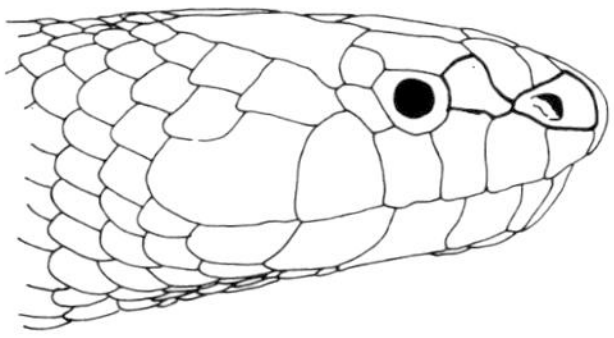

p

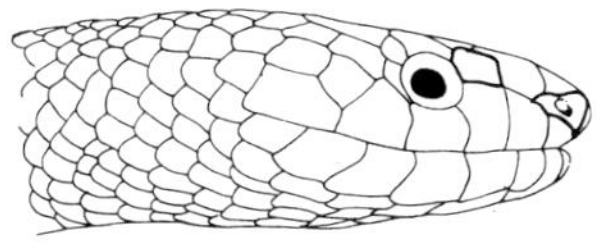

q

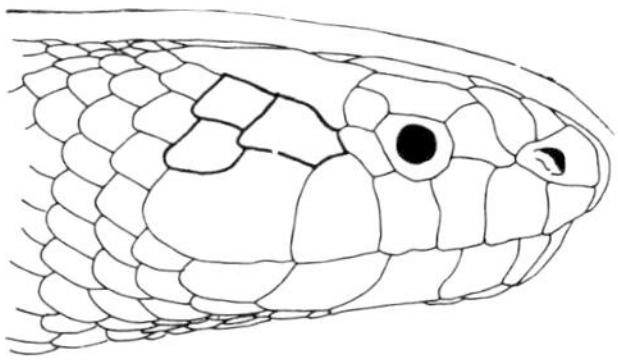

r

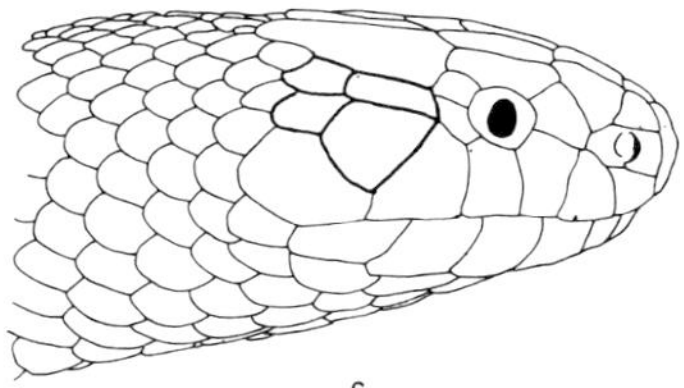

s

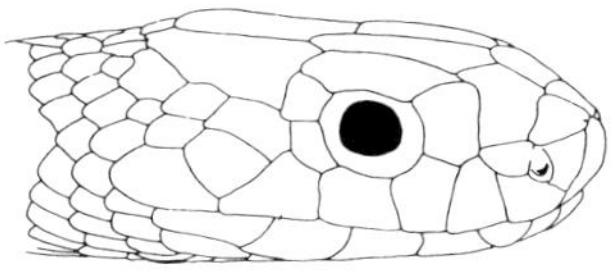

t

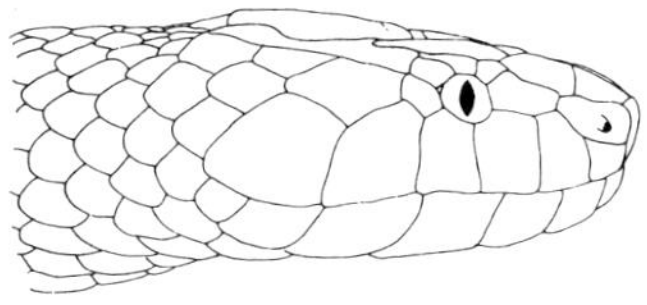

u

Genus ***Acanthophis*** Daudin, 1803

Death Adders, a group of viper-like snakes which are characterised by a broad, somewhat triangular head, narrow neck, short stout body and thin rat-like tail ending in a curved soft spine. The scales are usually at least slightly keeled. There may be either 21 or 23 mid-body scale rows, and there is a series of small subocular scales between the eye and the labial scales. Fang followed by two or three solid maxillary teeth. In appearance these snakes are unlike any other Australian snakes.

They are nocturnal, secretive snakes, which during the day are usually found half-buried in sand, soil or litter, often at the bases of trees or shrubs. Unlike other Australian elapids they tend to rely on cryptic coloration to avoid detection; they normally remain where they are when disturbed, and resort to flight only when strongly provoked and when their normal defense reaction — a tense, flattened, coiled position from which lightning-fast strikes are made — fails to deter an aggressor.

Death Adders have relatively large fangs and very toxic venom, and are among the most dangerous snakes in Australia and the world. An interesting habit noted by many writers is the ability of Death Adders to attract their prey to within striking distance by twitching the tip of the tail. At the approach of potential prey — perhaps a mouse or lizard — the insect-like movement of the tail acts as an effective lure.

Various forms — whether regarded as subspecies or full species — occur throughout continental Australia, New Guinea, and the islands west as far as Ceram. These snakes are also known commonly as 'Deaf Adders'

Acanthophis antarcticus

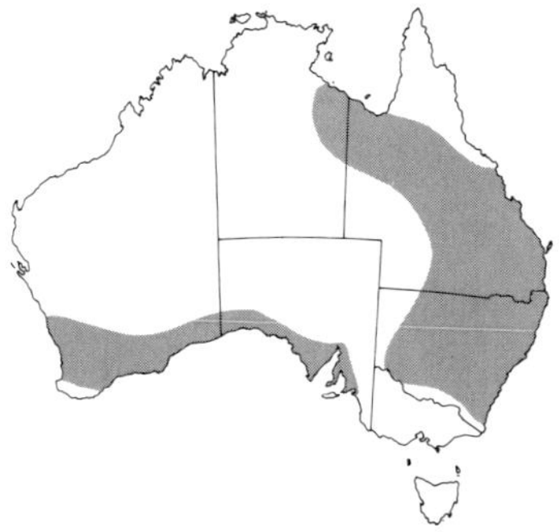

Acanthophis praelongus

Acanthophis pyrrhus

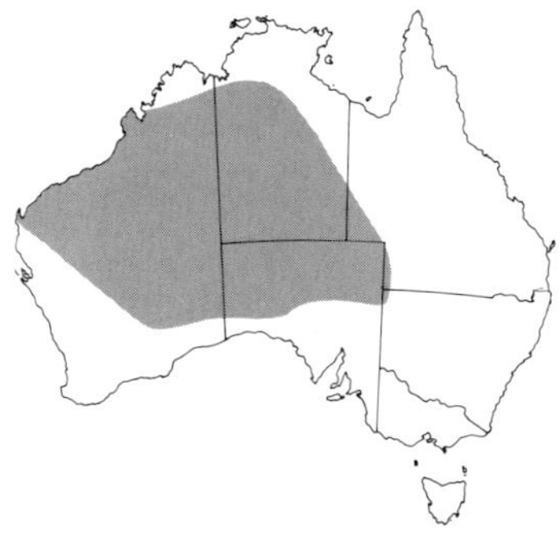

Key

TO THE AUSTRALIAN SPECIES OF ACANTHOPHIS

1 Anterior dorsal scales strongly keeled **2**

Anterior dorsal scales smooth or weakly keeled .... ***antarcticus***

2 Ground colour bright reddish-brown; ventrals usually more than 130, head shields strongly rugose....... ***pyrrhus***

Ground colour dark brown or grey-brown; ventrals usually fewer than 130; head shields moderately rugose.. ***praelongus***

Acanthophis antarcticus

(Shaw and Nodder, 1802)
Common Death Adder

Description: Variable in colour, ranging from pale grey to rich reddish-brown, usually with somewhat irregular cross-bands, often dark-edged, which depending on their colour and width may appear to be either dark or light in relation to the ground colour. Belly cream or greyish, with numerous dark brown or grey flecks and spots. Tail tip usually white or cream. Lips usually strongly barred with dark brown. Body shape, including the distinctive tail, as described for the genus. Mid-body scales smooth to moderately keeled, in 21 rows. Ventrals 110-135. Anal single. Subcaudals 35-60, mostly single, but a few posterior ones divided. Eye small, inconspicuous, with a vertical

Acanthophis antarcticus Brinerville, NSW DANGEROUS

Acanthophis praelongus Jabiru, NT DANGEROUS

Acanthophis pyrrhus Alice Springs district, NT DANGEROUS

pupil. Head shields, especially supraoculars, ranging from smooth to strongly rugose. Average size 40 cm, maximum about 1 metre. DANGEROUS.
Distribution: Throughout continental Australia except far north, central desert regions and wetter parts of Vic and south-eastern NSW.
Habit: Habits described under genus. Ovoviviparous, producing up to 20 young in a litter. Litters recorded from December until April. Adults feed largely on small mammals and birds, and juveniles feed on reptiles (Shine).

Acanthophis praelongus Ramsay, 1877

Northern Death Adder

Description: Status uncertain. Similar in most respects to *Acanthophis antarcticus,* from which it differs in its smaller size and much lighter build, its more rugose head shields (often a raised outer edge on each supraocular), and its strongly keeled scales on the neck and anterior part of the body. Average size 40 cm, maximum about 70 cm. DANGEROUS.
Distribution: Northern Australia, from the Kimberleys, WA, to Cape York Peninsula, Qld. Extra-limital in New Guinea.
Habit: Similar to that of *Acanthophis antarcticus.*

Acanthophis pyrrhus Boulenger, 1898

Desert Death Adder

Description: Differs from the Common Death Adder in its strongly keeled scales, rugose head shields, bright reddish-brown colour and somewhat more slender body. The lighter cross-bands may have their hind edges marked by black-tipped scales. Tail tip usually blackish. Belly cream or reddish. Mid-body scales in 19-21 rows. Ventrals 120-160. Anal single. Subcaudals 40-65, single anteriorly, divided posteriorly. DANGEROUS.
Distribution: Desert regions of central Australia, extending into the arid parts of all mainland states except Vic.
Habit: Probably similar in most respects to that of the Common Death Adder, but essentially unknown.

Genus **Austrelaps** Worrell, 1963

Currently a monotypic genus whose sole species is the Australian Copperhead, but three geographic forms have been recognised and proposed for full species status: a lowland or southern Copperhead *(superbus)*, a highland Copperhead *(ramsayi)*, and an isolated form from Kangaroo Island and the adjacent mainland of SA. While both available names have been used in the literature, a formal revision of the genus has yet to appear.

The genus is confined to south-eastern Australia and is characterised by undivided subcaudals; suboculars absent; internasals present; smooth scales usually in 15 rows at mid-body; anal undivided; frontal shield longer than broad, but less than one and a half times as broad as the supraocular; lateral scales noticeably enlarged. Fang followed by 3-5 solid maxillary teeth.

Austrelaps superbus New England district, NSW DANGEROUS

Austrelaps superbus (Günther, 1858)

Copperhead

Description: Very variable in colour, ranging from light grey, through reddish-brown or chocolate-brown to black above; the enlarged lateral scales may be cream, yellow or red, while the lips are often strikingly barred. Belly cream to leaden-coloured. The young are usually lighter in colour than the adults, and often possess a dark-coloured band across the nape and a dark vertebral stripe; occasionally one or both of these markings persists in the adult. Mid-body scales smooth, in 15 (rarely 17) rows. Ventrals 140-165. Anal single. Subcaudal 35-55, single. Head narrow, only slightly distinct from neck. Eye large, pupil round. 1.3 metres (total length). Maximum about 1.7 metres. DANGEROUS.

Distribution: Found in an arc along the highlands and adjacent slopes of south-eastern Australia from the region of the SA/Vic border almost as far north as the Qld border. Tas and the islands of Bass Strait. Kangaroo Island and the southern Mount Lofty Ranges, SA.

Habit: Usually found in or near marshes or swamps, where large aggregations may occur. Active both day and night, even at very low temperatures when no other reptiles are active. Usually inoffensive, bites are uncommon. Venom has strong neurotoxic action, but is also powerfully haemolytic and cytolytic. Feeds principally on cold-blooded vertebrates, especially frogs. Ovoviviparous. Worrell records litters of up to 20, while in the Armidale region Shine recorded litters of 9-31, with an average of 17.

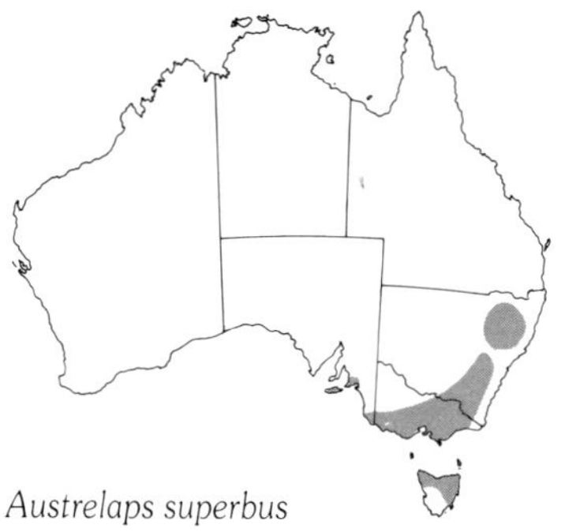

Austrelaps superbus

Genus ***Cacophis*** Günther, 1863

A group of small, secretive, nocturnal snakes, each of which has a characteristic yellowish or white band at least partly encircling the top of the head. The body is dark brown or greyish above, without any indication of banding. The belly is either coloured or has a distinctive pattern. Most are small but one species attains a length of nearly a metre. Internasals are present. No suboculars separate the eye from the labials. The anal scale is divided. Subcaudals number 25-50.

All species are venomous, but are not regarded as dangerous to humans. They usually hide under rocks or logs, or in crevices, etc. Little is known of their habits. Oviparous (Shine), usually laying 2-10 large, elongate eggs.

Key

TO THE SPECIES OF CACOPHIS

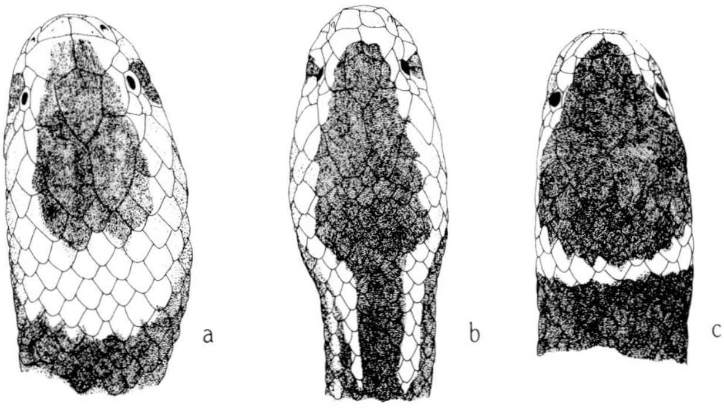

1 A complete white, cream or yellow nuchal band (a); belly not reddish........ **2**

Paler yellowish lateral head-marking not forming a complete nuchal band (b); belly reddish.... ***squamulosus***

2 Ventrals normally fewer than 165; white collar never more than two scales wide (c); belly white, at least medially........ ***krefftii***

Ventrals normally more than 165; white collar at least four scales wide (a); belly uniformly lead-grey......... ***harriettae***

Cacophis harriettae Krefft, 1869

White-Crowned Snake

Description: Dark brown or steely-grey above, with a white or light yellowish stripe around the side of the head, enclosing the snout, and forming a complete broad collar across the nape; this collar is at least four scales wide. Some body scales with pale, longitudinal centres forming narrow, paler stripes along the body, especially anteriorly. Belly uniformly lead-grey. Mid-body scales smooth, in 15 rows. Ventrals 170-200.

Cacophis harriettae Brisbane, Qld

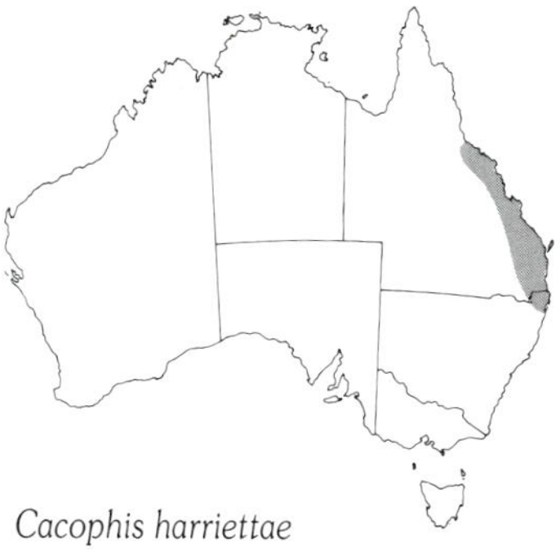

Cacophis harriettae

Cacophis krefftii

Cacophis krefftii Watagan State Forest, NSW

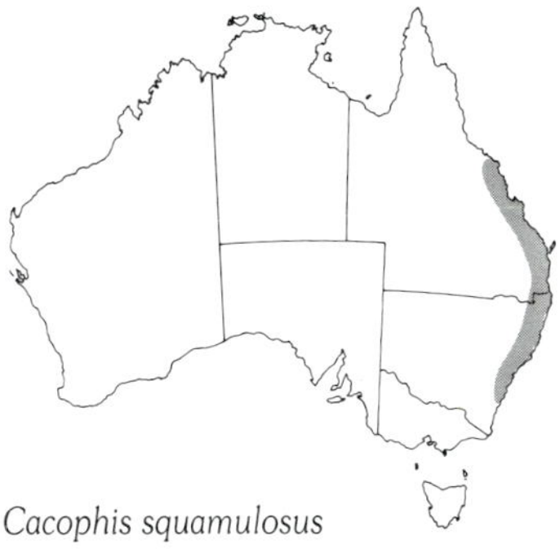

Cacophis squamulosus

Anal divided. Subcaudals 25-45, all divided. 40 cm (total length).
Distribution: Coastal and near-coastal areas from north of the Tropic of Capricorn to north-eastern NSW.
Habit: Secretive, nocturnal, it spends the day sheltering under leaf-litter, fallen timber, etc. Venomous, but not dangerous; its defence posture, which includes thrashing strikes, is essentially bluff, for it rarely attempts to bite. An egg-laying species; Worrell records a litter of four young. Shine records clutches of 2-10, with an average of 5. Food consists largely of small lizards.

Cacophis krefftii Günther, 1863
Dwarf Crowned Snake

Description: Steel-black above, with a narrow, white stripe around the side of the head enclosing the snout and forming a narrow, complete collar across the nape; this collar is scarcely more than one scale in width. Belly white medially, the ventral scales laterally edged with black to form a saw-toothed pattern; black stripe along the underside of the tail following the median division of the subcaudals. Mid-body scales smooth, in 15 rows. Ventrals 140-160. Anal divided. Subcaudals 25-40, all divided. 25 cm (total length).

Cacophis squamulosus
Wilson River, NSW

Distribution: Found from central coast of NSW to south-eastern Qld. Confined to coast and eastern side of ranges.
Habit: A secretive, nocturnal snake which is usually found under rotting logs, leaf-litter or bark. Venomous, but innocuous to humans, it rarely attempts to bite. Its threat display resembles that of *C. squamulosus*. Shine records clutches of 2-5 (average 3.2); the eggs are large and very elongate. Feeds on small lizards.

Cacophis squamulosus (Duméril, Bibron and Duméril, 1854)

Golden Crowned Snake

Description: Dark brown or steely-grey above, with a light fawn, brown or yellowish stripe around the side of the head, enclosing the snout and extending well back on to the nape on each side without meeting to form a collar. This light stripe is usually flecked with dark brown, especially on the sides of the face. Belly bright pink to red, with black patches and spots concentrated on the mid-line. A black stripe along the underside of the tail, following the median division of the subcaudals. Mid-body scales smooth, in 15 rows. Ventrals 165-185. Anal divided. Subcaudals 30-50, all divided. Head relatively large and distinct; eyes fairly small, with vertically elliptic pupil. 50 cm (total length), maximum length 75 cm.
Distribution: Coast and adjacent ranges from central NSW to south-eastern Qld
Habit: A secretive, nocturnal snake which shelters during the day under stones, logs, leaf-litter, etc. Although venomous it is not regarded as dangerous to humans; it adopts a fierce, raised, striking posture when alarmed, but rarely attempts to bite even when it strikes. Although abundant in sandstone areas in the southern part of its range, it more commonly inhabits deep forest in the north. Egg-laying, with an average clutch of about six (range 2-15: Shine). Feeds mainly on small skinks.

Genus *Demansia* Günther, 1858

Members of this genus are slender, whip-like, swift-moving, diurnal snakes, at least one species of which is likely to be encountered in most parts of continental Australia. One species also occurs in New Guinea.

The genus is characterised by its relatively large eye, its diameter markedly greater than the distance from the mouth; scales smooth, in 15 rows at mid-body; nasal and preocular scales in contact; subcaudals 35 or more, all divided; anal divided; no suboculars; 7-14 solid maxillary teeth following the fang.

Key

TO THE SPECIES OF DEMANSIA

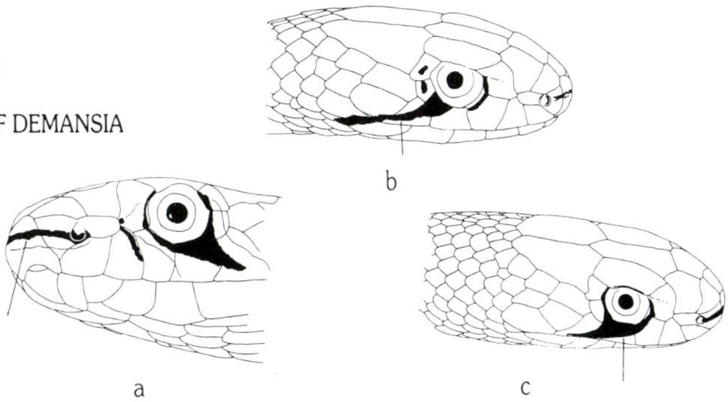

1 A narrow, usually pale-edged, blackish bar around front of snout from nostril to nostril (a)..**2**

No blackish bar around snout..**4**

2 Usually darker reticulations, spots or bars on throat and anterior ventral scales; dark comma-shaped mark below eye extending back almost on a level with the hind edge of the parietal scales (b) **3**

Throat and anterior ventral scales without dark reticulations or spots; dark comma-shaped mark below eye extending back only to about a level with the centre of the parietal scales (c)................................. ***psammophis***

3 Head with or without a dark, pale-edged nuchal bar; nuchal bar, if present, only in specimens from far-western WA... ***olivacea***

Head with one or more dark, pale-edged nuchal bars......... .... ***torquata***

4 Body black above, at least anteriorly.............................. **5**

Body dark grey above... ***simplex***

5 Anterior ventrals edged with black; head usually unspotted; ventrals plus subcaudals fewer than 280........... .... ***atra***

Anterior ventrals not edged with black; head usually spotted; ventrals plus subcaudals more than 280............... .... ***papuensis***

Demansia atra (Macleay, 1884)

Black Whip Snake

Description: Light to dark olive-brown or black above, lighter laterally, each body scale edged with darker to form a network pattern in lighter specimens, while dark pigment is often more pronounced posteriorly. Top of head usually without dark brown spots and flecks. No light-edged dark bar around front of snout. Side of face with at most a trace of strongly contrasting light and dark markings. Belly yellowish-grey to greenish-grey, underside of tail reddish. Mid-body scales smooth, in 15 rows. Ventrals 160-220, the anterior ones dark-edged. Anal divided. Subcaudals 70-95, all divided. Head narrow, deep and long; body slender; tail thin and whip-like. 1 metre (total length).

Distribution: Coast and adjacent areas of north-eastern and north Australia, from central-eastern Qld to the Kimberleys, WA.

Habit: A nervous, swift-moving, diurnal snake, it is more often found in drier habitats throughout its range. Venomous, but only larger specimens

Demansia atra Katherine, NT

Demansia olivacea Mt Isa, Qld

regarded as potentially dangerous to humans. **Oviparous:** Worrell records 'about 8 eggs'; Shine records clutches of 4-13, averaging 7.5. Feeds mainly on smaller vertebrates, especially lizards.

Demansia atra

Demansia olivacea

Demansia papuensis

Demansia olivacea (Gray, 1842)

Description: Grey-brown above, usually flushed with rich brown or russet on the post-temporal regions. Head above immaculate, or more often with distinct blackish marbling or blotching from the snout to the parietal region. Sides of the head distinctively marked; a dark purplish-brown streak from the lower hind corner of the eye to the angle of the mouth, bordered above by a narrow, white streak and below by a paler area continuous with a marbled supralabial region. Postoculars usually white-edged or marbled with white and brown, while the labials and many other head shields are narrowly edged with brown. Lower lips and chin shields and anterior ventrals whitish, margined or variegated with brown. Sometimes a dark, pale-edged bar across the nape. Remaining ventral surfaces white or cream, except for the tail, which may be yellow-green or even reddish below. Scales, smooth in 15 rows at mid-body. Ventrals 160-210. Anal divided. Subcaudals 65-105, all divided. 80 cm (total length).
Distribution: Coast and hinterland of northern Australia, from north-western Qld to northern WA.
Habit: Occurs in a variety of habitats from semi-arid, stony ranges (Qld) to coastal dunes, savannah woodlands and monsoon forests. Diurnal. Egg-laying, with a clutch size of 3-4 eggs; feeds on lizards (Shine).
Subspecies: *olivacea* (Kimberleys, WA, through the NT to western Qld); *rufescens* (Pilbara region, WA; *calodera* (coast and hinterland of WA, from North West Cape to Shark Bay region).

Demansia papuensis (Macleay, 1877)

Description: Black or very dark brown above, the head paler with numerous blackish spots or flecks and the body somewhat paler posteriorly; no dark, pale-edged bar around front of snout, and at most a faint trace of facial markings; ventral surfaces greyish. Scales smooth, in 15 rows at mid-body. Ventrals 192-220. Anal divided. Subcaudals 78-105. 1.3 metres (total length).
Distribution: Kimberley region of WA to north-eastern Qld; extra-limital in southern New Guinea.
Habit: Generally similar to *Demansia atra*.
Subspecies: *papuensis* (New Guinea); *melaena* (Australia).

Demansia papuensis Darwin, NT

Demansia psammophis (Schlegel, 1837)

Yellow-Faced Whip Snake

Description: Very variable in colour, tending towards uniform light steely-grey or olive-grey above in south-eastern populations; grey or greenish above, each scale dark-edged to form an overall network pattern, head and hind part of body reddish, in SA and WA populations (Wyree, subspecies *reticulata*); grey above, with an indefinite, broad, vertebral zone of reddish colour in north-eastern populations. A yellow-edged, narrow, dark bar around front of snout from nostril to nostril. A dark streak from eye to angle of mouth, edged on either side by bright cream or yellow. Belly grey-green to yellowish, the latter predominating under the tail. Scales smooth, in 15 rows at mid-body. Ventrals 165-230. Anal divided. Subcaudals 60-105, all divided. 80 cm (total length).
Distribution: Through most of continental Australia, except for the tropical north from the eastern Kimberleys to western Qld.
Habit: Found in a wide range of habitats from coast to arid interior. A swift-moving, diurnal snake. Venomous, but only very large specimens likely to be dangerous to humans. Oviparous, clutches of 5-6 (Worrell, McPhee) and 15-20 (Kinghorn) being recorded. McPhee also records communal egg-laying in this species. Feeds mainly on small diurnal lizards.
Subspecies: *psammophis* (eastern Australia); *cupreiceps* (arid interior to mid-western coast of WA and western Kimberleys); *reticulata* (coast and adjacent areas of WA south of Shark Bay).

Demansia simplex Storr, 1978

Description: Uniform dark greyish-brown above, contrasting sharply with the white ventral surface. Usually some indication of typical whip-snake facial markings: a pale-edged, dark, comma-shaped streak from beneath eye towards angle of mouth. Scales smooth, in 15 rows at mid-body. Ventrals 140-150. Anal divided. Subcaudals 50-65, all divided. 60 cm (total length).
Distribution: North-western Kimberley region, WA.
Habit: Open tropical woodland.

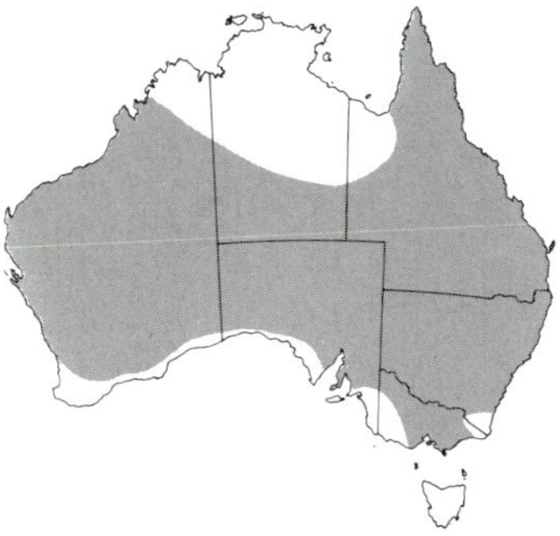

Demansia psammophis

Demansia simplex

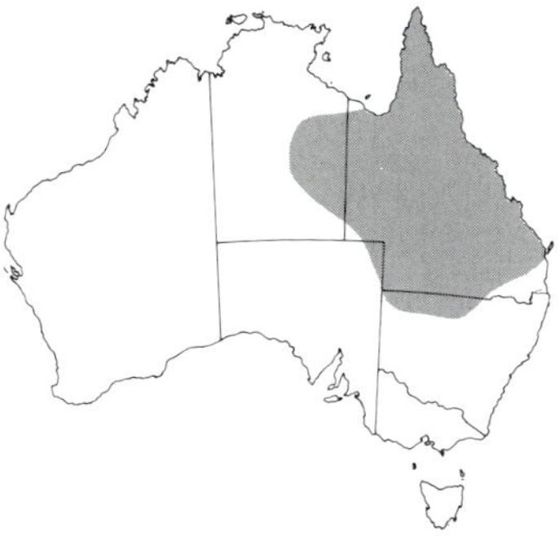

Demansia torquata

Demansia psammophis WA

Demansia psammophis Nymagee, NSW

Demansia torquata Townsville, Qld

Demansia torquata (Günther, 1862)

Collared Whip Snake

Description: Uniform medium grey-brown above. Top of head darker, bordered behind by a series of black and yellow cross-bands; in some specimens there is only a single black band, which is itself bordered in front and behind by narrower yellow bands; however, in other specimens these yellow bands are themselves bordered by additional black bands. All of these bands become more obscure in older specimens. A light-edged, narrow, dark bar around front of snout from nostril to nostril. A dark streak from the eye to the angle of the mouth, edged on either side with yellow. Belly greyish, darker medially. Scales smooth, in 15 rows at mid-body. Ventrals 185-220. Anal divided. Subcaudals 70-90, all divided. The most slender and whip-like member of the genus. 50 cm (total length).

Distribution: North-eastern Qld to far western and south-western Qld and adjacent areas of adjoining states.

Habit: Little is known of the habit of this species. Swift-moving and diurnal, it is found in a wide range of habitats from the tropical north-east to the arid interior. Oviparous; clutch size 2-8 (Shine). Venomous, but regarded as harmless to humans. Feeds mainly on small lizards, especially skinks. Sympatric in various parts of its range with *Demansia psammophis*, *D. olivacea* (to which it is closely allied) and *D.atra*.

Genus *Denisonia* Krefft, 1869

A genus of two small to moderate cryptozoic, nocturnal snakes widely distributed in eastern continental Australia.

These snakes are characterised by smooth scales in 17 rows at mid-body; preocular in contact with nasal; frontal longer than broad, at least one and a half times as broad as the supraocular; anal single; internasals present; subcaudals single, usually fewer than 40; suboculars absent; 3-5 small, solid maxillary teeth following the fang.

Key

TO THE SPECIES OF DENISONIA

Body with cross-bands.. ***devisi***
Body without cross-bands................................ ***maculata***

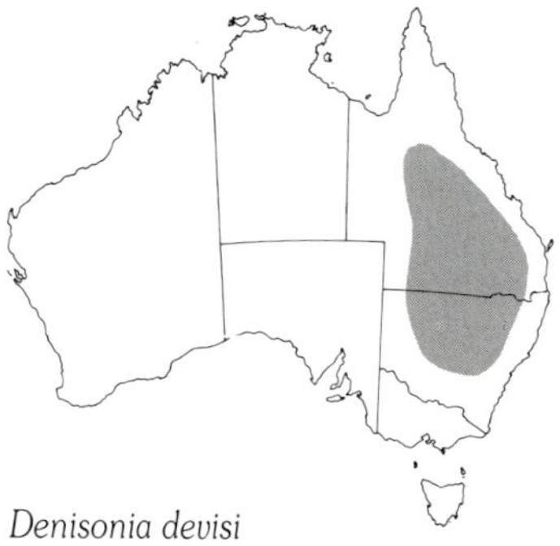

Denisonia devisi

Denisonia devisi Waite and Longman, 1920

De Vis Banded Snake

Description: Similar in most respects to *Denisonia maculata*, from which it is readily distinguished by colour and pattern. Light brown above, with a series of dark brown bands which are about twice as wide as the paler interspaces. The scales in the dark bands often have lighter brown centres, while anteriorly the dark bands are often interrupted on the vertebral line and fail to reach the ventral scales, so that they form a series of dorso-lateral blotches. Head dark brown with lighter brown flecks. Lips distinctly barred. Belly white or cream. Scales smooth, in 17 rows at mid-body. Ventrals 120-150. Anal single. Subcaudals 20-40, all single. A heavily built snake. 60 cm (total length).
Distribution: Western slopes and plains of southern Qld and northern NSW.
Habit: Found in a range of habitats from dry sclerophyll forest to savannah woodlands and grassy river floodplains. Usually found sheltering under ground debris during the day, it forages actively on warm nights.

Denisonia maculata (Steindachner, 1867)

Ornamental Snake

Description: Brown, grey-brown or almost black above, lateral scales lighter in colour, often with darker streaks or flecks and often with black hind edges. Crown of head darker brown to black, with lighter flecks or mottling. Lips distinctly barred. Belly white or cream, with dark spots or flecks on the outer edges of the ventral scales. Scales smooth, in 17 rows at mid-body. Ventrals 120-150. Anal single. Subcaudals 20-40, all single. A heavily built snake. 50 cm (total length).
Distribution: Central eastern Qld.
Habit: A nocturnal snake which shelters under litter and fallen timber during the day. Distinctive defence posture in which the body is greatly depressed and

Denisonia devisi Walgett, NSW

Denisonia maculata Rockhampton district, Qld

Denisonia maculata

held in a series of stiff curves, from which it will thrash about and bite savagely if approached. A bite can produce severe effects and the species should be regarded as potentially dangerous, although no deaths have been recorded. A live-bearing species: Worrell records 'about eight' young in a litter, while Shine records litters of 3-11 (average 6-8). Feeds principally on frogs.

Genus *Drysdalia* Worrell, 1961

A group of small, slender snakes confined to southern Australia. The genus is characterised by smooth scales in 15 rows at mid-body, the lower laterals not noticeably enlarged; frontal much longer than broad, usually less than one and a half times as wide as the supraocular; anal single; subcaudals single; internasals present; suboculars absent; 3-5 small, solid maxillary teeth following the fang.

Key

TO THE SPECIES OF DRYSDALIA

1 A pale band across the nape **2**
No pale band across the nape **3**

2 A distinct white labial stripe, edged above with black .... ***mastersii***
No white labial stripe .... ***rhodogaster***

3 Black band across the back of the head; south-western Australia .... ***coronata***
No band across the back of the head; south-eastern Australia .... ***coronoides***

Drysdalia coronata (Schlegel, 1837)

Crowned Snake

Description: Pale yellowish-brown, through grey or olive-brown to very dark brown above, often with a greenish tint. Tail often lighter than the rest of the body, yellowish or reddish. Head usually darker than body, and completely enclosed by a black crown which passes as a bar across the rostral and along each side of the head (through the eye) to the nape, where it forms a broader nuchal band. Labials white or yellowish. Mid-body scales smooth, in 15 rows. Ventrals 130-160. Anal single. Subcaudals 35-55, single. 40 cm (total length).
Distribution: South-western WA.
Habit: Little recorded. Nocturnal. Live-bearing, 3-9

Drysdalia coronata south-western WA

in a litter (Shine). Shine also records lizards as food items. Venomous, but not regarded as dangerous to humans.

Drysdalia coronoides (Günther, 1858)

White-Lipped Snake

Description: Very variable in colour. Light grey through various shades of brown and russet to almost black above; cream, grey, yellow, salmon or pink below. A thin, continuous or broken white stripe from the snout, along the upper lip and fading out on the side of the neck; this white line is bordered narrowly above by black. Mid-body scales smooth, in 15 rows. Ventrals 120-160. Anal single. Subcaudals 35-70, all single. 40 cm (total length).

Distribution: From higher parts of the northern tablelands of NSW, along the ranges to southern NSW (where it extends to lower altitudes and the coast), Vic and SA. Also Tas.

Habit: Little known. Mainly nocturnal, sheltering by day under rocks, logs or litter. However, sometimes

Drysdalia coronoides Snowy Mountains, NSW

Drysdalia coronoides Queenstown, Tas

forages during the day. Feeds on small skinks. 2-10 living young in a litter (Shine). Venomous, but not dangerous to humans.

Drysdalia mastersii (Krefft, 1866)

Masters' Snake

Description: Grey-brown, often tinged with reddish. The individual scales often have lighter lateral tips, producing a series of faint, light, longitudinal striations. Head usually dark grey above, flecked with darker, and bordered on the nape by a light yellow, orange or brown collar 2-3 scales in width. Snout and side of head lighter than above, with a narrow, black, light-edged streak from nostril to eye, and another narrow black streak, often broken, from the eye to the side of the neck. Labials spotted with black. Belly yellow, with dark spots and flecks along the outer edges of the ventrals. Scales smooth, in 15 rows at mid-body. Ventrals 140-160. Anal single. Subcaudals 40-55, all single. 40 cm (total length).
Distribution: North-western Vic and SA, extending as far as south-eastern WA.
Habit: As for *Drysdalia coronoides*. Number of live young 2-3 (Shine). Feeds on lizards.

Drysdalia rhodogaster (Jan and Sordelli, 1873)

Description: Olive-brown above, pale grey, yellow or orange below, each ventral scale edged with darker brown. Top of head very dark brown

Drysdalia coronata

Drysdalia coronoides

Drysdalia mastersii

Drysdalia rhodogaster

Drysdalia mastersii near Balladonia, WA

Drysdalia rhodogaster Kurrajong, NSW

posteriorly, sharply demarcated from a pale yellow or orange band 2-3 scales wide across the nape, but becoming paler anteriorly until the colour on the snout is the same as that on the body. A dark brown streak consisting of a series of short bars and dots, from the snout, through the nostril and eye. No white stripe along upper lip. Mid-body scales smooth, in 15 rows. Ventrals 140-160. Anal single. Subcaudals 40-55, all single. 40 cm (total length).

Distribution: NSW: south coast and adjacent ranges to highlands of the Great Dividing Range west of the central coast.

Habit: A secretive species found mainly in dry sclerophyll forests and montane heathlands. Nocturnal, but sometimes active in the late afternoon or during the day in deeply-shaded areas.

Genus ***Echiopsis*** Fitzinger, 1843

A genus whose two species are found in southern continental Australia. They are small, rather stumpy, nocturnal snakes, characterised by having smooth scales in 19 rows at mid-body; suboculars absent; anal single; subcaudals single; internasals present; two or three solid maxillary teeth following the fang.

Echiopsis curta Cape Leeuwin, WA. Female with new-born young. DANGEROUS

Key

TO THE SPECIES OF ECHIOPSIS

Ventrals fewer than 165; subcaudals fewer than 45; head not black.. ***curta***

Ventrals more than 165; subcaudals 45 or more; head black, contrasting with colour on neck and body................ ***atriceps***

Echiopsis atriceps

Echiopsis atriceps (Storr, 1980)

Description: Brown to dark brown above, pale reddish-brown below. Top and sides of head dull black, except for a narrow, white edge to the upper lips. Scales smooth, in 19 rows at mid-body. Ventrals 175-180. Anal single. Subcaudals 45-50, single. Average total length 50 cm (total length).
Distribution: Currently known only from the type locality: Lake Cronin, WA.

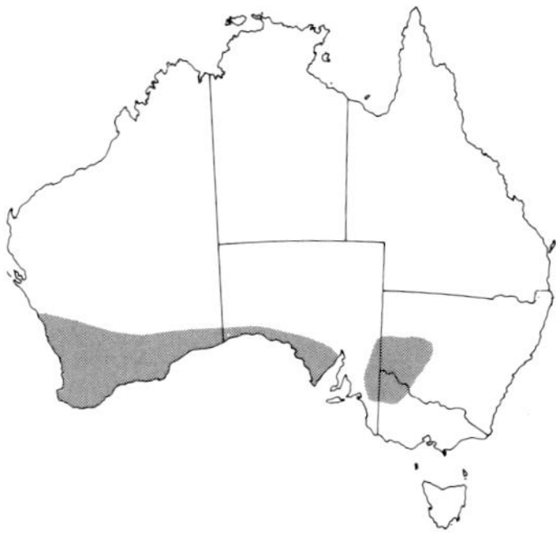

Echiopsis curta

Echiopsis curta (Schlegel, 1837)

Bardick

Description: Uniform grey-brown, olive-brown, reddish-brown or rich brown above, most of the lateral scales edged with paler reddish-brown; head usually with a few scattered pale flecks. Labials, lower temporals, nasal and rostral usually speckled with white, each white fleck edged with reddish-brown. Throat and anterior ventrals richly speckled with white and brown. Belly pale grey-brown, each ventral with a brown hind edge. Subcaudal region more yellowish than the belly. Scales smooth, in 19 rows at mid-body. Ventrals 130-145. Anal single. Subcaudals 30-40, single. Average total length 40 cm, maximum about 60 cm. DANGEROUS
Distribution: Widely distributed from coast and interior of south-western WA, through southern SA to western Vic and south-western NSW.
Habit: Poorly known. Usually found under logs and other ground debris on sandy or loamy soils. Nocturnal. Food items recorded are lizards, frogs, birds, mammals and insects. Litters of 8-10 live young have been recorded. Venomous, but although usually regarded as harmless to humans, the properties of its venom are poorly known, other than that its affinities lie with that of the Death Adders.

Genus ***Elapognathus*** Boulenger, 1896

A monotypic genus confined to far south-western Australia. It is characterised by having smooth scales, in 15 rows at mid-body; frontal shield longer than broad; suboculars absent; internasals present; anal single; subcaudals single; no solid maxillary teeth following the fang.

Elapognathus minor (Günther, 1863)

Little Brown Snake

Elapognathus minor

Description: Uniform brown above, tending to greenish-brown on the sides. Supralabials yellowish-brown, much lighter than remainder of head; supralabials of some specimens with black posterior margins giving a distinctly barred appearance to the

Elapognathus minor south-western WA

lips. A faint light (or dark) nuchal collar in some specimens, especially juveniles. Throat often bright yellow fading to yellowish-cream or greenish-yellow on belly. Ventrals each with a black, crescent-shaped area anteriorly, so that the belly has a median series of black bars becoming much fainter on the tail. Mid-body scales smooth, in 15 rows. Ventrals 120-130. Anal single. Subcaudals 50-70, single. 40 cm (total length).

Distribution: A rare snake confined to the lower south-western corner of WA, in an area centred at Albany. Type localities of Swan River and SA apparently in error.
Habit: Favours heathlands margining swamps, though also known from wet sclerophyll forests (Wilson and Knowles). Venomous, but regarded as innocuous to humans.

Genus ***Furina*** Duméril, 1853

A group of five snakes of small to moderate size, found throughout most of continental Australia, but with the majority of species confined to the north-eastern part of Australia and New Guinea. The genus is characterised by its smooth scales in 15-21 rows at mid-body; nasal divided or undivided, widely separated from the preocular; suboculars absent; subcaudals divided, 35 or more; anal divided; the head may be significantly darker than the rest of the body, and there is usually a contrasting red, orange, yellowish or pale cream patch or bar across the nape, especially in juveniles; seven or more solid maxillary teeth following the fang.

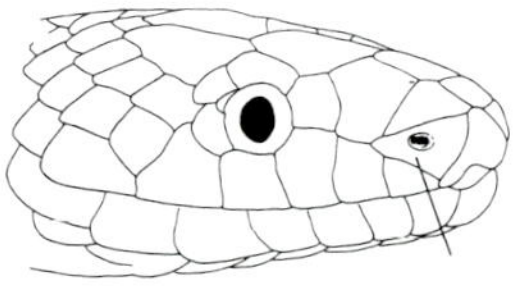

a

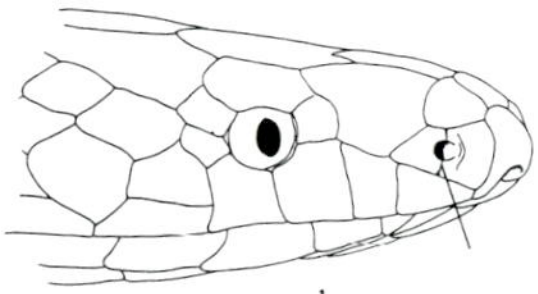

b

Key

TO THE SPECIES OF FURINA

1 A bright red or orange patch or bar on the nape; nasal undivided (a) **2**

Pale bar on nape, if present, never red or orange; nasal divided (b) 3

2 Head and neck black, completely enclosing a red or orange spot on the nape .... ***diadema***

Head and neck black or dark brown, with a pale yellow, orange or red occipital bar completely separating the dark colour of the head from that of the neck............... ***ornata***

3 Scales in fewer than 21 rows at mid-body **4**

Scales in 21 rows at mid-body .... ***dunmalli***

4 Scales in 17 rows at mid-body .... ***tristis***

Scales in 15 rows at mid-body .... ***barnardi***

Furina barnardi Qld

Furina barnardi (Kinghorn, 1939)

Yellow-naped Snake

Description: Status uncertain. Dark grey-brown to black above, the scales of the body light-edged, forming a reticulated appearance. Snout blackish, gradually becoming rich brown on top of the head, which colour in turn merges with a broad, yellow or light brown collar which extends from the back of the parietal scales for about six scale rows. This yellow collar is most conspicuous in juveniles and may almost disappear in old adults. Belly white or cream. Scales smooth, in 15 rows at mid-body. Ventrals 170-200. Anal divided. Subcaudals 35-50, all divided. 50 cm (total length).
Distribution: Coast and interior of north-eastern Qld, from about Port Curtis in the south to Cape York Peninsula.
Habit: A nocturnal snake which shelters under fallen timber and other litter during the day. Aggressive when alarmed, but although venomous is not regarded as dangerous to humans. Believed to be oviparous.

Furina diadema (Schlegel, 1837)

Red-naped Snake

Description: Rich reddish-brown above, each scale edged behind with black or dark brown giving a reticulated appearance. Head and nape shiny black, except for a white streak along the lower half of the supralabials and a bright red or orange crescent, oval or diamond-shaped patch on the back of the head; this patch is sharply defined and is contained within the black of the head and neck. Belly immaculate white or cream. Scales smooth, normally in 15 rows at mid-body. Ventrals 160-210. Anal divided. Subcaudals 35-70, all divided. 40 cm (total length).
Distribution: Found throughout many parts of eastern Australia, from coastal regions to the drier inland.
Habit: A nocturnal snake which hides by day under rocks, logs or litter, or in earth crevices. Often found in association with termite or ant colonies. When alarmed, the forepart of the body is raised high and held stiffly and the snake thrashes about, striking at any object presented to it, but usually with its mouth

closed! Venomous, but harmless to humans. An oviparous species, clutches of eight (Günther), ten (McPhee) and 1-5, average 3 (Shine) eggs having been recorded. Feeds on small skinks.

Furina dunmalli (Worrell, 1955)

Dunmall's Snake

Description: Uniform dark grey-brown above, white below. Scales smooth, in 21 rows at mid-body. Ventrals 175-190. Anal divided. Subcaudals 35-50, all divided. 60 cm (total length).

Distribution: Ranges and inland of south-eastern Qld.

Habit: Eucalypt and *Callitris* woodland and brigalow scrub. Nocturnal (Worrell).

Furina barnardi

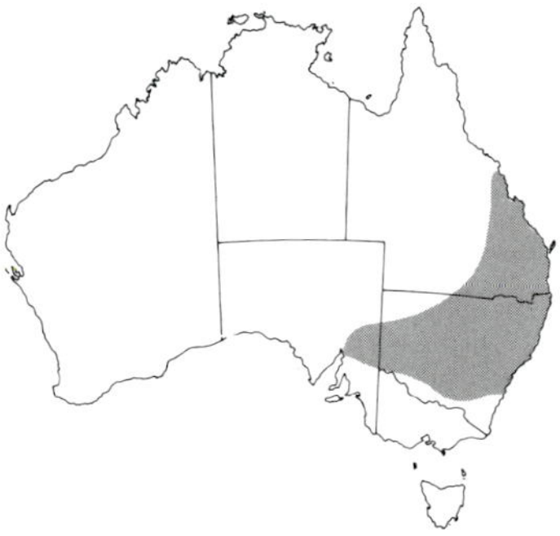

Furina diadema

Furina dunmali

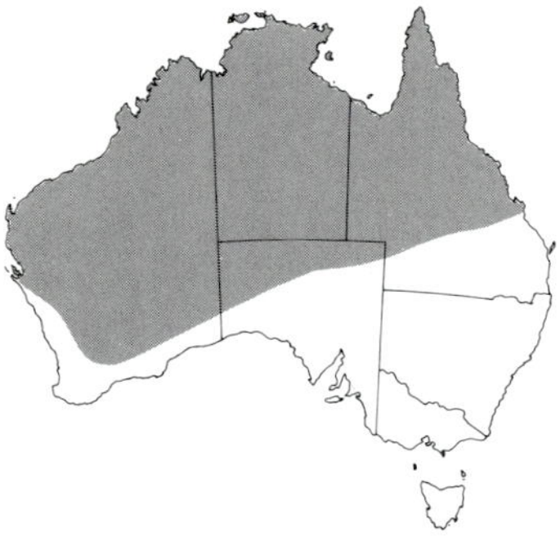

Furina ornata

Furina tristis

Furina diadema Sydney, NSW

Furina dunmalli Condamine River, Qld

Furina ornata (Gray, 1842)

Orange-naped Snake

Description: Pale to dark orange or reddish-brown above, each body scale edged with darker brown to form dark reticulations over the body. Head dark brown or blackish (somewhat paler on the snout), except for the lips which are pale cream; a broad yellow, orange or reddish bar across the nape separating the dark brown of the head from a similar dark brown area on the neck. Belly cream. Scales smooth, in 15 rows at mid-body in Qld and southern WA, but many specimens with 17 rows in the NT and north-western Australia. Ventrals 160-240. Anal divided. Subcaudals 35-70, all divided. 70 cm (total length).
Distribution: Most parts of continental Australia, except the south and south-east.
Habit: Similar in most respects to *Furina diadema,* except that it is found in a number of arid habitats ranging from savannah woodland to river floodplains and sandplain and sandridge deserts dominated by hummock grasses.

Furina ornata Weipa, Qld

Furina tristis (Günther, 1858)

Brown-headed Snake

Description: Iridescent blackish-brown above, somewhat paler on the head and with a distinct pale brown or yellowish collar, its edges merging with the ground colour. Lower labials and side of neck creamish. Most of the body scales with white hind edges becoming more conspicuous on the sides; outer edges of ventral scales with a brown patch, but the remainder of the ventral surface of the body white or cream. Usually some dark brown markings on the chin shields, while the margins of the subcaudals are strongly edged with brown. Scales smooth, in 17 rows

Furina tristis Weipa, Qld

at mid-body. Ventrals 160-190. Anal divided. Subcaudals 30-60, all divided. Average total length about 70 cm, maximum about 1 metre.
Distribution: Cape York Peninsula, Qld, and the islands of Torres Strait. Extra-limital in New Guinea.

Habit: Found in a range of habitats from rainforest to monsoon forest, seasonally dry woodlands, secondary growth, gardens, dense grasslands and even densely-vegetated beach dunes. Nocturnal, and aggressive when aroused.

Genus ***Hemiaspis*** Fitzinger, 1860

This genus currently includes two species of moderate size and build from eastern Australia. It is characterised by possessing smooth scales in 17 rows at mid-body; internasals present; anal divided; subcaudals single; suboculars absent; 3-5 small, solid maxillary teeth following the fang.

Key

TO THE SPECIES OF HEMIASPIS

Ventral surface black or grey, a narrow white or yellow bar behind the eye; no black collar.................................. ***signata***

Ventral surface yellowish, cream or white; no pale bar behind the eye; usually a black collar across the occiput........ ***damelii***

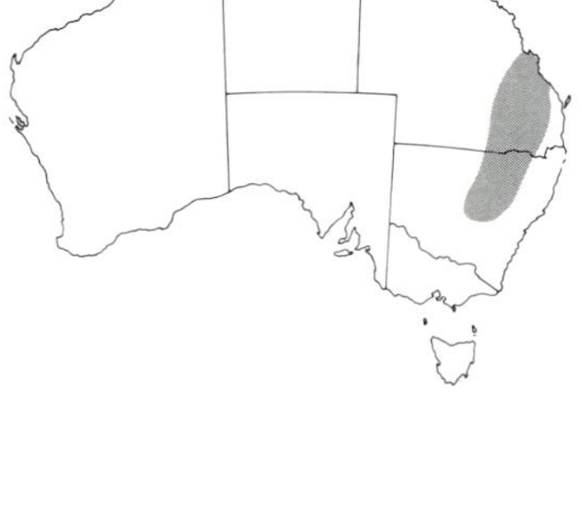

Hemiaspis damelii

Hemiaspis damelii (Günther, 1876)

Grey Snake

Description: Uniform olive-grey to grey above, except that each scale, especially on the sides, may

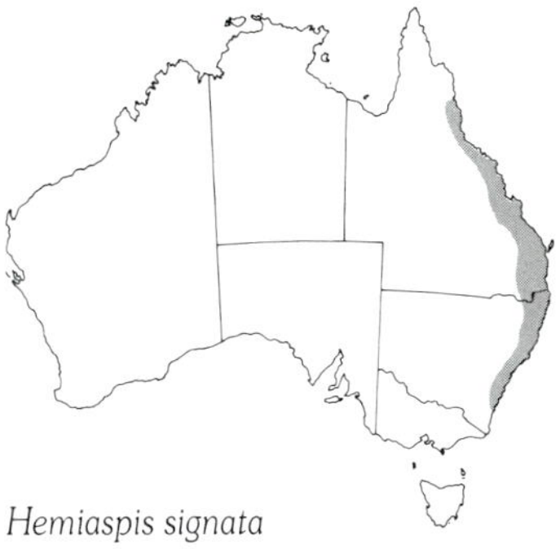

Hemiaspis signata

Hemiaspis signata Sydney district, NSW

be tipped with black anteriorly. Top of head to about second scale row behind parietals black in juveniles. In adults this usually fades to a black nuchal band or may disappear altogether. Belly white or cream with a few darker flecks. Scales smooth, in 17 rows at mid-body. Ventrals 140-170. Anal divided. Subcaudals 35-50, all single. 50 cm (total length).

Distribution: Central inland NSW, through the interior of south-eastern Qld to coastal areas near Rockhampton.

Hemiaspis damelii Quambone, NSW

Habit: Found in dry sclerophyll forests and woodlands throughout its range. Normally found under cover during the day, but Worrell records it as only 'partly nocturnal'. Worrell also records 6-12 live young in a litter. Feeds on lizards and frogs. Venomous, but not regarded as dangerous to humans.

Hemiaspis signata (Jan, 1859)

Black-bellied Swamp Snake

Description: Usually brown or olive-brown above, but black melanotic populations are common in NSW coastal areas. Head often darker than body, especially in juveniles; in new-born young the head is velvety-black. A narrow, white or yellow streak, dark-edged, from the eye to the side of the neck, and another narrow streak of the same colour, but usually flecked with darker, along the upper lip. Belly black or dark grey. Throat lighter. In some Qld populations the body may be russet or pink, while the belly may be cream or salmon. Scales smooth, in 17 rows at mid-body. Ventrals 150-170. Anal divided. Subcaudals 40-60, all single. 60 cm (total length).

Distribution: Coastal and near-coastal areas of eastern Australia, from far northern Qld to the south coast of NSW.

Habit: Found in a wide range of habitats from rainforest through wet and dry sclerophyll forests to coastal heaths. Although usually found in low-lying marshy areas, it is also found on dry rocky ridges and beach dunes. Normally diurnal and crepuscular, it can be nocturnal in hot weather. Produces live young, litters ranging from as few as four to about 20. A bite from a large specimen may be very painful, but it is not generally regarded as dangerous. Feeds largely on skinks and frogs.

Genus *Hoplocephalus* Wagler, 1830

This genus contains three species of broad-headed snakes confined to eastern continental Australia. All possess keeled ventral scales and are agile climbers, but only one species is more or less consistently arboreal.

All three species are characterised by their smooth dorsal scales in 19-21 rows at mid-body; ventral scales keeled or notched, more than 190; frontal shield noticeably longer than broad; internasals present; no suboculars; anal single; subcaudals single; two or three solid maxillary teeth following the fang.

Hoplocephalus bitorquatus Gloucester, NSW

Hoplocephalus bungaroides
Sydney district, NSW

Key

TO THE SPECIES OF HOPLOCEPHALUS

1 Body spotted or banded **2**
Body without spots or bands....................... ***bitorquatus***

2 Body banded with yellow and black, the former usually two or more scales in width; black bands often extending to sides of ventral scales................................ ***stephensii***
Body black with numerous, scattered, yellow or white scales; the latter often form irregular cross-bands which rarely exceed one scale in width; sides of ventral scales yellow or white ....***bungaroides***

Hoplocephalus bitorquatus

Hoplocephalus bungaroides

Hoplocephalus stephensii

Hoplocephalus bitorquatus

(Jan, 1859)
Pale-Headed Snake

Description: Body uniform light brown or grey above; a broad, white or cream band on the nape, immediately behind the parietal scales; this band is bordered behind by a narrow, blackish bar, which may be solid or broken in the middle; the top of the head is grey, with or without a series of black spots which are most prominent along the edge of the white nape patch and on the temporal region. Lips with or without black vertical bars. Belly creamy-grey, sometimes with darker flecks. Scales smooth, in 19 or 21 rows at mid-body. Ventrals 190-225. Anal single. Subcaudals 40-65, all single. 60 cm (total length).
Distribution: Patchy distribution along the coast, ranges and western slopes of eastern Australia, from about 80 kilometres north of Sydney, NSW, to Cape York Peninsula, Qld.

Habit: A partly arboreal, nocturnal snake found in a wide range of habitats, from rain or wet sclerophyll forest to the drier eucalypt forests of the western

Hoplocephalus stephensii
Port Macquarie, NSW

slopes of NSW and inland Qld. Live-bearing, with 2-11 young, average 5 (Shine). Bite is painful, but not regarded as potentially lethal. Feeds largely on frogs and lizards.

Hoplocephalus bungaroides

(Schlegel, 1837)
Broad-headed Snake

Description: Black above, with numerous bright yellow scales forming a series of irregular, narrow cross-bands. Other scales may link these cross-bands laterally to form a distinct, longitudinal, lateral stripe, straight or zigzagged, on each side. Head with numerous, irregular, yellow spots, while the upper labials are barred with yellow. Belly grey or grey-black, sometimes with yellowish blotches. Scales smooth, in 21 rows at mid-body. Ventrals 200-230. Anal single. Subcaudals 40-65, all single. Average total length 60 cm, maximum about 90 cm.
Distribution: Coast and ranges within an area approximately 250 kilometres from Sydney.
Habit: An aggressive, nocturnal snake largely confined to the Hawkesbury sandstone formation, where it is usually found under large slabs or rocky ridges, or in rocky crevices. Live-bearing, litters of eight (Worrell) to 20 (McPhee) having been recorded. Feeds largely on lizards and frogs. A bite may produce acute symptoms, but is not generally regarded as potentially lethal.

Hoplocephalus stephensii Krefft, 1869

Stephens' Banded Snake

Description: Brown (occasionally yellowish) above, almost invariably with a series of irregular, broad, dark cross-bands two or three times as broad as the lighter interspaces. However, occasionally specimens lack bands entirely, or the bands may change to form roughly longitudinal markings. Head black, with a brown crown and a brown or cream patch on either side of the nape. Lips barred with black and cream. Scales smooth, in 21 rows at mid-body. Ventrals 220-250. Anal single. Subcaudals 50-70, all single. 50 cm (total length).
Distribution: Coast and ranges from Gosford district, NSW, to southern Qld.
Habit: A nocturnal, partly arboreal snake usually encountered in the wetter sclerophyll or rainforests which occur within its range. Feeds on lizards, birds and small mammals. Live-bearing, with Shine recording an average litter of six (range 3-8).

Genus *Notechis* Boulenger, 1896

This genus is confined to southern Australia. The Tiger Snakes are probably the best known of Australian snakes, having been responsible for a significant proportion of snake-bite deaths in this country. Tiger Snake antivenene was the first to be developed in Australia, and the venom of this species has been very thoroughly studied.

The genus *Notechis* is characterised by a large, squarish frontal shield, not, or scarcely, longer than broad; the lower temporal is large and about as long as or longer than the frontal; scales smooth, in 17-21 rows at mid-body; suboculars absent; internasals present; ventrals more than 140; anal single; subcaudals single; four or five solid maxillary teeth following the fang.

The relationships of the various species and subspecies are obscure, especially as melanotic populations appear to have evolved independently in several areas. The treatment below is somewhat arbitrary, but follows the published scheme of Rawlinson.

Key

TO THE SPECIES OF NOTECHIS

Scales typically in 19 rows (17-21); typically not black; with or without bands .... ***scutatus***

Scales typically in 17 rows (17-21); jet-black dorsally......... ***ater***

Notechis ater

Notechis scutatus

Notechis ater (Krefft, 1866)

Black Tiger Snake

Description: Head and body black or very dark brown, sometimes (especially in juveniles) with faint darker or lighter cross-bands visible. Belly light to very dark grey. Scales smooth in 17 or 19 (very rarely 15 or 21) rows at mid-body. Ventrals 155-190. Anal single. Subcaudals 40-60, all single. 1.5 metres (total length). DANGEROUS.

Distribution: Flinders Ranges, Kangaroo and other offshore islands of southern SA; islands of Bass Strait and Tas; south-western WA.

Habit: Found in a wide range of habitats from dry, rocky areas to marshland and coastal dune grassland. Diurnal and crepuscular, but nocturnal in warm weather. Live-bearing. Feeds largely on frogs and small mammals. King Island snakes are cannibalistic (Worrell), while many island populations feed, in season, on the chicks of mutton birds (Mackay, Worrell).

Subspecies: *ater* (Flinders Ranges); *niger* (Kangaroo Island and other off-shore islands of SA); *humphreysi* (King and nearby islands, Bass Strait); *occidentalis* (south-western WA).

Notechis ater West Franklin Island, SA DANGEROUS

R. W. G. JENKINS

Notechis scutatus (adult) Collector, NSW DANGEROUS

Notechis scutatus (juvenile) Sydney, NSW

Notechis scutatus (Peters, 1861)

Eastern or Mainland Tiger Snake

Description: Very variable in colour, ranging from light grey through olive, brown and reddish to dark, blackish-brown, usually with (but often without) a series of narrow cross-bands formed by lighter yellow-edged scales. Belly cream, yellow, olive-green or grey, often with darker grey on the throat and under the tail. Scales in 17 (or 19, rarely 15) rows at mid-body. Ventrals 140-190. Anal single. Subcaudals 35-65, all single. 1.2 metres (total length). DANGEROUS.

Distribution: South-eastern Qld (where it is confined to a few montane populations), along the highlands of northern NSW to central NSW, where it extends to the coast and western slopes. Southern NSW including the Murrumbidgee area, Murray River Valley, Vic, and south-eastern SA.

Habit: Found in a broad range of habitats, from rainforest in the north to dry, open sclerophyll and river floodplains in the south. Feeds mainly on frogs. Aggressive only when aroused. Diurnal or crepuscular, but nocturnal in warm weather. Live-bearing, averaging about 30 young, but litters from 17 (Waite) to 109 (McPhee) have been recorded.

Genus *Oxyuranus* Kinghorn, 1923

This genus contains Australia's largest venomous snake and its two most dangerous species. The larger species, the Taipan, occurs widely in northern Australia, with an endemic subspecies in New Guinea, while the smaller Fierce Snake or Western Taipan is known only from the arid interior of eastern central Australia.

The genus *Oxyuranus* is characterised by possessing either smooth or keeled (at least on the neck) scales, in 21-23 rows at mid-body; suboculars absent; anal single; subcaudal divided; 1-4 solid maxillary teeth following the fang.

Key

TO THE SPECIES OF OXYURANUS

Scales keeled, at least on the neck; one solid maxillary tooth following the fang (a); anterior end of palatine bone splint-like, toothless (b) .... ***scutellatus***

Scales smooth; at least two solid maxillary teeth following the fang (c); palatine bone toothed along its length (d) .... ***microlepidotus***

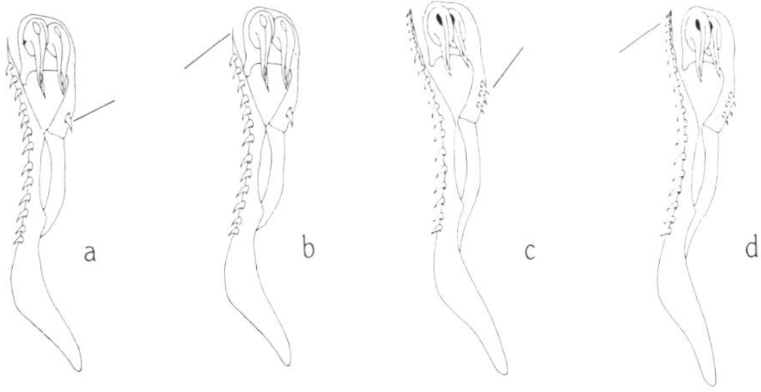

Oxyuranus microlepidotus near Windorah, Qld DANGEROUS J. WEIGEL

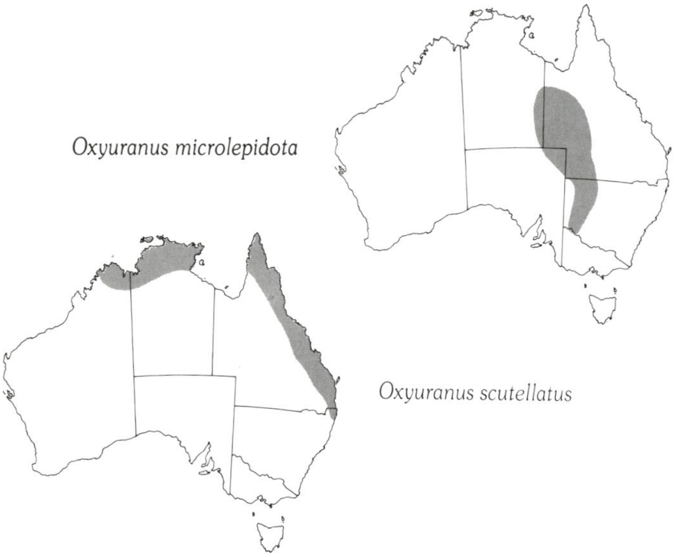

Oxyuranus microlepidota

Oxyuranus scutellatus

Oxyuranus microlepidotus
(McCoy, 1879)
Fierce Snake

Description: Rich brown or olive-brown above, many of the scales with dark brown or black anterior edges sometimes forming obscure cross-bands. Head with scattered, darker flecks. Ventral surface cream to bright yellow, the ventral scales with brown hind edges. Scales smooth, in 23 rows at mid-body. Ventrals 220-250. Anal normally single. Subcaudals 55-70, divided. Average total length 2 metres, maximum about 2.5 metres. DANGEROUS.
Distribution: Western and south-western Qld, north-western SA and western NSW, with old records extending to the Vic border.
Habit: A large, diurnal snake found on the cracked dark soils of the river overflows or flood plains or on lateritic gibber plains. Oviparous, with an average clutch of 16 (range 12-20); feeds on mammals, especially the local plague rat, *Rattus villosissimus* (Shine and Covacevich).

Oxyuranus scutellatus (Peters, 1867)
Taipan

Description: Uniform light to dark brown above, paling on the sides to creamy-brown. Head is often pale yellowish-cream, especially in juveniles, or pale colour may be confined to an indefinite nuchal bar and tip of snout. Belly cream to yellow, usually with irregular orange spots and flecks. Scales keeled (especially on the neck and vertebral region) to

Oxyuranus microlepidotus Morney Plains, Qld.

R. W. G. JENKINS

Oxyuranus scutellatus (adult) Weipa, Qld DANGEROUS

smooth, in 21 or 23 rows at mid-body. Ventrals 220-250. Anal single. Subcaudals 45-80, all divided. 2 metres (total length). DANGEROUS.
Distribution: Eastern Qld to extreme north-eastern NSW; northern part of the NT and Kimberley Division, WA.
Habit: Diurnal and crepuscular, though sometimes nocturnal. Found in a wide range of habitats, from tropical wet sclerophyll through dry sclerophyll forests and open savannah woodland. Australia's deadliest snake. Feeds mainly on small mammals. Oviparous, with clutches of three (McPhee) to 20 (Worrell) eggs recorded.
Subspecies: *scutellatus* (Australia); *canni* (New Guinea).

Oxyuranus scutellatus (hatching eggs)

Genus *Pseudechis* Wagler, 1830

Although members of this genus are generally termed 'black snakes', it is a singularly inappropriate name; as in most parts of Australia the genus is represented by the brown-coloured Mulga or King Brown Snake.

All species are very similar in form, structure and scalation, but are characterised by their smooth scales, in 17-19 rows; the condition of the anal and subcaudal scales is subject to considerable individual variation, but usually the anal is divided, and at least a few anterior subcaudals are single before giving way to divided subcaudals; suboculars absent.

Key

TO THE AUSTRALIAN SPECIES OF PSEUDECHIS

1 Scales in 17 rows.. **2**
Scales in 19 rows.. **4**

2 Black or brown above, without numerous pale spots on the individual scales **3**
Blackish above, the majority of scales black with sharply contrasting white, cream or yellow centres........... ***butleri***

3 Immaculate black above; crimson, pink or whitish below... .... ***porphyriacus***
Brown or reddish-brown above; white to orange below...... .... ***australis***

4 Ventrals 170-200 .... ***guttatus***
Ventrals 210-240 .... ***colletti***

Pseudechis australis (Gray, 1842)

Mulga or King Brown Snake

Description: Rich copper-coloured or reddish-brown to dark olive-brown above, the individual scales often with darker edges or tips forming an overall reticulated pattern. Belly cream to salmon-coloured, often with scattered, orange blotches. Scales smooth, in 17 rows at mid-body. Ventrals 185-225. Anal divided. Subcaudals 50-75, anterior ones single, posterior ones divided (occasionally all single). 2 metres (total length). DANGEROUS.
Distribution: Australia-wide except for coast, ranges and western slopes of south-eastern Australia from south-eastern Qld to SA and south-western WA.
Habit: Found in a wide range of habitats, from the tropical forests of northern Australia to the deserts of the interior. Often diurnal in southern parts of its range, it is often more nocturnal in the north or in hot weather. Feeds on small mammals, reptiles (including other snakes) and frogs. Oviparous, with an average clutch of about 12 (Shine).

Pseudechis australis
north-western NSW
DANGEROUS

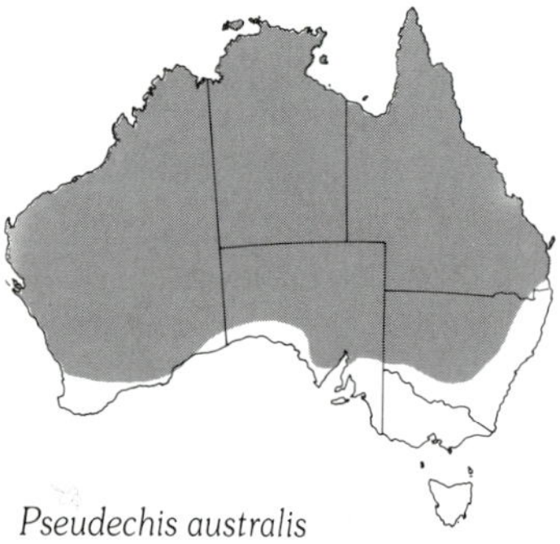

Pseudechis australis

Pseudechis australis near Oenpelli, NT DANGEROUS

Habit: Found '...on heavy (often stony) soils dominated by mulga *(Acacia aneura)* woodlands and shrublands' (Wilson and Knowles).

Pseudechis butleri Smith, 1982

Description: Black above, with groups of cream-, brown-or yellow-centred scales providing a generally spotted pattern which varies considerably between individuals, as in *Pseudechis guttatus*. Anterior head and throat usually distinctly reddish-brown. Ventral scales cream to bright yellow, sometimes flecked with black, and the base of each scale blackish. Scales smooth, in 17 rows at mid-body. Ventrals 200-220. Anal divided. Subcaudals 50-70, anterior ones single, the remainder divided. 1.6 metres (total length). DANGEROUS.
Distribution: 'Arid mid-west of Western Australia' (Smith).

Pseudechis colletti Boulenger, 1902

Collett's Snake

Description: Rich brown to black above, with numerous, irregular cross-bands formed by individual cream, pink or salmon-coloured scales, while the lower lateral scales may also be as brightly coloured as the cross-bands. Belly cream to yellowish-orange. Scales smooth, in 19 rows at mid-body. Ventrals 215-235. Anal divided. Subcaudals 50-70, anterior single, posterior divided. 1.5 metres (total length). DANGEROUS.

Pseudechis butleri
Yalgoo, WA
DANGEROUS

Pseudechis butleri

Pseudechis colletti Nonda, Qld DANGEROUS

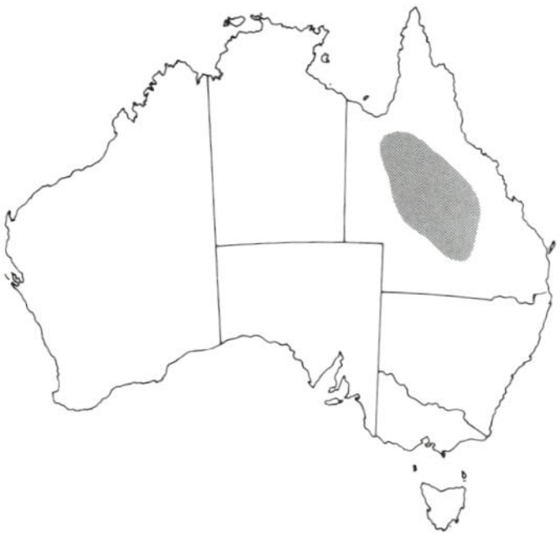

Distribution: Restricted to central Qld.
Habit: Blacksoil plains. Little is known of its habits. Oviparous, laying about 12 eggs (Charles, Watts and Shine).

Pseudechis guttatus De Vis, 1905

Spotted Black Snake

Description: Variable in colour, ranging from uniform black above, through various degrees of spotting in which many of the body scales have white or cream centres, to an extremely light phase in which all the scales are cream with black tips. Belly grey or blue-grey. Scales smooth, in 19 rows at mid-body. Ventrals 175-205. Anal divided. Subcaudals 45-65, anterior single, posterior divided. 1.5 metres (total length). DANGEROUS.
Distribution: From south-eastern Qld along western slopes and plains of northern NSW. Extends to NSW coast through the Hunter River Valley.
Habit: Found in a range of habitats from rocky hillsides to black-soil river floodplains and rich coastal forests. Largely diurnal. Feeds on small reptiles, mammals and frogs. Oviparous, producing 7-13 eggs (Charles and Shine).

Pseudechis guttatus near Gilgandra, NSW
DANGEROUS

Pseudechis porphyriacus Sydney, NSW
DANGEROUS

Pseudechis porphyriacus Brinerville, NSW DANGEROUS

Pseudechis porphyriacus (Shaw, 1794)

Red-bellied Black Snake

Description: Iridescent black above, except for the snout which is often light brown. The lateral scale row on each side adjacent to the ventral scales and the outer edges of the ventral scales are bright red or pink, fading to a duller red or pink in the middle of the belly. Underside of tail black. The red lateral and belly scales usually edged behind with black. Northern specimens usually much paler pink to almost white below. Scales smooth, in 17 rows at mid-body. Ventrals 170-215. Anal divided. Subcaudals 40-65, anterior single, posterior divided (occasionally all single). 1.5 metres (total length). DANGEROUS

Distribution: Eastern Australia, from far northern Qld to NSW, Vic and south-eastern SA.

Habit: A diurnal snake usually found associated with streams, swamps and lagoons, though sometimes ranging well away from these areas. Live-bearing, the young (numbering 8-40) are usually born in membranous sacs from which they emerge within minutes, or at most an hour or so, after birth. Feeds principally on frogs, but reptiles and small mammals are also eaten.

Genus ***Pseudonaja*** Günther, 1858

The classification of the members of this genus is in great need of revision. Existing species are poorly defined, and the present classification is uncertain and unreliable. There is a high level of individual and population variability in colour, pattern and scalation, while ontogenetic changes are very great in this genus. The classification presented below is a traditional one and should be regarded with scepticism, as should the distribution maps. Most species are probably composite.

The genus is characterised by its possession of smooth scales in 17-21 rows at mid-body; nasal and preocular scales in contact; suboculars absent; anal divided; subcaudals divided, 35 or more; 7-12 solid, maxillary teeth following the fang.

Members of the genus are widely distributed throughout continental Australia, with one species *(textilis)* also occurring in New Guinea.

Key

TO THE AUSTRALIAN SPECIES OF PSEUDONAJA

1 Scales in 17 or 19 rows **2**

Scales usually in 21 rows .... ***guttata***

2 Ventrals more than 175 .... **3**

Ventrals fewer than 175 .... ***modesta***

3 Scales in 17 rows; neck and head in adults uniform in colour or with scattered black scales tending to be concentrated along the vertebral region; young, if banded, usually with very regular, broad cross-bands **4**

Scales in 17 or 19 rows; if in 17 rows, adults regularly or irregularly banded, or with at least a few dark scales on the neck; young, if banded, usually with narrow, irregular cross-bands **6**

4 Nasal not or only partially divided, usually broadly contacting the preocular (a); inside of mouth flesh-coloured **5**

Nasal completely divided, usually not or in only point contact with the preocular (b); inside of mouth black .... ***ingrami***

5 Adults uniform pale to dark brown above .... ***textilis***

Adults with numerous scattered black scales, usually concentrated along the vertebral region, but sometimes almost covering the dorsum .... ***inframacula***

6 Scales normally in 17, sometimes in 19, rows; rostral large and strap-like, higher than broad, and conspicuous when viewed from above (c) .... ***nuchalis***

Scales normally in 19 rows; rostral normal, about as broad as high, and scarcely visible from above (d) .... ***affinis***

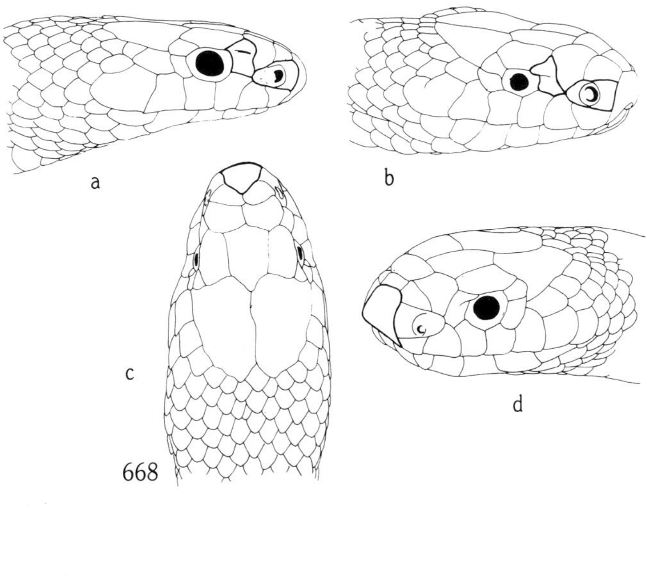

Pseudonaja affinis Esperance, WA DANGEROUS R. W. G. JENKINS

Pseudonaja guttata Winton, Qld

Pseudonaja affinis

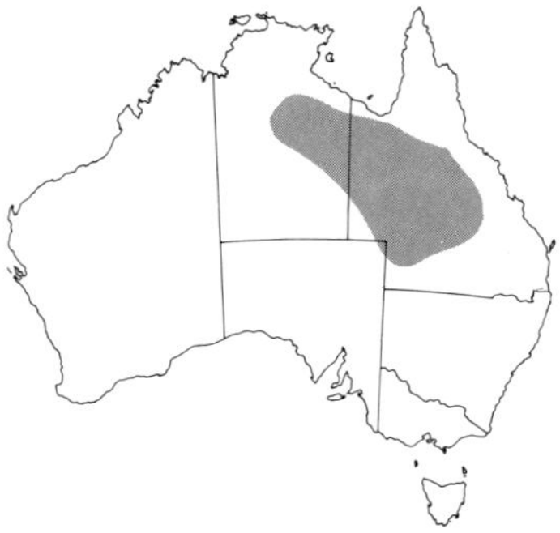

Pseudonaja guttata

Pseudonaja inframacula

Pseudonaja ingrami

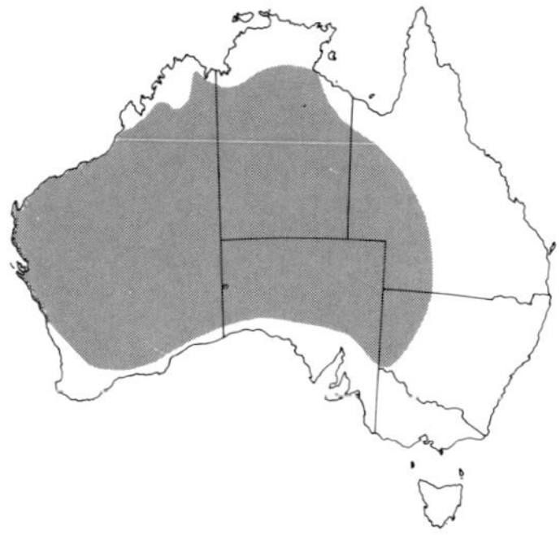

Pseudonaja modesta

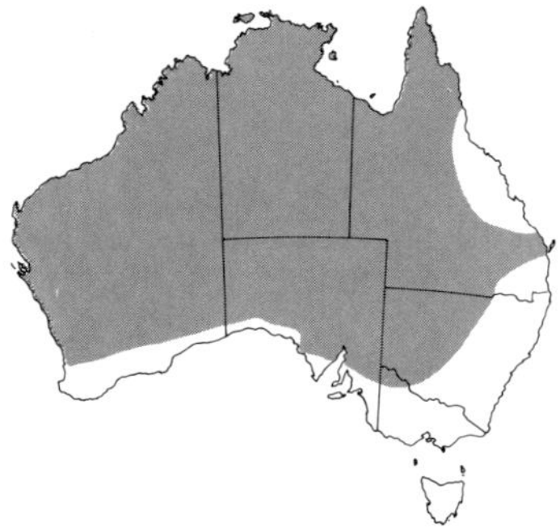

Pseudonaja nuchalis

Pseudonaja textilis

Pseudonaja affinis Günther, 1872

Dugite

Description: Grey, olive or brown above, the head often paler than the rest of the body. A series of blackish scales on the nape, often forming a ∧ or ⋀⋀ shaped mark. In some individuals black scales are scattered over the body. Belly olive or yellowish, with darker flecks and a series of orange or salmon-coloured blotches. Scales smooth, in 19 rows at mid-body. Ventrals 190-230. Anal divided. Subcaudals 50-70, all divided. 1.5 metres (total length). DANGEROUS.
Distribution: A narrow coastal and near-coastal strip of south-western WA.
Habit: From coastal dunes and heathland to the arid scrubs of the interior.
Subspecies: *affinis* (mainland of south-western WA); *tanneri* (offshore islands of south-western WA).

Pseudonaja guttata (Parker, 1926)

Description: Variable in colour and pattern. Some specimens are uniform pale fawn to bright orange-brown above, the concealed lower edges of many scales black, giving a speckled appearance when the snake moves or the skin is distended for any reason. In other specimens there are about 12-18 broad, blackish cross-bands or blotches on the body and tail, the first forming a black collar on the neck. Throat and most of the labials whitish, the belly creamy-orange to bright orange with irregular, obscure, brighter orange spots. Scales smooth, in 19-21 rows at mid-body. Ventrals 190-220. Anal divided. Subcaudals 45-70, all divided. Average total length 50 cm, maximum about 80 cm.
Distribution: Central Qld to eastern NT.
Habit: An inhabitant of the tussock grasslands of the cracked black soil plains of central Qld and the Barkly Tableland.

Pseudonaja inframacula (Waite, 1925)

Peninsula Brown Snake

Description: Similar in general body form and scalation to *Pseudonaja textilis*, of which it has until recently been regarded as a subspecies; however its colour pattern most closely resembles that of *Pseudonaja affinis*. Whereas adult *textilis* are usually uniform brown above, adults of *inframacula* are pale to rich brown above, with black flecks and patches on the head, and usually heavily spotted with

Pseudonaja ingrami near Camooweal, Qld DANGEROUS

black on the body, often with the black spots or black scales concentrated along the vertebral region. Some specimens may be almost entirely black above. The ventral surface is pale brown, with a grey central zone, and with blackish spots. Chromosomal studies by Mengden have shown that *inframacula* has a distinctive diploid chromosome complement of 36, compared with 38 in *textilis* and 34 in *affinis*. 1.2 metres (total length). DANGEROUS.
Distribution: Eyre Peninsula (and its offshore islands) and southern Yorke Peninsula, SA.
Habit: A swift-moving diurnal snake found in a variety of arid and semi-arid shrublands.

Pseudonaja ingrami (Boulenger, 1908)

Ingram's Brown Snake

Description: Status uncertain. Grey-brown to rich brown above, the head and neck, excluding the lips, blackish or speckled with dark grey. White or cream below, obscurely blotched with orange. Scales smooth, in 17 rows at mid-body. Ventrals 190-220. Anal divided. Subcaudals 55-70, divided. Nasal divided. Average total length 1.2 metres. DANGEROUS.
Distribution: Black soils and tussock grasslands of the Barkly Tableland of Qld and the NT.
Habit: A large, primarily diurnal snake which is nocturnal or crepuscular in hot summer conditions and which shelters in earth crevices on the Mitchell grass plains of the Barkly Tableland.

Pseudonaja modesta (Günther, 1872)

Ringed Brown Snake

Description: Pale grey-brown, through various shades of brown to rich reddish-brown above, with a black head (lighter on the snout), separated by a narrow, cream-coloured bar from a broad, black, nuchal band and 4-7 narrow, black cross-bands

Pseudonaja modesta
north-western NSW

Pseudonaja modesta Hamelin Pool, WA

evenly spaced along the body and tail. These bands may fade or even disappear with age. Belly cream to yellowish with orange blotches. Scales smooth, in 17 rows at mid-body. Ventrals 145-175. Anal divided. Subcaudals 35-55, all divided. 50 cm (total length).
Distribution: Drier parts of all mainland states except Vic.
Habit: Arid scrubs and shrublands, and hummock grasslands, where it shelters under fallen timber and other ground debris, or in spinifex. It has been recorded as diurnal (Worrell), but is also nocturnal in warm weather. Worrell also records that it feeds on skinks. Not regarded as dangerous.

Pseudonaja nuchalis Günther, 1858

Western Brown Snake or Gwardar

Description: Very variable in colour and pattern. Light brown to russet to almost black above. One or more of the following patterns may be present in an individual: head and nape black, a series of black scales on the neck, either irregular or in a distinct V- or W-shaped mark; a series of a few, broad, dark cross-bands; numerous irregular, narrow cross-bands formed by darker brown scales; a bright reticulated pattern formed by light-centred, dark-edged body scales. Belly cream, yellow, orange or grey, usually with dark grey and dark orange blotches. Scales smooth in 17 (or sometimes 19) rows at mid-body. Ventrals 180-230. Anal divided. Subcaudals 50-70, all divided. 1.5 metres (total length). DANGEROUS.
Distribution: Australia-wide, except extreme south-western WA and far-eastern and south-eastern Australia.

Pseudonaja nuchalis Hillston district, NSW. This photograph shows the distinctive lower surface colours; the spotting on the belly is typical of most members of this genus. DANGEROUS

Pseudonaja nuchalis Bourke, NSW
DANGEROUS

Habit: A swift-moving, primarily diurnal snake (although it is often nocturnal in hot, summer weather) which feeds largely on small mammals and reptiles. Inhabits a wide range of environments, from tropical and temperate sclerophyll forests and woodlands to the arid scrubs, spinifex-covered dunefields and sandplains, and stony plains and ranges of the central deserts.

Pseudonaja textilis (subadult) near Nelson's Bay, NSW DANGEROUS

Pseudonaja textilis (juvenile)
Blacktown, NSW

Pseudonaja textilis (adult)
Murrumbidgee River, NSW
DANGEROUS

Pseudonaja textilis (Duméril, Bibron and Duméril, 1854)

Eastern Brown Snake

Description: Variable in colour and pattern. Adults usually uniform in colour, ranging from light tan, through dark brown, russet and orange to almost black. Belly cream, yellow or orange, with scattered orange or dark grey blotches. Hatchling patterns vary enormously with locality (see illustrations); they generally include a black head (except for the snout) and black nuchal band in all individuals; the body may be uniform brown, or there may be a series of 50 or more black cross-bands along the length of the body; in others the body may be more indefinitely banded with alternate narrow and wide darker grey or black bands, or the dark-tipped scales may give a reticulated appearance. All of these patterns gradually disappear with age. Scales smooth in 17 rows at mid-body. Ventrals 185-235. Anal divided. Subcaudals 45-75, all paired (rarely several anterior subcaudals single). 1.5 metres total length. DANGEROUS.
Distribution: Eastern Australia from Cape York Peninsula, Qld, to south-eastern SA. Some specimens from arid areas of the NT, Qld, NSW and SA should probably be referred to this species. Extra-limital in eastern Papua New Guinea.
Habit: A swift-moving, diurnal snake. Occupies a wide range of habitats, from the wet and dry sclerophyll forests and heaths of the coast and ranges through savannah woodlands to inland grasslands and arid scrubs. Feeds primarily on small mammals and reptiles. McPhee records clutches of 10-35 eggs.

Pseudonaja nuchalis (juvenile) Wilcannia, NSW

Genus ***Rhinoplocephalus*** Müller, 1885

A genus containing several species found in the coastal and adjacent regions of the continent, with two species occurring in New Guinea.

Members of this genus are small to moderate in size and are characterised by uniform dorsal colour (except for a dark vertebral stripe in *nigrostriatus*); smooth scales in 15 rows at mid-body; frontal longer than broad, more than one and a half times as broad as the supraocular; supranasals present in all but one species (*bicolor*); anal single; subcaudals undivided; no subocular scales; two to five small, solid maxillary teeth following the fang.

Key

TO THE SPECIES OF RHINOPLOCEPHALUS

1 Internasals present **2**
Internasals absent .... ***bicolor***
2 Nasal contacting preocular **3**
Nasal not contacting preocular .... ***boschmai***
3 More or less uniformly black or dark brown above **4**
Predominantly pink or reddish above **5**
4 A distinct pale patch on the top of the head between the anterior edge of the frontal shield and the posterior edge of the parietal shields .... ***pallidiceps***
Head uniform shiny black or dark grey above .... ***nigrescens***
5 Uniformly bright pink above .... ***sp.***
Pink or reddish, usually with a distinct black or dark grey or brown vertebral stripe along the length of the body .... ***nigrostriatus***

Rhinoplocephalus bicolor Müller, 1885

Description: Uniform olive-grey to dark grey above, the lateral scales edged with darker. Belly creamish-white. Scales smooth, in 15 rows at mid-body. Ventrals 145-165. Anal single. Subcaudals 25-35, all single. Average total length 40 cm.

Distribution: Confined to the extreme south-western corner of WA.

Habit: '...sandy, seasonally saturated areas supporting ground cover of low shrubs....in stick-ant nests (*Iridomyrmex conifer*)...' and '...beneath granite slabs...and under fallen grass trees...' (Wilson and Knowles). Feeds mostly on scincid lizards (Shine).

Rhinoplocephalus bicolor south-western WA

P. RANKIN

Rhinoplocephalus bicolor

Rhinoplocephalus boschmai
Rockhampton, Qld

Rhinoplocephalus boschmai

(Brongersma and Knaap-van Meeuwen, 1964)
Carpentaria Whip Snake

Description: Uniform light tan, brown or very dark brown above, the lateral scales sometimes much lighter in colour than the remainder. Sides of head often yellowish to reddish-brown. Belly creamish-white. Prefrontals contacting upper labials, separating the nasals from the preoculars. Scales smooth, in 15 rows at mid-body. Ventrals 145-190. Anals single. Subcaudals 20-35, all single. 45 cm (total length).
Distribution: Eastern Qld, largely west of the Great Dividing Range.
Habit: A nocturnal, ground-dwelling snake found mostly in woodland habitats where it is usually found sheltering under bark, logs or other litter. Worrell records it as feeding on small lizards.

Unechis boschmai

Cryptophis nigrescens

Rhinoplocephalus nigrescens

(Günther, 1862)
Eastern Small-eyed Snake

Description: Closely allied to *Rhinoplocephalus pallidiceps*, from which it differs in always lacking a pale head, being uniform steely-black above. Belly cream to bright pink, often with blackish flecks and blotches. Nasal contacting preocular. Scales smooth, in 15 rows at mid-body. Ventrals 165-210. Anal single. Subcaudals 30-45, all single. 50 cm (total length), maximum about 1.2 metres. DANGEROUS.
Distribution: Coast and ranges of eastern Australia, from Cape York Peninsula, Qld to southern Vic.
Habit: Found in a range of habitats from coastal heathland to rainforest. A secretive, nocturnal snake,

Unechis nigrostriatus

Cryptophis pallidiceps

Rhinoplocephalus nigrescens Sydney, NSW DANGEROUS

it is usually found under rocks or logs, in rocky crevices or under ground litter. Feeds principally on lizards. Live-bearing, with recorded litters ranging from two (Worrell), to five (McPhee) and 2-8, average 4-5 (Shine).

Rhinoplocephalus nigrostriatus Weipa, Qld

Rhinoplocephalus nigrostriatus

(Krefft, 1864)
Black-striped Snake

Description: Bright reddish-pink to dark brown above, with a dark brown to black vertebral stripe, 1-2 scales wide, from the head to the tip of the tail. Top of the head is the same colour as the vertebral stripe. The individual scales may have a black base and light hind edges forming an overall reticulated pattern. Belly creamy-white. Nasal in contact with preocular. Scales smooth, in 15 rows at mid-body. Ventrals 160-190. Anal single. Subcaudals 45-70, all single. 50 cm (total length).
Distribution: Coast and adjacent ranges of north-eastern Australia, from Cape York Peninsula to southern Qld. Doubtfully recorded south of this region.
Habit: A secretive, nocturnal snake usually found sheltering under logs or ground litter in sclerophyll forests and woodlands. Feeds principally on lizards. Habit otherwise unknown.

Rhinoplocephalus pallidiceps

(Günther, 1858)
Northern Small-eyed Snake

Description: Uniform glossy black or grey-black above, sometimes with a paler zone on the head from about the front edge of the frontal to the hind edge of the parietals. Upper labials whitish, contrasting sharply with the darker colour on the top of the head. Belly cream, greyish or pink, often with darker flecks on the subcaudals (usually concentrated on the midline) and on the posterior ventrals. Nasal contacting preocular. Scales smooth in 15 rows at mid-body. Ventrals 160-180. Anal single. Subcaudals all single, 45-60. 50 cm (total length).
Distribution: Northern parts of the NT. Worrell suggests it may also occur in north-western WA.
Habit: A secretive, nocturnal snake usually encountered when active and foraging at night, or uncovered during the day under logs, stones or ground litter. Feeds principally on lizards. Habit otherwise unknown. Live-bearing.

Rhinoplocephalus sp.

Pink Snake

Description: Uniformly bright coral-pink above, pearly-white below. Nasal in contact with preocular. Scales smooth, in 15 rows at mid-body. Ventrals 180-185. Anal single. Subcaudals 50-65, all single. 40 cm (total length).
Distribution: Currently known only from Prince of Wales Island, Torres Strait.
Habit: A small-eyed nocturnal snake; the few known specimens have been found sheltering under flotsam along the upper strand line adjacent to open woodland on sandy soils. Habit otherwise unknown.

Rhinoplocephalus pallidiceps
Jabiru, NT

Rhinoplocephalus sp. Prince of Wales Island, Torres Strait

Rhinoplocephalus sp.

Genus *Simoselaps* Jan, 1859

An almost certainly composite group of small snakes, none of which exceeds about 60 cm (total length). All have a distinctive pair of black bars on the head — one between (and including) the eyes, and a broader one across the nape. All but two species have bands along the length of the body. Internasals are present. No suboculars separate the eye from the labials. The anal scale is divided. Ventrals number fewer than 240, and the subcaudals are divided and usually number fewer than 40. The nasal and preocular scales are in contact or separated, and the rostral is almost as long as broad, in some species with a sharp, anterior, shovel-shaped edge.

All species are burrowing snakes, seen above ground only at night. Though venomous, they do not normally attempt to bite and are regarded as harmless to humans and domestic animals. Little is known of their habits.

Key

TO THE SPECIES OF SIMOSELAPS

1 Three or more solid maxillary teeth following the fang . **3**

At most one solid maxillary tooth following the fang **2**

2 A black, longitudinal stripe, one scale wide and commencing on the nape, along the middle of the back; ventrals fewer than 165 .... ***calonotus***

No black, longitudinal stripe on the body; ventrals more than 165 .... ***bimaculatus***

3 Nasal not in contact with preocular (a) **4**

Nasal in contact with preocular (b) **5**

4 Mid-body scales in 17 rows; body banded along its length .... ***fasciolatus***

Mid-body scales in 15 rows; body without cross-bands, except on the nape .... ***warro***

5 Rostral shield sharp, projecting, shovel-shaped (c) **6**

Rostral shield rounded, not noticably projecting (d) **9**

6 Body with distinct cross-bands along its length **7**

Body uniform, without cross-bands (except for a dark collar) .... ***incinctus***

7 Frontal about as broad as long, about three times as broad as a supraocular (e) **8**

Frontal longer than broad, about twice as broad as a supraocular (f) .... ***australis***

8 Dark cross-bands at least 4-5 times as wide as pale cross-bands .... ***approximans***

Dark cross-bands at most about three times as wide as pale cross-bands .... ***semifasciatus***

9 Body banded along its length **10**

Body, except for bands on head and neck, without dark cross-bands .... ***minimus***

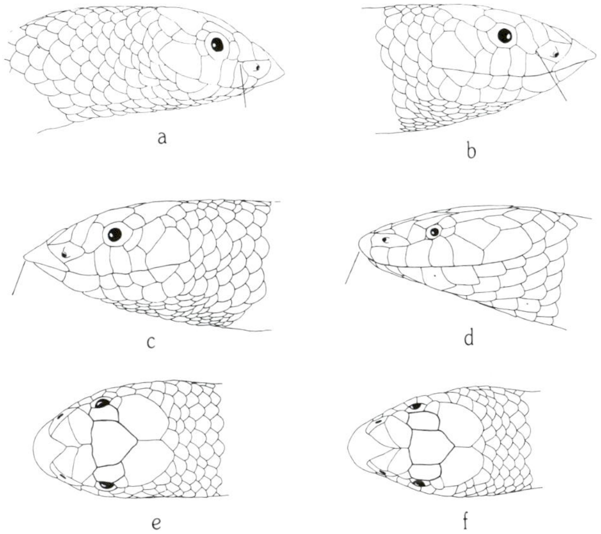

10 Six upper labials; head variegated with dark brown or black, the latter not sharply delineated from the narrow, pale, occipital band **11**

Five upper labials; head dark brown or black posteriorly, sharply delineated from the narrow, pale, occipital band .... ***anomalus***

11 Scales of pale occipital band not edged with dark brown or black; dark nuchal band less than four scales long .... ***littoralis***

Scales of pale occipital band strongly edged with dark brown or black; dark nuchal band more than four scales long .... ***bertholdi***

Simoselaps anomalus Alice Springs district, NT

G. SHEA

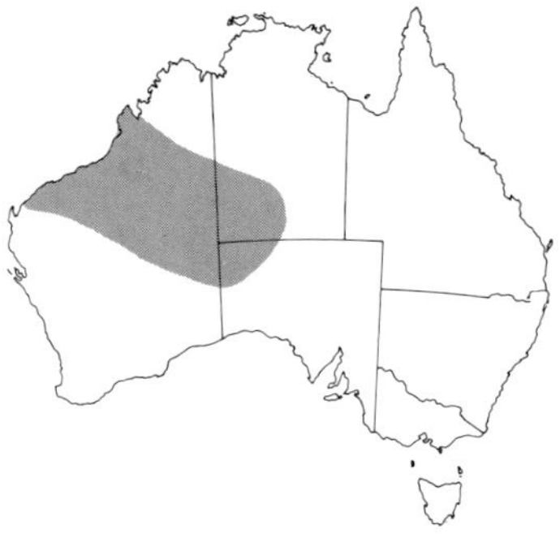
Simoselaps anomalus

Simoselaps approximans

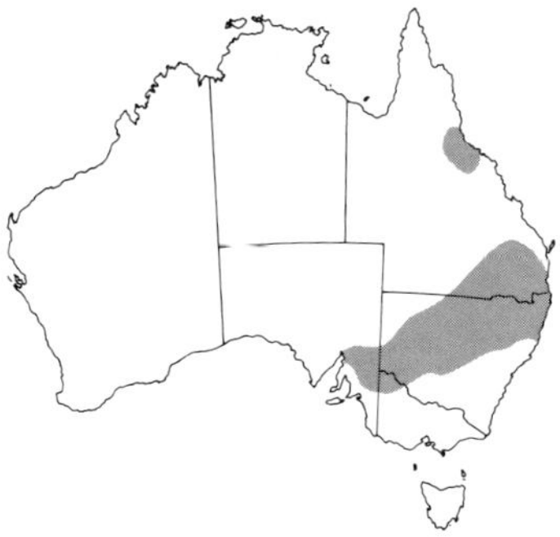
Simoselaps australis

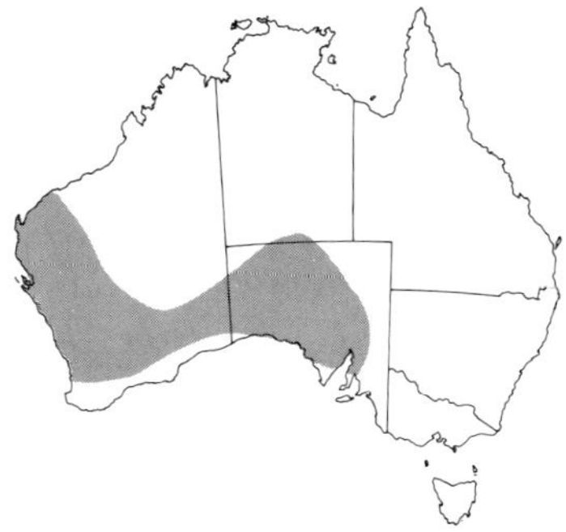
Simoselaps bertholdi

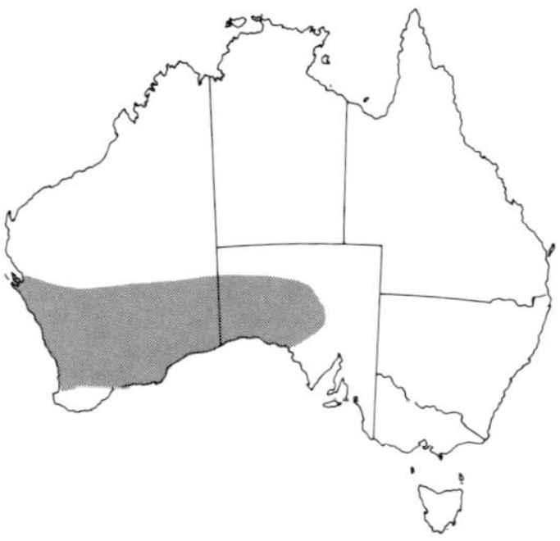
Simoselaps bimaculatus

Simoselaps calonotus

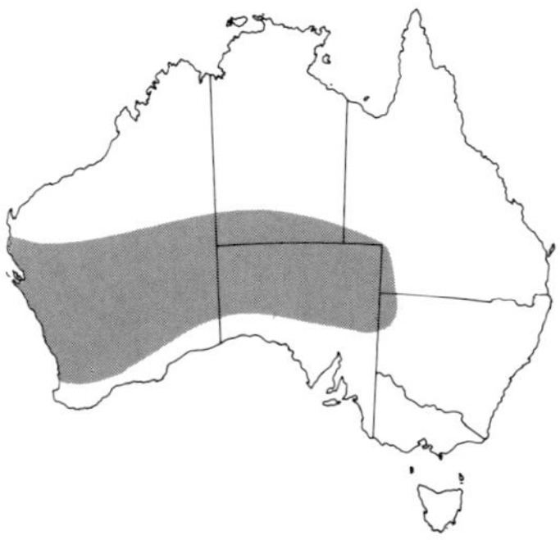
Simoselaps fasciolatus

Simoselaps anomalus (Sternfeld, 1919)

Description: Similar in most respects to *Simoselaps bertholdi*. Body pale creamy-yellow above, with about 25-40 narrow, black cross-bands on body and tail, the dark bands only slightly narrower than the paler interspaces; head black posteriorly, becoming paler (with dark flecks and blotches) on the snout and separated by a narrow, pale bar from a broad, black collar on the nape. Whitish below, except where dark cross-bands reach the belly. Scales smooth, in 15 rows at mid-body. Ventrals 115-130. Anal divided. Subcaudals 15-30, all divided. Average total length 25 cm.
Distribution: North-west coastal regions of WA to north-western SA.
Habit: A lizard-eating, burrowing snake found in sandy soils with a spinifex ground cover.

Simoselaps approximans (Glauert, 1954)

Description: Brown to reddish-brown above, the head with a broad, blackish bar between frontal and parietals, and a broad, blackish collar on the nape; body and tail with 50-80 obscure to well-defined narrow, dark cross-bands, slightly to markedly wider than the paler interspaces; dark cross-bands usually end on lower flanks. Ventral surfaces whitish. Scales smooth, in 17 rows at mid-body. Ventrals 165-190. Anal divided. Subcaudals 20-30, divided. Average total length 30 cm.
Distribution: Upper west coast to arid interior of WA.
Habit: '...heavy (often stony) reddish soils dominated by Acacia woodlands and shrublands' (Wilson and Knowles).

Simoselaps australis (Krefft, 1864)
Coral Snake

Description: Dull to bright pink or red above, with numerous, irregular, narrow cross-bands, one or two scales in width and made up of scales with cream or yellow centres and dark brown edges. A black bar across the head (enclosing the eyes), usually edged in front and behind with creamy yellow. Another broad, black bar across the nape, also narrowly pale-edged. Ventral surfaces whitish. Rostral with a sharply upturned, angular, projecting edge. Scales, smooth in 17 rows at mid-body. Ventrals 140-170. Anal usually divided. Subcaudals 15-30, divided. Average total

Simoseląps approximans,

Simoselaps australis
Round Hill, NSW

length about 30 cm, maximum about 50 cm.
Distribution: South-eastern SA to Qld, extending to the coastal areas of northern NSW and southern Qld. An apparent isolate in northern Qld.
Habit: A nocturnal, burrowing snake, found in a wide variety of habitats from coastal forests to open savannah woodland, mallee and arid eucalypt and acacia scrubs. Usually found under logs and other ground shelter during the day, or on the surface on warm nights. Oviparous, laying 4-6 eggs; feeds on lizards (Shine).

Simoselaps bertholdi (Jan, 1859)

Desert Banded Snake

Description: Body cream, yellowish or reddish-orange above, the individual scales edged behind with darker reddish-brown, and with numerous black cross-bands along the length of the body. These bands, which extend on to the belly, are about as wide as the paler interspaces. Belly creamish-white, except for dark cross-bands. Head grey-brown or black, usually lighter on the snout, and often with

Simoselaps bertholdi Bullsbrook, WA

dark or light flecks and separated from the first (nuchal) cross-band by a narrow, cream-coloured bar. Scales smooth, in 15 rows at mid-body. Ventrals 110-135. Anal divided. Subcaudals 15-30, all divided. Average total length about 30 cm.
Distribution: Southern WA to western SA and southern NT.
Habit: Occurs in a wide range of habitats from coastal dunes and heaths to the arid shrublands of the interior. Waite states that it basks in sunlight even in very hot sand. Oviparous, laying 1-8 eggs; feeds on lizards (Shine).

Simoselaps bimaculatus (Duméril, Bibron and Duméril, 1854)

Western Black-naped Snake

Description: Pale reddish-brown, orange or pinkish above, each scale edged with dark reddish-brown, with a dark, blackish head-blotch from about front edge of frontal to hind edge of parietals, and a black nuchal band about five scales long and starting about three scales behind the parietals. Belly white or cream. Five upper labials. Scales smooth, in 15 rows at mid-body. Ventrals 175-235. Anal divided. Subcaudals 15-35, all divided. Storr records marked sexual dimorphism in scalation: males have fewer ventrals and more subcaudals than females. 40 cm (total length).
Distribution: South-western WA and east to the western half of SA.
Habit: A small, burrowing snake of heath and low shrubland. Oviparous, clutch size ranging from 2-6 (Shine). Feeds on lizards, mostly of the burrowing skink genus *Lerista* (Shine).

Simoselaps calonotus (Duméril, Bibron and Duméril, 1854)

Western Black-striped Snake

Description: Reddish-brown above, each individual scale being cream-coloured, and edged narrowly to broadly with pink or reddish-orange. Snout tipped with black. A blackish head-blotch from about front edge of frontal to hind edge of parietals, and a black nuchal band, about three scales long and starting about three scales behind the parietals. A narrow, vertebral stripe to end of tail consisting of a single longitudinal row of light-centred but black-margined scales. Belly white or cream. Six upper labials. Scales smooth, in 15 rows at mid-body. Ventrals 120-150. Anal divided. Subcaudals 20-40, all divided. 30 cm (total length).
Distribution: Restricted to a narrow coastal and near-coastal strip of south-western WA, from about Lancelin to Rockingham and inland for about 90 kilometres.
Habit: A burrowing snake found in coastal heaths and low shrubland.. Oviparous, laying 2-5 eggs (Shine). Feeds on lizards, mostly of the burrowing skink genus *Lerista* (Shine).

Simoselaps fasciolatus (Günther, 1872)

Narrow-banded Snake

Description: A brightly coloured snake with ground

Simoselaps bimaculatus Shark Bay, WA

colour of light reddish-brown or cream, the individual scales narrowly or broadly tipped with darker reddish-brown or very dark brown-black. The black-tipped scales are arranged in groups to form 50 or more narrow, irregular cross-bands, becoming more indefinite posteriorly. Snout light brown or cream, speckled with darker. Remainder of top of head black, to about hind edge of parietals, separated by a narrow, light zone from a broad, black nuchal band 3-15 scales long. Belly creamy-white. Scales smooth, in 17 rows at mid-body. Ventrals 140-175. Anal divided. Subcaudals 15-30, all divided. Average total length 30 cm, maximum about 40 cm.
Distribution: South-western Australia and arid parts of all other mainland states except Vic.
Habit: Occupies a wide range of habitats from coastal dunes and heaths to the red spinifex-covered dunefields of central Australia. A nocturnal, burrowing snake usually found in sandy areas. Emerges on warm nights to forage on the surface. Feeds on lizards and their eggs (Shine).
Subspecies: *fasciolatus* (south-western Australia); *fasciatus* (central Australia).

Simoselaps incinctus (Storr, 1968)

Description: Pale brown to dull pink, the individual scales sometimes darker edged, resulting in an obscure, reticulated pattern. A dark brown or black

Simoselaps calonotus Lancelin, WA

bar across the head (enclosing the eyes), and another, broader, black bar across the neck. Ventral surfaces creamy-white. Rostral with an upturned, sharply angular, leading edge. Scales smooth, in 17 rows at mid-body. Ventrals 140-165. Anal divided. Subcaudals 18-30, divided. Average total length 30 cm.
Distribution: Central Australia to north-western Qld.

Simoselaps incinctus

Simoselaps littoralis

Simoselaps minimus

Simoselaps fasciolatus Innamincka, SA

Simoselaps incinctus Glen Helen, NT

Habit: A burrowing species which apparently prefers habitats associated with hummock grasses on stony hills and ranges.

Simoselaps littoralis (Storr, 1968)

Description: Pale creamy-yellow to whitish above, with a series of 20-45 narrow, black rings 1-3 scales wide, on body and tail, most of them extending to lower flanks and belly, and only slightly narrower than the paler interspaces; head pale brown on the snout, flecked with dark brown or black, but heavily blotched with black posteriorly to about the rear of the parietals; then a narrow, pale band separating the head from a broad, blackish, nuchal band 2-5 scales in width. White below, except where dark cross-bands extend on to belly; throat greyish. Scales smooth, in 15 rows at mid-body. Ventrals 100-125. Anal divided. Subcaudals 15-25, all divided. Average total length 30 cm.
Distribution: Mid-western coast of WA.
Habit: A burrowing, lizard-eating snake, found mostly in coastal dunes and low shrublands on pale sands.

Simoselaps minimus (Worrell, 1960)

Description: Body white or cream above, the

Simoselaps littoralis

Simoselaps warro Kuranda, Qld

individual scales narrowly edged with dark brown or black; a broad, black bar across the head, usually extending from rear of prefrontals to about the rear of the parietals; another black bar about 3-4 scales wide across the nape; some of the scales on the snout may be edged with dark brown. Ventral surfaces whitish, except for some fine brown flecking on the chin and throat. Scales smooth, in 15 rows at mid-body. Ventrals in only two specimens currently known 125-127. Anal divided. Subcaudals 19-22, all but the first few divided. Total length about 20 cm
Distribution: Dampier Land, WA.

Simoselaps semifasciatus (Günther, 1863)

Half-girdled Snake

Description: A species subject to considerable geographic variation. Many variants have been described as distinct species and may indeed prove to be so. Pale fawn or olive-brown to rich reddish-brown above, with numerous dark grey, dark brown or blackish cross-bands along the length of the body and tail; these cross-bands may be much wider than, to as wide as, the paler interspaces. The paler scales are often dark-edged. Always a blackish bar across the top of the head, enclosing the eyes. Ventral surfaces whitish. Rostral with an upturned, sharply angular, leading edge. Scales smooth, in 15 or 17 rows at mid-body. Ventrals 140-190. Anal divided. Subcaudals 14-30, divided. Average total length 30 cm, maximum about 40 cm.
Distribution: Most parts of WA, except the south-east; north-western SA and the adjacent border regions of the NT; northern and north-eastern Australia.
Habit: A nocturnal, burrowing snake found in a wide variety of arid and more mesic habitats, from arid scrubs and hummock grasslands to coastal dunes and heaths and tropical, seasonally-dry woodlands.

Simoselaps semifasciatus

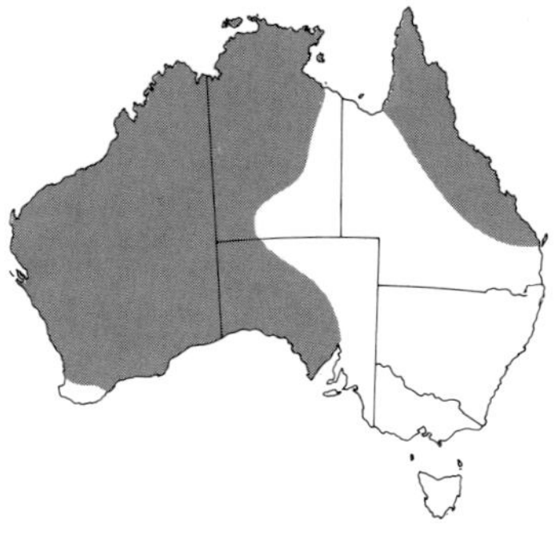

Simoselaps semifasciatus

Simoselaps warro

Sometimes found under logs or stones during the day. Frequently forages on the surface on warm nights. Feeds only on reptile eggs (Shine).

Subspecies: *campbelli* (north-eastern Qld); *roperi* (Kimberley region, WA, and northern NT); *semifasciata* (southern WA and SA).

Simoselaps warro (De Vis, 1884)

Description: Bright orange to orange-brown above, the individual scales edged behind with darker orange or brown to present a distinctly reticulated appearance. Head dark brown, flecked with lighter, and usually separated by a narrow, cream-coloured bar from a broad, black nuchal blotch, up to 12 scales long. Sometimes a black, median, caudal stripe. Belly creamish-white. Scales smooth, in 15 rows at mid-body. Ventrals 135-165. Anal divided. Subcaudals 15-25, all divided. Average size 30 cm, maximum about 40 cm.
Distribution: Coast and adjacent ranges of north-eastern Qld.
Habit: A nocturnal, burrowing snake usually encountered in sclerophyll forest and woodland habitats.

Genus *Suta* Worrell, 1961

A diverse genus, probably composite, with members found throughout continental Australia and extending to southern New Guinea. Characterised by smooth scales in 15-21 rows at mid-body; suboculars absent; frontal shield longer than broad; internasals present; ventrals not keeled or notched, between 125 and 190; anal single; subcaudals single; 3-7 small, solid, maxillary teeth following the fang.

Key

TO THE SPECIES OF SUTA

1 Scales in 17 or more rows at mid-body **2**
Scales in 15 rows at mid-body **6**

2 Scales in 17 rows at mid-body **3**
Scales in 19-21 rows at mid-body **5**

3 Head with a black hood contrasting sharply on the nape with the pale brown body colour .... ***flagellum***
Head with dark brown or black spots and lines, but without any indication of a dark, contrasting hood **4**

4 Body behind head uniformly rich reddish-brown above .... ***punctata***
Body with numerous irregular, narrow, dark cross-bands .... ***fasciata***

5 A dark streak from the nostril, through the eye to the temporal region, edged with white or cream below .. ***suta***
No dark, pale-edged canthal temporal streak .. ***ordensis***

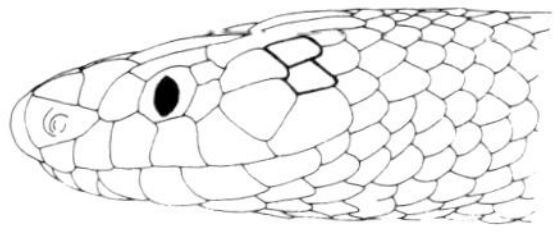

a

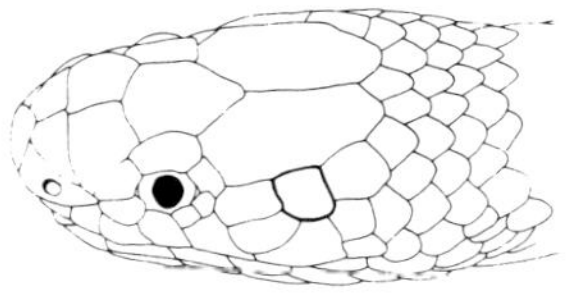

b

6 Two posterior temporals (a); black hood usually broken by a pale spot on the preocular and extending back to the first 3-9 vertebrals **7**
Single posterior temporal (b); unbroken black hood extending on to the first 1-6 vertebrals .... ***monachus***

7 Usually no indication of a vertebral stripe **8**
A conspicuous black vertebral stripe .... ***nigriceps***

8 Scales edged with dark brown or black, making a reticulated pattern .... ***gouldii***
Scales each with a dark basal spot, but not dark-edged .... ***spectabilis***

Suta fasciata Roy Hill, WA

Suta fasciata (Rosén, 1905)

Rosen's Snake

Description: The head and body are light brown. The head has scattered, dark brown flecks and patches, while there is a dark brown streak through the eye and along the side of the head to the neck. Lips not barred. Body with numerous irregular, dark brown cross-bands which are about as wide as the paler interspaces. Scales smooth in 17, rarely 19, rows at mid-body. Ventrals 140-185. Anal single. Subcaudals 20-40, all single. 40 cm (total length).
Distribution: Inland of south-western WA, from the Pilbara district in the north to Bruce Rock in the south-west and the Kalgoorlie and Laverton districts in the east (Glauert).
Habit: Arid scrubs and woodlands.

Suta flagellum (McCoy, 1878)

Little Whip Snake

Description: Light tan to brown above, each scale dark at its base, and with a light hind edge producing a marked reticulate appearance. Top of head black (including several scale rows on the neck), except for a light bar in front of the eyes. Lips cream or light brown, often extending up behind the eye. Belly creamish-white to brown. Nasal contacts preocular. Scales smooth in 17 (rarely 15) rows at mid-body. Ventrals 125-150. Anal single. Subcaudals 20-40, all single. 40 cm (total length).
Distribution: Vic, extending into south-eastern NSW and south-eastern SA.
Habit: A small, secretive, nocturnal snake. Feeds on

Suta fasciata

Suta flagellum

Suta flagellum Melbourne district, Vic

Suta gouldii Perth, WA

Suta punctata Mount Isa Qld.

small scincid lizards and frogs. Found mostly in eucalypt woodland and associated grasslands, especially on stony hills, where it shelters under rocks and logs. Viviparous, producing up to about 8 young.

Suta gouldii (Gray, 1841)

Black-headed Snake

Description: Rich reddish-brown above, the individual scales with darker bases, especially on the vertebral region, and sometimes finely edged with black, resulting in a reticulated appearance. Lower flanks very pale. Head and nape black, with a pale brown or cream preocular patch on either side; lips white or cream. Ventral surfaces white. Nasal contacting preocular. Scales smooth, in 15 rows at mid-body. Ventrals 150-180. Anal single. Subcaudals 25-40, all single. 40 cm (total length).
Distribution: South-western WA.
Habit: 'Heathlands, woodlands, shrublands, dry sclerophyll forests and rock outcrops...' (Wilson and Knowles).

Suta monachus (Storr, 1964)

Hooded Snake

Description: Bright reddish-brown above, the individual scales darker at the base, and sometimes

finely black-edged, giving a reticulated appearance. Head and nape black, normally without paler areas on the snout and preocular regions. Lips white. Ventral surfaces white. Nasal usually contacting preocular. Scales smooth, in 15 rows at mid-body. Ventrals 150-175. Anal single. Subcaudals 20-35, all single. 40 cm (total length).
Distribution: Mid-western coast of WA to western NSW.
Habit: Mulga and other arid shrublands. A secretive, nocturnal, ground-dwelling species usually found sheltering under rocks and logs, or in abandoned insect and lizard burrows.

Suta nigriceps (Günther, 1863)

Description: Head and neck black, usually continuous with a broad, blackish, vertebral zone extending to the tail; lateral scales pale brown, each with a black or dark reddish-brown base. Lips white. Ventral surfaces white. Nasal contacts preocular. Scales smooth, in 15 rows at mid-body. Ventrals 145-175. Anal single. Subcaudals 18-35, all single. 50 cm (total length).
Distribution: Southern Australia, from south-western WA to western Vic and south-western NSW.
Habit: Primarily mallee and saltbush. Nocturnal. Terrestrial.

Suta ordensis (Storr, 1984)

Description: Similar in most respects to *Suta suta*, from which it is said to differ in having 'little or no indication of hood or pale ocular stripe and with lower surfaces narrowly cross-banded with greyish-brown and white' (Storr). Scales smooth, in 19 rows at mid-body. Ventrals 165-185. Anal undivided. Subcaudals 30-40, all single. Total length to 75 cm.

Distribution: Northern WA/NT border region.

Suta punctata (Boulenger, 1896)

Little Spotted Snake

Description: Rich reddish-brown above, except for the upper labials which are white or pale cream. A short dark brown or black streak from the nostril through the eye. A few irregular black flecks and spots on the top of the head and on the neck, and several black blotches along the side of the neck; rows of black or black-tipped scales adjacent to the ventrals on each side. Belly immaculate white or cream. In some specimens, especially from WA, all of the body scales are black-centred or black-tipped. Mid-body scales smooth, in 15 rows. Ventrals 150-170. Anal single. Subcaudals 20-34, all single. 40 cm (total length).

Suta monachus Wiluna, WA

R. W. G. JENKINS

Suta nigriceps Mundaring Weir, WA

R. W. G. JENKINS

Suta spectabilis Port Wakefield, SA

Distribution: Through the drier inland parts of the northern half of Australia, from the coast of WA through central Australia to far western Qld.
Habit: Nocturnal. Live-bearing, producing 2-5 young; feeds on lizards (Shine). Venomous, but not regarded as dangerous to humans.

Suta spectabilis (Krefft, 1869)

Description: A probably composite species in which some of the described subspecies may represent distinct species. Brown or grey-brown above, the individual scales with darker bases and sometimes finely edged with black, those on the lower flanks usually much paler than those above; head and nape black, except for the lips, which are white, and a pale cream preocular patch on either side of the head and sometimes pale supraocular and postocular patches. Ventral surfaces white. Nasal contacting preocular. Scales smooth, in 15 rows at mid-body. Ventrals 135-170. Anal single. Subcaudals 20-40, all single. 40 cm (total length).
Distribution: Far south-western WA, through southern SA to western Vic, NSW and southern Qld.
Habit: Occupies a wide variety of habitats from acacia scrubs, mallee, low open shrublands to more mesic woodland in the east and north of its range. A nocturnal snake which is normally found sheltering under logs, rocks or ground litter, or in the abandoned borrows of insects and lizards.
Subspecies: *spectabilis* (eastern SA to NSW and Vic); *dwyeri* (NSW to southern Qld); *nullarbor* (Nullarbor Plain and adjacent coast); *bushi* (Esperance region, WA).

Suta suta (Peters, 1863)

Myall or Curl Snake

Description: Pale fawn to rich reddish-brown above, somewhat paler on the lower flanks, the concealed part of each scale sometimes dark brown and resulting in a distinct, reticulated pattern. Head

Suta suta Gigandra, NSW   DANGEROUS

and nape with a distinctive darker brown or blackish hood, complete except for a paler brown stripe along the canthus and over and through the eye to the temporal region, separated by an irregular, dark brown margin from the white or cream supralabials. Sometimes a narrow, black, vertebral stripe. Ventral surface creamy-white. Scales smooth in 19 (rarely 21) rows at mid-body. Ventrals 150-170. Anal undivided. Subcaudals 20-35, all single. Average total length 40 cm, maximum about 60 cm. DANGEROUS

Distribution: Widely distributed throughout the eastern two-thirds of continental Australia, excluding the eastern and northern coastal regions. Extends into far northeast of WA.

Habit: A nocturnal, ground-dwelling snake occupying a wide range of habitats from temperate and seasonally-dry tropical woodlands in the east and north of its range to eucalypt and acacia scrublands of the central deserts. Usually found during the day under fallen timber, stones, etc. Often seen on warm nights foraging in open areas. Found under a wide variety of conditions, from savannah woodland to sandy, arid scrubs, open saltbush plains and stony hills and ranges. Its characteristic offensive posture -a tense, spring-like curving of the body — has given rise to one of its common names. Venomous, its bite is not normally regarded as dangerous but it can be extremely painful. Feeds principally on lizards and mammals (Shine). Live-bearing, with clutches of 2-7 (Shine).

Suta gouldii

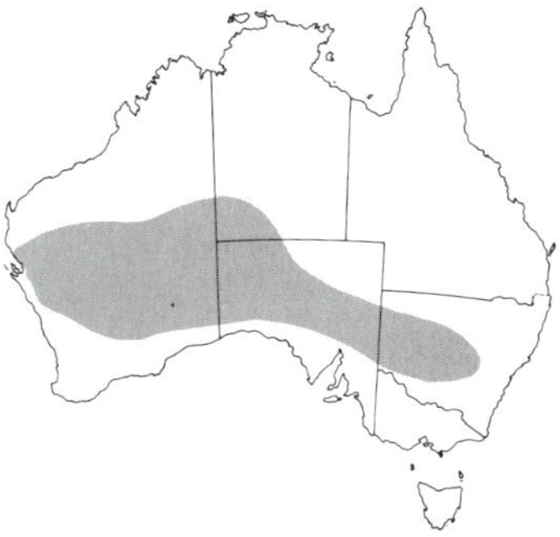

Suta monachus

Suta nigriceps

Suta ordensis

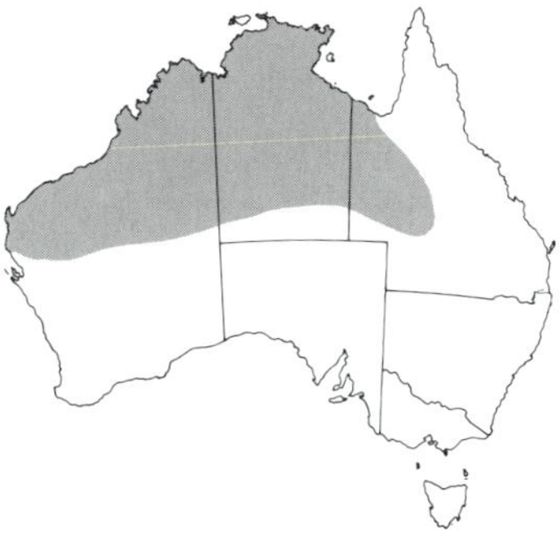

Suta punctata

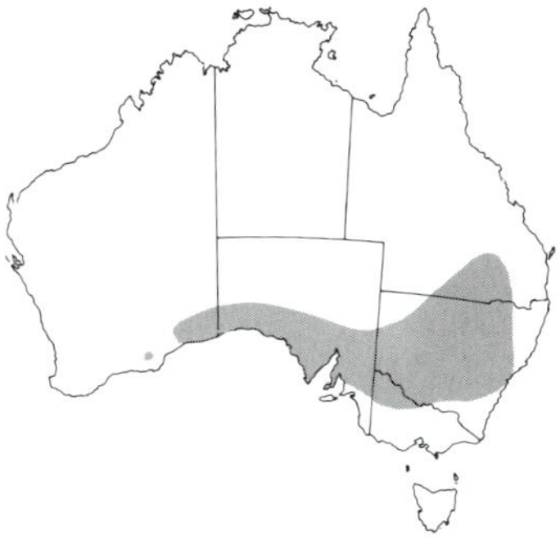

Suta spectabilis

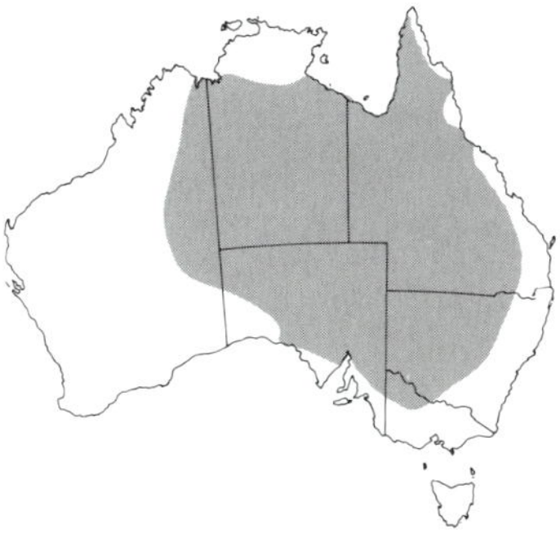

Suta suta

Genus ***Tropidechis*** Günther, 1863

A monotypic genus confined to the coast and ranges of central-eastern and north-eastern Australia. Readily distinguished from all other Australian elapid snakes by its strongly keeled body scales; single anal; subcaudals single; 3-5 small, solid, maxillary teeth following the fang.

Superficially similar to the Freshwater Snake *(Tropidonophis mairii),* a colubrid snake which is often a habitat associate of *Tropidechis* and which can be distinguished by its possession of a loreal scale (absent in *Tropidechis*).

Tropidechis carinatus (Krefft, 1863)
Rough-Scaled Snake

Description: Olive-brown to dark brown above, usually with narrow, irregular, dark cross-bands, which do not extend as far as the belly. Darker cross-bands most conspicuous anteriorly, sometimes disappearing posteriorly. Belly cream, yellow or olive-green, often with darker blotches. Body scales strongly keeled, in 23 rows at mid-body. Ventrals 160-185. Anal single. Subcaudals 50-60, all single. Average total length about 75 cm, maximum about 1 metre. DANGEROUS.
Distribution: Coast and ranges of eastern Australia from Barrington Tops in the south to the Cairns district in Qld. Northern and southern populations may be discontinuous as there are no records from central-coastal Qld.

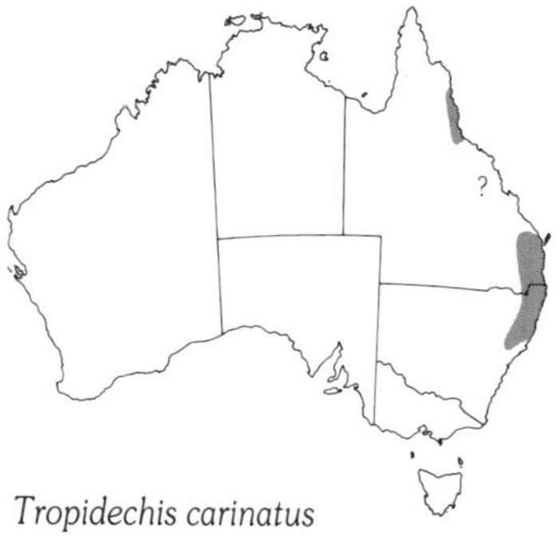

Tropidechis carinatus

Tropidechis carinatus Barrington Tops, NSW DANGEROUS

Habit: Shy, but very aggressive when aroused. Normally nocturnal, but sometimes seen basking or foraging during the day. Potentially very dangerous. Most often found in rain-or wet sclerophyll forests where it feeds on small mammals, birds, reptiles and frogs. Live-bearing, producing 5-8 young (Shine).

Genus ***Vermicella*** Günther, 1858

A genus of black and white banded snakes. The two species recognised below are closely allied and although Storr has regarded them as conspecific, the scalation and body proportions of *multifasciata* appear to set it quite apart from populations elsewhere in Australia.

Their colour pattern of alternate black and white rings distinguishes members of this genus from all other Australian land snakes. In addition they are characterised by their short tails, with fewer than 35 subcaudals, all of which are divided; scales smooth, in 15 rows at mid-body; suboculars absent.

The genus occurs throughout most of continental Australia.

Key

'TO THE SPECIES OF VERMICELLA

Internasals present (a) .... ***annulata***
Internasals absent (b) .... ***multifasciata***

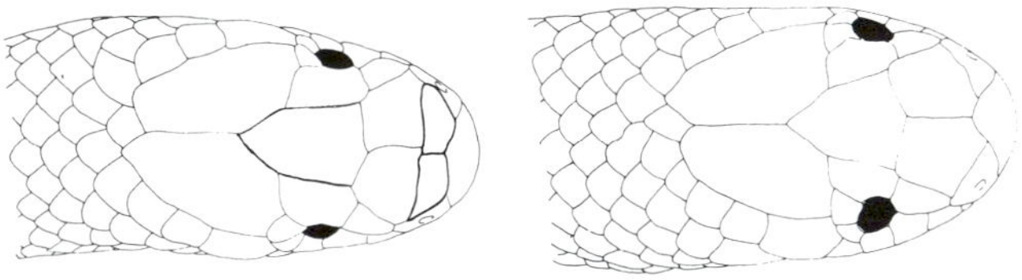

a b

Vermicella annulata Wallis Lake, NSW

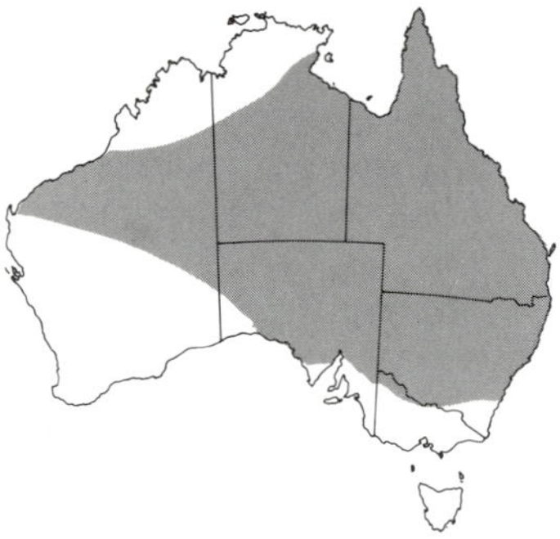

Vermicella annulata

Vermicella multifasciata

Vermicella annulata (Gray, 1841)

Bandy-Bandy

Description: A distinctive pattern of alternate black and white rings, commencing with a black snout, the black rings of the body usually extending well on to or even right across the belly. The number and relative width of the black and white rings varies sexually and geographically. Internasals present; smooth scales, in 15 rows at mid-body. Ventrals 180-320. Anal divided. Subcaudals 12-30, all divided. 60 cm (total length), maximum about 1 metre.
Distribution: Northern WA and throughout most other mainland States except extreme south-eastern Australia.
Habit: A nocturnal, burrowing snake, found in a great range of habitats from wet coastal forests, savannah woodland, mallee, mulga and other acacia scrubs to spinifex-covered desert sandhills. Numerous records suggest that Blind Snakes (family Typhlopidae) are major, if not sole, prey of the Bandy-Bandy. When alarmed it throws its body into one or more loops which are held high off the ground, a behaviour pattern subject to different and highly speculative interpretations. Oviparous (Worrell).
Subspecies: *annulata* (eastern and southern Australia); *snelli* (north-western, northern and central Australia).

Vermicella multifasciata (Longman, 1915)

Northern Bandy-Bandy

Description: Status uncertain, sometimes regarded as a subspecies of *Vermicella annulata*. Similar to latter in colour and pattern, but differs in having no internasals (i.e., internasals have fused with prefrontals), and relatively very small head and slender body (total length is about 75 times the diameter of the body, v. about 40 times in typical *V. annulata)*. Scales smooth, in 15 rows at mid-body. Ventrals 250-290. Anal divided. Subcaudals 15-25, all divided.
Distribution: North-western WA to north-western NT.
Habit: Found in seasonally-dry tropical woodlands and open eucalypt forests. Habits otherwise unknown, presumably similar to *V. annulata*.

Vermicella multifasciata Humpty Doo, NT

Family Hydrophiidae

The status and composition of this family have been critically reviewed in recent years, but no clear consensus view has yet emerged. Sea snakes are closely allied to the terrestrial Australasian elapid snakes, but have long been regarded as a distinct family, characterised by a suite of characters which reflect their adaptation to a marine, aquatic existence. The most obvious of these characters are valvular nostrils, a lingual fossa and a vertically compressed, paddle-shaped tail. All are viviparous.

Some of the characters utilised in the keys are not included in the descriptions.

Key

TO THE GENERA OF AUSTRALIAN SEA SNAKES

1 Ventrals large, at least three times as wide as the adjacent body scales (a) **2**

Ventrals small, at most scarcely more than twice as wide as the adjacent body scales (b) **5**

2 Six or more supralabials (c).......... **3**

Three supralabials (d).......... ***Emydocephalus***

3 Posterior chin shields not reduced and separated by a mental groove (e); portion of rostral scale bearing median valve-like fold continuous with remainder of scale (f)....... **4**

Posterior chin shields usually reduced and separated by one or more scales (g) and/or portion of rostral scale bearing median valve-like fold sometimes separated from remainder of scale by a suture (h) .... ***Aipysurus***

4 No preocular scale (i); rostral with a median lobe at its anterior-most end, this lobe fitting into a median notch in the mental and completely dividing the lingual fossa of the rostral into separate left and right grooves (j).......... ***Hydrelaps***

Preocular scale present (k); rostral with a median sharp fold located within the mouth, behind the median and undivided lingual fossa, this fold formed from the posterior edge of the portion of the keratinized scale extending within the lining of the lip (l) **11**

5 Head scales enlarged, regular, symmetrical, the supraoculars without projecting tubercles or spines (m) **6**

Head scales broken up into small, irregular and asymmetrical scales, the supraoculars with projecting tubercles or spines (n).......... ***Acalyptophis***

6 A distinct mental groove (o).......... **7**

No distinct mental groove (p).......... ***Pelamis***

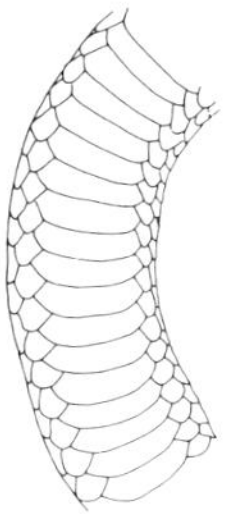
a

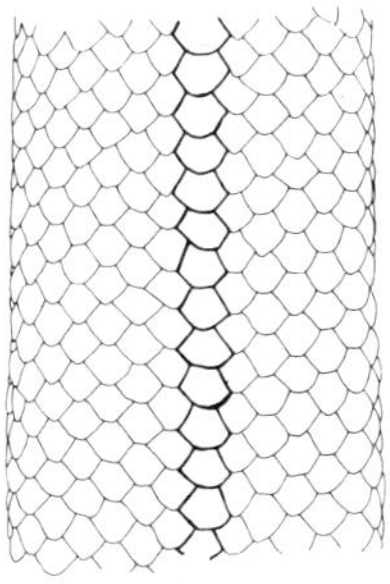
b

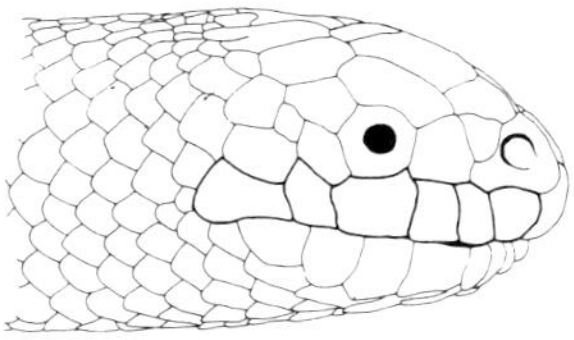
c

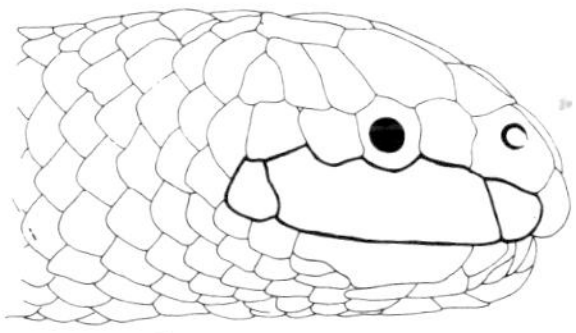
d

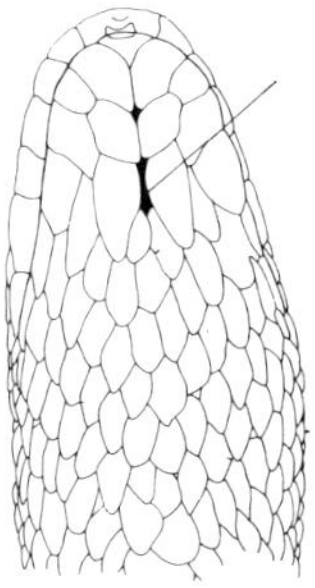
e

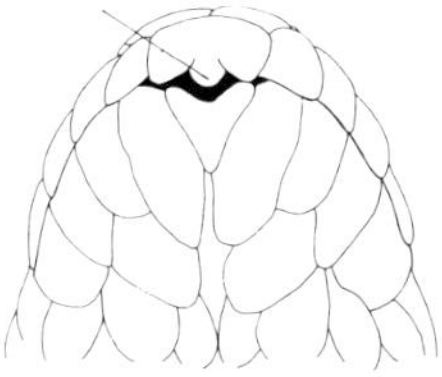
f

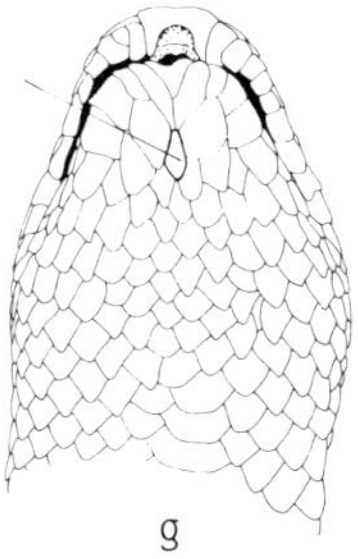
g

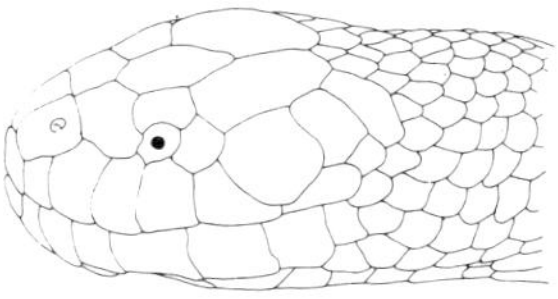
i

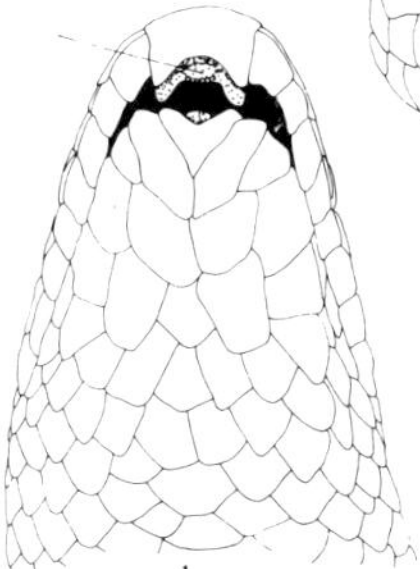
h

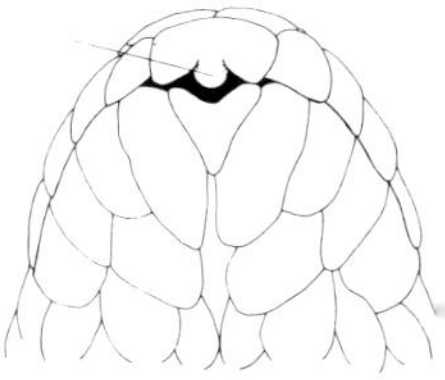
j

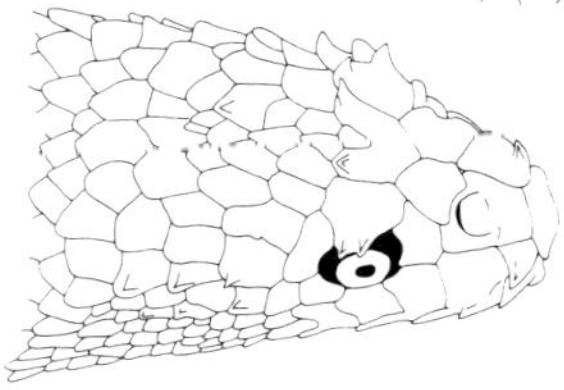
n

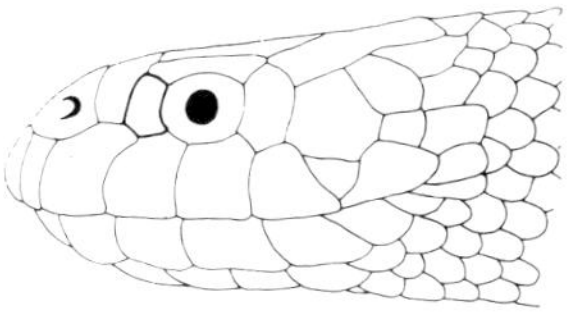
k

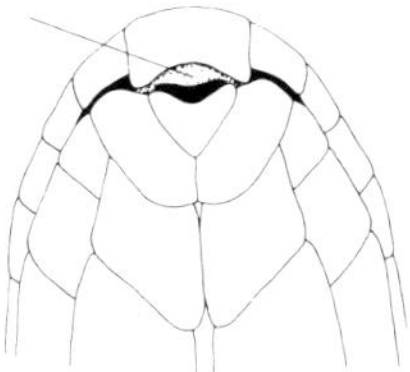
l

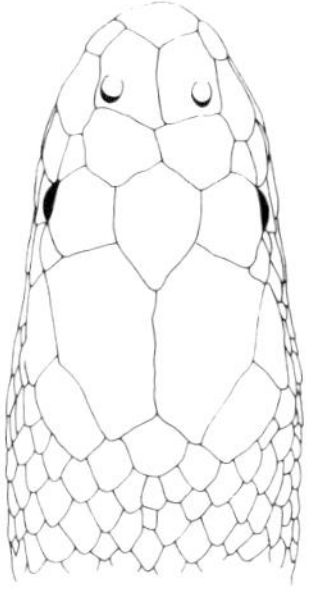
m

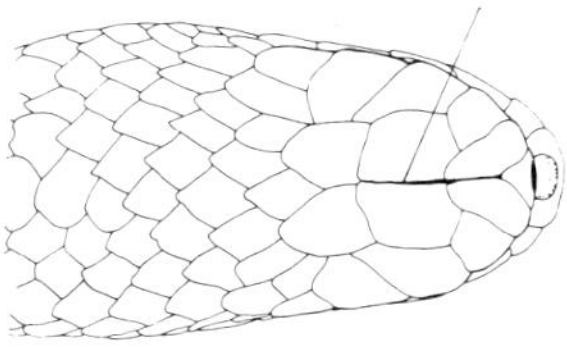
o

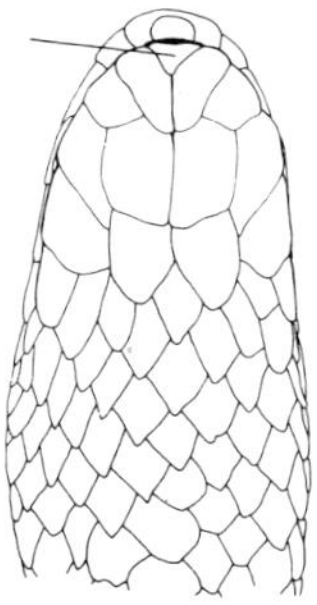
q

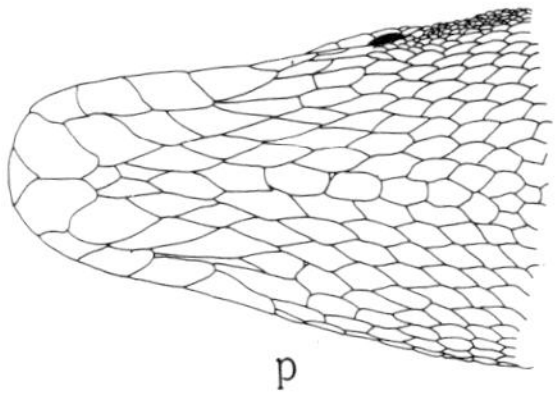
p

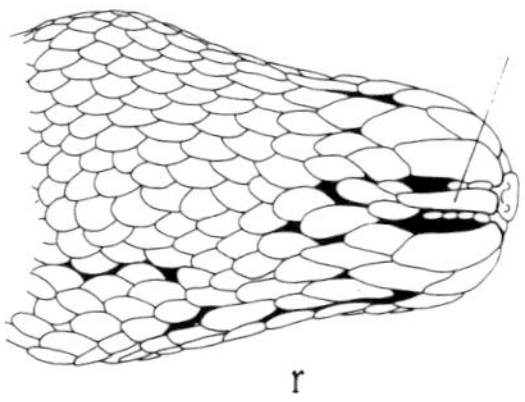
r

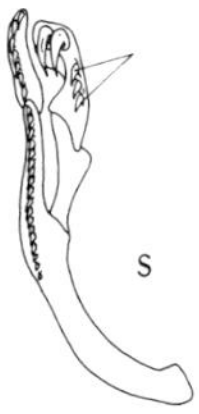
s

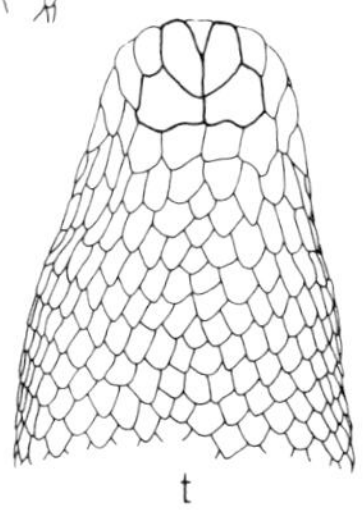
t

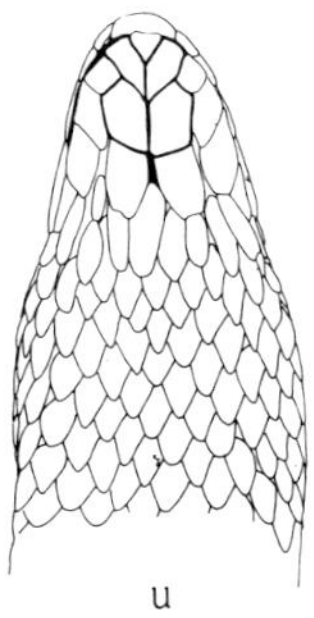
u

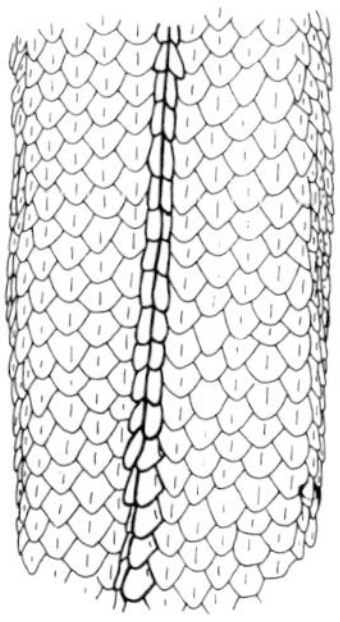
v

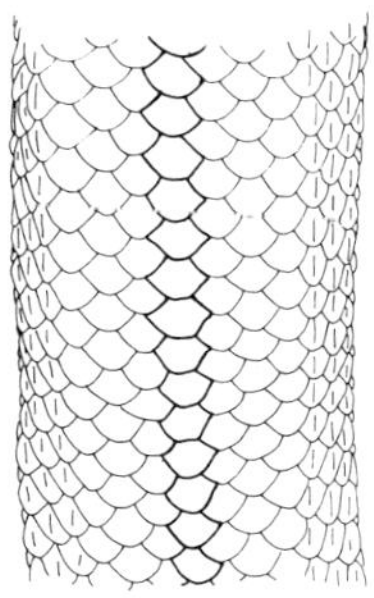
w

7 Mental normal, triangular, broader than long, and not partially hidden in the shallow mental groove (q) **8**

Mental narrow, splint- or dagger-shaped, much longer than broad, and partially hidden in the deep mental groove (r)... .... ***Enhydrina***

8 Either fewer than four solid maxillary teeth following the fang (s) or, if four or more, anterior chin shields reduced and not, or scarcely, contacting the mental groove, from which they are separated by the elongate first infralabials (t).. **9**

Four or more solid maxillary teeth; anterior chin shield large and mostly bordering the mental groove (u)............. .... ***Hydrophis***

9 Ventrals single or divided, but usually distinct posteriorly **10**

Ventrals not distinct posteriorly.......................... ***Lapemis***

10 Ventrals, except on throat, divided into pairs of foliform scales which in most specimens form a mid-ventral keel (v) .... ***Astrotia***

Ventrals mostly undivided, never foliform and never with a mid-ventral keel (w) .... ***Disteira***

11 Posterior dorsal scales smooth; scales in more than 30 rows at mid-body .... ***Parahydrophis***

Posterior dorsal scales with spine-like keels; scales in fewer than 30 rows at mid-body .... ***Ephalophis***

Genus ***Acalyptophis*** Boulenger, 1896

A monotypic genus more or less confined to the Australian region. Although most specimens are moderate in size, large and somewhat bulky individuals are found from time to time.

The genus is characterised by the presence of tubercles (young) or conspicuous projecting spines (adults) on supraocular and postocular scales; parietal and frontal shields fragmented into small scales. Prefrontal scales absent.

Acalyptophis peronii (Duméril, 1853)

Description: Cream, grey or pale brown above, the body with a series of about 25-30 dark brown cross-bands which are widest dorsally (nearly as wide as the paler interspaces), tapering on the flanks. Sometimes a series of secondary, incomplete, dark bands between the primary ones, while many of the scales on the paler parts of the body are dark-centred. The banding may become obscure in older adults, but at all ages the head is pale, while the bands on the tail are more obscure than those on the body. Head shields irregular, fragmented, many (but especially round the eye) raised posteriorly to form projections or spines; this condition is mostly developed in older adults. Prefrontal scales absent. 5-8 solid maxillary teeth following the fang. Scales moderate, imbricate (anteriorly) to almost juxtaposed (posteriorly), each with a short, central, and often darker, keel and in 21-31 rows at mid-body. 140-210 ventrals, about as wide as adjacent body scales; anal divided. 1 metre (total length).

Distribution: As for genus.

Habit: Poorly known. Often seen on surface in reef waters, especially at night. Feeds on a variety of fishes, and produces up to ten living young.

Acalyptophis peronii Ashmore Reef, NW Shelf

Acalyptophis peronii

Genus ***Aipysurus*** Lacépède, 1804

A group of moderate to very large snakes, all but one of which are confined to the Australian region including New Guinea and the Coral Sea east to New Caledonia.

The group is characterised by its large ventral scales, each at least three times as large as the adjacent body scales; nasals in contact; six or more supralabials; posterior chin shields usually reduced and separated by one or more small scales; preocular scale present.

Some members of this genus are rarely seen, others are known to congregate in large numbers on particular reefs. A small number, usually four or fewer, of large young are produced in a litter.

Key

TO THE SPECIES OF AIPYSURUS

1 Ventrals with (a) or without (b) a slight median notch on the hind edge **2**

Ventrals with a deep median notch on the hind edge (c).. **6**

2 Most head shields, but at least the parietals, broken up into a series of smaller scales (d).......... **3**

Head shields (including parietals) normal, enlarged, symmetrical (e) .... ***eydouxii***

3 Head shields more or less regular and symmetrical, larger than the scales on the neck (d).......... **4**

Head covered with small, irregular scales more or less equal in size to those on the neck (f).......... ***duboisii***

4 Ventrals fewer than 180.......... **5**

Ventrals more than 180.......... ***tenuis***

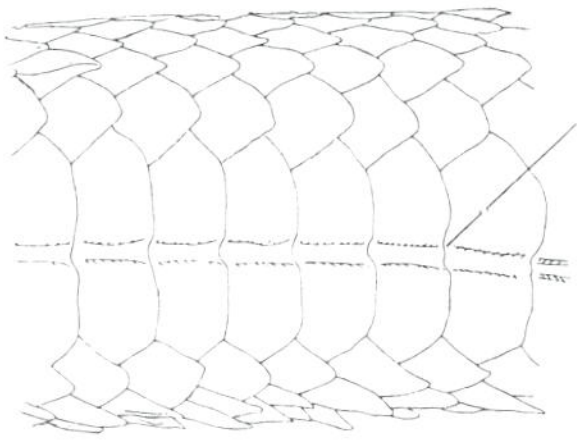

a

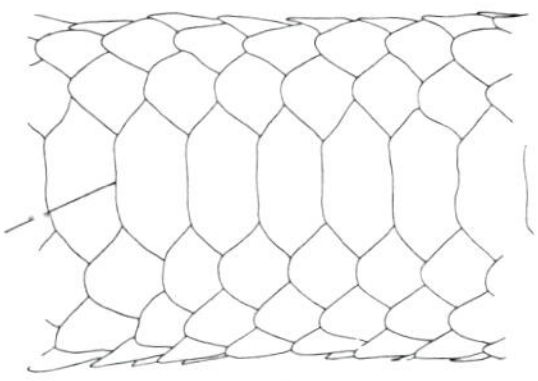

b

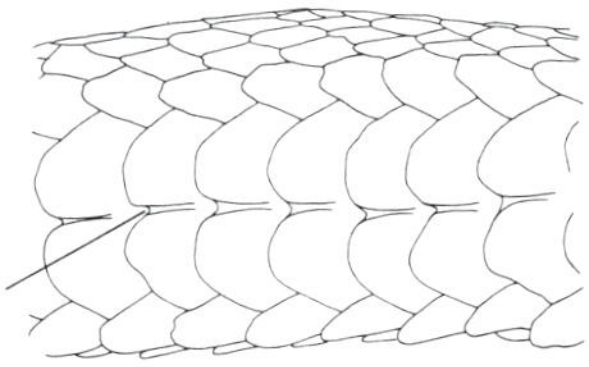

c

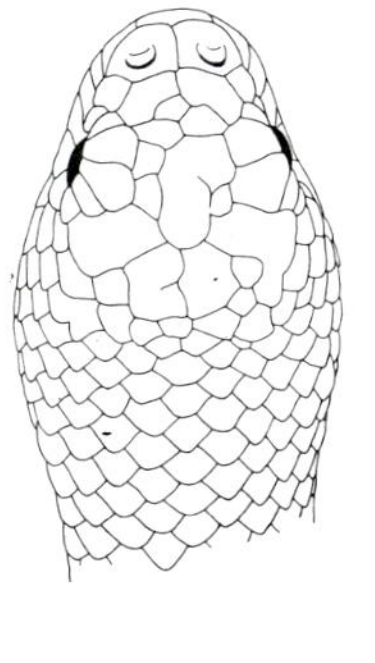

d

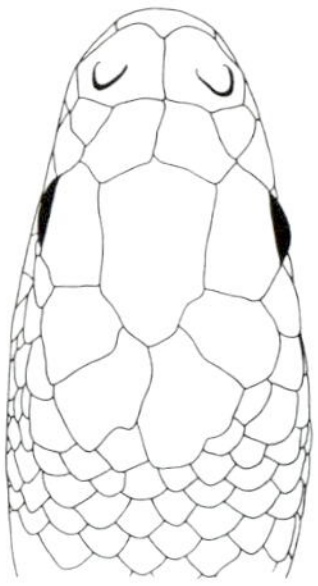
e

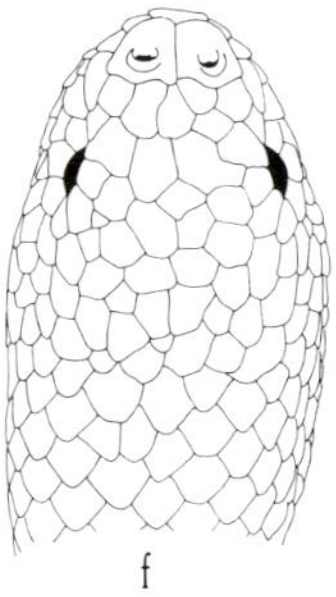
f

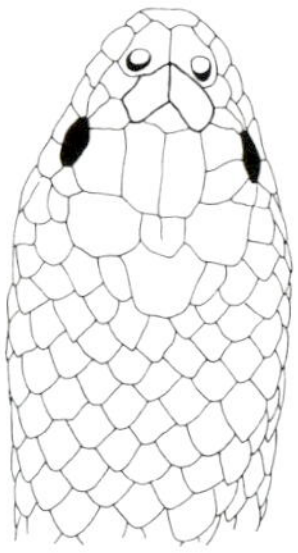
g

5 Scales normally in 19 rows at mid-body; ventrals more than 155.. ***fuscus***

Scales normally in 21 or 23 rows at mid-body; ventrals fewer than 155 .... ***laevis***

6 Prefrontals present (g); scales in 19 rows.... ***foliosquama***

Prefrontals absent (h); scales in 17 rows.. ***apraefrontalis***

Aipysurus apraefrontalis Ashmore Reef, NW Shelf

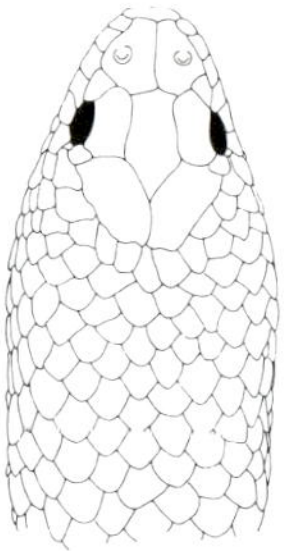
h

Aipysurus duboisii Ashmore Reef, NW Shelf DANGEROUS

Aipysurus apraefrontalis

Aipysurus duboisii

Aipysurus eydouxii

Aipysurus foliosquama

Aipysurus fuscus

Aipysurus apraefrontalis Smith, 1926

Description: Dark olive-brown or purplish-brown above, with either very faint olive-brown cross-bands (which are most conspicuous on the lower sides) or, in some specimens, with more conspicuous pale brown cross-bands and scattered creamy scales (with olive-brown tips), which are mostly confined to the lateral and lower lateral scale rows. Throat with small scales which are creamy-white anteriorly and dark brown posteriorly. Ventral surface more or less uniform grey-brown, with occasional white or white-blotched scales. The concealed part of each ventral scale is creamy-white. A small, rather slender snake with a small head and more or less pointed snout. Head shields enlarged and mostly symmetrical, but with some fragmentation in the parietal region, the fragmented scales larger than the scales on the neck. Prefrontals absent, the nasals contacting the frontal shield. Body scales smooth or each with a low tubercle or short keel posteriorly, imbricate, the hind edge of each scale extensively free and somewhat pointed or bifid, in 17 rows at mid-body. Ventrals 140-155, deeply notched behind and often with ragged hind margins. Anal divided. Subcaudals 18-25, all single. 60 cm (total length).
Distribution: Ashmore Reef and its nearby reef complexes, north-western WA. Also recorded in trawls made in the 'Timor Sea' (Shuntov).
Habit: Mostly found on the reef flat (hiding in cavities under dead coral debris at low tide) or in shallow waters along the outer reef edge.

Aipysurus duboisii Bavay, 1869

Description: Highly variable in colour and pattern. Usually dark purplish-brown above, the concealed surface of each scale pale cream and sufficiently visible to form a reticulated pattern over the dorsal surface. Some specimens are more or less uniform brown, but more often the scales of the lower flanks are creamy-white or white-spotted, forming wedge-shaped pale areas which extend upwards as a series of pale bands alternating with darker ones formed by downward expansions of the dorsal colour; occasionally the dark brown is confined to spots on the individual scales, so that the ground colour is pale cream or salmon, with obscure darker cross-bands. Scales of throat white, tipped with brown. Ventral surfaces range from cream to uniform dark brown. A moderately built snake. Head shields, except rostral and nasals, fragmented into small, irregular scales, the individual fragments not, or scarcely, larger than the scales on the neck. Scales usually smooth, occasionally with a slight central keel or series of tubercles, imbricate, in 19 rows at mid-body. Ventrals 150-165, slightly notched behind. Anal divided. Subcaudals 23-35, all single. 70 cm (total length).
DANGEROUS
Distribution: Waters of the continental shelf from WA to the Great Barrier Reef. Extra-limital in New Guinea waters and the Coral Sea east to New Caledonia.
Habit: A common species on coral reefs, from the reef flat to depths of about 50 metres.

Aipysurus eydouxii Thursday Island, Torres Strait DANGEROUS

Aipysurus eydouxii (Gray, 1849)

Description: Cream or salmon-coloured above, with a series of broad, often very irregular cross-bands which may taper and terminate on the sides or extend to the ventral surface. Scales of the paler interspaces usually with dark margins, while the interspaces may contain secondary darker bars or blotches, especially on the lower flanks. Ventrals range from black to pale cream with a dark median zone. Head uniform brown, or flecked with darker brown. A moderately built snake. Head shields enlarged, symmetrical, without any indication of fragmentation; prefrontals present; scales smooth, imbricate, in 17 rows at mid-body. Ventrals 124-150, not, or scarcely, notched behind. Anal divided. Subcaudals 23-35, all single. 1 metre (total length). DANGEROUS
Distribution: Seas of northern Australia. Extra-limital through the Indo-Malayan Archipelago.
Habit: Poorly known. Usually trawled in deeper (30-50 metres), more turbid waters.

Aipysurus foliosquama Smith, 1926

Description: Rich brown to dark reddish-brown or purplish-brown above, usually with obscure, paler brown cross-bands (which are most conspicuous on the lower flanks) and scattered white or cream-coloured scales. Ventral surface grey-brown, with occasional white or white-blotched scales. A small, rather slender snake with small head and more or less pointed snout. Head shields enlarged and mostly symmetrical, but with some fragmentation on the parietal region, and with paired prefrontal scales between the frontal and nasals. Body scales smooth, or each with a low tubercle or short keel, imbricate, the hind edge of each scale extensively free and somewhat pointed or bifid, in 19-21 rows at mid-body. Ventrals 135-155, each deeply notched behind. Anal divided. Subcaudals 20-30, all single. 60 cm (total length).
Distribution: Known only from the region of Ashmore and Scott Reefs, north-western WA.
Habit: Similar to that of *Aipysurus apraefrontalis.*

Aipysurus fuscus (Tschudi, 1837)

Description: Brown, blackish-brown or purplish-brown above, more or less uniform, but often with obscure, faint, paler cross-bands on the lower flanks. In some specimens the centre of each lateral scale is darker, resulting in faint, dark, longitudinal striations. Ventral surface brown. A small, moderately-built snake superficially resembling *Aipysurus foliosquama,* but with a blunter snout. Head shields, especially the parietals, partly fragmented, but major shields more

Aipysurus foliosquama Ashmore Reef, NW Shelf

Aipysurus foliosquama Ashmore Reef, NW Shelf

or less regular. Body scales smooth, imbricate, in 19 (rarely 21) rows at mid-body. Ventrals 155-180, slightly notched behind. Anal divided. Subcaudals 20-40, all single. 60 cm (total length).
Distribution: Ashmore Reef and its nearby reef complexes, north-western WA. The type specimen is said to have come from 'Celebes'.
Habit: Similar to that of *Aipysurus apraefrontalis.*

Aipysurus laevis Lacépède, 1804

Description: Highly variable in colour and pattern. Some specimens a rich dark brown or purplish-brown above, gradually fading to a paler brown ventral surface; more often there are numerous creamy-white or spotted scales scattered over the body. In some paler specimens the ventral and lateral scales are entirely creamy-white. The brown scales on the body often have darker centres which form faint, longitudinal striations. Tail uniformly brown to almost pure white, except for a dark brown dorsal ridge. The largest and bulkiest member of the genus. Head shields mostly large and regular, with only partial fragmentation of the parietal region. Body scales smooth, imbricate, in 21-25 rows at mid-body. 135-155 ventrals, slightly notched behind. Anal divided. Subcaudals 25-35, all single. 1.2 metres (total length), but commonly reaches nearly 2 metres. DANGEROUS

Aipysurus fuscus Ashmore Reef, NW Shelf

Distribution: Tropical coastal and reef waters of northern Australia. Extra-limital in New Guinea and the Coral Sea.
Habit: One of the most abundant sea snakes in coral reefs throughout its range. There have been many

Aipysurus laevis

Aipysurus tenuis

reports by divers of aggressive behaviour by this species, based largely, in my view, on its undoubted curiosity. Bites are unlikely, however, unless the snake is provoked, although this can easily happen when a diver tries to fend off a curious snake. It produces 2-5 large, living young. Feeds on a variety of reef fishes.

Subspecies: *pooleorum* (Shark Bay region, WA); *laevis* (remainder of species' range).

Aipysurus tenuis Lönnberg and Andersson, 1913

Description: 'Light brown with dark brown spots on tips of scales forming longitudinal lines on the back and more or less distinct cross-bars on the sides. Head above dark brown' (Smith). A moderately-built snake. Head shields enlarged and symmetrical, the parietals and frontal partly fragmented, but the fragments much larger than the scales on the neck. Body scales smooth, or outer rows with a small tubercle, imbricate, in 19 rows at mid-body. 185-195 ventrals, each with at most a slight notch behind, and each with a small median keel and a series of tubercles along the hind edge. Anal divided. Subcaudals 35-40, all single. Maximum known length 1.02 metres. DANGEROUS
Distribution: Known only from the vicinity of Broome, WA (Lünnberg and Andersson), and the Arafura Sea (Shuntov).
Habit: Not known.

Aipysurus laevis north-western WA DANGEROUS

Aipysurus laevis
Ashmore Reef, NW Shelf
DANGEROUS

Genus **Astrotia** Fischer, 1856

A monotypic genus whose sole member is one of the largest and bulkiest of all sea snakes and occurs throughout the Indo-Malayan and Australian regions.

It is characterised by having ventral scales (except on the throat) divided into pairs of foliform scales, each of which is scarcely larger than an adjacent body scale but which, in all but juveniles, form a deep, conspicuous, median ventral keel; nasals in contact.

Astrotia stokesii Darwin Harbour, NT DANGEROUS

Astrotia stokesii (Gray, 1846)

Astrotia stokesii

Description: Adults are uniform creamy-white to leaden-grey or almost black, sometimes with obscure, dark ocelli or a paler, reticulate pattern on the lower half of the body. Half-grown specimens with some obscure, transverse, dark-centred, pale blotches along the vertebral line. Below with two series of blotches or dark spots: one on the lower lateral surface, alternating with the second series along the mid-ventral line. This same pattern is well developed in the young. Head shields large, symmetrical, unfragmented. Nasals in contact. Body scales imbricate, each with a median keel or series of tubercles,in 46-63 rows at mid-body. Ventrals 226-286, those on the throat single, but remainder divided into pairs of elongate, pointed scales which form a strongly raised ventral keel in all except juvenile specimens. Preanal scales enlarged. 1.2 metres (total length), maximum nearly 2 metres. DANGEROUS

Distribution: Coastal and shelf waters of tropical Australia, often straying into more southern temperate seas in late summer. Extra-limital distribution in New Guinea and South-east Asian waters.

Habit: Usually seen on surface in turbid coastal waters, or deeper reef waters. Poorly known.

Astrotia stokesii Darwin Harbour, NT DANGEROUS

Genus ***Disteira*** Lacépède, 1804

Probably a composite genus whose species vary considerably in form and structure. As here recognised, the genus extends from the Persian Gulf to Australia and is characterised by its small ventrals, scarcely wider than adjacent body scales and most distinct and undivided. Fewer than four solid maxillary teeth following the fang, or if more than four, the anterior chin shields are reduced and at most in only narrow contact along the mental groove; head shield enlarged, regular; mental triangular, broader than long.

Key

TO THE AUSTRALIAN SPECIES OF DISTEIRA

Anterior chin shields not, or scarcely, contacting the mental groove from which they are separated by the elongated first infralabials (a); six or more maxillary teeth following the fang (b) .... ***major***

Anterior chin shields large and mostly bordering the mental groove (c); fewer than four maxillary teeth following the fang (d) .... ***kingii***

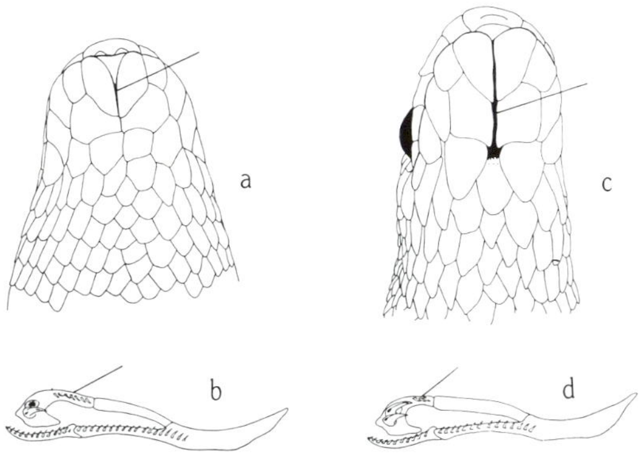

Disteira kingii (Boulenger, 1896)

Description: Head and throat black. Dorsal half of body grey, on which is superimposed a series of 45-50 darker grey rhombs or blotches extending lower on the sides than the grey dorsal colour. Lower half of body cream or pale brown, except for a blackish mid-ventral stripe and usually a series of dark, mid-lateral, triangular blotches below paler grey interspaces (and which may join with the darker blotches to leave a single, longitudinal series of pale, oval, upper lateral blotches) and a series of much smaller lower lateral dark spots. The dorsal blotches may form incomplete black rings on the neck, often with narrow, white or yellow interspaces. The dorsal pattern continues onto the tail. Head shields enlarged, symmetrical, unfragmented. Anterior chin shields large, mostly bordering the mental groove. Two or three solid maxillary teeth following the fang. Scales keeled, imbricate, in 37-39 rows at mid-body. 324-342 ventrals noticeably wider than adjacent body scales. Anals not enlarged. 1.5 metres (total length). DANGEROUS
Distribution: Confined to tropical coastal waters of northern Australia from WA to the eastern coast of Qld.
Habit: Poorly known. Most specimens have been taken from deeper water, on a variety of sea beds.

Disteira kingii Ashmore Reef, NW Shelf DANGEROUS

Disteira kingii

Disteira major (Shaw, 1802)

Description: Head olive or brown above with darker flecks. Body pale grey above, with a series of 25-30 dark dorsal blotches or cross-bars (the first on the nape), each slightly narrower than the paler interspaces, extending about halfway down each side on to the cream or yellowish lower half of the body. A narrow, dark bar, usually no more than one scale in width, in the middle of each pale dorsal interspace. A series of large, dark, lateral blotches, each below the narrow interspace bar, and a series of lower lateral blotches, each tending to lie below a large dorsal blotch. Most ventral scales dark grey, or tipped with

Disteira major

Disteira major Noumea, New Caledonia DANGEROUS

darker. Juveniles have a more conspicuous pattern than adults. Head shields large, symmetrical, unfragmented. Anterior chin shields not, or scarcely, contacting mental groove from which they are largely separated by the elongated first infralabials. Fang followed by 6-8 solid maxillary teeth. Scales imbricate, each with a low, blunt keel in 37-43 rows at mid-body. Ventrals 230-266, scarcely wider than adjacent body scales. Anals enlarged. 1.3 metres (total length). DANGEROUS

Distribution: Coastal waters of northern Australia from north-western WA and the Arafura Sea to eastern Qld. Extra-limital in New Guinea waters.

Habit: Poorly known, despite its apparent abundance. Usually trawled in deeper, more turbid waters throughout its range.

Genus ***Emydocephalus*** Krefft, 1869

A distinctive genus containing two closely related species, one of which is confined to Australian waters; the other occurs in the South China Sea.

The genus is unique in possessing only three supralabials, the second being very elongate and below the eye; ventral scales large, at least three times as wide as the adjacent body scales; nasals in contact; posterior chin shields usually reduced and separated by one or more scales; preocular scale present; a conspicuous rostral spine in adult males.

Emydocephalus annulatus Krefft, 1869

Description: Highly variable in colour and pattern, ranging from uniform black, dark brown or dark grey above and below, through various degrees of banding, in which more or less complete rings of creamy-white scales alternate with slightly wider complete, dark rings. Typically the dark rings contain some brown or brown-blotched scales, while black rings may contain some white-blotched scales. In banded forms the head is usually creamy-white or yellow above, speckled and blotched with dark brown, and with a

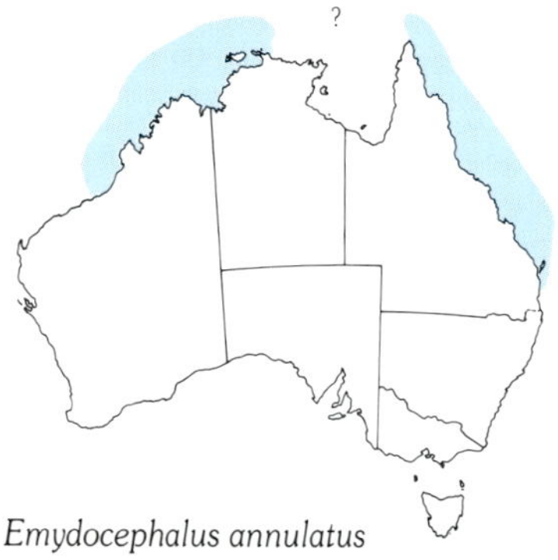

Emydocephalus annulatus

Emydocephalus annulatus Ashmore Reef, NW Shelf

dark brown band extending from behind each eye (sometimes continuing in front), which joins the first dark body ring on the nape. Head shields large and regular, unfragmented. The rostral shield often bears a conical projection, which in adult males is a conspicuous blunt spine. Three supralabials. Scales smooth, imbricate in 15-17 rows at mid-body. 125-145 ventrals, each with small tubercles and usually a median keel. Anal usually single, subcaudals 20-40, all single. Average total length 75 cm.

Distribution: Waters of tropical Australia from the Timor Sea to the Coral Sea.

Habit: Often occurs in large numbers on individual reefs, usually in shallower waters. Feeds exclusively on fish eggs (Voris), especially those of burrowing gobies and blennies. Non-venomous, the teeth and venom structures having atrophied.

Genus *Enhydrina* Gray, 1849

A genus of disputed status, recently included by McDowell in the genus *Disteira*. Monotypic, the species is a small to moderate snake, rather slender, the anterior body contrasting strongly with the deeply compressed rear portion.

Characterised by its greatly elongate mental shield which is much longer than broad, dagger-like, its posterior part lying partly concealed within the mental groove; head shields enlarged, regular; ventrals scarcely wider than adjacent body scales; 3-4 solid maxillary teeth following the fang.

It is found from the Persian Gulf to Australia.

Enhydrina schistosa (Daudin, 1803)

Description: A dark, more or less uniform grey above, whitish below; sometimes some obscure dark bars along the back, from as wide as, to much wider than, the paler interspaces and rarely extending more than halfway down the flanks. Head dark grey above, pale below. Australian juveniles have 45-55 blackish transverse bars which scarcely extend more than halfway down the flanks, but Smith records young from other parts of the range as having dark grey or black rings. Head shields enlarged, regular. Mental

Enhydrina schistosa Weipa, Qld DANGEROUS

shield as described for genus; anterior infralabials elongate — connected by highly extensile skin which forms a concertina-like anterior throat region. Body scales each with a short, low keel, imbricate, in 49-66 rows at mid-body. Ventrals 239-322, scarcely wider than adjacent body scales. Average total length 1.2 metres. DANGEROUS

Distribution: Known only from widely scattered localities in the waters between Australia and New Guinea.

Habit: Usually seen on the surface at night in the shallower waters of harbours, bays and estuaries. Extremely aggressive when disturbed or taken from the water. Frequently travels high up into the freshwater reaches of larger rivers. Feeds on fish.

Enhydrina schistosa

Genus ***Ephalophis*** Smith, 1931

A monotypic genus characterised by large ventral scales which are 3-5 times as wide as the adjacent body scales; the latter, at least posteriorly, with spine-like keels, in fewer than 30 rows at mid-body; large posterior chin shields bordering the mental groove, separated by a small scale; preocular scale present.

G. GOW

Ephalophis greyi

Ephalophis greyi

Ephalophis greyi Smith, 1931

Description: Cream or pale olive-brown above, the head blotched or mottled with dark grey, and with 25-40 dark grey dorsal blotches which are often more or less fused along the vertebral line to form an irregular and interrupted zigzag vertebral stripe. Tail with 7-8 dark grey rings. Head shields enlarged and regular. Lateral body scales smooth, but dorsal scales (at least posteriorly) with blunt keels, imbricate, in 19-21 rows at mid-body. Ventrals 159-169, nearly as broad as body. Anal divided. Subcaudals 28-33, single. Fang followed by 7-8 solid maxillary teeth. Tail shallow, not noticeably deeper than body. Average total length 50 cm.

Distribution: Known only from the vicinity of Broome, WA.

Habit: Mangroves and associated mudflats, especially in estuaries.

Genus *Hydrelaps* Boulenger, 1896

A monotypic genus whose single species is a small, banded snake, known only from shallow coastal waters in northern Australia and southern New Guinea, west of Torres Strait.

It is characterised by its large ventrals, at least three times as wide as the adjacent body scales; no preocular scale; nasal scales in broad contact; six or more supralabials; posterior chin shields at least as large as anterior chin shields, separated by the mental groove.

Hydrelaps darwiniensis NT

Hydrelaps darwiniensis

Hydrelaps darwiniensis Boulenger, 1896

Description: Cream or yellowish above, the body with 30-45 dark rings or cross-bands, each about twice as broad as the paler interspaces, and usually complete on the belly. Sometimes the bands are displaced on the vertebral line. 5-8 complete dark rings on the tail. The subcaudals occasionally entirely black. Head blackish, with cream or yellow variegations. Head shields enlarged, regular. Preocular scales absent, the prefrontal bordering the eye. Body scales smooth, imbricate, in 25-29 rows at mid-body. Ventrals 163-172, relatively narrow, only about three times as wide as the adjacent body scales. Anal divided. Subcaudals 27-39, usually single, but occasionally with a few divided anteriorly. Fang followed by 3-6 solid maxillary teeth. Average total length 50 cm.
Distribution: As for genus.
Habit: Most commonly encountered on mud flats associated with mangroves.

Genus ***Hydrophis*** Sonnini and Latreille, 1802

The largest group of sea snakes, with 12 species recorded from Australian seas, out of a world total of about 25 species. Recent major revision by McDowell has resulted in several subgenera, but these have not been used below; conversely, several species which had long been in the genus *Hydrophis* were removed by McDowell.

Members of this genus vary considerably in form and structure, but all are characterised by their small ventrals, never foliform, scarcely wider than adjacent body scales, and mostly undivided except in one species *(gracilis)* in which they are all divided posteriorly; four or more solid maxillary teeth behind the fang; anterior chin shields large and mostly bordering the mental groove; head shields enlarged, regular; mental triangular, broader than long.

Key

TO THE SPECIES OF HYDROPHIS

1 Posterior ventrals distinct and mostly undivided (a) **2**
Posterior ventrals all divided (b) .... ***gracilis***

2 Fewer than ten solid maxillary teeth behind the fang (c) **3**
Ten or more solid maxillary teeth behind the fang (d) . **10**

3 Anterior part of maxilla not arched upwards, the tip of the fang projecting conspicuously below a line connecting the tips of the solid maxillary teeth (e) **4**
Anterior part of maxilla arched upward, so that the tip of the longer fang is nearly or quite on a line with the tips of the solid maxillary teeth (f) **7**

4 Normally two or more supralabials contacting the eye (g) **5**
Normally a single supralabial contacting the eye (h) .... ***belcheri***

5 Tip of tail greyish, paler than darker cross-bands when the latter are present; dark cross-banding of adults more intense anteriorly, often either secondary bands or blotches between the main bands **6**
Tip of tail and most or all of the ventral side of the tail black at all ages; dark cross-banding of adults more or less equal in intensity along the length of the body, without secondary bands or blotches between the main bands .... ***coggeri***

6 Usually only third and fourth supralabials contacting the orbit; some indication, at least posteriorly, of dark scales, spots or blotches in the pale interspaces between the dark bands .... ***elegans***
Usually the third, fourth and fifth supralabials contacting the orbit; no indication of dark scales, spots or blotches in the pale interspaces between the dark bands .... ***pacificus***

7 Usually 25 or more scale rows on the neck; scales on neck as well as posterior part of body, each with central tubercle or short keel **8**
Fewer than 25 scale rows on the neck; scales on neck smooth but keeled posteriorly .... ***vorisi***

8 Head small; body very slender anteriorly; parietal bone not contacting prefrontal bone (i) **9**
Head moderate; body not noticeably slender anteriorly; parietal bone contacting the prefrontal bone (j) .... ***melanosoma***

9 Head black, even in adults, sometimes with a yellow spot behind the eye and/or nostril; rostral normal, triangular, broader than high (k); first infralabial normal, about as long as pregenial (l) .... ***atriceps***
Head black in young, with conspicuous yellow marking on the crown, but becoming much paler in adults; rostral large, oval, at least as high as broad (m); first infralabial large, strap-like, much longer than pregenial (n) .... ***mcdowelli***

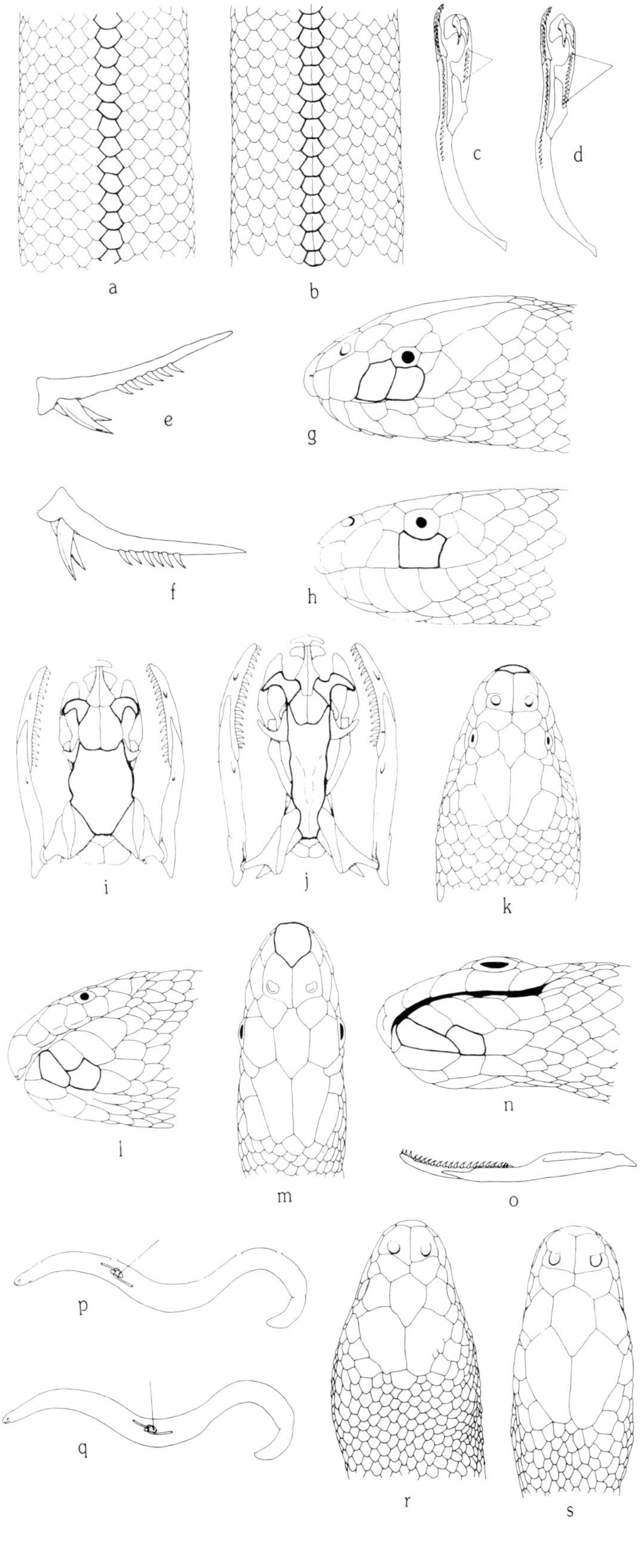

10 14 or fewer solid maxillary teeth; dentary teeth usually fewer than 23 (o); heart just behind anterior third of body (p) **11**

12 or more solid maxillary teeth; dentary teeth 22 or more; heart about midway along body (q) ***caerulescens***

11 Width of head between the eyes at least half the distance from the tip of the snout to rear edge of parietal scales (r); adults with dark dorsal blotches **12**

Width of head between the eyes less than half the distance from tip of snout to rear edge of parietal scales (s); adults without dorsal blotches .... ***inornatus***

12 Lateral pattern of obscure cross-bands or ocelli .... ***ornatus***

Lateral pattern of a connected chain of pale pentagons contrasting with the darker ground colour .... ***czeblukovi***

Hydrophis atriceps Günther, 1864

Description: In this species the head is very small, while the body is very slender anteriorly but deep and greatly compressed posteriorly. Pale fawn, brown or yellowish anteriorly. Young with 50-70 black cross-bands which sometimes form complete rings. In adults the bands may be reduced to a series of dorsal blotches. The head is black at all ages. Ventrals blackish, at least anteriorly. Head shields large, regular. Third and fourth supralabials contacting the eye. Five or six solid maxillary teeth following the fang. Body scales imbricate, in 35-49 rows at mid-body. Ventrals 323-514 (Smith), scarcely wider than adjacent body scales and mostly undivided. Average total length 1 metre. DANGEROUS
Distribution: Although widely distributed in South-East Asia and Indo-Malaysia, only one or two specimens are known from Australian waters between Darwin and the New Guinea coast.

Hydrophis belcheri (Gray, 1849)

Description: Status in Australian waters uncertain. Greyish above, with about 60 dark cross-bands on the body, broadest dorsally, almost fading on the belly, ventral surface pale grey. Posterior ventrals undivided. Fewer than 10 maxillary teeth following the fang. Anterior part of maxilla not arched upwards, the tip of the fang projecting well below a line connecting the tips of the solid maxillary teeth. A single supralabial contacting the eye. Scales in 34 rows at mid-body. Ventrals 300-320, mostly undivided. Total length about 1 metre. DANGEROUS
Distribution: Only 'Australian' record is the type specimen from 'New Guinea'. Appears to occur only to the north-west of New Guinea.

Hydrophis caerulescens (Shaw, 1802)

Description: Blue-grey above, the head blackish and the body with 41-43 blackish blotches or transverse bands, which may be divided or alternating, on either side of the vertebral line. Tail with 7-9 dark bands, or black with four pale blotches on its dorsal edge (McDowell). Head shields enlarged, regular. Third and fourth supralabials contacting the eye. Twelve or more solid maxillary teeth following the fang, dentary teeth 22 or more. Heart about midway along body. Body scales imbricate, in 37-39 rows at mid-body. Ventrals 266-287, scarcely wider than adjacent body scales and mostly undivided, except anteriorly. Average total length 0.6 metre. DANGEROUS
Distribution: All known Australian specimens from the lower south-east corner of the Gulf of Carpentaria. Otherwise a common species extending from India and China to the Moluccas.

Hydrophis coggeri (juvenile) Ashmore Reef, NW Shelf

Hydrophis coggeri (Kharin, 1984)

Description: A slightly-built snake, the adult having a small head, slender anterior part of the body, and being moderately deep and compressed posteriorly. Head black, with conspicuous yellow markings on the snout and postocular region in the young; olive-grey with darker flecks in adults. 30-40 blackish cross-bands on the body and tail, each band expanded dorsally and ventrally, and more or less equal in width to the pale yellowish (in young) or olive-grey (in adults) interspaces. End portion of tail and usually most of lower half, black. Anterior body bands usually joined below to form a black ventral surface. Head shields enlarged, regular. Usually only the third and fourth supralabials contacting the eye. 5-8 solid maxillary teeth following the fang. Body scales imbricate, in 29-34 rows at mid-body. Ventrals 280-360, scarcely wider than adjacent body scales, except anteriorly, and mostly undivided. Average total length 1 metre. DANGEROUS
Distribution: It is uncertain as to whether this species ranges continuously around the north Australian coast. Known populations are from the North-west Shelf/Timor Sea (where it is abundant) and from the Coral Sea, New Caledonia, Vanuatu and Fiji in the east. Western populations appear to inhabit deeper waters beyond the reef edges, whereas in the eastern populations specimens are often encountered on the reef flats and in the lagoons, especially over sea grasses.

Hydrophis coggeri (adult) Ashmore Reef, NW Shelf DANGEROUS

Hydrophis czeblukovi (Kharin, 1984)

Description: Dark grey above, with a series of narrow, pale cross-bars across the back which divide on the upper flanks to form a series of about 35-40 linked pentagons along the side of the body, their centres with scattered, pale spots and flecks; belly and lower lateral surfaces spotted and flecked with white or yellow. Body scales juxtaposed, each with a single, short keel, 51-58 at mid-body. Ventrals 288-304. Total length of largest known specimen about 1.2 metres. DANGEROUS
Distribution: Known only from a small area off the coast of north-western WA.

Hydrophis atriceps

Hydrophis belcheri

Hydrophis elegans Weipa, Qld DANGEROUS

Hydrophis elegans (Gray, 1842)

Description: This species is characterised by its greatly elongated body and its deep and compressed hind part in adults. Otherwise a highly variable species in which the young may differ markedly from the adults. Juveniles: pale brown with black head and strongly banded body, the 35-55 bands widest on the mid-dorsal and mid-ventral lines, narrowest laterally where all or some of the bands may be broken; usually at least some indication of secondary spots or narrow bands in the paler interspaces between the primary bands, at least on the neck and tail. Adults: bands reduced to a series of transverse vertebral bars or blotches and two series of spots on the flanks; a mid-lateral series on which each spot lies below a pale interspace, and a lower lateral series in which each spot lies below a dark dorsal bar. In addition there may be narrow secondary cross-bars or rows of dark scales. Ventrals usually blackish on the throat and forepart of the body. Head shields enlarged, regular. Third and fourth supralabial usually contacting the eye. Fewer than nine solid maxillary teeth following the fang. Anterior part of maxilla not arched upwards, the tip of the fang usually projecting noticeably below a line connecting the tips of the solid maxillary teeth. Body scales imbricate, in 37-49 rows at mid-body. Ventrals 345-432, scarcely wider than adjacent body scales (except anteriorly), and mostly undivided. Average total length 1.7 metres, maximum about 2 metres. DANGEROUS

Distribution: Confined to the waters off the northern coasts of Australia (and southern New Guinea), but individuals commonly found further south during late summer months.

Habit: A widespread and abundant species found in deeper reef waters and in the more turbid water of the Gulf of Carpentaria and the Arafura Sea.

Hydrophis elegans

Hydrophis gracilis (Shaw, 1802)

Description: A very small-headed species with a very slender body anteriorly, and deeply and strongly compressed posteriorly. Juveniles: 'black with a series of whitish dorsal bands or oval lateral spots on the slender part of the body, and more or less complete bands posteriorly, altogether from 40-60 in number' (Smith). Adults: usually with indistinct bars, but more or less uniform grey above and whitish below. The keels or tubercles on the lower lateral scales are often dark brown or black. Head shields large, regular. Third and fourth supralabials contacting the eye. Five or six solid maxillary teeth following the fang. Body scales juxtaposed, in 30-36 rows on the body, the lower lateral scales usually larger than the dorsals, and either tubercular or with prominent high keels. Ventrals 220-287. Average total length 70 cm. DANGEROUS
Distribution: Apparently rare in Australian waters, where it is known only from the Torres Strait region. Widely distributed extra-limitally from the Persian Gulf to Indonesia.

Hydrophis inornatus (Gray, 1849)

Description: A relatively moderately-built snake, the body more or less uniform along its length. Bluish-grey above, the young with 50-65 black bars or cross-bands, which sometimes form complete rings but which disappear or are reduced to obscure, dorsal blotches in adults. Lower half of body whitish. Head shields large, regular. Third and fourth supralabials contacting the eye. 10-13 solid maxillary teeth following the fang. Body scales imbricate, in 35-48 rows at mid-body. Ventrals 195-293, scarcely wider than adjacent body scales and mostly undivided. Average total length 70 cm. DANGEROUS
Distribution: Although widely distributed in Asia, only a few specimens have been recorded from northern Australian waters.

Hydrophis mcdowelli Kharin, 1983

Description: The head is very small, while the body is extremely slender anteriorly and deep and strongly compressed posteriorly. Head dark olive or black, body cream above, tending to become pale yellowish ventrally. A series of dark grey or blackish dorsal blotches, each blotch extending about one third of the way down the body. Flanks usually with three series

Hydrophis caerulescens

Hydrophis coggeri

Hydrophis czeblukovi

Hydrophis gracilis

Hydrophis inornatus

Hydrophis mcdowelli

Hydrophis ornatus
McCluer Gulf,
West Irian
DANGEROUS

of dark grey, sometimes black-edged, markings; an upper lateral series of inverted triangles or elongated rhombs, each series below the paler interspace between the vertebral blotches; a lower lateral series of small, irregular blotches, each lying below a vertebral blotch; an even smaller series of lower lateral spots or irregular vertebral bars, each below a pale dorsal interspace. In addition narrow, sometimes disrupted, secondary dorsal bars may be present in the pale interspaces. Tail with four or five obscure grey bands, usually with a narrow, disrupted band in each of the paler interspaces. Throat and anterior ventrals dark grey to black. Head shields enlarged, regular. Third and fourth supralabials contacting the eye. 5-6 maxillary teeth following the fang. Body scales imbricate, in 35-39 rows at mid-body. Ventrals 252-274, mostly undivided. Average total length 80 cm. DANGEROUS ?
Distribution: Apparently confined to the seas of northern Australia, where it has been taken from widely scattered localities.
Habit: A number of specimens have been taken from river estuaries and from other turbid, inshore waters. Produces only two or three young in a litter.

Hydrophis melanosoma Günther, 1864

Description: Status of Australian specimens uncertain. A moderately-built snake, the posterior part of the body only moderately compressed. Head black, body and tail cream or yellowish with 50-70 black cross-bands, each about twice as broad as the paler interspaces. Head shields enlarged, regular. 6-8 solid maxillary teeth following the fang. Third and fourth supralabials contacting the eye. Body scales imbricate, in 37-43 rows at mid-body. Ventrals 260-370, scales wider than adjacent body scales and mostly undivided. Average total length 1 metre. DANGEROUS
Distribution: Widely distributed in the waters of Malaysia and Indonesia. It has been reported as relatively abundant in shoal waters off the north-western coast of Australia (Shuntov).

Hydrophis ornatus (Gray, 1842)

Description: A moderate to heavily built snake, the body more or less uniform along its length. Grey or blue-grey above with 30-60 broad, blackish, transverse bars or blotches and a lateral series of dark-edged, ocellate markings and smaller dark blotches. Otherwise pale cream or whitish on the lower half of the body. In older specimens the dorsal markings are sometimes obscure, or reduced to a uniform blue-grey dorsum. Head shields large, regular. 10-14 solid maxillary teeth following the fang. Usually the third and fourth supralabials contact the eye. Body scales imbricate, in 39-59 rows at mid-body. Ventrals 240-340, about twice as broad as adjacent body scales. Average total length 1 metre. DANGEROUS
Distribution: Widely distributed throughout the coastal waters of northern Australia with many

individuals ranging further south in late summer, being one of only three species recorded from Tasmania. Extra-limital from Indonesia to the Persian Gulf.
Habit: Found in a variety of waters, from the clear waters of coral reefs to turbid inshore waters and estuaries.
Subspecies: Australian specimens have been referred to the subspecies *ocellatus*, but recent studies have raised doubts as to the status of the subspecies within this species.

Hydrophis melanosoma

Hydrophis ornatus

Hydrophis pacificus Boulenger, 1896

Description: A large snake with relatively large head, the body relatively slender anteriorly and rather deep and compressed posteriorly in adults. Young with well-defined black bands circling the body, the bands on the neck connected by a broad, black, ventral region to the black throat; head black above, with one or two pale yellow spots behind each eye and some small, pale spots on the snout. Adults dark grey above, whitish below, the two colours merging along a distinct mid-lateral zone; a series of dark transverse bands expanded as blackish blotches dorsally, continuing around the body as obscure, grey bands. The bands on the neck are usually connected by black ventrals, while some of the body bands may be divided or displaced on either side of the vertebral line. Head dark grey above, with obscure paler flecks. Head shields large, regular. 5-8 solid maxillary teeth following the fang. Third, fourth and fifth supralabials contacting the eye. Body scales imbricate, in 45-49 rows at mid-body. Ventrals 320-430, not much broader than adjacent body scales, and mostly undivided. Average total length 1.4 metres. DANGEROUS
Distribution: Known only from widely scattered localities in the seas of northern Australia and New Guinea.

Hydrophis pacificus

Hydrophis vorisi

Hydrophis vorisi Kharin, 1984

Description: Head very small and body very elongate. Slender anteriorly and moderately deep and compressed posteriorly. A series of 70-80 blackish cross-bands on body and tail, each band which circles the body broadest dorsally and narrowest laterally, where each band is about as wide as the whitish interspaces. Occasionally the dark bands are divided or displaced on either side of the vertebral line. Usually no indication of secondary dark markings in the pale interspaces, except on the tail and extreme hind part of the body. Head shields enlarged, regular. Third and fourth supralabials contacting the eye. Six solid maxillary teeth following the fang. Body scales imbricate, in 29-35 rows at mid-body. Ventrals 330-350, scarcely wider than adjacent body scales, except anteriorly and mostly undivided. Average total length 60 cm. DANGEROUS ?
Distribution: Only a handful of specimens have been recorded from northern Australian waters.

Genus *Lapemis* Gray, 1835

A genus with a single species represented in Australian waters. Characterised by: small ventral scales, no larger than adjacent body scales and rarely distinct posteriorly; head shields enlarged, regular, without projecting tubercles or spines; anterior chin shields reduced, in only narrow contact with the mental groove, more or less separated by the first infralabials; body scales juxtaposed, hexagonal or squarish, the lower laterals much larger than the remainder, and with grossly enlarged tubercles in adult males.

Genus with distribution from the Persian Gulf to Australia.

Lapemis hardwickii Weipa, Qld DANGEROUS

Lapemis hardwickii Gray, 1835

Description: Australian specimens usually pale to dark olive-grey above and uniform cream or pale yellowish below, the two colours meeting along an obscure zigzag line along the side of the body. In the young, and some adults, the pattern is more conspicuous with series of 30-55 dark mid-dorsal blotches usually joined to each other on the mid-vertebral line. Head shields enlarged, regular. Other scalation as described for genus. Scales in 23-45 rows at mid-body. Ventrals 110-240, virtually unrecognisable posteriorly. Preanal scales scarcely enlarged. Average total length 1 metre. DANGEROUS

Distribution: Found throughout the tropical waters of Australia's continental shelf and its outliers in the Coral Sea. Extra-limital in Asian waters.

Lapemis hardwickii

Habit: A common and widely distributed species, it has been found in a wide variety of habitats, ranging from shallow, clear reef waters to more turbid inshore waters of estuaries and the lower Gulf of Carpentaria.

Genus ***Parahydrophis*** Burger and Natsuno, 1974

A monotypic genus found only in the coastal waters of the Arafura basin between New Guinea and northern Australia. It is characterised by its relatively large ventral scales, each about three times as wide as the adjacent body scales; the latter are smooth and in more than 30 rows at mid-body; large posterior chin shields bordering the mental groove separated by a small scale; preocular scale present.

Parahydrophis mertoni Darwin, NT

Parahydrophis mertoni (Roux, 1910)

Description: Blue-grey or grey-brown above, with 40-50 irregular, blackish cross-bands or rings often joined on the midline, each slightly narrower to slightly broader than the paler interspaces, broadest above and broken only by the ventrals. The dark dorsal bands may be sometimes pale-centred. Head above brown with blackish variegations; snout and sides of head blackish. Ventrals brown anteriorly, paler posteriorly. Subcaudals sometimes blackish, linking 6-8 dark bands on the tail. Head shields enlarged, regular. Body scales smooth, imbricate, in 36-39 rows at mid-body. Ventrals 158-160. Anal divided. Subcaudals 29-35, all single except for one or two divided anterior scales. Fang followed by 5-8 solid maxillary teeth. Average total length 50 cm.

Distribution: Known only from the Aru Islands, the lower Gulf of Carpentaria and the coast of Arnhem Land, NT.
Habit: Principally coastal and estuarine mangroves and associated mud flats.

Pelamis platurus Noumea, New Caledonia DANGEROUS

Genus ***Pelamis*** Daudin, 1803

A monotypic genus whose sole species has a unique colour pattern among sea snakes. It is otherwise characterised by its small, juxtaposed scales, more or less hexagonal or triangular in shape; head shields enlarged, regular; mental groove absent; ventrals small, usually divided and scarcely wider than adjacent body scales.

This is the most widely distributed of all sea snakes, ranging from the east coast of Africa through the Indian and Pacific Oceans to the west coast of the Americas.

Pelamis platurus (Linnaeus, 1766)

Yellow-bellied Sea Snake

Description: Upper half of body black or dark brown, contrasting with a cream, yellow or paler brown lower half; these colours meet along a sharply differentiated midlateral line. Tail yellowish, with black bars or spots. Scales in 47-69 rows at mid-body. Ventrals 264-406. 70 cm average total length.
DANGEROUS

Distribution: Found in the seas surrounding Australia, except along the colder southern coastline.

Habit: Appears to reach greatest density of populations south of the tropics. One of only three species of sea snake recorded from Tasmania. A pelagic species, feeding mainly on surface fishes.

Pelamis platurus

Family Laticaudidae

A group of sea snakes characterised by their smooth, imbricate body scales; body with numerous black cross-bands; broad ventral scales (more than half the width of the body); laterally placed nostrils; nasals separated by internasals, and the maxillary bone extending forwards beyond the palatine bone. Usually called sea kraits, members of this family were long regarded as true sea snakes (family Hydrophiidae) and are still treated as such by some herpetologists.

These snakes are partly terrestrial, often being found in rocky or coral crevices along the shore, or in mangrove swamps, sometimes long distances from the sea. Unlike all other sea snakes, this group lays eggs on land.

Mostly nocturnal, but sometimes found foraging on reefs during the day. Inoffensive, not attempting to bite even when freshly captured. Nevertheless the venom is very toxic, and all should be regarded as dangerous. A single genus, although two species (*semifasciata* and *schistorhynchus*), neither of which occurs in Australian waters, are sometimes placed in a separate genus.

Neither of the species recorded from Australia is believed to have resident populations in this country.

Genus ***Laticauda*** Laurenti, 1768

Key

TO THE AUSTRALIAN SPECIES OF LATICAUDA

Scales in 21 or more rows at mid-body.................. ***colubrina***

Scales in 19 rows at mid-body............................ ***laticaudata***

Laticauda colubrina Kadavu, Fiji

Laticauda colubrina

Laticauda laticaudata

Laticauda colubrina (Schneider, 1799)

Description: Blue or blue-grey above, with from 20-65 black cross-bands each of which usually extends around the belly. Snout and upper lips yellow, rest of head black, except for a bar of yellow extending back above the eye to the temporal region. Belly cream or yellow. Usually a large azygous shield between the prefrontals. Body scales smooth, in 21-25 rows at mid-body. Ventrals 210-250. Anal divided. Subcaudals divided, 25-35 (females), 36-50 (males). Average length 1 metre, maximum about 1.4 metres.
Distribution: Occasional specimens have been recorded from the tropical and temperate coasts of Australia, although most specimens have been found east of Torres Strait; it is occasionally found in far southern waters. Extra-limitally the species ranges from India through Indo-Malaysia to New Guinea and the Pacific Islands.
Habit: As for genus.

Laticauda laticaudata (Linnaeus, 1758)

Description: Blue or blue-grey above with 25-70 black cross-bands, some or all of which may be incomplete on the belly. Head black above, except for a yellow bar over the eye and sometimes a yellow snout continuous with this bar. Upper lips brown. Belly cream or yellow. No azygous shield between the prefrontals. Body scales smooth, in 19 rows at mid-body. Ventrals 225-245. Anal divided. Subcaudals divided, 25-35 (females), 36-50 (males). Average length 80 cm, maximum about 1 metre.
Distribution: As for *Laticauda colubrina.*
Habit: As for genus.

Laticauda laticaudata Noumea, New Caledonia

The Terrestrial Reptiles of Australia's Indian Ocean Territories

The Cocos (Keeling) Islands and Christmas Island are small, isolated, oceanic islands lying far to the north-west of Australia and south of Indonesia. But whereas Cocos (Keeling) is a coral atoll of low sandy islets, Christmas Island is a large, rocky island covered for the most part in dense, tropical forest. Reptiles (but no amphibians) are found on both islands; these include both sea snakes and sea turtles as well as land reptiles. However, because the land reptiles, particularly of Christmas Island, are so distinctive, it will be easier for the visitor to these islands to identify the reptiles if the individual species descriptions are dealt with separately from those of Australia proper.

The following section offers brief descriptions of the reptiles of the Cocos (Keeling) and Christmas Islands, together with composite keys to the reptiles of each territory. With the exception of *Lygosoma bowringii* and *Lycodon capucinus*, all of the species found on Cocos (Keeling) and Christmas Islands belong to genera which occur on the Australian mainland and which are described elsewhere in this book. Two of the species occurring on these islands *Lepidodactylus lugubris* and *Hemidactylus frenatus* — are found on continental Australia and are also described elsewhere.

Key

TO THE SPECIES OF TERRESTRIAL REPTILES OF THE COCOS (KEELING) ISLANDS

1 Typical lizards, with four well-developed limbs **2**
Limbless, scaly, worm-like **_Ramphotyphlops braminus_**

2 Claws of digits free, arising from the upper surface of each expanded pad **3**
Claws of digits arising from within the outer edge of each expanded pad .... **_Lepidodactylus lugubris_**

3 Inner toe of each foot clawless .... **_Gehyra mutilata_**
Inner toe of each foot clawed .... **_Hemidactylus frenatus_**

Key

TO THE SPECIES OF TERRESTRIAL REPTILES OF CHRISTMAS ISLAND

1 Typical lizards, with four well-developed limbs **2**
Typical snakes, scaly, limbless, sometimes superficially worm-like **9**

2 Scales large (fewer than 50 round the middle of the body), smooth and glossy **3**
Scales small (more than 100 round the middle of the body), smooth or keeled but never glossy **6**

3 Lower eyelid moveable; tail not blue **4**
No moveable eyelid, the eye being covered by a snake-like spectacle; tail bright blue in life .... ***Cryptoblepharus egeriae***

4 Lower eyelid with a transparent window **5**
Lower eyelid scaly .... ***Lygosoma bowringii***

5 Scales in more than 37 rows at mid-body; a blackish dorso-lateral stripe .... ***Emoia atrocostata***
Scales in fewer than 37 rows at mid-body; no dark dorso-lateral stripe .... ***Emoia nativitatis***

6 Toes flattened to form expanded, adhesive pads **7**
Toes long, slender and bird-like, without obvious adhesive pads .... ***Cyrtodactylus* sp. nov.**

7 Claws of digits free, arising from the outer edge of the expanded pad .... ***Lepidodactylus listeri***
Claws of digits free, arising from the upper surface of each expanded pad **8**

8 Inner toe of each foot clawless .... ***Gehyra mutilata***
Inner toe of each foot clawed .... ***Hemidactylus frenatus***

9 Small, worm-like; no enlarged belly scales; eyes vestigial, consisting of dark spots beneath scales of head **10**
Large, typical snake; enlarged belly scales; eyes normal .... ***Lycodon capucinus***

10 Nasal cleft contacting the preocular .... ***Ramphotyphlops braminus***
Nasal cleft contacting the second labial .... ***Ramphotyphlops exocoeti***

Cyrtodactylus sp. Christmas Island

Gehyra mutilata Cocos (Keeling) Island

FAMILY GEKKONIDAE

Cyrtodactylus sp.

Description: This is an undescribed species which is endemic to Christmas Island. Dark grey, brown or blackish above, spotted and flecked with a mixture of darker and lighter patches and scales which coalesce to form a pattern of obscure, pale, cross-bands alternating with pairs of dark patches, the latter sometimes coalescing in the midline to form dark, transverse bands. Tail pattern consists of a series of broad, brown bands, alternating with narrow, whitish bands, usually with a dark spot or patch on the midline of each brown band. A blackish streak along the snout and continued behind the eye to the ear; ciliary scales pale cream; ventral surface whitish, or pale purplish-pink. A large, arboreal gecko, with a long, slender tail which is round in cross-section, and with long, slender, bird-like claws without obvious adhesive pads. Body scales small and heterogeneous. Pubic groove absent. Usually at least three (occasionally fewer) imperforate scales on each side separating the preanal and femoral pore series, of which there are 8-13 and 18-30 respectively 80 mm (snout-vent).
Distribution: Christmas Island, Indian Ocean.
Habit: Found in a wide range of habitats, from primary rainforest to secondary forest growth and scrubby regeneration between limestone pinnacles left after phosphate mining.

Gehyra mutilata (Wiegmann, 1835)

Description: Pale to dark brown above, usually with numerous, darker brown flecks and a few paler flecks; head, neck and anterior flanks usually with a series of obscure, pale spots, of which the most constant and conspicuous are several in a line on the temporal region, which may coalesce to form a pale postocular streak; tail above often more heavily flecked with dark brown; ventral surface whitish or pale fawn. Body moderately depressed with small homogeneous scales, and rather depressed tail with a distinct lateral fringe on each side. Pads of fingers and toes with divided subdigital lamellae. Third and fourth toes with some basal webbing. Anterior chin shields in contact only with first supralabials. A fold of skin along the hind edge of each hindlimb. 55 mm (snout-vent).
Distribution: Ranges from Madagascar through Asia to New Guinea and Oceania (with an introduced population in Mexico). On Cocos (Keeling) this species is now uncommon or absent from several of the larger islands on which it was once common. On Christmas Island it appears to be restricted to man-made structures and disturbed habitats (such as old coconut plantations).
Habit: Arboreal.

Hemidactylus frenatus Duméril and Bibron, 1836

Description and Distribution: see page 246. Found on both Christmas and Cocos (Keeling) Islands.
Habit: On Cocos (Keeling) this species appears to be a recent introduction (since the 1940's), and has colonised most of the islands in the atoll where it is found primarily on coconut palms and on man-made structures. On Christmas Island it appears to be confined to buildings and vegetation in heavily disturbed areas.

Lepidodactylus listeri (Boulenger, 1889)

Description: Brown above, usually with a broad, pale fawn or grey vertebral stripe which expands anteriorly to cover the top of the head and which is continuous with the colour and pattern on the tail; usually a few, scattered, darker brown flecks or blotches dorsally; ventral surfaces whitish. Body covered above with small, smooth, homogeneous scales. Tail moderate in length, round or oval in section and without lateral flanges. 50 mm (snout-vent).
Distribution: Found only on Christmas Island, Indian Ocean.
Habit: Virtually restricted to primary rainforest, where it is an arboreal species which forages from the high canopy almost to ground level.

Lepidodactylus lugubris (Duméril and Bibron, 1836)

Description and Distribution: see p. 249. Found on most of the islands of Cocos (Keeling) atoll, but absent from Christmas Island.
Habit: On Cocos (Keeling) this species is found in a wide range of habitats, from coconut palms and ironwood trees *(Cordia subcordata)* to low strand-line shrubs and in human habitations.

FAMILY SCINCIDAE

Cryptoblepharus egeriae (Boulenger, 1889)

Description: Rich, metallic-brown on the body, the dorsal scales edged with darker brown; a conspicuous white or silver dorso-lateral stripe from above and behind the eye to the base of the tail, where it turns brilliant metallic-blue, edged above with black; flanks and limbs brown, with darker brown and pale brown or white flecks (usually individual scales); ventral surfaces whitish; tail bright blue, this colour most conspicuous in juveniles and often extending on to the body and hindlimbs as a pale, blue flush. Nasals separated. Prefrontals in contact. Four supraoculars, the second usually largest. Supraciliaries 6 (rarely 7), the first usually largest. 7-9 supralabials, usually 8. 20-24 lamellae under the fourth toe. 26-30 mid-body scale rows. 45 mm (snout-vent).
Distribution: Found only on Christmas Island, Indian Ocean.
Habit: Most common in the settlement area, but also occurs in primary forest where it is usually seen basking on tree trunks and forest debris wherever there is a break in the canopy.

Emoia atrocostata (Lesson, 1830)

Description and Distribution: see page 476. Found on Christmas Island but absent from Cocos (Keeling); specimens from Christmas Island have at least 38 mid-body scale rows.
Habit: On Christmas Island this species is confined to the heavily eroded limestone foreshores, where it forages in the intertidal zone and rarely extends inland more than a few metres into the low vegetation of vines and shrubs of the supralittoral zone.

Emoia nativitatis (Boulenger, 1887)

Description: Rich, iridescent bronze-brown or chocolate-brown above, with numerous, scattered, darker brown, paler brown and cream scales; a faint indication of a paler dorso-lateral band, while the flanks are generally darker than the dorsum; rich cream or yellowish-brown below. Snout moderate, pointed, but only moderately depressed; nostril surrounded by the nasal, a small supranasal and small postnasal; prefrontals swell developed, separated (often narrowly); four supraoculars. Scales smooth, in 32-36 rows at mid-body. Limbs well developed, the hindlimb about 45-50% of snout-vent length. Subdigital lamellae under the fourth toe 29-34, smooth, normal, those under the basal phalanges not sharply differentiated from those under the distal phalanges. 70 mm (snout-vent).
Distribution: Found only on Christmas Island, Indian Ocean.
Habit: Largely restricted to forested habitats, where it forages mainly among litter. Specially abundant along the edges of tracks or roads, or wherever a break in the canopy allows sunlight to penetrate to the forest floor.

Lepidodactylus listeri (adult) Christmas Island

Lepidodactylus listeri (hatchling)
Christmas Island

Cryptoblepharus egeriae
Christmas Island

Emoia nativitatis Christmas Island

Genus ***Lygosoma*** Hardwick and Gray, 1827

A widespread genus containing about 32 species (Greer) in Africa and South-East Asia. It differs from all Australian skinks by the combination of moveable, scaly lower eyelid, postorbital bone present, supranasal scales present, subequal preanal scales and closed Meckelian groove.

Lygosoma bowringii (Günther, 1864)

Description: Rich bronzy-brown above, the individual scales dark-edged and often with a median, dark brown streak resulting in fine, longitudinal, dark brown lines on the back of some specimens; a black dorso-lateral stripe from behind the eye to the base of the tail, sometimes narrowly edged above with cream; a white stripe along the upper lip merging with white on the throat and side of the neck, the whole often heavily spotted with black; flanks the same colour as the dorsum, but often heavily spotted or flecked with black; usually a pale (white to bright lemon-yellow) patch on the flank behind the forelimb; tail brown, sometimes with a dark lateral stripe on each side and in mature males often flushed with deep reddish-brown on the base. Supranasals narrowly separated or in contact. Prefrontals widely separated. Four supraoculars. 6 or 7 labials. Ear-opening small, round, without lobules. Scales smooth or tri-striate in 24-28 rows around the middle of the body. Limbs moderately developed, not meeting when adpressed, the hindlimb about 25% of snout-vent length. 10-13 lamellae under the fourth toe. 45 mm (snout-vent), the tail only slightly longer than the snout-vent length.
Distribution: Widely distributed in South-east Asia. Found only in disturbed habitats on Christmas Island, where it appears to have been introduced by man only in recent decades.
Habit: A diurnal, ground-dwelling species, found active in litter and grass in open areas.

Lygosoma bowringii Christmas Island

FAMILY TYPHLOPIDAE

Ramphotyphlops braminus (Daudin, 1803)

Description and Distribution: see page 589. Found on both Christmas and Cocos (Keeling) Islands.
Habit: On Cocos (Keeling) this burrowing snake usually appears on the porous, sandy surface only after rain. On Christmas Island it is found in a variety of habitats including primary rainforest.

Ramphotyphlops exocoeti (Boulenger, 1887)

Description: Colour in life unknown. Preserved specimens brown above, pale brown below. Snout rounded from above and in profile. Nasal cleft meeting the second labial, extending forward beyond the nostril, but not visible from above. Rostral oval, about as long as broad from above. Scales in 20 rows at mid-body. Body diameter about 60 times in its length. 350 mm total length.
Distribution: Known only from Christmas Island, Indian Ocean.
Habit: Unknown. All specimens to date appear to have been collected during clearing of primary rainforest on the plateau, in preparation for phosphate mining.

FAMILY COLUBRIDAE

Lycodon capucinus Boie, 1827
Wolf Snake

Description: Variable in colour and pattern: some specimens a fairly uniform grey, brown or blackish, with only a few white or yellow spots or pale-edged scales on the nape, sometimes forming a collar; more commonly there are scattered white or yellow scales forming irregular, narrow, transverse bands; lips whitish, sometimes with dark bars; whitish below. Head somewhat flattened. Pupil of eye vertically elliptic. Loreal scale present. 17 mid-body scale rows. Ventrals 170-230, with distinct lateral ridges. Anal normally divided. Subcaudals 50-80, divided. 70 cm (total length). Non-venomous.
Distribution: Widely distributed throughout Indonesia and neighbouring countries; apparently accidentally introduced to Christmas Island, presumably in imported goods or produce, in early 1987, since when several specimens have been found (L.A. Smith). However, the finding of several adult or sub-adult specimens within a short period raises the possibility of either an earlier introduction with subsequent breeding or a later deliberate introduction.
Habit: Snakes of this genus are called wolf snakes

Ramphotyphlops braminus Christmas Island

because of their greatly enlarged front teeth, which are fang-like in appearance and which subsequently can cause an unpleasant, albeit harmless, bite. They are nocturnal, climbing snakes which are attracted to human dwellings and other buildings, especially where artificial lights attract insects which, in turn, attract the geckos that form a large part of the diet of this snake. Smith has pointed out that this species, if it becomes established on Christmas Island, poses a potential serious threat to the endemic lizards of the island, and to the Christmas Island shrew, the island's one endemic terrestrial mammal.

Lycodon capucinus Hong Kong

Appendix

Since the text of this edition was submitted to the Publisher in 1990, a number of changes have occurred in the names applied to Australian reptiles and frogs. These changes are listed below, and have resulted from the description of previously unrecognised species or genera, or from the resurrection of species from the synonymy of those with which they were previously confused. The following brief diagnoses are intended only to distinguish the new taxon from those others with which it is easily confused, and to make the reader aware of recent changes in the composition and nomenclature of the Australian herpetofauna.

Family Myobatrachidae

Geocrinia alba Wardell-Johnson and Roberts, 1989

Description: Most similar to *Geocrinia lutea* (p.66), *Geocrinia rosea* (p.67) and *Geocrinia vitellina* (p.733), from each of which it may be distinguished by its white ventral colouring, or white with pale yellow (bright, egg-yolk yellow in *vitellina*, pale yellow, fawn or orange in *lutea*, usually pinkish in *rosea*). Also distinguished on call and genetic differences. 25 mm
Distribution: Witchcliffe-Karridale area, south-western WA.

Geocrinia alba

Geocrinia vitellina Wardell-Johnson and Roberts, 1989

Description: Most similar to *Geocrinia lutea* (p.66), *Geocrinia rosea* (p.67) and *Geocrinia alba* (p.733). Adult males may be distinguished from those of *lutea* and *rosea* by the absence of black pigment on the submandibular skin (present in adult males of *lutea* and *rosea*) and from these and *alba* by the bright, egg-yolk yellow ventral surface (pale yellow, fawn or orange in *lutea*, usually pinkish in *rosea*, and white or white with a faint yellow wash in *alba*). Also distinguished on call and genetic differences. 25 mm
Distribution: Spearwood Creek area, south-western WA.

Geocrinia vitellina

Neobatrachus albipes Roberts, Mahony, Kendrick and Majors, 1991

Neobatrachus albipes

Litoria electrica

Description: Most similar to *Neobatrachus pelobatoides* (p.89), from which it is difficult to distinguish on external characters. Roberts, Mahony,

Kendrick and Majors report that apart from chromosomal (diploid), allozyme and call differences, it may be distinguished from all species of *Neobatrachus* other than *pelobatoides* by its unpigmented or light brown-edged metatarsal tubercle. From *pelobatoides* living specimens of *albipes* may be distinguished by white pigment on the skin of the upper surface of the foot (without pigment, flesh-coloured in *pelobatoides*).
Distribution: Southern WA, between Albany and Esperance, and north to Coolgardie.

Family Hylidae

Litoria electrica Ingram and Corben, 1990

Description: Most similar to *Litoria rubella* (p.152), to which it would key on p.124. Apart from differences in calls, it may be distinguished from *rubella* by its possession of three dark bars or blotches on the back (absent in *rubella*) and back of thighs with black and yellow blotching (more or less uniformly coloured in *rubella*). 35 mm
Distribution: Central-western and north-western Qld.

Litoria pearsoniana

Heteronotia planiceps

Varanus teriae

Litoria pearsoniana (Copland, 1961)

Description: Externally similar to *Litoria phyllochroa*, under which name it is included on p.150. Earlier reported to differ from *phyllochroa* in chromosomes and call, McDonald and Davies report that adult *pearsoniana* are distinguishable from those of *phyllochroa* by their possession of a brown tympanum (green in *phyllochroa*).
Distribution: South-eastern Qld and north-eastern corner of NSW.

Family Gekkonidae

Heteronotia planiceps Storr, 1989

Description: Similar in most respects to *Heteronotia spelea* (p.248), to which it would key on p.247. Storr reports that it may be distinguished from *spelea* by having the dark temporal stripe in contact with the occipital band, but not the nuchal band (in contact with the nuchal band in *spelea*).
Distribution: Kimberley region of WA, with a single record in the Pilbara region of WA.

Family Varanidae

Varanus teriae Sprackland, 1991

Description: This name has been applied to Australian specimens of *Varanus prasinus* (p.371). *Varanus teriae* is reported to be distinguishable from all other tree monitors, including *Varanus prasinus*, by its colour and pattern (blackish, "... with light bluish-green snout tip, yellow dorsal spots forming thin, paired chevrons and caudal rings, a pronounced temporal streak and a pale, yellowish venter ..." and by "... conical, not flat, gular scales, a more anterior nostril, and by a more robust appearance, especially the postocular region..." (Sprackland). 25 cm (snout-vent).
Distribution: Currently known only from the Nesbit River region, Cape York Peninsula, Qld.

Family Scincidae

Genus ***Bartleia*** Hutchinson, Donnellan, Baverstock, Krieg, Simm and Burgin, 1990

A genus erected to accommodate *Pseudemoia jigurru* (p.563). Distinguished externally from other Australian scincid genera by possession of parietal shields in contact behind the interparietal; transparent palpebral disk in a movable lower eyelid; frontoparietals paired; supraciliaries enlarged, as wide as long in dorsal view; head and body depressed.

Genus ***Bassiana*** Hutchinson, Donnellan, Baverstock, Krieg, Simm and Burgin, 1990

A genus erected to accommodate *Pseudemoia duperreyi* (p.561), *Pseudemoia platynota* (p.567) and *Pseudemoia trilineata* (p.571). Distinguished externally from other Australian scincid genera by possession of parietal shields in contact behind the interparietal; transparent palpebral disk in a movable lower eyelid; frontoparietals fused to form a single shield; interparietal reduced; supranasals absent; rostral-frontonasal suture almost as wide as frontal; limbs short, usually just touching when adpressed; breeding males with red throat coloration.

Genus ***Cautula*** Hutchinson, Donnellan, Baverstock, Krieg, Simm and Burgin, 1990

A genus erected to accommodate *Pseudemoia zia* (p.571). Distinguished externally from other Australian scincid genera by possession of parietal shields in contact behind the interparietal; transparent palpebral disk in a movable lower eyelid; frontoparietals paired; supranasals absent; rostral-frontonasal suture wider than frontal; limbs short, usually failing to touch when adpressed; venter of both sexes yellow in life.

Ctenotus nasutus Storr, 1969

Description: Previously regarded as a subspecies of *Ctenotus colletti* (p.420). It may be distinguished from *colletti* and *rufescens* (p.735; the latter was also previously treated as a subspecies of *colletti*) by having five dark dorsal stripes (seven subequal narrow dark stripes in *colletti* and *rufescens*) and from *nigrilineatus* (p.735) by having the dark vertebral stripe much wider than the others (five subequal dark stripes in *nigrilineatus*). 45 mm (snout-vent).
Distribution: Great Victoria Desert, WA and adjacent regions of NT.

Ctenotus nigrilineatus Storr, 1990

Description: Most similar to *Ctenotus colletti*, to which it would key on p.407. It may be distinguished from *colletti* (p.420) and *rufescens* (p.735) by having five dark stripes on the back (seven dark stripes in *colletti* and *rufescens*) and from *nasutus* (p.735) by having the vertebral dark stripe no wider than the other dark stripes on the back (dark vertebral stripe much wider than the others in *nasutus*). 45 mm (snout-vent).
Distribution: Known only from near Woodstock, WA.

Ctenotus rufescens Storr, 1979

Description: Previously regarded as a subspecies of *Ctenotus colletti* (p.420). It may be distinguished from *nasutus* (p.735; the latter was also previously treated as a subspecies of *colletti*) and *nigrilineatus* (p.735) by having seven dark dorsal stripes (only five in *nasutus* and *nigrilineatus*) and from *colletti* by having the dark upper lateral stripe split into two between the eye and the ear (this stripe does not split anteriorly in *colletti*). 45 mm (snout-vent).
Distribution: Exmouth Gulf region, WA.

Egernia arnhemensis Sadlier, 1990

Description: Most similar to *Egernia frerei* (p.461), under which it is mentioned as an outlying population

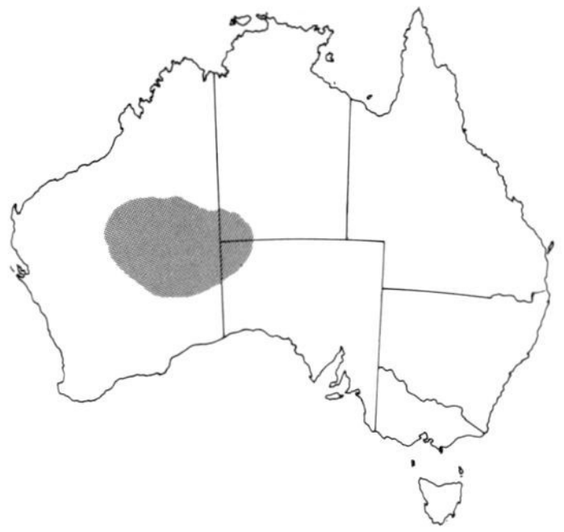

Ctenotus nasutus

Ctenotus nigrilineatus

Ctenotus rufescens

Egernia arhemensis

Lampropholis adonis

Lampropholis coggeri

Lampropholis colossus

in Arnhem Land. It may be distinguished from *frerei* by its uniform dorsal and lateral colouring (dark upper lateral pigmentation contrasting with colour of dorsum in *frerei*) and higher mid-body scale counts (more than 44, as against 30-36 in *frerei*). 180 mm (snout-vent).
Distribution: Alligator Rivers region, NT.

Lampropholis adonis Ingram, 1991

Description: Most similar to *Lampropholis delicata* (p.507), under which its populations are included, and from which (in its redefined form) it may be distinguished by having the interparietal fused with the frontoparietals to form a single scale (interparietal distinct in *delicata*). This same character distinguishes it from *Lampropholis couperi* (p.737), *Lampropholis coggeri* (p.736), *Lampropholis colossus* (p.736) and *Lampropholis robertsi* (p.737). 45 mm (snout-vent).
Distribution: Two apparently isolated populations in mid-eastern and south-eastern Qld.

Lampropholis coggeri Ingram, 1991

Description: Most similar to *Lampropholis delicata* (p.507), under which its populations are included, and from which (in its redefined form) it may be distinguished by having its darker upper lateral colour merge gradually with the paler lower lateral colour (the two areas sharply demarcated midlaterally in *delicata*). This character also distinguishes it from *Lampropholis colossus* (p.736) and *Lampropholis robertsi* (p.737). From *Lampropholis adonis* (p.736) it is distinguished by having the interparietal separate (fused in *adonis*), while from *Lampropholis couperi* (p.737) it is distinguished by its reddish to olive-brown dorsum with pale spots and black longitudinal dashes (uniform olive-brown in *couperi*). 35 mm (snout-vent).
Distribution: "Rainforests from near Cooktown south to Palm Island and Bluewater Range near Townsville", Qld (Ingram).

Lampropholis colossus Ingram, 1991

Description: Most similar to *Lampropholis delicata* (p.507), under which its populations are included, and from which (in its redefined form) it may be distinguished by its larger size (to 56 mm snout vent, as against a maximum 45 mm in *delicata*) and yellow venter (white in *delicata*). From *Lampropholis*

adonis (p.736) it is distinguished by having the interparietal separate (fused in *adonis*), while from *Lampropholis couperi* (p.737) and *Lampropholis coggeri* (p.736) it may be distinguished by having its darker upper lateral colour sharply demarcated midlaterally (the dark upper lateral colour merge gradually with the paler lower lateral colour in *couperi* and *coggeri*). From *Lampropholis robertsi* (p.737) it may be distinguished by its yellow ventral colour with black flecking on throat and tail (grey ventral colour with throat, chin, lower body and tail heavily spotted with black in *robertsi*). 50 mm (snout-vent).
Distribution: Bunya Mountains, south-eastern Qld.

Lampropholis couperi Ingram, 1991

Description: Most similar to *Lampropholis delicata* (p.507), under which its populations are included, and from which (in its redefined form) it may be distinguished by having its darker upper lateral colour merge gradually with the paler lower lateral colour (the two areas sharply demarcated midlaterally in *delicata*). This character also distinguishes it from *Lampropholis colossus* (p.736) and *Lampropholis robertsi* (p.737). From *Lampropholis adonis* (p.736) it is distinguished by having the interparietal separate (fused in *adonis*), while from *Lampropholis coggeri* (p.736) it is distinguished its uniform olive-brown dorsum (reddish to olive-brown with pale spots and black longitudinal dashes in *coggeri*). 45 mm (snout-vent).
Distribution: South-eastern Qld, from near Rockhampton south to Mount Glorious.

Lampropholis robertsi Ingram, 1991

Description: Most similar to *Lampropholis delicata* (p.507), under which its populations are included, and from which (in its redefined form) it may be distinguished by its grey ventral colour with throat, chin, lower body and tail heavily spotted with black. This feature also distinguishes it from *Lampropholis colossus* (p.736). It may be distinguished from *Lampropholis adonis* (p.736) by having the interparietal separate (fused in *adonis*), while from *Lampropholis couperi* (p.737) and *Lampropholis coggeri* (p.736) it may be distinguished by having its darker upper lateral colour sharply demarcated midlaterally (the dark upper lateral colour merges gradually with the paler lower lateral colour in *couperi* and *coggeri*). 40 mm (snout-vent).
Distribution: "... from rainforests of montane peaks from Thornton Peak south to Mt Bartle Frere ...", north-eastern Qld (Ingram).

Lerista arenicola Storr, 1972

Description: Similar to *Lerista microtis*, under which it is included as a subspecies on p.526, and from which it may be distinguished by its "greater size and narrow ragged-edged black upper lateral stripe" (wide, sharp-edged black upper lateral stripe in *microtis*). 55 mm (snout-vent).
Distribution: "Semiarid and arid sandy shores of Great Australian Bight ..." (Storr).

Lerista axillaris Storr, 1991

Description: Status uncertain; at time of writing, known only from a single specimen. Most similar to *Lerista desertorum* (p.518), with which it shares didactyle forelimbs and tridactyle hindlimbs, movable eyelids, narrowly separated nasals, separated frontoparietals, 20 mid-body scale rows and a dark upper lateral stripe. Said to differ from *desertorum* in having back and tail flecked with black or dark brown (longitudinal lines of dark spots or dashes, at least on tail, in *desertorum*). 87 mm (snout-vent).
Distribution: Near Kalbarri, WA

Lerista bunglebungle Storr, 1991

Description: At time of writing, known only from a single specimen. Most similar to *Lerista desertorum* (p.518), with which it shares didactyle forelimbs and tridactyle hindlimbs, movable eyelids, narrowly separated nasals, separated frontoparietals, 22 mid-body scale rows and a dark upper lateral stripe. Said to differ from *desertorum* in having nasals in contact (separated in *desertorum*) and six rows of dorsal spots (usually two, occasionally four, rows in *desertorum*). 59 mm (snout-vent).
Distribution: Bungle Bungle National Park, Kimberley region, WA.

Lerista concolor Storr, 1990

Description: Most similar to *Lerista frosti* (p.519) and *Lerista chalybura* (p.515), to either of which it could key on p.509. Distinguished from *frosti* by its possession of four conspicuous longitudinal series of dark grey-brown dashes (not or poorly developed in *frosti*), and from *chalybura* by its smaller ear-opening, patterned dorsum (unpatterned in *chalybura*), weak upper lateral stripe (strong in *chalybura*) and tail colour the same as the back (brightly coloured and contrasting with that of the back in *chalybura*). Limbs tetradactyle. Upper eyelid

movable. 20 mid-body scale rows. 52 mm (snout-vent).
Distribution: Known only from near Karratha, WA.

Lerista elongata Storr, 1990

Description: Most similar to *Lerista terdigitata* (p.533), to which it would key on p.509. Said to differ from *terdigitata* by its wider and sharper-edged upper lateral stripe and from *Lerista tridactyla* (p.740) by its paler reddish or grey-brown coloration. 60 mm (snout-vent).
Distribution: "Arid north-west of South Australia" (Storr).

Lerista ingrami Storr, 1991

Description: Most similar to *Lerista orientalis* (p.528), to which it would key on p.509, and from which it is said to be distinguished by the sharp lower edge to its dark upper lateral stripe (fuzzy-edged in *orientalis*). From *Lerista zonulata* (p.741) it is said to be distinguished by its smaller size, paler coloration, and lower number of mid-body scale rows (usually 18, sometimes 20; 20 or more in *zonulata*). Limbs tetradactyle. Upper eyelid immovable. 18-20 mid-body scale rows. 30 mm (snout-vent).
Distribution: "... south-east coast of Cape York Peninsula near mouth of McIver River", Qld (Storr).
Habit: Found in "... humid sandy coastal heaths" (Storr).

Lerista kendricki Storr, 1991

Description: Most similar to *Lerista nichollsi* (p.527), to which it would key on p.509, and with which it shares an immovable lower eyelid, forelimbs tubercular or absent, didactyle hindlimbs, 20 mid-body scale rows and second loreal not fused to prefrontal. Said to be distinguishable from *nichollsi* by its "... lesser size, relatively shorter tail, larger second loreal, larger presuboculars, darker head, wider vertebral stripe and narrower upper lateral stripe" (Storr). 60 mm (snout-vent).
Distribution: "Sandy country near mid-west coast of Western Australia ..." (Storr).

Lerista maculosa Storr, 1991

Description: Most similar to *Lerista uniduo* (p.534), to which it would key on p.509, and with which it shares an immovable lower eyelid, forelimbs absent, didactyle hindlimbs, 18 mid-body scale rows, three

Lampropholis couperi

Lampropholis robertsi

Lerista axillaris

Lerista bunglebungle

Lerista concolor

Lerista elongata

Lerista ingrami

supraciliaries and second loreal fused to prefrontal. Said to be distinguishable from *uniduo* by its heavily spotted body, the spots aligned longitudinally (the spots forming distinct vertebral and upper lateral stripes in *uniduo*). 40 mm (snout-vent).
Distribution: Near Shark Bay, WA.

Lerista petersoni Storr, 1976

Description: Similar to *Lerista nichollsi*, under which it is included as a subspecies on p.527, and from which it may be distinguished by its "much wider and paler vertebral stripe" (a dense, dark, narrow vertebral stripe in *nichollsi*). 65 mm (snout-vent).
Distribution: "Arid north-western interior ..." of WA (Storr).

Lerista puncticauda Storr, 1991

Description: Status uncertain. Most similar to *Lerista macropisthopus* (p.525) and *Lerista desertorum* (p.518), to either of which it might key on p.509, and with both of which it shares didactyle forelimbs and tridactyle hindlimbs, movable eyelids, narrowly separated nasals, separated frontoparietals and 20 mid-body scale rows. Said to differ from both of these species by the combination of no or poorly developed dark upper lateral zone, heavily dark-flecked upper surface of tail, and lower surface of tail with or without dark dots. 80 mm (snout-vent).
Distribution: South-western part of Great Victoria Desert, WA.

Lerista robusta Storr, 1990

Description: A stout species of *Lerista* most similar to *Lerista ips* (p.521) but, because of its reported possession of an immovable lower eyelid, it would automatically key to *Lerista onsloviana* (p.528) on p.509. From the latter it may be distinguished by the absence of even a forelimb groove, its much weaker vertebral and upper lateral stripes, and its lack of prefrontals. From *Lerista ips* it may be distinguished by its stronger colour pattern, rounded snout, larger eye, at least half as large as the subocular labial (at most a third the size of this scale in *ips*), two loreals (one in *ips*) and presence of one or two supraciliaries (none in *ips*). 60 mm (snout-vent).
Distribution: "... arid southern interior of Kimberley ..." region, WA.

Lerista kendricki

Lerista maculosa

Lerista puncticauda

Lerista robusta

Lerista speciosa

Lerista talpina

Lerista tridactyla

Lerista viduata

Lerista yuna

Lerista zonulata

Lerista speciosa Storr, 1990

Description: At time of writing, known only from a single specimen. Most similar to *Lerista terdigitata* (p.533), to which it would key on p.509 Said to differ from *terdigitata*, and from *Lerista tridactyla* (p.740) and *Lerista elongata* (p.738) by its possession of a conspicuous white mid-lateral stripe from upper lip to base of tail (absent in these other species) and four narrow black dorsal stripes (rows of dark dots in the other species). 51 mm (snout-vent).
Distribution: Musgrave Ranges, northern SA.

Lerista talpina Storr, 1991

Description: At time of writing, known only from a single specimen. Most similar to *Lerista nichollsi* (p.527), to which it would key on p.509, and with which it shares an immovable lower eyelid, forelimbs absent, didactyle hindlimbs, 20 mid-body scale rows and second loreal not fused to prefrontal. Said to be distinguishable from *nichollsi* by its "... lack of colour pattern and lack of ear aperture (only a small depression)" (Storr). 36 mm (snout-vent).
Distribution: Near Exmouth Gulf, WA.

Lerista tridactyla Storr, 1990

Description: Most similar to *Lerista terdigitata* (p.533), to which it would key on p.509 Said to differ from *terdigitata* by its wider and sharper-edged upper lateral stripe and from *Lerista elongata* (p.738) by its generally darker grey-brown coloration. 50 mm (snout-vent).
Distribution: "Semiarid eucalypt woodlands of south-eastern interior of Western Australia" (Storr).

Lerista viduata Storr, 1991

Description: Most similar to *Lerista microtis* (p.525), to which it would key on p.509, and to *Lerista arenicola* (p.737), and from both of which it may be distinguished by moderately widely separated nasals (nasal contacting or narrowly separated in *microtis* and *arenicola*) and absence of a white mid-lateral stripe (a conspicuous white mid-lateral stripe in *microtis* and *arenicola*). Limbs pentadactyle. Upper eyelid movable. 22 mid-body scale rows. 43 mm (snout-vent).
Distribution: Known only "... from the Ravensthorpe Range in the semiarid interior of ..." WA (Storr).

Lerista yuna Storr, 1991

Description: Most similar to *Lerista nichollsi* (p.527), to which it would key on p.509, and with which it shares an immovable lower eyelid, forelimbs tubercular or absent, didactyle hindlimbs, 20 mid-body scale rows and second loreal not fused to prefrontal. Distinguished from *nichollsi* by its wider vertebral stripe. From *Lerista petersoni* (p.739) it is said to be "... distinguishable by its larger second loreal, larger presuboculars and lack of yellow on flanks and venter" and from *Lerista kendricki* by its "... paler head and vertebral stripe and wider upper lateral stripe" (Storr). 60 mm (snout-vent).
Distribution: "Semiarid northern interior of South-West Division of Western Australia (north-east and south-east of Yuna)" (Storr).

Lerista zonulata Storr, 1991

Description: Most similar to *Lerista orientalis* (p.528), to which it would key on p.509, and from which it is said to be distinguished by the sharp lower edge of its dark upper lateral stripe (fuzzy-edged in *orientalis*). From *Lerista ingrami* (p.738) it is said to be distinguished by its greater size, darker coloration, and higher number of mid-body scale rows (20 or more; usually 18 in *ingrami*). Limbs tetradactyle. Upper eyelid immovable. 20-22 mid-body scale rows. 45 mm (snout-vent).

Distribution: "Mt Windsor Tableland south to Charters Towers", Qld.
Habit: Found "... mainly in semiarid hill country" (Storr).

Genus ***Niveoscincus*** Hutchinson, Donnellan, Baverstock, Krieg, Simm and Burgin, 1990

A genus erected to accommodate *Pseudemoia coventryi* (p.561), *Pseudemoia greeni* (p.562), *Pseudemoia metallica* (p.564), *Pseudemoia microlepidota* (p.566), *Pseudemoia ocellata* (p.566), *Pseudemoia orocrypta* (p.567), *Pseudemoia palfreymani* (p.567) and *Pseudemoia pretiosa* (p.568). Distinguished externally from other Australian scincid genera by possession of parietal shields in contact behind the interparietal; transparent palpebral disk in a movable lower eyelid; frontoparietals fused to form a single shield; supranasals absent; viviparous.

Glossary

The definitions provided below are by no means exhaustive and apply only in the context(s) in which they have been used in this book. For more comprehensive definitions of the strictly herpetological terms reference should be made to *A Dictionary of Herpetology* by J.A.Peters (Hafner Publishing Company, New York; 1964); for general biological terms *A Dictionary of Biological Terms* by I.F. Henderson and W.D. Henderson (Oliver and Boyd, London; 8th edition, 1963, by J.H. Kenneth) and *A dictionary of ecology, evolution and systematics* by R.J. Lincoln, G.A. Boxshall and P.F. Clark (Cambridge University Press, Cambridge; 1982 and subsequent reprints) are both valuable sources of information.

adpress: to press against the body; usually refers to the hindlimb alone being pressed forward against the body, but in some cases the forelimb is pressed backwards.
allantois: a membranous sac arising from the hind part of the gut in the developing embryo of a reptile or higher vertebrate, which in reptilian embryos is used partly to store waste products and also as an organ of respiration and nutrition (especially the absorption of calcium and albumen).
allopatric: populations or taxa which occur in separate or disjunct geographical areas.
alveolar ridge: a ridge on the crushing surface of the upper jaw of turtles.
amnion: a fluid-filled foetal membrane or sac in reptiles and higher vertebrates which surrounds the developing embryo.
anal: pertaining to the anal region; more specifically applied to one or more enlarged scales along the anterior margin of the vent. The paired anals in snakes are often referred to as a divided anal.
annuli: rings or ring-like markings.
anterior: situated at or near the front (head) end of the body
antivenine: = antivenom; typically blood serum containing antibodies to a snake venom, and produced by periodic small injections of venom to produce large numbers of antibodies.
apical: at or near the tip of a given structure (antonym: basal).
appendicular: of appendages; usually refers to the limb structures of the skeleton.
arboreal: dwelling, at least part of the time, in trees.
arciferal: of a frog pectoral girdle in which the epicoracoid of one side overlaps and can slightly slide across the epicoracoid of the other side.
arthropod: a member of the Phylum Arthropoda, a group which includes insects, spiders and crustacea.
auricular lobules: = ear lobules = lobules: enlarged scales projecting from the anterior rim of the ear opening.
auricular fold: a fold of skin, often bearing enlarged tubercles or spines, over or behind the ear (usually in lizards).
autotomy: loss of all or part of the tail, either as a result of spontaneous contraction of the tail muscles by the animal or as a result of the tail being seized or pressed by another animal; in some species the tail may fracture at a predetermined point, while in others it may fracture at any one of a number of potential breaking points.
axilla: armpit.
azygous scale: a scale usually on the midline and usually interposed between the paired scales on the top of the head.

---

barbels: soft, fleshy skin protuberances, usually believed to be sensory in function,on the chins of some turtles, especially those of the family Chelidae.
basal: at or near the base of a particular structure; antonym: apical.
bicarinate: bearing two keels.
bifid: symmetrically divided or forked
bifurcating: splitting or forking.
billabong: see oxbow lake.
bipedal: of lizards and crocodiles — running on hindlimbs only, with the forelimbs held off the ground.
bridge: that part of a turtle shell which connects the upper carapace to the lower plastron.

---

callus: a raised area of hard or corny skin, usually referring to the lower surfaces of fingers and toes.
canthal ridge: an angular or sharply differentiated canthus rostralis.
canthus rostralis: the ridge or angle between the side of the snout and the top of the head.
carapace: upper shell, including both horny and bony plates of a turtle or tortoise.
carinate: bearing ridges or keels, e.g. bicarinate.
casque: a helmet like thickening of skin over the head, often involving the deposition of bone in the skin.
caudal: relating to the tail.
choanae: the internal openings of the nasal passages situated in the roof of the mouth = internal nares.
chorion: a foetal membrane in reptiles and higher vertebrates which grows to enclose the yolk sac as well as the embryo within the amnion; the outer wall of the amnion is part of the chorion.
clavicle: a bone in the pectoral girdle (in frogs, see p.52).
cloaca: the common chamber in reptiles and amphibians into which the reproductive, intestinal and urinary ducts open. The external opening of the cloaca is the vent or anus.
cloacal spurs: one or more enlarged scales, often spinose, lying behind the vent on either side of the base of the tail.
cloacal bones: a pair of small bones, in geckos and snake lizards, each lying in a cavity on either side of the tail, immediately behind the vent.
coccygeal stripe: a longitudinal stripe over the centre of the rump in some frogs; strictly a stripe lying over that part of the vertebral column lying posterior to the sacrum (coccygum).

costals: those plates on a turtle carapace lying between the median centrals and outer marginals.
crenulate: of any pattern with a finely scalloped edge or border.
crepuscular: mostly active during twilight hours — evening or early morning.
cryptodirous: of turtles, in which the head is withdrawn under the shell by a vertical bending of the neck.
cryptozoic: living in hidden or darkened places, e.g. under stones, bark, logs, etc.
cutaneous fold: skin fold.

---

dentary pseudo-teeth: tooth-like structures at the tip of the lower jaw in some frogs. Genus Adelotus.
dentary: in reptiles and amphibians, the major bone making up the lower jaw.
dermal brood pouch: a fold of skin forming a sac, in which eggs or young are protected during development; found in males of the Marsupial Frog, *Assa darlingtoni*.
dermal fringe: a free, narrow and thin edging of skin on the digits of many frogs; also refers to series of scales in reptiles which project from the parts of the body such as the eyelids, digits or trunk to form a thin, free edge.
dermal fold: skin fold.
didactyle: having two digits.
digit: a finger or toe.
diploid chromosomes: the normal number of chromosomes found in sexually-reproducing animals, and consisting of a double set of homologous chromosomes.
discs: the enlarged expanded tips of the toes of many frogs.
distal: situated away from the point of attachment of a structure e.g. distal lamellae are those furthest away from the body; sometimes equivalent to apical (q.v.).
diurnal: primarily active during the day.
dorsolateral: situated more or less midway between the dorsal and lateral surfaces of the body.
dorsum: back or upper surface.

---

ectothermic: regulation of temperature largely by means of external heat sources.
emarginate: notched or scalloped.
endemic: restricted to a particular region.
epicoracoid cartilages: posterior element of the coracoids in the pectoral girdle (free, overlapping, in frogs, see p.52).
epiphytic: of plants which use other plants for physical support, but not directly for water or food.
extensile: capable of stretching.

---

femoral pore: a hole or pit in a scale on the lower surface of the thigh. Its function is more or less unknown. Usually better developed in males that females, the hole is typically filled with a waxy, cellular material which may protrude well above the surface of the scale. See also preanal pore and illustrations p.203.
firmisternal: of a frog pectoral girdle, in which the epicoracoids are fused in the midline of the sternum (see p.52).
foliform: leaf-shaped, and when applied to reptile scales indicates an extensive free edge.
foramen: an opening or perforation in any bony or cartilaginous structure
frontal: a large median shield or scale lying between the eyes in most snakes and lizards (see pp.203, 586).
fronto-parietal foramen: a large opening separating the paired frontoparietal bones in the skull of certain frogs.
frontoparietals: one or more shields or scales on the top of the head and lying between the frontal and parietal scales in lizards (see p.203).

---

gastralia: abdominal ribs, usually restricted to those of dermal origin which are not attached to other rib structures, and which occur between the pectoral and pelvic girdles. In modern reptiles found only in crocodilians and the tuatara.
gibber desert: an arid, stony plain, with ground cover consisting of scattered low herbs.
gular fold: transverse fold of skin across the throat, immediately in front of the forelegs, separating the throat and chest regions.
gular: pertaining to the throat but usually referring to the scales of the throat.

---

hemipenis: one of the paired copulatory organs found in lizards and snakes; each hemipenis normally lies in a cavity in the base of the tail, and either (but not normally both) is extruded like an inverted glove for insertion into the cloaca of the female when mating.
heterogeneous: refers to the condition in which the scales are of mixed size and/or form.
homogeneous: refers to the condition in which the scales are more or less similar in size and form.
humerals: the second pair of shields or laminae in the turtle plastron, lying between the gulars and the pectorals.

---

imbricate: overlapping; when referring to scales the hind edge of one scale overlaps the front of the scale behind it, rather like the tiles on a roof. cf. juxtaposed.
infra- (prefix): lower.
infralabial: one of a series of scales on the lower lips.
inframarginals: any small scales interpolated between the marginal scales (scutes) of turtles.
inguinal: lying in or near the groin. May refer to glands in certain frogs or in turtles refers specifically to the shield on the hind margin of the bridge.
intercalary cartilage: an extra cartilaginous element lying between the terminal and penultimate phalanges in hylid frogs.
intergular: one or two shields or lamellae at the front edge of the turtle plastron, lying between the gular laminae.
internarial distance: the distance between the centres of the nostrils or external nares.
internasals: those scales or shields on top of the snout lying between the nasal scales in snakes and lizards.
interocular: pertaining to that region of the head between the eyes, i.e. the area between the outer edges of the eyelids; sometimes used as a synonym of interorbital.
interorbital: pertaining to that region of the head between the orbits, i.e. the area between the eye bulges in frogs and reptiles.
interparietal: a median scale on top of the head lying between the parietal scales and containing the external opening of the parietal eye when present, in many lizards.
interpore scales: the scales, in those lizards in which preanal

or femoral pores are present, which are located *between* those scales carrying or penetrated by the pores.

---

juxtaposed: normally refers to the scales which are not overlapping but lying side by side. cf. imbricate.

---

karyology: study of chromosomes or chromosome complements.
keeled: a raised ridge: usually refers to the ridge(s) on individual scales, sometimes to a body or caudal crest.
keratinised: a horny thickening of the epidermis formed by a build-up of the protein keratin.
kinesis: movement occurring between the various bones of the skull. Great in most snakes, moderate in most lizards, absent in turtles and crocodiles.

---

labial: of the lips; usually refers to the scales bordering the lips.
lanceolate: shaped like the head of a spear or lance.
larva (pl. **larvae**)**:** An independent and self-sufficient stage in the development of an animal before it has aquired the characteristics of its parents; free-living tadpole stage in the development of a frog.
lateral: pertaining to the sides.
lingual fossa: the notch-like opening in the lower surface of the rostral scale of snakes through which the tongue is protruded when the mouth is closed.
littoral: pertaining to the shoreline.
loreal: separating the top from the side of the snout; usually refers to the scale lying on the side of the snout between the nasal and preocular scales in snakes (see p.586).

---

macrocephaly: as used here refers to a condition in some turtles in which older specimens may develop grossly enlarged heads.
mandible: the lower jaw.
mandibular symphysis: the line or area where the two halves of the lower jaw have fused together anteriorly.
marginals: the outer series of shields or laminae in the turtle carapace.
maxilla: the upper jaw.
median: lying on the midline.
melanotic: blackish, as a result of exceptional development of black pigment.
mental: the single scale at the anterior tip of the lower jaw in lizards and snakes.
mesic: living in, or adapted to, moist, temperate conditions.
metacarpal: any one of the small bones in the 'wrist' area of the hand or front foot.
metamorphosis: the change in body from the larval to adult stage, as in the change from tadpole to frog.
metatarsal tubercle: usually refers to one or more tubercles lying at the base of the underside of the hind foot in frogs.
metatarsal: any one of the small bones in the 'heel' area of the hind foot.
mid-body scale rows: in lizards, the number of scales counted in an imaginary line passing transversely around the middle of the body; in snakes, the number of scales along an imaginary line around the middle of the body, excluding the enlarged ventral scales. In snakes and many lizards the scales are most easily counted obliquely (see p.586).
monodactyle: having one digit.
monotypic: genus having one known species.
montane: of, or associated with, mountains or highlands.
morphological: pertaining to form or structure (as distinct from function).
morphology: the study of an animal's form and structure.
mucronate: ending in a sharp point or spine.

---

naris: an opening of the nasal passage. May be an external naris (= nostril) or an internal naris situated on the roof of the mouth (pl. nares); see also choanae.
nasal cleft: a deep groove partly or completely dividing the nasal scales in some snakes and lizards; = nasal groove.
nasal: a scale on the snout enclosing or bordering the nostril.
nuchal crest: a median longitudinal skinfold or row of enlarged scales on the nape.
nuchal shield: of turtles, a single, small median scale between the first (anterior) marginals (see p.177).
nuptial spines: a group of dark, dermal spines sometimes occurring as large individual spines, or more often as smaller spines forming a roughened area or nuptial pad in male frogs during the breeding season. Usually occurring on the first and second 'fingers' but may also occur on most other parts of the body in some species.

---

occipital region: pertaining to the back of the head.
occipital scale: is sometimes used to refer to the scale containing the parietal eye in many lizards.
occiput: occipital region of the head.
ocellate: with eye-like markings, usually large spots formed of concentric rings of colour.
ocellus (pl. **ocelli**)**:** a round, eye-like mark usually pertaining to colour pattern; a spot.
omnivorous: feeding on both animals and plants.
ontogenetic: pertaining to the development and growth of an individual throughout its lifetime.
osteoderm: a bony plate, embedded in the dermal layer of the skin.
oviparous: egg-laying (cf. viviparous, ovoviviparous).
ovoviviparous: as used here the production of living young which have developed usually in the oviduct, with little or no direct connection between foetus and mother.
ox bow lake: a lake formed when the circular meander of a river is isolated by the river cutting a new channel, with subsequent silting.

---

palmar: referring to the underside of the hand or, in the case of reptiles and frogs, the front foot.
palpebral disc: a transparent or translucent region or window in the lower eyelid of some scincid lizards.
palpebral: pertaining to the eyelids, as in palpebral venation (a fine network of lines in the lower eyelid of frogs of the genus *Nyctimystes*).
papilla: a small, fleshy, pimple-like projection.
paravertebral: lying to one side of the vertebral or mid-dorsal line.
parietal: pertaining to the part of the head in the region of the parietal body. May refer to particular scales on the head or bones in the skull.
parotid gland: = parotoid gland
parotoid gland: a swollen glandular region on the head usually commencing behind the eye and sometimes extending onto the neck.

parthenogenesis: reproduction without fertilisation by a male. Usually occurs throughout an entire population or species, in which males do not occur.
patronym: a zoological name derived from the name of a person.
pectoral girdle: that part of the appendicular skeleton supporting the chest and shoulders.
pectorals: the third pair of plates in the plastron of a turtle (see p.177); otherwise pertaining to chest region.
pelagic: inhabiting the water mass of the sea; ocean inhabiting.
pentadactyle: having five digits.
phalanx (pl. **phalanges**): one of the bones in a digit; in frogs the terminal phalanges (those at the tips of the digits) may be simple (ending in a rounded point) or T-shaped.
plantar: referring to the underside of the hind foot.
plastron: the lower half of the shell of a turtle or tortoise.
pleurodirous: of turtles, in which the head is withdrawn under the shell by a horizontal bending of the neck.
polyphyletic: originating from more than a single evolutionary line of descent.
porcupine grass: = 'spinifex'.Various species of grasses belonging to the genera *Triodia* or *Plechtrachne*. These grasses are characterised by their interlacing network of sharp, resinous or spiny leaves; various species constitute important reptile refuges in arid areas.
postanal tubercles: see cloacal spurs.
posterior: pertaining to the hind part of the body.
postmental: one or more scales on the chin lying immediately behind the mental scale.
postocular: one or more scales lying along the hind margin of the eye. Otherwise pertaining to that region of the head immediately behind the eye.
preanal pore: structure identical to femoral pore but situated in front of the anus.
prefrontal: one or more scales on top of the head lying immediately in front of the frontal shield. Also refers to the bone lying in the anterior margin of the orbital cavity.
pregenial: an anterior chin shield.
preocular: one or more scales lying along the front margin of the eye.
prepollex: a vestigial digit on the inside of the first finger in frogs, often used to enhance the grip of the male on the female during amplexus (q.v.), and so often better developed in males.
presubocular: one of up to several small scales continuous with the loreal(s) and lying below the preocular scale(s).
prevomer: a bone on the roof of the mouth immediately behind the premaxillary bone.
procoracoid cartilage: one of the bones making up the pectoral girdle in frogs (see p.52).
proximal: that part of a structure lying nearest to the body.

---

quadricarinate: bearing four keels.

---

reticulated: forming a network.
reticulum: a network.
retractile: able to be drawn in.
rhomb: diamond-shaped; rhombohedron or oblique equilateral parallelogram.
rhomboidal: rhomb-shaped (see **rhomb**)
rostral crease: a distinct groove or suture in the rostral shield.
rostral: scale found at the tip of the snout, its lower edge bordering the mouth.
rugose: a wrinkled or uneven surface.

---

sacral diapophyses: the transverse processes of the sacral vertebrae, which, especially in frogs, may be expanded (dilated) at their outer edges where each articulates with an ilium.
sacrum: the posterior vertebrae or vertebral elements which articulate with other bony elements of the pelvis.
savannah: tropical or subtropical grassland with scattered trees and shrubs.
saxicoline: living among rocks.
sclerophyll: pertaining to vegetation with hard, drought-resistant leaves, as typified by most eucalyptus (gum) trees.
sessile: attached or stationary; unable to move about.
sexual dimorphism: marked differences in the shape/colour/size, etc. between male and female of the same species.
shagreened: a smooth surface which is finely granulated or papillated and reflects light to give a satin-like appearance.
snout-vent length: the distance between the tip of the snout and the anterior opening of the vent measured along the vertebral line or its equivalent.
spectacle: the transparent scale covering the eye in snakes and those lizards lacking a movable eyelid.
sphagnum: peat or bog mosses of the genus *Sphagnum*, which form thick, dense and extensive water-saturated mats in many alpine and cool highland areas of high rainfall. An important habitat for frogs.
spicule: a small, pointed process; used here to refer to the minute, horny or keratinised epidermal spines which appear on the bodies or limbs of many frogs during the breeding season.
spinifex: *see* porcupine grass.
spinose: with spines.
sternum: a cartilaginous or bony plate lying on the ventral midline of the pectoral girdle.
striate: bearing lines or streaks of colour or texture which are different from the base colour or texture, but which are not raised above the surface.
style (adj. **stylar, styliform**): a slender, rod-like vestigial limb, in which none of the normal components of a limb (claws, digits, joints) are distinct externally.
sub- (prefix): (a) below, beneath; (b) approximately, more or less.
subapical lamellae: those soft, transverse plates lying on the undersurface of the digits of many geckos and excluding those enlarged, terminal plates, where the latter are present.
subarticular tubercles: small, rounded tubercles, lying below the joints between the bony phalanges of the digits of frogs.
subdigital lamellae: a series of transverse scales or plates lying along the lower surfaces of the digits on most lizards.
suctorial: sucking; applied here to describe the mouthparts of tadpoles which are especially adapted for maintaining the tadpole's grip on the substrate even in the strongest of currents.
supra- (prefix): upper.
supraciliaries: the small scales along the outer margin of the upper eyelid. (see p.203).
supralabial: = upper labial; one of a series of scales on the upper lip.
supralittoral: pertaining to the shoreline above high water mark.
supranasals: one or more scales adjacent to the upper edge

of the nasal scale and separated from their fellows on the other side by the internasals (qv.)
supraocular: one or more scales lying above the eyes.
supratympanic fold: a fold of skin from the temporal region to the side of the neck (usually in frogs) which borders the upper edge of the tympanic region and which often encloses the parotoid glands.
supratympanic ridge: a skinfold lying immediately above the tympanum in frogs and often extending back over the shoulder.
sympatric: populations or taxa which occur in the same geographical area.
symphysis: the junction between two pieces of bone. In this book it generally refers to the two halves of the lower jaw in turtles and lizards.

---

tarsal: pertaining to the 'sole' of the foot, i.e. between the digits and the ankle.
taxon: any category in a system of classification, i.e. any taxonomic group.
temporal: one of a series of scales in the region of the head bounded by the parietal scale, the postoculars and the supralabials; otherwise pertaining to the region of the temple.
terminal phalanx: the distal phalanx in each digit.
terraced: a condition described by G.M. Storr in some agamid lizards in which a disjunction in size and form between the inner and the outer scales of the chin results in a distinctive ridge below each lip.
tetradactyle: having four digits.
tetraploid chromosomes: twice the normal number of chromosomes found in sexually-reproducing animals, consisting of four sets of homologous chromosomes.
tibia: the larger of the two bones between knee and ankle.
tibial gland: a large swollen gland on the upper surface of the lower (tibial) region of each hindlimb in some frogs.
tricarinate: bearing three keels.
tridactyle: having three digits.
trilobed: having three lobes.
triodia: see porcupine grass.
tropicopolitan: found more or less throughout the world's tropical regions.
tubercle: any small, rounded protuberance on the skin.
turbid: murky, muddy.
tympanum: eardrum.

---

upper labial: see supralabial.

---

vagile: tending to disperse or move over time; may apply to an individual, a population or a taxon.
venter: the lower or ventral surface of the body.
ventral: pertaining to the lower surface of an animal.
vertebral: pertaining to the spine or vertebral column.
viviparous: livebearing; usually used only for those animals in which there is some form of placental connection between mother and embryo, but often loosely applied to all animals in which the young are born free-living, and not encased in an egg in which further development occurs before hatching.
vomerine teeth: small teeth or tooth-like structures lying on the vomer (or prevomer) in frogs.

---

xeric: of, or adapted to, arid conditions.

Selected References

After the first edition of this book was published in 1975, a complete catalogue of Australian amphibians and reptiles was published as: Cogger, H.G., Cameron, E.E. and Cogger, H.M. (1983). Zoological Catalogue of Australia. Volume 1. Amphibia and Reptilia. Australian Government Publishing Service, Canberra. 313 pp.

In the Catalogue, the original bibliographic references were provided for all species of frogs and reptiles described or recorded from Australia up until 30 June, 1982. In addition to references to the original descriptions, key references to the biology, ecology, natural history, taxonomy and distribution of each were included. The reader should consult this work (available from the Australian Government Publishing Service in each capital city) for a more thorough introduction to the literature on Australian herpetofauna, than can be included here. The references selected for this current edition of *Reptiles and Amphibians of Australia* are intended to fulfil two purposes — to provide a broad overview of the literature on Australian frogs and reptiles, and to list references to the original descriptions of all genera and species described since June 1982 (that is, to complement the references in the Zoological Catalogue).

In making the following selection I have tried to strike a balance between older classical books and monographs and recent papers on taxonomy and ecology. The references listed below should not be viewed as isolated studies; each of them includes bibliographic citations to a great variety of other research papers, thus providing the reader with many additional sources for further enquiry.

Reptiles and/or Amphibians — General

Adler, K. (1989). Herpetologists of the past. *in* Contributions to Herpetology No.5. *Contributions to the History of Herpetology* (K. Adler, ed.), pp. 5-141. Society for the Study of Amphibians and Reptiles.

Aslin, H.J. (ed.) (1985). *A list of vertebrates of South Australia.* Biological Survey Co-ordinating Committee and Dept of Environment and Planning, Adelaide. 74 pp.

Banks, C.B. (1980). *Keeping Reptiles and Amphibians as Pets.* Thomas Nelson Australia, West Melbourne. 129 pp.

Barrett, C. (1950). *Reptiles of Australia.* London, Cassell. 168 pp.

Bellairs, A.d'A. (1971). *La Grande Encyclopédie de la Nature, Vol.11. Les Reptiles.* Editions Rencontre, Lausanne. pp.385-768.

Bellairs, A.d'A. (1969). *The Life of Reptiles.* Weidenfeld and Nicholson, London. 2: 283-590.

Bradshaw, S.D. (1986). *Ecophysiology of Desert Reptiles.* Academic Press, Sydney. 324 pp.

Burbidge, A.A. and Jenkins, R.W.G. (eds) (1984). *Endangered Vertebrates of Australia and its Island Territories; Report of the Working Group on Endangered Fauna of the Standing Committee of the Council of Nature Conservation Ministers.* Australian National Parks and Wildlife Service, Canberra. 34 pp.

Carr, A. and the Editors of Life (1963). *The Reptiles.* Life Nature Library, Time Inc., New York. 192 pp.

Caughley, J. (1985). Effect of fire on the reptile fauna of mallee. pp. 31-34 in G.C. Grigg, R. Shine and H.F.W. Ehmann (eds.) *The Biology of Australasian Frogs and Reptiles.* Surrey Beatty and Sons with R. Zool. Soc. NSW, Sydney.

Chapman, A. and Dell, J. (1985). Biology and zoogeography of the amphibians and reptiles of the Western Australian wheatbelt. *Records of the Western Australian Museum* 12(1): 1-46.

Cochran, D.M. (1961). *Living Amphibians of the World.* Doubleday & Co., New York. 199 pp.

Cogger, H.G. (1984). Reptiles in the Australian arid zone. pp. 235-252 *in* H.G. Cogger and E.E.

Cameron (eds) *Arid Australia*. Australian Museum, Sydney.
Cogger, H.G. (1989). *Australian Reptiles in Colour*. Treasure Press, Sydney. 112 pp. 2nd revised ed.
Cogger, H.G. (1989). Herpetofauna. pp. 250-265 in J.C. Noble and R.A. Bradstock (eds) *Mediterranean Landscapes in Australia; mallee ecosystems and their management*. CSIRO Australia.
Cogger, H.G. and Cameron, E.E. (eds) (1984). *Arid Australia*. Australian Museum, Sydney.
Cogger, H.G. and Heatwole, H. (1981). The Australian reptiles: origins, biogeography, distribution patterns and island evolution. pp. 1331-1373 in A.J. Keast (ed.) *Ecological Biogeography of Australia*. Dr W. Junk, The Hague.
Cogger, H.G. and Lindner, D.A. (1974). Frogs and reptiles. in H.J. Frith and J.H. Calaby (eds) Fauna Survey of the Port Essington District, Cobourg Peninsula, Northern Territory of Australia. *CSIRO Division of Wildlife Research Technical Paper* 28: 63-107.
Cogger, H.G., Cameron, E.E. and Cogger, H.M. (1983). Zoological Catalogue of Australia. Volume 1. Amphibia and *Reptilia*. Australian Government Publishing Service, Canberra. 313 pp.
Cogger, H.G., Sadlier, R.A. and Cameron, E.E. (1983). *The Terrestrial Reptiles of Australia's Island Territories*. Australian National Parks and Wildlife Service, Canberra, Special Publication 11. 80 pp.
Copland, S.J. (1953). Recent Australian herpetology. *Proceedings of the Linnean Society of N.S.W.* 78: v-xxxvii.
Covacevich, J. (1987). Reptiles of far northern Cape York Peninsula. *Queensland Naturalist* 28(1-4): 22-30.
Covacevich, J. and McDonald, K.R. (1984). Frogs and reptiles of eastern Australian rainforests: distribution patterns and conservation. pp. 360-383 in G.L. Werren and A.P. Kershaw (eds) *Australian National Rainforest Study Report to the World Wildlife Fund (Australia). Vol. 1. Proceedings of a workshop on the past, present and future of Australian rainforests, Griffith University, December 1983.* Geography Dept., Monash University for Aust. Conservation Foundation, Melbourne.
Covacevich, J., Davie, P. and Pearn, J. (eds). (1987). *Toxic Plants and Animals; a guide for Australia*. Queensland Museum, Brisbane. viii + 504 pp.
Covacevich, J., Ingram, G.J. and Czechura, G.V. (1982). Rare frogs and reptiles of Cape York Peninsula, Australia. *Biological Conservation* 22: 283-294.
Duellman, W.E. and Trueb, L. (1986). *Biology of Amphibians*. McGraw-Hill Book Co., New York. 670 pp.
Ehmann, H.F.W. and Cogger, H.G. (1985). Australia's endangered herpetofauna: a review of criteria and policies. pp. 435-447 in G.C. Grigg, R. Shine and H.F.W. Ehmann (eds) *The Biology of Australasian Frogs and Reptiles*. Surrey Beatty and Sons with R. Zool. Soc. NSW, Sydney.
Friend, G.R., Smith, G.T., Mitchell, D.S. and Dickman, C.R. (1989). Influence of pitfall and drift fence design on capture rates of small vertebrates in semi-arid habitats of Western Australia. *Australian Wildlife Research* 16: 1-10.
Frith, C. and D. (1987). *Australian Tropical Reptiles & Frogs*. Tropical Australia Graphics, Paluma, Townsville. pp.i-iii, 1-71.
Fyfe, G. (1986 (1985)). Comparison of the ground-dwelling verbetrate faunas found in hummock grassland and mulga shrubland in central Australia. *Herpetofauna* 16(2): 49-52.
Gans, C. (ed.) (1969 *et seq.*). *Biology of the Reptilia*. Academic Press, London and New York. Vol. 1 (1969) — Vol. 16 (1988) (continuing series).
Gorham, S.W. (1974). *Checklist of World Amphibians*. New Brunswick Museum, Saint John. 172 pp.
Gow, G.F. (1981). Checklist of reptiles and amphibians of the southern sector of the N.T.; checklist of reptiles and amphibians of the northern sector of the N.T. *Northern Territory Naturalist* 4: 14-19.
Griffiths, K. (1987). *Reptiles of the Sydney Region*. Three Sisters Productions, Winmalee. 120 pp.
Grigg, G., Shine, R. and Ehmann, H. (eds) (1985). *The Biology of Australasian Frogs and Reptiles*. Surrey Beatty & Sons/ Zoological Society of New South Wales, Chipping Norton. pp. i-xvi, 1-527.
Heatwole, H. and Taylor, J.A. (1987). *Ecology of Reptiles*. Surrey Beatty and Sons, Chipping Norton. 325 pp.
Houston, T.F. (1973). Reptiles of South Australia: A Brief Synopsis. *South Australian Yearbook*, 1973. 11 pp.
Jenkins, R.W.G. (1985). Government legislation and conservation of endangered reptiles and amphibians. pp. 431-433 in G.C. Grigg, R. Shine and H.F.W. Ehmann (eds) *The Biology of Australasian Frogs and Reptiles*. Surrey Beatty and Sons with R. Zool. Soc. NSW, Sydney.
Jenkins, R.W.G. and Bartell, R.J. (1980). *A Field Guide to Reptiles of the Australian High Country*. Melbourne, Inkata Press. 187 pp.
Keast, A. (1959). The reptiles of Australia. pp. 115-135 in A. Keast (ed.) *Biogeography and Ecology in Australia*. The Hague, Dr W. Junk.
King, M. (1985). Chromosome markers and their use in phylogeny and systematics. pp. 165-175 in G.C. Grigg, R. Shine and H.F.W. Ehmann (eds.) *The Biology of Australasian Frogs and Reptiles*. Surrey Beatty and Sons with R. Zool. Soc. NSW, Sydney.
Lincoln, R.J., Boxshall, G.A. and Clark, P.F. *A Dictionary of ecology, evolution and systematics*. Cambridge University Press, Cambridge. pp.i-viii, 1-298.
Loveridge, A. (1934). Australian reptiles in the Museum of Comparative Zoology, Cambridge, Massachusetts. *Bulletin of the Museum of Comparative Zoology, Harvard* 77(6): 243-383.
Loveridge, A. (1935). Australian Amphibia in the Museum of Comparative Zoology, Cambridge, Massachusetts. *Bulletin of the Museum of Comparative Zoology, Harvard* 78(1): 1-60.
Loveridge, A. (1945). *Reptiles of the Pacific World*. New York. Macmillan. xii + 259 pp.
McPhee, D. (1979). *The Observer's Book of Snakes and Lizards of Australia*. Methuen of Australia, Sydney. 157 pp.
Mitchell, F.J. (1964). Reptiles and amphibians of Arnhem Land. pp. 309-343 in R.L Specht (ed.) *Records of the American-Australian Expedition to Arnhem Land. 4. Zoology*. Melbourne University Press, Melbourne.
Noble, G.K. (1931). *The Biology of the Amphibia*. New York, McGraw-Hill. xiii + 577 pp.
Parker, H.W. and Bellairs, A.d'A. (1971). *La Grande Encyclopédie de la Nature, Vol.10. Les Amphibiens et les Reptiles*. Editions Rencontre, Lausanne. pp.385-768.
Peters, J.A. (1964). *Dictionary of Herpetology*. Hafner Publishing Company, New York. pp.i-xii, 1-434.
Rawlinson, P.A. (1974). Biogeography and ecology of the reptiles of Tasmania and the Bass Strait area. pp. 291-338 in W.D. Williams (ed.) *Biogeography and Ecology in Tasmania*. Dr W. Junk, The Hague.
Romer, A.S. (1956). *Osteology of the Reptiles*. Univ. Chicago Press, Chicago. xxii + 772 pp.
Schmida, G. (1985). *The Cold-blooded Australians*. Doubleday, Sydney. 280 pp.
Schmidt, K.P. and Inger, R.F. (1957). *Living Reptiles of World*. London, Hamish Hamilton. 287 pp.
Shea, G.M. (1986 (1984)). Island herpetofaunas in New South Wales: a review. *Herpetofauna* 16(2): 30-38.
Shine, R. (1985). The reproductive biology of Australian reptiles: a search for general patterns. pp. 297-303 in G.C. Grigg, R. Shine and H.F.W. Ehmann (eds) *The Biology of Australasian Frogs and Reptiles*. Surrey Beatty and Sons with R. Zool. Soc. NSW, Sydney.
Shine, R. (1985). The evolution of viviparity in reptiles: an ecological analysis. pp. 605-694 in C. Gans and F. Billett (eds) *Biology of the Reptilia*, Vol. 15. Wiley Interscience, New York.

Shine, R. (1987). Parental care in reptiles. pp. 275-330 in C. Gans and R.B. Huey (eds) *Biology of the Reptilia*. Vol. 16. Wiley-Interscience, New York.

Sokolov, V.E. (ed.) (1988). *Dictionary of Animal Names in Five Languages: Amphibians and Reptiles*. Russky Yazyk Publishers, Moscow.

Storr, G.M. (1964). Some aspects of the geography of Australian reptiles. *Senckenbergiana Biologica* 45(3-5): 577-589.

Storr, G.M. (1978). Taxonomic notes on the reptiles of the Shark Bay Region, Western Australia. *Records of the Western Australian Museum* 6(3): 303-318.

Sutherland, S.K. (1983). *Australian Animal Toxins; the creatures, their toxins and care of the poisoned patient*. Oxford University Press, Melbourne. 527 pp.

Sutherland, S.K. (1985). *Venomous Creatures of Australia: a Field Guide with Notes on First Aid*. Oxford University Press, Melbourne. 112 pp. (rev. ed.).

Tyler, M.J., Watson, G.F. and Martin, A.A. (1981). The Amphibia: diversity and distribution. pp. 1275-1302 in A. Keast (ed.) *Ecological Biogeogaphy of Australia*. Dr W. Junk, The Hague.

Waite, E.R. (1929). *The Reptiles and Amphibians of South Australia*. Adelaide, Harrison Weir. 270 pp.

Weigel, J. (1988). *Care of Australian Reptiles in Captivity*. Reptile Keepers Association, Gosford. 144 pp.

Wells, R.W. and Wellington, C.R. (1985). A classification of the Amphibia and Reptilia of Australia. *Australian Journal of Herpetology* Suppl. Ser. 1: 1-61.

Wermuth, H. and Mertens, R. (1961). *Schildkroten, Krokodile, Bruckenechsen*. Gustav Fischer, Jena. 422 pp.

White, J., Pounder, D., Pearn, J.H. and Morrison, J.J. (1985). A perspective on the problems of snakebite in Australia. pp. 511-514 in G.C. Grigg, R. Shine and H.F.W. Ehmann (eds) *The Biology of Australasian Frogs and Reptiles*. Surrey Beatty and Sons with R. Zool. Soc. NSW, Sydney.

Wilson, S.K. and Knowles, D.G. (1988). *Australia's Reptiles; a photographic reference to the terrestrial reptiles of Australia*. Collins Publishers, Sydney. 447 pp.

Worrell, E. (1963). *Reptiles of Australia; Crocodiles, Turtles, Tortoises, Lizards, Snakes*. Angus and Robertson, Sydney. xv + 207 pp.

Frogs General

Barker, J. and Grigg, G.C. (1977). *A Field Guide to Australian Frogs*. Rigby, Adelaide. 229 pp.

Boulenger, G.A. (1882). *Catalogue of the Batrachia Salientia s. Ecaudata in the collection of the British Museum*. British Museum, London. 2nd edn. xvi + 503 pp.

Brook, A.J. (1983). *Atlas of Australian Anura*. Dept. Zoology, Univ. Melbourne Publ. 7.

Clyne, D. (1969). *Australian Frogs*. Lansdowne Press, Melbourne. 112 pp.

Duellman, W.E. (1985). Reproductive modes in anuran amphibians: phylogenetic significance of adaptive strategies. *South African Journal of Science* 81: 174-178.

Frost, D.R. (ed.) (1985). *Amphibian Species of the World; a taxonomic and geographical reference*. Allen Press and Assoc. Systematics Collections, Lawrence, Kansas. v + 732 pp.

Grigg, G.C. and Barker, J. (1973). *Explanatory Notes to Frog Calls of South Eastern Australia*. G. Grigg and J. Barker, Sydney. 9 pp. (with audio cassette of frog calls)

Kikkawa, J., Monteith, G.B. and Ingram, G.J. (1981). Cape York Peninsula; major region of faunal interchange. pp. 1695-1742 in A. Keast (ed.) *Ecological Biogeography of Australia*. Dr W Junk, The Hague.

Littlejohn, M.J. (1963). *Frogs of the Melbourne area*. *Victorian Naturalist* 79(10): 296-304.

Littlejohn, M.J. (1967). Patterns of zoogeography and speciation in south-eastern Australian Amphibia. pp. 150-174 in A.H. Weatherley (ed.) *Australian Inland Waters and their Fauna*. A.N.U. Press, Canberra.

Littlejohn, M.J. and Watson, G.F. (1985). Hybrid zones and homogamy in Australian frogs. *Annual Review of Ecology and Systematics* 16: 85-112.

Main, A.R. (1965). *Frogs of southern Western Australia*. West. Aust. Nat. Club Handbook 8: 1-73.

Main, A.R. (1968). Ecology, systematics and evolution of Australian frogs. *Advances in Ecological Research* 5: 37-86.

Maxson, L.R. and Roberts, J.D. (1984). Albumin and Australian frogs: molecular data a challenge to speciation model. *Science* 225: 957-958.

Moore, J.A. (1961). The frogs of eastern New South Wales. *Bulletin of the American Museum of Natural History* 121(3): 149-386.

Roberts, J.D. and Maxson, L.R. (1985). Tertiary speciation models in Australian anurans: molecular data challenge Pleistocene scenario. *Evolution* 39(2): 325-334.

Sanders, J. and Davies, M. (1984). Burrowing behaviour and associated hindlimb myology in some Australian hylid and leptodactylid frogs. *Australian Zoologist* 21(2): 123-142.

Savage, J.M. (1973). The geographic distribution of frogs: patterns and predictions. pp. 351-445 in J.L. Vial (ed.) *Evolutionary Biology of the Anurans*. Univ. Missouri Press, Columbia, Missouri.

Tyler, M.J. (1978). *Amphibians of South Australia*. South Australian Government Printer, Adelaide. 84 pp.

Tyler, M.J. (1982). *Frogs*. Collins, Sydney. (Australian Naturalists Library). 256 pp. (2nd ed.).

Tyler, M.J. (1985). Reproductive modes in Australian Amphibia. pp. 265-267 in G.C. Grigg, R. Shine and H.F.W. Ehmann (eds) *The Biology of Australasian Frogs and Reptiles*. Surrey Beatty and Sons with R. Zool. Soc. NSW, Sydney.

Tyler, M.J. (1989). *Australian Frogs*. Viking O'Neil, Penguin Books, Ringwood. pp.i-xii, 1-220.

Tyler, M.J. and Davies, M. (1986). *Frogs of the Northern Territory*. Conservation Commission of the Northern Territory, Alice Springs. vi + 77 pp.

Tyler, M.J., Crook, A.G. and Davies, M. (1983). Reproductive biology of the frogs of the Magela Creek System, Northern Territory, Australia. *Records of the South Australian Museum*, 18(18): 415-440.

Tyler, M.J., Smith, L.A. and Johnstone, R.E. (1984). *Frogs of Western Australia*. Western Australian Museum, Perth. xii + 109 pp.

Watson, G.F. and Littlejohn, M.J. (1985). Patterns of distribution, speciation and vicariance biogeography of southeastern Australian amphibians. pp. 91-97 in G.C. Grigg, R. Shine and H.F.W. Ehmann (eds) *The Biology of Australasian Frogs and Reptiles*. Surrey Beatty and Sons with R. Zool. Soc. NSW, Sydney.

Family Myobatrachidae

Blake, A.J.D. (1973). Taxonomy and relationships of myobatrachine frogs (Leptodactylidae): a numerical approach. *Aust. J. Zool.* 21: 119-149.

Corben, C. and Ingram, G.J. (1987). A new barred frog (Myobatrachidae: *Mixophyes*). *Memoirs of the Queensland Museum* 26(1): 233-237. [*Mixophyes fleayi*]

Czechura, G.V. (1986). A new species of *Taudactylus* (Myobatrachidae) from southeastern Queensland, Australia. *Memoirs of the Queensland Museum* 22(2): 299-307. [*Taudactylus pleione*]

Czechura, G.V. (1986). Kroombit Tops torrent frog *Taudactylus pleione*, with a key to the species of *Taudactylus*. *Queensland Naturalist* 27(1-4): 68-71.

Czechura, G.V. and Ingram, G.J. (1990). *Taudactylus diurnus* and the case of the disappearing frogs. *Memoirs of the Queensland Museum* 29(2): 361-365.

Davies, M. (1984). Osteology of the myobatrachine frog *Arenophryne rotunda* Tyler (Anura: Leptodactylidae) and comparisons with other myobatrachine genera. *Australian Journal of Zoology* 32; 789-802.

Davies, M. (1989). Ontogeny and the role of heterochrony in the myobatrachine genera *Uperoleia*, *Crinia* and *Pseudophryne* (Anura: Leptodactylidae: Myobatrachinae). *Journal of Morphology* 200: 269-300.

Davies, M. and Littlejohn, M.J. (1986). Frogs of the genus *Uperoleia* Gray (Anura: Leptodactylidae) in south-eastern Australia. *Transactions of the Royal Society of South Australia* 109(3): 111-143. [*Uperoleia martini*]

Davies, M. and McDonald, K.R. (1985). A redefinition of *Uperoleia rugosa* (Andersson) (Anura: Leptodactylidae). *Transactions of the Royal Society of South Australia* 109(2): 37-42.

Davies, M., Mahony, M. and Roberts, J.D. (1985). A new species of *Uperoleia* (Anura: Leptodactylidae) from the Pilbara region, Western Australia. *Transactions of the Royal Society of South Australia* 109(3-4): 103-108. [*Uperoleia glandulosa*]

Davies, M., McDonald, K.R. and Corben, C. (1986). The genus *Uperoleia* Gray (Anura: Leptodactylidae) in Queensland, Australia. *Proceedings of the Royal Society of Victoria* 98(4): 147-188. [*Uperoleia capitulata*; *Uperoleia fusca*; *Uperoleia littlejohni*; *Uperoleia mimula*]

Davies, M., Watson, G.F. and Miller, C.A. (1987). New records of *Uperoleia* (Anura: Leptodactylidae) from Western Australia with supplementary osteological data on *Uperoleia micromeles*. *Transactions of the Royal Society of South Australia* 111(4): 201-202.

Ehmann, H.F.W. and Swan, G. (1985). Reproduction and development in the marsupial frog, *Assa darlingtoni* (Leptodactylidae, Anura). pp. 279-285 in G.C. Grigg, R. Shine and H.F.W. Ehmann (eds) *The Biology of Australasian Frogs and Reptiles*. Surrey Beatty and Sons with R. Zool. Soc. NSW, Sydney.

Gorham, S.W. (1966). Liste der rezenten amphibien und reptilien. Ascaphidae, Leiopelmatidae, Pipidae, Discoglossidae, Pelobatidae, Leptodactylidae, Rhinophrynidae. *Das Tierreich* 85: 1-222.

Heyer, W.R. and Liem, D.S. (1976). Analysis of the intergeneric relationships of the Australian frog family Myobatrachidae. *Smithsonian Contributions to Zoology* 233: 1-29.

Hutchinson, M.N. and Maxson, L.R. (1987). Albumin evolution, paraphyly and the relationships of the Australian frog *Megistolotis lignarius* (Anura: Limnodynastinae). *Systematic Zoology* 36(4): 387-394.

Hutchinson, M.N. and Maxson, L.R. (1987). Biochemical studies on the relationships of the gastric-brooding frogs, genus *Rheobatrachus*. *Amphibia-Reptilia* 8: 1-11.

Lee, A.K. (1967). Studies in Australian amphibia. II. Taxonomy, ecology, and evolution of the genus *Heleioporus* Gray (Anura. Leptodactylidae). *Australian Journal of Zoology* 15: 367-439.

Leon, A. S.-Y., Tyler, M.J. and Shearman, D.J.C. (1986). Gastric brooding: a new form in a recently discovered Australian frog of the genus *Rheobatrachus*. *Australian Journal of Zoology* 34: 205-209.

Littlejohn, M.J. and Martin, A.A. (1965). The vertebrate fauna of the Bass Strait Islands: 1. The Amphibia of Flinders and King Islands. *Proceedings of the Royal Society of Victoria* 79(1): 247-256.

Littlejohn, M.J., Harrison, P.A. and MacNally, R.C. (1985). Interspecific acoustic interactions in sympatric populations of *Ranidella signifera* and *R. parinsignifera* (Anura: Leptodactylidae). pp. 287-296 in G.C. Grigg, R. Shine and H.F.W. Ehmann (eds) *The Biology of Australasian Frogs and Reptiles*. Surrey Beatty and Sons with R. Zool. Soc. NSW, Sydney.

Lynch, J.D. (1971). Evolutionary relationships, osteology, and zoogeography of leptodactyloid frogs. *Miscellaneous Publications of the University of Kansas Museum of Natural History* 53: 1-238.

MacNally, R.C. (1985). Habitat and microhabitat distributions in relation to ecological overlap in two species of *Ranidella* (Anura). *Australian Journal of Zoology* 33: 329-338.

Mahony, M.J. and Roberts, J.D. (1986). Two new species of desert burrowing frogs of the genus *Neobatrachus* (Anura: Myobatrachidae) from Western Australia. *Records of the Western Australian Museum* 13(1): 155-170. [*Neobatrachus fulvus*; *Neobatrachus kunapalari*]

Mahony, M.J., Tyler, M.J. and Davies, M. (1984). A new species of the genus *Rheobatrachus* (Anura: Leptodactylidae) from Queensland. *Transactions of the Royal Society of South Australia* 108(3): 155-162. [*Rheobatrachus vitellinus*]

Main, A.R. (1957). Studies in Australian Amphibia. 1. The genus *Crinia* Tschudi in south western Australia and some species from south eastern Australia. *Australian Journal of Zoology* 5: 30-55.

Malone, B.S. (1985). Mortality during the early life history stages of the Baw Baw frog, *Philoria frosti* (Anura: Myobátrachidae). pp. 1-5 in G.C. Grigg, R. Shine and H.F.W. Ehmann (eds) *The Biology of Australasian Frogs and Reptiles*. Surrey Beatty and Sons with R. Zool. Soc. NSW, Sydney.

Martin, A.A. (1972). Studies in Australian Amphibia. III. The *Limnodynastes dorsalis* complex (Anura: Leptodactylidae). *Australian Journal of Zoology* 20: 165-211.

Maxson, L.R. and Roberts, J.D. (1985). An immunological analysis of the phylogenetic relationships between two enigmatic frogs, *Myobatrachus* and *Arenophryne*. *Journal of Zoology* (A)207: 289-300.

Odendaal, F.J., Bull, C.M. and Telford, S.R. (1983). The vocabulary of calls of *Ranidella riparia* (Anura : Leptodactylidae). *Copeia* 1983(2): 534-537.

Osborne, W.S. (1989). Distribution, relative abundance and conservation status of corroboree frogs, *Pseudophryne corroboree* Moore (Anura: Myobatrachidae). *Australian Wildlife Research* 16: 537-547.

Parker, H.W. (1940). The Australasian frogs of the family Leptodactylidae. *Novitates Zoologicae* 42: 1-106.

Roberts, J.D. (1984). Terrestrial egg deposition and direct development in *Arenophryne rotunda* Tyler, a myobatrachid frog from coastal sand dunes at Shark Bay, W.A. *Australian Wildlife Research* 11(1): 191-200.

Roberts, J.D. (1985). Population density estimates for *Arenophryne rotunda*: is the Round Frog rare? pp. 463-467 in G.C. Grigg, R. Shine and H.F.W. Ehmann (eds) *The Biology of Australasian Frogs and Reptiles*. Surrey Beatty and Sons with R. Zool. Soc. NSW, Sydney.

Roberts, J.D. and Maxson, L.R. (1986). Phylogenetic relationships in the genus *Limnodynastes* (Anura: Myobatrachidae): a molecular perspective. *Australian Journal of Zoology* 34: 561-573.

Robertson, J.G.M. (1986). Female choice, male strategies and the role of vocalizations in the Australian frog *Uperoleia rugosa*. *Animal Behaviour* 34: 773-784.

Robertson, J.G.M. (1986). Male territoriality, fighting and assessment of fighting ability in the Australian frog *Uperoleia rugosa*. *Animal Behaviour* 34: 763-772.

Shea, G.M. and Johnston, G.R. (1988). A new species of *Notaden* (Anura: Leptodactylidae) from the Kimberley Division of Western Australia. *Transactions of the Royal Society of South Australia* 112(1): 29-37. [*Notaden weigeli*]

Straughan, I.R. (1968). A taxonomic review of the genus *Mixophyes* (Anura, Leptodactylidae). *Proceedings of the Linnean Society of N.S.W.* 93: 52-59.

Thompson, M.B. (1981). The systematic status of the genus *Australocrinia* Heyer and Liem (Anura: Leptodactylidae). *Australian Journal of Zoology* 29(1): 93-102.

Tyler, M.J. (1984). *There's a frog in my throat stomach*. Collins, Sydney. Tyler, M.J. (1985). Gastric brooding: a phenomenon unique to Australian frogs. *Search* 16(5-6): 157-159.

Tyler, M.J. (ed.) (1983). *The Gastric Brooding Frog*. Croom Helm, London. 163 pp.

Tyler, M.J. and Davies, M. (1985). The gastric brooding frog *Rheobatrachus silus*. pp. 469-470 in G.C. Grigg, R. Shine and H.F.W. Ehmann (eds) *The Biology of Australasian Frogs*

and Reptiles. Surrey Beatty and Sons with R. Zool. Soc. NSW, Sydney.
Tyler, M.J., Davies, M. and Martin, A.A. (1981). Australian frogs of the leptodactylid genus *Uperoleia* Gray. *Australian Journal of Zoology* Suppl. Ser. 79: 1-64.
Tyler, M.J., Martin, A.A. and Davies, M. (1979). Biology and systematics of a new limnodynastine genus (Anura: Leptodactylidae) from north-western Australia. *Australian Journal of Zoology* 27(1): 135-150.
Watson, G.F. and Martin, A.A. (1973). Life history, larval morphology and relationships of Australian leptodactylid frogs. *Transactions of the Royal Society of South Australia* 97(1): 33-45.
Williamson, I. and Bull, C.M. (1989). Life history variation in a population of the Australian frog *Ranidella signifera*: egg size and early development. *Copeia* 1989(2): 349-356.

Family Hylidae

Copland, S.J. (1957). Presidential address. Australian tree frogs of the genus Hyla. *Proceedings of the Linnean Society of N.S.W.* 82(1): 9-108.
Czechura, G.V., Ingram, G.J. and Liem, D.S. (1987). The genus *Nyctimystes* (Anura: Hylidae) in Australia. *Records of the Australian Museum* 39(5): 333-338.
Davies, M., Martin, A.A. and Watson, G.F. (1983). Redefinition of the *Litoria latopalmata* species group (Anura: Hylidae). *Transactions of the Royal Society of South Australia* 107(2): 87-108.
Davies, M., McDonald, K.R. and Adams, M. (1986). A new species of green tree frog (Anura: Hylidae) from Queensland, Australia. *Proceedings of the Royal Society of Victoria* 98(2): 63-71. [*Litoria xanthomera*]
Hutchinson, M.N. and Maxson, L.R. (1986). Immunological evidence on relationships of some Australian terrestrial frogs (Anura: Hylidae: Pelodryadinae). *Australian Journal of Zoology* 34: 575-582.
Hutchinson, M.N. and Maxson, L.R. (1987). Phylogenetic relationships among Australian tree frogs (Anura: Hylidae: Pelodryadinae): an immunological approach. *Australian Journal of Zoology* 35(1): 61-74.
Ingram, G.J., Corben, C.J. and Hosmer, W. (1982). *Litoria revelata*: a new species of tree-frog from eastern Australia. *Memoirs of the Queensland Museum* 20(3): 635-637.
Littlejohn, M.J. and Watson, G.F. (1983). The *Litoria ewingi* complex (Anura : Hylidae) in south-eastern Australia. VII. Mating-call structure and genetic compatibility across a narrow hybrid zone between *L. ewingi* and *L. paraewingi*. *Australian Journal of Zoology* 31: 193-204.
Maxson, L.R., Ondrula, D.P. and Tyler, M.J. (1985). An immunological perspective on evolutionary relationships in Australian frogs of the hylid genus *Cyclorana*. *Australian Journal of Zoology* 33: 17-22.
Robinson, M. and Cappo, M. (1990 (1989)). Comparison of feeding behaviours of the aquatic Australian hylid frogs *Litoria dahlii* (Boulenger, 1896) and *Cyclorana platycephala* (Günther, 1873) and the terrestrial hylid frog *Cyclorana novaehollandiae* (Steindachner, 1867). *Herpetofauna* 19(1): 8-24.
Tyler, M.J. (1968). Papuan hylid frogs of the genus *Hyla*. *Zoologische Verhandelingen (Leiden)* 96: 1-203.
Tyler, M.J. (1971). The phylogenetic significance of vocal sac structure in hylid frogs. *Miscelluneous Publications of the University of Kansas Museum of Natural History* 19(4): 319-360.
Tyler, M.J. (1974). The systematic position and geographic distribution of the Australian frog *Chiroleptes alboguttatus* Günther. *Proceedings of the Royal Society of Queensland* 85(2): 27-32.
Tyler, M.J. and Davies, M. (1985). A new species of *Litoria* (Anura:Hylidae) from New South Wales, Australia. *Copeia* 1985(1): 145-149 *Litoria piperata*.
Tyler, M.J. and Martin, A.A. (1977). Taxonomic studies of some Australian leptodactylid frogs of the genus *Cyclorana* Steindachner. *Records of the South Australian Museum* 17(15): 261-276.
Tyler, M.J. and Martin, A.A. (1975). Australian leptodactylid frogs of the *Cyclorana australis* complex. *Transactions of the Royal Society of South Australia* 99(2): 93-99.
Tyler, M.J., Davies, M. and King, M. (1978). The Australian frog *Chiroleptes dahlii* Boulenger: its systematic position, morphology, chromosomes and distribution. *Transactions of the Royal Society of South Australia* 102(1): 17-24.
Watson, G.F., Littlejohn, M.J., Gartside, D.F. and Loftus-Hills, J.J. (1985). The *Litoria ewingi* complex (Anura: Hylidae) in south-eastern Australia. VIII. Hybridization between *L. ewingi* and *L. verreauxi alpina* in the Mount Baw Baw area, south central Victoria. *Australian Journal of Zoology* 33: 143-152.

Family Microhylidae

Burton, J.C. (1986). A reassessment of the Papuan subfamily Asterophryinae (Anura: Microhylidae). *Records of the South Australian Museum* 19(19): 405-450.
Parker, H.W. (1934). *A Monograph of the Frogs of the Family Microhylidae*. London, British Museum (Nat. Hist.). viii + 208 pp.
Zweifel, R.G. (1962). A systematic review of the microhylid frogs of Australia. *American Museum Novitates* 2113: 1-40.
Zweifel, R.G. (1965). Revisionary notes on Australian microhylid frogs of the genus *Sphenophryne*. *American Museum Novitates* 2214: 1-9.
Zweifel, R.G. (1985). Australian frogs of the family Microhylidae. *Bulletin of the American Museum of Natural History* 182(3): 265-388. [*Cophixalus bombiens*; *Cophixalus crepitans*; *Cophixalus hosmeri*; *Cophixalus infacetus*; *Cophixalus mcdonaldi*; *Cophixalus peninsularis*; *Sphenophryne adelphe*]

Family Ranidae

Menzies, J.I. (1987). A taxonomic revision of Papuan *Rana* (Amphibia: Ranidae). *Australian Journal of Zoology*, 35:373-418.

Family Bufonidae

Covacevich, J. and Archer, M. (1975). The distribution of the cane toad, *Bufo marinus*, in Australia and its effect on indigenous vertebrates. *Memoirs of the Queensland Museum* 17: 305-310.
Easteal, S. (1985). The ecological genetics of introduced populations of the giant toad, *Bufo marinus*. III. Geographical patterns of variation. *Evolution* 39(5): 1065-1075.
Easteal, S., van Beurden, E.K., Floyd, R.B. and Sabath, M.D. (1985). Continuing geographical spread of *Bufo marinus* in Australia: range expansion between 1974 and 1980. *Journal of Herpetology* 19(2): 185-188.
Freeland, W.J. (1986). Populations of cane toad, *Bufo marinus*, in relation to time since colonization. *Australian Wildlife Research* 13: 321-329.
Freeland, W.J. and Martin, K.C. (1985). The rate of range expansion by *Bufo marinus* in northern Australia, 1980-84. *Australian Wildlife Research* 12: 555-559.
Freeland, W.J., Delvinquier, B.L.J. and Bonnin, B. (1986). Food and parasitism of the cane toad, *Bufo marinus*, in relation to time since colonization. *Australian Wildlife Research* 13: 489-499.
Straughan, I.R. 1966. The natural history of the "cane toad" in Queensland. *Australian Natural History* 15(7): 230-232.
Zug, G.R. and Zug, P.B. (1979). The marine toad, *Bufo marinus*: a natural history resumé of native populations. *Smithsonian Contributions to Zoology* 284: i-iv + 1-58.

Crocodiles

Bayliss, P., Webb, G.J.W., Whitehead, P.J., Dempsey, K. and Smith, A. (1986). Estimating the abundance of saltwater crocodiles, *Crocodylus porosus* Schneider, in tidal wetlands of the Northern Territory: a mark-recapture experiment to correct spotlight counts to absolute numbers, and the calibration of helicopter and spotlight counts. *Australian Wildlife Research* 13: 309-320.

Beal, A.M. and Webb, G.J.W. (1989). Effect of incubation temperature on tooth eruption in embryos of *Crocodylus johnstoni*. *Copeia* 1989(2): 325-331.

Bellairs, A.d'A. (1987). The Crocodilia. pp. 5-7 in G.J.W. Webb, S.C. Manolis and P.J. Whitehead (eds) *Wildlife Management: Crocodiles and Alligators*. Surrey Beatty and Sons, Chipping Norton, Sydney.

Brazaitis, P. (1987). The identification of crocodilian skins and products. pp. 373-386 in G.J.W. Webb, S.C. Manolis and P.J. Whitehead (eds) *Wildlife Management: Crocodiles and Alligators*. Surrey Beatty and Sons, Chipping Norton, Sydney.

Grigg, G.C, Farwell, W., Kinney, J., Harlow, P., Taplin, L.E. and Johansen, K. (1985). Amphibious behaviour and patterns of diving in a free-ranging crocodile, *Crocodylus porosus*. *Australian Zoologist* 21(7): 599-606.

Grigg, G.C. and Beard, L. (1985). Water loss and gain by eggs of *Crocodylus porosus*, related to incubation age and fertility. pp. 353-359 in G.C. Grigg, R. Shine and H.F.W. Ehmann (eds) *The Biology of Australasian Frogs and Reptiles*. Surrey Beatty and Sons with R. Zool. Soc. NSW, Sydney.

Grigg, G.C., Taplin, L.E. Green, B. and Harlow, P. (1986). Sodium and water fluxes in free-living *Crocodylus porosus* in marine and brackish conditions. *Physiological Zoology* 59(2): 240-253.

Groombridge, B. (1987). The distribution and status of world crocodilians. pp. 9-21 in G.J.W. Webb, S.C. Manolis and P.J. Whitehead (eds) *Wildlife Management: Crocodiles and Alligators*. Surrey Beatty and Sons, Chipping Norton, Sydney.

Guggisberg, C.A.W. (1972). *Crocodiles: their natural history, folklore and conservation*. Wren Publishing, Mount Eliza, Victoria. x + 195 pp.

Jenkins, R.W.G. and Forbes, M.A. (1985). Seasonal variation in abundance and distribution of *Crocodylus porosus* in the tidal East Alligator River, northern Australia. pp. 63-69 in G.C. Grigg, R. Shine and H.F.W. Ehmann (eds) *The Biology of Australasian Frogs and Reptiles*. Surrey Beatty and Sons with R. Zool. Soc. NSW, Sydney.

Johnson, C.R. (1973). Behaviour of the Australian crocodiles, *Crocodylus johnstoni* and *C. porosus*. *Zoological Journal of the Linnean Society* 52(4): 315-336.

Messel, H. and Vorlicek, G.C. (1986). Population dynamics and status of *Crocodylus porosus* in the tidal waterways of northern Australia. *Australian Wildlife Research* 13: 71-111.

Onions, V. (1987). Crocodile farming and ranching in Australia. pp. 345-348 in G.J.W. Webb, S.C. Manolis and P.J. Whitehead (eds) *Wildlife Management: Crocodiles and Alligators*. Surrey Beatty and Sons, Chipping Norton, Sydney.

Taplin, L.E., Grigg, G.C. and Beard, L. (1985). Salt gland function in fresh water crocodiles: evidence for a marine phase in eosuchian evolution? pp. 403-410 in G.C. Grigg, R. Shine and H.F.W. Ehmann (eds) *The Biology of Australasian Frogs and Reptiles*. Surrey Beatty and Sons with R. Zool. Soc. NSW, Sydney.

Webb, G.J.W. and Manolis, S.C. (1989). *Crocodiles of Australia*. Reed Books, Sydney. 160 pp.

Webb, G.J.W. and Manolis, S.C. (1988). *Australian Saltwater Crocodiles (Crocodylus porosus)*. G. Webb P/L, Darwin. 32 pp.

Webb, G.J.W. and Manolis, S.C. (1988). *Australian Freshwater Crocodiles (Crocodylus johnstoni)*. G. Webb P/L, Darwin. 32 pp.

Webb, G.J.W. and Smith, A.M.A. (1987). Life history parameters, population dynamics and the management of crocodilians. pp. 199-210 in G.J.W. Webb, S.C. Manolis and P.J. Whitehead (eds) *Wildlife Management: Crocodiles and Alligators*. Surrey Beatty and Sons, Chipping Norton, Sydney.

Webb, G.J.W., Beal, A.M., Manolis, S.C. and Dempsey, K.E. (1987). The effects of incubation temperature on sex determination and embryonic development rate in *Crocodylus johnstoni* and *C. porosus*. pp. 507-531 in G.J.W. Webb, S.C. Manolis and P.J. Whitehead (eds) *Wildlife Management: Crocodiles and Alligators*. Surrey Beatty and Sons, Chipping Norton, Sydney.

Webb, G.J.W., Manolis, S.C. and Whitehead, P.J. (eds) (1987). *Wildlife Management: Crocodiles and Alligators*. Surrey Beatty and Sons, Chipping Norton, Sydney and Conservation Commission of the Northern Territory. 552 pp.

Turtles and Tortoises

Boulenger, G.A. (1889). *Catalogue of the Chelonians, Rhynchocephalians, and Crocodiles in the British Museum (Natural History)*. British Museum, London. new edn. x + 311 pp.

Bustard, H.R. (1972). *Sea Turtles: Natural History and Conservation*. Collins, Sydney. 220 pp.

Cogger, H.G. and Lindner, D.A. (1969). Marine turtles in northern Australia. *Australian Zoologist* 15: 150-159.

Limpus, C.J. (1982). The status of Australian sea turtle populations. pp. 297-303 in K.A. Bjorndal (ed.) *Biology and Conservation of Sea Turtles*. Washington, Smithsonian Institution Press.

Marquez M., R. (1990). FAO species catalogue. Vol.11: Sea turtles of the world. An annotated and illustrated catalogue of sea turtle species known to date. *FAO Fisheries Synopsis*. No.125, Vol.11. Rome, FAO, 91 pp.

Nöllert, A. (1987). *Schildkröten*. Landbuch-Verlag, Hannover. pp.1-190.

Pritchard, P.C.H. (1967). *Living Turtles of the World*. T.F.H. Publications Inc., Jersey City. 288 pp.

Pritchard, P.C.H. (1979). *Encyclopaedia of Turtles*. T.F.H. Publicaions, Neptune, New Jersey. 895 pp.

Family Cheloniidae

Garnett, S.T., Price, I.R. and Scott, F.J. (1985). The diet of the green turtle, *Chelonia mydas* (L.), in Torres Strait. *Australian Wildlife Research* 12: 103-112.

Gyuris, E. and Limpus, C.J. (1988). The loggerhead turtle, *Caretta caretta*, in Queensland: population breeding structure. *Australian Journal of Wildlife Research* 15: 197-209.

Limpus, C.J. (1975). The Pacific ridley, *Lepidochelys olivacea* (Eschscholtz) and other sea turtles in northeastern Australia. *Herpetologica* 31(4): 444-445.

Limpus, C.J. (1980). Observations on the hawksbill turtle (*Eretmochelys imbricata*) nesting along the Great Barrier Reef. *Herpetologica* 36(3): 265-271.

Limpus, C.J. (1980). The green turtle, *Chelonia mydas* (L.) in eastern Australia. *James Cook University of North Queensland Research Monographs* 1: 5-22.

Limpus, C.J. and Nicholls, N. (1988). The Southern Oscillation regulates the annual numbers of green turtles (*Chelonia mydas*) breeding around northern Australia. *Australian Journal of Wildlife Research* 16: 157-161.

Limpus, C.J. and Reed, P.C. (1985). The green turtle, *Chelonia mydas*, in Queensland: a preliminary description of the population structure in a coral reef feeding ground. pp. 47-52 in G.C. Grigg, R. Shine and H.F.W. Ehmann (eds.) *The Biology of Australasian Frogs and Reptiles*. Surrey Beatty and Sons with R. Zool. Soc. NSW, Sydney.

Limpus, C.J. and Reed, P.C. (1985). The loggerhead turtle, *Caretta caretta*, in Queensland: observations on internesting behaviour. *Australian Wildlife Research* 12: 535-540.

Limpus, C.J., Fleay, A. and Baker, V. (1984). The flatback turtle, *Chelonia depressa*, in Queensland: reproductive periodicity, philopatry and recruitment. *Australian Wildlife Research* 11(3): 579-587.

Limpus, C.J., Gyuris, E. and Miller, J.D. (1988). Reassessment of the taxonomic status of the sea turtle genus *Natator* McCulloch, 1908, with a redescription of the genus and species. *Transactions of the Royal Society of South Australia* 112(1): 1-9.

Limpus, C.J., Parmenter, C.J., Baker, V. and Fleay, A. (1983). The flatback turtle, *Chelonia depressa*, in Queensland: post-nesting migration and feeding ground distribution. *Australian Wildlife Research* 10(3): 557-561.

Limpus, C.J., Reed, P.C. and Miller, J.D. (1985). Temperature dependent sex determination in Queensland sea turtles: intraspecific variation in *Caretta caretta*. pp. 343-351 in G.C. Grigg, R. Shine and H.F.W. Ehmann (eds.) *The Biology of Australasian Frogs and Reptiles*. Surrey Beatty and Sons with R. Zool. Soc. NSW, Sydney.

Zangerl, R., Hendrickson, L.P. and Hendrickson, J.R. (1988). A redescription of the Australian flatback sea turtle, *Natator depressus*. *Bishop Museum Bulletin in Zoology* 1: 1-69.

Family Dermochelyidae

Frazier, J.G., Meneghel, M.D. and Achaval, F. (1985). A clarification of the feeding habits of *Dermochelys coriacea*. *Journal of Herpetology* 19(1)159-160.

Hudson, D.M. and Lutz, P.L. (1986). Salt gland function in the leatherback sea turtle, *Dermochelys coriacea*. *Copeia* 1986(1): 247-249.

Limpus, C.J. and McLachlan, N.C. (1979). Observations on the leatherback turtle, *Dermochelys coriacea* (L.), in Australia. *Australian Wildlife Research* 6: 105-116.

Limpus, C.J., McLachlan, N.C. and Miller, J.D. (1984). Further observations on breeding of *Dermochelys coriacea* in Australia. *Australian Wildlife Research* 11(3): 567-571.

Lutcavage, M. and Lutz, P.L. (1986). Metabolic rate and food energy requirements of the leatherback sea turtle, *Dermochelys coriacea*. *Copeia* 1986(3): 796-798.

Family Carettochelyidae

Georges, A. (1987). The pig-nosed turtle Warradjan. *Australian Natural History* 22(5): 230-234.

Georges, A. and Kennett, R. (1988). Dry season distribution and ecology of the Warradjan, *Carettochelys insculpta* (Chelonia: Carettochelydidae), in Kakadu National Park. Australian National Parks and Wildlife Service, Canberra. *Unpublished report*. 50 pp.

Family Chelidae

Banks, C.B. (1987). Nesting, incubation and hatchling growth in captive Krefft's tortoise, *Emydura krefftii*. *Australian Wildlife Research* 14: 551-558.

Burbidge, A.A. (1983). A very rare Australian, the western swamp tortoise. *Australian Natural History* 21(1): 14-17.

Cann, J. (1978). *Tortoises of Australia*. Angus and Robertson, Sydney. 79 pp.

Cann, J. (1980). Notes on the reproduction of the northern longnecked tortoise (*Chelodina rugosa*). *Northern Territory Naturalist* 1(3): 4-5.

Chessman, B.C. (1983). Observations on the diet of the broad-shelled turtle, *Chelodina expansa* Gray (Testudines: Chelidae). *Australian Wildlife Research* 10: 169-172.

Chessman, B.C. (1984). Food of the snake-necked turtle, *Chelodina longicollis* (Shaw) (Testudines: Chelidae) in the Murray Valley, Victoria and New South Wales. *Australian Wildlife Research* 11(3): 573-578.

Chessman, B.C. (1986). Diet of the Murray turtle, *Emydura macquarii* (Gray) (Testudines: Chelidae). *Australian Wildlife Research* 13: 65-69.

Chessman, B.C. (1987). Atmospheric and aquatic basking of the Australian freshwater turtle *Emydura macquarii* (Gray) (Testudines: Chelidae). *Herpetologica* 43(3): 301-306.

Georges, A. (1983). Reproduction of the Australian freshwater turtle *Emydura krefftii* (Chelonia: Chelidae). *Journal of Zoology* 201(3): 331-350.

Georges, A. (1986 (1984)). Observations on the nesting and natural incubation of the long-necked tortoise *Chelodina expansa* in south-east Queensland. *Herpetofauna* 15(2): 27-31.

Georges, A. (1988). Sex determination is independent of incubation temperature in another chelid turtle, *Chelodina longicollis*. *Copeia* 1988(1): 248-254.

Georges, A., Norris, R.H. and Wensing, L. (1986). Diet of the freshwater turtle *Chelodina longicollis* (Testudines: Chelidae) from the coastal dune lakes of the Jervis Bay Territory. *Australian Wildlife Research* 13: 301-308.

Goode, J. (1964). *Freshwater Tortoises of Australia and New Guinea*. Landsdowne Press, Melbourne. x + 154 pp.

Grigg, G.C., Johansen, K., Harlow, P., Beard, L.A. and Taplin, L.E. (1986). Facultative aestivation in a tropical fresh water turtle, *Chelodina rugosa*. *Comparative Biochemistry and Physiology* 83A: 321-323.

Kennett, R.M. and Georges, A. (1990). Habitat utilization and its relationship to growth and reproduction of the eastern long-necked turtle, *Chelodina longicollis* (Testudinata: Chelidae), from Australia. *Herpetologica* 46(1): 22-33.

Legler, J.M. (1985). Australian chelid turtles: reproductive patterns in wide-ranging taxa. pp. 117-123 in G.C. Grigg, R. Shine and H.F.W. Ehmann (eds.) *The Biology of Australasian Frogs and Reptiles*. Surrey Beatty and Sons with R. Zool. Soc. NSW, Sydney.

McDowell, S.B. (1983). The genus *Emydura* (Testudines: Chelidae) in New Guinea with notes on the penial morphology of Pleurodira. pp. 169-189 in A.G.J. Rhodin and K. Miyata (eds.) *Advances in Herpetology and Evolutionary Biology*. Museum of Comparative Zoology, Harvard University, Cambridge, Mass.

Parmenter, C.J. (1985). Reproduction and survivorship of *Chelodina longicollis* (Testudinata: Chelidae). pp. 53-61 in G.C. Grigg, R. Shine and H.F.W. Ehmann (eds) *The Biology of Australasian Frogs and Reptiles*. Surrey Beatty and Sons with R. Zool. Soc. NSW, Sydney.

Lizards General

Arnold, E.N. (1984). Variation in the cloacal and hemipenial muscles of lizards and its bearing on their relationships. *Symposia. Zoological Society of London* 52: 47-85.

Baverstock, P.R. and Donnellan, S.C. (1990). Molecular evolution in Australian dragons and skinks: a progress report. *Memoirs of the Queensland Museum* 29(2): 323-331.

Boulenger, G.A. (1885). *Catalogue of the Lizards in the British Museum (Natural History)*. British Museum, London. Vol. 1. xii + 436 pp.

Boulenger, G.A. (1885). *Catalogue of the Lizards in the British Museum (Natural History)*. British Museum, London. Vol. 2. xiii + 497 pp.

Boulenger, G.A. (1887). *Catalogue of the Lizards in the British Museum (Natural History)*. British Museum, London. Vol. 3. xii + 575 pp.

Bustard, H.R. (1970). *Australian Lizards*. Collins, Sydney. 162 pp.

Dale, F.D. (1973). Forty Queensland Lizards. *Queensland Museum Booklet* 8: 1-64.

Glauert, L. (1961). *A Handbook of the Lizards of Western Australia*. Perth, West. Aust. Naturalists Club, Handbook 6. 100 pp.

Greer, A.E. (1990). *The Biology and Evolution of Australian Lizards*. Surrey Beatty and Sons, Chipping Norton. pp.i-xvi, 1-264.

James, C.D. and Shine, R. (1985). The seasonal timing of reproduction: a tropical-temperate comparison in Australian lizards. *Oecologia* (Berl.) 67: 464-474.

James, C.D. and Shine, R. (1988). Life-history strategies of Australian lizards: a comparison between the tropics and the temperate zone. *Oecologia* 75: 307-316.

Pianka, E.R. (1972). Zoogeography and speciation of Australian desert lizards, an ecological perspective. *Copeia* 1972(1): 127-144.

Pianka, E.R. (1985). *Ecology and Natural History of Desert Lizards; analyses of the ecological niche and community structure.* Princeton University Press, Princeton. 208 pp.

Swan, G. (1990). *A Field Guide to the Snakes and Lizards of New South Wales.* Three Sisters Productions, Winmalee, NSW. 224 pp.

Swanson, S. (1987). *Lizards of Australia.* Angus and Robertson, Sydney. 160 pp. (rev. ed.).

Family Gekkonidae

Bauer, A.M. (1990). Phylogenetic Systematics and Biogeography of the Carphodactylini (Reptilia: Gekkonidae). *Bonner Zoologische Monographien*, No.30, pp.1-218.

Bauer, A.M. and Russell, A.P. (1988). Morphology of gekkonid cutaneous sensilla, with comments on function and phylogeny of the Carphodactylini (Reptilia: Gekkonidae). *Canadian Journal of Zoology* 66: 1583-1588.

Bauer, A.M., Russell, A.P. and Rosenberg, H.I. (1989). Formal taxa, species groups, and perception of the genus *Diplodactylus* (Reptilia: Gekkonidae). *Zeitschrift für Systematik und Evolutionsforschung* 27: 44-48.

Brown, W.C. and Parker, F. (1977). Lizards of the genus *Lepidodactylus* (Gekkonidae) from the Indo-Australian Archipelago and the islands of the Pacific, with descriptions of new species. *Proceedings of the California Academy of Sciences* (4)41(8): 253-265.

Bustard, H.R. (1968). The ecology of the Australian gecko *Gehyra variegata*, in northern New South Wales. *Journal of Zoology* 154: 113-138.

Bustard, H.R. (1968). The ecology of the Australian gecko *Heteronotia binoei* in northern New South Wales. *Journal of Zoology* 156(4): 483-497.

Bustard, H.R. (1969). Population ecology of the gekkonid lizard (*Gehyra variegata* (Duméril and Bibron)) in exploited forests in northern New South Wales. *Journal of Animal Ecology* 38: 35-51.

Bustard, H.R. (1969). The ecology of the Australian geckos *Diplodactylus williamsi* and *Gehyra australis* in northern New South Wales. *Proceedings Koninklijke Nederlandse Akademie van Wetenschappen* (C)72(4): 451-477.

Cogger, H.G. (1957). Investigations in the gekkonid genus *Oedura* Gray. *Proceedings of the Linnean Society of N.S.W.* 82(2): 167-179.

Covacevich, J. (1975). A review of the genus *Phyllurus* (Lacertilia: Gekkonidae). *Memoirs of the Queensland Museum* 17(2): 293-303.

Delean, S. and Harvey, C. (1984). Notes on the reproduction of *Nephrurus deleani* (Reptilia: Gekkonidae). *Transactions of the Royal Society of South Australia* 108(3/4): 221-222.

Harvey, C. (1983). A new species of *Nephrurus* (Reptilia: Gekkonidae) from South Australia. *Transactions of the Royal Society of South Australia* 107(3-4): 231-235. [*Nephrurus deleani*]

How, R.A. and Kitchener, D.J. (1983). The biology of the gecko *Oedura reticulata* Bustard, in a small habitat isolate in the Western Austalian wheatbelt. *Australian Wildlife Research* 10(3): 543-556. How, R.A., Dell, J. and Gordon, S.J. (1987). Reproductive patterns in chromosomally distinct races of *Phyllodactylus marmoratus* (Lacertilia: Gekkonidae) in south-western Australia. *Records of the Western Australian Museum* 13(3): 413-418.

How, R.A., Dell, J. and Wellington, B.D. (1986). Comparative biology of eight species of *Diplodactylus* gecko in Western Australia. *Herpetologica* 42(4): 471-482.

How, R.A., Dell, J. and Wellington, B.D. (1990). Reproductive and dietary biology of *Nephrurus* and *Underwoodisaurus* (Gekkonidae) in Western Australia. *Records of the Western Australian Museum* 14(4): 449-459.

King, M. (1982). A new species of *Gehyra* (Reptilia : Gekkonidae) from Central Australia. *Transactions of the Royal Society of South Australia* 106(4): 155-158. [*Gehyra minuta*]

King, M. (1983). Karyotypic evolution in Gehyra (Gekkonidae: Reptilia). III. The *Gehyra australis* complex. *Australian Journal of Zoology* 31: 723-741.

King, M. (1983). The *Gehyra australis* species complex (Sauria: Gekkonidae). *Amphibia-Reptilia* 4: 147-169. [*Gehyra borroloola; Gehyra robusta*]

King, M. (1984). A new species of *Gehyra* (Reptilia: Gekkonidae) from northern Western Australia. *Transactions of the Royal Society of South Australia* 108(2): 113-117. [*Gehyra occidentalis*]

King, M. (1984). Three new species of *Oedura* (Gekkonidae, Reptilia) from the Mitchell Plateau of North Western Australia. *Amphibia-Reptilia* 5: 329-337. [*Oedura filicipoda; Oedura gracilis; Oedura obscura*]

King, M. (1987). Chromosomal evolution in the Diplodactylinae (Gekkonidae: Reptilia). I. Evolutionary relationships and patterns of change. *Australian Journal of Zoology* 35: 507-531.

King, M. (1987). Monophyleticism and polyphyleticism in the Gekkonidae: a chromosomal perspective. *Australian Journal of Zoology* 35: 641-654.

King, M. and Gow, G.F. (1983). A new species of *Oedura* (Gekkonidae: Reptilia) from the Alligator Rivers region of northern Australia. *Copeia* 1983(2): 445-449. [*Oedura gemmata*]

Kitchener, D.J., How, R.A. and Dell, J. (1988). Bioiogy of *Oedura reticulata* and *Gehyra variegata* (Gekkonidae) in an isolated woodland of Western Australia. *Journal of Herpetology* 22(4): 401-412.

Kluge, A.G. (1963). A review of the gekkonid lizard genus *Heteronota* Gray, with a description of a new species from Western Australia. *Journal of the Royal Society of Western Australia* 46(2): 63-67.

Kluge, A.G. (1967). Higher taxonomic categories of gekkonid lizards and their evolution. *Bulletin of the American Museum of Natural History* 135(1): 1-59.

Kluge, A.G. (1967). Systematics, phylogeny, and zoogeography of the lizard genus *Diplodactylus* Gray (Gekkonidae). *Australian Journal of Zoology* 15: 1007-1108.

Kluge, A.G. (1983). Cladistic relationships among gekkonid lizards. *Copeia* 1983(2): 465-475.

Kluge, A.G. (1987). Cladistic relationships in the Gekkonoidea (Squamata, Sauria). *Miscellaneous Publications of the Museum of Zoology, University of Michigan* 173: 1-54.

Mitchell, F.J. (1965). Australian geckos assigned to the genus *Gehyra* Gray. (Reptilia, Gekkonidae). *Senckenbergiana Biologica* 46: 287-319.

Moritz, C. (1983). Parthenogenesis in the endemic Australian lizard *Heteronotia binoei* (Gekkonidae). *Science*, 220:735-737.

Moritz, C. (1986). The population biology of *Gehyra* (Gekkonidae): chromosome change and speciation. *Systematic Zoology* 35(1): 46-67.

Moritz, C. (1987). The population biology of *Gehyra* (Gekkonidae: Reptilia). II. Individual movements and colonisation by *Gehyra variegata* and *Gehyra nana*. *Australian Journal of Zoology* 35: 587-596.

Moritz, C. and King, D. (1985). Cytogenetic perspectives on parthenogenesis in the Gekkonidae. pp. 327-337 in G.C. Grigg, R. Shine and H.F.W. Ehmann (eds) *The Biology of Australasian Frogs and Reptiles.* Surrey Beatty and Sons with R. Zool. Soc. NSW, Sydney.

Moritz, C., Donnellan, S., Adams, M. and Baverstock, P.R. (1989). The origin and evolution of parthenogenesis in *Heteronotia binoei* (Gekkonidae): extensive genotypic diversity among parthenogens. *Evolution* 43(5): 994-1003.

Pianka, E.R. and Pianka, H.D. (1976). Comparative ecology of twelve species of nocturnal lizards (Gekkonidae) in the Western Australian desert. *Copeia* 1976: 125-142.

Richardson, K.C. and Hinchliffe, P.M. (1983). Caudal glands and their secretions in the western spiny-tailed gecko, *Diplodactylus spinigerus*. *Copeia* 1983(1): 161-169.

Rosler, H. (1987). Observation on reproduction in *Diplodactylus williamsi* Kluge (Sauria: Gekkonidae). *Herpetofauna* 17(2):29-30.

Russell, A.P. and Bauer, A.M. (1987). Caudal morphology of the knob-tailed geckos, genus *Nephrurus* (Reptilia: Gekkonidae), with special reference to the tail tip. *Australian Journal of Zoology* 35: 541-551.

Storr, G.M. (1979). The *Diplodactylus vittatus* complex (Lacertilia, Gekkonidae) in Western Australia. *Records of the Western Australian Museum* 7(4): 391-402.

Storr, G.M. (1982). Two new *Gehyra* (Lacertilia: Gekkonidae) from Australia. *Records of the Western Australian Museum* 10(1): 53-59. [*Gehyra montium*; *Gehyra purpurascens*]

Storr, G.M. (1983). Two new lizards from Western Australia (genera *Diplodactylus* and *Lerista*). *Records of the Western Australian Museum* 11(1): 59-62. [*Diplodactylus wilsoni*]

Storr, G.M. (1987). The genus *Phyllodactylus* (Lacertilia: Gekkonidae) in Western Australia. *Records of the Western Australian Museum* 13(2): 275-284.

Storr, G.M. (1988). A new species of *Diplodactylus* (Lacertilia: Gekkonidae) from northern Australia. *Records of the Western Australian Museum* 14(2): 183-187. [*Diplodactylus jeanae*]

Storr, G.M. (1988). The *Diplodactylus ciliaris* complex (Lacertilia: Gekkonidae) in Western Australia. *Records of the Western Australian Museum* 14(1): 121-133. [*Diplodactylus assimilis*]

Storr, G.M. (1988). The subspecies of *Diplodactylus spinigerus* (Lacertilia: Gekkonidae). *Records of the Western Australian Museum* 14(2): 177-182.

Storr, G.M. (1988). Three new *Diplodactylus* (Lacertilia: Gekkonidae) from the arid zone of Australia. *Records of the Western Australian Museum* 14(2): 217-223. [*Diplodactylus immaculatus*; *Diplodactylus kenneallyi*]

Sumida, S.S. and Murphy, R.W. (1988). Form and function of the tooth crown structure in gekkonid lizards (Reptilia, Squamata, Gekkonidae). *Canadian Journal of Zoology* 65: 2886-2892.

Wermuth, H. (1965). Liste der rezenten Amphibien und Reptilien: Gekkonidae, Pygopodidae, Xantusiidae. *Das Tierreich* 80(1-22): 1-246.

Family Pygopodidae

Annable, T. (1983). Some observations on vocalization and the use of limb flaps in the pygopodid lizard, *Delma inornata* Kluge. *Herpetofauna* 14(2): 80-82.

Bauer, A.M. (1986). Saltation in the pygopodid lizard, *Delma tincta*. *Journal of Herpetology* 20(3): 462-463.

Bush, B. (1986 (1984)). Seasonal aggregation behaviour in a mixed population of legless lizards, *Delma australis* and *D. fraseri*. *Herpetofauna* 16(1): 1-6.

Hutchins, M. and Sleeper, B. (1989). Life without legs; the pygopodid lizards. *Australian Natural History* 22(11): 524-528.

Kluge, A.G. (1974). A taxonomic revision of the lizard family Pygopodidae. *Miscellaneous Publications of the Museum of Zoology, University of Michigan* 147: 1-221.

Kluge, A.G. (1976). Phylogenetic relationships in the lizard family Pygopodidae: an evaluation of theory, methods and data. Miscellaneous Publications of the Museum of Zoology, *University of Michigan* 152: 1-72.

Patchell, F.C. and Shine, R. (1986). Food habits and reproductive biology of the Australian legless lizards (Pygopodidae). *Copeia* 1986 (1): 30-39.

Patchell, F.C. and Shine, R. (1986). Feeding mechanisms in pygopodid lizards: how can *Lialis* swallow such large prey? *Journal of Herpetology* 20(1): 59-64.

Patchell, F.C. and Shine, R. (1986). Hinged teeth for hard-bodied prey: a case of convergent evolution between snakes and legless lizards. *Journal of Zoology* (A)208(2): 269-275.

Shea, G.M. (1987). Notes on the biology of *Paradelma orientalis*. *Herpetofauna* 17(1): 5-6.

Shea, G.M. (1987). Two new species of *Delma* (Lacertilia: Pygopodidae) from northwestern Queensland and a note on the status of the genus *Aclys*. *Proceedings of the Linnean Society of NSW* 109(3): 203-212. [*Delma labialis*; *Delma mitella*]

Shine, R. (1986). Evolutionary advantages of limblessness: evidence from the pygopodid lizards. *Copeia* 1986(2): 525-529.

Storr, G.M. (1987). Three new legless lizards (Pygopodidae) from Western Australia. *Records of the Western Australian Museum* 13(3): 345-355. [*Delma butleri*; *Delma haroldi*]

Wermuth, H. (1965). Liste der rezenten Amphibien und Reptilien: Gekkonidae, Pygopodidae, Xantusiidae. *Das Tierreich* 80(1-22): 1-246.

Family Agamidae

Badham, J.A. (1976). The *Amphibolurus barbatus* species-group (Lacertilia: Agamidae). *Australian Journal of Zoology* 24: 423-443.

Cogger, H.G. (1974). Thermal relations of the mallee dragon, *Amphibolurus fordi* (Lacertilia: Agamidae). *Australian Journal of Zoology* 22(3): 319-339.

Cogger, H.G. (1978). Reproductive cycles, fat body cycles and socio-sexual behaviour in the mallee dragon, *Amphibolurus fordi* (Lacertilia: Agamidae). *Australian Journal of Zoology* 26: 653-672.

Greer, A.E. (1987). Observations on the osteology and natural history of the agamid lizard *Ctenophorus clayi*. *Western Australian Naturalist* 17(1): 5-7.

Greer, A.E. (1987). Taxonomic and natural history notes on *Tympanocryptis butleri* and *T. parviceps*. *Western Australian Naturalist* 17(1): 13-16.

Greer, A.E. (1989). Observations on the osteology and natural history of the agamid lizard *Ctenophorus femoralis*. *Western Australian Naturalist* 18(1): 21-23.

Houston, T.F. (1974). Revision of the *Amphibolurus decresii* complex (Lacertilia: Agamidae) of South Australia. *Transactions of the Royal Society of South Australia* 98(2): 49-60.

Houston, T.F. (1977). A new species of *Diporiphora* from South Australia and geographic variation in *D. winneckei* Lucas and Frost (Lacertilia: Agamidae). *Transactions of the Royal Society of South Australia* 101(8): 199-206.

Houston, T.F. (1978). *Dragon Lizards and Goannas of South Australia*. South Australian Museum, Adelaide. 84 pp.

Kent, D.S. (1987). Notes on the biology and osteology of *Amphibolurus diemensis* (Gray, 1841), the mountain dragon. *Victorian Naturalist* 104(4): 101-104.

Mitchell, F.J. (1948). A revision of the lacertilian genus *Tympanocryptis*. *Records of the South Australian Museum* 9(1): 57-86.

Mitchell, F.J. (1973). Studies on the ecology of the agamid lizard *Amphibolurus maculosus* (Mitchell). *Transactions of the Royal Society of South Australia* 97(1): 47-76.

Pianka, E.R. (1971). Ecology of the agamid lizard *Amphibolurus isolepis* in Western Australia. *Copeia* 1971(3): 527-536.

Pianka, E.R. and Pianka, H.D. (1970). The ecology of *Moloch horridus* (Lacertilia. Agamidae) in Western Australia. *Copeia* 1970(1): 90-103.

Shine, R. and Lambeck, R. (1989). Ecology of frillneck lizards *Chlamydosaurus kingii* (Sauria: Agamidae). *Australian Wildlife Research* 16: 491-500.

Storr, G.M. (1964). The agamid lizards of the genus *Tympanocryptis* in Western Australia. *Journal of the Royal Society of Western Australia* 47(2): 43-50.
Storr, G.M. (1965). The *Amphibolurus maculatus* species-group (Lacertilia, Agamidae) in Western Australia. *Journal of the Royal Society of Western Australia* 48(2): 45-54.
Storr, G.M. (1966). The *Amphibolurus reticulatus* species-group (Lacertilia, Agamidae) in Western Australia. *Journal of the Royal Society of Western Australia* 49(1): 17-25.
Storr, G.M. (1974). Agamid lizards of the genera *Caimanops*, *Physignathus* and *Diporiphora* in Western Australia and Northern Territory. *Records of the Western Australian Museum* 3(2): 121-146.
Storr, G.M. (1977). The *Amphibolurus adelaidensis* species group (Lacertilia, Agamidae) in Western Australia. *Records of the Western Australian Museum* 5(1): 73-81.
Storr, G.M., Smith, L.A. and Johnstone, R.E. (1983). *Lizards of Western Australia. II. Dragons and Monitors.* Western Australian Museum, Perth. xiv + 114 pp.
Throckmorton, G.S., de Bavay, J., Chaffey, W., Merrotsy, B., Noske, S. and Noske, R. (1985). The mechanism of frill erection in the bearded dragon *Amphibolurus barbatus* with comments on the jacky lizard *A. muricatus* (Agamidae). *Journal of Morphology* 183: 285-292.
Webb, G.A. (1984). The distribution, ecology and status of the southern angle-headed dragon (*Gonocephalus spinipes*) in New South Wales. *Forestry Commission Rep.* 981: 1-13.
Wermuth, H. (1967). Liste der rezenten Amphibien und Reptilien: Agamidae. *Das Tierreich* 86: 1-127.
Witten, G.J. (1985). Relative growth in Australian agamid lizards: adaptation and evolution. *Australian Journal of Zoology* 33: 349-362.
Witten, G.J. and Coventry, A.J. (1984). A new lizard of the genus *Amphibolurus* (Agamidae) from southern Australia. *Proceedings of the Royal Society of Victoria* 96(3): 155-159. [*Amphibolurus norrisi*]

Family Varanidae

Bickler, P.E. and Anderson, R.A. (1986). Ventilation, gas exchange, and aerobic scope in a small monitor lizard, *Varanus gilleni*. *Physiological Zoology* 59(1): 76-83.
Carter, D.B. (1990). Courtship and mating in wild *Varanus varius* (Varanidae: Australia). *Memoirs of the Queensland Museum* 29(2): 333-338.
Copland, S.J. (1953). The blood vascular system of the trunk of the goanna *Varanus varius* (Shaw) *in* Recent Australian herpetology. *Proceedings of the Linnean Society of N.S.W.* 78: v-xxxvii.
Eidenmüller, B. (1986). Beobachtungen bei der Pflege und Nachzucht von *Varanus (Odatria) t. timorensis* (Gray, 1831) (Sauria: Varanidae). *Salamandra* 22(2/3): 157-161.
Eidenmüller, B. and Horn, H.-G. (1985). Eigene Nachzuchten und der gegenwärtige Strand der Nachzucht von *Varanus (Odatria) storri* Mertens, 1966. *Salamandra* 21(1): 55-61.
Green, B. (1972). Water losses of the sand goanna (*Varanus gouldii*) in its natural environment. *Ecology* 53: 452-457.
Green, B. and King, D. (1978). Home range and activity patterns of the sand goanna, *Varanus gouldii* (Reptilia:Varanidae). *Australian Wildlife Research* 5: 417-424.
Green, B., King, D. and Butler, C. (1986). Water, sodium and energy turnover in free-living perenties, *Varanus giganteus*. *Australian Wildlife Research* 34: 589-595.
Horn, H.-G. (1985). Beitrage zum Verhalten von Waranen: die Ritualkampfe von *Varanus komodoensis* Ouwens, 1912 und *V. semiremex* Peters, 1869 sowie die Imponierphasen der Ritualkampfe von *V. timorensis timorensis* (Gray, 1831) und *V. t. similis* Mertens, 1958. *Salamandra* 21(2-3): 169-179.
Houston, T.F. (1978). *Dragon Lizards and Goannas of South Australia.* South Australian Museum, Adelaide. 84 pp.
King, M. and Horner, P. (1987). A new species of monitor (Platynota: Reptilia) from Northern Australia and a note on the status of *Varanus acanthurus insulanicus* Mertens. *The Beagle* (Records of the Northern Territory Museum of Arts and Sciences) 4(1): 73-79. [*Varanus baritji*]
Mertens, R. (1942). Die Familie der Warane (Varanidae). Erster teil: Allgemeines. *Abhandlungen der Senckenbergischen Naturforschenden Gesellschaft* 462: 1-116.
Mertens, R. (1942). Die Familie der Warane (Varanidae). Zweiter teil: der Schadel. *Abhandlungen der Senckenbergischen Naturforschenden Gesellschaft* 465: 117-234.
Mertens, R. (1942). Die Familie der Warane (Varanidae) Dritter teil: Taxonomie. *Abhandlungen der Senckenbergischen Naturforschenden Gesellschaft* 466: 235-391.
Mertens, R. (1958). Bemerkungen uber die Warane australiens. *Senckenbergiana Biologica* 39: 229-264.
Mertens, R. (1959). Liste der Warane asiens und der indo-australischen Inselwelt mit systematischen Bemerkungen. *Senckenbergiana Biologica* 40(5-6): 221-240.
Mertens, R. (1963). Liste der rezenten Amphibien und Reptilien Helodermatidae, Varanidae, Lanthanotidae. *Das Tierreich* 79: i-x + 1-26.
Moehn, L.D. (1984). Courtship and copulation in the Timor monitor, *Varanus timorensis*. *Herpetological Review* 15(1): 14-16.
Pengilley, R. (1981). Notes on the biology of *Varanus spenceri* and *Varanus gouldii*, Barkly Tablelands, Northern Territory. *Australian Journal of Herpetology* 1(1): 23-26.
Peters, U.W. (1986). Gelungene Aufzucht von *Varanus spenceri* (Lucas and Frost). *Das Aquarium* 20(205): 377-379.
Schmutz, E. and Horn, H.-G. (1986). Der Lebensraum von *Varanus (Odatria) t. timorensis* (Gray, 1831) (Sauria: Varanidae). *Salamandra* 22(2/3): 147-156.
Shea, G.M. and Reddacliff, G.L. (1986). Ossifications in the hemipenes of varanids. *Journal of Herpetology* 20(4): 566-568.
Shine, R. (1986). Food habits, habitats and reproductive biology of four sympatric species of varanid lizards in tropical Australia. *Herpetologica* 42(3): 346-360.
Smith, K.K. (1986). Morphology and function of the tongue and hyoid apparatus in *Varanus* (Varanidae, Lacertilia). *Journal of Morphology* 187: 261-287.
Storr, G.M. (1980). The monitor lizards (genus *Varanus* Merrem, 1820) of Western Australia. *Records of the Western Australian Museum* 8(2): 237-293.
Storr, G.M., Smith, L.A. and Johnstone, R.E. (1983). *Lizards of Western Australia. II. Dragons and Monitors.* Western Australian Museum, Perth. xiv + 114 pp.
Weavers, B.W. (1988). Vital statistics of the lace monitor lizard (*Varanus varius*) in south-eastern Australia. *Victorian Naturalist* 105(6): 142-145.

Family Scincidae

Banks, C.B. (1986 (1983)). Notes on growth of the major skink (*Egernia frerei*) in captivity. *Herpetofauna* 15(1): 5-6.
Banks, C.B. (1988). Captive breeding of three species of the Australian skink genus *Egernia*. pp. 105-118 *in* K.H. Peterson (ed.) *10th International Herpetological Symposium on Captive Propagation and Husbandry.* San Antonio, Texas. June 25-28, 1986. Zoological Consortium, Thurmont, Maryland.
Bartlett, R.D. (1984). Notes on the captive reproduction of the Australian skink, *Tiliqua nigrolutea*. *British Herpetological Society Bulletin* 10: 34-35.
Bennett, A.F. and John-Alder, H. (1986). Thermal relations of some Australian skinks (Sauria: Scincidae). *Copeia* 1986(1): 57-64.
Brown, G.W. (1986). The diet of *Pseudemoia spenceri* (Lucas and Frost, 1894) (Lacertilia: Scincidae), a species endemic to south-eastern Australia. *Victorian Naturalist* 103(2): 48-50.
Bull, C.M. (1987). A population study of the viviparous Australian lizard, *Trachydosaurus rugosus* (Scincidae). *Copeia* 1987(3): 749-757.

Bush, B. (1983). Notes on reproduction in captive *Menetia greyii* (Lacertilia: Scincidae). *Western Australian Naturalist* 15(6): 130-131.

Bustard, H.R. (1970). A population study of the scincid lizard *Egernia striolata* in northern New South Wales. *Proc. K. Ned. Akad. Wet.* (C)73(2): 186-213.

Canfield, P.J. and Shea, G.M. (1988). Morphological observations on the erythrocytes, leucocytes and thrombocytes of blue tongue lizards (Lacertilia: Scincidae: *Tiliqua*). Zentralblatt für Veterinarmedizin. C. *Anatomie, histologia, embryologia* 17: 328-342.

Choquenot, D. and Greer, A.E. (1989). Intrapopulational and interspecific variation in digital limb bones and presacral vertebrae of the genus *Hemiergis* (Lacertilia, Scincidae). *Journal of Herpetology* 23(3): 274-281.

Covacevich, J. (1984). A biogeographically significant new species of *Leiolopisma* (Scincidae) from north eastern Queensland. *Memoirs of the Queensland Museum* 21(2): 401-411. [*Leiolopisma jigurru*]

Czechura, G.V. (1981). The rare scincid lizard, *Nannoscincus graciloides*: a reappraisal. *Journal of Herpetology* 15(3): 315-320.

Czechura, G.V. (1986). Skinks of the *Ctenotus schevilli* species group. *Memoirs of the Queensland Museum* 22(2): 289-297. [*Ctenotus astarte*; *Ctenotus serotinus*]

Czechura, G.V. and Wombey, J. (1982). Three new striped skinks, (*Ctenotus*, Lacertilia, Scincidae) from Queensland. *Memoirs of the Queensland Museum* 20(3): 639-645. [*Ctenotus arcanus*; *Ctenotus eurydice*; *Ctenotus ingrami*]

Daniels, C.B. (1987). Aspects of the aquatic feeding ecology of the riparian skink *Sphenomorphus quoyii*. *Australian Journal of Zoology* 35(3): 253-258.

Daniels, C.B., Heatwole, H. and Oakes, N. (1987). Heating and cooling rates in air and during diving of the Australian water skink, *Sphenomorphus quoyii*. *Comparative Biochemistry and Physiology* 87A: 487-492.

Daniels, C.B., Heatwole, H. and Oakes, N. (1987). Physiological diving adaptations of the Australian water skink, *Sphenomorphus quoyii*. *Comparative Biochemistry and Physiology* 88A: 187-199.

de Vree, F. and Gans, C. (1987). Kinetic movements in the skull of adult *Trachydosaurus rugosus*. *Zentralblatt für Veterinarmedizin. C. Anatomie, histologia, embryologia* 16: 206-209.

Donnellan, S.C. and Hutchinson, M.N. (1990). Biochemical and morphological variation in the geographically widespread lizard *Leiolopisma entrecasteauxii* (Lacertilia: Scincidae). *Herpetologica* 46: 145-155.

Ehmann, H.F.W. (1983). The natural history and conservation status of the Adelaide pigmy bluetongue lizard *Tiliqua adelaidensis*. *Herpetofauna*, 14(1): 61-76.

Ehmann, H.F.W. (1987). The habitat, microhabitat and feeding behaviour of the rainforest skink *Coeranoscincus reticulatus*. *Herpetofauna* 17(2): 14.

Ehmann, H.F.W. (1988). Post-oviposition egg care in three Australian skink lizards. *Herpetofauna* 18(1): 26-29.

Ehmann, H.F.W. and Swan, G. (1987). Microsympatry, limb characteristics and tail colour in burrowing skinks of the genus *Anomalopus*. *Herpetofauna* 17(2): 25-27.

Fergusson, B. and Algar, D. (1986). Home range and activity patterns of pregnant female skinks, *Tiliqua rugosa*. *Australian Wildlife Research* 13: 287-294.

Gans, C., de Vree, F. and Carrier, D. (1985). Usage pattern of the complex masticatory muscles in the shingleback lizard, *Trachydosaurus rugosus*: a model for muscle placement. *American Journal of Anatomy* 173: 219-240.

Greer, A.E. (1970). A subfamilial classification of scincid lizards. *Bulletin of the Museum of Comparative Zoology, Harvard* 139(3): 151-183.

Greer, A.E. (1974). The generic relationships of the scincid lizard genus *Leiolopisma* and its relatives. *Australian Journal of Zoology, Supplementary Series* 31: 1-67.

Greer, A.E. (1979). A phylogenetic subdivision of Australian skinks. *Records of the Australian Museum* 32(8): 339-371.

Greer, A.E. (1979). A new species of *Lerista* (Lacertilia: Scincidae) from northern Queensland, with remarks on the origin of the genus. *Records of the Australian Museum* 32(10): 383-388. [*Lerista ameles*]

Greer, A.E. (1979). *Eremiascincus*, a new generic name for some Australian sand swimming skinks (Lacertilia: Scincidae). *Records of the Australian Museum* 32(7): 321-338.

Greer, A.E. (1980). A new species of *Morethia* (Lacertilia: Scincidae) from northern Australia, with comments on the biology and relationships of the genus. *Records of the Australian Museum* 33(2): 89-122.

Greer, A.E. (1982). A new species of *Leiolopisma* (Lacertilia : Scincidae) from Western Australia, with notes on the biology and relationships of other Australian species. *Records of the Australian Museum* 34(12): 549-573. [*Leiolopisma baudini*]

Greer, A.E. (1983). A new species of *Lerista* from Groote Eylandt and the Sir Edward Pellew group in northern Australia. *Journal of Herpetology* 17(1): 48-53. [*Lerista carpentariae*]

Greer, A.E. (1983). The Australian scincid lizard genus *Calyptotis* De Vis: resurrection of the name, description of four new species and discussion of relationships. *Records of the Australian Museum* 35: 29-59. [*Calyptotis lepidorostrum*; *Calyptotis ruficauda*; *Calyptotis temporalis*; *Calyptotis thorntonensis*]

Greer, A.E. (1985). A new species of *Sphenomorphus* from northeastern Queensland. *Journal of Herpetology* 19(4): 469-473. [*Sphenomorphus cracens*]

Greer, A.E. (1986). Diagnosis of the *Lerista bipes* species-group (Lacertilia: Scincidae), with a description of a new species and an updated diagnosis of the genus. *Records of the Western Australian Museum* 13(1): 121-127 [*Lerista praefrontalis*].

Greer, A.E. (1987). Limb reduction in the lizard genus *Lerista* 1. Variation in the number of phalanges and presacral vertebrae. *Journal of Herpetology* 21(4): 267-276.

Greer, A.E. and Cogger, H.G. (1985). Systematics of the reduce-limbed and limbless skinks currently assigned to the genus *Anomalopus* (Lacertilia: Scincidae). *Records of the Australian Museum* 37(1): 11-54.

Greer, A.E., McDonald, K.R. and Lawrie, B.C. (1983). Three new species of *Lerista* (Scincidae) from northern Queensland with a diagnosis of the *wilkinsi* species group. *Journal of Herpetology* 17(3): 247-255.

Hauschild, A. (1988). Bemerkungen zu Haltnung und Zucht des Schneckenskinks *Tiliqua gerrardii* (Gray, 1845) (Sauria: Scincidae). *Salamandra* 24(4): 248-257.

Horner, P. and King, M. (1986 (1985)). A new species of *Ctenotus* (Scincidae, Reptilia) from the Northern Territory. *The Beagle* (Occassional Papers of the Northern Territory Museum of Arts and Science) 2(1): 143-148 [*Ctenotus borealis*].

Hutchinson, M.N. and Donnellan, S.C. (1988). A new species of scincid lizard related to *Leiolopisma entrecasteauxii*, from southeastern Australia. *Transactions of the Royal Society of South Australia* 112: 143-151 [*Pseudemoia rawlinsoni*].

Hutchinson, M.N., Robertson, P. and Rawlinson, P.A. (1989). Redescription and ecology of the endemic Tasmanian scincid lizards *Leiolopisma microlepidotum* and *L. pretiosum*. *Papers and Proceedings of the Royal Society of Tasmania* 123: 257-274.

Hutchinson, M.N., Schwaner, T.D. and Medlock, K. (1988). A new species of scincid lizard (Lygosominae: *Leiolopisma*) from the highlands of Tasmania. *Proceedings of the Royal Society of Victoria* 100: 67-73 [*Pseudemoia orocrypta*].

Ingram, G.J. and Covacevich, J. (1989). Revision of the genus *Carlia* (Reptilia; Scincidae) in Australia with comments on *Carlia bicarinata* of New Guinea. *Memoirs of the Queensland Museum* 27(2): 443-490.

Ingram, G.J. and Covacevich, J. (1988). Revision of the genus

Lygisaurus De Vis (Scincidae: Reptilia) in Australia. *Memoirs of the Queensland Museum* 25(2): 335-354.
Joger, U., Wallikewitz, E. and Hauschild, A. (1986). Hormon-. und serochemische Untersuchungen zur Bestimmung des Geschlechtes und zur Uberprufung des Gesundheitszustands bei *Trachydosaurus rugosus* (Gray, 1827) (Sauria: Scincidae). *Salamandra* 22(1): 21-28.
John-Alder, H.B., Garland, T. and Bennett, A.F. (1986). Locomotory capacities, oxygen consumption, and the cost of locomotion of the shingle-back lizard (*Trachydosaurus rugosa*). *Physiological Zoology* 59(5): 523-531.
Joss, J.M.P. (1985). Ovarian steroid production in oviparous lizards of the genus *Lampropholis* (Scincidae). pp. 319-326 in G.C. Grigg, R. Shine and H.F.W. Ehmann (eds) *The Biology of Australasian Frogs and Reptiles*. Surrey Beatty and Sons with R. Zool. Soc. NSW, Sydney.
Joss, J.M.P. and Minard, J.A. (1985). On the reproductive cycles of *Lampropholis guichenoti* and *L. delicata* (Squamata: Scincidae) in the Sydney region. *Australian Journal of Zoology* 33(5): 699-704.
Kendrick, P.G. (1989). Two new species of *Lerista* (Lacertilia: Scincidae) from the Cape Range and Kennedy Range of Western Australia. *Journal of Herpetology* 23(4): 350-355 [*Lerista allochira; Lerista kennedyensis*].
King, M., Horner, P. and Fyfe, G. (1988). A new species of *Ctenotus* (Reptilia: Scincidae) from central Australia, and a key to the *Ctenotus leonhardii* species group. *The Beagle* (Records of the Northern Territory Museum of Arts and Science) 5(1): 147-153 [*Ctenotus septenarius*].
Milton, D.A. and Hughes, J.M. (1986). Habitat selection by two closely related skinks, *Egernia modesta* Storr and *Egernia whitii* Lacépède (Lacertilia : Scincidae). *Australian Wildlife Research* 13: 295-300.
Mitchell, F.J. (1950). The scincid genera *Egernia* and *Tiliqua* (Lacertilia). *Records of the South Australian Museum* 9(3): 275-308.
Mitchell, F.J. (1953). A brief revision of the four-fingered members of the genus *Leiolopisma* (Lacertilia). *Records of the South Australian Museum* 11(1): 75-90.
Mittleman, M.B. (1952). A generic synopsis of the lizards of the subfamily Lygosominae. *Smithsonian Miscellaneous Collections* 117(4096): 1-35.
Phillips, J.A. (1986). Ontogeny of metabolic processes in blue-tongued skinks, *Tiliqua scincoides*. *Herpetologica* 42(4): 405-412.
Rankin, P.R. (1979). A taxonomic revision of the genus *Menetia* (Lacertilia, Scincidae) in the Northern Territory. *Records of the Australian Museum* 32(14): 491-499.
Rounsevell, D., Brothers, N. and Holdsworth, M. (1985). The status and ecology of the Pedra Branca Skink *Pseudemoia palfreymani*. pp. 477-480 in G.C. Grigg, R. Shine and H.F.W. Ehmann (eds) *The Biology of Australasian Frogs and Reptiles*. Surrey Beatty and Sons with R. Zool. Soc. NSW, Sydney.
Sadlier, R.A. (1984). A new Australian scincid lizard, *Menetia concinna*, from the Alligator Rivers region, Northern Territory. *Records of the Australian Museum* 36: 45-49.
Sadlier, R.A. (1985). A new Australian scincid lizard, *Ctenotus coggeri*, from the Alligator Rivers region, Northern Territory. *Records of the Australian Museum* 36: 153-156.
Sadlier, R.A. (1990). The scincid lizard genus *Nannoscincus* Gunther: a revaluation. *Memoirs of the Queensland Museum* 29(2): 487-494.
Sadlier, R.A., Wombey, J.C. and Braithwaite, R.W. (1986 (1985)). *Ctenotus kurnbudj* and *Ctenotus gagudju*, two new lizards (Scincidae) from the Alligator Rivers Region of the Northern Territory. *The Beagle* (Occasional Papers of the Northern Territory Museum of Arts and Science 2(1): 95-103.
Shea, G.M. (1981). Notes on the reproductive biology of the eastern blue-tongue skink, *Tiliqua scincoides* (Shaw). *Herpetofauna* 12: 16-23.
Shea, G.M. (1987). Oviparity in *Leiolopisma jigurru* and a brief review of reproductive mode in *Leiolopisma*. *Herpetological Review* 18(2): 29-32.
Shea, G.M. (1989). Diet and reproductive biology of the Rottnest Island bobtail, *Tiliqua rugosa konowi* (Lacertilia, Scincidae). *Herpetological Journal* 1: 366-369.
Shea, G.M. (1990). The genera *Tiliqua* and *Cyclodomorphus* (Lacertilia: Scincidae): generic diagnoses and systematic relationships. *Memoirs of the Queensland Museum* 29(2): 495-519.
Shea, G. , Millgate, M. and Peck, S. (1987). A range extension for the rare skink *Anomalopus mackayi*. *Herpetofauna*, 17(2):16-19.
Shea, G.M. and Peterson, M. (1985). The Blue Mountains water skink, *Sphenomorphus leuraensis* (Lacertilia: Scincidae): a redescription, with notes on its natural history. *Proceedings of the Linnean Society of NSW* 108(2): 141-148.
Simbotwe, M.P. (1985). Sexual dimorphism and reproduction of *Lampropholis guichenoti* (Lacertilia: Scincidae). pp. 11-16 in G.C. Grigg, R. Shine and H.F.W. Ehmann (eds) *The Biology of Australasian Frogs and Reptiles*. Surrey Beatty and Sons with R. Zool. Soc. NSW, Sydney.
Smyth, M. (1972). The genus *Morethia* (Lacertilia, Scincidae) in South Australia. *Records of the South Australian Museum* 16(12): 1-14.
Storr, G.M. (1967). The genus *Sphenomorphus* (Lacertilia, Scincidae) in Western Australia and the Northern Territory. *Journal of the Royal Society of Western Australia* 50(1): 10-20.
Storr, G.M. (1968). Revision of the *Egernia whitei* species-group (Lacertilia, Scincidae). *Journal of the Royal Society of Western Australia* 51(2): 51-62.
Storr, G.M. (1969). The genus *Ctenotus* (Lacertilia, Scincidae) in the Northern Territory. *Journal of the Royal Society of Western Australia* 52(4): 97-108.
Storr, G.M. (1971). The genus *Ctenotus* (Lacertilia, Scincidae) in South Australia. *Records of the South Australian Museum* 16(6): 1-15.
Storr, G.M. (1971). The genus *Lerista* (Lacertilia, Scincidae) in Western Australia. *Journal of the Royal Society of Western Australia* 54(3): 59-75.
Storr, G.M. (1972). The genus *Morethia* (Lacertilia, Scincidae) in Western Australia. *Journal of the Royal Society of Western Australia* 55(3): 73-79.
Storr, G.M. (1974 (1973?)). The genus *Ctenotus* (Lacertilia, Scincidae) in the South-West and Eucla divisions of Western Australia. *Journal and Proceedings of the Royal Society of Western Australia* 56(3): 86-93.
Storr, G.M. (1974). The genus *Carlia* (Lacertilia, Scincidae) in Western Australia and Northern Territory. *Records of the Western Australian Museum* 3(2): 151-165.
Storr, G.M. (1975). The genus *Hemiergis* (Lacertilia, Scincidae) in Western Australia. *Records of the Western Australian Museum* 3(4): 251-260.
Storr, G.M. (1975). The genus *Ctenotus* (Lacertilia, Scincidae) in the Kimberley and North-West Divisions of Western Australia. *Records of the Western Australian Museum* 3(3): 209-243.
Storr, G.M. (1975). The genus *Proablepharus* (Scincidae, Lacertilia) in Western Australia. *Records of the Western Australian Museum* 3(4): 335-338.
Storr, G.M. (1976). Revisionary notes on the *Lerista* (Lacertilia, Scincidae) of Western Australia. *Records of the Western Australian Museum* 4(3): 241-256.
Storr, G.M. (1976). The genus *Menetia* (Lacertilia, Scincidae) in Western Australia. *Records of the Western Australian Museum* 4(2): 189-200.
Storr, G.M. (1976). The genus *Cryptoblepharus* (Lacertilia, Scincidae) in Western Australia. *Records of the Western Australian Museum* 4(1): 53-63.
Storr, G.M. (1976). The genus *Omolepida* (Lacertilia, Scincidae)

in Western Australia. *Records of the Western Australian Museum* 4(2): 163-170.
Storr, G.M. (1978). Notes on the *Ctenotus* (Lacertilia, Scincidae) of Queensland. *Records of the Western Australian Museum* 6(3): 319-332.
Storr, G.M. (1978). The genus *Egernia* (Lacertilia, Scincidae) in Western Australia. *Records of the Western Australian Museum* 6(2): 147-187.
Storr, G.M. (1980). The *Ctenotus grandis* species-group (Lacertilia: Scincidae). *Records of the Western Australian Museum* 8(3): 415-422.
Storr, G.M. (1982). Four new *Lerista* (Lacertilia: Scincidae) from Western and South Australia. *Records of the Western Australian Museum* 10(1): 1-9.
Storr, G.M. (1984). A new *Ctenotus* (Lacertilia: Scincidae) from Western Australia. *Records of the Western Australian Museum* 11(2): 191-193. [*Ctenotus zastictus*]
Storr, G.M.. (1983). Two new lizards from Western Australia (genera *Diplodactylus* and *Lerista*). *Records of the Western Australian Museum* 11(1): 59-62. [*Lerista haroldi*]
Storr, G.M. (1984). A new *Lerista* (Lacertilia: Scincidae) from Western Australia. *Records of the Western Australian Museum* 11(3): 287-290. [*Lerista simillima*]
Storr, G.M. (1984). Revision of the *Lerista nichollsi* complex (Lacertilia: Scincidae). *Records of the Western Australian Museum* 11(2): 109-118. [*Lerista onsloviana; Lerista uniduo*]
Storr, G.M. (1985). Revision of *Lerista frosti* and allied species (Lacertilia: Scincidae). *Records of the Western Australian Museum* 12(3): 307-316. [*Lerista chalybura; Lerista dorsalis; Lerista flammicauda*]
Storr, G.M. (1985). Two new skinks (Lacertilia: Scincidae) from Western Australia. *Records of the Western Australian Museum* 12(2): 193-196. [*Ctenotus ehmanni; Lerista stictopleura*]
Storr, G.M. (1986). A new species of *Lerista* (Lacertilia: Scincidae) with two subspecies from central Australia. *Records of the Western Australian Museum* 13(1): 145-149. [*Lerista aericeps; Lerista taeniata*]
Storr, G.M. (1986). Two new members of the *Lerista nichollsi* complex (Lacertilia: Scincidae). *Records of the Western Australian Museum* 13(1): 47-52. [*Lerista gascoynensis; Lerista varia*]
Storr, G.M. (1988). A new *Ctenotus* (Lacertilia: Scincidae) from Western Australia. *Records of the Western Australian Museum* 14(1): 139-140. [*Ctenotus angusticeps*]
Storr, G.M., Smith, L.A. and Johnstone, R.E. (1981). *Lizards of Western Australia. I. Skinks*. Univ. West. Aust. Press and West. Aust. Mus. Perth. 200 pp.
Taylor, J.A. (1985). Reproductive biology of the Australian lizard *Ctenotus taeniolatus*. *Herpetologica* 41(4): 408-418.
Taylor, J.A. (1986). Food and foraging behaviour of the lizard, *Ctenotus taeniolatus*. *Australian Journal of Ecology* 11: 49-54.
Taylor, J.A. (1986). Seasonal energy storage in the Australian lizard, *Ctenotus taeniolatus*. *Copeia* 1986(2): 445-453.
Webb, G.A. (1985). Habitat use and activity patterns in some southeastern Australian skinks. pp. 22-30 in G.C. Grigg, R. Shine and H.F.W. Ehmann (eds) *The Biology of Australasian Frogs and Reptiles*. Surrey Beatty and Sons with R. Zool. Soc. NSW, Sydney.
Wells, R.W. and Wellington, C.R. (1984). A synopsis of the class Reptilia in Australia. [1983 on title page]. *Aust. Journal of Herpetology* 1(3-4): 73-129. [*Egernia mcpheei; Eulamprus heatwolei; Eulamprus leuraensis*]
Wineski, L. and Gans, C. (1984). Morphological basis of the feeding mechanics in the shingle-back skink *Trachydosaurus rugosus* (Scincidae, Reptilia). *Journal of Morphology* 181: 271-295.

Snakes General

Boulenger, G.A. (1893). *Catalogue of Snakes in the British Museum (Natural History)*. British Museum, London. Vol. 1. xiii + 488 pp.
Boulenger, G.A. (1894). *Catalogue of Snakes in the British Museum (Natural History)*. British Museum, London. Vol. 2. xi + 382 pp.
Boulenger, G.A. (1896). *Catalogue of Snakes in the British Museum (Natural History)*. British Museum, London. Vol. 3. xiv + 727 pp.
Cadle, J.E. (1988). Phylogenetic relationships among advanced snakes: a molecular perspective. *University of California Publications in Zoology* 119: i-x, 1-77.
Campbell, C.H. (1976). *Snake bite, snake venoms and venomous snakes of Australia and New Guinea; an annotated bibliography*. School of Public Health and Tropical Medicine, University of Sydney, Service Publication 13: 1-222.
Cann, J. (1986). *Snakes Alive! Snake Experts & Antidote Sellers of Australia*. Kangaroo Press, Kenthurst. 176 pp.
Cogger, H.G. (1971). The venomous snakes of Australia and Melanesia. pp. 35-77 in W.Bucherl and E. Buckley (eds.) *Venomous Animals and Their Venoms; Venomous Vertebrates. II*. Academic Press, New York. Vol. 2.
Cogger, H.G. (1980). *Snakes*. Longman Cheshire, Melbourne
Covacevich, J. (1980). *Snakes of Brisbane*. Queensland Museum, Brisbane. 20 pp. (rev. edn).
Dessauer, H.C., Cadle, J.E. and Lawson, R. (1987). Patterns of snake evolution suggested by their proteins. *Fieldiana Zoology* n.s. 34: 1-34.
Glauert, L. (1950). *A Handbook of the Snakes of Western Australia*. Western Australian Naturalists' Club, Perth. 50 pp.
Glodek, G.S. and Voris, H.K. (1982). Marine snake diets: prey composition, diversity and overlap. *Copeia* 1982(3): 661-666.
Gow, G.F. (1982). *Australia's Dangerous Snakes*. Angus and Robertson, Sydney. 80 pp.
Gow, G.F. (1983). *Snakes of Australia*. Angus and Robertson, Sydney. 118 pp. (rev. ed.)
Gow, G.F. (1989). *Graeme Gow's Complete Guide to Australian Snakes*. Angus and Robertson, Sydney. 171 pp.
Haas, C.P.J. de (1950). Checklist of the snakes of the Indo-Australian Archipelago (Reptiles, Ophidia). *Treubia* 20: 511-625.
Hunt, R.A. (1947). A key to the identification of Australian snakes. *Victorian Naturalist* 64(8): 153-167.
Kinghorn, J.R. (1964). *The Snakes of Australia*. Sydney, Angus and Robertson. rev. edn. 197 pp.
Klemmer, K. (1963). Liste der rezenten Giftschlangen; Elapidae, Hydropheidae, Viperidae und Crotalidae. *in Die Giftschlangen der Erde* N.G. Elwert Universitats- und Verlagsbuchhandl., Marburg. pp. 253-464.
Kochva, E. (1987). The origin of snakes and evolution of the venom apparatus. *Toxicon* 25(1): 65-106.
Lemen, C.A. and Voris, H.K. (1981). A comparison of reproductive strategies among marine snakes. *Journal of Animal Ecology* 50: 89-101.
Mirtschin, P.J. and Davis, R. (1982). *Dangerous Snakes of Australia: an Illustrated Guide to Australia's Most Venomous Snakes*. Rigby, Adelaide. 207 pp.
Mitchell, F.J. (1961). *Harmless or Harmful*. South Australian Museum, Adelaide. 30 pp.
Parker, H.W. and Grandison, A.G.C. (1977). *Snakes: a natural history*. British Museum (Natural History) & Cornell University Press, London. 108 pp. 2nd rev. ed.
Smith, M.A. (1926). *Monograph on the Sea Snakes*. (Hydrophiidae). British Museum, London. xvii + 130 pp.
Storr, G.M., Smith, L.A. and Johnstone, R.E. (1986). *Snakes of Western Australia*. Western Australian Museum, Perth. ix + 187 pp.
Swan, G. (1990). *A Field Guide to the Snakes and Lizards of*

New South Wales. Three Sisters Productions, Winmalee, NSW. 224 pp.

Underwood, G.L. (1967). A Contribution to the Classification of Snakes. *British Museum (Natural History) Publications* 653: 1-179.

Webb, G.A. and Rose, A.B. (1986 (1984)). The food of some Australian snakes. *Herpetofauna* 16(1): 21-27.

Weigel, J. (1990). *The Australian Reptile Park's Guide to the Snakes of South-East Australia.* Australian Reptile Park, Gosford, NSW. 103 pp.

Family Typhlopidae

McDowell, S.B. (1974). A catalogue of the snakes of New Guinea and the Solomons, with special reference to those in the Bernice P. Bishop Museum, Part I. Scolecophidia. *Journal of Herpetology* 8(1): 1-57.

Storr, G.M. (1981). The genus *Ramphotyphlops* (Serpentes: Typhlopidae) in Western Australia. *Records of the Western Australian Museum* 9(3): 235-271.

Storr, G.M. (1983). A new *Ramphotyphlops* (Serpentes: Typhlopidae) from Western Australia. *Records of the Western Australian Museum* 10(4): 315-317. [*Ramphotyphlops howi*]

Storr, G.M. (1984). A new *Ramphotyphlops* (Serpentes: Typhlopidae) from central Australia. *Records of the Western Australian Museum* 11(3): 287-290. [*Ramphotyphlops centralis*]

Waite, E.R. (1918). Review of the Australian blind snakes. *Records of the South Australian Museum* 1: 1-34.

Family Boidae

Banks, C.B. and Schwaner, T.D. (1984). Two cases of interspecific hybridization among captive Australian boid snakes. *Zoo Biology* 3: 221-227.

Charles, N., Field, R. and Shine, R. (1985). Notes on the reproductive biology of Australian pythons, genera *Aspidites*, *Liasis* and *Morelia*. *Herpetological Review* 16(2): 45-48.

Harlow, P. and Grigg, G. (1984). Shivering thermogenesis in a brooding diamond python, *Python spilotes spilotes*. *Copeia* 1984(4): 959-965.

McDowell, S.B. (1975). A catalogue of the snakes of New Guinea and the Solomons, with special reference to those in the Bernice P. Bishop Museum. Part II. Anilioidea and Pythoninae. *Journal of Herpetology* 9(1): 1-79.

Slip, D.J. and Shine, R. (1988). The reproductive biology and mating system of diamond pythons, *Morelia spilota* (Serpentes: Boidae). *Herpetologica* 44(4): 396-404.

Slip, D.J. and Shine, R. (1988). Thermoregulation of free-ranging diamond pythons, *Morelia spilota* (Serpentes, Boidae). *Copeia* 1988(4): 984-995.

Slip, D.J. and Shine, R. (1988). Habitat use, movement and activity patterns of free-ranging diamond pythons, *Morelia s. spilota* (Serpentes: Boidae): a radiotelemetric study. *Australian Wildlife Research* 15: 515-531.

Slip, D.J. and Shine, R. (1988). Thermophilic response to feeding of the diamond python, *Morelia s. spilota* (Serpentes: Boidae). *Comparative Biochemistry and Physiology* 89A(4): 645-650.

Slip, D.J. and Shine, R. (1988). Reptilian endothermy: a field study of thermoregulation by brooding diamond pythons. *Journal of Zoology* 216: 367-378.

Slip, D.J. and Shine, R. (1988). Habitat use, movement and activity patterns of free-ranging diamond pythons, *Morelia s. spilota* (Serpentes: Boidae): a radiotelemetric study. *Australian Wildlife Research* 15: 515-531.

Smith, L.A. (1981). A revision of the *Liasis olivaceus* species-group (Serpentes: Boidae) in Western Australia. *Records of the Western Australian Museum* 9(2): 227-233.

Smith, L.A. (1981). A revision of the python genera *Aspidites* and *Python* (Serpentes: Boidae) in Western Australia. *Records of the Western Australian Museum* 9(2): 211-226.

Smith, L.A. (1985). A revision of the *Liasis childreni* species-group (Serpentes: Boidae). *Records of the Western Australian Museum* 12(3): 257-276.

Stafford, P.J. (1986). *Pythons and Boas.* T.F.H. Publications, Neptune City. 192 pp.

Stimson, A.F. (1969). Liste der Rezenten Amphibien und Reptilien. Boidae. *Das Tierreich* 89: 1-49.

Underwood, G. and Stimson, A.F. (1990). A classification of pythons (Serpentes, Pythoninae). *Journal of Zoology* 221:565-603.

Worrell, E. (1951). Classification of Australian Boidae. *Proceedings of the Royal Zoological Society of NSW* 1949-50: 20-25.

Family Acrochordidae

Lillywhite, H.B., Smits, A.W. and Feder, M.E. (1988). Body fluid volumes in the aquatic snake, *Acrochordus granulatus*. *Journal of Herpetology* 22(4): 434-438.

McDowell, S.B. (1979). A catalogue of the snakes of New Guinea and the Solomons, with special reference to those in the Bernice P. Bishop Museum. Part III. Boinae and Acrochordoidea (Reptilia, Serpentes). *Journal of Herpetology* 13(1): 1-92.

Shine, R. (1986). Ecology of a low-energy specialist: food habits and reproductive biology of the Arafura filesnake (Acrochordidae). *Copeia* 1986(2): 424-437.

Shine, R. (1986). Sexual differences in morphology and niche utilization in an aquatic snake, *Acrochordus arafurae*. *Oecologia* 69: 260-267.

Shine, R. and Lambeck, R. (1985). A radiotelemetric study of movements, thermoregulation and habitat utilization of Arafura filesnakes (Serpentes: Acrochordidae). *Herpetologica* 41(3): 351-361.

Family Colubridae

Greene, H.W. (1989). Ecological, evolutionary, and conservation implications of feeding biology in Old World cat snakes, genus *Boiga* (Colubridae). *Proceedings of the California Academy of Sciences* 46(8): 193-207.

Ko Ko Gyi (1970). A revision of colubrid snakes of the sub-family Homalopsinae. University of Kansas. Kans. Publs Mus. Nat. Hist. 20(2): 44-223.

Malnate, E.V. and Underwood, G. (1988). Australasian natricine snakes of the genus *Tropidonophis*. Proceedings. *Academy of Natural Sciences of Philadelphia* 140(1): 59-201.

McDowell, S.B. (1972). The species of *Stegonotus* (Serpentes, Colubridae) in Papua New Guinea. *Zoologische Mededelingen (Leiden)* 47(2): 6-26.

Family Elapidae

Banks, C.B. (1983). Reproduction in two species of captive brown snakes, genus *Pseudonaja*. *Herpetological Review* 14(3): 77-79.

Banks, C.B. (1985). Observations on feeding and sloughing in a collection of captive snakes. pp. 495-501 *in* G.C. Grigg, R. Shine and H.F.W. Ehmann (eds.), *The Biology of Australasian Frogs and Reptiles.* Surrey Beatty and Sons with R. Zool. Soc. NSW, Sydney.

Barnett, B. and Schwaner, T.D. (1985). Growth in captive born tiger snakes (*Notechis ater serventyi*) from Chappell Island: implications for field and laboratory studies. *Transactions of the Royal Society of South Australia* 109(2): 31-36.

Baverstock, P.R. and Schwaner, T.D. (1985). Phylogeny of Australian elapid snakes: the genetic approach. pp. 159-164 *in* G.C. Grigg, R. Shine and H.F.W. Ehmann (eds.), *The Biology of Australasian Frogs and Reptiles.* Surrey Beatty and Sons with R. Zool. Soc. NSW, Sydney.

Cogger, H.G. (1987). The venomous land snakes. pp. 340-355 in J. Covacevich, P. Davie and J. Pearn (eds) *Toxic Plants and*

Animals; a guide for Australia. Queensland Museum, Brisbane.
Covacevich, J. (1987). Two taipans! pp. 480-485 in J. Covacevich, P. Davie and J. Pearn (eds) *Toxic Plants and Animals; a guide for Australia*. Queensland Museum, Brisbane.
Coventry, A.J. and Rawlinson, P.A. (1980). Taxonomic revision of the elapid snake genus *Drysdalia* Worrell 1961. *Memoirs of the National Museum of Victoria* 41: 65-78.
Fitzgerald, M. and Mengden, G.A. (1987). Captive breeding and oviparity in *Pseudechis butleri* (Serpentes: Elapidae). *Amphibia-Reptilia* 8: 165-170.
Hutchinson, M.N. (1990). The generic classification of the Australian terrestrial elapid snakes. *Memoirs of the Queensland Museum* 29(2): 397-405.
Johnston, G.R. (1987). Reproduction and growth in captive death adders *Acanthophis antarcticus* (Squamata: Elapidae). *Transactions of the Royal Society of South Australia* 111(2): 123-125.
Longmore, R. (ed.) (1986). *Atlas of Elapid Snakes of Australia*. Aust. Govt Publ. Service, Canberra. v + 115 pp.
Marshall, L.R. (1985). Positive cross reactivity of bardick snake (*Notechis curtus*) venom with death adder (*Acanthophis antarcticus*) antivenom and negative reactivity with tiger (*Notechis scutatus*) antivenom. *Copeia* 1985(1): 257-259.
Marshall, L.R. and Herrman, R.P. (1983). Coagulent and anticoagulant actions of Australian snake venoms. *Thrombosis and Haemostasis* 1983; 50: 707-711.
McDowell, S.B. (1967). *Aspidomorphus*, a genus of New Guinea snakes of the family Elapidae, with notes on related genera. *Journal of Zoology* 151: 497-543.
McDowell, S.B. (1969). *Toxicocalamus*, a New Guinea genus of snakes of the family Elapidae. *Journal of Zoology* 159: 443-511.
Mendgen, G.A. (1985). A chromosomal and electrophoretic analysis of the genus *Pseudonaja*. pp. 193-208 in G.C. Grigg, R. Shine and H.F.W. Ehmann (eds.) *The Biology of Australasian Frogs and Reptiles*. Surrey Beatty and Sons with R. Zool. Soc. NSW, Sydney.
Mengden, G.A. (1983). The taxonomy of Australian elapid snakes: a review. *Records of the Australian Museum*, 35:195-222.
Mengden, G.A. (1985). Australian elapid phylogeny: a summary of the chromosomal and electrophoretic data. pp. 185-192 in G.C. Grigg, R. Shine and H.F.W. Ehmann (eds.) *The Biology of Australasian Frogs and Reptiles*. Surrey Beatty and Sons with R. Zool. Soc. NSW, Sydney.
Mengden, G.A. and Fitzgerald, M. (1987). The paradoxical brown snakes. pp. 458-469 in J. Covacevich, P. Davie and J. Pearn (eds) *Toxic Plants and Animals; a guide for Australia*. Queensland Museum, Brisbane.
Mengden, G.A., Shine, R. and Moritz, C. (1986). Phylogenetic relationships within the Australasian venomous snakes of the genus *Pseudechis*. *Herpetologica* 42(2): 215-229.
Mirtschin, P.J. (1985). An overview of captive breeding of Common Death Adders, *Acanthophis antarcticus* (Shaw) and its role in conservation. pp. 505-509 in G.C. Grigg, R. Shine and H.F.W. Ehmann (eds.) *The Biology of Australasian Frogs and Reptiles*. Surrey Beatty and Sons with R. Zool. Soc. NSW, Sydney.
Morrison, J.J., Masci, P.P., Bennett, E.A., Gauci, M., Pearn, J., Whitaker, A.N. and Korschenko, L.P. (1987). Studies of the venom and clinical features of the Australian rough-scaled snake (*Tropidechis carinatus*). pp. 220-233 in P. Gopalakrishnakone and C.K. Tan (eds) *Progress in Venom and Toxin Research*. Proceedings of the First Venom and Toxin Research Group, National University of Singapore.
Morrison, J.J., Tesseraux, I., Pearn, J.H., Harris, J. and Masci, P.P. (1984). Venom of the Australian rough-scaled snake, *Tropidechis carinatus*: lethal potency and electrophysiological actions. *Toxicon* 22(5): 759-765.
Orange, P. (1986 (1983)). Observations on the mating of the bardick, *Notechis curtus*, in captivity. *Herpetofauna* 15(1): 24-25.
Pearn, J.H. (1987). The rough-scaled snake (*Tropidechis carinatus*). pp. 470-479 in J. Covacevich, P. Davie and J. Pearn (eds) *Toxic Plants and Animals; a guide for Australia*. Queensland Museum, Brisbane.
Pollitt, C.C. (1985). Australian snake venom toxicology. 23 pp. in *Intensive Care and Anaesthetic Management*. Univ. Qld Post-Grad. Vet. Sci. Committee, St. Lucia
Rowan, E.G., Harvey, A.L., Takasaki, C. and Tamiya, N. (1989). Neuromuscular effects of three phospholipases A_2 from the venom of the Australian king brown snake *Pseudechis australis*. *Toxicon* 27(5): 551-560.
Scanlon, J. and Shine, R. (1988). Dentition and diet in snakes: adaptations to oophagy in the Australian elapid genus *Simoselaps*. *Journal of Zoology* 216: 519-528.
Schmidt, J.J. and Middlebrook, J.L. (1989). Purification, sequencing and characterization of pseudexin phospholipases A_2 from *Pseudechis porphyriacus* (Australian red-bellied black snake). *Toxicon* 27(7): 805-818.
Schwaner, T.D (1985). Population structure of Black Tiger Snakes, *Notechis ater niger*, on offshore islands of South Australia. pp. 35-46 in G.C. Grigg, R. Shine and H.F.W. Ehmann (eds) *The Biology of Australasian Frogs and Reptiles*. Surrey Beatty and Sons with R. Zool. Soc. NSW, Sydney.
Schwaner, T.D. and Sarre, S.D. (1988). Body size of tiger snakes in southern Australia, with particular reference to *Notechis ater serventyi* (Elapidae) on Chappell Island. *Journal of Herpetology* 22(1): 24-33.
Schwaner, T.D., Baverstock, P.R., Dessauer, H.G. and Mengden, G.A. (1985). Immunological evidence for the phylogenetic relationships of Australian elapid snakes. pp. 177-184 in G.C. Grigg, R. Shine and H.F.W. Ehmann (eds) *The Biology of Australasian Frogs and Reptiles*. Surrey Beatty and Sons with R. Zool. Soc. NSW, Sydney.
Shine, R. (1983). Arboreality in snakes: ecology of the Australian elapid genus *Hoplocephalus*. *Copeia* 1983(1): 198-205.
Shine, R. (1983). Food habits and reproductive biology of Australian elapid snakes of the genus *Denisonia*. *Journal of Herpetology* 17(2): 171-175.
Shine, R. (1984). Ecology of small fossorial Australian snakes of the genera *Neelaps* and *Simoselaps* (Serpentes, Elapidae). pp. 173-183 in R.A. Seigel, L.E. Hunt, J.L. Knight, L. Malaret and N.L. Zuschlag (eds) *Vertebrate Ecology and Systematics — a Tribute to Henry S. Fitch*. Museum of Natural History, University of Kansas, Lawrence.
Shine, R. (1984). Reproductive biology and food habits of the Australian elapid snakes of the genus *Cryptophis*. *Journal of Herpetology* 18: 33-39.
Shine, R. (1985). Ecological evidence on the phylogeny of Australian elapid snakes. pp. 255-260 in G.C. Grigg, R. Shine and H.F.W. Ehmann (eds) *The Biology of Australasian Frogs and Reptiles*. Surrey Beatty and Sons with R. Zool. Soc. NSW, Sydney.
Shine, R. (1986). Natural history of the small elapid snakes *Elapognathus* and *Rhinoplocephalus* in southwestern Australia. *Journal of Herpetology* 20: 436-439.
Shine, R. (1987). Ecological ramifications of prey size: food habits and reproductive biology of Australian copperhead snakes (*Austrelaps*, Elapidae). *Journal of Herpetology* 21(1): 21-28.
Shine, R. (1987). Ecological comparisons of island and mainland populations of Australian tigersnakes (*Notechis*: Elapidae). *Herpetologica* 43(2): 233-240.
Shine, R. (1987). Food habits and reproductive biology of Australian snakes of the genus *Hemiaspis* (Elapidae). *Journal of Herpetology* 21(1): 71-74.
Shine, R. (1987). Intraspecific variation in thermoregulation, movements and habitat use by Australian blacksnakes,

Pseudechis porphyriacus (Elapidae). *Journal of Herpetology* 21(3): 167-177.
Shine, R. (1987). Reproductive mode may determine geographic distributions in Australian venomous snakes (*Pseudechis*, Elapidae). *Oecologia* 71: 608-612.
Shine, R. (1987). The evolution of viviparity: ecological correlates of reproductive mode within a genus of Australian snakes (*Pseudechis*, Elapidae). *Copeia* 1987(3): 551-563.
Shine, R. (1988). Food habits and reproductive biology of small Australian snakes of the genera *Unechis* and *Suta* (Elapidae). *Journal of Herpetology* 22(3): 307-315.
Shine, R. (1989). Constraints, allometry, and adaptation: food habits and reproductive biology of Australian brownsnakes (*Pseudonaja*: Elapidae). *Herpetologica* 45(2): 195-207.
Shine, R. and Covacevich, J. (1983). Ecology of highly venomous snakes: the Australian genus *Oxyuranus* (Elapidae). *Journal of Herpetology* 17(1): 60-69.
Shine, R. and Fitzgerald, M. (1989). Conservation and reproduction of an endangered species: the broad-headed snake, *Hoplocephalus bungaroides* (Elapidae). *Australian Zoologist* 25: 65-68.
Shine, R. and Schwaner, T.D. (1985). Prey constriction by venomous snakes: a review, and new data on Australian species. *Copeia* 1985(4): 1067-1071.
Smith, L.A. (1980). Taxonomy of *Denisonia punctata* and *Denisonia fasciata* (Serpentes: Elapidae). *Records of the Western Australian Museum* 8(2): 327-333.
Storr, G.M. (1968 (1967)). The genus *Vermicella* (Serpentes, Elapidae) in Western Australia and the Northern Territory. *Journal of the Royal Society of Western Australia* 50(3): 80-92.
Storr, G.M. (1978). Whip snakes (*Demansia*, Elapidae) of Western Australia. *Records of the Western Australian Museum* 6(3): 287-301.
Storr, G.M. (1979). *Dangerous Snakes of Western Australia.* Perth, Western Australian Museum Press, 3rd ed.
Storr, G.M. (1980 (1979)). Revisionary notes on the genus *Vermicella* (Serpentes, Elapidae). *Records of the Western Australian Museum* 8(1): 75-79.
Storr, G.M. (1981). The genus *Furina* (Serpentes: Elapidae) in Western Australia. *Records of the Western Australian Museum* 9(2): 119-123.
Storr, G.M. (1981). The *Denisonia gouldii* species-group (Serpentes, Elapidae) in Western Australia. *Records of the Western Australian Museum* 8(4): 501-515.
Storr, G.M. (1981). The genus *Acanthophis* (Serpentes: Elapidae) in Western Australia. *Records of the Western Australian Museum* 9(2): 203-210.
Storr, G.M. (1984). Revision of *Denisonia suta* (Serpentes: Elapidae) and the description of a new species closely related to it. *Records of the Western Australian Museum* 11(3): 249-257. [*Suta ordensis*]
Storr, G.M. (1988). A new *Rhinoplocephalus* (Serpentes: Elapidae) from Western Australia. *Records of the Western Australian Museum* 14(1): 137-138.
Tamiya, N. (1985). A comparison of amino acid sequences of neurotoxins and of phospholipases of some Australian elapid snakes with those of other proteroglyphous snakes. pp. 209-219 in G.C. Grigg, R. Shine and H.F.W. Ehmann (eds) *The Biology of Australasian Frogs and Reptiles.* Surrey Beatty and Sons with R. Zool. Soc. NSW, Sydney.
Wallach, V. (1985). A cladistic analysis of the terrestrial Australian Elapidae. pp. 223-253 in G.C. Grigg, R. Shine and H.F.W. Ehmann (eds) *The Biology of Australasian Frogs and Reptiles.* Surrey Beatty and Sons with R. Zool. Soc. NSW, Sydney.
White, J. (1987). Elapid snakes: venom toxicity and actions. pp. 368-389 in J. Covacevioh, P. Davie and J. Pearn (eds) *Toxic Plants and Animals; a guide for Australia.* Queensland Museum, Brisbane.
White, J. (1987). Elapid snakes: venom production and bite mechanism. pp. 356-367 in J. Covacevich, P. Davie and J. Pearn (eds) *Toxic Plants and Animals: a guide for Australia.* Queensland Museum, Brisbane.
White, J. (1987). Elapid snakes: aspects of envenomation. pp. 390-429 in J. Covacevich, P. Davie and J. Pearn (eds) *Toxic Plants and Animals; a guide for Australia.* Queensland Museum, Brisbane.
White, J. (1987). Elapid snakes: management of bites. pp. 430-457 in J. Covacevich, P. Davie and J. Pearn (eds) *Toxic Plants and Animals; a guide for Australia.* Queensland Museum, Brisbane.
Williams, V., White, J., Schwaner, T.D. and Sparrow, A. (1988). Variation in venom proteins from isolated populations of tiger snakes (*Notechis ater niger*, *N. scutatus*) in South Australia. *Toxicon* 26(11): 1067-1075.

Family Hydrophiidae

Burns, G.W. (1985). The female reproductive cycle of the olive sea snake, *Aipysurus laevis* (Hydrophiidae). pp. 339-341 in G.C. Grigg, R. Shine and H.F.W. Ehmann (eds.) *The Biology of Australasian Frogs and Reptiles.* Surrey Beatty and Sons with Royal Zoological Society of NSW, Sydney.
Cogger, H.G. (1975). The sea snakes of Australia and New Guinea. pp. 59-139 in W.Dunson (ed.) *The Biology of Sea Snakes.* University Park Press, Baltimore.
Dunson, W.A. (1975). Adaptations of sea snakes. pp. 3-19 in W. Dunson (ed.) *The Biology of Sea Snakes.* University Park Press, Baltimore.
Heatwole, H. (1987). *Sea Snakes.* New South Wales University Press, Kensington, with the Australian Institute of Biology. pp. i-viii, 1-85.
Kharin, V.E. (1983). A new species of the genus *Hydrophis sensu lato* (Serpentes, Hydrophiidae) from the north Australian shelf. *Zoologicheskii Zhurnal* 62(11): 1751-1753 [*Hydrophis mcdowelli*].
Kharin, V.E. (1984). A review of sea snakes of the group *Hydrophis sensu lato* (Serpentes, Hydrophiidae). 3. The genus *Leioselasma*. *Zoologicheskii Zhurnal*. 63(10): 1535-1546 [*Hydrophis coggeri; Hydrophis czeblukovi*].
Kharin, V.E. (1984). Sea snakes of the genus *Hydrophis* sensu lato (Serpentes, Hydrophiidae). On taxonomic status of the New Guinea *H. obscurus. Zoologicheskii Zhurnal* 63(4): 630-632 [*Hydrophis vorisi*].
Kharin, V.E. (1985). A new species of sea snakes of the genus *Enhydrina* (Serpentes, Hydrophiidae) from waters of New Guinea. *Zoologicheskii Zhurnal* 64(5): 785-787.
Limpus, C.J. (1978). The venom apparatus and venom yields of subtropical Queensland Hydrophiidae. pp. 39-70 in P. Rosenberg (ed.) *Toxins: Animal, Plant and Microbial; Proceedings of the 5th International Symposium.* Pergamon Press, London.
McCarthy, C.J. (1987). Adaptations of sea snakes that eat fish eggs; with a note on the throat musculature of *Aipysurus eydouxi* (Gray, 1849). *Journal of Natural History* 21: 1119-1128.
McDowell, S.B. (1969). Notes on the Australian sea-snake *Ephalophis greyi* M. Smith (Serpentes, Elapidae, Hydrophiinae) and the origin and classification of sea-snakes. *Zoological Journal of the Linnean Society* 48: 333-349.
McDowell, S.B. (1972). The genera of sea snakes of the *Hydrophis* group (Serpentes: Elapidae). *Transactions of the Zoological Society of London* 32: 195-247.
Smith, L.A. (1986). A new species of *Hydrophis* (Serpentes: Hydrophiidae) from north-west Australian waters. *Records of the Western Australian Museum* 13(1): 151-153.
Voris, H.K. and Jayne, B.C. (1979). Growth, reproduction and population structure of a marine snake, *Enhydrina schistosa* (Hydrophiidae). *Copeia* 1979: 307-318.

Family Laticaudidae

Cogger, H.G., Heatwole, H., Ishikawa, Y., McCoy, M., Tamiya, N. and Teruuchi, T. (1987). The status and natural history of the Rennell Island sea krait, *Laticauda crockeri* (Serpentes: Laticaudidae). *Journal of Herpetology* 21(4): 255-266.
Kharin, V.E. (1984). [Revision of sea snakes of subfamily Laticaudinae Cope, 1879 *sensu lato* (Serpentes, Hydrophiidae.)] Transactions of the Zoological Institute of the Academy of *Sciences of the USSR* 124: 128-139.
McCarthy, C.J. (1986). Relationships of the laticaudine sea snakes (Serpentes: Elapidae: Laticaudinae). Bulletin of the British Museum (Natural History) (Zoology) 50(2): 127-161.

Index

Note: an asterisk (*) following the page reference to a scientific name indicates that the species' description is accompanied by a photographic illustration, which will be found either with the description on the page indicated, or within a page or two on either side of the description.

aberrans, Diplodactylus ciliaris 217
Acalyptophis 698
Acalyptophis peronii 698*
Acanthophis 632
Acanthophis antarcticus 632*
Acanthophis praelongus 634*
Acanthophis pyrrhus 634*
acanthurus, Varanus 359*
acanthurus, Varanus acanthurus 361
Aclys 278
Aclys concinna 278*
Aclys concinna concinna 278
Aclys concinna major 278
acripes, Ctenotus pantherinus 436
ACROCHORDIDAE 615
Acrochordus 615
Acrochordus arafurae 615*
Acrochordus granulatus 616*
acutirostris, Taudactylus 105*
adelaidensis, Litoria 127*
adelaidensis, Morethia 546*
adelaidensis, Tiliqua 576
adelaidensis, Tympanocryptis 351*
adelaidensis, Tympanocryptis adelaidensis 352
Adelotus 55
Adelotus brevis 55*
adelphe, Sphenophryne 165*
adonis, Lampropholis 736
aeratus, Lygisaurus 538
aericeps, Lerista 512*
aethiops, Egernia stokesii 472
affinis, Pseudonaja 670*
affinis, Pseudonaja affinis 670
affinis, Ramphotyphlops 589
AGAMIDAE 298
Agamids 203
agassizii, Chelonia mydas 181
Aipysurus 699
Aipysurus apraefrontalis 701*
Aipysurus duboisii 701*
Aipysurus eydouxii 702*
Aipysurus foliosquama 702*
Aipysurus fuscus 702*
Aipysurus laevis 703*
Aipysurus laevis laevis 704
Aipysurus laevis pooleorum 704
Aipysurus tenuis 704
alacer, Ctenotus 412*
alanae, Menetia 542*
alba, Geocrinia 733
albertisii, Liasis 605*
albilabris, Diporiphora 328*
albipes, Neobatrachus 733
albofasciolatus, Eugongylus 480
alboguttata, Litoria 128*
alboguttatus, Diplodactylus 214*
albopunctatus, Heleioporus 70*
allanae, Lerista 512*
alleni, Ctenotus 412*
allochira, Lerista 512*
allotropis, Ctenotus 413*
alpina, Litoria verreauxii 157
amaura, Menetia 542
amax, Carlia 392
ameles, Lerista 512*
amethistina, Morelia 611*
amicula, Lampropholis 505*
ammodytes, Ramphotyphlops diversus 592
amphiboluroides, Caimanops 303*
Amphibolurus 300
Amphibolurus muricatus 301*
Amphibolurus nobbi 301*
Amphibolurus nobbi coggeri 302
Amphibolurus nobbi nobbi 302
Amphibolurus norrisi 302*
amplus, Eulamprus 482*
angusticeps, Ctenotus 413
annulata, Vermicella 696*
annulatus, Emydocephalus 708*
Anomalopus 382
Anomalopus brevicollis 383*
Anomalopus gowi 384*
Anomalopus leuckartii 384*
Anomalopus mackayi 385*
Anomalopus pluto 385*
Anomalopus swansoni 385*
Anomalopus verreauxii 386*
anomalus, Simoselaps 682*
antarcticus, Acanthophis 632*
apoda, Lerista 513
approximans, Simoselaps 682*
apraefrontalis, Aipysurus 701*
Aprasia 278
Aprasia aurita 279
Aprasia haroldi 279*
Aprasia inaurita 280*
Aprasia parapulchella 281*
Aprasia pseudopulchella 281*
Aprasia pulchella 281*
Aprasia repens 282*
Aprasia rostrata 282
Aprasia rostrata fusca 282
Aprasia rostrata rostrata 282
Aprasia smithi 282
Aprasia striolata 283*
aquilonius, Neobatrachus 87*
arafurae, Acrochordus 615*
arcanus, Ctenotus 413*
arenicola, Lerista microtis 526, 737
arenicola, Uperoleia 109
Arenophryne 56
Arenophryne rotunda 56*
ariadnae, Ctenotus 414*
arnhemensis, Ctenotus 415*
arnhemensis, Egernia 735
arnhemica, Diporiphora bennettii 329
arnhemicus, Glaphyromorphus darwiniensis 492
asper, Nephrurus 24*
asper, Trachydosaurus rugosus 584
aspera, Uperoleia 109
Aspidites 601
Aspidites melanocephalus 601*
Aspidites ramsayi 602*
Assa 57
Assa darlingtoni 57*
assimilis, Diplodactylus 214*
astarte, Ctenotus 415*
Astrotia 705
Astrotia stokesii 706*
ater, Notechis 659*
ater, Notechis ater 659
atlas, Ctenotus 415*
atra, Demansia 639*
atriceps, Echiopsis 649
atriceps, Hydrophis 714
atrocostata, Emoia 476, 728*
aurea, Litoria 128*
aurita, Aprasia 279
aurita, Cryptagama 307*
australiacus, Heleioporus 70*
australis, Ctenotus 416*
australis, Cyclorana 117*
australis, Delma 286*
australis, Diporiphora 329*
australis, Gehyra 236*
australis, Pseudechis 664*
australis, Pseudophryne 98*
australis, Pseudothecadactylus 271*
australis, Ramphotyphlops 589*
australis, Simoselaps 682*
Austrelaps 635
Austrelaps superbus 635*
axillaris, Lerista 737

badia, Egernia stokesii 472
badius, Ctenophorus maculatus 318
balbus, Mixophyes 83
baliola, Gehyra 236*
Bandy-Bandy 696
Northern 696
barbata, Pogona 347*
Bardick 649
baritji, Varanus 361*
barnardi, Furina 651*
barroni, Liasis olivaceus 608
Bartleia 735
Bartleia jigurru 735, 563
barycragus, Heleioporus 70*
basiliscus, Saproscincus 573
Bassiana 735
Bassiana duperreyi 735, 561*
Bassiana platynota 735, 567
Bassiana trilineata 735, 571
baudini, Pseudemoia 561
baynesi, Lerista picturata 529
belcheri, Hydrophis 714
bennettii, Diporiphora 329*
bennettii, Diporiphora bennettii 329
bennettii, Notaden 92*
bertholdi, Simoselaps 683*
bibronii, Pseudophryne 99*
bicolor, Litoria 129*
bicolor, Rhinoplocephalus 676*
bilineata, Diporiphora 330*
bilingua, Crinia 58*
bimaculatus, Simoselaps 684*
binoei, Heteronotia 248*
bipes, Lerista 513*
bitorquatus, Hoplocephalus 657*
bituberculatus, Ramphotyphlops 589*
Blind Snakes (see also Ramphotyphlops) 587
Blind Snakes (see Typhlopidae) 585
Blue-tongued Lizards (see Lizard) 576
Bockadam 619
BOIDAE 60
Boiga 617
Boiga irregularis 618*
bombiens, Cophixalus 160*
booroolongensis, Litoria 129*
borea, Delma 286*
borealis, Ctenotus 416
borealis, Lerista 514*
borealis, Uperoleia 109

borroloola, Gehyra 237*
bos, Egernia multiscutata 469
boschmai, Rhinoplocephalus 677*
bougainvillii, Lerista 514*
boulengeri, Morethia 546*
bowringii, Lygosoma 730*
boydii, Hypsilurus 337*
brachyonyx, Ctenotus 417*
brachysoma, Eulamprus tenuis 488
brachyurus, Varanus acanthurus 361
braminus, Ramphotyphlops 589, 731*
branchialis, Cyclodomorphus 452*
bredli, Morelia 611*
brevicauda, Varanus 361*
brevicollis, Anomalopus 383*
brevipalmata, Litoria 130*
brevipes, Ctenotus essingtoni 423
brevipes, Cyclorana 118*
brevis, Adelotus 55*
brongersmai, Glaphyromorphus 491
brongersmai, Tropidonophis mairii 628
brookeri, Hemiergis initialis 501
brooksi, Ctenotus 417*
brooksi, Ctenotus brooksi 418
broomi, Ramphotyphlops 591
brunnea, Chelosania 305*
Bufo 169
Bufo marinus 169*
BUFONIDAE 169
bungaroides, Hoplocephalus 658*
bunglebungle, Lerista 737
burbidgei, Ctenotus mastigura 434
burrowsae, Litoria 131*
burtonis, Lialis 294*
bushi, Suta spectabilis 693
butleri, Delma 286*
butleri, Morethia 547*
butleri, Notoscincus 553
butleri, Tympanocryptis parviceps 356
byrnei, Diplodactylus 215*

Cacophis 636
Cacophis harriettae 636*
Cacophis krefftii 637*
Cacophis squamulosus 638*
caerulea, Litoria 132*
caerulescens, Hydrophis 714
Caimanops 303
Caimanops amphiboluroides 303 *
caligula, Lampropholis 507*
calligastra, Dendrelaphis 620*
calodera, Demansia olivacea 640
calonotus, Simoselaps 684*
calurus, Ctenotus 418*
calx, Ctenotus pantherinus 436
Calyptotis 386
Calyptotis lepidorostrum 387*
Calyptotis ruficauda 387*
Calyptotis scutirostrum 388*
Calyptotis temporalis 389
Calyptotis thorntonensis 389
campbelli, Simoselaps semifasciatus 688
canni, Oxyuranus scutellatus 663
capitulata, Uperoleia 109
capricorni, Ctenotus 418
capucinus, Lycodon 731*
caretta, Caretta 178*
caretta, Caretta caretta 179
Caretta 178
Caretta caretta 178*
Caretta caretta caretta 179
Caretta caretta gigas 179
CARETTOCHELYDIDAE 186
Carettochelys 186
Carettochelys insculpta 186*

carinata, Egernia 457*
carinata, Morelia 612
carinatus, Tropidechis 694*
Carlia 389
Carlia amax 392
Carlia coensis 392*
Carlia dogare 392*
Carlia gracilis 392*
Carlia jarnoldae 393*
Carlia johnstonei 394
Carlia longipes 394*
Carlia munda 395*
Carlia mundivensis 395*
Carlia pectoralis 395
Carlia rhomboidalis 396*
Carlia rimula 396
Carlia rostralis 397*
Carlia rubrigularis 398
Carlia rufilatus 398
Carlia schmeltzii 399*
Carlia scirtetis 399*
Carlia storri 399*
Carlia tetradactyla 401*
Carlia triacantha 401*
Carlia vivax 401*
carnabyi, Cryptoblepharus 404*
carpentariae, Lerista 515
Carphodactylus 205
Carphodactylus laevis 207*
castanea, Litoria 132
castelnaui, Oedura 260*
casuarinae, Cyclodomorphus 452*
catenata, Gehyra 238*
catenifer, Ctenotus 419
caudiannulatus, Phyllurus 269*
caudicinctus, Ctenophorus 310*
caudicinctus, Ctenophorus caudicinctus 311
caudolineatus, Varanus 361*
Cautula 735
Cautula zia 735, 571*
cavaticus, Pseudothecadactylus lindneri 273
cavernicola, Litoria 132*
centralis, Neobatrachus 88*
centralis, Ramphotyphlops 591
cephalus, Tympanocryptis 352*
Cerberus 619
Cerberus rynchops 619*
challengeri, Saproscincus 574*
chalybura, Lerista 515
chapmani, Tympanocryptis adelaidensis 352
CHELIDAE 187
Chelodina 188
Chelodina expansa 189*
Chelodina longicollis 190*
Chelodina novaeguineae 191*
Chelodina oblonga 192*
Chelodina rugosa 192*
Chelodina steindachneri 193*
Chelonia 180
Chelonia mydas 180*
Chelonia mydas agassizii 181
Chelonia mydas japonica 181
Chelonia mydas mydas 181
CHELONIIDAE 176
Chelosania 304
Chelosania brunnea 305*
childreni, Liasis 606*
Chlamydosaurus 305
Chlamydosaurus kingii 305*
chloris, Litoria 133*
Chondropython 603
Chondropython viridis 603*
christinae, Lerista 516
Christinus 207
Christinus guentheri 207*
Christinus marmoratus 208*
ciliaris, Diplodactylus 215*
ciliaris, Diplodactylus ciliaris 217

cinctus, Nephrurus wheeleri 258
cinerea, Lerista 516
citrinus, Ctenophorus isolepis 317
citropa, Litoria 133*
clayi, Ctenophorus 311*
coensis, Carlia 392*
Coeranoscincus 402
Coeranoscincus frontalis 402*
Coeranoscincus reticulatus 402*
coggeri, Amphibolurus nobbi 302
coggeri, Ctenotus 419*
coggeri, Hydrophis 715*
coggeri, Lampropholis 736
coggeri, Oedura 260*
colletti, Ctenotus 420*
colletti, Ctenotus colletti 420
colletti, Pseudechis 665*
colossus, Lampropholis 736
COLUBRIDAE 617
colubrina, Laticauda 724*
concinna, Aclys 278*
concinna, Aclys concinna 278
concinna, Menetia 542*
concinnus, Cophixalus 161*
concolor, Lerista 737
connivens, Lerista 518*
conspicillatus, Diplodactylus 217*
continentis, Hemiergis decresiensis 500
convergens, Diporiphora 330
convexiusculus, Limnodynastes 75*
cooloolensis, Litoria 133
cooloolensis, Ophioscincus 555
Cophixalus 159
Cophixalus bombiens 160*
Cophixalus concinnus 161*
Cophixalus crepitans 161
Cophixalus exiguus 162
Cophixalus hosmeri 162*
Cophixalus infacetus 162*
Cophixalus mcdonaldi 162
Cophixalus neglectus 162
Cophixalus ornatus 163*
Cophixalus peninsularis 164
Cophixalus saxatilis 164*
coplandi, Litoria 134*
Copperhead 635
coriacea, Dermochelys 185*
coriacea, Pseudophryne 99*
cornutus, Phyllurus 269*
coronata, Drysdalia 645*
coronoides, Drysdalia 646*
corroboree, Pseudophryne 101*
couperi, Lampropholis 737
coventryi, Egernia 457*
coventryi, Niveoscincus 741, 561*
coventryi, Pseudemoia 561*
cracens, Glaphyromorphus 492
crassa, Uperoleia 110
crassicaudis, Glaphyromorphus 492*
Crenadactylus 209
Crenadactylus ocellatus 209*
Crenadactylus ocellatus horni 209
Crenadactylus ocellatus naso 209
Crenadactylus ocellatus ocellatus 209
Crenadactylus ocellatus rostralis 209
crepitans, Cophixalus 161
Crinia 57
Crinia bilingua 58*
Crinia deserticola 59*
Crinia georgiana 59*
Crinia glauerti 60
Crinia insignifera 60
Crinia parinsignifera 60*
Crinia pseudinsignifera 61
Crinia remota 61*
Crinia riparia 61*
Crinia signifera 62*
Crinia sloanei 63*

Crinia subinsignifera 64*
Crinia tasmaniensis 64*
Crinia tinnula 65
cristatus, Ctenophorus 311*
Crocodile, Estuarine 175
Freshwater 174
Saltwater (see Estuarine) 175
CROCODYLIDAE 173
Crocodylus 173
Crocodylus johnstoni 174*
Crocodylus porosus 175*
Cryptagama 307
Cryptagama aurita 307*
Cryptoblepharus 403
Cryptoblepharus carnabyi 404*
Cryptoblepharus egeriae 728*
Cryptoblepharus fuhni 405
Cryptoblepharus litoralis 405*
Cryptoblepharus megastictus 405*
Cryptoblepharus plagiocephalus 406*
Cryptoblepharus plagiocephalus plagiocephalus 406
Cryptoblepharus plagiocephalus ruber 406
Cryptoblepharus virgatus 406
cryptotis, Cyclorana 118*
Ctenophorus 308
Ctenophorus caudicinctus 310*
Ctenophorus caudicinctus caudicinctus 311
Ctenophorus caudicinctus graafi 311
Ctenophorus caudicinctus infans 311
Ctenophorus caudicinctus macropus 311
Ctenophorus caudicinctus mensarum 311
Ctenophorus caudicinctus slateri 311
Ctenophorus clayi 311*
Ctenophorus cristatus 311*
Ctenophorus decresii 312*
Ctenophorus femoralis 312*
Ctenophorus fionni 312*
Ctenophorus fordi 315*
Ctenophorus gibba 316
Ctenophorus isolepis 316*
Ctenophorus isolepis citrinus 317
Ctenophorus isolepis gularis 317
Ctenophorus isolepis isolepis 317
Ctenophorus isolepis rubens 317
Ctenophorus maculatus 317*
Ctenophorus maculatus badius 318
Ctenophorus maculatus dualis 318
Ctenophorus maculatus griseus 318
Ctenophorus maculatus maculatus 317
Ctenophorus maculosus 318*
Ctenophorus mckenziei 318*
Ctenophorus nuchalis 318*
Ctenophorus ornatus 320*
Ctenophorus pictus 320*
Ctenophorus reticulatus 322*
Ctenophorus rufescens 323*
Ctenophorus salinarum 323*
Ctenophorus scutulatus 326*
Ctenophorus vadnappa 326*
Ctenophorus yinnietharra 326*
Ctenotus 407
Ctenotus alacer 412*
Ctenotus alleni 412*
Ctenotus allotropis 413*
Ctenotus angusticeps 413
Ctenotus arcanus 413*
Ctenotus ariadnae 414*
Ctenotus arnhemensis 415*
Ctenotus astarte 415*
Ctenotus atlas 415*
Ctenotus australis 416*
Ctenotus borealis 416
Ctenotus brachyonyx 417*
Ctenotus brooksi 417*
Ctenotus brooksi brooksi 418
Ctenotus brooksi euclae 418
Ctenotus brooksi iridis 418
Ctenotus brooksi taeniatus 418
Ctenotus calurus 418*
Ctenotus capricorni 418
Ctenotus catenifer 419
Ctenotus coggeri 419*
Ctenotus colletti 420*
Ctenotus colletti colletti 420
Ctenotus colletti nasutus 420
Ctenotus colletti rufescens 420
Ctenotus decaneurus 420*
Ctenotus decaneurus decaneurus 421
Ctenotus decaneurus yampiensis 421
Ctenotus delli 421
Ctenotus dux 421*
Ctenotus ehmanni 422
Ctenotus essingtoni 423*
Ctenotus essingtoni brevipes 423
Ctenotus essingtoni essingtoni 423
Ctenotus eurydice 423*
Ctenotus eutaenius 424*
Ctenotus fallens 424
Ctenotus gagudju 425*
Ctenotus gemmula 425*
Ctenotus grandis 426*
Ctenotus grandis grandis 426
Ctenotus grandis titan 426
Ctenotus greeri 426
Ctenotus hanloni 426*
Ctenotus hebetior 427*
Ctenotus hebetior hebetior 427
Ctenotus hebetior schuettleri 427
Ctenotus helenae 427*
Ctenotus hilli 428
Ctenotus impar 428*
Ctenotus ingrami 428
Ctenotus inornatus 429*
Ctenotus joanae 429
Ctenotus kurnbudj 430*
Ctenotus labillardieri 430*
Ctenotus lancelini 432*
Ctenotus lateralis 432*
Ctenotus leae 433*
Ctenotus leonhardii 433*
Ctenotus mastigura 434
Ctenotus mastigura burbidgei 434
Ctenotus mastigura mastigura 434
Ctenotus militaris 434
Ctenotus mimetes 435*
Ctenotus monticola 435
Ctenotus nasutus 735
Ctenotus nigrilineatus 735
Ctenotus pallescens 435
Ctenotus pantherinus 436*
Ctenotus pantherinus acripes 436
Ctenotus pantherinus calx 436
Ctenotus pantherinus ocellifer 436
Ctenotus pantherinus pantherinus 436
Ctenotus piankai 437
Ctenotus piankai duricola 437
Ctenotus piankai piankai 437
Ctenotus pulchellus 437*
Ctenotus quattuordecimlineatus 438*
Ctenotus quattuordecimlineatus iapetus 438
Ctenotus quattuordecimlineatus quattuordecimlineatus 438
Ctenotus quinkan 438
Ctenotus rawlinsoni 438*
Ctenotus regius 438*
Ctenotus robustus 439*
Ctenotus rubicundus 440
Ctenotus rufescens 735
Ctenotus rutilans 440
Ctenotus saxatilis 441*
Ctenotus schevilli 441*
Ctenotus schomburgkii 442*
Ctenotus septenarius 442
Ctenotus serotinus 442
Ctenotus serventyi 443
Ctenotus severus 443*
Ctenotus spaldingi 444*
Ctenotus storri 446*
Ctenotus strauchii 446*
Ctenotus striaticeps 447*
Ctenotus taeniolatus 447*
Ctenotus tanamiensis 448
Ctenotus tantillus 449
Ctenotus uber 449*
Ctenotus uber orientalis 449
Ctenotus uber uber 449
Ctenotus vertebralis 449
Ctenotus xenopleura 450
Ctenotus youngsoni 450*
Ctenotus zastictus 450*
Ctenotus zebrilla 450
cucullatus, Stegonotus 627*
cultripes, Cyclorana 118
cunninghami, Egernia 157*
cupreiceps, Demansia psammophis 641
curta, Echiopsis 649*
Cyclodomorphus 451
Cyclodomorphus branchialis 452*
Cyclodomorphus casuarinae 452*
Cyclodomorphus maxima 453*
Cyclorana 116
Cyclorana australis 117*
Cyclorana brevipes 118*
Cyclorana cryptotis 118*
Cyclorana cultripes 118
Cyclorana longipes 119*
Cyclorana maculosa 119
Cyclorana maini 121
Cyclorana manya 121
Cyclorana novaehollandiae 121*
Cyclorana platycephala 121*
Cyclorana vagita 122*
Cyclorana verrucosa 123*
cyclorhyncha, Litoria 134*
Cyrtodactylus 210
Cyrtodactylus louisiadensis 210*
Cyrtodactylus sp. 727*
czeblukovi, Hydrophis 715
czechurai, Saproscincus 574*

daemeli, Rana 168*
dahlii, Litoria 135*
damaeum, Lucasium 250*
damelii, Hemiaspis 654*
darlingtoni, Assa 57*
darwiniensis, Glaphyromorphus 492
darwiniensis, Glaphyromorphus darwiniensis 492
darwiniensis, Hydrelaps 712*
davisi, Hemiergis decresiensis 500
dayi, Nyctimystes 158*
Deaf Adder (see Death Adder)
Death Adder, Common 632
Desert 634
Northern 634
decaneurus, Ctenotus 420*
decaneurus, Ctenotus decaneurus 421
decora, Lerista planiventralis 529
decresiensis, Hemiergis 500*
decresiensis, Hemiergis decresiensis 500
decresii, Ctenophorus 312*
deleani, Nephrurus 255*
delicata, Lampropholis 507*
delli, Ctenotus 421
Delma 284

Delma australis 286*
Delma borea 286*
Delma butleri 286*
Delma elegans 286
Delma fraseri 286*
Delma grayii 288
Delma haroldi 288
Delma impar 289*
Delma inornata 289*
Delma labialis 290
Delma mitella 290
Delma molleri 290*
Delma nasuta 291*
Delma pax 291*
Delma plebeia 292*
Delma tincta 292*
Delma torquata 292*
Demansia 638
Demansia atra 639*
Demansia olivacea 640*
Demansia olivacea calodera 640
Demansia olivacea olivacea 640
Demansia olivacea rufescens 640
Demansia papuensis 641*
Demansia papuensis melaena 641
Demansia papuensis papuensis 641
Demansia psammophis cupreiceps 641
Demansia psammophis psammophis 641
Demansia psammophis reticulata 641
Demansia simplex 641
Demansia torquata 643*
Dendrelaphis 620
Dendrelaphis calligastra 620*
Dendrelaphis punctulata 621*
dendyi, Pseudophryne 101*
Denisonia 643
Denisonia devisi 644*
Denisonia maculata 644*
dentata, Elseya 194*
dentata, Litoria 135*
depressa, Egernia 458*
depressus, Limnodynastes 75
depressus, Natator 183*
DERMOCHELYIDAE 184
Dermochelys 185
Dermochelys coriacea 185*
deserticola, Crinia 59*
desertorum, Lerista 518*
Devil, Thorny (see Moloch) 344
devisi, Denisonia 644*
diadema, Furina 651*
diemensis, Tympanocryptis 353*
Diplodactylus 211
Diplodactylus alboguttatus 214*
Diplodactylus assimilis 214*
Diplodactylus byrnei 215*
Diplodactylus ciliaris 215*
Diplodactylus ciliaris aberrans 217
Diplodactylus ciliaris ciliaris 217
Diplodactylus conspicillatus 217*
Diplodactylus elderi 217*
Diplodactylus, Fat-tailed 217
Diplodactylus fulleri 218
Diplodactylus galeatus 218*
Diplodactylus granariensis 219*
Diplodactylus granariensis granariensis 219
Diplodactylus granariensis rex 219
Diplodactylus immaculatus 219
Diplodactylus intermedius 219*
Diplodactylus jeanae 220
Diplodactylus kenneallyi 221
Diplodactylus maini 221
Diplodactylus mcmillani 221*
Diplodactylus michaelseni 222*
Diplodactylus mitchelli 222*
Diplodactylus occultus 222*
Diplodactylus ornatus 223*
Diplodactylus polyophthalmus 224*
Diplodactylus pulcher 224*
Diplodactylus rankini 225*
Diplodactylus savagei 225*
Diplodactylus spinigerus 225*
Diplodactylus spinigerus inornatus 226
Diplodactylus spinigerus spinigerus 226
Diplodactylus squarrosus 226*
Diplodactylus steindachneri 227*
Diplodactylus stenodactylus 228*
Diplodactylus strophurus 228*
Diplodactylus taeniatus 229*
Diplodactylus taenicauda 231*
Diplodactylus tessellatus 231*
Diplodactylus vittatus 232*
Diplodactylus wellingtonae 234*
Diplodactylus williamsi 234*
Diplodactylus wilsoni 234
Diplodactylus wombeyi 234
Diporiphora 327
Diporiphora albilabris 328 *
Diporiphora australis 329*
Diporiphora bennettii 329*
Diporiphora bennettii arnhemica 329
Diporiphora bennettii bennettii 329
Diporiphora bilineata 330*
Diporiphora convergens 330
Diporiphora lalliae 330*
Diporiphora linga 332
Diporiphora magna 332*
Diporiphora pindan 332*
Diporiphora reginae 333*
Diporiphora superba 334*
Diporiphora valens 334
Diporiphora winneckei 336*
Disteira 706
Disteira kingii 707 *
Disteira major 707*
distinguenda, Lerista 518*
diurnus, Taudactylus 105*
diversus, Ramphotyphlops 592
diversus, Ramphotyphlops diversus 592
dogare, Carlia 392*
dorsalis, Lerista 518*
dorsalis, Limnodynastes 75*
dorsalis, Litoria 136*
dorsalis, Litoria dorsalis 136
douglasi, Egernia 460
douglasi, Glaphyromorphus 492*
douglasi, Pseudophryne 101
Dragon, Bearded 347
  Boyd's Forest 337
  Central Netted 318
  Chameleon 305
  Crested 311
  Dwarf Bearded 349
  Eastern Water 345
  Lake Eyre 318
  Lozenge-marked 326
  Mallee 315
  Military 316
  Mountain 353
  Ornate 320
  Painted 320
  Ring-tailed 310
  Southern Angle-headed 338
  Spotted 317
  Two-lined 330
  Western Bearded 349
  Western Netted 322
Dragon Lizards (see Agamidae) 203
Drysdalia 645
Drysdalia coronata 645*
Drysdalia coronoides 646*
Drysdalia mastersii 647*
Drysdalia rhodogaster 647*
Dtella, Northern 236
  Pilbara 242
  Spotted 243
  Tree 244
dualis, Ctenophorus maculatus 318
duperreyi, Bassiana 735, 561*
dubia, Gehyra 238*
duboisii, Aipysurus 701*
Dugite 670
dumerilii, Limnodynastes 75*
dumerilii, Limnodynastes dumerilii 76
dunmalli, Furina 652*
duperreyi, Pseudemoia 561*
duricola, Ctenotus piankai 437
dux, Ctenotus 421*
dwyeri, Suta spectabilis 693

Echiopsis 648
Echiopsis atriceps 649
Echiopsis curta 649*
edelensis, Pletholax gracilis 296
edwardsae, Lerista picturata 529
egeriae, Cryptoblepharus 728*
Egernia 454
Egernia arnhemensis 735
Egernia carinata 457*
Egernia coventryi 457*
Egernia cunninghami 457*
Egernia depressa 458*
Egernia douglasi 460
Egernia formosa 460*
Egernia frerei 461*
Egernia hosmeri 461*
Egernia inornata 462*
Egernia kingii 465*
Egernia kintorei 465*
Egernia luctuosa 465*
Egernia major 465*
Egernia margaretae 466*
Egernia margaretae margaretae 467
Egernia margaretae personata 467
Egernia mcpheei 467*
Egernia modesta 468*
Egernia multiscutata 468 *
Egernia multiscutata bos 469
Egernia multiscutata multiscutata 469
Egernia napoleonis 469 *
Egernia pilbarensis 469*
Egernia pulchra 470*
Egernia pulchra longicauda 470
Egernia pulchra pulchra 470
Egernia richardi 470
Egernia rugosa 470*
Egernia saxatilis 471*
Egernia saxatilis intermedia 472
Egernia saxatilis saxatilis 472
Egernia slateri 472
Egernia slateri slateri 472
Egernia slateri virgata 472
Egernia stokesii 472*
Egernia stokesii aethiops 472
Egernia stokesii badia 472
Egernia stokesii stokesii 472
Egernia striata 472*
Egernia striolata 472*
Egernia whitii 473*
Egernia whitii moniligera 474
Egernia whitii whitii 474
ehmanni, Ctenotus 422
ELAPIDAE 629
Elapognathus 649
Elapognathus minor 649*
elderi, Diplodactylus 217*
electrica, Litoria 734
elegans, Delma 286
elegans, Hydrophis 716*
elegans, Lerista 518*
elongata, Lerista 738
Elseya 193

Elseya dentata 194*
Elseya latisternum 194*
Emoia 475
Emoia atrocostata 476, 728*
Emoia longicauda 477*
Emoia nativitatis 728*
Emydocephalus 708
Emydocephalus annulatus 708*
Emydura 196
Emydura krefftii 196*
Emydura macquarii 197*
Emydura signata 199*
Emydura subglobosa 199*
Emydura victoriae 199*
endoterus, Ramphotyphlops 592*
Enhydrina 709
Enhydrina schistosa 709*
Enhydris 623
Enhydris polylepis 623*
entrecasteauxii, Pseudemoia 562*
Ephalophis 710
Ephalophis greyi 711*
equalis, Saiphos 572*
Eremiascincus 477
Eremiascincus fasciolatus 477*
Eremiascincus richardsonii 478*
eremius, Varanus 362*
Eretmochelys 182
Eretmochelys imbricata 182*
Eretmochelys imbricata imbricata 182
Eretmochelys imbricata squamata 182
Eroticoscincus 479
Eroticoscincus graciloides 479*
essingtoni, Ctenotus 423*
essingtoni, Ctenotus essingtoni 423
euclae, Ctenotus brooksi 418
Eugongylus 480
Eugongylus albofasciolatus 480
Eugongylus rufescens 480*
Eulamprus 481
Eulamprus amplus 482*
Eulamprus heatwolei 483*
Eulamprus kosciuskoi 485*
Eulamprus leuraensis 485*
Eulamprus luteilateralis 485*
Eulamprus murrayi 486*
Eulamprus quoyii 487*
Eulamprus tenuis 487*
Eulamprus tenuis brachysoma 488
Eulamprus tenuis tenuis 488
Eulamprus tigrinus 489*
Eulamprus tympanum 489*
eungellensis, Taudactylus 106
eurydice, Ctenotus 423*
eutaenius, Ctenotus 424*
ewingii, Litoria 136*
exiguus, Cophixalus 162
exilis, Pseudonaja affinis 670
exocoeti, Ramphotyphlops 731
expansa, Chelodina 189*
exquisita, Morethia ruficauda 548
eydouxii, Aipysurus 702*
eyrei, Heleioporus 71*

fallax, Litoria 137*
fallens, Ctenotus 424
fasciata, Suta 689*
fasciatus, Simoselaps fasciolatus 685
fasciolatus, Eremiascincus 477*
fasciolatus, Mixophyes 83*
fasciolatus, Simoselaps 684*
fasciolatus, Simoselaps fasciolatus 685
femoralis, Ctenophorus 312*
File Snakes (see Acrochordidae) 585
filicipoda, Oedura 261*
fionni, Ctenophorus 312*
flagellum, Suta 689*
flammicauda, Lerista 519
flavirufus, Varanus gouldii 368
fleayi, Mixophyes 83*
fletcheri, Lechriodus 73*
fletcheri, Limnodynastes 76*
foliorum, Lygisaurus 539*
foliosquama, Aipysurus 702*
fordi, Ctenophorus 315*
Fordonia 624
Fordonia leucobalia 625*
formosa, Egernia 460*
fragilis, Lerista 519*
fraseri, Delma 286*
frenatus, Hemidactylus 246, 728*
frerei, Egernia 461*
freycineti, Litoria 137*
Frog, Baw Baw 96
  Bleating Tree 135
  Blue Mountains Tree 133
  Booroolong 129
  Brown-striped 78
  Brown Tree 137
  Centralian Tree 138
  Corroboree 101
  Dainty Green Tree 139
  Desert Tree 152
  Dwarf Rocket 136
  Eastern Banjo 75
  Eastern Dwarf Tree 137
  Eungella Torrent 106
  Fletcher's 73
  Freycinet's 137
  Giant Banjo 76
  Giant Barred 84
  Giant Burrowing 70
  Giant Tree 140
  Goldfields Bull 90
  Great Barred 83
  Green and Golden Bell 128
  Green-thighed 130
  Green Tree 132
  Humming 89
  Jervis Bay Tree 140
  Leaf Green Tree 150
  Lesueur's 143
  Long-thumbed 76
  Loveridge's 96
  Marbled 75
  Moaning 71
  Mount Glorious Torrent 105
  Northern Banjo 80
  Northern Barred 84
  Northern Dwarf Tree 129
  Northern Gastric Brooding 104
  Ornate Burrowing 77
  Peron's Tree 148
  Pouched 57
  Red-eyed Tree 133
  Rocket 145
  Salmon-striped 78
  Saxicoline Tree 134
  Shoemaker 90
  Slender Tree 127
  Sphagnum 97
  Sharp-snouted Torrent 105
  Spotted Grass 79
  Spotted-thighed 134
  Striped Burrowing 128
  Tasmanian Tree 131
  Torrent Tree 145
  Trilling 88
  Turtle 86
  Tusked 55
  Water-holding 121
  Western Banjo 75
  Western Green and Golden Bell 144
  Wood 168
Froglet, Common Eastern 62
  Wallum 65
Frogs, Narrow-mouthed 53
  Southern 53
  Tree 51
  True 53
frontalis, Coeranoscincus 402*
frosti, Lerista 519*
frosti, Philoria 96*
fryi, Limnodynastes dumerilii 76
fryi, Sphenophryne 165*
fuhni, Cryptoblepharus 405
fulleri, Diplodactylus 218
fulvus, Neobatrachus 88
Furina 650
Furina barnardi 651*
Furina diadema 651*
Furina dunmalli 652*
Furina ornata 653*
Furina tristis 653*
fusca, Aprasia rostrata 282
fusca, Uperoleia 110*
fuscicaudis, Glaphyromorphus 494*
fuscus, Aipysurus 702*
fuscus, Liasis 606*

gagudju, Ctenotus 425*
galeatus, Diplodactylus 218*
galgajuga, Nactus 251*
gascoynensis, Lerista 520*
Gecko, Beaded 250
  Beaked 274
  Bynoe's 247
  Chameleon 207
  Clawless 209
  Desert Cave 248
  Eastern Spiny-tailed 219
  Giant Cave 273
  Golden-tailed 231
  House 246
  Jewelled 217
  Lesueur's Velvet 263
  Marbled 208
  Marbled Velvet 263
  Northern Leaf-tailed 269
  Northern Spotted Velvet 260
  Northern Velvet 260
  Oceanic 240
  Ocellated Velvet 264
  Pelagic 253
  Reticulated Velvet 265
  Ring-tailed 210
  Robust Velvet 266
  Southern Leaf-tailed 271
  Southern Spotted Velvet 266
  Spiny-tailed 215
  Tessellated 231
  Thick-tailed 275
  Western Spiny-tailed 225
  Wood 232
Geckos (see Gekkonidae) 202
Gehyra 235
Gehyra australis 236*
Gehyra baliola 236*
Gehyra borroloola 237*
Gehyra catenata 238*
Gehyra dubia 238*
Gehyra minuta 239*
Gehyra montium 239*
Gehyra mutilata 727*
Gehyra nana 239*
Gehyra occidentalis 240*
Gehyra oceanica 240*
Gehyra pamela 242*
Gehyra pilbara 242*
Gehyra punctata 243*
Gehyra purpurascens 243*
Gehyra robusta 243*
Gehyra variegata 244*
Gehyra xenopus 244*
GEKKONIDAE 204
gemmata, Oedura 262*

gemmula, Ctenotus 425*
genimaculata, Litoria 138*
Geocrinia 65
Geocrinia alba 733
Geocrinia laevis 66*
Geocrinia leai 66
Geocrinia lutea 66*
Geocrinia rosea 67*
Geocrinia victoriana 68
Geocrinia vitellina 733
georgiana, Crinia 59*
gerrardii, Lerista 520*
gerrardii, Hemisphaeriodon 503*
gibba, Ctenophorus 316
giganteus, Varanus 362*
gigas, Caretta caretta 179
gilberti, Lophognathus 340*
gilleni, Litoria 138*
gilleni, Varanus 364*
glandulosa, Uperoleia 110*
Glaphyromorphus 490
Glaphyromorphus brongersmai 491
Glaphyromorphus cracens 492*
Glaphyromorphus crassicaudis 492*
Glaphyromorphus darwiniensis 492
Glaphyromorphus darwiniensis arnhemicus 492
Glaphyromorphus darwiniensis darwiniensis 492
Glaphyromorphus douglasi 492*
Glaphyromorphus fuscicaudis 494*
Glaphyromorphus gracilipes 495*
Glaphyromorphus isolepis 496*
Glaphyromorphus mjobergi 496*
Glaphyromorphus nigricaudis 496*
Glaphyromorphus pardalis 496*
Glaphyromorphus pumilus 498*
Glaphyromorphus punctulatus 498*
glauerti, Crinia 60
glauerti, Varanus 365*
glebopalma, Varanus 365*
Gnypetoscincus 498
Gnypetoscincus queenslandiae 499*
Goanna (see also Monitor) 202
Goanna Gould's 366
Goannas (see Varanidae) 202
gouldii, Myobatrachus 86*
gouldii, Suta 690*
gouldii, Varanus 366*
gouldii, Varanus gouldii 368
gowi, Anomalopus 384*
graafi, Ctenophorus caudicinctus 311
gracilenta, Litoria 139*
gracilipes, Glaphyromorphus 495*
gracilipes, Sphenophryne 166*
gracilis, Carlia 392*
gracilis, Hydrophis 716
gracilis, Oedura 262*
gracilis, Pletholax 296*
gracilis, Pletholax gracilis 296
graciloides, Eroticoscincus 479*
granariensis, Diplodactylus 219*
granariensis, Diplodactylus granariensis 219
grandis, Ctenotus 426*
grandis, Ctenotus grandis 426
granulatus, Acrochordus 616*
grayi, Limnodynastes dumerilii 76
grayii, Delma 288
greeni, Niveoscincus 741, 562*
greeni, Pseudemoia 562*
greeri, Ctenotus 426
greeri, Lerista 520
greyi, Ephalophis 711*
greyii, Menetia 543*
griffini, Lerista 521
griseus, Ctenophorus maculatus 318
grypus, Ramphotyphlops 592*
guentheri, Christinus 207*
guentheri, Pseudophryne 101*
guentheri, Ramphotyphlops 592
guichenoti, Lampropholis 507*
gularis, Ctenophorus isolepis 317
guttata, Pseudonaja 670*
guttatus, Pseudechis 666*
Gwardar 672*

hamatus, Ramphotyphlops 593
hanloni, Ctenotus 426*
hardwickii, Lapemis 720*
haroldi, Aprasia 279*
haroldi, Delma 288
haroldi, Lerista 521
harriettae, Cacophis 636*
haswelli, Paracrinia 94*
heatwolei, Eulamprus 483*
hebetior, Ctenotus hebetior 427
hebetior, Ctenotus 427*
Heleioporus 68
Heleioporus albopunctatus 70*
Heleioporus australiacus 70*
Heleioporus barycragus 70*
Heleioporus eyrei 71*
Heleioporus inornatus 71*
Heleioporus psammophilus 72*
helenae, Ctenotus 427*
Hemiaspis 654*
Hemiaspis damelii 654*
Hemiaspis signata 656*
Hemidactylus 246
Hemidactylus frenatus 246, 728*
Hemiergis 500
Hemiergis decresiensis 500*
Hemiergis decresiensis davisi 500
Hemiergis decresiensis decresiensis 500
Hemiergis decresiensis talbingoensis 500
Hemiergis decresiensis continentis 500
Hemiergis initialis 500*
Hemiergis initialis brookeri 501
Hemiergis initialis initialis 501
Hemiergis millewae 502*
Hemiergis peronii 502*
Hemiergis quadrilineatum 502 *
Hemisphaeriodon 503
Hemisphaeriodon gerrardii 503*
Heteronotia 247
Heteronotia binoei 248*
Heteronotia planiceps 734
Heteronotia spelea 248*
hilli, Ctenotus 428
Hoplocephalus 656
Hoplocephalus bitorquatus 657 *
Hoplocephalus bungaroides 658*
Hoplocephalus stephensii 658*
horni, Crenadactylus ocellatus 209
horridus, Moloch 344*
hosmeri, Cophixalus 162*
hosmeri, Egernia 461*
houstoni, Tympanocryptis lineata 354
howi, Ramphotyphlops 593
howittii, Physignathus lesueurii 346
humphreysi, Notechis ater 659
humphriesi, Lerista 521
Hydrelaps 711
Hydrelaps darwiniensis 712 *
HYDROPHIIDAE 697
Hydrophis 712
Hydrophis atriceps 714
Hydrophis belcheri 714
Hydrophis caerulescens 714
Hydrophis coggeri 715*
Hydrophis czeblukovi 715
Hydrophis elegans 716*
Hydrophis gracilis 716
Hydrophis inornatus 717
Hydrophis mcdowelli 717
Hydrophis melanosoma 718
Hydrophis ornatus 718*
Hydrophis ornatus ocellatus 719
Hydrophis ornatus ornatus 719
Hydrophis pacificus 719
Hydrophis vorisi 719
HYLIDAE 116
Hypsilurus 337
Hypsilurus boydii 337*
Hypsilurus spinipes 338*

iapetus, Ctenotus quattuordecimlineatus 438
imbricata, Eretmochelys 182*
imbricata, Eretmochelys imbricata 182
imbricata, Morelia spilota 614
immaculatus, Diplodactylus 219
impar, Ctenotus 428*
impar, Delma 289*
inaurita, Aprasia 280*
incinctus, Simoselaps 685*
indicus, Varanus 368*
inermis, Litoria 139*
infacetus, Cophixalus 162*
infans, Ctenophorus caudicinctus 311
infrafrenata, Litoria 140*
inframacula, Pseudonaja 670*
ingrami, Ctenotus 428
ingrami, Lerista 738
ingrami, Pseudonaja 671*
initialis, Hemiergis 500*
initialis, Hemiergis initialis 501
inornata, Delma 289*
inornata, Egernia 462*
inornatus, Ctenotus 429*
inornatus, Diplodactylus spinigerus 226
inornatus, Heleioporus 71*
inornatus, Hydrophis 717
insculpta, Carettochelys 186*
insignifera, Crinia 60
insulanicus, Varanus acanthurus 361
insularis, Limnodynastes dumerilii 76
interioris, Limnodynastes 76*
intermedia, Egernia saxatilis 472
intermedia, Tiliqua scincoides 582
intermedius, Diplodactylus 219*
intima, Tympanocryptis 353*
inundata, Uperoleia 111*
ips, Lerista 521
iridis, Ctenotus brooksi 418
irregularis, Boiga 618*
isolepis, Ctenophorus 316*
isolepis, Ctenophorus isolepis 317
isolepis, Glaphyromorphus 496*
iteratus, Mixophyes 84*

japonica, Chelonia mydas 181
jarnoldae, Carlia 393*
jeanae, Diplodactylus 220
jervisiensis, Litoria 140*
jigurru, Pseudemoia 563*
jigurru, Bartleia 735, 563
joanae, Ctenotus 429
johnstonei, Carlia 394
johnstoni, Crocodylus 174*

kalumburu, Lerista 521
karlschmidti, Lerista 522*
Keelback 628
kendricki, Lerista 738
kenneallyi, Diplodactylus 221
kennedyensis, Lerista 522*
kimberleyensis, Ramphotyphlops 593

kinghorni, Proablepharus 557*
kingii, Chlamydosaurus 305*
kingii, Disteira 707*
kingii, Egernia 465*
kingorum, Varanus 368*
kintorei, Egernia 465*
konowi, Trachydosaurus rugosus 584
kosciuskoi, Eulamprus 485*
krefftii, Cacophis 637*
krefftii, Emydura 196*
kunapalari, Neobatrachus 88
kundagungan, Philoria 96
kurnbudj, Ctenotus 430*

labialis, Delma 290
labialis, Lerista 523*
labillardieri, Ctenotus 430*
laevigata, Uperoleia 111*
laevis, Aipysurus 703*
laevis, Aipysurus laevis 704
laevis, Carphodactylus 207*
laevis, Geocrinia 66*
laevis, Lygisaurus 539
laevissimus, Nephrurus 256*
lalliae, Diporiphora 330*
Lampropholis 505
Lampropholis adonis 736
Lampropholis amicula 505*
Lampropholis caligula 507*
Lampropholis coggeri 736
Lampropholis colossus 736
Lampropholis couperi 737
Lampropholis delicata 507*
Lampropholis guichenoti 507*
Lampropholis mirabilis 508*
Lampropholis robertsi 737
lancelini, Ctenotus 432*
Land Mullet 465
Lapemis 720
Lapemis hardwickii 720*
lateralis, Ctenotus 432*
Laticauda 723
Laticauda colubrina 724*
Laticauda laticaudata 724*
laticaudata, Laticauda 724*
LATICAUDIDAE 723
latisternum, Elseya 194*
latopalmata, Litoria 142*
leae, Ctenotus 433*
leai, Geocrinia 66
Lechriodus 72
Lechriodus fletcheri 73*
leonhardii, Ctenotus 433*
Lepidochelys 182
Lepidochelys olivacea 183*
Lepidodactylus 248
Lepidodactylus listeri 728*
Lepidodactylus lugubris 249, 728*
Lepidodactylus pumilus 250*
lepidopodus, Pygopus 297*
lepidorostrum, Calyptotis 387*
leptosoma, Ramphotyphlops 593
Lerista 508
Lerista aericeps 512*
Lerista allanae 512*
Lerista allochira 512*
Lerista ameles 512*
Lerista apoda 513
Lerista arenicola 737
Lerista axillaris 737
Lerista bipes 513*
Lerista borealis 514*
Lerista bougainvillii 514*
Lerista bunglebungle 737
Lerista carpentariae 515
Lerista chalybura 515
Lerista christinae 516
Lerista cinerea 516
Lerista concolor 737
Lerista connivens 518*
Lerista desertorum 518*
Lerista distinguenda 518*
Lerista dorsalis 518*
Lerista elegans 518*
Lerista elongata 738
Lerista flammicauda 519
Lerista fragilis 519*
Lerista frosti 519*
Lerista gascoynensis 520*
Lerista gerrardii 520*
Lerista greeri 520
Lerista griffini 521
Lerista haroldi 521
Lerista humphriesi 521
Lerista ingrami 738
Lerista ips 521
Lerista kalumburu 521
Lerista karlschmidti 522*
Lerista kendricki 738
Lerista kennedyensis 522*
Lerista labialis 523*
Lerista lineata 524*
Lerista lineopunctulata 525*
Lerista macropisthopus 525*
Lerista maculosa 738
Lerista microtis 525*
Lerista microtis arenicola 526
Lerista microtis microtis 526
Lerista muelleri 526*
Lerista neander 527*
Lerista nichollsi 527
Lerista nichollsi nichollsi 527
Lerista nichollsi petersoni 527
Lerista onsloviana 528*
Lerista orientalis 528*
Lerista petersoni 739
Lerista picturata 528*
Lerista picturata baynesi 529
Lerista picturata edwardsae 529
Lerista picturata picturata 529
Lerista planiventralis 529*
Lerista planiventralis decora 529
Lerista planiventralis planiventralis 529
Lerista praefrontalis 530
Lerista praepedita 530*
Lerista punctatovittata 530*
Lerista puncticauda 739
Lerista robusta 739
Lerista separanda 530
Lerista simillima 531
Lerista speciosa 740
Lerista stictopleura 532*
Lerista storri 532
Lerista stylis 532*
Lerista taeniata 533
Lerista talpina 740
Lerista terdigitata 533*
Lerista tridactyla 740
Lerista uniduo 534*
Lerista varia 534*
Lerista vermicularis 535
Lerista viduata 740
Lerista vittata 536*
Lerista walkeri 536*
Lerista wilkinsi 536*
Lerista xanthura 536*
Lerista yuna 740
Lerista zonulata 740
lesueuri, Litoria 143*
lesueurii, Oedura 263*
lesueurii, Physignathus 345*
lesueurii, Physignathus lesueurii 346
leuckartii, Anomalopus 384*
leucobalia, Fordonia 625*
leucoproctus, Ramphotyphlops 593
leukops, Rheodytes 201*
leuraensis, Eulamprus 485*
levis, Nephrurus 256*
levis, Nephrurus levis 257
Lialis 293
Lialis burtonis 294*
Liasis 604
Liasis albertisii 605*
Liasis childreni 606*
Liasis fuscus 606*
Liasis maculosus 606*
Liasis olivaceus 608*
Liasis olivaceus barroni 608
Liasis olivaceus olivaceus 608
Liasis perthensis 608*
Liasis stimsoni 610*
lichenigera, Pseudemoia 563*
liemi, Taudactylus 106*
ligatus, Ramphotyphlops 593*
lignarius, Megistolotus 81*
Limnodynastes 73
Limnodynastes convexiusculus 75*
Limnodynastes depressus 75
Limnodynastes dorsalis 75*
Limnodynastes dumerilii 75*
Limnodynastes dumerilii dumerilii 76
Limnodynastes dumerilii fryi 76
Limnodynastes dumerilii grayi 76
Limnodynastes dumerilii insularis 76
Limnodynastes dumerilii variegatus 76
Limnodynastes fletcheri 76*
Limnodynastes interioris 76*
Limnodynastes ornatus 77*
Limnodynastes peronii 78*
Limnodynastes salmini 78*
Limnodynastes spenceri 79*
Limnodynastes tasmaniensis 80*
Limnodynastes terraereginae 80*
lindneri, Pseudothecadactylus 273*
lindneri, Pseudothecadactylus lindneri 273
lineata, Lerista 524*
lineata, Tympanocryptis 353*
lineata, Tympanocryptis lineata 354
lineoocellata, Morethia 547*
lineopunctulata, Lerista 525*
linga, Diporiphora 332
listeri, Lepidodactylus 728*
lithomoda, Uperoleia 112
litoralis, Cryptoblepharus 405*
Litoria 123
Litoria adelaidensis 127*
Litoria alboguttata 128*
Litoria aurea 128*
Litoria bicolor 129*
Litoria booroolongensis 129*
Litoria brevipalmata 130*
Litoria burrowsae 131*
Litoria caerulea 132*
Litoria castanea 132
Litoria cavernicola 132*
Litoria chloris 133*
Litoria citropa 133*
Litoria cooloolensis 133
Litoria coplandi 134*
Litoria cyclorhyncha 134*
Litoria dahlii 135*
Litoria dentata 135*
Litoria dorsalis 136*
Litoria dorsalis dorsalis 136
Litoria dorsalis microbelos 136
Litoria electrica 734
Litoria ewingii 136*
Litoria fallax 137*
Litoria freycineti 137*
Litoria genimaculata 138*
Litoria gilleni 138*
Litoria gracilenta 139*
Litoria inermis 139*
Litoria infrafrenata 140*
Litoria jervisiensis 140*
Litoria latopalmata 142*

Litoria lesueuri 143*
Litoria longirostris 143
Litoria lorica 143*
Litoria meiriana 143*
Litoria moorei 144*
Litoria nannotis 145*
Litoria nasuta 145*
Litoria nigrofrenata 146*
Litoria nyakalensis 146
Litoria olongburensis 146*
Litoria pallida 147*
Litoria paraewingi 148
Litoria pearsoniana 734
Litoria peronii 148*
Litoria personata 148*
Litoria phyllochroa 150*
Litoria piperata 151
Litoria raniformis 151*
Litoria revelata 151
Litoria rheocola 151*
Litoria rothii 152*
Litoria rubella 152*
Litoria spenceri 153*
Litoria splendida 155*
Litoria subglandulosa 155*
Litoria tornieri 155*
Litoria tyleri 155*
Litoria verreauxii 156*
Litoria verreauxii alpina 157
Litoria verreauxii verreauxii 157
Litoria wotjulumensis 157*
Litoria xanthomera 157
littlejohni, Uperoleia 112
littoralis, Simoselaps 686*
Lizard, Blotched blue-tongued 577
  Centralian Blue-tongued 577
  Eastern Blue-tongued 580
  Frilled 305
  Jacky 301
  Jew 347
  Pink-tongued 503
  Shingle-back 584
  Western Blue-tongued 579
longicauda, Egernia pulchra 470
longicauda, Emoia 477*
longicollis, Chelodina 190*
longipes, Carlia 394*
longipes, Cyclorana 119*
longirostris, Litoria 143
longirostris, Lophognathus 341*
Lophognathus 340
Lophognathus gilberti 340*
Lophognathus longirostris 341*
Lophognathus temporalis 342
lorica, Litoria 143*
louisiadensis, Cyrtodactylus 210*
loveridgei, Philoria 96*
Lucasium 250
Lucasium damaeum 250*
luctuosa, Egernia 465*
lugubris, Lepidodactylus 249, 728*
lutea, Geocrinia 66*
luteilateralis, Eulamprus 485*
Luth 185
Lycodon capucinus 731*
Lygisaurus 537
Lygisaurus aeratus 538
Lygisaurus foliorum 539*
Lygisaurus laevis 539*
Lygisaurus macfarlani 540
Lygisaurus rococo 540
Lygisaurus sesbrauna 540
Lygisaurus tanneri 540
Lygisaurus timlowi 541
Lygosoma 730
Lygosoma bowringii 730*

maccoyi, Nannoscincus 552*
macfarlani, Lygisaurus 540*
mackayi, Anomalopus 385*
macquarii, Emydura 197*
macra, Tympanocryptis lineata 354
macropisthopus, Lerista 525*
macropus, Ctenophorus caudicinctus 311
maculata, Denisonia 644*
maculatus, Ctenophorus 317*
maculatus, Ctenophorus maculatus 317
maculosa, Cyclorana 119
maculosa, Lerista 738
maculosus, Ctenophorus 318*
maculosus, Liasis 606*
magna, Diporiphora 332*
maini, Cyclorana 121*
maini, Diplodactylus 221*
maini, Menetia 544*
mairii, Tropidonophis 628*
mairii, Tropidonophis mairii 628
major, Aclys concinna 278
major, Disteira 707*
major, Egernia 465*
major, Pseudophryne 102*
manya, Cyclorana 121
margaretae, Egernia 466*
margaretae, Egernia margaretae 467
margaretae, Ramphotyphlops 594
marinus, Bufo 169*
marmorata, Oedura 263*
marmorata, Uperoleia 112
marmoratus, Christinus 208*
martini, Uperoleia 112
mastersii, Drysdalia 647*
mastigura, Ctenotus 434
mastigura, Ctenotus mastigura 434
maxima, Cyclodomorphus 453*
mcdonaldi, Cophixalus 162
mcdowelli, Hydrophis 717
mckenziei, Ctenophorus 318*
mcmillani, Diplodactylus 221*
mcpheei, Egernia 467*
megastictus, Cryptoblepharus 405*
Megistolotus 81
Megistolotus lignarius 81*
meiriana, Litoria 143*
melaena, Demansia papuensis 641
melanocephalus, Aspidites 601*
melanoscaphus, Notaden 92*
melanosoma, Hydrophis 718
Menetia 541
Menetia alanae 542*
Menetia amaura 542
Menetia concinna 542*
Menetia greyii 543*
Menetia maini 544*
Menetia surda 545*
mensarum, Ctenophorus caudicinctus 311
mertensi, Varanus 369*
mertoni, Parahydrophis 721*
Metacrinia 82
Metacrinia nichollsi 82*
metallica, Pseudemoia 564*
metallicus, Niveoscincus 741, 564
michaelseni, Diplodactylus 222*
microbelos, Litoria dorsalis 136
MICROHYLIDAE 159
microlepidota, Pogona 347
microlepidota, Pseudemoia 566
microlepidota, Oxyuranus 662*
microlepidotus, Niveoscincus 741, 566
micromeles, Uperoleia 112*
micromma, Ramphotyphlops 594
microtis, Lerista 525*
microtis, Lerista microtis 526
milii, Underwoodisaurus 275*
militaris, Ctenotus 434
millewe, Hemiergis 502*
mimetes, Ctenotus 435*
mimula, Uperoleia 113
minima, Pogona 349*
minimc, Uperoleia 113
minimus, Ramphotyphlops 595
minimus, Simoselaps 686
minor, Elapognathus 649*
minor, Pogona 349
minuta, Gehyra 239*
mirabilis, Lampropholis 508*
mitchelli, Diplodactylus 222*
mitchelli, Pogona 349
mitchelli, Varanus 369*
mitella, Delma 290
Mixophyes 82
Mixophyes balbus 83
Mixophyes fasciolatus 83*
Mixophyes fleayi 83*
Mixophyes iteratus 84*
Mixophyes schevilli 84*
mjobergi, Glaphyromorphus 496*
mjobergii, Uperoleia 113
modesta, Egernia 468*
modesta, Pseudonaja 671*
molleri, Delma 290*
Moloch 343
Moloch horridus 344*
monachus, Suta 690*
moniligera, Egernia whitii 474
monilis, Oedura 264*
Monitor (see also Goanna) 202
Monitor, Emerald 371
  Gould's 366
  Lace 379
  Long-tailed Rock 365
  Mangrove 368
  Merten's Water 369
  Mitchell's Water 369
  Pygmy Mulga 365
  Ridge-tailed 359
  Rusty 372
  Sand 366
  Spencer's 376
  Spotted Tree 377
monswilsonensis, Ophioscincus truncatus 556
monticola, Ctenotus 435
montium, Gehyra 239*
moorei, Litoria 144*
Morelia 610
Morelia amethistina 611*
Morelia bredli 611*
Morelia carinata 612
Morelia oenpelliensis 613*
Morelia spilota 614*
Morelia spilota imbricata 614
Morelia spilota spilota 614
Morelia spilota variegata 614
Morethia 545
Morethia adelaidensis 546*
Morethia boulengeri 546*
Morethia butleri 547*
Morethia lineoocellata 547*
Morethia obscura 548*
Morethia ruficauda 548*
Morethia ruficauda exquisita 548
Morethia ruficauda ruficauda 548
Morethia storri 548*
Morethia taeniopleura 550*
muelleri, Lerista 526*
multiscutata, Egernia 468*
multifasciata, Tiliqua 577*
multifasciata, Vermicella 696*
multifasciata, Vermicella multifasciata 469
munda, Carlia 395*
mundivensis, Carlia 395*
muricatus, Amphibolurus 301*
murrayi, Eulamprus 486*
mustelina, Saproscincus 574*
mutilata, Gehyra 727*
mydas, Chelonia 180*
mydas, Chelonia mydas 181

MYOBATRACHIDAE 53
Myobatrachus 86
Myobatrachus gouldii 86*
Myron 625
Myron richardsonii 625*

Nactus 251
Nactus galgajuga 251*
Nactus pelagicus 253*
nana, Gehyra 239*
Nannoscincus 552
Nannoscincus maccoyi 552*
nannotis, Litoria 145*
napoleonis, Egernia 469*
naso, Crenadactylus ocellatus 209
nasuta, Delma 291*
nasuta, Litoria 145*
nasutus, Ctenotus 735
nasutus, Ctenotus colletti 420
Natator 183
Natator depressus 183*
nativitatis, Emoia 728*
neander, Lerista 527*
neglectus, Cophixalus 162
Neobatrachus 87
Neobatrachus albipes 733
Neobatrachus aquilonius 87*
Neobatrachus centralis 88*
Neobatrachus fulvus 88
Neobatrachus kunapalari 88
Neobatrachus pelobatoides 89*
Neobatrachus pictus 89
Neobatrachus sudelli 90*
Neobatrachus sutor 90*
Neobatrachus wilsmorei 90*
Nephrurus 253
Nephrurus asper 254*
Nephrurus deleani 255*
Nephrurus laevissimus 256*
Nephrurus levis 256*
Nephrurus levis levis 257
Nephrurus levis occidentalis 257
Nephrurus levis pilbarensis 257
Nephrurus stellatus 257*
Nephrurus vertebralis 257*
Nephrurus wheeleri 257*
Nephrurus wheeleri cinctus 258
Nephrurus wheeleri wheeleri 258
nichollsi, Lerista 527
nichollsi, Lerista nichollsi 527
nichollsi, Metacrinia 82*
nichollsi, Notaden 93*
niger, Notechis ater 659
nigrescens, Ramphotyphlops 595*
nigrescens, Rhinoplocephalus 677*
nigricaudis, Glaphyromorphus 496*
nigriceps, Pygopus 298*
nigriceps, Pygopus nigriceps 298
nigriceps, Suta 691*
nigrilineatus, Ctenotus 735
nigrofrenata, Litoria 146*
nigrolutea, Tiliqua 577*
nigrostriatus, Rhinoplocephalus 679*
Niveoscincus conventryi 741, 561
Niveoscincus greeni 741, 562*
Niveoscincus metallicus 741, 564
Niveoscincus microlepidotus 741, 566
Niveoscincus ocellatus 7412, 566
Niveoscincus orocryptus 741, 567
Niveoscincus palfreymani 741, 567
Niveoscincus pretiosus 741, 568
nobbi, Amphibolurus 301*
nobbi, Amphibolurus nobbi 302
Nobbi 301
norrisi, Amphibolurus 302*
Notaden 91
Notaden bennettii 92*
Notaden melanoscaphus 92*
Notaden nichollsi 93*
Notaden weigeli 94*
Notechis 658
Notechis ater 659*
Notechis ater ater 659
Notechis ater humphreysi 659
Notechis ater niger 659
Notechis ater occidentalis 659
Notechis scutatus 660*
Notoscincus 553
Notoscincus butleri 553
Notoscincus ornatus 553*
Notoscincus ornatus ornatus 554
Notoscincus ornatus wotjulum 554
novaeguineae, Chelodina 191*
novaehollandiae, Cyclorana 121*
nuchalis, Ctenophorus 318*
nuchalis, Pseudonaja 672*
nullarbor, Pogona 350*
nullarbor, Suta spectabilis 693
nyakalensis, Litoria 146
Nyctimystes 158
Nyctimystes dayi 158*

oblonga, Chelodina 192*
obscura, Morethia 548*
obscura, Oedura 265*
occidentalis, Gehyra 240*
occidentalis, Nephrurus levis 257
occidentalis, Notechis ater 659
occidentalis, Pseudophryne 103
occipitalis, Tiliqua 579*
occultus, Diplodactylus 222*
oceanica, Gehyra 240*
ocellata, Pseudemoia 566*
ocellatus, Crenadactylus 209*
ocellatus, Crenadactylus ocellatus 209
ocellatus, Hydrophis ornatus 719
ocellatus, Niveoscincus 741, 566
ocellifer, Ctenotus pantherinus 436
ocreatus, Varanus storri 377
Oedura 259
Oedura castelnaui 260*
Oedura coggeri 260*
Oedura filicipoda 261*
Oedura gemmata 262*
Oedura gracilis 262*
Oedura lesueurii 263*
Oedura marmorata 263*
Oedura monilis 264*
Oedura obscura 265*
Oedura reticulata 265*
Oedura rhombifer 266*
Oedura robusta 266*
Oedura tryoni 266*
oenpelliensis, Morelia 613*
olivacea, Demansia 640*
olivacea, Demansia olivacea 640
olivacea, Lepidochelys 183*
olivaceus, Liasis 608*
olivaceus, Liasis olivaceus 608
olongburensis, Litoria 146*
onslowiana, Lerista 528*
Ophidiocephalus 294
Ophidiocephalus taeniatus 294*
ophioscincus, Ophioscincus 556*
Ophioscincus 554
Ophioscincus cooloolensis 555
Ophioscincus ophioscincus 556*
Ophioscincus truncatus 556*
Ophioscincus truncatus monswilsonensis 556
Ophioscincus truncatus truncatus 556
ordensis, Suta 691
orientalis, Ctenotus uber 449
orientalis, Lerista 528*
orientalis, Paradelma 296*
orientalis, Uperoleia 114
orientalis, Varanus tristis 379
ornata, Furina 653*
ornata, Rhynchoedura 274*
ornatus, Cophixalus 163*
ornatus, Ctenophorus 320*
ornatus, Diplodactylus 223*
ornatus, Hydrophis 718*
ornatus, Hydrophis ornatus 719
ornatus, Limnodynastes 77*
ornatus, Notoscincus 553*
ornatus, Notoscincus ornatus 554
orocrypta, Pseudemoia 567
orocryptus, Niveoscincus 741, 567
Oxyuranus 660
Oxyuranus microlepidota 662*
Oxyuranus scutellatus 662*
Oxyuranus scutellatus canni 663
Oxyuranus scutellatus scutellatus 663

pacificus, Hydrophis 719
palfreymani, Niveoscincus 741, 567
palfreymani, Pseudemoia 567*
pallescens, Ctenotus 435
pallida, Litoria 147*
pallidiceps, Rhinoplocephalus 679*
pamela, Gehyra 242*
panoptes, Varanus 370*
panoptes, Varanus panoptes 370
pantherinus, Ctenotus 436*
pantherinus, Ctenotus pantherinus 436
papuensis, Demansia 641*
papuensis, Demansia papuensis 641
Paracrinia 94
Paracrinia haswelli 94*
Paradelma 295
Paradelma orientalis 296*
paraewingi, Litoria 148
Parahydrophis 721
Parahydrophis mertoni 721*
parapulchella, Aprasia 281*
pardalis, Glaphyromorphus 496*
parinsignifera, Crinia 60*
parviceps, Tympanocryptis 355*
parviceps, Tympanocryptis parviceps 356
parvus, Stegonotus 627
pax, Delma 291*
pearsoniana, Litoria 734
pectoralis, Carlia 395
pelagicus, Nactus 253*
Pelamis 722
Pelamis platurus 722*
pelobatoides, Neobatrachus 89*
peninsularis, Cophixalus 164
Perentie 363
peronii, Acalyptophis 698*
peronii, Hemiergis 502*
peronii, Limnodynastes 78*
peronii, Litoria 148*
personata, Egernia margaretae 467
personata, Litoria 148*
perthensis, Liasis 608*
petersoni, Lerista 739
petersoni, Lerista nichollsi 527
Philoria 95
Philoria frosti 96*
Philoria kundagungan 96
Philoria loveridgei 96*
Philoria sphagnicolus 97*
phyllochroa, Litoria 150*
Phyllurus 268
Phyllurus caudiannulatus 269*
Phyllurus cornutus 269*
Phyllurus platurus 271*
Phyllurus salebrosus 271
Physignathus 344
Physignathus lesueurii 345*
Physignathus lesueurii howittii 346

Physignathus lesueurii lesueurii 346
piankai, Ctenotus 437
piankai, Ctenotus piankai 437
picturata, Lerista 528*
picturata, Lerista picturata 529
pictus, Ctenophorus 320*
pictus, Neobatrachus 89
pilbara, Gehyra 242*
pilbarensis, Egernia 469*
pilbarensis, Nephrurus levis 257
pilbarensis, Varanus 370
pindan, Diporiphora 332*
pinguicolla, Tympanocryptis lineata 354
pinguis, Ramphotyphlops 596*
piperata, Litoria 151
plagiocephalus, Cryptoblepharus 406*
plagiocephalus, Cryptoblepharus plagiocephalus 406
planiceps, Heteronotia 734
planiventralis, Lerista 529*
planiventralis, Lerista planiventralis 529
platurus, Pelamis 722*
platurus, Phyllurus 271*
platycephala, Cyclorana 121*
platynota, Bassiana 734, 567
platynota, Pseudemoia 567*
plebeia, Delma 292*
pleione, Taudactylus 107
Pletholax 296
Pletholax gracilis 296*
Pletholax gracilis edelensis 296
Pletholax gracilis gracilis 296
pluto, Anomalopus 385*
pluvialis, Sphenophryne 166*
Pobblebonk 75
Pogona 346
Pogona barbata 347*
Pogona microlepidota 347
Pogona minima 349*
Pogona minor 349
Pogona mitchelli 349
Pogona nullarbor 350*
Pogona vitticeps 350*
polygrammicus, Ramphotyphlops 596*
polylepis, Enhydris 623*
polyophthalmus, Diplodactylus 224*
pooleorum, Aipysurus laevis 704
porosus, Crocodylus 175*
porphyriacus, Pseudechis 668*
praefrontalis, Lerista 530
praelongus, Acanthophis 634*
praepedita, Lerista 530*
prasinus, Varanus 371*
pretiosa, Pseudemoia 568*
pretiosus, Niveoscincus 741, 568
primordius, Varanus 371*
Proablepharus 556
Proablepharus kinghorni 557*
Proablepharus reginae 557*
Proablepharus tenuis 559*
proximus, Ramphotyphlops 597*
psammophilus, Heleioporus 72*
psammophis, Demansia psammophis 641*
Pseudechis 664
Pseudechis australis 664*
Pseudechis butleri 665*
butleri, Pseudechis 665*
Pseudechis colletti 665*
Pseudechis guttatus 666*
Pseudechis porphyriacus 668*
Pseudemoia 559
Pseudemoia baudini 561
Pseudemoia coventryi 561*
Pseudemoia duperreyi 561*
Pseudemoia entrecasteauxii 562*
Pseudemoia greeni 562*
Pseudemoia jigurru 563*
Pseudemoia lichenigera 563*
Pseudemoia metallica 564*
Pseudemoia microlepidota 566
Pseudemoia ocellata 566*
Pseudemoia orocrypta 567
Pseudemoia palfreymani 567*
Pseudemoia platynota 567*
Pseudemoia pretiosa 568*
Pseudemoia rawlinsoni 569
Pseudemoia spenceri 569*
Pseudemoia trilineata 571*
Pseudemoia zia 571*
Pseudemydura 200
Pseudemydura umbrina 200*
pseudinsignifera, Crinia 61
Pseudonaja 668
Pseudonaja affinis 670*
Pseudonaja affinis affinis 670
Pseudonaja affinis exilis 670
Pseudonaja affinis tanneri 670
Pseudonaja guttata 670*
Pseudonaja inframacula 670*
Pseudonaja ingrami 671*
Pseudonaja modesta 671*
Pseudonaja nuchalis 672*
Pseudonaja textilis 675*
Pseudophryne 97
Pseudophryne australis 98*
Pseudophryne bibronii 99*
Pseudophryne coriacea 99*
Pseudophryne corroboree 101*
Pseudophryne dendyi 101*
Pseudophryne douglasi 101
Pseudophryne guentheri 101*
Pseudophryne major 102*
Pseudophryne occidentalis 103*
Pseudophryne semimarmorata 103*
pseudopulchella, Aprasia 281*
Pseudothecadactylus 271
Pseudothecadactylus australis 271*
Pseudothecadactylus lindneri 273*
Pseudothecadactylus lindneri cavaticus 273
Pseudothecadactylus lindneri lindneri 273
pulchella, Aprasia 281*
pulchellus, Ctenotus 437*
pulcher, Diplodactylus 224*
pulchra, Egernia 470*
pulchra, Egernia pulchra 470
pumilus, Glaphyromorphus 498*
pumilus, Lepidodactylus 250*
punctata, Gehyra 243*
punctata, Suta 691*
puncticauda, Lerista 739
punctulata, Dendrelaphis 621*
punctulatus, Glaphyromorphus 498*
punctatovittata, Lerista 530*
purpurascens, Gehyra 243*
PYGOPODIDAE 277
Pygopus 297
Pygopus lepidopodus 297*
Pygopus nigriceps 298*
Pygopus nigriceps nigriceps 298
Pygopus nigriceps schraderi 298
pyrrhus, Acanthophis 634*
Python, Amethystine 611
  Black-headed 601
  Carpet 614
  Children's 605
  Diamond 614
  Green 603
  Olive 608
  Water 606
Pythons (see Boidae) 585

quadrilineatum, Hemiergis 502*
quattuordecimlineatus, Ctenotus 438*
quattuordecimlineatus, Ctenotus quattuordecimlineatus 438
queenslandiae, Gnypetoscincus 499*
quinkan, Ctenotus 438
quoyii, Eulamprus 487*

Ramphotyphlops 587
Ramphotyphlops affinis 589
Ramphotyphlops australis 589*
Ramphotyphlops bituberculatus 589
Ramphotyphlops braminus 589, 731*
Ramphotyphlops broomi 591
Ramphotyphlops centralis 591
Ramphotyphlops diversus 592
Ramphotyphlops diversus ammodytes 592
Ramphotyphlops diversus diversus 592
Ramphotyphlops endoterus 592*
Ramphotyphlops exocoeti 731
Ramphotyphlops grypus 592*
Ramphotyphlops guentheri 592
Ramphotyphlops hamatus 593
Ramphotyphlops howi 593
Ramphotyphlops kimberleyensis 593
Ramphotyphlops leptosoma 593
Ramphotyphlops leucoproctus 593
Ramphotyphlops ligatus 593*
Ramphotyphlops margaretae 594
Ramphotyphlops micromma 594
Ramphotyphlops minimus 595
Ramphotyphlops nigrescens 595*
Ramphotyphlops pinguis 596*
Ramphotyphlops polygrammicus 596*
Ramphotyphlops proximus 597*
Ramphotyphlops tovelli 597*
Ramphotyphlops troglodytes 598
Ramphotyphlops unguirostris 598
Ramphotyphlops waitii 598
Ramphotyphlops wiedii 599*
Ramphotyphlops yampiensis 599
Ramphotyphlops yirrikalae 599
ramsayi, Aspidites 602*
Rana 168
Rana daemeli 168*
RANIDAE 168
raniformis, Litoria 151*
rankini, Diplodactylus 225*
rawlinsoni, Ctenotus 438*
rawlinsoni, Pseudemoia 569
reginae, Diporiphora 333*
reginae, Proablepharus 557*
regius, Ctenotus 438*
remota, Crinia 61*
repens, Aprasia 282*
reticulata, Demansia psammophis 641
reticulata, Oedura 265*
reticulatus, Coeranoscincus 402*
reticulatus, Ctenophorus 322*
revelata, Litoria 151
rex, Diplodactylus granariensis 219
Rheobatrachus 103
Rheobatrachus silus 103*
Rheobatrachus vitellinus 104*
rheocola, Litoria 151*
Rheodytes 200
Rheodytes leukops 201*
rheophilus, Taudactylus 107*
Rhinoplocephalus 676
Rhinoplocephalus bicolor 676*
Rhinoplocephalus boschmai 677*
Rhinoplocephalus nigrescens 677*
Rhinoplocephalus nigrostriatus 679*
Rhinoplocephalus pallidiceps 679*
Rhinoplocephalus sp. 679*
rhodogaster, Drysdalia 647*

rhombifer, Oedura 266*
rhomboidalis, Carlia 396*
Rhynchoedura 274
Rhynchoedura ornata 274*
richardi, Egernia 470
richardsonii, Myron 625*
richardsonii, Eremiascincus 478*
Ridley, Pacific 183
rimula, Carlia 396
riparia, Crinia 61*
robertsi, Lampropholis 737
robusta, Gehyra 243*
robusta, Lerista 739
robusta, Oedura 266*
robusta, Sphenophryne 167*
robustus, Ctenotus 439*
rococo, Lygisaurus 540
roperi, Simoselaps semifasciatus 688
rosea, Geocrinia 67*
rosenbergi, Varanus 372*
rostralis, Carlia 397*
rostralis, Crenadactylus ocellatus 209
rostrata, Aprasia 282
rostrata, Aprasia rostrata 282
rothii, Litoria 152*
rotunda, Arenophryne 56*
rubella, Litoria 152*
rubens, Ctenophorus isolepis 317
ruber, Cryptoblepharus plagiocephalus 406
rubicundus, Ctenotus 440
rubidus, Varanus panoptes 370
rubrigularis, Carlia 398
rufescens, Ctenophorus 323*
rufescens, Ctenotus 735
rufescens, Ctenotus colletti 420
rufescens, Demansia olivacea 640
rufescens, Eugongylus 480*
ruficauda, Calyptotis 387*
ruficauda, Morethia 548*
ruficauda, Morethia ruficauda 548
rufilatus, Carlia 398
rugosa, Chelodina 192*
rugosa, Egernia 470*
rugosa, Uperoleia 114*
rugosus, Trachydosaurus 584*
rugosus, Trachydosaurus rugosus 584
russelli, Uperoleia 115
rutilans, Ctenotus 440
rynchops, Cerberus 619*

Saiphos 571
Saiphos equalis 572*
salebrosus, Phyllurus 271
salinarum, Ctenophorus 323*
salmini, Limnodynastes 78*
Sand-swimmer, Broad-banded 478
Narrow-banded 477
Saproscincus 572
Saproscincus basiliscus 573
Saproscincus challengeri 574*
Saproscincus czechurai 574*
Saproscincus mustelina 574*
Saproscincus tetradactyla 575*
savagei, Diplodactylus 225*
saxatilis, Cophixalus 164*
saxatilis, Ctenotus 441*
saxatilis, Egernia 471*
saxatilis, Egernia saxatilis 472
scalaris, Varanus timorensis 377
Scaly-foot Common 297
Hooded 298
schevilli, Ctenotus 441*
schevilli, Mixophyes 84*
schistosa, Enhydrina 709*
schmeltzii, Carlia 399*
schomburgkii, Ctenotus 442*
schraderi, Pygopus nigriceps 298
schuettleri, Ctenotus hebetior 427
SCINCIDAE 380
scincoides, Tiliqua 580*
scincoides, Tiliqua scincoides 582
scirtetis, Carlia 399*
scutatus, Notechis 660*
scutellatus, Oxyuranus 662*
scutellatus, Oxyuranus scutellatus 663
scutirostrum, Calyptotis 388*
scutulatus, Ctenophorus 326*
Sea-kraits (see Laticaudidae)
Sea-snakes (see Hydrophiidae)
semifasciatus, Simoselaps 687*
semifasciatus, Simoselaps semifasciatus 688
semimarmorata, Pseudophryne 103*
semiremex, Varanus 372*
separanda, Lerista 530
septenarius, Ctenotus 442
serotinus, Ctenotus 442
serventyi, Ctenotus 443
sesbrauna, Lygisaurus 540
severus, Ctenotus 443*
Shingle-back 584
signata, Emydura 199*
signata, Hemiaspis 656*
signifera, Crinia 62*
silus, Rheobatrachus 103*
similis, Varanus timorensis 377
simillima, Lerista 531
Simoselaps 680
Simoselaps anomalus 682*
Simoselaps approximans 682*
Simoselaps australis 682*
Simoselaps bertholdi 683*
Simoselaps bimaculatus 684*
Simoselaps calonotus 684*
Simoselaps fasciolatus 684*
Simoselaps fasciolatus fasciatus 685
Simoselaps fasciolatus fasciolatus 685
Simoselaps incinctus 685*
Simoselaps littoralis 686*
Simoselaps minimus 686
Simoselaps semifasciatus 687*
Simoselaps semifasciatus campbelli 688
Simoselaps semifasciatus roperi 688
Simoselaps semifasciatus semifasciatus 688
Simoselaps warro 688*
simplex, Demansia 641
Skink, Alpine Water 485
Black Rock 471
Copper-tailed 447
Cunningham's 457
Desert 462
Eastern Water 487
Fire-tailed 550
Gidgee 472
Great Desert 465
Hosmer's 461
King's 465
Lord Howe Island 563
Major 461
Oak 452
Ocellated 566
Pigmy Spiny-tailed 458
Red-throated 567
Tree 472
Weasel 574
White's 473
Yakka 471
Skinks (see Scincidae) 202
slateri, Ctenophorus caudicinctus 311
slateri, Egernia 472
slateri, Egernia slateri 472
sloanei, Crinia 64*
smithi, Aprasia 282
Snake, Arafura File 615
Black-bellied Swamp 656
Black-headed 690
Black-striped 679
Black Tiger 659
Black Whip 639
Broad-headed 658
Brown-headed 653
Brown Tree 618
Carpentaria Whip 677
Collared Whip 643
Collett's 665
Common Tree 621
Coral 682
Crowned 645
Curl 693
Desert Banded 683
De Vis' Banded 644
Dunmall's 652
Dwarf Crowned 637
Eastern Brown 675
Eastern Small-eyed 677
Eastern Tiger 660
Fierce 662
Freshwater 628
Golden-crowned 638
Grey 654
Half-girdled 687
Hooded 690
Ingram's Brown 670
King Brown 664
Little Brown 649
Little File 616
Little Spotted 691
Little Whip 689
Macleay's Water 623
Mainland Tiger 660
Masters' 647
Mulga 664
Myall 693
Narrow-banded 684
Northern Small-eyed 679
Northern Tree 620
Orange-naped 653
Ornamental 644
Pale-headed 657
Peninsula Brown 670
Red-bellied Black 668
Red-naped 651
Ringed Brown 671
Rosen's 689
Rough-scaled 694
Slatey-grey 627
Spotted Black 666
Stephen's Banded 658
Western Black-naped 684
Western Black-striped 684
Western Brown 672
White-bellied Mangrove 625
White-crowned 636
White-lipped 646
Yellow-bellied Sea 722
Yellow-faced Whip 641
Yellow-naped 651
Snake-lizard, Burton's 294
Snake-lizards (see Pygopodidae) 202
spaldingi, Ctenotus 444*
sp., *Cyrtodactylus* 727*
sp., *Rhinoplocephalus* 679*
speciosa, Lerista 740
spectabilis, Suta 693*
spectabilis, Suta spectabilis 693
spelea, Heteronotia 248*
spenceri, Limnodynastes 79*
spenceri, Litoria 153*
spenceri, Pseudemoia 569*
spenceri, Varanus 376*
sphagnicolus, Philoria 97*
Sphenophryne 164
Sphenophryne adelphe 165 *

Sphenophryne fryi 165*
Sphenophryne gracilipes 166*
Sphenophryne pluvialis 166*
Sphenophryne robusta 167*
sphyrurus, Underwoodisaurus 276*
spilota, Morelia 614*
spilota, Morelia spilota 614
spinigerus, Diplodactylus 225*
spinigerus, Diplodactylus spinigerus 226
spinipes, Hypsilurus 338*
splendida, Litoria 155*
squamata, Eretmochelys imbricata 182
squamulosus, Cacophis 638*
squarrosus, Diplodactylus 226*
Stegonotus 626
Stegonotus cucullatus 627*
Stegonotus parvus 627
steindachneri, Chelodina 193*
steindachneri, Diplodactylus 227*
stellatus, Nephrurus 257*
stenodactylus, Diplodactylus 228*
stephensii, Hoplocephalus 658*
stictopleura, Lerista 532*
stimsoni, Liasis 610*
stokesii, Astrotia 706*
stokesii, Egernia 472*
stokesii, Egernia stokesii 472
storri, Carlia 399*
storri, Ctenotus 446*
storri, Lerista 532
storri, Morethia 548*
storri, Varanus 376*
storri, Varanus storri 377
strauchii, Ctenotus 446*
striata, Egernia 472*
striaticeps, Ctenotus 447*
striolata, Aprasia 283*
striolata, Egernia 472*
strophurus, Diplodactylus 228*
stylis, Lerista 532*
subglandulosa, Litoria 155*
subglobosa, Emydura 199*
subinsignifera, Crinia 64*
sudelli, Neobatrachus 90*
superba, Diporiphora 334*
superbus, Austrelaps 635*
surda, Menetia 545*
suta, Suta 693*
Suta 688
Suta fasciata 689*
Suta flagellum 689*
Suta gouldii 690*
Suta monachus 690*
Suta nigriceps 691*
Suta ordensis 691
Suta punctata 691*
Suta spectabilis 693*
Suta spectabilis bushi 693
Suta spectabilis dwyeri 693
Suta spectabilis nullarbor 693
Suta spectabilis spectabilis 693
Suta suta 693*
sutor, Neobatrachus 90*
swansoni, Anomalopus 385*

taeniata, Lerista 533
taeniatus, Ctenotus brooksi 418
taeniatus, Diplodactylus 229*
taeniatus, Ophidiocephalus 294*
taenicauda, Diplodactylus 231*
taeniolatus, Ctenotus 447*
taeniopleura, Morethia 550*
Taipan 662
talbingoensis, Hemiergis decresiensis 500
talpa, Uperoleia 115
talpina, Lerista 740
tanamiensis, Ctenotus 448
tanneri, Lygisaurus 540*
tanneri, Pseudonaja affinis 670
tantillus, Ctenotus 449
tasmaniensis, Crinia 64*
tasmaniensis, Limnodynastes 80*
Taudactylus 104
Taudactylus acutirostris 105*
Taudactylus diurnus 105*
Taudactylus eungellensis 106
Taudactylus liemi 106*
Taudactylus pleione 107
Taudactylus rheophilus 107*
temporalis, Calyptotis 389*
temporalis, Lophognathus 342*
tenuis, Aipysurus 704
tenuis, Eulamprus 487*
tenuis, Eulamprus tenuis 488
tenuis, Proablepharus 559*
terdigitata, Lerista 533*
teriae, Varanus 734
terraereginae, Limnodynastes 80*
tessellatus, Diplodactylus 231*
tetradactyla, Carlia 401*
tetradactyla, Saproscincus 575*
tetraporophora, Tympanocryptis 356*
textilis, Pseudonaja 675*
thorntonensis, Calyptotis 389
Thorny Devil (see Moloch) 344
Tiger Snake 659, 660
tigrinus, Eulamprus 489*
Tiliqua 576
Tiliqua adelaidensis 576
Tiliqua multifasciata 577*
Tiliqua nigrolutea 577*
Tiliqua occipitalis 579*
Tiliqua scincoides 580*
Tiliqua scincoides intermedia 582
Tiliqua scincoides scincoides 582
timlowi, Lygisaurus 541
timorensis, Varanus 377*
timorensis, Varanus timorensis 377
tincta, Delma 292*
tinnula, Crinia 65
titan, Ctenotus grandis 426
Toad, Cane 169
  Crucifix 92
  Desert Spadefoot 93
  Marine (see Cane Toad) 169
  Northern Spadefoot 92
Toadlet, Brown 99
  Gunther's 101
  Nicholl's 82
  Orange-crowned 103
  Red-backed 99
  Red-crowned 98
  Southern 103
Toads, True 51
tornieri, Litoria 155*
torquata, Delma 292*
torquata, Demansia 643*
Tortoise (see Turtle)
Tortoise, Long-necked 190
Tortoises, Side-necked 176
tovelli, Ramphotyphlops 597*
trachyderma, Uperoleia 115
Trachydosaurus 583
Trachydosaurus rugosus 584*
Trachydosaurus rugosus asper 584
Trachydosaurus rugosus konowi 584
Trachydosaurus rugosus rugosus 584
triacantha, Carlia 401*
tridactyla, Lerista 740
trilineata, Bassiana 735, 571
trilineata, Pseudemoia 571*
tristis, Furina 653*
tristis, Varanus 377*
tristis, Varanus tristis 379
troglodytes, Ramphotyphlops 598
Tropidechis 694
Tropidechis carinatus 694*
Tropidonophis 628
Tropidonophis mairii 628*
Tropidonophis mairii brongersmai 628
Tropidonophis mairii mairii 628
truncatus, Ophioscincus 556*
truncatus, Ophioscincus truncatus 556
tryoni, Oedura 266*
Turtle, Broad-shelled River 189
  Eastern Snake-necked 190
  Flatback 183
  Flat-shelled 193
  Green 180
  Hawksbill 182
  Krefft's River 196
  Leathery (see Luth) 176, 185
  Loggerhead 178
  Murray 197
  Northern Snake-necked 192
  Northern Snapping 194
  Oblong 192
  Pitted-shelled 186
  Saw-shelled 194
  Western Swamp 200
Turtles, Sea 176
tyleri, Litoria 155*
tyleri, Uperoleia 115
Tympanocryptis 350
Tympanocryptis adelaidensis 351*
Tympanocryptis adelaidensis adelaidensis 352
Tympanocryptis adelaidensis chapmani 352
Tympanocryptis cephalus 352*
Tympanocryptis diemensis 353*
Tympanocryptis intima 353*
Tympanocryptis lineata 353*
Tympanocryptis lineata houstoni 354
Tympanocryptis lineata lineata 354
Tympanocryptis lineata macra 354
Tympanocryptis lineata pinguicolla 354
Tympanocryptis parviceps 355*
Tympanocryptis parviceps butleri 356
Tympanocryptis parviceps parviceps 356
Tympanocryptis tetraporophora 356*
Tympanocryptis uniformis 356
tympanum, Eulamprus 489*
TYPHLOPIDAE 587

uber, Ctenotus 449*
uber, Ctenotus uber 449
umbrina, Pseudemydura 200*
Underwoodisaurus 275
Underwoodisaurus milii 275*
Underwoodisaurus sphyrurus 276*
unguirostris, Ramphotyphlops 598
uniduo, Lerista 534*
uniformis, Tympanocryptis 356
Uperoleia 108
Uperoleia arenicola 109
Uperoleia aspera 109
Uperoleia borealis 109
Uperoleia capitulata 109
Uperoleia crassa 110
Uperoleia fusca 110*
Uperoleia glandulosa 110*
Uperoleia inundata 111*
Uperoleia laevigata 111*
Uperoleia lithomoda 112
Uperoleia littlejohni 112
Uperoleia marmorata 112
Uperoleia martini 112
Uperoleia micromeles 112*

Uperoleia mimula 113
Uperoleia minima 113
Uperoleia mjobergii 113
Uperoleia orientalis 114
Uperoleia rugosa 114*
Uperoleia russelli 115
Uperoleia talpa 115
Uperoleia trachyderma 115
Uperoleia tyleri 115

vadnappa, Ctenophorus 326*
vagita, Cyclorana 122*
valens, Diporiphora 334
VARANIDAE 356
Varanus 356
Varanus acanthurus 359*
Varanus acanthurus acanthurus 361
Varanus acanthurus brachyurus 361
Varanus acanthurus insulanicus 361
Varanus baritji 361*
Varanus brevicauda 361*
Varanus caudolineatus 361*
Varanus eremius 362*
Varanus giganteus 362*
Varanus gilleni 364*
Varanus glauerti 365*
Varanus glebopalma 365*
Varanus gouldii 366*
Varanus gouldii flavirufus 368
Varanus gouldii gouldii 368
Varanus indicus 368*
Varanus kingorum 368*
Varanus mertensi 369*
Varanus mitchelli 369*
Varanus panoptes 370*
Varanus panoptes panoptes 370
Varanus panoptes rubidus 370
Varanus pilbarensis 370
Varanus prasinus 371*
Varanus primordius 371*
Varanus rosenbergi 372*
Varanus semiremex 372*
Varanus spenceri 376*
Varanus storri 376*
Varanus storri ocreatus 377
Varanus storri storri 377
Varanus teriae 734
Varanus timorensis 377*
Varanus timorensis scalaris 377
Varanus timorensis similis 377
Varanus timorensis timorensis 377
Varanus tristis 377*
Varanus tristis orientalis 379
Varanus tristis tristis 379
Varanus varius 379*
varia, Lerista 534*
variegata, Gehyra 244*
variegata, Morelia spilota 614
variegatus, Limnodynastes dumerilii 76
varius, Varanus 379*
Vermicella 695
Vermicella annulata 696*
Vermicella annulata annulata 696
Vermicella annulata snelli 696
Vermicella multifasciata 696*
vermicularis, Lerista 535
verreauxii, Anomalopus 386*
verreauxii, Litoria 156*
verreauxii, Litoria verreauxii 157
verrucosa, Cyclorana 123*
vertebralis, Ctenotus 449
vertebralis, Nephrurus 257*
victoriae, Emydura 199*
victoriana, Geocrinia 68
viduata, Lerista 740
virgata, Egernia slateri 472
virgatus, Cryptoblepharus 406
viridis, Chondropython 603*
vitellina, Geocrinia 733
vitellinus, Rheobatrachus 104*
vittata, Lerista 536*
vittatus, Diplodactylus 232*
vitticeps, Pogona 350*
vivax, Carlia 401*
vorisi, Hydrophis 719

waitii, Ramphotyphlops 598
walkeri, Lerista 536*
warro, Simoselaps 688*
weigeli, Notaden 94*
wellingtonae, Diplodactylus 234*
wheeleri, Nephrurus 257*
wheeleri, Nephrurus wheeleri 258
whitii, Egernia 473*
whitii, Egernia whitii 474
wiedii, Ramphotyphlops 599*
wilkinsi, Lerista 536*
williamsi, Diplodactylus 234*
wilsmorei, Neobatrachus 90*
wilsoni, Diplodactylus 234
winneckei, Diporiphora 336*
Woma 602
wombeyi, Diplodactylus 234
wotjulum, Notoscincus ornatus 554
wotjulumensis, Litoria 157*

xanthomera, Litoria 157
xanthura, Lerista 536*
xenopleura, Ctenotus 450
xenopus, Gehyra 244*

yampiensis, Ctenotus decaneurus 421
yampiensis, Ramphotyphlops 599*
yinnietharra, Ctenophorus 326*
yirrikalae, Ramphotyphlops 599
youngsoni, Ctenotus 450*
yuna, Lerista 740

zastictus, Ctenotus 450*
zebrilla, Ctenotus 450
zia, Cautula 735, 571
zia, Pseudemoia 571*
zonulata, Lerista 740